Feature Highlights of *Kleppner's Advertising Procedure* 18th Edition

Feature	Description	Benefit
Chapter Objectives	Numbered list outlining the major topics and issues addressed in the chapter, and linked to specific content within the chapter	Alert students to the major topics that they should recall after reading the chapter
Advantage Points	Examples of new marketing and creative practices in advertising today	Demonstrate to students how advertisers are responding to technological and economic change and connect key concepts from the book to real-life examples
Kleppner Viewpoints	Leading advertising professionals with expertise in digital advertising, media/communication planning, international advertising, research, account planning, traffic, and more, offering insight on chapter topics	Deepen student understanding of the professional application of specific advertising issues
End-of-chapter Summaries	Summaries of the key points in the chapter	Remind students of the chapter highlights
End-of-chapter Reviews	Assessment questions to challenge students' understanding of the theories and topics covered within the chapter	Assist students in confirming whether they know what they need to know about the key topics presented in the chapter

To Gain a Competitive Edge in Marketing or Advertising, Students Must "Get Media"

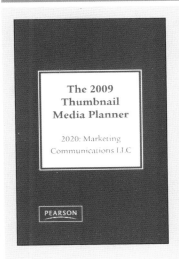

The 2009
Thumbnail
Media Planner

2020: Marketing
Communications LLC

PEARSON

Media is the Future.

We are in a media-marketing revolution brought about by new technologies and a rapidly changing market place.

If you want to work in marketing, chances are, you will need to "get media" pretty fast. For example, in an advertising agency you will propose target markets and integrated media solutions to clients. You will discuss traditional, digital, and new media options with clients.

Or, as a brand manager, you will review and approve (or disapprove) proposals from the agency or media. You will use media as a market segmentation tool or to create new channels of distribution. As the marketing director, you will manage your strategies and plans to maximize ROI.

Educate yourself. Media is your competitive edge.

Introducing the *Thumbnail Media Planner*

That's why Prentice Hall is offering the *Thumbnail Media Planner* to supplement your marketing or advertising textbook. Published annually since 2003 by a leading advertising agency executive, The *Thumbnail Media Planner* is a compact marketing/media reference already purchased by thousands of advertising and marketing professionals. The Planner contains key data about the U.S. marketplace and each of the major media, including audience and cost benchmarks. If your instructor hasn't yet adopted *Thumbnail* to supplement your text, ask for it or buy it at your bookstore using ISBN 0136118798. For more information, visit this Web site: **www.pearsonhighered.com**

KLEPPNER'S
Advertising Procedure
18th Edition

W. Ronald Lane
UNIVERSITY OF GEORGIA, EMERITUS

Karen Whitehill King
UNIVERSITY OF GEORGIA

Tom Reichert
UNIVERSITY OF GEORGIA

PRENTICE HALL

Boston   Columbus   Indianapolis   New York   San Francisco   Upper Saddle River
Amsterdam   Cape Town   Dubai   London   Madrid   Milan   Munich   Paris   Montreal   Toronto
Delhi   Mexico City   Sao Paulo   Sydney   Hong Kong   Seoul   Singapore   Taipei   Tokyo

Library of Congress Cataloging-in-Publication Data

Lane, W. Ronald, 1940-
    Kleppner's Advertising procedure / W. Ronald Lane, Karen Whitehill King, Tom Reichert. —
18th ed.
      p. cm.
    Includes bibliographical references and index.
    ISBN-13: 978-0-13-611082-8 (alk. paper)
    ISBN-10: 0-13-611082-7 (alk. paper)
     1. Advertising. I. King, Karen Whitehill. II. Reichert, Tom. III. Title. IV. Title:
Advertising procedure.
HF5823.K45 2011
659.1—dc22

2009046216

Editorial Director: Sally Yagan
Editor in Chief: Eric Svendsen
Acquisitions Editor: James Heine
Editorial Project Manager: Kierra Kashickey
Editorial Assistant: Karin Williams
Director of Marketing: Patrice Lumumba Jones
Senior Marketing Manager: Anne K. Fahlgren
Marketing Assistant: Melinda Jensen
Senior Managing Editor: Judy Leale
Senior Production Project Manager: Karalyn Holland
Senior Operations Supervisor: Arnold Vila
Creative Director: Christy Mahon
Senior Art Director: Kenny Beck
Interior and Cover Designer: Laura C. Ierardi
Manager, Visual Research: Beth Brenzel
Manager, Rights and Permissions: Shannon Barbe
Image Permission Coordinator: Annette Linder
Cover Art: Shutterstock/New York Times Square/© Emin Kuliyev; Blueprint image: Kenny Beck
Full-Service Project Management: Heather Willison/S4Carlisle Publishing Services
Composition: S4Carlisle Publishing Services
Printer/Binder: LSC Communications
Cover Printer: LSC Communications
Text Font: Times Ten

Credits and acknowledgments borrowed from other sources and reproduced, with permission, in this textbook appear on appropriate page within text (or on page 789).

Microsoft® and Windows® are registered trademarks of the Microsoft Corporation in the U.S.A. and other countries. Screen shots and icons reprinted with permission from the Microsoft Corporation. This book is not sponsored or endorsed by or affiliated with the Microsoft Corporation.

Many of the designations by manufacturers and seller to distinguish their products are claimed as trademarks. Where those designations appear in this book, and the publisher was aware of a trademark claim, the designations have been printed in initial caps or all caps.

Prentice Hall
is an imprint of

www.pearsonhighered.com

ISBN 10: 0-13-611082-7
ISBN 13: 978-0-13-611082-8

13 2023

To our valued colleague, mentor, and friend,
Dr. J. Thomas Russell, for masterfully guiding
Kleppner's Advertising Procedure from the eighth
to the seventeenth editions. RON, KAREN, AND TOM

Brief Contents

Contents

Preface

There are few areas of business and marketing that operate in a more dynamic atmosphere than advertising and promotion. The eighteenth edition of *Kleppner's Advertising Procedure* continues the 85-year tradition of providing new material capturing the dramatic changes affecting the planning and execution of advertising and marketing communication. This book introduces students to this exciting field through Viewpoints from advertising professionals and recent exhibits that highlight the best advertisements and promotional techniques.

What's New in This Edition?

- **New author.** This edition welcomes the perspective of new author Tom Reichert, a University of Georgia professor who has written extensively about advertising history, content, and effects. Dr. Reichert also brings his professional experience in media sales to this edition. His contributions are most evident in Chapters 1, 2, 4, 13, 23, and 24.

- **Expanded discussion and examples of digital advertising.** Chapter 13 includes an updated look at digital media. In addition, discussions of digital media and advertising are now integrated throughout the book, and we offer many examples of digital creativity. Chapter 19, now titled "Video and the Commercial," contains new content describing online and other uses of video.

- **The best of contemporary advertising.** More than 100 advertising exhibits throughout the book are new to this edition. They richly illustrate the best of today's commercial messages, from web sites to banner ads to traditional format magazine ads and TV commercials.

- **New industry Viewpoints.** More than a dozen new Viewpoints from advertising professionals with expertise in digital advertising, media/communication planning, international advertising, research, account planning, traffic, creative, and more appear throughout the book.

- **Innovative new cases.** An innovative new international media/communication case for P&G's Fairy brand appears in Chapter 12. In Chapter 15, there is a new Advantage Point for Virginia Tech University that highlights the role of research in the development of an advertising campaign for the university. A Viewpoint detailing the development of ad concepts for the Peabody Awards runs in Chapter 17, and Chapter 18 includes an unusual production concept case Advantage Point for the Richmond Catholic Diocese. Other new cases include Original Bike Spirits Advantage Point (Chapter 21) as well as Orlando/Orange County Convention and Visitors Bureau, Smokey Bones Bar & Fire Grill, and Western Hemisphere Travel Initiative, which all appear in Chapter 22.

- **New examples and brand stories.** This edition is loaded with recent examples of marketing and creative practices that demonstrate how advertisers are responding to technological and economic change. Each chapter contains stories of new marketing practices. For example, there is an Advantage Point from the *Little Red Book* series in Chapter 19.

Discussions of important changes in the advertising profession appear throughout the text, though we have kept the basic structure of the book similar to that of previous editions. The eighteenth edition is organized as follows:

PART I

The authors strongly believe that contemporary advertising should be studied from the perspective of the social, cultural, and economic foundations that created modern marketing and promotion. Part I offers a historical overview and situates advertising within the sphere of marketing communication.

- **Chapter 1** examines how advertising and marketing developed as part of the larger society. We look at the Industrial Revolution, a rising middle class, and the introduction of democratic principles in both politics and economics. The chapter brings the personalities and events that created the modern American marketing system to life.

- **Chapter 2** offers an overview of the multitude of channels currently used to reach prospective buyers and demonstrates the ways that advertising and marketing communication are used by advertisers as small as the neighborhood retailer and as large as global multinational corporations.

PART II

Part II introduces fundamentals of advertising planning and brand research, the basis for virtually all successful advertising.

- **Chapter 3** introduces the concept of the advertising spiral and the strategies needed to keep brands vigorous in a changing marketplace.

- **Chapter 4** outlines the fundamentals of identifying and understanding the target markets that are most interested in specific products and that may be the most profitable for the advertiser.

PART III

Part III emphasizes the business operations of advertising and the sometimes-fragile and contentious relationships between agencies and clients.

- **Chapters 5 and 6** explore how the advertising and management functions have become more complex. Today, advertising is more likely to be integrated into a total

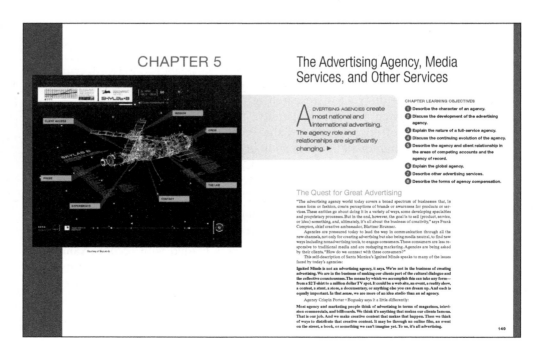

marketing communication program, resulting in changes in management relation-ships. The text also discusses the organization of the advertising industry from both advertiser and agency perspectives.

PART IV

In Part IV, we discuss the methods of reaching consumers with sales messages. The chapters in this part examine both traditional media and emerging methods of reaching customers.

- **Chapter 7** begins the consideration of media with an overview of the media planning function and the role of the media/communication planner in delivering advertising messages to consumers.

- **Chapters 8 to 14** discuss each of the basic media and communication methods used to reach consumers. We look at media as diverse as web sites, iPods, and cell phones. These chapters also address the communication strengths and weaknesses of each medium and how media are converging as consumers embrace new technology and media companies merge to form large multimedia conglomerates.

PART V

Ultimately, prospects are converted to buyers with the introduction of strong product benefits that solve consumer problems. The discussion of the creative function in this section highlights the need for creative ideas based on research that offers insight into consumer needs, product selection, and media preferences.

- **Chapters 15 to 22** emphasize the need for planning and research to bring rough ideas to fruition as a finished ad. Contrary to popular opinion, great advertising is rarely the result of spontaneous brilliance, but rather it is the byproduct of hours of hard work and study.

PART VI

Part VI covers global and multicultural advertising considerations as well as advertising's economic, social, and legal effects.

- **Chapter 23** underscores the global nature of advertising and marketing. Globalization is no longer a theory but rather it is part of the everyday strategy of companies throughout the world. In addition, advertisers increasingly must be aware of multi-cultural considerations within the United States.

- **Chapter 24** stresses the fact that advertising is constrained by a number of legal, regulatory, and ethical considerations as the public demands greater candor from advertisers and protections from governmental agencies. More than simply a discussion of rules and regulations, Chapter 24 emphasizes the new environment of public responsibility that major advertisers have embraced during the past half century.

Major Objectives of the Text

The text offers a clear and comprehensive examination of the roles that advertising practitioners play from three perspectives. First, we consider a firm's marketing and advertising department. Second, we look at an advertising agency professional. Third, we consider the perspective of media executives who provide the bridge between a company's products and its target audience. The skill set needed for a successful advertising career has never been more complex. So, we have brought together contemporary information from the fields of marketing, communication, psychology, sociology, anthropology, and social science research as it relates to the practice of advertising.

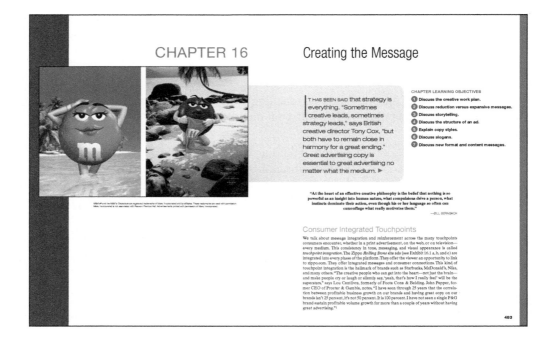

Student Resources

CourseSmart As an alternative to purchasing the print textbook, you can purchase an electronic version of the same content and save up to 50 percent off the suggested list price of the print text. This is an exciting new choice for students looking to save money. With a CourseSmart eTextbook, you can search the text, make notes online, print reading assignments that incorporate lecture notes, and bookmark important passages for later review. For more information or to purchase access to the CourseSmart eTextbook, visit www.coursesmart.com.

Acknowledgments

John Adams, *The Martin Agency, Richmond*

Annisa Mae Al-Timimi, *Blue Sky Agency, Atlanta*

Michele Barker, *The Martin Agency, Richmond*

Peter Bell, *Smokey Bones Bar & Fire Grill, Orlando*

Sheri Bevil, *Lane Bevil+Partners, Atlanta*

David Botsford, *The Botsford Group, Atlanta*

Chuck Brasfield, *Boy Scouts of America, Atlanta*

Kelly Caffarelli, *Home Depot Foundation, Atlanta*

Joel Cardwell, *The Florida Times-Union, Jacksonville*

Adam Carmean, *Schlotzsky's, Athens, GA*

Brett Compton, *Brunner, Atlanta*

Frank Compton, *Brunner, Atlanta*

John Conaghan, *Newspaper Association of America*

Phil Corley, *Pathway Communities, Atlanta*

Mary Beth Cowardin, *Elmer's, Columbus, OH*

Peter Cressy, Ph.D., *Distilled Spirits Council*

Lisa Delaney, *Arras Group*

Kelly Kenton Fink, *Bowen Family Homes, Atlanta*

Sylvia Fox, *Brunner, Atlanta*

Guy Gabriele, *Idea Engineering, Santa Barbara, CA*

Kimberly A. Greenia, *The Home Depot, Atlanta*

Jennifer Griffith, Ph.D., *Grady College, University of Georgia, Athens*

Steven Guyer, *Experian CheetahMail, New York*

Chris Hartley, *Blue Rhino, Winston-Salem, NC*

Chris Hooper, *Fitzgerald+Co., Atlanta*

Ron Huey, *Huey+Partners, Atlanta*

Mike Hughes, *The Martin Agency, Richmond*

Sarah Hughes, *Ignited Minds, Del Ray, CA*

Gilad Kat, *Mediacom, Tel Aviv, Israel*

Tom G. Kuypers, *Bed Bath & Beyond, Farmington, NY*

Steven Lang, *Cox Radio/Athens*

Jim Learned, *Elevation, Washington, DC*

Donna LeBlond, *Grady College, University of Georgia, Athens*

Amy Lokken, *McRae Communications, Atlanta*

John Ludwig, *Push, Inc., Orlando*

Monica Luck, *Georgia Department of Transportation, Atlanta*

Brad Majors, *Your Brand Rep, LCC., Greenville, SC*

Tim Mapes, *Delta Air Lines, Atlanta*

Rob Marbury, *Max2O, Atlanta*

Kelly Markey, *Neathawk Dubuque & Packett, Richmond*

Hugh Martin, Ph.D., *Ohio University*

Mike Martin, *Skylab-B, Atlanta*

Heather McBride, *Push, Inc., Orlando*

Andrew McLean, *Groupm*

Parker Middleton, Ph.D., *Grady College, University of Georgia, Athens*

Josslyn Mikow, *Ogilvy Worldwide, San Francisco*

Russ Mischner, *The Home Depot, Atlanta*

Ernie Mosteller, *Brunner Digital, Washington, DC*

Jim Mountjoy, *LKM, Charlotte, NC*

Roger Neathawk, *Neathawk Dubuque & Packett, Richmond*

Greg Nyilasy, Ph.D., *Hall and Partners*

Robert Passikoff, *Brand Keys Inc.*

Don Perry, *Chick-fil-A, Atlanta*

Tom Robinson, *Robinson & Associates, Tupelo, MS*

Sunayana Sarkar, *Starcom MediaVest Group, New York*

Scott Scaggs, *Trone, High Point, NC*

Megan Sovern, *Goodby. Silverstein & Partners, San Francisco*

Jeanne Spencer, *Idea Engineering, Santa Barbara, CA*

Gary Swain, *Orlando/Orange County Convention and Visitors Bureau, Orlando*

Richard C. Wahl, *Push, Inc., Orlando*

Robert Willett, *Willett Design, Athens, GA*

Matt Wilson, *SBC Advertising, Columbus, OH*

About the Authors

Otto Kleppner (1899-1982)

A graduate of New York University, Otto Kleppner started out in advertising as a copywriter. After several such jobs, he became advertising manager at Prentice Hall, where he began to think that he, too, "could write a book." Some years later, he also thought that he could run his own advertising agency, and both ideas materialized eminently. His highly successful agency handled advertising for leading accounts (Dewar's Scotch Whisky, I. W. Harper Bourbon and other Schenley brands, Saab Cars, Doubleday Book Clubs, and others). His book became a bible for advertising students, and his writings have been published in eight languages.

Active in the American Association of Advertising Agencies, Mr. Kleppner served as a director, a member of the Control Committee, chairman of the Committee of Government, Public and Educator Relations, and a governor of the New York Council. He was awarded the Nichols Cup (now the Crain Cup) for distinguished service to the teaching of advertising.

W. Ronald Lane

Ron has worked in all aspects of advertising. He began in advertising and promotion for a drug manufacturer. Later he was marketing manager for a drug store chain. He has worked in creative and account services for clients including Coca-Cola, National Broiler Council, Minute Maid, and for small clients like Western North Carolina Tourism and Callaway Gardens Country Store.

He was presented with the American Advertising Federation Distinguished Advertising Educator Award for service to advertising education and industry. He was coordinator of the Institute of Advanced Advertising Studies sponsored by the American Association of Advertising Agencies for six years. He was a partner in SLRS Communications, an advertising-marketing firm. He served 20 years on the American Advertising Federation's (AAF) Academic Committee. He has been AAF Academic Division Chair, a member of the AAF Board of Directors, Council of Governors, Executive Committee and the AAF Foundation. He has been an ADDY Awards judge numerous times, and been a member of the *Advertising Age* Creative Workshop faculty. He has also served as a member of the ACEMJC Accrediting Council. Currently, Ron is a senior partner at Lane Bevil+Partners.

Karen Whitehill King

Karen King is a professor of advertising and the head of the Department of Advertising and Public Relations in the Grady College of Journalism and Mass Communication at the University of Georgia. She received her Ph.D. in communications from the University of Illinois. While on the faculty at UGA, she has been a visiting communication researcher at the Centers for Disease Control and Prevention in Atlanta, working on their AIDS public service campaign, and a visiting professor at Lintas in New York.

Karen's research interests include advertising industry issues and health communication. She has published her research in leading academic journals including: *Journal of Advertising, Journal of Advertising Research, Journal of Public Policy and Marketing, Journal of Current Issues and Research in Advertising, Journalism and Mass Communication Quarterly, Journal of Newspaper Research, Journal of Health Care Marketing and Journalism,* and *Mass Communication Educator.* She was the editor of the *1994 Proceedings of the American Academy of Advertising Conference* and she co-authored a textbook supplement, *Media Buying Simulation.*

Prior to joining Grady College, Karen was a research supervisor and a media planner/buyer at FCB Chicago. Her clients included Kraft, Coors, Sears, Sunbeam, and International Harvester. In 1999, Karen was named the Donald G. Hileman Educator of the Year by the American Advertising Federation's Seventh District for her work with the UGA Ad Club and its AAF campaign competition team.

Tom Reichert

Tom Reichert is a professor of advertising in the Department of Advertising and Public Relations in the Grady College of Journalism and Mass Communication at the University of Georgia. He received his Ph.D. in communication from the University of Arizona and earned his journalism degree from the University of Missouri where he read *Kleppner's Advertising Procedure* in his first advertising course.

Tom's been teaching, researching, and writing about advertising since 1993. His areas of expertise include social marketing, sex in advertising, political advertising, and media sales. He has written or edited seven books about major issues and concerns regarding the uses and effects of advertising on professional practice and culture. He authored *The Erotic History of Advertising* and co-edited and contributed to *Sex in Advertising: Perspectives on the Erotic Appeal* and *Sex in Consumer Culture: The Erotic Content of Media and Marketing.* Also, Tom's research has been published in leading advertising and mass communications journals such as the *Journal of Advertising,* the *Journal of Current Issues and Research in Advertising,* and *Journalism and Mass Communication Quarterly.*

Prior to earning his Ph.D., Tom sold advertising for *The Orange County Register,* a major metropolitan daily newspaper in southern California. He also served as deputy press secretary for U.S. representative Jim Kolbe's 1994 re-election campaign and as a researcher for a political consulting firm. Before joining the faculty at the University of Georgia, he taught at the University of Alabama and the University of North Texas.

KLEPPNER'S
Advertising Procedure
18th Edition

PART 1

PART 2

PART 3

PART 4

PART 5

PART 6

THE PLACE OF ADVERTISING

Contemporary advertising should be studied from the perspective of the social, cultural, and economic foundations on which modern marketing and promotion are based. Part I offers an historical overview and situates advertising within the sphere of marketing communication.

■ **CHAPTER 1** examines how advertising and marketing developed as part of the larger society, especially in regard to the Industrial Revolution, a rising middle class, and the introduction of democratic principles in both politics and economics. The chapter brings to life the personalities and events that created the modern American marketing system.

■ **CHAPTER 2** offers an overview of the multitude of channels currently used to reach prospective buyers and demonstrates the ways that advertising and marketing communication are used by advertisers as small as the neighborhood retailer and as large as global multinational corporations.

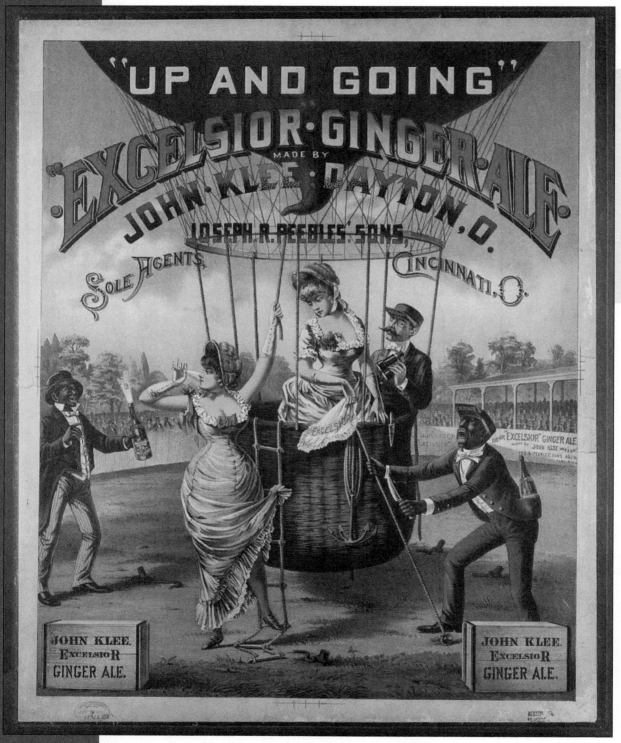

"Up and Going," 1885, Library of Congress, Prints and Photographs Division (LC-USZ62-2588).

Background of Today's Advertising

SUCCESSFUL advertisers are keenly aware of the historical forces that have shaped today's—and tomorrow's—advertising and its role in marketing communication. ▶

Loved, loathed, sought after, and avoided describe the range of reactions experienced by Americans toward advertising during the past 150 years. At one time advertisers were admired and held in high esteem as lords of capitalism and commerce. At other times they suffered the consequences of low public opinion and increased regulation because they betrayed public trust and hawked products that were harmful or did not work. Today, many Americans are cautious when approaching advertising. They can be cynical and resent marketers' intrusiveness into their lives, yet, consumers seek information when making purchase decisions and eagerly engage with advertising that is entertaining and relevant.

This chapter touches on the relationship between advertising and consumers; it lays the foundation for understanding advertising's historical roots and its development in the United States. We will see that advertising grows in concert with a dynamic and advanced economy as it adapts to social, political, and technological change. We will also examine the circumstances that contributed to its growth, including the development of mass media, a rising middle class, effective transportation, and the growth of mass production in the United States.

Forces in the Rise of Modern Advertising

1 Identify factors that contributed to the rise of modern American advertising.

The exchange of goods and the need to link buyers with sellers date to prehistoric times. We have evidence of messages offering goods for sale dating to 5000 B.C., and some of the earliest cave drawings refer to the makers of primitive objects. Modern advertising began in the United States in the mid 1800s, and, during the following century, advertising practitioners introduced sophisticated elements such as motivational research to define consumer behavior, media analysis to reach targeted consumers, and creative strategy to enhance selling messages. In order to understand the origins of modern advertising, we must examine the conditions that made it possible.

At the outset, it is necessary to understand that advertising is a communications tool that functions most efficiently in combination with two primary components:

1. *Centralized exchange.* When goods and services moved from a system of decentralized exchange in which buyers and sellers dealt directly with each other to one in which merchants functioned as intermediaries, advertising was needed to make potential consumers aware of the availability of goods.

2. *An economy in which supply surpasses demand.* The primary purpose of advertising is to create demand by introducing new products or suggesting how consumers can solve some problem with existing products. When consumers' problem(s) are obvious (demand) and a particular product is the clear solution to the problem, advertising's role is largely limited to letting buyers know the location and price of goods. However, in an economy with numerous brands fighting for the consumer dollar, advertising must not only inform and persuade potential customers that these products exist but also give consumers reasons to purchase one brand over those of competitors. "Societies of scarcity . . . need not advertise anything. Their people sign up to buy a car, wait three years or more and then gladly take whatever is assigned them."[1]

centralized exchange
A system of trade and marketing through specialized intermediaries rather than the direct exchange of goods between buyers and producers.

Although **centralized exchange** and excess supply were necessary ingredients for advertising, a number of other factors came together in the 50 years after the Civil War to create the foundations for this multibillion-dollar industry. The first was the beginning of the fulfillment of democratic ideals. Although eighteenth-century America had far to go before basic rights such as women's suffrage and full citizenship for Americans of African descent were a reality, public education was creating a literate population and interest in the political process created both the need and support for newspapers and magazines.

Second, advertising prospered as the Industrial Revolution swept across the United States during the latter part of the nineteenth century. Not only did mass production allow the efficient manufacturing of goods but this same technological expertise also created the high-speed presses that enabled the publishing of mass circulation magazines and newspapers that carried the advertising that provided the media's financial foundations. Just as important, industrialization created the need for skilled workers who earned high wages and moved from the farm to urban centers bringing with them the need for information provided by a growing print media.

Mass production efficiencies could only be realized if manufacturers were able to distribute goods beyond a limited geographic area. The introduction of the railroad not only created unity among a formerly divided country but also created a means of national distribution for the products of a growing manufacturing sector. The railroad, combined with instant telegraph communication, connected the country economically and culturally. However, it wasn't until the introduction of national brands that advertising and marketing began to fulfill their promise.

National brands, supported by a coast-to-coast system of railroad distribution and national magazines to advertise them, provided the impetus for a sophisticated advertising and marketing structure based on product differentiation and consumer loyalty to individual brands. Nationally branded goods changed the relationship between buy-

EXHIBIT 1.1

Does the appeal in this 1863 ad differ from those in contemporary cosmetic and lotion advertising?

ers and sellers from one based on the simple exchange of commodity goods to one with a marketing system based on consistent product quality and identification; these national brands gave manufacturers leverage over retailers that would continue for the next 100 years until the rise of mega-retailers during the 1990s. Although, Laird's did not stand the test of time, its 1863 ad for cosmetic brands "Bloom of Youth" and "Liquid Pearl" (see Exhibit 1.1) promised users beautiful and rejuvenated skin.

The era of national brands and the advertising and distribution systems to sell and market them cannot be underestimated. Although advertising did not create the centralized, efficient system of national marketing, it did provide one of the primary ingredients to make such a strategy practical. Entrepreneurs rushed to benefit from the advantages of being the first in the marketplace with branded goods. Quaker Oats cereal is generally considered to be the first national marketer, but men such as Daniel

Gerber, Dr. William Scholl, Gail Borden, Richard Sears, and Frederick Maytag have all left their legacies through the brands they established.

The convergence of the availability of branded products, the ability to provide national distribution, and a growing middle class with the income to provide a market for these products had evolved sufficiently by 1920 to support the creation of an advertising industry that demonstrated many of the basic functions found among modern agencies and corporate advertising departments today.

Advertising's Modern Era: Research and Responsibility

② Discuss the impor-tance of research and responsibility in advertising's development.

The two elements missing in most advertising during the early years of the twentieth century were the following:

1. An ethical framework for creating promotional messages
2. Valid and reliable research to measure advertising effects

At first glance, these may seem to be unrelated concerns. However, from a philosophical perspective, they are very much linked. Advertising was part of a rising democratic movement with foundations in Europe's eighteenth-century Age of Enlightenment, during which time, for the first time, a philosophy was introduced that held that the individual was fully capable of discerning truth from falsehood. In this open marketplace of ideas, falsehoods would be identified and rejected as part of some natural process. In such an environment, there would be little need for regulation of information. Furthermore, research to find underlying consumer motivations would be of scant value in influencing totally "rational" buyers.

However, by the late nineteenth century, public opinion shifted to a position calling for greater consumer protection. The initial battleground centered on the regulation of patent medicines. Not only did many of these concoctions provide no benefit to consumers in need of medical help but also in many cases they actually were harmful. Products containing high levels of alcohol, opium, and cocaine created a group of legal drug addicts rather than curing legitimate ailments. There is little question that greater control and regulation of these products and the advertising that promoted them were needed. However, many of the most zealous proponents of advertising regulation were as extreme in their criticism of advertising as the fraudulent advertisers themselves. These critics continued their condemnations of advertising throughout most of the twentieth century. Promoting false fears of the power of techniques such as subliminal advertising and motivational research, a host of advertising commentators demanded that both advertising research and the messages that resulted from it be curtailed or greatly limited.

As we look back on that time, it is obvious that the advertising research of the period held little danger of mind control, subliminal or otherwise, for the average consumer. If anything, most of the early research was almost laughable in its lack of sophistication. For example, "Several agencies boasted of . . . research into consumer attitudes in the late 1920s, but their crude, slapdash methods made these 'surveys' of questionable value in providing accurate feedback. One agency reported that it could obtain quick, inexpensive results . . . by having all members of the staff send questionnaires to their friends."[2]

Despite the rather primitive research methods of the period, a few advertising executives such as Claude Hopkins were conducting direct-mail and coupon-response research in the 1920s to gather information about effective advertising messages. Pond's was among a few enlightened advertisers that were analyzing audience response to advertising. However, it would not be until the 1950s that sophisticated advertising research gained widespread acceptance (see Exhibit 1.2).

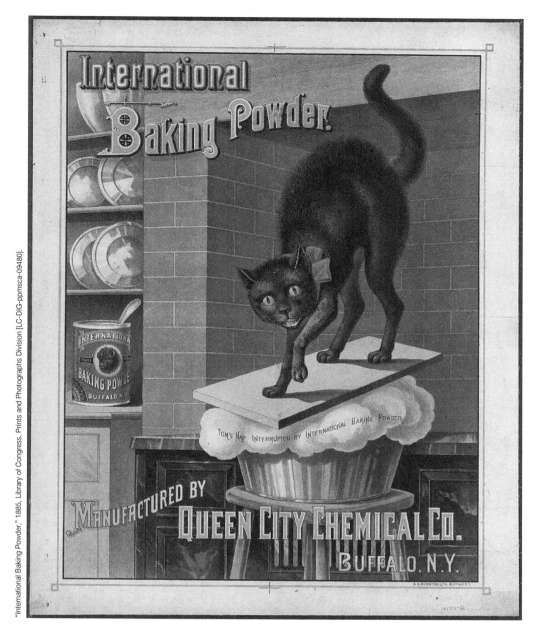

EXHIBIT 1.2

It is doubtful that research was involved in this 1885 ad for International Baking Powder.

Beginnings

The urge to advertise seems to be a part of human nature, evidenced since ancient times. Of the 5,000-year recorded history of advertising right up to the current satellite age, the period that is most significant begins when the United States emerged as a great manufacturing nation about 100 years ago. The early history of advertising, however, is far too fascinating to pass by without a glance.

Perhaps the earliest known evidence of advertising is a Babylonian clay tablet dating to 3000 B.C., which bears inscriptions for an ointment dealer, a scribe, and a shoemaker. Papyri exhumed from the ruins of Thebes show that the ancient Egyptians had a better medium on which to write their messages. (Regrettably, the announcements preserved in papyrus offer rewards for the return of runaway slaves.) The Greeks were among those who relied on town criers to chant the arrival of ships with cargoes of wines, spices, and metals. Often a crier was accompanied by a musician who kept him in

EXHIBIT 1.3

Do today's ads promoting new media compare to this ad for Edison's vitascope?

hoarding
First printed outdoor signs—the forerunner of modern outdoor advertising.

the right key. Town criers later became the earliest medium for public announcements in many European countries, and they continued to be used for centuries. (At this point, we must digress to tell about a promotion idea used by innkeepers in France around A.D. 1100 to tout their fine wines: They would have the town crier blow a horn, gather a group, and offer samples!)

Roman merchants, too, had a sense of advertising. The ruins of Pompeii contain signs in stone or terra-cotta advertising what the shops were selling: a row of hams for a butcher shop, a cow for a dairy, a boot for a shoemaker. The Pompeiians also knew the art of telling their story to the public by means of painted wall signs. These and other forms of outdoor advertising have proved to be some of the most enduring forms of advertising. Outdoor advertising survived the decline of the Roman Empire and became the decorative art of European inns in the seventeenth and eighteenth centuries. That was still an age of widespread illiteracy, so inns vied with one another in creating attractive signs that all could recognize. This explains the distinctive names of old inns, especially in England, such as the Three Squirrels, the Man in the Moon, and the Hole in the Wall. In 1614, England passed a law, probably the earliest pertaining to advertising, that prohibited signs from extending more than 8 feet out from a building (longer signs pulled down too many house fronts.) Another law required signs to be high enough to give clearance to an armored man on horseback. In 1740, the first printed outdoor poster—referred to as a **hoarding**—appeared in London. The 1896 poster shown in Exhibit 1.3 used marvelous color to demonstrate Thomas Edison's vitascope.

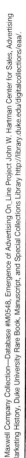
RC Maxwell Company Collection—Database #M0548, Emergence of Advertising On Line Project John W. Hartman Center for Sales, Advertising & Marketing History, Duke University Rare Book, Manuscript, and Special Collections Library http://library.duke.edu/digitalcollections/eaa/.

EXHIBIT 1.4

Similar to today, advertisers take advantage of any available outdoor space to appeal to consumers.

We begin our discussion of the foundations of modern advertising by examining its history, which we divide into four broad periods:

3 **List the four periods in advertising history.**

1. *The* **premarketing era**. From the start of product exchange in prehistoric times to the middle of the seventeenth century, buyers and sellers communicated in very primitive ways. For most of this period, "media," such as clay tablets, town criers, and tavern signs, were the best ways to reach potential prospects for a product or service. Only in the latter decades of the period did primitive printing appear as the forerunner of modern mass media.

premarketing era
The period from prehistoric times to the eighteenth century. During this time, buyers and sellers communicated in very primitive ways.

2. *The* **mass communication era**. From the 1700s to the early decades of the 1900s, advertisers were increasingly able to reach larger and larger segments of the population. Mass newspapers first appeared in the 1830s, and they were quickly followed by a number of national magazines. By the 1920s, radio had ushered in the broadcast era when advertising was delivered free to virtually every American household. The mass communication era also saw advertisers beginning to differentiate their brands with specific consumer benefits (see Exhibit 1.4).

mass communication era
The period from the 1700s to the early decades of the twentieth century, in which advertisers were able to reach large segments of the population through the mass media.

3. *The* **research era**. Beginning in the 1920s, advertisers used a number of techniques to reach and motivate mass audiences. From the 1990s to the present, reflecting the more personalized nature of media, advertisers have shifted their focus to ever more sophisticated techniques for identifying and reaching narrowly targeted audiences with messages prepared specifically for specific groups or individuals. Early advertising research emphasized general information concerning broad demographic information such as age, sex, and geographic location of consumers. Today,

research era
In recent years, advertisers increasingly have been able to identify narrowly defined audience segments through sophisticated research methods.

advertising research includes much more detailed information about the lifestyles and motivations of consumers. Rather than studying general audience characteristics, advertising research is more inclined to investigate the motivations behind purchase behavior.

interactive era
Communication will increasingly be controlled by consumers who will determine when and where they can be reached with promotional messages.

4. *The* **interactive era.** For the past century or more, the typical advertising model involved reaching passive consumers through one-way communications provided by the mass media. A new model, one based on interactive communication, is quickly being adopted. This model makes the consumer an active participant in the communication process. In 2008, for example, more than 82 million people in the United States created online content in the form of blog posts, podcasts, YouTube videos, or simply interacting with friends on social networking sites. By 2013, that number is expected to increase to 114 million, more than half of all Internet users. People are also in greater control of the media content they consume. Thanks to widespread broadband adoption and new technology consumers are not only free to watch their favorite TV program but now they can also download it, buy it on iTunes, or record it on their DVRs. Marketers are responding to these changes in a number of ways from being more sensitive to consumer feedback to integrating Internet-based promotions into advertising campaigns.[3] Obviously, the change from media to consumer control and the development of one-to-one communication channels will require major changes by both the mass media and advertisers. We discuss these implications throughout the media and creative sections of the text.

As we begin our discussion of the development of advertising, we must keep in mind the interrelationships among marketing, the general business climate, and social mores and conventions, as well as public attitudes toward advertising. As advertising has become an integral part of our economy, advertising practitioners have come under close public scrutiny and must work within a complex legal and regulatory framework. Perhaps the most important change in the business climate during the past 20 years has been the growing sense of social responsibility within the advertising community. Many advertising practices that were routine a century ago are universally condemned by the industry today. Advertisers realize that public trust is a key to successful advertising. Throughout the remainder of this chapter, we discuss the forces that have shaped contemporary advertising.

The Move to Creativity in Advertising

As we discuss in a later section, the original advertising companies were really no more than media space brokers—buying bulk space from newspapers and reselling small space allotments to advertisers. However, significant changes in the economic environment forced both agencies and their clients to emphasize the creative function. The first two decades of the twentieth century were marked by an emphasis on persuading consumers through creative advertising messages. Several factors led to the growing importance of persuasive advertising during the early decades of the century:

1. By 1900, the industrial output of products had reached a point at which serious brand competition was taking place in a number of product categories such as soap and food. Led by major companies such as Procter & Gamble, Kellogg, and H. J. Heinz, the shift from commodity products to branded goods was well established in a number of consumer goods categories. The competition among brands for the first time saw strong promotional offers accompanying product advertising, as well as the introduction of emotional appeals.

2. Innovative marketers such as John Wanamaker of Wanamaker Department Store in New York City realized the need to sell products on the basis of style and luxury

EXHIBIT 1.5

Advertisers early on recognized the need for consumer understanding.

rather than simple utility. He hired John Powers, considered by many to be the first true copywriter. By the turn of the twentieth century, agencies were emphasizing their creative expertise as they moved toward providing full-service advertising to their clients.

3. Advertising was beginning to draw from social science research to determine the most effective means of reaching consumers. In 1921, J. Walter Thompson hired John Watson from Johns Hopkins. Watson, the "father of **behavioral research**," was one of the earliest researchers to study the underlying motivations of consumer purchasing. Even at this early stage, agencies such as Thompson's recognized the importance of understanding the needs and wants of consumers (see Exhibit 1.5).

behavioral research
Market research that attempts to determine the underlying nature of purchase behavior.

4. Building on the work of Watson and others, Alfred Sloan Jr. made General Motors (GM) the preeminent carmaker by surpassing his major rival Henry Ford. Sloan viewed the automobile as a symbol of status, and GM advertising sought to transform Ford's idea of the car as low-cost transportation to one in which consumers were encouraged to trade up—to buy the newest tailfins and other flashy cosmetic options—as automobiles introduced model changes from year to year. Sloan is credited with introducing the idea of planned obsolescence in which products would be discarded not because of lost utility but because of lost status.

By the 1950s, virtually all national companies had accepted the concept that it was the position that a brand held in the mind of consumers more than real product superiority that would determine which firms would be successful. "If sales were not dependent either upon ever lower prices or real technological improvements but on status perceptions, artificial needs and superficial change, then focusing on the brand, rather than individual products, might prove the best way for a marketer to achieve lasting profitability. Products, after all, had life cycles and died. Brands, properly managed, could last forever."[4]

The Development of Print Media

4 **Describe the relationship between advertising and the development of print media.**

Although product availability and compelling selling messages are certainly necessary components for the growth of advertising, neither can be successful without a readily available means of reaching consumers and prospects with information concerning the quality, price, and availability of goods and services. The early history of advertising cannot be separated from the early print media that carried its messages. From our discussion, it will become obvious that the relationship between advertising and the mass media is a symbiotic one, with growing media circulations allowing advertisers to reach more and more buyers and increasing advertising dollars enabling the media to prosper in an environment largely free from government and special interest control.

THE NEWSPAPER AS AN ADVERTISING MEDIUM

siquis
Handwritten posters in sixteenth- and seventeenth-century England—forerunners of modern advertising.

Newspapers have historically been the primary medium for information and advertising. It has only been in the past century that other communication media have challenged the preeminent position of newspapers. As early as 59 B.C., the Romans posted daily government-published news sheets known as *acta diurna*, and the forerunners of modern want ads were **siquis**, notices posted by clergy seeking positions. The name comes from the Latin *si quis* ("if anyone"), which was the way the notices usually began. The name *siquis* continued for many years, although soon these notices covered a variety of subjects, including lost-and-found objects, runaway apprentices, and so on, much like modern classified advertisements.[5]

Although the Chinese probably developed some form of printing as early as the eighth century A.D., it was *Johannes Gutenberg*'s invention of movable type that brought printing to the West in 1440. Within a decade of Gutenberg's introduction of the printing press, forerunners of the newspaper in the form of pamphlets and broadsides opened the door to more formal publications. The first English newspaper, *The Oxford Gazette*, was published in 1665. The first colonial newspaper, Benjamin Harris's *Publick Occurrences*, was published in Boston in 1690 and was promptly banned by the governor after one issue. The first American newspaper to carry advertising was the *Boston Newsletter*, published in 1704. Soon newspapers were common throughout the colonies, and by 1800 every major city in the United States had several daily or weekly publications.

penny press
Forerunner of the mass newspaper in the United States; first appeared in the 1830s.

With the introduction of Richard Hoe's rotary press during the 1830s, Benjamin Day's *The New York Sun* ushered in the era of the so-called **penny press**, which provided inexpensive newspapers to the general population. For the first time, both readers and advertisers had extensive access to a mass medium. The Civil War created an unprecedented demand for current news and information, and by the 1880s more than 11,000 newspapers were being published in the United States (compared to approximately 8,000 daily and weekly newspapers today). By 1900, newspapers such as the *New York World* and the *Chicago Tribune* had circulations of more than 500,000. These high-circulation publications were supported by advertisers seeking more and more buyers for their goods. The newspapers of that era established the model for financial support from advertising that continues for the majority of media to the present day.

MAGAZINES

The earliest colonial magazines provided little promise of growing into major communication media. William Bradford published the first magazine in America in 1741. Aptly named the *American Magazine*, it lasted all of three issues. Its major competitor, Benjamin Franklin's *General Magazine* started in the same year, died a quiet death after only six issues.

Despite the barriers to financial success for magazines, a number of publications emerged during the latter part of the eighteenth century. By 1800, there were more than 100 magazines serving an educated and wealthy elite with articles and essays on matters of literary, political, or religious interest. Unlike newspapers, magazines were national or regional in scope and, therefore, poor transportation and high cost further prohibited the rapid growth of magazines. Although legislation providing low-cost mailing rates for magazines had passed in Congress as early as 1794, it was not until the Postal Act of 1879 that magazines enjoyed significant mail discounts.

Despite the hurdles for magazines, publications such as *Harper's Monthly*, *Atlantic Monthly*, and *Century* were widely read and some, such as *The Saturday Evening Post*, provided content of a more popular nature. However, the editorial and advertising foundations of the modern consumer magazines did not take shape until the latter part of the nineteenth century. Using the business plan developed by Benjamin Day and other publishers of penny newspapers and supporting a populist agenda, many magazines of the day began to address the concerns of the American family with articles on health, fashion, and food. In addition, some of the major writers of the time such as Mark Twain and Sir Arthur Conan Doyle were frequent contributors to these magazines. Unlike their newspaper counterparts, these magazines had a national audience with influence beyond the borders of a particular city.

In many respects, the magazine was a unifying means of communication and, serving as a slower version of the telegraph, gave the far-flung country a sense of common purpose after the Civil War. "The magazine was a vehicle which could present simultaneously identical facts, uniformly treated, in every locality. Men and women, North, South, East, and West, could read and judge the same materials, instead of forming their beliefs and reaching their decisions on the basis of varied accounts published in different sections and often distorted by regional prejudice."[6]

By the turn of the twentieth century, *Ladies' Home Journal* passed a milestone with a circulation of 1 million, and other major magazines such as *Munsey's* and *McClure's* had circulations of more than half a million. Many of the major publishers of the day also embarked on campaigns to address the abuses of patent medicine advertising as well as social reforms in industries such as meatpacking and industrial monopolies.

Advertising support for these publications came from manufacturers that were enjoying success with the distribution of national brands such as Quaker Oats and Uneeda Biscuit. It was very common for magazines of the time to carry 100 pages or more of advertising. For manufacturers, magazines provided the only means of reaching buyers throughout the country. Advertising was crucial to the success of most magazines; because subscription prices covered only a small portion of the costs of publishing, advertising was required to make up the revenue shortfall. During the 1920s, high-quality color advertisements were commonplace in most major publications. By 1923, when Henry Luce and Briton Hadden founded *Time*, magazines were the preeminent medium for national advertisers. They offered national circulation, both editorial and advertising credibility, color availability, and an extremely low-cost means of reaching millions of readers.

MASS PRODUCTION MATURES

By the mid-1700s, primitive forms of **mass production** were being introduced into the English textile industries. In America, the manufacture of firearms during the Revolutionary War was one of the earliest examples of production using interchangeable parts. By the end of the Civil War, American industry was rapidly adopting many of the

mass production
A manufacturing technique using specialization and interchangeable parts to achieve production efficiencies.

EXHIBIT 1.6

Outdoor advertising increased as Americans took to the road in their automobiles.

techniques of mass production as factories produced an array of goods such as textiles, furniture, and even food. For example, by the 1850s, Gail Borden was selling purified, airtight, sealed milk from his Connecticut plant.

Although the beginnings of mass production in the United States were impressive, it was the introduction of the automobile that created the foundations of American industry (see Exhibit 1.6). Innovators such as Henry Leland, who built the first Cadillac; Louis Chevrolet; Albert Champion; Walter Chrysler; and John and Horace Dodge all contributed to the growth of the automotive industry. However, it was Henry Ford and his Model T, selling for less than $600, that put a car within the reach of the ordinary family. The first Model T sold 10,000 cars in 1908; by 1913, sales passed 250,000. Ford was a visionary who saw that mass production was based on high volume, affordable price, and mass selling through advertising. Throughout the early 1900s, American industry was quick to adapt to the successful formula of Henry Ford.

The move to a manufacturing economy had dramatic effects on politics, culture, and society. The availability of goods created significant improvements in the lifestyles and standards of living of almost every American family. Virtually anyone could afford to own products that would have been available to only the wealthiest classes a few years earlier. A growing manufacturing sector required more and more consumption to keep factories humming. "To encourage such consumption, the advertising industry grew while rapid improvements in transportation, warehousing, and distribution led to giant department store chains and supermarkets. American society moved from a culture of 'Yankee thrift' to one of extravagant consumerism."[7]

"Associated Advertising Clubs of the World," 1920, Library of Congress, Prints and Photographs Division [pan 6a25847].

THE ADVERTISING AGENCY

Volney Palmer is generally credited with starting the first advertising agency in 1841. In reality, he was little more than a space broker, buying bulk newspaper space at a discount and selling it to individual advertisers at a profit. In 1869, George Rowell published *Rowell's American Newspaper Directory*, which provided newspaper circulation estimates and started the movement toward published rate cards and verified circulation. In today's fractured world of media, we are seeing a limited return to the brokerage model.

By the end of the nineteenth century, major agencies such as J. Walter Thompson, N. W. Ayer & Sons, and Batten and Company (the forerunner of BBDO) were providing creative services, media placement, and basic research as well as developing the functions of the full-service advertising agencies of the future. In 1917, the **American Association of Advertising Agencies (AAAA, 4As)** was founded with 111 charter members (see Exhibit 1.7). Today, the 4As has more than 500 member agencies that place approximately 75 percent of all advertising dollars. By the 1930s, agencies such as McCann-Erickson and J. Walter Thompson had established overseas offices, beginning the movement to global advertising.

Marion Harper, a legendary advertising innovator, founded the Interpublic Group in 1954, which sought to provide a holding company for separate agencies that could then serve competing accounts. By 1960, Interpublic not only controlled a number of agencies but also owned subsidiaries that conducted research, provided television production, and handled the public relations needs of clients. At the time, *Advertising Age* wrote that Harper's plan "may be a wholly new tactic for the agency business."[8] Certainly, Interpublic represented the first formal move to integrated marketing by a major advertising company. We devote Chapter 5 to the role of the contemporary advertising agency.

America Enters the Twentieth Century

The changes in American industry, advertising, and society during the nineteenth century were remarkable by any standard. In that short 100 years, the United States experienced the movement to urbanization, the abolition of the blight of slavery, railroads and instantaneous communication spanning the continent, and its emergence as a world power. However, as impressive as these changes were, they were only a harbinger of greater developments to come. In 1900, 60 percent of Americans resided on farms, including 2,000 within New York City. In 1895, the city had perhaps 300 automobiles—a figure that grew to 78,000 by 1905.[9] Neither American society nor business would ever be the same.

However, all the changes during the period were not positive. In the decades after the Civil War, a business atmosphere emerged that reflected laissez-faire policies in the extreme. The administration of Ulysses S. Grant (1869–1877) is still considered one of the most corrupt in American history. By the dawn of the twentieth century, the excesses of big business and the advertising that contributed to the environment of

EXHIBIT 1.7

Advertising clubs flourished as the profession matured.

5 **Describe the origins of advertising agencies and professionalism.**

American Association of Advertising Agencies (AAAA, 4As)
The national organization of advertising agencies.

6 **Identify two legislative acts that significantly affected advertising.**

immorality reached a stage where both the public and Congress demanded stricter regulation of advertising and other business practices.

THE PURE FOOD AND DRUG ACT (1906)

Pure Food and Drug Act
Passed in 1906 by legislation, it was one of the earliest attempts by the federal government to protect consumers.

Concerns about public safety in the food supply date to colonial times. However, it wasn't until after the Civil War that serious efforts were mounted for national legislation to protect consumers. As Americans moved from farms to cities, for the first time a majority of people were dependent on others for their food. Although mass production was bringing a host of economically priced products to American consumers, many food and drug products were notably lacking in purity and often placed the health of consumers in jeopardy.

Furthermore, the advertising claims for these products were often outrageous. A number of media had taken up the challenge of exposing the problem. Some, such as the *New York Herald Tribune* and the *Ladies' Home Journal*, restricted or completely banned medical advertising (see Exhibit 1.8). The primary catalyst for reform is often credited to *Colliers* magazine, which in 1905 published a 10-part investigative report of the patent medicine industry entitled "The Great American Fraud." Industry leaders such as H. J. Heinz who made food safety a primary attribute of all his products joined these media efforts. Heinz was among the first to sell products in clear glass jars to demonstrate to buyers that they were buying untainted food. By 1906, public opinion had reached the point that Congress moved to protect public health with passage of the **Pure Food and Drug Act**. President Theodore Roosevelt signed the act into law on June 30, 1906.

Although the 1906 act did much to protect the public health, it failed to address a number of important issues. For example, product content information on labels had to be truthful, but there was no requirement that such labels had to be used. In addition, false claims for patent medicines were outlawed, but enforcement required the government to prove that the manufacturer intended to swindle buyers. In other words, if defendants asserted that they believed the claims, no matter how absurd, there was little the government could do. In addition, apathetic enforcement and minor penalties for breach of Food and Drug Administration (FDA) regulations did little to control the problem. For example, Robert Harper, maker of a headache remedy called Cuforhedak BraneFude, was the first person cited under the act for instilling his product with caffeine and abundant amounts of alcohol—hardly a wise headache remedy. After a 16-day trial, he was found guilty and fined $700 despite having made some $2 million on the sale of the product.[10]

The modern era of food and drug enforcement began with passage of the Federal Food, Drug, and Cosmetic Act, which was signed by President Franklin Roosevelt on June 25, 1938. Among the several provisions of the 1938 act, drug manufacturers were required to provide scientific proof of new product safety and proof of fraud was no longer required to stop false claims for drugs. Since that time, a number of amendments including those dealing with pesticide, food additives, and color additives have continued to strengthen the role of the FDA in production and labeling of food, drug, and cosmetic products.[11]

THE FEDERAL TRADE COMMISSION ACT (1914)

Federal Trade Commission (FTC)
The agency of the federal government empowered to prevent unfair competition and to prevent fraudulent, misleading, or deceptive advertising in interstate commerce.

The original mandate of the **Federal Trade Commission (FTC)** was to protect one business owner from the unscrupulous practices of another. In 1914, when the Federal Trade Commission Act was passed, Congress and the public were increasingly alarmed over antitrust violations by big business. It was clear by the early 1900s that the antitrust actions of John D. Rockefeller and other business titans would soon drive their smaller competitors into bankruptcy and create monopolies in vital industries such as oil and steel. Basically, the law said that unfair business-to-business practices were now illegal and would no longer be tolerated.

In 1938, the Wheeler-Lea Act extended the FTC's original mission to offer protection to consumers as well as businesses. By combining both business and consumer protection activities, the FTC "seeks to ensure that the nation's markets function

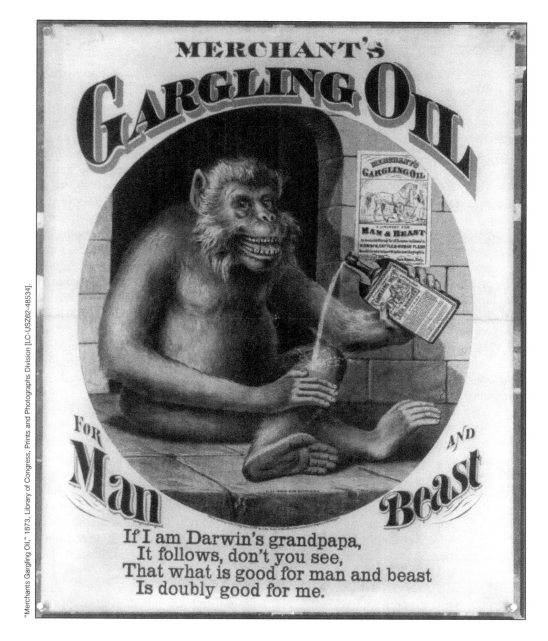

EXHIBIT 1.8

Patent medicine ads often contained questionable claims but the ads subsidized the growth of mass media in America.

competitively, and are vigorous, efficient, and free of undue restrictions. The Commission also works to enhance the smooth operation of the marketplace by eliminating acts or practices that are unfair or deceptive."[12] Today, the FTC is the primary federal enforcement agency to ensure that advertising claims and sales practices meet reasonable standards for honesty and truthfulness.

In Chapter 24, we discuss in detail not only the role of the FTC but also other regulatory and legal bodies that are concerned with truthful advertising. In addition, the advertising industry's self-regulatory mechanisms are examined and a number of criticisms of advertising's social effects are addressed.

Advertising Comes of Age

By 1900, both the public and legislators were increasingly concerned about unscrupulous businesses and the deceptive advertising they used to take advantage of consumers. It was during this time that a number of advertising executives recognized the need for the industry to do more to ensure honest advertising and to regain consumer confidence lost as a result of decades of fraudulent claims and inferior products. They gathered with like-minded peers in their communities to form advertising clubs to support truthful advertising.

These clubs subsequently became the Associated Advertising Clubs of the World (now the American Advertising Federation). In 1911, they launched a campaign to promote truth in advertising. In 1916, they formed vigilance committees that developed into today's **Council of Better Business Bureaus**, which continues to deal with many problems of unfair and deceptive business practices. In 1971, the bureaus became part of the National Advertising Review Council, an all-industry effort at curbing misleading advertising. The main constituency of the American Advertising Federation continues to be the local advertising clubs. On its board are officers of the other advertising associations.

In 1910, the Association of National Advertising Managers came into being. It is now known as the Association of National Advertisers (ANA) and has about 500 members, including most major national advertisers. Its purpose is to improve the effectiveness of advertising from the viewpoint of the advertiser. In 1917, the American Association of Advertising Agencies was formed to improve the effectiveness of advertising and the advertising agency operation. More than 75 percent of all national advertising is currently placed by its members, both large and small.

In 1911, *Printers' Ink*, the leading advertising trade paper of the day, prepared a model statute for state regulation of advertising, designed to "punish untrue, deceptive or misleading advertising." The ***Printers' Ink* Model Statute** has been adopted in its original or modified form by a number of states, where it is still operative.

Until 1914, many publishers routinely exaggerated their circulation claims. In the absence of reliable figures, advertisers had no way of verifying what they got for their money. However, in that year, a group of advertisers, agencies, and publishers established an independent auditing organization, the **Audit Bureau of Circulations (ABC)**, which conducts its own audits and issues its own circulation reports. Most major publications belong to the ABC, and an ABC circulation statement is highly regarded in media circles. As advertising became internationalized, similar auditing organizations began operating throughout the world. In June 1916, President Woodrow Wilson, addressing the Associated Advertising Clubs of the World convention in Philadelphia, was the first president to give public recognition to the importance of advertising. Advertising had come of age!

ADVERTISING IN WORLD WAR I

When the United States entered World War I, advertising was called on to support the war effort across a broad spectrum of initiatives. Advertising agencies turned from selling consumer goods to arousing patriotic sentiment, selling government bonds, encouraging conservation, and promoting a number of other war-related activities. Recruitment efforts were enhanced in 1917 with James Montgomery Flagg's poster featuring Uncle Sam (see Exhibit 1.9). The ad created an icon of Uncle Sam and was later adapted for recruitment efforts in World War II. One of the largest agencies of the era, N. W. Ayer & Sons, prepared and placed advertisements for the first three Liberty Loan drives and donated much of its commission to the effort.[13] The success of these initiatives demonstrated that advertising could be used effectively to sell products or as an instrument of direct social action. By the end of the war, these efforts by individual agencies were coordinated by the Division of Advertising of the Committee of Public Information, a World War I government propaganda office.

THE 1920S

Throughout most of the 1920s, America experienced enormous economic growth fueled by postwar euphoria and unprecedented business expansion. When World War I drew to an end, manufacturers of war goods turned to the task of meeting unfulfilled

---

Council of Better Business Bureaus
National organization that coordinates a number of local and national initiatives to protect consumers.

Printers' Ink Model Statute
The act directed at fraudulent advertising, prepared and sponsored by *Printers' Ink*, which was the pioneer advertising magazine.

Audit Bureau of Circulations (ABC)
The organization sponsored by publishers, agencies, and advertisers for securing accurate circulation statements.

7 **Discuss the role of advertising during World War I and World War II.**

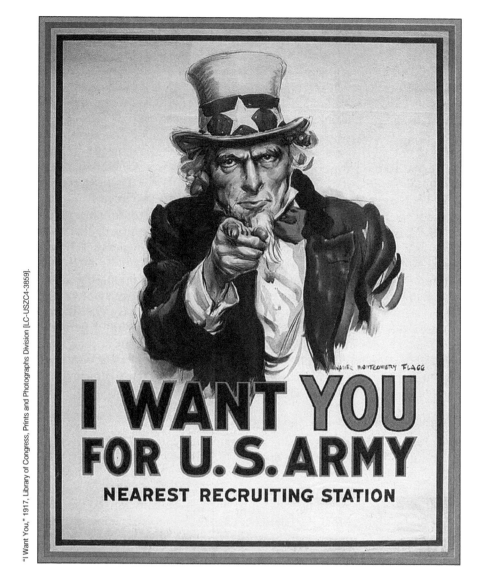

"I Want You," 1917, Library of Congress, Prints and Photographs Division [LC-USZC4-3859].

EXHIBIT 1.9

Uncle Sam became an icon because of the popularity of this 1917 recruitment poster.

consumer demand built up during the war. A newly created highway system fueled the need for personal automobiles, and demand for commercial trucks skyrocketed as overland transportation became an effective means of product distribution. Firestone spent $2 million promoting the generic "Ship by Truck" campaign. With truck manufacturers profiting by the good roads that had been built, production jumped from 92,000 trucks in 1916 to 322,000 in 1920. Door-to-door delivery from manufacturer to retailer spurred the growth of chain stores, which led, in turn, to supermarkets and self-service stores. Transportation was only one of the multitude of product categories that boomed during this period. New products appeared in profusion: electric refrigerators, electric washing machines, electric shavers, and—most incredible of all—the radio. Installment selling made tangible goods available to all. And all the products needed advertising. Unfortunately, the good times of the 1920s would come to a sudden halt with the devastation of a worldwide depression.

Radio was among the very few industries that actually grew during the Depression. Guglielmo Marconi invented radio in 1895; it was the first practical system of wireless communication. In the early years, radio was viewed as a means of maritime communication using Morse code and, with the first voice transmission in 1906, as a diversion for hobbyists. Prior to 1920, few investors saw any commercial potential for the medium.

KDKA, the first commercial station, was established in Pittsburgh by Westinghouse Corporation to provide programming to buyers of its radio sets.

The modern era of radio can be traced to the broadcast of the Harding-Cox presidential election results in 1920. Soon radio was broadcasting sporting events, such as the 1921 heavyweight title fight between Jack Dempsey and Georges Carpentier, and various local entertainment shows.[14] By 1922, there were more than 500 licensed stations on the air, but fewer than 2 million homes owned radio sets and the medium was still in the novelty stage. By the mid-1920s, the emphasis was shifting away from local radio to networks where several stations could simultaneously broadcast programs. In 1926, the Radio Corporation of America (RCA) established two NBC networks with 24 stations, and a year later, William Paley founded CBS with 16 stations.

Unlike most advertising media of the period, radio advertising revenues demonstrated healthy growth rising from $18.7 million in 1929 to more than $80 million by 1939.[15] Likewise, as the cost of radio sets became more affordable and listeners sought radio's free entertainment in a period of economic hardship, set ownership increased from 12 million households in 1930 to more than 28 million in 1939.[16] Regular programming featuring news, drama, and comedy was becoming standard at both the local and network levels. Radio came under government regulation with formation of the Federal Communication Commission (FCC) in 1934. By 1939, there were 1,464 stations in the United States; and by the end of World War II, 95 percent of households owned at least one radio.[17] Today, Americans average more than five radio sets per household and it is difficult to find an automobile or workplace without a radio. From its noncommercial beginnings, radio advertisers now spend approximately $18 billion annually.

THE GREAT DEPRESSION OF THE 1930S

The rapid growth of advertising was temporarily slowed by the Great Depression, beginning with the stock market crash of 1929 and continuing through much of the 1930s. The crash had a shattering effect on our entire economy: Millions of people were thrown out of work; business failures were widespread; banks were closing all over the country. Breadlines and high unemployment eventually moved the government to establish the Works Progress Administration (WPA) to put people to work on public service projects. However, even this extraordinary step offered only partial relief to a country in crisis.

Some of the major causes for the Depression, that is, excess industrial capacity, heavy consumer debt, and declining price levels, combined to discourage consumer spending and manufacturing output with a resulting negative impact on advertising. With few exceptions, the Depression was a time of catastrophe for advertising, businesses, and society in general. With the start of World War II, the economy recovered. However, wartime restrictions on consumer goods would not permit a rejuvenation of advertising until after the war.

ADVERTISING DURING WORLD WAR II

World War II saw a replay of the practices of World War I, only played on a larger scale and with even greater homeland sacrifices. As consumer goods turned to war goods, virtually all civilian material was rationed or in short supply. Although there were limited sales of household goods, many companies continued to advertise to keep their brand names before the public as they looked to a future of peacetime normalcy. Most advertising, even messages promoting specific brands, was created to encourage Americans to cooperate in the war effort through conservation and volunteerism.

However, the government needed the public to do more than simply adhere to the letter of rationing regulations. "Food, clothing and a variety of essential items were to be used wisely. Avoiding purchasing items through a black market and acting in the interest of the greater community were strongly encouraged, both to hold down inflation

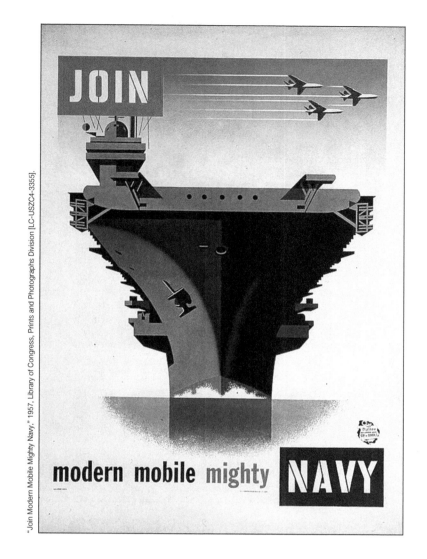

"Join Modern Mobile Mighty Navy," 1957, Library of Congress, Prints and Photographs Division [LC-USZC4-3355].

EXHIBIT 1.11

Although this 1957 ad isn't promoting "service" in the traditional sense, how does it compare to today's armed forces recruitment efforts?

Advertising and the Twenty-First Century

The 2000s have been marked by two significant developments in marketing and advertising:

1. *Defining and using new technology to reach prospects.* Advertisers are working in a marketing environment vastly different from that of only a decade ago. Technology has created a consumer empowered with interactive, two-way communication devices that allow them to determine when, where, and if they will invite advertisers to deliver their messages. This era of **permission marketing** requires companies to rewrite the old rules of marketing and fundamentally redefine exactly what constitutes advertising.

    One example of this new media landscape is so-called "third screen," or mobile advertising. Many marketers view the cell phone as a unique means of connecting with niche prospects through text messaging, music, and videos. Although mobile marketing is still evolving, a number of major advertisers are already finding success with the opportunities afforded by techniques to involve mobile audiences with games, music downloads, free ring tones, and a variety of other promotions.[23] Although the specific promotions demonstrate a wide variety of uses, marketers realize that audience involvement is the key to their success so the promotions

9 **Describe the factors influencing contemporary advertising.**

permission marketing
Asking consumers for permission or to "opt in" before sending them advertising and other forms of marketing communication.

EXHIBIT 1.12

How does this 1930s ad compare to the ads and promotional techniques used by today's aquariums and zoos to attract patrons?

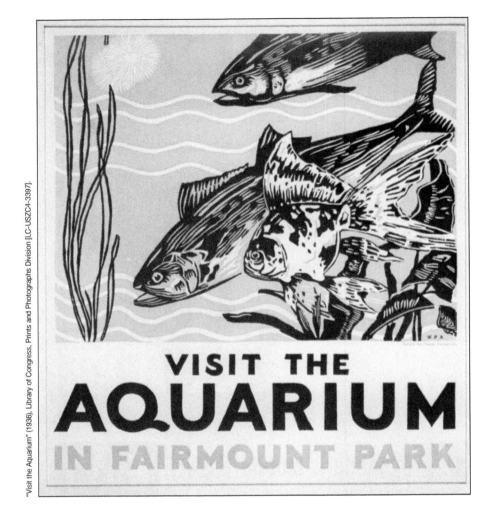

"Visit the Aquarium" (1936), Library of Congress, Prints and Photographs Division [LC-USZC4-3397].

function as participatory communications—that is, talking *with* consumers rather than talking *at* them.

2. *Measuring the value of investing in various communication channels as it relates to the changes in how we reach prospects.* Since the beginning of fragmentation in the late 1980s, measuring the return on investment (ROI) of advertising dollars has been a major problem. The prevailing media measurement metric during the twentieth century was audience delivery—that is, in broadcast ratings and print media circulation. Advertisers knew that these metrics were rough estimates at best. However, given the limited media outlets during most of that period, audience delivery seemed the best and most economical means of comparing competing advertising vehicles.

   As we entered the twenty-first century, advertisers knew that a system that worked marginally during a period of limited media was woefully inadequate in this era of expanded communication opportunities. "Continued media fragmentation and consumers' increased control over how, when and where they receive ad messages caused advertisers to look for new avenues. Strategies included product integration . . . viral marketing and contextual Internet advertising, out-of-home media, and co-branding and branded entertainment."[24] For example, today's large-scale aquariums and tourist venues must use a complex mix of promotional tools to attract audiences instead of simply relying on print ads like the one in Exhibit 1.12.

ASSESSING ROI AND VALUE

The transition from mass to class media saw huge increases in costs to reach customers. For example, in 1994, it cost $7.64 to reach 1,000 households with a prime-time television commercial. In 2008, it cost $26.22 to reach an equivalent number of households.[25] During the past decade, the television audience has declined approximately 2 percent annually. And computer usage and broadband household penetration has increased dramatically since 2000. However, new media audiences tend to be individualized and expensive to reach. Consequently, audience measures based on media delivery (as contrasted to some minimum communication) make these new communication vehicles appear prohibitively expensive compared to traditional "old media."

Perhaps the most apparent aspect of the transition from old to new media will be a change in advertisers' mind-set concerning audience measurement. It is a given that reaching individual consumers will continue to be more expensive. However, although they are resigned to accepting a higher expense ratio, advertisers are demanding that media offer evidence concerning audience engagement and outcomes of advertising. Simply counting eyeballs tuned to a network program or purchasers of a magazine or newspaper is no longer adequate to prove the value and efficiency of a company's advertising investment. A number of companies are developing media research models to measure audience involvement, attention, and/or media loyalty as alternatives to audience delivery.

CONTENT DELIVERY

Communication media are in a period of rapid transition. However, although the old media are clearly in decline, a fully implemented new order is some years off. Regardless of what the future holds, both advertisers and media know that content is king. As one media executive pointed out, "The key for us is to be able to come up with that unique, signature, compelling content for the Internet, the way television has been able to do over the years."[26] Bob Garfield, *Advertising Age* columnist, has coined the term "The Chaos Scenario" to refer to the current period of media transition. It will be interesting in coming years to see if media, advertising agencies, and clients can bring order to this chaos.

At one time, most observers viewed media consolidation and content convergence as a movement that would typify the current century. The proponents of convergence predicted great advantages for huge companies blending technologies such as television, cable, and the computer to create Internet interactivity with the technical speed of cable and the sight, sound, and motion of television. According to its proponents, convergence was going to offer advertisers the ability to reach audiences on a one-to-one basis with individualized commercial messages tailored specifically for their needs.

In recent years, many of the mega media companies are finding that some of the benefits of these consolidations were more illusion than reality. Clearly, the consolidation of media is a reality. During the past 20 years, fostered by liberalized laws and regulations that allow almost unlimited ownership of broadcast stations, more and more media are owned by fewer and fewer corporations. Companies such as General Electric (NBC, Telemundo, Universal Pictures, and approximately 30 television stations), Disney (ESPN cable networks, online services and ESPN *The Magazine*, ABC, Disney Channel), and Time Warner (AOL, CNN, local cable systems, and more than 150 magazines) increasingly brought numerous media outlets under their control. However, many of the optimistic predictions of greater profitability and efficiencies of cross-media advertising have not come to fruition or have not created profit centers for the parent companies. In many cases, overlapping media ownership has created competitive problems rather than cooperation among units.

There will be no return to a model of media ownership characterized by relatively small companies, each owning a few newspapers, magazines, or broadcast stations. However, we are seeing a recognition that media companies may be best served by concentrating in specific areas of expertise rather than trying to manage communication outlets with little in common in terms of audiences, content, or advertising. For example, Time Warner has begun to view each of its units (e.g., the cable channels TNT and TBS; AOL; and its magazine group, which includes *Time* and *Sports Illustrated*) as separate profit centers rather than emphasizing corporate-wide synergy. Other media conglomerates also are rumored to be exploring various types of unit independence or spin-offs.

BRANDING

Another aspect of advertising in the twenty-first century includes a return to strong branding, with companies searching for means to differentiate their products, and a move away from price competition and generic selling. Products that can successfully build their brand images will enjoy the luxury of fewer price-based promotions. With consumers increasingly in control of the communication channel, companies will find that strong brands are more important than ever. After all, we don't invite strangers into our house, and likewise, unknown brands will find it difficult to get an invitation in a consumer-controlled environment. It will be harder for companies to develop new markets based on the sheer weight of advertising, and we will probably see more brand extensions in the future aimed at taking advantage of established brand names. However, smaller companies with superior products may find that customized communication may make entry to the market possible at a lower cost than they might pay using traditional mass-media outlets.

GLOBALIZATION AND DIVERSITY

Finally, marketing in this century will involve globalization and diversity. One only has to look at the population projections for Latin America, the Far East, and Africa to see the potential for sales of virtually any goods but particularly consumer products. The smallest increase in the market share of Coca-Cola, Tide detergent, Huggies diapers, Gerber Baby Food, or Charmin toilet tissue in India or China would create a profit windfall for these brands.

Understanding the language, culture, economy, and political environment of countries throughout the world is already a prerequisite for most marketing executives. It will become even more important as new areas of the globe are opened to foreign investment. Multinational marketers will find that a locally oriented strategy for global marketing is essential. Corporations such as Coca-Cola, Sony, Ford, and Procter & Gamble will continue to increase their expansion into every part of the world. However, global strategies will increasingly be geared to each country or region.

An advertiser does not have to go abroad to see the necessity for marketing plans that consider a diversified marketplace. Marketing executives and advertisers must realize that in our own country, Hispanic, Asian American, and African American consumers are part of the fabric of our society, and they must be reached through messages that are sensitive to their needs. This sensitivity means supporting minority media owners with advertising dollars; hiring a diverse workforce in the advertising industry; creating advertising and commercials that fairly reflect the various ethnic and cultural groups within this country; and, when appropriate, developing products specifically for these markets. In Chapter 23, we discuss the globalization of advertising as well as the need for greater sensitivity to the issue of diversity in domestic advertising.

SUMMARY

If the study of advertising history tells us anything, it is that change is the norm. Every period of advertising has seen remarkable changes in the structure of the industry, whether in media, creative, or account planning. In addition, the public perception of advertising changes from one generation to the next resulting in differences in its effectiveness and importance within the marketing communication matrix. As we write this text, advertising continues to demonstrate its affinity for change. For example, the development of e-commerce, or Internet selling, has had major effects on marketing, promotion, and selling. As of 2010, Internet advertising revenues are expected to exceed $29 billion, a level that now surpasses radio and consumer magazine advertising. Of more far-reaching significance is the development of new technology that allows advertisers to reach prospects—and prospects to avoid advertisers—on a more personal basis, which is having a major impact on the way we communicate with consumers. We are beginning to look at consumers as individuals as opposed to large groups of buyers.

As we conclude this opening chapter, we should make three points about advertising, past and future:

① Although modern advertising with its sophisticated, segmented media and billion-dollar expenditures is primarily a creation of the past 100 years, the idea of using persuasive communication to sell goods and services is as old as trade and commerce.

② Advertising cannot be studied in the abstract. Virtually any development in advertising is the result of some advance in technology (e.g., printing presses, radio, television, the Internet), research (advances in psychology, sociology, and anthropology to better understand human behavior), or society as a whole (the acceptance of capitalism and consumerism by the majority of the American population). In the United States, advertising prospered because of a unique situation that included a democratic government, unfettered business institutions, sophisticated technology, an inexpensive media, and a receptive

culture. The move from an agrarian to an industrialized society brought with it unprecedented specialization. However, the efficiencies of mass production and specialization could only be achieved with effective use of mass advertising and promotion.

③ It is obvious that advertising and promotion are no longer confined to the traditional media that dominated the twentieth century. As we have noted, persuasive communication will take numerous forms in coming decades. Advertising and brand identification are ubiquitous. Commercial messages, to the chagrin of many critics, can be found in venues as diverse as NASCAR races; product placement is found in movies, television shows, and video games; and promotions abound on a multitude of caps and T-shirts. As we will see in our later discussions, the definition and implementation of traditional advertising have undergone and will continue to undergo dramatic changes in coming years.

Although we can't be certain about the specific advertising trends of the coming decades, we can predict that the twenty-first century will experience fundamental changes in marketing and mass communication not seen since the advent of high-speed presses and the introduction of broadcasting. As audiences take greater control of communication channels, advertisers will need to view themselves as invited guests rather than opportunistic intruders. Likewise, advertisers will have to adapt creative messages to the specific needs of smaller groups of homogeneous consumers. The Internet will be only one piece of the marketing puzzle. Marketers will have to coordinate a host of available communication and distribution channels to reach evermore demanding buyers.

REVIEW

1. What factors contributed to the rise of modern advertising during the past 100 years?
2. Advertising can rarely be successful in an economy in which demand is greater than supply. Why?
3. Discuss the importance of the introduction of national brands to the growth of advertising.
4. How has the so-called "interactive era" brought fundamental changes to the advertiser/customer relationship?
5. Discuss some of the factors that caused the emphasis on creativity in advertising during the early 1900s.

6. Briefly trace the development of the advertising agency from Volney Palmer to the early 1900s.
7. What societal changes led to passage of the Federal Trade Commission Act and the Pure Food and Drug Act?
8. Discuss the role of the War Advertising Council.
9. How did the Great Depression support the growth of radio?
10. How has new technology contributed to more personal relationships between advertisers and customers?

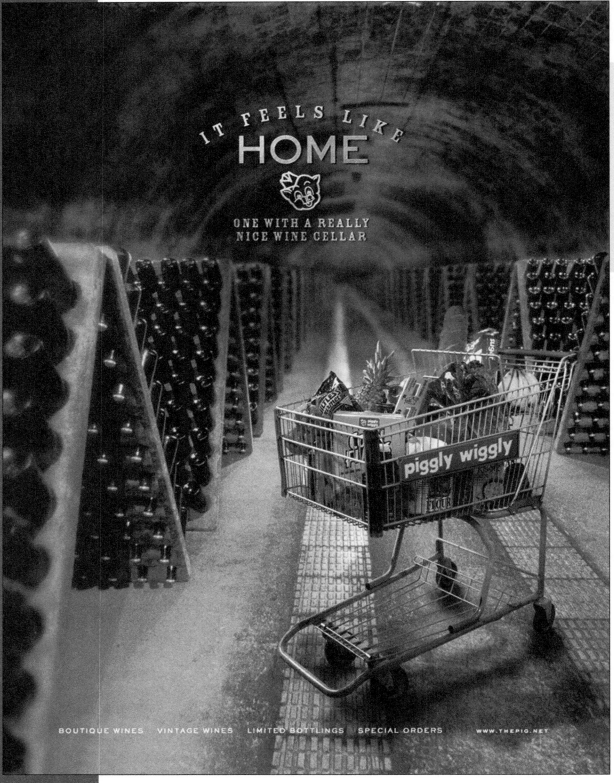

IT FEELS LIKE

HOME

ONE WITH A REALLY
NICE WINE CELLAR

BOUTIQUE WINES   VINTAGE WINES   LIMITED BOTTLINGS   SPECIAL ORDERS   WWW.THEPIG.NET

Courtesy of Rawle-Murdy and Piggly Wiggly Carolinas.

Roles of Advertising

ADVERTISING can take many forms and wear many hats but, at its core, advertising plays an integral role in the promotion and dissemination of brands. ▶

CHAPTER LEARNING OBJECTIVES

1. Identify advertising and marketing goals and objectives.

2. Explain the importance of advertising and return-on-investment (ROI).

3. Describe the four primary types of marketing communication.

4. Explain the institutional roles of advertising for consumers, business, and society.

5. Identify the primary components and considerations of advertising strategy.

6. List four types of advertising directed toward consumers.

7. List the types of advertising directed toward businesses and professionals.

As we discussed in the previous chapter, significant changes in advertising have accelerated in the past two decades. Fueled by new technology and demands from clients for more accountability for their advertising expenditures, media companies and advertising agencies have seen a number of modifications in the practice and execution of advertising. Regardless of these revolutionary changes, advertising's primary role continues to be to convey truthful information about products, services, or ideas to a targeted audience. For example, the role of this creative ad is to convey that Piggly Wiggly markets offer an extensive wine selection.

There is no question that new consumer-controlled communication technology will force advertisers to alter both their methods of reaching consumers and their messages. However, the basic communication goals of good advertising will remain constant whether they are used by companies to reach customers around the world or around the corner. This chapter discusses the basic goals of advertising and its role in contributing to the bottom line through integrated marketing and other considerations. Because advertising does not operate in a vacuum, its economic and social roles are reviewed, as well as the different types of advertising, including national and local advertising, trade advertising, and nonproduct advertising.

Advertising and the Changing Communication Environment

Reaching elusive consumers with meaningful messages at a reasonable cost has become more and more difficult. Advertisers are in a period in which some of the old rules don't work and they have yet to find new ones that guarantee success. "If marketers learned one key point . . . it is that reaching consumers by traditional means—TV, magazines, and newspapers—is getting harder. . . . They are seeking information from a broader range of sources than ever and, in the process, filtering out messages that don't resonate or speak to their specific needs."[1]

convergence
The blending of various facets of marketing functions and communication technology to create more efficient and expanded synergies.

Finding a cost-efficient plan for reaching increasingly in-control and demanding consumers is the major challenge of contemporary advertising. As we discuss the functions and procedures of advertising, we will see that the forces of convergence and consolidation dominate virtually every advertising, promotion, and marketing decision. The term **convergence** means coming together or intersecting different components of some related system. In mass communication, the term has come to refer to three distinct though related areas:

1. *Technological convergence.* For example, listening to radio programs over your home computer or watching movies through a DVD player connected to your television set.

2. *Business convergence.* Usually referred to as consolidation, one of the dominant trends of modern business is the merging of company after company, including, as we discuss later in the text, advertising agencies and media companies.

3. *Content convergence.* Content is the primary expense of most communication companies. Whether it is a network showing reruns to amortize its investment in its programs or an advertising agency using clip art or sharing footage with its global partners, companies try to stretch the use of communication content.

As you can see, these forms of convergence contribute to the multitude of ways today's consumers receive advertising messages. As a result, advertisers find they have a dual problem: On the one hand, they must choose a media plan from an ever-expanding number of options, and on the other hand, they must develop advertising messages that consumers will invite to share their time. "Advertising was once a simple mass-market media buy; now it is a dialog between a seller of soup, sneakers or cell phones and a particular media outlet's narrow audience. That media outlet is just as likely to be a computer screen or a mobile device as a television set . . ."[2]

Some have coined this new relationship between advertisers and consumers as *citizen media* implying more control by users of communication rather than by providers.[3] Another step in citizen media is participatory media in which the audience takes an active role in creating media content—also referred to as user-generated content. So-called blogs, which began as informal communication links among individuals with similar interests, have become an important part of the marketing plans of companies such as General Motors and Procter & Gamble (P&G). Commercially sponsored blogs not only provide an exciting means of reaching fragmented audience segments but also provide companies with information and research about their brands at virtually no cost.

Since the 1970s, futurists have predicted a communication revolution. But in the future, we might look back on 2000 as the benchmark when the revolution first became commercially viable. In 1985, cell phones cost approximately $1,000 and calls cost 45 cents per minute. The worldwide universe of cell phones was perhaps 200,000, including military and public safety officials. By 2009, it was projected that some 2.6 billion cell phones were in use, serving a third of the world's population.[4] The term *phone* is already becoming a misnomer as mobile technology is used for everything from music downloads to text messaging to program viewing—with much of the content sponsored by one or more brands.

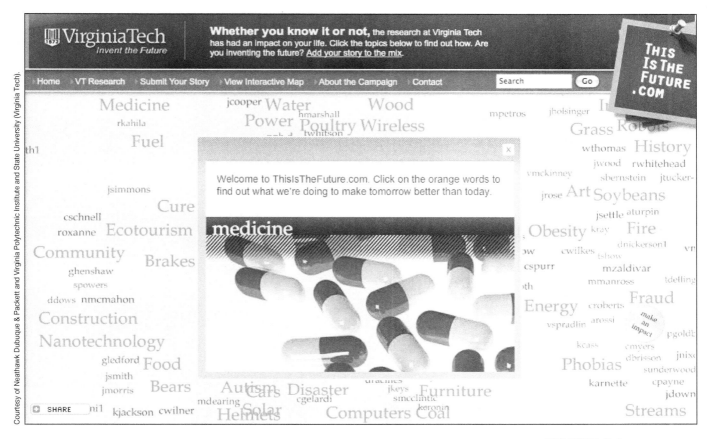

Courtesy of Neathawk Dubuque & Packett and Virginia Polytechnic Institute and State University (Virginia Tech).

EXHIBIT 2.1

Advertising drove citizens to enter their personal stories on this interactive microsite.

Advertisers vote with their dollars, and no better evidence exists of the importance of new technology than the shift in financial support by major advertisers away from traditional media to new and, especially, interactive technology. For example, a recent campaign used traditional, viral, and web media to promote a leading university's research activities (see Exhibit 2.1). Virginia Tech hired ad agency Neathawk Dubuque & Packet (ND&P) to raise awareness of how the university's research benefits Virginians. Direct mail, magazine ads, and banner ads drove citizens to an interactive microsite where they could enter their names and personal stories. So far the campaign has received much media attention and hundreds of personal stories have been entered on the site. ND&P's strategy exemplifies how interactive media has become a central component of many of today's advertising campaigns.

ADVERTISING AS A COMMUNICATION TOOL

With the significant changes in advertising practice, it is tempting to lose sight of the fact that advertising remains a communication tool. Regardless of the specific advertising plan or goals of a particular strategy, successful advertising depends on the use of effective communication (see Exhibit 2.2). Advertising objectives must be viewed from a *communication* perspective; advertising rarely can accomplish tasks that are not related to communication.

The fundamental principle of good advertising is that it must be built around the overall marketing plan and execute the communication elements of a more far-reaching marketing program. For example, increasing a dealer network by 10 percent is a marketing goal; increasing awareness of a brand by 25 percent among retailers is an advertising goal that we would expect to contribute to achieving a growth in dealers of 10 percent.

Because advertising objectives must complement the marketing plan, let's look at the primary factors in a typical marketing plan. As we do, consider those aspects that

1 Identify advertising and marketing goals and objectives.

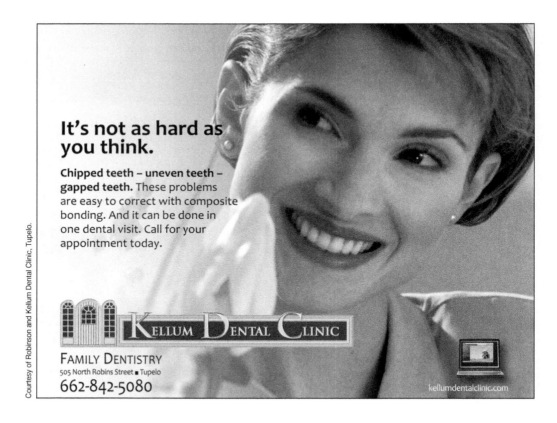

Courtesy of Robinson and Kellum Dental Clinic, Tupelo.

can be addressed by marketing communication and in what ways communication could complement the implementation of the plan:[5]

1. *Overall goal(s) of the plan.* Marketing goals are often expressed in financial terms such as expected sales revenues at the end of the first year or percentage increases over previous years.

2. *Marketing objectives.* Marketing objectives should be clearly stated and measurable. For example, we may want to show a significant increase in market share relative to specific competitors over a set time period.

3. *Marketing strategy.* The strategy outlines the general course of action to achieve our goals and objectives. These will include what each element of the marketing function (e.g., advertising and promotion, distribution, pricing) should contribute to achieving our goals.

4. *Situational analysis.* Situational analysis includes a statement of the product benefits as well as data concerning sales trends, the competitive environment, and industry forecasts.

5. *Problems and opportunities.* At this point, we outline the major current and anticipated future problems and opportunities facing the brand.

6. *Financial plan.* The financial plan is an outline of the expected profit or loss over various time frames. Projections are made concerning needed investments in various marketing functions before a product is profitable.

7. *Research.* Marketing planning is based on both primary and secondary research. This section outlines the data needed, where they can be obtained, their cost, and the time frame for availability.

With the marketing plan providing our blueprint, we begin to plan the advertising implementation needed to accomplish the communication tasks specific to brand and company objectives.

1. *Prospect identification.* The guiding principle of the advertising plan is the detailed identification of a company's prime prospects including who they are (e.g., basic demographic data) and the social, cultural, and psychological characteristics that predict purchase behavior.

2. *Consumer motivations.* Accurate insights about our core consumers will greatly enhance our chances of success as we move to determine the role that advertising can play in channeling consumer needs, wants, and aspirations into purchases of general product categories and, more important, specific brands of goods and services.

3. *Advertising execution.* Once we identify the role of advertising within the context of the marketing program, our next step is to develop overall creative themes and media plans that effectively deliver messages to set our brand apart from its competitors, recognizing that advertising does not communicate in a void; rather, it benefits from a synergism between message and medium.

4. *The advertising budget and allocation.* The share of the marketing program designated for advertising will be included in the marketing plan. However, allocation of the advertising budget to specific media, creative executions, and production will normally be a part of the advertising plan.

In the remainder of this chapter, we examine the many aspects of advertising and the planning and executions that result in success or failure for the companies that advertise.

Advertising and Profitability

The critical evaluation for any business activity is its contribution to profitability. The value of a particular marketing function is often expressed as **return-on-investment (ROI)**, that is, how many dollars are produced for every dollar spent. A number of research studies indicate a strong correlation among brand awareness, market share, and profits (see Exhibit 2.3). A leading marketing executive summed up the importance of advertising's role in profitability, "... [W]e believe that brand building is about sustaining price premiums. ... [O]ur experience is that advertising influences price more than sales. And yield improvements go straight to the bottom line."[6]

Reckett Benckiser, a packaged goods conglomerate with brands such as Woolite, Lysol, and Airwick, strongly believes in the ability of advertising to help build its brands and add to its bottom line. Reckett uses advertising to build brand equity even during economic hard times. During the recent recession, the company posted an 8 percent overall sales increase backed by a 9 percent boost in global advertising spending.[7] While some competitors are decreasing ad spending, Reckett believes it will be in an even stronger position during economic good times.

With this emphasis on brand building, clients are increasingly demanding that media and advertising agencies measure advertising success on the basis of effective communication rather than on audience exposure (i.e., circulation or ratings). Recently,

2 **Explain the importance of advertising and return-on-investment (ROI).**

return-on-investment (ROI)
One measure of the efficiency of a company is the rate of return (profits) achieved by a certain level of investment on various business functions including advertising.

EXHIBIT 2.3

How brand awareness aids profitability (the sequence of events).

Used with permission. *Cahners Advertising Research Report*, No. 2000.6, p. 6.

Previous Level of Brand Awareness	+	Changes in Brand Awareness	=	Current Level of Brand Awareness		Conversion Rate of Brand Awareness into Market Share	=	Level of Achieved Market Share	which strongly influences	ROI or Profitability
This is the net result of all past successes and failures.		Brand awareness decreases by the normal decay process, and increases by (a) doing an above-par volume of Marketing Expenditures/Sales (b) having a higher-than-average level of Advertising/Sales (c) being successful (recently) in converting previous brand awareness into market share.				The conversion rate is aided by (a) having available or developing new production capacity, and (b) advertising (and other actions) that establish product or company differentiation.				

advertising industry trade groups have sought to replace the concept of audience delivery with one that measures audience engagement. Although there is general agreement on the need to estimate audience involvement, there is a lack of consensus on how to define and/or measure it. As one advertising executive pointed out, "The issue is whether we can agree on what [audience] engagement is. . . . There are different levels of engagement and different levels of effectiveness."[8]

Despite attempts to change the method of buying and measuring the audience of various media, we are far from a consistent model for determining audience value across the hundreds of communication vehicles currently used by advertisers—not to mention those that will come online in future years. Advertising researchers realize that each communication outlet presents its own unique challenges for measuring audience response (see Exhibit 2.4). In addition, there are concerns by some media directors that the emphasis on short-term audience involvement runs the risk of devaluing the long-term value of advertising. Because brand building is a continuing process that often takes years to accomplish, involvement-based ROI measures may give advertising less than its full worth in the marketing process.

Integrated Marketing

Marketing consists of four primary elements: product, price, distribution, and communication. These are the primary elements in what is known as the **marketing mix**.[9] The communication component of marketing is further divided into four primary categories:

1. *Personal selling.* Personal communication is the most effective means of persuading someone. However, it is also the most expensive and, because of its expense, usually impractical at the initial stages of mass selling. The days of door-to-door selling at the retail level are largely over. As a primary technique, personal selling is most often used in business-to-business marketing. Even then, it is frequently employed as a follow-up to advertising to close a sale or develop a long-term relationship that will eventually result in a sale. In business-to-business marketing, advertising opens doors for personal salespeople, and in consumer marketing it introduces brands and retailers, which allows salespeople to make the final sale.

    Although traditional personal selling is a minor part of the promotional strategy of most companies selling directly to consumers, its techniques are becoming important factors in many selling tactics across a number of media platforms. For example, direct response and the Internet both incorporate the strengths of personal selling in communicating personalized messages and anticipating consumer resistance to sales approaches.

2. **Sales promotion**. Sales promotion is an extra incentive for a customer to make an immediate purchase. It is by far the most extensive category of promotional spending. Sales promotion may consist of a special sales price, a cents-off coupon, a colorful point-of-purchase display, or a chance to win a trip to Hawaii in a sweepstakes. The largest categories of promotions, those directed to wholesalers and retailers, are rarely seen by consumers. These promotions, known as *trade promotions*, are used to persuade the distributors to carry a brand or give it an advantage such as favorable shelf space.

    One of the fears, especially during recessionary periods, is that an overuse of short-term promotions such as coupons and various trade deals will not only cut into profits but also harm long-term brand equity by placing a major emphasis on price. Marketers are well aware of the potential downside of promotional offers, and the most astute companies incorporate strong brand messages in their promotions. By

3 **Describe the four primary types of marketing communication.**

marketing mix
Combination of marketing functions, including advertising, used to sell a product.

sales promotion
(1) Sales activities that supplement both personal selling and marketing, coordinate the two, and help to make them effective. For example, displays are sales promotions. (2) More loosely, the combination of personal selling, advertising, and all supplementary selling activities.

The groundswell of marketer demand for methods to measure the value of their advertising has hit an unprecedented level. *Ad Age* asked Aegis Group's Marketing Management Analytics to rate the measurability for ROI of various marketing media.

Medium	The Measurement Challenge	ROI Measurability Rating
Direct Response	Direct mail, telemarketing and other forms are the most measurable of media listed here. Direct can have a synergistic feel, especially on pharma, telecom and financial services.	5
Sales Promotion	Offers such as coupons and discounts generate a lot of consumer response and therefore a bounty of data. The data lend themselves to measurement, especially for package goods via syndicated scanner data. Free-standing inserts generate much valuable data.	5
Internet	The Internet can be very influential for big-ticket purchases like cars. Very measurable, with the cautionary note that "Internet is a very broad net," ranging from search engines to ads in content to Web sites such as in the auto market, where such marques as Saab get lots of hits, and all should be looked at separately. The goal is to understand how the consumer is interacting online with the brand.	5
TV	While promotions have very pronounced, short-term effects that allow precise measurement, TV has a more subtle and gradual effect that may show greater variability. But ROI can be measured with a high degree of accuracy, and there's no excuse for TV not to show a measurable effect. MMA clients have been using a lot more analysis to create a better mix between :15s and :30s, and better allocation across dayparts.	4 1/2
Print	The experts can slice and dice print by weekly vs. monthly publications, by targeted vs. general market, by promotional ads vs. equity-building. Print promotional materials, like free-standing inserts, are a separate—and much more measurable—matter. As with all other media, accuracy and timing of the data are crucial in determining how measurable the medium is. Print can play a strong role in expanding the reach of the media mix.	4 1/2
Public Relations	There are companies that specialize in the measurement of PR campaigns' quality; they can measure the number of impressions delivered—via positive or negative PR—for a brand name or category. PR can have a measurable impact on sales (think trans fats in food). The problem: Many marketers aren't buying these PR data.	4
Video Games	Whether the game is played online or offline is crucial. An ad embedded in a game cartridge is very hard to measure because there's no way to know how often it's played. Though there's no denying "True Crime's" Nick Kang is a big hit. With online games, there are great data available through the Internet.	Online: 4 Offline: 1
Radio	The available data typically aren't as strong as those for its traditional-media colleagues of TV and print, and this hampers radio.	3
Cinema	Movie advertising can be measured by the number of impressions delivered, much like outdoor or kiosk advertising would be measured.	3
Sponsored Events	Measurability depends on whether sponsorship is likely to spark short-term effect. A major recurring event like the Olympics is very measurable. Others can be difficult to measure short term. Measurement can be complex because events have so many pieces, including how the event is advertised, the PR buzz, signage and the recollection of event itself.	3
Product Placement in Content	There are companies that measure quality of placement as well as the quantity of exposures. Treated much like TV advertising, with the caveat that not every product placement is the same. Fox's "American Idol" is a great example: AT&T Wireless's tie-in, which involved voting by text message, is interactive—even part of the entertainment—while Paula Abdul drinking from a Coke cup is not. (P.S. AT&T Wireless, now owned by Cingular, isn't an MMA client.) So the question becomes: How do you score the quality of placement?	3
Outdoor	Available data are limited due to the nature of outdoor advertising; there's no syndicated vendor that sells the needed data on outdoor. And outdoor lacks "variance"—the billboard is up X number of months and is seen by an unchanging X number of people each day.	2
Guerrilla Marketing	Hard to measure if the variable you're using is sales. If 10,000 people at an event get free T-shirts, it's difficult to measure the effect on the 400,000 people living in that market. Because guerrilla can encompass so many different kinds of tactics, getting useful data can be a problem—it depends on how measurable the response is. Marketers' ROI expectations for guerrilla are lower than for other media, so the urgency to measure is less. Not to mention they spend a lot less on guerrilla than on traditional media like TV.	1

EXHIBIT 2.4

Rating Media for Their Accountability

From Dan Lippe, "Media Scorecard: How ROI Adds Up," *Advertising Age*, June 20, 2005, pg. 5–6. Copyright © 2005 Crain Communications, Inc. Used with permission.

public relations
Communication with various internal and external publics to create an image for a product or corporation.

doing so, they ensure that promotions remain short-term sales incentives rather than having consumers rely on them for their primary means of brand assessment.

3. **Public relations**. According to the Public Relations Society of America, "Public relations helps an organization and its publics adapt mutually to each other." In the past decade, public relations has become one of the fastest-growing sectors of marketing communication. A primary benefit of public relations is that it is perceived as having higher audience credibility than advertising. For most of its existence, public relations, as practiced by most companies, consisted primarily of issuing an occasional press release with little or no follow-up, coordination with other marketing elements, and virtually no attempt to measure either its short- or long-term value to profitability. In the past decade, the regard for public relations among major marketers has increased dramatically, and public relations has been fully integrated into the marketing communication plans of most major companies. Exhibit 2.5 reviews the numerous ways in which public relations can potentially function within marketing communication.

Since the 1930s, researchers have known that word-of-mouth endorsements by influential peers are an important method of getting ideas adopted by a greater population. Early work by researchers such as Paul Lazarsfeld and Elihu Katz demonstrated the relationship between media and personal influence in the political arena. In what is known as the *two-step flow*, the media provided information to opinion leaders who, in turn, influenced the opinions of less-involved voters. Contemporary marketers have adopted many of the techniques of the two-step flow and other public-relations practices to develop similar programs of influencing the purchase of brands.

In recent years, terms such as *buzz*, *guerilla marketing*, and *word-of-mouth marketing* have been added to the business lexicon. The techniques have many characteristics, including product placement in movies and television shows, company-sponsored blogs, having a book reviewed by Oprah, event marketing, and hundreds of other techniques to engage consumers. Regardless of their names, the key to success of word-of-mouth marketing is to engage marketplace influencers.

EXHIBIT 2.5

PR Effectiveness and Functionality

Firms are increasing their use of public relations as a marketing tool.

In which roles do you consider public relations effective?

Raising awareness	83%
Providing credibility	67%
Reaching influencers	63%
Educating consumers	61%
Prompting trial	28%
Persuading skeptics	22%
Driving sales	22%

From Paul Holmes, "Senior Marketers Are Sharply Divided about the Role of PR in the Overall Mix," *Advertising Age*, January 24, 2005, pg. C1. Copyright © 2005 Crain Communications, Inc. Used with permission.

Faced with negative public opinion toward pharmaceutical companies, industry giant GlaxoSmithKline enlisted its 8,000-member sales force as public-relations ambassadors. The aim of the campaign was to have these local representatives speak to civic clubs, senior citizen groups, and local media to spread the word about the work of drug companies. A company executive noted that information from rank-and-file employees would be more trusted than the same information imparted through formal communication media from company executives.[10]

The key to successful public relations is to view it as a complement rather than a competitor to advertising. "Sometimes you need one, sometimes the other. Ideally, you probably want both operating in harmony, orchestrated by the same conductor."[11] Advertising and public relations should work in concert to get the brand message to as many prospects as possible. For example, Chick-fil-A has greatly enhanced the value of its advertising through public-relations techniques related to its "eat more chicken" bovines. Because public relations is usually seen as news, it has credibility that is lacking in most advertising. However, even a unique product is news for only a short period of time. Public relations and especially word-of-mouth advertising tend to work best at the introductory stage of building brand awareness with advertising taking over to build long-term brand loyalty.

Best Buy introduced its in-home technical support unit with geekmobiles on high-traffic roads; Microsoft created buzz for the Xbox 360 by creating *Colony*, a community-based game; and Procter & Gamble scored a coup by having Super Bowl winning quarterback Ben Roethlisberger shave his beard on the *Late Show with David Letterman* the week following his big win using the just-introduced five-bladed Fusion razor. Furthermore, unlike advertising, a public-relations message is ultimately controlled by the media. The media make decisions concerning when, where, and if a particular product story will be carried. The elements of message control and credibility most distinguish public relations and advertising.

4. **Advertising**. Advertising is a message paid for by an identified sponsor and usually delivered through some medium of mass communication. Advertising is persuasive communication. It is not neutral; it is not unbiased; it says: "I am going to attempt to sell you a product or an idea." As in the case with other forms of marketing communication, advertising is undergoing dramatic changes as it adapts to new technologies—including those allowing the audience to delete advertisements. Throughout the remainder of this text, we discuss not only the principles of advertising but also how advertising interacts with other forms of marketing communication.

advertising
Advertising consists of paid notices from identified sponsors normally offered through communication media.

During the early development of modern marketing and advertising, marketing communication components were regarded as more or less discrete functions. Each had its own manager, and coordination of the various functions was not always as rigorous as it should have been. Today, many see the use of various elements of the marketing mix as a first step in changing the core mission of advertising agencies. An executive at a major agency said that his agency should look upon itself not as an advertising agency but as a media-arts company.[12] By that he meant that brand messages should be woven into the culture in such a way that art and commerce are seamless, using all aspects of communication technology to focus on consumer needs.

More important, the various elements of marketing communication, as they become more personal and move from mass to one-to-one contacts, can more accurately measure a campaign's ROI. The reliance on marketing mix strategy allows evaluations that view promotion as a coordinated mix of elements rather than judging each independently. In the past, a lack of coordination led many companies to address their customers with several different and sometimes confusing and contradictory messages. However, in recent years, companies have begun to move toward a consolidation of all areas of the marketing function, especially marketing communication.

The complexity of contemporary marketing communication plans has resulted in a demand for programs that *speak with one voice*, which refers to the fact that companies are demanding that all communication from their letterheads to product packaging demonstrate a consistent look and theme. The need for coordinating marketing communication is apparent when one realizes that 75 percent of *Fortune* 1,000 companies have more than 100 brands. As one marketing executive said, "Today's environment has created an overabundance of brands, messages, and delivery channels, and brand portfolios that fail at driving business performance. Unless someone is charged with 'minding the store,' individual brand management will remain as brand fiefdoms and brand proliferation will continue to drag the business down."[13]

integrated marketing communication (IMC)
The joint planning, execution, and coordination of all areas of marketing communication.

For approximately 20 years, companies have moved to organize the total communication program under the general heading of **integrated marketing communication (IMC)**. Although the application of IMC differs with each company, a primary outcome of the approach is less concern with how a message is delivered (e.g., advertising, public relations) and more emphasis on the effectiveness of the total marketing communication plan. The need for coordination and integration of marketing communication is apparent when you realize that a company like Toyota has 17 unique marketing plans for each of its models. "Each plan is designed to package information in the way customers want to get it and have it delivered when they need it."[14] Yet, within these targeted plans, there needs to be a consumer awareness that each is a member of the "Toyota family." Integrated marketing communication also has had significant implications for the way advertising agencies deal with clients. For example, one of the world's largest agencies, Ogilvy & Mather, has combined its advertising, direct marketing, public relations, health care, and sales promotion agencies into a single reporting structure and profit-and-loss statement.[15]

Today, major marketers are much more interested in the efficiency and benefits of their total marketing communication program than with the specific means of achieving these results. "Whatever the disciplines used . . . they all must work together to give a unified message to consumers. It is relationships with consumers that matter, and these are built by ideas that transcend individual media."[16]

In coming years, some form of IMC will be even more the norm in the marketing plans of virtually every company. See, for example, a few of the ways ND&P promoted Virginia Tech's microsite beyond traditional media. The campaign encouraged alumni to post yard signs, and use tree wraps and window stickers, and the agency even hired a plane to pull a banner with the web site's URL: ThisIsTheFuture.com (see Exhibit 2.6). Demands for marketing efficiency combined with new marketing communication channels and an increasingly diverse audience will combine to force greater integration and coordination of all aspects of the marketing function, especially those involved in the communication process. In later chapters, we discuss in more detail the execution of IMC.

Advertising: An Institutional Approach

4 Explain the institutional roles of advertising for consumers, business, and society.

Aside from very individual ads and campaigns developed to achieve specific goals, advertising has a much larger social and economic role. Society establishes institutions to bring order to vital activities. These social institutions control various behaviors within a society by setting standards and guidelines for what are both appropriate and required to promote the goals of a society (or at least goals agreed on by the majority). Institutions can be regarded as "evolving to address the separate needs of society (e.g., the military institution out of the need for defense; the family out of social needs for procreation, socialization and intimacy) . . ."[17]

Some would argue that advertising is not a stand-alone institution such as religion. However, an institutional consideration of advertising permits us to see that it is a

Courtesy of Neathawk Dubuque & Packett and Virginia Polytechnic Institute and State University (Virginia Tech).

EXHIBIT 2.6

Virginia Tech used a variety of tactics to drive citizens to its web site, including an aerial banner flown behind an airplane.

logical—some would say necessary—requirement for a capitalistic economic system. To the extent that advertising is an institution, it is "... primarily designed to provide information on economic goods and services, but which now, under the impact of modern conditions, finds broader, noneconomic applications."[18]

Advertising is viewed from two related perspectives: (1) its economic role and (2) its social and cultural role in communicating not only product information but also social values. The cultural role of advertising is often referred to as its *inadvertent role*. With the exception of advertising overtly intended to foster some idea or initiative, many of advertising's social consequences are often unintended by sponsors. For example, one of the major criticisms of contemporary advertising is its effect on the behavior of children. Advertising is so ubiquitous that children begin to develop strong brand preferences by the age of 2 and babies as young as 6 months are able to recognize certain corporate logos and mascots.[19] Critics charge that the epidemic of childhood obesity is a direct result of the advertising of unhealthy food to children, but their complaints go far beyond this hot-button topic. "... [J]unk food isn't the only potentially harmful product being marketed directly to children. Each day children are bombarded with sophisticated marketing for alcohol, tobacco, violent media, and precociously sexualized clothes, toys and accessories as well."[20]

Under the current level of scrutiny, advertisers must be aware of both economic and social aspects of their advertising. The public has proven itself to be unforgiving when it perceives that certain advertising is exploitive (whether the exploitation is intended or not).

Rob Marbury Founding Partner, Chief Creative Officer, Max2o Advertising, Atlanta

Jennifer Griffith, Ph.D. Lecturer, Grady College of Journalism and Mass Communication, University of Georgia

WELCOME TO THE JUNGLE: REAL-WORLD ADVICE FROM A CHIEF CREATIVE OFFICER

Rob Marbury

Rob Marbury is a founding partner and the chief creative officer at Max2o Advertising in Atlanta. He earned an ABJ from the Grady College of Journalism and Mass Communication at the University of Georgia (UGA) with a major in advertising and a minor in graphic design.

Before starting Max2o in 1992, Marbury served as the art director for Peachtree Advertising and was a partner at Art'oons. One day, Marbury and fellow UGA alum Tom Matte were eating in a Mick's restaurant in Atlanta; they were discussing how much they enjoyed the work for advertising they were doing but not necessarily the people with whom they were doing that work. The duo was looking for more job fulfillment and wanted to find it working for and with people they believed in and enjoyed. Max2o was born in that moment with the company's mantra being advertising can be both effective *and* enjoyable."

Since then, the agency has been fortunate in that the Max2o team can carefully choose who they work with, believing that it's far more important to love your work in advertising than it is to win awards or receive high pay for something you are miserable doing.

For students looking ahead to their own futures in the advertising industry, here are Marbury's "10 motivating thoughts to consider (before you start this wild ride)":

1. **Learning.** As you hone your craft of advertising, try to learn on someone else's dime; find an employer who can afford your mistakes. You need a place where you can learn quickly, and sometimes you will find this at a corporation rather than an agency. Once you develop your skills, however, then you can break out on the scene. And along the way, be nice to everyone you meet.
2. **Out-house versus in-house.** Decide whether you want to work out of house or in-house. According to Marbury, working in an out-house environment (e.g., at an agency) can be a lot more fun than in-house or corporate work, but, like a true outhouse, "it can get kind of funky." With an in-house position, you'll often earn better pay and have better benefits, and you'll have more consistency and job security. However, the benefits to working in an agency include the variety of accounts you'll have the opportunity to work on, the flexibility that often exists in an agency environment, and the opportunity to earn "creative respect" from other people in the industry.
3. **Life.** "Life," says Marbury "is too damn short for you to hate going to your job."
4. **Partnerships.** The crazy hair means you have great creative ideas; the

Most economists agree that advertising has a utilitarian function in the marketing system. That is, the basic economic functions of advertising—to disseminate product information that allows consumers to know that products exist, to give consumers information about competing brands, and to permit consumers to make intelligent choices among product options—are accepted by most observers. However, the effects of advertising, beyond these strictly functional characteristics, are viewed with suspicion in many quarters. Increasingly, critics and advertisers alike are examining advertising messages from a social perspective. Issues such as truthful messages; the inclusion and portrayal of women, ethnic groups, and the elderly; and the need for responsible consumption are among the issues contemporary advertising must confront that were minor considerations in the past. The current controversy about advertising to children is only one example that demonstrates that advertising is regarded by many as an institution that communicates

Jennifer Griffith

suit means those ideas are going to cost somebody money. A mix of creative *and* business sense is what helps an agency grow, as it did for the team at Max2o.

5. **Strippers.** Choose your clients for a variety of reasons (money, fun, principles, and so on) but realize that even though the assignment may be a blast, you might want to leave the execution out of your portfolio. That risqué condom T-shirt and the racy calendar featuring the ever-so-lovely ladies of the Cheetah Lounge might have made everyone laugh at the office, but what kind of response will they elicit when your portfolio makes the rounds?

6. **Reality.** Some work may not be pretty, but it pays the bills. Know that not everything you create will be fun and sexy. And as long as you enjoy the work, have a good time with it and make yourself some money. Just remember this: Often creatives are called on to generate work that is pretty generic and, truthfully, pretty boring. Get used to it. While you're at it, take on pro bono work for a cause you care about and to build up your portfolio with the kinds of ads you really like to do.

7. **Trust.** "Trust is the foundation you have to build on before you pitch the unconventional, yet brilliant, idea." And when you prepare to present your concepts to clients, win them over by offering choices such as the following: (a) The *industry norm* is the ad that is safest, but make sure you do indeed love it because that ad might be the one they go with. (b) The *stand-out* is brilliant. It will get noticed, get results, and could win you many awards. (c) You could present the ad that is undeniably unique. A client would be extremely bold to run this one, but it does get props for being unusual. Just remember that *all* the choices need to be tied to the client's brand.

8. **New Ideas.** Brainstorming is often a process of "throwing ideas to the wall and seeing which ones stick." When it comes to new ideas, know that sometimes the bad one sticks to the wall. That's the one the client loves. (Sigh.) Also, test your ideas physically, and do some research before making the client presentation. Marbury and his team actually had one idea for posters that, literally, would cling to the wall. They proudly stuck one to a wall behind a CEO's desk in his new office during a presentation and then promptly removed the paint while "easily" removing the poster.

9. **Burning bridges.** "It's always fun until you're a signature away from a $1,000,000 contract and you recognize the charred pile of remains holding the pen." Advertising is a smaller industry than you think. Don't burn bridges, and don't annoy Kevin Bacon (because he's never more than six degrees away from you).

10. **Ego.** Don't take criticism from clients personally. "Sometimes even the most perfect idea can be smashed to smithereens on a single whim of the client." Advertising is a business for tough skins. The client has to be happy to pay you and then to rehire you in the future. So keep on trying and trying and trying and trying.

social as well as economic messages even when the social aspects of advertising may be both unintended and undesirable from the advertiser's perspective.

The majority of both practitioners and consumers accept the fact that advertising has an ethical and moral responsibility to provide product information that is both truthful and socially appropriate. However, it is obvious that consumers make purchase decisions on the basis of psychological and social factors as well as strictly utilitarian considerations. People buy Cadillacs instead of Chevrolets, not only for basic differences in transportation needs but also because the Cadillac brand satisfies a need for prestige, social status, and a number of other psychological factors. It can be argued that advertising creates these wants (as opposed to needs). But, in fact, advertising mirrors the society in which it functions, but over time it probably contributes to subtle changes in the mores and behaviors of the public that is exposed to it.

Advertising's role as an institution has been studied by both critics and proponents. These perspectives about the roles of advertising generally fall into one of the following three categories.

WHAT ADVERTISING DOES FOR CONSUMERS

Consumer behavior is need driven. That is, we assume that a purchase is the culmination of a process that begins with the recognition that some problem can be solved by a particular product or service. The *problem* may be utilitarian (we buy a new car for transportation) or hedonistic (we buy a new car to impress our neighbors). To a large degree, our purchases have elements of both and consumers search for products that satisfy their needs and wants on both levels. Advertising's role in this process is to provide information as efficiently and economically as possible to potential buyers. Advertising is particularly proficient in providing information and introducing consumers to new products and services. With the advent of specialized media that can reach narrowly segmented audiences, advertising has an enhanced ability to provide even better information to selected consumers about products (see Exhibit 2.7).

Closely related to the function of consumer information is the belief that advertising promotes greater choice for the consumer. Effective communication provides a means for new products to enter the marketplace and, therefore, increases the number of products available to consumers. In the future, as technology and interactive media increase the practicality for consumer feedback, buyers will have even greater input into the marketing process.

WHAT ADVERTISING DOES FOR BUSINESS

For businesses, the primary roles of advertising include contributing to new-product launches, increasing consumer brand loyalty for existing brands, and maintaining the sales of mature brands. In other words, advertising creates awareness of useful products so that businesses can build shareholder value by profitably moving inventory. Advertising facilitates exchanges between buyer and seller such that advertising is an important element in a fundamental marketing process known as *exchange theory*. Simply put, exchange theory suggests that market transactions will take place only to the extent that both buyers and sellers see value in the process. One of the myths perpetrated

EXHIBIT 2.7

Advertising provides information that helps consumers make informed brand choices.

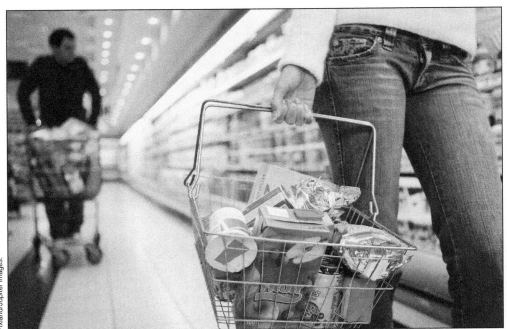

Pixland/Jupiter Images.

by advertising critics is that there is an adversarial relationship between businesses selling goods and consumers buying them with each side trying to "beat" the other. On the contrary, exchange theory suggests that the long-term success of a business is built on the positive and mutually beneficial relationship it develops with its consumers. This relationship can only be maintained if consumers perceive value in the goods they purchase and the business enjoys a reasonable profit for its efforts.

Just as mass production provides economies of scale in production, advertising provides similar efficiencies in communicating to mass audiences. Despite the introduction of specialized media reaching smaller and smaller audience segments, there remains a demand for mass advertising to promote widely distributed products and services. Without advertising, many businesses would not be able to bring new products to the attention of enough consumers fast enough to make the enormous cost of creating, developing, manufacturing, and distributing these products practical. In other words, advertising is both a tool and a requirement for an abundant economy.

WHAT ADVERTISING DOES FOR SOCIETY

If we accept the fact that advertising is a social institution (or at least interacts strongly with many other institutions), then its role in society should be considered. As we discussed earlier, advertisers convey subtle messages about society by the manner in which their advertising portrays products and services. In the current environment of social change and diversity, advertisers are hard-pressed to present effective sales messages that are at the same time compelling to the audience and noncontroversial to all segments of the population. In the United States, where people are continually undergoing changes in values and mores, advertisers are constantly challenged to develop effective marketing programs. Three challenges for contemporary marketing stand out:

1. Monitoring changes so that a company is aware of what is happening in society
2. Creating products and services compatible with changing values
3. Designing marketing messages that reflect and build on the values target markets and individual customers hold[21]

In a landscape of fragmented media and diverse audiences, it is more and more difficult to develop messages that appeal to specific target audiences without exposure to unintended consumers. For example, in 2005, Carl's Jr. promoted its BBQ Six Dollar Burger with a racy commercial featuring Paris Hilton. Although the spot was created for a target audience of young males, the advertisements drew criticism from a number of groups who took exception to the message.

In advertising's favor, the intended purpose of advertising is to contribute to the profitable sale of products and to the continued economic expansion that presumably benefits society as a whole. In addition to its economic role, advertising benefits society by providing revenues to support a diverse and independent press system protected from government and special interest control.

However, in carrying out these goals, advertising must be aware of its responsibility as a mirror and monitor of society. From a pragmatic standpoint, advertisers realize that "Consumers' reactions to a product are also influenced by their evaluations of its advertising, over and above their feelings about the product itself. Our evaluation of a product can be determined solely by our appraisal of how it's depicted in marketing communications—we don't hesitate to form attitudes toward products we've never seen in person much less used."[22]

Clearly, there are numerous opinions regarding the proper role of advertising as it relates to the overall social good. However, there is little question that advertisers have a new and different responsibility to society in the way they sell their products and services. New technology and sophisticated research methods have only increased the importance of issues such as consumer privacy and the potentially intrusive nature of advertising.

Advertising to Diverse Publics

Advertising, regardless of its intended recipients, communicates messages to various groups and individuals who in turn interpret these messages in the context of their own interests. For that reason companies must consider the effect of their messages on a number of publics beyond the narrow scope of the intended audience. For example, a company's advertising that is intended to demonstrate to consumers that it is a responsible corporate citizen by publicizing a lucrative employee health care program may raise questions among stockholders about expenditures of funds that could be used to raise dividends. Tyson Foods made available a free book of prayers entitled *Giving Thanks at Mealtime*. The booklet contained messages from a variety of religions from Christianity to Islam and was intended to carry out the company's mission statement as a "faith-friendly company." In the first month of the offer, the company had more than 25,000 requests for the booklet. It also gained a good deal of criticism that it was commercializing religion.

Although advertisers must be aware that they reach unintended audiences, they also often use a single advertising campaign to reach several publics at once. A single advertisement might be directed to a number of publics:

distribution channel
The various intermediaries, such as retailers, that control the flow of goods from manufacturers to consumers.

1. *The **distribution channel**. With the growth of huge national retailers such as Wal-Mart and Kmart, national advertisers often use consumer advertising to demonstrate to retailers that they are offering brands with high consumer demand and ones they are willing to support with significant advertising dollars at the consumer level. In fact, large retailers often demand a certain level of consumer advertising support before they will agree to stock a brand.

2. *Employees.* The most important assets of any company are its employees, and it is important to build loyalty and teamwork among rank-and-file workers. An advertising message may carry an overt appeal to employees by mentioning the quality workmanship that goes into a product or featuring company employees in advertising. More often, the message to employees is subtler but nevertheless can be an important function of advertising.

3. *Current and potential customers.* Obviously, the key to success for most companies is building brand awareness among new customers and enhancing brand loyalty among current buyers. Advertising is often the most efficient means of achieving both objectives.

4. *Stockholders.* Approximately 50 percent of American households currently own stock, up from 19 percent in 1983. For the first time in history, the majority of ordinary customers hold ownership in many of the companies they patronize. Not surprisingly, studies have shown that high brand awareness and a company's positive reputation contribute to maintaining higher stock prices than might otherwise be the case.

5. *The community at large.* Many companies operate local plants throughout the country. Advertising is often used to influence public opinion so that when the inevitable disputes about local tax assessments, excessive noise, or zoning ordinances arise, the company is viewed as a good neighbor.

Too often, firms take a short-term, narrow view of advertising. These companies view advertising from the perspective of the immediate (and intended) communication effects on the primary market for their products. However, advertising functions within a matrix of political, legal, economic, and cultural environments. Within each of these categories are interested parties who are judging companies and their products by the advertising messages they disseminate. It is important to consider the entire range of publics when developing advertising.

The Components of Advertising Strategy

With this section, we begin to discuss the fundamentals of advertising procedure. As we will see, the application of advertising techniques often demonstrates markedly different approaches from one company to another. Advertising should be designed to reach those consumers who are interested in the particular product features and benefits that a brand offers. The most successful brands are those with features and benefits unique within a product category and, consequently, those that hold a differentiated position in the minds of consumers. It is advertising's job to turn product benefits into an attention-getting story that appeals to prospective buyers. In this section, we discuss some of the primary elements of successful advertising. In subsequent chapters, we examine the various executions of these basic principles that set one brand apart from its competitors.

BRAND NAME

An established **brand name** that customers recognize and respect is one of the most valued assets of a company. Studies have shown that anywhere from one-third to one-half of the value of some companies comes from the brand names they own. Products are concrete objects; brands, however, represent attitudes and feelings about products. One of the principal uses of advertising is to enhance brand familiarity awareness in the minds of consumers by emphasizing consumer benefits of a product. James Spaeth, past president of the Advertising Research Foundation, said that "A brand name is the intangible benefit that differentiates an otherwise readily substitutable product in a highly consumer relevant way." For example, the McDonald's name is a primary difference between it and the thousands of fast-food restaurants that compete for consumers' dollars.

Although high brand recognition is important for any product, it is especially critical for product categories that have little inherent product differentiation; that is, for example, soft drinks, beer, cigarettes, and similar products are easily duplicated by competitors from a functional standpoint. What competitors cannot duplicate are the years of successful brand building, primarily through advertising, that the parent companies have invested in their brands. Exhibit 2.8 demonstrates how difficult it is for competitors to compete against established brands. As the table points out, only five product category leaders have been replaced among twenty-five product types over the past 80 years. Even among the five displaced leaders, several remain popular names in the marketplace.

BRAND EXTENSION

In the global market, companies are finding that overcoming entrenched local brands is very difficult as they expand into new markets. Although Asian companies dominate in the areas of home appliances and electronics manufacture, they often lack the name recognition of American brands. In the automotive sector, Japanese carmakers such as Nissan, Toyota, and Honda have a strong presence, but it is one that has taken more than 25 years to achieve. Hoping to jump-start the process, many foreign companies have bought U.S. brands or even entire companies. Familiar American brands now owned by foreign manufacturers include IBM personal computers (Lenovo of China) and Zenith Electronics (LG Electronics of Korea). When China's Haier Group bid more than $1 billion to take over Maytag—including brands such as Amana, Hoover, and Jenn-Air—the primary motivation was acquisition of the brand names.[23] Although Whirlpool Corporation eventually bought Maytag, the Haier bid demonstrated the importance and value of brands. As new companies enter the global marketplace, brands will take on even more importance as a competitive tool to differentiate one product from another.

The fierce competition and the difficulty of entering new markets—either geographic or target market based—have caused many companies to consider **brand extension** rather than brand innovation as a strategy for product introduction. As we have

brand name
The written or spoken part of a trademark, in contrast to the pictorial mark; a trademark word.

brand extension
These are new product introductions under an existing brand to take advantage of existing brand equity.

A study of 25 popular product categories and their leading brands shows that branding was an important concept over 80 years ago. And brands that were built then are still the dominant brands in the business today. Source: Proprietary research by Jack Trout, based on industry share data.

Rank	25 Product Categories	The Leading Brands in 1923	The Leading Brands of Today	Only Five Lost Their Leadership
1	Bacon	Swift	Swift	Swift
2	Batteries	Eveready	Duracell	Eveready
3	Breakfast Cereal	Kellogg's Corn Flakes	Cheerios	Kellogg's Corn Flakes
4	Cameras	Kodak	Kodak	Kodak
5	Canned Fruit	Del Monte	Del Monte	Del Monte
6	Canned milk	Carnation	Carnation	Carnation
7	Chewing gum	Wrigley's	Wrigley's	Wrigley's
8	Chocolate	Hershey's	Hershey's	Hershey's
9	Crackers	Nabisco	Nabisco	Nabisco
10	Flour	Gold Medal	Gold Medal	Gold Medal
11	Mint candies	Life Savers	Life Savers	Life Savers
12	Paint	Sherwin-Williams	Sherwin-Williams	Sherwin-Williams
13	Paper	Hammermill	Hammermill	Hammermill
14	Pipe Tobacco	Prince Albert	Prince Albert	Prince Albert
15	Razors	Gillette	Gillette	Gillette
16	Sewing machines	Singer	Singer	Singer
17	Shirts	Manhattan	Arrow	Manhattan
18	Soap	Ivory	Dove	Ivory
19	Soft Drinks	Coca-Cola	Coca-Cola	Coca-Cola
20	Soup	Campbell's	Campbell's	Campbell's
21	Shortening	Crisco	Crisco	Crisco
22	Tea	Lipton	Lipton	Lipton
23	Tires	Goodyear	Goodyear	Goodyear
24	Toilet soap	Palmolive	Dial	Palmolive
25	Toothpaste	Colgate	Colgate	Colgate

EXHIBIT 2.8

Solid Foundations

Reprinted with permission from *Advertising Age*, March 14, 2005, pg. 28. Copyright © 2005 Crain Communications Inc.

seen, high-profile brands are a major resource for companies in a competitive environment. Obviously, the cost and financial risk of introducing a new product under an established name are much less than those under a completely new name. For example, once Bic became an established brand with its ballpoint pens, it was much more efficient to market disposable lighters and razors under the Bic name than it would have been to build new brands. The problem faced by contemporary marketers is to determine when excessive brand extension begins to harm core brands that, in some cases, have been nurtured for a century or more.

"If you chase two rabbits, both will escape."

ANONYMOUS

Brand extensions are sometimes like the hunter chasing two rabbits. Companies want to keep their core audience while using an established brand extension to reach new markets. Soft drinks and automobiles have been among the most persistent users of brand extensions. When established brands such as Coca-Cola Classic and Pepsi began to demonstrate flat sales trends, the companies moved to boost sales by introducing numerous products under some version of the core brand. Since 2000, Coca-Cola and Pepsi together have introduced approximately 20 new beverages using some version of these brand names.

The decision to use a brand extension or introduce an entirely new product is not a trivial one. Major soft-drink makers know that many of these brand extensions will fail. A major consideration is whether a product failure will hurt the core brand in the minds of consumers. "There's also the danger of cannibalizing sales of existing brands when new products are pushed hard. Finally, . . . companies also run the risk of confusing consumers by introducing too many products."[24]

An overriding problem of brand extensions is that successful brands have defined a special niche in the minds of consumers. When companies attempt to significantly enlarge or alter the scope of these brand positions, it leads consumers to question the values and benefits of the original brand. For example, the Volkswagen Phaeton luxury model (with prices starting in the mid-$60,000 range) met with lukewarm interest from consumers accustomed to seeing the brand sell in the $20,000 range. Although brand extensions present challenges, most successful brands reach a point of saturation among their core consumers and see some form of brand extension—either through new products or different advertising positioning—as the only way to expand their markets.

In 1991, reacting to the healthy eating movement, executives at Kentucky Fried Chicken changed the name to simply KFC. To many, the change took an established brand that held a specific position in the marketplace—and in the minds of consumers—and substituted a meaningless set of initials that meant nothing to its market. Fast-forward to 2005: The company brought back the Kentucky Fried Chicken name along with its "Finger Lickin' Good" tagline in a 50-store test. The KFC experience underscores a fundamental tenet of branding: "KFC violated basic rules that ailing marketers often forget when a business and market are in flux. Marketers need to be what they are, be authentic, be real. If you sell a product, make it the best you can, be proud of it, and don't waffle. . . ."[25]

We can summarize our discussion of brand extension by looking at advantages and disadvantages of the strategy.

Advantages of a brand-extension strategy include the following:

1. Saving money by not needing to build awareness for a new and unknown brand name
2. Adding equity to an existing brand name with a successful extension

Disadvantages of a brand-extension strategy include the following:

1. Damaging a core brand in the minds of loyal consumers with a failed introduction
2. Losing marketing focus on your existing brand and/or diluting marketing efforts and budget across several brands

From these examples, we can see that no single brand strategy is right for every company. However, regardless of the approach, the development, protection, and maintenance of brand value will continue to be one of the driving forces in modern advertising. Building brand value or equity is one of the most important elements of advertising. Whether introducing a new product or maintaining the vitality of a mature one, brand identity is crucial to a product's success.

FULFILLING PERCEIVED NEEDS

The fundamental job of most businesses is to develop products that meet the need of some consumer segment (see Exhibit 2.9). Successful products are those that solve a consumer problem better and/or more economically than an available alternative. Products and services must also lend themselves to efficient promotion, distribution, and production that will produce a profit for the manufacturer or provider. The difficulty of the task of introducing successful products is underscored by the estimates that only one in seven product ideas that enter the developmental process are successful and nearly half of the dollars allocated to new product introductions go to products that either fail or are abandoned.[26]

If there is any doubt about the odds against new products, a trip to the closeout chain Big Lots provides a sobering experience. "Closeout retailer Big Lots is a microcosm of

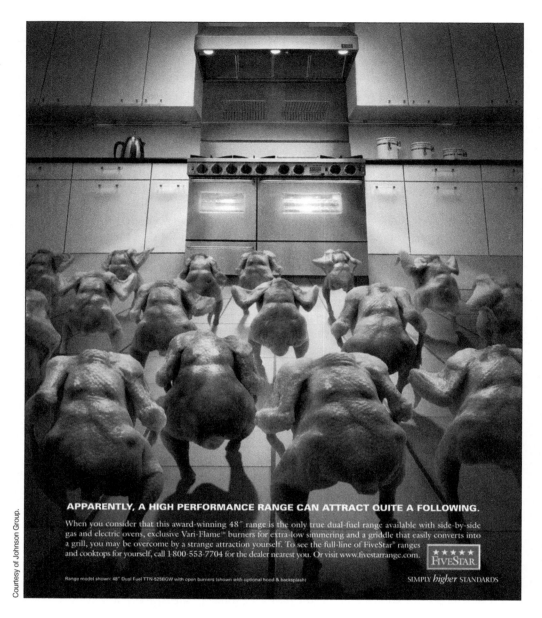

Courtesy of Johnson Group.

corporate America's mistakes, missteps and ambitions. The seemingly endless supply of new packaged-goods products—1,561 in 2004, according to Information Resources, Inc.—not to mention brand extensions—up 94% last year—has turned Big Lots into a $4.3 billion brand with 1,500 stores."[27] One of the goals of product planning may be to stay off the shelves of Big Lots!

To create one of the relatively few products that will be successful in the marketplace, companies must start with the premise that they are offering not a physical object but, rather, the means of solving a problem. The late Harvard professor Theodore Levitt is quoted as saying "People don't want a quarter-inch drill. They want a quarter-inch hole!" "When people find themselves with a job to be done, they essentially *hire* products to do that for them. Following this model, then, the marketer's fundamental task is not so much to understand the *customer* as it is to understand what *jobs* customers need to do—and build products that serve those specific purposes."[28] The more closely a brand is associated with a specific job, the more likely it will be the first choice of consumers faced with a particular task.

When evaluating the marketing potential for innovative products or product line expansions, firms often have to determine the social and psychological tendencies of their prospects before moving ahead. Successful products are those that are *perceived* by consumers as being best for a task, not necessarily those that are considered the winner according to some objective standard. For example, blind taste tests for soft drinks and beer have been notoriously unreliable in predicting what consumers will do in the marketplace.

Of course, attempting to determine the needs of consumers and actually doing so are two different things. For one thing, consumers may know what their problems are but they may not be able to enunciate the type of products that would solve these problems. This is particularly true of yet-to-be-marketed pioneering products. For example, before the invention of the microwave oven, consumers couldn't say they wanted a device that would stir up water molecules and provide a hot dinner in minutes. They could say that when they were tired and hungry they didn't want to wait 45 minutes for a conventional oven.[29]

Mercedes-Benz has found that rebuilding consumers' trust in a brand is much harder than gaining it in the first place. Long known for its quality, the carmaker experienced some quality-control problems during the early 2000s. Mercedes found that it was able to correct many of the defects relatively quickly. However, it may take much longer to win back consumers lost by the mechanical problems. In 2006, Mercedes launched an extensive advertising campaign aimed at explaining the steps it took to correct the problems while at the same time countering Mercedes' negative brand perceptions among many car buyers.[30]

ASSESSING NEEDS

A key ingredient in determining product success is reliable research. Companies constantly employ a host of research techniques to determine the most appealing products, advertising, and promotional messages that will be most interesting to target prospects, and they also examine information about pricing and distribution preferences. In a survey in the *Wall Street Journal*, readers were asked, "What factor is most important to you when buying a car?" Among the almost 3,500 respondents, no more than 20 percent cited a single reason (price and style tied for first).[31] The survey only reinforced what researchers have known for years—that product purchase decisions are the result of numerous factors. Research also has shown that buyers often indicate that they want an array of product features but that they are uncertain about the priorities they assign to these features and the prices they would be willing to pay for them.

During the past 20 years, a research technique known as **conjoint analysis** has been developed to address the numerous ways a consumer considers a product. "The rationale underlying the technique is that consumers weigh all the many elements of a product or service—such as price, ingredients, packaging, technical specifications, and on and on—when choosing, say, a sweater, airline ticket, stereo system."[32] Consumers may prefer a particular airline, but scheduling (one stop versus nonstop) or bargain pricing may move them to another normally less preferred carrier.

conjoint analysis
A research technique designed to determine what consumers perceive as a product's most important benefits.

Conjoint analysis considers the many individual elements that together determine consumer preference. By placing a value on these elements, it offers insight into the way consumers actually weigh considerations in making purchases. Done correctly, conjoint analysis can prevent costly mistakes when companies emphasize product characteristics that are of little value to consumers. By the same token, the technique allows product designers and marketers to concentrate on those factors that determine the characteristics of a "good product" in the minds of target prospects.

As we have seen in these examples, the key to successful advertising begins with product development and marketing from the consumer's perspective. For many companies, the idea of consumer empowerment in the marketing process has been given

KLEPPNER VIEWPOINT 2.2

John Adams Chief Executive Officer, The Martin Agency, Richmond, Virginia

Mike Hughes President and Creative Director, The Martin Agency, Richmond, Virginia

THE MARTIN AGENCY ON ADVERTISING

You can argue that the institution with the greatest influence on our culture today is not the federal government, not the church, but the corporation. And while that may be good or bad, what is not debatable is that the $300 billion that is spent annually to project the voice of the corporation makes it a very powerful voice.

AND IT MUST BECOME A BETTER VOICE.

SO I'M GOING TO ASK YOU TO SAVE ADVERTISING—from banality, self-absorption and uselessness. Save it also from mere usefulness. Instill it instead with power.

Save it from mere cleverness. Instill it with deep intelligence.

Save it from the mere call to action. Instill it with a call to lift ourselves up.

BY THE WAY, as you take on this task, you should know that you're outnumbered. There are legions of people who don't share our view.

For them the art of persuasion is just another science.

It's fad and fashion masquerading as real ideas.

For them it is impossible to underestimate the intelligence of the consumer.

For them it's just not worth that much trouble.

For them advertising is spelled with a lowercase "a" and is practiced with lowercase talent.

They are legion.

BUT YOU CAN—AND WILL—PREVAIL. You have the talent and you have the support.

Used with permission from, Mike Hughes, *Welcome to Our Beautifully Imperfect Company* (Richmond, VA: The Martin Agency, 2007).

John Adams

Mike Hughes

more than lip service. Procter & Gamble, the world's largest maker of consumer goods, has instituted an annual "Consumer Is Boss" event. As part of P&G's consumer emphasis, executives are required to man call-center phones to interact with customers and spend time with consumers in their homes or on shopping trips.[33] P&G is not alone in adopting a bottom-up, consumer-centric model of product development and maintenance as opposed to the top-down model of providing customers with products companies hoped they would buy. Obviously, the failure rate for the latter demonstrated that this new approach was long overdue.

SALES, REVENUES, AND PROFIT POTENTIAL

Marketing's contribution to profitability is achieved through a complex balance among sales, market share, promotional expenditures, and cost efficiency. Despite the contemporary demand for marketing accountability, there is no easy answer to the equation. For example, although strict accounting of expenditures and, when appropriate, making

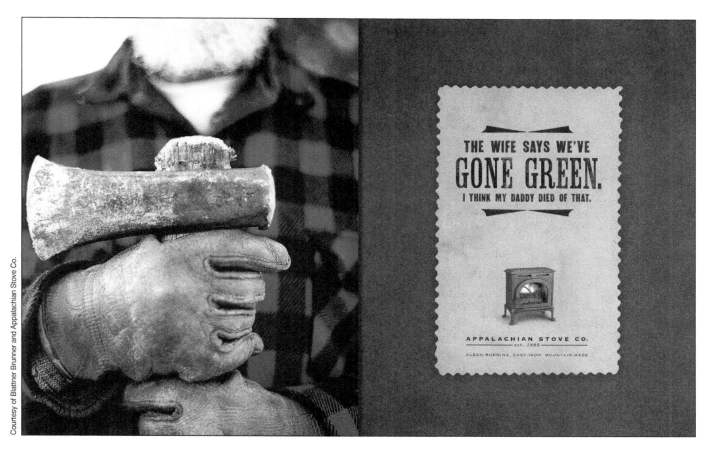

Courtesy of Blattner Brunner and Appalachian Stove Co.

THE WIFE SAYS WE'VE
GONE GREEN.
I THINK MY DADDY DIED OF THAT.

APPALACHIAN STOVE CO.
——— est. 1950 ———
CLEAN-BURNING CAST-IRON MOUNTAIN-MADE

EXHIBIT 2.10

What is the goal of this ad for Appalachian Stove Co. other than corporate profitability?

significant cuts in marketing and promotional outlays may contribute to immediate profits, no company achieves continuing success through protracted cost cutting. Likewise, gains in market share and gross sales may look good on the short-term balance sheet, but they can be misleading if this growth is not related to profitability. The cleverest advertisement or the most humorous, memorable television commercial is totally worthless unless it contributes directly to company profitability (see Exhibit 2.10).

Although only the most unsophisticated marketing executives would emphasize sales and revenue goals to the detriment of profits, a number of strategies are used to attain profitability. In this section, we examine four major approaches used by established companies to achieve long-term revenues and profits:

1. *Developing and expanding new-product niches to reach current customers.* Wal-Mart has long had a distinctive and dominant brand image. However, with 93 percent of households shopping at Wal-Mart at least once a year, the company held such a high level of market share that future increases in profitability were difficult to achieve. A recently announced strategy involves encouraging upscale customers who are currently purchasing household goods and underwear at Wal-Mart to think of the chain as a place to buy fashion clothing. Toward this end, Wal-Mart ran advertisements in *Vogue* featuring real customers but in much more stylish settings than in previous advertising. Although the results are still pending on the success of the campaign, most observers think that it holds little risk for the company of losing its current customer base. As one marketing consultant said, "You are never in danger when you make what you sell appealing."[34]

2. *Emphasizing profits over sales volume.* In 2006, Ford Motor Company chair William Clay Ford Jr. announced a 20 percent reduction in its workforce and the closing of 14 plants. In his announcement, Mr. Ford said that the company was moving away from a philosophy of "if you build it, they will buy it," in which product

planning was driven by available production capacity. The plan drastically cut production to match demand; furthermore, Mr. Ford indicated, "From now on, our vehicles will be designed to satisfy the customer, not just fill a factory."[35] Ford sought to redesign and introduce a number of new models with a strategy of giving emphasis to revenue and profitability over sales and market share, a move that ultimately kept Ford from bankruptcy in the subsequent recession.[36]

3. *Emphasizing short-term market share rather than profitability.* Faced with significant increases in advertising and promotion from archrival Procter & Gamble, Colgate-Palmolive decided to reduce profit levels in coming years in order to protect market share in a number of product categories. In commenting on the battle between Procter & Gamble and Colgate-Palmolive, the *Wall Street Journal* reported, "…a struggle for market share between big consumer goods companies will likely erode profit growth for the next several years."[37] The Colgate-Palmolive example underscores the need to take a long-term perspective in developing a marketing strategy.

4. *Customer tracking—are all customers created equal?* One of the goals of advertising is to grow the customer base of a firm. Some companies discourage continued patronage because some customers may be detrimental to a company's bottom line. For example, insurers cancel policies for those who "use" the product too often and banks impose significantly higher fees for customers who maintain low balances or write excessive checks. Now other mainline companies are beginning to identify and reward their best customers (i.e., most profitable) while discouraging less-valuable buyers with a number of tactics.

    Obviously, retailers do not refuse to sell to a customer; and, unlike insurance companies, they can't cancel their buying privileges. However, retailers initiate restrictive return policies for those who frequently take back merchandise; delete less-profitable buyers from direct mail and Internet promotion lists; and, with checkout scanning technology, provide coupons for future purchases only to A-list customers. As one marketing consultant pointed out, "It is controversial to redline [eliminate] customers. But done correctly, it really is simply about saying I have a limited pool of money, and I need as a business person to spend that money where I can get the most return."[38]

The emphasis on profit-based accountability in all areas of advertising and promotion has created major changes in many areas of advertising. For example, advertising agencies are being compensated on how their work contributes to a client's bottom line, not whether they produce award-winning advertisements, and media buys are evaluated from the perspective of their return on investment. At the corporate level, all marketing and promotional functions are being given much greater scrutiny than ever before and are increasingly being judged on the basis of return on investment.

This move to more precisely measure the contributions of advertising has led to a broader view of what advertising can and should accomplish. For example, advertisers are focusing on the role of advertising in *maintaining* sales and market share as a goal of equal importance to *increasing* sales. It is difficult to measure the value of advertising in terms of sales not lost versus sales gained. However, given the cost involved in finding new customers versus keeping current ones, the overall contributions to profitability may actually be greater in the former case. The emphasis on profitability and accountability—and the technology that allows them to be more precisely measured—has largely eliminated past mistakes made by viewing sales and revenues as substitutes for profits.

PRODUCT TIMING

Successful business ventures, including advertising, often depend on proper timing. From a strategic standpoint, advertising timing involves the interaction between two

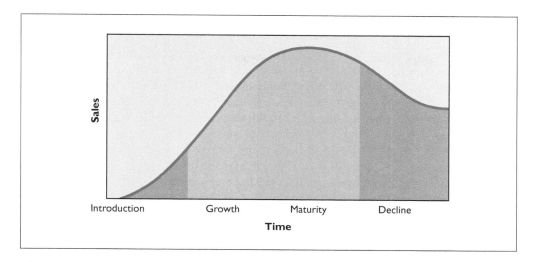

EXHIBIT 2.11

A Typical Life-Cycle Model

factors: stages of product development and the probability of marketplace acceptance. Both factors are critical timing issues in marketing and advertising decisions.

Advertising functions differently at various stages of the **product life cycle**. The typical life cycle of a brand is depicted in Exhibit 2.11 as linearly progressing through four distinct phases. During the introduction and growth phase of a product, businesses advertise to establish a beachhead against competition and to gain a level of consumer awareness. As products enter more mature stages of development, advertising strategies take longer perspectives and their goals are likely to be involved in brand equity and a longer horizon for sales development. With this in mind, businesses constantly evaluate their brands based, in part, on the maturity of the brands.

Product introduction and the advertising that accompanies it are among the most important decisions that determine the long-term success of a company. Few companies enjoy long-term survival without a steady flow of new products and product innovations. Likewise, how these improvements are communicated and to what market segments they are offered can have a major influence on their acceptance. The key is not simply to spot new trends but, rather, to creatively develop products and services to take advantage of them in the marketplace. "Don't confuse real trends with what's simply trendy. Trends are long-term economic, sociological, anthropological changes in the way people behave or believe."[39] Research conducted by Procter & Gamble found that men wanted to protect their skin but viewed most skin-care products as feminine. The company marketed a line of skin-care products under the Boss Skin brand. A crucial part of the introduction was print and television advertising that was decidedly manly with black backdrops and the tagline "Tested by Men."[40]

One of the great frustrations of marketers is that no matter how good a product is, it can rarely be forced on consumers before they are ready to accept it. Fuel-efficient automobiles have become a major area of competition in the past few years. However, without the current spikes in gasoline prices and more awareness of environmental issues by the public, it is doubtful that these cars would have been accepted. In fact, in a very short period, fuel economy has moved from a fringe benefit for many buyers to a major marketing tool. Virtually every domestic and foreign carmaker is marketing a fuel-efficient car and making conservation a key theme in its advertising. As a spokesman for Daimler-Chrysler said, "We've definitely stepped up efforts to advertise our fuel economy. You will see more on it in the future."[41]

Let's look at two other examples, one a "trend" that turned out to be decidedly a fad and another an example of products in development hoping to catch a trend. First, low-carb eating was going to revolutionize weight maintenance and create a new food industry built on a high-protein, low-carb diet. Developed by Dr. Robert C. Atkins, the Atkins diet and a host of related eating plans generated hundreds of products for followers of

product life cycle
The process of a brand moving from introduction to maturity and, eventually, to either adaptation or demise.

the plan. However, many people thought the diet was too restrictive for the long term, and soon one food maker after another withdrew low-carb products from grocers' shelves. Although many dieters gave up the Atkins plan, they didn't forsake their desire to lose weight. To cater to this audience, a number of companies are introducing "portion-control" products that allow eaters to indulge their cravings but still closely count calories. Nestlé and Hershey's have introduced 90-calorie candy products that attempt to cater to both weight consciousness and indulgence. As one marketing consultant observed, "Better-for-you eating is becoming a more consistent lifestyle choice for more people and rather than face the headwinds, many companies are trying to offer products that show how you can responsibly fit some indulgence into a weight-management program."[42] Only time will tell whether these products will resonate with consumers.

Market timing may be a matter of doing something first rather than doing something different. For example, makers of baby products know that their prime market is mothers of newborns. In the past, most strategies to reach this market involved contact with mothers shortly after the birth of their children. For example, mothers might be given a gift sampler of baby products when leaving the hospital. Kimberly-Clark Corporation, maker of Huggies disposable diapers, decided to get a jump on the competition by developing a relationship with expectant mothers shortly after they became pregnant. The key to the strategy was an expanded Internet presence that offered expectant mothers not only an introduction to the company's baby's products but also answers to questions and solutions to problems common to all new mothers and mothers-to-be. The company's ". . . $7 million marketing effort [is] designed to befriend women as soon as they get pregnant. The idea is to build a relationship so that Huggies will be top of mind as new moms buy their first package of diapers."[43]

Timing is often strategic, involving long-term decisions by both customers and marketers (see Exhibit 2.12). However, timing can also be tactical, involving sales related to specific events or occasions. For example, a major department store often substituted an umbrella and rainwear advertisement in the next day's newspaper when rain was predicted. Super Bowl Sunday is the biggest day for pizza delivery, especially in the cities whose teams are participating in the game. To accommodate sales that are sometimes 400 percent higher than normal, stores cancel vacations for drivers, stock extra supplies of dough and chicken wings, and pay workers overtime. Some stores reduce absenteeism by providing drivers with satellite radios so they don't miss the game during deliveries. Domino's stores provide television sets in stores so employees can anticipate orders, which spike during commercials and halftime.[44]

Finally, timing also is a major factor in the everyday function of advertising. Agency media planners deal with timing issues every day. Should television commercials be placed in prime time? Daytime? Late night? Should they be 30-second or 1-minute commercials? Should newspaper advertisements run on weekends or in midweek? Are magazine advertisements more effective in monthly or weekly publications, and, in either case, what is the most effective placement schedule? Every issue? Every fourth issue? As we discuss more fully in the next chapter, the level of product maturity and marketplace acceptance are important considerations for crafting sound marketing and advertising proposals.

PRODUCT DIFFERENTIATION

product differentiation
Unique product attributes that set off one brand from another.

Product differentiation is the circumstance in which a target audience regards a product as different from others in the category. Although this difference may be the result of some tangible attribute of the physical product, it also is often based on some intangible elements about the product including a brand image created in part by advertising. "The consumer's perception of brand value comes from many sources, but essentially it is based on ideas—rational or emotional—that set the brand apart from competitive brands."[45] Meaningful product differentiation exists only if consumers perceive it as an important distinction. If consumers *think* a product is better, then it is—regardless of any objective judgments to the contrary.

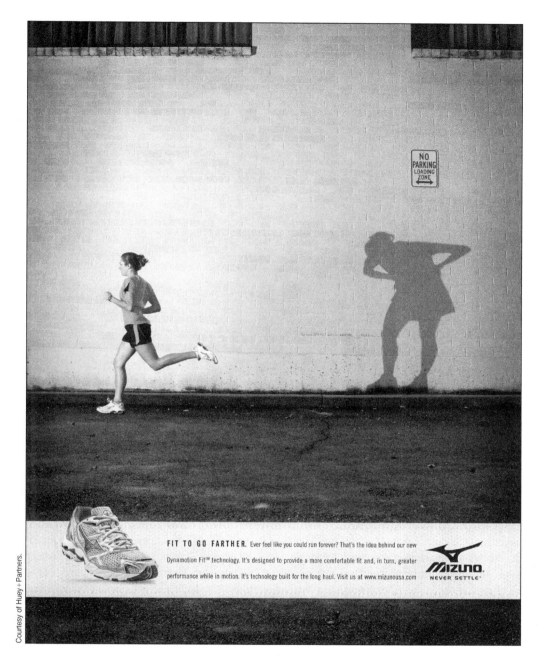

Courtesy of Huey + Partners.

EXHIBIT 2.12

At what product life-cycle stage would you advertise an athletic shoe's ability to enhance performance?

In the absence of a strong brand identity built on meaningful differentiation, buyers tend to view all brands in a category as interchangeable. When there are no real or perceived differences among brands, products are viewed as commodities and purchase decisions tend to be based on price. To the extent that price is the primary differentiating factor, profitability suffers as brands offer deeper and deeper price cuts to maintain market share. That is why brands built on an exclusive product attribute have such an advantage in the marketplace (see Exhibit 2.13).

As we mentioned earlier, attribute exclusivity is a matter of consumer perception. For example, if you did a survey and asked potential car buyers what brand is most closely associated with "safety," a majority of respondents would probably answer Volvo. In fact, the brand is so closely associated with safety that the carmaker felt safe in expanding its positioning to include performance and styling. In order to appeal to a broader customer base, Volvo introduced a new theme for its 2006 models: "Safety is a beautiful

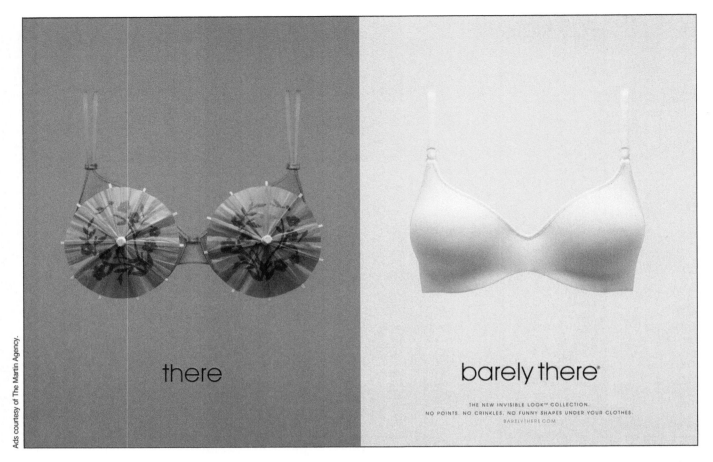

EXHIBIT 2.13

On what attribute or benefit is Barely There attempting to differentiate its intimate wear?

thing, especially when it's beautiful." As a Volvo executive commented, although its advertising may push other features, "... safety is always going to be part of our message."[46]

One of the most important elements of differentiation is keeping an open mind about how to achieve it. If a product is a bundle of benefits, we must look at the entire bundle when searching for a meaningful differentiation. Product differentiation often involves minor changes in either a product or the position communicated by advertising. For example, in a marketplace with a deli or sandwich shop on every corner, Quiznos created a distinctive position with toasted sandwiches. Since its start in 1981, Quiznos has established more than 3,000 stores in the United States and 15 foreign countries. One problem that the chain faces is that its distinctive toasted sandwich is also offered by larger chains such as Subway and a number of other franchises. Whether Quiznos can continue to "own" toasted sandwiches as a distinctive differentiation in the face of growing competition remains to be seen. The situation does point up the problem of product differentiation based on features that can be duplicated by competitors in a reasonably short period.

Too often when companies search for product differentiation, they concentrate on product function. Cell phones is a product category facing major problems of brand differentiation. Surveys indicate that most users are quite satisfied with their cell phones, provider service, and the calling area for their phones. In this type of product environment, price becomes the overriding motivation for selecting a brand—at the expense of corporate profits. Motorola, one of the major players in the cell phone industry, decided that because consumers regarded service and function as equal, it would compete on the basis of design. The RAZR cell phone was intended to capture the youth market. Its name adopted spelling used in text and Internet messaging shorthand. The RAZR propelled Motorola from a distant second in 2001 to the number one position with

36 percent of the market in the United States while making strong gains in international markets.[47] The RAZR example shows that any part of the "benefit package" is open to examination when searching for unique differentiations.

Before we leave the topic of product differentiation, we should mention two important elements involved in the process. First, as companies set about to differentiate their products, they should remember that product differentiation is also a means of target marketing. As they position their brands to appeal to a specific market segment, they often simultaneously surrender those consumers looking for features not emphasized in their brands to other manufacturers. A carmaker who markets a sports model that features high-performance handling, fancy design, glitzy colors, and an ornamental trim will eliminate cost-conscious, family-oriented buyers as it appeals more directly to the high-performance car market.

Second, firms have a special responsibility as they develop a brand-differentiation strategy. Advertisers have an obligation to promote meaningful product differences. Much of the criticism of modern advertising is that it tries to make obscure and inconsequential product variations important. There is no question that some advertising promotes unimportant product features. However, the best and most successful products demonstrate valuable differences from their competitors.

PRICE

The cost of producing and marketing a product plays a vital role in determining its price, but pricing strategy is much more complicated than simply covering costs and providing a reasonable profit. In fact, price is most often dictated by favorable consumer perceptions of the value of a product—a perception that is created in part by advertising. "Pricing power has long been the ultimate arbiter of brand value—a marketer's ability to charge consumers more than it costs them to provide a product or service is largely determined by perception of their product."[48] In this sense, price is closely related to product differentiation.

In many instances, the value of a brand has little to do with its objective worth. In fact, a primary function of advertising is to create, or enhance, a positive gap between the price of a product and the value the average consumer assigns to the product. The greater this **value gap**, the more insulated the product is from price competition. The concept of the value gap emphasizes the notion that price alone is not a particularly safe means of establishing a long-term, competitive advantage.

value gap
The perceived difference between the price of a product and the value ascribed to it by consumers.

A major part of positioning a product in the market and in the minds of consumers is setting the price. At least some segment of consumers in each product category equates price with value. These consumers gain a psychological benefit by the mere fact of paying more for a product. Price also defines who your competitors are. For example, the price-conscious buyers of the Ford Escort are not in the same market as customers for luxury-model BMWs or Mercedes. Rather than viewing pricing strategy as solely a means of covering costs, it should also be seen as an integral part of overall marketing strategy. ". . . [S]hould you charge more than your competitors? Or price below them? Should you pass cost increases along? And what message do these alternatives convey about you and your company?"[49] One only has to compare the advertising for a discounter such as Wal-Mart and an upscale retailer like Nieman-Marcus to see how price positioning dictates the tone and content of the message.

Although price has long been a major topic of concern for marketers, new technology is allowing them to be more flexible and precise in relating price to specific market segments, seasonal selling, and particular items within a product line (see Exhibit 2.14). Many marketers have long used a strategy known as **yield management** to even out supply and demand. Hotels offer special weekend rates to offset the loss of business travelers. Car-rental companies offer specials based on seasonal demand as a form of yield management. Too often these pricing strategies were hit or miss, based more on instinct than solid data. However, with software programs that identify consumer segments in

yield management
A product pricing strategy to control supply and demand.

EXHIBIT 2.14

Offering brand-name products at low prices can be an important strategy for many retailers.

Courtesy of Homer TLC, Inc.

terms of their sensitivity to price, the process has become much more sophisticated and reliable. At the retail level, research technology allows managers to analyze each store as its own discrete market. Known as *variable pricing strategy*, it offers "each customer a different price at a different point in time."[50] The goal is to neither lose sales by offering price-sensitive customers merchandise at too high a cost nor lose profits by selling goods below what premium buyers would be willing to pay.

We should make it clear that we are not disparaging a low-price strategy as a legitimate marketing tool and advertising strategy. It can be an important element in the marketing process. Many successful products cater to the low end of the price spectrum within a category. Depending on the product type, pricing strategy can be both a means of market entry for new products and a means of product differentiation for mature products. A new product can gain immediate visibility with a price advantage.

Pricing is one of the most studied areas of marketing and advertising. Proper pricing strategy is necessary for profitability and the continued existence of a business. However, it is a rare circumstance when a brand enjoys long-term success with a low-price strategy in the absence of some other brand value positioning. Price also plays a major role in advertising strategy. It is very difficult for a creative advertising plan to ignore the basic price/value perception held by a target audience. The pricing strategy for a brand determines to a significant degree the type of marketing strategy that can be used and the success that advertising will have in promoting and selling a specific brand.

Variations in the Importance of Advertising

Because companies differ in terms of their marketing goals, competitive situation, product line, and customer base, we would expect that advertising plans demonstrate markedly different approaches from one company to another. Exhibit 2.15 demonstrates the wide variance among major companies in terms of advertising-to-revenue ratios. Even within the same industry, companies often demonstrate large discrepancies in the use of advertising. Advertising investments fall along a continuum from the rare company that uses none to the equally unusual business that allocates its entire marketing communication budget to advertising.

Most firms use advertising in concert with a number of other promotional activities. The role that advertising plays in a company's promotional strategy depends on a number of factors including the following:

1. *Corporate preference for various segments of marketing communication channels.* In an era of greatly expanding communication options, marketers have more choices than ever before to effectively reach their target audiences. For example, the top five airlines reduced advertising spending by one-third from 1994 to 2004, opting instead for one-on-one communication with their best customers. "With a wide range of information about their customers—where they travel and how often, for starters—carriers can issue finely tuned offers to loyalty-program members."[51] Procter & Gamble, a company synonymous with the 30-second television commercial, has begun to shift significant spending from television commercials to product placement—paying to have its products on various television shows. Likewise, General Mills reduced its advertising budget as a percentage of sales from 4.8 percent in 2002 to 3.3 percent in 2005. According to the company, the reduction was a result of using nontraditional and new media approaches including the Internet and tests with cell phone messaging.[52] As a number of major companies experiment with marketing through the Internet, event marketing, word-of-mouth advertising, and public relations, we will continue to see a trend to supplement or replace dollars previously spent in traditional advertising media.

2. *High sales volume tends to lower advertising-to-sales ratios.* Companies with high sales volumes tend to spend less on advertising as a percentage of sales. In part, the

Advertising's share of worldwide revenue for selected 100 LNA marketers. Beauty seller Estée Lauder is at the top; Wal-Mart is most efficient.

EXHIBIT 2.15

Reliance on advertising.

Least Reliant			Most Reliant		
LNA RNK[1]	Marketer	'05 AD Spend. as % of Rev.	LNA RNK[1]	Marketer	'05 AD Spend. as % of Rev.
30	Estee Lauder Cos.[2]	28.6	40	Wal-Mart Stores	0.5
100	Molson Coors Brewing Co.	13.2	37	Hewlett-Packard Co.	1.3
20	Unilever	12.6	23	Home Depot	1.3
78	Mattel	12.1	48	Dell Inc.	1.4
3	Time Warner	11.8	57	IBM Corp.	1.4
65	Nike	11.7	86	BellSouth Corp.	1.5
41	Gillette Co.[3]	11.5	6	DaimlerChrysler	1.7
61	Diaego	11.3	5	AT&T Inc.	1.9
68	Coca-Cola Co.	10.7	36	Target Corp.	2.0
2	Procter & Gamble Co.	10.4	13	Toyota Motor Corp.	2.0

Figures for most recent available calendar or fiscal year for 100 LNA marketers that disclosed ad spending. 1. *Ad Age*'s '04 Leading National Advertisers, 2. Includes promotions, 3. 2004; P&G bought Gillette in '05.

consumers of these companies have often been saturated over a number of years with the brand story and need only to be reminded of the brand, not "sold" on it. In addition, the brands with the highest sales are also the most dominant in the market and the cost of attaining new customers through additional advertising may be nonproductive.

3. *Industries with a number of competing firms and/or extensive competition.* The acknowledged leader in the snack-food segment is PepsiCo's Frito-Lay division. In addition to the flagship Frito brand, Lay's, Cheetos, Doritos, and Tostitos are among the iconic brand names that allow the company to dominate the salty snack category. In spite of its dominant position in the category, Frito-Lay recently increased its ad budget by 50 percent.[53] The company's rationale for the increase was that a number of companies such as Nabisco have entered the market with snack-size packages of popular cookies, crackers, and candy. By increasing advertising support for its core brands, Frito-Lay hopes to prevent loss of market share by recognizing that competition in the snack category is not confined to salty snacks, which it dominates, but potentially comes from any snack product.

4. *Product categories with widespread competition and little perceived product differentiation.* Carmakers typically rank number one among all advertisers in total advertising spending. The high level of expenditures in the industry reflects the degree of competition among major manufacturers as they try to maintain or enhance market share. Interestingly, the number two spending category is telecommunications companies that face many of the same marketing challenges.

5. *Reversing sales or market share declines.* Advertising is generally seen as a tool to increase sales and expand customer usage. However, advertising also is used as a defensive weapon to halt declines in market share and sales volume. As we discuss in Chapter 6, often smaller brands in a category must allocate a significantly higher percentage of sales to advertising to compete with larger competitors. Companies such as Burger King and Wendy's spend at very high levels compared with most industries, but their dollars are dwarfed by McDonald's.

This list is not intended to include all the factors that might determine the level of advertising expenditures in a specific marketing communication plan. However, it does demonstrate the many variables that must be considered when a business is deciding what role advertising will play. Companies, even those with similar product lines, not only use different levels of advertising as part of their marketing communication mix but they also use vastly different advertising plans in terms of media used, scheduling of advertising placements, and the messages communicated. The allocation of advertising dollars is a continually changing dynamic of marketing management. Sometimes changes in advertising's role are made simply to avoid audience wearout after being exposed to the same marketing communication mix over a long period of time. However, most often, advertising is altered according to some specific change in the marketing environment.

Advertising and the Marketing Channel

5 Identify the primary components and considerations of advertising strategy.

One of the most important aspects of marketing is the development of the marketing channel. Exhibit 2.16 presents a traditional marketing channel model in which both products and communication flow from manufacturers to ultimate consumers. A well-organized marketing channel creates efficiencies through specialization in the movement of goods from producers, wholesalers, and retailers to ultimate consumers. Crucial to market channel efficiency is effective communication, including advertising. Most of the advertising that we see every day is called *consumer advertising* because it is directed to end-of-channel customers. However, advertising also plays a major role in

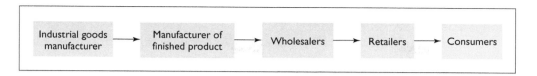

moving products through the various levels of production and distribution in the marketing channel.

For most of the twentieth century, the fundamentals of the marketing channel remained unchanged. Each product and service developed certain distribution methods for reaching consumers that were relatively consistent within an industry. However, in the past decade, new technology has started to change even longtime relationships among various elements of the marketing channel. For example, travel agents have seen their business decline as more and more travelers buy tickets directly from airline and hotel web sites. Digital cameras are quickly doing away with the need for film and film processing. More and more consumers are producing pictures on their home computer, sending them by e-mail, and bypassing hard copy prints altogether. Likewise, the ability to download music has affected all levels of the music marketing channel from major recording studios to the local music store. As we discuss the distribution channel, we should be aware that the "traditional" marketing channel has largely been replaced by distribution and marketing communication systems that are unique to each seller.

One of the fundamental changes has been the control of both marketing and communication channels by the consumer. For example, 68 percent of new-car buyers use nonmanufacturer-owned web sites to gain information and 37 percent of new-car sales are the direct result of online purchase decisions.[54] Research studies underscore the importance of the Internet as a marketing communications tool across a number of product categories and market segments. More than half of electronic goods buyers report they gathered information online before making a purchase, and approximately 25 percent spent as long as 3 hours researching their purchase. As one electronic marketer commented, "People are using the Internet not only to gather information about brands, but about product selection and variations of products and pricing."[55] A decade ago, the Internet was overwhelmingly a male-dominated communication channel. However, in recent years, that has changed dramatically as more and more women are using the convenience of Internet commerce. New mothers report that they have reduced their out-of-home shopping with the Internet, and 32 percent report fewer trips to shopping malls. Overall, 78 percent of women report they use the Internet to obtain product information.[56]

Although the Internet has increased the options for communicating and selling, it has not changed the fundamental decision-making process. Marketing strategy not only determines the role of advertising and its budget but also plays a major part in decisions concerning media choices. For example, a plan to use a coupon promotion will probably dictate a print media strategy. A decision to demonstrate product features may mean that television or the Internet will get the call. A complex sales message may take us to magazines, and a localized advertising strategy may move our message into newspapers or radio.

In the remainder of this chapter, we examine some of the ways advertising functions in various industries and stages of the marketing channel. Although you are most familiar with consumer advertising, it is only one of a number of categories that are used to bring products to market. Regardless of its audience, effective advertising must be successful on two levels: (1) communicating and (2) carrying out marketing goals.

DIRECTNESS AND DURATION

Perhaps the easiest way to evaluate advertising's role in the marketing process is to evaluate the *directness* of the intended communication effect and the anticipated *time* over which that effect is supposed to function. In other words, how much of the total selling job should be accomplished by advertising and over what time frame should we expect that task to be accomplished?

Advertising designed to produce an immediate response in the form of product purchase is called *direct-action*, *short-term* advertising. Most retail advertising falls into this category. An advertisement that runs in the newspaper this morning should sell some jeans this afternoon. Advertising used as a direct-sales tool but designed to operate over a longer time frame is called *direct-action*, *long-term* advertising. This advertising category is used with high-ticket items (washers and tires) in which the purchase decision is a result of many factors and the purchase cycle is relatively long.

Another category of advertising includes those advertisements that are used as indirect sales tools. Such indirect advertising is intended to affect the sales of a product only over the long term, usually by promoting general attributes of the manufacturer rather than specific product characteristics. Included in this category are most institutional or public relations advertising. The exception would be remedial public relations advertising designed to overcome some immediate negative publicity concerning product safety, labor problems, and so on.

The aim of most advertising is to move a product or service through the various levels of the marketing channel. The objectives and execution of advertising will change from level to level. The intended target audience will result in markedly different advertising strategies. In the following sections, we examine several categories of advertising to both consumers and businesses.

Advertising to the Consumer

NATIONAL ADVERTISING

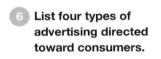

6 **List four types of advertising directed toward consumers.**

national advertising
Advertising by a marketer of a trademarked product or service sold through different outlets, in contrast to local advertising.

retail advertising
Advertising by a merchant who sells directly to the consumer.

The term **national advertising** has a special nongeographic meaning in advertising: It refers to advertising by the owner of a trademarked product (brand) or service sold through different distributors or stores. Thus, advertising for the dozens of regional beer brands is considered national advertising even though distribution might be confined to a single state or small area. Regardless of whether we are discussing a small regional company or a global brand such as Tide, Chevrolet, or Nike, all national advertising has a number of characteristics in common. For example, national advertising tends to be general in terms of product information. Because retailers often have varying policies and business practices, information concerning price, retail availability, and even service and installation is often omitted from national advertising or mentioned only in general terms. Conversely, **retail advertising** often includes price information, service and return policies, store locations, and hours of operation—information that national advertisers usually cannot provide. However, the need to communicate more closely with targeted consumers has caused national advertising to take on a more personalized tone during the past decade.

Beginning in the late 1980s, many national advertisers began to target their advertising on a geographic basis—first regionally and, increasingly, on a market-by-market basis. More recently, with a combination of better consumer research and advances in technology, national advertisers have begun to identify and reach more narrowly defined market segments and, in some cases, individual consumers (see Exhibit 2.17). Growth of Internet household penetration in concert with scanner data at the retail level allows national advertisers to offer specifically tailored messages to consumers based on individual lifestyle and product usage characteristics.

RETAIL (LOCAL) ADVERTISING

Retailing has undergone dramatic changes in the past 20 years, and these changes are reflected in its advertising and promotion. Without question, the most important change in retailing is the move from local and regional stores with anywhere from one to a dozen outlets to national chains operating throughout the country with more than 1,000

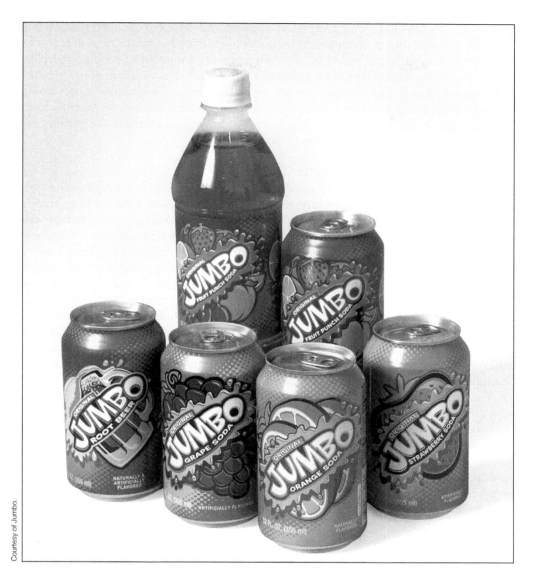

Courtesy of Jumbo.

stores. The consolidation of the retail industry has changed many of the retail practices of the past century. Consolidation has not only had the obvious effect of driving many locally owned, independent stores out of business but it also has had pronounced effects on the way retail marketing is conducted.

More and more, the retail category is dominated by one or two retailers. Rather than patronizing several independent retailers, customers more and more are doing "one-stop shopping," in which they can buy everything from groceries to eyewear, get a haircut, and service the family sedan under one roof. The new retail landscape makes it difficult to even categorize retailers. Does Wal-Mart more closely compete with Kroger as a grocery store or Target as a clothing store? Is Kroger a florist or a druggist? They sell more cut flowers and are the leading prescription drug seller in many markets. Is Target a high-end discounter or a low-end department store? Does a department store still fit that category if it employs shopping carts, centralized checkout, and few sales associates?

The move to national retailing has significant ramifications for newspapers and lo-cal radio stations. Newspapers, in particular, are seeing dramatic advertising spending shifts as retailers move to national promotional plans. A continuing trend over the past decade has seen declines in advertising pages in most major newspapers. Few observers see a quick turnaround given the continuing consolidation across virtually every seg-ment of the retail industry.

As we discuss later in the text, retail consolidation has also changed relationships between retailers and manufacturers. It has become so important for manufacturers to gain entry to these mega-stores that they often provide a number of product, merchandising, and promotional services specific to each retailer. For example, some products are manufactured to an individual retailer's specifications and both in-store promotions and advertising may be unique to a particular chain. At the same time, manufacturers find themselves increasingly competing with in-store brands. In effect, they are accommodating some of their strongest competitors.

END-PRODUCT ADVERTISING

end-product advertising
Building consumer demand by promoting ingredients in a product, for example, Teflon and NutraSweet.

What do products such as Intel computer chips, Lycra, and NutraSweet have in common? They are rarely purchased directly by consumers. Instead, they are bought as ingredients in other products. The promotion of such products is called **end-product advertising** (or *branded ingredient advertising*). End-product advertising is most commonly employed by manufacturers of ingredients used in consumer products. Successful end-product advertising builds consumer demand for an ingredient that will help in the sale of a product. The knowledge that manufacturers are creating consumer demand will encourage companies to use these ingredients in their consumer products.

End-product advertising began in the 1940s when DuPont began promoting its Teflon nonstick coatings. Soon consumers began to associate Teflon with a special benefit in cookware, and merchandise with the Teflon seal was marketed at a premium price and quickly built a loyal following among buyers. Despite the obvious benefits to the manufacturer, building demand through end-product advertising is not easy. It took Intel almost 5 years before computer buyers started actively seeking out the Intel brand when shopping for a computer. Regardless of the superiority of an ingredient, consumers must be convinced that it offers an added value to the final product. The selling task is made even more difficult by the fact that such ingredients usually are not obvious in the product; therefore, extensive advertising is required to make consumers aware of their advantages. Successful end-product advertisements are those that create meaningful differentiation for consumer purchase decisions. End-product advertising is a small part of total advertising, but it is extremely important in a number of product categories.

DIRECT-RESPONSE ADVERTISING

direct-response advertising
Any form of advertising done in direct marketing. Uses all types of media: direct mail, television, magazines, newspapers, radio. Term replaces mail-order advertising. See direct marketing.

Direct marketing and **direct-response advertising** are not new. In the United States, Benjamin Franklin is credited with the first direct-sales catalog, published in 1744, to sell scientific and academic books. The modern era of direct selling was ushered in with the publication of the Montgomery Ward catalog in 1872. The techniques and media of direct-response advertising have changed dramatically since those early days. However, what has not changed is the necessity to reach consumers with personal messages with offers designed to meet their specific needs. Although it has grown steadily throughout the past 50 years, the twenty-first century will be the era of direct-response marketing.

As more and more advertisers have shifted dollars from traditional mass media to more targeted vehicles, direct-response advertising has grown to more than $170 billion or almost half of all advertising expenditures. Consumer direct response accounts for 54 percent of the total with the remainder spent on business-to-business (B2B) advertising.[57] The largest sector of direct-response advertising is direct mail, which accounts for almost one-third of the total. Not unexpectedly, the fastest-growing area is Internet advertising. Although spending in telemarketing is still strong, it remains to be seen how the do-not-call list will impact the long-term health of the industry. With more than 90 million households signing up, it appears that consumer telemarketing may face serious hurdles in the future.

New technology, such as the Internet and other interactive media, provides a catalyst for future growth of direct response. In addition, advertisers in traditional media will increasingly adopt direct-response techniques. For example, it is quite common for advertisements and commercials to include 800-numbers to provide consumers with a way to buy directly or to obtain additional information about a product. In addition, cable television shopping channels and videocassettes and DVDs give consumers the opportunity to see merchandise "live" before ordering it from their living rooms. The future holds great promise for various forms of interactive media that will provide even more innovative ways of communicating with prospects.

Advertising to Business and Professions

The average person doesn't see a very important portion of advertising because it is aimed at retail stores, doctors, homebuilders, wholesalers, and others who operate at various stages of the marketing channel. However, B2B is one of the fastest-growing categories of advertising and it requires a much different strategy than consumer advertising. Although business publications remain a primary tool of B2B marketing, personal selling, telemarketing and other forms of direct response, and the Internet occupy a much higher share of expenditures directed to businesses compared to traditional media.

> **7** **List the types of advertising directed toward businesses and professionals.**

Another major difference between B2B and consumer advertising is the messages used in each. Although all advertising has to gain the audience's interest and attention, B2B tends to be fact oriented with few of the emotional appeals found in consumer advertising. Business-to-business messages are addressed not only to specific industries but also often to particular job classifications within these industries. Profit-oriented appeals are very common in B2B advertising. How a product will eliminate downtime, how it will decrease customer complaints, how it can save time and money, and how it can contribute to the overall efficiency and profitability of a business are among the primary themes of B2B marketing.

Business-to-business advertising also has to consider major differences in the buying process compared to consumer purchase behavior. Consumer purchases tend to be fairly straightforward. There may be some external influences on the purchase decision, such as children determining a family's fast-food or cereal preferences, but these causal relationships have little similarity with the formal purchasing models used in many B2B buys. The typical B2B purchase decisions tend to have distinct differences compared to typical consumer purchases. For example

1. Purchase decisions made by companies frequently involve many people, including those who do the actual buying, those who directly or indirectly influence this decision, and the employees who will actually use the product or service.

2. Organizational and industrial products are often bought according to precise, technical specifications that require significant knowledge about the product category on the part of both buyers and sellers.

3. Impulse buying is rare (industrial buyers do not suddenly get an "urge to splurge" on heavy machinery or silicon chips).

4. The dollar volume of purchases is often substantial, dwarfing most individual consumer grocery bills or mortgage payments.[58]

Categories of Business Advertising

TRADE ADVERTISING

Trade advertising is normally created by manufacturers and directed to middle components of the marketing channel—usually wholesalers and retailers. Trade advertising emphasizes product profitability and the consumer advertising support retailers will receive from manufacturers. In addition, trade advertising promotes products and services that retailers need to operate their businesses. Advertising for shelving, cleaning services, and cash registers, as well as the actual consumer products stocked for consumer purchase, is part of trade advertising.

trade advertising
Advertising directed to the wholesale or retail merchants or sales agencies through whom the product is sold.

KLEPPNER VIEWPOINT 2.3

Don Perry Vice President of Public Relations, Chick-fil-A

LEVERAGING PUBLIC RELATIONS

Don Perry

Throughout Chick-fil-A's history, public relations has played a critical role in building, maintaining, and protecting the brand. In fact, Truett Cathy himself could be considered the company's first "PR man." In addition to being a born entrepreneur, Cathy also was a natural showman. Although he had no formal marketing training, Cathy was a natural brand builder, not to mention a natural public relations practitioner and somewhat of a publicity hound.

Before the chain's inception, Cathy relied on his innate salesmanship and publicity-driving skills as he created the name for his new product, licensed his product, and eventually built a chain of restaurants around it. The early marketing efforts for the Chick-fil-A chain were predominantly public relations driven:

- Grand openings of new Chick-fill-A restaurants
- Development of the Leadership Scholarships ($1,000 scholarships provided to qualified restaurant team members)
- Creation of the "Symbol of Success" award (through a partnership with

Lincoln and Ford, Cathy offered cars as incentives for operators to reach aggressive sales goals)

As the company continued to grow, the strength of the Chick-fil-A brand continued to grow along with the need to formalize a public relations function to protect and enhance the brand. By the early 1980s, Chick-fil-A was achieving annual sales of more than $100 million.

Competitors were beginning to take notice of the success Chick-fil-A was enjoying, and one by one they began to introduce their own version of a chicken sandwich. These competitors included the major players—the members of the Big Three fast-food restaurants, which had multimillion-dollar advertising budgets to support their efforts. Chick-fil-A's advertising budget was—and still is—relatively minute in comparison to what its competitors spend. With no way to compete dollar for dollar for ad exposure, the chain relied predominantly on local marketing and public relations.

In 1983, with 281 stores spread out in malls from New Jersey to Atlanta to California that produced $136 million in total sales, Chick-fil-A hired Don Perry as its first public relations manager. As Perry recalls, "My directive from Steve Robinson was simple: put Truett Cathy and Chick-fil-A on the map."

Perry spent his first several years at Chick-fil-A on the road with Cathy, telling

the Chick-fil-A story and sampling the food, as the company spread its reach (both in terms of restaurants and publicity/brand building) beyond its original Southeast footprint.

Cathy made an effort to attend every opening and to conduct media interviews in each city. As Perry reflects, it was a public relations manager's dream to have the founder so available and so willing to work with the media.

As the chain increased its geographic reach and number of restaurants, it was necessary for the public relations function to adapt as well. Travelling with Truett to every grand opening was a logistical impossibility, with more and more stated each year. The size of the home office support staff was growing at a steady pace to keep up with the chain's continued growth.

With growth came the need for structure and processes. Amid all this change

Trade advertising has several objectives:

1. *Gain additional distribution.* Manufacturers are interested in increasing the number of wholesale and retail outlets that carry their brands.

2. *Increase trade support.* Manufacturers compete for shelf space and dealer support with countless other brands. Trade advertising can encourage retailers to give prominent positions to products or to use a manufacturer's point-of-purchase material.

in the chain as a whole, the role of public relations during this time went through a transition as well.

Public relations efforts in the early days at Chick-fil-A could generally be divided into three distinct categories:

- Acting as "publicist" for Cathy
- Event marketing logistics (primarily grand openings)
- Early stages of brand publicity (scholarships, product publicity)

Those categories quickly expanded to include a whole host of issues, initiatives, activities, and events that all require public relations support to maximize the positive impact on the chain's customers:

- Between 60 and 70 new restaurant openings per year
- Increased role and visibility of other Cathy family members involved in the business
- Marketing initiatives
  - Event marketing (*Chick-fil-A Bowl*; sponsorship of the ACC, SEC, and Big 12 conferences; and the *Chick-fil-A Kyle Petty Charity Ride*)
  - Family and kids marketing (Kids Meal program, *Core Essentials* and *Shake This Planet* character education programs)
  - Brand development (new products, brand expression)
  - Business development (licensing, outside sales)
  - Store marketing (systemwide promotions, in-store/local store marketing)

- Corporate initiatives (annual meeting, operator awards, etc.)
- Human Relations initiatives support (scholarships, trends, etc.)
- Issues management (crisis communications)

One area of support that has had a prominent place in Chick-fil-A's public relations plans since 1995 has been the "Eat Mor Chikin" Cows. The impact of the cow billboard campaign—and the significant role public relations would play in supporting it—was realized early on when one of the fiberglass cows was stolen in Chattanooga, Tennessee, by a group of bored teenagers. The "cow-napping" and subsequent "cow hunt" made national news. Perry's public relations team was on site to manage and disseminate the message through all media channels. From then on, the cows remained a public relations/branding staple for the chain.

The cows quickly became a key component in the chain's efforts to generate public awareness and to solidify the bond between the Chick-fil-A brand and its customers. Perry's team quickly learned to leverage the cows in many other ways to help enhance current programs. Costumed cow mascots were created to support all of Chick-fil-A's local marketing and event marketing efforts. Over time, the cows became a focal point for a majority of Chick-fil-A's marketing efforts (sports sponsorships, product launches, grand openings, merchandising and branding, their very own

calendar, even the title of Cathy's second book—*Eat Mor Chikin: Inspire More People*).

Public relations' place in Chick-fil-A's marketing mix is all but secured as the company continues to grow. Now in 37 states and Washington, DC, Chick-fil-A is moving ever closer to being a truly national brand—especially with its expansion into western markets (e.g., Southern California).

Consider where the brand is heading with the support of public relations:

- Mentioned on the *Regis & Kelly* show (During her pregnancy, Kelly Ripa spent several minutes during her show discussing her cravings for a Chick-fil-A Chicken Sandwich.)
- Truett Cathy was recently listed among the *Forbes* 400 richest people.
- Cathy has published four books and currently is working on a fifth book.
- WebMD profiled Chick-fil-A as an example to consumers on its segment about making healthy choices when dining out at quick-service restaurants.
- Chick-fil-A was named a "Customer Oriented Leader" by *Fast Company* magazine.

In slightly more than 4 decades, Chick-fil-A has grown to truly become part of the popular culture. Although much of the credit for this accomplishment rightly goes to Truett Cathy and to the success of the cows campaign, public relations has played a pivotal role in telling the Chick-fil-A story every step of the way.

3. *Announce consumer promotions.* Many trade advertisements offer a schedule of future consumer promotions and demonstrate to retailers that manufacturers are supporting brands with their advertising.

There are approximately 9,000 trade publications—several for virtually every category of retail business. The average consumer probably has not heard of most of these publications, but trade journals such as *Progressive Grocer* and *Drug Topics* play an important role in the advertising plans of many national advertisers.

INDUSTRIAL ADVERTISING

A manufacturer is a buyer of machinery, equipment, raw materials, and components used in producing the goods it sells. Companies selling to manufacturers most often address their advertising to the manufacturers in appropriate industry publications, by direct mail, through telemarketing, and by personal selling. This method is quite unlike consumer advertising and is referred to as **industrial advertising**. Industrial advertising is directed at a very specialized and relatively small audience. Examples of industrial magazines are *Plant Services*, *Rubber World*, and *Valve World*—only a few of the hundreds of publications that make up this category.

Industrial advertising rarely seeks to sell a product directly. The purchase of industrial equipment is usually a complex process that includes a number of decision makers. Often, industrial advertising is a means of introducing a product or gaining brand name awareness to make it easier for follow-ups from company sales representatives to close a sale.

industrial advertising
Advertising addressed to manufacturers who buy machinery, equipment, raw materials, and the components needed to produce the goods they sell.

PROFESSIONAL ADVERTISING

The primary difference between **professional advertising** and other trade advertising is the degree of control exercised by professionals over the purchase decisions of their clients. Whereas a grocery store encourages consumer purchases of certain goods by the brands it stocks, people can go to another store with more variety, lower prices, or better-quality merchandise. However, a person rarely will change doctors because a physician doesn't prescribe a certain brand of drugs, change banks because the bank orders checks for its customers from a particular printer, or choose an architect based on how designs are reproduced (see Exhibit 2.18). Publications in this category include the *ABA Journal* published by the American Bar Association, the *JAMA* published by the American Medical Association, *Public School Administrator*, and so on.

professional advertising
Advertising directed at those in professions such as medicine, law, or architecture who are in a position to recommend the use of a particular product or service to their clients.

CORPORATE OR INSTITUTIONAL ADVERTISING

To the average consumer, giant conglomerates such as United Technologies, ConAgra, and Unilever bring to mind few specific brands. However, these same consumers are very familiar with Dove soap, Lipton tea, and Birds Eye frozen food, all products of Unilever. Likewise, Healthy Choice, Chef Boyardee, and Orville Redenbacher's (ConAgra) and Otis elevators, Pratt & Whitney engines, and Carrier air conditioners (United Technologies) are household names. Although **institutional advertising** remains a long-term image-building technique, in recent years it has taken on a decided sales orientation in terms of the audiences reached and intent of communication. More and more, companies are attempting to bring their diverse inventory of products and brand names under a single corporate identity. In doing so, they are attempting to accomplish a number of corporate objectives, including:

institutional advertising
Advertising done by an organization speaking of its work views, and problems as a whole, to gain public goodwill and support rather than to sell a specific product. Sometimes called public relations advertising.

- Establishing a public identity
- Explaining a company's diverse missions
- Boosting corporate identity and image
- Gaining awareness with target audiences for sales across a number of brands
- Associating a company's brands with some distinctive corporate character

These are only a few examples of possible corporate advertising objectives. The competitive environment of recent years has brought about dramatic changes in corporate advertising.

Nonproduct Advertising

IDEA ADVERTISING

It is not surprising that the same marketing techniques so successful in selling products would be used to promote ideas. We are living in a period of conflicting ideas and special

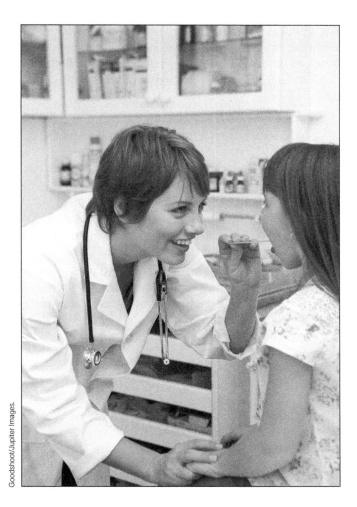

Goodshoot/Jupiter Images.

EXHIBIT 2.18

Among professionals, physicians are often targeted by prescription pharmaceutical advertisers.

interest groups. Marketing concepts and advertising have become important elements in swaying public opinion. As we saw in Chapter 1, advertising propaganda is not a new phenomenon. What is new are the number of public interest groups using advertising and the sophistication of the communication techniques being employed. In recent years, issues such as gun control, abortion, animal rights, and the environment have been debated in mass advertising.

Idea advertising is often controversial. Apart from the emotionalism of many of the topics being espoused, there are critics who think that advertising messages are too short and superficial to fully debate many of these issues. Proponents counter that advertising is the only practical way to get their messages before a mass audience. They point out that idea advertising may be the most practical means for these groups to use their First Amendment privileges. Regardless of one's position on idea advertising, the increasing ability of media to narrowly target audiences, by ideology as well as product preference, will make this type of advertising more prevalent in the future.

idea advertising
Advertising used to promote an idea or cause rather than to sell a product or service.

SERVICE ADVERTISING

We are becoming a nation of specialists with more and more Americans seeking advice and services for everything from financial planning to child care. Because service providers are basically people enterprises, **service advertising** almost always has a strong institutional component. Service companies tend to keep the same slogan, theme, or identifying mark over long periods of time to increase consumer awareness. Because service industries are so similar (and often legally regulated), it is difficult to develop a distinct differentiation among competitors. Banks and insurance companies have a particularly difficult time establishing an effective identity.

service advertising
Advertising that promotes a service rather than a product.

Fundamentals of good advertising are the same, regardless of whether a product or service is being promoted. However, many marketing experts point out that differences between the two categories require some care in the manner in which service messages are handled. Some basic principles of service advertising include the following:

1. *Feature tangibles.* Because service advertising has no tangible product to feature, it should be personalized in some way. For example, service advertisements often use testimonials. Service messages should show the benefits of the service, such as an on-time plane trip that results in closing a deal, or a contented older couple as a result of good investment advice by their broker.

2. *Feature employees.* Because the value of a service largely depends on the quality of a firm's employees, it is important to make them feel that they are an important part of the company and that they can and should develop trust with customers. Often, service messages feature real employees in their advertisements. This approach has the advantage of personalizing the service to customers and building employee morale.

3. *Stress quality.* Because the quality and performance of services are sometimes more difficult to measure than products, advertisements should emphasize consistency and high levels of competency. Hospitals use words such as *caring, professional,* and *convenient* in their advertising.

Government Advertising

All levels of government in this country have created various forms of propaganda and public policy messages since the Revolutionary War era. However, in the past 20 years, the growth of government services and programs has resulted in a greater use of traditional advertising by government agencies. The federal government spends millions of dollars each year promoting an array of agencies including the volunteer armed forces, consumer-protection programs, and environment and health initiatives. The new Medicare prescription drug program was launched with massive spending aimed at educating senior citizens about the options available to them. State governmental agencies also have taken advantage of advertising to create awareness regarding state beautification (see Exhibit 2.19).

EXHIBIT 2.19

State governments have become major advertisers in recent years.

Courtesy of Robinson.

SUMMARY

The roles of advertising are many, varied, and ever changing. The options open to advertisers have never been greater, and the costs of errors are significantly magnified compared to only a few years ago. With fragmented audiences and media, higher costs of reaching prospects, and the challenges of effectively using new media technology, the demands on advertisers and their agencies have never been greater. However, regardless of the changes in the advertising process, two fundamentals for successful advertising will remain constant:

1. Effective advertising can only function within the context of an organized marketing plan.

2. Advertising is a marketing communication tool and rarely will be successful if it is directed at noncommunication problems. It is difficult, if not impossible, for advertising to overcome deficiencies in the core marketing program.

An effective advertising plan is an extension of the marketing goals of a firm. Advertising typically is asked to help develop or maintain product awareness, build company and brand image, and provide product information that differentiates one brand from another. The execution of advertising varies based on the trade channel to which it is directed (e.g., retail, consumer, industrial, or professional). Furthermore, it can adapt to the primary product benefits and express them in a number of ways (e.g., testimonials, demonstrations, or long copy). Advertising also is modified according to budgetary considerations, as well as the corporate philosophy concerning the value of advertising within the marketing plan.

It is clear that advertising is only one of a number of possible sales tools. The advertising executive of the future will be a marketing communicator who is able to use an array of marketing communication elements including promotion, public relations, and personal selling in a coordinated fashion to bring synergy and unity to the overall corporate message.

Although major changes in advertising are on the horizon, the key to its success will continue to be the ability to develop an interesting message that will reach potential customers in an appropriate environment at the most opportune time. During the remainder of the text, we discuss the techniques of advertising against a backdrop of marketing, research, and planning.

REVIEW

1. Compare and contrast the three types of convergence discussed in this chapter and their effect on advertising.
2. How has the emphasis on return on investment changed the relationship between advertising and the media?
3. How does advertising complement other elements of marketing communication?
4. Discuss public relations from the standpoint of audience credibility and message control.
5. What role does brand equity play in a product's long-term success?
6. Why has integrated marketing communication become even more important in a period of media fragmentation?
7. Discuss the primary advantages and disadvantages of brand extension.
8. A product is a bundle of benefits. Discuss.
9. Discuss product differentiation in terms of target market segmentation.
10. Discuss price strategy as a means of marketing strategy.
11. Compare and contrast business-to-business and consumer advertising in terms of audiences, media, and promotional techniques.

PLANNING THE ADVERTISING

Part II introduces the fundamentals of advertising planning and brand research on which virtually all successful advertising is based.

- **CHAPTER 3** introduces the concept of the advertising spiral and the strategies needed to keep brands vigorous in a changing marketplace.
- **CHAPTER 4** outlines the fundamentals of identifying and understanding target markets that are most interested in and profitable for specific products.

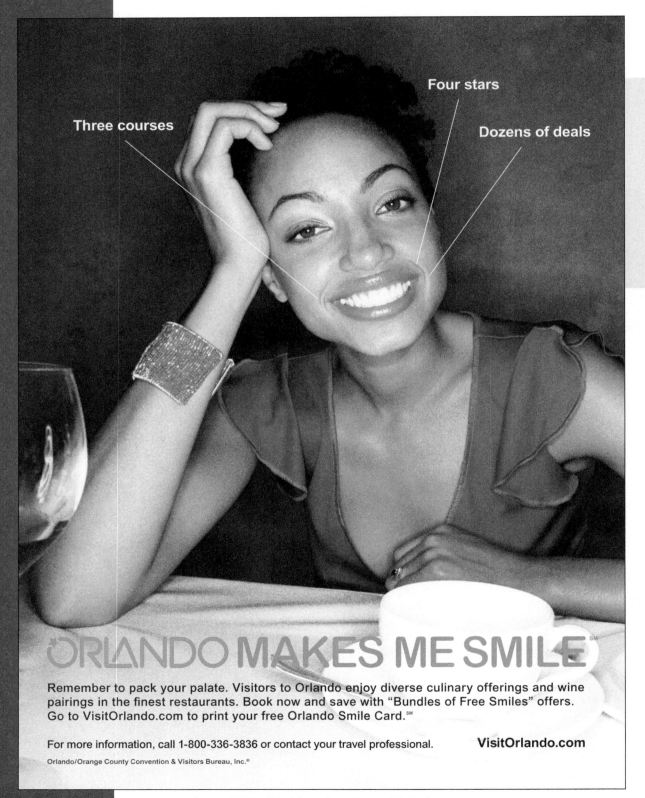

Three courses

Four stars

Dozens of deals

ORLANDO MAKES ME SMILE℠

Remember to pack your palate. Visitors to Orlando enjoy diverse culinary offerings and wine pairings in the finest restaurants. Book now and save with "Bundles of Free Smiles" offers. Go to VisitOrlando.com to print your free Orlando Smile Card.℠

For more information, call 1-800-336-3836 or contact your travel professional.

VisitOrlando.com

Orlando/Orange County Convention & Visitors Bureau, Inc.®

Brand Planning and the Advertising Spiral

O NE OF the critical aspects of marketing communications decision making is developing a strategy. It has been said that strategy is everything. ▶

CHAPTER LEARNING OBJECTIVES

1. Discuss the birth and basics of branding.
2. Explain brands and integrated marketing.
3. Discuss brand equity.
4. Explain IMC strategic planning.
5. Explain the importance of the product life cycle.
6. Discuss the relationship of the advertising spiral.

First, let's listen to the perspective of a brand expert at Landor Associates: "Brands matter, and never more so than today. In the escalating din of global choice and competition, brands are the most effective way of cutting through the racket to reach people's hearts and minds." And according to the global Amsterdam agency StawberryFrog, "Today, consumers don't want to buy brands, they want to BUY IN to what the brand believes in."

Building Strong Brands and Equity

Advertisers and their agencies don't agree on a lot of issues, but almost everyone agrees that brands are a company's most valuable assets, so we need to understand a little about them. The product is *not* the brand. A product is manufactured; a **brand** is created.

Yes, Orlando is a brand and has to compete with other cities for convention revenues (see the chapter-opening ad). A product may change over time, but the brand remains. A brand exists only through communication. Landor Associates' Antonio Marazza said, "A brand represents the most powerful link between the offer and consumer. What else is a brand if not what consumers (or more generally, stakeholders) perceive it to be? Familiarity, image, and trust drive a brand's reason to be and thus they are the building blocks of its capacity to generate value. It follows that to value a brand, you have to investigate not only within the company walls (or accounts), but above all else the mind of the consumer, where the real value of the brand resides." Landor's brand pioneer Walter Landor argued that "products are made in the factory, but brands are created in the mind."[1]

Every product, service, or company with a recognized brand name stands for something slightly different from anything else in the same product category (see Exhibit 3.1). Since 1933, Zippo has been a leading brand in its product category. If the product or service difference is a desirable one and is known and understood by consumers, the brand will be the category leader. Today, more than ever before, the perception of a quality difference is essential for survival in the marketplace.[2] According to Allen Adamson, managing director at Landor, a brand, for every intent and purpose, is a promise—a promise

brand
A name, term, sign, design, or a unifying combination of them intended to identify and distinguish the product or service from competing products or services.

EXHIBIT 3.1

Zippo has been a leading brand since the 1930s. This trade ad tries to convince retailers to carry the product because it is a leading brand.

that it will help the user make (or save) money, look better, or feel great. The Dove brand promises to make women feel gorgeous even if they aren't supermodels. Volvo, of course, vows to deliver your family safely from Point A to Point B. Honest Tea suggests that the ingredients are natural and free from preservatives. Today, marketers need to take a close look at their brand's promise and ensure its delivery. Everyone associated with that brand needs to understand its promise and how to bring it to life.[3] To gain consumer trust and to be perceived as credible, everything connected to that brand and every branded experience must be consistent.

1 Discuss the birth and basics of branding.

THE ORIGIN OF BRANDING

In the mid-1880s, there were no brands and little quality control by manufacturers. Wholesalers held power over both manufacturers and retailers. Manufacturers had to offer the best deals to wholesalers to get their products distributed. This created a squeeze of profits. As a result of this profit squeeze, some manufacturers decided to differentiate their products from the competition. They gave their products names, obtained patents to protect their exclusivity, and used advertising to take the news about them to customers over the heads of the wholesalers and retailers. Thus, the concept of branding was born. Among the early brands still viable today are Levi's (1873), Maxwell House Coffee (1873), Budweiser (1876), Ivory (1879), Coca-Cola (1886), Campbell Soup (1893), and Hershey's Chocolate (1900).[4] In 1923, a study showed that brands with "mental dominance" with consumers included Ivory (soaps), Gold Medal (flour), Coca-Cola (soft drinks), B.V.D. (underwear), Kellogg's Cornflakes (breakfast food), Ford (automobiles), Del Monte (canned fruit), and Goodyear (tires). Today, we have a whole new generation of brands fighting for value and a permanent place in consumers' lives, including TiVo, Starbucks, Panera, iPhone, Swiffer, eBay, ThermaCare, Expedia.com, Amazon.com, and others.

BRAND CONNECTIONS

Since brands started advertising in the mid-nineteenth century in newspapers, mass-media advertising has been about making connections. As technology brings areas of the modern world closer together, advertising is becoming more disconnected from its historical base, including its business models and its changing audiences. Thanks to all the digital changes and the Internet, advertising is going through its first true paradigm shift. As a result, there is a revolutionary change in media tools—social media, expanded web video, the promise of IPTV (Internet Protocol Television) that married television to the Internet—and a whole new way to connect.

BRANDING CHANNELS AND ENGAGEMENT

Branding today is not about the media; it's about the idea. Marketers have to dismiss conventional thinking and start with an understanding of the value of each communication channel and how—or if—it will engage people. The idea should be the organizing principle, and it should inform everything you do to help consumers grasp your brand promise in whatever channel you're using to reach them: blogs, banner ads, television, or word of mouth, according to Michael Mendenhall, chief marketing officer at Hewlett-Packard. In other words, in the digital age, it is absolutely critical to understand the value of each branding channel and its relevance to a particular audience.[5]

BRANDING AS A FINANCIAL DECISION

"Branding isn't an advertising decision. It's a financial decision," according to Howard, Merrell & Partners of Raleigh, North Carolina. "We have learned that creating brand leverage is about dealing correctly with strategic issues and financial commitments at the top management level—then taking the risks necessary to deliver category-dominating creative. It is about risk management. It is about a deep understanding of a brand's one-on-one relationship with people, considered in the context of a macro-competitive environment. We believe that perhaps our most important role is assisting our client partners to achieve the alignment needed to reinforce brand values at all points of human contact . . . ."[6]

DIGITAL INFLUENCE

Digital communication, alone, can influence how people think about brands in a way no other branding means can. Digital allows the world to determine whether a brand is practicing what it preaches. For instance, if you have a bad flight you can instantly Tweet the world about your experience. Word of mouth now acts like it is on steroids. If your brand is delivering on its promise in wonderful ways, be it creative execution or product performance, the world might know about it instantly. If your brand is screwing up badly, the world will know that too. In today's digital world, your brand and the brand organization must perform, behave, and satisfy the consumer's needs as they expect. As Allan P. Adamson of Landor Associates says, the promise your brand makes must be the promise it delivers.

Brands and Integrated Marketing Communications

Interbrand's branding experts indicate some marketers believe integrated marketing communications (IMC) is to marketing communications what digital convergence is to the world of technology—a revolutionary concept with great promise and hype. In theory, IMC is hard to debate because it is logical. The basic belief holds that integration of all communications emanates from a single strategic platform and will generate a significantly greater return on the communications investment than would be the case with traditional independent media executions. The theoretical benefits are clear. For the client, there is the potential for significant synergies and stronger connections with their customers.[8] Practice has fallen far short of theory.

In the past, many marketing functions—advertising, promotion, packaging, direct marketing, public relations, events—were created and managed independently in most organizations. Today, a brand's equity is best strengthened through the integrated use of all marketing communication tools working from a single strategy. It is imperative to

2 **Explain brands and integrated marketing.**

KLEPPNER VIEWPOINT 3.1

Brad Majors CEO, Brand Reps, LLC

BRAND DEVELOPMENT DEMYSTIFIED

There is a lot of talk about "branding" or "brand development" these days, as if it is the next "new thing" in marketing and sales. "Brand development" is not a new phenomenon. It has been around for at least 100 years.

Any marketer or ad agency worth its salt practices "brand development" every time they perform any marketing function. The history of advertising in America is, essentially, the history of branding. That is what good advertising (and the other communication disciplines) does—create good and consistent reputations for products or services and this consistent imagery is what converts a product into a "brand."

I say "consistent" because one of the greatest sins of marketing these days (especially for smaller businesses) is a lack of "integrated marketing." By this I mean that there may be mixed messages (from media advertising, public relations, the website, package copy, or whatever) that go out to consumers from a brand. And with these inconsistent messages comes an inconsistent image for the brand. Developing integrated marketing communications is one of the most important activities that can be done to enhance the value of a client's brand. It is nearly impossible to build a brand with inconsistencies in your marketing communications mix.

Business schools teach "the Marketing Mix," which is pretty basic stuff, but bear with me. This Marketing Mix includes the Four P's of marketing: the Product itself (and its structural packaging), the Price of the product, the Place

(of distribution) where the product can be purchased, and the Promotion of the product. Interestingly, the fourth P, Promotion, is simply the communication of aspects of the first three P's.

What else is critical to the sale other than what the product does, how much it costs, and where you can get it? Only one more "element" I can think of.

Enter the "Fifth P," which isn't discussed in B-School textbooks, but I doubt the idea is mine alone. What does the Fifth P stand for? The Prospect: The person who is going to buy this product or service, based on perceived needs and wants.

If the Fourth P, Promotion, connects Product, Price, and Place, it also performs another valuable function. Good Promotion, be it in the form of media advertising, packaging graphics, public relations, or in-store merchandising, also has the responsibility of connecting the Prospect to the Product, its Price, and the Place it can be found. In essence, the product is simply a collection of features and attributes until the Prospect arrives on the scene. When the Prospect's needs and wants begin to surface, so do the brand's marketing possibilities.

As the Prospect evaluates all the information he or she knows about the product (what it does, what it costs, where it can be purchased), a relationship may begin to form. However, this will only happen if the brand imagery has been consistently presented. This relationship is based on how the Prospect feels the product (or service) will meet his or her needs and wants. I call this "personal relevance." How does the Prospect relate

Brad Majors

emotionally to those rational product attributes? This "personal relevance" is not a new concept in marketing either. Marketers have been trying to figure out how to achieve the emotional bond between Prospect and brand since the 1920s when motivational research was first used by ad agencies. And we are still trying to crack the code on why consumers make the brand choices they make.

A final comment in the brand development demystification process: Sometimes the term *brand development* can suggest some type of inexpensive shortcut in marketing. I have spoken with entrepreneurs who wanted to do "brand development" because they didn't have money for advertising. Sorry, it doesn't really work that way. Although media advertising may not be the only way to promote your brand, developing a brand takes time and money. Strong brands do not come cheaply. Fortunately, if the "brand development" process is successful, that investment will pay out big as you go down the marketing road.

Courtesy of Brad Majors, yourbrandreps.blogspot. com.

Courtesy of Brunner Digital, Washington, DC, and Zippo.

EXHIBIT 3.2

This online storyboard shows frame by frame how this Zippo product will be seen on the web.

project a single, cohesive brand image into the marketplace and into the consumer's mind. This process could be called simply *common sense*. The result has been what is labeled *integrated marketing communications*.

To be perfectly clear, IMC refers to all the messages directed to a consumer on behalf of the brand: media advertising, promotion, public relations, direct response, events, packaging, web, and so forth. Zippo uses the web for a number of its products. Exhibit 3.2 is an online storyboard of how the online ad will move frame by frame. Each message from a company must be integrated or dovetailed in order to support all the other messages or impressions about the brand. If this process is successful, it will build a brand's equity by communicating the same brand message to consumers.

However, brand integration doesn't mean ensuring that your logo and end line are always the same. It doesn't mean persuading half a dozen agencies to work together. It is a result, not a process. When customers have a coherent experience whenever and wherever they come across your brand, you have achieved integration.[9] Ideas that can be captured in a nutshell can be understood more easily.

Today, most marketers realize the brand is their most important asset, and integrated programs and brand building are so important in building its value. The most important factor in determining the actual value of a brand is its equity in the market. We can define **brand equity** as the value of how people such as consumers, distributors, and salespeople think and feel about a brand relative to its competition.

Let us look at how Young & Rubicam assesses brand equity's value.

brand equity
The value of how such people as consumers, distributors, and salespeople think and feel about a brand relative to its competition over a period of time.

YOUNG & RUBICAM'S BRAND ASSET VALUATOR

One of the most respected proprietary tools in the industry for assessing a brand's stature among consumers is the Brand Asset Valuator (BAV) created by Young & Rubicam (Y&R). It is a diagnostic tool for determining how a brand is performing relative to all other brands. It explains the strengths and weaknesses of brands on measures of stature and vitality. It believes the relationship between these two factors tells the true story about the health of brand equity and can help diagnose problems and solutions.

The BAV demonstrates that brands are built in a very specific progression of four primary consumer perceptions: differentiation, relevance, esteem, and knowledge.

- Differentiation is the basis for choice: the essence of the brand, source of margin.
- Relevance relates to usage and subsumes the five P's of marketing related to sales.
- Esteem deals with consumer respect, regard, and reputation and relates to the fulfillment of perceived consumer promise.
- Knowledge is the culmination of brand-building efforts and relates to consumer experiences.

A brand's vitality lies in a combination of differentiation and relevance. A brand must be distinct, or it simply isn't a brand. But the fact that a brand is highly differentiated doesn't necessarily mean consumers have the desire or means to buy it. Unless a brand is also relevant, the consumer has no reason to select it. The lack of relevance is the reason so many fads come and go.

The two components of brand stature are esteem and familiarity, that is, whether people know and understand your brand and whether they like it. A brand that more consumers know than like is a clear warning signal. Similarly, a brand that is held in high esteem but ranks lower in familiarity suggests that increasing awareness is an appropriate objective.

Steve Owen, who helped create BAV, says BAV looks at brands from a logical perspective. The key challenge a brand has is how to increase its dominance. The most interesting thing about BAV is that it's based on the fact that almost every successful brand begins by being very simple. "It doesn't try to sell to everyone. It begins by selling one thing to a few people and ensures that it's different and better in a meaningful way."[10]

One of the keys to understanding brand equity is to recognize that there are differences between product categories.

From this discussion, you should be getting the sense that developing advertising strategy and building brand equity deal with many complex issues. Despite being a little deep, this discussion has given you a feel for the many issues and terms advertising practitioners face daily. Despite this complexity, the development of advertising isn't brain surgery. It is understanding all the ramifications in the market and the consumer's mind, so we can integrate communication and build brand equity better.

BRAND EQUITY AND DEVELOPING INTEGRATED MARKETING COMMUNICATIONS STRATEGIC PLANS

3 Discuss brand equity.

Before you start to think about creating advertisements for a brand, you need a strategic plan. Before you can develop a strategy, you need an understanding of the marketing situation and a clear understanding of the brand's equity. There are four logical steps in this process resulting in the creative brief or plan:

1. Brand equity audit analysis
2. Strategic options and recommendations
3. Brand equity research
4. Creative brief

Of course, these generally would be followed by evaluation or assessment of some nature. An outline of a strategic planning process is presented next to give you insight into what is required. Some of the concepts and terms are discussed in more detail throughout the text.

Push.

Courtesy of PUSH, Orlando.

When Push opened its doors in 1996 in Orlando, it was founded on the simple premise of giving amazing minds a place to do amazing work. Since its founding, the agency has grown to cover advertising in all disciplines and to produce award-winning work for international, national, and regional clients. Thanks to Push's unique approach, National ADDY, ReBrand 100, Pixel, Webby, and Silver Anvil awards line the Push mantel.

Push's success lies in its ability to be discipline neutral. The concept of discipline neutral is the foundation for what agency integration is truly about—bringing all agency disciplines (account planning, account management, creative, media, public relations, interactive) together under one roof and giving them all equality at the table to solve whatever problems or address whatever opportunities clients present. That is accomplished without preconceived ideas or agendas as to who has the best answer or which department or discipline needs the best-looking profit-and-loss statement.

To put this concept into practical use, the agency created a model that allows them to approach brands (and create revenue streams) from a holistic perspective. Push's proprietary Brand Convergence Model™ looks at brands in four quadrants—exposure (consumer-facing messaging that includes creative, interactive, public relations, etc.), environment (all physical designs including those in retail stores, sales centers, restaurant interiors, etc.), experience (the product or service itself), and expertise (all inward-facing communications to employees, such as, sales staff, customer service, waitstaff, etc.).

The most important idea about this model is that it gives Push the ability to approach both new and existing clients with brand ideas from all four of its quadrants. At the center of the model is the consumer, so Push's account planning staff plays a tremendous role in ensuring that the consumer is considered and connected through every step of the process. Push has hired design directors, public relations strategists, media directors, creative directors, and interactive directors based on this model, ensuring that all the work they do goes beyond a single campaign, a single social networking strategy, a single press release, or a single web site.

Although this model is primarily theory for most agencies, Push has put it into practice for a number of clients. A great example is Smokey Bones. In addition to the ad campaigns, web sites, and social media strategies (exposure), Push designed new Smokey Bones interiors (environment), affected menu items with both new products and new definitions (experience), and helped reenergize their staff through a variety of initiatives (expertise).

The Brand Convergence Model™ allows Push to do more than integrate at the agency level; it allows them to integrate with their clients, thereby allowing them to develop more relationships throughout their clients' companies. Not only does Push interact with marketing directors but it is also involved with directors of operations, human resources directors, development directors, and upper-level management as the agency constantly shows how a properly positioned brand affects business throughout an entire company.

BRAND EQUITY AUDIT ANALYSIS

There are a number of areas to examine in the first step, brand equity audit analysis. For instance, the context of the market, strengths and weaknesses, consumer attitude descriptions, and competitive strategies and tactics are of importance here.

MARKET CONTEXT   We begin by examining the existing situation of both the market and the consumer. What we are looking for are clues and factors that positively or negatively affect brand equity. The whole purpose is to set the scene. The types of questions that are asked include the following:

- What is our market and with whom do we compete?

- What are other brands and product categories?

- What makes the market tick?
- How is the market structured?
- Is the market segmented? If so, how? In what segment are we?
- What is the status of store and generic brands?
- Are products highly differentiated?
- What kind of person buys products in this category?
- In the minds of these consumers, what drives the market or holds it back (needs, obstacles, and so forth)? What are the key motivators?
- Do consumers perceive the brands as very much alike or different?
- Is the product bought on impulse?
- How interested are consumers in the product?
- Do consumers tend to be brand loyal?

These questions should help us understand the status and role of brands in a given market. For example, when the market consists of a few brands, the consumer will likely be more brand sensitive than if the market includes many brands.

We must look at the market from varying angles and select only the relevant ones so that we can set the scene for understanding and building brand equity.

BRAND EQUITY WEAKNESSES AND STRENGTHS   Now we have a better understanding of the market context and are ready to examine the current brand equity—how strong or weak consumer bias is toward our brand relative to other brands. The following is a list of weakness and strength indicators often used.

- Brand awareness—top of mind is best
- Market share, price elasticity, share of voice, and similar factors
- Brand sensitivity—the relative importance of the brand to other factors involved in the purchase, such as price, pack size, model
- Consistency of the brand's communication over time
- Image attribute ratings or ranking attributes
- Distribution, pricing, product quality, and product information
- Brand loyalty—the strength of a brand lies in the customers who buy it as a brand rather than only as a product

Once the key weakness and strength indicators have been identified, they are used for future tracking purposes.

BRAND EQUITY DESCRIPTIONS   Now that we understand the **market** in which our brand operates and have a clear understanding of the strengths and weaknesses of our brand equity, we need to identify and describe consumers' thoughts and feelings that result in their bias toward our brand relative to other brands. This personal relationship between the consumer and the brand provides the most meaningful description of brand equity. To accomplish this, we need an analysis from two points of view.

First, we need to review all the available research to get as close a feeling as possible on how consumers view the brand and how they feel about it. Second, we must analyze in depth our brand's and its competitors' communications over a period of time. It is from these communications that most of consumers' feelings (emotional elements) and opinions (rational elements) about the brand are derived (see Exhibit 3.3).

market
A group of people who can be identified by some common characteristic, interest, or problem; use a certain product to advantage; afford to buy it; and be reached through some medium.

EXHIBIT 3.3

The Basic Elements of a Brand

A brand equity description for the Golf GTI automobile might be as follows:

Emotional Elements	**Rational Elements**
My little sports car	Inexpensive
Sets me free	High gas mileage
It makes me feel and look good	Retains value
Simple	Durable
It's there when I want it	Dependable
I'm in control	Handles well
	Easy to park—small

COMPETITIVE STRATEGIES AND TACTICS This area of the audit is designed to provide a clear summary of the current communication strategies and tactics of our brand and of key competitors. It should include an analysis of all integrated communications in relation to brand equity. Is the strategy designed to reinforce current brand equity? Who is the target audience? Are there different target audiences? What are the themes and executional approaches? How are the marketing funds being spent (e.g., consumer pull versus trade push, advertising, promotions, direct marketing, others)? An assessment of problems and opportunities is also in order here.

STRATEGIC OPTIONS AND RECOMMENDATIONS

The second step draws on the conclusions from the analysis to develop a viable recommendation plan. The strategic options include the following:

- *Communication objectives.* What is the primary goal the message aims to achieve?
- *Audience.* To whom are we speaking?
- *Source of business.* Where are the customers going to come from—brand(s) or product categories?
- *Brand positioning and benefits.* How are we to position the brand, and what are the benefits that will build brand equity?
- *Marketing mix.* What is the recommended mix of advertising, public relations, promotion, direct response, and so on?
- *Rationale.* How does the recommended strategy relate to, and what effect is it expected to have on, brand equity?

BRAND EQUITY RESEARCH

In the third step, we do the proprietary, qualitative research. It is exploratory and task-oriented research. Here, we need to determine which elements or elements of brand equity must be created, altered, or reinforced to achieve our recommended strategy and how far we can stretch each of these components without risking the brand's credibility. This may give us a revised list of rational and emotional elements that describe how we want consumers to think and feel about our brand in the future.

CREATIVE BRIEF

The final step is a written creative brief (or work plan) for all communications. We synthesize all the information and understanding into an action plan for the development of all communications for the brand: advertising, public relations, promotion, and so forth.

The creative strategy (brief or work plan) is a short statement that clearly defines our audience, how consumers think or feel and behave, what the communication is intended to achieve, and the promise that will create a bond between the consumer and the brand. A typical strategy would include the following:

- *Key observations.* The most important market/consumer factor that dictates the strategy
- *Communication objective.* The primary goal the advertising or communication aims to achieve
- *Consumer insight.* The consumer "hot button" our communication will trigger
- *Promise.* What the brand should represent in the consumer's mind; what the brand is promising the consumer
- *Support.* The reason the promise is true
- *Audience.* To whom we are speaking and how they feel about the brand

There may be a need for an additional element:

- *Mandatories.* Items used as compulsory constraints, for example, a specific legal requirement or corporate policy that impacts the direction of the strategy

OTHER EXAMPLES OF STRATEGIC PLANNING

It is important to understand that there isn't only one approach to developing an integrated strategic plan for a brand. The basic steps are similar, but each agency approaches the process a little differently. Let's take a look at the basics of a couple of other strategic planning approaches.

AVRETT, FREE & GINSBERG'S PLANNING CYCLE   Avrett, Free & Ginsberg (AFG) uses a seven-step planning cycle that helps create strategic advertising. It uses the discipline of account planning at each stage of developing strategy. Briefly, the framework for its strategic planning cycle (see Exhibit 3.4) involves the following steps:

1. *Brand/market status.* AFG evaluates where the brand is in its marketplace and determines strengths, weaknesses, opportunities, and threats.
2. *Brand mission.* After determining brand status, AFG proposes and agrees on brand goals, that is, where it can take the brand.
3. *Strategic development.* Here, AFG explores various options to determine which of several strategies will empower the brand to achieve the mission. AFG uses a process called *needs mapping* (see Exhibit 3.5). The basic principle is that people respond or bond to products based on a wide range of psychological and rational needs. This process is loosely based on Maslow's hierarchy of needs.

EXHIBIT 3.4
AFG Planning Cycle

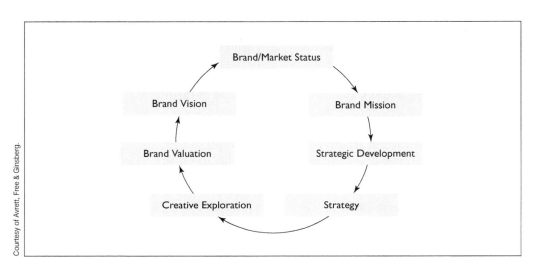

Courtesy of Avrett, Free & Ginsberg.

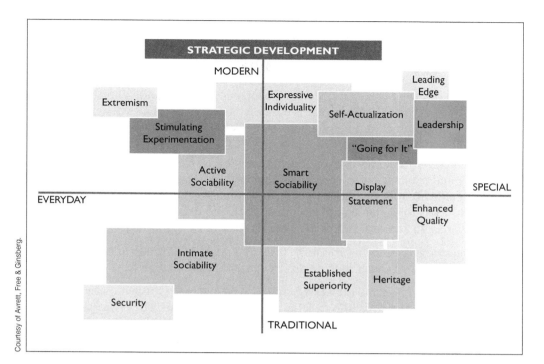

Courtesy of Avrett, Free & Ginsberg.

EXHIBIT 3.5

An Example of AFG's Need-Mapping Process

4. *Strategy.* AFG formulates a tight strategy to be used in developing a fully integrated marketing communication program.

5. *Creative exploration.* AFG develops, explores, and evaluates a range of executions to ensure that it maximizes the relevancy, distinctiveness, and persuasiveness of the strategy and final execution.

6. *Brand valuation.* AFG tracks marketplace performance and progress because it believes it must be accountable for the results its work generates. AFG constantly fine-tunes and improves communications in response to changing market conditions.

7. *Brand vision.* In building equities for a brand through effective communications, AFG plots long-range expansion plans for the base brand. AFG determines if the emerging brand equities can be line extended or translated to serve needs in other related categories.

These seven steps are constantly pursued in the evaluation of a brand's life cycle to ensure long-term growth and brand equity.

ANOTHER VIEW OF THE PLANNING PROCESS   Following are some of the typical steps agencies and clients take in the planning process.

1. *Current brand status.* In this step, there is an attempt to evaluate the brand's overall appeal. The brand is examined in the context of its marketplace, in its consumers' view, and in relation to its competitors. It answers the questions: Where do we stand in the marketplace? Who are our real competitors? What is the consumer attitude toward our brand? The category? Who are the consumers?

2. *Brand insights.* The agency may use a series of tools designed to help it develop insights to better understand the consumer's view. For example, it may attempt to capture the words that best describe the brand, the target audience, and the relationship between the two. This may include determining key attributes, benefits, and personality and answering these questions: How does it (the brand) make you feel? and What does it (the brand) say about you? This is the step in which strengths, weaknesses, opportunities, and threats (SWOT) are determined.

3. *Brand vision.* The strategic planners look for the consumer's hot button to identify the most powerful connection between the brand and the consumer. This is the bridge between the insight of planning and the magic of creative innovation.

4. *Big idea.* The next step is identifying the *big idea*, the creative expression of the *brand vision.* The *big idea* for branding becomes the foundation of all communication briefs. A communication plan is built on this idea. This plan is designed to reach the consumer target at a point where and when the consumer will be most receptive to the message.

5. *Evaluation.* An essential aspect of communications planning is accountability. The agency and client need to determine how well the objectives have been met and how to improve the communication the next time. Agencies may use their own proprietary tools to evaluate and learn from their performance, or they may use outside sources to accomplish this measurement.

Every agency has its own version of strategic brand building and understanding the consumer. After all, agencies have to differentiate themselves to attract clients:

- The word *disruption* and the TBWA agency have become synonymous with one another. Disruption helps TBWA define brands for its clients. The process challenges the underlying conventions that shape communication and marketing on every level in an attempt to break the status quo.

- Euro RSCG Worldwide looks at the marketer's need for ideas that apply to its business strategy. This strategic integration goes beyond advertising into such areas as "buzz" or word-of-mouth advertising that transfers brand information through social networks. This buzz concentrates not on the traditional trendsetters of society but on a group defined as *trend spreaders.* So when we talk about a strategic approach, it may include approaching the brand problem or solution from a different direction.

- Ogilvy & Mather takes a holistic look at communications and uses "what is necessary from each of the disciplines . . . to build a brand." Ogilvy calls this 360 Degree Branding. Under 360, every point of contact builds the brand. Building the brand is no longer solely the job of traditional advertising but also includes direct marketing, public relations, sponsorships, interactive services, customer relationship management, consulting, and promotion.

In short, the consumer (target) has to be an important part of the strategic planning process. How the advertiser engages consumers is critical to the process. In the past, marketers spoke and consumers listened. Today's consumers are proactive and speak loudly, and marketers have learned they need to listen. You can't plan integrated communications effectively without understanding the target more wisely than ever before.

WHAT GREAT BRANDS DO

Scott Bedbury, former senior vice president of marketing at Starbucks Coffee, said, "I walked through a hardware store last night and I came across 50 brands I didn't know existed. They may be great products, but they're not great brands." Scott should know brands. He's the man who gave the world "Just Do It," Nike's branding campaign. A few of Bedbury's brand-building principles are examined here:[11]

- *A great brand is in it for the long haul.* For decades, there were brands based on solid value propositions—they had established their worth in the consumers' minds. Then, in the 1980s and 1990s, companies focused on short-term economic returns and diminished long-term brand-building programs. As a result, there were a lot of products with very little differentiation. Today, a great brand is a necessity, not a luxury. By using a long-term approach, a great brand can travel worldwide, speak to multiple consumer segments simultaneously, and create economies of scale by which you can earn solid margins over the long term.

KLEPPNER VIEWPOINT 3.2

Mike Martin Owner/Creative Director Skylab-B and Principal at Owen+Martin

APPS SHOULD NEVER TRUMP IDEAS

Mike Martin

The world of communications is changing at lightning speeds. Blink your eyes and 10 new iPhone applications magically appear. With the emergence of social networking, consumers can stay in constant contact with each other as well as with their favorite brands. Handheld devices give us instantaneous access to information no matter where we go and keep us organized and entertained. It's no surprise that marketers are hungry to embrace emerging technology to keep their brands fresh and relevant to their customers.

The problem though is that using technology without a clear connection to the core brand idea often leads to an expensive exercise in futility and ultimately erodes the trust between client and agency. The challenge for advertising agencies is making sure that the need to use new technology doesn't trump the need for concepts that build brand equity.

Marketers are under constant pressure from management to deliver innovative ideas and give the appearance to the outside world that their brand is on the cutting edge. Ironically, an agency that presents a brilliant and highly strategic new print campaign that requires high-dollar production is scrapped because of budget constraints but a project that uses new technology that's devoid of branding and has an equally high production budget is quickly green-lighted.

Advertising agencies not only have the right but they also have a duty to say no to their clients if precious marketing dollars are being spent on new technology that will have limited gains or that could potentially damage the brand. Make no mistake; protecting clients from themselves is one of the most difficult jobs an agency has today. It requires tact, mutual respect, and resolve to look your client in the eye and tell that client an exciting new technology simply isn't right for a particular brand. It may feel like wrestling a giant lollipop out of the hands of a drooling kindergartener.

This is in not an excuse for agencies not to embrace new technology. After all, showcasing new media samples in an agency's portfolio is a must these days. The point is to step back occasionally and ask yourself if you're caught up in the excitement of getting to use that new toy or whether it is truly a worthwhile use of your client's marketing dollars and will likely grow the business and add equity to the brand. Your client will ultimately thank you.

Courtesy of Mike Martin, Skylab-B, Atlanta.

- *A great brand can be anything.* Some categories lend themselves to branding better than others, but anything is brandable. For example, Starbucks focuses on how coffee has woven itself into the fabric of people's lives, and that's an opportunity for emotional leverage. Almost any product offers an opportunity to create a frame of mind that is unique. Do you know what Intel computer processors do, how they work, or why they are superior to their competitors? All most people know is that they want to own a computer with "Intel Inside."

- *A great brand knows itself.* The real starting point is to go out to consumers and find out what they like or dislike about this brand and what they associate as the very core of the brand concept. To keep a brand alive over the long haul, to keep it vital, you have to do something new, something unexpected. It has to relate to the brand's core position.

- *A great brand invents or reinvents an entire category.* The common ground that you find among brands such as Disney, Apple, Nike, and Starbucks is that these companies made it an explicit goal to be the protagonists for each of their entire categories. Disney is the protagonist for fun family entertainment and family values. A great brand raises the bar—it adds a greater sense of purpose to the experience.

▥ *A great brand taps into emotions.* The common ground among companies that have built great brands is not simply performance. They realize consumers live in an emotional world. Emotions drive most, if not all, of our decisions. It is an emotional connection that transcends the product. And transcending the product is the brand.

▥ *A great brand is a story that's never completely told.* A brand is a metaphorical story that is evolving all the time. This connects with something very deep. People have always needed to make sense of things at a higher level. Levi's has a story that goes all the way back to the gold rush. It has photos of miners wearing Levi's dungarees. Stories create connections for people. Stories create the emotional context people need to locate themselves in a larger experience.

▥ *A great brand is relevant.* A lot of brands are trying to position themselves as "cool," but most of them fail. The larger idea is to be relevant. It satisfies people's wants; it performs the way people want it to. In the past couple of decades, a lot of brands promised consumers things they couldn't deliver. Consumers are looking for something that has lasting value. There is a quest for quality, not quantity.

The Advertising Stages of a Product

④ Explain IMC strategic planning.

Great importance is placed on the development of a product and its marketing objectives as part of a brand's strategic plan prior to creating advertisements. Here we examine several aspects of product development and the advertising implications that are important to creating the strategic plan. Despite the challenges to many marketing practices today, one constant is the need to have a clear understanding of the product and consumer wants and needs when making strategic advertising decisions.

In the previous chapter, we discussed stages in life. We are born; we grow up, mature, grow old, and, at some point, expire. As we said, products also pass through a number of stages. The developmental stage of a product determines the advertising message. As products pass through a number of stages—from introduction to dominance to ultimate demise—the manner in which advertising presents the product to consumers depends largely on the degree of acceptance the product has earned with consumers. The degree of acceptance can be identified as the product passes through its life cycle. *It is this degree of acceptance that determines the advertising stage of the product.* The life-cycle model as it relates to advertising discussed consists of three primary stages (see Exhibit 3.6):

▥ Pioneering stage
▥ Competitive stage
▥ Retentive stage

The nature and extent of each stage are discussed in the next sections.

Pioneering Stage

In 2008, 47,000 products filled a typical supermarket, up more than 50 percent from 1996. In the same year, 47,113 new products, variations, or sizes were launched.[12] In fact, in some years Procter & Gamble (P&G) alone brings 125 new products or brand extensions to market. Many new products are simply advertisers trying to get a piece of the pie in an established product category. The failure rate is staggering. During the past 25

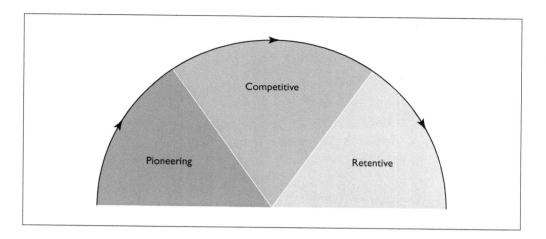

EXHIBIT 3.6

Primary Stages of the Life-Cycle Model

years, almost 60 percent of the companies appearing on the *Fortune* 500 list have been replaced by new companies. These new companies' success is based on the fact that they have created new markets or reinvented existing ones. One way of accomplishing this is to create new products or new product categories. Companies like Procter & Gamble have grown because of their ability to launch new products and create new product categories successfully. Procter & Gamble introduced Tide in 1941. It also introduced a new product category—the disposable diaper, or Pampers—in 1961, which became a billion-dollar product. In 1986, P&G introduced the first shampoo-conditioner combination. It also introduced the successful Swiffer mop.[13]

Consumer acceptance and understanding may take a long period of time—a few months, a number of years—or perhaps it may never be achieved. Just because manufacturers create revolutionary new products, consumers will not necessarily flock to buy them. Mike Martin's Skylab-B introduced a new service dubbed the Western Hemisphere Travel Initiative, or WHTI for short (see the case in Chapter 22), which created new travel document requirements for Americans and Canadians entering the United States by land or sea from Canada, Mexico, Bermuda, or the Caribbean. Exhibit 3.7 shows how advertising tries to educate travelers to the new service and requirements. Many times manufacturers have trouble accepting the fact that, despite all the money they spend developing and then promoting their product, consumers pay little or no attention to it. There are no guarantees that consumers will see a need for the product. It may never have occurred to consumers that they need or want the product, and, as a result, they don't feel compelled to buy it. Case in point: In 2009, the world celebrated the fortieth anniversary of the greatest product and technology innovation demo of all time. In a single day Douglas Engelbart demonstrated new hi-tech ideas that dominate our world today: the mouse, the hyperlink, hierarchical lists, user testing, and so on. What we often forget is that, despite the importance and success of his ideas, it took 20 years for many of them to become widely adopted and 40 years for them to become so ubiquitous that we no longer even think about them anymore. This reflects the fact that new ideas travel through cultures at much slower rates, especially if the ideas require (1) throwing something away and replacing it with something else, (2) relearning skills, or (3) coordination by large independent organizations.[14]

To capitalize on the growing foot-care market, Telebrands created a callous remover. Using short-form infomercials, it showed how the callous remover shaves skin close to make the foot smooth. The ads touted "For smooth, beautiful feet." Print and Internet ads suggest the same benefits from PedEgg's home pedicure product, touting it as a better way to get rid of rough skin. The product quickly sold more than $40 million in the retail environment, which does not include sales from direct-response infomercials. Will people continue to buy the product?[15]

EXHIBIT 3.7

WHTI tries to educate traveling consumers to new travel document requirements. This new service is a result of a recommendation from the 9/11 Commission about travel.

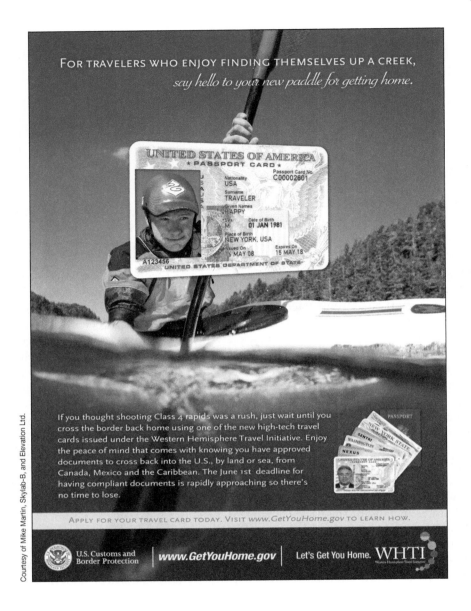

Here are two views on the introduction of the Kindle, a digital book reader. According to Steve Rubel, senior vice president and director of insights at Edelman Digital, "Like the iPod before it, the Kindle is a critical emerging device that actually encourages consumers to pay for content. When Apple launched the iTunes Music Store, some were skeptical that people would shell out cash for music they could snag for free from file-sharing networks. They did."[16] A critic of the Kindle digital book reader wrote, "And I admit that after a couple of days with the Kindle, I am still critical of the device . . . the Kindle remains an attractive niche device [for] book dweebs. Actually, I am a book dweeb myself, but the functional range of this device is too limited for my tastes. The storage (1,500 book capacity claimed), battery life, 3G wireless are all very impressive, but the electronic ink technology just is not there yet. The screen is too small and still slow." So is the Kindle a pioneering successful product today?[17]

And of course there is a long list of products not attracting consumers:

■ In 1993, Crystal Pepsi was launched. It was a clear cola (it looked like water) and tasted much like regular Pepsi. It attempted to create a "clear cola" category for those more health-conscious consumers. It lasted about a year in the United States. Oops.

- H. J. Heinz pitched funky fries—chocolate-flavored, blue-colored French fries—in 2002. Kids didn't think they were cool, and a year later Heinz pulled them off the shelves.

- And how many of you rode a Segway scooter to class today? Of course, it is still being sold.

Until people appreciate the fact that they need it, a product is in the **pioneering stage**.

Advertising in the pioneering stage introduces an idea that makes previous conceptions appear antiquated. It must show that methods once accepted as the only ones possible have been improved and that the limitations long tolerated as normal have now been overcome. It may be difficult to believe, but consumers didn't rush out to buy the first deodorants. Many consumers who were concerned with body odor simply used baking soda under their arms. So we can't take for granted that consumers will change their habits. Advertising in this stage must do more than simply present a product—it must implant a new custom, change habits, develop new usage, or cultivate new standards of living. In short, advertising in the pioneering stage of a product's life cycle must educate the consumer to the new product or service.

In 1973, Fleischmann's introduced Egg Beaters, a frozen egg alternative made from real eggs but without the yolks. The company had to convince consumers that they needed an egg alternative. It had to convert egg eaters into Egg Beaters customers. Its market was concerned about the high cholesterol and fat of egg yolks. The company had to change attitudes and habits to be successful. By accomplishing this, it became the dominating force in this new-product segment. In the early 1990s, Egg Beaters tried to expand the market with an advertising campaign built around the theme "When the Recipe Calls for Eggs" (see Exhibit 3.8). These advertisements tried to sell Egg Beaters as a substitute in cooking "because you're using the healthiest part of real eggs. No cholesterol. No fat." Do you and your family use Egg Beaters or egg substitutes?

The purposes of the pioneering stage of a product's life cycle, reduced to their simplest terms, are

- to educate consumers about the new product or service.

- to show that people have a need they did not appreciate before and that the advertised product fulfills that need.

- to show that a product now exists that is actually capable of meeting a need that already had been recognized but previously could not have been fulfilled.

Pioneering advertising generally stresses what the product can do, offer, or provide that could not have been done, offered, or provided by any product before.

A true pioneering product offers more than a minor improvement. It is important for the advertiser to remember that what determines the stage of the advertising is consumer perception of the product. In the pioneering stage, the consumer is trying to answer the question "What is the product for?" It does not really matter what the manufacturer thinks. Does the consumer think the improved changes in the product are significant? Or, does the product really offer a better way of doing things?

Often the copy, in this stage, focuses on the generic aspect of the product category in an attempt to educate or inform the consumer. In the late 1980s, Interplak introduced a revolutionary new home dental product—an automatic instrument that removed plaque using two rows of counterrotating oscillating brushes. Interplak had to convince consumers that this product cleaned teeth better than any kind of toothbrush—electric or otherwise (see Exhibit 3.9). This was no easy task because the product cost about $100 at introduction. The pioneering Interplak advertisements suggested that "Plaque is the real villain in oral hygiene. If not removed daily, its bacterial film can lead to early gum disease and tooth decay. But clinical studies have shown that manual brushing removes only some of the plaque buildup." Twenty years later, Interplak is still trying to

pioneering stage
The advertising stage of a product in which the need for such a product is not recognized and must be established or in which the need has been established but the success of a commodity in filling that need has to be established. See competitive stage, retentive stage.

EXHIBIT 3.8

Egg Beaters expands the market by trying to get the consumer to substitute Egg Beaters for eggs in cooking.

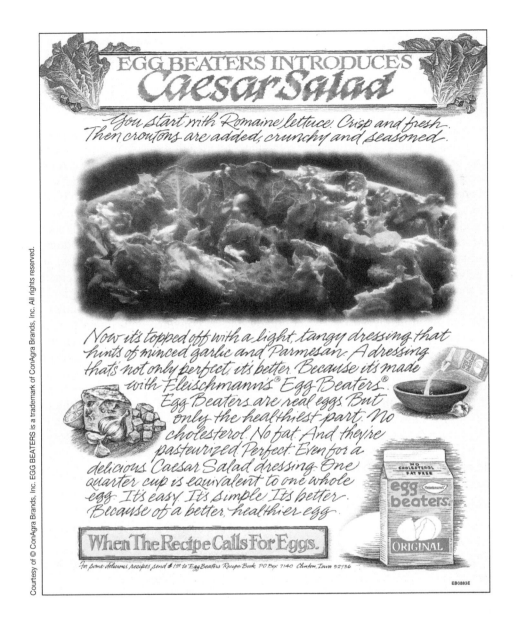

get the average household to try its product. And, of course, there is a new generation of less-expensive electric and battery-operated toothbrushes using the same idea.

THE PRODUCT ACCEPTANCE BATTLE

Snapple was created in 1972 as an all-natural juice drink line to be sold primarily in health-food stores. It didn't become a national beverage company until 20 years later. Originally, few consumers were interested in natural beverages and the idea took time to grow. Today, almost everyone buys bottled water products such as Aquafina or Dasani. This concept wasn't accepted overnight either. But once it was accepted by many consumers, along came products such as Propel offering enhanced water with vitamins and/or flavors. As an interesting contrast, Coca-Cola had a disastrous introduction of Dasani water in the United Kingdom. The drink was panned by the British media as recycled tap water and was withdrawn from shelves within weeks.

Nike's first attempt to sell runners a shoe that would tell them how far and fast they had run was called the Monitor. It had sonar detectors that attached to the runner's waist and calculated the speed of the runner, announcing it over a pair of headphones.

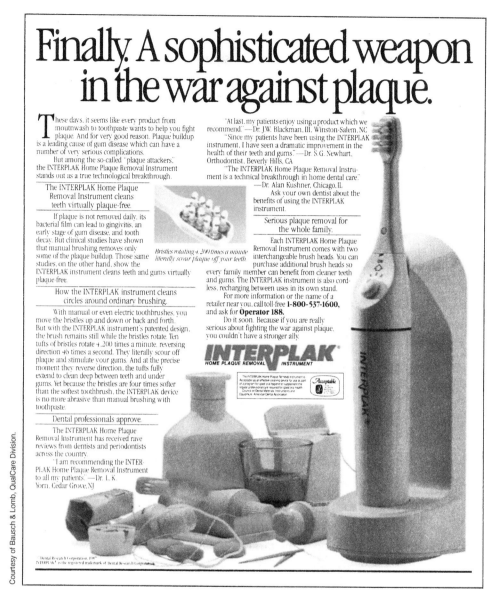

EXHIBIT 3.9

INTERPLAK introduces a new kind of home dental care.

Consumers thought it was impractical. Less than 2 years after its 1987 launch, Nike dropped the Monitor.

Another attempt to get consumer acceptance involved the Nike+ system of running. In 2008, you could attach a sensor to your Nike+ shoes, press the iPod, and track your every step. After each run, you sync the iPod to the Nike+ web site and get a visual representation of the workout. By combining a simple way to amass data with tools to use and share it, Nike attracted the largest community of runners ever assembled—more than 1.2 million runners have collectively tracked more than 130 million miles and burned more than 13 billion calories.[18] This was a new-idea success.

For these products, advertising will not exhort consumers to raise their standards of acceptance but rather will aim at convincing them that they can now accomplish something they couldn't before, through the use of the new product. For instance, the cellular phone industry told businesswomen that the cellular phone could not only keep them in touch with their clients but also could be used as a security device—especially if they had car trouble or were threatened in some way. Now it is more a matter of deciding on design, color, size, and other features than whether they should own one. For most people today, a cell phone is one of life's necessities.

PIONEERING EXPENSE

Usually, during the early introduction of a new product, heavy advertising and promotional expenses are required to create awareness and acquaint the target with the product's benefits. To expand, the manufacturer must gain new distribution, generate consumer trial, and increase geographic markets. The product in the pioneering stage usually is not profitable. In other words, there can be a number of factors involved in the acceptance and purchase of a new product. According to a U.S. study by Ernst & Young, there is a 67 percent failure rate among the truly new products that create a new product category.[19] According to other studies, it may be higher in specific categories.

DEVELOPING NEW PRODUCT CATEGORIES

Until 1997, consumers hadn't used antibacterial soaps outside a hospital environment. Purell Instant Hand Sanitizer for consumers to use at home and in the office was introduced in 1997 with a $15 million advertising budget. When a new pain product called Aleve, containing naproxen, was introduced, it created a new category in a very mature analgesic market. Consumers had many analgesic choices to fight pain: Aspirin was the first major product (i.e., Bayer) to fight pain, then came aspirin compounds (Anacin, BC tablets, among others), then acetaminophen (Tylenol), then ibuprofen (Advil), and then naproxen. Aleve's advertising support for the introduction was about $50 million. As you can see, pioneering advertisers incur heavy expenses in the process of educating the public about the advantages of a new type of product. If the advertiser has some success with the new idea, one or more competitors will quickly jump into the market and try to grab share from the pioneer.

Usually, the main advantage of being a pioneer is that you become the leader with a substantial head start over others. So a pioneering effort can secure customers before the competition can even get started. "When you're the market leader," says Ivan Seidenberg, Verizon CEO, "part of your responsibility is to reinvent the market."[20]

Competitive Stage

Once consumers accept a pioneering product, there is going to be competition. The consumer now knows what the product is and how it can be used. At this point, the main question the consumer asks is, "Which brand shall I buy?" When this happens, the product has entered the **competitive stage**, and the advertising for it is referred to as *competitive advertising*. (Note that this is a restrictive meaning of the term, not to be confused with the broader meaning that all advertisements are competitive with each other.)

In the short term, the pioneer usually has an advantage of leadership that can give dominance in the market. Red Bull started the caffeine-stoked energy drinks category decades ago in Europe. In 2006 alone, there were more than 500 new energy drinks launched worldwide to get a piece of the action. Generally, in the early competitive stage, the combined impact of many competitors, each spending to gain a substantial market position, creates significant growth for the whole product category. If the pioneer can maintain market share in this category during the initial period of competitors' growth, it can more than make up for the earlier expense associated with its pioneering efforts.

Among the many everyday products in the competitive stages are deodorants, soaps, toothpaste, cars, detergents, headache remedies, shaving creams, shampoos, televisions, cat food, computers, and packaged foods. The purpose of competitive stage advertising is to communicate the product's position or differentiate it to the consumer; the advertising features the differences of the product.

competitive stage
The advertising stage a product reaches when its general usefulness is recognized but its superiority over similar brands has to be established in order to gain preference. See pioneering stage, retentive stage.

Competitive headlines include the following:

All the sound without the wires.

BOSE WAVE MUSIC SYSTEM

There is a better way to soothe your skin.

NIVIA LOTION

**He spent decades researching the right wood for his wine barrels.
You can taste the results in just a sip.**

WOODBRIDGE WINE

The most fuel-efficient midsized sedan.

FORD FUSION+HYBRID

How to tell a pair of quality sunglasses from high-priced junk.

COSTA DEL MAR

These headlines don't educate you as to the product category advantages; they are taken for granted. Exhibit 3.10 is introducing a new restaurant brand. Despite being a new restaurant concept, it has to hit the ground running against all other food service

EXHIBIT 3.10

Despite being a new restaurant concept, the Rusty Rooster had to hit the ground running to compete with all food service organizations from day one.

companies. The headline builds on the credibility of the company's other restaurant brand, "Introducing a new restaurant by Folks."

Retentive Stage

retentive stage
The third advertising stage of a product, reached when its general usefulness is widely known, its individual qualities are thoroughly appreciated, and it is satisfied to retain its patronage merely on the strength of its past reputation. See pioneering stage, competitive stage.

Products reaching maturity and wide-scale acceptance may enter the **retentive stage**, or reminder stage, of advertising.

If a product is accepted and used by consumers, there may not be a need for competitive advertising. At this point, everybody knows about this product and likes or dislikes it—why advertise? The chief goal of advertising may be to retain those customers. Over the years, many manufacturers of successful products stopped advertising them and found that the public quickly forgot about them. Most advertisers try to retain their customers by keeping the brand name before them. The third stage through which a product might pass is sometimes called *reminder advertising*—it simply reminds consumers that the brand exists. This kind of advertising is usually highly visual and is basically name advertising, meaning that the advertisement gives little reason to buy the product. Most reminder advertisements look like posters—they have a dominant illustration of the product and a few words. Generally, there is little or no body copy because there is no need to give consumers this kind of information.

Few products are entirely in the reminder stage. There usually are other products in the pioneering and competitive stages challenging their leadership position. In fact, if your product is truly all alone in the retentive stage, that may be cause for alarm. It may mean the product category is in decline, and the competition sees little future in challenging you for consumers.

The advertiser's goal in the retentive stage is to maintain market share and ward off consumer trial of other products. Products in the retentive stage do not necessarily cut back on their advertising expenditures, but they adopt different marketing and promotional strategies than those used in the pioneering and competitive stages. When a brand is used by a large portion of the market, its advertising is intended to keep present customers and increase the total market, on the assumption that the most prominent brand will get the largest share of the increase.

Generally, products in the retentive stage are at their most profitable levels because developmental costs have been amortized, distribution channels established, and sales contacts made. The development of advertising and promotion may often be routine at this stage. Obviously, companies like to maintain their products in the retentive stage as long as possible.

The Advertising Spiral

5 Explain the importance of the product life cycle.

The advertising spiral (see Exhibit 3.11) is an expanded version of the advertising stages of products just discussed. The spiral provides a point of reference for determining which stage or stages a product has reached at a given time in a given market and what the thrust of the advertising message should be. This can be important information for deciding on strategy and giving the creative team a clear perspective on what information it needs to communicate to prospects. In many respects, the advertising spiral parallels the life cycle of the product.

COMPARISON OF STAGES

Naturally, there are fewer products in the pioneering stage than in the competitive stage. The development of new types of products or categories does not take place frequently. Most advertising is for products in the competitive stage. As already pointed out, such advertising often introduces features of a new product that is in the pioneering stage and gets the spotlight for a period of time.

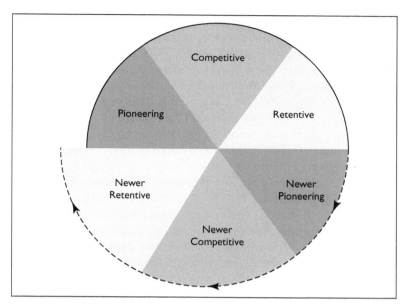

EXHIBIT 3.11

The Advertising Spiral

In using the advertising spiral, we deal with one group of consumers at a time. The advertising depends on the attitude of that group toward the product. A product in the competitive stage may have to use pioneering advertising aimed at other groups of consumers to expand its markets. Thus, pioneering and competitive advertising could be going on simultaneously. Each series of advertisements, or each part of one advertisement, will be aimed at a different audience for this same product. As hybrid automobiles became more popular, the number of car companies selling hybrids increased. The 2010 Toyota Prius had new competition from the Honda Insight. The Insight's selling proposition was this: Minicar mileage in a five-passenger compact with room enough to fit an adult's bike in the back, at a starting price roughly $2,000 to $3,000 below those other hybrid cars on the market. Most buyers didn't accept the hybrid car, so you had to sell the advantage of a hybrid and differentiate your hybrid from others on the market.

Products in the retentive stage usually get the least amount of advertising. This stage, however, represents a critical moment in the life cycle of a product when important management decisions must be made. Hence, it is important to create effective advertising in this stage.

PRODUCT IN COMPETITIVE STAGE, IMPROVEMENT IN PIONEERING STAGE

It is not unusual for a new brand to enter the competitive stage without doing any pioneering advertising. A new product entering an established product category must hit the ground running to differentiate itself from the competition. Every new brand thus enjoys whatever pioneering advertising has already been done in the product category. Despite the new product failure rates, marketers obviously see the value of new products. New brands entering an existing category experience a 50 percent failure rate and, perhaps most surprising, an 84 percent failure rate among brand extensions. Ernst & Young cited a fundamental lack of competitive differentiation as the reason for line extension failure.[21]

Earlier we said the consumer is the one who determines the stage of a product. In what stage would you place Coca-Cola Zero? Coca-Cola Zero—a sugar-free cola designed to taste like ordinary Coca-Cola—was described by the company as its most important new product since Diet Coke was launched in 1984. After introducing Coca-Cola Zero, several modifications to the advertising were made. It was introduced with advertisements containing the tagline "Everybody Chill." The key advertisement, called "Chilltop," was a remake of the famous Hilltop advertisement used for Coca-Cola in the 1970s. The introductory advertisements did not precisely tell consumers what the product was about, and consumers didn't understand the product proposition. Later, they added an explanatory line: "Real Coca-Cola Taste Plus Nothing." Another commercial showed Coca-Cola morphing into a bottle of Coca-Cola Zero, and the copy read: "Real Coca-Cola Taste, Zero Calories, No Compromise." More recently, the commercials featured Coke brand managers wanting to sue Coca-Cola Zero managers over "Taste infringement." Do consumers understand the product premise today?

One TV spot says, "Introducing Gold Bond Foot Swabs. Just snap to release . . . the only medicine proven to cure and prevent most athlete's foot. New Gold Bond swabs. The no-mess, no-touch cure." Gold Bond Foot Swabs created a new way to deliver athlete's foot relief (see Exhibit 3.12), the end of the messy athlete's foot creams.

A few years ago, manufacturers placed 150 new deodorant and antiperspirant products on store shelves within 12 months. Unilever brought its successful Axe line from Europe, sparking competitive sales. The category quadrupled. New formulas hit the market in all forms—gels, creams, sticks, and sprays. Manufacturers rushed to differentiate new products. Procter & Gamble created a "soft solid" that came out as a gritty mush that melted on the skin. Herbal Care introduced a deodorant with "anti-irritant and antioxidant" properties, aimed at women's sensitive skin. Gillette and Unilever introduced "odor-blocking technology." Take a look at the deodorant section the next time you're in a mass discounter, grocery store, or drugstore. See how manufacturers are attempting to differentiate their products. As you can see, simply selling deodorant is very competitive. Most new deodorants start in the competitive stage even when they are attempting to create a new subcategory.

Change is a continuum: As long as the operation of a competitive product does not change, the product continues to be in the competitive stage, despite any pioneering improvements. Once the principle of its operation changes, however, the product itself enters the pioneering stage. When a product begins to move into more than one stage, the changes are not always easy to categorize. Whenever a brand in the competitive stage is revitalized with a new feature aimed at differentiating it, pioneering advertising may be needed to make consumers appreciate the new feature.

Scramblers and Better 'n Eggs, Healthy Choice eggs, and Simply Eggs created non-frozen egg substitutes to compete with Egg Beaters' frozen product. Egg Beaters developed a refrigerated version to go with its frozen product. Exhibit 3.13 shows a television commercial that tells consumers they can find Egg Beaters in either the frozen food section or the egg section of their grocery. Was this new Egg Beaters in the competitive stage, the pioneering stage, or both?

THE RETENTIVE STAGE ISN'T THE END

The life of a product does not have to cease when it reaches the retentive stage. In fact, it may then be at the height of its popularity, and its manufacturer may believe the product can simply coast along. But a product can coast for only a short time before declining. No business can rely only on its old customers over a period of time and survive.

As noted earlier, the retentive stage is the most profitable one for the product. But all good things must come to an end. A manufacturer has a choice between two strategies when the product nears the end of the retentive stage.

In the first strategy, the manufacturer determines that the product has outlived its effective market life and should be allowed to die. In most cases, the product is not immediately pulled from the market. Rather, the manufacturer simply quits advertising it and withdraws other types of support. During this period, the product gradually loses market share but remains profitable because expenses have been sharply curtailed. This strategy is the one typically presented in textbook descriptions of the product life cycle, but it is not necessarily the one that corresponds to actual product development.

GOLD BOND | "LONG JUMPER"
:15 TV SPOT

V/O: Announcing an amazing achievement...

V/O:...In sport!

SFX: SPLAT

V/O: The end of the messy athlete's foot creams.

V/O: Introducing gold bond foot swabs.

V/O: Just snap to release...

V/O: ... the only medicine proven to cure...

V/O: ... and prevent most athlete's foot.

CURES

PREVENTS

THE NO MESS NO TOUCH CURE

V/O: New gold bond swabs. The no-mess, no-touch cure.

RESULTS

Per McCollum Spielman (MSW) testing

	CATEGORY NORM	GOLDBOND
Breakthrough	31	60
Persuasion	27	52

EXHIBIT 3.12

"Gold Bond Foot Swabs—just snap to release, . . . the no-mess, no-touch cure."

The problem with the typical life-cycle model (discussed in Chapter 2) is that it portrays an inevitable decline in the product life cycle, whereas most long-term products go through a number of cycles of varying peaks and duration before they are finally taken off the market. The advertising spiral depicted in Exhibit 3.11 shows these cycles. The advertising spiral—the second strategy for a product nearing the end of the retentive stage—does not accept the fact that a product must decline. Instead, it seeks to expand the market into a newer pioneering stage. General Mills's CEO's advice is, "Do not believe in the product life cycle. Innovate constantly." Tide detergent was introduced in 1946. Since then, Tide has gone through more than 60 product upgrades.

EXHIBIT 3.13

Egg Beaters expanded beyond the freezer with its refrigerated version. Advertisements told consumers where in the store they could find the product.

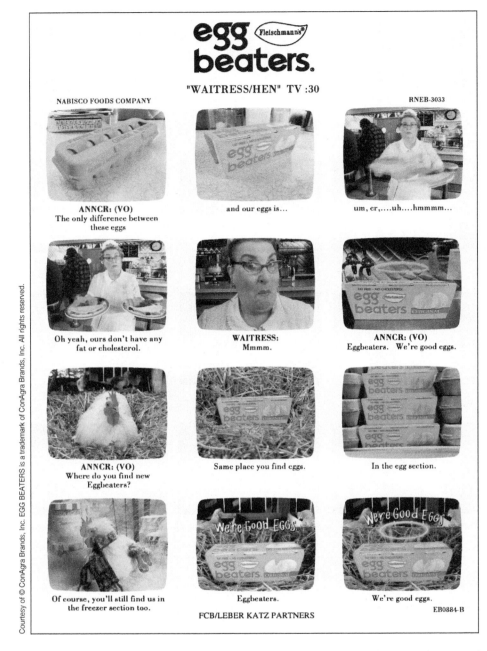

As a product approaches the retentive stage, management must make some important decisions:

- Can it make some significant improvements in the present product so that it virtually represents a new type of product or category (e.g., Clorox Cleaner)?
- Is there a possibility for line extensions (e.g., Diet Coke, Coca-Cola-Zero)?

As we have seen, the life cycle of a product can be affected by many conditions. If, however, the product is to continue to be marketed, its own advertising stage should be identified before its advertising goals are set.

The three basic stages of the spiral (pioneering, competitive, and retentive) are straightforward and easy to understand. However, the stages in the bottom half (newer pioneering, newer competitive, and newer retentive) are trickier. To continue to market an established product successfully and profitably, creative marketing is necessary.

The newer pioneering stage attempts to get more people to use the product. Basically, there are two ways to enter this new stage. The first is making a product change. This can be minor, such as adding a new ingredient to a detergent or adding deodorant to a bar of soap or—in the other direction—taking caffeine or sodium out of a soft drink or fat out of a food product. Alternatively, it may entail a complete overhaul of a product, such as a radical model change for an automobile. In some cases, advertising alone may be enough to get consumers to look at the product in a new light.

Advertisers cannot afford simply to rely on old customers because they die off, are lured away by the competition, or change their lifestyles. Smart advertisers will initiate a change in direction of their advertising when their product is enjoying great success. They will show new ways of using the product and give reasons for using it more often. For instance, if you are a successful soup company and your customers are eating your canned soup with every meal, you have reached a saturation point. How can you increase sales? Simply by encouraging people to use soup in new ways. You create recipe advertising that shows new food dishes and casseroles that require several cans of your product. You now have your customers eating your soup as soup, as well as making casseroles with it. Of course, this means more sales and a new way of thinking about soup. That's exactly what Egg Beaters did once the manufacturer got consumers to switch from eggs to Egg Beaters for breakfast: The company tried to get cooks to use Egg Beaters in their next recipe and emphasize taste.

NEW PIONEERING STAGE AND BEYOND

A product entering the new pioneering stage is actually in different stages in different markets. Longtime consumers will perceive the product to be in the competitive or retentive stage. New consumers will perceive it as being a pioneer. At this point, the advertising spiral will have entered still another cycle (see Exhibit 3.14), which we will call the *newest* pioneering stage, in which the focus is on getting more people to use this type of product. Today, the maker of Egg Beaters still advertises, "They taste like real eggs, because they are real eggs." The copy adds, "Look for Garden Vegetable and Southwestern, with real vegetables and special seasonings." The new "Garden Vegetable" adds a blend of green and red peppers, onions, celery, and seasonings, whereas the "Southwestern" adds red and green peppers, onions, chilies, and southwestern spices for burritos and omelets. It is also now part of ConAgra Foods (see Exhibit 3.15).

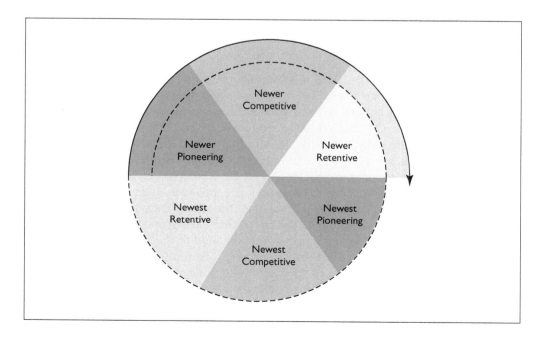

EXHIBIT 3.14

Expanded Advertising Spiral

EXHIBIT 3.15

Egg Beaters expanded into Garden Vegetable and Southwestern varieties.

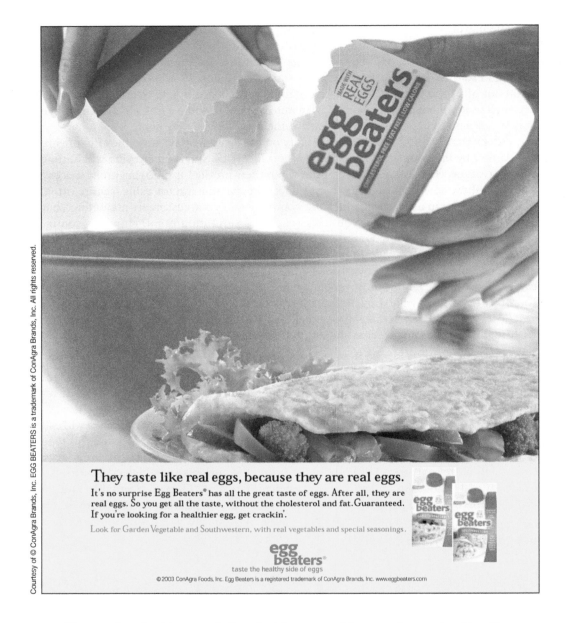

They taste like real eggs, because they are real eggs.
It's no surprise Egg Beaters® has all the great taste of eggs. After all, they are real eggs. So you get all the taste, without the cholesterol and fat. Guaranteed. If you're looking for a healthier egg, get crackin'.

Look for Garden Vegetable and Southwestern, with real vegetables and special seasonings.

egg beaters®
taste the healthy side of eggs
©2003 ConAgra Foods, Inc. Egg Beaters is a registered trademark of ConAgra Brands, Inc. www.eggbeaters.com

The product in this stage is faced with new problems and opportunities. Can you convince segments of your market who are not using your product that they should? Obviously, you have to understand why consumers were not interested in the product earlier. Creative marketing and a flexible product help this process.

McDonald's, Nike, Jell-O, Pepsi-Cola, Mountain Dew, Budweiser, Disney, ESPN, Google, and Gillette are a few of the brands that reached the retentive stage and began to look for ways to move beyond it. All of these companies moved into the new pioneering stage with product innovations. Hence, products such as Tropicana, Diet Coke, Coke Zero, Cherry Coke, Diet Pepsi, Diet Mountain Dew, and Bud Light were born. New pioneering can be the result of reworking the original product or a line extension—with a new formula and name—that is related to the original version of the product. What about Red Bull? Bartenders have created Friday Flatteners, which have been made with Red Bull and vodka for a number of years.

Creating product innovation does not always translate into brand share. Royal Crown Cola has been an industry innovator—first with national distribution of soft drinks in cans (1954), then a low-calorie diet cola (1962), then a caffeine-free diet cola (1980), and then a sodium-free diet cola (1983).[22] It had the innovation but didn't effectively manage its advertising against the larger companies of Coca-Cola and Pepsi, nor did it effectively communicate with consumers.

As with the pioneering stage, once an established product in the competitive stage begins to innovate successfully in a newer pioneering stage, competition isn't far behind.

The advertising focus in the newer pioneering stage must be on getting consumers to understand what the product is about. Advertising in the newer competitive stage aims at getting more people to buy the brand. Moving through these stages—newer pioneering, newer competitive, newer retentive—is not easy. It requires the manufacturer to develop either product innovations or advertising positioning strategies that make the product different in consumers' eyes. Also, as we move to the newer stages of the spiral, there are usually fewer prospects for the product. Therefore, a company must become most efficient at targeting smaller groups of prospects. H. J. Heinz Company introduced EZ Squirt, a line of colored, vitamin-C-fortified ketchup in packaging especially designed for kids. EZ Squirt was developed from insight that kids under age 12 are the biggest ketchup consumers. The advertising promoted the green-colored ketchup variety plus the product's easy-to-grip, squeezable bottles with a cap that allows kids to control the amount of ketchup they squirt.[23]

Since Bayer introduced and sold the first aspirin product in the late 1800s (first in powder form, then in 1915 as a tablet), it has become both a medical and marketing marvel. Its new pioneering stages have been endless. It has been sold for headaches, toothaches, muscle aches, back pain, and, more recently, to stave off first and repeat heart attacks. The Food and Drug Administration recently officially approved new uses, recommending aspirin for the prevention of heart problems, angina (severe chest pain), and stroke. In 2003, research showed daily aspirin use significantly reduced the incidence of colorectal tumors. Another study among postmenopausal women suggested the use of aspirin may reduce their risk of developing breast cancer by 21 percent. Each time a new use for the product is found, a new advertising campaign promotes the product to an appropriate group of consumers.

Consider this statement by Emory University professor and cardiologist, John Douglas: "Aspirin is the standard treatment for any person who has coronary heart disease," he said. "It should be standard therapy for anyone who's had a heart attack, has angina or coronary atherosclerosis—hardening of the arteries." Such comments are a marketer's dream. Obviously, most products aren't as versatile as this miracle product. But if marketers can find new uses for their products, then a new stage of pioneering advertising may result.[24]

NEW PIONEERING It is easy to understand the need for pioneering advertising when a new wrinkle in a product category is created. Just think of all the new technology advances over the past few years. Think of the recent changes in cell phone uses beyond talking. The cell phone has become an entertainment medium offering photos, games, music, and information. In these cases, a marketer must simply educate consumers about what the product will do for them. And think of the impact of Apple's iPod and iTunes. Many consumers are eagerly waiting for the advances in this product category.

As another example, look at the evolution of Procter & Gamble's Crest toothpaste: Crest was launched in 1955. It received American Dental Association approval in 1960. Crest Gel was introduced in 1980. Crest Tartar Control in 1985. Crest Sparkle for Kids was launched in 1988. Crest Multicare was introduced in 1996. And the product improvements continued with Crest Multicare Whitening Gel, Crest Pro-Health Whitening, and Crest Pro-Health Enamel Shield.

THE ADVERTISING SPIRAL AS A MANAGEMENT DECISION TOOL

6 Discuss the relationship of the advertising spiral.

A product may try to retain its consumers in one competitive area while at the same time seeking new markets with pioneering advertising aimed at other groups. We must remember that products do not move through each stage at the same speed. In some instances, a product may move quickly from one stage in one cycle to a newer stage in another cycle. This change may also be a matter of corporate strategy. A company may believe it can obtain a greater share of business at less cost by using pioneering advertising that promotes new uses for the product. It is possible that the same results could be obtained by continuing to battle at a small profit margin in a highly competitive market. A retentive advertiser may suddenly find its market slipping and plunge into a new competitive war without any new pioneering work. Like a compass, the spiral indicates direction; it does not dictate management decisions.

Before attempting to create new ideas for advertising a product, the advertiser should use the spiral to answer the following questions:

- In which stage is the product?
- Should we use pioneering advertising to attract new users to this type of product?
- Should we work harder at competitive advertising to obtain a larger share of the existing market?
- What portion of our advertising should be pioneering? What portion competitive?
- Are we simply coasting in the retentive stage? If so, should we be more aggressive?

To sum up, the life cycle of a product or brand may be affected by many conditions. If the brand is to continue to be marketed, its advertising stage must be identified before its advertising goals can be set.

SUMMARY

In the mid-1880s, there were no brands. Manufacturers differentiated their products and gave them names as the concept of branding was born. Brands are now among the most valuable assets a marketer owns. The product is not the brand. A product is manufactured; a brand is created and is made up of both rational and emotional elements. In today's marketing environment, it is essential that every communication reinforces brand personality in the same manner: advertising, public relations, promotion, packaging, direct marketing, and so forth. The most important factor in determining the actual value of a brand is its equity in the market: how consumers think and feel about the brand. Integrated marketing communications (IMC) uses all of the marketing tools working from a single strategy. BAV is a diagnostic tool for determining how a brand is performing relative to other brands. There are four steps in developing Integrated Marketing Communications Strategic Plans: brand equity audit analysis, strategic options and recommendations, brand equity research, and the creative brief.

Avrett, Free & Ginsberg (AFG) uses a seven-step planning cycle that helps create strategic advertising. It uses the discipline of account planning at each stage of developing a campaign: brand/marketing status, brand mission, strategic development, strategy, creative exploration, brand valuation, and brand vision.

Products pass through a number of stages—from introduction to ultimate demise—known as the product life cycle. Advertising plays a different role in each stage of product development. Until consumers appreciate the fact that they need a product, that product is in the pioneering stage of advertising. In the competitive stage, an advertiser tries to differentiate its product from that of the competition. The retentive stage calls for reminder advertising. The advertising spiral is an expanded version of the advertising stages of a product providing a reference for determining which stage or stages a product has reached in a given time in a given market. This may tell a marketer what the thrust of the advertising message should be.

A product's age has little to do with the stage it is in at any given time. Rather, consumer attitude or perception determines the stage of a product. As consumer perception changes, moving it from one stage to another, the advertising message should also change. In fact, the advertising may be in more than one stage at any given time. Creative marketing may propel a product through new pioneering, new competitive, and new retentive stages. And it is even possible for a product to continue on into the newest pioneering, newest competitive, and newest retentive stages. As a product ages, so do its users, which is why no product can survive without attracting new customers. Long-term success depends on keeping current customers while constantly attracting new ones.

REVIEW

1. What is brand equity?
2. What are the elements of the creative brief?
3. What are the key elements of the AFG planning cycle?
4. Briefly identify each stage in the first half of the advertising spiral.
5. What determines the stage of a product?
6. What is the essence of the advertising message in each stage of the spiral?

magimix **xL** | food processor

Target Marketing

S UCCESSFUL advertisers are those who identify and then direct resources toward the people who want or need what the brand has to offer. ▶

CHAPTER LEARNING OBJECTIVES

1. Define target marketing.

2. Identify important population trends revealed by the U.S. Census.

3. Define and provide examples of generational marketing.

4. Explain the importance of the marketing concept to advertising.

5. Identify the five ways markets are segmented.

6. Discuss the importance of positioning to advertising.

7. Discuss the role of heavy users in target marketing.

8. Explain why psychographic research is important to target marketing.

Advertisers can boast award-winning creative commercials and high-tech strategy, but such campaigns will ultimately fail if they are directed toward the wrong prospects. Good advertising is about getting your messages to people who are most interested in—and likely to want and benefit from—what it is you have to offer. Doing so involves conducting homework so that you carefully define the target audience, are aware of population trends and opportunities, and smartly segment the market based on a variety of factors. For example, the chapter-opening ad for Magimix food processors is designed to appeal to intended users. This chapter discusses the tools and concepts advertisers and marketers use to ensure that their messages are reaching the right people.

Targeting in a Changing Environment

As we've mentioned in previous chapters, *change* is absolutely everywhere: The kinds of people advertisers are trying to reach, their behavior, and the way we reach them are only part of the story. Even consumers are bewildered by the rate of change. Advertisers must keep up with the trends around them. If they don't understand their brands' environment, their advertising won't be on trend and directed to the right people.

Who do we think is going to buy our product? Men? Women? Teenagers? College students? Men and women? Seniors? Twenty-five- to forty-nine-year-olds? Primarily

Hispanic people? To whom are we going to aim our advertising? Is it going to be profitable? What is our rationale for selecting this target? Have there been any changes in this target? There are a lot of questions to be answered. We need a lot of answers. In the process, does that mean we don't aim at everybody who has money? We know that won't work—that's a shotgun approach. We need to be focused and direct, like a rifle shot, to hit our target.

The monolithic mass market of the mid-twentieth century has long been laid to rest, and smaller mass markets have taken its place. Coming up with new targeting approaches is critical to many advertisers. For example, Yahoo! developed approaches that allowed it to identify actual product or category purchases. They do this with behavioral tracking—matching the behavior of certain consumers with the Nielsen HomeScan database that captures consumers' actual buying habits. Yahoo! is then able to look for that web-user behavior pattern online, and it serves those particular users ads directed to those anonymous consumers. There is a high enough correlation with the web behavior and the purchasing of certain products.[1]

Marketing Generalization

As we discuss many factors and groups used by marketers, a word of caution is in order. We talk about baby boomers; seniors; and generations X, Y, and Z or limit discussions to demographics (age, income, sex) as if each is a uniform group of people who live, think, and act exactly the same. Do all 20-year-old women think and act alike? Do all Hispanic people? Do all boomers? Virtually no generalization encompasses an entire consumer segment, especially age groups.

If we stop to think about it, we know better than to generalize. Consider that seniors or matures can be wealthy or not, love the outdoors or not, be inclined to travel or be homebodies, own a vacation home or live in a mobile home. The same considerations apply to virtually every one of these catchall categories. Of course, these groupings or segments can be very useful in assessing potential markets; after all, they do have group behavior and lifestyle commonalities. These segments should be considered, but remember that they stereotype groups of people. We all know that all Russians drink vodka, Germans drink beer, and the French drink wine, right? Or that all Southerners eat grits? It is okay to start with a premise in narrowing to one of these groups, but it is important to dig deeper and create understanding.

A cardinal rule in marketing has always been to know your market. That doesn't mean segmenting young and old or rich and poor. It means defining your target in as much detail as circumstances allow and necessity requires. There is a reason that reliable market research looks at multiple factors such as age, gender, income, net worth, ethnicity, geography, lifestyle, and family status. It is very appropriate to use "families" as a partial descriptor of a given market, as long as it doesn't become a synonym for the market itself.[2] Now that we have sent up a red flag, let us look at some factors and segments used in target marketing. When possible, today's marketing aims at the individual and not at the mass market.

Defining Prime Prospects

① Define target marketing.

target marketing
Identifying and communicating with groups of prime prospects.

One of the decisions critical to success is defining prime prospects so you do not waste time and money advertising your product to people unlikely to buy it or to people you can't make a profit by attracting. This search for the best prospects among all consumers is called **target marketing**. For example, The Home Depot has likely discovered that sports fans represent a significant portion of home improvement shoppers (see Exhibit 4.1).

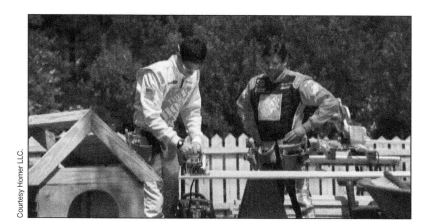

Courtesy Homer LLC.

WHERE DO WE START?

Different agencies and companies approach the process a little differently, as we saw in the previous chapter, but all have to answer the same important questions before advertising can be created. Brand equity research, for instance, seeks to answer a number of questions and examine the existing state of the brand in the context of market and consumers. Today, marketers have a host of informational sources to help plan integrated marketing programs aimed at individual users or groups. Let us look at some of the information sources and trends in America and their implications for advertising planning.

CENSUS DATA

Marketing executives must adapt to a constantly changing environment, especially evident are shifts in demographics and lifestyles. Census data offer marketers a wealth of information about people and how they live in the United States. Much of the database is online. The Topologically Integrated Geographic Encoding and Referencing system, known as TIGER, is one of the more sophisticated tools. The TIGER/Line Shapefiles contains coding of the country's natural, political, and statistical boundaries, including every street, road, and subdivision. TIGER provides the data for computer maps to plan sales territories and pinpoint direct-marketing prospects. This information can be linked to a number of relevant characteristics, such as age, income, and race. Custom research companies using these data have developed software for marketers to access geodemographic databases.

Now advertisers have a number of geodemographic sources that claim unprecedented precision and details about consumers and their purchasing behavior based on their home addresses. These services, using 2000 Census data clusters, promise advertisers that classifying geodemographics has grown from an art to a science (see Exhibit 4.2). Each service organizes America's households into 40 to 70 number-coded nicknames (Blue Bloods, Trailblazers, Penny Pinchers, Shotguns, and Pickups) to identify lifestyle segmentation. Nielsen Claritas' PRIZM, for example, steps beyond the ZIP code + 4 level of detail, a geographic area that encompasses 10 to 12 households, as opposed to blocks, which have 340 households, and ZIP codes, which include 3,600 households. These companies can zero in on smaller segments of the population than was previously possible. They also overlay precise demographic information with consumer behavior information giving advertisers a better consumer picture. Depending on the level of information, these geodemographic services can cost an advertiser from $500 to $100,000. Some of the services described here are discussed later in the text:[3]

- *Acxiom.* Acxiom has a life-stage-driven, household-level, consumer segmentation system representing more than 132 million U.S. households.

- *ESRI.* ESRI provides a demographic and lifestyle picture of neighborhoods, enabling businesses to profile their best customers.

EXHIBIT 4.2

Marketers geographically target consumers using sophisticated tools to analyze census data.

Photos.com/Jupiter Images.

- *Experian.* Experian is a global segmentation product accessing resources including automotive, retail, and catalog transactional information; household demographics; and so on.
- *MapInfo.* MapInfo ties location to behaviors and characteristics of the population, helping advertisers make decisions about market and product potential and store placement.
- *Nielsen Claritas.* By segmenting customers using demographic and behavioral traits, Nielsen Claritas can identify who the best customers are, what they are like, and where to find them.

POPULATION

2 Identify important population trends revealed by the U.S. Census.

The Census Bureau reports that, in 2010, the U.S. population will be 310 million people. We'll talk about the significance of that increase shortly. In the United States, marketers have always had to deal with population growth and shifts that influence advertisers' markets in some way. Obviously, we need to know who is out there in the marketplace. How many of them? Where and how do they live? What do they need? What are their buying patterns? We can't easily reach people if we don't know where they are. But population is more than simple numbers of people. Society tends to group people by age, ethnicity, generation, or some other factor.

The U.S. Census Bureau data projections indicate that by the year 2030, 70 percent of the growth will take place in the South and West. There will be single-digit growth in the Northeast and Midwest, but 40+ percent growth in the South and West. For example, Arizona will more than double its population from the year 2000 to 2030.

SELECTED CENSUS STATE POPULATION PROJECTIONS

Following is a look at the 10 most populous states, their populations in 2008, and the percent change from 2000. The second part of the table shows the population projections for the 10 states projected to have the most people by 2030:

2008		Change from 2000
1. California	36,756,666	8.5%
2. Texas	24,326,974	16.7%
3. New York	19,490,297	2.7%
4. Florida	18,328,340	14.7%
5. Illinois	12,901,563	3.9%
6. Pennsylvania	12,448,279	1.4%
7. Ohio	11,485,910	1.2%
8. Michigan	10,003,422	.7%
9. Georgia	9,685,744	18.3%
10. New Jersey	8,682,661	3.2%

2030	
1. California	46,444,861
2. Texas	33,317,744
3. Florida	28,685,769
4. New York	19,477,429
5. Illinois	13,432,892
6. Pennsylvania	12,768,184
7. North Carolina	12,227,739
8. Georgia	12,017,838
9. Ohio	11,550,528
10. Arizona	10,712,397

Source: Estimated U.S. Census Bureau projections.

Marketers may look at specific markets for numbers of people in a market or making media decisions. A narrower look might involve using Metropolitan Statistical Area (MSA) data, which are population estimates (see the accompanying table). These data examine the metropolitan areas where people actually live. You could also look at each of these MSAs by a number of demographic characteristics, which is discussed later.

Selected Rankings of U.S. Metropolitan Statistical Area (2005) Population Estimates	
1. New York–Northern New Jersey–Long Island, NY–NJ–PA	18,747,320
2. Los Angeles–Long Beach–Santa Ana, CA	12,923,547
3. Chicago–Naperville–Joliet, IL–IN–WI	9,443,356
4. Philadelphia–Camden–Wilmington, PA–NJ–DE–MD	5,823,233
5. Dallas–Fort Worth–Arlington, TX	5,819,475
6. Miami–Fort Lauderdale–Miami Beach, FL	5,422,200
7. Houston–Sugar Land–Baytown, TX	5,280,077
8. Washington–Arlington–Alexandria, DC–VA–MD–WV	5,214,666
9. Atlanta–Sandy Springs–Marietta, GA	4,917,717
10. Detroit–Warren–Livonia, MI	4,488,335
14. Phoenix–Mesa–Scottsdale, AZ	3,865,077
16. Minneapolis–St. Paul–Bloomington, MN–WI	3,142,779
22. Denver–Aurora, CO	2,359,994
25. Cincinnati–Middletown, OH–KY–IN	2,070,441
36. Charlotte–Gastonia–Concord, NC–SC	1,521,278
50. Salt Lake City, UT	1,034,484

CHANGE, CHANGE, CHANGE

The population for the next quarter century will be larger, older, and more diverse than ever before in the United States; it will present many opportunities and challenges for businesses. Of course, it is difficult to accurately predict the future. Speculation about its social and cultural—and even political—aspects is not so clear. By 2030, the U.S. population is expected to exceed 373 million. As this population grows, niche markets may become unwieldy for businesses to target with a single strategy. The niche market of today may become a mass market in its own right, segmented not only by nationality but also by spending behavior and other psychographic characteristics. This trend is called *beehiving*, says Vickie Abrahamson of Iconoculture, a trend consulting firm. Beehiving is the growth of tight-knit, alternative communities sharing common values and passions. Abrahamson says, "Marketers must tap in to beehive rituals, customs and language to build trust and patronage."[4]

A large opportunity for marketers in the next few decades will be in the age 65 and older set. The aging baby boomers group will cause this age group to nearly double in size. In addition to being focused on youth, marketers will also pay more attention outside the youth market. The key in the future will be to establish brands that attract older consumers without alienating younger ones.

We are not going to attempt to cover all the demographics that may be important, but these items should give you something to think about. Keep in mind that these may or may not be important to a specific marketing situation. It is imperative to fully understand the data that are important.

MULTICULTURAL OVERVIEW

Defining the multicultural market appears to be a problem for some. "We tend to forget that a culture means a culture, not necessarily a different language," says Lynn Adrian-Hsing, Asian segments marketing manager, multicultural marketing integration at Bank of America.[5] She encourages advertisers to "think outside the traditional 'multicultural box'" to include gay and lesbian consumers, senior consumers, and members of generation X and generation Y (gen X and gen Y, respectively). "These are cultural markets, not ethnic." Bank of America allocated 25 percent of its advertising budget to win business from African American, Hispanic, and Asian American consumers. The campaign's objective was to add mortgages and about a million new checking accounts during a 12-month period. Citigroup and JP Morgan Chase are other banking corporations that tailor campaigns to specific ethnic groups. The census indicates that the minority population totals more than 100 million, or about 30 percent of the total population. If a marketer included gay and lesbian people in the minority population mix, they would account for another 20 million potential consumers.[6]

Today's multicultural marketing has evolved since the term *minority marketing* was first used to describe targeting African American potential consumers during the 1960s. When marketers included Hispanic American efforts, it became known as *ethnic marketing*. Today, many marketers prefer the term *multicultural marketing* because it encompasses not only a range of ethnicities but also lifestyle-related targets such as the gay and lesbian markets.

SELECTED DEMOGRAPHIC SNAPSHOTS

The American Community Survey, a Census Bureau program, released its most recent findings in 2007. Among the new data were the following:

Ancestry. Seventeen percent of Americans say their roots are German, the largest ancestral group; 12 percent say their background is Irish; those saying their background is English (10 percent) rank third; and ranking fourth, 7 percent of the population say their ancestral background is "American."

Immigrants. One in eight residents (12.5 percent) are immigrants, up from 11 percent in 2000. Latin American residents account for more than half (53 percent) of the immigrant population; 27 percent came from Asian/Pacific areas. Nearly one-third (31 percent) of immigrants are from Mexico; there are an estimated 11 million Mexican-born residents in the United States, which is greater than the population of all but seven states.

Education. Seventeen percent of U.S. adults (age 25 and older) have bachelor's degrees; 10 percent have advanced degrees. Massachusetts ranks high among states in percentage of residents with bachelors' (21.4 percent) or advanced degrees (16 percent). Considering large cities, San Francisco is among the most educated: Fifty percent of its residents are college graduates.

THE AFRICAN AMERICAN POPULATION African Americans represent an integral part of our cultural, social, and economic landscape. In 2010, Census projections indicated that African American people constituted 13 percent of the U.S. population, or 37 million, ranking them as the second-largest minority segment—in 2003 they were surpassed by Hispanics.[7]

Economically, there are more than 823,500 African American–owned businesses generating $71 billion in revenues. Women own 38 percent of the nation's African American businesses, a higher percentage than that of any other minority ethnic group. More than 46 percent of the African American population own their own homes. The top five African American population cities are New York, Chicago, Detroit, Philadelphia, and Houston. Census data indicate that 55 percent of U.S. African American people live in the South, 18 percent live in the Northeast, 18 percent live in the Midwest, and only about 8 percent live in the West.

Homeownership and geographic location are important information for advertisers targeting African Americans. Marketers are very interested in this group for its economic prowess. According to 2008 data from the Selig Center for Economic Growth at the University of Georgia, African Americans represent more than $913 billion in consumer buying power (see Exhibit 4.3). By 2013, that figure is expected to reach $1.2 trillion. Some advertisers specifically appeal to African Americans with media buys in black media (more than $2 billion in 2008).[8] However, some advertisers prefer to address this segment with traditional general-market advertising: "A number of marketers still tend to think African-Americans are darker versions of white people, that they don't have to do anything different to reach them," says Howard Buford, chief executive officer (CEO) of Prime Access, a multicultural agency.[9]

THE HISPANIC POPULATION The U.S. Hispanic population in 2010, including immigrants and those born in the United States, total almost 50 million, or 16 percent of the nation's population. People of Mexican origin make up 64 percent of the U.S. Hispanic population; 9 percent of the Hispanic population in the United States have roots in Puerto Rico, 7 percent in Central America, 5 percent in South America, and 3 percent each in Cuba and the Dominican Republic. The Census Bureau uses the "non-Hispanic white" designation because Hispanics can be of any race. According to the Census Bureau, the term *Hispanic* is an ethnic classification. Hispanic purchasing power reached $870 billion in 2008 and is projected to reach $1.3 trillion by 2013, or almost 10 percent of the nation's buying power.

In addition to buying power, Hispanics have captured marketers' attention because it is the fastest-growing ethnic minority, accounting for 50 percent of growth in the United States, and it is projected to represent almost 30 percent of the U.S. population by 2050. Some marketers see Hispanics as essential to brand growth: "Walmart, a major marketer to Latinos, is pressuring its suppliers, such as GE, to develop their own Hispanic-marketing strategies. Johnson & Johnson says it will spend more on Hispanic

EXHIBIT 4.3

This anniversary ad for Colonial Mall is designed to speak to African American consumers.

Courtesy of Bright Ideas Group.

Bundle Up, Big Daddy!
Cool fall fashions are here.

30 Years of Style
1975-2005

marketing in 2009, adding brands that have never advertised to that segment before. And whole categories, such as pharmaceuticals, are assigning brands to Hispanic agencies for the first time."[10]

Coors' Hispanic marketing chief, Carl Kravetz, speaking to an Association of National Advertisers (ANA) multicultural marketing conference, hammered home the findings of a market study that paints a much more sophisticated, multifaceted, and nuanced picture of the country's broad Hispanic community. Kravetz said that the study's in-depth research found that traditional demographic markers such as Spanish-language usage, country of origin, and length of time in the United States are becoming much less relevant as the number of bilingual, bicultural households grows quickly. "If the heart is the core of Latino identity, then the four chambers [that] are responsible for its functioning are interpersonal orientation, time and space perception, spirituality, and gender perception. Interpersonal orientation is the way we live our relationships with other people, and is . . . radically different from non-Latinos," he said. For instance, individualism is important to Anglos, whereas Latinos have a

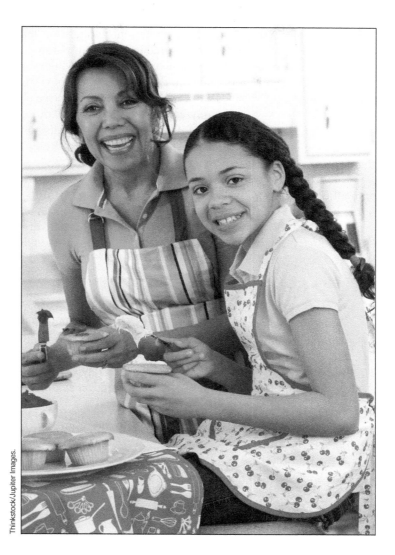

Thinkstock/Jupiter Images.

EXHIBIT 4.4

In the United States, generational differences are blurring among Hispanics.

collectivist culture that favors cooperation and values family needs over those of the individual (see Exhibit 4.4).[11]

For marketers, that means understanding the family as a unit, including group decision making, and avoiding conflict between individual needs and group expectations. Latino individuals perceive time and space very differently. They change plans easily, are more present- and past-oriented, and value friends and family more than privacy. In contrast, non-Hispanic people are future-oriented, have a rigid sense of space and privacy, and focus on results. Religion and spirituality affect how Latino individuals see the world and create a love of rituals and celebrations. Gender roles are also radically different. Machismo is about protecting and providing for the family.[12]

THE ASIAN AND PACIFIC ISLANDER POPULATION In 2010, the Census reported 14.5 million Asian and Pacific Islander people living in the United States, representing 5 percent of the population. Of the total, 51 percent live in the West, 19 percent live in the South, 12 percent live in the Midwest, and 19 percent live in the Northeast, with 95 percent living in metropolitan areas.

A high value is placed on education: Fifty-one percent of Asian men and 44 percent of Asian women earned at least a bachelor's degree compared to 32 percent of non-Hispanic white men and 27 percent of non-Hispanic white women. A glance at income in 2001 indicates that 40 percent of all Asian families had incomes of $75,000 or more.

Members of the Asian American population belong to at least one of fifteen distinct ethnic groups and national origins, including Bangladesh, Cambodian, Chinese, Filipino, Indian, Indonesian, Japanese, Korean, Laotian, Malaysian, Pakistani, Sri Lankian, Taiwanese, Thai, and Vietnamese, and others differing in culture, language, and history. Each of these factors drives what will be the most effective channel for reaching these consumers. "The Asian market will become increasingly more important over the next decade," says Bank of America's Adrian-Hsing, especially for high-end products. "It is slowly being discovered that this is an extremely wealthy, extremely affluent segment that is relatively untapped."[13]

Gilbert Davila, vice president–multicultural market for The Walt Disney Company, puts all of this into a marketing perspective, saying, "Multicultural marketing is not a fad. When you take a look at everything that's happening, at all the projections from the census, America is only going to become increasingly diverse, which will place more challenges on companies to figure out how to better market, be more relevant and target these constituencies."[14]

OTHER TARGET INFLUENCES

As you can see, there is a lot of information for marketers to digest. There are many additional factors a marketer can examine that might influence basic marketing decisions. For example, Home Depot may target women, do-it-yourselfers, contractors, and gardeners, requiring an understanding of many groups and lifestyles. Applebee's Carside To Go outdoor advertisement understands today's busy lifestyle (see Exhibit 4.5). Again, we'll sample some of the typical information available to marketers.

HOUSEHOLD INCOME   The Bureau of Labor Statistics' Consumer Expenditure Survey produces annual estimates of household spending on hundreds of items, crosstabulated by demographic characteristics. As with most data, you need to use these data wisely. In addition to looking at household income, advertisers often look at disposable and discretionary income. Disposable income is after-tax income. Discretionary income is the amount of money consumers have after paying taxes and buying necessities such as food and housing.

SPENDING   *American Demographics* found that the average U.S. metropolitan household devotes 16 percent of its spending to shelter, 17 percent to transportation, 14 percent to food, 6 percent to utilities, 6 percent to apparel, 5 percent to entertainment, 3 percent to household operations, and 11 percent to personal insurance. Spending patterns depend strongly on the unique age and income characteristics of individual markets.[15] Many products and services depend on disposable income of consumers for their existence.

EXHIBIT 4.5

Applebee's touts, "Make dinner before you even get home."

Courtesy of McRae Communications and AppleGrove Restaurants, an Applebee's Franchise company.

BIRTHRATE   To marketers, the number of births in a given year can be important in projecting market size. The birthrate in the United States has been in decline for decades. In 1960, the rate was 23.7 per thousand population, and it was 13.9 per thousand in 2002, the lowest since government records have been kept. There were 4,019,280 recorded births in America in 2002. Just think of the significance to companies selling baby items. If marketers marry knowledge of fluctuations in the birthrate with an understanding of how consumers tend to act at different stages of their lives, they can get a rough picture of the market challenges that lie in the future. Despite the declining numbers, this may be a terrific market for more than baby products, such as, for example, selling 529 Savings Plans (see Exhibit 4.6).

AGING   In 2010, more than one in eight Americans were 65 years or older (12.9 percent). It is estimated that by 2030, one in every six Americans will be 65 years or older (19 percent). Census estimates indicate that the seniors segment of the population will more than double by 2050. This will have a significant implication for both marketers and society as a whole.

WOMEN   For starters, there are 120 million women in the United States. They account for 47 percent of all workers and 51 percent of management positions. According to the U.S. Department of Education, in every state, in every income bracket, and in every racial and ethnic group, women earn close to 60 percent of the bachelor's degrees and master's degrees in the United States.[16]

Women purchase or influence 85 percent of all products. The demands on marketers will increase as women increase their wealth, education, and longevity. For decades, marketers have known that women drive all the obvious categories of food, beauty, and household products. Bridget Brennan, founder of Female Factor Communications, says that marketing to women as your leader is the way of the future in almost every product category. For example, research revealed that women, not male hobbyists, were frequent users of Krazy Glue. As a result, SBC Advertising created a campaign designed to speak to women and ran the ads in *People* and other publications with high female readership (see Exhibit 4.7).

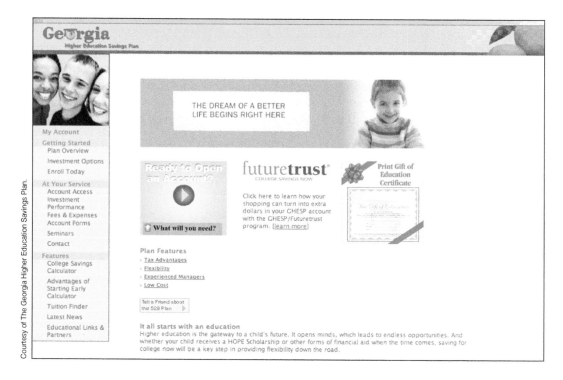

EXHIBIT 4.6

The ad for Georgia Higher Education Savings Plan is aimed at parents who are concerned about money for their children's college education.

EXHIBIT 4.7

Research revealed that women are frequent shoppers for products like Krazy Glue.

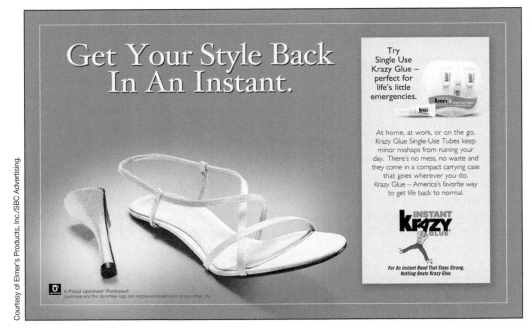

Women with children younger than age 18 account for nearly one-third of U.S. households, according to the Census Bureau, and are a rich target for marketers—especially when those women are online. Currently, there are more than 27 million "digital moms" and 65 percent of them social network online.[17] A recent survey by CafeMom revealed insights into five types of online moms so that marketers can better understand and engage with them: self-expressors, utility moms, groupsters, infoseekers, and hyperconnectors. For example, groupster moms are in their 30s, have young children in school, and actively blog and join and start groups. They are influenced by brand sponsorships and are more likely to share photos and respond to online polls.

MEN   Recently, advertisers and media buyers were wondering where the 18- to 34-year-old men had gone. They weren't in front of the television set. The answer was simply that their media habits had changed. This disturbed advertisers because single males have relatively high disposable incomes, are still forming brand loyalties, and are important to a number of product categories, for example, electronics, automobiles, beer, and personal items. Marketers have courted women more aggressively than men because women either buy or influence more purchases. *The Future of Man*, coauthored by an advertising man, looks at the stereotypes and changes taking place in the male culture.

SINGLE-PERSON HOUSEHOLDS   In 2005, the Census Bureau reported that single-adult households had displaced two-parent families with children as the most common kind of U.S. household. They project this group to total 34 million by the year 2010. The report indicated that people are most likely to live alone at either end of the life cycle—in youth or as senior citizens.

Apparently, most Americans still believe the typical household consists of a "mom, pop, and two kids." This nuclear-family household was the most common as recently as 1990, when there were 25 million such households. They are now the second-largest group. Married households without children remained third, with 20 million in 1990 and 22 million in 2000.

Understanding these numbers can be a complex issue. Peter Francese, who tracks trends for Ogilvy & Mather, says not all of those adults living alone are living completely alone. "There are many professional, commuter couples living alone during the week, but share weekends together. Single parents might regularly have their children

KLEPPNER VIEWPOINT 4.1

John Ludwig   Chief Executive Officer
and Founding Partner, Push

THE FORGOTTEN AUDIENCE

John Ludwig

I recently had a conversation with an editor from one of the top advertising trade publications and the discussion turned to why countless companies are so focused on speaking and listening to their "target audience" that they forget about one of the most important audiences of all—their employees. Now, ad agencies aren't doing much to help this either. After all, what's the fun of doing a corporate video about human relations issues when the ad agency could be doing a television spot that runs during the *Super Bowl*? Well, the fun lies in knowing that a brand can live or die by the way that their employees—whether salespeople, waiters and waitresses, customer service operators, field technicians, managers, or any other person who represents their brand—deal with and relate to their customers.

For example, let's say restaurant XYZ does an amazing commercial during the *Super Bowl*. It gets talked about by everyone, gets great reviews in the papers, and is watched a million times on YouTube. You, like everyone else, love it. So much so that you decide you need to get down to this particular restaurant right now. You get there and the service is horrible. The hostess forgets your party, the server spends more time in the kitchen than he does refilling your glass, and the check total is wrong at the end of the meal. Well, what's going to be your

lasting impression? The great *Super Bowl* ad you saw, or the awful experience you had? And guess what else? You'll probably talk about that horrible experience on Twitter or put it up on Facebook or Yelp about it—just plain tell all of your friends what a bad time you had. So all that time, money, and energy that went into making and airing that *Super Bowl* commercial simply went up in flames.

If there truly is an opportunity for ad agencies to become not only more integrated within themselves but also more integrated with their clients, this is it. After all, great brands are built from the inside out. If agencies are sincere about helping build brands, then they need to be helping not only the chief marketing officer but also they need to help the director of human relations, the chief operating officer, or even the chief technology officer. By integrating what we have to offer, whether it's strategy, our creative product, interactive, public relations, or media, we can affect the brand where it lives the most—with the people who day in and day out spend the most time with the customer. Because, at the end of the day, what's going to affect the brand more—30 seconds on TV, or 5, 10, or 15 minutes, or more, with a person who lives the brand every day?

I'm fortunate enough to be part of an agency that understands the need for and importance of communicating with

both the external consumer and internal stakeholders. And we've done a lot of fun, exciting, and important work for both. It simply depends on your attitude and belief in what truly makes a brand great. Sure, we do funny TV commercials, innovative web sites, and great magazine ads. But we've also done some pretty cool work for human relations directors, operations executives, and chief technology officers. Because at the end of the day, we are a creative, solutions-driven agency, and these are all creative opportunities.

So, as you move forward in this great business of ours and you start putting together that marketing plan that is going to win the world over for your company by persuading millions of people to buy your product or service, don't forget the troops who are going to be doing all the hard work for you—your company's employees.

in the home, and single adults might have lengthy visits from friends or lovers. There is a tremendous diversity in the living-alone group."

"The people who choose to live alone are creating their own communities without regret or unwanted claims made on their lives."[18]

Marketers need to realize that despite the potential of this group, like the others we have discussed, it is not a homogeneous target audience. For example, Looking Glass, Inc., lists 8 of its 30-plus key consumer segments as likely to live as one-person households. Among them are upscale mature women (56 percent of the segment lives alone), working-class women (63 percent), fit and stylish students (52 percent), well-to-do gentlemen (76 percent), and working-class men (78 percent).[19]

Generational Marketing

③ Define and provide examples of generational marketing.

The consumer society is really a twentieth-century phenomenon, and for the past century or so, many businesses have made decisions based on the assumption that one generation will grow up and make the same kinds of choices made by the group that went before it at the same stages of life.

Modern marketing's definition of *generation* is composed of two disparate parts. First, there's the traditional definition used by demographers as the number of people in any age group and what that portends about the size and shape of tomorrow's markets. Second, there's the issue of shared attitudes, a common history, and formative experiences. Both definitions are important to marketers of life. Most agree that a *generation* usually is defined as 30 years and extends past a single decade. However, if you look at the history of generations, you'll find some that are very short.

Marketers think experiences bind people who are born in continuous years into a *cohort*—a group of individuals who have a demographic statistic in common. Demographers like to package things in a way that's easy to measure, and date of birth is the easiest way to define generations. Generational marketing people take the statistical analysis of births and overlay major world events that occurred during a generation's formative years to construct a picture of a generation's personality.[20] Knowing how many babies are born and then tracing the numbers through different stages of their lives give marketers a rough idea of the challenges and opportunities over 10, 20, and even 30 years.

TARGET GENERATIONS

Demographers and marketers generally agree on the generation timeline but can disagree on generational titles and exact years. Generations living in 2009 include good warriors (those born from 1909 through 1928), lucky few/matures (those born from 1929 through 1945), baby boomers (born from 1946 through 1964), generation Xers (born from 1965 through 1982), generation Yers/new boomers (born from 1983 through 2001), and generation Zers (born since 2002). Researchers have concentrated on four generations (lucky few, baby boomers, and generations X and Y) and are beginning to learn about generation Z.[21] There are distinct differences in how each generation thinks and buys (see Exhibit 4.8).

The values of the lucky few generation are close to what are considered classic American values: The lucky few favor a kind of Puritan work ethic, with plenty of self-sacrifice, teamwork, conformity for the common good, and so forth.

The boomers, however, are self-assured and self-absorbed. They are much better educated than any generation before them, and they are aware of this. They think they are more sophisticated and believe they know better than their predecessors. They are very self-conscious about changing the world and fixing things. They are fighting the concept of *old*.

GENERATION X   The gen Xers were born in the post–baby boom. This generation was a longtime media whipping post, once decried as overeducated slackers, with a distrust for social institutions, politics, and religion. Recent Yankelovich Partners research finds Xers to be self-reliant, entrepreneurial, techno focused, media savvy, socially tolerant, and—slowly, but surely—parents. Growing up with skyrocketing divorce rates and with less than family stability, gen Xers have been more cautious about entering the life stage of family formation. As a result, today's Xers are reinventing the traditionalism they are bringing to family life.

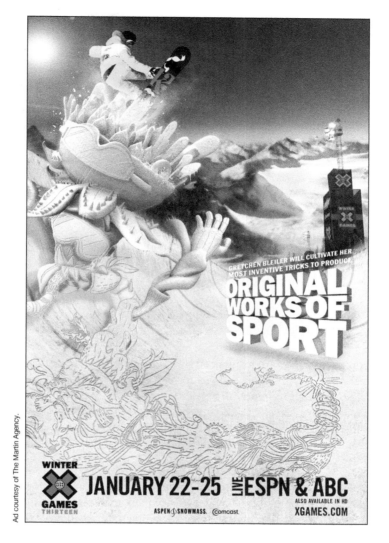

Ad courtesy of The Martin Agency.

EXHIBIT 4.8

What generation is most likely to tune in to watch the Winter X Games?

Marketers have begun shifting their views as these changing self-concepts evolve from carefree kids to obligation-bound parents. A recent advertising campaign cleverly highlighted markers of this life-stage transition, focusing on events such as the first time a man is called "Sir" and the first time one doesn't get carded at a bar; the advertisement touts sporty cars that will "make the other soccer moms talk." It seems that every generation is a catalyst for change as it moves through a new life stage.

GENERATION Y (NEW BOOMERS, ECHO BOOMERS, MILLENNIALS, IGENERATION)
Although demographers debate cutoff dates and labels, most calculations place generation Yers as those born from 1983 through 2001. By 2010, the 12-to-19 age group will have expanded to a historic peak of 35 million. However, members of this group outspend all previous generations. Research shows that teens spend more than $125 billion each year, about $5,000 per person each year. They spend money on gaming, music, coffee drinks at Starbucks, and food at Chipotle and McDonald's.[22] According to *USA Today*, they're techno savvy, coddled, optimistic, prone to abrupt shifts in taste, and tough to pigeonhole.[23]

Generation Y is the first generation to come along that's big enough to hurt a boomer brand simply by giving it a cold shoulder. This generation is more racially diverse: One in three is not Caucasian. Marketers will have to learn to think like they do—and not like their boomer parents.[24]

According to a new *Los Angeles Times*/Bloomberg poll that surveyed the habits of 12- to 24-year-olds, girls aged 12 to 14 are the most deeply motivated by television: Sixty-five

EXHIBIT 4.9

Even the youngest of consumers prefers certain brands.

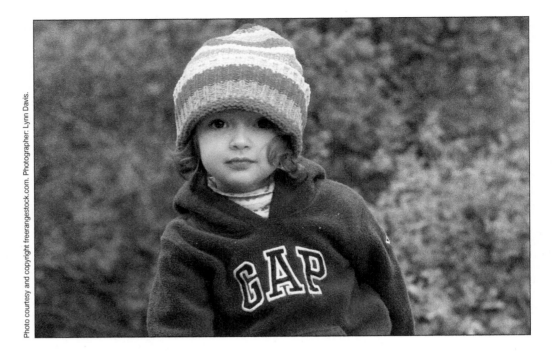

Photo courtesy and copyright freerangestock.com. Photographer: Lynn Davis.

percent say they are influenced by a television show or network, are more likely to multi-task than boys of their age group, and are easily bored; 41 percent say there are too few choices of entertainment. These kids are known by economists, sociologists, and marketing experts as optimistic team players and rule followers, born into "child-centered" families and raised as part of the most celebrated, protected, and overscheduled generation in memory. Technology has been so much a part of their lives that, to them, life before e-mail and the Internet was "the Stone Age."[25]

GENERATION Z   Generation Z is said to have begun with people born after 2001. This generation comes from a wider mix of backgrounds and will bring different experiences for marketers to understand. By 2010, marketers will have to start all over again to figure out how to impress this new generation. However, it's likely that they—like gen Yers—will have an affinity for branded goods (see Exhibit 4.9).

Paying attention to generational cohorts can make or break a brand. Without an accurate view of generations, you are likely to misinterpret what you see in the marketplace. No company provides a better object lesson in the importance of staying relevant than Levi Strauss & Co., one of America's great brands. Levi's lost more than half its share of the American jeans market during the 1990s. According to John Hancock Financial's CEO David D'Alessandro, Levi's failed to invest in gen X and the echo boom. It didn't keep tuned in to what kids wanted to wear. It didn't offer this target market anything of value to distinguish its potential consumers from the previous generation.[26]

Marketing Concept and Targeting

4   **Explain the importance of the marketing concept to advertising.**

marketing concept
A management orientation that views the needs of consumers as primary to the success of a firm.

Companies cannot operate in every market and satisfy every consumer need. Companies generally find that it is necessary to divide the market into major market segments, evaluate the segments, and then target those segments they can best serve. This focus on specific groups of buyers is called *market segmentation* (discussed later in this chapter). It is an extension of the **marketing concept**, defined by Philip Kotler, that achieving organizational goals depends on determining the needs and wants of target markets and delivering the desired satisfactions more effectively and efficiently than competitors. This idea has been stated as "find a need and fill it" or "make what you can sell instead of trying to sell what you can make." Advertisers have expressed this concept in colorful ways; for example, marketers at Burger King said, "Have It Your Way."

The old marketing concept—the management philosophy first articulated in the 1950s—is a relic of an earlier period of economic history. Most of its assumptions are no longer appropriate in the competitive global markets of today. The world is rapidly moving toward a pattern of economic activity based on long-term relationships and partnerships. The concept of customer value is at the heart of the new marketing concept and must be the central element of all business strategy.

As we look at the differences, we find that the old marketing concept had the objective of making a sale, whereas under the new marketing concept, the objective is to develop a customer relationship in which the sale is only the beginning. Under both marketing concepts, market segmentation, market targeting, and positioning are essential requirements for effective strategic planning. In the new marketing concept, the focus is sharpened by adding the idea of the value proposition.[27]

Market-driven companies need to understand how customer needs and company capabilities converge to form the customer's definition of value. This includes more than monitoring data. It includes listening to the consumer because they now control the communication process. That means using all the research techniques discussed in later chapters. It also means being attuned to the "blogosphere" and other informational technology and tracking systems. This is more than a philosophy; it is a way of doing business. It includes customer orientation, market intelligence, distinctive competencies, value delivery, market targeting and the value proposition, customer-defined total quality management, profitability rather than sales volume, relationship management, continuous improvement, and a customer-focused organizational structure.[28]

WHAT IS A PRODUCT?

Seems like a silly question, doesn't it? Let us define a *product* as a bundle of ingredients put together for sale as something useful to a consumer. People don't go into a store to buy alcohol denat., PPG-15 stearyl ether, butylenes glycol, aqua/water, propylene glycol, dipropylene glycol, cyclopean tasiloxane, and so on. Many people seeking a sunless tanning product do, however, go into a store and buy L'Oreal Sublime Bronze Any Angle Self-Tanning Spray. It is more than a physical object. It represents a bundle of satisfactions—a product that gives someone concerned about skin cancer (or because they work from 9 to 5) a chance to show up at the pool on the weekend with a tan.

Some of these satisfactions are purely functional—a watch to tell time or a car for transportation. Some of the satisfactions are psychological—a watch may represent a piece of beautiful jewelry and a car may represent status. Different people have different ideas about which satisfactions are important. Literally, a white respondent to a self-tanning suntan product said, "I work all day and can't get out in the sun, and when I go to the pool on the weekend, I want to be any shade other than white." Products are often designed with satisfactions to match the interests of a particular group of consumers. We are also judged in large measure by our physical possessions—think of your attitudes toward a Mercedes, a BMW, a Jaguar, a BlackBerry, a 120-inch plasma television, and so on. The products that we purchase say something about us and group us with people who seek similar satisfactions from life and products. As we match people and benefits, we create product loyalty that insulates us against competitive attack.

The 20,000-plus new products reaching the market each year often have a difficult time finding customers. Manufacturers must be selective in defining the most profitable market segments because introducing a new product can be expensive. New products need to be well thought out, and a key is to innovate brands that are sustainable.

WHAT IS A MARKET?

All advertising and marketing people could easily answer this question, but you might get different answers, depending on their perspectives. For our purposes, a *market* can

Courtesy of Blattner Brunner and Cub Cadet.

The ZTT Zero-Turn Tractor.

EXHIBIT 4.10

This ad demonstrates the competitive advantage of Cub Cadet's Zero-Turn Tractor.

be defined as a group of people who can be identified by some common characteristic, interest, or problem—who could use our product to advantage, who could afford to buy it, and who can be reached through some medium.

Markets can be defined differently and broadly or narrowly. Examples of potential markets include weight watchers, golfers, mothers of young children, singles, matures, newly marrieds, skiers, tennis players, Hispanic teens, do-it-yourselfers, runners, seniors, and tourists.

The *majority fallacy* is a term applied to the assumption, once frequently made, that every product should be aimed at and acceptable to a majority of all consumers. Research tells us that brands aimed at the majority of consumers in a given market will tend to have rather similar characteristics and will neglect an opportunity to serve the needs of consumer minorities. Take, for example, chocolate cake mixes. A good-size group of consumers would prefer a light-chocolate cake or a very-dark-chocolate cake, but the majority choice is a medium-chocolate cake. So, although several initial cake mix products would do best to market a medium-chocolate cake to appeal to the broadest group of consumers, later entrants might gain a larger share by supplying the smaller but significant group with its preference. What if the dark-chocolate cake was both calorie and fat free?

WHAT IS COMPETITION?

Stroll down the aisles of your favorite supermarket or drugstore and look at the toothpaste choices—they offer brighteners, abrasives, fresh breath, fluorides, pastes, gels, peroxides, and so on. Or look in the analgesic section. You will find many brands competing for your attention—Bayer, Aleve, Advil, Tylenol, Ascriptin, Empirin, Vanquish, Motrin IB, Goody's, BC, Excedrin, and the list goes on. Why does one consumer choose one brand and another consumer something else? How does one even get on the shelf to compete? These are very important questions to the makers of these products. Cub Cadet is anticipating that lawn tractor users will respond positively to the competitive advantage of its Zero-Turn Tractor (see Exhibit 4.10).

We are speaking of competition in the broadest sense to include all the forces that are inhibiting the sales of a product. They may be products in the same subclass as your product or in the same product class, or they may be forces outside the category of your product. Our list of analgesics includes products in different subcategories: Bayer, Tylenol, Aleve, and Advil are each in different analgesic categories, such as aspirin, acetaminophen, naproxen, and ibuprofen. Advil and Nuprin are in the same subcategory. Does that mean they compete with only themselves? The answer is generally no. Many consumers don't even consider the subclasses; they only think in terms of pain relief. If consumers are considering only the benefits of an ibuprofen product, then the answer is yes. Advil, Motrin IB, and Excedrin IB would all compete. The point is that advertisers and marketers need to try to find the answers as to which products in what categories compete for the consumer's attention and dollar. It may sound confusing because you don't know the category, but the seasoned marketer for these products knows its category and the products and the reasons people buy.

Marketers for all kinds of products and services must ask: Who are our competitors? What are their brands? What are other product categories? Are there many brands or only a few? Which are strong? Which are vulnerable? What impact, if any, do store brands and generics have? Are there any strong, long-established brands, or is the market volatile?

Planning the Advertising

MARKET SEGMENTATION

Marketers can't efficiently reach every person who has a dollar to spend. It is about maximizing your potential in the marketplace by targeting your product to certain segments of the population with similar behaviors, such as people your age, your gender, and with a similar lifestyle. From a communication standpoint, it is usually more difficult than you would imagine. You must understand each segment's cultural nuances and choose the right message so you don't stereotype the service or product you're selling as one designed only for a particular segment. It has been said, "If you try to talk to everyone, you'll end up talking to nobody." The division of an entire market of consumers into groups whose similarity makes them a market for products servicing their special needs is called **market segmentation**.

This classifying of consumers is generally one of the tasks of a marketing plan's **situation analysis** section, which consists of four components: a description of the current situation; an analysis of strengths, weaknesses, opportunities, and threats (SWOT); major issues; and assumptions about the future. Typically, the market-segmentation process runs through a number of steps:

1. *Segment* your market.

2. *Target* a segment.

3. *Position* your product for that segment.

4. *Communicate* your positioning.

A number of factors need to be considered in planning advertising to take advantage of market segmentation. The first step is to determine the variable to use for dividing a market. In addition to demographics, the major means of market segmentation are geographic, product-user, brand loyalty, and lifestyle segmentation. It is common for marketers to combine more than one segmentation variable in seeking their target. Of course, the segment has to be large enough in size to justify the marketing effort.

GEOGRAPHIC SEGMENTATION   Geographic segmentation is the oldest form of segmentation; it designates customers by geographic area. It dates back to early days when distribution was the primary concern of manufacturers. Today, geomarketing is of particular importance to media planners in deciding on national, regional, and local advertising campaigns. It is only recently that geomarketing has been elevated to a marketing discipline the way demographics was in the 1950s and psychographics was in the 1970s. In this instance, consumers haven't changed but marketers' awareness of regional and

market segmentation
The division of an entire market of consumers into groups whose similarity makes them a market for products serving their special needs.

situation analysis
The part of the advertising plan that answers the questions: Where are we today and how did we get here? It deals with the past and present.

5 **Identify the five ways markets are segmented.**

global marketing has. Geodemographical marketing is just another way of segmenting the market for companies in search of growth.

There has been a "data explosion" on local markets. Some of the information comes from an abundant number of research services for use on merchandising and buying decisions. Many retail companies such as supermarkets or fast-food feeders practice *micromarketing*—treating each individual store as its own market and trading area. Often, this approach translates into different advertisements for different markets. When thinking about geographic segmentation, advertisers can explore a number of categories:

- Census tract data/areas of dominant influence (ADI)
- ZIP codes/states
- Counties/census regions
- Metropolitan statistical areas/total United States

Companies that lack national distribution may consider geographic segmentation. Pro Balanced dog food is distributed primarily in the South but has to compete against national brands to survive. There are many local or regional brands that must be successful in their geographic areas to survive. Cheerwine is a cherry-cola-like soft drink that has a strong presence in its home area but would have problems in areas wherein its history and tradition were unknown. In the past, Cheerwine used the slogan, "It's a Carolina Thing." Cheerwine products can be purchased in grocery and convenience stores in North Carolina and South Carolina, as well as in some locations in Alabama, Georgia, Illinois, Indiana, Iowa, Kansas, Kentucky, Minnesota, Missouri, Nebraska, Tennessee, Virginia, West Virginia, and Wisconsin. In this case, geographic segmentation is a distribution strategy rather than a promotional one. Despite being small, Cheerwine is innovative with blogs, web games, road trips, and so on to help connect to prospects.

It is not unusual for national companies to divide their advertising and marketing efforts into regional units to respond better to the competition. McDonald's uses a major advertising agency (and media planning and buying agency) to handle its national advertising and numerous (generally smaller) agencies to handle franchise and regional efforts supplementing the national effort. Of course, we didn't mention their multicultural agencies that serve minority marketing. When McDonald's launched "i'm lovin' it," a global advertising campaign using Justin Timberlake, they used a German agency. This gives McDonald's the ability to react to the marketplace by cities, regions, or individual stores as well as globally.

product-user segmentation
Identifying consumers by the amount of product usage.

PRODUCT-USER SEGMENTATION   **Product-user segmentation** is a strategy based on the amount of usage and/or consumption patterns of a brand or category. The advertiser is interested in product usage rather than consumer characteristics. As a practical matter, most user-segmentation methods are combined with demographic or lifestyle consumer identification. Here, the advertiser is interested in market segments with the highest sales potential. Typically, a market segment is first divided into all users and then subdivided into heavy, medium, and light users and nonusers of the product. For example, let us look at the frequency of the weekly use of fast foods:

Frequency	Adults	Men	Women
Heavy (4+ visits)	11.4%	14.8%	8.3%
Medium (1–3 visits)	44.9	46.5	43.3
Light (less than weekly)	22.8	20.6	24.8

The definition of usage varies with the product category. For example, heavy fast-food use may be defined as four or more times per week, heavy luxury-restaurant use as once a week, and heavy seafood-restaurant use as once a week. As you can see, product-user segmentation can get quite complex, but these kinds of data allow marketers to use a rifle instead of a shotgun. The importance of heavy users is discussed later in the chapter.

BRAND LOYALTY SEGMENTATION   Users of a product also can be categorized by the brands they buy. There are numerous ways to estimate the chances of getting a heavy user of one brand to try a new brand. One technique is to define market segments according to their **brand loyalty** and preference for national over private brands. Studies of brand loyalty for packaged goods found six such segments:[29]

1. *National-brand loyal.* Members of this segment buy primarily a single national brand at its regular price.

2. *National-brand deal.* This segment is similar to the national-brand-loyal segment, except that most of its purchases are made on deal (that is, the consumer is loyal to only national brands but chooses the least expensive one). To buy the preferred national brand on deal, the consumer engages in considerable store switching.

3. *Private-label loyal.* Consumers in this segment primarily buy the private label offered by the store in which they shop (for example, CVS, Wal-Mart, Target, Publix, and other store brands).

4. *Private-label deal.* This segment shops at many stores and buys the private label of each store, usually on a deal.

5. *National-brand switcher.* Members of this segment tend not to buy private labels. Instead, they switch regularly among the various national brands on the market.

6. *Private-label switcher.* This segment is similar to the private-label-deal segment, except that the members are not very deal prone and purchase the private labels at their regular price.

Price, product distribution, and promotion also affect the share of market coming from each competing brand. However, a new national brand would expect to gain most of its initial sales from segments 2 and 5, whereas segments 1 and 3 would normally be poor prospects to try a new brand. There are many factors to consider. But remember: Today, a camera is not just a camera; markets change with the product, and products change with the market.

LIFESTYLE SEGMENTATION   **Lifestyle segmentation** makes the assumption that if you live a certain way, so do your neighbors and, therefore, any smart marketer would want to target clusters filled with these clones. Lifestyle clusters are more accurate characterizations of people than any single variable would be.

The concept of lifestyle segmentation is a viable one; however, researchers are having to adjust to a sea of changes taking place among America's shopping public. For example, old attitudes toward work and leisure or fitness don't fit today's realities. As a result, segmentation researchers are changing how they view many of the new lifestyle characteristics driving this new era.[30]

Marketers have used specialized segmentation techniques to find the most fruitful target audiences since PRIZM (Potential Rating Index for ZIP Markets) in 1974 grouped people who had similar demographics and lifestyles into neighborhood clusters on the theory that "birds of a feather flock together." A number of similar programs have popped up since—such as SRI's **Values and Lifestyle System (VALS™)**—all based on the premise that people in the same ZIP code or neighborhood tend to buy the same products. Each research company has its own terminology for the various clusters it identifies. Recently, Yankelovich Partners Inc. developed a psychographic-segmentation system called MONITOR MindBase. Its premise is the idea of segmenting individuals by values, attitudes, and mind-sets rather than by geography, demographics, and consumption patterns. It segments people into categories of consumers with varying degrees of materialism, ambition, orientation to family life, cynicism, openness to technology, and other elements.[31]

SummerGrove homes (see Exhibit 4.11) range from the $130,000s to $700,000s and are convenient to Atlanta and the airport. If you can afford them, those are good

brand loyalty
A consumer's preference for and commitment to a specific brand.

lifestyle segmentation
Identifying consumers by combining several demographics and lifestyles.

Values and Lifestyle System (VALS™)
Developed by SRI International to cluster consumers according to several variables in order to predict consumer behavior.

EXHIBIT 4.11

"The joys of SummerGrove will turn you into a kid again."

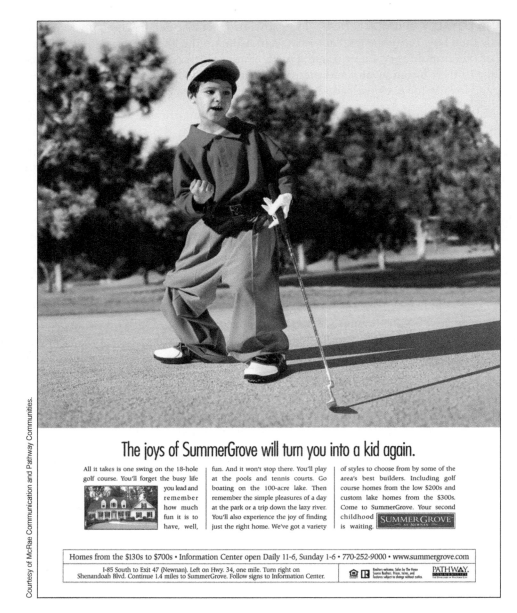

Courtesy of McRae Communication and Pathway Communities.

The joys of SummerGrove will turn you into a kid again.

attributes, but copywriter Amy Lokken knew the lifestyle appeal is what it is about, "All it takes is one swing on the 18-hole golf course. You'll forget the busy life you lead and remember how much fun it is to have, well, fun." And she ends with, "Your second childhood is waiting."

Researchers Kevin Clancy and Robert Shulman argue that "off-the-shelf segmentation studies cannot be as good as customized segmentation done with a specific product or service in mind. VALS™ will help break up the world into pieces, but the pieces may or may not have any relevance for any one brand."[32]

One approach to determining lifestyle characteristics is to identify consumers' activities, interests, and opinions (AIO). Typical AIO measures include the following:

- *Activities.* Hobbies or leisure-time preferences, community involvement, and preferences for social events
- *Interests.* Family orientation, sports interests, and media usage
- *Opinions.* Political preferences and views on various social issues

BENEFITS AND ATTITUDE SEGMENTATION   Not everyone wants the same thing from a product. There isn't only a single toothpaste because some people are interested in taste, some in fresh breath, others in whiteness of their teeth, or decay prevention, or tartar control for gums, or value, and so on. The objective here is to cluster people into groups based on what they want in a product.

SEGMENTATION RISKS   Although segmentation is very important to successful advertising, it isn't without risks. One problem is that once the outer limits of the niche are reached, sales growth will be limited unless the company can expand beyond its niche. By too narrowly defining a market—that is, by excessive segmenting—a marketer can become inefficient in media buying, creating different advertisements, and obtaining alternative distribution channels. A few years ago, Taco Bell was the first fast-food chain to target people with its Value Menu. It was so successful that most other fast-food companies followed with their own value menus. As a result of this competition, the pool of value-conscious consumers was split among numerous companies, diluting the profit.

TARGET MARKET SACRIFICE

Consultant Jack Trout says that staying focused on one target segment in a category enables your product to be different by becoming the preferred product by the segment: Pepsi for the younger generation, Corvette for the generation that wants to be young, Corona beer for the yuppies on their way up, Porsche for the yuppies who have made it. When you chase after another target segment, chances are you'll chase away your original customer. Whatever you do, you should not get greedy but stay true to your product type, your attribute, or your segment.[33]

NICHE MARKETING

Niche marketing can serve at least two purposes. It can gain a product entry into a larger market by attracting a small part of the larger market that is not being served by the competition. It can also cater to latent needs that existing products do not adequately satisfy.

In segmentation, marketers may slice the population very narrowly to find very specific groups. Niches usually are small groups of consumers with narrowly defined needs or unique combinations of needs. But *niche marketing* is not another buzzword for marketing segmentation, says Alvin Achenbaum.[34] It is essentially a flanking strategy, the essence of which is to engage competitors in those product markets where they are weak or, preferably, have little or no presence. The guiding principle of niche marketing is to pit your strength against the competitor's weakness. No-frill motels did not exist for many years, but they were logical means of competing against other motel segments. Red Roof Inn opened its motels with an advertisement claiming "Sleep Cheap" and positioned itself to value consumers not wanting to pay high prices for a place to sleep. Later, they even made fun of hotels placing a chocolate mint on your pillow for an extra $30 or $40. Today, most major hotel chains have moved into that niche with their own no-frills express motels.

niche marketing
A combination of product and target market strategy. It is a flanking strategy that focuses on niches or comparatively narrow windows of opportunity within a broad product market or industry. Its guiding principle is to pit your strength against their weakness.

HEART ATTACK NICHE   Niche marketers may create a specific product using variations of their product to meet a specific niche's needs. For example, Bayer Aspirin created an adult low-strength tablet for aspirin regimen users. As you know, research indicated that second heart attacks were greatly reduced by simply taking an aspirin daily. The only problem was that regular use of aspirin by some people resulted in stomach problems. A regular aspirin tablet consisted of 325 milligrams. The doctor-recommended daily therapy for patients having suffered an initial heart attack was 81 milligrams. Adults started taking children's aspirin, which was 81 milligrams, to prevent stomach problems and yet get the advantage of heart attack protection. As a result of this consumer action, Bayer introduced Bayer Enteric Aspirin, which is 81 milligrams and protects the stomach.

SOCIAL-NETWORKING NICHES   When Facebook and MySpace web sites became broad based, niche sites appealed to advertisers. For example, LinkedIn was aimed at career-oriented professionals; BlackPlanet attracted blacks; MiGente and Asian-Avenue attracted Hispanics and Asians. These niches attracted people of similar interests. Brand marketers seeking new niche opportunities should pay attention to marketing basics: changing shopping trends, demographics, marketing strategy, and delivery on commitments.[35]

Each niche offers challenges for advertisers. When advertisers try to develop niche marketing for Asians, an understanding of cultural and language issues is required, as we have indicated. Does the advertisement promoting Georgia tourism in Exhibit 4.12 appeal to animal lovers? Is this niche advertising?

Companies build growth by finding small niches to serve consumers' needs. For example, Kimberly-Clark launched Huggies Pull-Ups training pants in 1989. In 1994, it

EXHIBIT 4.12

Despite being part of the state's tourism advertising, is this advertisement aimed at animal lovers? Would you consider that a niche?

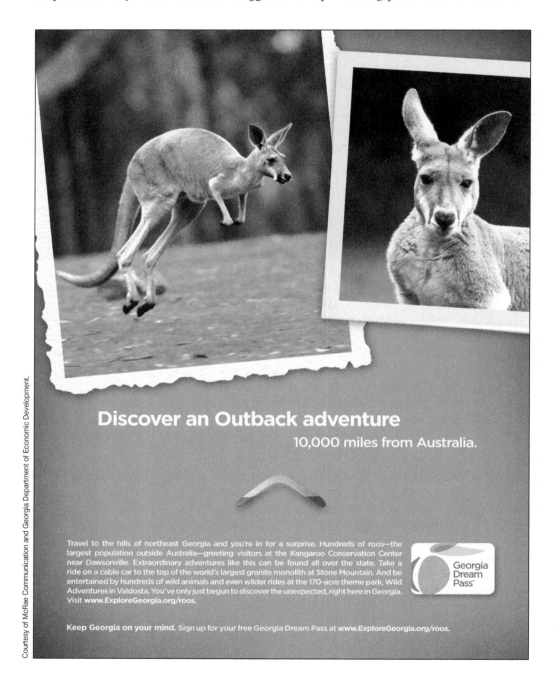

Courtesy of McRae Communication and Georgia Department of Economic Development.

launched Goodnites for older children who wet the bed. In 1997, it introduced Huggies Little Swimmers designed to survive swimming. The niche for Huggies Little Swimmers is a very narrow category segment. Originally, Procter & Gamble said the training pants niche was too small, but it has grown to a $400 million segment within the disposable diaper category.[36]

BOBOS Another example of niche segmentation is *bobos*, which is short for bourgeois bohemian. David Brooks coined this term in 2000 in his book *Bobos in Paradise*. Professor Richard Florida writes about bobos in *The Rise of the Creative Class*. We can try to define bobos as creative people who seem to have combined the countercultural 1960s and the achieving 1980s into one social ethos. This group is about 40 million strong. These people work in a range of fields from science to entertainment, but their jobs are to create new ideas, new technology, and new content. Typically, these people don't work 9-to-5 jobs because they are working on projects with deadlines. Generally, age isn't a defining factor and bobos are highly educated. Doug Cameron, strategist at Amalgamated advertising agency, says that bobos go for the functionally extreme; rather than buying any refrigerator, they'll buy an $8,000 Sub-Zero. Their individual incomes exceed $75,000 annually with many earning more than $150,000. The group favors brands such as JetBlue Airways, Volkswagen, and Apple Computer. The top 10 bobo market areas include San Francisco; Seattle; Boston; Austin; San Diego; Washington, DC; Chapel Hill–Raleigh–Durham, North Carolina; New York; Minneapolis; and Denver.[37] One method marketers use to find bobos involves looking at educational levels and Starbucks per capita, culled from census data.

Positioning

Positioning has to be done with a target in mind. You position a product in the mind of a specific prospect. **Positioning** is another term for fitting the product into the lifestyle of the buyer. It refers to segmenting a market in either or both of two ways: (1) creating a product to meet the needs of a specialized group and/or (2) identifying and advertising a feature of an existing product that meets the needs of a specialized group. The Coke Zero position was a new "Coca-Cola" drink with a great "Coke" taste but Zero Sugar; Coca-Cola Zero sits alongside regular Coke and Diet Coke, offering consumers a new, third way to enjoy the Coke brand.

Estrovite vitamins recognized a potential problem among women on birth-control pills and created a product positioned to fulfill that need. The headline read, "Your birth control pills could be robbing you of essential vitamins and minerals." The copy explained why.

Sometimes products don't quite work out in testing. The original Nyquil was created as a superior daytime cough suppressant. It had a slight flaw. The product made people drowsy. In an attempt to regain product-development costs, the side effect of drowsiness was transformed into a powerful positioning strategy. It became "the nighttime, coughing, sniffling, sneezing, so you can rest" medicine. As a result, Nyquil created a new category resulting in the ownership of the nighttime cold remedy market.

The purpose of positioning is to give a product meaning that distinguishes it from other products and induces people to want to buy it. Positioning is what you do to get into the mind of the consumer. Specifically, you position the product in the mind of the prospect. You want your positioning to be in harmony with the lifestyles and values we have discussed. It is necessary to understand what motivates people to buy in the product category—what explains their behavior. It is also necessary to understand the degree to which the product satisfies the target's needs.[38] One automobile may be positioned as a sports car, another as a luxury sports car, another as the safest family car, and still another as a high-performance vehicle.

6 Discuss the importance of positioning to advertising.

positioning
Segmenting a market by creating a product to meet the needs of a select group or by using a distinctive advertising appeal to meet the needs of a specialized group, without making changes in the physical product.

KLEPPNER VIEWPOINT 4.2

Chris Hooper Senior Vice President, Fitzgerald+CO

"SO, WHY DO YOU WANT TO WORK IN ADVERTISING?"

That's probably the most common question asked of folks interviewing for entry-level jobs at agencies. It's a good question. And the answer really does matter—not so much the answer you give in the interview, but the reason you want to be in this business has to be a good one if you hope to succeed.

Bad answers, and reasons, abound. "I'm really creative" is a clear signal to most agency veterans that you probably are not. "I love to watch television for the commercials" is odd behavior, at best. "It seems like a fun business" is certainly true some of the time but only if you're in it for the right reason.

There is one good reason to work for an agency—*it's the love of ideas*. It's the one trait that is common to those who excel in the business. If you're a person who loves ideas, it's probably a love that is bigger than simply advertising. You'll love ideas in many areas from the arts to pop culture to politics to the sciences.

Any time you come across a fresh perspective or a novel way to think about or look at any subject, you find it interesting and stimulating. It's a part of who you are that holds the key to what you can do with your career.

Star performers in good agencies not only love ideas but also they are skilled at helping generate them, nurture them, sell them, or implement them in the marketplace. Being able to play a role in bringing ideas to life is the common thread among the very best art directors, media planners, writers, account managers, producers, and brand planners. And it's what binds people from the different disciplines into the best teams who do the best work. Ideas are a constant in the ever-changing agency business, and now more than ever change is rampant. Television may become secondary to interactive, and in-store plasma screens may become the new media frontier. No one knows what the future really holds. But ideas always have been and always

Chris Hooper

will be the lifeblood of the business. If you enter the business for the love of ideas and can find your role in birthing and growing them, change will simply make your career more interesting.

So if you're interested in the agency business because of glamorous TV shoots, you may be disappointed. But if your heart races and your spirits lift over new ways of looking at the world around you, you have every reason to expect a great career in an advertising agency, built on your love of ideas.

It is possible for some products to successfully hold different positions at the same time. Arm & Hammer baking soda has been positioned as a deodorizer for refrigerators, an antacid, a freezer deodorizer, and a bath skin cleanser without losing its original market position as a cooking ingredient.

You might try to get the following reactions from consumers to a new line of frozen entrees that are low in calories, sodium, and fat and have larger servings than the competition's. Before seeing your advertising, the consumer thinks:

> I like the convenience and taste of today's frozen foods, but I don't usually get enough of the main course to eat. I would like to try a brand that gives me plenty to eat but is still light and healthy—and, most important, it has to taste great.

After being exposed to your advertising, the consumer thinks:

> I may buy Ru's Frozen Food entrees. They taste great and I get plenty to eat, and they are still low enough in calories that I don't feel I'm overeating. They're better for me because they have less sodium and fat than others. Also, there is enough variety so that I can eat the foods I like without getting bored by the same old thing.

How to Approach a Positioning Problem

As you would expect, not all products lend themselves to the type of positioning discussed here. The advertiser must be careful not to damage current product image by changing appeals and prematurely expanding into new markets. Jack Trout and Al Ries, who have written about positioning for several decades, say that the advertiser who is thinking about positioning should ask the following questions:[39]

- What position, if any, do we already own in the prospect's mind?
- What position do we want to own?
- What companies must be outgunned if we are to establish that position?
- Do we have enough marketing money to occupy and hold that position?
- Do we have the guts to stick with one consistent positioning concept?
- Does our creative approach match our positioning strategy?

According to David Aaker, the most-used positioning strategy is to associate an object with a product attribute or characteristic. Security Bank (see Exhibit 4.13) is associating itself with youth sports. Its advertising is primarily lifestyle. Its positioning is "... we believe that it's important to support the communities who support our company." Developing such associations is effective because when the attribute is meaningful, the association can directly translate into reasons to buy the brand or become a customer. Crest toothpaste became the leader by building a strong association with cavity control, in part created by an endorsement from the American Dental Association. BMW addressed performance with its tagline "The Ultimate Driving Machine." Mercedes with "The Ultimate Engineered Car." Hyundai with "Cars That Make Sense." The positioning problem usually involves finding an attribute that is important to a major segment and that is not already claimed by a competitor.[40] Philip Kotler says that many companies advertise a major, single-benefit position, for example, best quality, best performance, most durable, fastest, least expensive, and so on. In automobiles, Mercedes owns the "most prestigious" position, BMW owns the "best driving performance," Hyundai owns the "least expensive," and Volvo owns the "safest." Volvo also claims to be one of the most durable.[41]

Following up on this, David Martin, founder of the Martin Agency, suggests we think about Volvo for a minute. What is its core identity? Which benefits stand out and should be featured? What is the emotion the target feels from the brand? Would you agree with Volvo being the "safest" car? The car handles well and has speed and styling, with many built-in safety features that include sturdy construction. Reassurance is an appeal to the basic instinct of fear. *I feel better because my daughter drives a Volvo.* Martin also says if you do your homework on the brand, you may be able to fill in the following blanks for developing a brand positioning statement.[42]

To the (*target market*), (*brand name here*) is the brand of (*frame of reference*) with (*benefits and attributes*) that is (*sustainable and emotional point of difference*).

To the *car owner*, *Volvo* is the brand of *automobile* with *all the style, power, and comfort you want* that is *built to be safe*.

Positioning Examples

- Dove soap is the moisturizing beauty bar.
- Allstate insurance is the good hands people.
- Cheer is the detergent for all temperatures.
- Intel is the computer inside.
- Ace hardware is the helpful place.

EXHIBIT 4.13

How is Security Bank uniquely positioning itself?

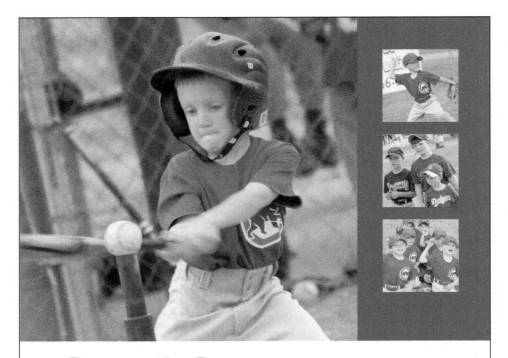

Courtesy of Bright Ideas Group.

Good Sports

At Security Bank, we believe that it's important to support the communities who support our company. We are proud to live, work and play in the neighborhoods we serve.

That's **my** bank.

Warner Robins
119 S. Houston Lake Road 722-7100
302 Russell Parkway 749-1320
849 Warren Drive (Hwy 96) 722-7170
1869 Watson Boulevard 749-1340
Perry
1208 Washington Street 722-7130

Security Bank

www.securitybank.net

Member FDIC

- It's not TV. It's HBO.
- Milk-Bone dog biscuits clean teeth and freshen breath.

Some marketers frequently alter a brand's positioning for the sake of change. This is especially unfortunate for those brands that are firmly entrenched and successful because their reason for being is widely accepted. In the past, a number of positioning statements were successful but were dropped; "Good to the Last Drop," "Pepperidge Farm Remembers," and "Two Mints in One" are examples. These campaigns were revised long after they were discontinued because they truly represented the consumer end benefit and character of the brand.[43]

market profile
A demographic and psychographic description of the people or the households of a product's market. It may also include economic and retailing information about a territory.

Market Profile

Up to this point, we have discussed market segments. Now we examine the overall **market profile** for a product. First, we determine the overall usage of the product type. This is usually defined in terms of dollars, sales, number of units sold, or percentage of

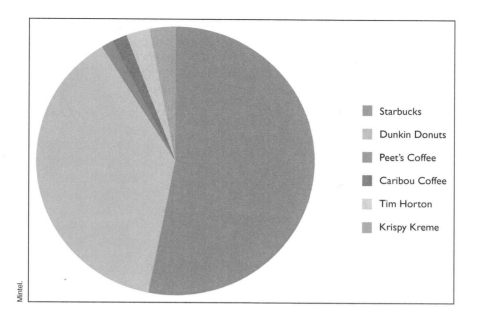

EXHIBIT 4.14

Market Share Analysis: 2008 National Sales of Coffeehouses and Donut Shops ($13.2 billion)

Legend:
- Starbucks
- Dunkin Donuts
- Peet's Coffee
- Caribou Coffee
- Tim Horton
- Krispy Kreme

households that use a product. Then we determine if the category is growing, stagnant, or declining. We compare our share of the market to the competition. Next we ask what the market share trends have been over the past several years. Finally, we want to know the chief product advantage featured by each brand.

Consider the recent surge of Americans buying coffee and coffee drinks such as lattes at coffeehouses and donut shops like Starbucks, Caribou, and Dunkin' Donuts. Since 2005, sales at top coffee and donut shops have increased more than 36 percent.[44] A market share analysis (see Exhibit 4.14) reveals that Starbucks has a commanding share of the nationwide market when it comes to sales in this product category. Conducting a market profile shows that coffeehouse sales has grown but it is dominated by a major brand. Despite recent growth, forecasts predict low, single-digit growth in the market category.

It is important for the advertiser to know not only the characteristics of the product's market but also similar information about media alternatives. In fact, approaching the market as media neutral is a good idea in the world of today's changing media habits. Most major interactive companies, newspapers, magazines, movies, and broadcast media provide demographic and product-user data for numerous product categories. Database marketing gives the marketer an abundance of information on which to base integrated promotional decisions.

PROFILE OF THE BUYER

Second, market profiles contain information about the people within the market with special attention directed toward current users. The size and scale of the market depends on the product's availability: national, regional, or local. Earlier in this chapter, we highlighted ethnic groups (Hispanics, African Americans, and Asians) that were largely ignored by advertisers in the past, but their increasing numbers demand attention in today's marketplace. Xers, boomers, teenagers, college students, and the 50+ markets are all studied by smart advertisers to understand their potential attraction to specific products and services. As indicated, these groups of consumers are not necessarily easy to understand or reach with effective integrated programs. Not all boomers act the same, and all gen Yers don't respond to messages in the same manner. Advertisers typically look at demographics and lifestyles, for starters, to understand any market.

Demography is the study of vital economic and sociological statistics about people. In advertising, demographic reports refer to those facts relevant to a person's use of a product.

7 **Discuss the role of heavy users in target marketing.**

HEAVY USERS   Take any product category and you will find that a small percentage of users is responsible for a disproportionately large share of sales. The principle of heavy usage is sometimes referred to as the 80/20 rule—that is, 80 percent of the units sold are purchased by only 20 percent of the consumers. Of course, the exact figures vary with each product and product category, but the 80/20 rule is a good rule of thumb.

However, a recent market study of 1,300 brands and 54 million shoppers suggests that heavy users are more important than commonly thought.[45] During the yearlong study, only 2 percent of customers accounted for more than 80 percent of sales for most packaged goods. For example, 1 percent of shoppers bought 80 percent of Iams pet food (see Exhibit 4.15). Similarly, 1.2 percent of Budweiser buyers accounted for 80 percent of sales. Based on these findings, it is clear that a brand's success is greatly influenced by heavy users.

Heavy users are identified not only by who they are but also by when they buy and where they are located. The following table shows that the heavy users of brand X are women aged 55 and older. In addition, the most effective selling is done from January through June in the East Central and Pacific regions. Obviously, heavy users are an important part of the market; however, they are also the group most advertisers are trying to target and, therefore, the competition can be fierce and expensive. Some advertisers find that aiming for a less lucrative segment—medium or light users—may offer more reasonable expectations. A marketer cannot simply assume the best prospects are 18- to 49-year-old women, heavy users, or people similar to current customers. Instead, marketers need to carefully study their target audience in great depth. In defining their market, then, they must determine who the heavy users are and identify their similarities, which would define the marketing goal.

USERS OF BRAND X

1. Target Audience: Current Consumers

Women	Pop. (%)	Consumption (%)	Index (100 = national (%) average)
18–24	17.5	5.0	29
25–34	21.9	10.1	46
35–54	30.1	24.0	80
55+	30.5	61.0	200
Total	100.0	100.0	

2. Geography: Current Sales

Area	Pop. (%)	Consumption (%)	Index
Northeast	24	22	92
East Central	15	18	120
West Central	17	16	94
South	27	24	89
Pacific	17	20	118
Total	100	100	

3. Seasonality

Period	Jan–Mar	Apr–Jun	Jul–Sept	Oct–Nov
Consumption (%)	30	36	20	14
Index	120	144	80	—

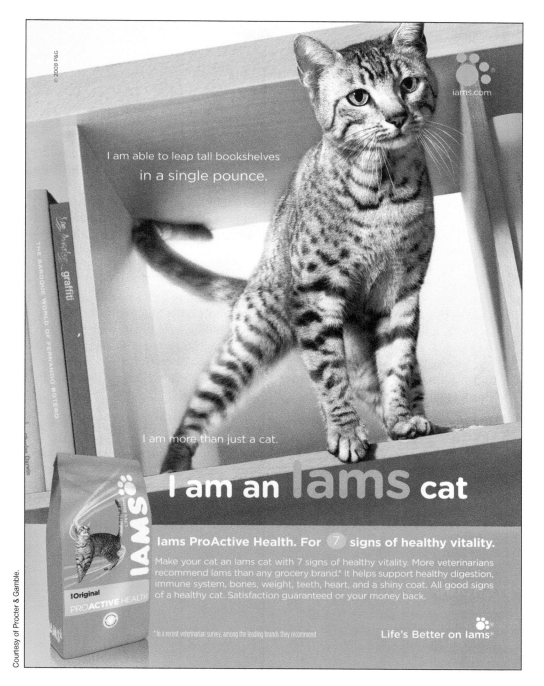

EXHIBIT 4.15

Who is buying all the Iams pet food?

Beyond Demographics: Psychographics

When driving through any suburban area past modest-size yards of middle-class homes, one is struck first by their similarity. But a closer look is more illuminating, for behind the similarities lie differences that reflect the interests, personalities, and family situations of those who live in such homes. One yard has been transformed into a carefully manicured garden. Another includes some shrubs and bushes, but most of the yard serves as a relaxation area, with outdoor barbecue equipment and the like. A third yard is almost entirely a playground, with swings, trapezes, and slides. A swimming pool occupies almost all the space in another yard. A tennis court occupies yet another. Still another has simply been allowed to go to seed and is overgrown and untended by its obviously indoor-oriented owners.

Although the neighborhood consists of homes of similar style, age, and value, the people are not all the same. If you want to advertise to this neighborhood, you would be addressing people with different interests and different tastes. There may be a big difference in the nature and extent of purchases between any two groups of buyers that have the same demographic characteristics. The attempt to explain the significance of such differences has led to an inquiry beyond demographics into psychographics. **Psychographics**—studying personality and lifestyles—sharpens the search for prospects beyond demographic data. It has been said that lifestyle information reveals the soul of the person. Good creative people can devise copy that appeals to a specific segment's lifestyle interest. The media are then selected, and advertising is directed to that special target group or groups. Put very simply, lifestyle information reveals the soul of a person; demographics alone present only a skeleton and not a whole person.

TARGET AUDIENCE: BEYOND DEMOGRAPHICS

Let us look at an example of a travel advertiser's defined target. This profile is based on the advertiser's research that helped define those people most likely to visit the area.

Research indicated that the basic demographic guideline for the consumer target is households with a combined household income of $80,000 or more. Households with less than $80,000 combined income simply do not have the discretionary income necessary for vacation travel. The other qualifiers in defining a consumer **target audience** are lifestyle and geography:

Primary vacation travelers. These are vacation travelers who take a 1-week-plus vacation during the primary season (summer).

Weekend travelers. These people live in states within close proximity to their vacation destinations to which they are attracted during the fall, winter, and spring seasons.

Mature market (50+). These people have both the discretionary income and available time to travel.

Business travelers. These are businesspeople coming to an area on business who can be encouraged to either extend their stay for pleasure travel purposes or to bring their spouse and family along.

PSYCHOGRAPHIC RESEARCH

Today, there is much more refined information available. Agency research information includes syndicated research from outside sources, the client's research, and the agency's own resources. Syndicated research services specialize in different types of information on what types of products people buy and which brands, who buys them and their demographic and psychographic distinctions, a comparison of heavy and light users, how people react to products and to advertisements, and people's styles of buying and what media reach them (see Exhibit 4.16).

Psychographic research also can help determine people's media preferences. A recent study found that personality is a good predictor of whether someone watches television, reads magazines, or reads newspapers.[46] For example, optimists spend more time with newspapers than any other medium. People who are leaders, dynamic, and open are less likely to watch TV. Advertisers who have insight into their target audience's personality can better determine how to reach them.

Lifestyle categories are numerous. Data categories are available through syndicated research to advertisers and their agencies to help them select the target market.

---

8 **Explain why psychographic research is important to target marketing.**

psychographics
A description of a market based on factors such as attitudes, opinions, interests, perceptions, personalities, and lifestyles of consumers comprising that market.

target audience
That group that composes the present and potential prospects for a product or service.

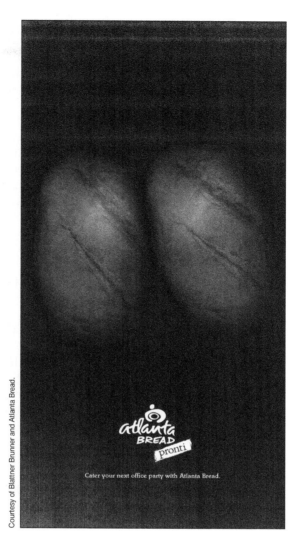

Courtesy of Blattner Brunner and Atlanta Bread.

EXHIBIT 4.16

"Pass the rolls, please." Would people differ in their reactions to this creative ad for Atlanta Bread?

This information is available on a market-by-market basis defining both demographic and lifestyle information. Some of the categories indicating the percentage of household activities include the following:

- Credit card usage for travel and entertainment, bank cards, gas and department store usage

- Good life activities, which include such activities as attending cultural or arts events, foreign travel, gourmet cooking and fine food interests, stock investments, antique interest, and interest in wines

- High-tech activities and usage, which involve home computers, watching cable television, VOD and viewing, and photography interests

- Sports and leisure activities by households, which include activities such as bicycling, boating, golf, bowling, tennis, and jogging

- Outdoor activities, which include the number of households in a specific market involved in camping, fishing, motorcycling, and environmental interests

- Domestic activities such as gardening, Bible and devotional reading, coin collecting, pet care, sewing, crafting, and reading

TEST MARKETING

Although extremely helpful, psychographic research cannot replace market testing as the ultimate guide to successful advertising and marketing. Manufacturers seldom introduce new products without doing some prior testing. This kind of testing helps determine if consumers will really purchase a product or react to specific advertising and promotional activities.

It is difficult to say which cities are best for testing. Ira Weinblatt, a Saatchi & Saatchi senior vice president, says, "You can't say one place represents everything because there are so many different lifestyles." Some cities are historically popular for test marketing. The Midwest has been popular because, geographically, it is the heartland of America. Each test market represents a kind of microcosm of America. Saatchi & Saatchi ranks the top-performing test markets. To make the list the following should apply:[47]

- A city's demographics must fall within 20 percent of the national average.
- The city should be somewhat isolated.
- Local media should be relatively inexpensive.
- Citizens should not be extremely loyal to any particular brand.
- Supermarkets should be impartial enough to give new products good display space on their shelves.

Milwaukee, one of the test market cities that historically makes the list, is popular because the newspapers offer marketers the flexibility to split production runs. This allows advertisers to test up to four advertisements at a time and to experiment with run-of-the-paper color or freestanding inserts. Typically, researchers examine purchases for a number of weeks before advertisements run, during the period of the test, and afterward.

Acxiom® Corporation, a database services company, ranks American's top 150 Metropolitan Statistical Areas (MSAs) based on their overall characteristics as a consumer test market. "If it plays in Peoria, it will play anywhere" is a traditional American marketing adage, but today's advertisers and direct marketers may want to look 800 miles farther east, to Albany, New York.[48]

The top 10 test market cities, which represent American consumers as a whole, are as follows:

1. Albany–Schenectady–Troy, New York
2. Rochester, New York
3. Greensboro–Winston-Salem–High Point, North Carolina
4. Birmingham, Alabama
5. Syracuse, New York
6. Charlotte–Gastonia–Rock Hill, North Carolina–South Carolina
7. Nashville, Tennessee
8. Eugene–Springfield, Oregon
9. Wichita, Kansas
10. Richmond–Petersburg, Virginia

The perils of introducing a product nationally without test marketing include failure. This can be extremely expensive, and most marketers are not willing to take that risk without some type of testing. In the late 1990s, PepsiCo took its lemon-lime Storm into 11 test markets during 2 years without success. PepsiCo also tested a lemon-lime cola called Pepsi Twist in mid-2000. The test was in Minneapolis and San Antonio using television and freestanding inserts (FSI) support. What makes Twist an interesting product is the fact that it was viewed as a possible in-and-out seasonal product and continues to be a niche product today. PepsiCo replaced Storm with caffeine-free Sierra Mist, which is now available nationally.

SUMMARY

The accurate identification of current and prospective users of a product will often mean the difference between success and failure. The targeting of advertising to these prospects in an efficient media plan with appropriate creativity is critical.

This chapter has concentrated on fundamentals: Who are the prospects? What is a market? What about competition? Positioning? Numerous methods of examining segmentation and other important considerations in planning integrated marketing programs have been discussed. Understanding these basic concerns through research is part of the process. Research is the key to successful target marketing. Market research to define prime market segments, product research to meet the needs of these segments, and advertising research to devise the most appropriate messages are mandatory for the success of a firm in a competitive environment. Also, we need to be familiar with the multitude of research services providing data for aiding our planning.

Advertisements are aimed at consumers with a rifle approach rather than with a shotgun approach. It is becoming easier to tailor messages through a variety of special-interest media vehicles.

Advertisers place more importance on lifestyle characteristics than on demographic factors. Advertisers recognize that purchase behavior is the result of a number of complex psychological and sociological factors that cannot be explained by a superficial list of age, sex, income, or occupational characteristics.

Finally, we need to keep abreast of changes in population and better understand such important segments as Hispanic, Asian, and African American populations as well as generational groups. This kind of knowledge will lead to better communications and targeting. We need to know more than simply numbers and location. We need to understand consumer lifestyles, identities, and motivations.

REVIEW

1. What is target marketing?
2. What are some important population trends that marketers should consider?
3. What is market segmentation?
4. What is multicultural marketing?
5. What is niche marketing and how does it affect advertising strategy?
6. What is positioning?
7. What information is needed when advertisers profile a market?
8. What is the 80/20 rule as it relates to target marketing?

PART 1

PART 2

PART 3

PART 4

PART 5

PART 6

MANAGING THE ADVERTISING

Part III emphasizes the business operations of advertising and the sometimes fragile and contentious relationships between agencies and clients.

■ **CHAPTERS 5 AND 6** explore the complexity of the advertising and management functions. Today, advertising is more likely to be integrated into a total marketing communication program resulting in management relationship changes than was the case in the past. The text also discusses the organization of the advertising industry from both the advertiser and agency perspectives.

CHAPTER 5

Courtesy of SkyLab-B.

The Advertising Agency, Media Services, and Other Services

ADVERTISING AGENCIES create most national and international advertising. The agency role and relationships are significantly changing. ▶

CHAPTER LEARNING OBJECTIVES

1 Describe the character of an agency.

2 Discuss the development of the advertising agency.

3 Explain the nature of a full-service agency.

4 Discuss the continuing evolution of the agency.

5 Describe the agency and client relationship in the areas of competing accounts and the agency of record.

6 Explain the global agency.

7 Describe other advertising services.

8 Describe the forms of agency compensation.

The Quest for Great Advertising

"The advertising agency world today covers a broad spectrum of businesses that, in some form or fashion, create perceptions of brands or awareness for products or services. These entities go about doing it in a variety of ways, some developing specialties and proprietary processes. But in the end, however, the goal is to sell (product, service, or idea) something, and, ultimately, it's all about the business of creativity," says Frank Compton, chief creative ambassador, Blattner Brunner.

Agencies are pressured today to lead the way in communication through all the new channels, not only for creating advertising but also being media neutral, to find new ways including nonadvertising tools, to engage consumers. These consumers are less responsive to traditional media and are reshaping marketing. Agencies are being asked by their clients, "How do we connect with these consumers?"

This self-description of Santa Monica's Ignited Minds speaks to many of the issues faced by today's agencies:

Ignited Minds is not an advertising agency, it says. We're not in the business of creating advertising. We are in the business of making our clients part of the cultural dialogue and the collective consciousness. The means by which we accomplish this can take any form— from a $2 T-shirt to a million dollar TV spot. It could be a web site, an event, a reality show, a contest, a stunt, a store, a documentary, or anything else you can dream up. And each is equally important. In that sense, we are more of an idea studio than an ad agency.

Agency Crispin Porter+Bogusky says it a little differently:

Most agency and marketing people think of advertising in terms of magazines, television commercials, and billboards. We think it's anything that makes our clients famous. That is our job. And we make creative content that makes that happen. Then we think of ways to distribute that creative content. It may be through an online film, an event on the street, a book, or something we can't imagine yet. To us, it's all advertising.

Okay, agencies don't publicly agree on what advertising covers today, and every agency tries to differentiate their viewpoint as a better approach. Some of us believe that anything created for a client can come under the umbrella of advertising. It probably isn't worth arguing about. We're talking about delivering marketing communication for clients in many forms. Despite the pressures from clients to do a better job, agencies continue to be the most significant companies in the development of advertising and marketing, not only in the United States but also globally. During a time when every business is being reinvented, agencies are grappling with a number of issues: media proliferation and fragmentation, compensation, client loyalty, short-term pressures on the bottom line, lean structures, use of talent, reorganization, and how to make integrated communication really work the way it was envisioned. And, yes, the new consumer is yet another issue.

The economy and corporate restructuring have pressured agencies to become stronger partners in reaching advertisers' marketing and sales goals. Agencies have undergone their own reengineering, adapting to the environment in which they operate. Not only have many agencies changed their structures but also many have gobbled up specialty firms such as health care, online, mail-order, interactive, and promotion companies and other units involved in integrated communication. Make no mistake about it—it's not business as usual. Roles and relationships are changing and probably will continue to do so for sometime to come.

As we indicated previously, each agency operates a little differently. Each tries to differentiate its approach. Here are a few more examples:

At JWT, we believe advertising needs to stop interrupting what people are interested in and be what people are interested in.

Huey+Partners insists

We believe. Brains will beat brawn every time. Fear is the mortal enemy of innovation. The world is too politically correct. Honesty is essential and arrogance is inexcusable. Ideas are fragile, but when constructed properly, can be indestructible. . . .

AFG says

We are Brand Soul searchers. We find a brand's deeper meaning. Beyond its architecture, beyond its DNA. We find its real relationship with the world within present day cultures. And create greater, longer-lasting connections with consumers.

The Agency

1 Describe the character of an agency.

An advertising agency, as defined by the American Association of Advertising Agencies (4As), is an independent business, composed of creative people and businesspeople, who develop, prepare, and place advertising in advertising media for sellers seeking to find customers for their goods or services. We'd probably like to incorporate Ignited's and Crispin's definitions as mentioned previously in this definition, but won't complicate the issue.

According to the U.S. Census Bureau, there are more than 10,000 advertising agencies in operation in the United States. The *LexisNexis Red Book of Advertising Agencies* (also known as the "Agency Red Book") lists more than 5,000 agency profiles, including full-service agencies, house agencies, media-buying services, sales promotion agencies, cyberagencies, and public relations firms. The *Adweek Agency Directory* lists about 6,000 agencies, public relations firms, and media-buying services, plus 22,000 personnel listings. There are about 2,000 agencies listed in the New York Yellow Pages alone. Unfortunately, there isn't a single printed or online directory listing every agency throughout the United States.

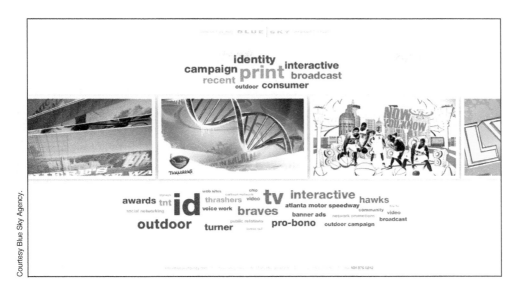

Courtesy Blue Sky Agency.

EXHIBIT 5.1

Blue Sky Agency Web Site

This is the opening page of the Blue Sky Agency's web site, where they attempt to describe what they do and what they are about.

The majority of agencies are small one- to ten-person shops (we talk about size and services later in this chapter). You will see advertisements for many specialized products and services throughout this text—from consumer, industrial products, and services to pro bono causes—in which the agency had to become an expert in marketing in addition to writing the advertisement. Agencies sometimes advertise themselves in all the appropriate media, as their client's might, but they also all try to explain themselves on their web sites. Exhibit 5.1 shows the opening page for Blue Sky Agency's web site.

How Agencies Developed

Before we discuss present-day agencies further, let us take a look at how advertising agencies got started and how they developed into worldwide organizations that play a prominent role in the marketing and advertising process.

> **2** Discuss the development of the advertising agency.

THE EARLY AGE (COLONIAL TIMES TO 1917)

It is not generally known that the first Americans to act as advertising agents were colonial postmasters:

> In many localities advertisements for Colonial papers were left at the post offices. William Bradford, publisher of the first Colonial weekly in New York, made an arrangement with Richard Nichols, postmaster in 1727, whereby the latter accepted advertisements for the *New York Gazette* at regular rates.[1]

SPACE SALESMEN   Volney B. Palmer is the first person known to have worked on a commission basis. In the 1840s, he solicited advertisements for newspapers that had difficulty getting out-of-town advertising. Palmer contacted publishers and offered to get them business for a 50 percent commission, but he often settled for less. There was no such thing as a rate card in those days. And the space asking price of $500 by the papers often was reduced, before the bargain was struck, to $50. (Today, we call that negotiation.) Palmer opened offices in Philadelphia, New York, and Boston. Soon there were more agents, and they offered various deals.

SPACE WHOLESALERS   During the 1850s in Philadelphia, George P. Rowell bought large blocks of space for cash from publishers at very low rates, less agents' commissions. He would sell the space in small "squares"—one column wide—at his own retail rate. Rowell next contracted with 100 newspapers to buy one column of space a month and

KLEPPNER VIEWPOINT 5.1

Anissa Mae Al-Timimi Director of Project Management
and Creative Services (and Reformed Traffic Manager),
Blue Sky Agency

REVAMPING A TRAFFIC DEPARTMENT

Anissa Mae Al-Timimi

The traffic department of an advertising agency ensures that no projects fall through the cracks. Traffic makes certain that deadlines are met, schedules critical meeting points, disseminates salient project information to all parties involved, and even proofreads the work before sending it to production. Traffic is the central hub of all project activity, from start to completion. And although a properly functioning traffic department can make profound, positive contributions to an advertising agency, a contrarily complacent, ineffective trafficking department can destroy a healthy agency infrastructure.

Almost 4 years ago, a well-known advertising agency (at which I no longer work) asked if I would be interested in "revamping their current traffic system." The agency omitted the part about account executives and creatives engaged in cross-cubicle screaming arguments over project deliverables and mandated deadlines. But like any professional looking to grow my resume and skill set, I (am supposed to) relish a challenge, so I probably wouldn't have rejected the opportunity, even if I had known the severity of their particular situation.

Three interviews later, I walked into a 100-person shop and ditched their old traffic system overnight. Within the first week, I found that the source of most internal conflict did not lie in the deadlines (there are always rush jobs) or the clients (they will always have unreasonable demands) or the work ethic of most of the folks there (there will always be slackers and there will always be people who work overtime). The crux of the issue was that the former traffic system did not monitor work allocation among the in-house art directors and copywriters.

Prior to my arrival, a request for creative work was presented to the traffic department and delivered to a writer or art director. The traffic director assigned the work based on the path of least resistance, that is, the creative team least likely to push back on timelines or deliverables was awarded the project. The director would place a stack of job orders on a creative's desk and walk away. So, although some people busted their butts and worked weekends to complete their overwhelming workloads, others spent the majority of their day on iChat or Facebook and walked out the door promptly at 5 P.M.

I began to assess the writers and art directors themselves. Some were fast but not incredibly talented. Others were highly skilled but not so expeditious. Some were slow and rather mediocre. And still others were rock stars, both incredibly talented and lightning-quick, with no ego or drama. So I began to allocate projects among the creatives accordingly, no matter whom the client happened to be.

If the series of teaser billboards required the absolute best creative product and had a protracted timeline, I gave it to my slower but more talented creatives. If a single print ad was a rush job and had highly restrictive parameters, I assigned it to a swift, less-skilled team. And if the campaign demanded a final product worthy of winning potential new business, I awarded the job to my best and brightest. Based on the scope of work and the capabilities of the team itself, I doled out assignments. And an art director might work with one writer on one project and a different writer on the next. Creative teams were no longer set in stone.

In addition, I began to monitor *who* had *which* assignments and the date of the next deliverable for each project, and I posted that information under each creative's name on a large white board for everyone to view. This public posting of everyone's schedule inspired the less-motivated creatives to near panic if they had consistently lighter workloads than their peers. It also served as a tool for both account services and the creatives so they would know when they would receive work for client presentation.

When I initially joined that agency, *traffic* had become a bad word. Work was shuffled from one person to the next and the accounts people had to seek out deliverables from the creative team, who probably hadn't even began the assignment because traffic didn't communicate when it was promised to the client or remind the creative that a critical due date was fast-approaching.

Within one year, all the agency drama had dwindled away. No one worked past 6 P.M.; the client's work was completed within or under budget; and, most importantly, folks stopped screaming at each other in the hallways.

Courtesy of Anissa Mae Al-Timimi.

sold the space in his total list at a fixed rate per line for the whole list: "an inch of space a month in 100 papers for $100." Selling by list became widespread. Each wholesaler's list was his private stock in trade. (This was the original media package deal.)

THE FIRST RATE DIRECTORY   In 1869, Rowell shocked the advertising world by publishing a directory of newspapers' rates and his own estimates of their circulation. Many publishers complained because his estimates of circulation were lower than their claims. Nevertheless, Rowell persisted in offering advertisers an estimate of space costs based on those published rates for whatever markets they wanted. This was the beginning of the media estimate.

THE AGENCY BECOMES A CREATIVE CENTER   In the early 1870s, writer Charles Austin Bates began writing advertisements and selling his services to whoever wanted them, whether advertisers or agents. Among his employees were Earnest Elmo Calkins and Ralph Holden, who in the 1890s founded their own agency, famous for 50 years under the name of Calkins and Holden. These men did more than write advertisements. They brought together planning, copy, and art, showing the way to combine all three into effective advertising. Not only was their agency one of the most successful agencies for half a century but also the influence of their work helped to establish the advertising agency as the creative center for advertising ideas. The business had changed from one of salespeople simply going out and selling advertising space to one of agencies that created the plan, the ideas, the copy, and the artwork; produced the plates; and then placed the advertising in publications from which they received a commission.

To this day, the unique contribution to business for which agencies are most respected is their ability to create effective advertisements.

AGENCY-CLIENT RELATIONSHIP ESTABLISHED   In 1875, Francis Ayer established N. W. Ayer & Son (which was merged into The Kaplan Thaler Group in 2002). Ayer billed advertisers for what he actually paid the publishers (that is, the rate paid the publisher less the commission), adding a fixed charge in lieu of a commission. In exchange, advertisers agreed to place all their advertising through Ayer's agents. This innovation established the relationship of advertisers as clients of agencies rather than as customers who might give their business to various salespeople.

THE CURTIS NO-REBATING RULE   In 1891, the Curtis Publishing Company announced that it would pay commissions to agencies only if they agreed to collect the full price from advertisers, a rule later adopted by the Magazine Publishers of America. This was the forerunner of no-rebating agreements, which were an important part of the agency business for more than 50 years. (Agency commissions, however, ranged from 10 to 25 percent in both magazines and newspapers.)

STANDARD COMMISSIONS FOR RECOGNIZED AGENCIES ESTABLISHED   In 1917, newspaper publishers, through their associations, set 15 percent as the standard agency commission, a percentage that remains in effect for all media (except for with local advertising, in which the media deal directly with the stores and pay no commission) to this day. However, the commission was granted only to agencies that the publishers' associations "recognized." One of the important conditions for recognition was an agency's agreement to charge the client the full rate (no rebating). Other criteria for recognition were that the agency must have business to place, must have shown competence in handling advertising, and must be financially sound. These three conditions are still in effect. Anyone may claim to be an agency, but only agencies that are recognized are allowed to charge commissions.

Today's agencies still receive commissions from the media for space they buy for clients. However, artwork and the cost of production are generally billed by the agency to the advertiser, plus a service charge—usually 17.65 percent of the net, which is equivalent to 15 percent of the gross. By preagreement, a charge is made for other services. This is covered in more detail later.

THE AMERICAN ASSOCIATION OF ADVERTISING AGENCIES   Founded in 1917, the American Association of Advertising Agencies (sometimes known as AAAA or 4As) is the national trade association representing the advertising agency business in the United States. Although virtually all of the large, multinational agencies are members of the AAAA, more than 50 percent of its membership bill less than $20 million annually. It is a management-oriented association that offers its members the broadest possible services, expertise, and information regarding the advertising agency business. In 2009, it simplified its name to 4As, and allowed associate member agencies from outside the United States.

THE NO-REBATE AGE (1918–1956)

The events of this era that left their mark on today's agency world are summarized here.

RADIO   One of the main news events in 1925 was the notorious *Scopes* trial, and the main advent was radio. Radio dramatized evolution-on-trial in Tennessee; it brought the issue of teaching scientific evolution home to Americans, and it brought people closer to their radios. Tuning in to radio soon became a major part of American life, especially during the Great Depression and World War II. Radio established itself as a prime news vehicle. It also gave advertising a vital new medium. A number of agencies handled the entire production of a radio program as well as its commercials. By 1942, agencies were billing more for radio advertising ($188 million) than they were for newspaper advertising ($144 million). The radio boom lasted until television came along.

TELEVISION   Television became popular after 1952, when nationwide network broadcasts began. Between 1950 and 1956, television was the fastest-growing medium. It became the major medium for many agencies. National advertisers spent more on television than they did on any other medium. Television expenditures grew from $171 million in 1950 to $1,225 million in 1956.

ELECTRONIC DATA PROCESSING   The computer entered advertising through the accounting department. By 1956, the computer was changing the media department, the marketing department, and the research department—all having grown in competence with the increasing number of syndicated research services. Agencies prided themselves on their research knowledge and were spending hundreds of thousands of dollars for research every year to service their clients better.

Business was good, and American consumers were attaining a better standard of living than they had ever previously enjoyed. The period from 1950 to 1956 proved to be the beginning of the biggest boom advertising ever had. Total expenditures jumped from $4.5 billion in 1950 to $9.9 billion in 1956. More than 60 percent of this spending was national advertising placed by advertising agencies.

THE AGE OF NEGOTIATION (1956–1990)

CONSENT DECREES   In 1956, a change occurred in the advertiser-agency relationship. The U.S. Department of Justice held that the no-rebating provision between media associations and agencies limited the ability to negotiate between buyer and seller and, therefore, was in restraint of trade and in violation of antitrust laws. Consent decrees to stop no-rebating provisions were entered into by all media associations on behalf of their members.

Although the Justice Department's ruling in no way affected the 15 percent that commission agencies were accustomed to getting from the media, it opened the way to review the total compensation an agency should receive for its services, with the 15 percent commission a basic part of the negotiations. Later we look at the effects this has had on the agency-client relationship.

THE REENGINEERING AGE (1990–2000)

MERGERS   During the 1980s, many corporations merged, thereby creating giant corporations. To be more competitive, agencies followed suit, many merging because of financial pressures to serve larger clients.

INTEGRATED SERVICES   The decade of the 1990s was about agencies reevaluating how they operate. *Integrated services* has been a buzzword relating to efforts to coordinate a client's entire marketing mix, including public relations, promotion, direct marketing, package design, and so on. Some agencies have expanded their communication services to clients by expanding departments or buying or creating subsidiary companies that enable them to offer sales promotion, public relations, direct marketing, logo and packaging design, and even television programming. One of the reasons is financial—clients have been moving dollars from advertising to promotion, and clients want their communications integrated. Agencies are trying to change to supply those needs.

MEDIA AND THE DIGITAL AGE (SINCE 2000)

Agency holding companies created mega-media buying and planning agencies (also called *media services agencies*) that became profit centers to attract global clients in an effort to become more efficient and cost effective. As a result, many clients unbundled their media from their agencies and gave them to a single-media agency to buy and place. Interactive agencies have risen in importance as clients have attempted to deal with the mobile, web, iPhone, blog, BlackBerry, consumer-generated advertising world. They have become mainstream.

The Full-Service Agency

3 Explain the nature of a full-service agency.

full-service agency
An agency that handles planning, creation, production, and placement of advertising for advertising clients. It may also handle sales promotion and other related services as needed by the client.

In the simplest terms, the **full-service agency** offers clients all the services necessary to handle the total advertising function—planning, creation, production, placement, and evaluation. Many have expanded this to include the management of all integrated marketing communications through a variety of disciplines—advertising, promotion, direct marketing, public relations, and so forth—with a tight strategic marketing focus so that the brand image is reinforced every time the consumer is exposed to a communication.

Almost everyone has taken to heart clients' needs to change the way they do business, which, of course, means that agencies have to change their models to survive. This typical attitude was reflected in a recent web site message from Luckie Advertising's agency, which said lightheartedly:

> No offense to the other conservative, 50-year-old Southern ad agencies out there, but that's just not who we are anymore. Luckie & Co. spent decades hammering out solid print and broadcast work for long-term clients, and that part hasn't changed. . . . Now we're all fully integrated, social media-savvy, cross-channel, content-producing, hungry sons-of-you-know-whats. Every time, out [of] the box, we have to prove we're smarter (we're in Birmingham, Alabama, for God's sake). We believe our job is to do whatever it takes, and we mean whatever it takes, to help your brand break through the clutter and take up permanent residence in the minds of your market. It all starts with being willing to rethink everything.

Large agencies need a new concept of their roles and responsibilities to meet the demands of their large clients. A new mission will demand a different organization. Some agencies have undergone a restructuring or reengineering in recent years, more than once. Small agencies love it because they can adjust more quickly than the large agencies, and this becomes a selling point. And some small agencies are getting much larger clients today.

Agencies generally believe that brand building is impossible without creative, persuasive advertising, which is, with few exceptions, the most potent component in the marketing communication mix. Despite looking for a new agency business model, most marketers find familiar department names in most restructured agencies: account management, creative, media, research or account planning, and administration. But many of these agencies have changed how they operationalize the work. It still isn't brain surgery, but it does require a managed process.

There is no universal agency structure model, because agencies have clients with specific and individualized needs. One structure doesn't fit all. That said, let's take a look at the functions full-service agencies perform. When a new account or a new product is assigned to a full-service agency, work on it will generally proceed as described in the following sections.

DIAGNOSING THE MARKETING AND BRAND STRATEGY

The process begins with the collection of all that you know about the product category, the brand, and its competitors. Research or brand planning takes the lead as the ad agency looks at consumer attitudes to develop penetrating insights into the prospects and to define the brand's core: Who are the prime prospects? Where are they? What are their demographics and psychographic characteristics? How does the product fit into their lifestyles? How do they regard this type of product, this particular brand, and competitors? What one benefit do consumers seek from this product and this particular brand? In what distinctive way can the product solve the prime prospects' problems? What media will best reach the target market? What will it take to reach this audience? At Crispin Porter+Bogusky, as John Winsor, vice president and executive director of strategy and product innovation, explains, the agency's emphasis on collaboration means that every department is involved in a brief. "It's fully integrated," he says. "So when there's a brief for a project, our planning department attacks the strategy and research side of things, and the guys from the design group look at that problem as a product problem versus an advertising and marketing problem. . . . I think it's the future."[2]

Some advertising agencies use their research capability to attract clients. According to one agency's self-advertisement, "…It's understandable that when you advertise, you tend to do it from your own perspective . . . we don't promote who you think you want to be. We explore through research who consumers will let you become. Then we apply that knowledge to the most important part of any communication plan, the ad itself."

SETTING OBJECTIVES AND DEVELOPING STRATEGY

Using the consumer insights discovered through the research as described in the previous section, a strategy is formulated that positions the product in relation to the prime prospect customer and emphasizes the attribute that will appeal to the prime prospect. Account management is responsible for leading this phase. Here, you define what is to be accomplished strategically, such as intensifying brand imagery and recapturing prior users, and plan how to do it. Strategic dialogues involve teams of account, creative, media, and research people.

CREATING THE COMMUNICATION

Once the overall strategy is determined, you decide on the creative strategy, write copy, and prepare rough layouts and storyboards. In advertising, the creative impulse is always disciplined—it is an imaginative and persuasive expression of the selling strategy and the character of the brand.

THE MEDIA PLAN   Large clients may separate out the media function, assigning it to a media service agency. In this event, both the creative and media agencies have to collaborate in developing the media plan. Either way, you define media strategy, checking objectives to ensure that they parallel your marketing objectives. Then you select media. All traditional and nontraditional options are explored, the goal being to avoid mere execution and, instead, to add value. Media schedules are prepared with costs. At this stage, you seek to coordinate all elements of the marketing communication mix to ensure maximum exposure. The choice of media leads the process by developing an environment that multiplies the impact of the creative team. This step may be implemented by the agency or by an independent media agency or buying service.

THE TOTAL PLAN   You present roughs of the copy, layouts, and production costs, along with the media schedules and costs—all leading to the total cost.

EVALUATION PLAN   The evaluation step in this process is both the end and the beginning. It is the moment of reckoning for the creative work, based on the objectives set in the beginning, and it provides the evidence needed to refine and advance future efforts. As such, it is an accountable system.

NOTIFYING TRADE OF A FORTHCOMING CAMPAIGN

For many product categories, you inform dealers and retailers of the campaign details early enough so that they can prepare to take advantage of the advertising campaign.

BILLING AND PAYMENTS

When advertisements are run, you bill the client and pay the bills invoiced by the media and production vendors. As an example of the billing procedure, let us say that through your agency an advertiser has ordered an advertisement in *Leisure Gourmet* magazine for one page costing $10,000. When the advertisement appears, the bill your agency gets from the publisher will read something like this:

1 page, August *Leisure Gourmet* magazine	$10,000
Agency commission @ 15% (cash discount omitted for convenience)	$1,500
Balance Due	$8,500

Your agency will then bill the advertiser for $10,000, retain the $1,500 as compensation, and pay the publisher $8,500.

The agency commission applies only to the cost of space or time. In addition, as mentioned earlier, your agency will send the advertiser a bill for production costs for such items as the following:

Finished artwork	Reproduction prints/films
Typography (typesetting)	Recording studios
Photography	Broadcast production
Printing collateral	

The items are billed at actual cost plus a service charge, usually 17.65 percent (which is equivalent to 15 percent of the net).

The Traditional Agency Organization

In this section, we first examine the traditional approach to the full-service agency structure, and then we look at the reengineering of this process.

Advertising agencies come in all sizes and shapes. The largest employ hundreds of people and bill tens of millions of dollars every year. The smallest are one- or two-person operations (usually a creative person and an account manager). As they grow, they generally must add to their organizational structure to handle all the functions of a full-service agency.

All agencies do not structure themselves in exactly the same manner. For discussion purposes, we have chosen a typical traditional organizational structure under the command of major executives: the vice presidents of (1) creative services, (2) account services, (3) marketing services, and (4) management and finance (see Exhibit 5.2). We discuss briefly how each department is organized.

EXHIBIT 5.2

**Organization of a Typical
Full-Service Agency**

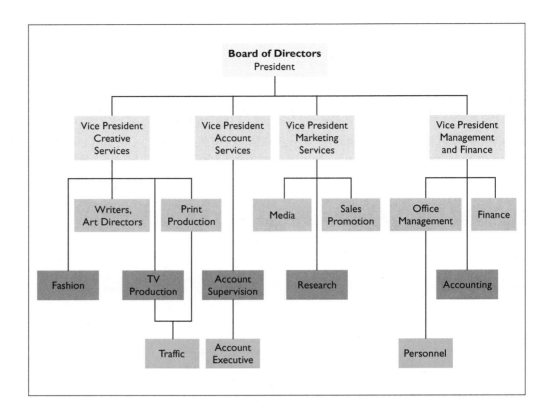

CREATIVE SERVICES

According to Ken Roman, former chair of Ogilvy & Mather Worldwide, "Agencies are generally hired on the basis of their creative abilities—the promise that they can create campaigns that will build business for the client." Every agency that exists is concerned with creating good advertising.[3] Yet only a small number of agencies are known for their creative work. In almost every agency, the agency creative director is almost a mythical, often legendary creature positioned near the top of the agency totem pole. The creative director is responsible for the care and feeding of its most prized possession—the creative product. Today success is measured by the client's results. The creative director is expected to have an opinion on everything interactive from promotion to public relations. In addition to being den mother, psychologist, cheerleader, arbiter of taste, basketball coach, team player, historian, jack-of-all-trades, showperson, social convener, architect, designer, and Renaissance person, today's more evolved species of creative director is also required to be a strategist, businessperson, planner, financier, and new-product developer. Bill Westbrook, on taking over as creative head of Fallon McElligott, stressed the importance of strategy: "If it's not a great strategy, it isn't a great campaign." Lee Chow, chair and chief creative officer of TBWA/Chiat/Day, says, "Managing an integrated campaign is different from doing just ads, as creative directors we've become joined at the hip with account planners."[4]

At first, all writers and artists work under one creative director; but as the business grows, various creative directors take over the writing and art activities of different brands. A traffic department will be established to keep the work flowing on schedule.

The print production director and the television manager also report to the creative director, who is ultimately responsible for the finished product—advertisements and commercials.

ACCOUNT SERVICES

The vice president in charge of account services is responsible for the relationship between the agency and the client and is, indeed, a person of two worlds: the client's

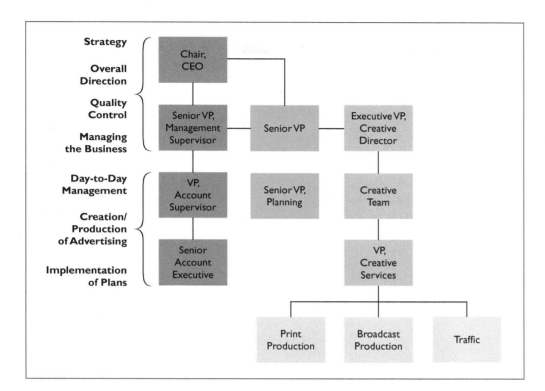

EXHIBIT 5.3

Typical Agency Team Responsibilities

business and advertising (see Exhibit 5.3). This vice president must be knowledgeable about the client's business, profit goals, marketing problems, and advertising objectives. He or she is responsible for helping to formulate the basic advertising strategy recommended by the agency, for seeing that the proposed advertising prepared by the agency is on target, and for presenting the total proposal—media schedules, budget, and rough advertisements or storyboards—to the client for approval. Then comes the task of ensuring that the agency produces the work to the client's satisfaction.

As the business grows and takes on many clients, an account supervisor appoints account executives to serve as the individual contacts with the various accounts. Account executives must be skillful at both communications and follow-up. Their biggest contribution involves anticipating the client's needs. And the account supervisor continually reviews the overall handling of the account, maintaining contacts with a counterpart at the client's office.

MARKETING SERVICES

The vice president in charge of marketing services is responsible for media planning and buying (if the creative agency handles media), for research, and for sales promotion. The media director (at the agency or a media services agency) is responsible for the philosophy and planning of the use of media, for the selection of specific media, and for buying space and time. As the agency grows, a staff of media buyers evolves, grouped according to media (print, television, radio, or interactive), accounts, or territory. The media staff includes an estimating department and an ordering department, as well as a department to handle residual payments due to performers. The media head may use independent media services, especially in the purchase of television and radio time.

The research director (or planning director) helps define marketing and copy goals. Agencies usually use outside research organizations for fieldwork, but in some agencies coordinate research and media planning under one person. The division of work among the executives may vary with the agency.

The promotion director takes care of premiums, coupons, event marketings, and all types of promotions.

KLEPPNER VIEWPOINT 5.2

Tom Y. Robinson   President, Robinson & Associates, Inc.

AFTER ALL, THEY DID BUY INTO THE SYSTEM!

Tom Y. Robinson

Working with franchises can be rewarding and challenging for the right advertising agencies, and a successful, long-term relationship with a franchise is as challenging as a successful marriage.

The reason that a franchisee "buys into a franchise" in the first place is because a system has been established that permits him or her greater opportunity for success and higher profitability than a de novo entrepreneurial venture. After all, someone has taken some of the risk out of the venture and created a plan of action that has proven successful in related markets with similar franchisees.

So where does the challenge come in? Many franchisees have contractual agreements with their franchiser to spend a preset percentage of sales on advertising and are encouraged to join an advertising cooperative for greater buying power and increased efficiency. The larger the advertising pool the greater the need for professional advertising and marketing—thus, the agency relationship begins. As group advertising develops where previously there was none, sales generally increase significantly from the advertising and all goes well.

There are a few challenges. Consultants provided by the franchise monitor the franchisee/agency relationship and advise both on corporate recommendations and suggestions for marketing. After all, the franchiser has been successful and is marketing savvy. However, the franchisee's entrepreneurial spirit makes him or her believe that he or she knows the local market better than anyone—after all the franchiser is paying the agency. Also, marketing is one of the few areas the franchisee feels autonomous.

But when the bloom wears off the new marketing effort or when a new competitor enters the area, the "wow" sales increase dwindles and the question becomes, "Is the agency really doing exactly what I need?"

Many large franchisers have a significant voice in their franchisees' businesses. By contract, the franchisers grade the operations and marketing execution of the franchisees; award additional franchises on their perception of the success of the franchisee; and provide a wealth of resources, including a corporate marketing team that "assists" the agency in serving their client.

Working with franchisees is not for the faint of heart. Entrepreneurs are special or they would not be entrepreneurs. Treat them special. They have "bought in" to the system, but they tug at the reins every time the franchisee tries to restrain them. Remember too, the franchiser brings a lot to the table, as do their representatives whose influence comes from the franchise and is based on their professional experience.

The relationship can be long, profitable, and often challenging. Do your job. Remember your role. Be flexible. Remember who pays you—the franchisee. Yet, remember the company representative can be your greatest ally with the franchisee. Learn to listen. Learn to compromise. It will make your relationships with all your other clients even stronger.

Courtesy of Tom Robinson, Robinson & Associates.

MANAGEMENT AND FINANCE

Like all businesses, an advertising agency needs an administrative head to take charge of financial and accounting control, office management, and personnel (including trainees).

4 Discuss the continuing evolution of the agency.

The Continuing Evolution of the Agency

Decades ago, clients sought agency powerhouse talents such as Leo Burnett, Bill Bernbach, David Ogilvy, Rosser Reeves, Howard Gossage, and Mary Wells. Then agencies that were less driven by famous individuals and more often driven by a collection of bright talent became popular. There has always been some sort of agency evolution taking place. In the 1980s, agencies followed the trend of clients and merged and restructured to be more financially competitive. The 1990s brought major agency reengineering as agencies changed to better serve the integrated and web needs of clients, and some no longer called themselves "advertising agencies." According to Peter Arnell, chair of Arnell Group, "The term ad agency needs a true and sincere facelift." He complicates this idea by defining his agency as a "brand-ideation and experience-marketing company specializing in integrated branding, strategy and communication solutions."[5]

J. Walter Thompson (JWT) identifies itself as a "brand communication company." It is now simply called JWT. The result is an integrated company with a number of companion companies offering marketing expertise beyond traditional advertising, digital, and marketing services.

Traditionally, agencies were trusted partners in the stewardship of the brand. They were key in developing products, and in serving as marketing and media experts and visionaries. Today, most major corporate marketing departments have the ability to manage these functions. Many agencies believe they are treated more like vendors—order takers—than partners as clients seek solutions from any place, once the exclusive territory of agencies.

Under the older agency structure, an account person met separately with creatives to discuss strategy and advertising copy, or with media people to review scheduling, or with the public relations person. Rarely did everyone meet together. In most reengineered operations, the key people on the team meet on a regular basis so that everyone knows what is going on in every aspect of the account. One of the significant changes is that creative staff, account managers, and media planners must work together as a team—a team of people working together to rapidly solve problems. Most agency teams consist of 8 to 12 people, although some use teams of about 20 people. Typically, key people meet every Monday morning to review the week's work—and they meet again when necessary. This means the sales promotion person knows about the public relations work, and the art director knows about media planning, and everyone knows about the interactive film. If necessary, the client participates in the review. In theory, a client could call anyone on the team to get an answer.

A few years ago, Jay Chiat, a pioneer in agency reengineering, said

> We believe the hierarchical structure [of the traditional agency], if not obsolete at present, is on its way. Most of the decisions are about the organization's needs— fiscal and administrative issues. An agency is a service organization whose sole existence depends on satisfying client needs.[6]

Today's reengineered agency structure is somewhat similar to the traditional structure. *It is how business works that is different.* People don't do their thing in isolation; they approach problem solving together. The team concept often helps younger people because it allows them to work side by side with senior people.

As with any new management trend, traditional agencies will copy and modify those structures that have been successful to meet their specific needs. There is little doubt that the agency structure in the future will not be a copy of today's.

SPECIALTY AGENCIES

Most advertising agencies are primarily general consumer agencies. However, some agencies specialize in certain kinds of business; for example, corporate and financial advertising (Doremus), health care (Ignite Health, Cline Davis & Mann, Common-Health, and Lowe Healthcare), entertainment, tourism, or other business specialties such as real estate marketing (Maximum Design & Advertising). There are also the multicultural agencies, for example, those who specialize in the Asian market (Kang & Lee, AdmerAsia, and IW Group), the African American market (Burrell Communications, Fuse, and Uniworld), the Hispanic market (Diesti, Bravo Group), and other groups such as the Arab market. Another big growth area includes digital agencies

(Digitas, Organic Ogilvy Interactive, Avenue A/Razorfish), which might think of themselves as mainstream agencies. There are even very narrow agencies specializing in social networks. Each of these specialty agencies operates pretty much as any other agency, but their expertise is narrower than those more generalized agencies who target all consumers.

BRAND INNOVATION COMPANIES

Most agencies are involved with their client's product development, but in 2006, Zag, a brand-invention company and a division of Bartle Bogle Hegarty advertising agency in London, developed and launched their own brands, bringing them to market with joint venture partners. They develop, find partners, then market.

AGENCY SIZE

Size always appears to be an issue. According to one argument, large agencies offer more services and expensive star talent than smaller agencies. According to a negative counterargument, the larger agencies generally charge more, are slower to react, and aren't very flexible because of their size. Small agencies promote the fact that small- to medium-size clients can be serviced by the agency's senior management and creative department, and they can react faster to client needs. This spirit is evident in successful small- to medium-size agencies that sell the fact that they aren't huge and complicated. Robinson & Associates was established in 1984 in Tupelo as a full-service agency, in which senior management works with clients. "The heart of our business is our clients' success. We work together to form an efficient, effective, creative force to meet their individual marketing challenges. A handshake is our contract." They have no long complicated contracts and seek marketers that can influence the client's bottom line (see Exhibit 5.4).

Brad Majors, CEO of Brand Reps, LLC, who has worked for agencies of all sizes in senior positions, offers these thoughts about agency size:

- Large/public agencies will, more than ever, be confined to large, multinational accounts. It will be nearly impossible for these large agencies to profitably service smaller clients. And because there will continue to be large, multinational clients (with growth primarily from the acquisitions of smaller competitors' brands), there should be room for the larger agencies to profitably handle them.

- Medium-size agencies, which have been the greatest source of creativity historically, will exist but will remain in the state of flux we see today. As they grow, they will have the resources to hire strong talent. Much of this talent, without the encumbrance of public ownership, will continue to produce provocative work. As the work is noticed and clients and prospects become more interested, these medium-size agencies will become attractive to larger agencies as acquisition targets. As the principals of the agency age, an immediate cash-rich buyout may seem more attractive than a deal with the next generation of the agency's management. Thus, the newly acquired agency will not be medium size any longer but will become only a part of the larger whole. Once acquired, it will be important for the medium-size agency to remain in the niche prescribed for it by the parent agency.

- Interestingly, smaller agencies not only will exist but also will thrive, if managed prudently. Historically, small agencies have either fared very well or gone under. To some extent, small-agency success was determined by the strength of the agency's financial management. Managing cash flow and accounts receivables has been a critical issue for most small agencies and it will continue to be so. But given the instability expected in medium-size agencies, there should be great opportunities for smaller agencies that combine a marketing-driven creative product with sound financial management.

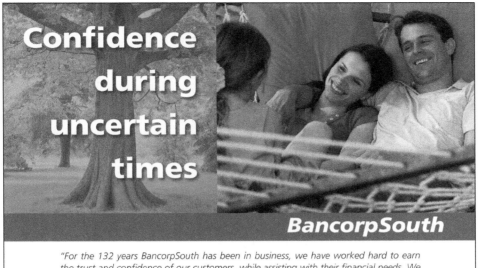

EXHIBIT 5.4

Robinson & Associates helps a regional bank market through tough times.

Competing Accounts

The client-agency relationship is a professional one. It may involve new product strategies, new promotions, sales data, profit or loss information, and new marketing strategies—information that is sensitive and confidential. As a result, most clients will not approve of an agency's handling companies or products in direct competition; Coca-Cola isn't going to allow its agencies to handle Pepsi products. In some cases, agencies will handle accounts for the same type of product or service if they do not compete directly—for example, banks that do not compete in the same market. Many agency-client conflicts result from mergers in which one merger partner handles an account for a product that competes with a product being handled by the other merger partner. When agencies consider merging, the first question is, "Will any of our accounts conflict?" There are a number of large, national agencies with independent offices around the country that hope clients will not view the same type of account in another office as a conflict.

5 **Describe the agency and client relationship in competing accounts and the agency of record.**

Client-Agency Relationship Length

Clients generally retain agencies as long as the relationship seems to be working. However, most contracts allow for a 90-day cancellation by either party if the relationship goes sour. At the same time, agencies can resign an account if they find their philosophies conflict with the client's goals and the account isn't profitable. 4As' data indicates the average tenure of client-agency relationships has declined from 7.2 years to 5 years since 1984. Yet today, some clients have been with their agencies for decades. Luckie Advertising in Birmingham client tenure averages 14 years. Pepsi was with BBDO Worldwide for almost 50 years and GE longer. Robinson & Associates have clients with more than 20-year relationships.

Agency of Record

The agency-of-record relationship offers marketers an advertising team to work solely on their brand, creating a stable team of experts in that particular industry.

In some instances, large advertisers may employ a number of agencies to handle their advertising for various divisions and products. To coordinate the total media buy and the programming of products in a network buy, the advertiser will appoint one agency as the agency of record. This lead agency will make the corporate contracts under which other agencies issue their orders, keep records of all the advertising placed, and communicate management's decisions on the allotment of time and space in a schedule. For this service, the other agencies pay a small part of their commissions (usually 15 percent of 15 percent is negotiated) to the agency of record.

Agency Multiple Offices

Many major agencies have offices in cities throughout the United States. McCann-Erickson is typical, with major offices in New York; Los Angeles; San Francisco; and Birmingham, Michigan. JWT USA's major offices include Atlanta, Dallas, Denver, Detroit, Houston, and Miami, with its headquarters in New York. It also has several JWT specialized communication offices in a number of other cities, as well as other offices throughout the world. BBDO has regional headquarters in Atlanta, Chicago, Detroit, Miami, Minneapolis, San Francisco, and Los Angeles, in addition to its New York worldwide headquarters. For the most part, each office functions as an autonomous agency that serves different clients and is able to draw on the talents and services of the other offices as needed. As a rule, these offices don't normally work on the same project for the same client. Whereas the parent organizations are busily marketing themselves as global networks, each local office fiercely tries to protect its unique culture. It may be said that because each office handles different kinds of accounts, each office has different specialties that could be leveraged on behalf of all clients. But, as a general rule, each office works primarily on its own accounts.

Keep in mind that the large media services agencies also have multiple offices in many of the same cities.

6 Explain the global agency.

Global Agencies and Global Markets

Globalization has become a necessary part of business and advertising. The demands on marketers to survive in a global economy place pressures on large- and medium-size agencies to become global partners. Companies and agencies need to learn cultural and market patterns to understand consumers from a global perspective. Someone trying to sell burgers, fries, and soft drinks outside of the United States may think there is no competition because there are no other burger outlets. The local version of fast food may

ADVANTAGE POINT 5.1

HUEY+PARTNERS AGENCY PROFILE

Advertising agencies, like brands, need a clear and distinguishable point of difference. With that in mind, Ron Huey and partner, Joe Paprocki, opened the doors of their Atlanta agency in 1997. Their distinguishable point of difference? Very simply, creative work that sets their clients' brands apart and grows their business. It was that sole focus on crafting emotionally compelling, arresting creative work that moved *Ad Age's Creativity* to name them one of the country's "Top 20 Agencies to Watch" in 2000. In the fall of 2004, *Communication Arts* featured the agency in an eight-page profile—one of only four agencies worldwide to be featured that year. The accompanying Advantage Point ad says, "H+P Strikes Gold at Addy Awards," copy states, ". . . For the third year in a row, Huey+Partners walked away as one of the night's biggest winners with 3 gold awards and 12 awards overall." They used this to promote themselves to potential clients and tout the fact that the ad generated a 25 percent increase in attendance at The Library of Congress.

What's the secret behind their success? Agency founder, Ron Huey, explains that he took the best of what he'd learned at some of the country's most-acclaimed shops, including The Martin Agency and Team One Advertising, where Ron's creative work for Lexus helped establish the brand as the number one luxury automobile in America. However, unlike larger shops, Huey+Partners is able to deliver that level of big brand and big agency experience to their clients in a much leaner, more responsive agency model.

Today, Huey+Partners continues in their steadfast belief that creativity is the key to setting brands apart. It's an approach that has yielded great results for their clients. In the

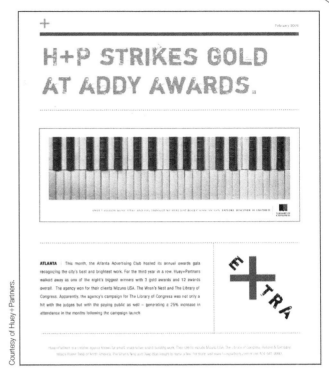

Courtesy of Huey+Partners.

H+P Strikes Gold at ADDY Awards.

agency's long relationship with Mizuno USA, the client has seen their market share in golf irons literally double. Thanks, in part, to a quirky, untraditional advertising campaign that recognizes the passion golfers share for the game. Meanwhile, other clients such as Hitachi Power Tools of North America, WeatherBug, Holland & Company, Do-It-Yourself Network, CBL Properties (shopping centers), *The Daily Report,* The Wrenn's Nest. The Library of Congress. and Russell Athletic have also reaped the benefits of Huey+ Partners' dedication to a singular mission: the work.

---

not include hamburgers at all; the real competition may be a rice shop or a tacqueria. Unless marketers understand competing sources for that same dollar, they won't be successful.[7]

Many small- to medium-size agencies that don't have the resources for international offices have made affiliations with agencies or independent agency networks throughout the world to service clients and give advice. If you're a Jacksonville agency without foreign offices, you might turn to one of the independent network agencies in Hong Kong for help marketing in Hong Kong. If an agency doesn't have the resources (offices or network) to help clients engage in international marketing, then the client is likely to turn to agencies that do have the resources and knowledge, or the client may seek a local agency in the country where it is doing business. Major agencies have been global in nature for many decades to service their clients' international needs.

JWT opened its first office outside the United States in 1891 in London. JWT is one of the world's best-known marketing communications brands. Headquartered in New York, JWT is a true global network with more than 200 offices in more than 90 countries

JWT GLOBAL AGENCY NETWORK

JWT Latin America (Regional Office Buenos Aires)	
Argentina	Honduras
Bolivia	Mexico
Brazil	Nicaragua
Chile	Panama
Columbia	Paraguay
Costa Rica	Peru
Dominican Republic	Puerto Rico
Ecuador	Uruguay
El Salvador	Venezuela
Guatemala	

JWT Asia Pacific (Regional Office, Singapore)	
Australia	Nepal
Bangladesh	New Zealand
China	Pakistan
Hong Kong	Philippines
India	Singapore
Indonesia	Sri Lanka
Japan	Taiwan ROC
Korea	Thailand
Malaysia	Vietnam

JWT EMEA (Regional Office, London)	
Algeria	Kuwait
Austria	Latvia
Bahrain	Lebanon
Belgium	Lithuania
Bosnia and Herzegovina	Macedonia
Bulgaria	Morocco
Croatia	Mozambique
Cyprus	Netherlands
Czech Republic/ Slovakia	Nigeria
Denmark	Poland
Egypt	Portugal
Estonia	Romania
Finland	Russia
France	Saudi Arabia
Germany	Serbia (including Montenegro)
Ghana	Slovenia
Greece	South Africa
Hungary	Spain
Ireland	Sweden
Israel	Switzerland
Italy	Syria
Ivory Coast	Tunisia
Kazakhstan	Turkey
Kenya	UAE
	United Kingdom

employing nearly 10,000 marketing professionals. Above is a list of its non–North American offices.

JWT Worldwide has an operating system to manage a client's global business that includes the following:

1. *Global teams.* JWT can help clients achieve their communications objectives virtually anywhere in the world.

2. *Director-in-charge system.* JWT uses an account director, who is the director-in-charge (DIC) on a global scale. These people operate as heads of an "agency within the agency," working with all offices to service global clients. The DICs work closely with their regional directors, local office CEOs, and account directors in each country to make sure the agency's network comes together seamlessly to execute a multinational advertiser's global communications efforts to build its business.

3. *Regional directors.* JWT regional directors are responsible for a specific group of countries. The CEOs of JWT's offices in that region report to the regional director.

4. *Global directors.* Each worldwide client is represented by a global business director, who sits on the JWT Worldwide executive group. The DIC reports to the global business director, whose role is to ensure that the full resources of the JWT global network are brought to bear in servicing multinational accounts.

WWP, the parent of JWT, sponsors a research study that interviews some 70,000 people around the world. This study asks consumers questions in 50 categories to understand how consumers view 3,500 brands. These insights are available to JWT clients.

In addition to JWT, WWP owns other major agency networks, which operate as independent companies, such as Ogilvy, with offices in 168 cities worldwide, and Y&R with

Courtesy of Adler Chomsky & Warshavsky (Grey Israel) and DeLonghi.

EXHIBIT 5.5

This ad was created by Adler Chomsky & Warshavsky (Grey Israel), part of the Grey Group agency network, owned by holding company WPP.

186 offices. Grey Groups' Israel agency ACW/Grey (WWP owned) created the clever Delonghi iron ad illustrating an ironed T-shirt and an un-ironed one in Exhibit 5.5.

Most global agencies have similar operations to JWT. For instance, DDB has 206 offices in 96 countries. BBDO has 316 offices in 77 countries. Sometimes agency offices are opened in a country because a client wants to do business there. In Chapter 23, we deal extensively with international operations.

GLOBAL AD CENTERS

The cities handling the most local advertising billings are New York and Tokyo—fighting neck and neck for world leadership. Other major advertising centers include London, Paris, Chicago, Los Angeles, Detroit, San Francisco, Minneapolis, Frankfurt, São Paulo, Düsseldorf, Madrid, and Seoul. Almost every country has an advertising agency center. For U.S. agencies, setting up a foreign office can be very complex. Each country is a different market, with its own language, buying habits, ways of living, mores, business methods, marketing traditions, and laws. So instead of trying to organize new agencies with American personnel, most U.S. agencies purchase a majority or minority interest in a successful foreign agency. Key members of the international offices regularly meet for intensive seminars on the philosophy and operation of the agency and share success stories. Remember, good marketing ideas can come from any place. The United States doesn't have a lock on great ideas.

GLOBAL MARKETING

Companies are continually attempting to become more globally integrated. Sometimes these efforts don't work as smoothly as the company wishes. As with U.S. advertising, success often stems from a product or positioning that is relevant to consumer needs, which often vary by culture. Although cultures and habits vary, people's emotions are remarkably similar. People are very much alike in their attitudes regarding love, hate, fear, greed, envy, joy, patriotism, material comforts, and family. Ogilvy & Mather found that strategies can and do move worldwide, but it is usually best to create advertising locally from a worldwide plan and strategy to maintain the desired brand image. If there is a local reason to vary strategy, it should be worked out in advance. For smaller companies, the promise of global branding has been a bumpy road. Global players face a common problem—virtually every global strategy now has a full complement of strong multinational and regional competitors. The promise of managing marketing from a single headquarters hasn't worked the way it was planned.[8] Jerry Judge, former CEO of Lowe Worldwide, says, "There really isn't much global marketing. There are companies that market globally." According to Ken Kaess of DDB Worldwide, "The benefit is consistency of product image or message, which is particularly true of service marketers like American Express, McDonald's, or Exxon Mobil. They have the same core values around the world."[9]

It is only logical that multinational clients want their agencies to know how to develop great advertising campaigns that can run across all the principal markets of the world. As the world gets smaller, there needs to be brand consistency so people don't get confused as they move from market [country] to market.[10] The result of this need is pressure on U.S. agencies to produce, place, and research global advertising.

GLOBAL PRODUCTION EFFICIENCIES

In theory, cost efficiencies in production of global advertising motivate advertisers to seek a single world execution for advertising concepts. A single execution also helps build the same global brand equity. However, "every international brand starts out as a successful local brand ... reproduced many times."[11] Being a global advertiser and having one global campaign sounds easy. But it is not. Despite being a global advertiser for many decades, Coca-Cola didn't launch its first global advertising campaign until 1992 with all the advertisements being similar in each country. Exhibit 5.6 shows an advertisement developed by Coca-Cola Company–Japan.

A brand and its advertising must be presented in relevant and meaningful ways in the context of local environments, or consumers won't care. As many experienced multinational marketers know, for any given brand, advertising that elicits the same response from consumers across borders matters much more than running the same advertising across borders. That may mean using the same brand concept or advertising concept and similar production format across borders, but the executions need to be customized to local markets so the consumers can relate to and empathize with the advertising. Simply translating American advertisements into foreign languages has proved dangerous. Perdue's (Chicken) Spanish translation of "It takes a tough man to make a tender chicken," actually said, "It takes a sexually excited man to make a chick affectionate." Language can be a barrier; for example, "Come alive with the Pepsi Generation" translated in Chinese as "Pepsi brings your ancestors back from the grave."

Agency Networks

Independent agency networks should not be confused with the multinational agency networks owned by huge holding companies. Remember JWT earlier in this chapter, with its hundreds of offices networked around the world. *Agency networks* include many small- and medium-size independent agencies that have working agreements with other independent agencies to help with gathering information from different markets and sharing it. Usually the relationship is centered around a single client's needs where the agency has the capabilities to serve without their agency network partner or partners. As a rule there is only one network member in each market or region. Agency networks provide information and financial skills to enhance agency operations.

THE MEGA-AGENCY HOLDING COMPANIES

Marion Harper set out his holding company vision for the Interpublic Group of companies in 1960, and the mega-agency was born. He understood that once an agency reached a certain size, account conflicts hindered the agency's growth. His solution was to create an organization that would own individual agencies that could handle competing brands. Each of these agencies would operate freely and independently. The definition still holds true today, by and large, but not quite as Harper envisioned. There are

EXHIBIT 5.6

Coca-Cola (Japan) Co. Ltd. tries to create a dialogue with young consumers in an attempt to develop a lasting relationship between the brand and the reader.

still account conflicts. And how is the integration of these agency brands working? Do clients really prefer one-stop shopping? Some of the holding companies are selling integrated services to a number of clients successfully.[12]

Mega-agency holding companies have huge networks (again, JWT, is an example) of their agencies, and they support companies around the world in serving clients. The modern version of the mega-agency holding company started in 1986 when a small London agency, Saatchi & Saatchi PLC, systematically grew over a 2-year period to become a mega-agency network with capitalized billings of more than $13.5 billion. Not a bad growth pattern. As a result, it became the world's largest advertising organization for a brief period and truly changed global advertising. Today, the largest organizations are Dentsu (Tokyo), WWP Group (London), Omnicom Group (New York), and Publicis Groupe (Paris). These and other mega-agency organizations own many advertising agencies and marketing service companies throughout the world. Some of the holdings of the Omnicom Group, founded in 1986, are listed in the accompanying Advantage Point 5.2.

Mega-agencies claim several advantages to their clients other than sheer size. Among the most important are a greater reservoir of talent and an ability to shift portions of accounts from one agency to another without going through the time-consuming, and often confusing, agency review. (Several Omnicom clients switched brand assignments from one of their national agencies to another, keeping the business in the family.) There are also some disadvantages for clients, the most important of which is conflicts with competing accounts.

Size, in itself, doesn't contribute to significant advantages or disadvantages in developing the advertisements themselves. All agencies—large or small—consist of small units or teams that work on an assigned account or group of accounts. The ability of the team and the dedication to creative and professional excellence are dictated by the talent and innovative abilities of individuals, not the size of their company. Obviously, size and structure of an agency will attract or repel clients, depending on what level and quality of services they are seeking. The agency business is simply mirroring business in general by diversifying, economizing, and becoming more efficient and profitable. Yet, some clients of mega-agencies complain they are more interested in selling more of their services than solving clients' problems.

OMNICOM GROUP

Founded in 1986, Omnicom Group is a strategic holding company that manages a portfolio of global market leaders. Our companies operate in the disciplines of advertising, marketing services, specialty communications, interactive/digital media, and media buying services. Omnicom Group includes the following:

OMNICOM'S THREE GLOBAL ADVERTISING BRANDS

BBDO Worldwide
DDB Worldwide
TBWA Worldwide

OMNICOM'S U.S.-BASED NATIONAL ADVERTISING AGENCIES

Arnell, New York
Goodby, Silverstein & Partners, San Francisco
GSD&M Idea City, Austin
Martin|Williams, Minneapolis
Merkley Newman Harty Partners, New York
Zimmerman Advertising, Miami
Element 79 Partners, Chicago

OMNICOM MEDIA GROUP (OMG)

- **OMD** is one of the largest media communications companies in the world. It was initially formed out of the media departments of three of Omnicom's global advertising agencies: BBDO, DDB, and TBWA. OMD is headquartered in New York.
- **PHD** has long been a leading media services company in the United Kingdom and North America. It is widely recognized for its pioneering and innovative work for clients.

MEDIA SPECIALIST SOLUTIONS

- **Full Circle Entertainment** is a branded entertainment company.
- **Icon International** is an asset barter company.
- **Novus Print Media Network** places billions in gross print advertising every year.
- **Outdoor Media Group** is one of the largest outdoor media specialists.
- **Resolution Media** delivers customized business solutions through search marketing strategy and integration.
- **Singer Direct** is a large U.S. provider of insert media buying and management services.

DIVERSIFIED AGENCY SERVICES (DAS)

DAS manages Omnicom's holdings in a variety of marketing disciplines, including customer relationship management, public relations, and specialty communications. DAS includes more than 160 companies, which operate through a combination of networks and regional organizations. They serve international and local clients through more than 700 offices in 71 countries. Examples of DAS companies include the following:

- **Branding/Consultants/Design:** Hall & Partners, Interbrand, Hornall Anderson Design Works
- **Direct Marketing/Relationship Management:** Rapp Collins Worldwide, Direct Partners
- **Entertainment:** AWE
- **Public Relations:** Fleishman-Hillard, Ketchum, and Porter Novelli, as well as specialist agencies including Brodeur, Clark & Weinstock, Gavin Anderson & Company, and Cone
- **Research:** M/A/R/C Research
- **Promotional Marketing:** Tracy-Locke
- **Nonprofit Marketing:** Grizzard Communication Group

Source: Omnicom Group, Inc., 2009.

Some clients have pressured mega-agency holding companies to create new agencies to primarily serve their single, large account. In some instances, the objective was to create a new agency organizational structure that better serves the client. For example:

- WWP, the communication services holding company, created a new 1,000-person agency, Enfatico, to serve Dell computer's $4.5 billion account globally; it replaced 800 agencies Dell previously used globally. The new agency was called the "agency of the future." Enfatico opened offices in Austin, New York, London, and Singapore to serve the global brand. After 16 months of lackluster performance, WPP merged the agency into their global Y&R Advertising.

- Omnicom Group, the advertising and marketing holding company, created Element 79 to serve Quaker's brands in its merger with Pepsico. They primarily created ads for Gatorade, Propel water, and other Quaker brands. They also pitched a few non-Quaker accounts. A number of years later, Quaker moved most of their brands to other Omnicom agencies. The agency continued with new clients despite losing Quaker's brands.

■   Agency DDB agreed to form a smaller dedicated agency, DDB Entertainment, to service the $12 million Blockbuster account. This consisted primarily of a regular account team.

Critics argue that this new client trend of demanding a personal, dedicated agency does work well. For one thing, top creative talent doesn't only want to work on one account all the time.

Other Advertising Services

7 **Describe other advertising services.**

New services are continually springing up in competition with advertising agencies. Each new service is designed to serve clients' needs a little differently. This competition has impacted agency structure and operations. Today, we're seeing a lot of innovation related to gaming, mobile, and interactive services.

TALENT AND PRODUCTION AGENCIES CREATING CREATIVE

A few major clients attempt to meld Hollywood talent sources into their advertising planning. Some production and talent agencies get entertainment stars, writers, and directors involved, and they develop advertising concepts and commercials for advertisers. They may have working agreements with marketers and their advertising agencies to provide creative and talent services. Some industry insiders believe such talent agency relationships can add another dimension to the advertising agency and client resources.

INDEPENDENT CREATIVE SERVICES

Some advertisers seek top creative talent on a freelance, per-job basis. Many creative people do freelance work. Some open their own creative shops or boutiques. In general, they have no media department, no researchers, and no account executives. The purpose of the shop is strictly to develop creative ideas for clients.

Creative services like Martin+Owen (MO) offer advertising and content services to clients and agencies. "MO [was] recently launched by Writer/Designer: Mike Martin and Writer/Director: Glen Owen. With a combined 20 years of experience creating award-winning advertising, Martin+Owen is a source for Branded Content and Original Programming," says their promotion (see Exhibit 5.7), "Quite simply we are storytellers. We

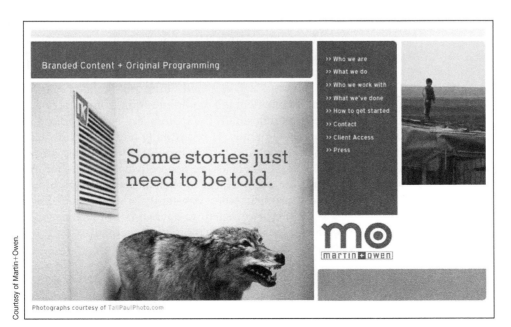

Courtesy of Martin+Owen.

EXHIBIT 5.7

Martin+Owen write and produce original content for television networks, web site marketers, and agencies.

write and produce original content for a variety of clients such as television networks, movie studios, websites, traditional marketers and even advertising agencies who don't have experience fulfilling this niche for their clients."

À LA CARTE AGENCY

There are agencies that offer for a fee only the part of their services that advertisers want. The à la carte arrangement is used mostly for creative services and for media planning and placement. Many agencies have spun off their media departments into independent divisions to seek clients interested only in media handling. Handling only the media portion of an account typically brings commissions that range from 3 to 5 percent.

ROLODEX AGENCY

An agency run by several advertising specialists, usually account and/or creative people, that has no basic staff is called a *Rolodex agency*. It hires specialists—in marketing, media planning, creative strategy, writing, and art direction, for example—who work on a project basis. The concept is similar to hiring freelance creative people to execute advertisements, except that the experts are hired as needed. The Rolodex agency claims to be able to give advertisers expertise that small full-service agencies cannot match.

IN-HOUSE AGENCY

in-house agency
An arrangement whereby the advertiser handles the total agency function by buying individually, on a fee basis, the needed services (for example, creative, media services, and placement) under the direction of an assigned advertising director.

The *in-house agency* is exactly what it sounds like, an agency developed in-house by a company, large or small. When advertisers found that all the services an agency could offer could be purchased on a piecemeal basis, they began setting up their own internal agencies. As a rule, the in-house agency is an administrative center that gathers and directs various outside services for its operation and has a minimum staff. The **in-house agency** can employ a creative service to originate advertising for a fee or markup. It can buy the space or time itself or employ a media-buying service to buy time or space and place the advertisements.

Folks Restaurant Management Group, Inc., had an agency. Then it created an in-house agency, which developed all creative concepts, copy, layout ideas, radio scripts, and so forth. It primarily used art studios and graphic design services to produce the finished art and used broadcast production companies for its broadcasts. It brought all print media in-house and used a media-buying service to place its broadcast buys. It also developed all direct mail, store marketing, public relations, and promotion. Later, it found a need for strategic marketing services and hired an agency to assist in strategic development for one of its restaurant concepts. The agency then created advertisements, produced advertising, and bought media.

Companies are always seeking the best means to deliver their marketing services efficiently and at lower costs. A few years ago, Broyhill Furniture's head of marketing, found their account wasn't big enough to demand major attention from larger national agencies, and the turnover of personnel in small- to medium-size agencies often made it difficult to work with knowledgeable people. He constantly had to educate account people about the furniture business. Broyhill solved its problem by building a strong in-house agency (see Exhibit 5.8). In-house agencies are generally created to save money or give advertisers more control over every aspect of their business. Many industrial companies have highly technical products that constantly undergo technological changes and advances; it may well be more efficient to have in-house technical people prepare advertisements. When the companies place their advertisements, they use their in-house agency or a media-buying service.

IN-HOUSE MEDIA SERVICES

A few large advertisers have taken the media-buying function in-house so they will have more control over the buying operation. It is more likely that advertisers will keep

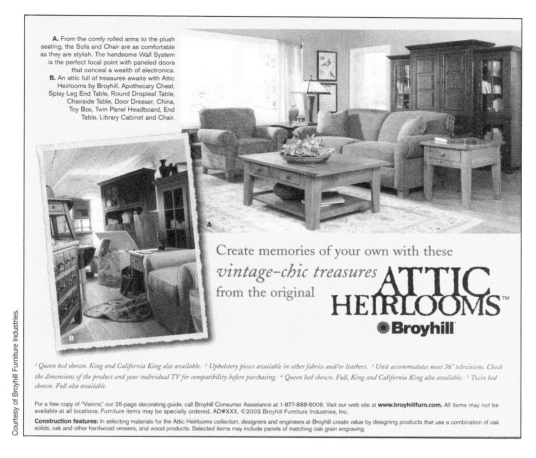

EXHIBIT 5.8

This was created by Broyhill's in-house agency.

a seasoned media consultant on staff to ride herd on their agency or media service's performance.

OUTSIDE MEDIA-BUYING SERVICES

There have been major changes in how advertisers handle their media since the mid-1990s. As all the new media developed, everyone had to be more creative in developing plans to meet the consumer's changing media habits. Some major advertisers chose to un-bundle media or give their media buys to independent media-buying services or new media agencies to try to gain buying efficiencies. At the same time, some agencies reinvented their media operations to remain competitive with the growing number of media-buying services and to develop their media operations as a stand-alone profit center.

MEDIA AS CLIENT CREATIVE RESOURCE

Companies such as Procter & Gamble, Johnson & Johnson, Kimberly-Clark Corp., Clorox Co., Hewlett-Packard, and Verizon have enlisted media companies lately, not only as conduits to reach consumers but also as co-creators of programs to do so. And they sometimes bypass their usual media and creative agencies in the process. Media companies were told by Procter & Gamble chair and CEO A. G. Lafley, "We want your creative ideas, and if we use them, we'll give you a piece of the action."[13]

Media Agencies

Not too long ago, there were large advertising agencies that created ads. They also planned and bought advertising space or time from media. Then many of the agencies added promotion, direct marketing, public relations, web promotion, e-marketing, and so on to the mix or bought firms that did. Because of all the money that was being spent on media, clients started placing more importance on media. As a result, agencies spun off their media departments into separate companies as profit centers. So the term *agency* took on new meaning. Now, if you hear the word *agency*, it could mean a "creative agency" or a "media agency." Each agency acting as a separate company could have different accounts. Each competes for clients for creative and clients for media.

Remember, for example, Omnicom's major national agencies BBDO, DDB, and TBWA. Each of these had its own media planning and buying department for its clients. The holding company, Omnicom, pulled together the media departments into a single, more efficient, separate company called Omnicom Media Group (OMD is one of the media services agencies). Being huge, it has more negotiating clout and resources.

JWT and Ogilvy, two global agencies owned by the same parent, WPP, followed the trend of creating joint media alliances and formed MindShare, a mega-media planning and buying agency to serve advertisers better. Both the Omnicom Media agency and WPP's media agency are free to seek clients that want to consolidate their media regardless of who handles their creative. "It is simply big business." Grey Group's Israel creative agency ACW/Grey (WWP owned) created the ad in Exhibit 5.9. Their media agency, Mediacom, was responsible for planning and buying. The original reasons for creating separate media companies included the following:

- Media agencies are stronger, with better resources to explore new areas within media.
- The fragmentation of target audiences and media vehicles has made media more important than ever before.
- A media company has the potential to be a major profit center. If the agency loses the creative responsibilities from a client, the media agency could continue serving the client because it is separate.
- The reciprocal action allows media agencies to acquire accounts that work with other parent agencies for their creative work.[14] One of the reasons for the consolidation is the fact that mega-advertisers have consolidated their multiple accounts to obtain better rates in their media buying.

In advertising, there is always change. Recently, there has been talk among some agencies of rebundling media back within the agency. Some executives are concerned that media and creative aren't working together efficiently as separate companies. As we've said, everyone is reinventing themselves to better serve client needs.

Other Services

BARTER

Barter is the original business model. Long before monetary systems came into existence, trade was the primary form of commerce. Known as **barter**, it allowed the advertiser or agency to buy media below the rate card price, especially in radio or television. Some agency holding companies own barter companies as part of their integrated offerings to clients. Especially in soft economies, both marketers and media may find they have stockpiles of unsold goods—including products in warehouses, depreciated real estate, unbooked hotel rooms, idle limousines, and so on. All media vehicles face similar problems. When media vehicles can't sell their ad inventories, they entertain cash trade arrangements.

The Atlanta Convention and Visitors Bureau (ACVB) bartered for commercial time from television and broadcast stations to advertise the city's accommodations, restaurants, and attractions. Its agency offered hotel rooms, tickets to local attractions, and meals at Atlanta area restaurants. The ACVB was able to turn a $165,000 budget into $1.5 million in promotions. A typical prize would be a 3-day trip to Atlanta for a family of four with tickets to four attractions; more than 900 packages were offered in exchange for airtime.[15]

barter
Acquisition of broadcast time by an advertiser or an agency in exchange for operating capital or merchandise. No cash is involved.

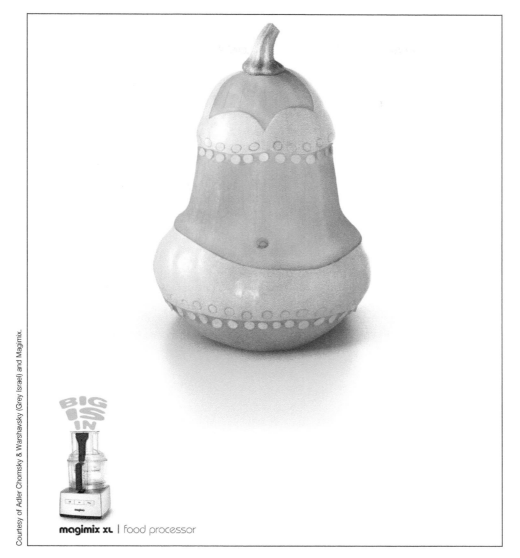

EXHIBIT 5.9

Adler Chomsky & Warshavsky (Grey Israel), created this ad. WPP's MediaCom was responsible for planning and buying.

In 2008, the 4As issued a position paper urging "that every agency, media and marketing executive re-examine [barter] with a fresh viewpoint to determine whether it can be applied effectively to assist present clients. . . . a recommendation from the agency to include corporate trade in the marketing plan as an effective way to create opportunities for the client."[16]

Barter houses often become brokers or wholesalers of broadcast time. They build inventories of time accumulated in various barter deals. These inventories are called *time banks*, and they are made available to advertisers or agencies seeking to stretch their broadcast dollars.

One of the drawbacks of barter is that the weaker stations in a market are more apt to use it the most. Some stations will not accept barter business from advertisers already on the air in the market. Generally, the airtime is poor time, although it is generally a good value at the low rate paid.

RESEARCH/PLANNING SERVICES

The advertiser, the agency, or an independent research firm can conduct any needed original research. (Research techniques are discussed in Chapter 15.) Large agencies may have substantial in-house research departments. In some, the research job title is "account planner." Account planning has a crucial role during strategy development, driving it from the consumer's point of view. Many smaller agencies offer little in-house research staffing, although some agencies have moved to add account planners as a selling tool to clients.

There are numerous techniques available to gather such information, including consumer surveys (using personal, telephone, or online interviews; self-administered questionnaires; or online surveys), focus groups, consumer panels, continuous tracking studies, cable testing of commercials, image studies, electronic questionnaires, opinion surveys, shopping center intercepts, and media-mix tests. Regardless of the technique used in collecting data for a research report, its real value lies in the creative interpretation and use made of its findings. Of course, media agencies do all kinds of media and audience studies.

MANAGING INTEGRATED BRANDS

A brand needs a single architect, someone who will implement and coordinate a cohesive strategy across multiple media and markets. According to David Aaker, the advertising agency is often a strong candidate for this role.[17] It regularly develops brand strategy and gains insights as a result of exposure to different brand contexts. An advertising agency inherently provides a strong link between strategy and executions because both functions are housed under the same roof. Strategy development in an agency is more likely to include issues of implementation. On the downside, many agencies still have a bias toward media advertising, and their experience at managing event sponsorships, social media, gaming, mobile, direct marketing, or interactive advertising may be limited.

The challenge for today's agency is to develop an integrated program that accesses and employs a wide range of communication vehicles. There are several approaches to managing this.

AGENCY CONGLOMERATE   Many agencies have approached the integrated communication program by acquiring companies with complementary capabilities. The usual mix includes promotions, corporate design, interactive, direct marketing, marketing research, package design, public relations, trade shows, and even event marketing. The hope is that advertisers will buy one-stop coordinated communications. The general consensus is that this approach doesn't work well because the units that make up the conglomerate often don't blend well with each other and are rivals for the advertiser's budget, and each unit within the conglomerate isn't necessarily best suited to solve the problem at hand.

IN-HOUSE GENERALIST AGENCY   Another option is to expand the agency's capabilities to include such functions as promotions and public relations. Brand teams spanning communication vehicles can then deal with the coordination issue. This approach works if the agency has the talent to handle the new services or has the clients or revenues to support such a diverse staff.

SERVICE CLUSTER   A service cluster team is a group of people drawn together from all the agency affiliate organizations. Strategically, the cluster's purpose is to service client needs, and the cluster has the flexibility to change with the needs of the client. A key characteristic of the service cluster team is that it focuses on creating ideas rather than advertisements.

COMMUNICATION INTEGRATOR   In the communication integrator approach, the agency draws from sources outside the agency and integrates these services for the brands.

BRAND STRATEGY IN-HOUSE

Many advertisers choose not to rely on the agency at all for managing brand strategy. Their view may be that agencies may be great at creating advertisements, but the brand management team may be better at planning brand strategy. If outside help is needed, their view may be that the agency may not be the best source—particularly if it has limited research resources. Some clients have found it beneficial to employ a team of specialized communication firms, each of which is the best in what it does. The advertiser may develop specialized expertise—including research, media buying, and strategy consulting.

Forms of Agency Compensation

Historically, agency compensation has been fairly standardized since the 1930s. An agency received a commission from the media for advertising placed by the agency. The commission would cover the agency's copywriting and account services charges. This method of compensation has been unsatisfactory during recent years because of the changing nature of business. The straight 15 percent remains in theory, but in most instances there are fixed commissions less than 15 percent (most large advertisers have negotiated a rate closer to 10 percent), sliding scales based on client expenditures, flat-fee arrangements agreed on by clients and agency, performance-based systems, and labor-based fee-plus-profit arrangements. Crispin Porter+Bogusky negotiated stock from clients in return for work. In other words, compensation arrangements now take many forms. Despite this change, there are only two basic forms of advertising agency compensation: commissions and fees.

- *Media commissions.* The traditional 15 percent commission remains a form of agency income, especially for modestly budgeted accounts. Clients and agency may agree to a relationship in which the rate is fixed at less than 15 percent. This generally applies to large-budget accounts—the larger the budget, the lower the rate for the agency. With a sliding-scale commission agreement, the agency receives a fixed commission based on a certain expenditure. After that level of spending, the commission is reduced (for example, there may be a 14 percent commission for the first $20 million spent by the client and a 7 percent commission on the next $15 million). Media payment is complicated by the independent media agency arrangements, but most of these negotiated contracts are similar to the foregoing. The combinations are endless.

- *Production commissions or markups.* As indicated earlier, agencies subcontract production work (all outside purchases such as type, photography, or illustrators) and charge the client the cost plus a commission—17.65 percent is the norm. This Folk's piece (Exhibit 5.10) involved different photos for each plate of food, plus the background. There had to be agreement on the method of charges.

- *Fee arrangements.* At times, the 15 percent commission is not enough for agencies to make a fair profit. For example, it may cost an agency more to serve a small client than a large one. The agency and client may negotiate a fee arrangement. In some cases, it is a commission plus a fee. There are a number of options: A cost-based fee includes the agency's cost for servicing the account plus a markup; a cost-plus fee covers the agency cost and a fixed profit; a fixed fee is an agreed-on payment based on the type of work being done (for example, copywriting at hourly fixed rates, artwork charges based on the salary of the involved personnel); and a sliding fee is based on a number of agreed-on parameters. Again, there are many possibilities based on agency and client needs.

- *Performance fees.* A predetermined performance goal may determine the compensation fee. For example, advertising-recall scores, unit sales, or market share may determine the level of compensation. If the agency meets the goals, compensation may be at the 15 percent level; if it exceeds them, a bonus could give the agency a 20 percent level. If it fails to meet the goals, compensation could be much less than 15 percent. And then the profit could be zero under the Coca-Cola model. Coca-Cola moved toward a "value-based" performance creative agency compensation model in 2009 after testing in five markets. It promised creative agencies nothing more than recouped costs if they didn't perform. However, if they hit their top targets, they could receive profit margins as high as 30 percent. Previously, Coca-Cola paid a flat fee based on hours worked. Procter & Gamble has been testing with about a dozen brands where a "brand agency leader" (BAL) is responsible for budget and payments to other agencies working on the brands. The BAL's compensation is based on a percentage of brand sales, and the other participating agencies' compensation is based on fees.[18]

EXHIBIT 5.10

This complex production piece involved many photos pieced together in PhotoShop. There had to be a mutual understanding between client and agency over production charges.

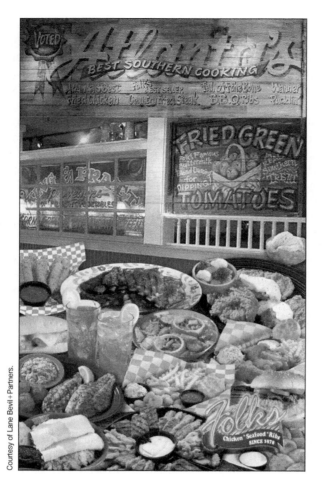

Courtesy of Lane Bevil+ Partners.

EXTENDING CLIENTS CREDIT

What happens to the bills, if clients don't pay? Always a sticky point in any business relationship. "Agencies need to be very careful about extending credit, and they need to go to the media [owners] and make it clear that they are not responsible for unpaid bills if a client goes into bankruptcy," said Rick Kurnit, a law partner at Frankfurt Kurnit Klein & Selz.[19]

In 2009, Omnicom standardized the language in its contracts to emphasize that "production companies will be paid when agencies are paid by marketers. Omnicom agencies will no longer assume liability for a project if the client doesn't pay." Known as sequential liability, the practice was put into place 20 years ago to protect agencies from unpaid media bills of troubled clients but was reemphasized as a result of the recent recession.

An example of a commission plus a fee is described in the following agency contract copy:

> Internal creative services provided by [agency] shall be applied against the monthly agency fee at the prevailing hourly rates [as distinguished from services bought outside our organization]. Such services include preparation of print, radio, television production, storyboards, special comprehensive layouts, booklets, catalogues, direct mail, sales representations, extraordinary research, package design, collateral materials, etc.

COST-BASED VERSUS PERFORMANCE-BASED FEES

The industry has moved in the direction of cost-based fee arrangements, rather than moving in the direction of value- and performance-based arrangements. This shift to cost-based arrangements, which are predominant today, is not optimal for either agencies or advertisers. Cost-based arrangements have resulted in an inappropriate and counterproductive client focus on agency salaries, overheads, and profits. The reasons why cost-based fee arrangements are counterproductive should be obvious, according to Nancy Hill, president of 4As:

■ Premium salaries attract and retain premium talent.

■ Growth lets agencies reinvest in technology and R&D.

■ Agency operating processes and cultural practices represent at least part of the reasons why a marketer selected an agency in the first place.

Campbell Mithun Esty's president says, "There's a broad acceptance among clients that it's in their best interest that their account be profitable for their agency. The smarter client understands that's what gets it the best people on their account. That's what gets it the best service."[20]

An advertising management consultant suggests that the key flaw of compensation based on the price of traditional media is the lack of a consistent relationship between income generated and the cost of providing services required by the clients. This will continue to be a problem as new media techniques are developed. He suggests that agencies align their compensation with their roles as salespeople, not buyers of media, and link agency profit goals to agreed-on performance standards.[21]

SUMMARY

The advertising agency is in a period of transition. It is being reevaluated and reengineered to be more responsive to client needs.

The first Americans to act as advertising agents were colonial postmasters.

A full-service agency works on many aspects of a client's marketing problems: strategy, creative response, media planning, and trade campaigns. Many agencies are organized into four divisions: creative services, account services, marketing services, and management and finance. In general, agencies do not handle competing accounts due to the broad business relationship. Clients generally retain agencies as long as the relationship works, or agencies resign accounts when they don't agree with client's goals. The agency-of-record relationship offers clients an advertising team solely committed to their brand. Some agencies have a domestic network of offices or affiliates to service their large accounts better. The growing importance of global marketing to some clients has led agencies to expand internationally. Mega-agency holding companies have huge networks of their agencies and support companies around the world to serve clients.

Other types of advertising services beside the traditional advertising agency include creative boutiques, à la carte agencies, Rolodex agencies, in-house agencies, and media-buying services. Agencies usually cannot and will not handle two accounts that compete in the same market.

Clients usually pay agencies by commission, fees, or a combination of the two, but there are numerous payment models to meet client needs.

REVIEW

1. What is a full-service agency?

2. Give an example of a global agency network.

3. What is an agency of record?

4. Describe the forms of agency compensation.

CHAPTER 6

SummerGrove is almost sold out. Hurry.

Slow and steady won't win this race. If you want to live in one of metro Atlanta's best-selling communities, now is the time to make your move. Choose from an impressive variety of traditional and custom homes, many with exceptional golf course and lake views. You'll love living in an established community filled with beautiful landscaping, friendly neighbors, and active amenity areas. Fill your days with a leisurely game of tennis, a swim at one of the pools, a trip with the kids to the playgrounds and parks, or a round of golf on the private course. SummerGrove has everything a person—or a turtle—could want. So do whatever it takes to get here today.

Homes from the mid $100s to $900s · Custom homes from the $500s · Information Center open Daily 11-6, Sunday 1-6 · 770-252-9000 · www.summergrove.com

I-85 South to Exit 47 (Newnan). Left on Hwy. 34, one mile. Turn right on Shenandoah Blvd.
Continue 1.4 miles to SummerGrove. Follow signs to Information Center.

Professional stunt turtle. Do not attempt. No animals were harmed in the making of this ad.

Courtesy of McRae Communications.

The Advertiser's Marketing/ Advertising Operation

Consumers control how they consume media and marketing. As marketers digest these changes, their companies restructure their marketing operations to be stronger in nontraditional media and to make their consumer communication efforts speak with one voice—and, in many cases, to communicate with consumers one-on-one. ▶

CHAPTER LEARNING OBJECTIVES

1. Discuss the marketing services system.
2. Explain integrated marketing brand management.
3. Discuss how advertising budgets are set.
4. Discuss agency-client relationships.
5. Identify advertising goals versus marketing goals.

Consumers are continually evolving. What makes this evolution so different today as opposed to in days past is the shift of control to consumers—and the speed of media and the degree of media fragmentation, which are discussed in detail in later chapters. "Research has demonstrated most people overestimate the speed of change in the marketplace and underestimate the significance of the changes taking place. Markets and consumer behavior don't change overnight, but over time these changes can be dramatic," says Ken Bernhardt, author and marketing professor.[1] What are the implications of these consumer and media changes? Simply put, it has become more difficult today to reach consumers with communication messages than it was even a few years ago. Marketers are attempting to integrate these problems and opportunities into their advertising and marketing organizational structure. In simple terms, we must always remember that advertising is a business. It is a marketing tool used by companies to reach consumers. It has a structure and an organization and must be managed, just like any business. Advertising is a financial investment in a brand or a company.

Corporate's Changing Climate

As we discussed in terms of brands in Chapter 3, digital relationships have altered the methods by which consumers absorb information and entertainment—the ways consumers perceive, retain, and engage with brands. Advertisers have increased their capabilities in digital technology, relationship marketing, and media innovation to supplement, or integrate, their traditional brand management apparatus.

During the past several decades, other major pressures have impacted corporations, for example, downsizing; cost cutting; mergers; and partnerships, both domestic and foreign. Companies restructured and reorganized divisions and departments to meet these challenges. Often this restructuring involved changes in marketing and advertising operations.

The advertising and marketing departments control the dollars and decide on the need for an advertising agency or, in some cases, multiple agencies for different products. At times, they may hire an agency to handle only creative or to place the advertisements in the media. As we discussed in the previous chapter, marketers may choose to use freelancers or creative boutiques or to use a media-buying service or combine their media-buying strength for all their products with one agency. They may decide to staff an in-house agency to develop advertisements, as discussed in Chapter 5. It is their ball game. They call the shots. There is no single business model.

Traditionally, all advertising functions are funneled through the advertising department, which is headed by an advertising manager or the director who operates under a marketing director. Broadly speaking, *the advertising manager controls the entire advertising strategy and operation*: budgeting, monitoring the creation and production of the advertising, research, planning the media schedule, and keeping expenditures in line. As the business grows and new product lines are added, assistant advertising managers, usually known as **product advertising managers**, are appointed to handle the advertising for different brands of the company; they work under the supervision of the advertising manager. Let's give a little better perspective of the scope of brands managed by large marketers. Frito-Lay lists 42 brands on its web site, including Lay's Potato Chips, Sun Chips, TrueNorth clusters, Maui Style chips, Quaker snack mix, Grandma's brand cookies, Cracker Jack brand snacks, Flat Earth crisps, and Chester's corn snacks, in addition to the brands you normally associate with the company. In your spare time, take a look at the web sites of Unilever (Knorr, Lipton, Dove, Pond's, etc.), Nestlé (Purina, Perrier, Stouffer's, Gerber, Lean Cuisine, etc.), and Kraft (Oreo, Jell-O, Maxwell House, Planters, Kool-Aid, Oscar Mayer, Breakstone's, Grape-Nuts, South Beach Living, Chips Ahoy!, etc.) and look at the number of brands they market. Following is a sample list of Procter & Gamble products that illustrates the complexity of P&G's marketing requirements.

product advertising manager
In package goods, the person responsible for the profitability of a product (brand) or product line, including advertising decisions. Also called a brand manager.

P&G Categories and Representative Product Brands

Antiperspirants	Old Spice, Secret
Baby care	Charmin, Children's Pepto, Dreft, Luvs, Pampers
Batteries	Duracell
Colognes	Old Spice
Cosmetics	CoverGirl, Max Factor
Dish washing	Cascade, Dawn, Ivory, Joy
Feminine care	Always, Clearblue Easy, Tampax
Hair care	Aussie, Head & Shoulders, Herbal Essences, Infusium 23, Pantene
Hair color	Clairol
Health care	Fibersure, Metamucil, Pepto-Bismol, Prilosec OTC, PUR, Vicks
Household cleaners	Bounty, Febreze Air Fresheners, Mr. Clean, Mr. Clean AutoDry Carwash, Swiffer
Laundry and fabric care	Bounce, Cheer, Downy, Dreft, Era, Febreze Air Fresheners, Gain, Ivory, Tide
Oral care	Braun, Crest, Crest Glide Floss, Crest Whitestrips, Fixodent, Gleem, Glided, Oral-B, Scope

Paper products	Bounty, Charmin, Puffs
Body wash & soap	Camay, Clairol, Herbal Essences, Ivory, Noxzema, Olay, Old Spice, Safeguard, Zest
Pet nutrition	Eukanuba, Iams
Prescription drugs	Actonel, Asacol, Didronel, Enablex, Macrobid, Macrodantin
Prestige fragrances	Anna Sui, Baldessarini, Giorgio Beverly Hills, HUGO, Jean Patou, Lacoste, Mexx, Naomi Campbell, Puma, Replay, Tom Tailor
Shaving	Braun, Gillette Fusion, Gillette M3Power, Gillette SatinCare, Gillette Venus, Gillette Complete Skincare
Snacks	Pringles

Obviously, it takes major efforts by P&G to coordinate all the advertising and marketing of its brands. Because companies vary in size and structure, it only makes sense that advertising and marketing staffs also differ from organization to organization. They may have a large department controlling all marketing activities, or they may have limited personnel in marketing, or they may rely on operation managers or the president to make the marketing decisions. As recently as 2005, the Coca-Cola Company named its first chief marketing officer (CMO) to manage all its brands. Since then, it has appointed a vice president of global marketing to coordinate their ad campaign in every market and across every channel. This global marketing position works with all of Coca-Cola's advertising and marketing agencies and will work on all Coca-Cola brands, overseeing the soft-drink giant's multibillion-dollar marketing budget.

Companies are making operational changes to handle the changing consumer landscape and manage all the new technology options, especially large complex companies.

Marketing Services System

The structural changes in a company are reflected in the way advertising and marketing departments function. Historically, the advertising department structure—the traditional system—worked well for most companies. Exhibit 6.1 illustrates this organizational structure. As companies such as Procter & Gamble grew with a multitude of brands, this structure needed to change.

1 Discuss the marketing services system.

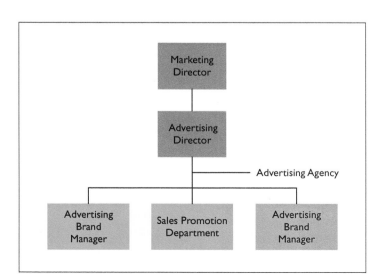

EXHIBIT 6.1

Simple organization chart for advertising department.

An Interview with Peter Bell

Vice President of Marketing, Smokey Bones Bar & Fire Grill

Peter Bell

Peter Bell has had a marketing career spanning more than 2 decades. After graduating from Gettysburg College in Pennsylvania, Peter managed client accounts at advertising agencies such as J. Walter Thompson, Foote Cone & Belding/Leber Katz Partners, and Ketchum. On the agency side, Peter acquired his first taste in marketing for the restaurant industry while working on the accounts for Friendly's Restaurants and Pizza Hut. Later on, he switched to the corporate side, leading marketing efforts for Boston Market and his former client, Friendly's. In early 2008, Peter took the marketing helm at Smokey Bones, joining a key team of executives responsible for the future direction of the restaurant following a change of hands from Darden Restaurants to Sun Capital Partners.

WHAT POTENTIAL DID SUN CAPITAL PARTNERS PERCEIVE FOR SMOKEY BONES AS A BRAND THAT DARDEN RESTAURANTS HAD LAUNCHED AND PROMOTED FOR 8 YEARS?

The leadership of Sun Capital Partners saw Smokey Bones as a great opportunity. Although it is true that sales were declining at Smokey Bones prior to their acquiring of the restaurant, Sun Capital believed there was excellent potential to grow an established brand by expanding its offerings. In particular, they were intrigued by Smokey Bones's bar, which was not actively marketed by Darden. By placing more of a focus on the bar, we believed that alcohol sales could become a major source of revenue for the brand.

WHAT DO YOU IDENTIFY AS THE MAJOR CHALLENGE IN CHANGING THE FOCUS OF AN ESTABLISHED RESTAURANT?

The biggest hurdle from the get-go for Smokey Bones was having to overcome

---

William Procter and James Gamble founded Procter & Gamble in 1837 as a maker of soap and candles. They formalized their business relationship by investing $3,596.47 apiece. Twenty-two years after the partnership was formed, P&G sales reached $1 million. P&G launched Tide in 1946 and won the American Dental Association's approval for Crest as an effective cavity fighter in 1960; Pampers, the first disposable diaper, was created in 1961. The first shampoo-conditioner was P&G's Pert Plus. P&G is known as a marketing innovator. It even invented the soap opera, a perfect consumer-sales vehicle. P&G has long been known as the world's finest marketing training ground. Remember that in Chapter 3 we talked about the pioneering and competitive stages. P&G is a master at marketing and product innovation. Recently, Tide Simple Pleasures, Gain Joyful Expressions, Febreze Noticeables, a variety of gadget Swiffer products, and Crest Pro Health toothpaste have been introduced.

THE BIRTH OF THE MARKETING SERVICES SYSTEM

In 1931, P&G developed a new organizational structure to solve its growing brands and marketing problems. The idea of brand management—setting up marketing teams for each brand and urging them to compete against each other—was the birth of the marketing services system. It became the model for handling brands. This concept has been a restaurant's lifetime of positioning. All of Smokey Bones's advertising, promotions, and team training by Darden positioned the brand as a national barbeque restaurant for family-friendly dining. Unfortunately, although this positioning did not resonate with guests, it became ingrained in their minds. The change of focus of Smokey Bones would challenge any company. You need to really think out your strategy and the meaning of the change.

WITH SUCH A PERCEPTION CHALLENGE, HOW WERE YOU ABLE TO IMPACT SMOKEY BONES?

Expanding our alcohol offerings was a major step, but we also had to give consumers a reason to come to our bar and not to go elsewhere. In repositioning Smokey Bones from Smokey Bones BBQ & Grill to Smokey Bones Bar & Fire Grill, we recreated the brand as a social experience, where guests could come to kick back, watch a game, hang out with friends, and enjoy a beer.

Moving forward, we didn't only have to focus on changing outward appearances but also internally by thoroughly educating the Smokey Bones team on the new branding we were to put in place.

AS A MARKETER, HOW DO YOU DETERMINE WHAT WILL SELL WELL OR SERVE FOR A GOOD PROMOTIONAL IDEA?

First, no matter what we do, we always need to take a step back and evaluate whether what we're offering to guests is credible for the Smokey Bones brand. For instance, we have a grill, but you shouldn't serve lobster in a bar environment.

Second, when we rebranded the restaurant, we hosted a number of focus groups to determine if we should add new products to the menu. All of these products suited the new brand and even had a bit of spice to exemplify the new "fired up" and more energetic mentality of the brand.

Of course, because we're trying to focus more on alcohol sales, we now regularly run a series of drink promotions to further create awareness of Smokey Bones as a "come as you are" place to drink.

WHAT RECOMMENDATIONS DO YOU HAVE TO SHARE WITH YOUNG PROFESSIONALS LOOKING TO FOLLOW THE SAME PATH?

I love the restaurant business because it's more fast paced than in the marketing for most other industries. It is also a highly competitive landscape. If you are considering a future career in restaurant advertising or marketing, you must be quickly adaptable. Each time we put out a new brand or campaign, it seems the landscape changes along with it. It's a stressful field, but with success comes great rewards.

To truly succeed you need to be well versed in the industry. Understand your consumer and your competitors, and be willing to take risks. This is a risky business, so sometimes you need to take large leaps to set your brand apart.

Relationships are also integral. Be a team player and fortify strong relationships with your operators. Without them and your frontline team, you don't have a restaurant.

Courtesy of Peter Bell and Smokey Bones Bar & Fire Grill.

widely adopted or modified, especially in the packaged-goods fields and by a number of service-oriented companies. Under this concept, each brand manager is, in essence, president of his or her own corporation-within-the-corporation. The brand manager is charged with developing, manufacturing, marketing, promoting, integrating, and selling the brand.

The marketing services system has two parts (see Exhibit 6.2). One is the marketing activity, which begins with the product manager assigned to different brands. The other part is a structure of marketing services, which represents all the technical talent involved in implementing a marketing plan, including creative services, promotion services, media services, broadcast services, advertising controls, and marketing research services. All of these services are available to the product manager, as is help from the advertising agency assigned to that manager's brand. The product manager can bring together the agency personnel and his or her counterpart in the marketing services division, giving the company the benefit of the best thinking of both groups—internal and external. Each group has a group product manager who supervises the individual product managers.

The product manager is responsible for planning strategy and objectives, obtaining relevant brand information, managing budget and controls, and getting agency recommendations and is the primary liaison between the marketing department and all other

EXHIBIT 6.2

A large company with a marketing services division may be organized into (a) a marketing department and (b) a marketing services department, where specialists in creative, media, and research advise product managers and consult with counterparts in the agency.

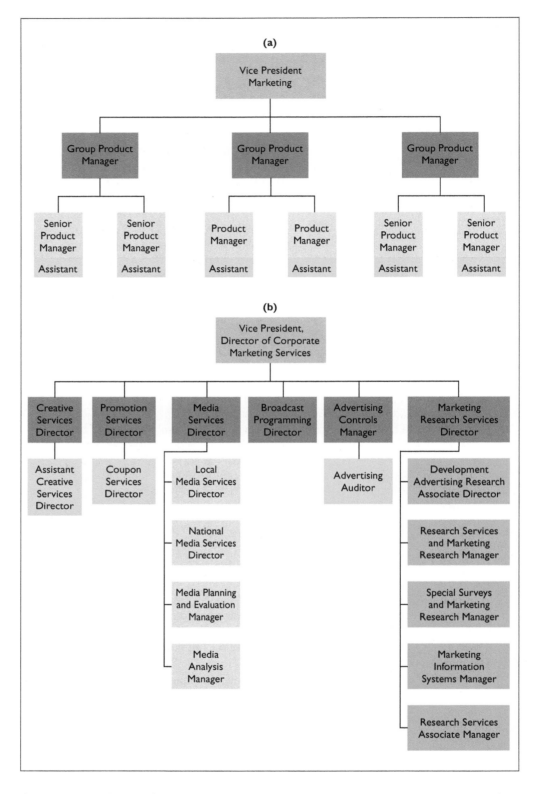

departments. The product manager's plans must be approved by the group product manager, who then submits the plans for approval to the vice president for marketing and finally to the executive vice president.

    The advertising department is a branch of the marketing services division. The vice president for advertising, responsible for the review and evaluation of brand media plans, attends all creative presentations to act as an adviser and consultant on all aspects of advertising. The vice president for advertising reports to the senior vice president, director of marketing (or the CMO).

CHIEF MARKETING OFFICER'S ROLE

Those who observe the chief marketing officer position say it's unrecognizable from a few years ago. Although crunching numbers was always part of the job, new sources of data—from nontraditional media such as interactive TV, mobile media, and social media—along with a need to show ROI have swamped the CMO in data. Some industry observers predict there will be a digital CMO in the future, a liaison between the company, its digital agencies, and the company's information technology (IT) department. Despite being rewarding, the CMO position is a short-tenure position in most companies. In general, the average tenure of a CMO is less than 2 years and this tenure has been shrinking. Macy's department store recently parted with its CMO after only 13 months, which isn't much time to create significant change or make a contribution. There is increasing pressure on results, which are measured quarterly, with sales numbers as the primary measure of success or failure.

Under this system, the advertising does not all come through one huge funnel, with one person in charge of all brands. The advantages to the corporation are that each brand gets the full marketing attention of its own group and that all brands get the full benefit of all the company's special marketing services and the accumulated corporate wisdom. The more important the decision, the higher up the ladder it goes for final approval (see Exhibit 6.3).

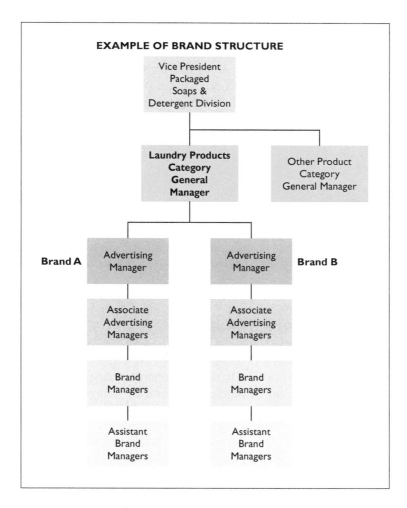

EXAMPLE OF BRAND STRUCTURE

EXHIBIT 6.3

The category manager is responsible for all aspects of the brands in his or her category. Each product's advertising manager reports to the category manager.

category manager
A relatively new corporate position, the category manager is responsible for all aspects of the brands in a specific product category for a company, including research, manufacturing, sales, and advertising. Each product's advertising manager reports to the category manager. Example: Procter & Gamble's Tide and Cheer detergent advertising managers report to a single category manager.

Large companies with many categories of products can have another layer of management called the **category manager**. All disciplines—research, manufacturing, engineering, sales, advertising, and so on—report to the category manager. The category manager follows the product line he or she is in charge of and decides how to coordinate each brand in that line. The category manager decides how to position brands in each category.

Here's a typical example of how companies restructure: Procter & Gamble restructured its global marketers earlier this decade. It reclassified about half of its global marketing directors to associate marketing directors. Brand managers report to either a marketing director or an associate director. Senior brand managers were promoted to associate directors instead of directors. These managers now stay in their position longer under the new system, giving them a broader experience with sales teams, research and development, and other areas. Under this system, a product's general manager is likely to remain in that position for 5 years. Brand managers' tenure in a position would be about 3 years, and assistant brand managers' jobs would last about 2.5 years. The P&G restructuring was an attempt to streamline the marketing organization.[2]

2 Explain integrated marketing brand management.

Integrated Marketing Brand Management

Previously, we discussed integrated marketing, or one-voice marketing, from the agency perspective. There has been debate about whether agencies can effectively implement this concept because of their structure. One of the major problems is that agencies are set up as separate profit centers, which results in competition among their own units for a strong bottom-line showing.

Research involving marketing executives indicates that integration of advertising, promotion, public relations, and all other forms of marketing communications is the most important factor influencing how strategies will be set. Larry Light, the former chair of the international division of Bates Worldwide, says, "The reason integrated marketing is important is consumers integrate your messages whether you like it or not. The messages cannot be kept separate. All marketing is integrated in the mind of consumers. Your only choice is how that message is integrated."[3] He's talking common sense.

An IMC study report found that "organizations are taking charge of the integration process themselves rather than looking to ad agencies or other suppliers to provide the integration."[4] According to Professor William Swain, "While there is some agreement that corporations are better equipped than their agencies to oversee IMC, there is no universal agreement where within the organization IMC leadership does or should reside."[5] Most companies generally agree that traditional advertising agencies are not staffed or organized to efficiently manage integrated thinking. Another reason that agencies fail to properly provide integrated marketing services is that they primarily concern themselves with communicating to the end customer/consumer. They often omit nonadvertising marketing tactics (sales/training materials, incentive programs, etc.).

INTEGRATED FUNCTIONS

Today many marketers believe IMC is to marketing communications what digital convergence is to the world of technology—a revolutionary concept with great promise and hype. In theory, IMC is hard to debate because it is logical. The basic belief holds that integration of all communications emanates from a single strategic platform and will generate a significantly greater return on the communications investment than would be the case with traditional independent media executions. The theoretical benefits are clear.[6]

This system can function within the marketing services system if there is management of the process among all the departments involved—advertising, sales promotion, public relations, and other existing departments. Some organizations call the process *integrated brand communication* (IBC). Radical organizational changes don't seem to work well with regard to implementation. Many organizations have found that inte-grated functions become evolutionary. However, there are marketers who believe that this kind of management isn't practical because the resistance to change by managers is simply too great. Don Schultz, author of *Integrated Marketing Communications*, sug-gests that changing the communications function and structure is sometimes necessary. He suggests the following functions:[7]

1. Start with the customer or prospect and work back toward the brand or organiza-tion. That's the outside-in approach. Most organizations are structured to deliver inside-out communications, which allows the budget cycle to dictate when commu-nications can be delivered.

2. Good communications require knowledge of customers and prospects. Without specific customer information, the marketing organization will continue to send out the wrong message and information to the wrong people at the wrong time at an exorbitant cost.

3. A database is critical to carry out the IMC task.

4. Brand contacts—all the ways the customer comes in contact with the organization—are the proper way to think about communications programs. This goes beyond traditional media. It includes managing the impact and influence of packaging, employees, in-store displays, sales literature, and even the design of the product so that the brand clearly or concisely communicates with the right person, at the right time, in the right way, with the right message or incentive through the right delivery channel.

There are three forms of adaptation to integrated marketing within corporate structures:[8]

- *Marcom (marketing communications) manager.* Adapting a business-to-business or-ganizational structure called marcom management centralizes all the communica-tion activities under one person or office (see Exhibit 6.4). Under this structure, all communication is centralized. Product managers request communication programs for their products through a marcom manager. The manager develops the strategy and then directs the communication programs either internally or externally.

- *Restructured brand management approach.* The restructured brand management approach reduces the layers previously involved in the process. All sales and

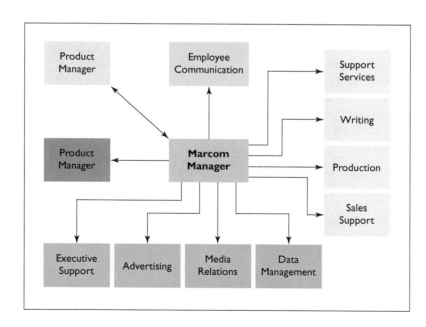

EXHIBIT 6.4

Marcom management centralizes all the communication activities under one person or office.

EXHIBIT 6.5

The communications manager approves or coordinates all communications programs for the entire organization.

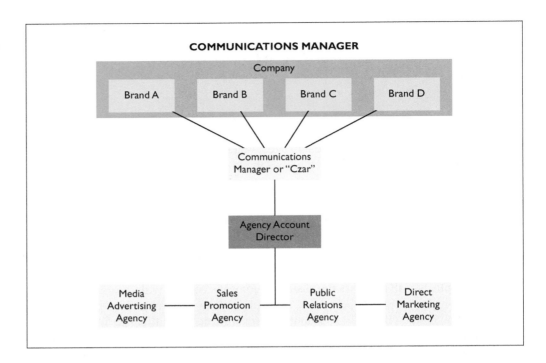

marketing activities for the brand, category, or organization are reduced to three groups, all reporting to the CEO, and all are on the same organizational level. They are marketing services/communications (MSC), marketing operations, and sales. Marketing operations is responsible for developing and delivering the product to MSC, which works with sales to develop and implement all sales and marketing programs (including advertising).

■ *Communications manager.* The communications manager approach names a communications manager who is responsible for approving and coordinating all communications programs for the entire organization. The various brands develop their own communications programs, as they have traditionally done. These plans go to the communications manager, who is responsible for coordinating, consolidating, and integrating the programs, messages, and media for the organization (see Exhibit 6.5).

IMC STRATEGY

Using IMC to coordinate all messages a company communicates helps to create a unified image and support relationship building with customers. The key, however, is to determine exactly what your IMC strategy should achieve.

One of the first steps is to identify the specific target (such as users or influencers) and understand what each needs from your IMC campaign. To sharpen the focus, concentrate on one or two goals to avoid stretching the strategy or budget. Three such possible goals are the following:[9]

■ *Build brand equity.* By using IMC to reinforce your brand's unique value and identity, you increase awareness and encourage stronger preference among customers and prospects. The business-to-business advertisements for Scotchgard, the stain protector, are aimed at the textile and garment industry, for example, stating that the product keeps apparel in good shape by adding stain-shedding qualities.

■ *Provide information.* Business customers need a lot of information. Differentiate products or features if applicable.

■ *Communicate differentiation/positioning.* What does the product stand for and how is it better than the competitors' products? IMC helps convey your most significant points.

DIFFERENT THOUGHTS

Al Ries, of Ries & Ries consultants, takes issue with the term *marcom*, saying, "The name encourages advertising people to go in the wrong direction. Advertising is not communication; advertising is positioning. What the best advertising does, however, is to establish and reinforce a position in the prospect's mind." Of course, this thought is from one of the people who created the concept of positioning decades ago. He makes a point:[10]

"Better ingredients, better pizza," says Papa John's.

As a result of this positioning, Papa John's has become one of the largest pizza chains in America. Ries asks, "Do you know what the better ingredients are? Do you know that Papa John's uses fresh crushed tomatoes, real mozzarella cheese and distilled water in the preparation of its pizzas? Most people don't. Does it matter? Probably not. Better ingredients, better pizza is enough to position Papa John's a step above Pizza Hut and Domino's."

Despite the structural quibbling among advertisers and agencies, in general, the concept of IMC itself has become a fundamental goal of most marketers and advertising agencies.

Advertising agency TBWA also believed that integration is no longer enough to help companies compete. Its goal was not about taking one discipline and extending into other channels but about how to connect big ideas across all channels of communication.

ADVERTISING EXPENDITURE EXPECTATIONS

John Wanamaker, founder of a department store in Philadelphia, is credited with saying decades ago, "I am certain that half the money I spend in advertising is wasted. The trouble is, I do not know which half." Today, companies rely on imperfect metrics, despite there being more metrics, and anecdotes to guide their marketing programs to answer questions such as these: What works best—sustained brand advertising or targeted retail promotion? Is likable media advertising a more effective vehicle than hard-sell direct marketing? Or, is social media as effective as webisodes?

Companies can know how and where to apply marketing expenditures to achieve significant and lasting lifts in a product's or service's profitability. It is referred to as return on investment (*ROI*) *marketing*, which is the application of modern measurement technologies and contemporary organization design to understand, quantify, and optimize marketing spending. ROI marketing is not a fix but a philosophy.[11]

Briggs and Stuart studied some 30 *Fortune* 200 companies (including P&G, Johnson & Johnson, McDonald's, Unilever, Ford, etc.) to determine advertising effectiveness. They believe a "70/20/10 approach" could work in the new world order of marketing to guide marketers to better manage their investment resources. They suggest the following:[12]

- Seventy percent of the budget should go toward marketing strategies and tactics that are proven to work.

- Twenty percent should go for sustaining innovation—to provide a framework to force innovation and learning on how to optimize within a media type.

- Ten percent is speculative, trying new models of advertising and systematically learning from experiments.

Today, organizations view how they allocate and use marketing communication expenditures differently from in the past. Each tries to solve its interpretation of how to become more efficient and not waste half of its money, as Wanamaker (at the beginning of this section) was convinced was happening to his company. They also are trying to measure the impact of some digital communications such as the ever-changing social community media and related ROI issues.

Remember the spiral in Chapter 3? In the competitive stage, you might try to improve the product to appeal to the consumer in a new way. Elmer's School Glue created

EXHIBIT 6.6

Elmer's launched an ad to demonstrate the efficacy of this new formula with a side-by-side demonstration as the primary creative platform. They had to determine how much to spend to accomplish the needed results.

 Discuss how advertising budgets are set.

a new formula that was designed to eclipse the biggest challenge teachers and moms had with their students' craft projects: mess. Elmer's wanted a launch ad (see Exhibit 6.6) that would simply demonstrate the efficacy of this new formula with a side-by-side demonstration as the primary creative platform. Of course, they had to determine how much the communication was going to cost to be effective in reaching the target.

Setting the Budget

What is an investment in an advertisement or campaign supposed to accomplish? Launch a new product? Increase a brand's awareness level? Neutralize the competition's advertising? Educate? Increase sales?

A key question is how much money will it take to accomplish the objective? Even if we have been successful with the product, do we know whether we are spending too much on advertising—or not enough? Each 1 percent increase in advertising produces a roughly 0.1 point change in sales or market share. As a result, an optimal ad budget is about 10 percent of gross profits. That rule doesn't necessarily hold for all marketers (if followed strictly, P&G would have to cut its global ad spending by half or more). More effective advertising, or ads for new products, produce as much as 250 percent greater lift than average and justify correspondingly much larger outlays.[13]

Despite all the technology available to help us determine how much should be spent, the final decision is a judgment call by corporate management. The person who is responsible for the budget decision varies across companies and according to objectives. Historically, the vice president of marketing and the vice president of advertising are the people most responsible for setting the advertising budget. Two-thirds of advertising budgets are submitted for approval in September or October; almost 80 percent are approved during the period of September to November. As you might expect for such an important decision, most presidents or chief operating officers strongly influence the approval process.

Budgeting can be complex and may not be an exact science. Budgets are usually drawn up using one of four approaches: percentage of sales, payout plan, competitive budgeting, and the task method.

PERCENTAGE OF SALES

The percentage of sales method simply means the advertising budget is based on a percentage of the company's sales. For instance, a family restaurant chain might budget 5 percent of its sales for advertising. A company using this method to determine its advertising budget will not spend beyond its means because the advertising budget will increase only when sales increase. If sales decrease, so will the company's advertising; however, if competitive pressures are severe, the company may have to maintain or increase the budget to retain market share, even though there is no prospect of increased profit. This method can actually reverse the assumed cause-and-effect relationship between advertising and sales; that is, because the budgeting is based either on the previous year's sales—usually with some percentage of increase added—or next year's anticipated sales, then it can be said that the sales are causing the advertising rather than advertising causing the sales.

A *BusinessWeek* study of start-up businesses' marketing budgets found that most followed the percentage-of-sales approach, devoting some percentage of their revenue to the marketing function. The amount they spent ranged from 1 percent on the low end to 12 percent or more on the high end. There's no magic to determining "how much," but there are rules of thumb. And you can find published norms for most industries. Determine whether the company will be margin driven or volume driven. Businesses such as supermarkets and hospitals are volume driven and spend a very small percentage of sales on marketing because their sales are high and their margins are low. They may spend between 1 and 2 percent on marketing. By contrast, margin-driven companies such as those in high tech and specialty retail have a smaller revenue base but more flexibility to build a higher percentage into their margins.[14]

PAYOUT PLAN

The payout plan looks at advertising as an investment rather than as an expenditure. It recognizes that it may take several years before the company can recover start-up costs and begin taking profits.

Exhibit 6.7 and Exhibit 6.8 are examples of typical payout plans. Let us go briefly through Exhibit 6.7, a payout plan for a new fast-food operation. In the first year of operation, the company spent the entire gross profits ($15,274,000) on advertising. In addition, the company invested $10,300,000 in store development for a first-year operating loss.

In the second year, the company again invested gross profits ($48,122,000) in advertising and carried over the $10,300,000 debt from the first year. By the third year, sales had increased to the point where advertising as a percentage of gross sales had dropped to 13 percent, or $46,312,000, leaving a profit of $35,625,000. After covering the first-year debt of $10,300,000, the payout was $25,625,000.

If the company had demanded a 10 percent profit in the first year (0.10 $\times$ $84,854,000 = $8,485,400), it would have had to curtail advertising drastically, reduce corporate store investment, or do some combination of the two. In that case, the company would have made a profit the first year but risked future profits and perhaps its own long-term survival.

COMPETITIVE BUDGETING

Another approach to budgeting is to base it on the competitive spending environment. In competitive budgeting, the level of spending relates to the percentage of sales and

EXHIBIT 6.7

New Fast-Food Company Investment Payout Plan— 36-Month Payout

Investment Introduction—36-Month Payout					
	Year 1	Year 2	Year 3	3-Year Total	Year 4
Size of market (MM cases)	8	10	11		12
Share goal:					
Average	12%	25%	30%		30%
Year end	20	30	30		30
Consumer movement (MM Cases)	1.0	2.5	3.3	6.8	3.6
Pipeline (MM Cases)	.3	.2	.1	.6	—
Total shipments (MM Cases)	1.3	2.7	3.4	7.4	3.6
Factory income (@ $9)	$11.7	$24.3	$30.6	$66.6	$32.4
Less costs (@ $5)	6.5	13.5	17.0	37.0	18.0
Available P/A (@ $4)	$5.2	$10.8	$13.6	$29.6	$14.4
Spending (normal $2)	$12.8	$10.0	$6.8	$29.6	$7.2
Advertising	10.5	8.5	5.4	24.4	5.7
Promotion	2.3	1.5	1.4	5.2	1.5
Profit (Loss):					
Annual	($7.6)	$0.8	$6.8	—	$7.2
Cumulative	($7.6)	($6.8)	—	—	$7.2

other factors: whether the advertiser is on the offensive or defensive, media strategies chosen (for example, desire to dominate a medium), or answers to questions such as, Is it a new brand or an existing one? The problem here is that competition dictates the spending allocation (and competing companies may have different marketing objectives). For example, a carmaker based its budget solely upon what its competition was spending. As it turned out, the competitor was doing the exact same thing. Both were using bad logic as to any ROI.

THE TASK METHOD

The task method of budgeting is possibly the most difficult to implement, but it may also be the most logical budgeting method. The method calls for marketing and advertising managers to determine what task or objective the advertising will fulfill over the budgetary period and then calls for a determination of how much money will be needed to complete the task. Under this method, the company sets a specific sales target for a given time to attain a given goal. Then it decides to spend whatever money is necessary to meet that quota. The task method may be called the "let's spend all we can afford" approach, especially when launching a new product. Many big businesses today started that way. Many businesses that are not here today did too.

EXHIBIT 6.8

Example of Package-Goods Product-Payout Plan

		Systemwide Payout (Fiscal Years 1, 2, 3)				
		Year 1		Year 2		Year 3
Sales		$84,854,000		$218,737,000		$356,248,000
Food cost	34%	28,850,000	34%	74,371,000	34%	121,124,000
Paper cost	5	4,245,000	5	10,937,000	5	17,812,000
Labor	22	18,668,000	20	43,747,000	20	71,250,000
Overhead	21	17,819,000	19	41,560,000	18	64,125,000
Total op. exp.	82	69,580,000	78	170,615,000	77	274,511,000
Gross profit	18	15,274,000	22	48,122,000	25	81,937,000
Advertising/Promo		$15,274,000		$48,122,000	13	$46,312,000
Store profit		0		0	10	35,625,000
Corp. invest.		10,300,000		0		0
Corp. profit		(10,300,000)		0		35,625,000
Cumulative		(10,300,000)		(10,300,000)		25,625,000

The approach can be complex. It involves several important considerations: brand loyalty factors, geographic factors, and product penetration. Advertisers who use this method need accurate and reliable research, experience, and models for setting goals and measuring results.

The task method is used most widely in a highly competitive environment. Budgets are under constant scrutiny in relation to sales and usually are reviewed formally every quarter. Moreover, they are subject to cancellation at any time (except for noncancelable commitments) because sales have not met a minimum quota, money is being shifted to a more promising brand, or management wants to hold back money to make a better showing on its next quarterly statement.

No one approach to budgeting is always best for all companies.

The Marketing Environment Shifts

The retail universe has consolidated, and the media universe has exploded. It is harder for an advertiser to reach consumers with traditional advertising. In 1995, it took three television spots to reach 80 percent of the women in the United States. Five years later, it took 97 spots to reach the same group. Some admit the mass market is basically dead because consumers are more in control of media, especially digital media.

Companies, often through their advertising agencies, are creating content—movies, television shows, Internet sites, online games, social and mobile entertainment, and so on—that they hope will be entertaining enough to endear viewers to the brands behind them. According to Martin+Owen, content agency, the challenge for today's marketers is how to engage consumers who have become numb to traditional messaging. This is where branded content comes in. Its purpose, first and foremost, is to entertain, and by holding a consumer's attention long enough, we can weave a brand into the content and market that product or service to the consumer without it feeling so invasive.[15]

"We're continuing our traditional advertising—TV, radio, print, online—but we're adding content to that," said Vic Walia, the senior brand manager for Snickers, a Mars brand that created a minitelevision show that it posted online. "What we're trying to do is find new ways to continue to be relevant to teens and to young adults."[16] These views indicate that marketers are looking for new marketing and communication formulas. Today, the winning brand marketers are those learning to reconfigure their efforts in several ways:[17]

- Shift spending and management attention to digital and social media, and use those media effectively to influence consumer purchase behavior.
- Develop formats using any available tools to promote interactions with audiences, especially the most likely consumers.
- Create new research approaches and metrics that measure outcomes, not inputs.
- Combine "above-the-line" advertising (television, radio, and print) and "below-the-line" marketing (promotions, sponsorships, events, public relations) in new two-way, integrated campaigns.
- Create branded entertainment.
- "In-source" new skills and capabilities (new media, technology).

Managing Brands

RETAILER CONTROL

There is no doubt about who controls shelf space and entry into supermarkets, discounters, and mass merchandise stores today. And it isn't the manufacturer. It is the mass channel, not the media, that is demanding most of the marketing dollars. It is estimated that almost 60 percent of the manufacturers' marketing budgets goes to the retailer in the form of trade spending (advertisements for shoppers, displays, etc.). The adoption of product-tracking technology—radio frequency identification (RFID)—has the potential to allow manufacturers to track individual packages, not only stock units, and some speculate that the technology might eventually give manufacturers more say about how and where their products are marketed. For example, Mini Cooper mailed owners RFID chips with customized messages that flash up on minibillboards as they pass by.[18] RFID may, unlike the universal product code (UPC), shift power back to the manufacturer in some meaningful manner. We will know if this is happening based on the mix among advertising, consumer promotion, and trade incentives (now 25, 25, and 50 percent, respectively). Twenty years ago, the mix was 50, 25, and 25 percent. If the share of advertising increases, power will have shifted to manufacturers.[19] Today manufacturers are somewhat at the mercy of big retailers. Category managers must understand the needs of these retailers as well as they understand the needs of consumers. They must be sure that their promotions are integrated into the retailer's total marketing program.

SLOTTING ALLOWANCES

Every square foot in a supermarket costs money and needs to pay for itself by holding products and brands that move off the shelves quickly. There is only so much shelf space for the category manager to obtain from grocers. Slotting allowances began because manufacturers were creating more new products than the retailers' shelf space could accommodate, so to add a new product an old product had to be removed. Grocers control the space and many charge slotting allowances for shelf space. This admission fee, which comes primarily from the marketer's trade promotion funds, ensures space for a period of about 3 to 6 months. Supermarkets use the slotting allowance to pay for slow-moving products and for administrative overhead for placing a new product into their system, including warehouse space, computer input, communications to individual stores about the product's availability, and the redesign of shelf space. Think about the frozen-food section in your favorite supermarket. It has a finite amount of space and almost always demands slotting allowances. Fees are negotiated separately for each item and can vary based on where in a store or on a shelf the new product is placed.

DIGITAL EXPERIMENTATION

Many marketers are spending 10 to 20 percent of their advertising budgets on what amounts to lab experiments. They are trying to deal with new technologies and a fresh wave of creativity. Many agencies are responding to new technologies. TBWA\Chiat\Day, for example, created a laboratory for clients (especially Apple) to find new ways of applying digital and traditional means of engaging consumers.

CONSUMER CONTROL: THE NEED TO MANAGE VIRAL TECHNOLOGY

Because neither corporations nor media control the communication revolution, there is, at best, a dialog. Consumers "talk" to friends about products and companies using their social sites, blogs, podcasts, moblogs, vBlogs (or vlogs), chat rooms, and e-mail; they follow brands and personalities on Twitter—the good and the bad, the truth and the lie. And, of course, there will always be the next new digital thing that consumers adore and use as part of their conversations. Marketers can't control what consumers say, but many marketers scan digital conversations for brand insights. Many companies are developing technology to analyze all kinds of "consumer-generated media," including blogs, chat rooms, message boards, and forums. They monitor what is being said about their brands as an early warning system. You can't have a dialog if you don't know what consumers are saying and thinking. And any dialog is risky because you don't control it. Smart companies can influence the discussion, or open forum, and harness consumer trust. Business blogs can include conversations with consumers, employees, and media. We discuss digital messages in greater detail in Chapter 16.

Today, marketers are forced to find the right formula and be innovative in marketing new and established products. Finding the right path can be risky. Breaking through the chatter can be risky. The discussion of risk is not new with agency people. Years ago, Bill Borders of Borders, Perrin and Norrander said, "Risk taking is the lifeblood of an agency." However, according to a former director of creative at PepsiCo, "The problem with most clients is that they are not willing to join the agency in the risk. Through the years Pepsi-Cola has told their agency to take the risk. If you miss, we understand that not everything is going to be a home run. But it could be a single. Occasionally, we have burned the film knowing that we tried and it just didn't work."[20] Unfortunately, most clients can't find the courage to join PepsiCo in taking chances or risks to seek cutting-edge advertising.

Bob Moore, creative director of Fallon, Minneapolis, says, "I am a believer that you have to do strong ads that stand out. A lot of times that leads you to something that is different. By its very nature, different is going to lead you to something risky. What's risky gets people talking. You can do work that feels good, but no one notices it. It is like wallpaper. That's far riskier."[21]

THE NO RISK CULTURE

Many clients are looking for advertising home runs to drive their brands from anyplace or media. Remember, earlier we said chief marketing officers, generally, stay in their jobs for about 18 months. As a result, marketing managers (product, brand, CMOs, etc.) mostly only care about what's happening now with their brands because their performance is being measured. The brand management system attempts to prevent failure by relying strongly on research and testing. The brand managers are promoted if they don't make mistakes—as well as if they hit a home run. This creates brand managers who play it safe and don't take risks. Some companies are extending the length of time brand managers stay on a particular assignment. Advertising never pays for itself in the short term. Promotions always do (we'll discuss this in detail later in the promotion chapter).

AGENCY-CLIENT RELATIONSHIPS

It has been said that agency-client relationships are much like interpersonal relationships: If you don't like each other, you move apart. If you like each other, you gravitate toward each other and great stuff gets produced. The agency should be trusted as an employee—it is in business with the client. The relationship between the agency and the client is that of a partnership. A self-promotion from Ames Scullin O'Haire agency said,

4 **Discuss agency-client relationships.**

> There was a time when ad agencies were partners, not vendors. They were trusted, not suspected. They added value, not expenses. Then agencies got greedy. In pursuit of hefty fees, ad agencies began to pay more attention to their own business than their clients'. Merger mania began as conglomerates gobbled agencies like Pac Man with the munchies. Soon agencies became little more than order-takers. Ironically, today clients pay consultants tens of millions for marketing advice while beating up their ad agencies over courier charges. Where's the love, babe, where's the love? We're Ames Scullin O'Haire, an ad agency built around you.[22]

Some would say they are close to the heart of the problem.

Continental Consulting Group reported that many clients are not satisfied with their advertising agencies, claiming their shops are understaffed, overcompensated, and not as creative as agencies were 2 decades ago. The report also complained about less-experienced account management personnel and weak strategic thinking. Clients responded that the quality of agency staffers is less than it was 5 years ago, and more than half said the person heading their account is less experienced than an account manager would have been 5 or 10 years ago. Some 81 percent of those surveyed believed agency people are stretched too thin.

Nancy L. Salz Consulting, which, since 1986, has sponsored what is known as the Salz Survey of Advertiser-Agency Relations, found in 2006 that when advertisers were asked to predict the effect on sales if their agencies were always able to do the best work possible, the respondents estimated an increase of 24.7 percent. By contrast, as recently as 2003, the response was as low as 20.8 percent.

Advertisers who were asked to assess the quality of the advertisements produced by their agencies gave the work a rating of 7.3 on a scale of 1 (terrible) to 10 (excellent). The survey average has been 7.2, and 7.3 was the highest response since 1998, when the figure reached 7.4. In response to another question about the tenseness of relationships with their agencies, the number who said the relationship grew tenser during 2008 fell to 17 percent, a record low for the question. In 2005, the response was 41 percent. Advertisers are now saying, "No one knows the best way to use the Internet or how to get ads to people over their mobile devices." "And we're both in this together, facing a common challenge neither of us has a history with." "There's no business-as-usual, no been-there, done-that," Salz added. "This sort of thing turns people on."[23]

Agencies have always prided themselves on selling the creative product; however, many people believe today's agencies are not producing the strongest creative product. Some clients hire advertising agencies because they believe they can help them persuade customers to do or think something. Clients may select an agency based on the agency's ability to be persuasive. The real task for the agency is to become a persuasion partner.

When advertisers develop a new product or become disenchanted with their existing advertising, they will conduct advertising reviews in which their current agency and others can compete for the account. This review process may take several months. The advertiser will evaluate which agencies it wants to participate in the review. Keep in mind that there are agencies that specialize in certain types of accounts.

In moving from his role as president of Coca-Cola North America to chair and CEO of Clorox Co., Donald R. Knauss was asked about his agency relationship philosophy. He responded, "First of all, my philosophy of agencies is that the people you work with over a long period of time are those who deliver great results. I'm not for the flavor-of-the-month club. I like to have long-standing relationships. And certainly we had that approach at [Procter & Gamble, where Mr. Knauss began his career]. And it depends at Coke which categories you're talking about—we've had a similar approach as well."[24]

With competitive pressures mounting, companies are more enamored with brand strategies and solutions—regardless of whether they are "advertising" driven—than with creative work. As a result, companies seek solutions from a coterie of other advisers, not exclusively from advertising agencies. Today, agencies are again trying to find their place at the table. Many are changing their direction or focus: "Clients don't care where good ideas come from," says WPP Group chief executive Martin Sorrells.[25] Agencies seek to be full-service partners, as opposed to being vendors, where clients go for any and all business solutions. Brunner Digital works hard to keep client DeVry happy with their efforts. Exhibit 6.9 illustrates a digital effort aimed at attracting women to their many programs.

AGENCY SEARCH CONSULTANTS

The trend continues of clients hiring consultants to help them seek out the best agency to handle their accounts (this is similar to the process of companies hiring headhunters to find executives or other employees). It is usual in account reviews for major advertisers to involve consultants, whose job is to do the initial screening; manage the search process; and, in some cases, negotiate compensation agreements. This may cost a client between $35,000 and $100,000. In the past, clients relied more heavily on their own marketing departments to conduct searches. Consultants have been hired more in recent years because fewer clients find they are qualified to do it themselves and because there have been so

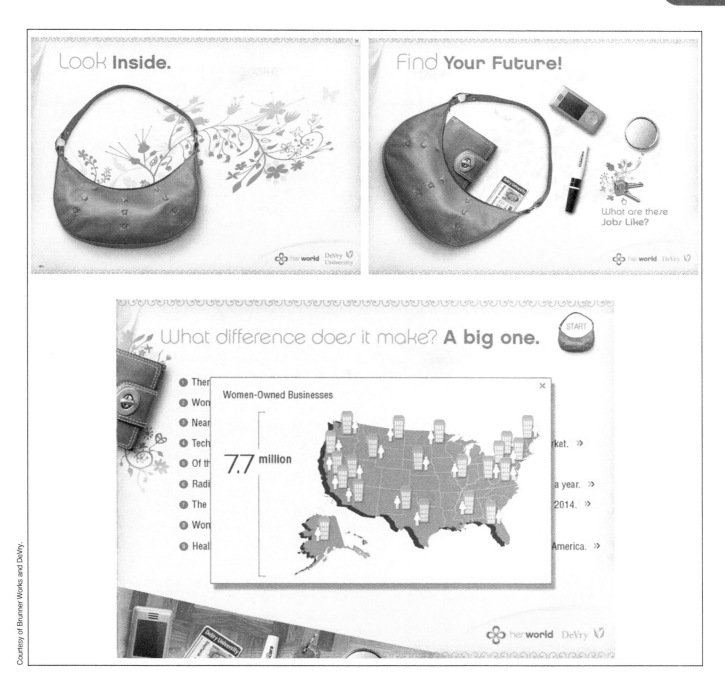

Courtesy of Brunner Works and DeVry.

EXHIBIT 6.9

DeVry's digital effort aimed at attracting women to their many programs.

many changes in the agency landscape, according to an agency principal.[26] The consultant has been characterized as a "marriage broker" between client and agency.

There has been a continued increase in clients reviewing their agencies. This is a natural result of the restructuring of businesses. When marketing departments are restructured and people change jobs, there is a tendency to start from scratch and this includes reviewing or changing advertising agencies. They send out a request for proposal (RFP) to potential agencies that asks a number of questions the client needs answered. The driving forces on account reviews include pressure on advertisers' marketing departments to sell more units and a fixation on quarterly financial results. That position deemphasizes the importance of long-standing relationships and spotlights how well agencies can deliver quick fixes to sales problems. Because marketers will already have done as much downsizing as is practical, increases will now have to be achieved through "real unit growth."[27] This creates pressure on both clients and agencies.

SELECTING AN AGENCY

Choosing an agency can be a complicated matter. Do you need a full-service agency, one with integrated services, one with strong media departments, or a specialized agency? After deciding whether you want a large, medium, or small; specialized or full-service; domestic or global agency, the following points may help you in evaluating specific agencies:

1. Determine what types of service you need from an agency and then list them in order of their importance to you—for instance, (a) marketing expertise in strategy, planning, and execution; (b) creative performance in television, print, radio, or outdoor; (c) media knowledge and clout, if media is part of the equation; (d) promotion and/or trade relations help; (e) public relations and corporate- or image-building ability; (f) market research strength; (g) fashion or beauty sense; (h) agency size; (i) location in relation to your office; or (j) web or new media capabilities. Your special needs will dictate others.

2. Establish a five-point scale to rate each agency's attributes. A typical five-point scale would be (1) outstanding, (2) very good, (3) good, (4) satisfactory, and (5) unsatisfactory. Of course, you should give different values or weights to the more important agency attributes.

3. Check published sources and select a group of agencies that seem to fit your requirements. Use your own knowledge or the knowledge of your industry peers to find agencies responsible for successful campaigns or products that have most impressed you. Published sources include the annual issue of *Advertising Age*, which lists agencies and their accounts by agency size, and the "Red Book" (*Standard Advertising Register*), which lists agencies and accounts both alphabetically and geographically. In case of further doubt, contact the American Association of Advertising Agencies, New York, for a roster of members. Of course, you can do this online.

4. Check whether there are any apparent conflicts with accounts already at the agency. When agencies consider a new account, that is the first question they ask (along with the amount of the potential billings).

5. Now start preliminary discussions with the agencies that rate best on your initial evaluation. This can be initiated with a letter asking if they are interested or a telephone call to arrange an appointment for them to visit you or for you to visit the agency. Start at the top. Call the president or the operating head of the agency or office in your area; this person will appoint someone to follow up on the opportunity you are offering.

6. Reduce your original list of potential agencies after the first contact. A manageable number is usually no more than three to five. Many can be eliminated by their RFP answers.

7. Again prepare an evaluation list for rating the agencies on the same five-point scale. This list will be a lot more specific. It should cover personnel. Who will supervise your account and how will the account be staffed? Who are the creative people who will work on your business? Similarly, who will service your interactive, production (television), research, and promotion needs, and how will they do it? What is the agency's track record in getting and holding on to business and in keeping personnel teams together? What is the agency's record with vendors and media? Make sure again to assign a weighted value to each service aspect.

8. Discuss financial arrangements. Will your account be a straight 15 percent commission account, a fee account, a combination of both, or will it be based on some performance formula? What services will the commission or fee cover, and what additional charges will the agency demand? How will new product work be handled from both a financial and an organizational point of view? What peripheral service does the agency offer, and for how much?

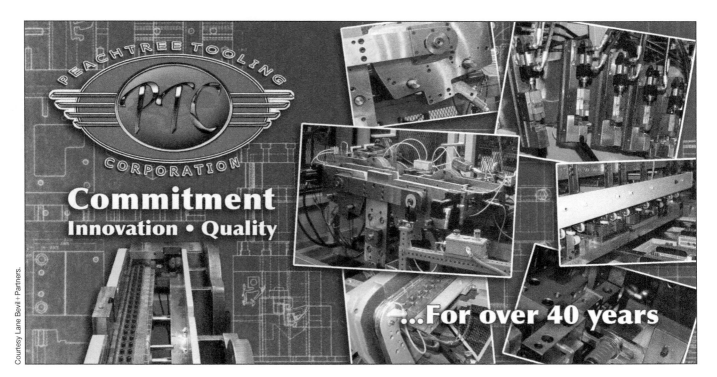

Courtesy Lane Bevil+Partners.

9. Do you feel comfortable with the agency?

10. If your company is a global one, can the agency handle all of your nondomestic business, and if so, how will they do it?

CLIENT REQUIREMENTS

Agency workloads vary significantly for each client. Agencies may produce only a few advertisements for a client during a year, which isn't taxing on their creative and management abilities. Ogilvy & Mather creates about 6,000 advertisements for IBM around the world, which requires excellent creative and management skills. However, industrial company Peachtree Tooling generates only a few ads during the year to reach its potential B2B clients (see Exhibit 6.10).

USING MULTIPLE AGENCIES

Many large clients may hire several agencies and give them different assignments for the same product or different brands. In some cases, this is changing the agency-client relationship by treating agencies as vendors and not as full marketing partners. One of the reasons for this change is that new marketing executives are under pressures from their CEOs. The message is this: "I don't care about your situation. I need an idea and people who are passionate about my business."

In the 1950s, the agency-client relationship was defined in *The Encyclopedia of Advertising*:

> An advertising agency is an organization which provides advertising, merchandising and other services and counsel related to the sale of a client's goods or services. It is understood that the client agrees not to engage a second agency to handle part of the advertising of the product without the consent of the first agency.

Traditionally, a marketer used one agency per brand. As companies got bigger and marketing more complex, this changed. For example, a number of years ago, Coca-Cola decided that its longtime agency wasn't creating enough big ideas. For additional creative ideas, it hired outside freelancers for a while and then hired about 40 agencies and boutiques to create advertisements. Coca-Cola's contention was this: *We know and understand our strategy better than our agencies do. So their job is to do the best execution of the strategy they can.*

Today, Coca-Cola has a number of different agencies working on its brands. It is not the only company to use multiple agencies. Many use a major global agency, plus a number of smaller creative shops. "The size of our business is such that it demands the expertise and attention of a number of agencies," said the national director of marketing communications at AT&T. "There are so many projects and assignments to be handled that one agency couldn't do it all. But using multiple agencies puts the onus on us to make sure all the messages are coordinated and represent one consistent voice coming from the company." These needs are different from a client having one agency partner to handle everything.[28]

The advertising business is famously cyclical, so it remains to be seen whether this multiple-agency trend is a permanent shift or a temporary blip. Right now, advertisers are looking for the best custom-made solutions to their marketing problems.

THE DIGITAL LIBRARY

Global clients and major advertising agencies build creative digital libraries for agencies in different parts of the globe to use. For example, the McDonald's digital commercial archive holds commercials from the chain's advertising since 1967 that may be used by local co-ops and agencies. It is a password-only system, so consumers or the competition can't access the files. Most of the archive includes still graphic assets, such as logos, product shots, text custom advertisements, point-of-purchase displays, and other print material. It allows for integration of visuals to all agencies around the globe working on the account.

Appraising National Advertising

The big questions that national advertising and marketing management must answer are these: How well is our advertising working? How well is our investment paying off? How do you measure national advertising, whose results cannot be traced as easily as those of direct-response and some interactive advertising?

ADVERTISING GOALS VERSUS MARKETING GOALS

5 Identify advertising goals versus marketing goals.

Measuring national advertising is not simple. Much of the discussion on the subject centers around a report prepared for the ANA, the industry's premier trade association dedicated exclusively to marketing and brand building. The thesis of this study is that it is virtually impossible to measure the results of advertising unless and until the specific results sought by advertising have been defined. When they are asked exactly what their advertising is supposed to do, most companies have a ready answer: increase their dollar sales or increase their share of the market. However, these are not advertising goals, they are **marketing goals**. In the digital world, messages (search, e-mail, banners, videos, etc.) have analytics that provide marketers with all kinds of information.

marketing goals
The overall objectives that a company wishes to accomplish through its marketing program.

advertising goals
The communication objectives designed to accomplish certain tasks within the total marketing program.

The first step in appraising the results of traditional advertising is to define specifically what the company expects to accomplish through advertising. The ANA report defines an **advertising goal** as "a specific communications task, to be accomplished among a defined audience to a given degree in a given period of time"[29] (see Exhibit 6.11).

As an example, let's look at a branded detergent. The marketing goal is to increase market share from 10 to 15 percent, and the advertising goal is set as increasing, among the 50 million housewives who own washing machines, the number who identify Brand X as a stain-removing detergent that gets clothes clean. This represents a specific communications task that can be performed by advertising independent of other marketing forces.

There may be a marketing communication spectrum ranging from unawareness of the product to comprehension to conviction to action. According to this view, the way to appraise advertising is through its effectiveness in the communication spectrum, leading to sales.

Based on their research, Briggs and Stuart say Wanamaker was wrong—only 37 percent of advertising is wasted. The authors pin much of the blame on marketers' failure to even define success for campaigns at the outset—much less measure it properly at the end. In the study, P&G clearly defined success for each marketing effort at the outset. In Briggs and Stuart's book *What Sticks*, they outline a program—the Communication Optimization Process—to help the marketing team see what it might otherwise miss. The authors suggest that you go through the 4Ms—motivation, message, media mix, and maximization—to get everyone on the same page. Then link the gold standard marketing effectiveness measurement of each M to the action plan. In other words, measure everything to see if it works.[30]

Researchers disagree on whether the effectiveness of national advertising—or, for that matter, of any advertising—should be judged by a communication yardstick rather than by sales. As a matter of fact, in Chapter 15 we discuss whether an advertisement's effectiveness should be measured by some research testing score.

Changes in Marketing

We remain in the midst of a revolution. This period of change has been compared to the French and Russian revolutions. The truth is that we are in the midst of several revolutions at once, including globalization, technology, management, an uncertain economy, and consumers' controlling messages. We are in competition with everyone, everywhere in the world. Today's management buzzwords are *reengineering*, *downsizing*, and *eliminating hierarchy*. Small, flexible organizations have the advantage in today's world. Finally, we are undergoing a revolution in our business structure.

THE TRADITIONAL FIVE P's OF MARKETING

As Brad Majors discussed in Chapter 3, the traditional five Ps of marketing consist of the elements product, price, place, promotion (which includes positioning, advertising, sales promotion, public relations, and so forth), and prospect. With a strategy in each of these areas, a person can put together an effective marketing plan. In the packaged-goods category, the general belief is that promotion accounts for about 90 percent of the marketing equation. Each product category may be different, as seen with automobiles, where price and product are key, with promotion being a small percentage. So the advertiser must understand what is important.

THE NEW FIVE P's OF MARKETING

Longtime advertising executive Tom Patty says the old five Ps served us well in a world dominated by stability and a growing economy with much less competitive pressures than we have today. Patty's new five Ps are aimed at helping us succeed in a world where chaos has replaced stability, where the fast-growing economy has slowed, and where global competition demands even greater levels of effectiveness and efficiency. The new five Ps are more abstract and conceptual than the traditional ones. They include paradox, perspective, paradigm, persuasion, and passion.[31]

■ *Paradox.* A paradox is a statement or proposition that, on the face of it, seems self-contradictory. Example: "All cars are the same; all cars are different." The paradox always contains within it an opportunity. An advertiser must exploit the differentiation. Miller used the paradox of "lite" beer to help focus on the dual benefits of

Tim Mapes Senior Vice President—Marketing, Delta Air Lines, Inc.

AGENCY SIDE OR CLIENT SIDE?

To be or not to be? Who knew Shakespeare's Hamlet was an ad major, soon to graduate, struggling with the decision to go client side or agency side?

Of course, in today's business environment, you may be happy (and lucky) to find a job at either. But what draws people to one rather than the other? What enables success once you're there? And how, based on a better understanding of life at each, might you make the best career decision and, in the process, improve the world of advertising management?

THE AGENCY SIDE

Professional life on the agency side is frequently depicted in glamorous ways with stylish, fashionable people creating stylish, fashionable advertising for their clients. Agency offices are sleek and modern. The atmosphere is electrically charged with creativity as ad execs go about the sexy business that is advertising. "Power lunches" abound. This can in fact be accurate. But beyond the veneer Hollywood tends to apply to the ad agency business, life on the agency side is not so superficial. Ad agency staffers, particularly those in entry-level roles, deal with demanding clients, unreasonable deadlines, competitiveness from other staffers looking to make a name for themselves, and a host of other factors that can lead to a stressful work environment.

And that stress varies by the disciplines represented at each agency. Account management people strive to remain knowledgeable about brand strategy issues, overall process management, and clients themselves. Creative people look to stay abreast of fashion and design trends, the latest production techniques, and ways to develop that next big idea. And media planners and buyers have to stay on top of syndicated research, emerging media vehicles

themselves, and measures of audience delivery. This collective effort to stay on top drives a fast-paced, energetic organizational culture in agencies that is best suited for like-minded, resilient souls whom no one would ever describe as "wall flowers."

Creatively driven agencies have been known to say, "it is all about the work" referring to the quality of their output as visible in the advertising and marketing communications activities they craft and churn out. Organizational emphasis is thus placed on the quality of the consumer insight achieved and the expression of the idea—as well as retention and advancement of people who can deliver either but better still both. The best, and most successful, agencies go well past concern for themselves (e.g., creative awards won) and focus instead on how their work as an agency directly or indirectly leads to success in their client's business. Agencies tend to be measured on the clients they keep and the work they do for them over time. Clients do not stay long at agencies that do not deliver desired business results, and agency staffers not seen by clients as key to their business depart even faster.

THE CLIENT SIDE

Staying within the Hollywood metaphor, client-side people are frequently perceived as mean-spirited tyrants who boss agency personnel around without regard for the people involved and without respect for the process at hand. Clients are also often portrayed as overly conservative oafs who fail to recognize, let alone act on, the agency's "big idea." They are considered power-hungry boars whose self-regard displaces their understanding of the very customers they seek. This may, regrettably, be based in fact. But life in client organizations tends to revolve around definitive business metrics such as total sales generated, revenue

Tim Mapes

generated, costs avoided, and other traditional definitions of market success. Staffers in client ad and marketing organizations deal with "the work" (advertising creative) but, like the best agencies, they must see it in the broader context of delivering business success and not simply attaining creative awards.

Life on the client side involves similarly long hours and the requisite "payment of dues" to move up. Paradoxically, clients can, at times, look to agencies for greater insight to their customers than they as clients have themselves. This is not always an abdication of responsibility. Client organizations can focus so much on "running the factory" that they lose touch with who is buying the product. But the best clients learn to function like agencies themselves in that they must have a commanding knowledge of consumer trends and research findings, brand strategy, media trends, production values and techniques, and the estimating and billing processes—all the while leading their own organizations and being accessible to agency representatives and members of the media.

Perhaps of greatest value to those considering life on the client side is the ability to exert influence over advertising outcomes. Agencies can lead the client horse to the water but they cannot make her or him drink. Thirsty clients get the best from their agencies by saying "yes" to the right recommendations, and, as an agency superior once told me, "clients get the advertising they deserve." Clients that contribute to, fight on behalf of, and say yes to the best agency ideas get more of them.

REQUIREMENTS FOR SUCCESS AT EITHER

So although there are clear differences in a day in your life as an ad person at an ad agency or a client organization, there are foundational elements in the work itself that can, and should, make the roles more alike than dissimilar. In fact, success on either the agency side or the client side requires the same five strategies.

Obsessive focus on the customer. It has been said that the business of selling begins with "no." As a form of selling, advertising and advertisers (regardless of whether on the client side or the agency side) must know as much as possible about the prospective customer. Entire companies exist that conduct forms of "ethnographic" research by following targeted customers around to learn more about where they live, what they drive, how they dress, where they eat, what they read, and about all of the values and behaviors that drive purchase decisions. The closer to the customer you are, the more likely you are to know, and therefore meet, their needs.

Innate curiosity. Although people tend to think of advertising as "art," it has components that are much more like "science." Curiosity in what drives consumer behavior, why scientifically the eye is drawn to red faster than to any other color, why black type on a white background is the most legible, and any variety of other otherwise seemingly disparate bits of information can enable success. It never ceases to amaze me how something I read or heard related to a field that has nothing to do with my own actually applies if I think it through fully. In fact, some of the greatest advertising breakthroughs resulted from "disruptions" to conventional wisdom. If you are not open to, or curious about, these pieces of information, your ability to process them and contribute most fully can be limited.

Attention to detail. An account supervisor once told me, "the client never sleeps." Another, at a different agency, advised that when proofreading a mechanical, "assume there is a mistake in it and that you have to be the one to find it no matter how many other signatures are already on the mechanical." There are rarely small mistakes in advertising—they go from big to bigger as campaigns run locally to globally. But attention to detail goes beyond the "downside" of mistakes to the "upside" of insights. Attention to detail can be the key to gaining better consumer insight than your competitor and thus will be more likely to lead to market success. And in categories as competitive as colas, airlines, and wireless communication, even the smallest of advantages can yield large-scale benefits.

The ability to connect with people. Agencies tend to say that their greatest assets leave the company each night. It is no less true in client organizations. Inherently, advertising is a business that is about people—people as customers, people as colleagues; people as bosses and people as subordinates; and people who devote themselves to serving clients as agency people and people who, if wise, do everything in their power to motivate their agencies as clients. It is a business, as Barbara Streisand sang, of "people who need people" and those who can understand, empathize, connect with, and captivate others will succeed.

Those who do not rarely make it past an initial interview.

A "love of the game." If you do not love, and I mean LOVE advertising, the question of agency versus client side is irrelevant. Advertising inherently requires lots of time. Time spent in the office. Time spent in meetings. Time spent in focus groups and on market research. Time spent traveling. And time spent with people you may not particularly care for! A love of the process (and of course the final output and resulting business success) is necessary to sustain you when things become challenging or, worse yet, tedious.

ONE PERSON'S VIEW

For these and other reasons, in my personal view, the best clients are former agency people, and, in turn, the best agency people are former clients. Stephen Covey suggests we "seek to understand before we seek to be understood." True understanding of what concerns or motivates your client is best developed by walking a mile (or miles!) in her or his shoes. Similarly, actual client experience—seeing what goes on in an agency in developing an idea in the first place, then transforming it into an "ad-like object" or "comp" and finished, produced work appearing in the medium for which it was intended—can be an invaluable way of ensuring that timelines are reasonable and praise is forthcoming when great work appears.

Clients who "get" the demands of the agency business are more likely to show respect for processes employed and timelines required—and to recognize great teams and great work knowing just how challenging agency work can be. Similarly, agency professionals who know what it is like as a client to lose sleep at night because your paycheck depends on the success of a new product launch think more thoroughly about how to ensure the benefits of that product's performance are clearly communicated in the advertising.

A former business-oriented yet creatively minded boss of mine used to employ the phrase, "when you come to a fork in the road, take it." Such guidance is brilliant on a number of levels but if for no other reason than that it challenges us to break with conventional wisdom.

If you happen to be facing a professional version of Hamlet's conundrum involving an opportunity at an agency or with a client, it might comfort you to know that in reality you will not make a bad decision—experience at one is invaluable to your success at the other should you ultimately ever wish to make a change.

Courtesy of Tim Mapes, Senior Vice President—Marketing, Delta Air Lines, Inc.

EXHIBIT 6.11

What is the advertising objective of this highly creative ad?

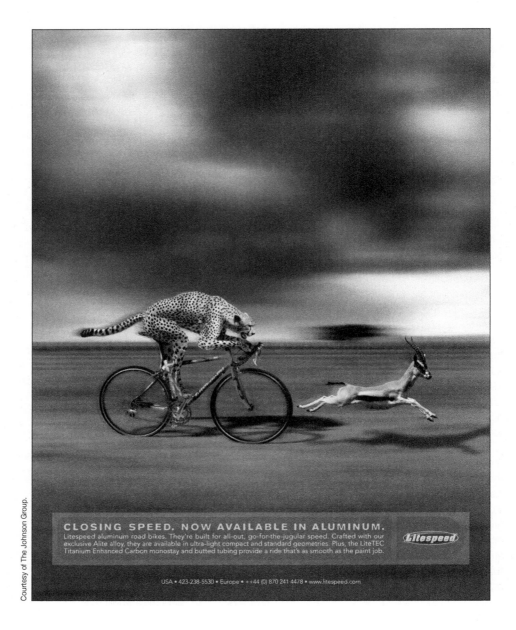

Courtesy of The Johnson Group.

the lite paradox, "Tastes Great, Less Filling." Everyone knows what a sports car is, but Nissan created a new category of sports cars in which it ranked first—the four-door sports car. To master the paradox, you first have to find or identify an opportunity and then exploit the changes. One way to create this unique identity is to be the first in something. For years, advertising told us that trucks are tough and rugged and durable, whereas cars are comfortable, luxurious, and safe. The new Dodge Ram exploits the paradox of combining many car-type features with the rugged look and performance of a Mack truck.

■ *Perspective.* Perspective is the ability to see things in relationship to each other. The manufacturer's perspective isn't the proper perspective. Advertisers must look at every issue—whether it's a product issue, a pricing issue, or a distribution issue—from the consumer's perspective. The only perspective is the consumer's perspective. Here, several questions need answers: What consumer need does my product or service satisfy? How does it satisfy this need differently from and better than competitors? Similarly, as it relates to advertising, are we in the advertising business or are we in the persuasion business? We should be in the business of persuading consumers to think or to do something.

COMPANY OPERATING PHILOSOPHY AND PROFILE

Chick-fil-A

Founded by entrepreneur and restaurateur S. Truett Cathy, Chick-fil-A® rose from rather humble beginnings to become America's second-largest quick-service chicken restaurant chain in the country.

Courtesy of Chick-fil-A.

BACKGROUND

Cathy started in 1946 in the Atlanta suburb of Hapeville with a single location called the Dwarf Grill. Cathy now presides over a chain of some 1,300 restaurants in 37 states and Washington, DC, generating annual sales of more than $2 billion.

The Chick-fil-A brand owes its success to three key factors:

- **Great food, consistently prepared.** Chick-fil-A uses only natural, all-white chicken breast meat, often considered the best part of the chicken. The signature Chick-fil-A sandwich is seasoned and breaded using a recipe that Cathy created in the early 1960s for his Dwarf Grill customers. Much as Cathy prepared his own menu items by hand, team members at Chick-fil-A restaurants across the country still bread chicken breasts by hand, squeeze lemons for Chick-fil-A lemonade, and hand-spin their milkshakes.
- **Adherence to sound, proven business principles.** Truett Cathy based his business on hard work, providing great food fast with a service-driven attitude that had customers returning as much for the hospitality as for the great food. As a chain, Chick-fil-A adheres to the basic biblical principles of fairness, honesty, and treating others as you would like to be treated. For example, every Chick-fil-A restaurant is closed on Sunday, allowing employees to spend time with friends and family and to worship if they choose. Other more secular business principles also have driven success at Chick-fil-A. For example, Chick-fil-A's franchise agreement with its restaurant owner-operators is unique to the industry. For a relatively small commitment fee, their unique operator agreement provides franchisees with an opportunity to sublease a Chick-fil-A chain restaurant, each month paying 15 percent of gross sales and 50 percent of net profits to Chick-fil-A, Inc., as a franchise fee. This profit-sharing system ensures that each operator has the incentive to succeed—and operators' success translates into success for the chain and the brand.
- **The creation and marketing of a memorable brand.** As the man who introduced the chicken sandwich to the quick-service industry, Cathy was determined to give his product (and later the chain that would bear his name) a meaningful—and memorable—name.

The name "Chick-fil-A" was derived from the part of the chicken from which the sandwich is made: the breast fillet. Determined to give the name additional flair, Cathy added the "A" at the end, to reinforce top quality ("grade A"). After the launch of the Chick-fil-A chain in 1967, the brand grew one restaurant at a time and one market at a time. Marketing efforts were public-relations driven and locally focused, allowing restaurant franchisees (called operators) and their employees—not to mention the food—to be the stars. As the brand grew beyond the southeastern and Sun Belt states in its bid to become a truly national brand, Chick-fil-A began to branch out, using more aggressive marketing strategies, including event sponsorship, sports marketing, and advertising to supplement local initiatives. Most notable among these new marketing strategies—and the biggest contribution to the development of the Chick-fil-A brand next to Cathy himself—was the creation in 1995 of the chain's Eat Mor Chikin® Cow campaign.

HISTORY

Chick-fil-A did not actually start off as a restaurant chain; rather, it started as a simple chicken sandwich. Tinkering with a recipe for a boneless breast of chicken sandwich at his original Dwarf Grill restaurant, Cathy quickly realized he created a hit when sales for the new chicken sandwich quickly began to outsell hamburgers (the former top seller). In 1963, Cathy decided to trademark his signature sandwich, branding it the "Chick-fil-A" sandwich.

In 1967, the first Chick-fil-A restaurant—a modest, 384-square-foot unit—opened in Atlanta's Greenbriar Shopping Center, the South's first enclosed shopping mall. Although small in stature, the restaurant represented a huge leap for the quick-service industry: the concept of mall-based dining (which evolved into the modern food courts found in most malls today). At that time, mall managers were reluctant to allow dining concepts in their venues because of concerns about smoke and fumes. In addition to providing assurances about the impact on the mall's air quality, Cathy stressed the potential economic impact of keeping mall

(continued)

shoppers in the mall during peak shopping times rather than losing them to nearby restaurants. With this sales pitch, Chick-fil-A quickly became synonymous with malls across America.

During the next 4 decades, the physical aspects of the Chick-fil-A chain—number of locations, restaurant types, geographic reach, menu items, and the sheer size of the organization—continued to evolve. The 1970s saw the expansion of the Chick-fil-A concept throughout Georgia and into neighboring states (including North Carolina, Florida, South Carolina, and Texas). In 1986, the chain developed its first stand-alone Chick-fil-A restaurant. In 1996, Chick-fil-A introduced Truett's Grill—a 1950s diner-themed restaurant featuring retro décor and counter, table, and drive-thru service—to commemorate Cathy's 50 years in

the business. During that same period, the chain established its licensing program to enable food-service partners to operate Chick-fil-A restaurants in settings such as college campuses, hospitals, airports, and business and industry locations. Since 2000, the chain has concentrated on geographical expansion, moving into key regions in the Northeast and Midwest and on the West Coast.

Anchored by the signature Chick-fil-A chicken sandwich, the menu has retained its focus on chicken as the main menu item, but the chain continues to develop new menu items and expand its menu offerings to appeal to its increasingly diverse customer base.

In Chapter 22, you'll see Chick-fil-A's marketing strategy and famous cows advertising and integrated marketing examples.

- *Paradigm.* Here we need a pattern example, a model way of doing things. We need to understand that we may not need to do business the "old" way. Certainly, the marketing bundle of Saturn reflects a new automotive paradigm. Instead of believing that product and price are the main ingredients of the marketing equation, Saturn believes that the major components are issues such as the experience of buying and owning a Saturn. They place much less emphasis on the product and much greater emphasis on the experiential component. There are also different advertising paradigms. In the model advertising paradigm, advertising has a simple task: Show the product and communicate the product features and benefits. A very different paradigm is called the brand advertising paradigm, for which Saturn again is a good example. In this paradigm the task is to communicate who and what you are.

- *Persuasion.* Here we attempt to induce someone to do or think something. All marketing and sales jobs are in the business of persuasion. The advertising agency's role is to help the client persuade potential consumer audiences either to do or to think something. To be persuasive, you have to understand three essential components: the credibility of the speaker, the content of the message, and the involvement of the audience. Credibility and trust are emotional, not rational. You can't make someone trust you. You have to earn it over time. The Honda brand has credibility. Consequently, the advertising tends to be simple and sparse. For a brand with less credibility, you need to provide more content, more information to be persuasive. The content includes the position of the brand. It needs to address the consumer need or desire this product satisfies. Remember, consumers do not buy products; they buy solutions to their problems. They buy holes, not drill bits; they buy hope, not perfume. The third and final element in any attempt to persuade is that you must understand the motivation of your customers so you can create an emotional connection with them. You also need to select the right persuasion tool. For example, if the brand has a credibility problem, the most persuasive tool might be public relations, although it is more difficult to control the content of the message in public relations. In advertising, you get complete control of content.

- *Passion.* Passion is an aim or object pursued with zeal or enthusiasm. We no longer have products for the masses. Instead, products are designed for specific needs and wants. Marketers are moving into a new paradigm in which advertising creates exciting, stimulating dialogs with consumers designed not only to make a sale but also to create a relationship. In this new marketing environment, you need passion.

SUMMARY

Procter & Gamble first developed the marketing services system. Today it has two parts: (1) brand management, under a brand manager, who is assigned a brand; and (2) marketing services, comprised of the technical talent involved in implementing the marketing plan, including creative services, promotion services, media services, advertising controls, and marketing research.

As companies consider implementing integrated marketing communications into their firms, there are three basic structures available: a centralized communication function under a marcom manager, a restructured brand manager approach, and the structure involving a communication manager who is responsible for approving and coordinating all communication programs.

Advertising budgets are usually devised using the task method, the payout plan, competitive budgeting, and the most commonly used percentage-of-sales method.

Advertisers are seeing the advantage of allowing their agencies more creative freedom and encouraging them to take more creative risk as long as it is on strategy. As Bill Borders said, "Risk taking is the lifeblood of an agency."

Agency search consultants are sometimes hired to help find the best agency for a client. The consultant has been characterized as a marriage broker between client and agency. Many clients hire several agencies for multiple products or for the same product. Many brand executives retain their jobs an average of only 18 months, and CMOs average little less than 2 years in their jobs, which hampers the client-agency relationship.

The traditional five Ps of marketing consist of product, price, place, promotion, and prospect. According to Tom Patty, the new five Ps are paradox, perspective, paradigm, persuasion, and passion.

REVIEW

1. In how many product categories do Procter & Gamble products compete?
2. What is the marketing services system?
3. What is a category manager?
4. What are the major methods of developing an advertising budget?
5. Who in the corporation prepares most of the advertising budgets?
6. What is a slotting allowance?

MEDIA

In Part IV, we discuss the methods of reaching consumers with sales messages. The chapters in this part examine both traditional media and emerging methods of reaching customers.

- **CHAPTER 7** begins the consideration of media with an overview of the media planning function and the role of the media/communication planner in delivering advertising messages to consumers.

- **CHAPTERS 8 TO 14** discuss each of the basic media and communication methods used to reach consumers. "Media" as diverse as web sites, iPods, and cell phones are included in the examination. This part also addresses the communication strengths and weaknesses of each medium and how these media are converging as consumers embrace new technology and media companies merge to form large multimedia conglomerates.

CHAPTER 7

Shutterstock/fineartfotography.

Media Strategy

T HE DEMAND for efficiency, effectiveness, and creativity in the media-planning process has never been greater. The steady increase in the number of media and promotional options and unprecedented audience fragmentation have combined to create both excitement and uncertainty for advertisers and media executives. ▶

The media function, whether executed by an advertising agency, an independent media-buying and planning firm, an unbundled media shop, or a company's in-house media department, is becoming increasingly complex. Let's begin our discussion by examining the primary characteristics of the media function.

Organization of the Media Function

Following are some of the key roles involved in the organization of the media function:

1. *Media/Communication planner.* The role of the **media/communication planner** is to supervise all areas of the advertising campaign as it relates to the use of media. Contemporary media planners have added the role of marketing specialist and strategist to their other duties; this is reflected in the title communication planner that is used by many media agencies. The media environment is changing so rapidly that it is part of the media planner's job to anticipate future trends in communication and media and keep agency management and clients abreast of major changes. In such an atmosphere, media planners have come to occupy a pivotal position in the advertising process.

2. *Media research.* The media research function coordinates both primary and secondary research data and analysis as a support group for media planners. Often, the media researchers are responsible for gauging and anticipating future trends in media.

1 Understand the basic organization of the media function and the role it plays in the total advertising function.

media/communication planner
Person responsible for the overall strategy of the media plan.

Sometimes the media researchers are also responsible for estimating the likely audience for new magazines, television programs, or newer, nontraditional media.

media buyers
Those who execute and monitor the media schedule developed by media planners.

3. *Media buying.* The role of media buyers is to execute the overall media plan. **Media buyers** select and negotiate specific media placements, and they are responsible for monitoring postplacement executions. Depending on the size of a media unit, there may be separate buying groups for broadcast and print or even for local and national broadcasts, or the media planners may execute the media buys themselves. Some media departments have established units to research and buy Internet advertising or to construct client web sites, although the current trend is to bring the digital planning and buying functions back into the main buying and planning unit.

Few areas of marketing and advertising have experienced the change demonstrated by media planning in the past decade. The media function has been driven by changes in the number of media options as well as by the increasing expenditures in media and the financial risk associated with media-buying mistakes. When a medium-size company invests as much as $3 million in a single Super Bowl spot, careers may ride on the outcome!

In 2008, total advertising expenditures in measured and unmeasured media were more than $396 billion, according to ZenithOptimedia.[1] The media planner of 2020 will be dealing with media outlets that probably don't exist today. Yet, these planners will have to provide clients with buying rationales, budget efficiencies, and measurable audience delivery in this unbelievably complicated environment.

The New Media Function

2 **Describe the trends that have set the tone for changes in the media planning function and the role of media in the total advertising function.**

As the media adapt to new technology and methods of planning, there are a number of trends that set the tone for these changes and provide an assessment of the future of media planning and buying. Among the most important are convergence, interactivity, creativity, and engagement.

CONVERGENCE

convergence
The blending of various facets of marketing functions and communication technology to create more efficient and expanded synergies.

One of the primary trends will continue to be media **convergence**. Simply stated, convergence is the blending of distribution, content, and/or hardware from a number of media companies to create a new or significantly expanded communication system. Examples of convergence are numerous—cell phone companies offering Internet connections, newspaper companies creating web sites, or NBC and Microsoft combining to create MSNBC. These types of collaborations are important for the businesses involved and may even expand promotional opportunities for advertisers. However, the audience is more interested in convergences such as webTV, in which the home television becomes a computer link, or online selling that combines catalog merchandise, television-like product demonstrations, and immediate buying capabilities.

Consumers will continue to see numerous types of convergence. For example, when ESPN publishes a magazine or *ABC News* creates a popular web site, the media that are created are the result of convergence. Most experts believe that marketing, media content, and technological convergences are in their embryonic stage. Although we are not certain where it will lead in the next 20 years, convergence is certainly a trend of the present and even more so of the future.

INTERACTIVITY

Audiences will control the future of advertising to a great extent. Technology will allow consumers to deal directly with marketers for their entertainment, purchases, and other services, bypassing traditional media and marketing channels. The system will allow buyers and sellers to deal on a one-to-one basis with communication and products tailored to the interests of specific households and individuals.

In many cases, technological capabilities will probably outpace consumer use of these services. However, interactive media are dramatically changing marketing opportunities.

CREATIVITY

Interactivity not only will change the media function but also will most likely have dramatic effects on the creative process. The need for attention-getting creative techniques and interest-building advertising formats will be greatly diminished. When a person with a previously determined product demand actively seeks out an advertiser, the dynamics of the relationship are dramatically different from the mass advertising of past years.

Clients are demanding more creativity from their media planners. Media planners are being asked to think of and evaluate new and different media options to build additional exposure to consumers in effective and efficient ways.

Media expertise is becoming increasingly important in developing and evaluating entertainment and experience marketing opportunities. Innovative uses of nontraditional media are generally designed to work with the more traditional media campaign for a brand. For example, GM obtained placements of its new Chevy Camaro in the original *Transformers* movie as well as in the summer 2009 sequel. Along with some innovative television spots using stars from the movies, these placements helped to create a flashy sports car image for the Camaro at a time when GM cars, in general, were not perceived to be exciting.[2]

According to Judy Franks, former executive vice president at Energy BBDO, "Great ideas can come from anywhere: an idea can be borne from a highly creative solution to a business problem, an idea can stem from the core values of the brand, itself. Creative teams of copywriters and art directors often spark ideas that blossom into integrated, multi-platform campaigns. And, the media channels, themselves, are often great catalysts for compelling ideas."[3]

ENGAGEMENT

With the shrinking of television audiences and the proliferation of new media, advertisers and media planners are becoming more and more interested in the concept of **engagement**. The term *engagement* means slightly different things to different people, but it is commonly thought to take into account the ability of an advertising vehicle to deliver a receptive audience to the advertising in it. Joseph Plummer, chief research officer of the Advertising Research Foundation, has said that engagement is turning on a prospect to a brand idea enhanced by the surrounding context. As put by media guru Erwin Ephron, engagement is the "hand-off of attentive consumers from media content to advertising."[4] Advertisers are interested in knowing which media make the advertising for their brand effective. In Viewpoint 7.1, Bob Gilbreath discusses the importance of choosing media with which the target audience actively engages to make meaningful connections. (See Exhibit 7.1).

engagement
The delivery of attentive consumers from a media vehicle to the advertising.

If there is a commonality in these trends, it is that they clearly demonstrate that media executives must be analytical, creative, and strategic in their approach to the media process. Knowledge of statistics, mathematical skills, and organized thinking are minimum requirements for media planners. For those people with the interest, imagination, and competency, media planning offers an extremely exciting, lucrative, creative, and challenging career in advertising.

Media Unbundling and Independent Media-Buying Firms

In a media environment characterized by convergence and creativity, one of the common approaches to the media function in recent years is known as *unbundling*. Basically, unbundling refers to the establishment of agency media departments as independent units apart from their traditional role as departments in full-service agencies.

The idea of firms established solely to carry out the media function is not new. The first U.S. media-buying company, Time Buying Services, was founded in 1960. During

KLEPPNER VIEWPOINT 7.1

Bob Gilbreath   Chief Marketing Strategist,
Bridge Worldwide, and author of *The Empowered Consumer Demands Marketing with Meaning*

MARKETING WITH MEANING

Bob Gilbreath

You would probably not be surprised to learn that most people do not like advertising. They are subjected to more than 3,000 advertising messages per day—mainly for brands and products that are irrelevant to their lives. Marketers used to be able to hold consumers hostage to these messages in return for free content on a handful of television channels and magazines—until now.

The rise of digital technology has empowered people to throw off the yoke of interruptive advertising. They use DVRs to skip television commercials, they hit "shuffle" on their iPods instead of tuning into radio stations, and they are playing *Madden '09* on Xbox instead of watching *Monday Night Football*.

A few brands have found a way to survive and thrive through this consumer-empowered media revolution. These winners have discovered success by creating marketing with which people choose to engage, marketing that itself improves people's lives. We call it "marketing with meaning."

For example, Abbott Nutrition created an online educational resource for people with diabetes. Tylenol advertisements advise people that skipping meals can cause headaches. Samsung has placed laptop-recharging stations in airports. Domino's Pizza allows customers to track the progress of their orders online. And Dove generated a conversation and cause around improving girls' self-esteem.

The idea of marketing with meaning is not completely new. The Michelin Guide

started in 1900 as a way to encourage early car owners to hit the roads and travel, wearing out sets of tires. The difference now is that Michelin's model is mandatory for a successful marketing program. Today, consumers expect much more from the brands they purchase, and their attention cannot be bought or sold—only earned.

We have found that there are generally three categories of meaningful marketing, which in turn correspond to the types of needs that people seek to fulfill:

- **Meaningful solutions.** Meaningful solutions advertising includes valuable information, incentives, and services. Folgers provides free samples of its new flavors, and Bank of America educates its customers on how to avoid banking fees.
- **Meaningful connections.** Meaningful connections include entertaining experiences that people can share with others. Burger King created a set of branded Xbox games, and Häagen-Dazs launched a contest for consumers to create its next flavor.
- **Meaningful achievements.** Meaningful achievements help consumers improve themselves, their families, and the world. Home Depot classes help people remodel their homes, and Pedigree found homes for more than 100,000 shelter dogs.

Programs such as these continuously show both a positive impact on consumers and a strong ROI. Because meaningful marketing is valuable, people are much more likely to spread positive

word-of-mouth. Research suggests that these deep brand engagements drive long-term loyalty. And because most of these programs are valuable assets instead of mere ads, they can literally pay off. For example, Sam Adams charges $30 for its specially designed beer glasses, and Kraft receives $.99 for each download of its iFood application at the iPhone store.

Aside from serving as a path to survive the shift in consumer media habits and drive a positive return on investment, meaningful marketing makes individuals and organizations feel better about the work they do every day. Studies show that people who are proud of their work are more loyal and productive.

Although the new empowered consumer is upsetting the old advertising models and forcing nearly every business to fundamentally change its practices, the shift to marketing with meaning offers a promising path toward greater sales, unprecedented loyalty, and the kind of work of which we all can be proud.

Courtesy of Bob Gilbreath.

Courtesy of Brunner and Cub Cadet.

The ZTT Zero-Turn Tractor. *Cub Cadet* YOU CAN'T GET ANY BETTER™

EXHIBIT 7.1

When would be a good time of year to run this ad?

the 1960s, a number of other media specialists opened for business, including Western International Media in 1966 and SFM Media in 1969. These early independents concentrated on television, which had the most negotiable rates and was the major medium for most national clients. The premise of these companies was that their media experts could obtain better commercial rates than could be obtained through full-service agencies, which often concentrated on creative services.

Although major advertising agencies took exception to this claim, the idea of breaking out the media function as a separate business has become an important reality during the past decade. With the increased focus on the media function, there are two major areas of disagreement:

■ *Where media planning (as contrasted with media buying) should take place.* Some independent media firms have control of the overall media function including both planning and buying. In other cases, firms only execute the media plan provided by an agency or client. Some argue that by divorcing planning strategy from buying tactics you lose many of the efficiencies promised by the new emphasis on media.

■ *The degree of coordination between the creative and media strategies.* Some agencies that have unbundled their media departments are now having second thoughts about this trend. Many who had separate units for traditional media planning and interactive or digital media services have moved to combine these units for more seamless delivery of media services to clients. With the media selection as the driver in some cases of the creative strategy, it is difficult to imagine that the creative department can be far-removed from the media planning experts.

The concept of a totally unbundled media department is a core issue for many agencies. Historically, advertising agencies have promoted themselves to prospective clients on the basis of their being able to offer a complete menu of advertising services. Creative strategy and execution; account management and interface with a client's marketing department; and media research, planning, and placement could all be handled within a single agency. Until the late 1980s, most agency reputations were determined by creative expertise and the number of award-winning advertisements and commercials they produced. Media departments (and the few independent media-buying firms that existed) were generally regarded as ancillary functions to the creative departments.

However, a number of factors changed the role of media and eventually led to the era of unbundling:

1. *Integrated marketing.* As clients began to view advertising as only one element in a complex marketing communication program, they began to see that advertising agencies were not the only source of communication expertise. To gain specialization in diverse areas, large companies often hired public relations firms, sales promotion agencies, and direct-response companies, in addition to their advertising agencies. As clients became comfortable dealing with a number of communication agencies, it was natural that they would look to specialization within the advertising function—such as unbundled media-buying companies.

2. *Cost factors.* As the cost of media time and space escalated, clients paid more attention to the media-buying function. Clients were demanding greater cost efficiencies, better identification of narrowly defined target markets, and accountability of media expenditures.

   The primary problem of achieving media cost efficiencies is that the goal of low cost is largely contradictory to the current move toward specialized media. Until a few years ago, advertisers were faced with a limited number of media choices. In an environment controlled by a few mass circulation magazines, dominance by three major networks, and largely monopolistic daily newspapers, advertisers sought to reach as many people as possible, even when the strategy carried high waste circulation. In today's world of fragmented media with much smaller but homogeneous audiences, advertisers are routinely paying much more for each person reached than they did only a few years ago.

3. *Globalization.* As clients began to market throughout the world, the expertise and demands on agency media departments grew exponentially. Major clients recognized that without strategic media planning, global brands could not achieve worldwide recognition and dominance no matter how well the creative function was executed.

4. *Complexity of the media function.* Media planning has moved light-years away from the days of dominance by mass circulation media. Large corporations such as AT&T and Procter & Gamble have invested advertising dollars in a diversified media schedule including the Internet, numerous niche cable networks, and prototype interactive media on an experimental basis. In addition, companies are demanding that this advertising be monitored and coordinated with event marketing opportunities, sales promotion, and public relations. Often, there is a significant role for media planning in the execution of these programs. This type of expertise requires a much greater level of knowledge and specialization than can be provided by a traditional media department.

5. *Profitability.* In addition to the benefits that unbundling accrues to clients, it also has added a profit center for the agencies engaging in it. Now agencies can compete for clients' media accounts even when another agency handles the creative side. Unbundled companies such as MediaCom, Starcom MediaVest Group, and ZenithOptimedia are playing a significant role in the media plans of major advertisers. Only a few years ago, the clients being served by these independent media buyers would have been handled by full-service agencies such as JWT, FCB, and Leo Burnett, all of which have unbundled their media departments (see Exhibit 7.2).

Unbundling has given media executives a greater role in the overall planning of advertising strategy. It also has highlighted the importance of media as part of the advertising mix. It is obvious that, in a world of fragmented audiences and niche media, media decisions will continue to occupy a primary position in advertising planning. Advertisers increasingly realize the wasted effort and money in delivering even the most creative messages to the wrong audience.

Media Specialist—2008 Estimated Revenue		
Rank	Agency	U.S. Revenue 2008 ($ millions)
1	OMD Worldwide [Omnicom (OMG)]	$216,700
2	Starcom USA[1] [Publicis (SMG)]	179,300
3	Mindshare Worldwide [WPP (Group M)]	176,200
4	Mediaedge:cia [WPP (Group M)]	175,400
5	MediaVest USA[2] [Publicis (SMG)]	134,600
6	Zenith Media USA [Publicis ZOG)]	129,600
7	MediaCom WPP [Group M]	121,900
8	Carat [Aegis Group (Aegis Media)]	109,600
9	Universal McCann [(Interpublic (Mediabrands)]	102,100
10	Initiative [(Interpublic (Mediabrands)]	78,900

[1] Starcom USA including Tapestry
[2] MediaVest USA including MV42

Source: Reprinted with permission from the April 27, 2009, issue of *Advertising Age.* Copyright, Crain Communications Inc. 2009.

EXHIBIT 7.2

World's Top Media Specialist Companies by Worldwide Billings in 2008

What are professionals at media agencies looking for when hiring people? According to Jeff Totaro, managing partner at Americas Region at MediaCom, there are five areas of expertise that MediaCom looks for when hiring media/communication professionals:

- *Market analysts* who can identify business and marketing growth opportunities
- *Strategic insight planners* who can develop consumer insights
- *Communication/media planners* who understand all forms of consumer communication
- *ROI analysts* who can set measurable objectives, evaluate results, and make recommendations to improve ROI
- *Media buyers/optimizers* who are skilled at negotiating media opportunities for clients.

In larger offices, a media agency may hire separate individuals to handle these functions. In smaller offices, the agency may look for individuals who possess abilities in all or most of these areas of expertise.

Mr. Totaro also states, "I think strong media education as part of a robust marketing/advertising program is absolutely critical to the industry." Sound exciting?!

Basic Media Strategy

Traditionally, media planners used a *building block strategy* to develop a media schedule. Keeping in mind cost efficiencies, they started with the medium that reaches the most prospects and worked down to those that reach the smallest portion of the audience. In the past, the first or second "blocks" were relatively easy to determine. National advertisers often used network television or magazines as the dominant medium. The media planner then considered other vehicles to reach smaller audience segments.

As mentioned earlier, the media options available to supplement an advertiser's primary vehicles have increased dramatically. The introduction of vehicles such as the Internet, video games, in-store media, guerrilla marketing, and interactive television have significantly altered the job of the media planner. These options also have created new ways to view the media function and media buying. Media planners are forced to think beyond costs in developing plans. When dealing with these specialized media, planners must consider factors such as additional weight against prime prospects, ability to deliver a communication message in a unique manner, and the prestige of a medium that may outweigh low audience delivery. Increasingly, media planners are examining qualitative factors of the media such as the communication interactions between the audience and the individual media.

When OMD designed a campaign to launch the second season of *Gossip Girl*, they used their understanding of the fact that the young female audience of the show doesn't simply watch television but also tends to multitask while doing so. OMD allowed the audience to sign up to receive real-time text messages on their mobile devices from the *Gossip Girl* narrator during the season's opener. This novel idea brought new viewers to the show, increased hits to the show's web site, and spurred buzz about the show on the Internet.[5]

Historically, the advertising process began with development of broad marketing and advertising strategies, moved to creative execution, and finally to media placement, which was often viewed as simply a channel for creative messages. Today, that notion has changed in some fundamental ways:

1. *Qualitative factors of media.* Media planners are increasingly working with account planners and/or the creative team to understand the qualitative core attributes of each medium to their target audience. These core values interact with advertising messages to enhance or diminish the advertising.

   For example, newspapers are about information, television scores better as an emotional medium, and direct mail is about personalization. The brand message is likely to work best when it is not in conflict with these qualitative factors.

   The experienced media buyer must be able to look beyond personal media preferences to determine the media vehicles that will best reach prospects. A network television spot might be needed or the best ad placement may be a stock car carrying a sponsor's logo. In any case, media planners must be able to step away from their personal biases and put themselves in the place of a client's prime prospects.

2. *Fading distinctions among media.* Technology is changing the fundamental relationships among media, audiences, and advertisers and creating an environment where distinctions among media are fading. For example, is the delivery of newspaper content over a computer still a "print" medium even though it has video content? Likewise, are text messages available through television still "broadcast" signals?

   In this new environment, media planners must be creative in the use of media vehicles and look less at the distribution system and more at the audiences and communication effectiveness. Even the traditional organizations of agency media departments and media agencies have been realigned to comply with changing media technology.

3. *Media accountability.* Changes in media buying and scheduling are putting pressure on media planners to become more knowledgeable in areas that were not part of their responsibility only a few years ago. As mentioned earlier, at many agencies, job functions such as media planner and media buyer have been replaced by more inclusive titles such as marketing communication specialist or communication planner. The change in terminology is more than semantic; rather, it more accurately reflects both the job function and the expectations for the advertising media executive (see Viewpoint 7.2).

   Research has shown that networks also have distinctive brand identities that appeal to certain demographic and buyer categories. High brand identification for a network does not always translate into short-term viewership. For example, two "brands" among television networks are the Discovery Channel and the Weather Channel, but neither averages 1 percent of the viewing audience. However, it bodes well for these networks as audience fragmentation drives more and more viewers to niche vehicles.

Ultimately, advertising accountability means that businesses want to be able to link their advertising to specific sales of their brands. In other words, they are looking for ROI. As noted earlier, it is difficult to determine exactly what contribution advertising makes to total sales, much less how it influences a single buyer or group of buyers. There are software programs available that try to make this link. Scanner data from the checkout counter are used to attempt to relate television viewing with purchase behavior to estimate the sales volume produced by viewers of specific shows.

4. *Value-added opportunities.* These are incentives offered by the media to advertisers to try to entice them to purchase more advertising time or space in their media vehicles. To provide an extra benefit to advertisers, added value is a way to encourage advertisers to spend more money while providing them with things that have worth to the advertiser. These value-added opportunities can include, for example, product placements, event sponsorships, or cross-media promotions with tickets to sporting events or remote broadcasts.

Value-added opportunities are limited only by the collective imagination of the media planners and the media sales representatives. For example, when Butler, Shine, Stern & Partners was creating a breakthrough campaign for BMW's Mini Cooper in the New York area, they enlisted the assistance of local radio stations to reach their male 35-to-54-year-old target audience. Each of the stations on which advertising was purchased worked together with the agency to develop unique opportunities for their audiences. At one station, local Mini dealers called in to the station. After identifying themselves, the dealers introduced the upcoming song: "This year the Mini turns 50. When Mini was first born, this song was on the charts." During a period of particularly high gas prices, another radio station told listeners the locations of the gas stations with the cheapest gas prices closest to local Mini Cooper dealers. The radio station also highlighted the stations with the cheapest prices on their web site. Both the on-air mentions and the web site included sponsorship identification by Mini Cooper.[6]

Everyday with Rachael Ray magazine offered advertisers some enticing value-added opportunities in conjunction with some of their other media properties. For purchasing a certain amount of advertising space in the magazine, advertisers were given placements on CBS Outernet, the digital out-of-home network that reaches supermarket shoppers and other retail customers. The 30-second video spots were produced for advertisers by the network. The spots look similar to the *Rachel Ray* show and showed celebrity guests using the products.[7]

The need to find ways to better link advertising and product sales becomes even more important as technology continues to change the nature of both mass media and advertising. We are no longer dealing with distinct media vehicles. Rather, there is a trend toward a convergence of media into fewer multimedia sources making traditional media categories obsolete. Consumers increasingly have much greater control over communication outlets, selecting only certain entertainment, information, and advertising messages to attend to. Waste circulation will be limited because, by definition, self-selected communication will only go to prospects.

MEDIA CHARACTERISTICS

Before a media strategy can be planned and implemented, we must have a basic knowledge of the characteristics and functions (both editorial and advertising) of the major media. Faced with a multitude of media choices, one of the most important attributes of a media planner is an open mind. From established message-delivery systems such as network television to the Internet and various nontraditional media, media planners must be able to sort out the media options that best fit the marketing and promotional goals of individual clients.

KLEPPNER VIEWPOINT 7.2

Gilad Kat Director of Communication Planning, MediaCom Tel Aviv

THE EVOLVING ROLE OF COMMUNICATION PLANNING WITHIN THE ADVERTISING PROCESS: FROM SCHEDULING TO RECEPTIVITY PLANNING

Gilad Kat

have a confession to make; I have been working in advertising media planning throughout most of my professional career. Still, many times I have a feeling that people around me (not to mention even my wife . . .) don't exactly know what I do for a living.

But they are not to blame. When I started out, we called ourselves media planners (which more or less fit the tactical role that "media" filled in the advertising process). Later on, at some point, we changed the job title to "communication planner" (which supposedly tried to capture the more strategic, all-encompassing role that "media" was required to fulfill). But lately, I am beginning to hear more and more voices in the industry calling for the return to the old "media planner" job title; this is because of the increasing complexity of the media scene as audiences and media grow more fragmented (no more "mass media"). Are you confused?

When he was asked a couple of years ago in a *Fortune* magazine interview, "What do media agency people do?" Irwin Gotleib, CEO of the WPP's Groupm (the largest advertising media placement company in the world), had a simple answer: "We devise communication strategies for our clients and then we implement them . . . ." I guess that hasn't changed a lot over the years, but what is involved in this task has transformed significantly. Gone are the days when the media were treated merely as the delivery system in the advertising process, sending out to the target audience the message that was formed by the creative department. In fact, given the complexity of the media scene and the multitude of available advertising platforms, we are getting closer to the day when media people will direct the creatives as to the format of messages they need to create.

There is a growing understanding that the media and the message need to go hand-in-hand as part of a holistic

We must remember that advertising budgets are not growing as fast as the increase in media options, so hard budget choices are the rule of the day for agencies and their clients. "In broad terms, we cannot sell more cars, sneakers or boxes of cereal to . . . people as a result of new technology. To fund these new media efforts, marketing executives will need to take a fresh look at the macro-level allocation of budgets as new media forms begin to take on some of the blended attributes of traditional advertising media, promotion, and direct marketing."[8] Future chapters discuss the various strengths and weaknesses of media vehicles from an advertising perspective.

3 Discuss the characteristics of a typical media plan.

4 Discuss relationships between media planning and target marketing.

Putting It All Together: The Media Plan

Knowing the characteristics of the various media is only a necessary first step. Not having a plan to organize media buys into a meaningful whole is analogous to trying to speak a language knowing many words but not knowing the grammar to make sense of it. Media planners must be able to use the distinctive attributes of each medium as part of a sophisticated analysis that leads to a complete media plan for an advertising campaign. Although there is no standard format, we offer a brief outline of a typical plan and then discuss in detail some of the most important elements:

communication product; creativity in advertising is no longer seen as the sole domain of the message creators. Media creativity has gained recognition and importance in recent years with the understanding that the *how* can significantly impact the effect of the *what*. This is also evident in the growing number of international advertising festivals that now feature a media category (including the best of them like the Cannes Lions and the Clios).

Media people are not only invading the creative part of the advertising process but we are also well into the strategic *who* (target audience) analysis realm. When it is no longer sufficient to arbitrarily flash a print ad or TV commercial in front of the eyes of our target audience and expect them to react to the brand's message, we need to better understand how we can reach them at a time when our client's message is more relevant to them.

Enter "receptivity planning." Similar to what advertising strategic planners do when it comes to message planning, we look to perform these tasks for media planning. Put simply, we must determine *when*, *where,* and in what *mind-set* we should reach our prospects, understanding that if we manage to become relevant with our message (based on a specific when, where, and prospect mind-set), the effect of our message will be multiplied. Just as strategic planners are looking for insights into the consumer's life, we also try to generate receptivity insights because insights into the *who* can impact both aspects of the *how*—content and contact.

So when MediaCom Canada tried to reach their "on the go" female, young adult target prospects with a new Covergirl Outlast 24-hour lipstick message, it was only natural to use mirrors in public restrooms and to ask young women via a motion sensor voice chip, "Is your lipstick still on?" at exactly the moment they were checking whether the current choice was performing. Or in Israel, when P&G's relatively new brand, Fairy, was facing the 25-year-long dish washing liquid category leader, we realized that in order to convince these loyal Palmolive users to switch brands, we needed to connect via a public relations driven campaign. The focus was on the traditional Friday night (Shabat) family dinner, where family members were encouraged to call "Mom, come sit with us," urging their perfectionist moms to leave the kitchen and the dishes and join the rest of family visiting with each other after dinner. A Friday-focused campaign coming from Fairy and accompanied by the brand's superior grease-cutting message (which actually means less time with the dishes and more time with family . . .) lead to Fairy becoming and maintaining the new market leadership position. (See Case 12.1 in Chapter 12.)

Receptivity planning is increasingly becoming the main role of the media agency as it is believed to be a key to a campaign's success, and it is, more than any other role, an indicator of how the media function within the advertising process has transformed over the years.

Courtesy of Gilad Kat.

A TYPICAL MEDIA PLAN

I. Marketing Analysis
   A. Fundamental marketing strategy: Sales, share of market, and profitability goals
      1. Demographic characteristics
      2. Lifestyle characteristics
      3. Geographic location
      4. Level of product usage
   B. Product benefits and differentiating characteristics
   C. Pricing strategy
   D. Competitive environment
      1. Number and competitive market share of product category firms
      2. Regulatory and economic situation facing product category
II. Advertising Analysis
   A. Fundamental advertising strategy
      1. Product awareness goals
      2. Target audience(s) advertising weight
   B. Budget
      1. Allocation to marketing communication mix
      2. Allocation by media category
      3. Allocation by media vehicle

III. Media Strategy
   A. Match media vehicles (*Time*, *Monday Night Football*, country music radio, etc.) with target audience media preferences
   B. Creative and communication considerations
      1. Need for product demonstration
      2. Need for complex message
      3. Daypart and/or seasonal requirements
      4. Media compatibility with message themes and competitive considerations
IV. Media Scheduling
   A. Print insertion dates and production requirements
   B. Broadcast allocations and availabilities
   C. Budget allocation for each medium (magazines) and media vehicle (*Sports Illustrated*)
   D. CPM estimates (by total audience, prime prospects, etc.)
V. Justification and Summary
   A. Statement of advertising goals in terms of measurable results
   B. Research plan to measure achievement of advertising goals
   C. Contingencies for media schedule adjustments

No two media plans will have exactly the same components nor will they give the same weight to those media that they include. However, the following section discusses those elements that are found in virtually every plan.

TARGET AUDIENCE

media plan
The complete analysis and execution of the media component of a campaign.

As we have discovered, a **media plan** encompasses a number of factors involving both marketing strategy and advertising tactics. However, nothing is more crucial to the ultimate success of an advertising campaign than the proper identification of the prime target market(s) for a brand. If errors are made at this stage of the advertising process, it is virtually impossible for the advertising program to be successfully executed. The foundation of media planning is the identification of prime prospect segments within the audience of various media. More often than not, this process is aimed not only at finding demographic niches but also at identifying consumer needs and the product benefits that meet these needs (see Exhibit 7.3).

Throughout the media-planning operation, buyers and planners must keep their focus on the total picture of consumer, product, and benefit rather than considering only reaching the target market at the lowest cost. In recent years, the process of evaluating media's contribution to the advertising message (in addition to the message itself) has become a major research track. Advertising researchers are constantly seeking more sophisticated tools to get a clear picture of consumers and the ways in which they interact with media and advertising messages.

In viewing these interactions, media planners are looking at cost efficiencies in more sophisticated ways than in previous years. At a minimum, this broader approach to cost efficiency requires that media plans maximize delivery of prospects as opposed to people or households. Until recently, media planners tended to concentrate on overall audience delivery by various media. The hope was that by reaching the greatest audience at the lowest cost, the media schedule would also reach a fair share of prospects. This strategy worked in the day of mass circulation magazines and network television domination of the airwaves. The most common measure of efficiency during that period was **cost per thousand (CPM)**. We offer a definition of CPM as we begin our discussion of the relationship between cost and targeting prospects. Cost per thousand is a means of comparing media costs among vehicles with different circulations. The formula is stated:

cost per thousand (CPM)
A method of comparing the cost for media of different circulations. Also, weighted or demographic cost per thousand calculates the CPM using only that portion of a medium's audience falling into a prime-prospect category.

$$CPM = \frac{Ad\ cost \times 1,000}{circulation}$$

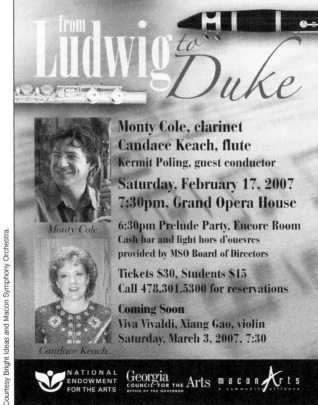

EXHIBIT 7.3

Who Would Be the Prime Prospects for This Advertisement for the Macon Symphony?

If we assume that *People Weekly* magazine has a circulation of 3,691,819 and a four-color page rate of $266,780, then its CPM is calculated:

$$People\ Weekly\ \text{CPM} = \frac{266{,}780 \times 1{,}000}{3{,}691{,}819} = \$72.26$$

Obviously, no medium provides an audience in which every member is of equal benefit to a specific advertiser, that is, with zero waste circulation. Also, keep in mind that there tends to be several readers per copy of every issue of a magazine. Let's assume that our client is a toy manufacturer and only wants to reach women with children 3 years old or younger. In order to measure *People Weekly*'s efficiency in reaching this audience, we might use some variation of the weighted or demographic CPM. Let's look at an example of the weighted CPM.

In this case, we find that from *People Weekly*'s circulation of 3,691,819, there are 1.4 million readers who are between the ages of 18 and 34. Now we calculate the CPM weighted to consider only our target audience rather than the total circulation of the magazine. Therefore,

$$People\ Weekly\ \text{CPM} = \frac{266{,}780 \times 1{,}000}{1{,}400{,}000} = \$190.56$$

You will recall that in Chapter 4 we discussed a number of different means of identifying target markets. In the preceding weighted CPM example, a media planner can substitute any number of lifestyle, product user, or psychographic data for the demographic category we used in the *People Weekly* magazine example. It is important to note that CPM figures are important only as comparisons with those of other media. *People Weekly*'s weighted CPM of $190.56 is of interest only to the extent that it might be compared to another magazine with a CPM of $150.90.

Media planners are constantly attempting to fine-tune cost efficiencies against more useful and targeted client prospects. An important research focus of recent years involves adding a communication component to the CPM mix. Rather than simply measuring the number of prospects who are potential readers or viewers of our advertising, we now add some measure of communication impact and audience awareness to the mix.

Among the primary communication considerations by media planners are the following:

1. *Creative predispositions of the audience.* For example, teens are predisposed to radio in a different way than to print.

2. *Qualitative environment for the message. Car and Driver* magazine reaches readers who are in the proper frame of mind for automobiles and accessory advertisements.

3. *The synergistic effect.* Advertisers seek a combination of media, which results in a communicative effect that is greater than the sum of each one. For example, cell phone manufacturers use outdoor advertising to gain brand recognition, magazines for detailed product information, newspapers for dealer location and price, and television for demonstration and image. The net effect is greater than any single medium used alone.

4. *The creative approach.* Does the need for long copy or quality reproduction require print, even if other media might be more cost efficient?

Intuitively, we can understand that these and other communication components should not be ignored in developing a media plan. However, the conversion of intuition into hard data is not an easy process. In recent years, a great deal of attention has been given to quantifying the value of communication in the media plan. Without going into the complex methodology involved, let's examine a few of the possible weighted CPM adjustments that might be made to take into account communication factors:

- *Probability of exposure to a medium.* Should a magazine reader and a person who passes an outdoor sign be given equal exposure weight?

- *Advertising exposure weights to equalize the probability of an advertisement being seen.* Are the readers of *Time* more likely to see the average message for your product than the viewers of *ABC Evening News*?

- *Communication weights to equalize the probability of an advertising message communicating.* What is the communication impact of a four-color magazine advertisement compared to a television commercial or a web site banner?

- *Frequency of exposure weights in the same medium.* Does the first exposure in a medium have the same or greater value than subsequent exposures?[9]

Research has shown that high levels of audience involvement with a medium are positively related to advertising response. These and other methods of audience communication weighting are attempts to address this relationship in the media-planning process as well as to give accurate estimates to the value of the audiences of various media.

NIELSEN CLARITAS'S POTENTIAL RATING INDEX BY ZIP MARKET (PRIZM)

A shortcoming of many audience analysis methods is that they consider only a single variable. In our earlier *People Weekly* example, we designated women with children under age 3 as our target market for toys. However, we know that within this broad category there are a number of differences. For example, a working woman might purchase toys from an Internet web site. Some women may buy children's toys from salespeople who come to their homes to demonstrate the toys rather than watching television commercials for toys. Likewise, income, education, and other factors might change the purchase behavior of a woman in this general category. Media planners realize that a multivariable approach is often needed to correctly identify a particular target segment.

One of the most innovative methods of segmenting markets on a multivariable basis is the **Potential Rating Index by ZIP Market (PRIZM)** system developed by Nielsen Claritas Inc. PRIZM NE divides the population into 14 social groups and further subdivides these large segments into 66 subcategories (see Exhibit 7.4 a and b). The primary variables for determining these social groups are lifestyle and income.

The PRIZM segments are arranged in descending order of affluence from the "upper crust," who reside in the elite suburbs social group, to the "low-rise living," whose

Potential Rating Index by ZIP Market (PRIZM)
A method of audience segmentation developed by Nielsen Claritas Inc.

EXHIBIT 7.4a
PRIZM Social Groups

Courtesy of http://www.nielsen.com, 15 April 2009.

LIFESTYLE			
URBAN Mega-Cities 18.7% US Population	**SUBURBAN** Cities and Big Towns 18.3% US Population	**SECOND CITY** Suburbs 21.4% US Population	**TOWN & COUNTRY** Exurbs and Towns 39.6% US Population
Urban Uptown	Elite Suburbs	Second City Society	Landed Gentry
Midtown Mix	The Affluentials	City Centers	Country Comfort
	Middle-burbs		Middle America
Urban Cares	Inner Suburbs	Micro-City Blues	Rustic Living

INCOME (vertical axis label)

EXHIBIT 7.4b

PRIZM NE Nielsen Claritas Segmentation Groups

Urban Uptown
04 Young Digerati
07 Money & Brains
16 Bohemian Mix
26 The Cosmopolitans
29 American Dreams

Midtown Mix
31 Urban Achievers
40 Close-in Couples
54 Multi-Culti Mosaic

Urban Cores
59 Urban Elders
61 City Roots
65 Big City Blues
66 Low-Rise Living

Elite Suburbs
01 Upper Crust
02 Blue Blood Estates
03 Movers & Shakers
06 Winners Circle

The Affluentials
08 Executive Suites
14 New Empty Nests
15 Pools & Patios
17 Beltway Boomers
18 Kids & Cul-de-Sacs
19 Home Sweet Home

Middle-burbs
21 Gray Power
22 Young Influentials
30 Suburban Sprawl
36 Blue-Chip Blues
39 Domestic Duos

Inner Suburbs
44 New Beginnings
46 Old Glories
49 American Classics
52 Suburban Pioneers

Second City Society
10 Second City Elite
12 Brite Lites, L'il City
13 Upward Bound

City Centers
24 Up-and-Comers
27 Middleburg Managers
34 White Picket Fences
35 Boomtown Singles
41 Sunset City Blues

Micro-City Blues
47 City Startups
53 Mobility Blues
60 Park Bench Seniors
62 Hometown Retired
63 Family Thrifts

Landed Gentry
05 Country Squires
09 Big Fish, Small Pond
11 God's Country
20 Fast-Track Families
25 Country Casuals

Country Comfort
23 Greenbelt Sports
28 Traditional Times
32 New Homesteaders
33 Big Sky Families
37 Mayberry-ville

Middle America
38 Simple Pleasures
42 Red, White & Blues
43 Heartlanders
45 Blue Highways
50 Kid Country, USA
51 Shotguns & Pickups

Rustic Living
48 Young & Rustic
55 Golden Ponds
56 Crossroads Villagers
57 Old Milltowns
58 Back Country Folks
64 Red Rock America

Courtesy of http://www.nielsen.com, 15 April 2009.

residents live in the most urban and lowest socioeconomic areas of the country. The value of PRIZM groups is that these general segments can be matched with those products and media that members of a particular group are most likely to use. For example, inhabitants of the upper crust are older, have higher incomes, and are more highly educated. They are more likely to drive luxury cars, read the *Washington Post*, watch the *Golf Channel* on television, and shop at Saks Fifth Avenue. By identifying these groups geographically, companies can develop efficient marketing and advertising plans without the wasted circulation of a less-targeted campaign.[10]

Communication Requirements and Creative Elements

As discussed earlier, media planners are interested increasingly in the differential value of various media and the value they add or subtract to specific advertising messages, that is, the engagement these media provide. Another dimension of this process is the manner in which art directors, copywriters, and media planners have begun to engage in the process at the strategic level rather than simply seeing their role as executing someone else's advertising plan.

There is growing recognition by both account supervisors and clients that the earlier in the process that media and creative functions are brought on board, the greater the opportunity for creative input into unique ways to position and advertise a brand. This early involvement also allows a more thoughtful approach to the various problems that will have to be addressed inevitably as the campaign goes from strategy to tactics to execution. Particularly now that **value-added opportunities** are usually an important part of the media-buying and planning process, it is necessary for both the creative and media teams to know what opportunities are most desirable for a brand to pursue.

value-added opportunities Extra things a medium will do for or provide to an advertiser that adds value to the purchase of time or space in the medium.

There is a wide gap between advertising exposure and advertising communication. The greater the input from the account team to both media and creative, the better the communication and coordination. Often, the creative and media teams must make compromises among those media with the best cost efficiencies and those with the best creative attributes to properly communicate the brand's core message. The earlier these decisions can be made, the better it is for media buyers who must negotiate prices and determine availabilities of space and time.

In the past, a major criticism of advertising execution was the fact that media and creative functions did not have enough knowledge of what each other was doing within the campaign strategy. The result, according to critics, was advertising that did not fully use the communicative strengths of the various media vehicles. As mentioned earlier in this chapter, the separation between the creative and media functions seems to have diminished in recent years. Among major advertising agencies, there seems to be a heightened sensitivity that creative/media cooperation is necessary for effective advertising.

In part, this cooperation has been necessitated by the convergence of media outlets, new media technology, and greater opportunities for interactive approaches to audiences. For example, when businesses experiment with Internet advertising, the integration of message, medium, and audience requires different approaches from that in traditional media advertising. The process of planning advertising in new technologies and interactive media demands that all the advertising functions work in concert to make the greatest impact with an audience that is very much in control of the communications process.

Geography—Where Is the Product Distributed?

Geographical considerations are among the oldest factors in buying media. Long before advertisers were knowledgeable about the importance of demographics and target markets, they knew the areas in which their products were distributed and bought as well as those promotional vehicles that best reached those regions. Even in an era of narrowly defined audiences, geography remains a primary consideration of the planner.

Today, the geographic media-planning boundaries are often much smaller than in previous years. Instead of states or regions, the planner may be dealing in ZIP codes and block units or even individuals, especially in direct mail and Internet advertising.

Geographical considerations also are becoming more important as advertisers find that consumers in different parts of the country demonstrate markedly different attitudes and opinions concerning various product categories. Sometimes these geographic differences are obvious—food preferences in the South are distinctly different from those in the Northeast, just as the demand for snow tires is different in Orlando from that in Chicago. Other reasons for differences in brand demand are less apparent.

Adding to the complexity of the media planner's job is the fact that media distribution demonstrates some of the same unpredictable distribution patterns as those of products. Some but not all of these differences can be explained when you look at the age or ethnic makeup of a particular market. For example, according to Nielsen data, Atlanta tends to have different television-viewing patterns than those in the country as a whole. The larger concentration of younger adults and African American viewers can account for some of the differences. These varying patterns of product usage and media preferences must be considered by planners as they develop a media schedule that will reach prime prospects. Planners must begin with the location of buyers and prospective buyers and their concentration in specific areas

Regional differences in product use require many firms to develop a secondary, localized media plan to supplement a national media schedule. National advertisers are increasingly using regional advertising options such as local cable and specialized product-specific publications (for example, restaurant guides). As research data that allow advertisers to define their markets and media technology more narrowly to reach these segments become more readily available, we will see an even greater use of localized media. In some cases, this localization will be supplemental to national campaigns; in other instances, national brands will adopt an area-by-area media schedule as the primary strategy.

Media Tactics: Reach, Frequency, Continuity, and Budget

5 **Understand the tactics used to obtain the desired levels of reach, frequency, and continuity in a media plan.**

The media planner deals with four primary elements in developing the final media schedule:

1. *Reach (also called coverage).* Reach is the number of different people exposed to a single medium or, in the case of a multimedia campaign, the entire media schedule. It may be expressed as the number of prospects or as a percentage of the target audience, but in either case, it represents a nonduplicated audience. For example, if the target audience is 500,000 18- to 24-year-old males and 200,000 are exposed to the advertising, it may be expressed as a reach of 40 percent.

frequency
In media exposure, the number of times an individual or household is exposed to an advertising vehicle for a specific brand within a given period of time.

2. *Frequency.* **Frequency** is the number of times that each person in the audience is exposed to the media schedule. In our earlier example, if the 200,000 men reached in the campaign generated 1 million exposures, the frequency would be 5.0:

$$\frac{1{,}000{,}000}{200{,}000} = 5.0$$

3. *Continuity.* Continuity is the length of time a campaign will run or the length of time that reach and frequency will be measured. In other words, a 20 percent reach and 5.0 frequency might be accumulated over 1 week, 1 month (which is most typical), or 1 year. In evaluating reach and frequency, it is important that the continuity over which these elements are measured be clearly stated.

4. *Budget.* The budget is the major constraint of any advertising plan. The core consideration in all media planning is the budget. Although the relative weight given reach and frequency can be adjusted, the overriding constraint on the total weight of the advertising schedule is the budget.

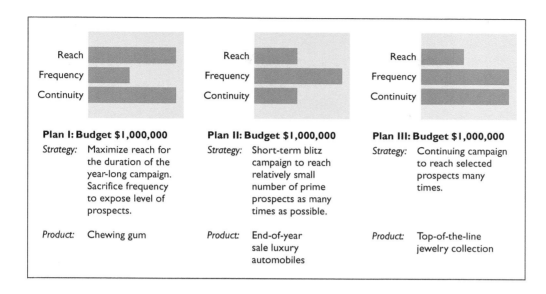

Plan I: Budget $1,000,000

Strategy: Maximize reach for the duration of the year-long campaign. Sacrifice frequency to expose level of prospects.

Product: Chewing gum

Plan II: Budget $1,000,000

Strategy: Short-term blitz campaign to reach relatively small number of prime prospects as many times as possible.

Product: End-of-year sale luxury automobiles

Plan III: Budget $1,000,000

Strategy: Continuing campaign to reach selected prospects many times.

Product: Top-of-the-line jewelry collection

As the media-planning process progresses, the planner moves from general strategy considerations to specific tactics. The planner must determine the most efficient and effective media to achieve previously determined marketing and advertising objectives.

The value of each media vehicle should be measured according to three criteria:

1. The cost of the vehicle
2. The number of target market members or the weighted target market quality of the audience reached by the vehicle
3. The effectiveness of the advertising exposures the vehicles deliver (e.g., the communications or qualitative component)

Reach, frequency, and continuity must be balanced against the demands of a fixed budget. From a practical standpoint, the media planner has control over reach and frequency. The budget is a strategic decision largely determined by the client. Likewise, the length of most campaigns is 1 year. The media planner must also consider the balance between the least-expensive media (efficiency) and those most able to communicate the core message and reach the best prospects (effectiveness). Exhibit 7.5 shows the relationship among the three elements in some typical media strategies.

The tactics associated with reach and frequency are a direct result of the previously agreed-on marketing and advertising objectives and strategies. The decision to emphasize reach or frequency in the communication strategy will most definitely influence the media tactics. A number of tactics can be used when reach or frequency is desired.[11]

Reach Tactics

▪ Prime-time television reaches a large mass audience but is very expensive, so the budget may be expended quickly.

▪ Daily newspapers reach approximately 50 million homes and cover from 30 to 50 percent in many markets.

▪ Large circulation magazines, such as *Better Homes and Gardens* or *Readers Digest,* serve similar functions as network television but with smaller overall audiences.

Frequency Tactics

▪ Cable television, particularly specialized outlets such as the History Channel or the Discovery Channel, can be purchased at relatively low cost and tends to build frequency by reaching the same core viewers over a long period.

- Special interest magazines, as opposed to mass circulation publications, can reach the same audience over several issues.
- Radio listeners tend to have one or two favorite stations and listen up to several hours daily.

Regardless of the specific techniques used by media planners to determine proper levels of reach and frequency, the overriding motive remains the same—to achieve cost efficiency with media dollars. However, a medium is not efficient if it is not first effective at communicating the message to the target audience. One of the most significant changes in media planning in recent years is a move away from the goal of audience accumulation to one of measuring the effectiveness of the audience reached. In other words, advertisers realize that every member of a medium is not equal to every other member, even those with similar demographic characteristics.

The measurement of effective audiences takes various forms. Planners use a number of techniques to exclude waste circulation. For example, they develop estimates of communication impact versus exposure, and they add qualitative variables such as media/message compatibility to their equations. Regardless of how they approach the issue, the overriding motive is to more precisely gauge the value of a particular prospect, medium, or message to the overall measure of advertising effectiveness.

The Media Schedule

media schedule
The detailed plan or calendar showing when advertisements and commercials will be distributed and in what media vehicles they will appear.

One of the final steps in the media-planning process is the development of a detailed **media schedule**. The media schedule is the calendar or blueprint for the media portion of the campaign. It also is the guide for media buyers to execute the media strategy developed by the planner. The schedule must offer in specific detail exactly what media will be bought, when they will be purchased, and how much time or space will be used for each advertisement or commercial. For example, if we decide to purchase space in *Sports Illustrated*, will we use four-color or black-and-white advertisements? Will we use the entire circulation of the publication or one of the numerous geographic editions offered? Which weekly editions will we buy?

The advertising schedule for a national brand may entail dozens or even hundreds of similar decisions. If local broadcast is a primary medium, there may be separate groups of media buyers who negotiate and purchase hundreds of radio and television stations. If cable or broadcast networks are a primary building block of the schedule, senior media executives with extensive television buying experience will negotiate buys that may run into the millions of dollars. Such advertising giants as General Motors and Procter & Gamble may spend an average of more than $2.5 million daily on network television alone. Television media budgets at this level are executed in close coordination among senior marketing executives on the client side, their counterparts at agencies, independent media-buying firms, and, of course, the networks.

Another concern at all levels of broadcast buys, but especially among networks and major affiliates, is time availability. As discussed in Chapter 8, just because you want to buy spots on the *Super Bowl* or *American Idol* doesn't mean they will be available. It is not unusual for a media-buying group to spend several days negotiating for time on a single network program.

flighting
Flight is the length of time a broadcaster's campaign runs. Can be days, weeks, or months—but does not refer to a year. A flighting schedule alternates periods of activity with periods of inactivity.

FLIGHTING

One of the most used advertising scheduling techniques is flighting. **Flighting** consists of relatively short bursts of advertising followed by periods of total or relative inactivity. For example, a company might run a heavy schedule of advertising for 6 weeks and then run only an occasional advertisement to its best prospects during the next 6 weeks. The idea is to build audience perception for the product so that brand awareness continues through periods of inactivity. Done correctly, the advertiser achieves

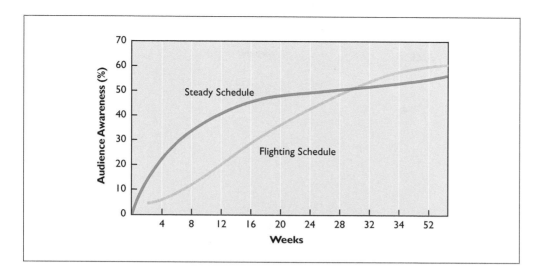

EXHIBIT 7.6

Steady versus Flighting Media Schedules

the same brand awareness at a greatly reduced cost compared to a steady advertising schedule.

The concept is obviously appealing to advertisers that rarely think they have enough funds to reach all their prospects with a consistent advertising program. The problem facing the advertiser is that available research on flighting cannot predict precisely the awareness levels needed to achieve any particular flighting strategy. One thing is certain—advertisers must guard against significant erosion of brand awareness during breaks between flights. Exhibit 7.6 demonstrates the ideal outcome of a properly executed flighting strategy compared to a steady schedule with both using the same advertising budget.

In the steady schedule, audience awareness peaks fairly quickly (after about 20 weeks) and afterward shows little if any increase. The flighting schedule grows much more slowly, but because of budget savings, it is able to reach more prospects and, therefore, actually achieve higher levels of brand awareness in the long term. As we cautioned earlier, an advertiser must be careful to consider the communication component of the media plan. Some media planners think that a flighting plan may sacrifice depth of communication even though minimal awareness may be achieved.

Regardless of the flighting schedule used, the following factors should be considered before using the strategy:

1. *Competitive spending.* How does your plan coincide with primary competitors? Are you vulnerable to competition between flights? (See Exhibit 7.7.)

2. *Timing of flights.* Does the schedule go contrary to any seasonal features found in the product-purchase cycle?

3. *Advertising decay.* Are you spending enough in peak periods to maintain awareness between flights?

4. *Secondary media.* Should secondary or trade media be used between flights to maintain minimal visibility?

A less extreme form of flighting is called *pulsing.* Pulsing schedules use advertising more or less continuously throughout the year but with peaks during certain periods. These peaks coincide with primary sales periods or a special promotion during contests or sweepstakes.

THE PRESSURE OF COMPETITION

Advertising operates in a competitive environment, usually with a number of companies vying for the same consumers. Advertisers must be constantly aware of competitors'

EXHIBIT 7.7

Who Would Be the Likely Competitors for This Zoo?

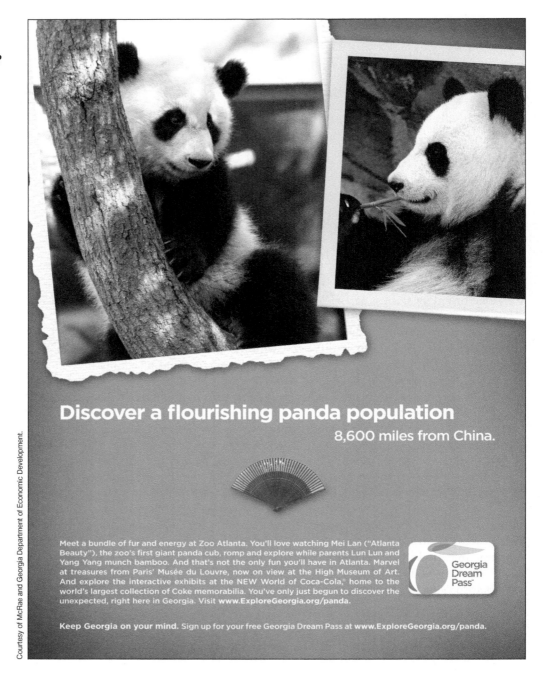

Courtesy of McRae and Georgia Department of Economic Development.

advertising strategy, product development, pricing tactics, and other marketing and promotional maneuvers. The media planner must not only develop an effective campaign for a product but also do so in a way that distinguishes his or her client's brand from the competition.

The media planner also must walk a tightrope between a healthy respect for competitors' actions and blindly reacting to every competitive twist and turn. Rather than operating from a defensive mentality, advertisers should take a practical stance in determining what their marketing and advertising plans can reasonably accomplish and how they meet the inroads of competing brands.

Many advertisers find it extremely difficult to analyze the market environment objectively. One of the primary functions of an advertising agency is to bring an objective voice to the table. Companies sometimes unrealistically judge the value and quality of their products. However, a key to successful marketing is an objective appraisal of both your products and those of the competition from the consumer's perspective.

For example, consumers who are aware of your brand but have never used it are probably satisfied with the product they are currently buying. Both the creative and media plans will have to work hard to give these consumers a reason to switch. In fact, we may have to recognize the fact that some market segments cannot be captured regardless of the quality of our advertising. In such cases, brand switching would be an inappropriate strategy; instead, we might target another market segment with new advertising appeals, creatively positioned products, or both.

A competitive analysis must also consider various media alternatives and how they might be used to accomplish specific marketing goals. For example, a smaller company in a product category may find that television is impractical if it is dominated by advertisers with budgets that are beyond the smaller company's reach. Likewise, we might find that certain media are so saturated with competitors' advertising that it will be difficult to gain attention for our message in the midst of high levels of competitive advertising. Media buyers must be aware of a number of marketing conditions in preparing the plan. The key point is that advertisers should undertake a thorough and candid appraisal of all aspects of the competitive situation. In doing so, a media buyer becomes an integral member of the campaign team.

THE BUDGET

If there is any advertising axiom, it is that no budget is ever large enough to accomplish the task. With the spiraling cost of media during the past several years, media planners view the budget with a growing sense of frustration. In addition, media planners are constantly caught between large media (especially the major television networks) demanding higher and higher advertising rates while their audience sizes are declining and clients demanding more efficiency for their advertising dollars. Because the allocation of dollars to media is by far the largest portion of the advertising budget, it is the media planner who is expected to gain the greatest cost efficiencies.

Advertisers and their agencies have reacted to this cost squeeze by instituting more stringent cost controls and accountability for their advertising dollars. In addition to these stricter controls on media costs, advertisers are constantly looking for alternative methods of promotion and advertising to hold down costs. Already, consumer sales promotion (sweepstakes, coupons, price-off sales, etc.) has passed advertising in terms of total share of promotional dollars. Advertisers also are using media such as cable and first-run syndicated programming to circumvent the high cost of network television. In addition, media planners and buyers will continue to put pressure on the media to provide them with a variety of value-added options. As media continue to fragment, we will see advertisers experiment with nontraditional media vehicles, some of which did not even exist only a few years ago.

In response to increases in advertising costs, advertisers are more precisely defining their prospects to cut down on waste circulation and are negotiating more aggressively with media for time and space. The fragmentation of media and audiences is driving up CPM levels to a point that it is costing more and more to reach selected target audiences.

The media schedule is normally summarized in a flowchart that presents the overall media to be included as well as their audience estimates and costs. Exhibit 7.8 presents an example of a media schedule for a packaged-goods product. The focus of this plan is largely on vehicles that reach women ages 25 to 54.

Sample of Possible Flowchart for a Packaged-Goods Product

TARGET: Women 35–54

TELEVISION

	Sep		Oct			Nov		Dec		Jan					Feb				Mar	TRPs
:30s																				
Prime	10	10	18	18	18	8	8	8												98
Early/Late Fringe	11	11	18	18	18	8	8	8												112
Early Morning	6	6	20	20	20	10	10	10												45
Late Night	5	5	6	6	6	5	5	5												40
Cable	20	20	5	5	5	5	5	5												40
:15s																				
Day	20	20	14	14	14	18	18	18	14	14	14	12	12	12	12	12	12	12	12	312
Cable	39	39	27	27	27	38	38	38	35	35	35	28	28	28	28	28	28	28	28	693
Prime	17	12	12	12	12	15	15	15	14	14	14	12	12	12	12	12	12	12	12	286
News	8	8	8	8	8	8	8	8				8	8	8	8	8	8	8	8	144
Early/Late Fringe	20	20							25	25	25									100
TRPs	136	131	110	110	110	107	107	107	88	88	88	60	60	60	60	60	60	60	60	1,870

TV—Total Cost ($M): $6,295 | $2,438

Digital

Search, Mobile, Lifestyle & Broad Reach Sites

Total Online Cost $(000): $3,000

EXHIBIT 7.8

Media Flowchart for a Packaged-Goods Brand

SUMMARY

The media function is undergoing rapid and significant changes at all levels. The competition for media dollars has never been greater, and the growing importance of new media technology promises to add even more options to the media mix. The trend toward localized media strategies, accompanied by the expansion of global markets, places even greater strains on the research, planning, and execution of media buys. As clients, agencies, and media attempt to make sense out of the mix of traditional and new media opportunities, the role of the media planner takes on even more importance.

While dealing in an unpredictable environment, a number of trends are certain to occupy the media community in coming years:

1. **Developing media/creative strategies to fully use interactive media.** After many decades of the media controlling the communication process, advertisers must quickly adjust to greater audience feedback and control.

2. **Measuring media synergism.** Research technology must account for a complex mix of communication techniques vying for consumer time. The Internet and mobile media online versions of traditional media will require creative planning by media planners.

3. **Controlling media costs and accountability will become driving forces in the media process.** As the costs of reaching narrowly defined audience segments or even individual consumers increase, so does the demand for accountability from clients. What were acceptable levels of waste circulation in a period of mass media and low CPMs are no longer tolerable in a stage of individual marketing.

4. **Evaluating the value and impact of value-added options.** Value-added options have become more important in the media-planning and buying process, requiring planners to develop ways of evaluating the importance and effectiveness of the value-added options offered by the media.

These are only some of the many complex issues facing the media executive of tomorrow. Regardless of what the future brings, it is clear that the media-planning function will occupy an even more important role in an era of targeted advertising. The tension between increased media costs and a search for cost efficiencies by clients will result in planners becoming more willing to try new media or spin-offs of existing media. If there is one sure trend in an otherwise unpredictable area, it is that the advertising media function will continue to look for narrowly defined markets and, with few exceptions, disregard those media vehicles that promise substantial but largely undefined or unmeasured audiences.

REVIEW

1. How has the fragmentation of media audiences affected media planning?
2. In what significant ways has the responsibility of media planners changed during the past decade?
3. Briefly define reach, frequency, and continuity.
4. Discuss the role of value-added options in advertising planning.
5. What effect has unbundling of media departments had on the media planning process?
6. Discuss why media planning is becoming more creative.

CHAPTER 8

Peter Gudella/Shutterstock.

Using Television

F ROM A MARKETING standpoint, television is not a single medium; rather, it is comprised of a number of related broadcast and cable entities that exhibit significant diversity as both advertising and programming sources. From large broadcast events such as the Super Bowl to local cable programming, each of the segments of the television industry has its special characteristics. ▶

CHAPTER LEARNING OBJECTIVES

1. Understand the diversified nature of the television industry.

2. Describe the multiple roles of television as an advertising medium.

3. Describe syndicated rating services and television research methodologies.

4. Discuss the changing position of network television.

5. Identify the various segments of television viewing.

PROS

1. Approximately 99 percent of all U.S. households have a television. Television viewing is particularly popular with many market segments that are primary target markets for advertisers.
2. Television's combination of color, sound, and motion offers creative flexibility for virtually any product message (see Exhibit 8.1).
3. Despite recent audience declines, television remains extremely efficient for large advertisers needing to reach a mass audience. Utilizing selected cable outlets and local broadcast stations, advertisers are able to provide a local or regional component to national television schedules.
4. Government-mandated moves to digital television in 2009 opened more opportunities for advertising and programming.

CONS

1. The television message is short-lived and easily forgotten without expensive repetition.
2. The television audience is fragmented and skewed toward lower-income consumers. Daily viewing time declines significantly as income increases.
3. Shorter spots, some as short as 10 to 15 seconds, have contributed to commercial clutter.

EXHIBIT 8.1

Television offers creative flexibility for product messages.

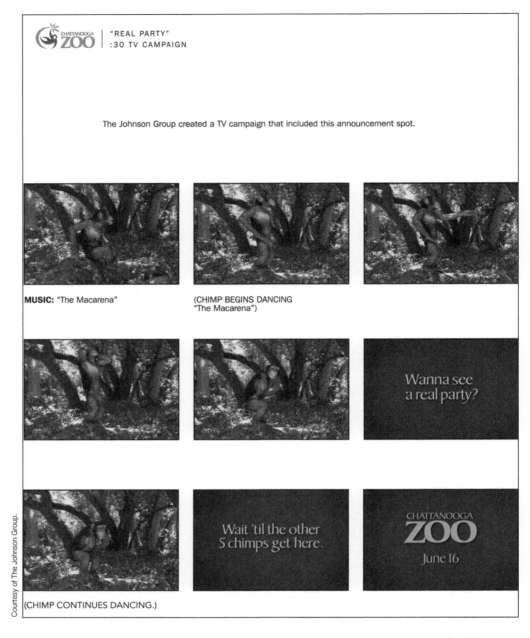

The Johnson Group created a TV campaign that included this announcement spot.

MUSIC: "The Macarena"

(CHIMP BEGINS DANCING "The Macarena")

Wanna see a real party?

Wait 'til the other 5 chimps get here.

CHATTANOOGA ZOO
June 16

(CHIMP CONTINUES DANCING.)

Courtesy of The Johnson Group.

4. With remote control use, channel surfing by viewers, and the VCR and DVR (digital video recorder), the amount of time spent viewing commercials by the average television user has been greatly reduced (see Exhibit 8.2).

Television, so ubiquitous and pervasive in our everyday lives, had very humble beginnings. In the 1920s when Philo Farnsworth, an Idaho teenager, envisioned the transmission of pictures over radio waves, he could not have imagined the medium that he was helping to launch. Unlike many scientists of the time who were experimenting with spinning disks similar to early film technology, Farnsworth was working on an all-electronic system. On September 7, 1927, Farnsworth and his team transmitted a line from one room to another. In his journal entry for the day, he stated:

> The received line picture was evident this time. Lines of various widths could be transmitted and any movement at right angles to the line was easily recognized. This was experiment #12.[1]

And so the age of television began.

Courtesy of Karen King.

EXHIBIT 8.2

Television remote controls make it easy for viewers to channel surf.

For more than 60 years, television has been a major advertising medium. However, at an age when most institutions are maturing, television continues to exhibit dramatic changes and innovations. Television-viewing levels are at their highest, and advertising costs are also high even as audiences spend more time on the Internet than in the past. Television has long been one of the most influential media for many people; it can even influence those who watch little or no television. Television news can set the political agenda; entertainment programming creates fads, such as hairstyles and fashions, and introduces new words and phrases into common use; and television advertising slogans become part of our everyday vocabulary.

In May 2004, 52.5 million people in the United States tuned into the final episode of *Friends*. Many of the viewers had come to identify with Rachel, Ross, Monica, Chandler, Joey, and Phoebe as their friends and wanted to see what the future held for the group. Such is the power of television. It is more than a simple channel of communication. In a real sense, it connects on an emotional basis with the viewing audiences and makes them part of the event they are watching.

The numbers of television viewers are stunning. Approximately 99 percent of households have at least one television set, and average household viewing is about 8 hours daily. In fact, Americans spend more than twice as much time with television than with the Internet or radio, the second and third most used media.[2] As impressive as the sheer numbers are, it is the qualitative dimensions of television as a source of news, entertainment, and advertising that are even more significant.

According to the Television Bureau of Advertising (TVB), television is regarded as the primary source of news by 65 percent of respondents, with newspapers coming in second at less than 14 percent. Obviously, advertisers want to be associated with a medium that not only reaches all segments of the population but also is highly regarded. TVB research found that television's credibility as a news source carries over to positive attitudes toward television advertising. For example, when asked about the image of media advertising, television ranked first as the most authoritative (49.2 percent), most exciting (77.9 percent), most influential (79.1 percent), and most persuasive (69.7 percent).[3]

Over the years, the complexion of television has changed dramatically. Television is moving from a mass medium to a niche medium, similar in some respects to radio and magazines. Beginning with the VCR and moving toward the introduction of a number of interactive formats, audiences have become active participants in the communication process rather than passive receivers. A major catalyst for the introduction of two-way television communication is the Internet. With the growth in Internet use among consumers, it is imperative that television continue to move toward interactivity to combat the appeal of the Internet. Many television network executives and station managers have realized that the Internet presents opportunities—as well as challenges—for broadcasters to expand their audiences.

Television as an Advertising Medium

1 **Understand the diversified nature of the television industry.**

The business of television—and advertising is a major part of that business—is to function as an audience delivery system. Commercial television programming decisions are rarely made on the basis of aesthetics, entertainment value, or which news personality is most credible. Instead, "These are merely the vehicles for pricing and delivering the real product in the television business: eyeballs. . . . [T]elevision is a business for the mass manufacture, collection, and distribution of viewers to advertisers. . . . Not stars and stories, eyeballs and households."[4]

Federal Communications Commission (FCC)
The federal authority empowered to license radio and television stations and to assign wavelengths to stations "in the public interest."

With an annual investment of more than $65.137 billion in all forms of television advertising, it is difficult to imagine the medium without commercials.[5] However, in the earliest days of experimental television, commercials were actually illegal. It wasn't until May 2, 1941, that the **Federal Communications Commission (FCC)** granted 10 commercial television licenses and allowed the sale of commercial time. The first commercial aired on July 1, 1941, during a Dodgers–Phillies baseball game. It was sponsored by Bulova watches and cost $4 for airtime and $5 for station charges. It is estimated that 4,000 people saw it.[6]

For a number of years, television has been adding program options at a growing rate. In the 1970s, a few independent stations offered sports and off-network reruns as an alternative to network affiliate programming. By the 1980s, cable was expanding the number of stations available to the average household, and a limited number of superstations such as TBS and WGN were accessible to most cable homes. However, although the number of channels increased, the variety of programming—most, network retreads—remained relatively stagnant except for sports, which proliferated at a quickening pace. By the 1990s, this situation took a dramatic turn as cable networks realized that in order to sustain their audiences and compete with the major broadcast networks for advertisers, they had to develop original programming.

2 **Describe the multiple roles of television as an advertising medium.**

Led by premium cable services such as Showtime and HBO, cable began to produce a number of original movies and even an occasional series. During the 1990s, major cable outlets such as TNT and USA joined the premium channels in producing a number of made-for-television films. In addition, basic cable networks were producing highly acclaimed programs such as A&E's *Biography*. More important, they were beginning to compete for the prime-time audience long dominated by the broadcast networks. Because both advertisers and audiences were attracted to these new programs, television fragmentation accelerated and became the order of the day. In about 25 years, television moved from basically three program and advertising options to a point where house-holds received more than 50 channels.

With digital capabilities, networks can deliver a number of services to a household over the same conduit. Not only are there more options available but also they can be tailored to the entertainment, news, and buying preferences of individual viewers on an interactive basis. In this interactive environment, viewers can participate in their favorite game shows and order merchandise directly from commercials. The vertical integration and capital resources of conglomerates, such as Disney and Time Warner, make this new interactive media landscape closer to a reality than many believe. It also will change the traditional relationships between the television industry and its advertisers.

Although many of the technological changes are at least a few years in the future, television remains the primary medium for many advertisers. In addition to its high household penetration, television offers creative flexibility not found in any other medium. With its combination of sight, sound, color, and motion, television is equally adept at communicating humorous, serious, or tongue-in-cheek commercials. Television is a 24-hour medium with an ability to reach viewers of every lifestyle from homemakers to third-shift workers. Television also offers a number of advertising formats from the 10-second station ID to the 30-minute, program-length infomercial.

LIMITATIONS OF TELEVISION

COST   Advertising and promotion, regardless of the medium or methods of distribution, are expensive. In recent years, there has been a great deal of publicity about the cost of television and commercials—especially those carried in blockbuster programs such as the *Super Bowl*, *American Idol*, or *Grey's Anatomy*. However, most people would be surprised to learn that even the most costly television commercials are much less expensive than print media on a CPM basis. For example, the average prime-time television commercial has a CPM of about $26 compared to about twice that for a typical daily newspaper.[7] Even with the highest-rated series charging more than $400,000 for a 30-second spot, television is still cost efficient for businesses needing to reach large numbers of people.

As household viewing hours remain fairly constant, the growing number of options for television audiences has created an extremely fragmented audience and generally lower ratings for all segments of the industry. As discussed earlier, this trend will probably accelerate in future years. In the slower economy of 2009, network CPMs in the upfront season actually decreased as advertisers held out for lower rates from the networks.[8] However, network television advertisers know that in spite of high costs and decreases in audience size, there is still no more efficient method of reaching a broadly based consumer market than through television.

However, with the competitive environment for viewers' time and attention, it also is imperative to make attention-getting commercials, which are often the most costly. Consequently, it is important to consider not only the cost of television time but also the production cost associated with commercials. Chapter 19 discusses in detail the process of commercial production. With some network television commercials budgeted for more than $1 million, production expenses are another important cost consideration for any television advertiser.

CLUTTER   Television **clutter** is defined as any nonprogram material carried during or between shows. Commercials account for more than 80 percent of this material with the other time devoted to public service announcements and program promotional spots. In recent years, the issue of television commercial clutter has become a major topic among advertisers and their agencies. There is a great deal of pressure on networks to increase the number of advertising minutes they sell in the highest-rated shows.

clutter
A proliferation of commercials in a particular medium. This reduces the impact of any single message.

According to WPP Group's MindShare media group, network television runs an average of about 15 minutes of nonprogram content per hour.[9] Advertisers are left to wonder if the commercials are as valuable now that there is so much clutter. Consumers may increase their avoidance of commercials if they are annoyed by all of the clutter. "Americans spend an average of four hours a day watching TV, an hour of that enduring commercials. That adds up to an astounding 10 percent of total leisure time; at current rates, a typical viewer fritters away three years of his life getting bombarded with commercials."[10]

Advertisers also point out that not only has the total nonprogram time increased but also the number of commercials has grown with the use of shorter spots. In 1980, almost 95 percent of network television commercials were 30-second spots. By 2008, more than 40 percent of commercial spots were 15 seconds or less.[11] Research has shown that the number of commercials contributes to the perception of clutter even when overall commercial time remains constant.

To try to combat this problem and break through the commercial clutter, some television networks have experimented with reducing the number of commercials and advertisers. They have allowed some advertisers to buy all of the commercial time within a particular program. "American Express Co., for example, sponsored an entire episode of *The West Wing* with a limited number of ads. Nissan North America and Time Warner Inc.'s Warner Brothers movie studio respectively sponsored debut episodes of *Heroes* on NBC and *Smith* on CBS—with limited ads."[12] This experiment represents a return to the days when program sponsorship was common among advertisers.

The Rating-Point System

3 **Describe syndicated rating services and television research methodologies.**

rating point
The percentage of television households in a market a television station reaches with a program. The percentage varies with the time of day. A station may have a 10 rating between 6:00 and 6:30 P.M. and a 20 rating between 9:00 and 9:30 P.M.

Television advertisers evaluate the medium according to the delivery of certain target audiences. In the case of networks and large affiliates, advertisers tend to look for exposure to fairly broad audience segments, such as women aged 18 to 49. Cable networks and some independent stations are evaluated by their ability to deliver more narrowly defined audiences that are both smaller in size and more expensive to reach on a CPM basis but that have less waste circulation.

The basic measure of television is the **rating point**. The rating, expressed as a percentage of some population (either television households or a specific demographic group such as women aged 18 to 49), gives the advertiser a measure of coverage based on the potential of the market. The rating is usually calculated as follows:

$$\text{Rating} = \frac{\text{program audience}}{\text{total TV households}}$$

When ratings are expressed as percentages of individuals, the same formula is used, but the population is some target segment rather than households. For example, if we are interested only in 18- to 34-year-old males, the formula would be

$$\text{Rating} = \frac{18 - 34 \text{ males viewing program}}{\text{total } 18 - 34 \text{ males in population}}$$

A household rating of 10 for a program means that 10 percent of all households in a particular area that have a television set tuned their sets in to that station. Prime-time network programs usually achieve a rating of between 4 and 10.

As we discuss later in this chapter, television advertising is rarely bought on a program-by-program basis. Instead, advertisers schedule a package of spots that is placed in a number of programs and dayparts. The weight of a schedule is measured in terms of the total ratings for all commercial spots bought—the **gross rating points (GRPs)**.

gross rating points (GRPs)
Each rating point represents 1 percent of the universe being measured for the market. In television, it is 1 percent of the households having television sets in that area.

Gross rating points were calculated by multiplying the insertions by the rating. In the case of *All My Children*, the rating was 5.5 × 20 (the number of insertions) = 110 GRPs (see Exhibit 8.3).

Vehicle	Rating	Cost	Spots	GRP
All My Children	5.5	$25,000	20	110
General Hospital	4.5	21,000	20	90
Guiding Light	3.3	19,000	11	33
One Life to Live	4.2	19,500	10	42
Total GRPs				275
Reach – 50.0				
Average Frequency = 5.5				

EXHIBIT 8.3

GRPs measure weight of an advertising broadcast schedule.

Advertisers also use GRPs as the basis for examining the relationship between reach and frequency. These relationships can be expressed mathematically:

$$R \times F = GRP$$
$$\frac{GRP}{R} = F \text{ and } \frac{GRP}{F} = R$$

where R = reach, and F = frequency.

To use these relationships, you must know (or be able to estimate) the unduplicated audience. In the television schedule in Exhibit 8.3, we estimate that we reached about 50 percent of the entire target market and that the average number of times we reached each person in the audience was 5.5. We can check the formulas using the solutions previously calculated:

$$R \times F = GRP \text{ or}$$
$$\frac{GRP}{R} = F \text{ or } \frac{275}{5.5} = 50$$
$$\frac{GRP}{R} = F \text{ or } \frac{275}{50} = 5.5$$

One of the principal merits of the GRP system is that it provides a common base that proportionately accommodates markets of all sizes. One GRP in New York has exactly the same relative weight as one GRP in Salt Lake City. GRPs cannot be compared from one market to another unless the markets are of identical size. However, Exhibit 8.4 shows that the cost of television commercial time varies by city size. Here is an idea of the use of GRPs in two markets, Los Angeles and Boston: The advertiser has to decide how much weight (how many GRPs) to place in his or her markets and for how long a period. This is a matter of experience and of watching what the competition is doing. Suppose the advertiser selects 100 to 150 per week as the GRP figure. Within this figure, the advertiser has great discretion in each market. How shall the time be allocated? Put it all on one station? Divide it among all the stations? What yardstick should be used to decide? The answers depend on whether the goal is reach or frequency.

Look at the hypothetical pricing structure in Exhibit 8.4.

If we buy three prime-time spots in these markets, we would expect to receive 24 GRPs (3 spots × 8 average rating). However, it would be a serious mistake to equate a 24-GRP buy in Los Angeles with the same level in Boston. In Los Angeles, 24 GRPs would deliver 1,344,000 household impressions (0.24 × 5,600,000 HH [households]) at

	TV Homes (000)	Average Cost per Spot	Average Prime-Time Rating
Los Angeles	5,600	$25,100	8
Boston	2,370	9,500	8

EXHIBIT 8.4

Television cost efficiency is measured on a cost-of-audience-delivered basis.

a cost of $75,300 (3 spots $\times$ $25,100 per spot). However, a 24-GRP buy in Boston would deliver 568,800 household impressions at a cost of $28,500. To estimate buys, advertisers often use the **cost per rating point (CPP)** calculation to estimate the cost of a particular schedule they are thinking of buying or a particular spot:

$$CPP = \frac{\text{Cost of schedule or commercial}}{\text{GRPs}}$$

In this case

$$\text{Boston: CPP} = \frac{28{,}500}{24} = \$1{,}187.50$$

$$\text{Los Angeles: CPP} = \frac{75{,}300}{24} = \$3{,}137.50$$

If we make the mistake of comparing GRPs from markets of different sizes, it would appear that a rating point costs more than 260 percent more in Los Angeles than in Boston. However, a rating point represents 56,000 households (1 percent of 5,600,000) in Los Angeles versus only 23,700 in Boston. A rating point in Boston costs $1,950 less than in Los Angeles. However, the advertiser is getting more than 236 percent more households for a 264 percent higher cost in Los Angeles. This means that it is also costing more per person to advertise on television in Los Angeles.

In addition to the problem of intermarket comparisons, the GRP has other limitations. It does not tell us the number of *prospects* for the product who are being reached by a program. Still, the GRP concept does provide a unified dimension for making scheduling judgments.

It must also be remembered that GRPs alone cannot tell how effectively a broadcast schedule is performing. If an advertiser's target audience is women aged 18 to 49, for example, 5 household GRPs may deliver more women in that group than 10 household GRPs will. This, as you would expect, is a function of where the GRPs are scheduled. Five GRPs during a Sunday night movie will almost always deliver many times more women aged 18 to 49 than will 10 GRPs scheduled on a Saturday morning.

Share of Audience

Although the rating is the basic audience-measurement statistic for television, another measure, the **share of audience** (or simply, share), is often used to determine the success of a show. The share is defined as the percentage of households using television that are watching a particular show. Advertisers use share to determine how a show is doing against its direct competition.

Let us assume that the *Good Morning America* show has 5,000 households watching it in a market with 100,000 households. In this case, we know that the *rating* for *Good Morning America* would be 5.

$$\text{Rating} = \frac{\textit{Good Morning America} \text{ viewers}}{\text{total TV households}} \times 100 = \frac{5{,}000}{100{,}000} \times 100 = 5$$

The *share* calculates the percentage of *households using television (HUT)* that are tuned to the program. Let us assume that of the 100,000 households, 25,000 are watching television. In this case, the share for *Good Morning America* would be 20:

$$\text{Share} = \frac{\textit{Good Morning America} \text{ viewers}}{\text{HUT}} \times 100 = \frac{5{,}000}{25{,}000} \times 100 = 20$$

It is understood that both the rating and share of audience are expressed as percentages (hence, the factor of 100 in the equations). Therefore, we do not use decimal points to refer to the measures in the example as "5 percent" and "20 percent." Instead, we say that the rating is 5 and the share is 20.

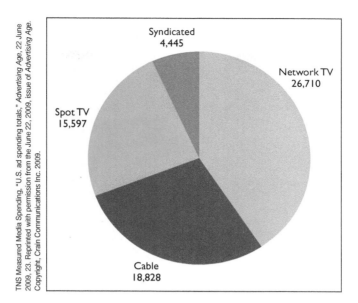

TNS Measured Media Spending. "U.S. ad spending totals," *Advertising Age*, 22 June 2009, 23. Reprinted with permission from the June 22, 2009, issue of *Advertising Age*. Copyright, Crain Communications Inc. 2009.

Syndicated
4,445

Network TV
26,710

Spot TV
15,597

Cable
18,828

EXHIBIT 8.5

Advertising Spending by Types of Television, 2008 (in million $)

The Many Faces of Television

Although the average viewer probably makes little distinction among cable, premium cable, broadcast networks, syndicated programs, daytime, or any of the other permutations of television, they are, in many respects, unique marketing vehicles. Each of the various segments of the medium has its own advertising pricing structure, programming, target audience, and rating expectations. Exhibit 8.5 shows how advertising spending is distributed among the different types of television.

Except for the fact that they appear on the television screen, there is little similarity between the Travel Channel and the Cartoon Network or between Home Shopping Network and MTV. Television has become primarily an individual-user medium, with the majority of the audience viewing alone during most dayparts. The use of television as a personal medium is further demonstrated by the number of multiset households and the increased viewing of television programming on Internet sites such as Hulu. com (see Exhibit 8.6).

As television technology continues to evolve, the medium will demonstrate even more diverse advertising opportunities. To some viewers, it will be primarily a source of immediate information such as stock quotes; for others, it will remain the primary entertainment outlet; and, as we are increasingly a wireless society, for still others, it will be an out-of-home companion serving multiple purposes.

The process of media planning and buying of television has become extremely complex. Besides the proliferation of programming options, you may recall from Chapter 7 that there is often a variety of value-added options for agency media experts to consider. This section examines the many aspects of this extremely complex medium, which occupies so much of our time and advertisers' dollars.

Network Television

In the 1987–88 television season, *The Cosby Show* was the top-rated program with an average audience share of 44. That same year, *Hunter*, a predictable police drama, had a respectable 19 rating with an average share of 34. Now, fast-forward 10 years to the top-rated, award-winning *Seinfeld*, a show that many people would regard as a cult classic. In reality, *Seinfeld* finished behind the largely forgotten *Hunter* in average audience share for almost its entire run. Exhibit 8.7 shows the top network programs over the

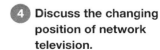

4 Discuss the changing position of network television.

EXHIBIT 8.6

More and more consumers are watching their favorite television shows on the Internet.

Courtesy of Gigi and Nick.

years. Note that the top-rated show in the 2008–2009 season, *American Idol*, had a rating that was less than half the rating size of *Gunsmoke*, the top-rated show in 1960–61, and less than a third as large as the top-rated show in 1950–51, *Texaco Star Theater*.

Although much has been written about the decline of network television numbers, why should anyone be surprised? Given the proliferation of television options, it would be an impossible task for **networks** to maintain earlier audience levels. As the television landscape is peppered with competition from the Discovery Channel to the Disney Channel, it is amazing that the big four (ABC, CBS, FOX, and NBC) have sustained the share levels they currently enjoy. This section discusses some of the key elements necessary to understand television networks as an advertising medium.

networks

Interconnecting stations for the simultaneous transmission of television or radio broadcasts.

EXHIBIT 8.7

Historical Ratings

Top-Ranked Regular
Program Series Based on Household Ratings

Year	Program	Network	Rating (Household)	Share (Household)
1950–51	*Texaco Star Theatre*	NBC	61.6	81
1955–56	*$64,000 Question*	CBS	47.5	65
1960–61	*Gunsmoke*	CBS	37.3	62
1965–66	*Bonanza*	NBC	31.8	48
1970–71	*Marcus Welby MD*	ABC	29.6	52
1975–76	*All in the Family*	CBS	30.1	44
1980–81	*Dallas*	CBS	31.2	52
1985–86	*The Cosby Show*	NBC	33.8	51
1990–91	*Cheers*	NBC	21.6	34
1995–96	*E.R.*	NBC	22.0	36
2000–2001	*Survivor*	CBS	16.9	27
2005–2006	*American Idol*	FOX	17.7	NA
2008–2009	*American Idol*	FOX	16.4	NA

Source: 1950–1996 data: *Nielsen 2000 Report on Television*; 2000–2001 data: Nielsen Media Research, www.chez.com/fbibler/tvstats/ recent_data 2002; 2005–2006 data: www.nielsenmedia.com, 5 January 2007; 2008–2009 data: www.neilsenmedia.com, 30 June 2009. Copyrighted information of The Nielsen Company, licensed for use herein.

CLEARANCE AND AFFILIATE COMPENSATION

Networks are comprised of local stations that contract to carry network programming. The exceptions are the so-called O&O (owned-and-operated) stations of the networks. These stations (e.g., KABC in Los Angeles and WNBC in New York City) are located in a few major markets and make up a small minority of any network's station lineup. The four major networks have affiliates in most television markets. The newest networks, WB and UPN, have affiliation agreements with smaller stations in most markets. In fact, some of the CW affiliates (formerly WB and UPN) are secondary affiliates, which means they belong to another network and air CW shows on a delayed basis, often during non-prime-time hours.

Networks sell national advertising on the basis of station clearance. Network **clearance** is expressed as the percentage of the network's station lineup that has agreed to clear their schedules for network programming. In the case of the top four networks, clearances normally run close to 100 percent. The new networks often express their clearance rates as a percentage of the U.S. population that is potentially reached. Clearance rates are crucial to the economics of the smaller networks. For example, if a network fails to get clearance in New York City, it is shut out of 10 percent of the total national audience. Until a network reaches 70 percent potential coverage, it is usually not considered a national program by major advertisers.

Another primary factor in the relationship between networks and affiliates is station compensation. **Compensation** is a system whereby networks share advertising revenues with their affiliates in return for using local station time for their programs. At one time, station compensation was a major profit item for most stations. However, as the cost of network programming has increased and audience levels have fallen, the relationship between networks and stations over compensation has become contentious. Basically, networks have taken the position that the value of a station's local advertising spots is in large measure a result of the audience gained through popular network programming. Consequently, the networks are demanding that their affiliates share in the cost of this programming. For their part, the stations contend that without availability to stations, there would be no networks. In the future, stations may find that rather than being a source of profit, affiliation may be an expense. Regardless of the form the compensation debate takes, the root causes of costly programming and falling revenues will make compensation a continuing issue for discussion between networks and their affiliates.

clearance
The percentage of network affiliates that carry a particular network program.

compensation
The payment of clearance fees by a television network to local stations carrying its shows.

NETWORK OWNERSHIP

Despite the fact that the major television networks are very large companies with revenues in the billions of dollars, each of them is a relatively small part of a major conglomerate. The network may not even be the most profitable media holding of the corporation. For example, the Walt Disney Company owns the ABC Television Network and a number of local affiliated stations. It also owns, among many other holdings, ESPN's television and radio networks and its magazine; Lifetime and A&E networks; and, of course, the Disney Channel. In addition, the company owns theme parks, as well as Marimax, Touchstone, and Disney film studios and production facilities. A similar situation exists for each of the other networks.

The accelerated pace of acquisitions and mergers among media companies has raised some troubling questions in a number of quarters. For example, will the concentration of broadcast and cable ownership restrain the free flow of news and information, especially in the case of stories that relate to their parent companies? Will a lack of competition among media affect the economic marketplace in setting advertising rates? Will television content be restricted if networks are pressured to buy programming from production studios owned by the same parent company? Some have argued that Congress should prohibit companies from owning both the means of distribution (a station or network) and the production of content (a program production studio).

This is unlikely to happen, but advertisers are concerned with the consequences of a marketing environment dominated by a few companies.

NETWORK COMMERCIAL PRICING AND DECLINING AUDIENCE SHARES

As we noted earlier, television is in the business of delivering prospects to advertisers. The networks find themselves in the difficult position of encountering higher and higher program costs at a time when audience levels do not justify significant commercial price increases. Prime-time spots vary according to ratings and audience demographics, but an average 30-second commercial cost was less than $125,000 in 2008 on the four major networks.[13] At the high side, a spot on shows such as *Monday Night Football* and *American Idol* may be more than $400,000, whereas ABC's *Supernanny* with its lower ratings will bring about $82,000.[14]

In the past few seasons, network advertising revenues have grown significantly. However, media buyers complain that these increases are a result of more commercials (the clutter problem) and unjustified rate increases that have resulted in higher CPMs. The networks are often in a dilemma, caught between advertisers clamoring for better cost efficiencies and stars of top-rated series demanding higher salaries. A further complication is that as popular shows age, there is an inevitable slippage in ratings. However, each year the stars earn higher salaries and networks are reluctant to cancel even their more expensive series, fearing that the odds are slim that potential replacements would fare as well.

BLOCK PROGRAMMING

Network executives not only have to choose programs that will appeal to a large segment of households and at least a handful of major advertisers but also their work is made even more difficult by the fickle television audience. Research has consistently shown that shows do not stand on their own but instead are greatly influenced by the programs on directly before them, called the *lead-in*, and the total daypart schedule, called a *block*.

The importance of lead-ins can be seen in the investment local stations make to schedule the most popular programming they can buy prior to their early evening news shows. The demand for strong news lead-ins is, in large measure, responsible for the enormous prices paid for off-network syndicated programs. The same principle is at work in building a network schedule. Programmers strive to make sure that individual programs will attain high ratings, but just as important, they want to ensure that the block will work together to attract consistently high audience levels.

Network programmers are very aware of the ebb and flow of audiences as they move from one program to another. The pricing of new network shows depends, in large measure, on their placement in the network schedule. Advertisers know that programs that follow proven hits have a high probability of success. An even better situation is the occasional new show that is scheduled between two popular returning programs. This is called a *hammock position*—the analogy being that the new program is placed between two trees (hit shows). Once a new show is on the air, it is judged by how it keeps the audience from its lead-in and sustains the strength of the block.

NETWORK TELEVISION ADVERTISING CRITERIA

Clients and their advertising agencies apply a variety of criteria in determining if, and to what extent, they will use network television spots. However, buying decisions are largely determined by three factors: demographics (demos), CPM, and demand by advertisers.

- *Demos.* Whereas at one time households were the unit of measure, today television advertisers place major emphasis on the demographics of television audiences. This change in criteria has altered the manner in which networks choose shows and the pricing structure for advertisers. For most advertisers, the makeup of the audience of potential network buys has become more important than the size of the audience. Of course, both advertisers and the networks demand that a show attain a certain minimum rating, but the price for shows with favorable demographics usually exceeds what their ratings alone would bring.

■ *CPMs.* Although most advertisers are seeking favorable demographics and are willing to pay a premium to get them, other advertisers are driven primarily by cost considerations. Of course, no advertiser ignores the audience profile of its advertising buys. However, there are a number of advertisers who evaluate cost efficiencies and CPM levels on an equal basis with audience demographics. Advertisers of widely distributed package goods are more likely to take this approach than are advertisers for a product with more limited appeal. These companies take the position that, within certain broad audience criteria, they gain some benefit from virtually any audience because their product usage is so universal.

■ *Demand.* The third criterion that determines the relationship between networks and advertisers is the demand for certain programs. Of course, demand is a function of both demographics and CPMs, but there are also qualitative factors—for example, an association with a special event such as the final episode of *American Idol* or with a star who has unique appeal to a particular target market such as Oprah Winfrey— that create a pricing structure over and above the objective numbers.

AVAILS   Next Thanksgiving, begin to take note of the number of pages in your favorite magazines. Some November and December issues of popular publications swell to catalog size as advertisers compete for holiday sales. After the first of the year, these same publications will be very thin, with many advertisers standing on the sidelines after spending a sizable percentage of their budgets during the previous 2 months.

The broadcast media do not have the advantage of flexible advertising inventory. Every day, 365 days a year, each local station and network must sell more than four hundred 30-second spots. Television advertisers, like their print counterparts, want to heavy-up in peak buying seasons and on the most popular shows. Combined with the problem of high demand and finite network commercial time is the practical restraint that this amount of time cannot be sold on a spot-by-spot basis.

Networks must ration prime commercial spots among their major advertisers. The availability (called *avails* in network jargon) problem is solved, in part, by combining top-rated avails with less popular ones as advertisers buy packages of commercial time from each network. Whether an advertiser will gain availability to a top-rated show depends largely on the company's total advertising investment on that network. Package plans allow the networks to work with agencies to place commercials across their entire schedule, with the understanding that each advertiser will have to accept some lower-rated (but demographically acceptable) spots in order to obtain some very desirable spots.

UP-FRONT AND SCATTER BUYS   Each May, major advertisers begin the negotiation process to buy commercials on the network prime-time lineup for the coming fall season. This is the so-called **up-front buying** season in which most prime-time spots are bought. Usually, in a period of only a few weeks, advertisers will purchase prime-time commercials worth several billion dollars. The up-front period opens with each network previewing its shows, followed by the actual negotiation for time. There is a separate negotiating period for cable and syndication. At one time, the up-front period consisted primarily of negotiation between major agencies and the three major networks. Today, the up-front buying process has become much more complex with a number of new players and different approaches by advertisers. See Exhibit 8.8 for a list of the top 10 advertisers on network television.

The up-front season is followed by a second phase known as **scatter plan** buys.[15] Scatter plans are usually bought on a quarterly basis throughout the year. They are

up-front buying
The purchase of network television time by national advertisers during the first offering by networks. The most expensive network advertising.

scatter plan
The use of announcements, over a variety of network programs and stations, to reach as many people as possible in a market.

EXHIBIT 8.8

Top 10 Network Television Advertisers, 2008 (in million $)

Network TV

Rank	Marketer	2008
1	Procter & Gamble Co.	$985.6
2	AT&T	751.3
3	General Motors Corp.	704.9
4	Verizon Communications	564.8
5	Ford Motor Co.	455.7
6	Sprint Nextel Corp.	433.6
7	Toyota Motor Corp.	407.3
8	GlaxoSmithKline	407.1
9	Johnson & Johnson	402.8
10	Timer Warner	370.2

Source: TNS Media Intelligence, "Top U.S. advertisers in 10 media," *Advertising Age*, 22 June 2009, 18. Reprinted with permission from the June 22, 2009, issue of *Advertising Age*. Copyright, Crain Communications Inc. 2009.

designed for larger advertisers that want to take advantage of changing marketing conditions or, more often, for smaller advertisers that are shut out of up-front buys. Generally, scatter plans will sell at a higher CPM than up-front spots because there is less time inventory and smaller advertisers don't have the leverage to negotiate the CPM levels of huge network advertisers.

There also are up-front markets for other dayparts, children's programming, and prime-time cable. Early morning and midday programming each has its own up-front season, special advertising categories, and pricing structure. It is important to understand that network avails are often largely filled through the up-front seasons in each daypart.

NEGOTIATION   As mentioned in the previous section, negotiation is the key to network buying. Because each advertising package is unique to a particular advertiser, there are no rate cards for network television advertising. During the past several years, network rate negotiation has undergone a number of changes. The decline in network rating and share levels has created a more contentious atmosphere. But the fact is that network television, despite decreasing audiences, remains the best way to reach a mass market.

Advertisers are concurrently negotiating for time across a number of television options. As we mentioned, up-front negotiation still takes place among more or less discrete television formats (e.g., daytime, prime time, broadcast networks, cable networks). However, a number of media planners are looking to a diversity of options to reach particular target markets. As they negotiate network time, they are considering the cable, syndication, and even Internet markets that will be used as supplements to the network or to keep overall costs down. With billions of dollars at stake, agencies and their clients know that an extremely small difference in the cost of a rating point has great significance when a large national advertiser is involved. In addition, they are often seeking value-added opportunities across multiple media properties owned by a network.

make-goods

When a medium falls short of some audience guarantee, advertisers are provided concessions in the form of make-goods. Most commonly used in television and magazines.

MAKE-GOODS   One of the major elements of network negotiation concerns **make-goods**. As the name implies, make-goods are concessions to advertisers for a failure to achieve some guaranteed rating level. Make-goods are normally offered on the basis of total GRPs for an advertiser's television advertising schedule. That is, when the advertiser fails to achieve a certain agreed-on cost per point, the make-good provisions are initiated. At one time, make-goods were part of most advertising negotiations—they were always part of the up-front market. Make-goods usually take the form of future commercials to make up for a shortfall in ratings. Monetary refunds are virtually never given as part of a make-good plan.

The new competitive environment has changed the make-good situation dramatically. With most network shows achieving sub-10 ratings, the make-good has become a major negotiating point with agencies and a high-risk endeavor for networks. If a prime-time network schedule includes a number of low-rated or canceled shows, it may well mean the network will give up a significant portion of its inventory during the winter and spring to accommodate make-goods. In part because of make-goods, networks are reluctant to support low-rated shows. Each season, there are a few shows that are canceled after one or two airings to prevent a significant demand for make-goods.

Spot Television

When national advertisers buy from local stations, the practice is known as **spot television** or spot buys. The term comes from the fact that advertisers are spotting their advertising in certain markets as contrasted to the blanket coverage offered by network schedules. The primary disadvantages of spot television are that it requires a great deal more planning and paperwork than network because each market must be bought on a one-to-one basis and it is more costly on a CPM basis than network buys.

Spot advertising is an extremely competitive market. Not only are more than 1,300 local stations competing for spot dollars but also the several thousand local cable outlets are becoming important players with many spot advertisers. Broadcast stations face a number of new competitive options from wireless and Internet services and other forms of local, interactive media. Large increases in spot dollars are not projected in the near future as advertisers divert budgets to other forms of local television.

Today, most spot advertising is placed through station **representatives (reps)**. The rep is paid a commission by the station based on the time sold. A good sales rep is both a salesperson and a marketing specialist for advertisers. The rep must be able to show a national advertiser how a schedule on WSB-TV in Atlanta or WTNH-TV in New Haven, Connecticut, will meet a national company's advertising objectives.

Rep firms may have 100 or more station clients on a noncompetitive basis. Reps go to agencies and advertisers to convince them that the markets in which their client stations broadcast are prime sales areas for their brands. To make the purchase of spot buys more efficient, a rep will allow advertisers to buy all or any number of stations it represents. Because the idea is to provide one order and one invoice, it offers similar advantages to a network buy. However, the stations sold through a rep are not linked in any way other than being clients of a particular rep firm. These station groups are called **nonwired networks**. The commercials bought on a nonwired network, unlike a real network, are not necessarily broadcast at the same time or on the same programs. The nonwired concept is simply a means of providing buying efficiency and convenience for spot advertisers.

The rep's role in the spot market is undergoing changes as the move to consolidation in the television industry accelerates. For example, at one time, a single owner could only hold seven television licenses. In 2004, the rules changed to allow "a single entity to own any number of television stations on a nationwide basis as long as that station group collectively reached no more than 39 percent of the national TV audience."[16] Today, the rules allow a person or corporation to control stations with total television household coverage of up to 35 percent of the U.S. population. With this loosening of ownership rules, we have seen a significant growth in the number and size of station groups, some now owning dozens of stations. Some of these groups are large enough to support their own national sales force.

Regardless of changes in the manner in which spot advertising is bought and sold, the primary purposes for spot buys remain the same:

1. To allow network advertisers to provide additional GRPs in those markets with the greatest sales potential.

2. To provide businesses with less than national or uneven distribution a means of avoiding waste circulation incurred by network television.

---

5 **Identify the various segments of television viewing.**

spot television
Purchasing of time from a local station, in contrast to purchasing from a network.

representative (rep)
An individual or organization representing a medium selling time or space outside the city of origin.

nonwired networks
Groups of radio and television stations whose advertising is sold simultaneously by station representatives.

EXHIBIT 8.9

Television Ratings Vary by Ethnic Group

Top 10 Prime-time Broadcast TV Programs,
Week of 6/8/09–6/12/09

Rank	Program	Origin	HH Rating (Live + SD)
1	*America's Got Talent*—Wed 9PM	NBC	7.2
1	*NCIS*	CBS	7.2
3	*America's Got Talent*—Tues	NBC	6.2
3	*Mentalist, The*—Tues	CBS	6.2
5	*Primetime: Family Secrets*	ABC	6.0
5	*Two and a Half Men*	CBS	6.0
7	*60 Minutes*	CBS	5.9
8	*CSI: Miami*	CBS	5.7
9	*Mentalist, The*	CBS	5.5
10	*Bachelorette, The*	ABC	5.3
10	*Big Bang Theory, The*	CBS	5.3

Top 10 Broadcast TV Programs Among African American TV Households,
Week of 6/8/09–6/12/09

Rank	Program	Origin	HH Rating (Live + SD)
1	*Primetime: Family Secrets*	ABC	8.5
2	*America's Got Talent*—Wed 9PM	NBC	6.5
3	*20/20 Special Edition*—(7/7)	ABC	6.3
4	*NCIS*	CBS	6.2
5	*48 Hours Mystery*—Tues	CBS	6.1
5	*Dateline NBC* (7/7)	NBC	6.1
7	*CSI: NY*	CBS	6.0
8	*Mentalist, The*—Tues	CBS	5.4
9	*CSI: Miami*	CBS	5.3
10	*60 Minutes*	CBS	5.2

Source: TNS Media Intelligence, "Top U.S. advertisers in 10 media," *Advertising Age*, 22 June 2009, 18. Copyrighted information of The Nielsen Company, licensed for use herein.

3. To allow network advertisers to control for uneven network ratings on a market-by-market basis. For example, a network program with a 9 rating may demonstrate huge rating variances from one market to another. Ratings can vary widely based on demographic and viewing preferences of audiences within individual television markets. One reason that ratings can vary widely between markets is the viewing patterns of different racial and ethnic groups. Exhibit 8.9 shows the ratings for the top 10 shows during the first week of July. The first part of the chart shows the top 10 shows among total television households. The bottom half of the chart shows the top 10 shows during the same week among African American households. It is interesting to note the variations between the lists.

4. National advertisers can use spot advertising to support retailers and provide localization for special marketing circumstances. Automobile companies are the leaders in spot advertising. As shown in Exhibit 8.10, five of the top ten spot television advertisers are automobile companies. Automobile companies have extensive local dealer networks that have traditionally been supported through spot television advertising.

DEFINING THE TELEVISION COVERAGE AREA

Before the advent of television, companies generally established sales and advertising territories by state boundaries and arbitrary geographical areas within them. However, television transmissions go in many directions for varying distances. Television

EXHIBIT 8.10

Top 10 Spot Television Advertisers, 2008 (in million $)

Spot TV		
Rank	Marketer	2008
1	Chrysler Group	$330.1
2	Honda Motor Co.	304.7
3	Verizon Communications	288.3
4	AT&T	288.1
5	Nissan Motor Co.	253.8
6	Toyota Motor Corp.	233.7
7	Comcast Corp.	230.4
8	General Mills	213.9
9	General Motors Corp.	210.5
10	Yum Brands	164.5

Source: TNS Media Intelligence, "Top U.S. advertisers in 10 media," *Advertising Age*, 22 June 2009, 18. Reprinted with permission from the June 22, 2009, issue of *Advertising Age*. Copyright, Crain Communications Inc. 2009.

research uses three levels of signal coverage to designate potential station coverage of a market area:

1. **Total survey area**. The total survey area is the largest area over which a station's coverage extends.

2. *Designated market area (DMA). Designated market area* is a term used by the A. C. Nielsen Company to identify those counties in which home market stations receive a preponderance of viewers.

3. *Metro rating area.* The metro rating area corresponds to the standard metropolitan area served by a station.

Local television stations also provide advertisers with signal coverage maps to show the potential audience reach of the station. The signal coverage designations have become less important in recent years because cable has greatly extended the area over which a television station can be viewed.

total survey area
The maximum coverage of a radio or television station's signal.

LOCAL TELEVISION ADVERTISING

Local advertisers increasingly purchase television advertising. Businesses as diverse as restaurants and banks place advertising on local stations. However, local franchise outlets of national companies also place a significant portion of the dollars invested in local television. For example, Yum Brands, the company that owns Pizza Hut and KFC, is a large local advertiser (see Exhibit 8.10).

BUYING AND SCHEDULING SPOT AND LOCAL TELEVISION TIME   Because advertisers have shifted more of their budgets to local markets, media buyers must be familiar with the specifics of buying spot and local television time.

THE TELEVISION DAY   Spot and local television advertising is often purchased by daypart rather than by specific program. Each daypart varies in audience size and demographic profile. Media planners must be familiar with the audience makeup of various dayparts. Some typical daypart designations for East and West Coast time zones are as follows.

1. Morning: 7:00–9:00 A.M. Monday through Friday
2. Daytime: 9:00 A.M.–4:30 P.M. Monday through Friday
3. Early fringe: 4:30–7:30 P.M. Monday through Friday
4. Prime-time access: 7:30–8:00 P.M. Monday through Saturday
5. Prime time: 8:00–11:00 P.M. Monday through Saturday and 7:00–11:00 P.M. Sunday

6. Late news: 11:00–11:30 P.M. Monday through Friday

7. Late fringe: 11:30 P.M.–1:00 A.M. Monday through Friday

PREEMPTION RATE   A considerable portion of spot television advertising time is sold on a preemptible (lower-rate) basis, whereby the advertiser gives the station the right to sell a time slot to another advertiser that may pay a better rate for it or that has a package deal for which that particular spot is needed. Whereas some stations offer only two choices, nonpreemptible and preemptible advertising, others allow advertisers to choose between two kinds of preemptible rates. When the station has the right to sell a spot to another advertiser any time up until the time of the telecast, the rate is called the *immediately preemptible (IP)* rate (the lowest rate). When the station can preempt only if it gives the original advertiser 2 weeks' notice, the rate is designated *preemptible with 2 weeks' notice* and is sold at a higher rate. The highest rate is charged for a non-preemptible time slot, the 2-week preemptible rate is the next highest, and the immediately preemptible rate is the lowest.

The following table is an excerpt from a rate card.

	I	**II**	**III**
Tuesday, 8–9 A.M.	$235	$225	$215

Column I is the nonpreemptible rate, column II is the rate for preemption with 2 weeks' notice, and column III is the rate for preemption without notice. Notice how the rate goes down.

SPECIAL FEATURES   News telecasts, weather reports, sports news and commentary, stock market reports, and similar programming are called *special features*. Time associated with special features is sold at a premium price.

RUN OF SCHEDULE (ROS)   An advertiser can earn a lower rate by permitting a station to run commercials at its convenience whenever time is available rather than in a specified position. (This is comparable to run of paper in newspaper advertising; see Chapter 10.)

PACKAGE RATES   Every station sets up its own assortment of time slots at different periods of the day, which it sells as a package. The station creates its own name for such packages and charges less for them than for the same slots sold individually. The package rate is one of the elements in negotiation for time.

PRODUCT PROTECTION   Every advertiser wants to keep the advertising of competitive products as far away from its commercials as possible. This brings up the concern about what protection against competition an advertisement will get. Although some stations say that they will try to keep competing commercials 5 to 10 minutes apart, most say that although they will do everything possible to separate competing advertisements, they guarantee only that they will not run them back to back or in the same pod or group of commercials in a break.

SCHEDULING SPOT AND LOCAL TIME   *Rotation of a schedule* refers to the placement of commercials within a schedule to get the greatest possible showing. If you bought two spots a week for 4 weeks on a Monday-to-Friday basis, but all the spots were aired only on Monday and Tuesday, your rotation would be poor. You would miss all the people who turn to the station only on Wednesday, Thursday, or Friday. Your horizontal rotation should be increased. Vertical rotation ensures there will be differences in the time at which a commercial is shown within the time bracket purchased. If you bought three spots on the *Tonight Show*, which runs from 11:30 P.M. to 12:30 A.M., but all your spots were shown at 12:15 A.M., you would be missing all the people who go to sleep earlier than that. To avoid this situation, you would schedule one spot in each half hour of the program, vertically rotating your commercial to reach the largest possible audience.

Television Syndication

Television syndication is the sale of television programming on a station-by-station, market-by-market basis. Syndication companies have programming to sell, and they seek to sell individual programs to at least one station in every market. Most major syndicated shows are sold on an advertiser-supported or barter basis. **Barter syndication** refers to the practice of offering the right to run a show to stations in return for a portion of the commercial time in the show, rather than selling the show to stations for cash. A majority of the commercial time on syndicated shows is packaged into national units and sold to national advertisers. The typical syndicated show comes with spots presold on a national basis, and the station sells the remaining time to local and spot advertisers.

Syndication began when producers sold their canceled network shows to stations for inexpensive "fillers" during late afternoon or other time periods not programmed by the networks. During the early days of syndication, no one thought that it was anything but a method for producers to pick up a few extra dollars by selling programs that had completed their network runs to local stations. During this period, syndication was a minor portion of television advertising.

Currently, syndication accounts for close to $4.4 billion in advertising revenues, and major syndicated shows provide coverage comparable to the broadcast networks (see Exhibit 8.11).[17] For example, leading syndicated shows such as *Wheel of Fortune* and *Everybody Loves Raymond* have potential coverage in excess of 90 percent of television households. Syndication is theoretically available in every television household, whereas cable programs can come into only the 88 percent of homes wired to receive cable channels through cable operators or alternative delivery systems such as satellite television.[18]

Like any television format, the key to syndication's success is quality programming. Syndicated programs are either *first-run* programs made for syndication, such as *Entertainment Tonight* and *The Oprah Winfrey Show*, or **off-network syndication** reruns such as *Friends* and *The X-Files*. Most long-running shows such as *Everybody*

barter syndication
Station obtains a program at no charge. The program has presold national commercials, and time is available for local station spots.

off-network syndication
Syndicated programs that have previously been aired by a major network.

EXHIBIT 8.11

New technology has made it possible for households to receive many more television stations than ever before. This has created the need for more program content such as syndicated programs.

Courtesy of Karen King.

Loves Raymond and *Friends* entered the syndication market during their original network runs.

Off-network shows have built-in audiences and reach predictable demographic segments. Advertisers also feel more comfortable with the known content of a high-quality rerun versus the less predictable talk and entertainment first-run product. In fact, advertisers are willing to pay a significant premium for most off-network syndicated programs compared to first-run shows with comparable ratings. In fact, a 30-second spot on *Friends* or *Seinfeld* in syndication can cost more than many prime-time network shows.

Syndication advertising costs vary much more than other types of television programming. Essentially, there is a three-tier pricing structure for the top 50 syndicated shows:

1. The top 10 blockbusters include proven off-network reruns, such as *Law and Order*, and a handful of proven first-run winners, such as *Entertainment Tonight* and *Wheel of Fortune*. Typically, the off-network reruns command the highest prices for 30-second spots.

2. The second tier includes a small number of shows that fall short of the top 10 but still have a sizable, loyal audience. *Judge Judy* and *Dr. Phil* fall into this category.

3. Finally, there are a number of talk shows and less popular reruns that will be the least expensive of the available syndicated options.

The demand for syndicated shows is driven by television's insatiable demand for programming—any programming. For local stations and cable networks with 24 hours to fill, there is simply not enough programming for the thousands of hours required to fill their schedules. In addition, as more and more cable networks are added, the demand continues to increase. Nickelodeon, Lifetime, TNT, the Family Channel, and a host of other cable networks are competing with local stations for off-network programs and driving up the price of those that remain in the syndication market. Adding to the demand for syndicated time are a number of national advertisers that use syndicated programming as a means of extending reach on a demographic and/or geographic basis. Generally, broadcast syndication will surpass cable networks in achieving significant levels of audience reach because the average over-the-air station has higher audience levels than cable networks.

The demand for syndicated programming has moved some stations to sign long-term contracts with program producers to guarantee continued access to certain shows. With the relatively few shows that can generate high audience levels, stations sometimes have had to make long-term commitments to ensure that some of the more popular syndicated shows are on their schedule in future seasons.

THE AUDIENCE FOR SYNDICATED TELEVISION

Syndication has some of the same characteristics as cable. For example, although syndication generates high aggregate audience levels, it does so over multiple programs and showings rather than delivering a mass audience in a single showing as in the case of broadcast networks. In fact, syndicators sell programs on the basis of multiple airings known as *gross average audience* ratings. For example, let's assume that an airing of *CSI: Miami* on CBS has a local market affiliate rating of 9 and a *CSI: Miami* syndicated version has a rating of 3.0. If ACME, Inc., runs one spot on the network version and three spots on the syndicated version, the total rating points would be 9 for both options. However, it's very difficult to compare the two because on network you're achieving your audience all at once. The network audience exposures are unduplicated exposure. In syndication, your ratings are based on spots running within a week.

The future of syndication is extremely bright because local stations find it highly lucrative. In the typical network show, stations may only be allowed to sell 1 minute of commercial time. In a syndicated show, the station can sell from 6 to 12 minutes of

Syndicated TV

EXHIBIT 8.12

Top 10 Syndicated Television Advertisers, 2008 (in million $)

Rank	Marketer	2008
1	Procter & Gamble Co.	$270.0
2	GlaxoSmithKline	156.3
3	Johnson & Johnson	149.2
4	L'Oréal	95.6
5	Pfizer	65.6
6	SC Johnson	64.8
7	Chattem	64.1
8	Kellogg Co.	63.2
9	Verizon Communications	62.8
10	Reckitt Benckiser	62.0

Source: TNS Media Intelligence, "Top U.S. advertisers in 10 media," *Advertising Age*, 22 June 2009, 18. Reprinted with permission from the June 22, 2009, issue of *Advertising Age*. Copyright, Crain Communications Inc. 2009.

commercials, depending on how the program was bartered to the station. Consequently, a syndicated program does not have to generate huge ratings to be a financial success for a station.

As shown in Exhibit 8.12, the top 10 syndicated television advertisers include large package-goods companies such as Procter & Gamble and Johnson & Johnson as well as L'Oréal and the pharmaceutical giant GlaxoSmithKline.

Because local stations find syndication profitable and because the demand for new syndicated programming continues to grow, there is every reason to believe that syndication will be a major advertising vehicle for the foreseeable future. If anything, syndication will be an even stronger competitor to the traditional networks, and the relationship between syndicators and stations may become more formal with long-term contracts and stations buying equity shares in syndicated programs to ensure continued access.

STRIPPING

Most local stations schedule syndicated shows on a basis of five nights a week. That is, they will run *Jeopardy* or *Inside Edition* Monday through Friday in the same time slot. This practice is called **stripping** because the show is stripped across a time period. It is cost efficient to buy fewer shows for multishowings and allows a station to build a consistent audience for selling commercials to potential advertisers. Because most syndication is used as a lead-in either for early news or prime-time programs, stations don't want huge rating or audience composition swings from one day to another.

stripping
Scheduling a syndicated program on a 5-day-per-week basis.

Cable Television

Cable television has its roots in the small Pennsylvania town of Mahanoy City. In the 1940s, John Watson, an appliance store owner, was having difficulty selling television sets because of poor reception caused by a mountain range between Philadelphia stations and Mahanoy City. By placing an antenna on a surrounding peak combined with coaxial cable and amplifiers, cable television (then known as community antenna television or CATV) had begun.

Soon cable systems were importing a variety of signals from different cities to rural households. By the 1970s, cable had become attractive to viewers throughout the country and it moved from remote areas to major cities. In 1972, pay television was launched when Home Box Office (HBO) began service. HBO initiated the era of original programming as opposed to simply extending the signals of over-the-air stations. Of equal importance, HBO's programming was delivered by satellite and provided universal availability for cable networks.[19]

cable television
Television signals that are carried to households by cable. Programs originate with cable operators through high antennas, satellite disks, or operator-initiated programming.

From its humble beginnings, cable television has become a major medium in its own right, with household penetration of more than 88 percent. Both local and national cable advertising revenues continue to grow at a rate higher than many other forms of advertising.

THE CONTEMPORARY CABLE TELEVISION INDUSTRY

For the first 2 decades of its existence, cable customers were satisfied with a wide option of over-the-air broadcast programs and cable operators were making satisfactory profits from cable subscription fees. However, cable industry executives realized that they were missing a major source of revenue by failing to open the medium to advertisers. Cable has matured into a medium serving both viewers and advertisers. The success of cable can be traced to two related elements:

1. Brand identification based on unique and selective networks and programs that appeal to targeted demographic audience segments
2. The investment by cable networks in first-run programming

Unlike broadcast networks that reach huge audiences for mass advertisers, cable provides advertisers with much smaller niche audiences that exhibit both common demographic characteristics and interests. Advertisers know that Lifetime, MTV, the Cartoon Network, and the Discovery Channel will deliver predictable groups of viewers. Cable networks define their brands in the same way that product manufacturers do. For both, brand identification and awareness create a consistent environment for the users of these brands.

It is favorable brand recognition that provides the major impetus to cable success in bringing large national advertisers to the medium. As shown in Exhibit 8.13, with leading advertisers such as Procter & Gamble, Johnson & Johnson, and AT&T, cable is competing for the same advertisers as the broadcast networks.

Cable networks know that it is original programming that will bring both viewers and advertisers to a particular network. Only a few years ago, the majority of cable network programming consisted of off-network reruns and theatrical films that had usually been run several times on both broadcast networks and local stations. Today, cable networks annually invest billions of dollars in original programming, some of which is among the most popular on television. From ESPN's *Monday Night Football* games to A&E's *Biography*, cable networks are appealing to a larger share of the total viewing audience.

EXHIBIT 8.13

Top 10 Cable Television Advertisers, 2008 (in million $)

Cable TV Networks

Rank	Marketer	2008
1	Procter & Gamble Co.	$783.4
2	Johnson & Johnson	312.6
3	AT&T	251.7
4	Verizon Communications	248.9
5	Yum Brands	244.6
6	Walt Disney Co.	243.6
7	General Mills	231.5
8	General Electric Co.	228.0
9	Time Warner	224.5
10	General Motors Corp.	214.8

Source: TNS Media Intelligence, "Top U.S. advertisers in 10 media," *Advertising Age*, 22 June 2009, 18. Reprinted with permission from the June 22, 2009, issue of *Advertising Age.* Copyright, Crain Communications Inc. 2009.

THE FUTURE OF CABLE ADVERTISING

A number of factors make cable television an attractive medium for advertisers:

1. *Ability to target audiences.* When advertisers consider cable television, its ability to reach specific demographic and lifestyle segments is almost always the prime consideration.

2. *Low cost.* The cable industry is faced with a competitive environment that prevents significant increases in CPMs. With an abundance of cable channels, many trying to prove themselves to advertisers, it is very unlikely that we will see the type of advertising increases that have been so prevalent among the major broadcast networks in recent years.

3. *A strong summer season.* In recent years, cable has counterprogrammed the networks by presenting some of their strongest programs opposite network summer reruns. Many advertisers have taken advantage of the audience shifts inherent in this strategy to move dollars into cable during what is typically a down viewing time for networks.

4. *Opportunity for local and spot cable advertising.* The majority of cable advertising dollars are spent at the network level. However, local cable advertising is growing at a rate significantly higher than network advertising. Local cable spending comes from national spot buyers looking to enhance advertising weight in specific markets and a wide variety of local firms such as restaurants, video stores, and small retailers. Because of cable's low advertising rates, these retailers now have a chance to use television.

One interesting trend of the past few years has been for cable networks to branch out and begin their own magazines. ESPN launched its highly successful *ESPN: The Magazine* to sports fans in 1998. Nickelodeon has successful spin-offs with *Nick Jr.*, and *Nick Jr. Family Magazine (NJFM)*. *NJFM*, geared to families with children under age 12, has been named to *Adweek*'s magazine "hot" list several times in recent years.[20] These types of magazines offer advertisers the opportunity to negotiate cross-media deals with the potential for more impact on their target audiences.

Current technology offers advertisers some sophisticated coverage alternatives in cable advertising. The first innovation is the use of *cut-ins* on network cable programs. Cable networks, like their broadcast counterparts, provide some advertising spots to local system operators to sell to local advertisers. Rather than having a spot appear on a largely unwatched local channel, commercials for the local pizza shop now can air on network cable programs such as CNN's *Larry King Show* or ESPN's *Sports Center* in select markets (see Exhibit 8.14).

A further strengthening of local cable advertising comes from the use of **interconnects**. "An interconnect exists where two or more cable systems [in the same market] link themselves together to distribute a commercial advertising schedule simultaneously."[21] In larger markets, an advertiser can simultaneously air several different commercials in various areas of the city. The agency gets a single bill from all the systems, which facilitates individual client billing. The use of interconnects has helped some national brands such as Guinness back up their national television plan in key markets. Interconnects have also been used with success by automotive dealers, such as Ford, to target spots to consumers in specific counties where various dealers do business.[22] The use of interconnects greatly enhances the prospects for bringing more spot advertisers to cable.

interconnects
A joint buying opportunity between two or more cable systems in the same market.

As cable has garnered more advertising dollars, research has improved to help advertisers measure the cable audience and plan the cable portions of their advertising campaign. In particular, Nielsen Media Research provides a number of services, including overnight household ratings and local audience composition data. In addition, Mediamark Research Inc. (MRI) offers national product and cable media usage

EXHIBIT 8.14

Most local cable operators can insert commercials such as this one into their local systems.

information. Advertisers also are able to obtain customized data for local market commercials and information about optimum local commercial efficiencies.

Videocassette Recorders and Digital Video Recorders

Since its introduction in the 1970s, the *videocassette recorder (VCR)* has allowed viewers access to theatrical movies, made-for-VCR films, promotional and educational tapes, and, of course, it has permitted them to record television shows for later viewing—called **time-shift viewing**. At one time, it was anticipated that the primary use of VCRs would be off-air recording. Advertisers thought that the VCR would provide a method to increase the audience of a show (viewers too busy to watch the show during its originally scheduled time could record it to watch later at their convenience). However, studies showed that more than half of recorded shows were never watched, the audiences for time-shift viewing tend to be demographically different from original audiences, and the VCR allowed viewers to fast-forward through commercials—hardly an advantage for advertisers!

time-shift viewing
Recording programs on a VCR for viewing at a later time.

Many industry observers think the VCR is an outdated relic, replaced by digital technology that allows much greater flexibility than the VCR. The *digital video recorder (DVR)* allows viewers to take control of their viewing in a manner never before possible. The DVR digitizes all incoming signals and stores many more hours of programming than a VCR. The viewer can then pause in a program to answer the telephone, provide instant replay or slow motion on demand, and record for later viewing any program just as with a VCR, but it can be done much more quickly and easily, and it doesn't require a tape. It also allows advertisers to customize commercials for individual viewers. For example, let's say your favorite show is *Monday Night Football* but you are not a beer drinker. Therefore, instead of the network Coors commercial, you receive a commercial for Coca-Cola that is digitally stripped into the program. Furthermore, the commercial may be one that fits your age and interests, which are known to Coca-Cola from information you previously provided the cable provider.

Obviously, a number of issues among network advertisers, secondary advertisers, program providers, and the networks would have to be addressed before the technology could be used to refit commercials. Advertisers also worry that technology, such as that of DVRs, makes skipping commercials very easy. According to a study conducted by Juniper

Research, 53 percent of DVR subscribers skip at least some commercials.[23] This can allow them to watch a half-hour program in 23 minutes. However, one advantage of the system is that it can measure the households that are zapping commercials and measure actual commercial audience. This, in turn, brings up the issue of viewer privacy. Another concern of advertisers is that the technology may make pay-for-view movies a more viable option for viewers, which would further decrease commercial viewing.

In the beginning, DVRs were not as popular as originally predicted. One of the reasons was the high cost of a unit. However, many satellite and cable television companies now offer DVRs in their set-top boxes in order to lure subscribers. According to Nielsen research, by March of 2009, DVR penetration of U.S. television households reached an estimated 30.6 percent.[24] The DVR provides technical convergence of computers, interactive communication, and multiple options for standard television. If DVRs achieve predicted levels of household penetration, advertisers will have to better target their commercials to audiences that are most likely to watch them and/or seek alternatives to the 30-second commercial. In 2006, Nielsen began measuring and reporting DVR usage in their People Meter households. Data indicate that some shows such as *House* and *The Office* can achieve a significant lift in their ratings when playback data are included.[25]

Brand Integration or Product Placement

Product placement is when a real brand or product is included in a media vehicle (i.e., program, film, video game) in exchange for goods, services, and/or money. The idea is that the brand is integrated into the programming such that it appears realistic to the viewer and may lead to a positive impression of the brand in the minds of the audience. Product placement is not new in television programs or movies, but more recently product placements have been showing up in songs, Broadway shows, and video games.

Fueled in part by advertisers' desires to increase the value of their television advertising and to recapture some of the audience lost to both network audience erosion and DVRs, advertisers have been more aggressive in seeking ways to integrate their brands into television programs. Brand integration can involve a range of activities from simply having the product appear in one episode of a television program to sponsorship of entire shows. The broadcast and cable networks have become very creative in the kinds of opportunities they offer advertisers. The following are some recent examples of successful brand integration:

- Sometimes the placement is somewhat subtle. For example, Florida Citrus worked with *Good Morning America* to sponsor a contest for Mother's Day called "Emeril's Breakfast in Bed."

- For the program *American Idol*, cups clearly labeled with the Coca-Cola logo are sitting on the table in front of the judges, Randy Jackson, Paula Abdul, Simon Cowell, and Kara DioGuardi, throughout the competition.

- Sometimes the product placement is blatant and part of the show's setting. The 2008–2009 season of *Gossip Girl* began with a Vitamin Water White Party that provided a perfect send-up of Hampton's society.[26]

- Occasionally, the product even becomes part of the show's comedy sketch. On an episode of *30 Rock*, a character played by Alec Baldwin, Jack Donaghy, talks about the wonders of his Verizon wireless service. When he finishes, the main character played by Tina Fay, Liz Lemon, turns to the camera and says, "Well sure, that Verizon wireless service is just unbeatable. Can we have our money now?"[27]

New technology has now made virtual product placements possible. This process uses digital editing to insert brand images in television programming and other video

EXHIBIT 8.15
Advertisers

Top 10 Brands Appearing in a TV Program (1/1/09–1/31/09)

Rank	Brand	Total Number of Times Brand Appeared on TV
1	Coca-Cola Soft Drinks	838
2	24-Hour Fitness Centers/Clubs	598
3	National Football League Association	210
4	Indianapolis Colts Football Team	162
5	Chicago Bears Football Team	138
6	Free Motion Fitness Exercise Equipment	119
7	Precor Exercise Equipment	98
8	NBC Web Site, nbc.com	95
9	Apple Computer Systems Laptop	92
10	Reebok Apparel	91

Top 10 TV Programs Using Product Placement (1/1/09–1/31/09)

Rank	Program	Network	Total Number of Times Brand Appeared in Program
1	*Deal Or No Deal*	NBC	1,522
2	*The Biggest Loser*	NBC	1,351
3	*American Idol*	FOX	963
4	*The Apprentice*	NBC	886
5	*CW Now*	CW	474
6	*Extreme Makeover Home Edition*	ABC	339
7	*One Tree Hill*	CW	309
8	*CSI Crime Scene Investigation*	CBS	302
9	*Just for Laughs*	ABC	255
10	*Amazing Race*	CBS	240

Source: Nielsen Product Placement, http://en-us.nielsen.com/rankings/insights/rankings/advertisers, 7 July 2009. Copyrighted information of The Nielsen Company, licensed for use herein.

content that has already been filmed. This makes it possible for production companies to change the brands that are visually featured on a program to other brands when the show goes into syndication. It also allows the creation of new advertising inventory that cannot be time-shifted without giving up more programming time for commercials.

The value of such integration is debated among advertisers. Most industry experts seem to believe that the value of the integration depends on how well the brand fits into the program and how well it is integrated into the campaign.[28] Traditional CPM comparisons do not provide an adequate assessment. Some measurement services are beginning to look at ways to measure the effectiveness of product placements. More value is placed on characters using the brand and/or saying the product name than on simply showing the product. Product placements are not seen as something that will replace commercials.

Some programs and products lend themselves to product placements better than others. Exhibit 8.15 shows the top 10 brands appearing within a television program and the top 10 programs using product placements.

Syndicated Rating Services

As mentioned earlier in this chapter, from an advertising perspective, television is simply an audience delivery system. Needless to say, it is crucial for advertisers and their agencies to have reliable data on which to make buying decisions and to use to determine whether they are paying fair prices. The problems of accurately accounting for the increasingly fragmented television audience have become more and more difficult. At the same time, as audiences for each television outlet decrease, the magnitude of any error increases as a percentage of the total viewing audience. For example, a 1 rating-point error for a program with a 20 rating is 5 percent; the same error for a program with a 5 rating is 20 percent. Because advertising rates are determined directly by ratings, these errors are a cause for considerable concern among advertisers.

THE NIELSEN RATINGS

The primary supplier of syndicated television ratings is Nielsen Media Research.[29] The company was founded in 1923 by A. C. Nielsen to collect radio audience information, and it initiated television ratings in 1950. The Nielsen Television Index (NTI) provides network ratings on a national basis. Data are provided from more than 9,000 households. In these households a **People Meter** is attached to each television set. The People Meter has buttons assigned to each person living in the home and additional buttons for visitors.

People Meter
Device that measures television set usage by individuals rather than by households.

Many advertisers are interested in local viewing levels, and Nielsen provides ratings for all markets through its Nielsen Station Index (NSI). In the 56 largest markets, Nielsen uses set meters (not People Meters) to measure household television set usage on a continuous basis. In each of the 210 television markets, Nielsen provides diaries in which individuals record their viewing habits. These diaries are administered four times a year during February, May, July, and November. These four periods are known as *sweeps*, and they are used to set the price of local commercials for the coming quarter. Paper dairies are used to collect this information in smaller markets from one to four times per year.

In recent years, the ratings system has come under a great deal of scrutiny by both advertisers and broadcasters. Although a number of issues have been raised, we discuss three major areas of concern:

1. *Sweeps weeks.* In theory, **sweeps weeks** (or simply *sweeps*) are an efficient and relatively inexpensive means of estimating quarterly local market ratings. In fact, local market stations have sometimes used the period to artificially distort their ratings by airing sensational news exposés and special promotions and pressuring networks to program their best miniseries, movies, and specials to support their affiliates during sweeps.

   sweeps weeks
   During these periods, ratings are taken for all television markets.

   The result is that the sweeps period ratings of local stations may have little relation to the 36 "unrated" weeks. Advertisers are extremely frustrated by what they see as inflated ratings and the accompanying higher commercial rates they pay for them. The alleged abuses of sweeps week programming have resulted in increasing calls for measuring of local audiences on a continuing basis.

2. *Diaries.* Everyone agrees that in an era of 50-channel-plus household reception and with the trend toward individualized viewing, the diary is an antiquated measurement tool. A number of major advertisers have called for People Meters in at least the top 125 markets, which would include approximately 75 percent of television households. It also would largely eliminate the current sweeps problem by providing ongoing audience measurements for most of the country. The major obstacle to implementing local People Meter ratings is cost. It is estimated that each metered market would require a minimum of 300 sampled households, or almost 40,000 homes, at a cost of several hundred million dollars—much more than either advertisers or broadcasters are currently willing to pay.

3. *Exposure value.* Another area generating great interest is estimating exposure levels for television commercials versus set usage. Advertisers only want to pay for audiences who are watching their commercials. Television networks want to get credit for audiences that record and playback their programs. Although controversial, Nielsen now reports C3 ratings, a mix of average commercial ratings and three days of program DVR playback.

Arbitron is engaged in a study using a Portable People Meter (PPM). As discussed in Chapter 9, the PPM is a device about the size of a pager that measures inaudible signals from the audio portion of television, radio, cable, and the Internet. It eliminates the nuisance of keeping a diary, and the PPM is particularly valuable in measuring the out-of-home audience of radio. The major barrier to its use is the cost associated with its introduction.

Regardless of what form changes in syndicated ratings take in the future, it is clear that methods that served the television industry well in a period of three networks and a few stations in each market will not work in the fragmented landscape of the twenty-first century. A primary issue is how much the major players—stations, networks, and advertisers—are willing to pay to gather these elusive data.

Nielsen is currently working on a new television/media research product that will combine their television ratings data, their Internet streaming video measurement service, Videocensus, and data on consumer product purchases. The hope is that this will help advertisers to better assess the ROI they are getting for their advertising.

QUALITATIVE RATINGS

As you will recall in our discussion of cable television, we commented on the need for cable networks to sell the quality and lifestyle of their audiences in contrast to the basic numbers reported by most major rating reports. Another type of qualitative audience measure seeks to offer insight into audience involvement or degree of preference for particular television shows or personalities. These measures can be used to determine if a person can be successfully used as a testimonial spokesperson or to see if a popular show is beginning to wear out.

The best-known qualitative research service is Marketing Evaluations, which compiles a number of "popularity" surveys called "Q" reports. The most familiar of these are **TVQ** and Performer Q.

Let us assume that a television show, *House*, is familiar to 50 percent of the population and that 30 percent of the people rank it as one of their favorite shows. The Q score would be calculated as follows:

$$Q = \frac{FAV}{FAM} \text{ or } \frac{30}{50} = 60$$

Interestingly enough, the fragmentation of television has taken its toll not only on average program ratings but also on the TVQ scores. Because the number of people watching any particular show is so much lower now than in past years, the general recognition level of television personalities has fallen significantly in recent years. A generation ago, Lucille Ball and Jackie Gleason were as well known as the president. Today, many television stars have a loyal following among their fans but are not necessarily household names.

TVQ
A service of Marketing Evaluations that measures the popularity (opinion of audience rather than size of audience) of shows and personalities.

SUMMARY

In the near future, television will become more than a medium of information, entertainment, and advertising. Television, in its various permutations, will be an interactive system that will allow viewers to pay bills, make airline reservations, receive pay-per-view programming on demand, and even play computer games with other viewers. How long it will be before these systems are generally available and what their final form will take are still very much in question. However, programmers, advertisers, and the general public will all be dealing with a dramatically changed television medium in the not-too-distant future.

In addition to its functional options, television is becoming a gateway to a world of communication never before imagined. Every aspect of the medium from audience research to news must be reevaluated in terms of viewer control and a changing economic base. Throughout most of the past century, it was understood that American mass media would be largely financed by advertisers using a business plan of reaching the largest audience possible at the lowest cost per person. The fragmentation of the television audience has changed programming, financing, and the criteria of what constitutes a "mass" medium.

Although television advertising faces an uncertain future, it is an uncertainty filled with opportunities for those who have the creativity and insight to operate in an era of an audience-driven medium. Nowhere will the customer-oriented notion of the marketing concept be more apparent than in interactive television. It appears certain that both advertisers and viewers will soon pay a higher price for access to the numerous options offered by television. In return, astute advertisers will be reaching customers and prospects on a one-to-one basis with some form of permission marketing being the rule rather than the exception.

REVIEW

1. Discuss major changes in network television advertising during the past 25 years.
2. Define the following terms:
   a. Rating
   b. Share of audience
   c. People ratings
   d. TVQ ratings
   e. Clutter
3. Compare and contrast syndication and spot television buying.
4. Discuss the relationship between networks and their affiliates.
5. Describe the up-front television buying market for prime time.
6. Compare and contrast cable networks with broadcast networks.

CHAPTER 9

Shutterstock/U.P.images_photo.

Using Radio

RADIO PROVIDES advertisers with options to reach very narrowly defined niche prospects with a host of formats and numerous stations in even the smallest towns. Among the most popular media, radio has high levels of listenership throughout the day. It offers the opportunity for advertisers to reach some audiences, such as teenagers, working women, and light television viewers, that are sometimes hard to reach with other media. ▶

CHAPTER LEARNING OBJECTIVES

1. **Describe radio's strengths as an advertising medium.**
2. **Understand the limitations and challenges faced by radio.**
3. **Discuss how radio commercial time is bought and sold.**
4. **Identify different roles of AM and FM radio.**
5. **Explain the rating systems used in radio.**

PROS

1. Radio is a primary medium for targeting narrow audience segments, many of who are not heavy users of other media.
2. Radio is a mobile medium, going with listeners into the marketplace and giving advertisers proximity to the sale.
3. Radio, with its relatively low production costs and immediacy, can react quickly to changing market conditions.
4. Radio has a personal relationship with its audience. This affinity with listeners carries over to the credibility it offers many of the products advertised on radio.
5. With its low cost and targeted formats, radio is an excellent supplemental medium for secondary building blocks to increase reach and frequency to specific target markets.

CONS

1. Without a visual component, radio often lacks the impact of other media. Also, many listeners use radio as "background" rather than giving it their full attention.

In the early days, radio listening was often a group activity.

R. Gino Santa Maria/Shutterstock

2. The small audiences of most radio stations require numerous buys to achieve acceptable reach and frequency levels.

3. Adequate audience research is not always available, especially among many small market stations.

During the week of March 6, 1949, the top-rated radio show was the *Lux Radio Theater*, which reached almost 30 percent of American households.[1] By contrast, the most popular television show of the 2008–2009 season, *American Idol*, received an average household rating of 14.4 on its highest rated night.[2] Until the 1950s when television became the major broadcast medium, radio was the primary national medium for both advertisers and audiences.

Radio was the most prestigious of the national media from 1926, when the first network (the National Broadcasting Company) was formed, until the mid-1950s. During those golden years of radio, the family gathered around the living room radio set to listen to Jack Benny, Fred Allen, and Bob Hope entertain them while news personalities such as Edward R. Murrow enlightened them. All of this programming was brought to the audience by the major advertisers of the day. The advent of coast-to-coast television broadcasts and the introduction of instant hits such as *I Love Lucy* and *The $64,000 Question* during the early 1950s accelerated radio's decline as a national medium.

Despite its minor position on the national scene, as a local medium, radio advertising revenues are about $9.5 billion and the medium demonstrates impressive reach. Each week, radio reaches about 94 percent of all adults and 90.6 percent of teenagers.[3]

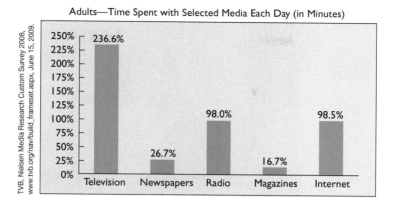

Adults—Time Spent with Selected Media Each Day (in Minutes)

TVB, Nielsen Media Research Custom Survey 2008, www.tvb.org/nav/build_frameset.aspx, June 15, 2009.

Television 236.6% · Newspapers 26.7% · Radio 98.0% · Magazines 16.7% · Internet 98.5%

EXHIBIT 9.1

The Average Consumer Will Spend About 1 Hour and 40 Minutes a Day Using Radio

Each day adults spend about as much time listening to the radio as they do on the Internet (see Exhibit 9.1). By reaching prospects with targeted formats from urban to all-talk, radio commercials can create an intimate, one-to-one relationship with prospects. In addition, radio can achieve effective creative effects at a lower production cost than virtually any other medium.

The Contemporary Radio Industry

Like most media, radio has had to adapt to a new competitive environment and a very different economic structure. Only a few years ago, the FCC limited ownership of radio stations to seven FM and seven AM stations with only one of each in a single market. However, the FCC gradually loosened ownership restrictions and the Telecommunications Act of 1996 allowed corporations or individuals to control as much as 35 percent of the U.S. market (with other rules governing local station ownership determined by the size of a market). The new ownership rules changed the radio industry from one of numerous small groups to one comprised of a few huge conglomerates.

With companies such as Clear Channel with more than 800 local stations and CBS Radio, Inc., with more than 130 stations, more and more radio stations belong to these mega-owners. Many radio stations are owned by large media companies that also own television stations or newspapers. Accompanying this new movement to large group ownership is a revival of radio as a preferred advertising medium for a number of major businesses. As many advertisers seek to reach more narrowly defined targets, radio offers them the opportunity to more efficiently reach a niche market.

RADIO AND NEW TECHNOLOGY

Some observers think that the audio platform of the next decade will be computers and satellites, rather than a radio dial. More and more radio executives see the future of radio as an Internet business with numerous options for reaching niche audiences and eventually individuals with tailored programming, music, and advertising. Web sites have become the new business model for radio as Internet radio listening continues to grow. Broadcasters are facing copyright regulations regarding the performance fees they must pay for streaming their on-air programming over the Internet.

HD radio and **satellite radio** also pose challenges for traditional broadcast radio. Satellite radio is available by subscription and contains few, if any, commercials. It requires a special receiver but offers near-CD-quality sound. Penetration of satellite radio is still small. HD radio offers terrestrial radio stations the ability to deliver additional programming on the same bandwidth with higher-quality sound. Some say that this could help revitalize AM stations. Although HD radio also requires a special receiver, there is no subscription fee for consumers.

HD radio
Offers terrestrial radio stations the ability to deliver additional programming on the same amount of bandwidth with higher-quality sound. It requires a special receiver.

satellite radio
Available by subscription and contains few, if any, commercials. It requires a special receiver but offers near-CD-quality sound.

A look inside a radio studio.

Courtesy of Ron Lane.

Predicting precisely the future of radio, even in the near term, is difficult. However, we can examine some of the major trends that will drive the medium during the coming years.

1. The size of the audience listening to radio stations over the Internet is growing rapidly. In 2000, 11 percent of Americans aged 12 and older said that they had listened to radio stations over the Internet. By June 2009, almost half said they had listened to radio stations on the Internet at least once (see Exhibit 9.2).

2. More listeners to Internet radio are becoming habitual listeners. As of 2009, 27 percent of Americans aged 12 and older said they listened to radio stations online in the past month. About 17 percent said they listened to radio stations over the Internet in the past week.

3. Many teens prefer to listen to their favorite music online. According to a study conducted by the Nielsen research company, 33 percent of 12- to 17-year-olds consider the Internet their primary source for music.[4]

EXHIBIT 9.2

Almost Half of Americans Have Listened to Radio Stations Online

"The Infinite dial 2009," Arbitron Inc./Edison Research, 7.

The future of radio as a medium for the delivery of more specialized and personalized programming is very bright. However, the form that this transmission will take, whether local stations can survive satellite and Internet systems, and how advertisers will use the new technological options fully are very much up in the air.

Features and Advantages of Radio

Radio is an ideal medium for the segmented marketing of the twenty-first century. In many respects, radio was the forerunner of many of the localized marketing and advertising strategies so much in use today. As the **Radio Advertising Bureau (RAB)** points out, "Radio gives you the opportunity to take advantage of the most powerful form of communication—the human voice. The right combination of words, voices, music, and effects on radio can help you establish a unique 'one-on-one' connection with your prospects that lets you grab their attention, evoke their emotions, and persuade them to respond. All this at a fraction of the production cost of other broadcast media."[5]

According to the Radio Marketing Bureau, radio offers a number of advantages not found in most other media. Some of the primary elements of interest to advertisers are the following:

1. *Radio targets.* One of the greatest strengths of radio is its ability to deliver advertising to a very selective audience. It would be difficult to find a market segment whose needs, tastes, and preferences are not reached by some station's programming.

   Radio's combination of high overall reach and its ability to provide numerous formats makes it a multifaceted medium. In some sense, each programming category, whether country, classical, all-talk, or rhythm and blues, can be treated as a distinct medium for marketing purposes. From a marketing perspective, radio has the ability to reach prospects by gender, age, race, or interest with a format that adds an even greater dimension to its already strong personal communication environment. For example, Exhibit 9.3 shows the gender, education, race, and age of the audience for four popular radio formats.

2. *On average, radio reaches Americans (age 12 and older) more than 2.6 hours per day.* According to Arbitron, there are more than 600 million radios in use in the United States.[6] Radio can even deliver higher-income and educational segments that are of prime importance to many advertisers.

   Radio reaches more than 94 percent of college graduates 25 to 54 years of age. According to Arbitron research, 95 percent of adults aged 25 to 54 with college degrees and annual incomes of $50,000 or more tune into the radio over the course of a week.[7]

3. *Radio advertising influences consumers closest to the time of purchase.* No major medium can compete with radio as a means of reaching prospects as they approach a purchase decision. Although both outdoor and point-of-purchase advertisements also reach consumers in the marketplace, neither can deliver a sales message the way radio can.

4. *Radio reaches light users of other media.* Light viewers of television spend more time with radio than they do with television. In addition, radio can fill in gaps in both newspaper and magazine coverage of prime audiences.

5. *Radio works well with other media.* Radio can reach light users of other media and fill in gaps in a media schedule. For many years, a fundamental marketing strategy for radio has been to promote its ability to successfully work with other media to increase reach and frequency or to reach nonusers or light users of other media. The radio industry realizes that the majority of its revenue comes from advertisers that use radio as a secondary medium. Radio provides affordable repetition that delivers high levels of awareness—a key component in gaining market share.

---

1 **Describe radio's strengths as an advertising medium.**

Radio Advertising Bureau (RAB)
Association to promote the use of radio as an advertising medium.

EXHIBIT 9.3

There Is a Radio Format for Everyone

	Country	Mexican Regional	Adult Contemporary	Urban Adult Contemporary
Gender (persons 18+)				
Women (18+)	53.7%	42.1%	65.3%	57.6%
Men (18+)	46.3%	57.9%	34.7%	42.4%
Education (persons 18+)				
Less than 12th Grade	11.6%	48.1%	6.1%	11.1%
HS Grad	37.6%	33.7%	27.4%	31.5%
Some College	35.3%	14.6%	38.7%	38.4%
College Grad	15.5%	3.6%	27.8%	19.0%
Age				
12–17	5.1%	5.1%	3.0%	4.4%
18–24	11.0%	19.9%	7.1%	7.9%
25–34	15.1%	35.0%	13.4%	15.0%
35–44	18.0%	20.4%	20.1%	24.0%
45–54	19.7%	10.2%	25.1%	25.6%
55–64	15.5%	5.5%	18.3%	15.2%
65+	15.8%	3.9%	12.9%	8.0%
Race				
African American	1.9%	.3%	8.5%	90.1%
Hispanic	5.7%	95.4%	13.0%	3.0%
Other	92.4%	4.3%	78.5%	6.9%

Source: Arbitron's *Radio Today 2008 Edition.*

6. *Much of radio listening takes place on an out-of-home basis.* This means that radio can reach consumers where they are and where other media are sometimes not readily available (see Exhibit 9.4).

7. *Radio delivers consistent listening patterns.* Unlike television, radio offers year-round coverage with little or no summer audience drop-off. Likewise, radio maintains high audience levels throughout the day.

EXHIBIT 9.4

Radio Reaches Customers Everywhere

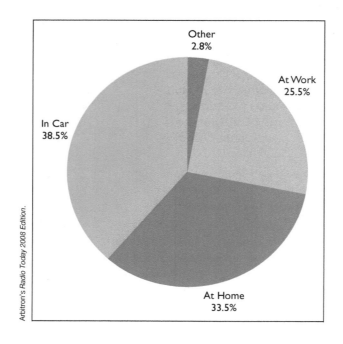

Arbitron's *Radio Today 2008 Edition.*

Other 2.8%

At Work 25.5%

In Car 38.5%

At Home 33.5%

8. *Radio delivers its messages at a very low CPM level.* Advertisers are increasingly giving more attention to cost efficiencies. Radio delivers its audience at a CPM level below that of virtually any other medium. Not only are the CPM levels low, but radio's recent increases also have been below that of major competitors.

9. *Radio provides advertisers with both immediacy and flexibility.* Radio advertising has the ability to react quickly to changing market conditions. With relatively short production deadlines and inexpensive creative techniques, radio is an excellent medium to take advantage of fast-breaking opportunities.

   The ability to anticipate or react to changing conditions cannot be underestimated. For example, when the Indianapolis 500 ends on Memorial Day afternoon, radio commercials touting the winner's tire and oil brands begin running that evening. The simplicity of radio can be a major advantage in making tactical marketing decisions. Radio's sense of immediacy and flexibility, all at a cost within the budget of even the smallest advertiser, has made it an important part of the advertising strategy of many advertisers.

Limitations and Challenges of Radio

No medium is suited for every marketing and advertising situation. Like all media, radio has special strengths and weaknesses that must be considered by advertisers considering placing radio in their media schedule. Radio has a number of characteristics that make it an ideal vehicle for numerous advertisers as either a primary or secondary medium. By the same token, advertisers need to be aware of some of the major disadvantages that must be considered before scheduling a radio buy. Four of the major problems facing advertisers using radio are (1) the sheer number of stations, which creates a very fragmented environment especially for those advertisers needing to reach a general audience; (2) clutter; (3) the medium's lack of a visual element; and (4) increased use of MP3 players and digital radio.

2 **Understand the limitations and challenges faced by radio.**

AUDIENCE FRAGMENTATION

One of the great strengths of radio is its ability to reach narrowly defined audience niches with formats of particular interest to specific listeners. However, some advertisers wonder if the extent of segmentation has resulted in an overly fragmented medium with audience levels for most stations so small that it is difficult to reach a brand's core prospects. For those product categories with broad appeal, **audience fragmentation** has made it difficult to gain effective reach and frequency without buying several radio stations or networks. Radio executives respond that although there are a few major markets in which competition has forced stations into continually narrowing their program formats, for the most part, radio remains among the most effective means of achieving the target marketing desired by the majority of advertisers. However, to put the situation in perspective, in 2009, there were more than 13,500 commercial registered radio stations on the air in the United States.[8] Exhibit 9.5 shows a breakdown of these stations by format.

audience fragmentation
The segmenting of mass-media audiences into smaller groups because of diversity of media outlets.

CLUTTER

As discussed in Chapter 8, clutter is a major concern to advertisers. The more commercials and other nonprogram content, the less likely it is that listeners will recall any particular advertising message. The number of commercials on radio has always been significantly greater than that on television. However, with deregulation, the time devoted to commercials has steadily increased. Some radio stations are running more than 30 percent advertising during peak listening periods. The use of shorter commercials is also contributing to clutter on some radio stations.

EXHIBIT 9.5

U.S. Radio Station Format Analysis

Number of Stations by Radio Format			
228	Adult Alternative	472	New stations (no designated formats yet)
782	Adult Contemporary	288	New Rock—Modern Rock
332	Adult Standards	1,162	News/News—Talk
312	Album Rock	766	Oldies
93	Black Gospel	56	Pre-teen
2	Bluegrass	284	R&B—Urban
4	Blues	0	Reading Service
299	Classic Hits	1,014	Religion
512	Classic Rock	768	Religious—Contemporary
550	Contemporary Hit Radio (Top-40)	147	Religious—Gospel
2,066	Country	168	Soft Adult Contemporary
40	Easy Listening	249	Soft Urban Contemporary
102	Ethnic	221	Southern Gospel
2	Farm News and Talk	812	Spanish
266	Fine Arts/Classical	527	Sports
23	Financial News	563	Talk
1	Folk	5	Travel Info
447	Hot Adult Contemporary or "Adult CHR"	806	Variety
70	Jazz	28	Weather/Traffic
36	Modern Adult Contemporary		

Source: ©News Generation, Inc., 2009. Obtained from http://www.newsgeneration.com/radio_resources/stats.htm, 13 April 2009.

LACK OF A VISUAL ELEMENT

A fundamental problem for advertisers is radio's lack of a visual component. At a time when advertisers are attempting to enhance brand image and build consumer awareness, many advertisers find radio's lack of visuals a difficult problem to overcome. With the growth of self-service retailing and competitive brand promotions, package identification is crucial for many advertisers.

Radio has long used a number of creative techniques to substitute the ear for the eye and to attempt to overcome the lack of visuals. Sound effects, jingles, short and choppy copy, and vivid descriptions attempt to create a mental picture. Radio has attempted to show that images familiar to consumers from television commercials can be transferred to consumers through radio.

INCREASED USE OF MP3 PLAYERS

Although most teens still listen to the radio at least once per week, there has been a dramatic increase in the use of MP3 players and digital music listening, particularly among younger audiences. According to a study conducted by the Nielsen research company, 39 percent of 12- to 17-year-olds say that they would choose MP3 players as their primary source of music.[9]

Technical Aspects of Radio

THE SIGNAL

The electrical impulses that are broadcast by radio are called the *signal*. If a certain station has a good signal in a given territory, its programs and commercials are clear to listeners in that area.

FREQUENCY

All signals are transmitted by electromagnetic waves, sometimes called *radio waves*. These waves differ from one another in frequency (the number of waves that pass a

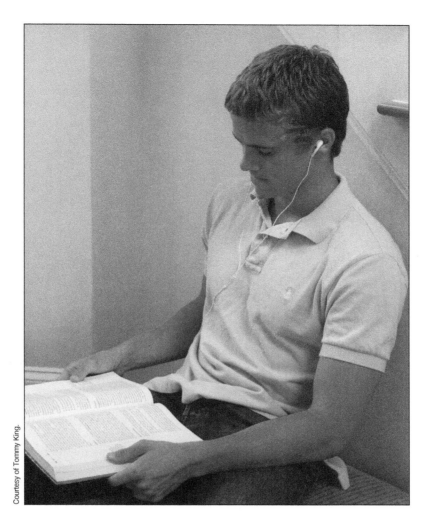

Courtesy of Tommy King.

Many teens prefer to listen to music on their MP3 players.

given point in a given period of time). Frequencies for AM stations are measured in kilohertz or kHz and FM stations' frequencies are measured in megahertz or MHz. The FCC has assigned the following frequencies to all radio stations:

AM: 540 to 1,700 kHz

FM: 88.1 to 107.9 MHz

AMPLITUDE

All electromagnetic waves have height, referred to as *amplitude*, whose range resembles the difference between an ocean wave and a ripple in a pond; and speed, measured by the frequency with which a succession of waves passes a given point per minute. If, for example, a radio station operates on a frequency of 1,580 kHz, this means that 1,580,000 of its waves pass a given point per second.

On the basis of these two dimensions—amplitude and frequency—two separate systems have been developed for carrying radio waves. The first system carries the variations in a sound wave by corresponding variations in its amplitude; the frequency remains constant. This is the principle of **amplitude modulation (AM)**. The second system carries the variation in a sound wave by corresponding variations in its frequency; the amplitude remains constant. This is the principle of **frequency modulation (FM)** (see Exhibit 9.6a and b).

amplitude modulation (AM) Method of transmitting electromagnetic signals by varying the amplitude (size) of the electromagnetic wave, in contrast to varying its frequency. Quality is not as good as frequency modulation but can be heard farther, especially at night.

frequency modulation (FM) A radio transmission wave that transmits by the variation in the frequency of its wave rather than by its size (as in amplitude modulation [AM]). An FM wave is 20 times the width of an AM wave, which is the source of its fine tone. To transmit such a wave, it has to be placed high on the electromagnetic spectrum, far from AM waves with their interference and static, hence its outstanding tone.

EXHIBIT 9.6

In amplitude modulation (a), waves vary in height (amplitude); frequency is constant. Frequency modulation (b) varies the frequency but keeps the height constant. These drawings, however, are not made to scale, which would reveal that width is the significant difference between AM and FM. The FM wave is 20 times wider than the AM wave. This fact helps to explain how FM captures its fine tones.

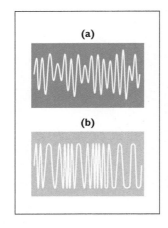

(a)

(b)

The technical structure of AM and FM radio has created, in effect, two distinct media, each offering different values to the listener and the advertiser. AM signals carry farther but are susceptible to interference. FM has a fine tonal quality, but its signal distances are limited. A particular station's quality of reception also is determined by atmospheric conditions and station power (broadcast frequency).

Selling Radio Commercial Time

3 Discuss how radio commercial time is bought and sold.

4 Identify different roles of AM and FM radio.

Radio advertising dollars are very much concentrated at the local level. Despite significant growth in both radio network and spot advertising, local advertising continues to dominate industry revenues.

Buying radio can be a difficult task because of the number of stations and formats available to advertisers. For example, there are more than 850 stations in Texas alone. Even the most sparsely populated state, Wyoming, has more than 155 commercial stations.[10] In addition, there are dozens of distinct formats throughout the country from which to choose. Recent consolidation of radio ownership offers the potential for major changes in the radio rate structure and the way radio time is bought. From the outset of the move to group ownership, major radio group executives promised advertisers better service and more efficient buying procedures. Rather than dealing with many individual stations or independent rep companies, a media buyer in a streamlined environment could negotiate time availability and rates for hundreds of stations while dealing with a single person and submitting one insertion order.

Although ownership consolidation may have the potential to drive up local radio rates and give stations more leverage with advertisers, it does not eliminate the fierce competition that radio faces for local advertising dollars. Radio advertising continues to operate in a challenging environment as it competes for local advertisers. Radio must compete with traditional selective media, such as newspapers, the Yellow Pages, and direct response, that also reach targeted audiences. In addition, radio is competing with newer media such as the Internet and both broadcast and cable television, which see local advertising as major profit centers.

NETWORK RADIO

The demise of network radio as a major national medium and the beginning of local radio began in 1948 with the introduction of television. Average ratings for Bob Hope's radio show dropped from 23.8 in 1948 to 5.4 in 1953. Soap operas left radio for television throughout the 1950s until *Ma Perkins*, the last survivor, went off the air in 1960. The last major radio dramas, *Suspense* and *Have Gun Will Travel*, ended in 1962 and the era of network radio was essentially over. For the next decade, network programs were largely confined to news and occasional short features.

Network radio was huge in the late 1940s.

Courtesy of Karen King.

Network radio is a minor source of advertising dollars. However, media planners continue to look to network radio as a means of extending reach to workingwomen and light users of other media and building greater brand awareness through inexpensive additional frequency to prime target segments. Network radio advertising only accounts for $975 million of the more than $9.5 billion spent annually in radio.[11] Leading advertisers on network radio include national retail chains, telecommunications, and entertainment companies (see Exhibit 9.7).

Radio networks are much different from those in television as is the relationship between radio networks and their affiliates. Radio networks are basically program providers, but unlike television, a single radio station may belong to several radio networks simultaneously. For example, a station might get sports reports from one network, personality profiles and news from another, and entertainment fare from yet another. Whereas in television local stations sell advertising time on the basis of the

Rank	Marketer	2008
1	Verizon Communications	$107.4
2	Home Depot	79.2
3	Berkshire Hathaway	78.9
4	Walmart Stores	76.1
5	General Motors Corp.	51.6
6	AT&T	43.3
7	Safeway	41.6
8	Walt Disney Co.	40.9
9	News Corp.	37.8
10	General Electric Co.	36.0

EXHIBIT 9.7

Top U.S. Advertisers in National Radio

Source: "Top U.S. advertisers in 10 media," *Advertising Age*, 22 June 2009, 18. Reprinted with permission from the June 22, 2009, issue of Advertising Age. Copyright, Crain Communications Inc. 2009.

strength of the network programming, in radio the networks must depend on local ratings to garner national advertising support.

Regardless of the way a radio station uses network programming and the many differences with television, radio networks do offer some of the same advantages as their television counterparts. For example, an advertiser prepares one insertion order for multiple stations, pays one invoice, and is guaranteed uniform production quality for the commercials scheduled on all stations. Radio networks also provide economical reach and, like all radio, target special audience segments who often are light users of other media.

Radio networks have benefited from the use of satellite technology. The availability of satellite links for national radio programmers offers a number of advantages for their local station affiliates:

1. Stations are guaranteed quality programming based on the latest audience research for a particular format.

2. Radio networks bring celebrities to the medium that local stations could not afford.

3. Even the smallest stations can obtain national advertising dollars as part of a network. Stations that would not be considered by national advertisers as part of a local spot buy may now be included in a network radio schedule.

4. The cost efficiencies of sharing programming with several hundred other affiliates keep both personnel and programming costs to a minimum.

Network radio will never return to its former status as a primary medium for national advertisers. However, as a source of program services, with its ability to target narrow audience segments, it will continue to play an important role for a number of national advertisers.

SPOT RADIO

spot radio
Buying radio time on local stations on a market-by-market basis by national advertisers.

Recall from our discussion in Chapter 8 that *spot advertising* is the buying of local stations by national advertisers. Advertisers spent approximately $8.5 billion in **spot radio** advertising in 2008.[12] It is almost always a second medium for national companies to build added reach and frequency against selected target markets. Spot radio offers these advertisers an opportunity to react quickly to changing competitive challenges and hit narrowly segmented markets with little waste circulation. As shown in Exhibit 9.8, for example, Verizon Communications ranks among the top users of radio with expenditures of $98.9 million. However, this expenditure represents less than 3 percent of the company's annual advertising budget.

Despite the relatively low percentage of total advertising dollars, spot radio serves important functions for a number of advertisers. To those companies with a national

EXHIBIT 9.8

Top U.S. Advertisers in Local Radio

Rank	Marketer	2008
1	AT&T	$130.8
2	Verizon Communications	98.9
3	General Electric Co.	78.4
4	McDonald's Corp.	68.5
5	Comcast Corp.	57.7
6	Berkshire Hathaway	56.4
7	News Corp.	53.8
8	Safeway	51.8
9	Walt Disney Co.	47.9
10	Kroger Co.	37.6

Source: "Top U.S. advertisers in 10 media," *Advertising Age,* 22 June 2009, 18. Reprinted with permission from the June 22, 2009, issue of *Advertising Age.* Copyright, Crain Communications Inc. 2009.

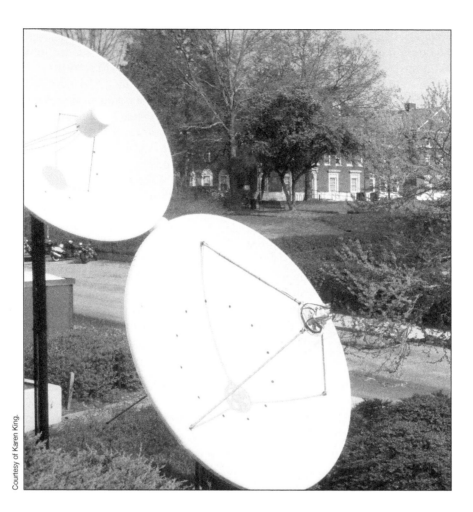

Courtesy of Karen King.

Satellite technology has helped radio networks regain popularity.

presence that have widely differentiated market potential, spot radio can provide added weight in selected regions or individual markets. A second group of heavy spot radio users are national companies with extensive retail outlets. Spot radio commercials allow these companies to build on their national brand awareness with localized spots directed at the local community. For example, Home Depot and McDonald's are advertisers that depend on spot radio to augment their national advertising. As is the case in other categories of the medium, advertisers take advantage of the flexibility and low cost offered by spot radio.

Just as with television, most spot radio broadcast purchases are made through reps. In principle, radio reps serve the same function as those in television. The best reps are those who serve as marketing consultants for their client stations. They work with agencies to match target audiences with the appropriate stations on their client list. Sometimes this is done on a market-by-market basis. In other cases, buys are made through nonwired networks in the same manner as they are made through television nonwired networks, which we discussed in Chapter 8. It remains to be seen what effect consolidation within the radio industry will have on the relationship between reps and stations. As more and more local stations are bought by major groups, it may mean that a significant amount of spot advertising will be sold directly by group salespersons bypassing rep firms and that reps will be left primarily to sell smaller market stations through their nonwired networks. The rep/station relationship is only one more area of potential change in an industry where reorganization has become the rule.

AM VERSUS FM AS AN ADVERTISING MEDIUM

FM dominates the overall listening audience and is the clear leader in most formats. With the exception of several major all-talk stations, most AM stations are far down the list of stations in terms of ratings and audience share. In fact, AM stations tend to reach an older audience with talk, news, and specialty formats such as gospel and nostalgia.

The growth of FM radio audiences and advertising revenues during the past 30 years is one of the most important trends in the industry. FM technology was adapted for radio shortly before World War II. During the war, all broadcast station construction was halted, but a few stations that had gone on the air prior to the start of the war continued to operate. For almost 3 decades after the end of the war, FM was largely confined to noncommercial and classical stations with few listeners and little or no advertising. The exceptions were the jointly owned AM/FM stations, which usually duplicated programming on both stations. Because AM and FM radio sets were sold separately and there was little original programming, few incentives existed for listeners to purchase the more expensive FM sets.

In 1975, FM independent stations (those without an AM partner) reported a combined loss of almost $10 million. Only 3 years later, these same stations had profits of slightly less than $25 million. Obviously, this type of economic turnaround did not happen by accident. A number of factors contributed to the vitality of FM with both advertisers and audiences. Among the major elements are the following:

1. In 1972, the FCC ruled that owners of both AM and FM stations in the same market had to program different formats. This ruling opened the way for FM as a separate medium.

2. The sound quality of FM is markedly better than that of AM. Because music formats dominate radio, FM steadily gained audience share at the expense of AM.

3. The decline in the cost of FM sets coincided with the popularity of the medium. Thirty years ago, radio sets with an FM band were much more expensive than AM-only sets. Also, few cars were equipped with an FM radio. Currently, about 9 out of 10 car radios are AM/FM and virtually all radio sets are equipped with both AM and FM bands.

4. As radio audiences turned to FM for the most popular music formats, AM was left with an audience skewed to older listeners, a less than prime market segment for most advertisers. Therefore, the switch to FM by audiences was followed quickly by an increase in advertising dollars.

A typical "recording" sign at a radio station announces that the station is broadcasting a transmission on the air.

Courtesy of Ron Lane.

FM is likely to continue to be the dominant radio medium as AM stations search for those formats that will attract niche audiences. In fact, many observers say that it was only the popularity of talk radio in the past 20 years that saved AM from economic disaster. HD radio may make it possible for AM stations to see a resurgence in listenership with its promise of high-quality sound.

TYPES OF PROGRAMMING   As we previously discussed, radio is a medium constantly searching for targeted audiences to deliver to advertisers. It also is a medium overwhelmingly devoted to music. The typical radio station depends on a music format and unique talent to appeal to the largest audience in a particular listener demographic. Unlike television, where viewers tune to a certain program for a half-hour or hour and then move to another station for another show, radio audiences tend to demonstrate loyalty to a station because of the type of music, sports, or information it programs.

For a number of years, more stations have carried the "country" format than any other radio format. More than 2,000 stations report that they program some form of country music as their primary format. The number of country music stations can be attributed, in part, to the large quantity of small stations in rural and small-market areas where country music is most popular. Although many of the newer country styles have brought country into the mainstream and larger markets, it has its roots in small-town America.

To advertisers, it is often the quality of the audience as much as its size that is of most importance. For example, those relatively few stations with "children," "public affairs," or "agriculture and farm" formats might be exactly the advertising vehicle for particular advertisers seeking to reach small but (for them) profitable prospects.

One of the problems for radio stations is that they function in an environment of economic Darwinism in which only the strongest survive. Although every station would like to be the leader in a popular format, radio executives know that it is extremely difficult for more than one or two stations in a market to be financially successful in any particular format. Why would an advertiser buy a market's third- or fourth-rated country station?

Consequently, second- and third-tier stations are constantly searching for niche formats that will allow them to be the leader among some audience segment that is of value to advertisers. Specialty formats, such as classical or jazz, usually depend on an upscale audience that is difficult for advertisers to reach in other media. However, with dozens of stations in some large markets, developing niche formats is not only cutthroat but also often gets a little silly. For instance, stations without impressive total numbers may resort to calling themselves the number-one station in a particular daypart (e.g., midnight–6 A.M.) or developing subcategories of a format to differentiate themselves from other stations (easy listening country). (See Exhibit 9.9.)

Radio should be considered a quasi-mass medium. Despite its high aggregate audiences, the number of people listening to any particular station at a given time is very small. Even the top stations in a market will be lucky to achieve ratings of 5 or 6, and a rating of 1 to 3 is more common. Consequently, an audience increase that would be insignificant in other media might make a major difference in the financial health of a radio station. For example, a change of one rating point for a station with an average rating of 3 is an increase of 33 percent, a figure that often will move a station significantly up in the rankings among stations in a market.

		EXHIBIT 9.9
Morning Drivetime	6:00 A.M. to 10:00 A.M.	**Radio Dayparts**
Midday	10:00 A.M. to 3:00 P.M.	
Afternoon Drivetime	3:00 P.M. to 7:00 P.M.	
Evening	7:00 P.M. to 12:00 A.M.	
Overnight	12:00 A.M. to 6:00 A.M.	

Radio Ratings Services

5 **Explain the rating systems used in radio.**

As discussed in Chapter 8, the growth of television has created some significant problems in determining accurate audience-rating data. However, the problems in television research pale in comparison to those facing radio. Not only are there more than 10 times the number of radio stations compared to television but also the lack of specific programming on most stations makes respondent recall much more difficult than that in television. As we have discussed, television recall is not a problem for the majority of viewers where meters are used. In addition, much of the radio audience listens out-of-home where it is impractical to keep a diary or reach respondents by telephone.

Dozens of companies provide research services for radio. However, most of these firms are engaged in program consulting or custom research for individual stations and advertisers. The major source of local syndicated radio ratings and the dominant company in radio research is **Arbitron Inc.**, which provides audience data through its Arbitron Radio division.

Arbitron Inc.
Syndicated radio ratings company.

Arbitron measures radio audiences in approximately 300 local markets primarily through the use of listener diaries. All members of diary-sampled households over the age of 12 have a personal diary in which they record listening behavior during a 7-day period. Rating periods in a specific market last for 12 weeks. The number of weeks that a market is sampled is determined by its size, with most of the largest metropolitan areas sampled on a continuous basis throughout the year. The smallest markets are sampled for only one 12-week period, and the ratings are published in a condensed version of the larger ratings books.[13] Nielson, long the dominant company for television ratings data, has begun audience measurement of radio audiences in more than 50 smaller and mid-sized markets. The diaries used by Nielson use stickers rather than requiring panelists to write down which station they listened to. This is considered by some to be more accurate than Arbitron's method and is also less costly for radio stations. The latter is a key selling point for broadcasters.[14]

Because much of radio listening occurs outside of the home, and advertisers and radio stations are interested in capturing data on radio listening throughout the day, Arbitron has developed a Portable People Meter (PPM). There are PPM panels of users in more than 20 of the largest radio markets. The PPM can track what consumers listen to on the radio, watch on television, stream on the Internet, or hear in stores. This small mobile device is worn by Arbitron panel members and detects identification codes that can be embedded in the signal transmission. This signal is collected automatically by the device and sent daily to Arbitron for analysis.[15] The hope is that this device will eventually eliminate the need for diaries and permit more accurate data collection that is less intrusive for the respondents.

Station ratings are much more critical to most advertisers than those for networks because of the local nature of radio. However, as we discussed earlier, network radio is important to a number of national advertisers. As major businesses move into network radio advertising, the demand for accurate ratings will become even more important. The primary source of radio national network ratings is the **Radio's All-Dimension Audience Research (RADAR)** reports, also a service of Arbitron. Research data for RADAR reports are collected through 7-day listening diaries kept by consumers or by PPMs in larger metered markets.[16]

Radio's All-Dimension Audience Research (RADAR)
Service of Statistical Research, Inc., that is the primary source of network radio ratings.

An overriding problem in dealing with radio ratings is money. The funds available to solve an advertising research problem are directly related to the level of advertising expenditures by major advertisers. For example, when Procter & Gamble invests more than $2.1 billion annually in television, there is a major incentive to invest millions of dollars in research.[17] However, even though the problems may be more difficult in media such as radio and outdoor, the overall advertising investment will simply not support a research expenditure comparable to that of television.

Michael Pettigrew/Shutterstock.

Buying Radio

Radio demonstrates a number of characteristics as an advertising medium:

- Advertising inventory is perishable, and when a spot goes unsold, revenue is permanently lost.

- Radio is normally used as a supplement to other media. Therefore, coordination with the total advertising plan is crucial for most radio sales.

- Every radio buy is unique. Almost all radio advertising is sold in packages of spots that are tailored, to some degree, to each advertiser.

- Because of the unique nature of each buy, a fixed rate card rarely exists for radio advertising. Pricing is largely the result of negotiation between media buyers and radio salespersons.

Despite the complexity of buying radio advertising, the fundamentals of buying radio are very similar to those used with other media. For example, as with most advertising plans, we must examine a number of elements before we proceed to an advertising execution:

1. Review product characteristics and benefits and decide whether these benefits can be effectively communicated through radio.

2. Decide who the target market is and whether they can be reached effectively with radio and, if so, using what formats and during what dayparts. For example, Hispanic audiences are more likely to spend time listening to radio—particularly to one of several Spanish radio formats—than are non-Hispanic audiences.[18] According to Arbitron reports, African American audiences are more likely to spend their radio listening with urban adult contemporary, gospel, urban adult contemporary hit, urban contemporary, or religious radio formats.[19] The ability to reach audience segments with this type of pinpoint precision remains radio's major strength.

3. Determine who the competition is. How are they using radio and other media? Will radio provide a unique differentiation for our product or will we be up against strong competing messages?

4. Determine what the basic advertising and marketing strategy is and whether it can be effectively carried out with radio.

In virtually all advertising situations, we start with a clear delineation of our target market. This audience definition is particularly important in buying radio because of the narrowly defined formats that are offered by the medium. We then must look at the cost of alternative radio outlets and must compare the options available against the CPM/prospects or CPP. Radio, from both a marketing and creative standpoint, must be considered in terms of the advertising objectives we have set for our advertising. For example, radio in general or a specific station may meet our objectives for reach and cost but fail in terms of the creative strategy. Because radio advertising is often used as a secondary medium, it may be the case that we will evaluate radio in terms of how it complements other more primary media in our advertising schedule and what proportion of our budget should be devoted to radio in this complementary role.

Once we have decided that radio can play a role in our advertising plan, we must begin the task of selecting particular stations that both reach our target audience and provide a program environment that fits our product image. As we discussed, the number of radio stations provide advertisers, particularly those with national distribution, with many options from which to choose. For some advertisers, network radio is a better option—in terms of cost and guaranteed quality of editorial services—than a spot or local schedule. Nevertheless, radio is one of the most challenging aspects of media planning.

The final step in radio buying is the actual scheduling of the spots. Because most advertisers use a great number of spots to achieve reach and/or frequency, the scheduling process can be difficult. Although radio spots are often 60 seconds, some advertisers use shorter messages to gain frequency while a few opt for longer-form commercials to achieve greater impact. Some advertisers also use shorter 15-second spots for simple messages that allow them to increase frequency (see Exhibit 9.10). In addition, decisions such as whether to use specific dayparts or a combination of time periods and, in a few instances, whether to take advantage of program sponsorship or on-site event promotions must be considered. Regardless of the final determinations of these and other questions, radio can provide great flexibility and fit into the plans of virtually every advertiser.

Because of the complicated nature of radio, buyers must often rely on the expertise of radio sales personnel—at the station, network, or rep level. Given the nature of radio buys, it is imperative that both buyers and sellers understand the relationship involved in the process. This starts with credibility. One of the primary ways a radio salesperson gains trust is by positioning radio as a part of the marketing plan. This

EXHIBIT 9.10

Fifteen-second Radio Spots for Georgia 511, a Traffic Hotline

Thanksgiving

Music	Dramatic Announcer
1950s instructional movie music underneath.	An important Thanksgiving safety tip. Do *not* drive while in a turkey-induced coma. *Do* drive after alertly calling Georgia 511. 511 is fast, free, real-time traffic information. 511—We'll get you there.

Holiday Shopping

Music	Dramatic Announcer
Action movie music underneath.	You are on a mission. Reach the mall before the Super Ninja Robot Doll sells out. You need Georgia 511. Just call 511 for fast, free, real-time traffic information. 511—We'll get you there.

Source: Courtesy of McRae Communications and Georgia Department of Economic Development.

entails walking a fine line between aggressively selling the medium and your station and, at the same time, acknowledging the strengths and contributions of other media.

Rather than trying to convince heavy newspaper advertisers to move out of the medium, it is more reasonable to show how radio can make newspaper advertising more effective. The key to successful selling is identifying with the problems of the clients. To do this, the salesperson needs to show advertisers that radio can solve their specific marketing problems. Remember, advertisers are not interested in buying time—they are interested in finding prospects and demonstrating major product benefits to these prospects.

Using Radio Ratings

We defined both television ratings and share of audience in Chapter 8. Radio ratings and share figures are calculated in the same way. However, the size of the radio audience and the highly fragmented nature of programming and formats have created a system in which ratings are used differently from that in television. This section discusses some uses of ratings that are unique to radio.

Among the primary differences between the use of ratings in television and their use in radio are the following:

1. Radio advertisers are interested in broad formats rather than programs or more narrowly defined television scatter plans.

2. Radio ratings tend to measure audience accumulation over relatively long periods of time or several dayparts. Most television ratings are calculated for individual programs.

3. The audiences for individual radio stations are much smaller than those for television, making radio ratings less reliable.

4. Because most radio stations reach only a small segment of the market at a given time, there is a need for much higher levels of advertising frequency in order to increase reach compared to other media. Consequently, it is extremely difficult to track ratings information accurately for national radio plans that include a large number of stations.

Let's begin our discussion by examining several definitions used in radio-rating analyses.

GEOGRAPHIC PATTERNS OF RADIO RATINGS

Radio audience ratings use two geographic boundaries to report audiences: Metro Survey Area (MSA) and Total Survey Area (TSA). Typically the majority of a station's audience comes from within the MSA.

- *Metro Survey Area.* An MSA always includes a city or cities whose population is specified as that of the central city together with the county (or counties) in which it is located.

- *Total Survey Area.* The TSA is a geographic area that encompasses the MSA and certain counties located outside the MSA that meet certain minimum listening criteria.

DEFINITIONS OF THE RADIO AUDIENCE

The basic audience measures for television are the rating and share of audience for a particular show. It would be a serious mistake to buy radio and television on the same basis without considering major differences in the way audience figures are considered between the two media. In radio, audience estimates are usually presented as either **Average Quarter-Hour (AQH)** audiences or the cumulative or unduplicated audience (Cume) listening to a station over several quarter hours or dayparts.

Average Quarter-Hour (AQH)
Manner in which radio ratings are presented. Estimates (AQHE) include average number of people listening (AQHP), rating (AQHR), and share (AQHS) of audience. The Metro Survey Area (MSA) population can be used to determine share.

AVERAGE QUARTER-HOUR ESTIMATES (AQHE)

1. *Average Quarter-Hour persons.* The AQH persons are the estimated number of people listening to a station for at least 5 minutes during a 15-minute period.

2. *Average Quarter-Hour rating.* Here, we calculate the AQH persons as a percentage of the population being measured:

   (AQH persons/population) $\times$ 100 = AQH rating

3. *Average Quarter-Hour share.* The AQH share determines what portion of the average radio audience is listening to our station:

   (AQH persons to a station/AQH persons to all stations) $\times$ 100 = AQH share

CUME ESTIMATES   Cume estimates are used to determine the number or percentage of different people who listen to a station during several quarter-hours or dayparts.

1. *Cume persons.* Cume persons include the number of different people who tuned in to a radio station for at least 5 minutes.

2. *Cume rating.* The cume rating is the percentage of different people listening to a station during several quarter-hours or dayparts.

   (Cume persons/population) $\times$ 100 = Cume rating

Let's look at a typical station's audience and calculate these formulas.

Station XYZQ

Friday 10 A.M.–3 P.M., Adults 12+

AQH persons = 20,000

Cume persons = 60,000

Metro Survey Area population = 500,000

Metro Survey Area AQH persons = 200,000

For station XYZQ

AQH rating = (20,000/500,000) $\times$ 100 = 4

Cume rating = (60,000/500,000) $\times$ 100 = 12

MSA AQH share = (20,000/200,000) $\times$ 100 = 10

Using our XYZQ example, we can also calculate the following:

1. Gross impressions (GI) = AQH persons $\times$ Number of commercials
   If we buy six commercials on XYZQ, we have purchased 120,000 impressions:

   20,000 AQH persons $\times$ 6 spots = 120,000 GI

   Remember, these are impressions, not people.

2. Gross rating points = AQH rating $\times$ Number of commercials
   Again, six commercials would deliver 24 GRPs (4 AQH rating $\times$ 6 spots).

The media planner must be able to manipulate the various radio data to develop a plan most suited to a particular client. Although the computer makes these manipulations quickly, it doesn't substitute for a basic understanding of the process. The same budget, and even the same number of spots, used in different dayparts and across multiple stations, can deliver vastly different levels of cumes, reach, frequency, and demographics.

SUMMARY

Every day more Americans use radio than any other medium. With thousands of stations, multiple formats, inexpensive production, and low commercial cost, it can provide effective reach and frequency for a number of product categories.

Technology is taking the immediacy and person-to-person nature of radio to another level. With satellite transmission and out-of-home capability, radio can reach individual customers with programs and commercials tailored to their demographics and lifestyle. New audience-measurement technology holds the promise of being able to track some of this out-of-home audience enjoyed by radio.

Radio has a significant advantage in achieving high penetration among light users or nonusers of other media. Given the current demand by advertisers for narrowly defined audience segments, radio is increasingly becoming at least a secondary option in more and more media plans.

Despite the opportunities for radio to become more important in the advertising plans of both large and small advertisers, the medium faces four major problems. First, the audience delivered by radio is very fragmented. It is better at delivering frequency than reach. Second, commercial clutter is a problem. A third major problem with radio is the lack of a visual element. Many advertisers think that without strong visual brand identification the medium can play little or no role in their advertising plans. The industry has sponsored a number of research studies to show that radio can work effectively with television to remind consumers of the commercials they have seen previously. Probably the biggest problem currently facing radio, however, is the increased use of the Internet and MP3 players, which threatens to diminish the size of the traditional radio audience. Since the delivery systems for radio content are changing, the future success of the medium will likely depend on the ability of radio content providers to adapt to the notion that they are in the business of delivering audio content through a variety of delivery systems.

REVIEW

1. Define the following:
   a. Drivetime
   b. Satellite radio
   c. HD radio
2. What is the major disadvantage of radio for most advertisers?
3. What are the primary advantages of radio to advertisers?
4. What is spot radio?
5. What is the role of radio networks?
6. Who are the listeners of AM radio? To what do they listen?
7. Where do most advertisers obtain radio audience information?
8. What is the difference between an AQH rating and a Cume rating?

U.P. images_photo, Shutterstock.

Using Newspapers

NEWSPAPERS have long been a leader in terms of local advertising revenue, trailing only television in terms of total advertising revenue. Each day approximately 48.5 million newspapers are distributed, providing a large segment of the population with news, entertainment, and advertising.[1] Newspapers also enjoy a reputation for credibility that creates a positive advertising environment. ▶

CHAPTER LEARNING OBJECTIVES

1. Describe the changing character and role of local and national newspapers in the marketing mix.

2. Explain the marketing of newspapers to readers and advertisers.

3. Identify the many categories of newspaper advertising.

4. Describe the newspaper advertising planning and buying process.

5. Discuss the role of newspaper-distributed supplements.

6. Discuss the role of ethnically oriented newspapers and weeklies.

Newspaper advertising offers a number of advantages to businesses from large national corporations to the smallest retailer. Among the most important advantages of newspaper advertising are the following:

Pros

1. Newspapers are especially useful in reaching upscale households and opinion leaders, especially adults aged 35 and older. However, compared to most other media, newspapers have significant reach in many major demographic segments.

2. Newspapers offer significant flexibility of advertising formats and audience coverage. Advertisers can buy space ranging from a full-page, four-color advertisement to a small classified notice. In addition, virtually every newspaper offers a variety of specialized advertising plans, including coupons and online options, to allow advertisers to reach selected portions of the newspaper's total circulation through special sections and targeted editions. Newspapers offer advertisers a number of creative options including preprinted inserts and product samples.

3. With coupons and sophisticated tracking techniques, it is much easier to measure newspaper response rates than response rates of many other media.

4. Newspapers provide an environment of credibility and immediacy unmatched by most media. A number of surveys have shown that consumers regard newspaper advertising as an important and reliable source of both information and advertising—just the type of medium with which advertisers want to be associated.

Disadvantages for using newspapers as an advertising medium include the following:

Cons

1. Many newspapers have as much as 60 percent advertising content. This high ratio of advertising, combined with average reading time of less than 30 minutes per day, means few advertisements are read.

2. Overall newspaper circulation has fallen far behind population and household growth. Readership among a number of key demographics such as teens and young adults has not kept pace with population growth.

3. Advertising costs have risen much more sharply than circulation in recent years.

On an average weekday, newspapers are read by about 43 percent of the adult population and by an even greater percentage of readers from households with higher-than-average income and education levels.[2] Annual advertising revenues in print and online newspapers are more than $37.8 billion with approximately 84 percent coming from local advertisers.[3] In addition, national advertisers are looking increasingly to local and regional advertising strategies to communicate with target consumers in the most effective manner.

So, why is the newspaper industry so concerned about its future? The fact of the matter is that a number of trends pose challenges for newspaper publishers.

1 Describe the changing character and role of local and national newspapers in the marketing mix.

1. *Circulation.* According to the Newspaper Association of America (NAA), in 1976, newspaper circulation was 77 million; by 2008, this figure was approximately 48.6 million in spite of significant increases in both population and households during that period.[4]

   The reasons given for the decline in newspaper circulation vary from not enough time in single-parent and two-income families to devote to newspaper reading; to younger demographic segments who don't like to read or who never developed the habit of reading newspapers; to other media, especially television and the Internet, that have encroached on the newspaper's position as the preferred method of getting news and information. All of these factors have probably played a role in the decline of newspaper readership.

   Different newspapers have attacked the readership problem with diverse approaches. In some cases, newspapers engage in aggressive subscription sales campaigns including setting up booths in grocery stores or on college campuses (see Exhibit 10.1, for example). Others have set up programs to provide newspapers to middle and high schools in an attempt to give young readers experience with the medium.

2. *Advertising revenues.* Obviously, the advertising community has not ignored newspaper circulation problems. As recently as 1980, newspapers' share of total advertising revenue was 28 percent. Currently, the figure is about 18 percent.[5]

   Several problems have beleaguered newspapers in maintaining their share of advertising dollars. First, a number of retail chains have turned to direct mail and inserts to reach customers. Even the inserts that are distributed through newspapers provide lower profits for newspapers than traditional advertising. Second, newspapers have been unable to increase support from national advertisers. Although many national advertisers look to regional and local strategies, newspapers have had a difficult time gaining significant support from major national advertisers. Despite a number of newspaper initiatives to overcome national advertisers' reluctance to use the medium, dollars in the sector remain small.

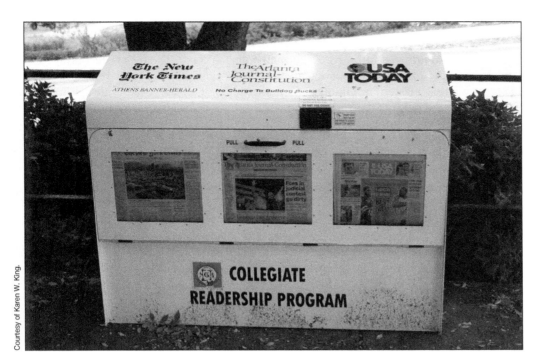

EXHIBIT 10.1

Some newspapers are trying to increase their readership among college students.

Although newspapers have never enjoyed a large amount of revenue from national advertisers, currently their franchise with local advertisers is being threatened from a number of quarters. Local television; local cable cut-ins; free niche advertising books featuring real estate, automobiles, and the like; regional and city editions of magazines; and, of course, radio continue to fight for local advertising dollars that 30 years ago would have gone automatically to newspapers. Later in this chapter, we discuss some of the ways that newspapers are countering these problems.

3. *Changing technology.* Newspapers, like all media, face challenges from new media technology. In fact, many believe that the newspaper as we know it will be changed dramatically by this technology—not the many functions it serves but the method of distribution. The argument is that the cost of paper, ink, postage, and physical distribution is simply not going to be viable in a world of electronic communication. Going back no further than 1990, virtually no one outside the scientific community had ever heard of the Internet.

In light of the foothold enjoyed by the Internet, with continued improvements in instantaneous delivery, clarity and reliability of content, and portability of technology over the next 20 years, it is hard to imagine thick wads of paper being thrown in the driveways of the 2025 household! It is more likely that many households will be reading up-to-date news content on their computers or wireless reading devises. This gloomy prediction for newspapers does not mean the functions of newspapers will be dead or even that the companies that provide these services will be gone. It certainly does not mean that there will not be reporters, advertising salespeople, and most of all businesses with dollars to spend to reach a literate audience. It does mean that the methods of reaching these customers and "readers" will change dramatically.

Currently, most newspapers provide web sites for their readers and/or advertisers. But as we discuss later in this chapter, the immediacy of newspapers is being replaced by electronic formats—many developed by newspapers themselves. In addition, newspaper classified advertising, which used to provide more than 35 percent of newspaper advertising revenue, now provides about 26 percent of total revenues for the newspaper industry.[6] Newspaper classified advertising is being challenged by dozens of online web sites, such as Craigslist, seeking a share of the classified market.

The continuing challenge for both newspaper publishers and newspaper advertising executives is to provide the audience with readers to look to the daily paper as a primary source of information, advertising, and entertainment. The task is becoming more difficult as newspapers try to serve a diverse audience of readers who are young or old, readers who are affluent or middle class, and readers of a variety of ethnic cultures. It is clear that newspapers face growing competition from other media and information sources as they attempt to retain their position as a leading medium. The newspaper industry faces both problems and opportunities. As evidenced by the demise of some large metropolitan dailies and the move of some dailies to online-only versions (e.g., the *Seattle Post-Intelligencer*), it is obvious that long-term trends will continue to endanger the basic foundation of newspaper readership and advertising. In the meantime, newspapers, despite declines in readership, remain one of the most effective means of reaching a broad, heterogeneous audience.

As can be seen throughout the remainder of this chapter, newspapers need innovative initiatives to function successfully in this competitive environment. As we discuss major aspects of contemporary newspaper advertising, we must keep in mind the evolving and dynamic nature of the industry.

The National Newspaper

Historically, the United States, unlike most other developed countries, did not have a national newspaper. When the first newspapers were founded, distances were too great and unique regional concerns made nationally distributed newspapers impractical. However, a number of newspapers now have national circulation, national stature, or both. The Internet has made it possible for newspapers that were previously only available locally to reach a regional or national audience for the first time.

A national newspaper is generally defined having the following characteristics:

- It publishes at least 5 days per week.
- It has printed copies that are sold, distributed, and available nationwide.

Based on these criteria, there are three national newspapers: the *Wall Street Journal*, *USA Today*, and the *New York Times*. The *Wall Street Journal* is an upscale, specialized paper with an emphasis on financial news but with great influence in politics and public policy issues. With a circulation of more than 2 million, it is the second-highest-circulation newspaper in the country. It also is among the most respected newspapers in the world, and it reaches readers with the most elite audience demographics of any U.S. newspapers.

All three of the leading national publications have extensive web sites. However, not all newspaper web sites are profitable. The *Wall Street Journal* has a profitable web site largely because of its reputation and specialized business content; it is able to charge an annual subscription fee of $129 (or lower if a person subscribes to the print edition). By comparison, many other newspaper sites are free, advertising supported, and only marginally profitable.

In 1982, the Gannett Company made a commitment to develop *USA Today* as a general-readership national newspaper. Although newspaper purists often criticized the paper's lack of depth, *USA Today* was popular with readers from the beginning with a mix of bright colors, short articles, and extensive business and sports coverage. The paper now has a circulation of more than 2.2 million. Exhibit 10.2 shows the U.S. newspapers with the largest circulations.

The problem facing all newspapers that aspire to national circulation is finding a profitable advertising niche. A national newspaper is a hybrid vehicle for most advertisers. Unlike other newspapers, national papers are unlikely to gain advertising from grocery stores, department stores, and other local product categories that have been

Rank	Publication	Average Daily Circulation
1	*USA Today*	2,113,725
2	*Wall Street Journal*	2,082,189
3	*The New York Times*	1,039,031
4	*Los Angeles Times*	723,181
5	*The Washington Post*	665,383
6	*Daily News (New York)*	602,857
7	*New York Post*	558,140
8	*Chicago Tribune*	501,202
9	*Houston Chronicle*	425,138
10	*The Arizona Republic*	389,701
11	*The Denver Post*	371,728
12	*Newsday*	368,194
13	*The Dallas Morning News*	331,907
14	*Star Tribune (Newspaper of the Twin Cities)*	320,076
15	*Chicago Sun-Times*	312,141
16	*San Francisco Chronicle*	312,118
17	*The Boston Globe*	302,638
18	*The Plain Dealer (Cleveland)*	291,630
19	*Detroit Free Pass*	290,730
20	*The Philadelphia Inquirer*	288,298

EXHIBIT 10.2

Top 20 U.S. Daily Newspapers by Circulation

Source: Audit Bureau of Circulations, *Editor and Publisher,* 3 April 2009, http://www.editorandpublisher.com/eandp/news/article_display.jsp?vnu_content_id=1003966608, accessed 7 June 2009.

traditionally major profit centers for newspapers. Instead, *USA Today* and other national newspapers depend on national automotive, computer, and communication companies and financial services for much of their revenue.

Although the *New York Times* is now classified as a national newspaper, most large metropolitan newspapers such as the *Washington Post* and the *Chicago Tribune* are considered regional advertising media. They are bought much like spot broadcast to reach specific high-potential markets as a supplement to other primary media. Despite attempts by some newspapers to broaden their coverage, most advertisers classify all newspapers other than the *Wall Street Journal*, the *New York Times*, and *USA Today* as regional.

Newspapers will probably continue to have a difficult time reaching out to national advertising as a primary medium. Newspapers have a long tradition as a local vehicle, which is a difficult perception to change. The key to a move toward national newspapers is not how papers define themselves but how readers and advertisers define the papers. Until a number of newspapers achieve widely dispersed, upscale audiences (not likely for any but a handful of papers), advertisers will continue to regard the medium as a local vehicle with occasional national advertising opportunities. The Internet now offers newspaper publishers an opportunity to reach a national and even an international audience.

Marketing the Newspaper

It is obvious from our discussion thus far that newspapers are a product in need of extensive marketing to both readers and advertisers. Like any product with declining sales, newspapers must make a number of strategic and tactical decisions to reverse the trends they are seeing. Despite being one of the leading sources of advertising dollars, the traditional retail base of newspaper revenues is being challenged by a number of new and traditional media competitors. At the same time, newspapers are finding it more difficult to maintain the broad base of readership that has made them such a powerful medium for more than 200 years.

2 **Explain the marketing of newspapers to readers and advertisers.**

A positive trend among newspapers is the desirability of newspaper readers to advertisers. Newspapers are popular among college graduates and households with incomes in excess of $100,000. Unfortunately, newspaper circulation also skews toward the oldest portion of the population. Newspaper readership is inversely related to age, with those in the 18 to 34 age group (prime prospects for the majority of advertisers) the least likely to read newspapers on a regular basis.

Newspapers have taken a number of steps to identify their customers and advertisers, as well as the preferences of both. This process starts with marketing research. It is rare for any newspaper not to conduct at least one readership or market survey each year. Large newspapers annually sponsor several studies of their markets. A number of concerns have become apparent as a result of these studies.

Among the most important of these concerns is the fact that readers are obtaining their information from a number of sources, including television and the Internet. They no longer see the newspaper as an indispensable source of information. Although many advertisers regard newspapers as an economical means of reaching a mass audience, especially at the local level, many are adopting strategies that replace newspaper advertising with direct mail and other forms of promotion such as product sampling and the Internet. On the positive side, these same studies demonstrate that newspapers maintain their reputation for integrity and prestige as sources of both advertising and editorial information.

Although newspapers face some formidable challenges, they will remain an important advertising medium in the foreseeable future as they continue to offer unique advantages to both readers and advertisers. However, because newspapers dominated the local market for so long, they did not develop a marketing mentality. Unfortunately, the industry is now playing catch-up with its more aggressive media competitors. The next sections discuss how newspaper publishers are marketing the medium to both readers and advertisers. We examine some of the approaches that newspaper publishers are using to protect and extend their franchises with both readers and advertisers.

MARKETING TO READERS

Newspapers are fully aware that they cannot reverse the decline in advertising share unless they first address the problem of falling readership. Advertisers will only buy newspaper space when they are convinced that the medium will deliver prospects for their brands. Some elite newspapers may be able to survive decreasing readership by marketing the quality of their audience. However, most newspapers will continue to depend on a broadly based audience and high household penetration for their financial success.

Because the current problems facing newspaper advertising are caused by a number of factors, publishers must address several issues if they are to compete with other media in the future. Among the primary steps that newspapers should take are the following:[7]

1. Maintaining good circulation numbers through print or online editions should be a high priority. Newspapers should continue to emphasize getting newspapers into the hands of younger readers. Many newspapers have put in place programs that provide newspapers to grade schools and make it easy for college students to get newspapers.

2. Editors and reporters should be free of control by marketing departments. The news staff should understand that the newspaper is a business enterprise and that even they can make use of market research in the development of a more reader-friendly newspaper, but this does not mean that the editorial product should be directed by advertising or business concerns. To do so will undermine the newspaper's editorial credibility, which is one of its major strengths.

3. Continue to pursue opportunities in national advertising. Newspaper advertising departments must continue to explore creative approaches to demonstrate that newspapers can provide national advertisers with desirable audiences that cannot be reached effectively with other media.

4. More newspapers consider their web sites as a distinctive product rather than a mere spin-off from the printed paper. The Internet can offer profitable opportunities to exploit a fuller range of information and advertising than what is printed in the newspaper. The Internet accessed through either computers or wireless mobile reading devices can reach specific readers (and nonnewspaper readers) with selective news, digital video content, and advertising and—properly marketed—make a newspaper's web site a profit center rather than merely a value added to both readers and possible advertisers.

5. Give readers a choice and market to diverse audience segments. The marginal costs are often worth the expense, even if only a relatively few new readers are added. Newspaper web sites offer newspapers an inexpensive way to provide targeted content to specific readers.

6. Invest in research and explore ways to make Internet sites complement the information provided in the newspaper. This will allow the newspaper to remain competitive over the long term even though it may not contribute to short-term profits.

Despite the medium's many strengths, newspapers will continue to see a need to aggressively market themselves to readers. Most newspaper readers and potential readers see the value of a newspaper in local news and sports and other information with relevance to their lives. Readers want information about things to do and places to go, self-help articles, local news of personal interest, and national and international news that has an effect on their lives. In a diverse, multicultural society, appealing to diverse reader interests is extremely difficult. But newspapers will have to find ways to address this heterogeneous population if they are to maintain their position as a primary source of news and advertising.

MARKETING TO ADVERTISERS

Traditionally, advertising constitutes more than 70 percent of all newspaper revenues, and more than 50 percent of total newspaper space is devoted to advertising. Clearly, newspapers must continue to attract a number of business categories if they are to remain financially viable. In a fragmented media market, newspapers are finding it more difficult to maintain their share of advertising. As shown in Exhibit 10.3, leading advertisers in newspapers include department stores and communication and entertainment companies.

One of the problems facing newspapers is the dramatic increase in the cost of printing and delivery. This has lead to increases in advertising rates charged to advertisers. Obviously, other media have had significant advertising cost increases, but few were higher on a percentage basis than newspapers.

In order to stem the decline in newspaper advertising revenue, it is imperative that newspapers continue to convince advertisers that they are an efficient means of meeting a variety of marketing and advertising objectives. In order to accomplish this goal,

Rank	Marketer	2008 (in billion $)
1	Verizon Communications	681.9
2	Macy's	583.3
3	General Motors Corp.	320.9
4	AT&T	288.6
5	Fry's Electronics	205.0
6	Time Warner	204.2
7	News Corp.	197.9
8	Sears Holdings Corp.	191.2
9	Procter & Gamble Co.	187.1
10	General Electric Co.	171.0

EXHIBIT 10.3

Top 10 Advertisers in Newspapers

Ranked by measured spending in 2008.

Source: "U.S. ad-spending totals by medium," TNS Measured Media, *Advertising Age*, 22 June 2009, 18. Reprinted with permission from the June 22, 2009 issue of *Advertising Age.* Copyright, Crain Communications Inc. 2009.

KLEPPNER VIEWPOINT 10.1

Jim Conaghan Vice President/Research,
Newspaper Association of America

THE STRENGTH OF NEWSPAPERS IN THE TWENTY-FIRST CENTURY

Jim Conaghan

n the first chapter of Charles Dickens's novel, *Hard Times*, Mr. Gradgrind proclaimed, "In this life, we want nothing but Facts, sir; nothing but Facts."

There's no doubt that the facts about newspaper advertising today are daunting, as the economy continues to struggle. Structural changes in advertisers' businesses, the attraction of digital platforms, and the consumer recession have weighed on ad performance for all media and will continue to do so for some time. (For facts about advertising spending in newspapers in print and online, see www.naa.org/TrendsandNumbers/. It's all there.)

While you're reviewing past performance and the outlook for newspaper advertising, consider some of the facts that the critics and the promoters of other media are overlooking:

- Digital revenues have become an important part of the sustaining business model for newspapers. For example, in 2008, newspapers' online products generated about $3 billion in advertising revenue. Meanwhile, newspapers' digital audience has grown more than 60 percent since 2005. More than 40 percent of active Internet users visit a newspaper web site in a typical month.
- Scarborough Research reports that more than 100 million adults read a printed newspaper on an average weekday (and more than 115 million on Sunday). Compare that to 94 million

who watch the *Super Bowl*, 23 million who have viewed *American Idol,* and 64 million who typically watch the late local news.

- Newspaper readership in the top 50 markets has declined about 6 percent in the past 5 years (according to Scarborough). Compare that to a 10 percent decline in the prime-time television audience and a 6 percent decline in early evening local TV news in 2007 alone.
- Sixty-two percent of 18- to 24-year-olds and 25- to 34-year-olds read a newspaper in an average week. In addition, 64 and 66 percent, respectively, visited a newspaper web site in the past 7 days.
- According to consultant John Morton in a recent article in the *American Journalism Review*, newspaper companies that have reported results for the first 9 months of 2008 had a weighted average operating profit margin of 11.3 percent, clearly down but still above what is typical for most nonmedia businesses. He concludes that article by saying "Overall, the beleaguered newspaper industry's financial health has been weakened but remains healthy by most measures. In this environment, that is an achievement."

It's important to keep these facts in perspective. It's true that pessimists see newspapers as a declining ink-on-paper summary of news and information,

dropped at the doorstep every morning or waiting to be picked up at the newsstand. Optimists see an ink-on-paper product at the center of a collection of platforms, reaching different kinds of people with diverse kinds of content, how, when, and where they want it.

Which view is correct? Old industry or new industry?

Right now, they both are. We are in the process of moving from one to the other. It's a time of transition and transformation. Challenges abound, but this also is an exciting time for newspapers. We are not simply standing still. We're innovating, creating, pushing into digital platforms, and developing new ways to serve advertisers and consumers.

The strength of newspapers—their quality, credibility, and the powerful engagement they create with readers and online users—will be at the core of successful business models for tomorrow's newspapers and their digital companions.

Courtesy of Jim Conaghan.

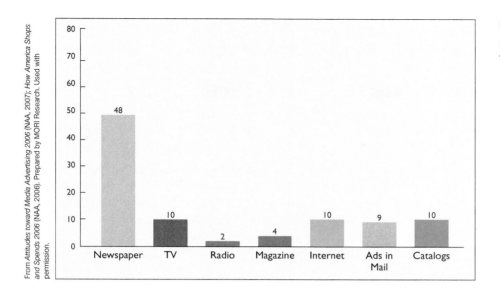

From *Attitudes toward Media Advertising 2006* (NAA, 2007); *How America Shops and Spends 2006* (NAA, 2006). Prepared by MORI Research. Used with permission.

EXHIBIT 10.4

Most Believable and Trustworthy Advertising

newspapers must develop a plan that shows a diverse group of current and potential advertisers that newspapers should be a part of their media plans.

The marketing task for newspapers is a twofold undertaking: (1) to deliver the audience and (2) to compete for advertisers. Research by the newspaper industry has shown that newspaper advertising is considered high on believability and trustworthiness relative to other major media types (see Exhibit 10.4).

The newspaper industry must convince advertisers that it represents the best local medium and at the same time demonstrate to national advertisers that it should constitute an important element of their advertising strategy. To accomplish these goals, newspapers must retain local retailers that have traditionally comprised the bulk of newspaper revenues and must gain more support from national advertisers that have not used newspapers previously to a great extent. In the current media climate, neither job will be easy. However, newspapers have an advantage in providing readers with localized, in-depth information concerning products and services in their communities.

Newspapers have taken a number of steps to position themselves more favorably in the eyes of advertisers. One approach has been to provide information about readership and paid circulation data. Virtually all media report readership or total viewers, whereas newspapers have traditionally reported only the number of newspapers distributed. Obviously, this difference in reporting standards relative to other media places newspapers at a significant disadvantage. As mentioned earlier, in 2008, daily newspaper circulation was approximately 48.6 million. However, when including pass-along readers, the newspaper audience is likely more than twice that number.

Many of the past complaints of media buyers centered around the difficulty of making multipaper buys across a number of markets. This is a particular problem for media buyers who are accustomed to the relative ease of buying national broadcast spots and magazines. To address the buying problem, newspapers developed information centers to make it easier for national and regional advertisers to know what services and products are available for advertisers. The **Newspaper Association of America (NAA)**, in cooperation with *Editor & Publisher* magazine, provides advertisers with a database indicating which newspapers provide special editions, targeted inserts, and other advertising options to make it easier to plan multinewspaper media buys.

As we discuss in later sections, newspapers are developing advertising strategies that try to meet the demands of the smallest retailer as well as the largest national firms.

Newspaper Association of America (NAA)
The marketing and trade organization for the newspaper industry.

Newspaper Inserts, Zoning, and Total Market Coverage

3 **Identify the many categories of newspaper advertising.**

Newspaper advertising executives must provide service to a number of advertisers, many with distinctly different marketing and advertising problems. Although there are a number of variations of newspaper advertising strategy, we discuss four approaches here:

1. *Full coverage of a newspaper's circulation.* In the past, most newspapers simply sold advertising space in their pages and advertisers received whatever circulation the paper provided. Large department stores, grocery stores with a number of locations, and national businesses with widely distributed products could take advantage of the majority of a newspaper's readers whereas other advertisers had to accept some level of waste circulation.

2. *Zoned preprints.* By the early 1980s, targeted direct mail began to offer advertisers a viable alternative to newspaper advertising without its inherent waste circulation. Newspapers countered by offering advertisers the opportunity to have advertising circulars and preprinted inserts delivered with the paper. The first businesses to make significant use of inserts were grocery stores and major retailers. In recent years, newspaper preprints have become the major vehicle for the distribution of coupons for businesses such as fast-food franchises.

The next step in the evolution of newspaper preprints, again in reaction to direct-mail competition, was the zoned distribution preprints. Rather than simply being inserted in every issue of the newspaper, zoned preprints could be delivered to specific ZIP codes within a metropolitan area. Initially, most papers offered these so-called zoned preprints only in upscale ZIP codes, but in recent years, advertisers have been able to buy any ZIP code within a newspaper's primary circulation area. In some instances, newspapers have begun to distribute preprints to even smaller, sub-ZIP-code circulation clusters called *microzones*.

Preprints are popular with some advertisers and have replaced traditional advertising or run-of-paper (ROP) for newspapers. (See Exhibit 10.5 for an example of a preprinted insert.) Today, the majority of newspapers provide ZIP-code zoning for advertising inserts. The largest advertisers in free-standing inserts tend to be consumer packaged goods such as household cleaning products, pet foods, and personal care products.

Although preprinted inserts allow newspapers to compete with direct mail, they also create problems for the newspaper industry. Following are some of the major issues:

- Inserts are less profitable than ROP advertising.
- Although surveys show that newspaper inserts attain higher reach and are preferable to direct mail, the newspaper is no more than an advertising delivery system for these inserts.
- As ROP advertising decreases, the space for news and editorial matter (the so-called *news hole*) shrinks and, ultimately, it may change the character of newspapers as both an advertising and information medium.

Despite any associated problems, **zoning** has offered newspapers a compelling weapon against direct mail and other forms of targeted media. It also holds the potential for bringing an increased number of national advertisers to newspapers:

1. *The zoned newspaper.* In addition to preprint zoning, many metropolitan newspapers are providing suburban weekly or even daily sections in the newspaper to

zoning
Newspaper practice of offering advertisers partial coverage of a market, often accomplished with weekly inserts distributed to certain sections of that market.

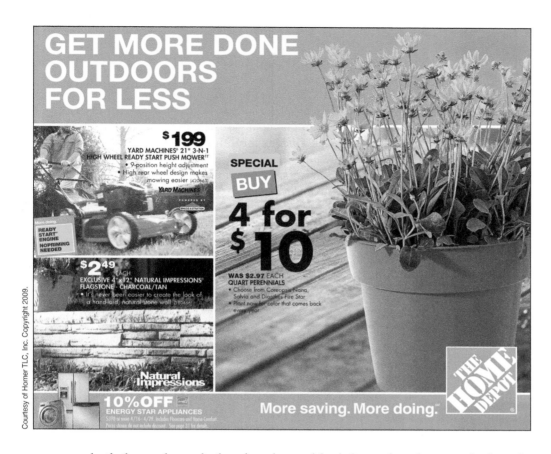

EXHIBIT 10.5

Why are preprinted inserts such as this one popular with many large advertisers?

serve both the reader and advertiser demand for information about particular suburbs of a city. In the past, many newspapers devoted limited resources to these sections. Today, most newspapers are making meaningful investments in their zoned editions and, in many cities, publishers have been rewarded with significant readership and advertising increases.

The zoned newspaper has major advantages for both advertisers and publishers. Advertisers can gain the advantages of zoning but still run ROP advertising, which has greater prestige and credibility. The zoned newspaper also overcomes the problem of insert clutter. Some major newspapers, especially their Sunday editions, carry dozens of inserts, which drastically decreases their readership and impact.

2. *Total market coverage.* Ironically, although newspapers seek to serve advertisers that are interested in a narrowly defined group of readers, they also find that a number of advertisers are seeking total penetration of a market. Because no newspaper has complete coverage of its market (in many markets, it is as low as 30 percent), other means must be used to augment regular circulation and achieve **total market coverage (TMC)**. Total market coverage may be accomplished in a number of ways:

    ▪ Weekly delivery of a nonsubscriber supplement carrying mostly advertisements

    ▪ Using newspaper-supported direct mail to nonsubscribers

    ▪ Delivering the newspaper free to all households once a week

Regardless of the method used to achieve total market coverage, the aim is the same, that is, to reach all the households in a market regardless of whether they are newspaper subscribers. The objective is to combine the regular daily paper with a supplemental TMC product and, thus, allow advertisers to reach virtually 100 percent of the households in a market.

total market coverage (TMC)
Newspapers augment their circulation with direct mail or shoppers to deliver to all households in the market.

Categories of Newspaper Advertising

4 **Describe the newspaper advertising
planning and buying
process.**

classified advertising
Found in columns so labeled,
published in sections of a
newspaper or magazine that
are set aside for certain
classes of goods or services—
for example, help wanted
positions.

display
Newspaper ads other than
those text-only ads in the
classified columns. Display ads
are generally larger and can
include color, photos, or
artwork to attract reader
attention to the product.

Newspapers provide a number of categories and subcategories of advertising. This section discusses some of the primary types of newspaper advertising.

All newspaper advertising is divided into two categories: *classified* and *display*. **Classified advertising**, which is carried in a special section, is comprised of a variety of advertisements from a small notice announcing a yard sale to those for the largest automobile dealers and real estate firms. **Display** is all the nonclassified advertising in a newspaper. Within the display category, advertising is considered either *local* (also called *retail*) or *national*. The percentage of newspaper revenue generated by online advertising on newspaper web sites is growing rapidly. According to the NAA, newspaper advertising revenues amount to more than $37 billion and come from the following sources:[8]

Percentage of Total	
Classified	26.4
Local	49.6
National	15.8
Online	8.2

As we mentioned earlier, marketing research is an important element of newspaper advertising. Newspaper executives have sponsored a number of research studies showing that newspapers are equal to or better than their media competitors on a number of measures. Much of this research has been oriented toward audience delivery data, demonstrating the quality and/or the size of newspaper readership.

CLASSIFIED ADVERTISING

Classified advertising (commonly referred to as the "want ads") is often ignored unless you are looking for a car, house, or job. Newspapers also carry advertisements with illustrations in the classified section. These are known as *classified display* advertisements and normally are run in the automotive and real estate sections. All these notices are included under the heading of *classified advertising*, which has its own rate card and is usually operated as a separate department within the newspaper. Classified revenues account for almost $10 billion annually, and generally the classified department is the most profitable department of most newspapers (see Exhibit 10.6). The revenue generated by classified advertising for newspapers has decreased significantly in recent years.[9]

Competition for classified advertising constitutes one of the most serious financial threats to the newspaper industry. To understand the problem facing newspapers, we have to examine a number of factors that are rapidly changing the face of classified advertising. First, the classified advertising sector is very concentrated in three areas: employment, real estate, and automotive. This concentration among so few advertisers has allowed specialized online services to gain a foothold in competition

EXHIBIT 10.6

**Newspaper Classified Ad
Revenue, 1980–2008**

Year	Revenue in Million $
1980	$4,222
1985	8,375
1990	11,500
1995	13,742
2000	19,608
2005	17,312
2008	9,975

Source: NAA Business Analysis & Research, http://www.naa.org/
TrendsandNumbers/Advertising-Expenditures.aspx, 5 June 2009.

with newspapers' more broadly defined classified sections. That is, a person wanting a car can look at web sites that are dedicated to only automobiles.

Second, the initial competition for newspaper classified advertising came from online services that introduced two concepts to the world of classifieds: *aggregation* and *vertical sites*. Newspapers regarded classifieds as local advertising and catered more or less exclusively to the local employment and real estate markets and so forth. However, new web competitors offered vertical services, that is, a single category of classified advertising, such as jobs, and, perhaps more important, they compiled (or aggregated) classified advertising from across the country. Prospective job seekers, particularly those looking to relocate from other areas, now could look at a single site and see employment opportunities anywhere in the country (or even internationally) without going to the trouble of subscribing to a number of out-of-town newspapers.

Newspapers have countered these incursions from independent online classified sites in two ways. First, the vast majority of newspapers have created their own web sites, most with classified sections. Second, newspapers have established a number of aggregate sites, such as www.CareerBuilder.com, which is owned by Gannett Company, Inc., Tribune Company, and Microsoft Corporation, a consortium of media companies that handles job listings and related information for more than 9,000 web sites including 140 newspapers and broadband portals such as AOL and MSN. Founded in 2002, CareerBuilder.com has a presence around the country and has a monthly reach of more that 23 million unique visitors.[10]

Newspaper advertising executives know that significant dollars are going to be shifted to online classified services. For them, the key is to use their strong franchise in the classified market to capture the lion's share of the dollars being diverted from print classified advertising.

It is important to emphasize that despite the recent challenges to newspaper classified advertising, newspapers remain an important source of such notices. Nevertheless, in only a few years time, the Internet has brought dramatic changes to classified advertising. Some predict that in the near future—and we are already seeing this on a limited basis—print classified advertising will be devoted largely to a directory of web sites, a starting place for further shopping and gathering detailed information. Regardless of where classified advertising moves, it seems that newspapers will need to continue to position themselves to take advantage of future changes.

DISPLAY ADVERTISING

Virtually all nonclassified newspaper advertising falls into the category of display advertising. The general segment of display advertising is divided into two subgroups: local and national.

LOCAL ADVERTISING Newspaper advertising has an overwhelmingly local focus. The financial structure of the newspaper industry is built on retailer support, and, by any measure, newspapers are the most popular local advertising medium with both readers and advertisers. Local advertising refers to all nonclassified advertising placed by local businesses, organizations, and individuals. Traditionally, major retailers have provided a large percentage of newspaper advertising revenues and that continues to this day. See Exhibit 10.7 for an example of a local display advertisement.

Because of their dependence on retail advertising, newspapers are acutely aware of any changes in the local advertising landscape that might impact advertising dollars. Some of the major retailing trends and the potential impact on newspaper advertising are the following:

- Consolidation of general merchandising and discount retailers will continue to reduce the number of retail advertisers, and this has the potential to reduce the amount of total retail advertising dollars. Mergers and acquisitions as well as stresses put on smaller retailers from the recession that began in 2008 have

EXHIBIT 10.7

A local display advertisement.

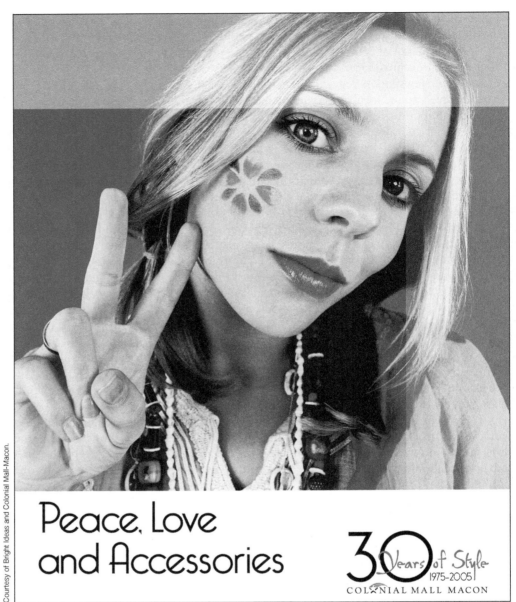

Courtesy of Bright Ideas and Colonial Mall-Macon.

Peace, Love
and Accessories

resulted in a greater concentration of sales among leading retailers. Fewer retail outlets present two problems for newspapers. First, consolidation of retail ownership can result in a decrease in total retail advertising dollars. Second, because each of these retail conglomerates accounts for a greater share of dollars, the risk associated with the loss of any account is much greater than in past years when the number of retailers spread total newspaper advertising revenues among numerous businesses.

▪ In addition to a concentration of traditional retail outlets, they also have created a concentration of services not usually associated with these types of outlets. For example, rather than having separate outlets for automotive repairs, banking, home decorating, and eye care, many of the new mega-stores are housing all these services under one roof.

▪ Retailers will continue to add shopping options to cater to the changing preferences of consumers. Online marketing, catalogs, and other options will augment in-store selling and may result in a shift of advertising dollars to other media.

■ As retailers move to promote themselves as brands and consumers look for more ways to save money, we will see more emphasis on store brand and private-label merchandising. Traditionally, a private-brand marketing strategy has resulted in a reduction in advertising budgets, and newspapers fear that this might happen if there is significant movement to house brands among national retailers.

Although predicting the future of retail advertising is difficult, newspaper advertising directors can anticipate continuing changes in the near term.

NATIONAL ADVERTISING   One of the recent success stories in newspaper advertising is the increase in national advertising. Despite these increases, national newspaper advertising remains a relatively small contributor to overall revenues. In 2008, national advertising represented almost 16 percent of all newspaper advertising revenue.

Placing advertising in newspapers has become more common for national advertisers with the success of the Newspaper National Network (NNN). The NNN was formed in 1994 when 23 major U.S. newspaper chains gave funds to the NAA to provide an avenue for national advertisers to gain easy access to national newspaper buys. The NNN provides a network of participating newspapers, which could be bought using one insertion order and one invoice. The intent of the NNN was to duplicate for national media buyers the convenience they experience in buying network television.

Many national advertisers do not consider newspapers equal to other media. When they think of national media, media planners often think of network and cable television and magazines. If the NNN and other industry-wide efforts do no more than create a higher profile and greater consideration of newspapers among national advertisers, they will have served an important purpose.

The NNN also provides national advertisers with **Standard Advertising Units (SAUs)** from one newspaper to another (see Exhibit 10.8). Standardization allows national advertisers to purchase space in virtually every major U.S. newspaper and prepare one advertisement that will be accepted by all of them. As you can see, NNN formats are flexible enough to provide virtually every advertiser a design that will fit any creative execution.

Standard Advertising Unit (SAU)
Allows national advertisers to purchase newspaper advertising in standard units from one paper to another.

Overcoming some of the more cumbersome buying procedures has helped newspapers to market the medium more effectively on a national basis. However, these procedural changes have not addressed one of the most serious points of disagreement between national advertisers and newspapers—the continuing debate over the so-called local/national rate differential. Most newspapers charge a substantial premium to national advertisers. This differential generally ranges from 40 to 60 percent. Newspapers defend the difference on the basis that they must pay an agency commission for national advertising and many of these advertisers are only occasional users of their papers, unlike retailers from whom they enjoy continuing support.

In summary, newspapers must overcome several obstacles if they are to increase their national advertising share. Given the tight retail market and the potential for growth in the national sector, newspapers must continue to make it easier for national advertisers to buy the medium. An effective system of national newspaper advertising will take time. In addition, it seems clear that some accommodation must be made concerning the national/local rate issue. Perhaps the ultimate catalyst for finding solutions to the problems of national advertisers will be the mutual self-interest of both groups.

COOPERATIVE ADVERTISING

One of the historical outgrowths of the newspaper local/national rate differential was the development of a relationship between national advertisers and their retail distributors called **cooperative (co-op) advertising**. We discuss cooperative advertising more fully in Chapter 14, but it is such an important part of newspaper advertising that we need to mention it here.

cooperative (co-op) advertising
Joint promotion of a national advertiser (manufacturer) and a local retail outlet on behalf of the manufacturer's product on sale in the retail store.

EXHIBIT 10.8

Why are standardized advertising formats crucial to national newspaper advertisers?

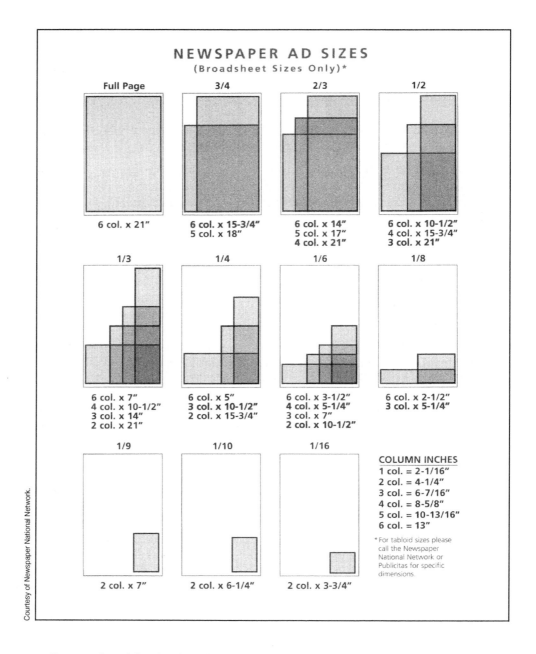

NEWSPAPER AD SIZES
(Broadsheet Sizes Only)*

Courtesy of Newspaper National Network.

Co-op advertising is placed by a local advertiser but paid for, all or in part, by a national advertiser. The national manufacturer usually provides the advertisements, allowing space for each participating retailer's logo. The original reason for the development of co-op advertising was that it allowed national advertisers to place advertisements at local rates.

Today, co-op is a huge source of advertising funds. Co-op also is a source of building goodwill with distributors and retailers and exercising some creative control over local advertising, as well as saving money for national advertisers.

Because national advertisers pay anywhere from 50 to 100 percent of the cost of locally placed co-op, it extends the budgets of local advertisers as it saves money for national firms. It is ironic that a system that was developed largely to circumvent the national/local newspaper rate differential is strongly supported by the newspaper industry. Because co-op dollars are an important revenue source for newspapers, their sales staffs are extremely aggressive in helping retail accounts find and use co-op money.

THE RATE STRUCTURE

The local advertiser, dealing with one or two newspapers, has a fairly easy job buying newspaper space. The rate structure and discounts for any one newspaper are usually straightforward. However, as we have seen, the national advertiser has a much more difficult time. An advertiser buying space in a number of newspapers confronts an unlimited set of options and price structures, including discounts, premium charges for color, special sections, preferred positions, and zoned editions. In the following discussion, we look at some of the primary options and rate decisions that an advertiser must make.

DISCOUNTS Newspapers are divided into two categories: those with a uniform **flat rate** offering no discounts and those with an **open rate** providing some discount structure. The open rate also refers to the highest rate against which all discounts are applied. The most common discounts are based on *frequency* or *bulk* purchases of space. A bulk discount means there is a sliding scale so that the advertiser is charged proportionally less as more advertising is purchased. A frequency discount usually requires some unit or pattern of purchase in addition to total amount of space.

flat rate
A uniform charge for space in a medium, without regard to the amount of space used or the frequency of insertion. When flat rates do not prevail, time discounts or quantity discounts are offered.

open rate
In print, the highest advertising rate at which all discounts are placed.

Frequency within 52-Week Contract Period Full-Page Contract		Bulk within 52-Week Contract Period	
Open Rate	$2.50/Column Inch	No. of Column Inches	Rate
10 insertions	2.30	500	2.40
15 insertions	2.20	1,500	2.30
20 insertions	2.10	3,000	2.20
30 insertions	2.00	5,000	2.10
40 insertions	1.90	10,000	2.00
50 insertions	1.80	15,000	1.90

ROP AND PREFERRED-POSITION RATES The basic rates quoted by a newspaper entitle the advertisement to an ROP position anywhere in the paper that the publisher chooses to place it, although the paper will be mindful of the advertiser's request and interest in getting a good position. An advertiser may buy a choice position by paying a higher, preferred-position rate, which is similar to paying for a box seat in a stadium instead of general admission. A sporting goods advertiser, for example, may elect to pay a preferred-position rate to ensure getting on the sports page. A prescription drug advertiser may buy a preferred position in the health and lifestyle section. There are also preferred positions on individual pages. An advertiser may pay for the top of a column or the top of a column next to news reading matter (called *full position*).

Each newspaper specifies its preferred-position rates; there is no consistency in this practice. Preferred-position rates are not as common as they once were. Now many papers simply attempt to accommodate advertisers that request a position.

COMBINATION RATES A number of combinations are available to advertisers. What they all have in common is the advantage of greatly reduced rates for purchasing advertising in several papers as a group. The most frequently seen combination rate occurs when the same publisher issues both a morning and an evening paper. By buying in both papers, the advertiser can pay as little as one-third to one-half for the second paper. This type of combination may involve as few as two papers in a single metropolitan market or many papers bought on a national basis. In either case, the advertiser has to deal with only one group and pays a single bill.

THE RATE CARD

For most media, the advertising rate card, if it exists at all, is simply a starting point for negotiation. As discussed earlier, most radio and television stations don't publish formal rate cards because rates are determined by negotiated scatter plans that are unique to each advertiser. During the 1980s, many consumer magazines also initiated a system of rate negotiation. Today, newspapers are one of the few media to generally maintain rate integrity by offering all advertisers the same rates and discounts. Many newspapers do offer frequent advertisers value-added options such as featured positions on their web sites.

Unlike broadcast media with their fixed time inventory and magazines with their lengthy advertising production cycles, newspapers can adjust quickly to whatever advertising space is needed. We only have to look at the typical newspaper's bulky Sunday and Wednesday (best grocery day) editions compared to the lightweight Saturday edition to see the flexibility enjoyed by newspapers.

Despite the existence of a traditional rate card, we should not leave the impression that newspapers do not accommodate advertisers with flexible rates in the face of competitive pressure. For example, the following options are available:

- *Multiple rate cards.* Many newspapers offer a number of rate cards for different categories of advertisers. For example, package goods, travel, business, and retail stores may all qualify for different rates. Some advertisers think that the array of different rates makes the buying process unnecessarily complex, and, for national advertisers and other multiple-paper advertisers, it has the same effect as individual rate negotiation. Newspapers see the process as a type of yield management in which a premium is charged for high-demand space. (See Exhibit 10.9.)

- *Newspaper merchandising programs.* Many newspapers, while refusing to negotiate rates directly, are willing to make other types of merchandising concessions. These programs, also known as value-added programs, may include sharing of detailed audience research, providing free creative or copy assistance to advertisers, or inclusion in special promotion programs created by the newspaper.

- *Offer pickup rates.* An advertiser that agrees to rerun an advertisement may receive a lower rate. This encourages return business and passes along some of the savings that the newspaper enjoys from not having to deal with the production process involved with a new advertisement. (See Exhibit 10.10.)

COMPARING NEWSPAPER ADVERTISING COSTS

National advertisers, many of whom consider hundreds of newspapers in a single media plan, want to make cost comparisons among their potential newspaper buys. Advertisers use CPM for the purpose of making comparisons between advertising cost and audience delivery.

Using the CPM for newspaper rate comparisons has two advantages:

1. It reflects the move to page and fractional-page space buys. Media planners are much more comfortable using the standardized space units of the NNN than lines or column inches in space buys.

2. Comparisons among media are more easily calculated using a standard benchmark such as the CPM. Although qualitative differences among newspapers and other media must still be considered, the CPM does offer a consistent means of comparison:

Newspaper	Open-Rate Page Cost	Circulation	CPM
A	$5,400	165,000	$32.72
B	3,300	116,000	28.45

Example: $\dfrac{\$5,400 \times 1,000}{165,000} = \$32.72$

THE SPACE CONTRACT, THE SHORT RATE

If a paper has a flat rate, obviously there is no problem with calculating costs—all space is billed at the same price regardless of how much is used. However, space contracts in open-rate papers must have flexibility to allow advertisers to use more or less space than

Growing to Meet the Changing Times

In the late 1800s Japan's Sakichi Toyoda invented an automatic power loom and then set up his own spinning company, originally named the "Toyoda Automatic Loom Works." In 1918, the company's name was changed to Toyoda Boshoku Corporation. And just as the company changed names, it began an evolution that carried it from a company that produced textiles to a world-class supplier of automotive interiors and manufacturer of automotive filters.

An ocean away, in tiny Verona, Mississippi, a new bank began in a hardware store in 1876 as Raymond Trice and Company and now spreads from just east of Dallas to St. Louis to west of Atlanta. Similarly, this company changed names to reflect the times. BancorpSouth's tremendous market expansion has been matched by the continuous growth in new products and services to help clients meet and exceed their financial goals.

Changing to meet the times has been a cornerstone to the growth of Toyota Boshoku and BancorpSouth. BancorpSouth welcomes Toyota Boshoku to Itawamba County and the Northeast Mississippi industrial community.

TOYOTA BOSHOKU AMERICA

BancorpSouth®
Member FDIC
Right Where You Are

Courtesy of Robinson and BancorpSouth.

EXHIBIT 10.9

Who is the target audience for this national ad?

originally contracted. Normally, an advertiser will sign a space contract estimating the amount of space to be used during the next 12 months. Such a space contract is not a guarantee of the amount of space an advertiser will run but rather an agreement on the rate the advertiser will pay for any space run during the year in question.

The space contract involves two steps: First, advertisers estimate the amount of space they think they will run and agree with the newspaper on how to handle any rate adjustments needed at the end of the year; then they are billed during the year at the selected rate. Second, at the end of the year, the total linage is added. If advertisers ran the amount of space they had estimated, no adjustment is necessary, but if they failed to run enough space to earn that rate, they have to pay the higher rate charged for the number of lines they actually ran. That amount is called the **short rate**.

As an example, let us assume that a national advertiser plans to run advertising in a paper with the following rates:

- Open rate, $5.00/ column inch
- 1,000 column inches, $4.50/column inch
- 5,000 column inches, $4.00/column inch
- 10,000 column inches, $3.50/column inch

short rate
The balance advertisers have to pay if they estimated that they would run more advertisements in a year than they did and entered a contract to pay at a favorable rate. The short rate is figured at the end of the year or sooner if advertisers fall behind schedule. It is calculated at a higher rate for the fewer insertions.

EXHIBIT 10.10

Is this an ad that the advertiser might want to run multiple times?

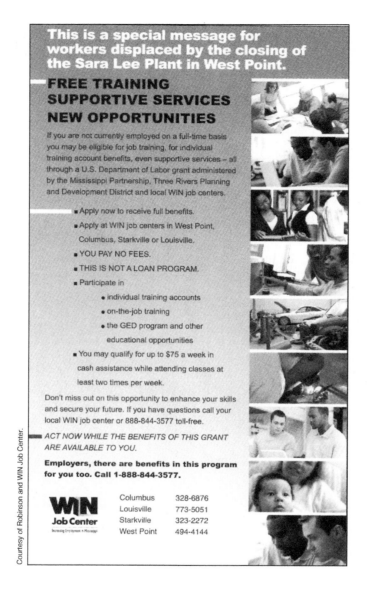

Courtesy of Robinson and WIN Job Center.

The advertiser expects to run at least 5,000 column inches and signs the contract at the $4.00 (5,000-column-inch) rate (subject to end-of-year adjustment). At the end of 12 months, however, only 4,100 column inches have been run; therefore, the bill at the end of the contract year is as follows:

Earned rate:	4,100 column inches @ $4.50 per column inch	= $18,450
Paid rate:	4,100 column inches @ $4.00 per column inch	= <u>$16,400</u>
		Short rate due = $ 2,050

or

$$\text{Column inches run} \times \text{Difference in earned and billed rates}$$
$$= 4{,}100 \text{ column inches} \times \$.50$$
$$= \$2{,}050$$

If the space purchased had qualified for the 10,000-column-inch rate ($3.50), the advertiser would have received a **rebate** of $5,000. The calculation then would be as follows:

rebate
The amount owed to an advertiser by a medium when the advertiser qualifies for a higher space discount.

Paid rate:	10,000 column inches @ $4.00 per column inch	= $40,000
Earned rate:	10,000 column inches @ $3.50 per column inch	= <u>$35,000</u>
		Rebate due = $ 5,000

Newspapers will credit a rebate against future advertising rather than actually paying the advertiser. Some papers charge the full rate and allow credit for a better rate when earned.

Circulation Analysis

THE AUDIT BUREAU OF CIRCULATIONS

Prior to the founding of the **Audit Bureau of Circulations (ABC)** in 1914, those newspaper publishers that bothered at all provided advertisers with self-reported circulation figures. Obviously, many publishers grossly inflated their circulation and created an adversarial relationship among newspapers, advertising agencies, and clients.[11]

The ABC serves advertisers, agencies, and publishers. It is a self-regulating and self-supporting cooperative body. Revenues for the ABC come from annual dues paid by all members and auditing fees paid by publishers. It should be noted that the information in ABC reports is constantly changing in response to subscribers' needs. The ABC report includes the following primary information:

1. Total paid circulation

2. Amount of circulation in the city zone, retail trading zone, and all other areas (*Note:* The *city zone* is a market made up of the city of publication and contiguous built-up areas similar in character to the central city. The *retail trading zone* is a market area outside the city zone whose residents regularly trade with merchants doing business within the city zone.)

3. The number of papers sold at newsstands

The ABC reports have nothing to do with a newspaper's rates. They deal with circulation statistics only. Publishers have always been glad to supply demographic data on their readers, but the ABC now has its own division for gathering demographic data for many of the markets in the United States. All data are computerized and readily available.

Although the verification of newspaper circulation seems to be a relatively straightforward process, it has been surrounded by controversy in recent years. In particular, two areas are of primary concern to the newspaper industry:

1. *Discounted circulation and bulk sales.* ABC rules require that in order to qualify as paid circulation, copies must be sold for 50 percent or more of the standard subscription price. The rule was initiated to prevent newspapers from simply giving away unsold papers and counting them as normal circulation in determining advertising rates.

   Newspaper publishers, while admitting that strict controls must be applied to deep discounts or free circulation, argue for greater flexibility. They point out that newspapers delivered free to rooms in upscale hotels, made available on airplanes or at special events such as trade shows, or sold at greatly discounted prices to college students are reaching prime advertising prospects. Many advertisers take the position that the liberal interpretation of circulation advocated by some publishers would take the industry back to pre-ABC days when newspapers counted any distribution as quality circulation.

   Ultimately, the debate will be settled by advertisers, not newspaper publishers. The basic ABC auditing process is the standard by which most media buyers judge newspapers. Advertisers may accept some changes in the requirements for audited circulation. However, it is doubtful that they will agree to the most liberal changes in bulk and discount circulation advocated by some in the industry.

2. *Readership versus paid circulation.* Newspapers are at a significant disadvantage in that they measure audiences by circulation or newspapers distributed rather than

Audit Bureau of Circulations (ABC)
The organization sponsored by publishers, agencies, and advertisers for securing accurate circulation statements.

the total readers of these newspapers. Most large- and mid-size papers routinely commission readership and market research from a number of companies. Again, whether readership replaces or supplements circulation will be up to advertisers.

The ongoing debate over circulation simply emphasizes the competitive environment in which newspapers are operating. Regardless of how these issues are settled, the decline in paid circulation, the loss of household penetration, and the decrease in newspapers' share of total advertising dollars are all concerns that must be addressed by the industry.

TECHNOLOGY AND THE FUTURE OF NEWSPAPERS

As we discussed in an earlier section, the Internet is significantly changing the way in which readers search and respond to classified advertising. It is clear that new technology must be a factor in the marketing plans of any media company.

Newspaper executives are beginning to view themselves as information providers, not newspaper editors and publishers. This distinction is not one of simple semantics. Rather, it allows people to think beyond the newspaper as a print-on-paper product and to consider alternative delivery systems as well as the type of information that is provided. Most daily newspapers have web sites. The need to have an effective web presence may be underscored by the fact that young adults are spending far less time than older adults with the printed newspaper. The amount of time that readers spend on newspaper web sites varies; however, research by Nielsen Online suggests that most Internet users do not spend more than 11 minutes per month on the top 30 newspaper web sites. Some newspapers, such as the *Minneapolis Star Tribune,* have been successful at keeping readers on their web sites for longer periods of time. According to Terry Sauer, assistant managing editor for digital at the *Star Tribune,* this is likely because of the publishers placing homepage links on articles accessed through search engines, for example, or providing links to bring readers to the newspaper homepage itself or including blog applications.[12]

Despite its potential threat, the daily printed newspaper has advantages over the Internet, including convenience and portability. They can also be a very effective way for advertisers to deliver their own web addresses to potential consumers. With the increased use and access consumers have to the web via cell phones and other mobile devices, these and other forms of new media will likely become a decided threat to traditional newspapers. The fact that newspapers are moving aggressively into the world of new media is testimony to the changing world of both advertising and communication.

Newspaper-Distributed Magazine Supplements

5 **Discuss the role of newspaper-distributed supplements.**

One of the most enduring newspaper traditions is the Sunday magazine supplement. For years, most major dailies published a Sunday magazine with features on gardening, local lifestyles and fashion, and personalities. Today, only a few survive. Most of these are concentrated in major newspaper markets where they attract national advertisers and the newspapers are large enough to invest millions of dollars annually in these upscale publications. From a marketing perspective, national supplements appeal to advertisers because they gain network buying efficiency, a broad-based newspaper circulation, a magazine format, consistent quality reproduction, and a CPM lower than both newspapers and most magazines.

Individual newspapers view the expense of production combined with declining advertising support as the primary reasons to move to syndicated national publications.

Courtesy of USA Weekend Magazine.

EXHIBIT 10.11

Parade and *USA Weekend* are the two leading magazines delivered through newspapers.

The two leaders in the category are *USA Weekend* and *Parade* (see Exhibit 10.11). Both magazines deliver huge readership (at a cost to both newspapers and advertisers that is less than most independent supplements). *Parade* tends to be more popular at larger newspapers with a circulation of 33 million in 470 papers.[13] In fact, *Parade* is the largest circulation consumer magazine by a wide margin. *USA Weekend* is distributed by more than 650 newspapers but has a lower circulation of 23 million.[14] As is the case with most consumer magazines, both publications offer numerous opportunities for regional buys. Although several advertisers such as the Franklin Mint advertise on a national basis, some form of less-than-full-run buy is very common in Sunday supplements.

A number of other supplements reach ethnic markets in newspapers directed toward these readers. Among the most well known is *Vista*, a magazine carried in almost 30 newspapers with large Hispanic audiences. It is published 11 times per year and has a rate base of more than 500,000.

COMICS

Any discussion of newspaper special features would have to include a mention of the comics. The newspaper comic traces its origins to 1889 when the *New York World* used newly installed color presses to build circulation with a comic section. The importance of comic strips became obvious in 1895 when two titans of journalism, Joseph Pulitzer and William Randolph Hearst, waged a fierce battle over ownership of the most popular cartoon of the day, *The Yellow Kid*.

In 1897, *The Katzenjammer Kids* was introduced as the first modern comic strip with separate panels and speech balloons. In 1912, Hearst's *New York Evening Journal* published the first full page of comics. From the 1920s on, comics became a major source of readership with the introduction of *Blondie*, *The Phantom*, *Beetle Bailey*, and *Peanuts*.

Although not a major advertising vehicle, comics are used by a number of advertisers to reach millions of readers. Editors constantly evaluate comics as they choose among the hundreds of available strips. For those advertisers that want to use the comic sections, there are networks that sell the Sunday comic sections in a variety of combinations so that advertisers can place an advertisement simultaneously in a number of papers.

The Ethnic and Foreign Language Press

6 Discuss the role of ethnically oriented newspapers and weeklies.

With the changing multicultural environment in the United States, it is not surprising that a number of media are being introduced to reach these audiences with information, entertainment, and advertising. The role played by newspapers varies among the major ethnic markets. The largest and fastest-growing group of ethnic newspapers is Spanish-language newspapers. This growth coincides with a Hispanic population that is outpacing all other segments in the United States. Hundreds of Hispanic newspapers are available in the United States. Unlike other members of the ethnic press, many successful Hispanic-oriented newspapers are dailies. The best evidence of the importance of the Hispanic press is the support and investment in these publications by major newspaper companies.

Despite healthy circulation growth, Hispanic newspapers face a number of problems reaching a very fragmented Spanish-language population with roots in a variety of countries with different cultures and product preferences. In addition, surveys show a wide disparity in language preferences. Some would like their information in Spanish, some prefer English, and still others prefer a bilingual publication. Despite these problems, the Hispanic press is among the fastest-growing sectors of the newspaper industry in both readers and advertising revenues (see Exhibit 10.12).

The African American press has not shown the same economic vitality as its Hispanic counterpart. The African American press was at its height from the 1930s to the early 1960s with almost 300 papers and a total circulation of 4 million. These newspapers were sources of news, political action, and advertising. They contributed to much of the social progress made during this period. Among their significant legacies was the drive for passage of the Voting Rights Act and other civil rights legislation during the term of President Lyndon Johnson.

Ironically, the African American press has suffered financially as opportunities have opened to African American citizens. During the 1960s and 1970s, the majority press began to incorporate coverage of African American readers into its papers. As time went on, it was less viable to have separate newspapers to cover news of African American readers.

A continuing problem for traditionally African American newspapers is the preference among the African American population for television and a few selected magazines. Given this trend, it is not surprising that advertisers, particularly major national companies, have shifted significant dollars from newspapers to television, radio, and magazines with high African American audiences.

The Asian press faces many of the same problems of both the Hispanic and African American press—only more so. Like the Hispanic population, the Asian population comes from dozens of different cultures and languages from Chinese to Indian. Lumping Asian consumers into a single category is the same mistake as considering all Hispanic consumers to be alike. Added to the problem is that the Asian population in the United States is not nearly as large as the Hispanic population so the large population centers to support a national Asian press system are not as readily available.

EXHIBIT 10.12

The Spanish version of this ad can run in Spanish-language newspapers.

Still, a number of newspapers serve the Asian population. New York City's Chinese-language *Brooklyn Chinese Monthly* and Japanese-language *Rafu Shimpo* have circulations of from 20,000 to 50,000. Interestingly enough, the foreign language press in the United States is not a new phenomenon. Beginning in 1732 when Benjamin Franklin published *Philadelphische Zeitung (Philadelphia Newspaper)*, the foreign language press has played a major role in this country. The increasingly multicultural nature of the United States is reflected in a growing number of newspapers available in more than 40 languages. Virtually every language is represented by at least one newspaper. From French, Italian, and German to Vietnamese, Chinese, and Arabic, every part of the world is represented by a publication unique to an ethnic group.

Ultimately, the success of the ethnic press is largely determined by the same formula used by mainstream media—advertising support. As population diversity increases along with growing economic power among these groups, we should expect to see growth in advertising-supported media directed at these cultural and ethnic members. The degree to which newspapers will fill this communication gap remains to be seen.

Weekly Newspapers

Weekly newspapers fall into a number of categories: suburban papers covering events within some portion of a larger metropolitan area, traditional rural weeklies providing local coverage, specialty weeklies covering politics or the arts, and free shoppers with little editorial content. According to the NAA, there are several thousand weekly newspapers in the United States. During the past 30 years, the complexion of the weekly newspaper field has changed dramatically. Far from its rural, small-town roots, the typical weekly is more likely to be located in a growing suburb and, rather than covering weddings and family reunions, its major topics are probably zoning disputes, overcrowded schools, crime, and how to control future growth while increasing the county's tax base.

As important as their content is the marketing strategy employed by many weeklies. More and more weeklies are part of networks. These networks are sometimes owned by a single company, including the major local daily newspaper, or they may be independent weeklies that joined a consortium to sell their space through a single media rep. These groups recognize that the core city trade zone is no longer as economically viable as in previous years. Today, many cities exist only as suburban clusters with one or two large malls anchoring the advertising base. Retailers in these malls depend on a narrowly defined suburban area or neighborhood for their customers rather than on an entire metropolitan area. In some cases, these suburban newspaper groups exist as a supplement to the daily metropolitan newspaper.

From an advertising standpoint, the strength of suburban weekly newspaper networks is that they can serve equally well small, local advertisers that may buy a single member of the group and national advertisers or major retailers that want high penetration into most of the suburban market. Weekly growth will be concentrated in suburban and urban areas for the foreseeable future. Weeklies, once rarely considered by large metropolitan retailers or national advertisers, now play a more important role in the localized marketing strategies of many advertisers.

SUMMARY

Newspapers remain an important advertising medium, particularly for local advertisers. However, newspaper publishers recognize that they face a number of serious challenges if they are to maintain their historical position as a major source of news and advertising.

As newspapers attempt to increase national advertising, their local advertising franchise is coming under increasing attack from a number of quarters. For example, local cable companies provide advertisers opportunities to cut in to major cable networks that provide targeted opportunities to reach viewers interested in news, music, or sports, often at a CPM less than that of the newspaper. Metropolitan newspapers are competing with suburban weeklies and with shoppers intent on exploiting the move to the suburbs by both consumers and retailers.

Add to the traditional advertising competitors the threat posed by the Internet and other new wireless digital-based media formats that take away both readers and the lucrative classified advertising market. Finally, newspapers are continuing to deal with a declining reader base as younger market segments are increasingly finding alternative sources for information and entertainment.

When marketing their medium to advertisers, newspapers have a major advantage over most of their competitors in that they are perceived as among the most believable and trustworthy mass communication vehicles. They have an established brand that most competitors look on with envy. There are a variety of ethnic and foreign language papers available as well, making it possible for advertisers to target more specific audiences. As we discussed in this chapter, there are several different categories of newspaper advertising including insert, zoned editions, classified, display, dailies, weeklies and cooperative advertising. Many newspapers offer both ROP and preferred position rates.

REVIEW

1. What are some of the factors that have eroded the local newspaper advertising base?

2. What are the two major problems in newspapers gaining national advertising?

3. Contrast zoned editions and total market coverage programs.

4. What are three major categories of newspaper advertising and for how much advertising revenue does each account?

5. What is the difference between short rate and rebate?

6. In what area have newspapers been most successful in achieving standardization?

7. What are the primary advantages of newspaper magazine supplements?

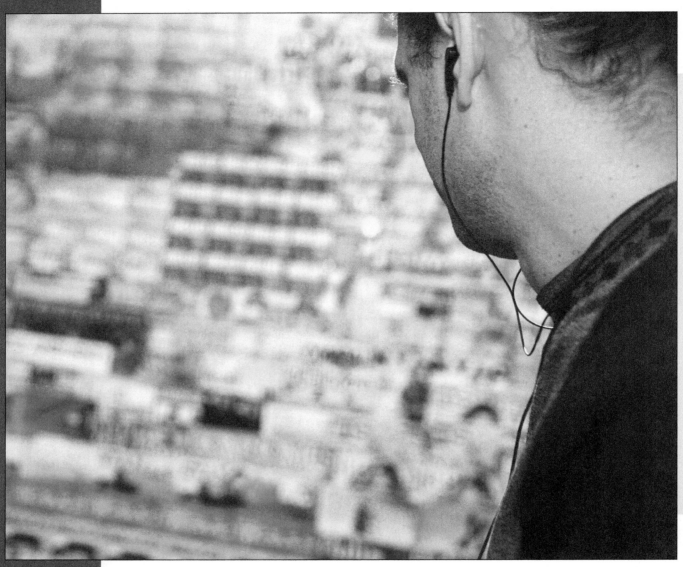

iStockphoto.com.

Using Magazines

MOST MAGAZINES today appeal to niche readers, particularly those in categories with special value to advertisers. Virtually all magazines are targeted to the special interests, businesses, demographics, or lifestyles of their readers. Magazines have adopted Internet technology to provide Web versions of their publications as a way to reach new readers, to increase loyalty among their readers, and to generate advertising revenue. ▶

CHAPTER LEARNING OBJECTIVES

1. Describe the history and development of the American magazine.

2. Discuss the usefulness of magazines in national media plans.

3. List the characteristics of consumer and trade publications.

4. Explain how magazine space is sold to advertisers.

5. Describe the role of magazines as a targeted advertising medium.

6. Explain how magazine audiences are measured.

7. List the characteristics of business publications.

8. Describe the role of the agribusiness press.

Pros

1. The number and range of specialized magazines provide advertisers with an opportunity to reach narrowly targeted audiences that are otherwise hard to reach.
2. Magazines provide strong visuals to enhance brand awareness, and they have the ability to deliver a memorable message to their niche audiences.
3. Most magazines offer some form of regional and/or demographic editions to provide even greater targeting and opportunities for less-than-national advertisers to use magazines.
4. Magazines are portable, they have a long life, and they are often passed along to several readers. Business and farm publications are especially useful as reference tools, and leading publications within various industries offer advertisers an important forum for their messages.

Cons

1. In recent years, magazine audience growth has not kept up with increases in advertising rates. Magazines are among the most expensive media per prospect. The growth in advertising rates has exceeded growth in audience size.

2. Advertising clutter is a concern of many magazine advertisers. Many magazines approach 50 percent advertising content; consequently, time spent with any single advertisement is often minimal.

3. Most magazines have relatively long advertising deadlines creating a lack of immediacy of the message. This long lead time can reduce flexibility and the ability of advertisers to react to fast-changing market conditions. In the age of the Internet during which consumers are used to getting up-to-date information on demand, this poses a problem for some advertisers.

4. Despite the obvious advantages of magazine specialization, a single magazine rarely reaches the majority of a market segment. Therefore, several magazines must be used or alternative media must supplement magazine buys. With thousands of consumer magazines from which to choose, advertisers often have difficulty choosing the correct vehicle.

Advertising and Consumer Magazines

1 Describe the history and development of the American magazine.

In 2008, approximately 20.1 percent of U.S. measured advertising dollars was spent in all forms of magazines including consumer, business, Sunday, and local magazines. The top 10 advertisers in magazines include package-goods companies, an automobile manufacturer, a pharmaceutical company, and a media company (see Exhibit 11.1).

With the introduction of television as a national advertising medium in the 1950s, magazines began to market themselves as a specialized medium to reach targeted prospects within the more general population. Unable to duplicate the huge numbers that the three television networks at the time could deliver, magazines based their economic future on the quality of audience they could deliver rather than the quantity. The modern niche magazine evolved in much the same way as narrowly formatted radio stations, and both did so as a reaction to the ultimate mass appeal of television.[1]

Magazines today find that they must continue to change and adapt to a marketplace that exhibits both competitive and economic pressures. The magazine industry is undergoing changes in all aspects of the way it does business. In fact, there is little in the way of magazine production, distribution, circulation, or advertising that is not undergoing some type of transition.

The contemporary magazine faces many opportunities and challenges in the twenty-first century. Some of these problems are also concerns in both the radio and newspaper industries. The segmented and fragmented nature of magazine publishing means that publications are constantly seeking to define their audiences in narrower ways. Like the radio industry, magazines find that marketers invest an overwhelming percentage of their advertising dollars in the two or three leaders in a category, leaving

EXHIBIT 11.1

Top 10 Magazine Advertisers Ranked by Measured Spending, 2008 (in million $)

Rank	Marketer	2008
1	Procter & Gamble Co.	$956.2
2	General Motors Corp.	447.5
3	Kraft Foods	401.6
4	Johnson & Johnson	399.6
5	L'Oréal	324.3
6	Walmart Stores	266.1
7	Campbell Soup Co.	234.1
8	GlaxoSmithKline	231.7
9	Time Warner	230.2
10	Unilever	218.4

Source: TNS Media Intelligence, "Top U.S. advertisers in 10 media," *Advertising Age*, 22 June 2009, 18. Reprinted with permission from the June 22, 2009 issue of *Advertising Age*. Copyright, Crain Communications Inc. 2009.

a small share of advertising dollars to the others. This has led magazines to attempt to create editorial differentiation directed to interest groups that are often too small to support them financially. More than two-thirds of magazine titles have a circulation of less than 500,000 readers.

Just as magazines are similar in some respects to radio, they also have characteristics in common with newspapers. The costs of paper, delivery, and marketing to readers and advertisers are creating profitability problems even as gross revenues increase. The *National Directory of Magazines* reports that there were more than 7,300 consumer magazines in the United States.[2] Many of these have very small circulations. In such a competitive marketplace when the economy is weak, gaining and maintaining readership are constant challenges for publishers. One only has to look at the number of discounted subscriptions for even the most popular magazines to see the extent of the problem.

It is estimated that five or more magazines are introduced each week covering topics as diverse as shopping, aviation, and competitive swimming. Although consumer magazines have a number of attributes in common, in many respects each magazine or category of magazines has unique problems and opportunities. In this atmosphere, simultaneous successes and failures exist among different categories of publications. Women's service magazines, long a leading consumer magazine category, have experienced a number of significant changes in the past decade in an attempt to fend off competition from women's lifestyle magazines such as *O The Oprah Winfrey Magazine*, and *Real Simple*.[3]

In order to understand the contemporary consumer magazine industry, we have to examine two primary factors: (1) selectivity and (2) cost versus revenue considerations.

SELECTIVITY

Although magazines represent an eclectic continuum of titles and interests, the success stories are almost universally confined to narrow editorial interests and audience segments. A sampling of some of the top magazines in terms of advertising revenues and advertising pages demonstrates this range of interests. For example, *Women's Health*, *Fast Company*, *People Stylewatch*, and *Everyday with Rachael Ray* are among the leaders in advertising revenue growth in recent years.[4] Virtually the only thing these publications have in common is that they have been able to find a distinctive niche among both readers and advertisers.

Magazines are searching for the right editorial formula in a market that is increasingly fragmented (see Exhibit 11.2). Although there are very few large homogeneous groups, there are homogeneous segments within more general groups. For example, publishers have long tried to effectively reach the valuable teen market. However, they find that no market as such exists. Boys and girls differ markedly not only in what they read but also in the amount of magazine reading they do, with teen girls reading significantly more than boys.

THE EVOLUTION OF THE MODERN MAGAZINE Although selectivity is one of the keys to contemporary magazine success, audience and editorial selectivity is actually rooted in the historical development of magazines. The magazines of the mid-nineteenth century were targeted to audiences of special interests, were sold at a high cost, and carried little advertising. Most magazines were literary, political, or religious in content and depended on readers or special interest groups to provide most of their financial support.

In the latter years of the nineteenth century, a rising middle class, mass production, and national transportation combined to provide the opportunity for nationally distributed branded goods. The opportunities offered by national brands could be exploited only with the efficiencies of mass promotion. During the 1890s, a number of publishers provided the foundation for today's advertising-supported, mass circulation magazine. Frank Munsey (*Munsey's*) and S. S. McClure (*McClure's*) were among the most successful publishers of the period. However, it was Cyrus H. Curtis who "developed the

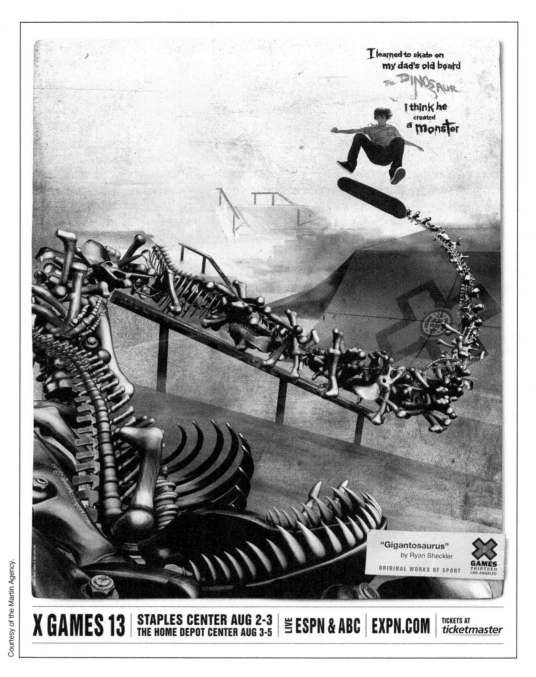

Courtesy of the Martin Agency.

magical possibilities of national advertising, and demonstrated more clearly than anyone else that you could lose millions of dollars on your circulation by selling at a low price yet make more millions out of your advertising. . . ."[5] The formula was so successful that by 1900 his *Ladies' Home Journal*, under the editorship of Edward Bok, was the first magazine to achieve a circulation of 1 million.

Until the advent of radio in the 1920s, magazines remained the only national advertising medium. With the introduction of radio, magazines had to share the national advertising dollar. Still, magazines were the only visual medium available to national manufacturers. However, when television came on the scene in the 1950s, people's reading habits became viewing habits, and national magazines had to change to survive.

The change from a mass to a class medium, which began in the competitive turmoil of the 1950s, continues to this day. Perhaps the most dramatic indication of this change was the March 2000 demise of the monthly version of *Life* after 64 years of publication.

Today, even the largest circulation publications tend to appeal to a fairly narrowly defined market segment. For example, *Sports Illustrated*, *Time*, *Better Homes and Gardens*, and *Modern Maturity*—all among the circulation leaders—would not be classified as general editorial magazines. Only newspaper-distributed *Parade* and *USA Weekend* have both large circulations and general appeal. However, as discussed in Chapter 10, they are hybrid publications that many advertisers consider more as newspapers than as magazines.

COSTS AND REVENUES

Consumer magazine revenues are huge, and these publications largely depend on advertising for their existence. Typical consumer magazine content consists of slightly more than 46 percent advertising pages.[6] Although the advertising industry as a whole was hit hard by advertising cancellations following the September 11, 2001, tragedy, many publications were hit again when tobacco advertisers substantially curtailed or eliminated their advertising in magazines. As with other media, magazines were dealt a further blow in lost revenue with the recession that began in 2008. Publishers are increasingly concerned about profitability.

Magazine cost concerns can be summarized largely in four primary categories:

1. *Marketing costs.* With the number of publications and a sometimes-fickle readership, publishers are seeing significant increases in the cost of gaining and maintaining readers. Currently, approximately 68 percent of consumer magazine circulation revenue is from subscriptions as opposed to newsstand sales. Consequently, it is imperative for publishers to invest huge sums of money in gaining new readers and keeping current ones. Likewise, escalating printing and postage costs have made direct-mail campaigns increasingly expensive. The competitive economic environment of magazine publishing prevents many publishers from raising the cost of subscriptions to cover higher expenses. About 60 percent of magazine revenue comes from advertising.[7]

2. *Postage and distribution costs.* Since 1995, the U.S. Postal Service (USPS) has imposed several rate increases on magazine publishers. These increases have been far greater than the rate of inflation, and they have caused a major rift between publishers and the USPS.

   At the same time that publishers are facing hefty increases in postal charges, they are witnessing similar boosts in the cost of newsstand distribution. Consolidation at both the retail and wholesale levels has created a more streamlined—and limited—distribution channel. Retailers, concerned with profit margins, are insisting that wholesalers limit the number of titles sent to them. Wal-Mart, which accounts for 15 percent of all single-copy magazine sales, for example, dropped close to 1,000 titles from its shelves in 2008. Industry sources say that part of the reason for dropping titles was concern for the environment. Wal-Mart executives used retail sales as their criteria for eliminating titles.[8] The result has been an even greater reliance on subscription sales and a continuing upward cost spiral for publishers.

3. *Concentration of advertisers.* Although a primary strength of magazines is their selectivity, it works against them in terms of broadly based advertising appeal. Magazines receive a disproportionate percentage of their advertising revenues from a very few product categories. Twelve categories account for 87 percent of all magazine advertising (see Exhibit 11.3). Only 50 companies provide almost one-third of all consumer magazine revenues. In fact, Procter & Gamble, the top magazine advertiser in 2008, accounted for 3.8 percent of total advertising revenue in consumer magazines.

   If even one of these major advertisers decreased its magazine spending, it could have a significant impact on a number of publications. Advertising cutbacks are even more damaging to magazines geared to a very narrow interest such as

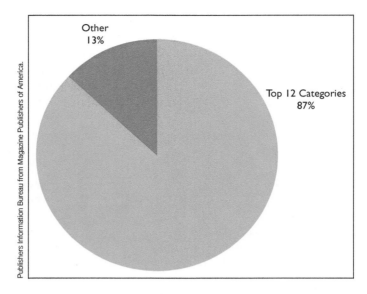

computing or golf. In these cases, a magazine has few practical alternatives to make up for the loss of even one large advertising client.

During the past 20 years, magazines have tried to insulate themselves from their dependence on advertising by shifting a disproportionate percentage of the cost of magazines to readers. The increasing popularity of free magazine Internet sites has made it difficult for publishers to significantly increase the cover price of magazines. There has been a 78 percent increase in the number of consumer magazine web sites since 2005.

4. *Increases in discounting.* Growth in the amount magazines charge advertisers has slowed with the slowing of the economy. Many magazines are offering large discounts off of their regular rate card to regular advertisers. As advertisers push for more efficiencies in their media plans, magazines have been pushed to provide a wider array of discounts and value-added opportunities on their print as well as their digital versions.

CROSS-MEDIA BUYS

There are few magazine, television, or newspaper companies in the United States today. They have been replaced by multimedia companies with interests in all traditional media as well as the Internet, interactive media, and various forms of direct response. Magazines are major players in many of these huge conglomerates, and they form a symbiotic relationship with their media partners. From an advertising standpoint, it can be of great benefit for a magazine to be sold as part of a multimedia package—known as a **cross-media buy**.

cross-media buy
Several media or vehicles that are packaged to be sold to advertisers to gain a synergistic communication effect and efficiencies in purchasing time or space.

Because magazines reach niche audiences, they can often reach prime prospects who are light users of other media. Companies such as Time Warner and Disney can offer advertisers hundreds of options for their advertising messages—often at a significant discount compared to buying the same properties on an individual basis. One of the most creative cross-media sellers is Disney. In the sports arena, for example, Disney can offer package deals with ABC, ESPN, *ESPN: The Magazine*, and ESPN radio programming.

In another example of cross-media planning opportunities, the magazine publisher Condé Nast leveraged its connection with the entertainment industry to create original digital programming for its advertiser, Verizon, as part of a multiplatform advertising package deal. This original programming was made available to Verizon cellular subscribers via their mobile phones.

One of the appealing features of cross-media buys for national advertisers is the complementary nature of magazines and television in reaching different segments of the general population. Television simply does not reach those prospects who are the heaviest users of magazines. There is such a strong inverse relationship between magazine readership and television viewing that mass advertisers are almost compelled to use both media. Not only does the combination of magazines and television extend reach but it also provides a welcome diversity of advertising themes and creative executions.

Despite some obvious advantages to advertisers in terms of lower media costs, advertisers should be careful in analyzing cross-media buys. Marketers have to realize that a package of media owned by a single company is not necessarily the best choice in each category. For instance, even though we buy spots on ESPN's *Monday Night Football*, are we sure that *ESPN: The Magazine* is a better fit for our target audience than *Sports Illustrated*, or is ESPN.com a better web choice than CNN/SI.com? There is nothing inherently wrong with cross-media buys as long as advertisers realize that they are put together largely for the benefit of the media companies. As single media companies come to control more and more media properties, the possibilities of building tailored media packages for individual advertisers increase.

Magazines as a National Advertising Medium

ADVANTAGES OF MAGAZINE ADVERTISING

Depending on the product and advertising objectives, magazines may offer a number of advantages as primary or secondary media vehicles. This section examines the primary considerations that determine whether magazines in general—or a particular title—will be included in a media plan.

2 **Discuss the usefulness of magazines in national media plans.**

1. *Does it work?* An advertiser is interested in the various advantages and characteristics of a medium only to the extent that these elements allow the medium to contribute to sales and profits. In recent years, Magazine Publishers of America (MPA) has commissioned a series of studies conducted by independent research firms to determine the value of magazines as an advertising tool.

   In one study, results showed that more than half of magazine readers said they took or plan to take action as a result of exposure to magazine advertisements. About one-fifth of magazine readers said they had considered purchasing the advertised product or service, and about 12 percent said they gathered more information about the product or service. Eleven percent said they visited the advertiser's web site (see Exhibit 11.4).

2. *Audience selectivity.* Assuming that magazines can accomplish the required communication task, the next question is whether they can reach a specific target market. It is here where magazines excel. There is a magazine targeted to virtually every market segment and almost everyone reads a magazine during a given month. There are magazines for almost every demographic and interest group (see Exhibit 11.5). With magazines, total readership is often a secondary advertising consideration to how the magazines reach target audiences. As mentioned earlier, two out of every three magazines have a circulation of less than 500,000.

Percentage of Readers Taking/Planning to Take Specific Actiions	
Consider purchasing the advertised product or service	21%
Have a more favorable opinion about the advertiser	12
Gather more information about advertised product or service	12
Visit the advertiser's web site	11
Visit a store, dealer or other location	9
Purchase the advertised product or service	8
Save the ad for future reference	7
Recommend the product or service to a friend, colleague or family member	5
Took any action (net)	56%

Source: Affinity's VISTA Print Effectiveness Rating Service, 2008 from *MPA Handbook* 2009.

EXHIBIT 11.4

Actions readers took or plan to take as a result of exposure to specific magazine ads.

EXHIBIT 11.5

Latina is a fashion and lifestyle magazine targeted to bilingual women in the United States.

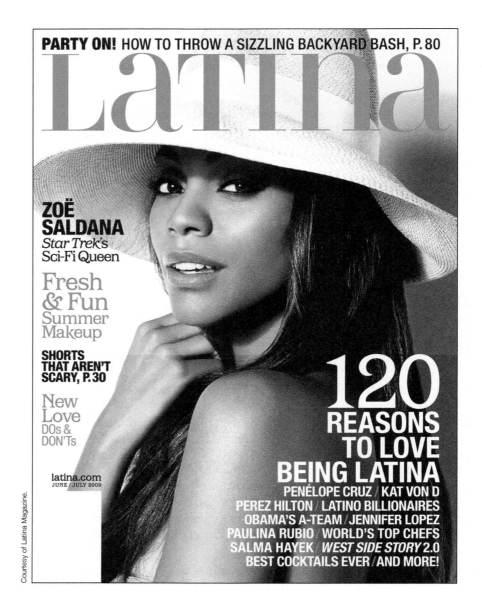

Courtesy of Latina Magazine.

PARTY ON! HOW TO THROW A SIZZLING BACKYARD BASH, P. 80

Latina

ZOË SALDANA
Star Trek's Sci-Fi Queen

Fresh & Fun Summer Makeup

SHORTS THAT AREN'T SCARY, P. 30

New Love DOs & DON'Ts

latina.com
JUNE / JULY 2009

120 REASONS TO LOVE BEING LATINA
PENÉLOPE CRUZ / KAT VON D
PEREZ HILTON / LATINO BILLIONAIRES
OBAMA'S A-TEAM / JENNIFER LOPEZ
PAULINA RUBIO / WORLD'S TOP CHEFS
SALMA HAYEK / *WEST SIDE STORY* 2.0
BEST COCKTAILS EVER / AND MORE!

3. *Long life and creative options.* Unlike a short-lived broadcast message or the daily newspaper, many magazines are saved and referred to over a long period of time, whereas others are passed along to or shared with other readers. In addition, magazines are portable, with more than three-fourths of magazine readers saying they sometimes read magazines in such places as doctors' offices, someone else's home, or at work.[9] In this disposable media world, magazines are almost alone as a long-term medium. Magazines are often used as reference sources—articles are clipped, back issues are filed, and readers may go back to a favorite magazine numerous times before finally discarding it. Advertisers potentially benefit from each of these exposures.

   The magazine is also a visual medium with a number of creative options. Magazines offer advertisers a wide range of flexible formats such as double-page spreads, bright colors, and even product sampling. Magazines are particularly well suited to long copy. Discussions of detailed product attributes for automobiles and consumer electronics as well as advertising for financial services lend themselves to magazines (see Exhibit 11.6).

4. *Availability of demographic and geographic editions.* In Chapter 10, we discussed newspaper zoning as a reaction to advertiser demand for selected segments of a

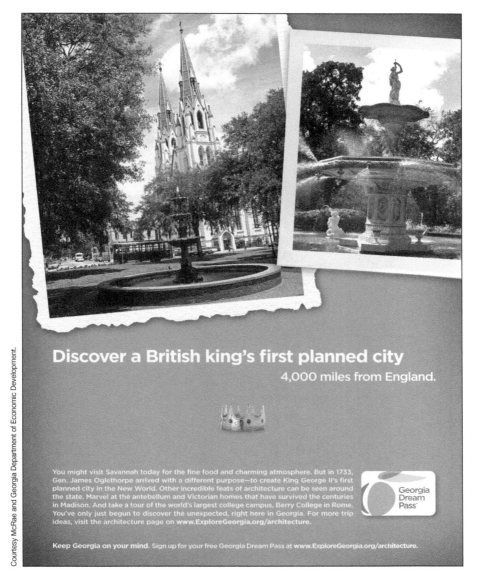

Courtesy McRae and Georgia Department of Economic Development.

EXHIBIT 11.6

What magazines do you think the target audience for this ad would read?

publication's circulation. On a national scale, magazine demographic and geographic editions meet the same demands of large advertisers. It is very rare that a national magazine does not offer some type of regional or demographic breakout of its total circulation. These special editions are called partial runs and are so common and important to magazine advertising that they are discussed separately in a later section of this chapter.

5. *Qualitative factors and engagement.* Advertisers are interested in the demographics of the audience, but they are also interested in how audience members think of themselves when they read a particular publication. The *Playboy* man and the *Cosmopolitan* woman are as much a matter of readers' perception as a reality. Unlike many other media, magazines offer advertisers relatively high levels of audience involvement or engagement. Consequently, magazine advertisers are more apt to use understated creative approaches as contrasted to the hard-sell advertising found in so many other media. Few media connect with their audiences to the degree that magazines do. According to a recent report by Dynamic Logic, more than half of all consumers say that they have a positive attitude toward magazine advertising.[10] This is higher than for any other medium (see Exhibit 11.7).

EXHIBIT 11.7

This ad was designed specifically for *Sports Illustrated*. Can you guess in which issue of the magazine it ran?

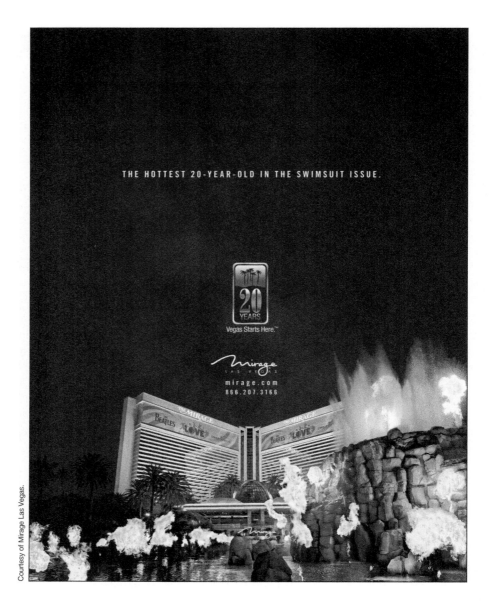

Courtesy of Mirage Las Vegas.

In Chapter 7, we discussed the PRIZM system of categorizing people according to their lifestyle characteristics. Magazines use psychographic and lifestyle research to sell advertisers on the qualitative aspects of their audiences. Take a moment to review the various PRIZM categories in Exhibit 7.4 and try to match these audiences with the primary readers of some major magazines. Research indicates that magazines are preferred by a wide margin as a source of ideas and information on topics as diverse as automobiles, fashion, and fitness. This editorial connection with readers should carry over to a connection between readers and advertisers. When readers pick up *Parents*, *Money*, *Splash*, or *Wired*, there is little doubt about their interests. These same readers also watch prime-time television, listen to the radio on the way home from work, and see numerous billboards each day. However, it is difficult to anticipate what they are thinking about at these moments. On the other hand, specialized magazines can practically guarantee a synergism between the reader and editorial content, which in many cases will carry over to advertising content.

Despite the recent attention given to the qualitative nature of magazines, the ultimate measure of magazines as an advertising vehicle will be determined by their ability to deliver prime prospects at a competitive cost. Media planners will continue to judge magazines on a cost-efficiency basis using criteria such as CPMs, reach, and frequency. The final evaluation of magazines, as with any medium, is whether they can deliver the right audience, at the right price, and in the right environment to help contribute to the achievement of the communication objectives.

DISADVANTAGES OF MAGAZINE ADVERTISING

Despite the many advantages that magazines offer advertisers, there are some important considerations for advertisers contemplating buying magazines.

1. *High cost.* As we have discussed, magazines generally are the most expensive medium on a CPM basis. It is not unusual for specialized magazines to have CPM levels of more than $100 compared to $30 to $40 on average for prime-time shows. However, in an era of niche marketing, the CPM is important only in relation to the prospects reached and the waste circulation of a medium. A related problem to overall cost is the fact that, as magazines have refined their audiences, many advertisers have determined the need to use several publications to achieve acceptable reach levels. As the number of magazines in a media schedule increases, so does the risk of duplicated audience levels, which often results in an unacceptable overlap in readership.

2. *Long* **closing dates**. Because of the printing process, most magazine advertisements must be prepared well ahead of publication. Unlike the spontaneity associated with radio and newspapers, magazines tend to be inflexible in reacting to changing market conditions. For example, a monthly magazine advertisement may run 8 to 10 weeks after an advertiser submits it. This long lead time makes it difficult for advertisers to react to current marketing conditions either in scheduling space or developing competitive copy. The long closing dates are one reason why most magazine copy is very general.

closing date
The date by which all advertising material must be submitted to a publication.

Many magazines have one date for space reservations and a later date for when material must be submitted. Normally, the space contract cannot be canceled. It is not unusual for a magazine to require that space be reserved 2 months prior to publication and that material be sent 6 weeks before publication. Some publications require that material be submitted with the order.

Many magazines have sought to overcome the competitive disadvantage of long closing dates by providing **fast-close advertising**. As the name implies, fast-close advertising allows advertisers to submit advertisements much closer to publication dates than standard closing dates allow. At one time, fast-close advertising was very expensive, carrying a significant premium compared to other advertising. However, competitive pressure and improvements in print technology have seen many publications offer fast-close advertising at little or no extra expense.

fast-close advertising
Some magazines offer short-notice advertising deadlines, sometimes at a premium cost.

The remaining sections of this chapter examine some specific features and techniques involved in buying advertising in magazines.

Features of Magazine Advertising

PARTIAL-RUN MAGAZINE EDITIONS

Partial-run editions refer to any magazine space buy that involves purchasing less than the entire circulation of a publication. The oldest and most common partial-run edition is the geographic edition, followed by demographic and vocational/special interest editions. Basically, the partial-run edition allows relatively large-circulation magazines to compete with smaller niche publications for specialized advertisers.

As advertiser demand for more and more narrowly defined audiences has increased in recent years, magazines with fairly small circulations and/or specialized editorial formats have begun to offer some form of partial-run edition. Again, the smaller

3 List the characteristics of consumer and trade publications.

partial runs
When magazines offer less than their entire circulation to advertisers. Partial runs include demographic, geographic, and split-run editions.

KLEPPNER VIEWPOINT 11.1

Andrew McLean Chief Development Officer, Groupm

"MIRROR, MIRROR ON THE WALL...." THE IMPACT ON MEDIA CAUSED BY CHANGES IN CONSUMER BEHAVIOR

Andrew McLean

The realities of the media and communications landscape as we close out the first decade of the twenty-first century are significant. There is a massive difference between the volume of media outlets and inventory (supply) and ad dollars (demand). As any economist will point out, such differences create competition that drives down pricing and that will result in "survival of the fittest."

It is easy to spot the dual forces that have led to this imbalance: One is the explosion in digital ad opportunities; the second is the pull back in spending whereby the consistent 5 percent annual global rise in ad budgets is, at least for now, a thing of the past.

So who is the "fairest of them all" and in which media do clients invest their budgets? The answer is not to be found by studying media but by studying the consumer. Media (despite its occasional arrogance) does not dictate consumer behavior but rather mirrors it. For example, spending online will reach $70 billion by the end of 2010 as people spend more time online and less time with printed media. The impact on newspapers and magazines is obvious and the cause was simple—a change in individual behavior.

In addition, it's our perspective that technology and its influence on consumers have expanded business functions so they now have a media agency component. Originally, we may have been hired by clients to take creative work and distribute it with optimal reach and frequency, but now the potential is much greater. Today, we have to find a way to send messages to active consumers and determine how to encourage engagement so that viewers move through the purchase process. At the same time, we have to consider that empowered consumers can be either powerful advocates or vicious enemies of a brand and find roles for commercial engagement in those channels of advocacy while recognizing the high risks and rewards that this approach entails.

Implementing these strategies gives us a different view of media. For example, we are now reclassifying media into three broad types—earned, paid, and owned—based on how today's consumers use and react to media.[1]

What's interesting for us in the media-buying business is that the brands we serve now have to look beyond the confines of the paid media channels we relied on in the past. Today, we have "earned" media, such as social networks, and our

clients "own" web properties, which are very important and measurable components of the communications ecosystem that demand the same levels of message management and optimization as other channels. Importantly, we don't simply see client web sites (as in "owned" media) as destinations, we also see them as (1) repositories of content (video, images, data) that can be distributed elsewhere and (2) indicators of the performance of marketing activity in general.

When all is said and done, those who seek to understand and work with media must transition from an inward to an outward perspective of how we and those around us consume media and react to it.

[1]These thoughts were originally presented by Rob Norman, CEO Groupm Interaction in 2008.

the circulation and the more specialized the content of a magazine, the more likely it is that the geographic edition will be the only partial run offered.

Some magazines that offer partial-run editions offer only geographic ones. However, major publications, especially large-circulation weeklies such as *Time*, *Newsweek*, and *People*, offer dozens of options to advertisers. These publications combine both geographic and demographic editions so that an advertiser can reach *Time* readers who occupy positions in top management throughout the country or in selected locations. *Time*, for example, offers dozens of ways to buy advertising in the magazine, including both demographic and regional editions.

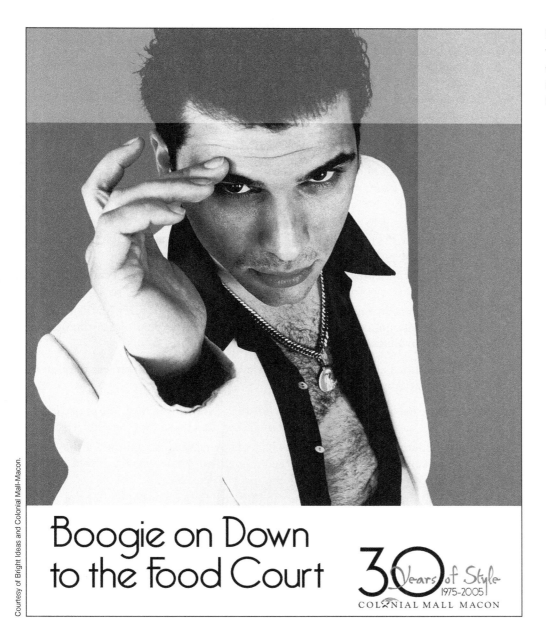

Courtesy of Bright Ideas and Colonial Mall-Macon.

Boogie on Down
to the Food Court

30 Years of Style
1975-2005
COLONIAL MALL MACON

As advertisers continue to demand that all media deliver narrowly targeted audiences and the techniques honed by direct mail and other direct-marketing media become more prevalent, we will see the majority of magazines offering some form of partial-run circulation. Computer technology and advances in high-speed printing also are allowing magazines to meet these advertiser requirements. (See Exhibit 11.8.)

SPLIT-RUN EDITIONS A special form of the partial-run edition is the split run. Whereas most partial-run editions are intended to meet special marketing requirements of advertisers, split-run editions normally are used by both advertisers and publishers for testing purposes. The simplest form of split-run test is when an advertiser buys a regional edition (a full run is usually not bought because of the expense) and runs different advertisements in every other issue.

Each advertisement is the same size and runs in the same position in the publication. The only difference among the advertisements is the element being tested. It may be a different headline, illustration, product benefit, or even price. A coupon is normally included, and the advertiser, based on coupon response, can then determine the most productive version of the advertisement. This split-run technique is called an *A/B split*. Half of the audience gets version A and half gets version B.

As the competition for readers has grown, so has the use of split-run tests by magazines themselves. Magazines occasionally experiment with different covers for the same issue—either for testing purposes or to take advantage of some story of regional interest. The split-run technique has been instrumental in providing both publishers and advertisers with insight into how magazine advertising can be most effective. Partial-run and split-run editions offer a number of benefits to advertisers (and, in some cases, publishers):

1. Geographic editions allow advertisers to offer products only in areas in which they are sold. For example, snow tires can be promoted in one area, regular tires in another.

2. Partial runs can localize advertising and support dealers or special offers from one region to another. As advertisers increasingly adopt local and regional strategies, the partial-run advantages will become even more apparent.

3. Split-run advertising allows advertisers to test various elements of a campaign in a realistic environment before embarking on a national rollout.

4. Regional editions allow national advertisers to develop closer ties with their retailers by listing regional outlets. This strategy also provides helpful information to consumers for products that lack widespread distribution.

Partial-run editions also have some disadvantages that make them less than ideal for all advertising situations:

1. CPM levels are usually much higher than full-run advertising in the same publication, and close dates can be as much as a month earlier than those for other advertising.

2. In the case of demographic editions, the lack of newsstand distribution for these advertisements can be a major disadvantage if single-copy sales are significant for the publication.

3. Some publications bank their partial-run advertising in a special section set aside for such material. There also may be special restrictions placed on partial-run advertising. For example, such advertising often must be full page and only four-color advertising is accepted by some publications.

SELECTIVE BINDING   The customization of partial-run editions can be even more sophisticated thanks to selective binding. Although it is essentially the same as partial-run advertising, **selective binding** refers to different editorial material or large advertising sections that are placed in less than the full run of a publication. Using computer technology and sophisticated printing techniques, advertisers and publishers can develop advertising and editorial material specifically for one group or even for individual readers.

Selective binding first gained popularity among major farm publications in the early 1980s. Articles and advertisements were published only in editions delivered to farmers who raised certain types of crops or livestock. In recent years, selective binding has been offered to advertisers by more and more consumer magazines.

Advertisers find selective binding most useful when there are significant subgroups of larger target markets within a publication's audience. Occasionally, a magazine will offer selective binding that is fully integrated into the editorial format of a magazine. More commonly, the technique is used with multipage advertising inserts distributed to a select audience segment identified by age, income, and so forth.

Selective binding is an example of a technology that, in order to be successful, must be advertiser driven. That is, advertisers must be convinced that it offers enough value to justify the additional expense. Many advertising executives think that the practical applications of selective binding are more apparent for business and farm publications than for consumer magazines, which have a number of selective publications.

selective binding
Binding together different material directed to various reader segments in a single issue of a magazine.

Obviously, the widespread use of selective binding has major implications for direct mail. If the technique becomes widely used, advertisers could combine the individual characteristics of direct mail with the high-prestige environment of the magazine. Just as important, selective binding costs the advertiser about double what a normal magazine advertisement costs, but direct-mail CPMs generally run several times that of consumer magazines. Like most partial-run techniques, a major drawback of selective binding is that it can be used only for subscribers.

Because selective binding adopts some of the techniques of direct response, it also raises the same questions of readers' concerns with invasion of privacy. If subscribers are targeted by anything more than name and address, they may regard selective binding as inappropriate, with negative consequences to both the advertiser and magazine. Still, the idea that each reader can have a custom-made magazine, including both editorial and advertising material of specific interest to that individual, is an intriguing concept.

CITY MAGAZINES Magazines directed to readers within a particular city are not a new idea. *Town Topics* was published in New York City in the late nineteenth century, but most observers credit *San Diego Magazine*, first published in the 1940s, as the forerunner of the modern city magazine. Today, city magazines are available in virtually every major city—and most of the largest cities have several.

At one time, city magazines were often regarded as nothing more than booster publications for a city. Many of them were published by a local business or tourism organization and they offered little in terms of hard news or in-depth reporting. Although most city magazines continue to feature lifestyle and entertainment stories, a growing number of publications report on local business, technology, and medical issues. Many publishers are combining the traditional strengths of the city magazines with specialized publication content and initiating such titles as *Chicago Bride*; *Atlanta Business Chronicle*; or the *Fulton County Reporter*, a publication devoted to the Atlanta legal scene.

Because of the generally upscale readership of city magazines, they are popular with upscale local and regional firms and even some national advertisers that want to target individual markets. Advertising revenues are very cyclical. A soft economy often leads to a decrease in advertisement pages because of the downturn in retailing and automobile sales, traditionally two prime categories of city magazine advertising. In addition, city magazines are normally a supplement to mainline advertising for many of these magazines' clients. Consequently, when the advertising market goes soft, they are often among the first medium to be dropped. Whereas the city magazine was formerly a domain of large metropolitan centers, we now find successful publications in cities with populations of about 100,000 (e.g., Macon, Georgia; see Exhibit 11.9).

City publications are in some ways a hybrid between small-circulation specialty publications and the partial-run editions of national magazines. However, they have an advantage over both in reaching upscale local audiences with editorial and advertising content specifically directed to the special, local interests of their prime prospects. More than ninety-five city and regional magazines have come together to sell their space to advertisers as a magazine network. Advertisers can buy space in groups of these magazines with one single insertion order at a cheaper price than if they were buying space in each separately. This allows the magazines to compete effectively with national magazines.[11]

CUSTOM PUBLISHING

Another growing and specialized area of magazine publishing is custom publishing. It is one of the fastest-growing sectors of the magazine business and consists of advertiser-produced publications intended to reach prospects or current customers in a communication environment totally controlled by the marketer. These publications are a cross between direct mail and traditional magazine publishing.

EXHIBIT 11.9

This advertisement is for a regional business-to-business development publication in Macon, Georgia.

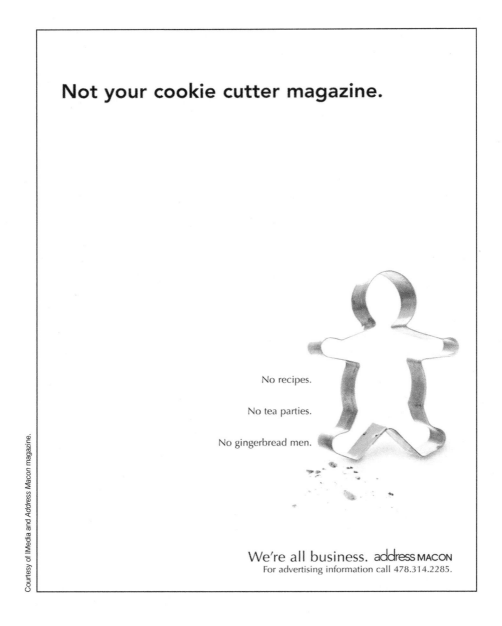

Courtesy of IMedia and *Address Macon* magazine.

Custom publishing is not a new concept. In 1949, General Motors commissioned its agency, Campbell-Ewald, to publish *Friends*, a magazine sent to Chevrolet car and truck owners. However, since those early days, custom magazines account for expenditures of several hundreds of millions of dollars with more and more companies seeing them as an extension of their direct-response marketing. Most mainline magazines offer custom publishing services to their advertisers.

Regardless of the specific use of custom publishing, to be successful it needs to function as part of a planned and integrated marketing program. The objectives of custom publishing vary from company to company. The U.S. Postal Service, for example, uses *Deliver* magazine to keep marketers informed about the benefits and uses of direct mail in marketing campaigns. Custom magazines can be a valuable tool for companies to speak directly to their customers and prospects. The current status of custom publishing is made possible through market research. "People and their buying patterns have never been segmented so precisely before. Most marketers today know a lot about the individual man, woman, or child buying their products, and custom media is considered the best way to talk to them."[12]

Some custom-published magazines are evolving to look much like traditional publications. One of the most obvious features of this transition is the acceptance of outside (albeit noncompetitive) advertising by some publications. It is sometimes hard to tell them from other magazines on the magazine racks.

Magazine Elements

Once an advertiser has made the hard choice of which magazine to select for its business among the hundreds of options, the job is not over. Now the media planner must decide the size, color, placement, and format that will best serve the advertiser's marketing goals and the creative message.

SIZE

The page size of a magazine is the type area, not the size of the actual page. For convenience, the size of most magazines is characterized as standard size (about 8 by 10 inches, like *Time*) or small digest size (about 4 3/8 by 6 1/2 inches, like *Reader's Digest*). There also are a few oversized publications, but they are the exception. When you are ready to order advertising space and send creative materials to a publication, you must get the exact sizes from the publication because sizes may have changed.

POSITION, COLOR, AND SIZE OF MAGAZINE ADVERTISING

Space in magazines is generally sold in terms of full pages and fractions thereof (half pages, quarter pages, three columns, or one column; see Exhibit 11.10). The small advertisements in the classified pages of many magazines are generally sold by the line.

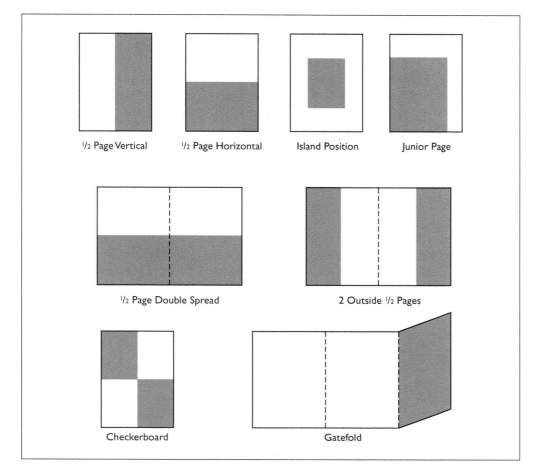

EXHIBIT 11.10

Various Ways of Using Magazine Space

1/2 Page Vertical 1/2 Page Horizontal Island Position Junior Page

1/2 Page Double Spread 2 Outside 1/2 Pages

Checkerboard Gatefold

Impact of Magazine Ads (average)

Type of magazine	Advertisement	Recall index
UNIT*	Full page	100
	Inside front cover	109
	Inside back cover	106
	Back cover	116
	Multiple-page units	115
	Two-page spread	109
	Less-than-full-page	84
COLOR	Black and white	100
	Spot color(s)	96
	*4-Color	108
POSITION	Second half of issue	100
	First half of issue	102

*Four color (including 5th color or metallics)

Source: Magazine Publishers of America.

Magazine covers are the most expensive positions in most magazines, although some magazines offer deep discounts for large advertisers. The front cover of a magazine is called the first cover, which is seldom, if ever, sold in American consumer magazines (although it is sold in business publications). The inside of the front cover is called the second cover, the inside of the back cover is the third cover, and the back cover is the fourth cover.

Advertisers constantly are trying to determine the optimum combination of color, size, and placement that will achieve the highest readership. Exhibit 11.11 shows 12 different combinations of elements and the effect that they have on recall compared to a standard four-color advertisement. These findings are consistent with most research, which has determined that four-color advertising is worth the additional cost in terms of added attention and readership. By the same token, this same research indicates that a two-color advertisement fails to add to reader attention levels and is usually not worth the additional expense.

Another concern of many advertisers is the placement of an advertisement within a magazine. Traditionally, many advertisers have regarded right-hand pages at the front of the book, preferably near related editorial matter, as the ideal advertising placement. "FFRHPOE" or "far forward, right-hand page opposite editorial" is routinely stamped on many insertion orders delivered to magazines in spite of no evidence that these positions add any value to an advertisement.

As the size of an advertisement increases, the audience does not grow proportionately (nor does the cost). For example, in Exhibit 11.11, note that an advertisement that is less than a full page achieves 84 percent of the impact of a full-page unit. If we run a two-page spread, we increase readership by 9 percent (even though we have increased the space by 100 percent). The reason, of course, is that as size increases there are not enough nonexposed readers remaining to continue to increase readership at the same rate.

Although the increase in audience exposures is not proportionate to increases in magazine advertisement size, larger space allows more creative flexibility. Advertising objectives that require long copy can be presented much more effectively in larger spaces. Larger advertisements have greater impact and stronger recall rates over time, even though in the short term they don't score significantly higher than smaller space advertisements. It is important to remember that these studies held creative content constant whereas in reality the quality of the message is perhaps the most important variable in advertising readership and recall. These findings point out again that the specific objectives and creative approach must be considered in designing magazine advertising.

BLEED PAGES

Magazine advertising is able to use a number of formats and designs unavailable or impractical in other media. A common technique is bleed advertising in which the advertisement runs all the way to the edge of the page with no border. **Bleed** advertisements are used to gain attention and use all the available space. Without a border, the advertisement does not have the appearance of being confined to a particular space (see Exhibit 11.12). Typically, bleed advertising will be seen by 10 to 15 percent more readers than nonbleed advertising.

There is no standardization for premium charges for bleed advertising. In the competitive marketplace for magazine advertising, a number of publications offer bleed advertising at no charge as a value-added or extra incentive for advertisers. Even when a magazine has a standard charge for bleed advertising, large advertisers often make these charges a point of negotiation with publishers. With modern printing equipment, most advertisers contend that bleed charges are an unjustified anachronism and many resent even minimal charges for bleed.

MULTIPLE-PAGE UNITS AND INSERTS

Multiple-page advertising covers a broad spectrum of insertions. The most common form of multipage advertising is a facing, two-page spread. Among the most frequent users of multipage inserts and spreads are automobile manufacturers. They face an extremely competitive environment, they need to show their cars in the most favorable, larger-than-life fashion, and they often have an in-depth story to tell about the features of their brands—all reasons to use large-space advertising. A spread increases the impact of the message and eliminates any competition for the consumer's attention. Gatefold spreads come off the front cover and usually are either two or three pages.

One problem with the growing use of multiple-page advertising is that it has lost much of its novelty for consumers. When a reader can turn to practically any consumer magazine and find numerous examples of such advertising, they come to be taken for

bleed
Printed matter that runs over the edges of an outdoor board or of a page, leaving no margin.

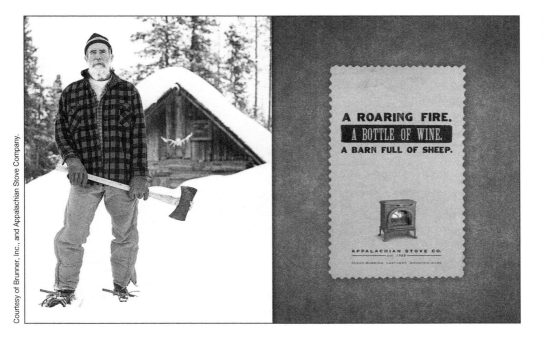

Courtesy of Brunner, Inc., and Appalachian Stove Company.

EXHIBIT 11.12

Two-Page Spread Bleed Advertisement

EXHIBIT 11.13

This one-and-a-third-page ad takes advantage of the production flexibility of magazines to handle ads in a variety of sizes.

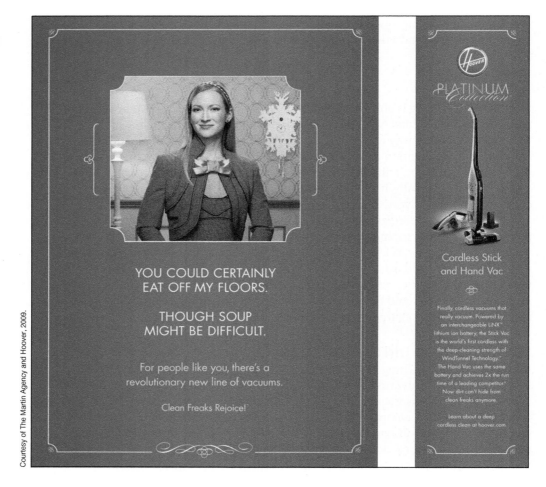

Courtesy of The Martin Agency and Hoover, 2009.

granted, even by serious prospects. It is important to work closely with the creative team to ensure that such expensive space is going to be fully used with a meaningful message. The most effective multiple-page units are for advertisers with an interesting product, a new story to tell, and an interested and involved group of prospects (see Exhibit 11.13).

Cost is a major consideration when planning inserts. Although the insert will be less expensive per page than run-of-publication advertising, the advertiser is still concentrating significant dollars in the publications that carry the inserts. This expense will reduce the number of media vehicles that can be included in a media schedule. Because an advertiser is putting a disproportionate share of advertising into one or a few vehicles, the likely result is a reduction in reach and frequency compared to a more traditional media plan.

How Space Is Sold

ADVERTISING RATES, NEGOTIATION, AND MERCHANDISING

4 Explain how magazine space is sold to advertisers.

In the competitive world of magazine advertising, it is not surprising that publishers are constantly seeking merchandising and value-added programs to differentiate their publications from others in a particular category. Unfortunately, many publishers find themselves in a situation in which advertising rates are the primary consideration for most advertisers.

Scheduling and buying full-run magazine advertising was, at one time, the easiest function for a media planner. Clients usually bought full-page advertisements, circulations were audited, discounts for frequent usage were obtainable from straightforward rate cards, and rates were consistent for every advertiser that qualified for available discounts. In addition, most advertisers bought only a few high-circulation publications.

The rate situation underwent fundamental changes when magazine advertising experienced a downturn in revenues during the 1980s. Faced with flat advertising revenues and new publications continually entering the market, magazines began to negotiate with individual advertisers for special rates. This practice of one-to-one negotiation is called *going off the card*. Starting as a short-term fix during a period of weak advertising spending, negotiation has become a common practice among magazines, with many advertisers regarding the rate card as simply a point at which to start negotiation.

Obviously, publishers would like to maintain rate integrity and they attempt to do so with a number of merchandising and value-added plans. One of the most common means of magazine merchandising is through brand extensions. The Good Housekeeping Seal is one of the oldest and most recognized merchandising tools. The publication sponsors research laboratories that review or evaluate products. Only advertisements for products that pass the evaluations conducted by the Good Housekeeping Research Institute are accepted by the publication. Readers are offered a money-back guarantee if the product is found to be defective within 2 years of purchase.[13] The program is almost 100 years old and is still going strong.

Magazine merchandising services take numerous forms, and they are used by virtually every major magazine. *Better Homes & Gardens* produces greeting cards, provides real estate services, and franchises garden centers. Meanwhile, consumers can buy *Family Circle* classical CDs, *Field & Stream* bass lures, and *Popular Mechanics* work boots. In order to promote its *Parenting* magazine, Time Inc. bought a product-sampling company, First Moments, that delivers products to new mothers in hospitals. Ownership of First Moments allowed the delivery of *Parenting* magazine, subscription offers, and related samples to build relationships with both readers and advertisers.[14]

The key to merchandising programs is to coordinate a magazine's reputation and expertise with marketing techniques that help advertisers sell their products. Among the more traditional merchandising programs are trade shows, conferences, newsletters, database services, and co-promotions such as point-of-purchase displays that highlight certain advertisers that are using a publication. For example, in 1999, *Cooking Light* began sponsoring a series of *Cooking Light* Supper Club dinners around the country to demonstrate the products of its advertisers. Attendees were charged between $49 and $59 for a value of $100 or more. Each dinner was attended by as many as 250 people who were given door prizes and goody bags full of merchandise and information from advertisers as well as their *Cooking Light* meal.[15] These supper clubs have now evolved into smaller groups of readers who organize their own clubs. The *Cooking Light* advertiser-supported web site provides recipes, an e-newsletter, and tips to clubs throughout the year. This helps strengthen the magazine's and its advertisers' relationship with readers and keeps readers coming back to the web site for more information.

In another example of value-added opportunities available to advertisers, *Bon Appetit* magazine partnered with Premier Retail Network's Checkout TV to provide content to their checkout screens in supermarkets and other outlets such as Wal-Mart. The magazine provided custom food-related content that featured products from some key advertisers.[16]

All of these techniques allow advertisers to extend the message of their advertising into related areas and provide an added value to their magazine advertising buy.

MAGAZINES AND THE INTERNET

Magazines were among the earliest media to use the Internet as part of their overall marketing and merchandising plans, and they remain heavily involved in online endeavors. The most common use of the Internet by publishers is the online version of print publications. Hundreds of publications offer full or edited online versions of their

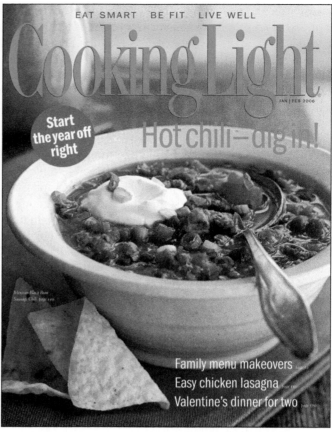

EXHIBIT 11.14

Cooking Light magazine sponsors supper clubs for its readers.

magazines. They are often designed to help build brand loyalty among readers. These online vehicles are generally advertiser supported, used as a value-added mechanism for advertisers, and/or intended to extend the audience reach of the core magazine to online users as in the *Cooking Light* preceding example. Smart publishers have recognized the opportunity that the Internet offers to enhance the value of their titles and build an online community with their brand. The challenge facing magazine publishers now is to find a way to make their magazine web sites profitable as both magazines and advertisers can benefit from this multiplatform tie-in (see Exhibit 11.14).

MAGAZINE RATE STRUCTURE

In the examples that follow, we assume the advertiser is making a full-run magazine buy. That is, the entire circulation of the publication is being purchased. An advertiser buying a partial-run edition will consider a number of other options. A typical rate card for a monthly publication might look like this:

Details Magazine Color Rates (four color)				
Space	1 time	3 time	6 time	12 time
1 page	$59,000	$57,230	$56,050	$52,510
2/3 page	$47,480	$46,056	$45,106	$42,257
1/2 page	$36,980	$35,871	$35,131	$32,912
1/3 page	$25,720	$24,948	$23,662	$22,891

An advertiser buying this publication will pay $59,000 for a one-time, four-color, full-page insertion. The advertiser that buys at least 12 four-color full-page insertions in the publication will pay only $52,510 per advertisement for the same space.

Before placing a magazine on its advertising schedule, the advertiser will compute the cost efficiency of that publication against others being considered. Let's assume that *Details* has an average paid circulation of 440,840. Using the CPM formula discussed earlier, we can calculate the efficiency of the publication as follows:

$$\text{CPM} = \frac{\text{Cost per page}}{\text{Circulation}} \times 1{,}000 \quad \frac{59{,}000}{440{,}840} \times 1{,}000 = \$133{,}835.40$$

DISCOUNTS

FREQUENCY AND VOLUME DISCOUNTS   The one-time, full-page rate of a publication is referred to as its basic, or open, rate. In the case of *Details*, its open rate is $59,000. All discounts are computed from that rate. Most publications present their discounts on a per-page basis in which rates vary according to frequency of insertion during a 12-month period, as we have done here. However, some publications use either **frequency** or volume discounts based on the number of pages run. For instance, frequency discounts offered by a magazine might look like this:

Frequency	Discount Percentage
3 times to 5 times	4
6 times to 8 times	6
9 times to 11 times	9
12 times to 17 times	12

In a similar fashion, the volume discount gives a larger percentage discount based on the total dollar volume spent for advertising during a year. The volume discount is convenient for advertisers that are combining a number of insertions of different space units or that are using a number of partial-run insertions. Volume discounts offered by *People* magazine might look like this:

Volume, $	Discount Percentage
2,700,000 or more	10
2,100,000–2,699,999	8
1,500,000–2,099,999	6
800,000–1,499,999	4

OTHER DISCOUNTS   In addition to discounts for volume and frequency, individual magazines offer a number of specialized discounts, usually for their largest advertisers. Among the more common discounts in this category is a lower per-page price for advertisers that combine buys with other publications or media owned by the same magazine group. We previously discussed these arrangements in the section on cross-media buys. As media companies become larger, the opportunities for these buys will be more numerous. Cross-media discounts operate similarly to volume discounts except advertisers accumulate credit across a number of media vehicles.

THE MAGAZINE SHORT RATE

As we have seen, most magazine discounts are based on the amount of space bought within a year. However, the publisher normally requires that payment be made within 30 days of billing. Therefore, an advertiser and a publisher sign a space contract at the beginning of the year and agree to make adjustments at the end of the year if the space usage estimates are incorrect. If the advertiser uses less space than estimated, the publisher adjusts using a higher-than-contracted rate. If more space is used, the publisher adjusts using a lower rate.

Let's look at a typical short rate, using the rate card for *Details*. A wristwatch manufacturer contracted with *Details* to run six pages of advertising during the coming year.

frequency
In media exposure, the number of times an individual or household is exposed to a medium within a given period of time.

At the end of the year, the manufacturer had run only five pages. Therefore, it was short the rate for which it had contracted and an adjustment had to be made, as follows:

$$\text{Ran five times. Paid the six-time rate of \$56,050 per page} = (5 \times 56,050)$$
$$= \$280,250$$
$$\text{Earned only the three-time rate of \$57,230 per page} = (5 \times 57,230)$$
$$= \$286,150$$
$$\text{Short rate due (\$286,150} - \$280,250) = \$5,900$$

Some publishers charge the top (basic) rate throughout the year but state in the contract "rate credit when earned." If the advertiser earns a better rate, the publisher gives a refund. If the publisher sees that an advertiser is not running sufficient pages during the year to earn the low rate on which the contract was based, the publisher sends a bill at the short rate for space already used and bills further advertisements at the higher rate earned. Failure to keep short rates in mind when you are reducing your original schedule can lead to unwelcome surprises.

Much of the consumer magazine cost, circulation, contact, and other advertising-specific information needed by advertisers (including online links to magazines) can be found in the ***Standard Rate and Data Service*** **(SRDS)** *Consumer Magazine Advertising Source. SRDS* provides information on more than 3,000 consumer and farm publications. With both printed and online versions available, it is a useful resource for media planners. (See Exhibit 11.15.)

Standard Rate and Data Service (SRDS)
SRDS publishes a number of directories giving media and production information.

MAGAZINE DATES

There are three sets of dates to be aware of in planning and buying magazine space:

1. *Cover date.* The date appearing on the cover
2. *On-sale date.* The date on which the magazine is issued (the January issue of a magazine may come out on December 5, which is important to know if you are planning a Christmas advertisement)
3. *Closing date.* The date when the print or plates needed to print the advertisement must be in the publisher's hands in order to make a particular issue

For example:

***Self* (published monthly)**
- March issue
- On sale February 24
- Closes December 31

***People* (published weekly)**
- March 9 issue
- On sale February 27
- Closes January 19

MAGAZINE NETWORKS

The term *network*, of course, comes from broadcast when affiliated stations cooperated to bring audiences national programming as early as the 1920s. A special adaptation of the network concept has been employed by virtually every medium as a means of offering advertisers a convenient and efficient means of buying multiple vehicles. There are newspaper networks, outdoor networks, and even networks for direct-mail inserts and comic strips. Magazines are no exception.

As we mentioned earlier, one of the problems of the growing specialization in magazines is that advertisers increasingly need to buy a number of titles to achieve reach and frequency goals. Another consequence of smaller circulations is that magazine

EXHIBIT 11.15

SRDS lists ad rates and other information of interest to advertisers for more than 3,000 magazines.

CPM levels have increased. Many large national advertisers have complained about both the difficulty of buying numerous magazines and the higher CPMs. In order to accommodate these advertisers, a number of publishers have established **magazine networks**. As with networks in other media, their intent is to make it possible for an advertiser to purchase several publications simultaneously with one insertion order, one bill, and often significant savings compared to buying the same magazines individually.

Currently, there are dozens of magazine networks, some representing dozens of different titles. The network concept allows several magazines to compete for advertisers by offering lower CPMs and delivering a larger audience than any single publication. Networks must be carefully tailored to reach a particular audience segment with as little waste circulation or audience duplication as possible. Although there are a number of magazine networks, they generally fall into two categories:

1. *Single publisher networks.* Here a network is offered by a single publisher that owns several magazines and will allow advertisers to buy all or any number of these publications as a group. For example, Hearst Magazine Group publishes more than 20 magazines and allows advertisers that use multiple titles to build network discounts.

   The publisher network can be especially effective in encouraging a media buyer to choose among similar magazines. For example, let's assume a media buyer has decided to purchase space in *Cosmopolitan* and *Marie Claire*, both Hearst magazines. A third option is to purchase either *O, The Oprah Magazine*, another Hearst magazine, or *Glamour* to complete the schedule. Assuming that both magazines meet the advertising criteria of a particular client, the discounts available from buying *O, The Oprah Magazine* as part of the Hearst network may well sway the media buyer in that direction.

   To a degree, the single publisher network is being replaced by cross-media buying. As more and more magazines become part of media conglomerates, they no longer confine a "network" buy to magazines but broaden the concept to all media vehicles owned by a particular company.

2. *Independent networks.* The second type of magazine network is made up of different publishers that market magazines with similar audience appeals. A rep firm that contracts individually with each publisher and then sells advertising for magazines

magazine networks
Groups of magazines that can be purchased together using one insertion order and paying a single invoice.

within the group usually offers these networks. The concept is similar to the space wholesaling that George Rowell began in the 1850s. Media Networks, Inc., the largest independent network firm, offers several networks, each geared to a specific audience. For example, the MNI Business Network consists of seven magazines including *Forbes, Inc., Fortune Small Business, Money, Fast Company*, and *Business Week*. Even though different publishers own these magazines, they know that there are advantages to cooperating in selling space to large advertisers.

Magazine Circulation

5 **Describe the role of magazines as a targeted advertising medium.**

As with any medium, accurate magazine readership measurement is extremely important to advertisers. Media planners don't buy magazines, television spots, or outdoor signs—they buy audiences. More specifically, they buy certain groups of people who are customers or prospects for their products. In the magazine industry, there are two distinct methods of determining audiences: *paid circulation* and *the rate base*.

The more commonly used and reliable method of audience measurement is paid circulation. Most major consumer magazines have their circulations audited by an outside company. Magazine rates are based on the circulation that a publisher promises to deliver to advertisers, referred to as the *guaranteed circulation*. Because the guaranteed circulation is the number of readers advertisers purchase, it also is referred to as the **rate base**, or the circulation on which advertising rates for a specific magazine are based.

rate base
The circulation level on which advertising rates are based.

You will recall from our earlier discussion that magazine publishers are finding it increasingly expensive to maintain high readership levels. Increased circulation for a magazine is sometimes caused by marginally interested readers who subscribed because of special introductory deals, among other things. Publishers usually find it very expensive to keep these fringe readers when it is time to renew subscriptions. Added to this problem is the fact that major auditing organizations, such as the ABC, require that a subscriber pay at least 50 percent of the full subscription price to be counted as a reader. Consequently, magazines are limited in the marketing promotions they can use and still count readers as paid for auditing purposes.

In the past few years, a number of major magazines have lowered their rate bases substantially. Rate base management is fundamentally a financial consideration. As circulation rises, advertising rates also will increase. However, if publishers are spending more on marketing to keep circulation figures artificially higher than they can gain in increased advertising revenue, it doesn't make economic sense to continue to do it.

Magazine circulation figures can vary a great deal from month to month largely because of newsstand sales. In the past, many publishers have averaged their circulation over a 6- or 12-month period. Many publishers argue that ABC should judge them on an average monthly circulation basis rather than on the circulation of individual issues.

Of course, advertisers would rather buy space in magazines with a quality readership, that is, with readers who are interested in both the magazine and its advertising. By the same token, advertisers generally will gravitate to those publications with the largest number of readers within their target audience. Common sense tells us that publishers, particularly those of second-tier magazines, will continue to explore whatever steps are necessary to keep circulation levels as high as possible within their profit constraints.

A magazine does not necessarily offer a guaranteed rate base to advertisers. In fact, a number of audited publications do not make a specific guaranteed circulation claim. These publishers provide advertisers with accurate circulation for past issues, but they don't take any risk for circulation shortfalls in the future. In the volatile world of magazine advertising, many smaller magazines do not want to deal with the financial problems of make-goods related to audience decreases.

READERSHIP

In magazine terminology, *readership* usually combines paid circulation (subscribers and newsstand purchasers) with pass-along readers. For example, according to ABC, *Elle* magazine has a paid circulation of 1.1 million. According to Mediamark Research Inc., *Elle* has 5.1 million readers. This means that there are approximately 4.6 readers per copy (RPC).[17] The more general the publication's editorial, the more likely it is to have significant pass-along readership.

Many advertisers and even magazine publishers are concerned about the use of readership as a substitute for paid circulation. Historically, the use of readership is rooted in the magazine industry's competition with television. Publishers want to keep readership surveys to take into account fairly their total readers.

It would seem that total readership, accurately measured, would be a reasonable approach to measuring magazine audiences. But a problem arises because many media buyers regard pass-along readers of consumer magazines as inherently inferior to paid circulation. Between those advertisers that see no value in readership and those that view it as equal to paid circulation, there is probably a middle ground. As in most marketing and advertising questions, the real answer is determined by the specific objectives of the publication and its readers. However, regardless of the value that one places on readership, most acknowledge that it is different from paid circulation.

Measuring Magazine Audiences

We now turn to the issue of how publishers verify the circulation and readership of their magazines. Advertisers normally will not purchase a magazine unless its publisher can provide independent verification of the magazine's readership. In magazine terminology, readership has two distinct meanings. One refers to the time spent with a publication. The other, and the one we discuss here, includes all readers of a magazine as contrasted to only those who buy a publication.

6 **Explain how magazine audiences are measured.**

THE AUDIT BUREAU OF CIRCULATIONS

The Audit Bureau of Circulations (ABC) is the largest of several auditing organizations that verifies magazine circulation. The ABC provides two basic services: the publisher's statements or "pink sheets" (because of their color), which report 6-month periods ending June 30 and December 31, and the ABC audits, or "white sheets," which annually audit the data provided in the publisher's statements. The ABC reports total circulation, as well as circulation figures by state, by county size, and per issue during each 6-month period. ABC reports also state the manner in which circulation was obtained—for example, by subscription or by newsstand sales—and any discounts or premiums provided to subscribers.

The ABC reports are matter-of-fact documents that deal only with primary readers. They do not offer information about product usage, demographic characteristics of readers, or pass-along readership. Both publishers and advertisers rely on the accuracy of the ABC audience data.

SYNDICATED MAGAZINE READERSHIP RESEARCH

Advertisers are, of course, interested in the primary readers of magazines. But they are also interested in who these readers are and what they buy, as well as pass-along readers who are given the publications. Currently, there are two principal sources of syndicated magazine readership research: **Simmons Market Research Bureau (SMRB)** and **Mediamark Research Inc. (MRI)**.

Mediamark Research Inc. (www.mediamark.com) methodology consists of selecting a sample of 26,000 people and eliciting media usage, demographic characteristics, lifestyle, and product-purchase information. Using a combination of personal interviews and self-administered questionnaires, respondents report on magazine readership and product usage. Simmons Market Research Bureau (www.smrb.com) samples more than 25,000 adults, including more than 7,500 Hispanic/Latino adults. The data are collected via mailed questionnaires and measure media usage, including data on several hundred magazines, with an emphasis on audience and product-usage information.

Simmons Market Research Bureau (SMRB) and Mediamark Research, Inc. (MRI)
Two competing firms that provide audience data for several media. Best known for magazine research.

The Business Press and Business-to-Business Advertising

Professional Candy Buyer, *Auto Body Repair News*, *The Science Teacher*, *Mediaweek*, and *Journal of Athletic Training* are only a handful of the more than 10,000 publications that make up the business press. Business-to-business (B2B) communication is a marketplace where million-dollar deals are commonplace and the methods for sales, marketing, and advertising are markedly different from those in consumer advertising. A number of media and promotions are used to reach business buyers. We discuss them in this chapter because traditionally business magazines have constituted the primary source of B2B expenditures.

Prospects for most business advertisers are fewer and more concentrated, audiences tend to be experts concerning the products they purchase, and audience selectivity is much more important than the CPMs or reach measures used in consumer media. Another feature of business publications is their efficient reach of major decision makers. Given the specialized audience of these publications combined with their moderate cost, the business magazine continues to be a cost-efficient medium. (See Exhibit 11.16.)

Both the tone and advertising of business publications differ significantly from those of consumer magazines. The business press is a medium of reference and commerce, whereas consumer magazines are vehicles of entertainment, news, and leisure reading. Many business publications are used on a regular basis to keep up with the latest industry trends, competitive activity, and product category marketing strategy. Because of this, business executives are likely to be more engaged and involved with business-to-business publications than with more general media.[18]

COMMUNICATING THE BUSINESS-TO-BUSINESS MESSAGE

business-to-business advertisers
Advertisers that promote goods through trade and industrial journals that are used in the manufacturing, distributing, or marketing of goods to the public.

Business-to-business advertisers must consider a number of factors in addressing their specialized audiences. First and foremost, the message must be directed at the profitability of the customer. Whereas few consumer advertisements contain technical product specifications and details about equipment compatibility and delivery terms, these are the types of information commonly contained in business publications.

In communicating with the business community, there are a number of considerations:

1. Advertisers must appeal to prospects in terms of specific job interests and demands. The advertisement should address how a product or service can increase the productivity and enhance the job performance of a particular function.

2. The advertisement must sell the benefits to the buyer, not the features of the product. Again, these benefits need to be couched in terms of sales and productivity.

3. The job of business advertising, particularly for high-end products, is to support and facilitate the sales function. Business transactions, unlike their consumer counterparts, are rarely completed with a single advertisement or even solely through advertising. Most business advertising is a means of moving prospects into the personal sales channel or to seek more information. That is, advertising should function to make the job of personal selling or prospect follow-up easier.

4. Advertisements should avoid product puffery. Remember, the readers of your advertising are trained professionals with high levels of expertise in their fields. They expect to see product information, often with detailed diagrams, charts, and technical specifications. The type of appeals common in consumer media will not work in the business and trade press.

5. Business advertising, just like consumer advertising, needs to have clear objectives that are measurable in terms of specific target publics.

6. Advertisers must consider pass-along readership. A significant number of business publication readers receive their magazines on a pass-along basis. We noted earlier

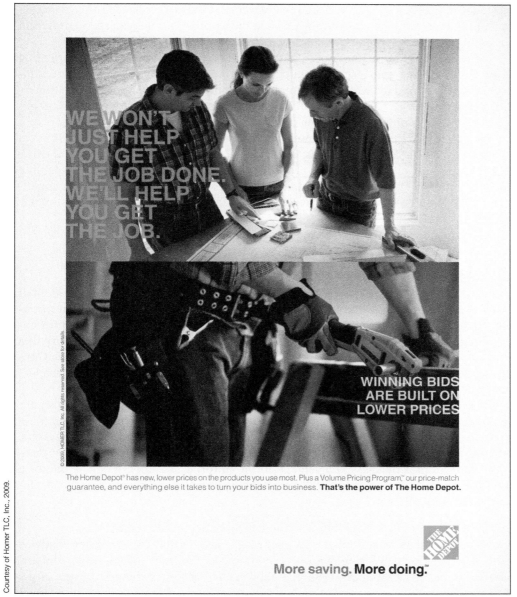

EXHIBIT 11.16

What type of businessperson would be the target for this B2B ad?

that such readership among consumer magazines is generally regarded as inferior to paid circulation. However, one of the notable differences between business and consumer publications is the way advertisers view pass-along readership. The typical consumer medium has a relatively short life and low pass-along readership. Occasionally, a recipe will be clipped or a magazine will be passed on to a neighbor, but consumer magazines are read largely for pleasure and tossed aside. In any case, advertisers view pass-along readership of consumer magazines as vastly inferior to primary readership. Business publication advertisers, in contrast, view pass-along readership as quite valuable. For one thing, readers don't normally browse through *The Journal of Cell Biology* or *Plastics Engineering*; they pay close attention to the copy. For another, some business publications limit their circulation in a way that forces pass-along readership.

CORPORATE BRANDING

Although business-to-business selling is about buying products, it also is about buying the reputation of the companies with which other companies do business. A general consumer may take a chance with an unknown company for a product costing even several hundred dollars. The same is rarely true in the world of business marketing wherein the future of a business can be at stake when major purchases are made.

In recent years, more and more emphasis has been placed on corporate branding by companies. As companies grow and become more complex in terms of different divisions, products, and distribution channels, it becomes difficult to approach customers with a single message. Corporate branding attempts to integrate a company's total image through a coordinated marketing communications process.

Ideally, corporate branding allows a company to speak with its various customers through advertising, public relations, the Internet, and even product design and other identity programs such as logos and product trademarks. Effective corporate branding allows a company to establish its reputation and set its brands apart from the competition. It also allows a company to provide a consistent message to prospects, customers, stockholders, and employees.[19]

The remainder of this section examines some of the special features of the business-to-business sector and the differences and similarities with consumer advertising.

AUDIENCES OF THE BUSINESS PRESS

There are both important qualitative and quantitative differences between readers of business publications and the typical audiences of consumer magazines. Most important, trade publications are part of the job for most readers. They are not read for entertainment, but rather will be judged on the basis of how well they improve the readers' ability to do their jobs, market their products, and improve their profits. Consequently, business magazines must develop a depth of understanding of their readers that typically is not required in the consumer press.

In addition to the approach that readers take to the business press, there also are significant differences in the audience composition of business versus consumer magazines. In terms of age, income, job categories, education, and other basic demographic data, business publications skew far higher than typical consumer magazines.[20] Basically, the tone of a business magazine, both in editorial and advertising, is one of a problem solver. There is a special relationship between business magazines and the industries they serve.

COMPETITION FOR BUSINESS-TO-BUSINESS ADVERTISING

Television, newspapers, radio, and consumer magazines are the core of consumer advertising. On a national basis, television is in fierce competition for consumer dollars, whereas radio and newspapers serve local retailers in reaching these same buyers. However, business selling and marketing have devoted most of their dollars to personal sales, trade and business publications, and direct mail.

As discussed earlier, for most major accounts, marketing communication is used as a means of providing entry for personal selling. Studies show that, by an overwhelming margin, executives with purchasing authority will not make appointments with salespersons unless they have a thorough knowledge of the companies and products they represent. In many respects, the environment of business marketing was unchanged for the 50 years from the end of World War II to the mid-1990s. Then—you guessed it—the Internet became a major force in business marketing.

THE INTERNET AND BUSINESS-TO-BUSINESS MARKETING

The Internet gained acceptance faster in B2B marketing than in consumer marketing. For one thing, businesses were mostly computer savvy long before the Internet came along, so it represented just another phase in the development of computer integration into the business world. The Internet also was more functional for B2B marketing because the number of customers was infinitesimal compared to most consumer products. Both customers and their e-mail addresses could be identified easily, and the Internet

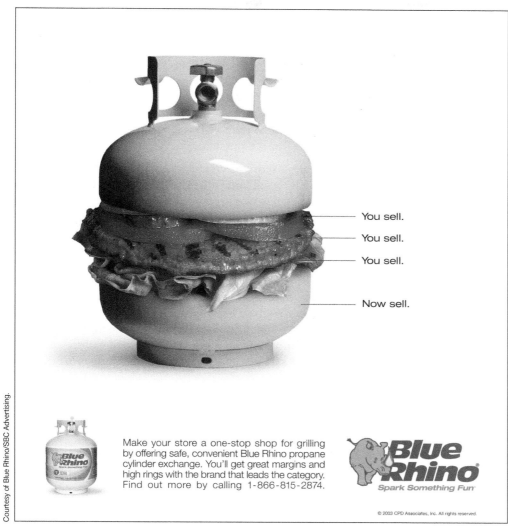

You sell.
You sell.
You sell.

Now sell.

Make your store a one-stop shop for grilling by offering safe, convenient Blue Rhino propane cylinder exchange. You'll get great margins and high rings with the brand that leads the category. Find out more by calling 1-866-815-2874.

Blue Rhino®
Spark Something Fun

Courtesy of Blue Rhino/SBC Advertising.

EXHIBIT 11.17

The visual in this business-to-business advertisement is sure to grab the reader's attention.

quickly became part of the integrated marketing communication plans of most companies. (See Exhibit 11.17.)

BUSINESS PUBLICATION EXPANSION OF SERVICES

You will recall that we discussed the fact that many consumer magazines have introduced a number of merchandising and ancillary services. Because of the specialized nature of business-to-business publications, they are even better positioned to engage in ancillary services than their consumer counterparts. As the competition for B2B advertising and promotional dollars increases, business publications have increasingly engaged in a number of ventures to reach their core readers and at the same time increase the profitability of their companies:

1. *Subscriber list rentals.* Major business publications find that their subscriber list is one of the most valuable commodities they own. In fact, depending on the degree of specialization and the industry they service, business publications make as much as 10 percent of their total revenue from list rentals.

2. *Event-related publications.* Golf tournaments, car shows, and conventions from religious denominations to service organizations often provide an advertiser-supported program with the schedule of the event as well as information about the group. An independent trade publisher usually publishes these publications.

3. *Custom publications.* As we discussed in an earlier section, custom publishing is a very lucrative business. These custom magazines are a major source of revenue for many trade publishers.

4. *Trade shows.* In Chapter 14, we discuss the role of trade shows in the marketing channel. Major trade shows bring buyers and sellers from an entire industry together to view new products and methods of doing business. In some cases, business publications organize and sell sponsorship to these shows usually under the name of the publication. A named trade show demonstrates leadership in the field and can also be a profitable enterprise for the publication.

Entry into ancillary services usually is more successful for established magazines than for their smaller competitors that are less well known. Magazines provide credibility and high visibility to these ancillary events, which would be lacking without the tie-in to a major publication. Seeing the growth of promotional techniques in business-to-business advertising, many magazine publishers use ancillary vehicles to add to their overall profitability and decrease their dependence on advertising from their publications.

Regardless of their format, ancillary activities offer a number of advantages to a publisher. First, they use the publisher's knowledge of a particular industry to help clients develop a coordinated promotional and advertising campaign. Second, they gain revenue from companies that do not use advertising as a primary business-to-business marketing tool. Finally, they increase a magazine's credibility by demonstrating far-reaching expertise in a number of promotional areas. In the future, we will see publishers developing a variety of information services and promotional techniques in addition to their basic magazines.

Business publications are different from consumer magazines in several ways. This section briefly discusses the more important ones.

TYPES OF BUSINESS-TO-BUSINESS PUBLICATIONS

Despite the wide array of business publications, they can generally be placed in one of four categories:

- Distributive trades (trade)
- Manufacturers and builders (industrial)
- Top officers of other corporations (management)
- Physicians, dentists, architects, and other professional people (professional)

TRADE PAPERS   Because most nationally advertised products depend on dealers for their sales, we discuss advertising in **trade papers** first. Usually, this advertising is prepared by the agency that handles the consumer advertising, and in any new campaign both are prepared at the same time. The term *trade papers* is applied particularly to business publications directed at those who buy products for resale, such as wholesalers, jobbers, and retailers. Typical trade papers are *Supermarket News*, *Chain Store Age*, *Hardware Retailer*, *Women's Wear Daily*, and *Home Furnishings Retailer*.

Almost every business engaged in distributing goods has a trade paper to discuss its problems. Trade papers are a great medium for reporting merchandising news about the products, packaging, prices, deals, and promotions of the manufacturers that cater to the particular industry. The chain-store field alone has more than 20 such publications. Druggists have a choice of more than 30, and there are more than 60 different publications issued for grocers. There are many localized journals, although several of these are now offered only in digital format as e-magazines or e-newsletters.

INDUSTRIAL PUBLICATIONS   As we move into the world in which a company in one industry sells its materials, machinery, tools, parts, and equipment to another company for use in making a product or conducting operations, we are in an altogether different ballpark—the industrial marketing arena.

trade paper
A business publication directed to those who buy products for resale (wholesalers, jobbers, retailers).

There are fewer customers in this arena than in the consumer market, and they can be more easily identified. The amount of money involved in a sale may be large— hundreds of thousands of dollars, perhaps even millions—and nothing is bought on impulse. Many knowledgeable executives with technical skills often share in the buying decision. The sales representative has to have a high degree of professional competence to deal with the industrial market, in which personal selling is the biggest factor in making a sale. Advertising is only a collateral aid used to pave the way for or to support the salesperson; hence, it receives a smaller share of the marketplace budget.

Advertising addressed to people responsible for buying goods needed to make products is called *industrial advertising*. It is designed to reach purchasing agents, plant managers, engineers, controllers, and others who have a voice in spending the firm's money.

MANAGEMENT PUBLICATIONS   The most difficult group for a publication to reach is managers. After all, even the largest companies have only a relatively few decision makers. When these decision makers are widely dispersed across a number of industries and job descriptions, publications find they must be extremely creative to reach them.

The management category is one that straddles a gray area between consumer and business-to-business publications. Magazines such as *Business Week*, *Fortune*, and *Nation's Business* have characteristics that would place them in either the business or the consumer category. Even magazines such as *Time* have at least some of their partial-run editions listed in the *Business Publications SRDS*.

PROFESSIONAL PUBLICATIONS   The *SRDS*, in its special business publication edition, includes journals addressed to physicians, surgeons, dentists, lawyers, architects, and other professionals who depend on these publications to keep on top of new developments in their professions. The editorial content of such journals ranges from reports about new technical developments to discussions on how to meet client or patient problems better and how to manage offices more efficiently and profitably. Professional people often recommend or specify the products their patients or clients should order. Therefore, much advertising of a highly technical caliber is addressed to them. (See Exhibit 11.18.)

CONTROLLED CIRCULATION   Magazines are sometimes distributed free to selective readers. Free circulation is known as **controlled circulation**. The term *controlled* refers to the fact that publishers distribute only to a carefully selected list of people who are influential in making purchase decisions for their organization. They use the same database techniques that direct mailers use in building their mailing lists. Controlled circulation makes sense when dealing with an easily defined audience of decision makers. To some media planners, the logic of controlled circulation is not very different from that of direct mail except that the advertising is delivered in an editorial environment. Despite the fact that controlled circulation is widely used in the trade press, it is not universally embraced. In the past, most research indicated that a high percentage of both clients and media directors prefer the reader commitment inherent in paid circulation.

The number of controlled publications in the business field plays a major role in their share of advertising-to-circulation revenues compared to consumer magazines. A number of publications use a mix of controlled and paid circulations in which qualified readers receive the magazine free and others can buy it if they wish.

Controlled circulation creates a significant dependence on advertising support. Unlike consumer magazines, business publications have been largely unsuccessful in shifting to a reader-driven revenue stream. This dependency on advertising is another reason why business publications suffer so much during economic downturns.

VERTICAL AND HORIZONTAL PUBLICATIONS   Industrial publications are usually considered to be either horizontal or vertical. A **vertical publication** is one that covers an entire industry. An example is *Snack Food & Wholesale Bakery*, which contains

controlled circulation
Publications sent without cost to people responsible for making buying decisions. To get on such lists, people must state their positions in companies; to stay on them, they must request it annually. Also known as qualified-circulation publications.

vertical publication
Business publications dealing with the problems of a specific industry, for example, *Chain Store Age*, *National Petroleum News*, and *Textile World*.

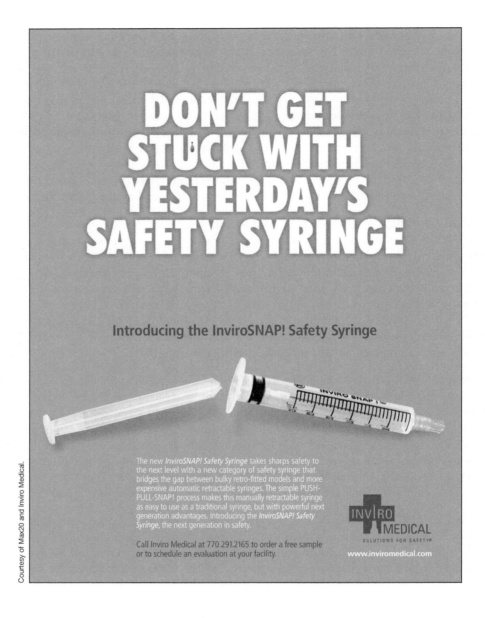

Courtesy of Max20 and Inviro Medical.

information concerning research and development, manufacturing, product quality, marketing, warehousing, and distribution.

A **horizontal publication** is edited for people who are engaged in a single function that cuts across many industries. An example is *Purchasing Magazine*, which is circulated to purchasing managers. It discusses trends and forecasts applicable to all industries.

horizontal publication
Business publications for people engaged in a single job function regardless of the industry, for example, *Purchasing Magazine*.

CIRCULATION AUDITS

Business-to-business advertisers are keenly interested in the circulation of the publications in which they advertise. In some respects, the readership numbers are more important than those in general consumer magazines. The total audience is smaller, the CPM for most publications is significantly higher than that for consumer magazines, and the competition makes it imperative that business-to-business marketers reach their target audience in a timely fashion.

Because of the number and diversity of audiences contacted by the trade and business press, business publishers and advertisers use a number of auditing organizations. The Business Publications Audit (BPA) of Circulation International, the leading business auditor, audits more than 500 trade and industrial magazines. Because many business publications are circulated to a general business audience, the ABC is used for publications such as *Business Week*, and a few publications use both auditing firms.

A third auditing organization is the Verified Audit Circulation (VAC). Founded in 1951, VAC provides circulation audits for a wide variety of newspapers, shoppers, magazines, and even Yellow Pages directories. There are a number of publications in the business area that are not audited. Although an unaudited publication can survive, there are a number of business-to-business advertisers and agencies that, as a matter of policy, will not consider an unaudited publication.

Agribusiness Advertising

At one time, farm media, both print and broadcast, were geared largely to the millions of families who lived and worked on small farms. In recent years, the farm press has had to adapt to dramatic changes in the way agriculture is conducted in the United States. Between 1940 and 1991, the number of farm workers declined by almost 70 percent. During that same period, the number of farm residents dropped from 31 million to 5 million.[21] These numbers have continued to decline in the past 15 years.

Contemporary agribusiness media and advertisers are tailoring their messages to a concentrated industry of huge farm cooperatives and farm managers with income and educational levels that rival those of the CEOs of any major business. Although weather and crop prices are still major topics of the farm press, these publications are likely to discuss the weather in Russia, price controls, and export policies as opposed to what is happening in a local community.

The farm press is facing many of the problems of the business press. A number of media competitors have come on the scene in recent years to take advertising dollars from the print media. Unlike business-to-business advertising in which television and radio have only recently been used by advertisers, farm broadcasting has a long history of serving the farm community.

There are a number of local and regional farm broadcasters, but on a national level the primary sources of agribusiness news and advertising are those that follow:

- *AgDay*, a daily syndicated television show, reaches an average of 260,000 households each morning and is carried by about 120 stations (www.agday.com).
- The weekly *U.S. Farm Report*, which is syndicated to more than 180 of the nation's television stations, is the nation's longest-running agricultural news program (www.farmjournalmedia.com).
- *National Farm Report* is a syndicated 3-minute daily farm report airing on more than 200 radio stations (www.tribuneradio.com).

In addition, a number of web sites have been established by the farm media and agribusiness advertisers.

Advertising products to the agribusiness community uses many of the same techniques demonstrated by other sectors of business marketing. However, agribusiness promotional techniques are even more specialized than those of traditional business-to-business selling. The relatively small agribusiness population makes sophisticated information readily available. Agribusiness advertising can target audiences and deliver a message that solves specific problems of the farm industry.

The business of farming has been hit hard during recent years with an uncertain farm economy, high prices for feed and other supplies, and unpredictable weather. These factors have combined to make it very difficult for farm magazines and agribusiness advertising in general. A continuing consolidation of farms has reduced the number of farmers and companies involved in agribusiness. This trend toward consolidation has been reflected in the farm press by lower circulation and fewer advertising dollars during the past quarter century.

8 **Describe the role of the agribusiness press.**

Ironically, as the number of farms and major agribusiness suppliers has decreased, the number and diversity of media competing for advertising dollars in the sector have grown dramatically. In order to compete in this environment, farm publications have used many of the techniques of the business press in expanding the means they use to reach their audiences. For example, these magazines have accumulated sophisticated databases to develop subscriber list rentals, do their own direct mail to nonsubscribers, and publish special catalogs and other material. Like the business press, farm magazines will probably see more revenue coming from nonpublishing sources as they become more successful in promoting these ventures.

THE ORGANIZATION OF THE FARM PRESS

Farm magazines fall into three classifications: general farm magazines, regional farm magazines, and vocational farm magazines.

GENERAL FARM MAGAZINES   The three major publications of general farm magazines are *Farm Journal*, *Successful Farming*, and *Progressive Farmer*. In recent years, each of these publications has experienced circulation decreases reflecting the consolidation of the farming industry. The general farm publications are designed to address all aspects of farm life but with a clear emphasis on business.

REGIONAL FARM MAGAZINES   A number of farm publications are directed to farmers in a particular region. These publications tend to be general in nature, but they contain little of the family-oriented topics found in the large-circulation farm magazines. They address issues of crops, livestock, and government farm policy unique to a particular region. Among the publications in this category are the *Prairie Farmer*, the majority of whose readers live in Indiana and Illinois; the *Western Farmer-Stockman*; and the *Nebraska Farmer*.

VOCATIONAL FARM MAGAZINES   The last category of farm publications comprises those devoted to certain types of farming or livestock raising. Typical of these publications are *The Corn and Soybean Digest*, *The Dairyman*, *American Fruit Grower*, and *The Tomato Magazine*. Many of the vocational magazines combine elements of both regional and vocational publications—for instance, *The Kansas Stockman*.

Whatever farmers' interests may be, a number of publications are edited to cater to them. Many farm homes subscribe to several publications.

SUMMARY

The challenges and opportunities facing consumer magazines cover a wide range of concerns. From practical considerations of cost management in distribution and printing to the ways in which the Internet can be integrated into traditional magazine practices, publishers must deal with an ever-changing marketplace.

In spite of these challenges, magazines offer many advantages to advertisers. Magazine readers are among the most upscale of any media audience. They show great strength among Internet users that, combined with the selective nature of most publications, may offer a profitable convergence for many publishers. New technology aside, magazines are well positioned as a major marketing and advertising tool.

Magazines can play a role as either the primary medium for a national advertiser or as a niche medium to reach prime prospects. Magazines will continue to be a major source of news, information, and entertainment for millions of prime prospects. It is this combination of prestige and segmentation that gives magazines a major qualitative advantage over most other media. The fact that magazines are asking readers to carry a major share of the financial support of magazines also has enhanced their value to advertisers.

The combination of upscale readers, opportunities for targeted advertising, editorial involvement, and both reach and frequency among a number of qualitative and quantitative audience segments of importance to advertisers will work to the advantage of magazines in the future. Despite these positive characteristics, magazines will continue to face a number of economic problems. Some, like postage increases and newsstand distribution concerns, are beyond their immediate control. In the long term, it may be that financial elements will determine the future of the medium as much as readership.

Business-to-business publications are facing a number of challenges now and in the future. Among the most obvious is the consolidation of many industries into fewer and fewer firms. This merging of firms has resulted in a decrease in both the number of potential advertisers to support the business press and in the number of companies that are being reached with advertising.

A second major trend in the business press has been the growth of competition for advertising dollars. At one time, trade and business publications had a virtual monopoly in the business sector and the farm press had only radio as a major competitor. Today, that situation has changed dramatically. Business advertisers are putting their marketing communication dollars in numerous vehicles as well as the Internet and using sophisticated database technology to demand immediate and measurable results from their advertising.

Because of the relatively low price of trade magazine advertising, it is possible to appeal to specialized job interests with different messages in a variety of publications. The messages of these publications are also specialized. Factual copy with product information is presented to a knowledgeable audience in a manner that would be impractical in most consumer magazines.

Business-to-business publications are an ideal medium for reaching the targeted audience segments that advertisers seek in an environment suited to the mood of that audience. Business magazines also provide audience involvement to a degree impossible in most other media formats and the affinity for these magazines carries over to the advertising messages.

With the ability of computers to track employment demographics and new technology to reach readers through partial-run editions and selected binding, business magazines can compete in an increasingly competitive media environment. On the negative side, business magazines face the same problems of rising postage, printing, and marketing costs as their consumer counterparts. Quality, credibility, believability, and audience selectivity are the elements that will continue to make the business press a primary choice of business-to-business advertisers.

REVIEW

1. Two of the major concerns of the magazine industry are costs and selectivity. Explain.
2. Why would an advertiser want to use both television and magazines?
3. What are some qualitative features of importance to magazine advertisers?
4. Contrast full-run and partial-run magazine editions.
5. What is selective binding?
6. What is the role of negotiation in setting magazine advertising rates?
7. Contrast circulation and readership in magazines.
8. What are the major competitors for business magazines?
9. What has been a primary method for business magazines to extend their services and increase profits?
10. What are vertical and horizontal publications?

CHAPTER 12

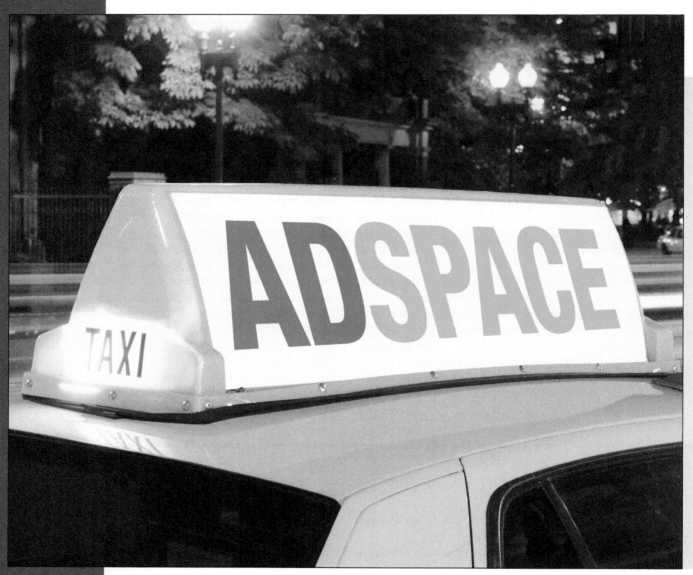

Jorge Salcedo, Shutterstock.

Out-of-Home Advertising

W ITH THE current move to targeted formats in most advertising vehicles, out-of home advertising is fast becoming the last of the truly mass media. Out-of-home advertising can grab the attention of consumers in places and at times of day that are difficult for other media to reach them. There has been a dramatic change in the definition of out-of-home media in recent years as the standard highway billboard is being joined by many innovative out-of-home approaches. ▶

CHAPTER LEARNING OBJECTIVES

1. Understand the basic marketing strategy of out-of-home advertising.
2. Describe the legislative environment of outdoor advertising.
3. Identify various types of out-of-home media.
4. Explain how outdoor advertising is bought and sold.
5. Describe measurement of the outdoor audience.

Out-of-home advertising offers a number of advantages to businesses from large national corporations to the smallest retailer. Among the most important advantages of out-of-home advertising are the following:

Pros

1. Outdoor can provide advertising exposure to virtually every adult in a geographic market with high frequency and at a very low cost per exposure.
2. With 24-hour exposure, outdoor is an excellent means of supplementing other media advertising for product introduction or for building brand-name recognition.
3. With the use of color and lighting, outdoor is a medium that gains immediate audience attention and can provide reminder messages in proximity to retail outlets such as fast-food franchises.

4. The outdoor industry has diversified the product categories using out-of-home in an attempt to lose its image as a "beer and cigarette" medium.

Disadvantages of using out-of-home media for advertising include the following:

Cons

1. With a typical audience of high-speed drivers, outdoor is unable to communicate detailed sales messages. Copy is usually limited to headline length—seven to ten words.

2. Outdoor advertising is extremely difficult to measure, making audience comparisons with other media almost impossible.

3. Outdoor has been attacked in many communities as a visual pollutant, which has made it the topic of some controversy. It also faces a number of additional legal restrictions in selected jurisdictions. In a few states (e.g., Alaska, Hawaii, and Vermont), some local governments have banned the medium altogether. This negative image may discourage some advertisers from using outdoor.

Outdoor is the oldest form of promotion. Evidence of outdoor messages can be found in prehistoric carvings on bronze and stone tablets in the Middle East. In ancient Egypt, outdoor was a popular means of posting public notices as well as sales messages. Placed on well-traveled roads, they became the forerunner of the modern highway billboard. Painted advertising dates to Pompeii where elaborately decorated walls promoted local businesses.

In the United States, outdoor "broadsides" announced the Boston Tea Party and reported the Boston Massacre, and posters publicized the presidential campaign of Andrew Jackson. The first American commercial billboard was a poster by Jared Bell for the 1835 circus season. Throughout the 1800s, posters promoted a number of products and political causes. In 1850, signs were first used on streetcars in major cities and by 1870 some 300 bill-posting firms served advertisers throughout the East and Midwest.

In 1900, the first standardized outdoor sign format was introduced, and national advertisers such as Kellogg's and Coca-Cola began to share the outdoor market with local advertisers. The modern era of outdoor advertising was introduced when the automobile created a mobile society early in the twentieth century. In addition to a population on the move, outdoor benefited from new printing techniques and a growing advertising industry that was always looking for effective means of reaching prospective customers. During this period, the industry adopted standardized signs; formed the forerunner of its national trade association, the **Outdoor Advertising Association of America (OAAA)**; established what is now the **Traffic Audit Bureau for Media Measurement (TAB)** to authenticate audience data; and initiated a national marketing organization, OAAA Marketing.[1]

The variety of outdoor advertising vehicles available today has resulted in the term *out-of-home advertising* replacing the more familiar term *outdoor advertising* in recent years; *out-of-home advertising* more fully reflects the scope of this industry. Today, *outdoor* normally has a narrower meaning, referring only to highway posters and large signs. The change is more than simply semantic because it reflects the diversity of the industry and its marketing strategy.

Although traditional billboards are still the primary source of industry revenues, they constitute only 66 percent of the industry's total income (see Exhibit 12.1).

The growth of alternative advertising options offered by out-of-home is a major reason for the growth of the industry. Overall, the OAAA estimates that there are more than 40 types of out-of-home media, including everything from the largest outdoor signs to airport and shopping mall kiosks, stadium signs, and airplanes towing banners (see Exhibit 12.2).

Outdoor Advertising Association of America (OAAA)
Primary trade and lobbying organization for the outdoor industry.

Traffic Audit Bureau for Media Measurement (TAB)
An organization designed to investigate how many people pass and may see a given outdoor sign, to establish a method of evaluating traffic measuring a market.

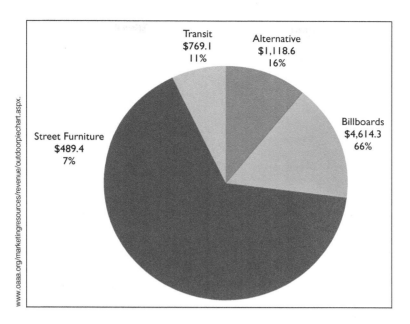

www.oaaa.org/marketingresources/revenue/outdoorpiechart.aspx.

Transit
$769.1
11%

Alternative
$1,118.6
16%

Billboards
$4,614.3
66%

Street Furniture
$489.4
7%

EXHIBIT 12.1

Categories of Out-of-Home Advertising, 2008

Media executives predict that the future of the out-of-home industry will continue to be one of consistent growth. Among the contributing factors to out-of-home's popularity are the following:

1. *An increasingly mobile population.* Americans rarely stay in one place for long. Millions of people commute to work each day, placing them in the out-of-home market ready to receive a variety of messages. Consumers are spending more time

EXHIBIT 12.2

Types of Out-of-Home Media

Billboards[1]	Street Furniture[2]	Transit[3]	Alternative[4]
Bulletins	Bicycles and Bicycle Racks	Airports	Airborne
Digital Billboards	Bus Benches	Buses—Exterior and Interior	Beach Advertising
Spectaculars	Bus Shelters	Mobile Billboards and Truckside	Blimps & Custom Inflatables
Wall Murals	Convenience Store Advertising	Rail Systems and Subways	Cartons & Cups
Posters	In-Store Advertising	Taxicabs	Cinema
Wrapped Posters	Kiosks: Information and Telephone		Dry Cleaning Bags
Junior Posters	Newsstands and Newsracks		Gas Station Advertising
	Pedestrian Panels		Golf Course Advertising
	Shopping Malls		Marine Vessels
			Parking Garage Advertising
			Place-Based Advertising
			Postcards
			Projection
			Rest Area Advertising
			Ski Area Advertising
			Stadium & Arena Advertising
			Trash Receptacles
			Vending Cart Umbrellas
			Place Based Digitial Networks

[1] Standardized large format advertising displays intended for viewing from extended distances, generally more than 50 feet.

[2] Advertising displays, many that provide a public amenity, positioned in close proximity to pedestrians and shoppers for eye-level viewing, or at curbside to influence vehicular traffic.

[3] Advertising displays affixed to moving vehicles or positioned in the common areas of transit stations, terminals and airports.

[4] Alternative is just about anything you could imagine. New products are constantly being developed.

Source: www.oaaa.org, 2009.

EXHIBIT 12.3

Top Outdoor Advertisers

Rank	Marketer	2008
1	AT&T	$108.6
2	Verizon Communications	63.7
3	Sprint Nextel Corp.	60.5
4	Time Warner	54.3
5	Walt Disney Co.	48.0
6	McDonald's Corp.	45.7
7	General Motors Corp.	45.2
8	Anheuser-Busch Cos.	36.8
9	General Electric Co.	28.5
10	Coca-Cola Co.	27.4

Source: TNS Media Intelligence; "Top U.S. advertisers in 10 media," *Advertising Age*, 22 June 2009, 18.

today than ever before traveling to their jobs. According to the OAAA, consumers spend about 15 hours per week in their cars.[2] Average round-trip commute times are estimated to be about 46 minutes per day.[3]

2. *Cost of out-of-home advertising.* No major medium comes close to matching the inexpensive CPM levels of out-of-home advertising. The relatively low cost of out-of-home advertising means that advertisers can generate extremely high levels of both reach and frequency at inexpensive prices. These affordable CPM figures mean that out-of-home advertising provides an ideal medium to fill in gaps among target segments who are missed or underexposed to by other media.

3. *Media fragmentation.* Outdoor advertising is benefiting from the growing audience fragmentation witnessed in other media. In the past 3 decades, the dramatic increase in the number of television channels available per household and the number of magazines and radio stations consumers could access during the same period has resulted in a more fragmented audience than ever before for most media. Although the ability to target prospects is a major benefit for many advertisers, widely distributed package goods and other mass-appeal brands need high levels of exposure to virtually everyone. Outdoor advertising can inexpensively deliver massive audience exposures.

4. *Advertiser diversification.* Once heavily used by tobacco and alcohol beverage companies, the outdoor industry now appeals to a more diversified roster of advertisers. As shown in Exhibit 12.3, only one beer or wine was included in the top 10 categories of outdoor advertising in 2008. Companies such as McDonald's, Verizon, AT&T, Sprint, and Coca-Cola all have made major investments in outdoor. The result has been increased revenues and an improved public image for the outdoor industry.

Strategic Advertising and Out-of-Home

1 Understand the basic marketing strategy of out-of-home advertising.

Out-of-home advertising is one of the most flexible and adaptive of all media. It provides one of the last opportunities to reach consumers prior to purchase. In this regard, it combines the best features of radio and point-of-purchase advertising. Out-of-home advertising has many characteristics that set it apart from other media types. With its ability to command attention, out-of-home also is well suited to enhance the effectiveness of other advertising media. It can function as an economical supplement to a media plan, or it can stand alone as a primary medium. Although there are some opportunities to reach particular portions of a geographic or demographic market with outdoor advertising, its major strength is its ability to reach broad population centers quickly and cheaply.

As is the case with other media, individual advertisers have specific marketing objectives when they select out-of-home. However, there are a number of primary

Courtesy of The Johnson Group.

INSURING 15 MILLION AMERICANS.

ChattanoogaCanDo.com

EXHIBIT 12.4

Outdoor advertising can enhance direct response from consumers by providing web sites.

marketing advantages that are common to most out-of-home buys. Among these are the following:

- It quickly builds awareness for new brands and maintains and reinforces brand identity for established products.
- It creates continuity for a brand or message by extending basic advertising themes beyond traditional media.
- It offers a localized approach for national advertising campaigns.
- It is adaptable to virtually any advertising message or brand with multiple formats.
- It provides local support by offering directions to retail outlets.
- It serves as a point-of-purchase reminder to customers in the shopping and buying process.
- It can enhance direct-response offers by providing web addresses and/or telephone numbers (see Exhibit 12.4 for example).

Despite the fact that a number of high-profile national advertisers are using out-of-home currently, the medium remains essentially a local vehicle. The majority of outdoor advertising revenue comes from local advertisers. However, a number of changes in the out-of-home industry have taken place that make it more attractive to national advertisers to consider out-of-home as part of their future advertising schedule. For example:

1. *Consolidation of ownership.* Only a few years ago, the outdoor business was made up primarily of local companies that provided little audience research, had no national force, or had limited funds to upgrade their facilities. Today, the industry is dominated by large conglomerates that control hundreds of sites throughout the country. These companies are in a position to deal effectively with large national and regional advertisers to gain a larger share of their advertising budgets.

2. *Research.* National advertisers routinely expect sophisticated audience and creative effectiveness research to justify their expenditures. In past years, out-of-home research fell far short of other major media. Even basic demographic data were unavailable in some markets. The out-of-home industry has made major strides in providing meaningful research to prospective advertisers. As we discuss later in this chapter, the industry provides audited audience information as well as eye movement research and demographic segmentation information in areas as small as ZIP codes. Obviously, the outdoor research investment does not compare to that of media with 10 times its advertising revenues, but marketers are being given reasonable information on which to base their media decisions.

3. *Increased and improved creative opportunities.* The quantity and quality of out-of-home production and options have improved dramatically in the past decade. Rather than simply printed or painted signs, advertisers have the choice of options such as

EXHIBIT 12.5

Outdoor advertising is most effective when the message takes advantage of the strengths of the medium.

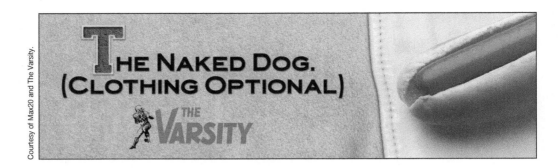

backlit dioramas, vinyl surfaces for outdoor and transit, a number of building-size signs, and interactive and digital mobile media.

4. *Terminology.* Over the years, outdoor developed terminology that was unique to the industry. Not only did media buyers feel uncomfortable dealing in a "foreign" language when buying outdoor but also, more important, the terminology made intermedia comparisons difficult. With the adoption of the GRP as the basic measure of outdoor audience reach, the industry has taken steps to address this issue.[4]

Although outdoor can achieve a number of advertising goals, it is not suitable for every advertiser or every advertising or marketing situation. Like other advertising media, outdoor is most successful when it is used in accordance with narrowly defined marketing objectives that take advantage of the strengths of the medium. In some respects, outdoor presents special challenges because in almost every case it is used as a supplemental medium in a more general campaign (see Exhibit 12.5).

Because out-of-home is rarely a primary campaign building block, it must be coordinated, both creatively and in terms of audience reach, with other media. It is important that the main advertising themes be translated properly to outdoor, so that the target audience is exposed to a seamless message. Outdoor is rarely effective as a standalone medium. Its major strength is the extension and reinforcement of the more detailed advertising messages carried in other media.

Of course, no amount of planning can overcome some of the inherent weaknesses in a medium. While analyzing the strengths of out-of-home, advertisers also must consider its shortcomings and how these may influence a particular marketing, media, or creative strategy. Because exposure to outdoor is both involuntary and brief, there is little depth of communication, even among a product's most loyal customers. It is estimated that the average person sees most signs for less than 10 seconds.

In addition, most out-of-home vehicles provide little audience selectivity. The major disadvantage of most out-of-home advertising is that it is more a shotgun than a rifle. Even though advertisers can tailor their messages to reach specific audiences by pinpointing certain neighborhoods or specific streets, such as roads that lead to stadiums or shopping malls, targeting specific audiences is not considered a primary attribute of the medium.

Finally, as the popularity of out-of-home advertising has grown, it has encountered availability problems. In major markets, demand for premium outdoor sites means some advertisers cannot have access to choice locations. Despite these disadvantages, properly executed outdoor advertising can be an inexpensive method of gaining immediate product visibility.

Outdoor Regulation and Public Opinion

2 Describe the legislative environment of outdoor advertising.

Outdoor advertising's major advantage—its size—is also a significant public relations problem. For years, environmentalists and public activists have argued for strict limits or complete removal of all outdoor signs. However, a number of research studies suggest that many consumers see value in outdoor advertising and think that its positive aspects outweigh the negatives. Given the controversies that surround outdoor, it may be well to examine some of the primary areas of criticisms and the reaction of the outdoor industry to them.

FEDERAL LEGISLATION

The most comprehensive attempt at regulating outdoor advertising dates to the **Highway Beautification Act of 1965** (known as the "Lady Bird Bill" because Mrs. Lyndon Johnson lobbied for the legislation). The act restricted the placement of outdoor signs along interstate highways and provided stiff penalties for states that failed to control signs within 660 feet of interstates. Since passage of the legislation, the number of signs has been reduced from 1.2 million to approximately 400,000. Most of the remaining signs are concentrated in commercially zoned areas. Exhibit 12.6 outlines some of the major provisions of the act.

Highway Beautification Act of 1965
Federal law that controls outdoor signs in noncommercial, nonindustrial areas.

TOBACCO ADVERTISING

Historically, one of the most criticized aspects of outdoor advertising was the promotion of tobacco. Critics charged that the uncontrolled exposure of cigarette messages encouraged usage by underage smokers. In April 1999, the issue became moot when outdoor advertising of tobacco was banned as part of the Master Settlement Agreement with 46 state attorneys general and the major tobacco companies.

In the 1980s, one-third of all billboards promoted tobacco products. This concentration of dollars not only made the outdoor industry too dependent on one product category but the controversy surrounding outdoor also discouraged other product categories from buying the medium. "Conventional wisdom once dictated that the outdoor industry couldn't survive without the . . . dollars from U.S. tobacco marketers. Now it seems not only can the industry survive the loss of that revenue, it can thrive in a nicotine-free world . . . outdoor's day of reckoning is fast becoming its day in the sun."[5]

EXHIBIT 12.6

Federal and State Controls

The Highway Beautification Act of 1965 (23 U.S.C. 131).

Summary of Existing Outdoor Advertising Control Programs

- Billboards are allowed, by statute, in commercial and industrial areas consistent with size, lighting, and spacing provisions as agreed to by the state and federal governments.

- Billboard controls apply to Federal-Aid Primaries (FAPs) as of June 1, 1991; interstates, and other highways that are part of the National Highway System (NHS). The FAP routes were highways noted by state DOTs to be of significant service value and importance. Approximately 260,800 FAP Miles existed as of June 1, 1991 (226,440 rural miles and 34,360 urban miles). These roads have full HBA protections and controls are very important. Maps can be obtained from your state DOT or FHWA Division office or from the OAAA in Washington, D.C.

- States have the discretion to remove legal nonconforming signs along highways; however, the payment of just (monetary) compensation is required for the removal of any lawfully erected billboard along the Federal-Aid Primary, interstate, and other National Highway System roads.

- States not complying with the provisions of the HBA are subject to a 10 percent reduction in their highway allocations.

- States and localities may enact stricter laws than stipulated in the HBA.

- No new signs can be erected along the scenic portions of state-designated scenic byways of the interstate and federal-aid primary highways.

THE OAAA CODE OF INDUSTRY PRINCIPLES

The industry has moved on a number of fronts to improve its image and create positive public relations in the communities it serves. One step to counteract negative publicity toward the industry has been the enactment of a voluntary *Code of Industry Principles* by the OAAA. As part of this code, outdoor companies are asked to limit the number of billboards in a market that carry messages about products that cannot be sold to minors. Specifically, the code asks that member companies establish "**exclusionary zones**" that prohibit advertisements of all products illegal for sale to minors that are either intended to be read from, or within 500 feet of, established places of worship, primary and secondary schools and hospitals."[6]

OUTDOOR INDUSTRY PUBLIC SERVICE

Each year, the outdoor industry contributes hundreds of millions of dollars worth of donated space to a number of charities and public service campaigns. Many of these messages are posted in connection with local service projects. However, the OAAA has formed a number of partnerships to coordinate national projects with organizations such as the Ad Council and the National Center for Missing and Exploited Children. The outdoor industry donates several hundred million dollars worth of outdoor space and production each year to nonprofit organizations.

THE OUTDOOR ADVERTISING PLAN

Successful outdoor advertising depends on both a strategic marketing plan and effective execution of the creative, media, and research elements of this strategy. A number of strategic issues should be considered before we move ahead with the creation of outdoor messages. Among the most important are the following:

1. *Clearly state objectives.* As we discussed earlier, most outdoor advertising is used as either an introduction for a new product or event (such as a sale) or as a reminder to keep consumers continually aware of a brand. With its headline format, outdoor is rarely suited to offer a complete sales message. Furthermore, national advertisers do not usually use outdoor as their primary medium. Consequently, it is extremely important to plan the outdoor portion of the total advertising campaign in a manner that will ensure maximum efficiency and support to other advertising and promotional vehicles.

2. *Define the target market.* Generally, outdoor media have broad coverage throughout a market. However, outdoor does offer some opportunities for geographic targeting (see Exhibit 12.7). "Most products and brands have distinct regional and local-market purchase patterns. It is common to find that a large group of local markets [or areas within a single market] will index at or above 130 in per-capita brand purchases. Geo-targeting with outdoor is a fine complement to demo-targeting with television or print."[7] It is also a great way to put special emphasis in areas of cities or neighborhoods that contain a large number of residents who belong to specific ethnic groups that may be important to a brand.

3. *Specify measurable goals.* An outdoor plan needs to specify what objectives it hopes to accomplish and how these goals will be measured. For example, do we want outdoor to contribute to increases in brand awareness, increases in sales, or higher market share? Finally, what research methodology will be used to determine if these goals were met and what was the contribution of outdoor?

4. *Coordinate the buy.* Outdoor advertising is purchased from local outdoor companies known as **plants**. Increasingly, most local plants are part of large national outdoor companies that provide network buying options to national and regional advertisers. With today's tight marketplace, it is more important than ever for agencies and advertisers to work with plants well ahead of the starting date for a campaign. Ideally, space should be purchased at least 4 months in advance; some markets require

exclusionary zones (outdoor)
Industry code of conduct that prohibits advertising within 500 feet of churches, schools, or hospitals of any products that cannot be used legally by children.

plant
In outdoor advertising, the local company that arranges to lease, erect, and maintain the outdoor sign and to sell the advertising space on it.

EXHIBIT 12.7

Outdoor can help regional brands such as this one achieve broad reach in specific geographic markets.

even more time. Like spot television and radio, out-of-home is a supply-and-demand business with site availability a recurring problem in some locations.

5. *Postbuy inspection (called riding the boards).* After the posters are up, an in-market check of poster locations should be made. This inspection determines that proper locations were used and that the signs were posted or painted properly. It also helps ensure that billboards containing the client's message are not obstructed by such things as trees or poles.

All this only emphasizes that successful outdoor advertising demands the use of the same fundamental principles of advertising planning that apply to other media. In some respects, planning in outdoor is even more complex than in other media. Media planners must make certain that the characteristics and objectives of outdoor mesh properly with those of more dominant media. The complementary nature of outdoor is an overriding concern in most outdoor schedules. The planner must be certain that outdoor can, in fact, reinforce the media schedule in a cost-efficient manner.

Forms of Outdoor Advertising

As we mentioned at the outset of this chapter, outdoor is only one of several categories of out-of-home advertising. However, in terms of revenues, public familiarity, and long-term usage, the two basic forms of outdoor are posters and painted bulletins (see Exhibit 12.8). In either case, the message is designed by the advertising agency. The creative design is then reproduced on paper or vinyl and posted on panels. The larger painted bulletins are prepared by outdoor company artists either in a studio or on site. Even large posters that once were painted are now being reproduced in vinyl (see Exhibit 12.9).

3 Identify various types of out-of-home media.

POSTER PANELS

The 30-sheet poster is the most widely used form of outdoor advertising. The most common type of poster is really two posters in one. Bleed and 30-sheet posters, which use the same frame, constitute the typical highway billboard with which we are so familiar. Poster buys can be made for a single location or for total national coverage.

The primary use of most posters is to reach the majority of a market quickly and inexpensively. However, with geomarketing, posters also can be used to reach more targeted prospects. For example, posters placed in financial districts or on routes to the airport reach more affluent customers and business travelers.

EXHIBIT 12.8

Posters and bulletins make up the standardized outdoor industry.

Standardized Outdoor Advertising

The two structures which comprise standardized Outdoor advertising are the poster panel and the bulletin. For the most part, these structures are built on leased property and are rented to advertisers by independent Outdoor advertising companies. In the United States there are hundreds of Outdoor companies operating coast-to-coast in thousands of markets.

This primer is intended to give the advertiser a working knowledge of standardized Outdoor so that he/she can understand the medium more fully and utilize it most profitably.

The standard poster panel measures 12 feet by 25 feet. The bleed poster either prints to the edge of the frame or uses blanking paper matching the background of the poster. The term *bleed* is, of course, borrowed from the magazine advertisement that has no border. The term *sheet* originated in the days when presses were much smaller and it took many sheets to cover a poster panel.

Today, posters are often printed on vinyl instead of paper. The vinyl-wrapped poster uses the standard 30-sheet board, but by "wrapping" or covering the entire board, it expands the coverage area. Wrapped posters are usually available at any 30-sheet location. Although it lasts longer and retains color better than paper, vinyl is more expensive to produce so it is used at high-traffic locations and for longer contract periods than paper posters.

EXHIBIT 12.9

Every outdoor ad has to attract attention and compete with distractions in the environment.

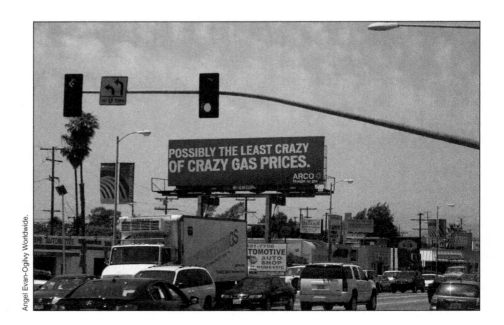

Poster displays are sold on the basis of *illuminated* and *nonilluminated* panels. Normally, poster contracts are for 30 days with discounts for longer periods. Those panels in locations with high-traffic volume are illuminated normally for 24-hour exposure. A typical poster showing will consist of 70 to 80 percent **illuminated posters**, but major advertisers often request full-illuminated postings. When buying an outdoor showing, the advertiser is provided information about the number of displays, the number that are illuminated and nonilluminated, the monthly and per-panel cost, and total circulation or exposure.

illuminated posters
Seventy to eighty percent of all outdoor posters are illuminated for 24-hour exposure.

THE EIGHT-SHEET POSTER

Another important type of outdoor advertising is the eight-sheet poster. **Eight-sheet posters** (also called *junior posters*) measure 5 feet by 11 feet, slightly less than one-third the size of 30-sheet posters. Eight-sheet posters are bought by small, local businesses as well as by national companies. Often they are placed immediately adjacent to the point of sale as the last customer contact before a purchase decision. These compact posters add enormous reach and frequency to advertising plans at a modest cost.

eight-sheet poster
Outdoor poster used in urban areas, about one-fourth the size of the standard 30-sheet poster. Also called *junior poster*.

Eight-sheet posters rapidly build brand awareness, announce new products and services, and provide reminder messages for a brand. In addition, eight-sheet space costs are much lower than traditional billboards and, because of their smaller size, production costs are significantly lower as well. The average CPM of eight-sheet posters is approximately half that of 30-sheet posters.

In most markets, zoning regulations are more favorable for the smaller eight-sheet posters than for traditional billboards. Therefore, they can be used in a cost-effective way to reach various target audiences without expensive waste circulation. Like billboards, eight-sheet posters generally are bought to support a larger advertising campaign. Eight-sheet posters can enhance television by adding frequency and recall, and they add a visual element to radio messages. They also can offer reminder messages to print media. Eight-sheet posters are handled by special poster plants but frequently appear concurrently with 30-sheet showings in a market.

PAINTED BULLETINS

Painted bulletins are the largest and most prominent type of outdoor advertising. Painted bulletins are of two types: *permanent* and the more popular *rotary*. The permanent bulletin remains at a fixed location and can vary in size because it is never moved. The **rotary bulletin (outdoor)** is a standardized sign that is three times larger (14 feet by 48 feet) than the standard poster, and it is placed at high-traffic locations for maximum visibility. Rotary bulletins can be moved from site to site to ensure maximum coverage of a market over a period of months. Both types of bulletins are almost always illuminated.

rotary bulletin (outdoor)
Movable painted bulletins that are moved from one fixed location to another in the market at regular intervals. The locations are viewed and approved in advance by the advertiser.

Bulletins are approximately four times more expensive than posters. In recent years, the basic bulletin has been augmented with special embellishments, such as cutouts, freestanding letters, special lighting effects, fiber optics, and inflatables. Painted bulletin contracts usually are for a minimum of 1 year; however, short-term contracts are available at a higher monthly rate.

Rotary bulletins offer advertisers the advantages of the greater impact of the painted bulletin combined with more coverage and penetration than a single site could deliver. A rotary bulletin can be moved every 30, 60, or 90 days, so that during a 12-month period consumers throughout the market will have seen the advertiser's message.

SPECTACULARS

As the name implies, outdoor spectaculars are large, one-of-a-kind displays designed for maximum attention in urban centers. They may consist of special lighting or other types of ingenious material and innovations. In some cases, they use a building as the canvas for the message. Spectaculars are very expensive, and both production and space rentals are negotiated normally on a one-time basis with the minimum contract for most spectaculars being a year.

With the advent of new technology in outdoor advertising, what was once a spectacular may soon be the norm. Currently, the outdoor industry is using a variety of digital and laser technology for computerized painting/printing systems. More and more outdoor advertising is printed on flexible vinyl, which provides consistent, magazine-quality reproduction in all markets. In the future, outdoor planners envision the ability to provide satellite-distributed video images similar to giant television screens on which computerized messages can be changed immediately. Regardless of the new technology becoming available to outdoor advertising, it is obvious that the traditional paper poster billboard soon may be history.

A growing segment of the spectacular category is the *wall mural* (also called *wallscapes*). Actually, it was ancient Roman wall paintings that gave outdoor advertising its start. Wall murals, done properly and in selected areas, can add a sense of urban art to an area. Many building surfaces will not hold paint well and, from a practical standpoint, most building owners will not allow someone to paint their building.[8]

The Elements of Outdoor

Outdoor advertising is a visual medium with creative elements playing a much greater role than in most other advertising vehicles. The creative options available for outdoor and out-of-home advertisers are almost limitless with dozens of shapes and sizes offered to carry persuasive messages. As the OAAA points out, "Designing outdoor advertising is visual storytelling. The expression of an idea can surprise viewers with words or excite them with pictures . . . designing for the outdoor medium is a challenging communication task that requires the expression of a concept with clarity and austere focus."[9]

OUTDOOR DESIGN

Designing an outdoor display is among the most difficult tasks for a creative team. Creating a picture and a few words to be seen by fast-moving traffic at distances of up to 500 feet is hard enough—to do so in a manner that moves customers to buy a product adds an obstacle not found in other media. However, outdoor also is one of the most enjoyable media to work with from a creative standpoint. Its size and color allow maximum creativity without the space constraints of other advertising vehicles.

COPY   Outdoor only allows a headline, usually no more than seven words. Unlike copy in traditional media, there is no theme development and copy amplification. Conciseness is not only a virtue but also a necessity. Advertisers have learned to work with these constraints to provide not only interesting but also motivating sales messages.

COLOR   Color is one of the primary advantages of outdoor. However, colors must be chosen carefully to ensure readability. Outdoor designers use those colors that create high contrast in both hue (red, green, etc.) and value (a measure of lightness or darkness). For example, Exhibit 12.10 demonstrates 18 combinations of colors with 1 being the most visible and 18 the least visible.

OUTDOOR ADVERTISING AND DIGITAL TECHNOLOGIES

One of the difficulties facing outdoor advertising is developing a way to have clients visualize creative concepts in a realistic environment. Most other media can demonstrate how an advertisement or commercial will look or sound in finished form. Translating an 8 1/2 inches × 11 inches piece of paper to a 300-square-foot billboard is more difficult. However, a growing number of outdoor plants are providing Internet systems that allow advertisers and media planners to see how their posters will appear in actual locations. The systems offer a driver's view of a poster location. Using computer scanning, any creative execution can be superimposed on the board. The system can also be used to make riding the boards a thing of the past as advertisers can now view posters from their office computers.

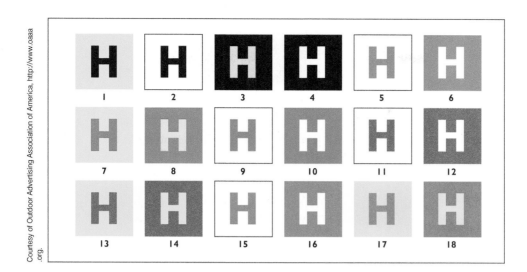

Courtesy of Outdoor Advertising Association of America, http://www.oaaa.org.

EXHIBIT 12.10

Some color combinations are much more effective than others for outdoor advertising.

Computer technology also offers the potential for a number of creative innovations in outdoor advertising. Computers for some time have directed the design and painting process on vinyl, which is used in most of the larger bulletin displays. In addition, individual advertisers and plants are beginning to use digital technology on billboards that offer changing messages, for example, the amount of money in a lottery jackpot. As we mentioned earlier, some outdoor executives envision a day when most high-traffic signs will consist of digital displays that are similar to large television screens and programmed from a central location.

Buying Outdoor

Both the methods and terminology used in buying outdoor advertising are different in a number of ways from those used in other media. Poster advertising is purchased on the basis of *gross rating points (GRPs)*. Recall from our earlier discussion of television that 1 GRP is equal to 1 percent of the population. Similarly, GRPs normally are bought in units of 50 or 100 and measure the duplicated audience reached by a poster allotment. An allotment is the number of posters used in an individual buy. To achieve a showing of 50 GRPs in a market means that an advertiser will have daily exposures to outdoor messages equivalent to 50 percent of the adult population of the market.

The audience for outdoor is called the *daily effective circulation (DEC)* and is calculated by using the following formula:

$$\text{24-hour traffic count} = 36{,}000$$

For nonilluminated posters, the traffic count is multiplied by 0.45; therefore,

$$0.45 \times 36{,}000 = 16{,}200 \text{ adult DEC}$$

For illuminated posters, the traffic count is multiplied by 0.64; therefore,

$$0.64 \times 36{,}000 = 23{,}040$$

Let's examine a market and work through these calculations:

Market: Hometown

Population: 800,000

Audience level purchased: 50 GRPs

Allotment: 26 posters (20 illuminated, 6 nonilluminated)

4 **Explain how outdoor advertising is bought and sold.**

Explanation: Our 26-poster allotment generated a DEC of 400,000. We calculate this by the following formula:

$$\text{GRPs} = \frac{\text{Daily effective circulation}}{\text{Market population}}$$

$$50 \text{ GRPs} = \frac{400,000}{800,000}$$

You may not compare GRP levels in markets of different size, except as a measure of advertising weight and intensity. For example, 50 GRPs might require an allotment of 50 or 100 posters in a large market, whereas in a very small market 50 GRPs might be achieved with one or two posters. By the same token, in a market of 2 million population, a 50 GRP buy would generate a DEC of 1 million, whereas the same weight in a market of 50,000 would show a DEC of only 25,000.

Verifying

5 Describe measurement of the outdoor audience.

The success of outdoor advertising depends on providing advertisers and agencies with reliable research data on which they can base their media-buying decisions. The outdoor industry, dealing with an audience that is entirely out-of-home and on the move, faces significant challenges in developing audience research.

THE TRAFFIC AUDIT BUREAU FOR MEDIA MEASUREMENT

The primary source of out-of-home audience information is the Traffic Audit Bureau for Media Measurement (TAB). Founded in 1933, this nonprofit organization audits the circulation of 30-sheet posters; bulletins; eight-sheet posters; shelter advertising displays; and, most recently, truck advertising. The TAB provides market-based traffic data on a designated marketing area (DMA) by designated marketing area basis. These data give advertisers audited traffic counts to give them an idea of the numbers of people in a market who pass their displays. The TAB updates data annually and checks visibility of signs as well as traffic flow.[10]

Nielsen and Arbitron have both been working on new ratings systems for outdoor that can provide some of the demographic audience data desired by advertisers. Nielsen and Arbitron have both explored the possibility of using a passive Portable People Meter and personal Global Postioning System (GPS) device, such as the one being tested for television and radio, to track outdoor audiences. Expansion of this system could potentially allow the tracking of outdoor exposure in an affordable way.

COMMUNICATION EFFECTIVENESS

In addition to traffic audits, which are primarily measures of potential audiences, advertisers are interested in the communication effectiveness of outdoor advertising. In order to address this issue, Perception Research Services (PRS) was engaged by the OAAA to conduct eye-tracking studies to determine the levels of outdoor visibility and the impact of this visibility. Using a technique that recorded drivers' and passengers' eye movements, PRS found that 74 percent of subjects noticed outdoor signs and 73 percent of those read the copy. Results also showed that the size of boards and creative enhancements, such as three-dimensional figures and board extensions, increased attention levels. Overall, the study showed that outdoor can be effective in building brand recognition and it is able to draw attention from all target groups. Chick-fil-A has successfully used eye-catching billboards to help build the image of its brand (see Exhibit 12.11).

Another approach to measuring outdoor communication uses personal computers to measure the potential audience exposed to an outdoor campaign. This system combines cost and audience information in order to determine if specific campaign objectives have been met with a particular outdoor campaign.

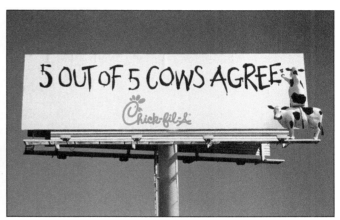

Courtesy of Chick-fil-A.

EXHIBIT 12.11

Outdoor is becoming a popular choice among advertisers who want to increase brand awareness.

MARKETING AND RATE DATA

- The Experian Simmons company conducts the Simmons National Consumer Survey (NCS) annually. The Simmons NCS reports the reach of target audiences, media usage habits, and outdoor delivery for several thousand consumer products and services.[11]

- The *Buyer's Guide to Outdoor Advertising* contains rate guides for 30- and eight-sheet posters and bulletins. The *Buyer's Guide* provides information concerning costs, number of panels in a showing, and market population.

As the outdoor industry has sought to encourage more advertising from package-goods and retail advertisers, it has adopted many of the buying practices used by other media. One of the potential benefits of consolidation within the outdoor industry is a movement toward more industry-wide support for a number of research and audience measurement studies. As outdoor continues to appeal to major national advertisers, it will become necessary to provide standardized audience data and research.

TRENDS IN OUTDOOR ADVERTISING

Out-of-home advertising is becoming a popular choice with a number of advertisers seeking increased brand awareness and a means of differentiating themselves from traditional media messages. In an environment in which people are bombarded by hundreds of messages every day, outdoor is a means of gaining high attention levels in a mass audience.

Outdoor complements and enhances other media advertising by providing high levels of reach and frequency at a lower cost than most other media. Research shows that outdoor can create a synergistic effect when combined with other media. In particular, out-of-home offers advertisers a last chance to create brand awareness among potential prospects. The influx of product categories such as package goods, cellular companies, retailers, and high-profile fashion brands has given the outdoor industry much-needed diversification.

Research and reliable audience measurements continue to be a challenge to the industry. In recent years, outdoor has sponsored a number of new and innovative approaches to verifying the reach and communication effectiveness of the medium. Computer technology has permitted researchers to undertake a number of studies that would have been impossible only a few years ago.

Finally, the industry is able to provide even better creative approaches for advertisers. The use of computer design, vinyl and other new materials, online visualization of final creative products, and new digital technologies combine to make outdoor even more appealing to advertisers. The many formats of out-of-home are motivating a number of advertisers to use the medium—even those who resist traditional outdoor posters. The remainder of this chapter discusses some of the out-of-home formats beyond billboards.

Transit Advertising

Transit advertising is designed to accomplish many of the same tasks as traditional outdoor messages. It builds brand awareness and provides reminder messages to a mobile population. Transit provides extensive reach and high repetition at a fraction of the cost of other media. Because transit audiences demonstrate repetitive travel patterns, transit advertising provides extremely high levels of frequency and consistent reach year-round. Transit is one of the fastest-growing segments of out-of-home advertising. It accounts for almost 11 percent of outdoor advertising revenue.

The transit advertising category is defined by the OAAA as "advertising displays affixed to moving vehicles or positioned in the common areas of transit stations, terminals and airports."[12] The basic marketing strategy of transit advertising is that it reaches a mobile urban population on an out-of-home basis. Unlike billboards, exposure often takes place in an environment where there is more time to read a message and, in the case of interior displays, where the audience is exposed over a relatively long period of time during the average commute. An advertiser can either get broad or very targeted reach depending on its needs.

EXTERIOR DISPLAYS

Exterior displays provide the largest revenue source in transit advertising. These messages are carried on the outside of buses; subway cars; taxis; and, increasingly, on the sides of trucks or on mobile billboards (see Exhibits 12.12 and 12.13).

Whereas exterior signs are generally available on all sides of a bus, the basic units are the king-size bus posters and the queen-size posters. King-size posters are carried on both the curb and street sides of buses, whereas queen-size posters are displayed on the curbside

EXHIBIT 12.12

Exterior displays provide exposure to both pedestrians and vehicular traffic.

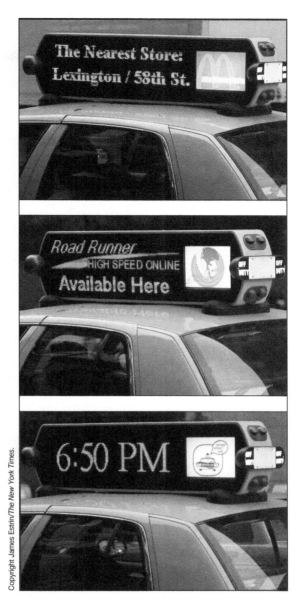

Copyright James Estrin/*The New York Times*.

EXHIBIT 12.13

Taxi toppers can be seen in many large metro areas.

only (see Exhibit 12.14). A more recent innovation is the full-bus or subway wrap in which an entire vehicle is covered by a single advertising display. Material is used to cover the windows so that passengers can see out from the inside, but a continuous design is viewed from the outside. All exterior signs are printed on vinyl and either placed in frames or, more often, affixed with adhesive. In most markets, advertisers can choose from a number of bus routes to create all or only a portion of a market. The intent of exterior signs is to reach both pedestrian and vehicular traffic primarily during daylight hours.

Exterior vehicle advertising can offer much needed cash to urban transit systems that are feeling pressure to be profitable. For example, the Metropolitan Transit Authority (MTA) in New York City began selling ad space on the exterior of their subway cars in the fall of 2009. The History Channel, the first client to buy this space, covered the cars with ads for its series, "Cities of the Underworld." The New York MTA has also begun selling advertising space on their turnstiles.[13]

INTERIOR DISPLAYS

Interior signs, often referred to as *car cards*, come in a number of sizes and they are fitted into racks inside buses and subway cars. The advantage of interior signs is that they can be

EXHIBIT 12.14

Two of the Most Popular Exterior Transit Formats

KING-SIZE BUS POSTERS

QUEEN-SIZE BUS POSTERS

seen over a relatively long period of time, especially compared to most other forms of outdoor advertising. Interior signs are ideal for building high levels of frequency because most commuters travel the same routes on a daily basis. Occasionally, interior signs include cards or tear-off slips that riders can take—thus combining features of both transit and direct-response advertising. Interior displays can also be found in some taxis.

Some major transit systems in the United States have experimented with the use of transit television in their fleets. The Milwaukee bus transit system has also tested the use of location-based text messaging services. Riders on the Milwaukee system were prompted via in-bus advertising to send a text message for a chance to win a $500 shopping spree to the grocery chain, Sentry Foods. The company generated a large number of contest entries with this campaign.[14]

AIRPORT DISPLAYS

There are many different options available for airport displays. Among familiar formats are backlit panels, courtesy phone centers, wall wraps, baggage carousels, baggage carts, airport bus shelters, and kiosks in terminals and at the gates. Regardless of the specific format, airport displays are intended to reach pedestrian traffic in a captive environment. This medium's ability to generate significant audience levels and reach an upscale audience has resulted in a number of advertisers moving into the medium.

Street Furniture Advertising

A specialized sector of the outdoor medium is street furniture advertising. This category of out-of-home advertising is defined by the OAAA as "advertising displays, many of which provide a public amenity, positioned at close proximity to pedestrians and shoppers for eye-level viewing, or at curbside to influence vehicular traffic." Included in this category of out-of-home advertising are such options as bus benches, in-store displays, shopping mall displays, kiosks, bicycle racks, and bus shelter panels. (See Exhibits 12.15 and 12.16.)

Shelter posters are a fast-growing medium in major metropolitan areas. Shelter displays are approximately 4 feet by 6 feet and provide attention-getting messages for both commuters and pedestrian traffic. The backlit panels provide 24-hour exposure with no clutter from competing media. Shelter operators offer full market coverage or geographic targeting in selected sections of a metropolitan area (see Exhibit 12.17).

Like station posters and interior transit, shelter advertising generates extremely high frequency among commuters (see Exhibit 12.18). The cost of individual panels varies with the population, the number of displays purchased, and the length of contracts (space contracts run from 1 to 12 months). The CPM for shelter is comparable to other forms of transit with CPMs running at only a few cents. Even though the posters are small by outdoor standards, ". . . when you take into account that they're seen at eye level, they have every bit as much . . . impact as the big boards which obviously are viewed from a much greater distance."[15]

Shelter advertising is a large medium within the street furniture category. It is used by a number of major advertisers, and it has been a leader in developing the type of diverse advertising support sought by other forms of out-of-home. Shelter advertising, although accounting for a small portion of total advertising, will continue to grow at a faster rate than overall advertising expenditures. Finally, rather than facing the regulatory problems of outdoor, the revenues generated by shelter posters are often shared with municipal transit companies, making the medium a welcome revenue producer to many cities facing tight budgets.

Mall advertising is another important form of advertising in the street furniture category. Recent research by Scarborough indicates that mall advertising is particularly effective at reaching the hard-to-reach teenage market. In their study, the majority of teens indicated that they spend more than 2 hours at the mall per visit. In addition, teens also reported noticing ads at the mall including posters, digital video screens, interactive kiosks, and moving images on the floor or walls.[16]

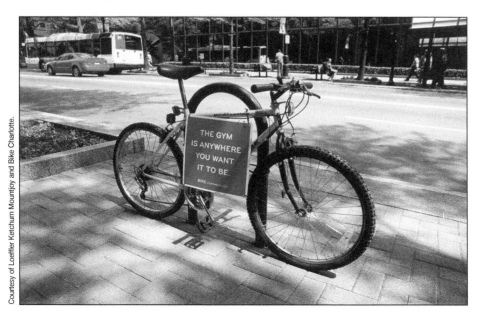

Courtesy of Loeffler Ketchum Mountjoy and Bike Charlotte.

EXHIBIT 12.15

Advertising on bike racks puts an advertiser's message at street-level with pedestrians.

Courtesy Max20 and Landmark Midtown Art Cinema.

Alternative Out-of-Home Advertising

Alternative out-of-home advertising includes a variety of formats that reach audiences when they are engaged in specialized activities. This is the broadest form of out-of-home advertising and includes everything from parking meter, cinema, and stadium advertising to trash bins, health clubs, and subway tunnels. It also includes shopping bags, roadside logos, beach sand impressions, and commercial restrooms.

There are many opportunities for advertisers within some of these alternative options. For example, cinema advertising can include advertisements in a slideshow or 1- to 2-minute commercials run before the movie, interactive kiosks, or posters in the theaters. Cinema advertising revenue has increased in recent years as it gains popularity with advertisers.[17] Stadium advertising includes scoreboard, restroom, trashcan, or concession stand signage. Fitness club advertising permits access to an active hard-to-reach target through flat panel posters in gyms, full-video opportunities, and health club sampling networks with relatively low CPMs.

Digital placed-based media opportunities have grown as wireless and broadband Internet access have made it more efficient for content and advertising delivery. Digital place-based media represent an intersection between broadcast and out-of-home advertising that offers an array of advertising opportunities for advertisers.[18] For example,

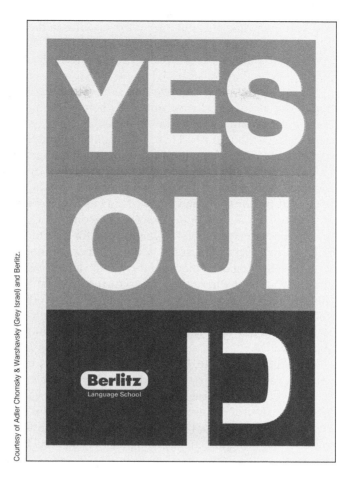

Courtesy of Adler Chomsky & Warshavsky (Grey Israel) and Berlitz.

EXHIBIT 12.17

A wide range of products and services can be effectively promoted on transit posters.

EXHIBIT 12.18

Bus shelter advertising can be seen by drivers and pedestrians.

Courtesy of Josslyn Mikow.

Wal-Mart launched a digital format for its stores in the Wal-Mart Small Network in September 2008. They expect to have the network available in all 27,000 stores in 2010. This new network allows advertisers to program content to specific stores and even to specific screens within the stores.[19]

Many of the most creative and innovative media plans in recent years have included the use of alternative out-of-home advertising options, and some of the media in the out-of-home category are more similar to promotions than to traditional advertising (see Exhibit 12.19). These less-traditional media types sometimes offer the best opportunity for reaching hard-to-reach target audiences. See Case Study, for example, which describes the creative media plan designed by MediaCom Israel for Procter & Gamble's Fairy dishwashing liquid. This plan uses a combination of television teaser ads, ads at flower stalls, and egg-vertising as well as product giveaways. "As technology provides consumers with ever-increasing control of the advertising messages they receive, access to consumers, so long taken for granted, can no longer be assumed. No matter how good the message is, if consumers do not receive it, the creative genius is wasted."[20] Strategically placed out-of-home advertising can help provide access to consumers when and where they are most receptive to the selling message. According to Gilad Kat, director of communication planning, MediaCom Tel-Aviv, "The moment in which the message was received is what we call a high-receptivity moment."[21] If you can hit the consumer with your message at that point in time, your message is more likely to be effective.

In another example, Procter & Gamble (P&G) had the "Pottypolooza" created to bring to events such as festivals and fairs where consumers might be in need of a restroom. The Pottypolooza is a truck painted with signage for Charmin toilet tissue inside and out. It contains several extremely clean flush toilets and is stocked with Charmin, Safeguard soap, Pampers changing tables, and Bounty paper towels. It has been very popular with consumers. During the holiday shopping period, P&G brought a Wall-Street themed mobile public restroom truck to Times Square. It was a big hit with holiday shoppers.[22]

Some of the newer forms of alternative out-of-home media involve putting advertising messages in places where we aren't used to seeing them. LCD screens mounted in elevators play commercials. Sanitation trucks have carried advertisements for Glad trash

EXHIBIT 12.19

This alternative out-of-home ad can travel to various locations in the city.

Courtesy of Loeffler Ketchum Mountjoy and Bike Charlotte.

bags.[23] Dry-cleaning bags carried advertisements for *Desperate Housewives*.[24] Even eggs and bananas have been used to carry stickers promoting movies and television programs.

Another form of alternative out-of-home advertising is interactive digital outdoor media. Interactive outdoor advertising is a fast-growing segment of the alternative outdoor media segment in large part because of its ability to engage the consumer. According to the OAAA, three interactive technologies that are receiving a lot of attention are short message service or multimedia messaging service (SMS/MMS), Bluetooth, and WiFi. Content can be delivered in text form with images and audioclips, as well as with web-based content. Several different types of devices can receive these messages, including computers, mobile phones, personal digital assistants (PDAs), and some portable game consoles. Even some static billboards are becoming interactive. According to *Advertising Age*, "With more cellphones equipped with Bluetooth, consumers can request more information or download music, while 'digital ink' lets marketers change their messages and video screens respond to touch."[25]

SUMMARY

Although out-of-home advertising currently comprises a small but growing percentage of total advertising revenues, it is likely to continue to grow in the next decade. Outdoor advertising offers opportunities for advertisers to provide brand reminders to current customers and to introduce brands to prospective customers at a cost of less than virtually any other medium.

In many respects, out-of-home can function in the same way as point-of-purchase advertising to reach consumers immediately before purchase. With the many options available in out-of-home, there is a format for almost every advertising objective. As traditional media become more fragmented, outdoor remains a medium that can provide both reach and frequency to a mass audience. At a time when outdoor is appealing to national advertisers, industry consolidation is creating efficient means of buying multiple markets. Many advertisers are finding the new interactive out-of-home media options to be particularly appealing.

Out-of-home media also are enjoying the benefits of more sophisticated research addressing both audience measurement and communication effects of the medium. As more national advertisers begin to consider out-of-home advertising, it will be necessary for the industry to provide research similar to what is available from other media competitors.

REVIEW

1. Why is a diversity of product categories important to the outdoor industry?
2. Why has the term *out-of-home* partially replaced *outdoor*?
3. What are the primary categories of out-of-home advertising?
4. What is the function of the Traffic Audit Bureau for Media Measurement (TAB)?
5. Why has transit advertising grown significantly in recent years?
6. What are the primary uses of outdoor for most advertisers?
7. What are the major advantages of the eight-sheet posters?
8. What are the major disadvantages of outdoor posters?

Fairy Dishwashing Liquid—P&G

INNOVATIVE MEDIA STRATEGY

Fairy had enjoyed growth in Israel since its 2002 launch. But market leader Palmolive, who had been the markets number one dishwashing liquid for 25 years, seemed to have an impenetrable hold on the market. Within this tight market, our challenge was to grow Fairy even more.

Our target group, "traditional perfectionists," are mature moms at the hearts of their families. They have established brand choices. Although they want the best performance from cleaning brands, they are not easily swayed by newcomers. They trust the proven veteran Palmolive.

We realized we weren't simply fighting for higher awareness; we were fighting tradition. We had to move away from performance-related communication and win trust on a different level.

Our insight: The perfectionist target group feels torn between priorities—spending time with family and keeping a perfect house. How can Fairy help our perfectionist target group do both?

CREATIVE EXECUTION

Mature moms are determined to retain stability in their families, but they are confronted with uncertainties such as grown-up children leaving home for the mandatory Israeli military service.

The traditional Friday Shabbat dinner is the pinnacle of reuniting the family each week. But despite the desire to be with the family, these mothers can't overcome their perfectionist guilt, so they end up washing the dishes while the rest of the family congregate, sharing valuable time with each other.

We decided to introduce Fairy dishwashing soap into the Friday agenda. Our mission was to let these mothers know that Fairy's superior grease-cutting formula will help them wash dishes faster so they can get out of the kitchen and enjoy spending time with their families. Our communication idea was a purposeful call to action: "Mom, come sit with us!" And we let these moms' families help make the appeal to their mothers.

MEDIACOM
People First ►► Better Results

TARGET AUDIENCE

We took advantage of the time leading into Shabbat:

- Television teasers implored the family, "Turn up the volume; mom's still in the kitchen!" (implying that with Fairy mom would already be out of the kitchen).
- Homecoming sampling at train stations included greeting students and soldiers coming home for the weekend and giving them notes for the young people to give to their mothers, asking their moms to spend more time with their "weekend kids."
- Sampling, signs, and reminders at flower stalls—flowers being typical Friday gift purchases for moms—also helped drive home the "Fairy for the Sabbath" theme.

- Egg-vertising, with "Mom, come sit with us!" printed on 20 million eggs, helped to remind moms as they prepared the Shabbat dinner of the importance of family time.

Nonprofit organizations and public figures helped promote the importance of Friday night family get-togethers, widening the Fairy theme to an even larger social conversation.

EFFECTIVENESS

The mom-focused campaign achieved a first: Fairy leapfrogged past Palmolive to achieve the number one spot in less than 4 months and took sustainable market leadership in what had been a 25-year Palmolive stronghold. Awareness, purchase intent, and "top of mind" scores achieved all-time highs. And Fairy became a new tradition in Israel.

Courtesy of MediaCom Tel-Aviv, and Procter & Gamble.

CHAPTER 13

Khlobystov Alexey, Shutterstock.

Digital and Direct-Response Advertising

DIGITAL TECHNOLOGY and new opportunities for direct response advertising are revolutionizing how advertisers and consumers communicate with one another. ▶

Since the mid-1990s, every aspect of direct response from selling techniques to consumer information acquisition has undergone dramatic change. Today, virtually every advertiser is using the techniques of direct response as a key ingredient of marketing strategies. Advertising in digital media is often, but certainly not always, used by marketers as a form of direct-response advertising. Digital media was discussed in Chapters 7 through 12 as it has implications and is being used in various ways by all of the traditional media. In the discussion of the Internet and other forms of interactive advertising, this chapter principally focuses on the uses of digital media not previously discussed.

Digital Media Pros and Cons

1 List the pros and cons of digital media for advertisers.

Digital—Pros

1. Digital media offers advertisers a relatively inexpensive, quick, targeted, measurable, and easily available interactive medium, especially among niche markets such as the business-to-business market.

2. Digital provides advertisers with a combination of interactive audio and video capabilities that can engage the consumer.

3. Digital is among the most flexible media with an ability to change messages immediately in reaction to market and competitive conditions.

Digital—Cons

1. To this point, some types of digital advertising are just beginning to perform for marketers. Early failures made some advertisers cautious about exploring the unique possibilities offered by this medium.

2. Despite the growing popularity of the Internet as a means of informal communication, some consumers are still reluctant to use the service for purchasing products and services. In particular, consumers are reluctant to give their credit card numbers over the Internet even though secure sites are available.

3. The sheer number of commercial and noncommercial web sites makes it difficult for consumers to know what is available or, once known, to have much time to spend with any single site.

Direct Contact with Consumers

2 Describe the development of direct-response advertising.

There is nothing new about the concept of selling directly to consumers. Benjamin Franklin sold scientific books by mail in the 1740s, and more than 100 years ago, Montgomery Ward had a thriving mail-order business through its catalog (see Exhibit 13.1). For the past 25 years, marketers have moved toward a more personal relationship with their customers. They have progressed steadily

- From mass marketing wherein prospects were reached relatively indiscriminately at the lowest possible cost per impression
- To category marketing wherein prospects who belong to some broad demographic category, such as women aged 18 to 34, were targeted
- To niche marketing wherein these broad categories were more narrowly defined (e.g., women aged 18 to 34 with children)
- To group (or community) marketing wherein prospects who regard themselves as part of a group with common interests (e.g., tennis players, opera lovers, antique collectors) are reached with messages and product benefits that acknowledge these interests
- To one-to-one marketing wherein products and messages are tailored to the expressed interest of the individual

From the first direct-mail research of the 1920s to computer-driven technology of the Internet, direct-response marketers have been able to refine their identification and outreach more precisely to various customer groups. It was not too many years ago that people were amazed when direct-mail offers addressed customers by name in the body of letters. Now, almost all of them are individually addressed.

At the same time this technological renaissance was taking place, the competitive environment was reducing the distinction among brands, resulting in (1) price competition with shrinking profit margins for sellers and/or (2) a reliance on trusted brands to provide customers with a perception of consistent quality. For example, the local Ford

Courtesy of Montgomery Ward & Co. Catalogue (1895) 1969. Reprint, New York: Dover.

EXHIBIT 13.1

Mail-order catalogs have been thriving for more than 100 years.

dealer faced with an informed customer armed with the latest dealer invoice information from edmunds.com is faced with a choice of lowering the profit margin or increasing after-sale service. In fact, the dealer probably will have to do some of both because a large percentage of car buyers are using the Internet as an information source. According to research conducted by the Polk Center for Automotive Studies, more than one-third of first-time car buyers listed the Internet as their most important informational tool compared to 8.2 percent for television, 4.4 percent for magazines, 3.6 percent for newspapers, and 1.1 percent for radio.[1]

Marketers are increasingly asking their marketing communication programs to blend old and new communication strategies. On the one hand, television commercials and other traditional media messages are establishing or maintaining brand visibility and positioning. On the other hand, high brand identity makes contact through e-mail and web sites much more effective. Although new technology can reach consumers with interactive media at a time of the prospect's choosing and with messages crafted to meet the needs of each individual, alone it can be difficult to create brand image.[2]

CUSTOMER RELATIONSHIP MANAGEMENT

Customer relationship management or **customer relationship marketing (CRM)** is a core principle of both direct-response and digital marketing. The concept of CRM should be viewed from both the customer and marketer perspective. From the standpoint of consumers, it is clear that the audience feels empowered by interactive media, and they use this empowerment in a proactive manner. From a lifestyle standpoint,

customer relationship marketing (CRM)
A management concept that organizes a business according to the needs of the consumer.

research shows that online audience members use some traditional media less than they did before gaining Internet capability and less than those who are not online. In addition, some audiences, particularly teens and young adults, use the Internet at the same time they are using traditional media.

In addition to media usage, consumers also are embracing online couponing, entering sweepstakes online, and participating in other targeted sales promotion activities. It is not surprising that consumers would respond to targeted promotions tailored to their interests. Likewise, businesses are happy to avoid the expense of waste circulation by reaching this selective audience.

The CRM concept offers several other advantages to businesses. Although sacrificing some control to consumers, marketers are dealing with a much higher percentage of prospects than in mass advertising or even in the direct-response methods used only a few years ago (see Exhibit 13.2). For example, the combination of sophisticated software and the Internet allows companies to achieve the following:[3]

3 Identify five advantages of customer relationship marketing.

- More effective cross-selling and upselling from current customers
- Higher customer retention and loyalty
- Higher customer profitability
- Higher response to marketing campaigns
- More effective investment of resources

None of these benefits should be surprising. As a company develops a closer relationship with each of its customers, we would expect that it would use the greater

EXHIBIT 13.2

Zippo and Rolling Stone are co-marketing to create social space for music enthusiasts.

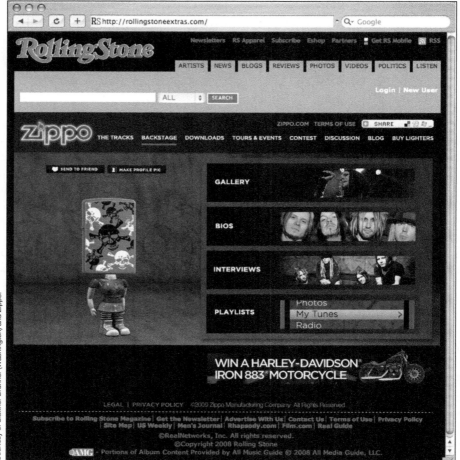

Courtesy of Blattner Brunner (Washington) and Zippo.

understanding to approach consumers with offers that fit their particular interests and tastes. The use of interactive technology allows businesses to deal with the unique purchasing, lifestyle, and behavioral histories of each customer. Rather than dealing with statistical aggregations of groups of customer data, a business now has the capability of one-to-one marketing. Communication and product offers can be based on predetermined consumer needs and can be differentiated from similar competitive offers. The end results are that the consumer gains better value and the company engenders continued customer loyalty.[4]

Advertising and Digital Media

Throughout this text, we offer examples of ways in which the Internet and other forms of digital media have dramatically changed the way marketers and the media do business. In this section, we discuss the primary types of advertising opportunities on the Internet and mobile devices, including a look at ways it is being used by firms to promote products and services.

It is estimated that in 2009 almost 74 percent of the U.S. population—or more than 227 million citizens—use the Internet.[5] Given this high percentage, it is not surprising that advertisers are continuing to look for new and better ways to use the medium. As you can see in Exhibit 13.3, the list of the largest Internet advertisers includes a range of marketers from financial institutions such as Bank of America, Fidelity, and Capital One to carriers and entertainment companies such as Verizon and Walt Disney. According to a recent research study on advertising industry trends conducted by the American Advertising Federation, more than half of the agency respondents said that they expect to shift at least 20 percent of their television budgets into online video by 2010.[6]

Seeing the potential of the Internet as an advertising medium, large advertisers such as McDonald's, Estée Lauder, and Procter & Gamble have all used the full complement of digital media for advertising campaigns as well as for direct-marketing.[7] Interactive advertising in 2010 is estimated at $29 billion and is expected to exceed $55 billion by 2014.[8] Exhibit 13.4 contains a list of the top agencies specializing in digital marketing. These agencies specialize in using digital media in new and inventive ways to reach today's digitally connected consumers. Following is a list of major forms of advertising in digital media and their proportion of 2010 expenditures:

Major Types of Interactive Advertising ($29 billion), 2010	
Digital Media	Expenditure Percentage
Search marketing	61%
Online display advertising	29%
E-mail marketing	5%
Social media marketing	3%
Mobile marketing	2%

Source: Forrester Research.

4 Identify five primary types of advertising in digital media.

SEARCH

Search, or keyword advertising, dominates all forms of digital advertising, and revenues are expected to double by 2015. Marketers, from global brands to local mom-and-pop businesses, can bid through auction systems on words or phrases related to their offering. When consumers enter those terms in a search, sponsored links appear at the top and right-hand side on the search result page. Advertisers only pay the search engine a fee when consumers click on sponsored links. Major search providers include Google, Bing, Yahoo!, Dogpile, and Comcast Search, among many others. Currently, Americans

EXHIBIT 13.3

Top 10 Display Advertisers on the Internet

Rank 2008	Marketer	Measured Spending in Medium		
		2008	2007	% Change
1	Bank of America Corp.	$223.2	$158.3	41.0
2	FMR Corp. (Fidelity Investments)	212.7	193.9	9.7
3	General Motors Corp.	187.5	158.6	18.2
4	Experian Group	151.1	190.6	−20.7
5	Verizon Communications	143.3	157.8	−9.2
6	Walt Disney Co.	108.7	84.5	28.6
7	Apollo Group	107.1	99.9	7.2
8	News Corp.	100.8	138.1	−27.1
9	Capital One Financial Corp.	83.6	101.0	−17.2
10	Expedia	79.4	104.9	−24.4

Source: Reprinted with permission from *Advertising Age. Advertising Age,* June 22, 2009, p. 18/Top Ten Display Advertisers on the Internet.

EXHIBIT 13.4

Top Digital Agencies

Digital agencies are experiencing high growth.

Rank	Agency [Parent]	Headquarters	U.S. Revenue	% Change
1	Digitas* [Publicis]	Boston	$345.0	34.2
2	Razorfish [Microsoft Corp.]	Seattle	299.3	27.1
3	Rapp* [Omnicom]	New York	204.0	90.5
4	OgilvyInteractive* [WPP]	New York	203.9	16.3
5	IBM Interative* [IBM Corp.]	Chicago	188.0	NA
6	Sapient [Sapient Corp.]	Cambridge, Mass.	164.0	10.8
7	Wunderman* [WPP]	New York	162.3	11.7
8	AKQA	San Francisco	128.0	30.6
9	Organic* [Omnicom]	San Francisco	125.3	45.0
10	R/GA* [Interpublic]	New York	102.2	33.4

Dollars in millions for 2007. *estimates.

Source: Reprinted with permission from *Advertising Age. Advertising Age,* December 29, 2008, p. 49/Top Ten Digital Agencies.

conduct more than 11 billion searches a month, with Google representing 65 percent of those searches.

Search is a viable option for small advertisers with limited budgets. Instead of investing in traditional advertising, such as newspaper advertising with wasted coverage, local marketers can target search results by city and ZIP code. In addition, mobile search provides an effective means for consumers to access information about local services. Hugh Martin, a media economist, discusses search opportunities in Kleppner Viewpoint 13.1.

ONLINE DISPLAY

The second-largest type of digital advertising is online display. Banners and buttons represent the vast majority of these ads, but many other formats also exist (e.g., skyscrapers, full banners, microbars). These ads can be static, animated, or contain video, but most contain the direct-response feature of a link to the advertiser (see Exhibits 13.5 and 13.6). Rich-media display ads contain video, audio, and/or Flash as long as it plays within the web page, not on a separate video player. Advertising behemoth Procter & Gamble attracted attention in 2008 when it increased online display advertising more than 200 percent while decreasing its network television advertising more than 44 percent.[9] As previously mentioned, many companies are following Procter & Gamble's move from traditional advertising to online display and other forms of digital advertising.

Click-through rate (CTR) is the traditional measure of success for online display ads. CTR is defined as the number of clicks an ad receives divided by the number of times it is seen. Rates are often in the 1- to 2-percent range—or as low as 0.1 percent for some products—but can be much higher depending on the execution, offers, and technological features. Although easy to conceptualize and measure, CTR fails to consider a display ad's influence on branding and other forms of marketing communication: "... a display ad can increase a search ad's click-through rate 25% to 30%. If [the advertiser] had simply measured the clicks from search, he would have missed the display ad's influence," notes one online researcher.[10]

Display ads for national advertisers are often handled through online ad networks. These companies place ads in various content sites to maximize exposure to a desired audience. Display ads are monetized in several ways, but cost-per-impression (more commonly referred to as CPM) still represents the industry norm. A study in 2008 revealed that CPMs on ad networks ranged from $.60 to $1.10.[11]

Online video advertising represents another class of display advertising. It can range from repurposed television commercials streamed online to outtakes from commercial shoots to long-form branded videos. Estimates vary, but up to $1 billion was invested in online video ads in 2010 with most of them shown on broadcast network sites (e.g., ESPN.com, NBC.com) instead of consumer-generated video sites such as YouTube.

E-MAIL MARKETING

E-mail remains an effective means of cultivating and maintaining relationships with prospects and customers. With 2010 spending on e-mail marketing at $1.4 billion, it is an established means of online marketing, with newfound resurgence during the recent economic downturn. According to one industry expert, e-mail is "the rock star of direct marketing ... because it's the most cost-effective and most trackable." A recent study revealed that, on average, 22 percent of e-mails from marketers are opened and about 6 percent result in a click-through to the sender. These rates vary by sender and product type. For example, e-mail for financial services is opened more frequently (32 percent of the time) than e-mail for apparel (14 percent of the time). Similarly click-through is higher for consumer products (9.7 percent) and financial services (7.8 percent).[12]

Marketers are moving from mass e-mailings to much more targeted and personable approaches: "Enhancing e-mail lists with demographic data . . . can improve performance threefold."[13] In addition to enhancing performance, marketers are facing a number of concerns about how and under what circumstances they can contact a person online. The debate has created a new vocabulary for online marketers:

- **Spam** refers to unsolicited and usually unwanted online advertisements or promotional messages. *Spammers* are those companies that send these messages.

- **Opt-in** is a form of permission marketing in which online customers are sent messages only after they have established a relationship with a company. The customer may have purchased a product previously from the company or signed up on a company web site giving the firm permission to send product announcements or promotional material. Ford Motor Company has an opt-in program known as "The Connection." The online system offers various promotions and discounts to Ford owners. However, only customers who have granted permission are contacted and Ford assures them that no information is shared with other companies.

- **Opt-out** is a mechanism by which customers can notify online promoters that they do not want to receive spam.

Congress passed legislation—the Controlling the Assault of Non-Solicited Pornography and Marketing Act (CAN-SPAM) Act of 2003—that establishes requirements for those who send commercial e-mail and gives consumers the right to ask e-mailers to stop spamming them. E-mail that facilitates an agreed-on transaction or updates a customer in an existing business relationship may not contain false or misleading routing information, but otherwise is exempt from most provisions of the CAN-SPAM Act.

In addition, the direct-marketing industry has come out strongly against e-mail spam. According to H. Robert Wientzen, president and CEO of the Direct Marketing

spam
Online advertising messages that are usually unsolicited by the recipient.

opt-in
A form of permission marketing in which online customers are sent messages only after they have established a relationship with a company. Only consumers who have granted permission are contacted.

opt-outs
Procedures that recipients use to notify advertisers that they no longer wish to receive advertising messages. A term usually associated with online promotions.

KLEPPNER VIEWPOINT 13.1

Hugh J. Martin, Ph.D. Associate Research Professor,
E.W. Scripps School of Journalism, Ohio University

OF SEARCH ENGINES, AD PRICES, AND BLIND SALES

Hugh J. Martin

A report that Google and Yahoo! are losing ad sales to an upstart might, at first glance, raise doubts about the search giants' understanding of the advertising business. However, a closer look suggests the famously smart people at Google and Yahoo! know exactly what they are doing.

The article in the *New York Times*[1] reports a new company, Quigo Technologies, convinced FOX, ESPN, and Cox Enterprises to abandon the search giants as providers of text advertising. These ads appear beside your search results in response to the words you are searching for.

Quigo, unlike Yahoo! and Google, tells advertisers where ads appear on the web and allows advertisers to buy ads on specific sites, the *Times* reports.

It may seem odd for search giants to conceal this information because advertisers target people likely to buy their products. So most advertisers want to appear on web sites with content that attracts large numbers of people potentially interested in their products—if you sell sporting goods, you want to be on the big sports sites.

HOW SEARCH ADVERTISING WORKS

According to *Advertising Age*,[2] the search giants make most of their money from these text ads.

Advertisers buy key words, and their ad appears when those words are typed in a search engine. The advertiser only pays if someone clicks on an ad. Advertisers bid a certain amount for each click, and that determines how often and where their ads appear.

The search giants display the ads on their pages and on innumerable other web sites participating in their advertising programs. The advertiser knows how many clicks it paid for but not where the clicks came from.

If advertisers knew ads were appearing on sites they wanted to target, wouldn't they buy even more ads? So why is this information concealed?

CONCEALING INFORMATION INCREASES AD REVENUES

I am indebted to Roy W. Kenney and Benjamin Klein, authors of a 1983 article

Association (DMA), "It recently occurred to me that spammers are to e-mail users what weeds are to gardeners."[14] In addition, the AAAA, the ANA, and the DMA worked together to establish a set of nine self-regulatory guidelines to help protect the use of legitimate e-mail marketing. These guidelines encourage members to[15]

1. Use an honest subject line.
2. Include a valid return e-mail address as well as a physical address for those who wish to contact the company.
3. Clearly identify the subject and the sender at the beginning of the e-mail.
4. Provide a clear and conspicuous e-mail option for consumers to remove themselves from the list.
5. Ensure that electronic name-removal features are prompt and reliable.
6. Offer options for removal of consumers from commercial e-mail lists for each brand or product featured.
7. Not acquire e-mail address through automated systems (i.e., spiders and robots) without the consent of the consumer.
8. Not provide e-mail lists to unrelated third parties for their use.
9. Provide the sender's privacy policy in the body of the e-mail or via a link.

in the *Journal of Law and Economics*,[3] for this explanation:

Advertisers consider some web sites to be better than others. They may be attracted by the large number of sites available through Google and Yahoo!, but most advertisers would probably like to select some sites and ignore the rest.

But advertisers cannot select sites, so they must instead estimate the average value of a click from all sites, desired or not. Many people who click on an ad will not buy anything. And sites with small amounts of traffic probably have smaller proportions of buyers among those who do click on ads.

So the best sites will generate large numbers of clicks and many more likely buyers. Another way to think of this is that average sales per click will be much higher on the desirable sites.

If advertisers could identify the desirable sites, they would bid more for those, and advertising would be concentrated there. But Google and Yahoo! would be forced to sell ads for much less on the undesirable sites, and their total advertising revenue would decline.

TWO ALTERNATIVES

What if Google and Yahoo! instead offered to sell advertisers web sites in groups—or bundles—and included some less desirable sites in each bundle? Buyers would look for bundles they considered bargains, and only bid for those. The search giants would be forced to sell ads on the remaining bundles for less than buyers would pay if they did not know what bundle they were getting.

Another alternative would allow buyers to experiment, buying ads on a variety of sites to see which sites produced the best results. Advertisers would make adjustments after their initial purchase, asking the search giants to redirect ads to sites generating the most sales. But this would be costly for the search giants. It would also have the same effects on ad prices and revenues as the other alternatives.

A CHANGE IS (PROBABLY) GONNA COME

The existing arrangements also make it possible for Google and Yahoo! to distribute ads differently than expected. For example, an ad on 1,000 blogs might generate 1,000 clicks but few buyers. The same ad on a few big news sites might generate the same 1,000 clicks and deliver far more potential buyers. Google and Yahoo! are asking buyers to trust that this is not happening.

The *Times* article also reports some buyers are worried about click fraud. This happens when people click on ads simply to generate revenue for the sites where they appear (Google and Yahoo! share some of the revenue with the site).

The article says Google is planning to give advertisers more information about where ads appear. The search giant is feeling competitive heat from companies like Quigo. It will be interesting to see what happens next.

[1]Louise Story, "An ad upstart forces Google to open up a little," *New York Times*, 26 February 2007, C1.

[2]*Advertising Age*, *Search Marketing Fact Pack 2006* (New York: Crain Communications, 2006); available from http://adage.com/images/random/searchfactpack2006.pdf, accessed 4 March 2007.

[3]Roy W. Kenney and Benjamin Klein, "The economics of block booking," *Journal of Law and Economics* 26, no. 3 (October 1983), 497–540.

The idea of spam, opt-in, and opt-out seems relatively straightforward. However, specific implementation can be very difficult. For example, the first message in an online promotion is spam—it was unsolicited. Marketers, even the most ethical ones, are pushing to continue to allow mass online messages with the proviso that consumers can then opt out of future communication. However, consumers are often receptive to e-mail messages when they have opted in to an e-mail list. A survey conducted by the e-mail firm Bigfoot Interactive found that when consumers have opted in to receive regular e-mail from a business, they derive more satisfaction from the relationship than those consumers who did not choose to receive the messages.[16]

SOCIAL MEDIA MARKETING

Although small in relation to other forms of digital marketing ($716 million in 2010), the potential of advertising on social networks and other forms of social media is capturing marketer's attention. Americans are flocking online to network, socialize, and create and share content, and advertisers are eager to get involved in these social interactions (see Exhibit 13.7). Social media include blogs, social network sites, chat rooms, message boards, podcasts, and video and photo sharing sites.

SOCIAL NETWORKING Facebook and MySpace are the largest social networking sites. Facebook alone has more than 250 million members with more than 120 million

EXHIBIT 13.5

Animation can be cleverly used to deliver a brand message in a display banner ad.

logging in at least once a day. The site generated more than $300 million in advertising revenue in 2008.

There are two primary ways advertisers use Facebook to reach prospects.[17] First, many businesses set up a profile page and actively enlist friends and fans to sign up who are then sent bulletins about special events and discounts. Brands with the most fans include Starbucks with 3.7 million fans, Coca-Cola with 3.6 million fans, and Nutella at 3.2 million fans. In addition to building a fan base, companies can run traditional online display ads on member pages. Advertisers target their ads based on information users choose to share on the site such as college affiliation, groups, age, and where they live. Similar to Google's AdWords program, advertisers can choose to pay-per-click (PPC)—get charged a fee when the ad generates a click—or pay by the number of impressions generated (CPM). According to one retailer, "You can target your ad better on Facebook than anywhere else. I know my customer's age, where they live, what their interests are, and only those who fit my target see the ads."[18]

Other social media sites generating attention include Twitter and LinkedIn. Twitter was originally developed as a way for people to follow friends. Increasingly, however, marketers are using it to create a following for their brands and to enhance customer service. Kraft is creatively using Twitter to build a following for its Oscar Meyer Wienermobile. Drivers tweet when and where followers can next sight the distinctive vehicle.[19] LinkedIn, with more than 36 million members, is a connection site for colleagues, employees, and business contacts.

VIDEO SHARING　Video is a popular type of content people like to view and share online. YouTube is the leading video-sharing site. At last count, YouTube had more than 90 million unique visitors per month who viewed more than 6 billion videos during the same time period. More daunting is users' desire to share video: More than 20 hours of video content are uploaded each minute, equating to more than 28,000 hours of video content each day.[20] YouTube sells display advertising, search, and other features. For example, GEICO, in 2009, paid $175,000 to dominate YouTube's front page for one day and buy related search keywords for its videos. However, Ford paid nothing to YouTube to have 100 "social-media influencers" upload their experiences with the Ford Fiesta to the "Fiesta Moment" channel.[21]

Americans have an insatiable desire not only to share but also to view online video. The Pew Internet and American Life Project reported in 2009 that 62 percent of adults

EXHIBIT 13.6

The use of animation adds humor to this banner ad.

online view video on video-sharing sites, with 19 percent of all Internet users doing the same each day.[22] Who can forget the much-cited user-generated video "Diet Coke and Mentos Experiment" that accumulated millions of views as news about it created a viral buzz? Advertisers have found ways to join the viral trend primarily by producing intriguing videos around their brands and letting consumers share them with family and friends. In the summer of 2009, for example, Evian's "Live Young" video of roller skating babies generated more than 11 million views a week.

The Internet makes it possible for advertisers to run edgier and more consumer-produced content than they would be able to run in the broadcast media. According to advertising guru Stuart Elliot, "Major marketers believe they can take greater risks online because users tend to be younger and more accustomed to irreverent humor. Procter & Gamble has underwritten viral campaigns for mainstream brands such as Folgers coffee, Crest toothpaste, Febreze fabric spray and ThermaCare heat wraps."[23]

Some marketers also are capitalizing on the user-generated-video trend by running video contests: A recent study revealed that 20 percent of interactive marketers asked contestants to submit video about brands.[24] Notable in 2009 were the Doritos' "Crash the Super Bowl" and the A1 Steak Sauce "Sing for your Beef" contests. Aside from engaging consumers and creating awareness, contests "let marketers listen to their customers and learn about their needs. . . . Contests can help marketers energize users and drive a viral marketing effort. . . . And they can give marketers access to cheap, original online video content."[25] Even Huddle House is getting in on the act. Users must create a Huddle House fan video and post it to YouTube to be eligible to win a flat screen TV and other electronic prizes (but no free breakfast).

As noted, advertisers are finding ways to leverage the popularity of social media. This must be done in such a way as to engage consumers rather than making them feel as though the advertiser is invading their personal space. "It's a switched-on crowd with a huge amount of time who hold brands close to them. The difficulty is that they regard this as their space. We have all become our own source of entertainment. . . . But there is a resistance to being advertised at in our own spaces."[26]

MOBILE MARKETING

Mobile advertising is an area of promise that is finally gaining traction. Spending on mobile advertising is expected to almost triple from 2009 to 2014. In 2009, *eMarketer*

EXHIBIT 13.7

Seniors represent a fast-growing segment on social network sites.

estimated there were more than 280 million U.S. mobile phone subscribers.[27] Smartphones are fast becoming the norm as more people use their phones to check weather, find movie schedules, search, e-mail, socialize, bank, watch video, and trade stocks. For example, if a particular stock drops to a certain level, you can be alerted automatically so that you can place a sale order online (or with your broker)—all from a fishing dock in the Bahamas!

Advertisers see the potential in mobile but must tread carefully because research shows that consumers are annoyed by unwanted mobile solicitations. As a result, mobile marketers are sponsoring content such as sports scores so that their brand names or slogans appear on the screen when accompanied by requested information. Using behavioral tracking tools, Porsche created a highly successful mobile campaign with the tagline "You can own one, click to see how." Users whose surfing behavior suggested they were searching for luxury cars were shown Porsche's message when they visited Weather.com or checked sports scores on their smartphone.[28]

SMARTPHONE APPS   With more than 30 million iPhones sold since 2007, Apple's App Store is fast becoming a marketer's dream. Apps is short for applications, most of which are not created by Apple, that can be downloaded to the phone. Apps are either free or cost a token amount and range from games, to news gathers, to entertainment. At last count, more than 65,000 apps are available at the App Store and more than 1.5 billion have been downloaded. Kraft created its own "killer app" for the iPhone; it provides recipes containing Kraft products (and Kraft ads). Kraft's iFood Assistant costs $.99 and quickly became one of the top 100 most popular apps.[29] As Kraft demonstrates, advertisers can use mobile in creative ways to deliver value and advertising to users while developing new customer databases.

Digital as a Complement to Other Media

As discussed in the previous media chapters, for most media categories, including other direct-response media, digital advertising can stand alone but more often serves a complementary role in integrated campaigns. As evidence of this, next time you flip through a magazine, take note of the number of advertisements that send readers to a company's web site for more information or to place an order.

Television seems to work well with online messages. The medium's high credibility can build brand equity among large groups of prospects very quickly. Television reaches a mass audience in a typical advertising environment of formal programming interspersed with 30-second commercials. During the same time that a person is viewing a television show, a typical Internet user may have visited five or six web sites, and the advertising he or she was exposed to may have been more like outdoor than, traditional print or broadcast. Research suggests that many television audience members are surfing the web at the same time they are "watching" television. This is particularly true of young adult and youth audiences.

Television networks are getting more creative in their use of the Internet and cross-media deals to attract advertisers. In 2006, for example, NBC began an online-only series called *StarTomorrow*. The online audience could view, on demand, episodes of bands trying out to win a record deal with a successful producer. In the style of *American Idol*, viewers cast votes for the people they wanted to move on to the next round. NBC ran a prime-time special on its television network before the show started to promote it to viewers. Nissan signed on as a title sponsor and received a 15-second spot on each Internet video as well as prominent placement of its logo on the stage where the bands performed. Nissan had banner and display advertisements on the web site and a marker on the homepage as well as exposure and product placements on the NBC network in promotion spots.[30]

Many online promotions must deal with three groups of prospects. The first, and by far the largest, group for most sites consists of surfers and casual users. For these consumers, web advertising must gain attention quickly if the consumers are going to click a banner or spend time with a commercial message (see Exhibit 13.8). The second group consists of the entertainment/information-oriented regular users of a site. This group of users is looking for an interactive activity and will return to a web site often if it provides the entertainment and information they seek. The third group of users consists of those who are actively in the market for a product or service. They are information seekers who may have seen the web site in a media advertisement, run across the site on a search engine, or actively sought out a specific site because of familiarity with a brand. In any case, the site should provide relevant, up-to-date product information including price,

Courtesy of Hyunjae Yu.

EXHIBIT 13.8

Banner advertisements on the Internet must gain attention quickly.

purchase instructions, warranties, and so forth. If you think about it, the process is much the same for media advertising in which advertisements and commercials first gain awareness and attention for a brand and retailers close the sale. The media-Internet relationship is, in some respects, the same as that of the media and retailers.

Some research has shown that the average online user will not wait long for a connection before moving to another site. The sheer number of online options has created a level of impatience unseen in other communication technology. The effect of this impatience is a heightened need by companies for brand awareness. Branding accomplishes two goals in the online world:

dot-coms
A generic designation that refers to companies engaged in some type of online commerce.

1. It gains awareness for the web site itself. In the early years of online commerce, the *Super Bowl* might well have been named the "**dot-com**" Bowl given the number of commercials bought during the game by online companies. Some products such as prescription drugs send consumers to their web sites to read a full disclosure of the possible negative side effects of their products in order to satisfy FDA requirements.

2. Branding is important for the companies that want high visibility on the web. Online consumers, like their offline counterparts, will gravitate to companies, products, and brands with which they are familiar. The difference is that the online attention span makes branding more important than ever before.

A number of companies have found that traditional advertising works better than online messages to encourage web site visits. As long as this is the case, the complementary relationship between online and traditional media will continue. As one leading online executive pointed out, "At the end of the day, [interactive advertising] is just one more way to communicate with the consumer. It needs to be integrated in everything that an agency does for a brand or a business because treating it as a separate part of the mix ultimately doesn't work."[31]

The Role of Digital Media and Marketing

5 Describe four ways marketers can use commercial web sites.

From an advertising and marketing perspective, there are a number of uses for the Internet and commercial web sites:

1. *As a source of direct sales.* Internet direct sales may be accomplished as stand-alone e-businesses, such as Amazon.com, or as an ancillary to an established business, such as cataloger Crate and Barrel (www.crateandbarrel.com), or as a traditional retailer, such as Home Depot, which augments walk-in traffic with a merchandising web site (see Exhibit 13.9).

2. *As a source of advertising-supported communication.* Virtually every magazine, newspaper, and major broadcast outlet has some Internet presence. Often newspapers or television news programs give their web site address at the end of news stories so that interested readers can obtain more in-depth information about a specific story. There also are a number of Internet-only media, such as Salon, that have only Internet audiences. Most of these communication outlets have attempted to be advertising supported, but few have been able to turn a profit from their Internet-only services.

3. *As a source of marketing and promotion information.* Thousands of businesses large and small have established web sites to provide product information, enhance stockholder relations, and report current company news. Advertising agencies have scrambled to find a way to service clients' Internet demands effectively. Many major agencies, for example, Leo Burnett, have established separate interactive divisions to offer interactive marketing to clients. Other agencies have integrated online and offline advertising strategies within the traditional advertising agency account team, but this is becoming more rare.

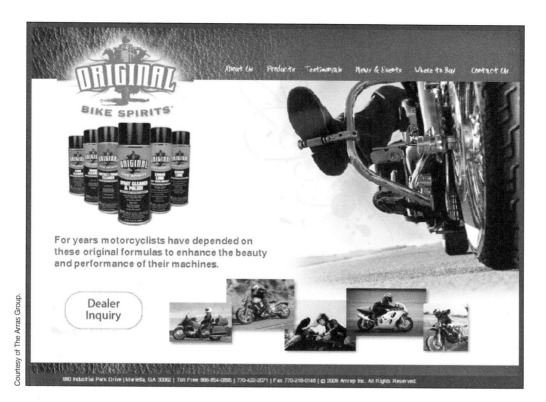

EXHIBIT 13.9

Media drive prospects to brand web sites for more information or to conduct transactions.

4. *As builders of consumer engagement.* Increasingly, advertisers are finding ways to engage consumers when they visit the advertisers' web sites in attempts to help build brand connections and encourage consumers to regularly visit the sites. Some products such as the BMW Mini Cooper (www.miniusa.com) have included video games or contests whereas others have social networks or blogs set up for consumers to interact with each other or with company personnel.

Digital Media and Marketing Research

Clearly one of the primary benefits of Internet marketing is the ability to gain information about individual buying habits and product preferences. These data are, of course, collected as part of the consumer search and transaction process (see Exhibit 13.10). However, one of the emerging advantages of Internet technology is the ability to collect market research quickly and inexpensively from a larger respondent base than might be possible with conventional research methodology. The Internet allows marketers to reach samples of specific consumers to determine a number of product, marketing, or advertising responses. Instead of being confined to a few locales, a marketer can now sample globally. Even something as relatively simple as getting response data back from product testing is faster and demonstrates higher levels of cooperation than other methods.

There are several dangers associated with conducting research online. For example, there are questions about samples and perceptions in online testing. An important concern is that online respondents may be different in some relevant way from the general public: Online survey participants are typically younger and less techphobic than other members of the population. There are also troubling questions about whether persuasion and brand concepts are evaluated differently during online surveys. As online transactions become more common and Internet household penetration continues to increase, the differences between online and offline testing likely will diminish.

Metric	Total	Percent Responding Advertisers	Agencies
Increased traffic volume	76%	70%	80%
Conversion rate	76	65	83
Click-through rate	70	65	73
Return on investment	67	53	76
Cost per click	62	58	64
CPA (cost per action or acquisition)	55	41	64
Cost of generating sales offline	55	41	64
Total number of online sales	55	41	64
Overall revenue increase	55	43	62
Return on adspend	44	37	49
Rank of link on search engine	33	26	37
Boss satisfaction	31	33	31
Brand impact	26	16	32

Source: Reprinted with permission from *Advertising Age. Advertising Age,* 2008 Search Marketing Fact Pack, p. 26/Top Performance Metrics.

PRIVACY CONCERNS

The same technology that allows marketers to reach consumers on a one-to-one basis is creating major public relations problems over privacy concerns about the collection and use of personal information. The problem is so great that many observers think that the potential of new technology and online direct response will not be fulfilled until consumers are satisfied about the use and security of personal data.

In response to growing public concerns, the FTC has launched a number of inquiries about online policies and practices. The FTC advocates four elements for online privacy policies:

1. Disclosure of what information is collected
2. Choice for customers to opt-out
3. Access by consumers to their personal information
4. Security standards for information use and access

Consumers are likely to feel more comfortable doing business with companies that have good consumer privacy policies. Recently, online advertisers announced their own self-policing guidelines in the face of concerns about consumer privacy and behavioral tracking. The guidelines were co-developed by the AAAA, the ANA, the Council of Better Business Bureaus, and the DMA. Efforts are designed to both enhance transparency and educate citizens about online behavioral advertising.

Digital Branding, Audience, and Daypart

The Internet is instant, intrusive, and international. It is a medium with no boundaries; consequently, it presents a challenge to international advertisers. As we discuss in Chapter 23, global companies realize they must adapt to local market conditions, but at the same time it is important for them to maintain a consistent presence and identification if they are to be truly worldwide companies.

Although the Internet presents problems for multinational companies attempting to execute localized strategies on a global basis, it does offer a number of major advantages to them. For example, companies can provide information about their products as well as receive orders from consumers in other countries without incurring additional expense. An example of a service that has benefited from being able to communicate to a broader international audience is higher education. Most colleges and universities in the United States provide information about themselves to an international audience on the Internet. In addition, most of these academic institutions put application materials and forms online, which saves them a great deal of money in materials and mailing costs.

YOUTH AUDIENCES

The amount of time the Internet is used by audiences varies by age. Teens and young adult audiences who have grown up with the Internet—sometimes referred to as the Internet generation—report spending more time using the Internet than watching television (see Exhibit 13.11). According to research conducted by Harris Interactive and Teenage Research Unlimited, 13- to 24-year-olds spend 16.7 hours per week online (excluding e-mail) and 13.6 hours watching television. By contrast, they spend only about 12 hours per week listening to the radio, less than 7 hours talking on the phone, and 6 hours reading either books or magazines that are not related to their studies.[32]

Youth audiences report that the control over the content offered by the Internet is the primary reason that they prefer to use the Internet. Teens and young adults are better able than other demographic groups to use more than one form of media at a time, and they often surf the web while they are watching television.[33] As pointed out by Wendy Harris Millard, chief sales officer for Yahoo!, "Our industry needs to evaluate and change our communications approach to successfully reach this key target market. This generation is a revolutionary consumer group, actively in control and entrenched in their media experience, and their patterns will influence the future of media spending."[34]

INTERNET DAYPARTS

As with radio and television, there appear to be distinctive daypart usage patterns on the Internet. According to a study conducted by the Online Publishers Association, there are five distinct Internet dayparts:

1. Early morning (Monday–Friday, 6 A.M.–8 A.M.)
2. Daytime (Monday–Friday, 8 A.M.–5 P.M.)

EXHIBIT 13.11

Young audiences spend most of their media time online.

Courtesy of Tommy King.

3. Evening (Monday–Friday, 5 P.M.–11 P.M.)

4. Late night (Monday–Friday, 11 P.M.–6 A.M.)

5. Weekends (Saturday–Sunday, all day)

Although the use of search engines and e-mail don't seem to vary much based on time of day, content sites experience distinct differences in usage by daypart. During the early morning and daytime dayparts, news and information sites receive more attention relative to other dayparts. During evening and weekend dayparts, there is an increased concentration on entertainment and sports sites relative to daytime. In contrast to television, Nielsen/NetRatings reports that daytime has the largest audience in terms of size and number of minutes of usage. However, evening and weekend dayparts are a better time to reach those younger than age 18. Use of the Internet at work peaks between 10:00 A.M. and noon. At-home usage is the highest between 5:00 P.M. and 9:00 P.M.[35]

As pointed out by Assistant Media Director Sunayana Sarkar of Starcom MediaVest Group in Kleppner Viewpoint 13.2, understanding and embracing these changes in the media landscape are essential for those who want to work in advertising.

Direct-Response Marketing: An Overview

Although direct-response marketing has embraced many of the techniques and technologies of interactive media, it would be a mistake to think that traditional means of direct response from direct mail to infomercials are going away in the near future. Direct marketing and advertising will continue to use a number of options to reach consumers and prospects. The next section discusses some of the pros and cons of direct response.

Direct Response Pros and Cons

6 **List of the pros and cons of direct-response marketing.**

Direct Response—Pros

1. Direct response has the potential to reach virtually any prospect on a geographical, product use, or demographic basis.

2. Direct response is a measurable medium with opportunities for short-term, sales-related response.

3. Direct response allows advertisers to personalize their messages and build ongoing relationships with prime target audiences that are often impossible in traditional mass media vehicles.

Direct Response—Cons

1. High cost per contact is a major problem with many forms of direct response, especially direct mail. Expenses for printing, production, and postage all have increased significantly in recent years.

2. To keep up with an increasingly mobile population, prospect lists must be updated constantly at considerable expense to advertisers.

3. Public and government concerns with privacy issues have become a major problem for the direct-response industry. Internet marketers, in particular, are facing restrictive legislation and regulations at both the state and federal levels that have limited their ability to reach new prospects through certain types of contacts.

OBJECTIVES OF DIRECT RESPONSE

7 **Identify three objectives of direct-response marketing.**

Most direct-response campaigns have at least one of the following objectives:[36]

1. *Direct orders.* Direct order includes all direct-response advertising that is designed to solicit and close a sale. All the information necessary for the prospective buyer to make a decision and complete a transaction is provided in the offer.

KLEPPNER VIEWPOINT 13.2

Sunayana Sarkar Associate Media Director,
Starcom MediaVest Group, New York

FIVE TIPS TO HELP YOU SURVIVE YOUR FIRST YEAR IN A MEDIA AGENCY

Sunayana Sarkar

1. **Excel in Excel.** Knowledge of Microsoft Excel—knowing how to toggle through a pivot table, import external data, or filter through thousands of rows of data—is critical. It will not only increase your efficiency by reducing your working time on a project but it also will help you survive when you have to crunch numbers at record speed to answer those urgent questions from your client and supervisors.

   The ability to use Microsoft PowerPoint to create an effective presentation goes a long way too. Always remember that your presentation slides need not have every single sentence outlined. The presentation should be the visual that brings your ideas to life and highlights the key points you want your client to take away. Remember that a good presentation can make or break an idea—however good your ideas are, if your client can't visualize them, you stand a chance of losing out on a brilliant strategy.

2. **Be a trend expert.** While developing target profiles, agencies rely on syndicated research data for demographics and psychographics. But often our own social observations can help in understanding the consumers and developing key targeting insights. For example, it could be as simple as watching teenagers in a mall: How are they dressed, what brands they are buying, what beverages are they drinking, what CDs are they browsing in a music store? Keeping up with the latest news, watching TV, reading magazines, and browsing the Internet also help in understanding

social phenomena and consumer trends!

3. **Embrace the changing media landscape.** Technology has revolutionized the media landscape. About 2 decades ago, there were three major television networks, 7,000-plus radio stations, and 2,000-plus print vehicles. Today, the choices are endless and consumers have control—television offers 7 networks, more than 50 cable networks, 500 channels, digital cable, satellite TV, high definition, and interactive TV. Television is now portable on your mobile phone, iPod, and is available "on demand" through devices such as digital-video-recorders,video-on-demand, and webcasts on your computer. Radio has leapt forward as well with online streaming, podcasting, satellite radio, and so on. There are more than 12,000 print vehicles that can be accessed online and even on your mobile phone. The mobile phone is the new powerful medium—a medium in your pocket. It is making possible interactivity that is exponential in comparison with television. Gaming has also emerged in recent years as new media for marketers to reach a captivated audience through in-gaming placement and brand integration. With the increasing household penetration of broadband Internet, consumers will have even more control, and user-generated content such as blogging, chats, and social networking represents a growing opportunity for marketers.

4. **Think beyond traditional flow-charts.** Traditional media planning often refers to "number of on-air-weeks on TV," "reach," "frequency,"

and "impressions." Although these are still very integral parts of any media plan, the focus has moved away from "exposures" to "engagement." The key is to create a strategy that makes an emotional connection with consumers, captures their attention in a more engaging manner, and evokes consumer participation. With the many media choices available, consumers are media multitasking and marketers have to compete even harder for their attention—requiring them to find creative solutions by creating an engaging experience for the target.

5. **Find a mentor.** A few agencies proactively assign mentors for recent college graduates who join the company. It is smart to find a mentor at the beginning of your career. This could be someone at work whom you respect and whose footsteps you would like to follow in—someone who has been in the company or industry for some time. Make an appointment with that person, introduce yourself (if he or she doesn't know you well), and let him or her know your career goals. Mentors can make a big difference by helping you identify your next steps, giving you an experienced perspective on the important career decisions.

2. *Lead generation.* Lead generation includes all direct-response advertising that is designed to generate interest in a product and provide a prospective buyer with a means to request additional information about an item or to qualify as a sales lead for future follow-up.

3. *Traffic generation.* Traffic generation includes all direct-response advertising conducted to motivate buyers to visit a business to make a purchase. The advertisement provides detailed information about a product but usually no order form.

Traditional advertising often works in concert with direct response. For example, direct-response advertisements and commercials offering a number of products and services are a major source of revenue for virtually every medium. In addition, direct-response offers, whether by mail or other media, are enhanced by brand advertising that gives consumers confidence to order goods directly.

FEATURES OF DIRECT RESPONSE

8 Discuss three important features of direct response.

Regardless of the means of reaching consumers with direct-response offers, there are a number of characteristics that these approaches have in common:

1. *Direct response is targeted communication.* With the exception of mass media direct response, the advertiser determines exactly who will be reached by the sales message. The copy can be tailored to the demographic, psychographic, and consumption profile of the audience. In addition, both the timing and production of advertising are totally under the control of the advertiser.

2. *Direct response is measurable.* One of the disadvantages of most traditional advertising is that only the results can be estimated. However, in many forms of direct response the results can be computed to the penny. Furthermore, the advertiser is able to measure precisely various messages and other creative alternatives.

3. *The message of direct response is personal.* Whether by mail, media, or computer, the direct-response marketer is able to identify consumers better than ever and reach them with targeted, personalized messages. Many in the direct-response industry think it is only a matter of time before one-to-one advertising will be commonplace.

In part, the growth of direct response is directly attributable to a changing marketplace. We have moved from a manufacturer-driven economy to one that is dominated by huge retailers. In the twenty-first century, we are finding that consumers are increasingly in charge. Home computers and high-speed connectivity are making it practical for consumers to avoid traditional media and make purchasing decisions on a one-to-one basis with sellers. Soon consumers will no longer be limited by traditional market channels; rather, whether they live in a major city or a remote village, they will have immediate availability to goods and services. This is a marketing environment in which direct response will prosper.

In an environment of increasing accountability for marketing and advertising dollars, direct response can provide measured results. However, because of the expense of much direct response, it is imperative for most direct-response offers to reach a narrowly targeted audience. Many direct-response formats (e.g., mail catalogs, mail-distributed product samples, etc.) can be extremely expensive if directed at nonprospects. On a CPM basis, any type of direct-mail solicitation is much more costly than traditional media exposure. However, a properly executed direct-response campaign will reach a significantly higher percentage of prospects with much less waste circulation than mass advertising (see Exhibit 13.12). In addition, a major portion of the investment in direct response is intended to create an immediate sale whereas advertising investment is usually only one step in a process of building awareness and brand equity with the hope of leading to a sale sometime in the future.

As we see in this chapter, direct-response advertising takes many forms and is expected to accomplish a number of marketing objectives.

EXHIBIT 13.12

Creative executions directed to target prospects enhance response rates.

Database Marketing

The key to successful direct response is a thorough knowledge of each business's customers. This information includes not only consumers' demographic characteristics but also their purchase behavior and their interests and lifestyles. Not long ago, a consumer database consisted largely of basic information about the person, perhaps some information about recent purchases, and a lot of guesswork about what product might be bought next.

Businesses are looking for methods of combining personal information with purchase behavior to predict future purchases and the type of offers and advertising messages that will move an individual to a future purchase. Seeking this information has required marketers to undertake much more sophisticated research and data cross-checking than in previous years. Many refer to this process as *data mining*. Using computer technology, businesses are sorting through large amounts of data to look for new consumer insights, market segments, and patterns of behavior. Data mining attempts to find those characteristics of current customers that relate most meaningfully to prospects. It allows companies to enhance profitability by examining how they have been successful in the past and apply those lessons in the future.

The primary consideration of database marketing involves using information to predict future purchases. A number of predictive models are used by businesses. These models are referred to as *behavior maps*, and they allow marketers to combine recent purchasing activity and consumer profiling to offer a relatively accurate picture of what will be purchased in the future and what offers will move that customer to make a purchase. For example, it is senseless for the local video store to offer a "Fifth Movie Free" promotion to a customer who usually rents five movies at a time. "When marketers understand individual purchase patterns, they learn what circumstances, if any, are necessary to spur sales. They also find out which offers may be exercises in futility—before they waste lots of time and money in the discovery process."[37]

In order to accomplish behavior mapping and other sophisticated consumer purchasing identification methods, consumer data must be managed centrally. This need for

9 Explain the concept of database marketing.

data management has led to the development of *data warehouses*, which are centralized company-wide data storage and retrieval systems.

The ACME Catalog Company has the following information on a customer:

Sonya I. Buyer, married, 39, two children: boy 7, girl 9

Lives in an affluent ZIP code

Address: 677 Brookhaven Dr., Evanston (June 2001–present)

101 Sunny Lane, Chicago (April 1994–June 2001)

44 Olive Blvd., Miami (May 1991–March 1994)

777 Main St., St. Louis (September 1989–May 1991)

Purchases from ACME:			
	Diamond bracelet	$ 750	8/3/98
	Perfume	124	10/4/98
	Dress	98	12/10/99
	Desk set	49	12/10/99
	Snow skis	233	3/25/00
	Woman's sweater	99	4/11/00
	Man's leather jacket	340	5/22/01
	Crystal glasses	210	9/12/01
	Perfume	168	11/30/06
	Diamond pendant	1,025	6/07/07

From this very simple database example, you can tell several things about the customer. She comes from an upwardly mobile household and, based on the items she purchased, she has a reasonably high level of discretionary income. From a marketing standpoint, she does not purchase children's items from ACME. (Is she a potential customer for these items?) The most troubling part of the data is that she has not made a purchase for some time. Should ACME make a special offer to renew the relationship or contact her by phone or by e-mail? We know that keeping her as a customer will be much less expensive than gaining a new customer with her profit potential.

The key to CRM and the benefits of database marketing is to provide information that allows a company to maintain the loyalty (and profitability) of its customers. The primary element in data mining is that the end result is a relationship that is beneficial to both the company and the consumer.

The Direct-Response Industry

The direct-response advertising industry has grown dramatically in the past 25 years, and this growth is likely to continue. This growth was fueled in part by Internet advertising; however, there are many other forms of direct response including catalogs, inserts, coupons, direct television and radio, and direct mail. Exhibit 13.13 lists the leading agencies specializing in direct marketing. In this section, we review some of the key forms of direct response and discuss some of the opportunities and challenges they present.

TELEVISION AND DIRECT-RESPONSE MARKETING

10 Identify four types of direct-response marketing.

Like all television advertising, direct response has the advantage of sight, sound, and motion, coupled with toll-free 800 numbers and/or Internet ordering capability to make it a seamless sales process. Television direct response also has benefited from the growth of cable outlets, which offer firms a number of additional options to use the medium for direct selling. In 2008, it was estimated that more than $13 billion was invested in direct-response commercials.[38]

Rank	Agency [Parent]	Headquarters	U.S. Revenue	% Change
1	Epsilon/Purple@Epsilon* [Alliance Data Systems]	Irving, Texas	$360.0	55.2
2	Rapp* [Omnicom]	New York	351.9	15.0
3	DraftFCB* [Interpublic]	Chicago/New York	298.4	4.6
4	Wunderman* [WPP]	New York	295.0	11.7
5	G2* [WPP]	New York	189.2	8.1
6	Harte-Hanks Direct	Langhorne, Pa.	181.9	0.6
7	Merkle	Lanham, Md.	180.7	20.9
8	MRM Worldwide* [Interpublic]	New York	140.0	16.7
9	OgilvyOne Worldwide* [WPP]	New York	134.5	9.8
10	Aspen Marketing Services*	West Chicago, Ill.	111.8	18.3

Dollars in millions for 2007. *estimates.

Source: Reprinted with permission from *Advertising Age. Advertising Age,* December 29, 2008, p. 49/Top Ten Direct Marketing Agencies.

EXHIBIT 13.13

Top 10 Direct Marketing Agencies

Direct-response television (DRTV) comes in a variety of formats, but the most familiar are the short-form spot (30 seconds to 2 minutes) and the program-length infomercial. With the linkage of traditional television and the Internet or toll-free calling, television is becoming more and more a primary direct-response medium. The convergence of the Internet and television is moving us one step closer to interactive television, as discussed in Chapter 8. DRTV marketers are designing their messages with a twofold purpose: (1) immediate sales response and (2) bringing prospects to a company's web site in order to have them bookmark the site and become regular customers. The most used forms of DRTV are the following:

- *The traditional 30-second format with a tagline allowing consumers to order merchandise.* With DRTV being combined with Internet selling, the 30-second format is becoming increasingly popular, especially with well-known products and brands with established demand. This traditional advertising commercial format can be fairly expensive relative to the number of sales leads it generates.

- *The 2- or 3-minute commercial.* The 2- or 3-minute spot usually has problems gaining clearance during peak periods and, consequently, most often is scheduled in fringe-time programming such as during late-night movies. This format has the advantage of allowing more sales time and the opportunity to provide information about ordering the product.

- *The infomercial.* In the past decade, the **infomercial** has become a multibillion-dollar advertising format. Using well-known personalities, slick production techniques, and blanket coverage during certain dayparts, the infomercial has created a number of legendary product success stories. However, with the advent of various forms of interactive and convergent technology, it remains to be seen whether infomercials will continue to be as prevalent in the future.

infomercial
Long-form television advertising that promotes products within the context of a program-length commercial.

Regardless of its format, DRTV has certain inherent advantages as an advertising tool:[39]

1. It shows the product in use and provides opportunities for product demonstrations in realistic circumstances.

2. DRTV can create excitement for a product. For example, *Sports Illustrated* has used sports clips for what would otherwise be an advertisement for a static magazine.

3. DRTV offers immediate results. Within 15 minutes of a commercial spot, a company will receive 75 percent of its orders.

4. Because most DRTV spots are not time sensitive, they can be scheduled in fringe dayparts for significant discounts. In addition, production costs of most DRTV are less than traditional television commercials.

5. DRTV complements retail sales. For generally distributed products, businesses find that they sell as many as eight units at retail for every one ordered through direct response.

6. DRTV is a great technique for testing various product benefits and measuring sales response.

per inquiry (PI)
Advertising time or space for which medium is paid on a per-response-received basis.

Direct-response advertising is sold both on a paid and **per inquiry (PI)** basis. In fact, with the competitive environment so prevalent in the broadcast area, PI is relatively common in television, especially in fringe time. Basically, PI advertisers share their risk with a television station or cable channel. There are no initial costs for time, but the television outlet will divide the profits (if any) when the orders come in. PI advertising can be very beneficial, especially to companies with good products but little capital. The Snuggie—a blanket with sleeves—was a DRTV hot-seller. More than 4 million Snuggies were sold in the first 3 months of its introduction, which left suppliers scrambling to meet demand.[40] Other popular DRTV brands include Proactiv, Rosetta Stone, Nutrisystem, and Video Professor. In 2008, the marketer of Proactiv invested nearly $210 million in DRTV advertising.[41]

TELEVISION SHOPPING NETWORKS

The logical extension of long-form infomercials is an entire network devoted to selling. Home shopping channels have been a major source of product sales for the past decade. It is not unusual to see name-brand merchandise being sold on QVC or the Home Shopping Network and a diverse group of celebrities appearing to sell products such as dolls, sports memorabilia, and jewelry. A number of major retailers and designers use home shopping networks to sell their products to this niche consumer market.

Although home shopping has grown significantly in recent years, the executives involved in these ventures see the full potential for home shopping being in interactive systems. The most optimistic proponents of shopping networks predict that they will change retailing fundamentally in the next 2 decades. Some experts estimate that sometime in the next 20 years traditional retailing will be all but replaced by interactive home shopping. Of course, we have seen similar predictions for the Internet in recent years. Nevertheless, there is little question that these networks will continue to grow and occupy a larger place in general retailing.

RADIO AND DIRECT RESPONSE

Radio, despite its targeted audiences and niche programming, has not been a major player in direct-response marketing. Traditional radio has suffered from its lack of visualization. Radio is deficient in many of the elements so familiar to direct response in other media. Radio cannot show a product, no coupons can be provided, and a toll-free number cannot be flashed on a screen.

As discussed in Chapter 9, all of this may change with the growth of streaming audio. With the introduction of computer-based audio programming, an advertiser can incorporate all the missing elements of traditional radio in this new convergent medium. As in the case with interactive television, electronic coupons can pop up on the screen; offers can not only be seen along with the music but also downloaded at the request of the listener; and, with database technology, listeners can be prompted about products that fit their consumer profiles (see Exhibit 13.14).

Although the economic promise of "visual" radio is in the near future, for the present, radio can serve as a valuable supplement for a variety of direct-response marketers. The combination of low commercial rates and tightly targeted audience composition can saturate prime prospects with frequently occurring ads. Even with competition from other forms of direct response, radio can continue as a niche medium for direct-response marketing. For example, it can be fairly effective at delivering 800 numbers and web addresses to potential customers.

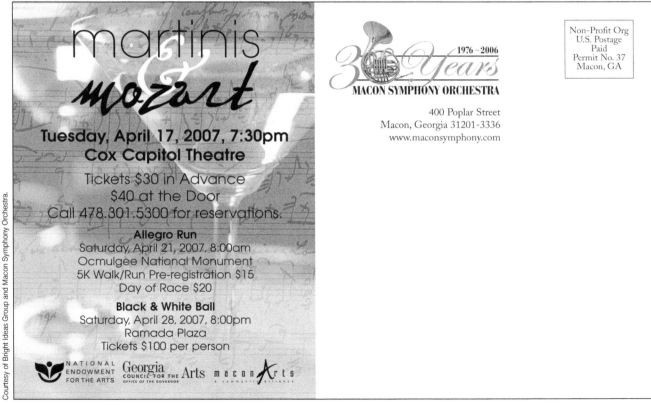

EXHIBIT 13.14

This invitation is targeted to music enthusiasts, many of whom listen to the local classical music station.

Per inquiry also makes radio a bargain for many direct-response advertisers. Radio stations often find that PI advertising is a means of moving unsold commercial inventory. With the number of stations and commercial spots available, it is almost impossible for even the most prosperous stations to sell all of their time. Unsold inventory can be especially acute during certain months, such as the after-Christmas period. Rather than using this time for public service announcements or station promotions, the sales manager may be willing to run PI spots at significant discounts.

MAGAZINES AND DIRECT RESPONSE

Magazines provide a targeted medium for a number of direct-response advertisers. As discussed in Chapter 11, the success of most magazines depends on their ability to reach a targeted group of readers with common interests, demographics, or vocations. It is in the area of business and trade publications that direct response is especially important. Magazines with editorial objectives geared specifically toward some particular business or profession can be extremely beneficial for direct-response marketers. In the business press, the majority of direct-response messages attempt to gain leads for personal salespersons and telemarketers or are used as a means of follow-up.

Despite the importance placed on business-to-business magazine direct response, consumer magazines also can provide an important means of reaching prospects. You only have to look in the back of many major publications to find lengthy classified sections offering a number of direct-response products. In addition, the majority of regular magazine advertisements carry some form of direct response either to provide additional information to consumers or to provide opportunities for direct orders.

Many of the magazine characteristics discussed in Chapter 11 are of primary importance to direct-response advertisers. Audience selectivity, combined with high reach among prospects who are not heavy users of other media (especially television), makes magazines ideal for many direct marketers. Magazines also appeal to a number of major advertisers because of the prestige associated with national publications. Magazine direct response provides the intimacy of direct response with the traditional advertising virtues of magazines.

CATALOGS

One of the oldest and most popular forms of direct-response selling is the catalog. The use of catalogs dates at least to 1498 when Aldus Manutius published his book catalog containing 15 titles. Since its humble beginnings, the catalog has become a keystone of direct marketing. As early as 1830, New England companies were selling fishing and camping supplies by mail. By the end of the 1800s, both Sears, Roebuck and Company and Montgomery Ward brought retail merchandise to every household in the country through their catalogs. By 1904, Montgomery Ward was mailing more than 3 million catalogs to potential customers in the United States. Consumers could even buy homes through catalogs. Sears, Roebuck and Company sold more than 100,000 homes by catalog from 1908 to 1940.[42]

Today, the catalog industry is facing many of the uncertainties and challenges that other forms of marketing and advertising are facing. The role of the Internet has huge potential for the industry, and many in the industry see the need to make important long-term decisions regarding how interactive media will fit into their future. Whether the Internet is a curse or an opportunity is in the eye of the beholder.

The role of the Internet is a chief concern of catalogers that mail billions of catalogs each year. However, it is only one of the several challenges facing traditional catalog sales companies. Another challenge is presented by the increasing number of companies, including mainline retailers such as Nordstrom and Gap, that are entering the ranks with either catalog sales or Internet sales or, in many cases, both. The growing number of catalogs has significantly increased the players in an already-crowded field. Some—like L.L.Bean, the longtime marketer of outdoor gear and clothing—have reacted to competition from mainline retailers by opening new retail stores themselves (see Exhibit 13.15). Since 1998, L.L.Bean has expanded from one headquarters outlet in Freeport, Maine, to a number of retail sites.

Victoria's Secret owes much of its success (and revenue) to its popular catalog. In 2008, the company's direct marketing subsidiary, Victoria's Secret Direct, was responsible for more than $1.5 billion in sales or about 30 percent of Victoria's Secret's total sales.[43] It's been estimated that the iconic intimate-wear marketer mails more than 395 million catalogs a year. Given its distribution of such a large number of catalogs, advocacy groups are pressuring Victoria's Secret to use more recycled materials in producing its catalogs.

Victoria's Secret, and, for that matter, virtually every cataloger, have strong e-commerce sites. Many traditional catalogers such as Lands' End see a number of benefits in e-commerce. Online systems can easily adjust to changing trends in merchandising or weather. For example, if a particular winter proves milder than usual, a company may change its focus to lightweight outerwear. The Internet may offer catalog companies relief from catalog-related production and postage costs that account for a large percentage of their total operating costs. Catalog companies realize that the Internet, traditional brand advertising, and the core catalog are all part of multiple channels that must work together to reach consumers. Different customers prefer different channels, and the same customers will use various channels at different times. Earlier, we discussed data warehouses. Catalogers must embrace the concept of the data warehouse as they integrate information into a single transaction history regardless of what channels a customer uses.

As catalogers begin to take advantage of online options, they are discovering that their basic marketing techniques must be adapted to these new channels. One of the primary challenges involves dealing with the customer-controlled online environment and finding ways of encouraging prospects to visit the cataloger's web site. Catalog companies find that there are fundamental differences between online and offline selling. For

EXHIBIT 13.15

These popular catalogs are available online.

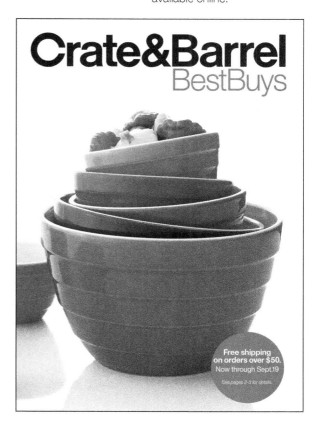

example, "Paper catalogs are intrusive by nature, online catalogs are passive by nature. Once businesses understand this fundamental limitation of e-cataloging, they can become creative in the ways that generate more traffic and, importantly, more sales, through the Web."[44]

Regardless of the channel(s) used by a catalog seller to reach prospects and customers, there are a number of keys to the successful process of moving a person from a prospect to a buyer:

1. *The right product.* As with any product or service, the selling process must begin with merchandise that appeals to consumers. Quality, price, consumer benefits, and range of merchandise are all elements in successful selling. However, catalogers often find that an added consideration is uniqueness of products. Generally, catalog sellers have a difficult time moving merchandise that is easily obtainable at retail outlets. Product differentiation is always important, but it is doubly so for catalog products.

2. *Exciting creative execution.* Remember that the customer can't try on clothes, handle camping gear, or sample a food item. The sales story has to be conveyed in attention-getting messages that grab the imagination of the reader (see Exhibit 13.16).

3. *Reach a targeted group of prospects.* No element of direct selling is more important than the prospect list. Waste circulation is even more expensive in direct marketing than in other forms of promotion, and every effort has to be made to keep it to a minimum.

4. *Fulfillment and customer service.* Nothing will kill a catalog company faster than a reputation for faulty customer service. The process begins with knowledgeable customer service representatives; then the right merchandise must be shipped promptly; and, finally, when mistakes are made, they need to be dealt with fairly and quickly.

5. *The process of successful selling doesn't end with a single purchase.* Catalogers must establish a means of database management that will allow product inventory management as well as a means of determining the quality of customers on a lifetime value basis.

Direct-Mail Advertising

11 Describe the opportunities and challenges of direct mail.

Despite recent competition from e-mail, telemarketing, and other direct-marketing options, direct mail remains a primary advertising vehicle. More than $58 billion a year is invested in direct-mail advertising, which represents about 23 percent of estimated advertising expenditures in the United States.[45] Because of the rising expenses associated with direct mail, it is anticipated that direct mail's share of direct-response advertising will decrease in the future. However, it remains an important direct-response advertising tool.

One of the problems facing direct mail is that the sheer volume of mail coming to households makes gaining a competitive advantage very difficult. Clearly, the number of mailing pieces combined with the "junk mail" perception held by many people is a challenge for direct mailers. This challenge is all the more reason that direct mailers must take steps to reach targeted prospects with an interesting message and a worthwhile product (see Exhibit 13.17). Assuming that a business has a quality product and a competitive offer, the success of direct mail usually hinges on the mailing list.

In direct mail, the advertiser determines the circulation. The list is the media plan of direct mail. Just as the media planner must carefully analyze the audiences of the various vehicles that will make up the final media schedule, the advertiser must carefully choose the list(s) that will provide the greatest number of prospects at the lowest cost. Most lists are compiled lists; that is, they are developed from a number of existing sources. The problem for the direct-mail advertiser is developing these names into a

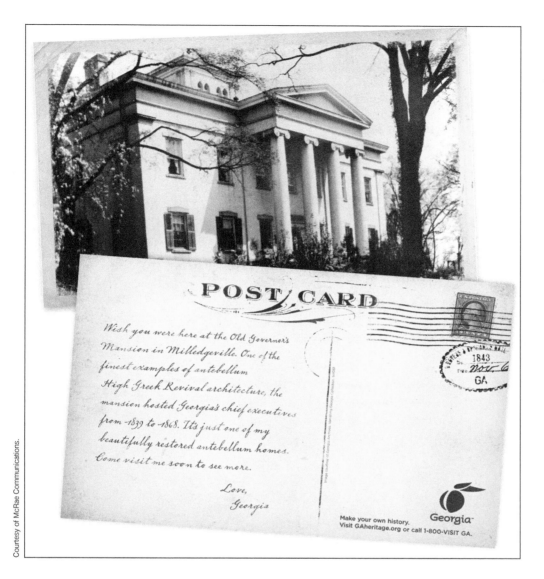

EXHIBIT 13.16

Direct mail can be used to encourage tourism as well as to promote products and services.

single list and then fine-tuning it for accuracy, nonduplication, and so forth. There are a number of organizations that are involved in the direct-mail list process:

- *List brokers.* Some of the key figures in direct mail are **list brokers**. Brokers function as liaisons between mailers who need lists of particular target prospects and those with lists to rent. The primary functions of list brokers include determining the availability of appropriate lists, negotiating with list owners on behalf of their clients, and offering general marketing advice. The list broker is generally paid a commission of approximately 20 percent by list owners.

- *List compilers.* The list compiler is usually a broker who obtains a number of lists from published sources and combines them into a single list and then rents them to advertisers. The first format list compiler is considered to be Charles Groves, superintendent of Michigan City schools. In the late 1800s, he compiled lists of teachers by writing to other school superintendents throughout the United States. He then sold the lists to textbook publishers and other companies wanting to reach teachers.[46] Compilers tend to specialize in either consumer or business lists, although a few do both.

- *List managers.* The **list manager** represents the list owner just as the broker is the agency for the mailer. The primary job of the list manager is to maximize income

list broker
In direct-mail advertising, an agent who rents the prospect lists of one advertiser to another advertiser. The broker receives a commission from the seller for this service.

list manager
Promotes client's lists to potential renters and buyers.

Matt Wilson General Manager, SBC Advertising

UNIVERSITY OF DIGITAL MARKETING— WHAT YOU NEED TO TEACH YOURSELF

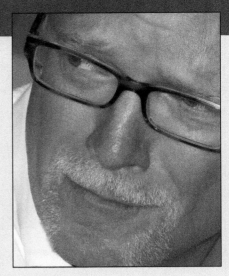

Matt Wilson

We are entering another golden age of advertising and marketing. And you will own it.

I grew up in an era where the rules were simple. Aggregate a large audience, pound it with great creative, and a percentage of that audience will buy, and buy again. It was a probability game. It still is a probability game.

But the rules have changed; the winners will find, build, and attract an audience with new tools and new media. By the time this book goes to print, you most likely will be consuming three to four types of media simultaneously.

Your laptop will feature an interface that links all social marketing applications, you will catch up with your favorite shows on Hulu.com, SMS and RSS feeds will ping in every few seconds to alert you to news and happenings both locally and nationally, and you will be teleconferencing internationally with Skype and texting with friends and co-workers.

Wait a minute . . . that's happening now.

Universities, colleges, and tech schools are catching up to this rapidly changing landscape. However, the wise student will supplement education that is available at school with a program designed by their own hand.

Stephen Covey wrote in his book *Seven Habits of Highly Effective Executives* that a *must* for professional development is what he calls "sharpening the saw." He means that you must continue to learn, read, and research new skills and leading technologies that affect your livelihood.

Here's what you should have mastered by the time you enter the advertising or public relations world:

- Audience composition and online behavior
- Online marketing: SEO/SEM, site takeovers, microsites, RSS/SMS
- Online media planning and buying
- The third screen: text and phone applications for marketing
- Information architecture, basic web programming and design, and web analytics
- Interactive campaign integration
- Content creation and management
- Database creation, analysis, and e-mail deployment
- Online events/virtual public relations press conferencing
- Interactive and e-marketing law
- Online research, consumer research, and virtual press conferences

The best part is that all of this information is available online. Go to Twitter, Facebook, MySpace, BlackPlanet, Hulu, Comscore, Forrester, Google, Yahoo!, MSN, AOL, YouTube, MarketingCharts. org, or Rapleaf, Nielsen, among many sources, and click the "advertise with us" or research links. Sign up for webinars and watch them. It's all free and it's *your* University of Digital Marketing.

Good luck. Sharpen your saw. You are on your way.

---

merge/purge
A system used to eliminate duplication by direct-response advertisers who use different mailing lists for the same mailing. Mailing lists are sent to a central merge/purge office that electronically picks out duplicate names. Saves mailing costs, especially important to firms that send out a million pieces in one mailing. Also avoids damage to the goodwill of the public.

for the list owner by promoting the list to as many advertisers as possible. List managers are usually outside consultants, but some large companies have in-house list managers. Most national magazines, DVD clubs, and other direct marketers offer their lists for rent. These lists are ideal direct-response vehicles because most have been accumulated through sales to narrowly defined, specialized audiences. They also have the benefit of providing prospects who are proven direct-mail buyers.

Service bureaus. Service bureaus engage in a number of functions. One of the primary jobs of the service bureau is to improve the quality of lists. This function is called list enhancement; it includes a number of steps. One of the most important steps is the **merge/purge**. Basically, merge/purge systems eliminate duplicate names from a list. Such duplication is costly to the advertiser and annoying to the

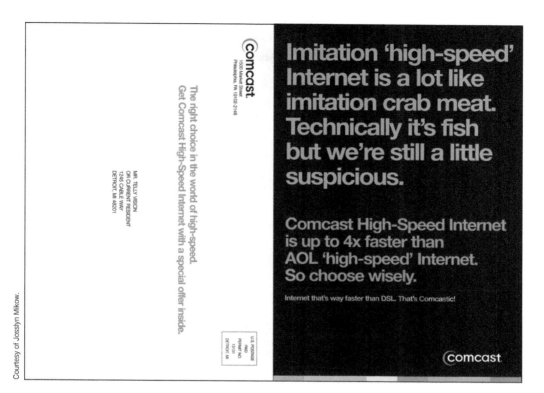

EXHIBIT 13.17

Direct mail can be especially effective with creative sales messages.

Courtesy of Josslyn Mikow.

customer. For example, duplicate mailings offset any personal contact with the customer by portraying the message as a mass mailing—and one done with little care. Merge/purge is accomplished by computers that are so sophisticated that they can cross-check names against those with the same addresses and similar spellings.

- *Lettershop.* The **lettershop** is, in reality, a mailing house. Lettershops coordinate the mailing of millions of pieces of mail, from printing labels to keeping abreast of the latest postal regulations. Large lettershops even have a representative of the U.S. Postal Service on the premises to work with every aspect of the delivery of mail in a timely fashion.

- *Response lists.* The majority of mailings are sent to people on existing lists. However, a number of mailing-list houses sell or rent lists of people who have responded previously to a direct-mail offer or demonstrated some interest in doing so. People on **response lists** are those who are prone to order by mail; therefore, these lists are more productive and the rental charges are higher than for compiled lists. By combining response and compiled lists, a mailer can reach both previous customers and a larger pool of prospective customers.

Response lists are often obtained from previous customers of a company (see Exhibit 13.18). These are called *house lists* and they are among the most valuable commodities of a direct mailer. Owners of house lists rent their lists to noncompeting companies, and they are often a major source of revenue. Advertisers can find an endless number of response lists of people who have gone on cruises, hunted specific animals, or bought books on psychoanalysis in the past 6 months.

LIST PROTECTION

Because mailing lists are so valuable, companies go to great lengths to protect them from misuse. The most common list abuse is multiple mailings beyond an agreed-on

lettershop
A firm that not only addresses the mailing envelope but also is mechanically equipped to insert material, seal and stamp envelopes, and deliver them to the post office according to mailing requirements.

response lists
Lists of prospects who have previously responded to direct-mail offers.

EXHIBIT 13.18

Retailers can send direct-mail special offers to existing customers.

limit. For example, one direct mailer reported that a company rented its list on a one-time basis and used it 13 times.

The traditional protection for such misuse is to include a number of fictitious names so that the list owner can trace the number of mailings. This is known as *list decoying*. In addition to protecting the list itself, list renters should also ask for a sample of the mailing material. Occasionally, a mailing may be in bad taste or contain a deceptive offer. However, the much greater problem is that the mailing offer may be too closely competitive with the list owner's products. Renting a list should provide additional profit, not additional competition!

TESTING DIRECT-MAIL ADVERTISING

In 1926, Claude Hopkins published *Scientific Advertising*, which many advertisers credit with providing the foundation of formal advertising research. Hopkins based his findings on the results of direct-mail and direct-response offers, and testing and research remain core elements of modern direct-mail advertising. The same is true for all forms of direct-response advertising. For example, a recent survey revealed that 63 percent of e-mail marketers test their campaigns. The most commonly tested e-mail elements in descending order of importance include subject lines (85% tested), calls to action (55%), design (51%), body copy (49%), offers (42%), and timing (37%).[47] The key elements in testing direct mail are the list, the offer (or featured consumer benefit), and the creative presentation. Let's look at some examples of the type of elements most commonly tested in direct mail:

1. *List tests:*
   Various list sources, including response lists
   Demographic segments
   Geographic segments

2. *Offer tests:*
   Guarantee wording
   Free-trial, send-no-money-now offers
   Use of incentives

3. *Format tests:*
   Single mailing versus series
   Window versus closed envelope
   Live postage versus meter
   Envelope size

4. *Copy tests:*
   Personalization
   Letter length
   Use of testimonial
   Various opening paragraphs

5. *Layout and design tests:*
   Photographs versus line art
   Four color versus one or two color
   Type size and font
   Product alone or with models

Direct-mail testing can be expensive so it is important to concentrate on major elements that normally determine the success or failure of a mail campaign (see Exhibit 13.19). It is extremely crucial to research validity to test only one element at a time. Too many mailers try to cut corners by testing several items in a single mailing. Obviously, if you change the format, the mailing list, and the offer, it is impossible to determine what factor created any changes in test results.

OTHER DIRECT-MAIL TECHNIQUES

Because of the expense of stand-alone direct mail, many advertisers are looking at alternative means of distribution of their sales pieces. Some of the primary print alternatives are the following:

- *Package inserts.* A number of companies will allow the insertion of sales messages when they ship merchandise. These messages, called *bounce-back circulars*, are delivered to customers who are proven direct-marketing users. In addition, the cost is much less than solo mailings because the sales message is being delivered as part of another package. Generally, package inserts are limited to five offers.

- *Ride-alongs.* One form of package insert is the ride-along, which is included in a company's own packages. **Ride-alongs** have many of the same advantages of package inserts except they are going to a company's loyal customers with whom a company has a proven and recent sales relationship. Depending on the product, ride-alongs can be extremely profitable because the overhead is so low.

ride-alongs
Direct mail pieces that are sent with other mailings, such as bills.

- *Statement stuffers.* Few companies miss an opportunity to include a message with your monthly bill. The idea behind statement stuffers is the same as ride-alongs, and they have several advantages. First, they cost nothing to deliver because the mailing expense is being incurred anyway. Second, they are at least seen, because everyone eventually gets around to opening their bills. Finally, most recipients are credit qualified and have already dealt with the company before or they would not be getting a statement.

EXHIBIT 13.19

Direct mail, as in this invitation, can be very creative and engaging.

■ *Ticket jackets.* A popular form of ride-along is promotions on airline, bus line, or train ticket jackets. Companies such as car rental firms find that ticket jackets are an ideal way to reach their prime target audiences.

■ *Cooperative (joint) mail advertising.* With the cost of postage continuing to increase, direct mailers often attempt to share expenses through cooperative mailings. A number of firms specialize in joint mailings. These mailings may include as many as 20 different advertising offers in one envelope. Each advertiser provides a coupon or other short message, and the joint mailer handles the mailing and divides the cost among the advertisers.

Cooperative mailings have two major drawbacks. First, they are extremely impersonal because each advertiser's message must be very short. Second, it is difficult to reach specific customers through joint mailings with the same precision that marketers would have with their own lists. The dilemma of joint mailings is that as the number of participating advertisers increases, the cost per advertiser goes down, but, likewise, the unique feature of the mailing decreases.

The use of inserts is big business and is growing as the cost of postage increases. It is estimated that annually as many as 25 billion inserts are distributed in various venues. The insert's position as an alternative "medium" can be demonstrated in the number of sources that are seeking to track the advertising options available to advertisers. For example, both SRDS and the DMA's Alternative Response Media Council have devoted resources to tracking the choices open to advertisers in placing inserts.

SUMMARY

Direct-response marketing is targeted, personal, and measurable. In an era of increasing accountability, these traits have moved it center stage as a means of reaching and selling to a diverse universe of consumers whether with e-mail, infomercials or direct mail. In terms of sales produced and expenditures, it represents more dollars than all other forms of advertising combined. It is rare for a company not to include direct marketing and direct-response advertising as major elements in its marketing mix. Companies have come to realize that the ability to combine personal messages with highly selective audience segmentation gives direct response advantages seen in few other media. The tremendous strides in digital technology have made the future of direct response both exciting and uncertain.

Although not all forms of digital advertising are direct response, the emergence of the Internet and mobile technology has given a new focus to many of the practices of direct marketing. The Internet and other forms of interactive media are changing the landscape of marketing dramatically. The challenge is to make the obvious advantages of e-commerce profitable for general selling and take advantage of the ability of this interactive medium to engage the consumer.

Regardless of the channel that direct response uses, its flexibility makes it practical for virtually every advertiser. In addition, the ability to test and verify direct marketing is vitally important in the current era of accountability and measured results. Not only does measurement of direct response provide a major advantage to advertisers but it also creates the type of audience databases so valuable to companies in all their advertising, marketing, and promotion endeavors.

There is little question that direct advertising will continue to outpace most other forms of media advertising. Not only will direct response become more important in the marketing plans of many companies but also because of its influence even more sophisticated forms of audience segmentation will emerge in the future. History will probably mark the 1990s as the end of the era of mass media and mass audience delivery. In the future, even the one-to-one communication of today will slowly give way to some form of interactive media. There is little question that direct response will play a major role in this transition.

Perhaps the greatest challenge facing direct marketing is public skepticism, especially concerns over privacy issues. However, industry-wide efforts sponsored by the Direct Marketing Association and other organizations have made great strides in improving the industry's image. The fact that most *Fortune* 500 companies routinely include some form of direct marketing in their promotional plans is testimony to its growing respectability among advertisers and improved credibility among consumers. Nevertheless, the industry is aware that legislation affecting its operation is constantly being introduced and presents a threat to future growth.

REVIEW

1. What is direct marketing?
2. What are the fastest-growing forms of advertising in digital media?
3. What is a major obstacle to mobile advertising?
4. How can marketing effectiveness be measured in digital media?
5. What are some of the major factors that contributed to the growth of direct-response advertising?
6. What steps have been taken to improve the image of direct-response advertising?
7. What role does database marketing play in direct-response advertising?
8. What is the key element in direct mail?
9. What is the difference between a list broker and a list manager?

FINAL   1:30
HIBBERT   93.06
LAVALLEE ◄

FIND THE BEST LINE,
EVADE SINKHOLES
THAT RESEMBLE JAWS.

- WINTER X RULES OF THUMB
  BY LEVI LAVALLEE

WINTER X GAMES 12 • JAN 24-27 • LIVE ON ESPN & ABC

Courtesy of The Martin Agency.

Sales Promotion

W HEN STRATEGICALLY planned and implemented, sales promotion and advertising should interact in a complementary fashion. In other words, to achieve successful promotions you must know the desired result *and* understand the marketing context within which this goal is being sought. ▶

CHAPTER LEARNING OBJECTIVES

After reading this chapter, you will be able to

1. Discuss the complementary roles of sales promotion and advertising.

2. Discuss the general forms of promotion available to marketers.

3. Explain the basic approaches to product association and tie-ins.

4. Discuss the varied types of couponing today.

5. Discuss the uses of sales promotion as consumer and trade incentives.

Pros

1. Sales promotion provides a means of encouraging consumer sales response.

2. Sales promotion is extremely flexible with a number of techniques to reach consumers across demographic and lifestyle categories. There are few product categories that cannot benefit from some form of sales promotion.

3. Sales promotion functions at both the consumer and trade levels to encourage high levels of distribution and goodwill with the distribution channel.

Cons

1. If not executed properly, sales promotion can damage brand equity by replacing the image of a product with price competition.

2. Because of the variety of formats and techniques of promotion, care must be taken to coordinate the various messages of advertising and sales promotion. High levels of promotion demand some form of integrated marketing communication if the company is to speak with a single "voice."

3. Some forms of promotion such as couponing have become so prevalent that they no longer provide a competitive differentiation for a brand and, in fact, may become a consumer expectation rather than a temporary sales boost.

Promotion Context

Historically, sales promotion has been considered an activity that offers customers, salespeople, or resellers a direct inducement for purchasing a product. And it still is.

However, promotion may be more than a sales inducement today. As marketing communicators' tools have changed and the goal of integrated communications has evolved, the definition has broadened. Momentum, a global promotion company, says it moves "brand-in-mind" to "brand-in-hand" by using core disciplines such as event marketing, promotional and retail marketing, and sponsorships. WPP Group's classification of services lumps "direct, promotional and relationship marketing" together. Other companies also talk about adding brand value through promotion—about creating communications with a compelling sales stimulus and building promotional campaigns that build market share and executions that increase brand value. These ideas aren't really in conflict. They are actually holistic because integrated marketing is concerned with—to use Ogilvy's 360-degree branding model—every point of contact building the brand—including promotion. New technology is changing marketers' ability to communicate—from using in-store television networks to text messaging. We've talked about many of these technologies in the media chapters.

Transactional and Relational Promotion

Craig McAnsh, a senior level marketer with a number of top companies, believes experience has shown that promotion is primarily used to accomplish results across two main categories: *transactional* and *relationship*. As the names imply, *transactional* promotional tactics are associated with the actual purchase of a product or service or a visit to a distributor/retailer, whereas *relationship* tactics are focused on the customer's relationship with the product, service, or distributor/retailer. Understanding the differences between these two strategic uses of promotion is significant as we work toward identifying what makes a promotion excellent.

TRANSACTIONAL PROMOTION

Loss leaders, money-off coupons, and price rollbacks are all effective ways to execute a discount promotion. These tactics become excellent when their implementation is well branded and simple and meets the right customer motivation thresholds.

Value-added promotional tactics include (among many other tactics) gift with purchase, two for one, percentage more free, free delivery, and toys in cereal boxes. Because even getting the *chance* to receive something free is an added value, sweepstakes and contests fall into this category as well. Promotion excellence occurs when the presentation of the value being added is simple, fits the brand image and target audience, and is the *perfect* amount to drive the sale without impacting long-term profitability of the business. If the promotion tactic helps redefine an entire industry, that's good, too.

The Church's Kids' Meal is an example of a value-added promotion in which the promotion became the product. Church's chicken uses three-dimensional glasses and promotion in both English and Spanish to attract customers to the "kids' meal." "Get a SPY Kids 3-D Spy Guide with 3-D Glasses in each Church's® Kids' Meal while supply lasts." (See Exhibit 14.1.) One of the primary reasons for the consistent and pervasive use of discounting and value-added tactics is that their success or failure is immediate and measurable. Old-school marketers still believe that direct and immediate results are the only reasons to use promotions. Savvy marketing professionals use innovative promotional strategies to achieve a variety of results beyond transactions.

RELATIONAL PROMOTION

Relationship-building promotions are becoming more popular because traditional (i.e., one-way) communication has reached the point of oversaturation. Traditional marketing messaging has been applied to every possible media vehicle from television to fruit to bathroom walls. The Internet has been firing messages at consumers in all sorts of creative ways—e-mail spamming, adver-gaming, pop-up windows, banners,

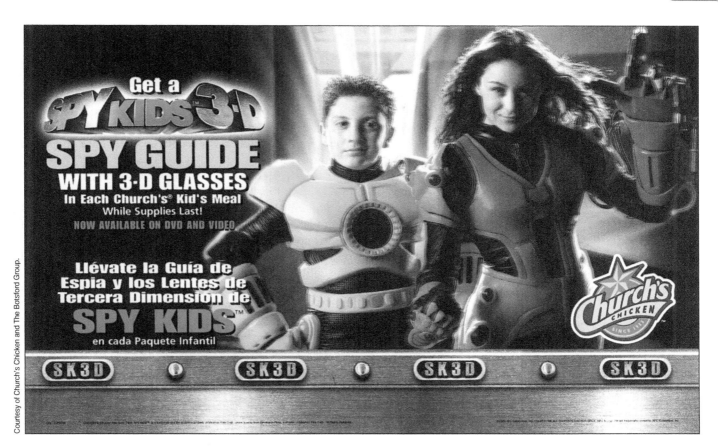

links, chat room infiltration, search engine optimization, and literally hundreds of other variations.

Connecting with the consumer is the goal of relationship promotional strategies. There are four stages of connection within relationship-building promotional strategies: introduction, sharing, friendship, and love. Each of these relationship stages is important at some point in the life cycle of a brand (remember our discussion in Chapter 3).

Introductions are the first stage in building a relationship. This is when promotion is used to develop awareness for a product, service, or distributor/retailer. First impressions are very important in establishing company-to-consumer relationships because you don't often get a second chance. These promotional introductions should be infused with your product or service brand personality. Publicity, street marketing, and even cross-promotion are very simple promotional tactics employed to make introductions that are direct and personal.

Sharing is the stage most conducive to promotional activation. Here promotion is used to educate and involve the customer. Extensive product knowledge and brand positioning can be shared in a memorable way through such experimental marketing tactics as sampling, demonstrations, life style infiltration, interactive mobile marketing, and events. Sharing an experience with your customers is the strategy that will help create promotional excellence. For example, inviting thousands of kids to a local park to watch a movie on a 30-foot-tall inflatable screen while they win prizes, eat popcorn, and stay up late, or an apparel marketer's traveling fashion exhibit that gives people free makeovers, the experience of sharing will result in a deep brand knowledge.

The *friendship* stage is what you have (or should have) with your customers. It is hard to build and harder to maintain, but promotional tactics can work at building this. You need to reward loyal customers and give them special attention. Having a unique dialogue with customers is another friendship tactic. *Fast Company* magazine developed a fan base called "Company of Friends," who meet in cities across the country to

EXHIBIT 14.1

This promotion promotes the "Kids' Meal" with Spy Guide and three-dimensional glasses and the DVD and video. It is promoted in English and Spanish.

share and learn. The Pepsi-Stuff promotion was a way of rewarding existing friends and an exciting way to attract new ones.

The final stage is *love*. The best reason to nurture a relationship is that it may lead to love. Love is rare and can only result when all the marketing "P's" discussed earlier are meshed in unity. It is said that love is best communicated through an unexpected gift, or "doing good" for others, and in B2B promotions involving incentive travel experiences, go a long way toward building love.

To ensure an excellent promotion marketers must create an excellent connection between the brand and the consumer.

We all come into contact with numerous examples of **sales promotion** each day. The various forms of sales promotion remind us of brands and persuade us to make purchases in subtle ways that often make little or no conscious impression. A hallmark of Bed Bath & Beyond is their famous 20 percent coupon. However, all marketing that surrounds the distribution of the coupon must reinforce the quality of goods available in the store. Bed Bath & Beyond is not a discounter and they do not want to be painted with the brush of having lower-quality products. Thus, the headline: "It's not 20% less. It's 20% off." (See Exhibit 14.2.) When technical support managers tee up golf balls

sales promotion
(1) Sales activities that supplement both personal selling and marketing, coordinate the two, and help to make them effective. For example, displays are sales promotions. (2) More loosely, the combination of personal selling, advertising, and all supplementary selling activities.

EXHIBIT 14.2

Bed Bath & Beyond provides a 20 percent off coupon and tries to get customers to sign up online for other promotions.

Courtesy of SBC Advertising.

given to them by their computer vendor, they are reminded of the vendor's services. And when doctors write prescriptions with the pen left behind by the pharmaceutical rep, a particular drug is being promoted. All of these items and thousands more are examples of sales promotion.

A Little Background

Before we talk about promotion tactics, let's review where we came from. Many sales promotion techniques were well established by 1900, but they often consisted of gimmicks and trinket giveaways rather than the well-planned promotional campaigns we see today. However, many modern methods of sales promotion were initiated by retailers and manufacturers of the nineteenth century. In 1895, both Asa Candler and C. W. Post were offering coupons for free Coca-Colas and reduced prices on boxes of Grape-Nuts cereal. At the same time, Adolphus Busch was promoting his beer with free samples; lithographs of "Custer's Last Stand"; and red, blue, and gold pocket knives. By 1912, Kellogg's was including rag dolls, cartoons, and spoons in its cereal boxes.

These and the other forerunners of modern sales promotion recognized that brands need attention and differentiation to gain sales and that customers react positively to extra incentives when making purchase decisions. Sales promotion provided both. What most sales promotion of the period failed to do was complement a company's overall marketing program and provide long-term strategies for brand building. In fact, on occasion the giveaways and promotions overshadowed the product. A classic example is Topps bubble gum baseball cards. After years of promoting the cards as an incentive to buy gum, in 1990 the company dropped the gum and simply began marketing the baseball cards as collectibles.

By the 1960s, promotion firms were offering marketing advice to complement their promotional programs. Promotion firms, in response to client demand, were transformed from companies developing stand-alone incentive programs to full-service marketing consultants. They began to offer expertise in consumer marketing, merchandising, and branding. During this period, the full-service promotion shop took root and integration with advertising and marketing became the norm.[1]

Today, in order to provide better balance between advertising and sales promotion, we are finding that a number of companies are consolidating overall responsibility for both under a single corporate executive. Despite the fact that advertising and sales promotion are different in many respects, coordination between them is imperative. More and more sales promotion and advertising agencies are consolidating, or at the very least coordinating their efforts to retain clients who demand a synergistic approach to their total advertising and promotional programs. "Ad agencies, promo shops, and even premium suppliers are feverishly buying or cultivating disciplines to complement their core expertise. Promo execs sitting at the pitch table with their sister ad agencies find themselves more central to the conversation as ad shops turn to promo types for their expertise at retail."[2]

Despite the merging of advertising and sales promotion in terms of both management responsibility and creative execution, we should be aware that they differ in both execution and objectives. Yet, it is impossible to be successful as an advertiser, marketing executive, or promotion manager without a knowledge of the broad concepts involved in the total system of **marketing communication.**

This chapter discusses the primary types of sales promotion and how they complement media advertising. As with advertising, the opportunities for successful execution of sales promotion programs depend on an understanding of the marketing objectives of a particular firm or individual brand. Both advertising and sales promotion failures are most often a direct result of poor planning and a lack of integration with the elements of the marketing mix.[3]

marketing communication
The communication components of marketing, including public relations, advertising, personal selling, and sales promotion.

Promotion and Advertising

1 Discuss the complementary roles of sales promotion and advertising.

Effective sales promotion has two basic functions: (1) to inform and (2) to motivate. Normally, sales promotion is most effective when its message is closely related to advertising themes. Point-of-sale displays may feature a testimonial spokesperson who simultaneously appears in television commercials; counter displays often use the same headlines and copy style as print advertisements; and product sampling may offer miniature packages to enhance brand identification as promoted in the company's advertising. Although the means of communication may be different from that in advertising, consistent information and formats are key ingredients in successful promotions.

The second aspect of promotion—motivation—differs in some major respects from advertising. Motivation, in a marketing sense, involves the means used to move a customer to purchase a brand. This process usually moves across a continuum from awareness (initially hearing about a product) to purchase. In Exhibit 14.3, we can see that advertising and sales promotion have markedly different responsibilities in the communication and purchase process.

The key to successful marketing communication is determining the purposes and objectives of advertising, sales promotion, and other components and how best to coordinate and integrate these objectives. In the past, a major distinction between advertising and sales promotion was that sales promotion was viewed as a short-term sales incentive, whereas advertising was intended to build brand equity over time. Today, most marketers recognize that it is counterproductive for sales promotion to gain short-term sales at the expense of long-term brand equity. One only has to look at a number of package-goods categories that have used coupons and other price-oriented deals to realize that consumers see little inherent value in the brands and simply purchase the one with the lowest cost at any given moment. In this environment where promotion must work with advertising and contribute to the overall marketing goals, objectives for promotion might include the following:[4]

- To gain trial among nonusers of a brand or service
- To increase repeat purchase and/or multiple purchases
- To expand brand usage by encouraging product uses in addition to the traditional use
- To defend share against competitors
- To support and reinforce an advertising campaign/theme or specific image
- To increase distribution and/or retailer/dealer cooperation

Note that none of these objectives advocates short-term sales increases except when these sales are part of a larger marketing strategy. For example, when we encourage product trial by nonusers or expansion of uses by present customers, the implication is that these trials will lead to long-term consumer relationships. In turn, consumer relationships, initially gained through promotion, will be reinforced over time by advertising.

PROMOTION STRATEGY

An analysis of a product's performance considers both surface indications and underlying problems facing the brand. In-depth situation analyses and strategy development

EXHIBIT 14.3

Advertising and sales promotion should function in a complementary fashion.

THE CONSUMER COMMUNICATION AND PURCHASE PROCESS

| Awareness | Positioning | Consideration | Preference | Shopping | Purchase |

Primarily the Role of Advertising

Primarily the Role of Sales Promotion

can help determine the incentive needed, the type of promotion likely to have the greatest appeal, and the media required to reach the desired audience. Partners & Levit suggests the following considerations in establishing strategy:[5]

1. *Customer attitudes and buying behaviors.* Determine who your customers are demographically and psychographically. Establish what it is about your brand that attracts them and how they make their buying decisions.

2. *Brand strategy.* Consider your level of dominance in the product category. How will sales promotion factor into performance? What are the strengths and time period before returns are realized?

3. *Competitive strategy.* Evaluate past performance, both yours and your competitors', and determine what activities, levels of spending, and time periods produced the best results.

4. *Advertising strategy.* How do you currently promote your product in your existing markets? Which media best suit your needs?

5. *Trade environment.* What are your distributors' attitudes toward the brand? What are your competitors' attitudes?

6. *Other external factors.* What resources are available and what unpredictable factors may influence a product's availability or pricing (e.g., weather, raw materials)?

Total promotion budgets are generally divided into three categories: consumer advertising, consumer promotion (usually referred to as either sales promotion or simply promotion), and trade promotion (known as dealer promotion or merchandising). Whereas coordination among these promotional classifications is important, they each serve a distinct purpose. Let's examine the role of each in the marketing mix and the share of promotional budgets spent in these promotional categories.

1. **Consumer advertising.** The role of measured media advertising is to build long-term brand equity and promote basic product attributes, provide locations of dealers, and/or provide comparisons with other products. The percentage of total promotional budgets spent on advertising has declined steadily during the past decade. Approximately 25 percent of promotional dollars are currently spent in advertising.

2. *Consumer sales promotion.* Consumer sales promotional incentives are directed to the consumer. Cents-off coupons are the most common consumer promotion, but premiums, rebates, and sweepstakes also are used frequently. Driven primarily by a decrease in the use of coupons, consumer sales promotion has fallen slightly to 25 percent of spending. Great South Catering mails out their catering menu (see Exhibit 14.4) and includes a coupon for $25 off on catering orders of $250.

3. *Trade promotions.* Accounting for about half of the promotional budget, trade incentives are designed to encourage a company's sales force or retail outlets to push their products more aggressively. These are the most expensive types of promotion on a per-person basis. Winning dealers or retailers may be awarded a trip to Hawaii, a new car, or a cash bonus. Behind the significant increase in trade promotions is the fact that companies think they get a more immediate payout for their spending in this sector and that they have more control over expenditures than in other forms of promotion.

consumer advertising
Advertising directed to people who will use the product themselves, in contrast to trade advertising, industrial advertising, or professional advertising.

Despite some movement of dollars among the three categories, the long-term trend seems to be a ratio of 75 percent of promotional dollars in trade and sales promotion and 25 percent in advertising. The relatively low figure for advertising might be even further depressed if we had an accurate measure of the advertising dollars that are allocated to support major promotions such as sweepstakes, rebates, or sales. For example, it is estimated that as much as 20 percent of total advertising expenditures are devoted to supporting some form of promotion. Most marketing executives predict minimal future increases in advertising's share of total promotion budgets.

EXHIBIT 14.4

This catering mailer gives product information and a discount.

Forms of Sales Promotion

The remainder of this chapter discusses the primary types of sales promotion. Priority is given to those techniques most associated with advertising, especially at the consumer level. However, we also briefly discuss trade-oriented promotions. In all cases, we need to keep in mind the complementary purposes of advertising and promotion. The most frequently used forms of sales promotion are the following:

2 **Discuss the general forms of promotion available to marketers.**

- Event marketing
- Virtual advertising
- Sponsorships
- Point-of-purchase advertising
- Premiums and incentives
- Interactive and digital
- Product sampling
- Sweepstakes and contests
- Cooperative advertising
- Trade shows and exhibits
- Directories and Yellow Pages
- Trade incentives

EVENT MARKETING

Event marketing spending is about $19.18 billion. The largest event sponsorship segment is sports, accounting for approximately $7.61 billion, followed by entertainment, road shows, and mobile marketing. The average event-marketing budget is estimated to be about $800,000. Some 96 percent of national marketing executives say they use events in their marketing mix. To give you an idea of how much they spend on events, note that budgets vary significantly: About a third of marketers spend less than $50,000 a year on events, some 20 percent spend $100,000 to $500,000, and roughly 25 percent spend more than $500,000.

How do marketers know if they are getting their money's worth from a marketing event? A *PROMO* survey indicated that about half of marketers measure event results by sales volume, and others track headcount. They also measure purchase intent, and some count Internet hits after an event. The push for higher ROIs has marketers cutting street-team budgets.

Most brands rely on buzz marketing to drive event traffic; that's likely to grow as marketers co-op pop culture (think film screenings and concerts) and recruit brand ambassadors. There is also much competition for mind share—podcasts, social networking, socialized content via new media.

Mountain Dew slashed its measured-media budget to $21.6 million in 2008 from $57 million in 2006 and moved more toward branded entertainment. In the past few years it has invested heavily in branding subcultures such as the Dew Tour, Green Label Sound, and video games like Game Fuel. Frank Cooper, chief marketing officer of sparkling beverages at Pepsi North America, said, "We clearly have moved from impressions as the primary determinate of whether something's successful to answering the question, 'Are we building relationships with the right group of people?' Whether it's a blogger at these events, influencers talking about it, those are more indicators of whether we're reaching the right consumer."[6]

What do Tide detergent, Home Depot, Hot Wheels, Coca-Cola, Viagra, and DuPont have in common? Besides being among the largest and most sophisticated brands in the world, they are primary sponsors of NASCAR racing teams. Is NASCAR worth the $20 million investment primary sponsors pay for a hood logo, or the $10 million associate

EXHIBIT 14.5

Home Depot is a sponsor of NASCAR and integrates that sponsorship in its advertising.

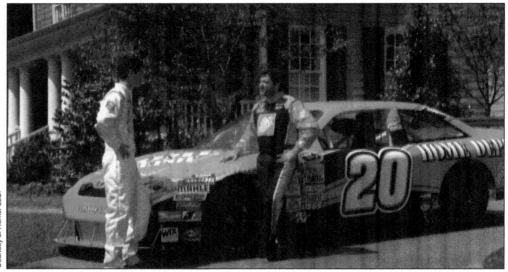

sponsors fork over for space on a rear panel or above a back tire? And, of course, there is all the television coverage of major races. Typically, there are 200,000 fans at an event, many wearing souvenir team jackets honoring drivers such as Tony Stewart and advertisers such as Home Depot (see Exhibit 14.5). Once inside the gates, there is a Sprint Fan Zone plaza, where visitors can buy refreshments from Coca-Cola or Budweiser kiosks while listening to bands playing on a Sprint-branded stage or picking through a variety of NASCAR literature.[7] There is a lot of exposure for sponsors.

③ Explain the basic approaches to product association and tie-ins.

BENEFIT BY ASSOCIATION   One of the oldest types of advertising is the testimonial by which a brand gains from an association with a celebrity through a product endorsement. The idea, of course, is that the star power of famous sports or entertainment figures will rub off on the brand. It is this idea of benefit by association that has driven event-marketing and product-licensing deals to multibillion-dollar levels.

There are three basic approaches to product association and tie-ins:

1. *Event marketing.* There is hardly a sporting event, musical concert, or art exhibit that does not enjoy some form of corporate sponsorship. From sponsored scoreboards at football stadiums to the Nike swoosh on players' uniforms, every aspect of public events is open to purchase by a business. We have even divided up parts of events for sponsorship. The Olympics is among the most high-profile event-marketing venues, with companies making multimillion-dollar investments in return for being named an official sponsor.

   Advertisers understand that sports fans and patrons of the arts are extremely loyal to their special favorites. Sponsors hope that an association with these events will increase brand visibility and foster goodwill for their products. Event marketing is most effective when it involves a long-term relationship that offers advertisers a chance to develop a continuing connection with a loyal audience.

2. *Staged promotions.* A staged promotional event differs from event marketing in that the sponsor not only sponsors an event but also initiates it. Concerts are among the most sponsored events of this type. These events combine product sampling, couponing, interviews with local media, and in-store publicity to maximize brand identification with the band. For example, Flossie.com, a New Zealand-based, female-centric web site full of fashion, beauty, sex and dating, entertainment, and career tips, was recently launched. To promote itself, it staged an event on a busy New Zealand street using a vending machine that dispensed living, breathing, single men. Using the tag line, "Whatever you need, it's on us," a vending machine

asked women to choose the type of man they preferred: classic, action, romantic, rich, foreign, or Mr. Perfect. The machine functioned like a soft drink vending machine: Women pushed a button indicating their preferences for the type of man they would desire most. To their surprise, a real, in-the-flesh man matching their characteristic preferences opened the door and walked out of the vending machine in a puff of smoke, ready to take them on a date. The "date man" matched the stereotype of the man chosen. For example, women might be treated to a bungee jump or a romantic meal date. The event was created by TBWA/Whybin/Tequila. The agency recruited the single men, ran them through a series of interviews, and then grouped them into their appropriate categories.[8]

3. *Product licensing.* Related to event marketing is the concept of commercial relationships with movies, television shows, cartoon characters, and so forth to gain recognition for a brand. Examples of licensing agreements cover numerous opportunities. Sometimes it involves product placement in a film.

Movie licensing often involves a marketing tie-in between a fast-food company and a toy manufacturer or some other children-related item. It is common for fast-food companies to join with movies, television shows, or networks, using the popularity to bring customers into their restaurants for toys, books, cups, and so forth.

The biggest beneficiaries of licensing agreements are toy manufacturers. It is estimated that nearly half of toy revenues come from licensed figures. They include movie personalities, children's television characters, and so on. Action toys have become a core income source for most toy manufacturers. These companies invest millions of dollars in these agreements, and their success largely depends on the popularity of a particular entertainment project. Not all licensing agreements involve entertainment, and some involve cross-licensing contracts between two brands.

In 2009, retail sales for licensed products totaled almost $108 billion. The royalties from those products were almost $6 billion. Character licensing, which includes entertainment, movie, and television licensing, is about $49 billion and accounts for about 45 percent of the revenue. The licensing of trademarks and brands is estimated at $19 billion in sales and slightly more than a million in royalties.

As you can see from our discussion, the opportunities for event sponsorship and licensing agreements are endless. However, their success depends on a positive connection with a brand's target market. In order to accomplish this goal, it is imperative that the image of the event and that of the product are compatible and that there is a logical relationship between the product and the event.

VIRTUAL ADVERTISING

Throughout the text, we have discussed advertising and marketing via the Internet. Among the most interesting are the so-called virtual advertisements. Computer-generated advertisements, logos, and products are superimposed on a live video feed or inserted into a completed movie or television show. These computer-inserted brand messages are not seen and, in fact, don't exist at the actual event. Using technology and creativity, it is now possible to seamlessly integrate an image into a live event or program after filming has taken place, and this virtual advertising can target a specific demographic in any given market. You may have seen the yellow first-down markers while watching football on your television screen or the advertisements behind home plate at a ballgame that change. The fans at the games don't see these advertisements because they are electronic.

The technique has been adapted for product placement in movies and television shows. In some instances, producers are able to insert local or regional brands in films and television shows. As you might imagine, purists are not particularly happy about the intrusion of product promotions into entertainment content, but virtual advertising does open up interesting possibilities to reach target audiences. There are also potential legal ramifications with the use of this technique.

SPONSORSHIPS

Some people include sponsorships under event marketing, but some companies include it as a separate item. For clarity, we'll briefly mention some aspects. IEG, a division of WPP PLC, projected that sports sponsorships in North America will grow slowly because of the slow economy. It is estimated to be about $11.48 billion.[9] A few examples of their sponsorships include the *Super Bowl* half-time show, NASCAR racing events, golf tournaments, and tennis tournaments. There are also sponsorships of entertainment tours and attractions, cause-related activities, festivals, fairs, and the arts.[10]

Research shows that "true" online sponsorship programs generate significantly better results for marketers in terms of intent to purchase, brand recognition, and ROI than traditional advertisements. In separate programs, Sony and Intel sponsored online courses teaching people how to be better digital photographers. In both cases, for every dollar spent on the promotion, the marketer received $50 in retail spending. ROI for traditional media advertisements is roughly two to one.[11]

POINT-OF-PURCHASE ADVERTISING

point-of-purchase
Displays prepared by the manufacturer for use where the product is sold.

The retail industry is slowly changing the way it reports some promotional activities. All in-store marketing services are now referred to as *retail marketing services*. Retail marketing includes **point-of-purchase** (POP), retail merchandising, and in-store services. Restaurants such as Folks often use in-store merchandising to promote specific products or services. Exhibit 14.6 illustrates the promotions of their new breakfast. The biggest portion of retail spending, POP, is estimated to be $20.3 billion. "Marketing-mix modeling still reinforces that trade spending has the highest level of return on investment and then within consumer support . . . those [efforts] closer to the point of consumption and point-of-sale tend to have the higher return," according to Rick Lenny, Hershey's CEO. In general, he said, Hershey uses advertising to create awareness for new brands and new platforms but views in-store support—whether through sampling or through activities tied in with retailers' own strategies—as the best way to capitalize on high-return investments.

Many retailers have expanded their in-store services, including in-store television viewing. For example, Wal-Mart updated its in-store TV network to the Wal-Mart Smart Network, a system powered by Internet protocol television. Advertisers can offer short promotional clips on screens at eye level to catch shoppers' eyes.

POP is tailor-made for a retail environment in which almost 60 percent of consumer purchases are unplanned. In recent years, the industry has sponsored a number of studies to help retailers and manufacturers better use POP advertising. Findings of these studies demonstrate that POP has several primary advantages as a sales promotion technique:

1. *Motivates unplanned shopping.* One major study indicated that displays at the ends of aisles and at the checkout counter were most conducive to promoting sales. The same study also found that factors such as the age of the shopper, predilection to influence by in-store deals, and time pressure all played roles in the influence of POP advertising. It also showed that retailers could influence impulse buying by encouraging shoppers to go down as many aisles as possible.[12]

2. *Offers brand and product reminders.* One of the major roles of POP advertising is to remind consumers about product categories and brands that they might overlook. The POP industry is upgrading the creative options available for in-store selling. In addition to the familiar cardboard signage, more and more displays are using computer technology to change messages electronically and target selective demographic shopper segments.

3. *Influences brand switching.* Consumers show remarkably low levels of brand loyalty in food categories. In a study by the Meyers Research Center, "more than half of grocery shoppers would switch brands if their preferred items were not available,

Courtesy of Lane Bevil + Partners.

EXHIBIT 14.6

This poster represents an example of an in-store promotion.

compared to only a third of shoppers who would do the same if their favorite non-food items were unavailable."[13]

This research not only shows the need for POP but also indicates that the use of such displays will be an ongoing necessity to motivate unpredictable consumers.

One of the historical problems facing POP advertising has been guaranteeing that the displays were properly displayed or even displayed at all. In the past, manufacturers' sales-persons were largely responsible for maintaining in-store displays. Particularly among small companies, signs were simply placed by manufacturers' reps in those stores that would give them space. Now, marketing in-store displays is a much more sophisticated process and is highly coordinated at both the local and national levels. For huge retailers such as Home Depot and Wal-Mart, some POP signs are made exclusively for their outlets.

To ensure better usage of in-store displays, a number of companies have hired independent firms called retail merchandising service companies to work with retailers to gain maximum POP coverage on an outsourcing basis. Many companies find that "hiring merchandising companies may mean extra costs, but the expense is offset by the fact that crack sales forces don't need to waste valuable selling time setting up displays, doing store sets and out-of-stock correction, or updating merchandise."[14]

In the future, we will see even more innovations in the uses of POP and retail services. The in-store industry will provide better research as well as use a number of electronic, interactive, and broadcast media.

Increasingly, POP advertising is dominated by retailers and manufacturers who are required to meet rigid requirements to gain retail shelf and floor space. Retail space is the most valuable commodity that merchants have, and they will allocate POP spots only to those companies and brands that provide the highest-quality displays, the greatest merchandising and advertising support, and, most importantly, the most significant profit potential.

Not only are these innovations in in-store retailing interesting in themselves but also they point out once again that advertising, promotion, and marketing are increasingly becoming interrelated to the point that it is difficult to tell when one stops and another begins. Rather than trying to decide in what category a promotion element belongs, managers are becoming more concerned with using whatever techniques work.

PREMIUMS AND INCENTIVES

premium
An item other than the product itself given to purchasers of a product as an inducement to buy. Can be free with a purchase (for example, on the package, in the package, or the container itself) or available with proof of purchase and a payment (self-liquidating premium).

Premiums are items given to customers in exchange for a purchase or some other action such as a store visit or test drive. In other words, they are rewards given with strings attached. Premiums and incentives are among the most common sales incentives with spending at about $46 billion.

Premiums are not only one of the largest categories of sales promotion but also they are among the oldest. Premiums date to the mid-1700s when calendars, wooden specialty items, and other promotional products were quite common. According to the industry's major trade association, Promotional Products Association International (PPAI), by the 1850s specialty printers had established a relatively formal business for premium items.

Premiums are comprised of a number of types of merchandise, with writing instruments, calendars, and clothing being the most popular. The key to successful premium promotions is that the merchandise has some logical connection to the product and the target market. Remember that premiums are not traditional gifts; they are marketing gifts. Premium offers are generally categorized by either the purpose or the method of distribution. Among the major sectors of the premium industry are the following:

traffic-building premium
A sales incentive to encourage customers to come into a store where a sale can be concluded.

1. **Traffic-building premiums**. Most premiums are offered at the time of purchase. However, other premiums, particularly those associated with high-cost products and services, are given for merely visiting a retailer, real estate development, or automobile dealer.

2. *Continuity premiums*. Continuity premiums build in value as a consumer continues to buy a product. The key to successful continuity premiums is that "programs shouldn't neglect the brand. Frequent flyers or rewards cards for restaurants, or points to redeem gifts for credit card purchases, etc., are a great chance to build brand image by getting consumers actively involved with them for months, or even years. If prizes, too, are related to the brand, so much the better."[15]

   In recent years, continuity premium programs have been widely adopted by e-commerce companies. Various incentive web sites use continuity programs to encourage return visits and brand awareness. Consumers who visit these sites are offered points toward rewards for clicking on sponsoring merchant sites, searching for information, or making purchases.

direct premium
A sales incentive given to customers at the time of purchase.

3. *In- or on-pack premiums*. Also called **direct premiums**, in- or on-pack premiums are among the most popular items with both advertisers and customers because they offer an immediate incentive and instant reward in return for a purchase. The direct premium has become so popular that advertisers are constantly searching for ways to differentiate their offers.

   Many direct premiums are offered as a co-promotion so that compatible brands can cooperate and extend promotional opportunities while at the same time reducing costs to the participating companies. Pizza companies frequently co-promote with a soft drink company. When your pizza is delivered you get a large drink or two.

4. **Self-liquidating premiums**. Regardless of the method of distributing the premium, the most popular type of premium is the self-liquidating offer (SLO). As the name implies, these premiums are designed to require that customers pay all or a major portion of their cost. On average, customers are required to pay approximately 75 percent of the premium. It is not surprising in this era of tight budgets that self-liquidating premiums are the most popular and the fastest-growing category. During the past decade, self-liquidating offers have increased by more than 30 percent and the average cost to consumers has risen sharply.

> **self-liquidating premium**
> A premium offered to consumers for a fee that covers its cost plus handling.

At one time, it was thought that SLOs could only be marketed successfully for inexpensive low-end merchandise. However, marketers are finding that consumers will pay considerably more for items that have high-perceived value or interest.

In some cases, the premiums have become so popular that they have actually become major profit centers for a company. Coca-Cola and Harley-Davidson are but two of the many examples in which branded merchandise is so popular that it is sold as "stand-alone" stock. This merchandise is no longer a premium, but it shows the popularity that some brands (and their premiums) have achieved.

With the thousands of available items for premium markets, it is extremely important that great care be given to the selection of this merchandise. The primary concern is that any premium promotion is complementary to the overall marketing goals of a firm and that the relatively high investment in such an endeavor can be justified.

LOYALTY INCENTIVES Loyalty has become the mantra of marketers, moving strategies far beyond the one-time purchase, the sample, or the sweeps. It's all about getting to know those customers, earning and keeping their business, and staying in touch. The Coca-Cola North America's "My Coke Rewards" is Coca-Cola's largest rewards program. A Spanish-language version marks the company's first fully bilingual, Internet-based initiative. The program plays on a tactic Coca-Cola uses in some of its most successful promotions: hiding a code under the cap. Players then register online to redeem rewards.

Loyalty "programs" have even begun to creep into the corporate world as employee incentives. Just like a frequent flyer can build points to redeem for merchandise or an airline flight, employees can now earn points based on a variety of job performance criteria to redeem for lifestyle experiences, gift cards, or merchandise. The programs keep employees engaged, focused on performance, and dedicated, hopefully for the long haul, says Karen Renk, the executive director of the Incentive Marketing Association.[16]

INTERACTIVE AND DIGITAL

Major marketers use some form of interactive or digital promotion. For Dole Foods, the standard promotion of its Fruit Parfaits would have been to provide a national free-standing insert (FSI, discussed later in the chapter) and maybe deploy some in-store materials. But the online social world, where women gather in droves and recommend—or not—products and services beckoned Dole's efforts. Bloggers also played a big role in the Dole parfait promotion. A number of bloggers who focus on moms and health and wellness were asked to talk about Dole parfaits and the Sweet Retreat contest. Bloggers not familiar with the product were sent samples to try.[17] Purina offered audio podcasts of its *Animal Advice* radio program topics, including animal training, pet care, pet insurance, and behavioral theories. The audiocasts were followed later by video podcasts of Purina's Incredible Dog Challenge. Purina divided the program into free 5-minute downloadable segments on iTunes and Purina.com. Good podcasting should support a marketer's objectives, strategy, and message, and it should build its consumer relationship. According to the report, marketers used interactive channels to build brand loyalty, prompt a sale, drive consumers to web sites, collect personal data, and offer incentives.[18]

KLEPPNER VIEWPOINT 14.1

Steven Guyer Project Lead, Experian CheetahMail

RENEWING CUSTOMERS WITH REMARKETING

Steven Guyer

Chances are, if you are reading this textbook for a class, you are younger than e-mail—but not by much. E-mail, as we know it, was born in the early 1980s. It may seem old compared to Twitter and Facebook, but it's still young compared to direct mail, radio, or even direct television. E-mail continues to grow among clients because it is incredibly fast, yields high ROI, and is trackable. E-mail is growing among younger and older customers because of its usefulness as a digital receipt, to confirm purchases, or to resolve questions. Given these advantages, e-mail is, arguably, the backbone media channel for the new digital one-to-one customer relationship. E-mail service providers (ESPs), such as Experian CheetahMail, are creating more and more ways to help clients make the relationship between customers and brands stronger. And customers are taking notice.

One way ESPs are strengthening the brand-to-customer relationship is through behavior-targeted messaging. Experian CheetahMail refers to this as *remarketing*. Remarketing takes into consideration customer preferences, actual shopping activity, and product availability. To get an idea of how remarketing works, imagine that you visit a shop online and have a personal shopper hold onto a few items for possible future purchase. Now imagine that a few days later, your personal shopper reminds you about your favorite items (and even recommends some other items you might like). This low-pressure, highly relevant customer contact is cost prohibitive for in-store shopping, but e-mail is emerging as the new method to reengage customers with more relevance and personalization than before.

Experian CheetahMail has implemented these types of personalized remarketing programs for a range of *Fortune* 500 clients, and e-mail performance data prove not only that customer involvement increases with these messages but also that it increases future purchases. Remarketing e-mails enhance the overall shopping experience, reinforcing the online brand experience for both young and old.

Courtesy of Steven Guyer, Experian CheetahMail, New York.

Marketers have had mixed experiences on the social networking sites. Consumers have not been happy with those on YouTube, for example, that hide the fact that they are promoting something. So marketers must be careful how they promote on new technology sites, or risk a backlash.

Anheuser-Busch (A-B) launched a new marketing venture, a web-based television network, after the 2007 *Super Bowl* called Bud TV. The 24/7 "network," featuring both live and on-demand programming, was carried on up to seven channels. It used branded content for A-B products—but it also used independent offerings, such as webisodes, celebrity interviews, comedy, short films, consumer-generated content, and even sports events. The channels also were dedicated to specific genres, while music downloads were also available.[19]

At a pre–*Super Bowl* event, Sprint conducted an on-stage event during the NFL Experience in which 24 NFL players greeted fans and sent them messages during a 6-hour period over handsets provided by Sprint. The goal was to expose consumers to the Sprint brand while the fans had fun with NFL players, said Dawn Ridley, senior vice president for Players, Inc., the licensing and marketing subsidiary of the NFL Players Association, which arranged the event.[20]

Consumer-generated advertisement-making contests have been successful. A Chipotle winner was posted on YouTube. "Dady" stars a bald-headed father who is presented with a handmade drawing from his young son, only to criticize the tyke for not doing justice to the shape of his head or even spelling his name correctly. The kicker? Chipotle customers don't settle for anything but the best. "Dady" (catch the clip on YouTube to understand the intentional misspelling) amassed 2.25 million views on YouTube only 2 weeks after its initial posting.[21]

DEALS

Deals are a catch-all category of promotional techniques designed to save the customer money. The most common deal is a temporary price reduction or "sale." The cents-off coupon is also a consumer deal because it lowers the price during some limited period. A deal also may involve merchandising. For example, a manufacturer may offer three bars of soap wrapped together sold at a reduced price. Another deal possibility is attaching a new product to a package of an established product at little or no extra cost—an effective way of new-product sampling. Among the most familiar deals are rebates toward the purchase of a product. They can be instant rebates or mail-in rebates and are among the most common deals offered by manufacturers. Premium offers are offers of free or discounted merchandise used as an incentive for the customer to purchase more.

The downside of offering frequent deals is that a promotion may start off as a temporary incentive and become, to some buyers, an expectation. Deals can be extremely effective in building sales at the trade level. Trade deals offered to retailers, wholesalers, and others in the trade channel were discussed earlier in the chapter as a type of trade incentive.

FULFILLMENT

The physical work of handling, organizing, and responding to requests for merchandise is normally managed by **fulfillment firms**. Customer satisfaction and efficiency remain top priorities for brands and their fulfillment shops. Marketers' fulfillment budgets have been static for the past several years. As a result, fulfillment houses are trying to take on more roles for each brand client. For example, marketing and fulfillment services typically provide clients with warehousing, real-time order processing, inventory control, and distribution systems to enable timely delivery to end users. Fulfillment firms usually operate on a fee basis according to the number of requests. Their work is crucial to the success of any promotion. Sloppy fulfillment services can virtually guarantee an unsuccessful promotion as well as long-term damage to customer goodwill. Fulfillment is an extension of customer service and it is your company, not the fulfillment firm, that will be blamed if something goes wrong.

fulfillment firm
Company that handles the couponing process, including receiving, verification, and payment. It also handles contest and sweepstakes responses.

SPECIALTY ADVERTISING

The same items used in premium promotions—clothing, writing instruments, calendars—are among the most popular with specialty advertisers.[22] However, there are two major differences between premiums and specialties:

1. Advertising specialties are imprinted with the advertiser's name, logo, or short advertising message. Premiums are not normally imprinted because the customer is being given a reward for purchasing a product.

2. Unlike premiums, specialties are given with no obligation on the part of the recipient.

The uses and formats of advertising specialties are almost limitless with more than 15,000 items available to carry out virtually any marketing objective. Specialties also complement other media and can be targeted to prime prospects with little waste circulation. The ideal specialty is one that is used on a regular basis, thereby creating continuing frequency with no additional cost.

The disadvantages of specialties include their significant expense on a CPM basis and, like outdoor, the fact that they offer little opportunity for a sales message. In addition, there is no natural distribution system for specialties and, depending on the item selected, production time may take up to 6 weeks.

specialty advertising
A gift given to a consumer that
encourages a purchase.

Specialty advertising has experienced significant growth in recent years as businesses have attempted to establish brand identities in an increasingly competitive environment. The selling techniques of specialties to companies has changed. Instead of using expensive catalogs, some reps show an array of targeted merchandise using portable computers or provide their selections online.

Because a major role of specialty advertising involves providing long-term brand awareness, it is not surprising to find its heaviest users in markets with little perceived product differentiation and a number of competitive brands. Financial institutions, such as banks and stockbrokers; hospitals and health-care providers; and telecommunication and Internet companies are examples of categories that spend heavily on specialty advertising.

Specialty advertising, like all forms of promotion, should be planned in terms of specific marketing goals and objectives. One survey of advertisers found some of the primary reasons for using specialties:[23]

1. To promote customer retention and appreciation
2. To use in connection with trade shows
3. To build goodwill and enhance company image
4. To create awareness for new products and services
5. To generate sales leads and responses

In choosing a specialty item, it is important to determine that the item has some logical relationship to both the target market and the product or service being promoted. The item needs to have some useful function if the specialty is going to be kept as a reminder of a brand. Because the advertising message can be no more than a few words, a specialty needs to adapt the theme of a company's overall advertising campaign to offer an integrated communications approach to consumers.

COUPONS

**4 Discuss the varied
types of couponing
today.**

coupon
Most popular type of sales-
promotion technique.

free-standing inserts (FSIs)
Preprinted inserts distributed
to newspaper publishers,
where they are inserted and
delivered with the newspaper.

Coupon promotions are among the oldest forms of sales promotion, and they are without question the most pervasive category within the promotion industry. Marketers give consumers more than 302 billion coupons a year. The value of those coupons is about $388 billion. Yep, *billion*. Redemption rates at about 2.6 percent have been basically flat for a number of years. The average value of the offer per coupon is $1.28.

Free-standing inserts (FSIs) continue to lead the way marketers distribute coupons. They are by far the most preferred method of coupon distribution and are usually included in Sunday newspapers. FSIs are responsible for more than 88 percent of total coupon distribution, whereas handouts, in-ad, in-pack, in-pack cross ruff, instant redeemable, and the Internet follow as distribution methods. Interestingly, Internet distribution accounted for only 0.4 percent of coupons. If you look at their reach, FSIs are an inexpensive way for marketers to motivate consumers. To put these numbers into perspective, FSIs reach more than 60 million households a week. The average expiration date on coupons has decreased slightly to 2.5 months from just less than 3 months.

Folks Southern Kitchen uses FSIs to distribute coupons on a quarterly basis (see Exhibit 14.7). This promotion is selling baskets of smaller portions with four coupons and promotes their holiday meal.

There are two basic approaches to coupon marketing and distribution. Traditionally, the primary marketing objectives for distributing coupons are to encourage product trial by prospective customers and to combat competitive encroachments against present customers. Both of these goals were normally addressed through mass coupon distribution.

One of the recurring complaints about the number of coupon promotions is that they create price competition at the expense of building brand loyalty. In recent years, a number of major advertisers have taken steps to include coupon promotions within a

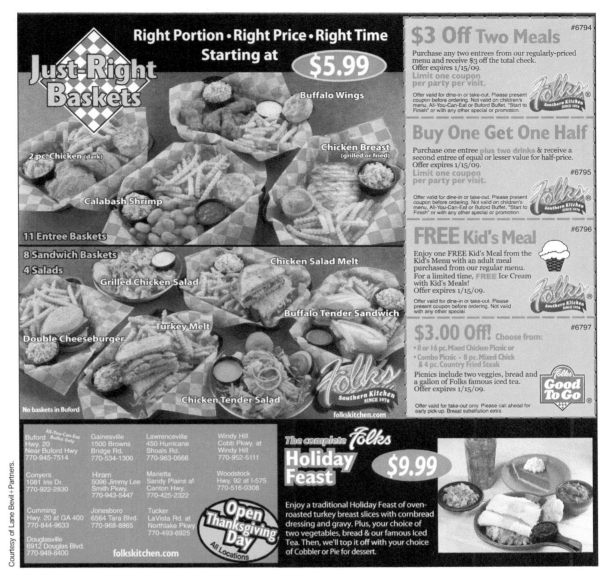

EXHIBIT 14.7

Folks provides free-standing insert promotions.

traditional advertising environment. Such an approach serves to encourage product trial and build brand equity.

In addition to FSI and other blanket coupon distribution methods, we are starting to see a number of more targeted efforts. These more narrowly defined approaches to coupon promotions have one of two goals:

1. To reach targeted prospects based on lifestyle and demographic information
2. To build loyalty among current customers

In both cases, scanning checkout data and information from other computer-based data-retrieval systems gives manufacturers insight into the past purchasing behavior of individual buyers. Using this information, retailers and manufacturers can provide offers that reflect specific consumer behavior and brand preferences.

INTERNET AND MOBILE COUPONS

Despite low numbers of coupons currently obtained online, the combination of consumer convenience and manufacturers' ability to build customer databases makes the growth of web couponing inevitable. Sometimes getting a coupon for a free meal creates problems.

In one instance, Oprah Winfrey wanted to give everyone a free meal, and KFC was looking to promote its latest product. They offered consumers coupons that could be downloaded that were good for two pieces of grilled chicken, two sides, and a biscuit. The coupons could be downloaded at www.unthinkkfc.com and www.oprah.com. The Oprah-KFC coupons were the fifth most popular search on Google.com the day of her show.

KFC crowed in a tweet on its Twitter site when publicity from its "*Oprah Winfrey Show* 2 Piece Meal Coupon" deal led to KFC reaching the top 10 trending topics on the social media site. But the company seems to have been unprepared for the reach of this promotion. As KFCs around the country were inundated with customers, bloggers and tweeters complained about long lines and stores refusing to honor the coupons. The coupons were good at about 5,200 stores. The company had to apologize for the mess as stores ran out of chicken or stopped honoring the coupons. One expert called it a "tsunami" brought on by the endorsement. Was it a success despite the nightmare? Would people forgive and remember the product's popularity in light of Oprah's endorsement.[24] Apparently they have.

Procter & Gamble's web site typically tells consumers, "Don't forget to look for the P&G brandSAVER coupon insert in your home-delivered paper on Sunday—you could save more than $30 on some of your favorite P&G brands!" Online services such as Catalina Marketing's valupage.com and Val Pak Direct Marketing's valpak.com offer coupons in exchange for some consumer information. As online services continue to develop consumer databases, they will begin providing services such as e-mail offers tailored to a person's past buying behavior. (Exhibit 14.8 is an example of a Val Pak promotion. Coupons are on the reverse side.)

same-day coupons
Coupons designed to be used almost instantly, or same day.

Same-day coupons are getting a little exposure. For example, Yahoo! offered coupons for a free Baskin-Robbins ice cream cone, and Toys "R" Us ran a series of same-day offers via e-mail. Some mobile coupons have made similar offers.

There has been resistance to mobile ads, but mobile coupons are more acceptable to some. Research indicates that one-third of consumers who get text-message ads are more likely to respond if they also received an incentive, such as a coupon or music offer. Recently, Coupons.com made an agreement to put its coupons on the Yahoo! Mobile service. In some markets, Kroger grocery shoppers browse for coupons on their phones, choose the ones they want to redeem, and have the discounts linked to their loyalty cards at checkout.

EXHIBIT 14.8

This small Val Pak promotion has coupons on the reverse side.

COUPON REDEMPTION FRAUD

When we redeem our 50-cent coupons, we give little thought to the significant investment for manufacturers offering them. Unfortunately, those interested in defrauding

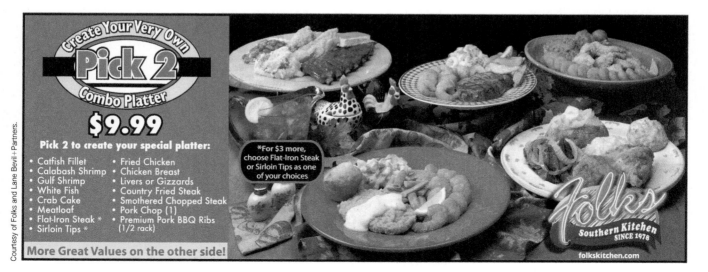

Courtesy of Folks and Lane Bevil+Partners.

manufacturers through the illegal redemption of coupons are very much aware of their value. The most common type of fraud occurs when a person sends in coupons for which no product purchase has been made. There have been instances in which criminals have obtained thousands of coupons and sent them to manufacturers using the name of supermarkets and other retailers. In some cases, manufacturers have spent millions of dollars on redemptions for fraudulent claims.

The industry is working with bar code technology and other techniques to address the problem. However, regardless of the distribution method, coupon fraud and misredemption remain problems.

PRODUCT SAMPLING

Recently, sampling has moved from inside stores to more targeted environments. Online sampling is growing as web communities bring together people looking for new products, then blog about the products, and tell how to get samples. Other companies have worked directly with web communities to promote trials of new products.

We have emphasized throughout the text that regardless of the quality of the advertising and promotion, ultimately the product must sell itself. This is the philosophy behind product sampling. **Sampling** is the free distribution of a product to a prospect. In recent years, product sampling has grown significantly, and in many cases it has replaced coupons as a manufacturer's primary method of gaining product trial. The sampling expenditure by marketers is estimated at $2.3 billion. Experts say sampling's growth will continue, fueled by its measurability.

Sampling has always been a successful tactic for trial and conversion. The tactical side of sampling has changed as companies move from goody boxes to **experiential sampling**, which include tours with big trucks or buses (for example, the Weinermobile from Oscar Meyer) to get consumers into the whole experience. Mobile sampling events seem less sterile (and goodies raise consumers' participation). For example, Kimberly-Clark launched an extensive sampling program of its Kleenex brand's new product—tissue enhanced with lotion. It gave away 60 million samples in places you couldn't previously find a Kleenex. Free-standing and shelf displays provided dispensers with the new product so shoppers could sample a Kleenex with lotion. They sampled in magazine spreads (in *O* and *Good Housekeeping*) and with newspaper coupon inserts. They also had a mobile sampling van that toured selected cities.

Coca-Cola gave away free samples of its Vault brand to anyone who bought PepsiCo's Mountain Dew. The aggressive "Don't Dew It" promotion was aimed at die-hard Dew-ers to get them to try Vault. After 3 years on the market they only achieved a 4 percent share, versus Mountain Dew's 80 percent share of the citrus soft drink segment.[25]

Advertisers are increasingly using creative approaches to get samples into the hands of prospective buyers. One of the significant changes in sampling is the move away from mass distribution campaigns and toward narrowly targeted dissemination. Targeting of prospects allows manufacturers to drastically decrease waste and obtain more accurate results from sampling tests. Some of the growing areas of sampling include the following:

1. *Newspaper distribution.* Many newspapers define their delivery areas in small geographic areas (e.g., ZIP codes and block units), giving marketers a more targeted demographic for sampling.

2. *Event/venues marketing.* Because events such as rock concerts and sporting events tend to appeal to specific demographic and/or lifestyle segments, they offer ideal venues for sampling. In many cases, venue sampling—for example, suntan lotion at the beach—gives an immediate opportunity for product usage.

3. *In-store sampling.* Usually, in-store sampling is combined with a coupon incentive encouraging immediate purchase of the product. It is rare that a trip to the grocery store doesn't include at least one opportunity to sample some food product and receive a coupon.

sampling
The method of introducing and promoting merchandise by distributing a miniature or full-size trial package of the product free or at a reduced price.

experiential sampling
A company's use of specialty vehicles to engage consumers and give them samples to enhance the contact experience.

4. *In-pack/co-op programs.* On-pack and in-pack distribution is popular when one product has a natural affinity to another. Washing machines often are delivered with a box of detergent, or shaving cream might come with a razor attached. In other cases, a multibrand manufacturer might want customers to inexpensively sample a new product by including it with one of its established brands.

5. *Internet sampling.* Many of the same characteristics that offer substantial advantages for Internet coupon distribution apply to sampling over the Internet. Samples woo consumers online, too, where they swap data for products. One study indicated that 70 percent of consumers have completed a survey to get a sample. A major advantage of this approach is that by sending samples only on request, manufacturers drastically decrease waste distribution.

SWEEPSTAKES AND CONTESTS

The primary goal of most promotions is to gain immediate sales and consumer involvement. Recently, the need to keep consumers engaged fueled technology gains as a prime tool for games, contests, and sweepstakes. Whether it's a text-messaging campaign, online sweepstakes, or an interactive game, the Internet continues to dominate the field. Marketers prefer cyberspace largely for its cost efficiency, immediate data-collection capabilities, and ability to keep consumers engaged. They spend approximately $1.86 billion a year building games, sweepstakes, and contests.

contest
A promotion in which consumers compete for prizes and the winners are selected strictly on the basis of skill.

sweepstakes
A promotion in which prizewinners are determined on the basis of chance alone. Not legal if purchaser must risk money to enter.

The methods in which games, **contests**, and **sweepstakes** are deployed are changing to ensure a more engaging consumer experience across multiple touch points, says a representative of Archway Marketing.[26] In addition, the level of interactivity has increased and prizes are not only bigger but also more customized and lifestyle based.

Each year, more than 70 percent of American businesses sponsor a game of some kind, and it is estimated that almost 30 percent of the population enters a commercially sponsored contest or sweepstakes. The major marketers of these games are soft drink companies, fast-food franchises, and movie studios. Participants get game pieces in stores in addition to major prizes. Obviously, one objective with contests and sweepstakes is to drive traffic to the store. A contest or sweepstakes is an ideal marketing strategy for these companies.

Companies want to build ongoing relationships with consumers, and they use games and contests to obtain consumer data. For example, Subway used the database of opt-in subscribers from its Scrabble game to promote their new products and programs. Customers peeled off game pieces from drink cups and wrappers for instant prizes. Then they went online to play an instant-win game or spell out words for a chance at other prizes. In Exhibit 14.9, Church's chicken game piece could win a customer an automobile or one of 100,000 other prizes.

Because contests call for some element of skill, there must be a plan for judging and making certain that all legal requirements have been met. The typical contest is much more expensive than a sweepstakes. When millions of entries are anticipated, even the smallest overlooked detail can be a nightmare for the contest sponsor. It is estimated that almost 30 percent of the public enter either a sweepstakes or contest each year. A major contest can place a tremendous burden on a company to properly administer and judge. Most games are handled by outside firms specializing in these promotions.

Another limitation of contests is the time (and skill) required of participants. The majority of consumers will not devote the time necessary to complete a contest. Therefore, if the intent of the promotion is to gain maximum interest and participation, a sweepstakes will probably be better suited to the objective. However, a cleverly devised contest that complements the product and appeals to the skills of prime prospects can be extremely beneficial and encourage greater involvement than a sweepstakes.

Kleenex tissues had a contest to get some Latin flavor onto its packaging to celebrate Hispanic Heritage Month. The brand ran a contest to find up to three artists to

EXHIBIT 14.9

Peel to Win

The game piece could make a customer a winner of an automobile.

provide Hispanic-themed motifs for Kleenex boxes. The contest was titled "Con Kleenex, Expresa tu Hispanidad" ("With Kleenex, Express Your Hispanic Culture") and sought package designs and artwork that would be culturally relevant to Hispanic consumers. A panel of judges selected by Kleenex parent Kimberly-Clark Global Sales chose 12 finalists based on authenticity, creativity, workmanship, Hispanic relevance, and alignment with Kleenex brand values. Those dozen submissions were posted to the contest web site and put to a public vote.[27]

THE DECEPTIVE MAIL PREVENTION AND ENFORCEMENT ACT   Sweepstakes that require a purchase (known as *consideration*) by an entrant are considered lotteries and, with the exception of state-sponsored lotteries, are usually illegal. The next time you receive a sweepstakes offer, notice that there is some language indicating that no purchase is necessary to enter. Despite these disclaimers, it has been alleged that a number of people, especially the elderly, have assumed that a purchase would enhance their chances of winning. In 1999, Congress passed the Deceptive Mail Prevention and Enforcement Act, which addressed a number of these issues. Industry criticism of the bill has been directed largely at the provision for a national opt-out list in which recipients can remove their name from all sweepstakes solicitations. As one promotion executive commented, "I don't think you will see marketers abandoning sweepstakes, but they may proceed more cautiously."[28]

COOPERATIVE ADVERTISING

Historically, co-op advertising was initiated primarily as a means of overcoming the significant rate premiums charged to national advertisers by newspapers. Although

KLEPPNER VIEWPOINT 14.2

David Botsford CEO, The Botsford Group

GETTING THE RETAIL SUPPORT YOU WANT

No matter how much time and money a packaged-goods manufacturer pours into its brands, what happens—or doesn't happen—on the sales floor can quickly turn dreams into nightmares on the market share front.

With 70 percent of all brand purchase decisions made at the retail level, according to the Point-of-Purchase Advertising Institute, the store is more than simply a place to win a battle. It's an opportunity to win the war.

Increased display activity, more in-store merchandising, and additional retail ad support are three major avenues for influencing these purchase decisions.

Of course, the importance of your category to the retailer, as well as your brand's position in the category, determines the degree of retailer support possible. I've never met a manufacturer, however, whose retail support couldn't be increased. It comes down to three things: Motivate retailers to authorize incremental support for your brand, ensure the support you get builds the brand (all support is not created equal), and get the

support promised implemented at the store level (which only happens 40 percent of the time).

The good news is you don't need a SWAT team to get this done. Just follow the five rules listed here and you'll see measurable results every time.

Rule 1: Collaborate
If you don't help the retailer build his business, he isn't going to be motivated to build yours. Don't take programs to your retailers that simply induce brand switching. Develop ideas that expand the category or increase profitability—or both if you can pull it off. Start by becoming familiar with each retailer's distinct needs, wants, and rules. Ditto for the retailer's brand personality and merchandising style.

Integrate with the retailer's brand and you'll earn the opportunity to talk about yours (don't, however, leave creative development in the retailer's hands!). Additionally, you should factor store employees, the gatekeepers of implementation, into your program. If your field force or agency doesn't know the lay of the land at the store level, get them educated

David Botsford

quickly. Talk to a representative sampling of key employees (two or three people per chain). Most appreciate being asked, plus you'll learn something.

Rule 2: Differentiate
Retailers don't want the same program you gave their competitor down the street. They need promotions that set them apart from rivals. Differentiation doesn't have to be a budget buster. Lightly customized creative is one way to accomplish this in a cost-effective manner. For example, by using different photography for competing retailers in overlapping markets we were able to

that is still a purpose of co-op advertising, it also has become a major category of trade promotion with annual expenditures of more than $30 billion. The marketing goals and objectives differ from one manufacturer or retailer to another, but some of the primary purposes of co-op include the following:

1. It benefits retailers by allowing them to stretch their advertising budgets. Most co-op advertising is offered on a 50 percent basis; that is, the national firm pays half of the local advertising costs. However, some co-op plans will reimburse retailers at a rate of 100 percent. In other cases, a manufacturer will place some limit on the amount of reimbursement according to a formula based on sales of the product by the retailer. Federal law requires that regardless of the formula of reimbursement, manufacturers must treat all retailers proportionately the same.

2. National manufacturers build goodwill with retailers; encourage local support of their brands; and, by having the retailer place the advertising, qualify for lower local rates, especially in newspapers. Manufacturers also gain a positive association between local retailers and their products, thus enhancing the brand equity among

increase retailer support of a recent outdoor campaign. The return on investment for co-marketing can also be very high, especially if you focus on high-volume retailers. We've seen clients use this avenue to achieve double-digit volume lifts, increases that resulted in the program paying for itself many times.

Rule 3: Motivate

Even though some retailers will tell you it isn't necessary, find ways to tie store-level incentives to in-store implementation—they can make you look like a hero. Make sure the programs are flexible enough to meet retailer guidelines. For retailers that don't allow direct employee rewards, consider staging special events for top-performing associates, awarding the store's own gift certificates, or offering store-specific promotions (it's hard for a chain's headquarters to argue with this one).

Rule 4: Communicate

About a week before a program starts, make sure to check in with the folks who are physically responsible for getting displays and merchandising out of the back room and into the store. Clearly mark shipping containers with the program name, start date, and exact store location desired. Do the same thing with merchandising materials.

Chiquita: The Official Banana of U.S. Soccer.

Rule 5: Participate

Let the retailer become part of your account-specific planning without relinquishing control of your creative, brand positioning, and marketing strategies. Most retailers not only have fun doing so but also will be flattered at the offer and will begin to view you as a partner, not simply a vendor.

At the close of a recent meeting of our agency and a client with marketers at one of the top 10 U.S. food chains, the retailer thanked us profusely for including them in the process, adding: "I wish other manufacturers approached account specific marketing this way."

That's a wake-up call to manufacturers and agencies if I've ever heard one.

Courtesy of David Botsford and The Botsford Group.

customers of specific retailers. Many co-op advertisements are prepared by national advertisers and require only that retailers add their logo.

3. The media are among the strongest supporters of co-op advertising. Co-op allows current advertisers to place more advertising and, at the same time, brings new advertisers into the marketplace. Because co-op involves local advertising, it is not surprising that the majority of co-op dollars is spent in newspapers. However, in recent years, co-op has reflected the diversity of local media. About 60 percent of co-op budgets are spent in newspapers, followed by direct mail, television, and radio, each with approximately 10 percent. In the future, we will see significant dollars going into local cable co-op programs and this will increase the share of television co-op.

One of the surprising aspects of co-op advertising is the amount of money that is available but goes unspent. It is estimated that as much as one-fourth of co-op dollars goes unspent. The main reasons for the failure to fully use co-op primarily involves a lack of knowledge on the part of retailers as to how to use co-op dollars and an unwillingness to meet the restrictions placed on their expenditure by manufacturers.

vendor program
Special form of co-op
advertising in which a retailer
designs the program and
approaches advertisers for
support.

VENDOR PROGRAMS   A special form of co-op normally used by large retailers is the **vendor program**. The primary difference between vendor programs and other forms of co-op is that they are initiated by retailers. Vendor programs are custom programs designed by retailers (often in cooperation with local media). In vendor programs, manufacturers are approached by retailers to pay all or a share of the program.

For example, a department store might plan a summer "Beach Party" promotion. The store would then approach manufacturers of swimwear, sunglasses, suntan preparations, and so forth and request funds to support the advertising and promotion of the event. Often, manufacturers fund vendor programs from their unspent co-op money.

INGREDIENT MANUFACTURER CO-OP   Most co-op programs are set up between manufacturers and retailers. However, many companies make ingredients that they sell to other manufacturers for inclusion in finished products. The strategy of advertising for both the ingredient and the final product is called end-product advertising (for example, Intel computer chips: Intel doesn't make computers) and represents another opportunity for co-op. Often, the ingredient manufacturer will contract with finished-product manufacturers to co-op with retail outlets or even to co-op in the manufacturer's national advertising to promote the ingredient.

MANUFACTURER-TO-WHOLESALER CO-OP   Occasionally, distribution in an industry is dominated by a relatively few wholesale outlets, and manufacturers have little direct relationship with retailers. In this situation, it often is worthwhile for manufacturers to allocate co-op dollars to wholesalers that then make co-op arrangements with individual retailers. Most manufacturers avoid going through wholesalers because they lose both the goodwill and control achieved by direct allocation of co-op dollars by the national company.

CONTROLLING CO-OP DOLLARS   Retailers are paid for advertising when they submit documentation or proof of performance. The advertisements or proof can be matched with the media invoice. For radio and television cooperative advertisements, the Association of National Advertisers, the RAB, and the TvB developed an affidavit of performance that documents in detail the content, cost, and timing of commercials. The adoption of stricter controls in broadcast co-op has been a contributing factor in the growth of co-op dollars for both radio and television. Stations provide manufacturers with the actual on-air commercial and the context in which it ran online.

Despite attempts to improve the process, expenditures of co-op dollars still are allocated improperly out of neglect or inexperience by retailers. In a few cases, there is evidence of outright fraud. Co-op fraud usually takes one of two forms. In the first, retailers bill manufacturers for advertisements that never ran, using fake invoices and tear sheets. The second type of fraud, called double billing, occurs when manufacturers are overcharged for the cost of advertising. Basically, retailers pay one price to the medium and bill the manufacturer for a higher price using a phony (double) bill. It should be noted that double billing is regarded as an unethical (and, in most circumstances, illegal) practice, and only a small minority of retailers and media engage in it.

TRADE SHOWS AND EXHIBITS

It is estimated that more than 100 million people will attend more than 5,000 trade and consumer shows this year. Products as diverse as boats and cosmetics will be promoted through these shows. In some cases, a show will be open to both the trade and the public and might be visited by 100,000 prospects. In other cases, the shows are extremely selective and open by invitation only to a few dozen prospects.

Trade shows are one of the best examples of integrated promotion. They combine a number of media and other forms of marketing communication. Trade show sponsorship is almost never used as a stand-alone marketing tool. A trade show can fulfill a number of objectives, including product introduction, lead getting, and direct selling. Research shows that trade shows are most successful for those sponsors with high brand recognition. The use of trade magazines and other forms of promotion and communication, including e-commerce, work both before and after the show to encourage the final sale.

The higher the level of brand recognition created before a show, the less time sales reps have to spend creating a product image and the more time they can devote to selling. By the same token, trade shows create opportunities for on-site market research as well as follow-up by personal or online selling.

Overall, trade shows are a major component in the marketing strategy of many firms. However, trade shows are normally only one piece in a total marketing program rather than an end in themselves. Trade shows provide a number of advantages for both buyers and sellers. They allow face-to-face selling at a cost much lower than traditional personal sales calls. In addition, trade shows are a self-selecting process with only serious prospects attending. Although some sales take place at these exhibits, they are more likely to provide leads for future sales calls or introduce new product lines to prospective customers.

Many companies or organizations have reason to have exhibits away from trade shows. Robinson & Associates created this exhibit to promote a nonprofit to encourage education (see Exhibit 14.10).

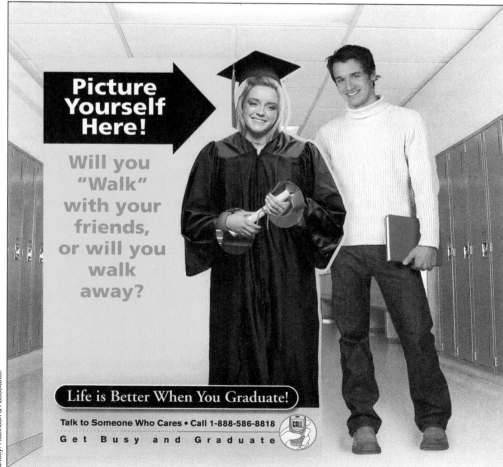

Courtesy: Robinson & Associates.

EXHIBIT 14.10

There are all types of trade shows and exhibits, even for nonprofit promotional events.

DIRECTORIES AND YELLOW PAGES

At one time there was a single Yellow Page provider in each town. This made it simple for retailers to buy advertising in the Yellow Pages and for consumers to use them. Now the Yellow Pages is being attacked on all sides by the explosion of web-based information and directories. MagicYellow, AOL Yellow, onlineyellowpages.com, dexknows.com, Google, Yahoo!, Craigslist, and local sites offer advertisers a lot of directory choices. Buying directories isn't as simple as it was. However, it is still an important advertising vehicle for local businesses. Directories may be a cost-efficient medium reaching serious prospects who are in the mood to purchase. There are more than 10,000 printed directories aimed at both consumers and trade buyers (and many of these are also available online). Because directory advertising is available when the purchase decision is being made, there are few companies that do not include at least some directory advertising in their marketing plans. Many retailers, particularly service businesses such as plumbers, rely on directories as their only type of promotion.

According to research, 76 percent of all U.S. adults refer to the Yellow Pages monthly, and 88 percent of those who use the Yellow Pages ultimately make or are likely to make a purchase.[29] Research also shows the average Yellow Pages user looks at more than five advertisements when scanning the directory, so it's even more important to make your company stand out.

Directory advertising (online and off) has many of the characteristics of the more expensive direct-response media but with none of their intrusiveness. It also offers advertisers a continuing presence and high frequency without continuing advertising expenditures. Specialized directories are a major medium for business-to-business advertising and frequent reference sources for business buyers. Directories, printed or online, are an important complement to other forms of advertising and promotion.

TRADE INCENTIVES

5 **Discuss the uses of sales promotion as consumer and trade incentives.**

incentives
Sales promotion directed at wholesalers, retailers, or a company's sales force.

Although the average consumer is not familiar with trade promotions, businesses will spend some $25 billion in promotions to reach wholesalers, retailers, and company sales personnel. These promotions are referred to as sales incentives or simply **incentives**. Incentives include everything from cash bonuses to travel offers, with various types of merchandise (clothing leads the list) being the most popular type of incentive.

Sales promotions directed to the trade channel are called incentives. There are two types of incentives: *dealer incentives*, which are directed to retailers and wholesalers, and *sales incentives*, which are directed to a company's sales force. Almost 80 percent of incentives are offered directly to salespeople. The most common incentives to wholesalers or retailers are price reductions in the form of promotional allowances. In effect, these incentives are comparable to cents-off promotions at the consumer level. In addition, sweepstakes, contests, and continuity promotions (some with prize catalogs) based on sales volume are all used at the trade level.

The primary objectives of incentives are to motivate either members of the distribution channel or company reps to achieve higher sales and profitability. Dealer and trade incentives are becoming more and more crucial as retailers take greater control of the distribution channel. Most dealers have the option of selling a number of brands from different manufacturers. Manufacturers have to compete for retail distribution and, once achieved, for dealer support for their brand (e.g., premium shelf space, co-op advertising agreements, and in-store recommendations to customers). As one incentive consultant pointed out, the relationship between a manufacturer and a dealer is similar to that of a tenant and a landlord. "The dealer actually owns the distribution channel. The manufacturer is really just a tenant in the channel. Just like anything else in life, the power lies with the owner."[30]

The key to successful incentive programs is to have them complement overall business strategy. The goals that the incentive programs are intended to address should be very specific. For example, a company may use incentives to gain support for a new

CHICK-FIL-A'S COW INTEGRATED CAMPAIGN

In Chapter 6, Chick-fil-A's operating philosophy was discussed. Here, we want to share one of the world's great integrated marketing campaigns.

BACKGROUND

Atlanta-based Chick-fil-A, founded by entrepreneur and restaurateur S. Truett Cathy, has risen from rather humble beginnings to become America's second-largest quick-service chicken restaurant chain.

Cathy started in 1946 in the Atlanta suburb of Hapeville with a single location he named the Dwarf Grill. Cathy now presides over a chain of some 1,300 restaurants in 37 states and Washington, DC, generating annual sales of more than $2 billion.

MARKETING

Chick-fil-A's marketing strategy throughout the chain's history can be summed up in two words: maximizing resources. From the beginning, the Chick-fil-A's brand was built on people, product, and purpose.

Necessitated by limited marketing budgets, Chick-fil-A's early marketing efforts were locally focused. One early marketing program Cathy adopted that still is employed today is product sampling. Leveraging their location within malls,

Chick-fil-A operators and team members frequently offer free product samples of the Chick-fil-A Chicken Sandwich (and later other products, such as Chick-fil-A Nuggets, Chick-fil-A Chick-n-Strips, etc.). In those early days, the chain's marketing slogan was: "Taste It! You'll Love It For Good." Even as the chain grew, expanding into a regional—and eventually, a national—brand, Chick-fil-A maintained a local focus for its marketing efforts.

In 1981, Steve Robinson joined Chick-fil-A as director of marketing (currently, he serves as senior vice president of marketing) and was charged with developing the company's overall marketing strategy. Realizing that the brand's strength was in its local store's efforts and recognizing that the chain's marketing budgets were limited relative to other quick-service brands, Robinson created a marketing strategy that turned convention on its head—literally.

Although most quick-service chains focused most of their marketing spending on national programs and allotted proportionally smaller amounts to regional (and even smaller amounts to local) efforts, Robinson proposed the opposite. He knew he did not have the advertising dollars to compete with other brands on a national level, so he focused those dollars in the cities and the immediate market areas where the restaurants were located.

Chick-fil-A initiated a field marketing strategy that leveraged this model. At the store level, unit marketing directors (UMDs) were hired who were responsible for all marketing activities within a 3- to 5-mile radius of their restaurant. For larger markets with multiple restaurants (e.g., Atlanta, Dallas, Orlando, etc.), Robinson recommended hiring area marketing directors (AMDs). An AMDs would report directly to the group of operators in their market, and their duties would include marketwide sponsorships, partnerships, events, promotions, and public relations.

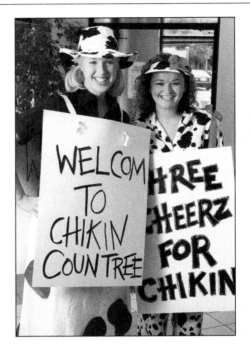

On a national level, Chick-fil-A focused the remainder of its marketing dollars on systemwide promotions and sports sponsorships (which today includes the *Chick-fil-A Bowl*, as well as sponsorship of the Southeastern Conference, the Atlantic Coast Conference, and the Big 12 Conference championship events). At all levels, Chick-fil-A relied heavily on public relations as a cost-effective means to support the brand locally, regionally, and nationally.

In terms of advertising dollars, Chick-fil-A typically focused locally. Point-of-purchase materials and local print and radio ads made up the bulk of the chain's advertising arsenal for many years. But as the chain grew—both geographically and in terms of sales—the need to support the brand with a memorable campaign grew as well.

In 1995, Chick-fil-A brought in a new advertising agency—The Richards Group, which is based in Dallas. Stan Richards, the agency's founder and chief creative officer, recommended a unique approach to advertising for Chick-fil-A that would not work for just any company:

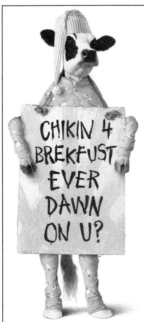

Concentrate on billboards. Given its limited budgets, Chick-fil-A could not make much of an impact in television advertising (national or local), radio, or even print. But billboards were a truly local advertising medium, and the exposure to local traffic was just what the chain needed to drive customers to their restaurants. And the price was right to allow Chick-fil-A to "own" billboards.

The now-famous "Cow" billboard (featuring two, three-dimensional cows perched atop a billboard, painting the words: "Eat Mor Chikin") was not the first "edgy" billboard concept developed, but it certainly was the campaign that stuck. With the cows, Chick-fil-A had an irreverent, humorous, and extremely memorable campaign with creative messages that helped cut through the clutter and maximize the chain's use of outdoor advertising. It did not take long for the "Cow" campaign to extend far beyond billboards and into every aspect of Chick-fil-A's marketing efforts, including:

- Point-of-purchase materials
- Print advertising
- Radio advertising
- Television advertising (local and in support of national sponsorships)
- Merchandise sales
- Event support
- Its popular *Cow Calendar*. Now the number one selling calendar in the nation.

Leveraging such a memorable campaign, Chick-fil-A has had an impact in all advertising media without having to commit huge advertising budgets to generate exposure through repetition. The campaign also has won several awards.

Courtesy of Chick-fil-A.

product line, to motivate salespersons to increase sales to current retailers, or to expand distribution to new retailers or in new territories.

There is no question that trade incentives can be extremely effective in increasing sales, productivity, and morale. However, increasingly, regulatory agencies are questioning the ethics of some trade incentives that do not provide full disclosure to customers. For example, in a retail store, consumers may seek objective information from a salesperson about one brand over another. How objective can retailers be if they are receiving significant rewards for promoting a particular brand? Currently, there is no effective system of providing consumer disclosure for trade incentives. However, as competition in many industries grows more intense and the financial value of incentives increases, we may see both state and federal regulators take a new look at the entire system of trade incentives.

SUMMARY

It is clear that distinctions among the various elements of marketing communication are becoming less evident and less important to both marketers and their customers. Businesses are increasingly demanding accountability for the dollars invested in promotion. Whether a customer is reached through traditional media, e-commerce, or one-to-one selling is less important than the contribution to profits that these elements make.

Remember that promotion is a powerful and versatile tool in the marketing arsenal. Promotions can be successfully implemented to achieve both transactional and relationship goals. By understanding this and identifying the life-cycle stage a brand is experiencing (remember the spiral in Chapter 3), skillful marketers can maximize the effectiveness of promotions within the overall marketing mix.

Another notable change in recent years in sales promotion is the concept that promotion, like advertising, must contribute to brand image and brand equity. Astute marketers reject the idea that sales promotion is intended only for a quick fix or immediate sale at any cost. Today, promotion and advertising have a complementary relationship that works to develop a seamless relationship with consumers. Not only must advertising and promotion be coordinated but also it is crucial that promotion be used in a manner that will enhance, rather than erode, brand equity.

In addition to consumer sales promotion, companies usually use some combination of trade and retail promotions to carry out overall marketing objectives. In fact, by far the largest segment of marketing communication involves trade promotions. To a significant degree, the increase in trade promotions reflects the growth of large retail chains that require national manufacturers to compete for shelf space and divert funds from promotions and advertisements that encourage consumer loyalty. The consequence of this emphasis on trade promotion is an erosion of brand equity in some product categories and an emphasis on price as the primary factor in consumer purchases.

Finally, we are beginning to see the impact of the Internet on sales promotion. Technological convergence has created new ways to reach and cultivate prospects. It also has created concerns about privacy, the practicality of permission marketing, and how to deal with growing trends toward consumer opt-out programs. We may not be able to predict the twists and turns of new and old media, but as we see the growth in online couponing, sweepstakes, and games accessed through the computer and electronic versions of the Yellow Pages, it is certain that advertising and promotion will never be the same.

REVIEW

1. Contrast sales promotion and advertising.
2. What is the primary disadvantage of sales promotion?
3. What are the major advantages and disadvantages of event marketing?
4. What are the primary purposes of co-op advertising?
5. What is the primary regulation of co-op?
6. Why is point-of-purchase advertising so important to many advertisers?

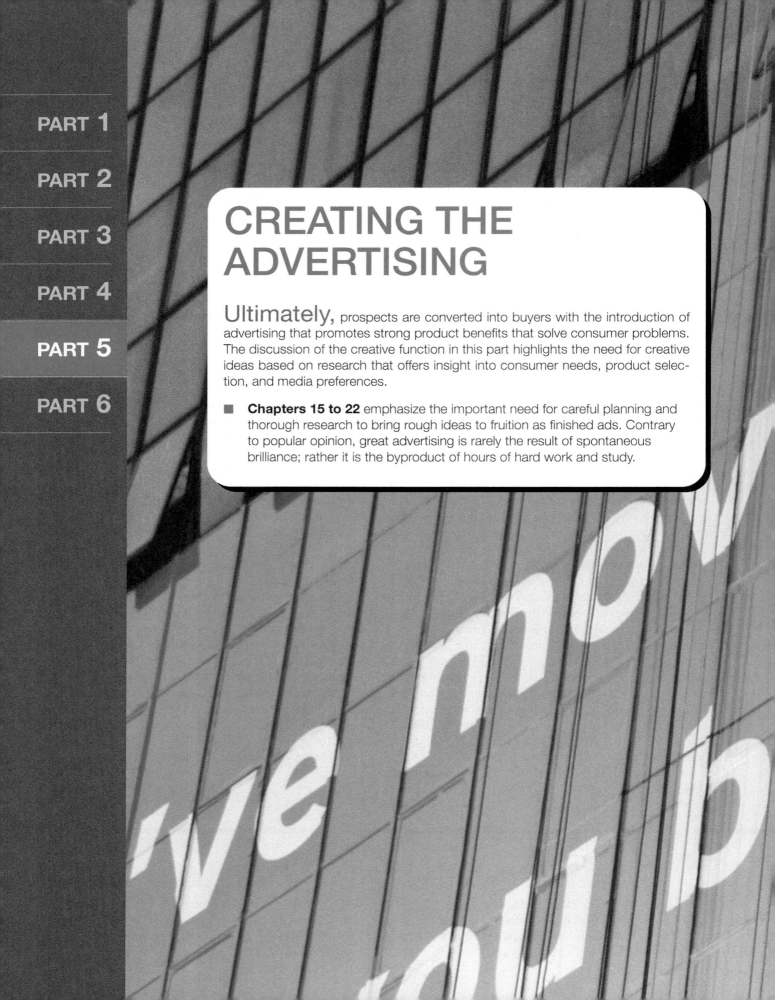

PART 1

PART 2

PART 3

PART 4

PART 5

PART 6

CREATING THE ADVERTISING

Ultimately, prospects are converted into buyers with the introduction of advertising that promotes strong product benefits that solve consumer problems. The discussion of the creative function in this part highlights the need for creative ideas based on research that offers insight into consumer needs, product selection, and media preferences.

■ **Chapters 15 to 22** emphasize the important need for careful planning and thorough research to bring rough ideas to fruition as finished ads. Contrary to popular opinion, great advertising is rarely the result of spontaneous brilliance; rather it is the byproduct of hours of hard work and study.

We make it like you'd make it.

The all-natural goodness of ripe tomatoes and fresh basil.
Just what you'd put in your homemade sauce.

classico.com

Courtesy of Heinz.

KLEPPNER VIEWPOINT 15.1

Robert Passikoff, Ph.D. Founder and President,
Brand Keys, Inc.

Co-author of *The Certainty Principle: How to Guarantee Brand Profits in the Consumer Engagement Marketplace*

DEFINING "BRAND EQUITY" AND "ENGAGEMENT"

Engagement's been a tough metric for marketers to define. It's tougher if you insist, as Brand Keys does, on a behavior-centric view based on something positive actually happening to the brand.

Engagement with the brand is the ultimate objective. Nothing substitutes for it; nothing else ensures brand survival. Yes, brands need to employ outreach of all kinds—conversations, experiences, advertising, and every touch point possible—and that outreach requires engagement also. But that's not engagement with the brand. That's engagement with *the method* the brand is using to get the consumer to engage with the brand. Ultimately, there are four engagement methods: (1) platform (TV, online, print, sponsorship), (2) context (program, web page, magazine, game), (3) message (ad or communication), and (4) experience (store or event). But there is only one objective: brand engagement.

We define *brand equity* as the brand's strengths compared to the consumer's ideal. How well does the brand meet—or even exceed—expectations for the drivers of the category in which it competes? That definition is a leading indicator of profits. The stronger the brand is seen as versus the ideal, the

more sales result. Always. "Engagement," then, logically can be defined as the *consequence* of any marketing or communication effort that results in an increased level of brand equity for the product or service.

This is our working definition, and it was the definition we provided to a consortium of representatives of the Advertising Research Foundation, the Association of National Advertisers, and the American Association of Advertising Agencies, seeking to define the anatomy of engagement.

Definitions offered up by the major media and client companies ranged from "awareness" to "time spent," and from "visitors per month" to "positive attitudes." Definitions included "relevance" and "the consumer connection," "getting the right message in front of the right audience at the right time" and "the audience (remaining) at the commercial break." Our word-of-mouth brethren suggested, "buzz was an indicator, a form, and a result of engagement," forgetting that buzz comes in two frequencies: good *and* bad!

Only Brand Keys advocated a direct relationship between engagement and positive consumer behavior and sales. ARF president, Bob Barocci, offered the

Robert Passikoff

only other definition that tied engagement to commerce: "A prospect's interaction with a marketing communication in a way that can be proven to be predictive of sales effects."

Any definition that does not mention positive marketplace behavior or sales or profitability is not talking about real *brand* engagement but probably simply about methods that drew a consumer's attention to a brand. Cool platforms running hot programming with funny ads can get the brand attention—and that's why definitions about engagement from a media and advertising perspective are so loosely tied to in-market performance, if at all. Breakthrough is not engagement. Neither is entertainment. Virtually anything about the brand and its planned activities can be measured for the level of engagement it *will* produce, predictively and in advance of spend, with absolute certainty. You simply have to define your terms properly.

Courtesy of Robert Passikoff, Ph.D.

The Right Kind of Research

The kind of research and how much research is needed are always legitimate questions. And there are dangers. Former chair of Roper Starch Worldwide's Roper division commented on a classic failure—the Ford's Edsel—and the misuse of research. In the case of the Edsel automobile, the research was used to make people believe something that wasn't true, not to design a product to meet consumers' tastes. Ford designed a powerful, flashy car with a horse-collar grille before doing any consumer research. After the car was designed, research found consumers wanted a quietly styled, conservative, American-made, Mercedes-Benz-like vehicle. Ford then tried to make consumers fit the car by marketing Edsel as a conservatively styled automobile. It generated interest, but when consumers saw the car they were disappointed.

However, Roper cited the launch of new Coca-Cola in the 1980s as an example of research overreliance and overkill. In several taste tests, new Coca-Cola beat Pepsi, but other studies showed that sweeter products often are preferred initially. In-house and outside research for Coca-Cola failed because it didn't run normal usage taste tests on consumers. If the researchers had given consumers a case of new Coca-Cola and asked them what they thought 2 or 3 weeks later, more accurate responses would likely have been generated. Roper concluded that marketers shouldn't always follow the findings of a research study, whether it be a consumer-products study or a political campaign. There are dangers despite the potential rewards.

Account/Brand Planners and Consumer Insights

2 **Explain the role of the account planner.**

account planner
An outgrowth of the British agency structure in which a planner initiates and reviews research and participates in the creative process. In some agencies, the planner is considered a spokesperson for the consumer.

A British concept of research has become fundamental for many worldwide agencies. In the 1980s, some U.S. agencies moved toward copying the British restructuring of the research department. British agencies found clients doing much of their own research, yet the agency research function remained necessary to understand the information on consumers and the marketplace. The agencies restructured or reduced the size of their research departments and added **account planners**. Their task was to discern not only who buys specific brands but also why. The account planners are usually responsible for all research including quantitative research (usage and attitude studies, tracking studies, advertisement testing, and sales data) as well as qualitative research (talking face-to-face with their target audiences). See Exhibit 15.2.

Account planning is based on a simple premise. A client hires an advertising agency to interpret its brand to its target audience. The account planner is charged with understanding the target audience and then representing it throughout the entire advertising development process, thereby ensuring that the advertising is both strategically and executionally relevant to the defined target. The account planner sorts through the multiple layers that develop around marketing a brand, eliminating the irrelevant and highlighting the relevant. According to British account planning guru Chris Crowpe, "Account Planning is the discipline that brings the consumer into the process of developing advertising. To be truly effective, advertising must be both distinctive and relevant, *and* planning helps on both counts."[2]

Jon Steel says, "If the agency has a true planning philosophy, it is interested in only one thing, and that is getting it right for its clients."[3] Account planning plays a crucial role during strategy development, driving it from the consumer's point of view. During creative development, account planners act as sounding boards for the creative team. They are responsible for researching the advertising before production to ensure it is as relevant as it can be; and finally, once the work is complete, they monitor its effect in depth with a view to improving it the next time around.

The key benefit account planners contribute to the creative teams is usable research—they provide information that explains and communicates, giving the creatives useful insights. The key benefit to clients is a consumer-focused advertising strategy that speaks directly to the target audience in a persuasive way. According to Dr. Greg Nyilasy, senior research and development executive at Hall & Partners, "Research at its best is the highest-grade fuel for brand building imagination, it can add enormously to the creative product itself, and it was the greatest tool to break through the

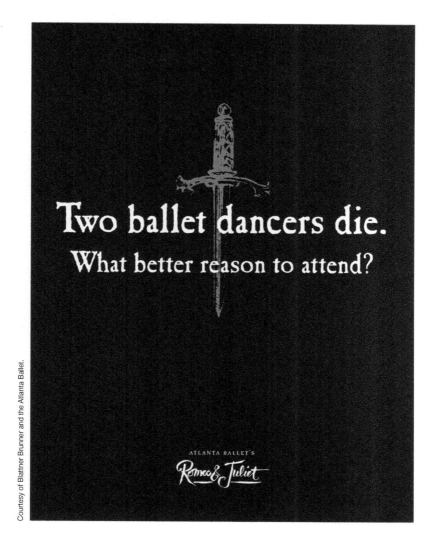

Courtesy of Blattner Brunner and the Atlanta Ballet.

EXHIBIT 15.2

What consumer insight might have lead to the creation of this ad?

subjectivity of any one decision maker and enter the consumer's mind, the most important one in the whole marketing communications game."

Because many marketers direct much of the needed research themselves, the agency is not necessarily a partner in planning the type and direction of research studies conducted for a specific brand or company. However, agency researchers or planners are available to the account groups to help them get the needed information and may be involved in all kinds of advertising research.

The account planners work with account management, media, and creative, covering most research functions. They are more like partners to the account and creative teams than traditional researchers. The planner is considered the team's spokesperson for the consumer and an interpreter of available research. To work, advertising must deeply understand, empathize with, and speak the same language as the consumer (see Exhibit 15.3).

What Kind of Research Is Needed?

Now that we have a better understanding of the research structure, let us look at the kinds of research available and some specific examples. Keep in mind that marketing has become far more complex than it was in the past because of the tremendous increase in new products, the high cost of shelf space, the expansion of retailer control

3 **Understand anthropology, sociology, and psychology as they relate to advertising.**

EXHIBIT 15.3

What consumer insight likely drove the development of this ad?

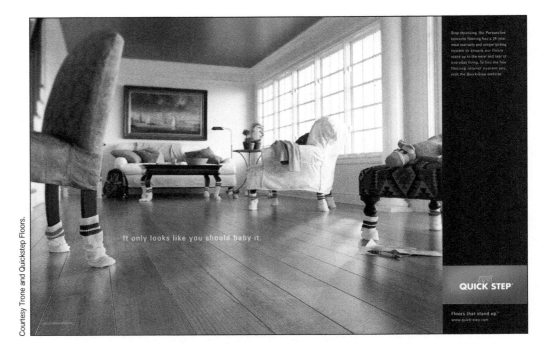

Courtesy Trone and Quickstep Floors.

It only looks like you should baby it.

over the distribution system, changing media habits, overload of information, and the bewildering array of communication choices.

Marketing research—up-front research—tells us about the product, the market, the consumer, and the competition. There are four basic considerations in any market research undertaking: (1) maintaining a consumer-behavior perspective; (2) being sure the right questions are asked; (3) using appropriate research techniques and controls; and (4) presenting the research findings in a clear, comprehensible format that leads to action. After completing market research, we do advertising research—principally pretesting advertisements and evaluating the campaign—to get the data we need to develop and refine an advertising strategy and message. The behavioral sciences—anthropology, sociology, and psychology—have had a strong influence on up-front research.

ANTHROPOLOGY AND ADVERTISING

4 Discuss values, lifestyle, and life-stage research.

Today, marketers employ anthropologists and ethnographers who use direct observation to understand consumer behavior. They study the emotional connection between products and consumer values. When Warner-Lambert wanted to find out what consumers thought of Fresh Burst Listerine, a mint-flavored product designed to compete with Scope, they paid families to set up cameras in their bathrooms and film their routines around the sink. Users of both brands said they used mouthwash to make their breath smell good, but they treated their products differently. Users of Scope typically swished and spat it out. Devotees of the new Listerine felt obliged to keep the mouthwash in their mouths longer; one went so far as to keep it in his mouth until he got to his car. (See Kleppner Viewpoint 15.2 for another example of observing consumers.)

Ogilvy & Mather's Discovery Group has used cameras to record observations of consumers. It sent researchers with handheld cameras into homes to get up-close pictures of how people behave in various aspects of their lives. Hours of footage were then condensed into documentary-like 30-minute videos that gave marketers and agency staff the chance to see how people really communicate and interact in certain situations. The videos may give marketers a clearer sense of how people use their products and what their motivations are, which in turn can influence marketing decisions and help craft creative strategy.[4]

Anthropologists have found that certain needs and activities are common to people the world over. Body adornment, cooking, courtship, food taboos, gift giving, language, marriage, status, sex, the meaning of various colors, and superstitions are present

KLEPPNER VIEWPOINT 15.2

Brad Majors Former CEO, SOCOH Marketing LLC,
and Senior Vice President, Lintas Worldwide

LESSONS IN BRAND LOYALTY AT THE POINT OF SALE

Brad Majors

confess—I'm a stalker. Not the kind that makes women nervous. The kind that bothers store managers.

I stalk people shopping for goods and services. And when watching them doesn't answer my questions about their purchasing decision processes, I ask questions. Generally speaking, I only question friends and acquaintances, so don't worry about being accosted in a store when all you want to do is buy shampoo in peace.

Are people brand loyal and if so, why? How much more will they pay for one brand before they select another? What would make them try another brand? Unfortunately, we marketers are learning that buyers are much less loyal than we would like them to be.

Here's an example. Traditional marketing wisdom holds that brand preferences are formed early in life, when consumers are young and willing to experiment. As consumers age, they become more loyal to brands that perform according to their expectations. Thus, if anyone in a brand's franchise is loyal, it's the seniors.

The Roper Report's Public Pulse (April 2002) explored "The Myth of Brand Loyalty and the Reality." Roper looked for loyalty patterns among categories and age groups and found some behavior worth noting. One of their key findings was that "categories themselves drive brand loyalty a lot more than age does." In fact, Roper makes the point that older consumers have a certain savvy gained by their many life experiences, making them more inquisitive and adventurous regarding brand choices. The double whammy is that many seniors now have enormous disposable income. Losing them when they have all that money to spend hurts twice as much.

That brings me to Gloria, my neighbor. She's a senior and as savvy as the Roper folks say she is. We went shopping together Friday night, as we do from time to time. As I pushed my cart around the store to cover my stalking behavior, I watched different people read packaging copy, examine in-store displays, and make their brand choices. I kept an eye on Gloria as she considered various brands of ice cream, studying flavors and ingredient information on the packages. After she made her decision, I asked what had influenced her choice. "Well, I knew I wanted peach ice cream and usually get Breyers," she said. "But I've heard that Mayfield was very good and wanted to try their peach flavor." Sorry, Breyers, but don't take Gloria and her money for granted. She's enjoyed your product for years, but not without a regular assessment of its value.

In addition to that new brand trial, the raspberry vinaigrette flavor offered by Ken's Steakhouse intrigued Gloria enough for her to ignore her usual Wish-bone and Kraft salad dressings. And recently, Gloria tried an alternative cleaning product, OxiClean, because of its multipurpose flexibility and its advertised stain-removing claims. This is particularly interesting because Roper says that household cleaning products have traditionally had high brand loyalty among seniors. Well, they better not depend on Gloria to stick with those brands when something new just might work better.

Quantitative studies can tell us a lot about brand loyalty. They're a valuable tool for marketers. However, nothing beats observing real shoppers in the selling environment. This adds a human face to the insights of that research. You can take this a step further—instead of critiquing the ads you see on TV or in magazines, try withholding your own assessment and, instead, simply watch the reactions of others as they review the advertisements. You might be surprised at what you see and hear.

Courtesy of Brad Majors.

in all societies, although each society attaches its own values and traditions to them. Anthropologists see the United States as a pluralistic society made up of an array of subcultures. In each subculture lives a different group of people who share its values, customs, and traditions. Think about the cultural differences among Italian, Polish, African American, and Hispanic populations as a starting point.

EXHIBIT 15.4

The ad on the left announces that "Heinz Ketchup has a Kosher certificate." The ad on the right says that the brand has a "A taste that kids would love."

We are all aware of regional differences in the English language in the United States. For example, a sandwich made of several ingredients in a small loaf of bread is a "poor boy" in New Orleans, a "submarine" in Boston, a "hoagie" in Philadelphia, and a "grinder" in upstate New York. Geomarketing allows advertisers to use these cultural differences in food preferences, terminology, and subgroup identities when they advertise their products. See Exhibit 15.4 (a and b).

SOCIOLOGY AND ADVERTISING

Sociology examines the structure and function of organized behavior systems. The sociologist studies groups and their influence on and interaction with the individual. Advertisers recognize group influences on the adoption of new ideas, media use, and consumer purchase behavior. They use sociological research to predict the profitability of a product purchase by various consumer groups.

SOCIAL CLASS AND STRATIFICATION   We are a society that is clustered into classes determined by such criteria as wealth, income, occupation, education, achievement, and seniority. We sense where we fit into this pattern. We identify with others in our social group ("these are my kind of people"), and we generally conform to the standards of our group. Experienced advertisers have recognized that people's aspirations usually take on the flavor of the social group immediately above their own. It is important to remember that the state of the economy can have a big impact on consumption patterns of even the most affluent consumers. (See Viewpoint 15.3.)

Social-group structure helps explain why demographic categories sometimes fail to provide helpful information about consumers. A professional person and a factory worker may have the same income, but that doesn't mean their interests in products will coincide. In today's marketing environment, research has shown that no single variable, for example, age, income, or sex, will accurately predict consumer purchases. Advertisers have discovered that using several variables gives a more accurate prediction of consumer behavior. Think of the differences between homemakers and working women of the same age, income, and education in their food preferences for themselves and their families, usage of convenience goods, child care, and media habits.

TREND WATCHING Quantitative research is as important as ever, but there seems to be a premium on nuggets of more attitudinal, psychographic market smarts with which marketers hope to base the creative approach to their communication.

Trends come from all forms of media and advertising. They come from music, from politics, from travel, and from the Internet. They develop everywhere. Fads, however, are like crushes; they burn fast and hot but die quickly and often leave a bitter taste. Pokémon cards, the Macarena and Beanie Babies represented fads that came and went quickly. Trends are a product of society. They reflect our changing attitudes, behaviors, and values. They are the most obvious and most concrete signs of the times. Trends can be of two sizes: macro and micro.

Macrotrends are about the "big issues"—our definitions of happiness, success, and fulfillment. Macrotrends develop from the way people think. They emerge when people feel dissatisfaction with the status quo in their own lives and in society. They announce our new definitions of happiness. Some of the neotraditionalism is reflected in the return to traditions—people setting new priorities in the balance among work, family, and friends.

Microtrends are the details in the big picture. They are the tangible manifestations of the macrotrends in fashion, music, and sports activities. For example, the macrotrend of neotraditionalism will foster microtrends such as cooking schools cropping up as members of the microwave generation try to behave like their grandparents and throw dinner parties.

Generally, young people set trends, but not every young person is a trendsetter. Those most comfortable on the cutting edge are the ones called *early adopters*, *trendsetters*, *leading edgers*, and *innovators*, and all these terms mean the same thing. These are the people who are willing to experiment. Not all trends will work for a brand. Yet, look at what Mountain Dew did by using extreme sports and over-the-top imagery to become the extreme brand despite being around for more than 30 years. Many companies spend a lot of money trying to track trends. Are coffee shops such as Starbucks fads or trends? (See Exhibit 15.5.)

COHORT ANALYSIS Using a research technique called *cohort analysis*, marketers can assess consumers' lifelong values and preferences and develop strategies now for products these consumers will use later in life. Cohorts are generations of people with the same birth years and core values. According to advertising executive Natalie Perkins, these values are formed by significant events between the ages of 13 and 20 and endure throughout one's life. For example, such events as the Great Depression, the Korean War, the Vietnam War, the sexual revolution, the Gulf War, and the war in Iraq, or the influence of Martin Luther King Jr., McCarthyism, television, computers, divorced and single families, and environmental crises can form a value system.

Generally, we study consumers using demographics, psychographics, lifestyles, and behaviors. Cohort analysis combines these data and adds to the consumer profile by examining the past as well as the present. By identifying a generation's collective hot buttons, mores, and memories, advertisers can hone messages and create persuasive icons to better attract that generation.[5] This kind of research can aid in developing a product marketing plan that follows the lifetime of a consumer.

LIFE-STAGE RESEARCH Advertisers have traditionally considered the family as the basic unit of buying behavior. Most traditional households pass through an orderly progression of stages, and each stage has special significance for buying behavior.

KLEPPNER VIEWPOINT 15.3

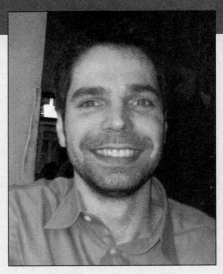

Greg Nyilasy

Greg Nyilasy, Ph.D. Senior Research and Development Executive, Hall & Partners New York Communication and Brand Research (www.hall-and-partners.com)

RECESSIONARY REASSESSMENT

Unprecedented. Catastrophic. Once-in-a-century. Adjectives are piling up in media reports to describe the economic crisis that began in the latter half of 2008. Consumer behavior, marketing, and advertising are experiencing significant changes as a result of the economic crisis. Hall & Partners was among the first to invest in an ongoing research and development (R&D) project about the recession. We wanted to make sure we keep our clients as close as possible to the cutting edge of changes in consumer attitudes and behavior. Although it always has been the case, now with the volatility we see, it's indeed a question of life and death for marketers to stay tuned in.

So what have we discovered through this research? The current mind-set of consumers is best described as panicky:

- **Young adults don't know what to expect.** The promises and rules that young adults lived by are coming into question. They believe they are entitled to a good job and the "good life." When the implicit promises do not turn into reality (because of a tightening job market and narrowing opportunities), they are surprised and disappointed.
- **Gen Xers are used to uncertainty.** Gen Xers are accustomed to extreme volatility and ambiguity. They have time to recover until retirement, but they see the future as chaotic. Some see new opportunities (to start new businesses, buy cheap assets, etc.), but others are reluctant to take additional risks and choose to "stay put" instead.
- **Boomers are especially scared and angry and they are running out of time.** The boomers can't retire because their investments have been hit hard by the crisis. Increasing health care expenses (despite the general deflation scare) are a prime concern. Some have both children and elderly parents depending on them.
- **The elderly are used to being frugal but worry about their kids.** The elderly believe that this recession is going to be as deep and long as the Great Depression. Although they worry about their children and grandchildren, they also remember that time fondly: What mattered was spending time with friends and family and memorable experiences; a sense of community and pulling together.

family life cycle
Concept that demonstrates changing purchasing behavior as a person or a family matures.

Knowledge of the **family life cycle** allows a company to segment the market and the advertising appeal according to specific consumption patterns and groups. Of course, the concept of the family has significantly changed over the past decades. Yet, there are still crucial points in the lives of consumers—they leave home, get married or stay unmarried, bear children, raise children, and launch adult children into lives of their own. As a result of these life transitions, people suddenly or gradually go from one stage of life to another.

According to census data, the nature of the traditional family life cycle has changed in the past 30 years. For example, people are waiting longer to get married, women are postponing childbearing, the incidence of divorce has multiplied, the proportion of single-parent households has significantly increased, and more young adults are living with their parents than in the past. As a result, some advertisers have reevaluated the way they look at the family life cycle. By examining these segments' subgroups, advertisers begin to get a clearer picture of buying behavior and lifestyles. Researchers refer to these subgroup studies as *life-stage research*. As with the family life cycle, life-stage research examines the crucial points in consumers' lives. Advertisers can find syndicated

- **Some of us do feel stable—for now.** People with recession-proof jobs (in health care, some forms of education, or government, for example) feel safe. They have stable, predictable incomes. One traumatic event (unexpected job loss, illness, family trouble) can tip them out of stability.

So how do consumers react to the panic they are experiencing? We started to track five key trends, some of which, in fact, appeared way before the current crisis:

1. **Consumers are delaying big purchases.** This is particularly acute in big-ticket categories (cars, electronics, and other expensive durables). Consumers are putting off unnecessary upgrades, planning to "leap-frog" a few versions.

2. **Consumers are weighing options more deliberately.** The sphere of impulse buying and whimsical shopping is narrowing. Consumers are more cautious and conscious about how they spend their tightening budgets (the lack of easy credit is also a key driver of this readjustment). The concept of value (the most benefits for the cheapest price) is coming to the foreground.

3. **Consumers are bargaining at the point of sale.** The redefinition of value means that consumers are more proactive than ever—comparing, selecting, and cherry-picking. They take pride in finding ways to get more for their money. They are rediscovering a set of "recessionary shopping" behaviors: coupon clipping, buying in bulk, trying out sample sizes, and buying private labels.

4. **We're bonding; we are all in this together.** Even if we're not personally affected, we want to fit in and be seen as sensitive to others. Conspicuous consumption is perceived as vulgar. Consumers take pride in "good housekeeping": In-house consumption and entertainment are in. We want to share tips and ideas for saving; we feel like we are part of something positive and inclusive.

5. **Consumers are still indulging in small pleasures.** Indulging provides a sense of relief from bad news and the unforgiving economic necessity of trading down. Indulgence is a rebellion against the new constraints. We splurge on small things: lipstick, a manicure, ice cream, wine, takeout food, and reduced-price getaways.

What do all these changes in consumer attitudes and behaviors mean for brands and marketers? Consumers don't want to lose the brands they love. It is more important than ever for marketers to stay close to their consumers. It is imperative for brands to

- Clearly define what they stand for: proven quality, distinctiveness, and meaningfulness. The redefinition of value is a necessity for many.
- Demonstrate shared values with their consumers: a deep understanding and realignment with shifts to the "new normal" in consumer behavior.
- Reestablish trust in an era of skepticism toward and disappointment in big business.
- Have real conversations with people: allowing a two-way flow of communication, potentially using the social media space.

The winners in this recession (and the subsequent recovery) are brands that really understand their consumers through intelligent research and sensitivity and engage them through relevant conversations.

Courtesy of Greg Nyilasy, Ph.D.

research services that analyze young singles, newlyweds, young couples, mature couples, and teenage households. Advertisers need knowledge of the life stages to help them develop and understand the changes taking place today in the twenty-first century so they can create more effective integrated marketing communications (see Exhibit 15.6).

CONSUMPTION RESEARCH   Advertisers often find it useful to study consumers' consumption patterns to help them learn more about their target audience. Recently, politicians have also studied these personal buying habits in an effort to determine where they can find higher concentrations of likely supporters. This can give them insight into where to focus their advertising efforts. According to the *International Herald Tribune*, some political strategists, including those working for former president George Bush and California governor Arnold Schwarzenegger, believe that this type of research can tell more than their party label about a voter's political views. "In simplest terms: A homeowner who drives a Volvo, reads the *New Yorker* and shops at Whole Foods Market is likely to lean Democratic. A pickup driver with a hunting and fishing license who reads *Time* magazine probably leans to the right."[6]

EXHIBIT 15.5

What trend do you think this ad is trying to tap into?

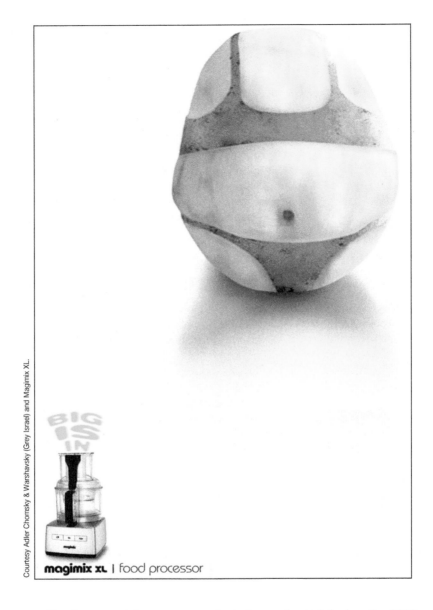

Courtesy Adler Chomsky & Warshavsky (Grey Israel) and Magimix XL.

magimix XL | food processor

By the same token, a research study conducted during the 2008 presidential campaign, "2008 Presidential Image Power Survey," found that voters associated certain specific brands with the candidates. John McCain was associated with AOL, Ford, Wal-Mart, and Jack Bauer (from the television series *24*). Voters associated Barak Obama with Google, BMW, Target, and James Bond.[7]

Research has also examined consumption patterns of some consumer groups based on their stage of acculturation. For example, Spectra Marketing has developed a consumption-driven model called the Culture Point Model™ to identify three consumer segments in the U.S. Hispanic population. These three groups are called: least acculturated, most acculturated, and bi-cultural. Using a combination of demographic variables including income, age, and language preference, marketers can explore variations in consumption patterns among these groups to help identify message strategies for each group.[8]

PSYCHOLOGY AND ADVERTISING

Psychology is the study of human behavior and its causes. Three psychological concepts of importance to consumer behavior are motivation, cognition, and learning. *Motivation*

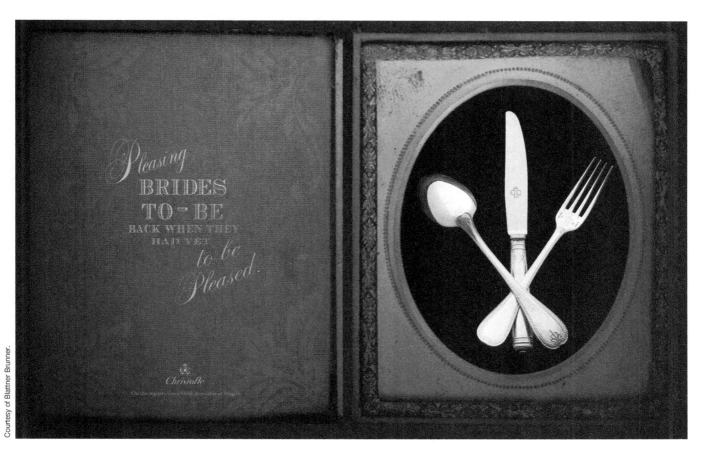

EXHIBIT 15.6

An advertiser may test the power of this lifestyle appeal.

refers to the drives, urges, wishes, or desires that initiate the sequence of events known as "behavior." *Cognition* is the area in which all the mental phenomena (perception, memory, judging, thinking, and so on) are grouped. *Learning* refers to those changes in behavior relative to external stimulus conditions that occur over time.[9] These three factors, working within the framework of the societal environment, create the psychological basis for consumer behavior. Advertising research is interested in cognitive elements to learn how consumers react to different stimuli, and research finds learning especially important in determining factors such as appropriate advertising frequency levels. However, in recent years, the major application of psychology to advertising has been the attempt to understand the underlying motives that initiate consumer behavior. Companies are also interested in studying emotions.

Barry Goldbatt, marketing director at Trojan, states that his company is increasing their use of clinical psychologists, psychiatrists, and cultural anthropologists to moderate focus groups because of the sensitive nature of their product category and the tendency of consumers to lie when talking about it. Goldbatt says, "You've got to be a very special person to discuss the subject matter and not pass judgement."[10]

VALUES AND LIFESTYLES   The research company that popularized psychographic segmentation developed Values and LifeStyle (VALS™) classification system. SRI Consulting Business Intelligence's VALS is designed to predict consumer behavior by profiling the psychology and demographics of U.S. consumers. It segments respondents into eight clusters of consumers, each with distinct behavioral and decision-making patterns that reflect different primary motivations and available psychological and material resources

VALS classifies consumers along two key dimensions: primary motivation (what in particular about the person or the world governs his or her actions and activities) and resources (the range of psychological and material resources available to sustain that self-concept).[11]

This classification takes into account an individual's primary motivation, such as ideals, achievement, or self-expression. Resources, however, include both material and acquired attributes (e.g., money, position, education) as well as psychological qualities (e.g., inventiveness, interpersonal skills, intelligence, energy). (See Exhibit 15.7.)

According to VALS, an individual purchases certain products and services because he or she is a specific type of person. VALS is a network of interconnected segments. Neighboring types have similar characteristics and can be combined in varying ways to suit particular marketing purposes.

Advertisers can use the VALS typology to segment particular markets, develop marketing strategies, refine product concepts, position products and services, develop advertising and media campaigns, and guide long-range planning.

EXHIBIT 15.7

VALS Lifestyle Categories

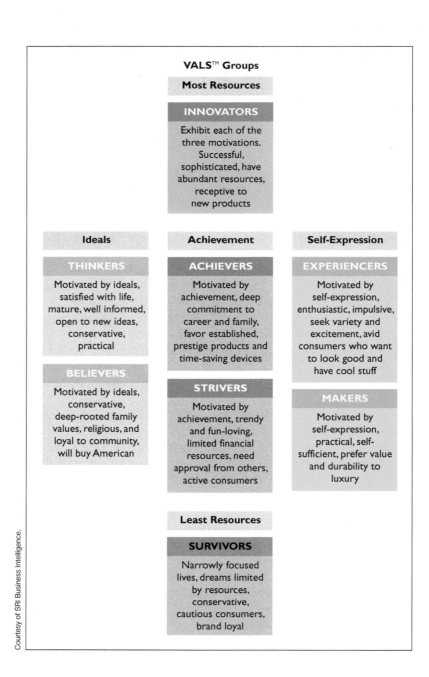

Courtesy of SRI Business Intelligence.

VALS™ Groups

Most Resources

INNOVATORS

Exhibit each of the three motivations. Successful, sophisticated, have abundant resources, receptive to new products

Ideals

THINKERS

Motivated by ideals, satisfied with life, mature, well informed, open to new ideas, conservative, practical

BELIEVERS

Motivated by ideals, conservative, deep-rooted family values, religious, and loyal to community, will buy American

Achievement

ACHIEVERS

Motivated by achievement, deep commitment to career and family, favor established, prestige products and time-saving devices

STRIVERS

Motivated by achievement, trendy and fun-loving, limited financial resources, need approval from others, active consumers

Self-Expression

EXPERIENCERS

Motivated by self-expression, enthusiastic, impulsive, seek variety and excitement, avid consumers who want to look good and have cool stuff

MAKERS

Motivated by self-expression, practical, self-sufficient, prefer value and durability to luxury

Least Resources

SURVIVORS

Narrowly focused lives, dreams limited by resources, conservative, cautious consumers, brand loyal

Yankelovich's MindBase, a segmenting tool, identified eight major consumer groups with shared life attitudes and motivations and an understanding of consumers' generational cohorts. These eight groups are each divided into three subgroups that reflect distinctions in how they react in the marketplace and to marketers' efforts. Here are the eight major MindBase segments:[12]

- I am Expressive.
- I am Driven.
- I am at Capacity.
- I am Rock Steady.
- I am Down to Earth.
- I am Sophisticated.
- I Measure Twice.
- I am Devoted.

See if you can tell to which Mindbase segment this ad for Lifesavers would appeal. (See Exhibit 15.8).

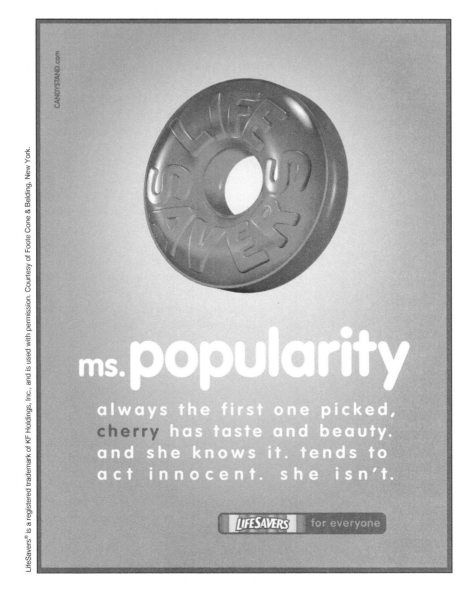

EXHIBIT 15.8

To which MindBase segments do you think this ad would appeal?

BIOMETRIC RESEARCH

Marketers have explored the use of physiological measures such as galvanic skin response, eye movements, and pulse rates to better understand consumers for a number of years. Recently, as a result of the slowing economy, they have increased their use of physiological measures and have begun exploring the use of brain wave research. Although this research may sound Orwellian at first blush, according to Harvard professor Gerald Zaltman, brain wave research involves trying to understand consumer motivation and not simply inserting "ideas into people's thinking."[13] The theory behind this type of research is that it can provide marketers with an honest consumer reaction to a product or an advertisement.

According to Frank Stagliano, executive vice president for the Nielsen Entertainment Television Group in New York, "In many ways, we're testing advertising the way we were testing advertising when I was at Procter & Gamble 22 years ago." Neuroscience can provide "a more accurate way to understand what consumers really like," Mr. Stagliano said, which helps to produce ads that "break through the clutter" rather than contribute to it.[14]

With the help of neuroscientists, marketers can use a functional magnetic resonance imaging (fMRI) scanner to determine how much oxygen different parts of the brain use when a person is exposed to an advertisement or a product. Different colors show up on the scan depending on which part of the brain is stimulated with thought. Electroencephalograms (EEGs) also are used by some marketers to monitor consumers' brain activity while they are viewing advertisements. Through a special cap worn by subjects, the EEG measures electrical impulses produced by the brain. EEGs can be used to assess reactions to all or parts of a commercial message because different parts of the brain react to attraction, revulsion, recall, and level of attention, for instance. However, it can be difficult to interpret what this activity means.[15]

electroencephalography
The recording of the brain's electrical activity via electrodes placed on the scalp.

According to author and advertising industry expert Martin Lindstrom, physiological measures such as **electroencephalography** can be used to measure sensitive brainwaves to help determine consumers' emotional engagement. In describing how he and his team used EEG data to help determine the effectiveness of product placements in the popular *American Idol* television program, Lindstrom says, "Using this method, we would be able to measure how interested consumers were in what they were watching. We could find out what penetrated their long-term memories and what attracted or repelled them." The researchers determined that Coca-Cola did well; the Ford placement did not do well and the placement almost seemed to have a negative effect on the brand.[16]

In another application of neuroscience, Google and MediaVest used the Nielsen Company's NeuroFocus research unit to investigate the effectiveness of overlay ads appearing in YouTube videos at grabbing consumers' attention and boosting brand awareness. The measures used in this assessment included measures of brainwave activity, eye tracking, and skin response. The videos were rated based on multiple criteria including attention level, emotional engagement, and memory retention.[17]

These kinds of tests can be very costly. EEGs are comparatively less expensive than fMRI scanners. According to Caroline Winnett, vice president of marketing for NeuroFocus, these tests cost about the same as a typical focus group.[18]

MARKETING ENVIRONMENT

Companies and agencies want to accumulate as much information about their markets as possible before making crucial integrated marketing decisions. Technology has been assisting marketers in getting more information faster.

UNIVERSAL PRODUCT CODE   Universal product code (UPC) information has greatly enhanced the process of tracking product sales. When the grocer scans a price into the register at the checkout, that information is instantly available to the retailer. Scanner reporting systems have allowed marketers to track their performance quickly—rather than monthly or bimonthly—and at local levels. UPC information allows marketers to determine what their share of the market is, if one kind of packaging or in-store advertising sells better, and which retailers sell the most units. Grocery store rewards cards can be scanned into the system to keep a record of what kind of products consumers buy. This offers the retailer and manufacturer the opportunity to target promotions directly to people who have used the product in the past. This information can contribute to any database marketing effort by the retailer.

SINGLE-SOURCE DATA   For single-source data, retail tracking scanner data are integrated with household panel data on purchase patterns and advertisement exposure. The information comes from one supplier and is extracted from a single group of consumers. These data can be combined with other research sources to supply micro-marketers with a wealth of information on who, what, and how. Despite these micromarketing capabilities, research firms are far more adept at generating data than most clients are at using the information.

DATABASE MARKETERS   Database marketers use sweepstakes entries, rebate information, merchandise orders, free-product offers, requests for new-product information, and purchase information to build consumer databases telling them a great deal about how consumers live. This information offers many opportunities for database marketing (see Exhibit 15.9).

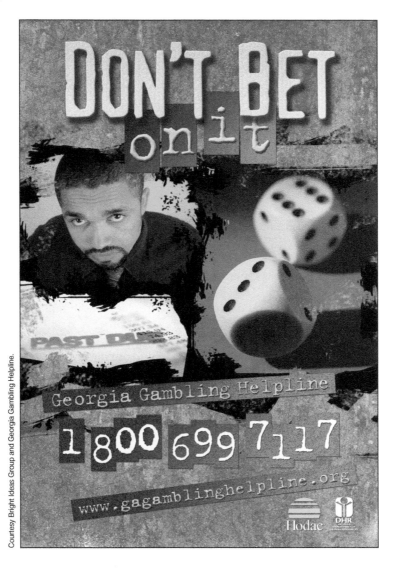

Courtesy Bright Ideas Group and Georgia Gambling Helpline.

EXHIBIT 15.9

One way to test the success of this advertisement is by evaluating the number of calls to the phone number provided.

EXHIBIT 15.10

This direct-mail piece was one in a series aimed at history buffs trying to get them to vacation in Georgia and explore the state's heritage. What are two ways that you could test the effectiveness of this direct-mail ad?

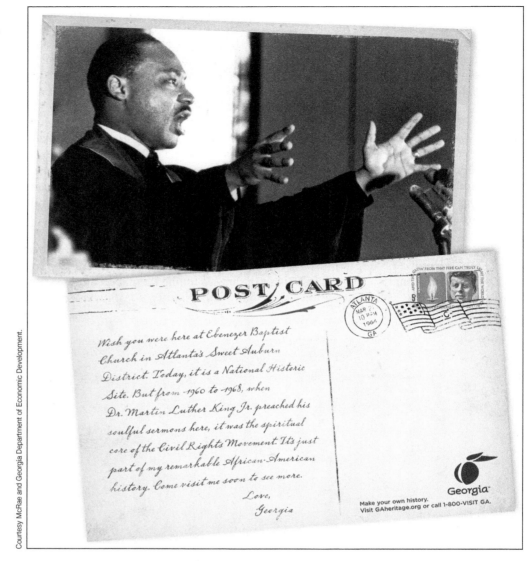

Courtesy McRae and Georgia Department of Economic Development.

INTERNET DATA Many advertisers and research companies have embraced the Internet for online focus groups, surveys, and other marketing research, despite the Internet's flaws and problems (e.g., how representative web users are of the overall population). Online research shouldn't completely replace traditional marketing research, but harnessing the Internet improves the research process. Web-based research should be part of the mix (see Exhibit 15.10).

Online surveys have been used to find out more about brands and products but also to gain insight into how consumers use different media. For example, the digital and market design company Razorfish conducted an online survey of digital moms to find out more about how they were using the Internet for themselves and their kids. Based on this survey, Razorfish learned that mothers' use of the Internet was primarily for themselves and secondarily for their children. According to Terri Walker, vice president of emerging media at Razorfish, "They're most interested in fashion and food, regardless of age, and their use of online video, blogs and DVRs have become mainstream, in the 29 percent to 36 percent range, while podcasting, RSS feeds and mobile-web browsing remain niche channels, used by 10 percent to 21 percent of respondents."[19]

Advertisers can also learn a lot about consumers from searching the information available on social media sites. Monitoring online "conversations" on Facebook and Twitter, for example, can allow advertisers to "listen" in on how consumers "talk" about their brands. According to Ben Kunz, director of strategic planning at Mediassociates, "The ultimate payday for Facebook and Twitter won't come from ad insertions, but instead by mining the relationships and conversations between people. Organizations can use the resulting analytical models to learn, to design products, to serve customers, to put out fires, perhaps even to predict the future."[20]

The Series of Research Steps in Advertising

The term *advertising research* is broadly defined as including research that contributes to all four stages of the advertising process:

5 **Describe the research steps in advertising.**

1. *Advertising strategy development.* Research tries to answer many questions: Who is the market and what does it want? What is the competition we are specifying? What communication do we want our selected market to get from our advertising? How will we reach the persons selected as our market?

2. *Advertising execution development.* There are two kinds of research used at the execution stage of advertising. The first is exploratory research to stimulate the creative people and to help them know and understand the language used by consumers. The second is research to study proposed creative concepts, ideas, roughs, visuals, headlines, words, presenters, and so forth to see whether it can do what the creative strategy expects of it.

3. *Evaluating pretesting executions.* Pretesting is the stage of advertising research at which advertising ideas are tested. Partly because of the finality of much pretesting, it is the most controversial kind of advertising research.

4. *Campaign evaluation.* Campaign evaluation usually involves a tracking study to measure the performance of a campaign.

The primary goal of advertising research is to help in the process of creative development. Before we examine the research process advertisers use in developing advertising strategy for campaigns, let us get a better perspective on using research information.

TRANSLATING INFORMATION INTO STRATEGY

Information isn't enough by itself to answer marketing problems. A few years ago, Mc-Cann Erickson researcher, Jack Dempsey, said, "By itself information has no value." It acquires value only when the strategist takes "a point of view" about what the information means—a point of view that is relevant to the marketing and advertising issues. You have to get involved in all the data at your disposal and, if necessary, fill in some gaps by acquiring more information. But then you have to step back from it. The secret of effective strategy formation lies in deciding which data are important and which are not. It is a process of organizing simplicity out of complexity, for the best strategic insights are usually the very simple ones.

Take the consumer's point of view. Ask yourself what the consumer is really buying. Is he or she buying the product because of its functional benefits? How important are the psychological benefits? The corporate landscape is littered with examples of companies and industries that failed to appreciate what their consumers were really purchasing. Because of this, they defined their markets inappropriately and often disastrously. Begin with an analysis of how people behave rather than an analysis of how they feel or what they believe. You will probably get into these issues, but behavior is the foundation from which you build. And above all, try to see the world with the consumers' eyes.

MARKET, PRODUCT, COMPETITIVE, AND CONSUMER RESEARCH

Basic information is gathered and analyzed to determine the marketing strategy for a product or service, projected sales, the source of business, pricing and distribution

EXHIBIT 15.11

Situation Analysis

factors, geographic information, and how to develop data to identify the size and nature of the product category. This kind of research includes data on competitors, sales trends, packaging, advertising expenditures, and future trends. A situation analysis helps to define clearly the market in which the product or service competes (see Exhibit 15.11).

Prospect research is critical to define clearly who is expected to buy the product or service. Studies may identify users, attitudes, lifestyles, and consumption patterns—all of which identify the prime prospect.

The amounts and kinds of information required will vary according to the product category and marketing situation. Exhibit 15.12 outlines strategy choices indicated by different levels of brand trial and awareness. It is difficult to talk about strategy until you have information on awareness levels for each brand in the market. "Brand trial" will occur if what consumers know about the brand fits in with their needs and is sufficiently important or motivating. The relationship between a brand's level of awareness and its trials may be expressed as a ratio. A high ratio suggests one strategy option; a low ratio suggests another. For example, a ratio of high awareness to low trial (lower-left box of Exhibit 15.12) clearly indicates that what people know about the brand is not sufficiently motivating or relevant, and the brand may need repositioning.

Research does not always tell us what we want to hear, which can create problems if we think an advertising idea is really strong. Take the classic "Avis. We try harder" campaign. It tested poorly in research. Consumers said the "We're number two" concept meant Avis was second rate. Research was against running it, but creative genius Bill Bernbach fervently believed in the idea and convinced Avis to take a chance with it. Today, the Avis campaign is considered one of the most powerful and most memorable advertising campaigns in history.

EXHIBIT 15.12

Brand Trial/Awareness Ratios: Strategic Options

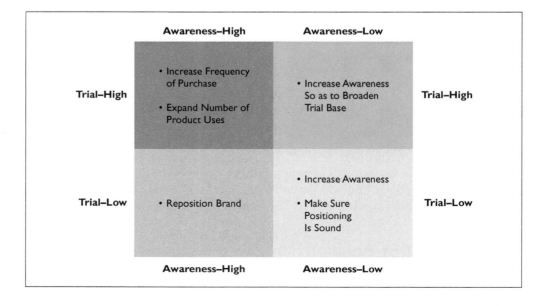

ADVERTISING STRATEGY OR MESSAGE RESEARCH

Most products have a number of positive appeals that could be successfully promoted, so how do we go about making the decision as to which direction to go with an advertisement or appeal? The idea is to choose the one that is most important to the majority of our target. Because selecting the primary appeal is the key to any advertising campaign, many research techniques have been developed to find which appeal to use. Message research is used to identify the most relevant and competitive advertising sales message. It may take many forms, but focus groups and concept testing are frequently used to evaluate creative ideas and strategies.

FOCUS GROUP RESEARCH   **Focus groups** became fashionable in the late 1960s as a **qualitative research** tool that was often used to provide a more in-depth way to explore creative ideas than through rigid quantitative tests. Later account planners saw the use of focus groups as a way of getting early consumer feedback to an idea without putting it through the artificiality of a formal test. Focus groups have also become an important qualitative tool used by marketers and account planners to find out why consumers behave as they do. The focus group offers a means of obtaining in-depth information in a discussion-group atmosphere. This process is designed to probe into the behavior and thinking of individual group members and can elicit spontaneous reactions to products or advertisements. A trained moderator leads a group of eight to twelve consumers, usually prime prospects. The typical focus group interviews last 1½ to 2 hours. The number of different group sessions varies from advertiser to advertiser based somewhat on expense, topic being discussed, diversity of the target audience, and time considerations. The client and other members of the account team often watch the interviews from behind a one-way mirror so as not to disrupt the normal functioning of the group.

> **focus group**
> A qualitative research interviewing method using in-depth interviews with a group rather than with an individual.
>
> **qualitative research**
> This involves finding out what people say they think or feel. It is usually exploratory or diagnostic in nature.

As we indicated earlier, researchers are using more online focus groups to gather consumers' responses to questions and products.

Videoconferencing links, television monitors, remote-control cameras, and digital-transmission technology allow focus group research to be accomplished over long-distance lines. Many advertising agencies believe videoconferencing enriches the creative process because it gives more people input. This technique allows more agency and client people to watch groups from all over the country without having to travel.

There are critics of the overemphasis on focus groups. They point to the fact that many good ideas—whether a 30-second commercial or a new product or concept—may get killed prematurely because they did not do well with a focus group. One increasing criticism is the growing number of "professional" respondents who are savvy enough to go from focus group to focus group, speaking the marketers' language and picking up an easy $50 or $75 each time. Most account planners agree that focus groups should never be used as a replacement for quantitative research. But these groups are useful to determine consumer reaction to certain language in a television commercial or in the development process for creative.

CONCEPT TESTING   **Concept testing** is a method to determine the best of a number of possible appeals to use in your advertising. A *creative concept* is defined as a simple explanation or description of the advertising idea behind the product. A tourism association developed several appeals that might motivate prime prospects to drive 2 hours to the mountains from a large metro area in another state:

> **concept testing**
> The target audience evaluation of (alternative) creative strategey. Testing attempts to separate good and bad ideas and provide insight into factors motivating acceptance or rejection.

1. Only 2 hours to relaxation
2. Mountain fun in your own backyard
3. The family playground in the mountains
4. Escape to white-water rafting, fishing, and the great outdoors
5. Weekend vacation-planner package

By using cards with the theme statement and/or rough layouts, the advertiser tries to obtain a rank order of consumer appeal to the various concepts and diagnostic data explaining why the concepts were ranked as they were. The tourism group found that targets had not realized they were so close to these mountain areas. As a result, mountain areas had not been considered in their vacation or recreation plans. In the case of a car rental company, a test of vacation travelers found that one benefit stood out: the lowest-priced full-size car. The second most important benefit was no hidden extras.

One drawback of concept testing is that consumers can react only to the themes presented to them. You may find that they have chosen the best of several bad concepts.

PRETEST RESEARCH The client wants assurances that the advertising proposed will be effective. In pretesting, a particular advertisement passes or fails or is selected as being better than others. The only alternative is for the client to depend solely on the judgment of the agency or its own personnel.

In general, there are two levels of research aimed at helping advertisers determine how well an advertisement will perform. **Copy testing** is done in two stages:

1. Rough copy research is needed to determine if the copy is effectively achieving its goals in terms of both message communication and attitude effects.

2. Finished copy research is done on the final form of the copy to evaluate how well the production process has achieved communication and attitude effects (see Exhibit 15.13).

Pretesting is the stage of advertising research in which a complete advertisement or commercial is tested. It is important that the objectives of pretesting research relate back to the agreed-on advertising strategy. It would be wasted effort to test for some characteristic not related to the goal of the advertising.

A number of variables can be evaluated in pretesting, including the ability of the advertisement to attract attention, the comprehension of the ad by the reader/viewer, playback of copy points (recall), persuasion (the probability that the consumer will buy the brand), attitude toward the brand, credibility, and irritation level.

Pretests should be used as guides and not as absolute predictors of winners or losers. In copy testing, a higher score for one advertisement over another does not guarantee a better advertisement. Sometimes the results are a reflection of the way the questions are asked. Norm Grey, former creative director and now head of the Creative Circus, once commented on creative testing, "If you don't like the score an ad gets, demand another test. The only thing that's certain is that you'll get another score." This comment does not imply that creative testing is bad. It simply points to the fact that it is controversial and simply another tool for the advertiser.

There have been arguments about the value of testing advertisements for years. In general, clients demand them and agency creatives are suspect of the process. Ed McCabe of McCabe & Company made a distinction between research and testing: "Without great research, you can't make great advertising. However, testing is the idiocy that keeps greatness from happening. Testing is a crutch the one-eyed use to beat up the blind." He points to his Hebrew National hot dog campaign in which an actor portraying Uncle Sam is brought up short by the company's insistence on exceeding federal regulations because its products are kosher and must "answer to a higher authority." The advertisements did not test well, and the client was reluctant to run them. After much discussion, the advertisements ran. Some 2 decades later, the advertisements were still running. The point is that testing can be useful, but it is not a foolproof science. If you were spending millions of dollars on a creative idea, wouldn't you do everything possible to reduce the risk and maximize the chance for success?

CAMPAIGN EVALUATION RESEARCH In evaluating advertising within the total marketing effort, an advertiser should analyze the market and competitive activity and look at advertising as a campaign—not as individual advertisements. This information can

copy testing
Measuring the effectiveness of advertisements.

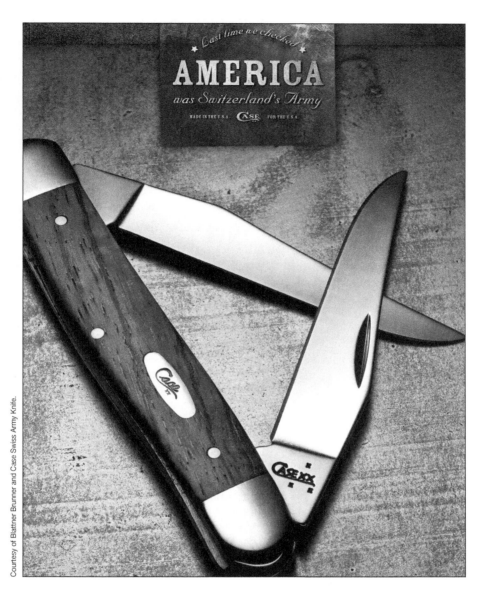

Courtesy of Blattner Brunner and Case Swiss Army Knife.

EXHIBIT 15.13

Research can test the power of this visual.

help determine whether changes in the advertising strategy are needed to accomplish the objectives established for the campaign or to deal with a changed situation (see Advantage Point 15.1).

Advertisers frequently conduct tracking studies to measure trends, brand awareness, and interest in purchasing, as well as advertising factors. The research at the end of one campaign becomes part of the background research for selecting the next campaign strategy.

Testing Creative Research

Creative research takes place within the context of the research stages discussed previously. Creative research aids in the development of what to say to the target audience and how to say it. Copy-development research attempts to help advertisers decide how to execute approaches and elements. Copy testing is undertaken to aid them in determining whether to run the advertising in the marketplace.

6 **Explain types of advertising research.**

1. A good copy-testing system provides measurements that are relevant to the objectives of the advertising. Of course, different advertisements have different objectives (for example, encouraging trial of a product).

VIRGINIA TECH AND NEATHAWK DUBUQUE & PACKETT

Virginia Tech approached Neathawk Dubuque & Packett (ND&P), a marketing and public relations firm, in 2008 with a proposal to create a campaign that would focus on Virginia Tech's wide-ranging research efforts and the resulting impact on the daily lives of Virginians. The goal of the campaign was to shift the conversation about Virginia Tech from one of tragedy, referring to the April 16 massacre, to one of triumph, demonstrating that Virginia Tech is moving forward, leading the state in research, outreach, and an educated workforce.

The challenge for ND&P was to create a campaign that was buzz worthy and highly conversational—one that created a heightened sensory awareness of Virginia Tech's research and the outcomes resulting from it.

RESEARCH

Research completed as recently as 2007 indicated that Virginia Tech is known as a research university, and since the tragedy, it also became known as a close-knit, innovative community. However, there is suspicion that the target audience is not aware that Virginia Tech is *the* top research university in the Commonwealth of Virginia or that the

university impacts Virginians' everyday lives across the state with its research.

EXECUTION

ND&P developed a unique multimedia campaign centered on driving traffic to a newly created microsite focused on Virginia Tech research—www.ThisIsTheFuture.com.

The campaign kicked off September 4 with a direct-mail drop to 54,000 Virginia Tech alumni. The direct-mail piece, entitled "The Future Has Your Name On It," encouraged alumni to "be part of the most innovative campaign in Virginia Tech's history." It instructed them to go to ThisIsTheFuture.com and tell their story of how they are making Virginia a better place to live.

The direct mail was immediately followed by an e-mail blast to alumni with the same message and then another e-mail blast a few days later reminding the alums that the campaign launch date was September 8. On September 8, banner ads began running on Washingtonpost.com/Newsweek.com, InRich.com, and Roanoke.com. These banner ads were primarily simply the URL, ThisIsTheFuture.com, with the exception of expandable leader board ads that had the Virginia Tech logo and the added message: "All across the Commonwealth, Virginians are doing things to make tomorrow better than today. Visit ThisIsTheFuture.com to learn more."

2. A primary purpose of copy testing is to help advertisers decide whether to run the advertising in the marketplace. A useful approach is to specify action standards before the results are in. Examples of action standards are the following:
   - Significantly improves perceptions of the brands as measured by _____.
   - Achieves an attention level no lower than _____ percent as measured by _____.

3. A good copy-testing system is based on the following model of human response to communications: the reception of a stimulus, the comprehension of the stimulus,

In addition to the banner ads, airport duratrans went up in Norfolk, Roanoke, Richmond, and Dulles airports with a visual of one of the viral media elements and the same message from the expanding leader board banner ads.

Print ads were placed in *Washington Business Journal* and *Virginia Business Magazine*.

In addition to the traditional media messages, the Hokie Nation alumni were invited to participate in the campaign and distribute a variety of viral media across their communities to willing businesses and neighbors. These viral elements included tens of thousands of window statics, handout cards, yard flags and tree/pole wrappers. All of these items simply spelled out the URL ThisIsTheFuture.com with the intent to peak curiosity and drive visitors to the site.

Included in the teaser campaign were gas toppers and hose talkers in the Roanoke and Blacksburg markets as well as banner plane flyovers in Blacksburg (over the nationally televised VT/GT football pregame activities and interstate traffic), Roanoke, Richmond, Virginia Beach, and Northern Virginia.

THE MICROSITE: THISISTHEFUTURE.COM

This user-generated microsite is all about encouraging interactive communications. The first visitors to the site were greeted with scrolling images that corresponded to a cloud of floating orange words. When they clicked on one of the words, the corresponding research story appeared in the center window. When they submitted their own story on how they were contributing to life in the commonwealth, the visitors' names joined the orange words and new visitors could click on their names and read their stories. There is also an interactive map indicating where all of the stories have come from, which also offers the ability to click on a name and view that person's story. The site informs viewers about the campaign and provides a downloadable portable document format (pdf) document that fully details all of the exciting research projects ongoing at the university.

RESULTS

The campaign has successfully generated quite a buzz, garnering media attention from newspapers, TV, online news sites, multiple blogs, social media mentions, and even a French online article! More than 200 stories were submitted by users in only the 2 weeks following the campaign launch with the site receiving an impressive number of hits. Follow-up research will be conducted to measure the awareness/perception of Virginia Tech as a research institution at the close of this campaign.

and the response to the stimulus. In short, to succeed, an advertisement must have an effect:

- On the eye and the ear—that is, it must be received (reception)
- On the mind—that is, it must be understood (comprehension)
- On the heart—that is, it must make an impression (response)

4. Experience has shown that test results often vary according to how complete a test is. Thus, careful judgment should be exercised when using a less-than-finished version of a test. Sometimes what is lost is inconsequential; at other times, it is critical.[21]

FORMS OF TESTING

Each advertiser and agency use similar but modified steps in the testing of creative research. The following are examples of this process.

CONCEPT TESTING   As mentioned earlier, concept testing may be an integral part of creative planning and is undertaken for most clients as a matter of course. Creative concept testing can be defined as the target audience evaluation of (alternative) creative strategy. Specifically, concept testing attempts to separate the "good" ideas from the "bad," to indicate differing degrees of acceptance, and to provide insight into factors motivating acceptance or rejection. There are a number of possible concept tests:

1. *Card concept tests.* With card concept tests, creative strategies are presented to respondents in the form of a headline followed by a paragraph of body copy on a plain white card. Each concept is on a separate card. Some concepts cannot be tested in card form (for example, those requiring a high degree of mood, such as concepts based on humor or personalities).

2. *Poster tests.* Poster tests are similar to card tests except that small posters containing simplified illustrations and short copy are used rather than plain cards without illustrations.

3. *Layout tests.* A layout test involves showing a rough copy of a print advertisement (or artwork for a television commercial with accompanying copy) to respondents. Layout tests are more finished than poster tests in that they use the total copy and illustration as they will appear in the finished advertisement. Additionally, whereas a card or poster test measures the appeal of the basic concept, the purpose of the layout test may be to measure more subtle effects such as communication, understanding, and clarity.

FINISHED PRINT TESTS   Finished print tests can take many forms; they measure the finished advertisement as it will appear in print. One such testing procedure used for finished print advertisements goes something like this: Test advertisements, finished or unfinished, are inserted into a 20-page magazine in a folder containing both editorial and control advertisements. Prospects preview the magazine during one-on-one interviews in high-traffic malls. Respondents are questioned regarding unaided, aided, and related recall of the test advertisement. Next they are asked to focus on the test advertisement only and are probed for reactions. Agencies are furnished with diagnostic data to improve the advertisement. The advertisements may be measured for stopping power, communication effectiveness, relevance, and persuasion. Likes and dislikes about the advertisement are also provided (see Exhibit 15.14).

TESTING UNFINISHED COMMERCIALS   Generally, commercial testing falls into one of three categories:

1. *Animatics.* Animatics is artwork, either cartoons or realistic drawings, that are computer generated or hand drawn. Some animatics show limited movement; those that do not move are usually called video storyboards.

2. *Photomatics.* Photomatics are photographs shot in sequence on film. The photos may be stock (from a photo library) or shot on location.

3. *Livamatics.* Livamatics involves filming or taping live talent and is very close to the finished commercial.

FINISHED COMMERCIAL TESTING   Television testing techniques can generally be classified into two categories:

1. Those that attempt to evaluate a commercial's effectiveness in terms of viewers' recall of a certain aspect of the commercial

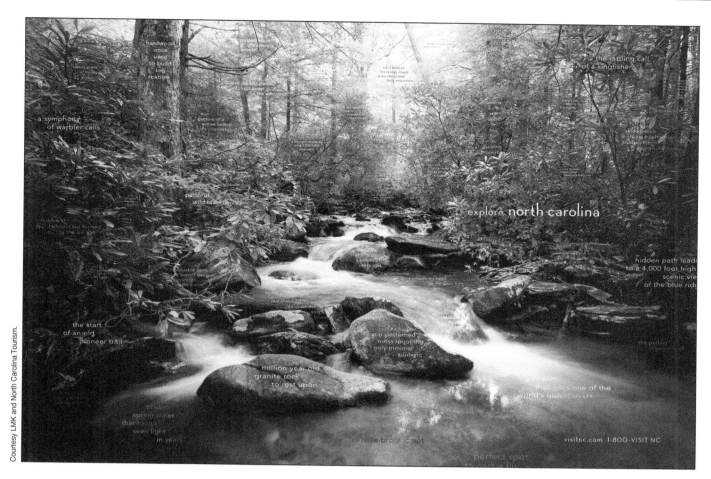

Courtesy LMK and North Carolina Tourism.

EXHIBIT 15.14

Do you think that this visually appealing ad would test well in rough form?

2. Those that attempt to evaluate a commercial's effectiveness in terms of what it motivates a viewer to say or do

Recent advances in production technology are helping the testing process. The more closely the test spot resembles the finished commercial, the more accurate the test results will be. Computer animation has become less expensive, so there is more computer-generated artwork in commercial testing.

READERSHIP

Advertisers face mounting competition both in the market and on the printed page. It is important to have the ability to determine if an advertisement is being seen. One such readership service that supplies this kind of information is the Starch Readership Service from Roper Starch.

The Starch Readership Service is designed to measure the extent to which advertisements are being seen and read and the level of interest they arouse. Starch interviews thousands of consumers each year to determine their responses to print advertisements. Starch uses the recognition method of interviewing. With the publication open, the respondent explains the extent to which he or she has read each advertisement prior to the interview. For each advertisement, respondents are asked, "Did you see or read any part of this advertisement?" If yes, a prescribed questioning procedure is followed to determine the observation and reading of each component part of each advertisement—illustration, headline, signature, and copy blocks. After these questions are asked, each respondent is classified as follows:

- *Noted reader.* A noted reader is a person who remembers having previously seen the advertisement in the issue being studied.

- *Associated reader.* An associated reader is a person who not only noted the advertisement but also saw or read some part of it that clearly indicated the brand or advertiser.
- *Read most.* A person who read half or more of the written material in the advertisement fits the "read most" class of person.

Clients receive Adnorm data with the Starch Readership Reports. Adnorms enable advertisers to compare readership data of their advertisement in a given magazine issue to the norm for advertisements of the same size and color in the same product category. These data can help advertisers identify the types of layouts that attract and retain the highest readership as well as the level of engagement consumers have with their ad in a specific magazine. They can also compare current advertisements against those of competitors, compare the current campaign against previous campaigns, compare the current campaign against a competitor's previous campaign, and compare current advertisements against the Adnorm tables.[22] (See Exhibit 15.15.)

EXHIBIT 15.15

This ad would likely score well on a Starch Readership test among football fans.

CRITICISMS OF COPY TESTING RESEARCH

Standard copy-testing techniques have long been criticized by advertising agency personnel. They see many of these techniques as giving an unfair advantage to boring and/or irritating advertisements while penalizing more innovative approaches. According to John Kastenholz, vice president of consumer and market insights at Unilever, "There is a feeling, particularly among creative directors, that copy testing can undermine the ability to produce breakthrough creative ideas."[23] Many marketers and advertising agency executives recognize that most of the commonly used techniques do not adequately assess consumers' emotional response to advertising, and they don't feel as though there have been adequate advances in the methods used. The chief research officer of the Advertising Research Foundation, Joe Plummer, says, "there's been no fundamental advance in copy testing since the early 1980s. So much new information is available today on how the mind works and processes emotional responses to stories, metaphors and symbols."[24] Several companies have new techniques under development that hold promise for future copy-testing research.

SUMMARY

Advertising is a people business. Successful advertisers know who their prospects are and—to whatever extent is practical—their needs and motives, which result in the purchase of one product or service and the rejection of another. Consumer behavior is usually the result of a complex network of influences based on the anthropological, sociological, and psychological makeup of the individual. Account planners are often the individuals on an advertising team who are responsible for being knowledgeable about all of the consumer research for the brand.

Advertising rarely, if ever, changes these influences but rather channels needs and wants of consumers toward specific products and brands. Advertising is a mirror of society. The advertiser influences people by offering solutions to their needs and problems, not by creating these needs. The role of the advertiser is to act as a monitor of the changing face of society.

Advertisers pay special attention to what we call up-front research or market research that reflects the market, the consumer, and the competition. Such information as cohort analysis, VALS, and MindBase can help us understand consumer lifestyles and values, which aids in developing strategies.

Once all of this information is digested, it is used in the four stages of advertising development: strategy development, execution development, pretesting of executions, and campaign evaluation. By itself, information has no value. It acquires value only when we take a point of view about what the information means.

There are a number of testing stages available in creative research ranging from concept testing and commercial testing techniques to finished print and commercial tests. It is much less expensive to test concepts and advertisements prior to buying expensive media schedules.

REVIEW

1. Why are sociology, psychology, and anthropology important to advertising?
2. What kind of research is used in advertising execution development?
3. What is the role of the account planner?
4. What is biometric research, and how is it used by some advertisers in advertising development?
5. How are focus groups used in advertising research?

M&M's® and the M&M's Characters are registered trademarks of Mars, Incorporated and its affiliates. These trademarks are used with permission. Mars, Incorporated is not associated with Pearson Prentice Hall. Advertisements printed with permission of Mars, Incorporated.

Creating the Message

IT HAS BEEN SAID that strategy is everything. "Sometimes creative leads, sometimes strategy leads," says British creative director Tony Cox, "but both have to remain close in harmony for a great ending." Great advertising copy is essential to great advertising no matter what the medium. ▶

CHAPTER LEARNING OBJECTIVES

1. **Discuss the creative work plan.**
2. **Discuss reduction versus expansive messages.**
3. **Discuss storytelling.**
4. **Discuss the structure of an ad.**
5. **Explain copy styles.**
6. **Discuss slogans.**
7. **Discuss new format and content messages.**

"At the heart of an effective creative philosophy is the belief that nothing is so powerful as an insight into human nature, what compulsions drive a person, what instincts dominate their action, even though his or her language so often can camouflage what really motivates them."

—BILL BERNBACH

Consumer Integrated Touchpoints

We talk about message integration and reinforcement across the many touchpoints consumers encounter, whether in a print advertisement, on the web, or on television—every medium. This consistency in tone, messaging, and visual appearance is called *touchpoint integration*. The Zippo *Rolling Stone* site ads (see Exhibit 16.1 a, b, and c) are integrated into every phase of the platform. They offer the viewer an opportunity to link to zippo.com. They offer integrated messages and consumer connections. This kind of touchpoint integration is the hallmark of brands such as Starbucks, McDonald's, Nike, and many others. "The creative people who can get into the heart—not just the brain—and make people cry or laugh or silently say, 'yeah, that's how I really feel' will be the superstars," says Lou Centlivre, formerly of Foote Cone & Belding. John Pepper, former CEO of Procter & Gamble, notes, "I have seen through 25 years that the correlation between profitable business growth on our brands and having great copy on our brands isn't 25 percent, it's not 50 percent. It is 100 percent. I have not seen a single P&G brand sustain profitable volume growth for more than a couple of years without having great advertising."[1]

EXHIBIT 16.1

The Zippo message is integrated into every aspect of the *Rolling Stone* web site.

So little of advertising is still actually advertising. But fortunately ideas are still ideas, according to Trone's Scott Scaggs.[2] As we've said, the term *advertising* is considered much broader than actual traditional pure advertising. We discuss ideas in greater detail in the next chapter. But the truth is, everything in the world appears to be changing, so there are new rules for developing advertisements. Or, are there? Earlier we said that long-held tenets sometimes distort our view of what might be and what should be. It has been asked, "What will replace the old rules? Anarchy?" In some ways, new rules haven't been written, especially in new technology communication. There is more scope for intuitive thinking, for experimentation, for innovation, for connecting. Oh, once again I forgot to tell you, there are no rules. There have never been "rules." That said, we need to understand that there are nonrules, guidelines that are generally accepted and that sometimes draw on years of research results or accumulated wisdom of creative communicators. You might say they are similar to fashion rules—some things simply work better. And it's your job to figure this out. This probably sounds like a contradiction, but it really isn't.

In this chapter we discuss some "how to" issues and these words will form what appear to be rules. It is a means of sharing and analyzing. Ken Roman, former CEO of Ogilvy & Mather Worldwide, says, "Recipes don't work for a very simple reason: This is a business of ideas. Ideas don't derive from rules; they derive from principles."[3] The real challenge is to use this knowledge in the context of your specific communication problem. Remember that earlier in this text we discussed creative risk. Consider taking smart risks, where you know what the norm of thinking is, and go from there—with caution. The goal is to communicate.

Creative Risk Taking

As media and advertising businesses move through this period of transition, marketers are trying to discover insights to tap into consumers' emotional connections. The advertisers want to narrow the field and move away from the traditional mass audience quantifications of reach and frequency. They want to build relationships.[4] Many of the fundamental beliefs are under siege, but certain rules, beliefs, and methodologies have served the business well, and restraint is called for. Agencies owe their clients effective advertising and must find ways to accomplish this. "An idea that hasn't been done before might, on the surface, look really risky," argues Bob Isherwood of Saatchi & Saatchi. "It's an area where no one has gone before. There is no precedent. But usually the biggest risk lies in ideas that are predictable." Ideas that are predictable don't get noticed. As Oscar Wilde once said, "*an idea that does not involve risk does not deserve to be an idea.*" David Jones, CEO of global agency network Euro RSCG Worldwide,

EXHIBIT 16.2

How do you sell a legal newspaper full of legal matters? Be creative.

READ ABOUT WHERE ALL YOUR LAWYER PALS ARE GOING. BESIDES HELL, OF COURSE.

No one keeps better tabs on movement within our industry than we do. But now you can turn to us for expanded coverage of transactional law, general business and coming soon, a new leisure section. There's never been a better time to subscribe, so call 404-521-1227. THE FULL STORY.

says rather than talking about how to redefine creativity in a fast-changing world, "[w]e should just get on and do it."[5] Some of the most well liked advertisements were based on a creative director's gut instinct of what consumers would like. He says creatives should "trust your gut." Advertising is changing fast, and not to take a risk is risky—even though it's scary to do so. Risk is about breaking rules or guidelines.

"A lot of creative people think creative risk taking means doing ads that scare the life out of you," says Singapore creative director Garry Abbott. "Good ads don't rely on borrowed ideas. Risk is about *freshness*." Finding out from consumers what it really is like being them so that ads can respond to their needs is a risk many don't take. According to Hugh Mackay, one way to accomplish this is to "take a set of familiar elements and rearrange them in an unfamiliar way so that the reader recognizes both the familiar and the unfamiliar. In other words, present something the readers recognize as themselves, their lives, their dreams, but with a twist, so they're a bit startled by it, or get an extra insight from it."[6] Is this a rule? No. It is a way of thinking about how to solve a problem. Maybe, create a web site that impacts people's lives like Nike+ did with runners. Huey+Partners had to sell a typical legal newspaper and had fun with the target (see Exhibit 16.2).

All creatives have a responsibility. Erik Veruroegen, executive creative director at a number of global shops, says, "I am against advertising where people just show crap and say 'but it works.' We have a mission to stop that. The consumer does not like advertising at all. It interrupts. It is pretentious to believe that the consumer will give you a chance just because you're there. Advertising must earn the right to be paid attention to, but you can't be different for the sake of being different."[7]

The Creative Work Plan

1 **Discuss the creative work plan.**

Before most agencies start creating an advertisement, they develop a creative work plan to guide them in the right direction. A creative brief (sometimes called a creative work plan) is like a road map. A great brief leads to imaginative on target ads, web sites, videos, and so on. The brief is the starting point for the creative process. Recall from Chapter 3 that the creative brief consists of the following elements:

- Key observations
- Communication objective
- Consumer insight
- Promise
- Support
- Audience
- Mandatories

What does a brief accomplish? In simple factual terms, a good brief should accomplish three main objectives. First, it should give the creative team a realistic view of what the advertising really needs to do and is likely to achieve. Second, it should provide a clear understanding of the people that the advertising must address, And third, it needs to give clear direction as to the message to which the target audience seems most likely to be susceptible. In some agencies, there is a creative briefing in which an account planner outlines the nature of the advertising problem for the creative team and suggests ways of solving it.[8]

The purpose of the work plan is to provide proper direction for the creative team prior to developing ideas, heads, and copy. Exhibit 16.3 shows a work plan format originally developed by Young & Rubicam that is widely used by a number of agencies. Note that the work plan emphasizes factual information and research data. The creative process is not a "shot in the dark"; rather, it depends on knowing as much as possible about the product, the consumer, and the expected benefits. The advertising professional is able to channel objective information into a creative, attention-getting sales message. Many agencies and clients have their own format and style for specific information that they think is necessary for creative strategy development.

A Challenge and Creative Vision

2 **Discuss reduction versus expansive messages.**

We know we are living in an explosive information age. It is also true to say that knowledge is power, and the speed with which marketers use that knowledge in the future will determine success or failure. Because advertising is, in its most basic form, a conveyor of information, it will be at the center of this revolution. But there are a number of factors working against that happening.

According to global creative director John Hegarty, we already have to deal with a major communication problem. It's called *time famine*. How do consumers assimilate the ever-growing mass of messages being directed at them? How do they cope with the volume of traffic going through their brains? How do they process this valuable

CREATIVE WORK PLAN

PRODUCT: **NEW ORLEANS**

KEY FACT
Bevil Foods is a 30-year-old New Orleans–based frozen food company. In 1993, Bevil Foods will introduce a new line of premium frozen entreés to be distributed nationally.

PROBLEM THE ADVERTISING MUST SOLVE
Currently there is **NO awareness** of the New Orleans product among potential consumers.

ADVERTISING OBJECTIVE
To achieve 70% awareness of the product at end of year 1. To communicate the taste and low-calorie/low-fat benefits of the product.

CREATIVE STRATEGY

PROSPECT DEFINITION
1. Women 25–54, professional/managerial, with household incomes of $25,000 plus.
2. Adults 25+, professional/managerial, with household incomes of $25,000 plus.

   Psychographically, these people tend to be active, concerned with their health, and "on the go" a lot.

PRINCIPAL COMPETITION
Lean Cuisine, Weight Watchers, Healthy Choice.

KEY PROMISE
New Orleans are lite entreés with the great taste of New Orleans.

REASON WHY
Less than 300 calories; low fat, great tasting, original New Orleans recipes, served in fine restaurants for 30 years.

MANDATORIES
Must use logo, calorie and fat information, and original New Orleans recipes in each ad.

EXHIBIT 16.3

A Creative Work Plan

information as opposed to allowing it to pass straight through unnoticed? A related issue that has been debated for years is media clutter. Are consumers reaching the point of "overchoice," as futurist Alvin Toffler predicted? "We are racing against overchoice—the point at which the advantages of choice and individualization are canceled by the complexity of the buyer's decision-making process."[9]

How do we get consumers to want to turn us on? They certainly have the ability to turn us off. Advertisers interrupt viewing and listening; they shout in printed material for attention. As electronic media take a greater hold on the distribution of information, consumers will have greater control over turning us, the advertisers, off, unless we are compelling and necessary. Unless we recognize the change in the balance of power and consider our consumers' aspirations, we will be cut out of the loop and become irrelevant. What can we do as communicators?

STRATEGY AND GREAT WRITING

Don't forget the importance of strategy as you read about how to create. Often there are dangers in our decision process. Frederick Smith, founder of Federal Express, said, "We thought we were selling the transportation of goods; when in fact, we were selling peace of mind. When we finally figured that out, we pursued our goal with vengeance."[10]

REDUCTIVE MESSAGES

For the past 50 years or so, successful brands have had to reduce their sales messages to be instantaneously seen on TV or read in print and outdoor. These brief brand stories created an emotional bond that, in theory, translated into sales at the cash register.

A brilliantly simple idea was created for *The Economist*. The typical advertisement for *The Economist* (a British publication read in more than 140 countries) has been three columns of copy. The advertisements present the benefits of reading the publication—much information aimed at a sophisticated, well-educated target. Yet, a simple poster reads,

I've never read *The Economist.*

SIGNED, MANAGEMENT TRAINEE. AGE 42.

The concept was even integrated in a longer T-shirt message:

**My dad reads *The Economist* and all I got was this lousy tee shirt,
a penthouse apartment in New York, two Ferraris, an eighty foot yacht,
my own private jet, and an island retreat in the Caribbean.**

There is a valuable message in this example for those creating advertising: The faster ideas get across, the more powerful they become. As you reduce the idea down, as you hone it to its essential structure, its power increases. The faster it penetrates the mind, the longer it stays there. You aren't trying to buy newspaper, magazine, or web space or time in a commercial break. The space you are trying to buy is in the consumer's head. That is the most valuable space. That is what you are trying to influence. Ogilvy & Mather Singapore carried *The Economist* advertising a step further. The head read "Money back guarantee." That was the advertisement. Their simplistic advertisements have become so famous as a technique that some advertisers mock them. Wonderbra copied the layout and the copy read:

"I never read *The Economist.*"

LINDA FOSTER, CEO. AGE 29.
WONDERBRA

Luke Sullivan, long-time executive creative director at a number of popular agencies, speaking of creating advertising ideas, says it is simple: simplicity, simplicity, simplicity. Tony Cox says, "Inside every fat ad is a thinner and better one trying to get out." Maurice Saatchi on simplicity says: "Simplicity is all. Simple logic, simple arguments, simple visual images. If you can't reduce your arguments to a few crisp words and phrases, there's something wrong with your argument."[11]

Fallon Worldwide's self-promotion says, "The crucial part of the creative process is what we call relentless reductionism. It means having the discipline and will to drive for focus. A focus that results in a single-mindedly compelling idea. Then Fallon expands the idea. This is where creativity takes over, as we take this single-minded idea and apply it to every step of the consumer's path to purchase." You're getting the idea.

Was it Oscar Wilde—it doesn't really matter—who understood that an idea got better as it got faster? How do we do that? The brilliance of our craft is to reduce, to distill messages down, not to elongate. Remember Abraham Lincoln's quote, "You can fool all the people some of the time, and some of the people all the time, but you cannot fool all the people all of the time." He captured the essence of modern politics in one sentence, and most of us remember it. Great writing is about using fewer words to be more compelling. When you do that, you liberate your ideas to become more powerful, more involving, and hopefully more memorable. Brevity not only allows us to become more powerful but it also allows us to become more stimulating. Creative director, Scott Scaggs used a simple concept meshing the illustration and the headline, "As you wish," with copy driving the reader to CenturyFurniture.com (see Exhibit 16.4). If you are more stimulating, there is a good chance you are becoming more relevant. We have to change because our audience is demanding it.

The Greeks said that information is taken through the heart. As we have moved from the unique selling proposition (USP) to the *emotional selling proposition*, we need to understand that the way we talk to consumers must also change. Advertising still needs to be based on the foundation of product or corporate attributes. But we must remember that it may no longer be unique nor will it necessarily be obvious.

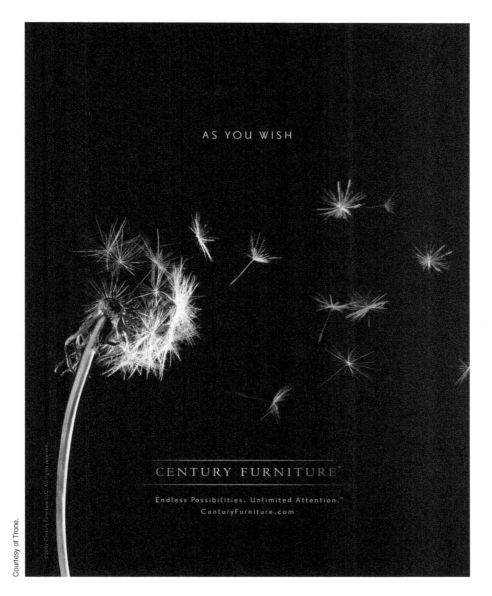

EXHIBIT 16.4

The headline and visual are simple concepts. The copy drives people to more information on the Internet.

EXPANSIVE MESSAGES

We have just made a case for reduction. However, with web sites and other online and social media, we also can make the case that consumers seek more information. Online advertising offers marketers the opportunity to give unlimited detail and content. So both concepts can co-exist in their appropriate arenas. According to Barry Wacksman, executive vice president, chief growth office at digital agency R/GA, the reductive messages era began to give way to the expansive era in the 1990s. The growth of the Internet meant brand messages no longer needed only to be reductive. Traditional media was expensive and limited brands to brief messages, whereas the web provided brands with cheap, unlimited space to give consumers more information. Today, consumers are more deliberate about how they purchase things as the 3 billion-plus daily Google searches indicate.[12]

Online and Off: Storytelling

Whether it's reductive or expansive, a story may be the key. Brunner's creative storytelling guru, Frank Compton, says, "Storytelling is the oldest and most powerful form of communication known to man. People love stories. People get stories. People interact

3 **Discuss storytelling.**

with stories. True brand loyalty happens when people believe your story so much that they become a part of it. Your story becomes a chapter in theirs. When that happens, they tell other people. Then the story gets repeated, again and again.

As Compton indicates, there's something magical about stories. They can be marketing stories involving brands. There are great brand stories. Think of Starbucks. What's the story there? Stories may be nothing more than the presentation of a sequence of events. They have been characterized as "about motion or moments of reflection." Brand stories always have a point. They are thought out in such a way as to leave a lasting impression. They are true to the brand's promise. Sometimes we use suspense to hold attention; no one likes a boring story. Because stories can be used for any medium (okay, maybe not so easy in outdoor), they can be long or short, humorous or factual.

Seth Godin says, "I think that while markets are conversations, marketing is a story. Starbucks creates conversations among customers, so does Apple. But great marketing is storytelling. Great marketers listen relentlessly. They engage in offline conversations constantly. They poll and they do censuses and most important, they have true conversations with small groups of real people. But *then*, they tell a story."[13]

TELLING STORIES

Maybe you can remember your grandmother's stories? Think about it. Storytelling is relatively simple. It is basically a sequence of events or actions. For starters, think of one of Starbucks' stories. "Many years ago Starbucks' founder was thinking coffee. . . . He had a mission to educate consumers about the joys of coffee. . . . He had a vision to create an atmosphere. . . . And he had a vision for employees and the good earth. . . ." Okay, Tom Ehrenfeld says, "The test of a good story isn't its responsibility to the facts as much as its ability to provide a satisfying explanation of events."[14] There should be one event after another. Building to a big event is important. Make a point. Remember, the story is about the creative brief's promise you are trying to share with the reader.

Should there be conflict? According to Scott Scaggs of Trone, without conflict, there's not much of a story. It's just Batman living in a crimeless Gotham City. (Yawn.) It's Harry Potter without He Who Must Not Be Named. ("Your parents seem nice, Harry.") It's GEICO in a world that actually embraces the complexities of auto insurance. The real point here is to engage your audience the way one human being engages another in conversation. If you can get your target nodding along by using only positive statements, then by all means do it. But sometimes the more interesting way to start the conversation is to poke at the problem a little.[15]

Another storytelling technique involves simply raising questions. And then answering each question. Is there suspense, or drama, or characters to give it spice and feeling?

SOCIAL STORYTELLING ONLINE

We're starting a lot of stories today, online and off. But typical web ads are awful. At a 2008 industry conference, Lee Clow, chair and chief creative officer of TBWA/Media Arts Lab, deplored the state of online ad creativity as "semi-nowhere." A year later he said, "Most online advertising still feels like it is a result of a conversation about click rates and the tactics of grabbing attention through gimmicks, as if tricking people to engage is a measure of true success. But I believe creativity should be our filter. I want to see artists and idea people find more influence in this space."[16] In Mr. Clow's mind, it's not simply about embracing the rational utilities of this space—search, information, and functionality—something most brands are still trying to figure out but it's also about creating desirable content that works for the audience and the environment.

Part of the reason early web ads were so bad was because of how they evolved. In the beginning, the web had little to offer besides two-way interaction via the mouse; thus, the click was born as a proxy for effectiveness. Now, the conversation about clicks is not a pretty one—fewer than 0.1 percent of display ads are clicked on, according to ComScore. And bemoaning dropping click-through rates as a sign display ads are dying is a big part of the problem.

This is changing slowly. The Apple "Mac versus PC" ads worked, both online and off, because they were *the starting point of a story*. AKQA co-chief creative officer Lars Bastholm called this concept "**social storytelling**" and said it's even more essential online because the watercooler is built into the system.[17] Social storytelling can be the basis for that dialogue between the marketer and the consumer.

Okay, this isn't a story writing course. But in today's marketing, successful advertising typically is about storytelling.

How Do We Create Great Advertising?

Creativity isn't simply about putting a strategy down on a piece of paper. It is also about capturing the essence of that strategy and giving it a creative vision that is both compelling and competitive. What worked yesterday isn't necessarily going to work today or tomorrow. The consumer has not only less time to listen to us but also less inclination.

Saatchi & Saatchi's Kevin Roberts said, "Do you really want a great ad? If you want a quiet life—no highs, no lows, no struggle, no passion—forget great ads." The opposite of a great ad is not a bad ad but an average one. The response to good ads? "Let's analyze." The response to great ads? "I want more."

We've already heard this, but we need to hear another viewpoint. Ron Huey, award-winning creative director of Huey+Partners, says, "Simplicity is the key to great advertising. Take the single most salient feature of your product or service and communicate that in a simple, thought provoking or entertaining way. Good copy speaks to the common man. It should be smart, entertaining and conversational, not fancy or frilly. Today's best creative people are resilient. Great ideas are killed every day for sometimes stupid reasons. The best creatives accept that and come back with something even better." Huey's thoughts on advertising through the years: "The great ads from Bernbach in the '60s, Fallon McElligott in the '80s, Wieden [Wieden & Kennedy], Goodby [Goodby, Silverstein & Partners] and The Martin Agency today, all have a common thread—The headline, visual and logo communicate the idea immediately." He also believes, "Three quarters of today's best ads use humor. But it's wry humor. Not a bathroom joke or humor that's intended to shock people."[18] Huey says, "One path we always investigate when concepting print is a 'visual solution.' By that, I mean an ad where the idea is really imbedded in the visual and usually communicates 90% of what you're trying to say. In this approach, the headline is more of straight payoff to complete, or bullet-proof, the communication."

The Nature and Use of Appeals

Advertising motivates people by appealing to their problems, desires, and goals, and by offering a means of solving their problems. Let us look at the value of using a psychological **appeal** in advertising. David Martin, founder of The Martin Agency, points to decades of research indicating the relative strengths of motives and appeals in advertising. He believes human desires are woven into our basic nature. They do not change with lifestyles or external environmental stimuli. Consumers will always have a desire for food and drink; for rest, comfort, and security; and for a sense of social worth, independence, power, and success. Parental feelings to protect and provide are basic. Human nature is a constant. Humans are born with certain instincts: fear (self-preservation), hunger (need for food and drink), sex (love), and rage (anger). People also have five senses: sight, touch, smell, hearing, and taste. The instincts and senses are

social storytelling
Storytelling is a powerful way of social bonding. Social storytelling is open-ended. You try to tell a story in a way that leaves room for the consumers to fill in the blanks, to add their own tendrils to the main storyline.

appeal
The motive to which an advertisement is directed; it is designed to steer a person toward a goal the advertiser has set.

KLEPPNER VIEWPOINT 16.1

Ron Huey President/Executive Creative Director, Huey+Partners, Atlanta

GETTING YOUR MESSAGE THROUGH? IT'S SIMPLE.

Ron Huey

The average person is blindsided by more than 3,000 messages a day. Not only with television commercials, magazine and newspaper ads but also with outdoor boards, radio spots, Internet pop-ups, signs on trucks, signs on trees, signs on just about anything that will stand still. It's a deafening roar for the consumer's attention to say the least. So how do you create communication that actually communicates in this environment? The key, for me at least, has always been simplicity. Make a simple point in a very compelling and simple way and, chances are, people may actually pay attention. The tendency, however, is to try and say everything. Put forth every conceivable product benefit. That's okay; it's a natural inclination. After all, they're probably all things worth saying. It's a fast car, a luxurious car, a safe car, a well-engineered car, a stylish car, a car that fits your needs. The problem is that now no one knows what kind of car you're offering. You've made a lot of pertinent points, but no one point has penetrated with any meaning. So the first step is to put a single strategic stake in the ground. Stand for something rather than trying to stand for everything. Now you must bring your simple strategy to creative life in an arresting, impacting way. Remember, consumers aren't eagerly awaiting the next advertisement from you, or from anyone else for that matter. (They've already been hit by 3,000 today.) In fact, you will be an uninvited guest; you will be interrupting their day. So it's important that you intrigue them and invite them in. Make your point and do so in a way that entertains them and rewards for spending time with your message. It's that simple.

Courtesy of Huey+Partners.

often a starting point for advertising appeals.[19] The creative genius of the late 1960s, the late Bill Bernbach, put it this way:

> There may be changes in our society. But learning about those changes is not the answer. For you are not appealing to society. You are appealing to individuals, each with an ego, each with the dignity of his or her being, each like no one else in the world, each a separate miracle. The societal appeals are merely fashionable, current, cultural appeals, which make nice garments for the real motivations that stem from the unchanging instincts and emotions of people—from nature's indomitable programming in their genes. It is the unchanging person that is the proper study of the communicator.[20]

John Hegarty says, "There was always one word that came through [when defining great advertising]: irreverence. Because what you are doing is changing the rules. You are trying to do something in an incredibly different way which captures the imagination." Jeff Goodby of Goodby, Silverstein & Partners adds, "Great advertising scrabbles logic a little bit, it jumps beyond that by being likable and watchable and captivating. It surprises you." Someone once said that great advertising is great ideas simply executed.[21]

Most products have a number of positive appeals that could be successfully promoted, so how do we go about making the decision as to which direction to go with an advertisement or appeal? The idea is to choose the one that is most important to the majority of our target audience. Because selecting the primary appeal is the key to any advertising campaign, many research techniques have been developed to find which appeal to use, as discussed in Chapter 15.

Whether created by research or in other ways, the appeal provides the basis of the advertising structure. This appeal can be expressed in many ways. Here, we discuss how to make use of words, called *copy*, in presenting the appeal.[22]

Great Advertising Elements

The creative council of Ogilvy & Mather Worldwide found that examples of great advertising have certain elements in common (the same fundamental principles apply to direct-response and sales promotion):[23]

- *Potent strategy.* The strategy is the heart of advertising. It is impossible to create great advertising if the strategy is weak or does not exist at all.
- *Strong selling idea.* Great advertising promises a benefit to the consumer. The idea must be simple, and it must be clear. The brand must be integrated into the selling idea.
- *Stands out.* A great advertisement is memorable, even when competing for attention with news and entertainment.
- *Always relevant.* Prospects can easily relate the advertising to their experience and to the role of the product in their lives.
- *Can be built into campaigns.* No matter how clever one idea may be, if you cannot make it into a campaign, it is not a great idea.

Structure of an Advertisement

In some instances, the promise is the whole advertisement. Usually, however, a fuller exposition is required, in which case the promise can act as the headline—the first step in the structure of the advertisement. All of the following references print, but may be applicable to most display ads used in any medium. Most advertisements are presented in this order:

4 **Discuss the structure of an ad.**

- Promise of benefit (the headline)
- Spelling out of promise (the subheadline, optional)
- Amplification of story (as needed)
- Proof of claim (as needed)
- Action to take (if not obvious)

Nobody reads body copy in an advertisement. "Lies, lies, and more lies," say Steve Lance and Jeff Woll. Long copy isn't needed when a picture can tell a thousand words. Borrow a page from your Internet site. If you're giving people a benefit and relevant information, long copy can work. But you have to work hard to make it work.[24] People tend to scan advertisements in the following manner: illustration first, then the headline, followed by the first line of the body copy, and then the logo. If they are still interested, they will go back and read the rest of the copy. Yes, you can get people to read the copy, but the first sentence and first paragraph are extremely important in attracting and keeping readers. As a matter of fact, the drop-off rate of readers is pretty significant during the first 50 words, but not so great between 50 and 500 words.

THE HEADLINE

The headline is the most important part of a print advertisement. It is the first thing read, and it should arouse interest to entice the consumer to keep on reading and get to know more about the product being sold. If the headline does not excite the interest of the particular group of prime prospects the advertiser wants to reach, the rest of the advertisement

EXHIBIT 16.5

The short headline connects the benefits put forth in the visual images in this ad.

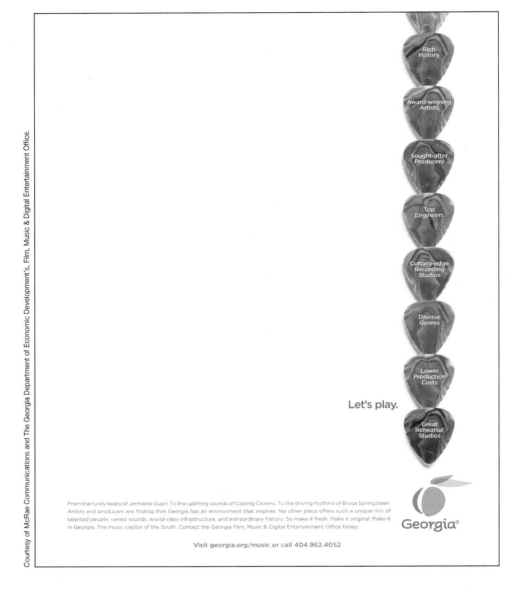

probably will go unread. The ad for the Film, Music & Digital Entertainment Office at the Georgia Department of Economic Development says, "Let's Play." But the visual "picks" tout the benefits (and the ad was in *Billboard* magazine): top engineers, cutting-edge recording studios, lower production costs, diverse genres, and so on. So, "Let's play" takes on more meaning without ever getting to the body copy (see Exhibit 16.5).

Get prospects' attention by telling them what they want to know immediately. Don't make them guess the brand's benefit. You certainly should consider using a benefit in the headline. Ask yourself, "What's our promise and what's our proof?" Why do so many advertisements get it wrong, when it isn't that hard to get it right? Figure out why people would really benefit from your brand or service. Then tell 'em. Make it interesting. Make it readable.[25]

No formula can be given for writing a good headline. However, several factors should be considered in evaluating an effective headline:

■ It should use short, simple words, usually no more than 10.

■ It should include an invitation to the prospect, primary product benefits, name of the brand, and an interest-provoking idea to gain readership of the rest of the advertisement.

▨ The words should be selective, appealing only to prime prospects.

▨ It should contain an action verb.

▨ It should give enough information so that the consumer who reads only the headline learns something about the product and its benefit.

Not every headline is going to adhere to these guidelines. However, when you write a headline that excludes any of these points, ask yourself: Would this headline be more effective if it did adhere to the guidelines? You want to be sure you have thought through the process. Many headlines fall into one of four categories:

1. *Headlines that present a new benefit.* The moment of peak interest in a product is when it offers a new benefit. That is why, in our innovative society, you often see headlines such as these for online banners:

> **The new ORECK Halo. The world's only UV-C germ-killing vacuum.**
>
> ORECK HALO

> **New Covergirl Outlast Lipstain**
>
> COVERGIRL

Or these for print ads:

> **Introducing Gillette Fusion. Breakthrough technology on the front and back.**
>
> GILLETTE FUSION

> **Introducing a new restaurant by Folks.**
>
> RUSTY ROOSTER CAFÉ (see Exhibit 16.6)

2. *Headlines that directly promise an existing benefit.* Products cannot be offering new benefits all the time, of course, so headlines often remind consumers of a product's existing features, as, for example, this online banner ad:

> **More Fun Close to Home.**
>
> SIX FLAGS

Or this print ad:

> **Cheerios can lower cholesterol 4% in 6 weeks.**
>
> CHEERIOS

WORDPLAY

Gary Knutson, former executive creative director at Howard Merrell & Partners, would send memos to creatives to get them to think. He sent the following entitled "Wordplay."

RE: If this is what we want to say, why can't we just say it?

How many times have you heard this from a client?

The answer is that if that was all there was to this business, we wouldn't need all you high-paid employees. It would be more like a civil service job, sort of like working at the post office.

You'd do what you're told, do it on time, and everyone would be happy. We wouldn't need fancy writers or art directors, certainly not for those clients who know exactly what they want to say and probably have a pretty good idea of how the ad should be laid out, too.

Imagine that Don Solomon's goal is to get all the single women in the agency to think that he's a wonderful, bright, handsome guy.

Now suppose that Don goes up to a girl and says, "I'm a wonderful, bright, handsome guy."

He has said what he wanted to say. Why wouldn't it work?

The reason, of course, is that there is a big difference between persuasion and flatulent braggadocio, and we're being paid to create the former.

Q: Who decides what constitutes a good ad?

A: I do. There has to be a final say, one.

EXHIBIT 16.6

This ad presents a direct headline introducing a new restaurant.

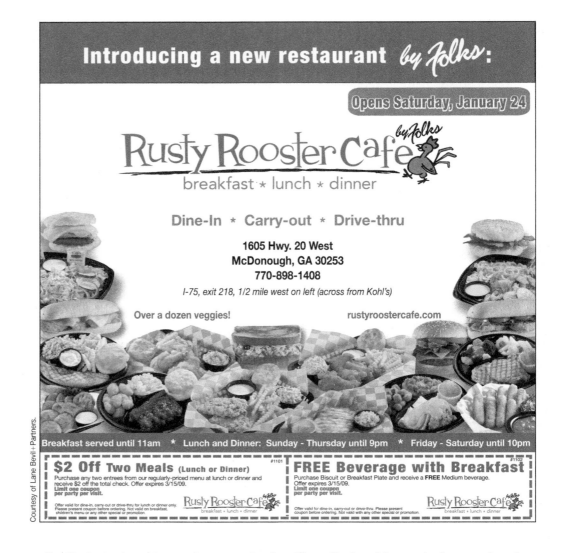

3. *Curiosity-invoking and provocative headlines.* By invoking curiosity, an advertiser may grab attention from an otherwise-disinterested audience by challenging the curiosity of the readers, thereby prompting them to read further and leading them into the key message. David Ogilvy warned against using heads that don't communicate the benefits because of the large numbers of readers that don't read the body copy. It can work, but the writer must be careful to build a strong relationship between the curiosity point and the brand.

Forget the hair of the dog.

ALKA SELTZER WAKE-UP CALL

Not pictured: the weaker sex.

HARLEY-DAVIDSON

Thanks for nothing.

KNOB CREEK BOURBON

The question headline that works best is the kind that arouses curiosity so the reader will read the body copy to find the answer. Readers do not like being tricked. They want a strong relationship between the curiosity and the product. Knob Creek Bourbon's head said "Thanks for nothing" And the accompanying illustration showed an almost empty bottle pouring literally a drop of product. So, what is the take-away from seeing the ad? Well, we could guess. But if you read the copy, you would know.

You see, because we have so many loyal customers out there, demand for Knob Creek Bourbon has finally outstripped the supply. And rather than compromise quality, we're letting it run out. Until the next batch is finished aging for its *full* 9 years. So you may experience something of a shortage at your local liquor store very soon. But not to worry, the next batch will be bottled and on the shelf in November. We appreciate your understanding. . . .

They wanted to tell customers that their choice of bourbon is a popular one and about their quality standards and so on. So the purpose of the head was to get people to read the story because it was too complicated to communicate in a head or a head and subhead.

4. *Selective headlines.* Readers looking through a magazine or newspaper are more likely to read an advertisement they think concerns them personally than one addressed to a broad audience. The selective headline aimed at a particular prime prospect who would be more interested in the product is often used. If the head says, "condominium owners," and you don't own a condominium, you probably won't pay attention; conversely, if you do own a condominium, you might read it. A Pampers advertisement head reads, "Babies absorb everything around them. Wetness doesn't have to be one of them." Obviously, if you don't have a baby in your life, you probably aren't going to read this advertisement. However, if you do have a baby, you may be attracted to the copy. Four such headlines that specifically reach out to special groups are the following:

- To All Men and Women
- To All Young Men and Women
- To All College Men and Women
- To All College Seniors

The first headline is addressed to the greatest number of readers, but it would be of the least interest to any one of them. Each succeeding headline reduces the size of the audience it addresses and improves the chances of attracting that particular group. What about "All College Seniors Who Need Jobs"? You get the idea!

Besides addressing a particular group directly, headlines can appeal to people by mentioning a problem they have in common:

Cancer. Where you're treated first can make all the difference.

MEMORIAL SLOAN-KETTERING CANCER CENTER

Most baby bottoms stink. (And their tops aren't great, either.)

HEALTHTEX

Another vital quality in headlines is specificity. Remember, consumers are more interested in the specific than the general. Therefore, the more specific you can be in the headline, the better: "A Peppermint Peroxide Toothpaste That Will Help Kill Bacteria and Keep Tartar from Your Teeth" is better than "A Nice-Tasting Toothpaste That Cleans Your Teeth."

A headline must say something important to the reader. The actual number of words is not the deciding factor; long or short headlines may work well. But say what you need to say in as few words as possible. Remember, simple is better, but it can be more than one sentence.

Number One in heart care for ~~13, 14,~~ 15 years.

THE CLEVELAND CLINIC

**If you wouldn't want anyone in this magazine to see you naked,
you need to drink this stuff.**

MUSCLE MILK

THE SUBHEADLINE

If the message is long, it can be conveyed with a main headline (with large type) and a subheadline (with smaller type but larger than the body copy). The subheadline can spell out the promise presented in the headline. It can be longer than the headline, it can invite further reading, and it serves as a transition to the opening paragraph of the copy. Orlando uses the headline and the visual to attract you (see Exhibit 16.7). The subheadline gives more information.

Headline: **Orlando makes me smile.**
Subhead: **More smiles. More values. More Orlando for less with our "Bundles of Free Smiles" offers.**

ORLANDO/ORANGE COUNTY CONVENTION & VISITORS BUREAU, INC.

Headline: **Would you rather have a claim or a guarantee?**
Subhead: **Only Valvoline guarantees your engine for up to 300,000 miles.**

VALVOLINE

EXHIBIT 16.7

The subheadline gives more information about the product to the reader. It serves as a transition between the main headline and the following copy.

Courtesy of PUSH and The Orlando/Orange County Convention & Visitors Bureau, Inc.

AMPLIFICATION

The headline and, if used, the subheadline are followed by the body copy of the advertisement. It is here that you present your case for the product and explain how the promise in the headline will be fulfilled. In other words, the body copy amplifies what was announced in the headline or subheadline. What you say and how deep you go depend on the amount of information your prime prospect needs at this point in the buying process. An HD plasma television screen probably calls for more explanation than a low-cost product, such as a barbecue sauce with a new flavor. If a product has many technical advances, there probably is not sufficient room to detail all the features. In this case, the objective is to create enough interest to get the prime prospect to go to the store for a demonstration or to the web for more information. If you said, "Discover a clinically proven way to treat cold sore symptoms up to 3 1/2 days faster," you are presenting a clear benefit.

Amplification should emphasize those product or service features that are of primary importance but cannot be included in the headline. Take, for example, the Krystal trade advertisement (see Exhibit 16.8).

These are dangerous times to be just another clown in the burger biz.

And then the amplification:

Krystal is the small, square burger that packs a big wallop in the competitive world of fast food. To find out how you can become a part of QSR Magazine's Top 50 Franchisors, call 1-800-458-5912, or visit www.krystal.com

EXHIBIT 16.8

The brief copy talks to people about franchising a store. It is not consumer directed.

Courtesy of The Johnson Group.

PROOF

The body copy amplifies what the headline promised. At times the process acts to reassure the consumer that the product will perform as promised. Consumers may look for proof in an advertisement, and proof is particularly important for high-priced products, health products, and new products with special features. Here are a few ways in which proof can be offered to the reader.

SEALS OF APPROVAL   Seals of approval from such accredited sources as *Good Housekeeping* and *Parents* magazines, the American Dental Association, the American Medical Association, the American Heart Association, and Underwriters Laboratories allay consumers' fears about product quality. Such endorsements distinguish a product, and a seal of approval can give a new product an edge of credibility in the marketplace. Aiming at seniors, Verizon Wireless promoted the Samsung Knack, "Introducing a sleek and uncomplicated phone that fits nicely into your active lifestyle. Enjoy effortless calling with raised and readable number keys . . . And the knowledge your phone is backed by the Good Housekeeping Seal. . . ."

GUARANTEES   Zippo lighters uses its guarantee as a major selling point in print advertisements (see Exhibit 16.9). Many companies offer consumers money-back guarantees for trying specific products to reduce the risk and get trial by consumers. The Bose QuietComfort Acoustic Noise Canceling Headphones has a 30-day trial period and guaranteed satisfaction. "Crest Whitestrips and Crest Whitestrips Premium provide you with a beautiful, visibly whiter smile—guaranteed. If you are not satisfied with your results, Crest Whitestrips will refund your purchase."

TRIAL OFFERS AND SAMPLES   KFC and Oprah Winfrey created a nightmare and near riots when people downloaded free online coupons and stores ran out of the new chicken product for their "KFC UnFried Campaign." Procter & Gamble has used direct mail to sample consumers as well as online coupon offers. Obviously, a sample or a trial offer reduces the consumer risk.

WARRANTIES   Sherwin-Williams SuperPaint is advertised with a 20-year warranty against peeling. James Hardie Building Products touts a 50-year warranty for its siding.

REPUTATION   Copy for V8 juice touts its American Heart Association approval. And Spring Air mattress says, "The award winning mattress more people prefer for 5 straight years" (and also has the Good Housekeeping Seal).

DEMONSTRATIONS   "Before" and "after" demonstrations are used to show how a product works. Research says showing models demonstrating cosmetic products is powerful. In one advertisement, Almay showed a supermodel from the neck up, making it easy to see her facial imperfections—or lack thereof—after using Almay's line of hypoallergenic cosmetics. Find a way to tell consumers about a benefit, and you will do well; find a way to show them, and you will fare even better.

TESTIMONIALS   The ability to attract attention to advertisements and offer a credible source has made testimonials a popular device. Testimonials should come from persons viewed by consumers as competent to make judgments on the products they are endorsing. BB&T bank used a campaign of business customers' stories to attract more business customers. One advertisement read: "As far as I'm concerned, if your word's no good, nothing else about you is good. . . . They're in the bank ready to answer our needs. That sets them apart."

The "Got Milk" campaign has been a big fan of testimonials over the years. Some of the personalities from all walks of life include Danica Patrick, Serena Williams, Sheryl

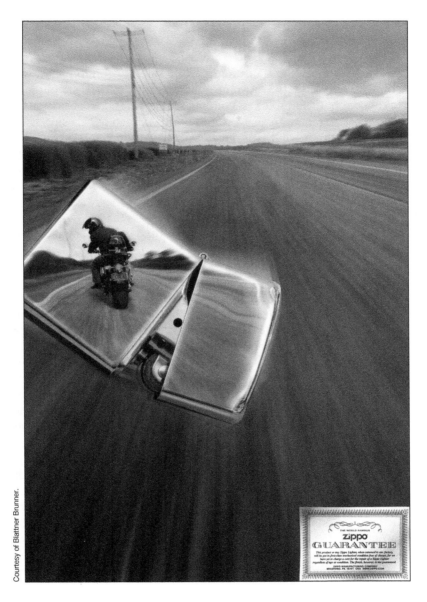

Courtesy of Blattner Brunner.

EXHIBIT 16.9

Zippo features its guarantee.

Crow, Kathy Smith, Christie Brinkley, Brooke Shields, Dara Torres, Suze Ormond, Mariska Hargitay, Michelle Aguilar, and Ellie Krieger.

Dean Rieck, president of Direct Creative, promotes the use of testimonials and suggests that companies actively collect testimonials and success stories. He says they support advertisers' claims and build confidence. He also suggests the following:[26]

- Use testimonials from people who are similar and relevant to prospects. A teacher will believe other teachers; a business owner will believe other business owners; seniors will believe other seniors. Testimonials are more effective if they are from experts or people with relevant experience.

- Don't try to rewrite or fabricate testimonials. The real words of real people are always more believable than anything a writer can come up with. Besides, making them up isn't ethical.

- Testimonials are a form of proof, so increase the credibility of that proof whenever you have a chance. Use full names when possible. Appropriate titles may be an indication of a person's experience or expertise.

Copy Style

5 Explain copy styles.

As with a novel or a play, good advertising copy has a beginning, a middle, and an end. And, like a novel, the transition must be smooth from one part to another. Up to this point, we have discussed how the building blocks of copy are put together. Now we need to think about what it takes to create special attention and persuasion. It takes style—the ability to create fresh, charming, witty, human advertising that compels people to read. Remember what Ron Huey said: "Take the single most salient feature of your product or service and communicate it in a simple, thought-provoking or entertaining way." See the product in a fresh way, explore its possible effects on the reader, or explain the product's advantages in a manner that causes the reader to view the product with a new understanding and appreciation.

Most advertisements end with a close by asking or suggesting that the reader buy the product. The difference between a lively advertisement and a dull one lies in the approach to the message at the outset.

The lens through which a writer sees a product may be the magnifying glass of the technician who perceives every nut and bolt and can explain why each is important, or it may be the rose-colored glasses of the romanticist who sees how a person's life may be affected by the product. That is why we speak of **copy approaches** rather than types of advertisements. The chief approaches in describing a product are the factual, the imaginative, and the emotional.

copy approach
The method of opening the text of an advertisement. The chief forms are the factual approach, the imaginative approach, and the emotional approach.

FACTUAL APPROACH

In the factual approach, we deal with reality—that which actually exists. We talk about the product or service—what it is, how it is made, and what it does. Focusing on the facts about the product that are most important to the reader, we explain the product's advantages.

One of the interesting things about a fact, however, is that it can be interpreted in different ways, each accurate but each launching different lines of thinking. Remember the classic example of an 8-ounce glass holding 4 ounces of water, of which can be said: "This glass is half full" or "This glass is half empty." As you know, both are correct and factual. The difference is in the interpretation of reality, as the Mitsui O.S.K. advertisement headline for shipping seafood says, "We cater to the best schools." Their copy talks facts: "MOL takes a great deal of pride in catering to the needs of the world's most discriminating shippers. Salmon, shrimp, crabs, mussels and other gourmet seafood, for example, are delivered in 409-high-cube reefer containers so that they arrive fresh and delectable in Asian and American markets." Skill in presenting a fact consists of projecting it in a way that means the most to the reader.

The factual approach can be used to sell more than products or services. Facts about ideas, places—anything for which an advertisement can be written—can be presented with a fresh point of view.

IMAGINATIVE APPROACH

There is nothing wrong with presenting a fact imaginatively. The art of creating copy lies in saying a familiar thing in an unexpected way. The Johnson Group took herbs from Kettleby Herb Farms and made them interesting. Their curiosity approach just makes you want to find the answers. The headline reads, "Quite possibly the most delicious toilet bowl cleanser you've ever put in your mouth." Part of the body copy answers questions and puts the benefit in place, "Rosemary. For centuries it's been one of the world's most popular herbs in the kitchen and bathroom. Chefs praise its singular ability to liven any meat dish, particularly lamb and pork roast. And while less well known, boiling a handful of rosemary in two cups of water makes a powerful antiseptic cleaning solution. . . ."

KLEPPNER VIEWPOINT 16.2

Amy Lokken Senior Writer,
McRae Communications, Atlanta

MY CAREER AS A COPYWRITER

Amy Lokken

You. The person who's actually reading every word in this book because you enjoy learning, appreciate the English language, like to see how people communicate, and think there might be a career for you in this thing called advertising. I've got a suggestion for you. Become a copywriter.

To help you on your way, I offer the following tidbits. Maintain curiosity with the world around you. Explore as many topics as you can. Stay current with culture. Listen to what others have to say. And always be willing to learn something new. Why? Because you never know on what account you might be working next. Or what nugget of information just might come in handy.

I've found this to be especially true at the agency where I work. I'm constantly juggling several clients at once, which means I have to quickly get up to speed and cogently write about a wide range of topics, from hiking boots to lawn mowers, from fishfinders to foreign currency exchange, or from tourism to text messaging. On one particular account, our client was entering the new field of digital energy. The only problem was, none of us knew what the heck that meant. In only a few days I had to sift through all of the information from the client and become (somewhat of) a digital energy expert to produce the needed brochure. (See, all that practice you get doing research papers *can* come in handy one day!)

You may have noticed I said "brochure," not "ad campaign." This brings me to another point: There are lots of different types of writing to be done. When I first thought, "I'll have a career in advertising!" I had grand visions of writing 60-second movies that delighted both clients and consumers. But you soon discover lots of clients don't have budgets for big campaigns. Others can't reach their targets with a TV spot, especially business-to-business clients. And as new technologies keep changing the way we communicate, companies keep reexamining how to slice up their ad budget pies.

So be prepared to write anything and everything. It could be six lines of tight body copy; 20 pages of a product catalog; a five-part direct mail campaign; two lines on a blog; a three-word tagline; and, sometimes, even a glorious 60-second movie because for certain clients it is the most effective way to reach their audience and show what they have to offer.

You'll also need to be ready to write to all sorts of target audiences. I've had to address 50-year-old affluent men about buying a dream motorcycle and 30-year-old moms about finding a dream home. Just be sure to talk to them as people, not targets, and never talk down to them. Think about how you would tell your best friend, your brother, or your grandmother about a product or service they might like. You want to inform, help, and entertain, but don't be overbearing.

You never know what type of account or project you might end up working on. But you'll always be learning. You'll always be growing as a writer. And you'll certainly never be bored.

Courtesy of Amy Lokken.

EMOTIONAL APPROACH

Emotion can be a powerful communicator. The feelings about your product or company can be an important plus or minus. Copy using psychological appeals to love, hate, or fear has great impact. "When other hospitals told Dawn Buxbaum her unborn baby would not survive, our doctors said he could be saved. Talk about a second opinion." The illustration and headline in Exhibit 16.10 bring out not only warmth and maternal instincts but also emotion—every parent can identify with the photo. "Life's biggest events are necessarily the ones seen on the nightly news." Often the copy will continue the emotional appeal, although at times it will take a factual direction to inform the reader about specific features of the product to convince the reader of its value.

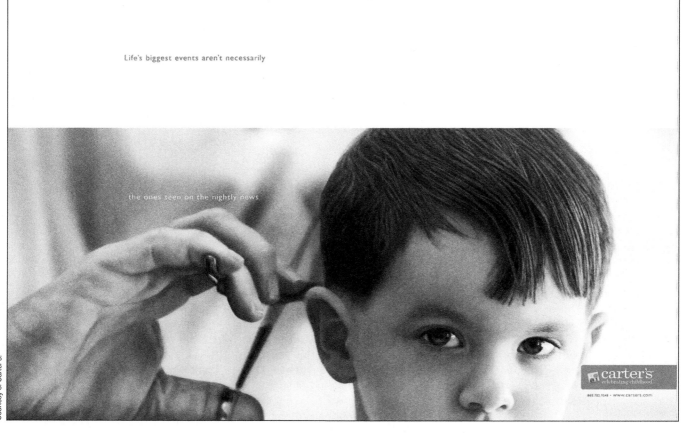

Life's biggest events aren't necessarily

the ones seen on the nightly news.

carter's

Courtesy of Carter's.

EXHIBIT 16.10

Every parent can identify with the emotional pull.

Research indicates that emotion can create positive feelings, such as warmth, happiness, and delight, which work best for low-involvement goods. For higher-involvement, higher-ticket items, such as televisions or automobiles, emotions must be unique and mesh with the brand.

Kevin Roberts, CEO Worldwide of Saatchi & Saatchi, tells us that human beings *think* with feeling and emotion. We just can't help it. Emotion is the *key* to every decision we make, every thought we have, whether it's to click on an attached file or reach for our usual brand of soap powder. Human beings tend to take everything personally and respond with feeling. Joseph Ledoux, one of the world's leading researchers into the emotional brain, had this to say: "Emotions are mostly processes at an unconscious level."

They are quick and focused on what really matters. They acknowledge that intuition, loyalty, and emotion can't be quantified, and then move on.

All the stuff we've been told about "think before you act" and "think it through" is rubbish. It doesn't happen. Rational man is a myth. Women, of course, have always been too smart to have gotten into the rationality arena because in reality it doesn't work. Humans have the ability to focus. People focus on new events, on changes in their environment. They disregard the everyday and the routine. They pay attention until a need is satisfied and then they move on. How do we attract attention? Kevin Roberts believes we can only do this with emotion.

The Center for Emotional Marketing Research shows that advertising that provokes a strong emotional response without providing sufficient product information often breaks through the clutter but is unlikely to change behavior and increase market share. Such advertising connects with consumers but then fails to make use of that connection with the credible information needed to change people's minds. This is "emotional undersell"—a situation in which advertising captures consumers' attention and engages them emotionally but fails to close the deal.[27]

Comparative Advertising

Comparing your product directly with one or more competitors is called **comparative advertising**. It is actually encouraged by the Federal Trade Commission, but it has risks:[28]

comparative advertising Directly contrasts an advertiser's product with other named or identified products.

> *Commission policy in the area of comparative advertising encourages the naming of, or reference to competitors, but requires clarity, and, if necessary, disclosure to avoid deception of the consumer. Additionally, the use of truthful comparative advertising should not be restrained by broadcasters or self-regulation entities.*
> The Commission has supported the use of brand comparisons where the bases of comparison are clearly identified. Comparative advertising, when truthful and nondeceptive, is a source of important information to consumers and assists them in making rational purchase decisions. Comparative advertising encourages product improvement and innovation, and can lead to lower prices in the marketplace.

Some advertisers think it isn't smart to spend money to publicize your competition. Others think it creates a bad atmosphere for the company that demeans all advertising. Pepsi has frequently run advertisements in *Nation's Restaurant News* featuring "Coke and Pepsi View Your Business Two Different Ways," and the copy talks about how it does business differently. Campbell Soup, in a campaign for its Select Harvest line, attacks Progresso by name. Dunkin' Brands goes after Starbucks, promoting a web site that features the results of a taste test that favored its coffee. "We wanted consumers to know our coffee is better-tasting," said Frances Allen, brand marketing officer at Dunkin' Donuts. Even their web site name created for the campaign is combative: dunkinbeatstarbucks.com. Site visitors can send friends e-cards bearing statements like "Friends don't let friends drink Starbucks" and similar greetings.[29]

Comparative campaigns run the risk of being perceived as overly negative, a judgment that can hurt a brand. It is necessary to walk that fine line of not turning consumers off. Often, humor is used to soften the message.

Despite each comparative advertisement being different, there are certain rules of thumb that can be applied: (1) The leader in the field never starts a comparative campaign. (2) The most successful comparison advertisements are those comparing the product with products identical in every respect except for the special differential featured in the advertisement. The stronger the proof that the products are identical, the better. (3) The different features should be of importance to the consumer.

Slogans

Originally derived from the Gaelic *slugh gairm*, meaning "battle cry," the word *slogan* has an appropriate background. A slogan sums up the theme for a product's benefits to deliver an easily remembered message in a few words—"It's the Real Thing."

6 **Discuss slogans.**

There have been many very memorable slogans in advertising over the years, for example, "Just Do It" (Nike); "Tastes Great, Less Filling" (Miller Lite); "Good to the Last Drop" (Maxwell House); "Does She . . . Or Doesn't She?" (Clairol); "When It Rains It Pours" (Morton Salt); and "We Try Harder" (Avis). Even though not all effective slogans are etched in every consumer's mind, many slogans do help communicate the essence of the product position, for example, "Pawleys Island. Arrogantly Shabby."

Used even more often on television and radio than in print, slogans may be combined with a catchy tune to make a jingle.

Slogans are created to communicate something specific and defined by strategy. In general, they may be either institutional or hard sell. Institutional slogans are created to establish a prestigious image for a company. Relying on this image to enhance their products and services, many firms insist that their slogans appear in all of their advertising and on their letterheads. An entire advertisement may feature the slogan, for example, "You're in good hands with Allstate." Hard-sell slogans epitomize the special or significant features of the product or service being advertised, and their claims are strongly competitive. For example, Home Depot's slogan is "More saving. More doing."

General Electric (GE) purged its 24-year-old slogan "We Bring Good Things to Life" for "Imagination at Work." It is difficult to change a slogan in which you have invested millions of dollars for one that isn't proven. The reason for the change was that the old slogan no longer represented the corporate direction. Research about "Good Things" brought surprises. "Nearly everybody said it meant only two things: lighting and appliances," says GE's Judy Hu, general manager for corporate advertising and marketing communications. The company ranks as one of the world's largest and most diversified technology and service organizations. Its holdings range from aircraft engines and power generators to financial services and a television network.

"Most companies want a really great tagline that can crystallize the brand across different audiences," says Tracey Riese, president of branding consulting firm TG Riese.[30]

Some marketing gurus argue that large marketing firms, such as Anheuser-Busch and Coca-Cola, should forget one-size-fits-all themes and come up with different slogans to reach different audiences. Most marketers, however, haven't bought into this theory.

Slogans are widely used to advertise groceries, drugs, beauty aids, and liquor. These are products that are bought repeatedly at comparatively low prices. They are sold to consumers in direct competition on the shelves of supermarkets, drugstores, and department stores. If a slogan can remind a shopper in one of those stores of a special feature of the product, it certainly has served its purpose. Slogans can also remind shoppers of the name of a product from a company they respect. Not all advertising needs slogans. One-shot announcements—sale advertisements for which price is the overriding consideration— usually do not use slogans. Creating a slogan is one of the fine arts of copywriting.

Companies sometimes need to change because of competition or market changes. Here is a brief history of Coca-Cola's slogans:

> **Open Happiness (2009)**
>
> **The Coke Side of Life (2006)**
>
> **Life Tastes Good (2001)**
>
> **Always Coca-Cola (1993)**
>
> **Can't Beat the Real Thing (1990)**
>
> **Red, White and You (1986)**
>
> **Coke Is It! (1982)**
>
> **Have a Coke and a Smile (1979)**
>
> **I'd Like To Buy the World a Coke (1971)**
>
> **It's the Real Thing (1969)**

RECYCLING OLD POPULAR TAGLINES

"We believe that great taglines are things that people connect with," says legend Jeff Goodby, co-chair of Goodby, Silverstein & Partners, San Francisco, "And I think it takes a certain amount of selflessness to think this out and figure what is best for your client. People could say we're just being lazy and opportunistic—which, of course, we are—but we're also smart enough to know a great piece of equity when we see it."[31]

The "Citi never sleeps" tagline, was written in 1977 by Wells, Rich, Green, the bank's agency at the time. It was resurrected in 2008, replacing the extremely short-lived "Let's get it done," but the agency used a newer, more creative logo.

During the past several years, The New York Times Media Group, brought back a tagline not used for 20 years: "These times demand the Times." Hair-brand Finesse brought back, "Sometimes you need a little Finesse. Sometimes you need a lot." In 2004, agency Richards Group revived "For the seafood lover in you" for Red Lobster after testing its popularity in 2003.[32] It scored high points with consumers and the decision was made to bring it back. Nationwide Insurance traded in their humorous "Life comes at you fast" tag for their classic, "Nationwide is on your side."

ELEMENTS OF A GOOD SLOGAN

A slogan differs from most other forms of writing because it is designed to be remembered and repeated word for word to impress a brand and its message on the consumer. Ideally, the slogan should be short, clear, and easy to remember.

Advanced Medicine for Pain

ADVIL

Where Shopping Is a Pleasure

PUBLIX MARKETS

Can You Hear Me Now?

VERIZON

Zoom-Zoom

MAZDA

Love the skin you're in.

OLAY

It is an advantage to have the name of the product in the slogan:

Kroger. For Goodness Sake.

KROGER

The Milk Chocolate Melts in Your Mouth—Not in Your Hands.

M&M

It pays to Discover.

DISCOVER CARD

Tested Guidelines for an Advertisement

Philip W. Sawyer, editor, *Starch Tested Copy*, after years of studying readership studies, shares some of his findings:[33]

> What follows are 10 guidelines that I believe advertisers should keep in mind whenever they sit down to create an ad. As we offer these, we are well aware that any number of ads ignore these guidelines yet are very successful. That's fine. Mark Twain broke almost every rule of grammar when he wrote *The Adventures of Huckleberry Finn*. But he had to know the rules before he could break them effectively.

1. *Keep it simple, stupid.* The KISS principle, as this is called, has no better application than in advertising, yet it is probably the most abused principle of all. Simplicity is a virtue. Traditional advertising (and some online) needs to catch the eye quickly and deliver its message quickly, or it will be missed.

2. *You're not selling the product; you're selling the benefits of the product.* Robinson & Associates created a trade ad for Ceco Building System's "Cool Roof" (see Exhibit 16.11). Some of the copy reads, ". . . cool is smart. Cool is an energy-efficient, sustainable, low life-cycle cost, durable, fire and wind resistant, lightweight Ceco metal roof." In reality, most readers do not enter the advertiser's realm readily. They do so only when convinced that the product will do something

KLEPPNER VIEWPOINT 16.3

Sarah Hughes   Copywriter, Ignited Minds, Marina del Ray

Sarah Hughes

THINGS TO WORK ON BESIDES YOUR PORTFOLIO

Creatives often get caught up perfecting their beloved book. But frankly, getting a job done goes far beyond that. Here are a few tips I've learned on my journey as a copywriter and really, simply as a business professional. They apply to any and all disciplines and are good ideas to keep in mind at any stage of your career.

SHAKE HANDS, WITH EVERYONE

Arm yourself with a bottle of hand sanitizer and start shaking. Get to know your peers in class. Meet your professors during their office hours. Get the business cards of every single person who speaks at your marketing or advertising club. Introduce yourself to the person sitting next to you on the bus reading *Adweek*. Make the rounds to every ad agency in your city. These people are your greatest assets. They should know your name and recognize your face.

THEN LET THEM JABBER ON AND ON AND ON . . .

If there's one thing I've learned over the years, it's this: People love to tell their story. They love to talk about how they got started, how they became successful, and what they learned along the way. And it's a good thing too, because you can glean a lot of helpful information from their successes and their mistakes. So prepare a barrage of questions and start listening. You'll be amazed by many interesting insights people have to share.

FOLLOWING THROUGH MEANS FOLLOWING UP

But all these people you're meeting and shaking hands with don't mean anything if they don't know your name from Adam. That's why following up is key. Send a quick e-mail every 3 to 6 months with an update on what you're doing. Keep a record of who you've followed up with and when. After having worked in advertising, there's nothing more obnoxious than meeting someone once and then 4 years later, getting an e-mail from that person asking for a favor. If you've done your due diligence keeping in touch, then you'll have no problems asking someone to help you once that time comes around.

EVERYONE NEEDS A SHTICK

Anyone can write a generic introductory e-mail. But can you make the person you're contacting pay attention to you? Can you raise a question that drives him or her to find an answer for you? I once sent an e-mail to a creative director at East/West Creative in New York City. Not recognizing my address, he thought my message was junk mail at first. And so I followed up with a package of newspaper ads and coupons, along with a note that said, "You sounded disappointed that my e-mail wasn't junk mail, so I thought I'd send you some anyway." I landed an interview a week later.

Courtesy of Sarah Hughes.

for them. If an advertiser does not answer the reader's implicit question—What's in it for me?—the ad is unlikely to attract any real interest.

Many of the best ads directly address the problems that the product or service solves and suggest how that solution makes life better for the potential consumer.

3. *When appropriate, spice it up with sex.* Sawyer's Copy Research says sex still sells, or at least in appropriate circumstances. Some believe that men are interested in sex and women are not. In truth, the publications that carry the sexiest advertising are those aimed at women and they attract considerable notice and readership.

   At the same time, it should be emphasized that sexy ads tend to be simple ads—perfectly reasonable because clutter and salaciousness are not really compatible. The best ads of this type may feature nudity but are not explicitly erotic.

4. *Use celebrities.* Opinion surveys indicate that Americans do not believe an ad simply because it features a well-known person hawking the product. However,

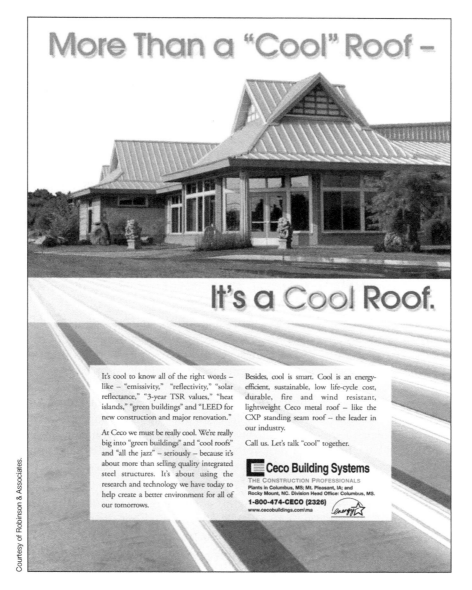

Courtesy of Robinson & Associates.

EXHIBIT 16.11

Ceco sells the benefits of its cool roof in this trade ad.

according to our data, ads with celebrities earn "noted" scores that are 13 percent higher than average. They are particularly effective with women readers, scoring 15 percent higher than average, compared with 10 percent higher for men. Overall, ads with testimonials from celebrities score 11 percent above the average, whereas testimonials from noncelebrities actually earn below-average scores. Celebrities may not be believable, but they are very effective at attracting reader attention, which is the first job of any advertisement.

5. *Exploit the potential of color.* Print advertising has the potential to contend with television. The moving image is a profoundly effective means of communication, and anyone who has ever tried to amuse a baby knows that the eye has an inherent attraction to motion. At the same time, the eye is also attracted to bold, bright, and beautiful color. Our data indicate that one-page color ads earn "noted" scores that are 45 percent higher on average than comparable black-and-white ads; two-page color ads earn scores that are 53 percent higher than similar black-and-white ads. Generally, the more colorful, the better (as long as the advertiser keeps in mind the other nine principles).

Television has a lock on the moving image, but print's ability to generate astonishing, eye-catching colors is substantial, and publications should do everything possible to stay current with new advances in color technology.

6. *Go with the flow.* Every ad has flow to it, and the flow is determined by the positioning of the various creative elements. Ads with good flow send the reader's eye around the page or screen to take in all the important elements: the illustration, headline, body copy, and brand name. Ads with bad flow may attract a fair amount of attention at first, but send the reader on their way. For example, a number of advertisers make the mistake of placing a flashy illustration toward the bottom of the page and the copy and headline at the top. In such cases, the most powerful element of an ad can turn out to be the most detrimental because that alluring illustration steals attention away from the copy.

7. *Avoid ambiguity.* Although it appears that Europeans accept, if not welcome, ambiguous themes and symbols, we have found that Americans have little tolerance for advertising that does not offer a clear and distinct message.

   Americans like it straight. They choose not to spend a great deal of time thinking about the messages in their advertising. If the point of the ad is not clear, the typical American reader will move on.

8. *Heighten the contrast.* We live in a visual culture, and one thing that delights the eye is contrast. So advertisers would do well to employ what might be called "visual irony" in their advertising. One suggestion is to contrast the content of the ads. Be sure to read Sheri Bevil's comments about the elephant in the cornfield in the next chapter.

   Another way to fulfill this principle is to contrast the elements constituting the form of the ad—color, for example. Data indicate that using black as a background makes elements in the foreground pop off the page. Stolichnaya earned average scores with a horizontal shot of the product against a white background. When the same layout was produced with a change only in the background, from white to black, the scores increased by 50 percent on average.

9. *Use children and animals.* Almost any advertising can succeed with an appeal to the emotions, and children and animals appeal to all but the most hard-hearted. But you better make a connection; if people feel "had," they will leave you.

10. *When an ad has a good deal of copy, make it as inviting as possible.* Some people present copy over a mottled background, making it almost impossible to read easily (sometimes we get too cute will our PhotoShop abilities). We need to make the process as easy for the reader as possible. Good content alone will not attract readers. The best-written, wittiest, and most powerful copy will be overlooked in any medium unless it is well spaced and sufficiently large and clear to invite the reader. The Home Depot ad in Exhibit 16.12 uses bold type in reverse to communicate "Cost issues." The body copy is easily read and has contrast built in. Its simple clean layout helps readership.

Outdoor Messages

New production technologies offer the opportunity to create something bigger than life. Here you can create disruption from the ordinary. A giant peach sitting in a field will attract attention because it is a thousand times larger than a peach should be. The Richards Group in Dallas created an outdoor poster that had a cow on a billboard threatening to jump (Exhibit 16.13). We all know that cows don't climb up on billboards or jump off, yet we look.

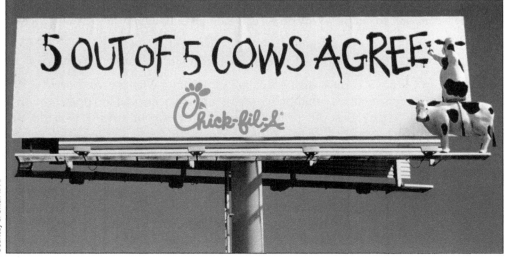

EXHIBIT 16.12

Home Depot strives for attention and readership.

EXHIBIT 16.13

Climbing cows are a disruption to the norm, especially up on outdoor boards.

TRONE

If you wanted someone's attention at a party, you wouldn't scream at them from across the room. You'd get closer to them and have your conversation face-to-face. More so, you probably wouldn't do all the talking; you'd also listen. When you did talk, you'd do your best to make sure the person you were talking to actually wanted to hear what you had to say. The same applies to marketing today.

Trone is a midsize agency in North Carolina that connects people and brands by getting to know both as well as possible. We call it Unmass the Message—making communications personal, timely, relevant, and engaging.

Our understanding of the target audience has to go beyond demographic profiles and media consumption habits.

We are constantly asking people from our online consumer panel (opinion.trone.com) questions about their attitudes, motivations, and behavior. This data helps us develop insights that shape our communication strategies for our clients.

But an insightful strategy isn't the agency's final product. It merely points us in the right direction to develop a brand's communication. Increasingly, that communication includes far more than ads. Trone regularly creates campaigns that use some combination of direct-response marketing, web sites, social media, online advertising, ambient media, trade shows, and public relations in addition to traditional media.

The result? A brand that connects to its target audience in a meaningful way and maintains a long-term relationship.

Just a few thoughts on outdoor. First, you have a responsibility to create something wonderful because most people dislike ads cluttering up the environment. You should ask, as with any medium, how the ad will be integrated into other kinds of communications. In Chapter 12, an overview of creative was given. Generally, there should be no more than seven words in the main head. We're not saying an ad won't communicate with more than seven words in the head, but the more words you have, the harder the message is to grasp quickly. This is truly a medium in which simple is better. Reduce all the elements, if possible. If you have a bottle of Sobe energy drink as your illustration, do you also need to have a logo? Maybe, but if the bottle is large enough, you'll easily see the logo on it. The point is to reduce the visual and verbal elements down to their simplest form. And digital technology, where available, offers creatives other creative ways to attract consumers' attention.

Today's Message Tools

7 Discuss new format and content messages.

Today's communication tools offer advertisers many ways to attract attention and hopefully communicate with people who want the message. And they are changing every day. Did iPhone change the way we think of phones? How have Apps changed the way we market to people? Why do we call them phones anymore? Let's take a look at a few of these.

SOCIAL SUCCESS

According to Carnet Williams, chief executive of Sprout, "What we've learned is that social media success involves common sense, listening to peers and looking at things in a different light" Here's a list of best practices for creating your own social media success story:"[34]

1. *Appeal to what people love the most—themselves.* When I get an e-mail notification that I have been tagged in a photo, I immediately race to Facebook.

2. *Measurement is very important, but don't lose the forest for the trees.* Companies shouldn't delay adding social media components to their campaigns while waiting for the perfect ROI scenario. Social media is about engagement and with 20 percent engagement rates, brands would be served well to find a good social media partner and take the leap.

3. *Plan for success, but know you won't always hit home runs.* Social media has the power to exceed your wildest goals because of the viral features of social networks. People love to share with their friends and if you hit on an idea that resonates, it will take off. But if you don't hit a home run right away, try again. Social media is easy to tweak and optimize. Don't be afraid to try different things until you get it right.

4. *What they are saying is true; social media is about conversations.* When is the last time you met a friend for a drink and showed up at the bar with a script? Hopefully, you wouldn't think about scripting your conversations with your customers, either.

SOCIAL MEDIA MARKETING

BLOG STORIES   There have been discussions about the ethics of marketers paying bloggers to review their products, which is a valid conversation to have. But that is only a small part of the blog story.

Marketers are getting involved with every kind of social media, including blogging. Yes, bloggers may seem so 2005, but they're far from unnoticed by marketers. For example, the BlogHer network has 1,200 blogging members and touts a unique visitor reach of 15 million moms; they may be an important part of social media for marketers' efforts.

Moms' buying habits changed during the economic downturn and this has affected brands. How do marketers address the issues with new mom, since many of the old ways of connecting with this market segment are obsolete to her? Many marketers aren't interested in buying banners on blogs like BlogHer, but using them as part of their conversation is important. PepsiCo sees its participation in blogs and social media generally as a combination of listening to its consumers and reaching consumers through influencers. PepsiCo global chief marketing officer Jill Beraud said at the BlogHer 2009 Conference that Pepsi believes social media is the way of communicating in the future, and shouldn't be considered a short-term ROI. She indicated Pepsi's blogging support is really an investment in our brands and understanding our consumers. Everyone is looking for a new dialog.

TELLING THE STORY   There are many means to tell a marketing story, and talented creative people explore all of these to find the best approach to engage potential consumers. "We create demand for our brand by being flexible about how we tell the story," says Nike's Trevor Edwards, vice president, global brand and category management. "We do not rigidly stay with one approach. We do not start with the medium," Mr. Edwards says. "We always start with the consumer and then look for the best ways to connect with them."[35]

Here are a couple of definitions of tools used by creative people in the changing world of marketing technology:

Webisodes: A series of minimovies created for the web. Today, there isn't really a standard. Each tells its story as the creatives see fit. Many are 3-minutes stories. Check out martinowens.com to see some examples. As content providers, Martin+Owen provide webisodes for a number of clients. In 2001, Fallon advertising revolutionized the Internet with the BMW film series, *The Hire.* Five years later, they were back with a low-interest commodity Brawny Paper Towels film series. The theme was lack of performance—about how women are basically disappointed in their husbands. Each 10- to 12-minute reality episode was compelling and full of laughs. Today, webisodes are not unusual; they're one of the tools.

Rich media: Method of communication that incorporates animation, sound, video, and/or interactivity that is going to overtake search marketing as the dominant form of web advertising by the end of the decade. In general, consumers will click on a rich media ad five times compared to once for a banner ad.

ONLINE MISSION

Maxine Clark, founder and CEO of Build-A-Bear-Workshop says, "Selling on the Internet shouldn't be your priority. Instead, focus on building an online community that enhances your ability to communicate with customers. Unless you have only an online presence, the number one goal of your site should be to drive business to your physical locations, where you can deliver on your brand promise."[36]

Mar's M&M chocolate candy uses e-mail to bring you to their microsite. Recently, they sponsored *Transformers,* with a game that asked you to "Help stop the M&M deceptions." There were a number of other activities and information on the site: M&M characters, Fun & Games, Recipes & Ideas, M&M Racing, Newsletters, History. This is obviously more than simply storytelling by a marketer; it is an attempt to engage people while building their online community—and hopefully furthering the conversation. From our standpoint, all of this is advertising (see the opening print ads at the beginning of this chapter).

Brown-Forman's Southern Comfort brand—weary of the narrow window on which they are permitted to advertise on cable—took its entire media buy digital, allowing it access to programs online it couldn't touch on TV. They used online properties such as Facebook, Spin, Fader, Pitchfork, ThrillistBreak.com, My Damn Channel, NBC, CBS, FOX, FX, and Hulu.[37] Each offers a new creative opportunity.

SUMMARY

Start planning an advertisement with the creative work plan or the creative brief for any advertising format. If it is written properly, the creative work plan will tell you what the message should be in the advertisement and what the advertisement is to accomplish. It tells you the advertisement's specific purpose. However, no work plan will tell you how to execute the copy—that's part of the creative process.

For years good advertising was the result of reductive writing. Today, new media offers the opportunity to provide the information consumers seek. We call that expansive writing. With all the advertising formats and tools, simplicity is still a key to either reductive or expansive writing because consumers want the information. Good copy speaks to all people. The great creative shops of today have a common thread running through their advertising—the headline, the visual, and the logo communicate the idea immediately.

Advertising motivates people by appealing to their problems, desires, and goals and by offering them solutions to their problems, satisfactions of their desires, and a means of achieving their goals.

In general, advertisements have a definite structure consisting of the promise of a benefit in the headline (and maybe the spelling out of the promise in a subheadline), amplification of the story or facts, proof of claim, and action to take. Effective heads can be long or short, but they need to clearly communicate the message. The subheadline can expand on the promise presented in the headline and can provide transition between the headline and the first sentence of the body copy. The body copy is where you build your case for the product with consumers and where you support the promise in the head or subhead. The details about the product or service are presented in the body copy, along with support for your claim.

The creative essence of copywriting involves seeing a product in a fresh, unique way. The chief approaches used to describe products are factual, imaginative, and emotional. A slogan sums up the theme for a product's benefits. It needs to be a memorable message with few words.

REVIEW

1. What is social storytelling?
2. How can advertisers use psychological appeals?
3. How do reductive and expansive copy work?
4. What's the purpose of the headline?
5. What is the purpose of amplification?
6. What is meant by "copy style"?
7. What are the characteristics of an effective slogan?
8. What is time famine?

Bluegrass

Alternative Rock

Country

R&B

Rock

Pop

Jazz

Hip-Hop

Where music thrives.

Welcome to Georgia, music capital of the South. A friendly place that inspires fresh, original music across every genre. You'll be drawn here to work with top producers, artists, and engineers in our state-of-the-art recording and rehearsal studios. And you'll become part of a rich recording history that spans from a wildly successful album in 1923 to the chart-toppers of today. Find out more about the one state that hits all the right notes. Contact the Georgia Film, Music & Digital Entertainment Office today.

Visit georgia.org/music or call 404.962.4052

Georgia®

The Total Concept: Words and Visuals

IDEAS AND advertisements. How does a creative team get from an idea to a finished advertisement? What kinds of visuals are best? How do we generate fresh ideas? ▶

CHAPTER LEARNING OBJECTIVES

1. Define concepts and executional ideas.
2. Discus left- and right-brain ideas.
3. Explain how a creative team works.
4. Explain visualizing the idea.
5. Identify the principles of design.
6. Discuss types of visuals.

More and more clients are realizing that creative advertisements work better, are more memorable, and make their point more effectively in the marketplace. You can run a good creative ad fewer times. People remember it after seeing it three times rather than 30 times. Any unique selling proposition (USP) advantage is gone in 15 minutes if you don't create an emotional bond with consumers. "Advertising is not art. It is a business masquerading as art," claims John Butler, creative director of Butler, Shine, Stern & Partners. He has told this to many good art directors and writers when they balked at a layout comment or an editorial mandate and refused to budge. He suggests they can go to a craft store and buy a canvas and some oils, because this is advertising, and "it is not a spectator sport."[1] Grey Worldwide's chief creative officer says, "You should bring together art and commerce. But you can do some of the most engaging, funny work in the world and if it doesn't motivate the consumer to do something or stimulate some part of their brain, then it doesn't work."[2] So again we find that there isn't a simple set of rules that works for creating strong advertisements or other marketing communications. But all agree that strategic concepts, insights, and ideas are the foundation.

Create Relevant Ideas

All advertising, regardless of where and how it appears, can only be successful if it has an impact on the audience it is addressing. And the only way you can be sure of achieving this is if the content (idea) is so compelling that it creates a desire among those exposed to it to want more information—to want to know more.[3]

> 1 Define concepts and executional ideas.

What are some of the great ads you remember from your growing-up years? Why do you remember them? There probably was an idea that was relevant or entertaining to you. Our minds work in mysterious ways. We have to learn to take the reader or viewer beyond the strategy. We also need to go beyond style into a magical dimension. You probably remember "Just Do It." It helped define a company. "I can't believe I ate the whole thing" is another classic for those who are old enough to remember or fortunate enough to have seen it as part of advertising history. Brylcreem's "Greasy Kid's Stuff"; Avis's "When You're Only No. 2, You Try Harder"; Volkswagen's "Lemon"; Wendy's "Where's the Beef?"; and AT&T's "Reach Out and Touch Someone" were all

EXHIBIT 17.1

Yes, readers get the idea.

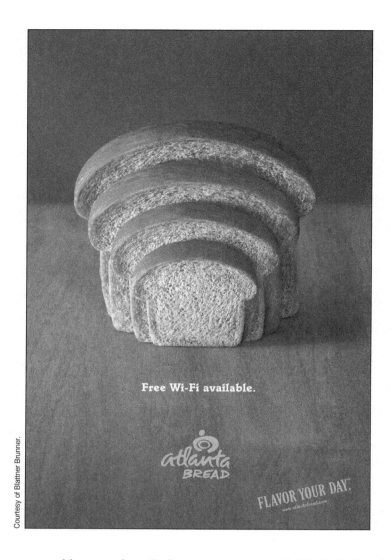

memorable campaigns. Before we can create this kind of advertising, we have to learn to develop the idea behind the strategy.

George Lois, the outrageous art director, was once asked, "What is advertising?" He answered, "Advertising is poison gas. It should bring tears to your eyes, and it should unhinge your nervous system. It should knock you out." He admitted that his description is probably excessive but regards it as forgivable hyperbole because it certainly describes the powerful possibilities of advertising. Great advertising should have the impact of a punch in the mouth. Great advertising should ask, without asking literally, "Do you get the message?" And the reader (viewer) should answer, without answering literally, "Yeah, I got it!" Lois says all of this can be accomplished with the "big idea." Atlanta Bread delivers it message visually (see Exhibit 17.1).

And today, that big idea may be aimed at consumers in television, magazines, mobile, short-content films, or any other medium. Ideas are an obsession at Crispin Porter+ Bogusky (CP+B). Jeff Benjamin, the agency's interactive director, is one of its idea stars. He developed the web element that would go along with a series of television spots for the Subservient Chicken campaign. "Even if another agency had thought to bring back the 'Have It Your Way' slogan, it probably would have just replayed the original Burger King (BK) song from 30 years ago and shot some spots around that," says Pete Favat, executive creative director for Boston-based advertising shop Arnold Worldwide. "They are like pitbulls when it comes to finding creative ways to deliver a message." The BK site attracted more than 460 million visitors in 2 years.[4] Obviously, that was a big idea.

The creative process can be broken down into four basic areas: concepts, words, pictures, and the medium or vehicle used to present them. The dictionary defines a *concept* as a general notion or idea, an idea of something formed by mentally combining all its characteristics or particulars. In advertising, the total concept is a fresh way of looking at something—a novel way of talking about a product or service, a dramatic new dimension that gives the observer a new perspective. A concept is an idea. Many in advertising, including Lois, call it the big idea—one that is expressed clearly and combines words and visuals. The words describe what the basic idea is, and the visuals illustrate what the words say or, even better, reinforce the words or provide a setting that makes the words more powerful.

Your creative concept must not only grab attention but it also must get across the main selling point and the brand name. How often has someone seen a compelling advertisement only to later say, "I don't remember the brand name or product."

Ideas Come from the Left and Right Brain

The brain is divided into two completely separate hemispheres. Each hemisphere processes different information. The left hemisphere provides reasoning, controls verbal skills (a characteristic of good talkers), and processes information. It thinks in language. It works linearly and methodically. The right hemisphere provides intuition, processes information in parallel, controls the creative process, thinks in mental images, thinks nonverbally, responds to color, and is artistic. It "sees" the big picture. Usually, we have a left-brain person and a right-brain person work together to develop concepts. Each comes to the table with a different point of view.

One side of the brain is dominant. Some people are left-handed and some people are right-handed. In a similar fashion, some people are left brainers and some people are right brainers. Al Ries says, "Ambibrainerity" is extremely rare. Although you can learn to exercise the less-favored half of your brain, working both sides equally is almost impossible. Depending on how you were born, you will live your life as either a left brainer or a right brainer.[5]

Long-time creator of memorable ad campaigns—for example, "Millertime," "Soup Is Good Food," "Things Go Better with Coke," and "Tastes Great, Less Filling"—Bill Backer defines a *basic idea* or *concept* as an abstract answer to a perceived desire or need. An **executional idea** is a rendering in words, symbols, sounds, colors, shapes, forms, or any combination thereof of an abstract answer to a perceived desire or need. We use the word *execute* in advertisement development. It is a schizophrenic verb. It means to complete or put into effect or to use according to a pattern—as a work of art. Of course, it also means "to put to death."

It is the idea that drives things. John Hegarty has an enlarged quote up on his wall from a dictionary and it says, "An idea is a thought or plan formed by mental effort." In other words, the color blue is not an idea. However, when you are trying to promote a new movie studio production stage that holds 280,000 gallons of water, maybe blue is part of an idea. The award-winning agency LKM created this strong visual ad (see Exhibit 17.2), which is aimed at a very specific target—people in the film industry. The copy at the top right says, "A 280,000 gallon tank. Now on one of the world's biggest production stages. EUE/Screen Gems Stage 10." The floating bottle says, "Cut."

The Creative Team

In general, the art director is responsible for the visuals, layouts, and graphics in an advertisement. The copywriter creates the words for the advertisement and maybe the advertising concept. We say "maybe" because when creative teams are used, it is the responsibility of the team to develop a concept. The copywriter needs to understand art

2 **Discus left- and right-brain ideas.**

executional idea
A rendering in words, symbols, shapes, forms, or any combination thereof of an abstract answer to a perceived desire or need.

3 **Explain how a creative team works.**

EXHIBIT 17.2

The copy reads, "A 280,000 gallon tank. Now on one of the world's biggest production stages. EUE/Screen Gems Stage 10." The floating bottle says, "Cut." This ad was aimed at people in the film industry.

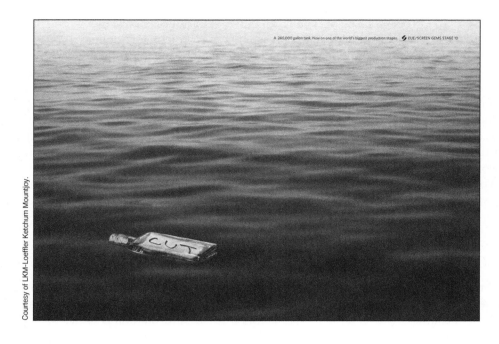

Courtesy of LKM-Loeffler Ketchum Mountjoy.

direction, and the art director needs to appreciate the impact of words. Together they need to have a rapport to be successful. Both are concept thinkers. Both think in terms of words and pictures, after team members arm themselves with all the information they need. When they have settled on a target audience and a creative strategy, these left- and right-brain people begin to create.

This relationship between the copywriter and the art director is almost like a marriage. You spend an average of 8 hours a day with your partner—that's 40 hours a week, or 2,080 hours a year. The truth is that better teams feed off each other. Each has its own method of developing big ideas. But there probably isn't a single best method. Dick Lord, creative legend, says, "I get my biggest drawing pad and I'll draw little thumbnails and I'll just do headlines or visual ideas. I'll brainstorm myself. I'll sit by myself and do 60, 70—I don't edit them. And then you go over them a little later and you find maybe 10 or 12 that you could look at again. Then, you get with your art director partner, and say, 'Well, what have you got? I have this.'" Some art directors and copywriters like to work by themselves first.

The Idea

Strong ideas may be difficult to develop, but they're worth fighting for when you find one. Strong ideas are simple ideas (see Exhibit 17.3). People do not remember details as clearly as they recall concepts. In advertising, simple concepts become great advertisements through attention to detail—the words, type style, photography, and layout. A great advertising concept might survive poor execution, but the better crafted the advertisement, the better the chances that prospects will become customers.

We are not necessarily talking about hitting home runs with breakthrough advertising. We are not talking about Nike, Coca-Cola, or Pepsi, iPhone, or glamorous products. We are talking about ideas that solve problems and communicate to consumers. Ogilvy & Mather took the declining Lever Brothers' Surf detergent brand and increased its sales by more than 20 percent by telling it like it is—doing laundry is a drag and there's no point in trying to deny it. Research showed that 45 percent of all laundry-doers do laundry only as a last resort. Lever's even has a name for them—the un-laundry people. The campaign's idea was to accentuate the negative by playing up the drudgery of doing laundry in a lighthearted way.

KLEPPNER VIEWPOINT 17.1

Scott Scaggs

Scott Scaggs Group Creative Director, Trone

THE FIRST AD YOU CREATE WILL BE TOTAL GARBAGE

Sorry. Don't take it too hard. It takes a while to get through all the first thoughts, corny wordplay, and yawn-inducing ideas. But the bigger obstacle aspiring writers and art directors need to overcome is the inclination to create ads that look and sound like other real ads. They copy what they've seen. Too bad most ads aren't worth copying.

The best thing to do this early in your ad career is to fill your brain with as much great advertising as you can. True, some of the 3,000+ advertising messages you're exposed to every day might actually be brilliant. But I'm going to assume you want to have a life and would like someone to cull the stack of brand communications down to a digestible set of expertly crafted ads—ads that you can absorb, dissect, analyze, and mimic. (By mimic, I certainly don't mean steal. I mean figure out what makes them great so you can apply that kind of thinking or approach to your own creative work.)

So where do you find the good ones? Here's a by-no-means-complete list of places you can look to find award-winning creative work:

- *Communication Arts* (advertising and design magazine, commarts.com)
- *The One Show* (awards annual, oneclub.org)
- *Lürzer's Int'l Archive* (magazine with cutting-edge ads)
- *AdCritic* (creativity-online.com)
- *Adweek* (adweek.com/creative)
- *I Believe In Advertising* (ibelieveinadv.com)
- *CMYK* (magazine for aspiring creatives)

Visit the bookstore and spend some time in the magazine section that includes *Communication Arts, Print*, and *Lürzer's Int'l Archive*. See what else is there. You'll probably notice many of the same ad agencies showing up in these awards annuals and showcases over and over. Take note of who they are and visit their web sites to see what new work they're featuring.

Once you get a sense of what great advertising is, expand your inspiration pool to include things outside of existing ads, for example, fine art, photography, YouTube videos, discarded gum wrappers, or anything. Fill your creative well with life experiences that you can draw from every time you sit down with a blank page.

But for all the time and energy you spend studying the great work that's already been done, don't expect every idea you come up with to be on that level. For every ad that appears in those awards annuals, you can bet that the creative team had 50 to 100 more ideas for the very same assignment. Maybe more. If you want to end up with better ideas, start by coming up with more ideas. Don't stop when you get to the first good one because there's likely a great one you haven't thought about yet.

Soon you'll be on the same roller coaster writers and art directors ride their whole careers—the one where you alternately think you're a miserable hack and you're a freakin' genius.

Courtesy of Scott Scaggs.

A few years ago, BBDO presented a concept to KFC based on the old joke about the chicken crossing the road to illustrate customers' preference for KFC. But, in 1989, KFC had used a "Cross the Road" campaign from Young & Rubicam that franchises disliked. Also, rival Wendy's International was using a "Why People Cross the Road" campaign for chicken nuggets.[6] This is one of the reasons advertisers must do research and both agencies and clients maintain libraries of their work (and research the history of the category). At times, using an old idea may work but it could have risks. You could argue whether there actually are original ideas, but certainly we seek fresh executions.

In an ideal world, the idea needs to come alive, leap off the page, or grab your senses while you watch television. In addition, creative ideas do two important things:

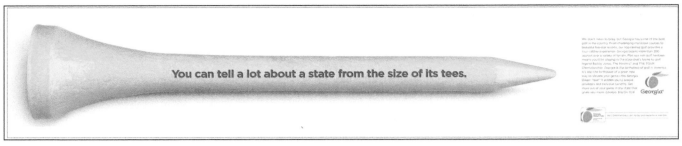

You can tell a lot about a state from the size of its tees.

EXHIBIT 17.3

McRae created a surprising ad about Georgia based on a simple idea.

4 Explain visualizing the idea.

(1) They make the prime prospect consider your product first. (2) They implant your brand name indelibly in the prospect's mind and connect it to the positive attributes of your products.

VISUALIZING THE IDEA

It is time to execute the big idea. At this stage in the process, the creative team forms mental pictures of how the basic appeal can be translated into a selling message. Just as a good novel has various subplots that are brought together in a creative and interesting, cohesive story line, a good advertisement has a well-coordinated layout that flows freely to create a compelling message about the product and its benefits.[7] You might visualize a sports car speeding on a mountain road and around hairpin curves. You might see a sedan of understated luxury in front of a country club. Or you might simply see a close-up of the grill.

These mental pictures can be shown in words or in the crudest form. The crucial thing is to imagine the kind of mental picture that best expresses your idea. While thinking in the visual form (remember, a picture is worth a thousand words), find the words that work with the visual for the most powerful effect. Show it, if you can. Make as many versions of the basic idea as you can. Tweak or stretch your idea to the limit. Remember, Dick Lord said he sketched about 70 rough ideas with heads. And, yes, they could be done on the computer, but Fallon's Tom Lichtenheld believes sketching on paper and tweaking on his Mac work best for him. There is no magic number of sketches. Try every possibility, but remember that your end result must deliver the basic message and the brand name. Do the illustration and copy deliver the creative work plan promise?

MARKETING APPROACH TO VISUALIZATION

We know that advertisements are not created for the sake of creativity. Each advertisement is created for a specific marketing purpose. All advertisements for a product should conform to the same set of objectives, even though some advertisements may not appear to be related, and usually, they use the same theme or slogan in each advertisement.

Using all the information you have about the product or service, write a statement of the one thing you need to say about the product to the prime prospect. This is your promise or the basic theme. A family restaurant might shift to low-fat menu items and promise, "We offer you all the things you like about family-style restaurants—convenience, great-tasting foods, and reasonable prices, with the added benefit of fitting into your lifestyle since you want food that is nutritious and good for you." The illustrations must reflect these marketing concepts. The promise is a consumer benefit statement that tells the prospects what the product will do for them.

The Creative Leap

Are we about ready to begin to create an advertisement? Yes, if we have done our homework. Joseph Wallas, a creative theorist, said creativity is the product of four developmental stages: preparation, incubation, illumination, and verification or evaluation.

A Leo Burnett creative director has said, "The best creative comes from an understanding of what people are thinking and feeling. Creativity is a sensitivity to human nature and the ability to communicate it." Starch Research suggests that we have to evaluate the consumer, address the consumer's needs, and suggest the clear benefit of using the product: "Tell her how her life will change for the better if she uses the product, and she'll pay close attention."

From where does the inspiration come? Some think brainstorming or free association is the answer to creative inspiration, but others say very few ideas come from these techniques. A crazy idea may be the spark for a great campaign. The idea usually comes when you are not looking.

Former creative director Jim Aitchison gives a few suggestions for the source of inspiration for an idea:[8]

- Is there an idea in the packaging—shape, color, label, or material the product is made of?
- How is the product made? Where is it made?
- How about the product's history?
- Can you show what happens with the product?
- Are there any new ideas from the product's old advertising?

The process is one part reason, one part heart, and one big part simple intuition, say others. So the creative leap is not necessarily the same for everyone. There may be some truth in the fact that you spend more time on the logical process, and then the emotional part comes more easily. Once you get the idea—the concept and visual and words that work together—you've made the creative leap. Leonard Monahan developed a visual idea for North protective work gloves that got right to the point of product advantage by using a wet sponge cut out in the shape of a hand as the illustration. The headline read, "This is what your hand looks like to most toxic chemicals." The headline and visual spoke to the reader as one. A mundane product became the most talked-about advertisement in its industry.

LAYOUT

The creative leap is only the first step in advertisement making. The advertisement itself has a variety of elements: headlines, illustration, copy, logotype, maybe a subheadline, several other illustrations of varying importance, a coupon—the number of components varies tremendously from advertisement to advertisement. Putting them all together in an orderly form is called *making up the layout of the advertisement.* **Layout** is another of those advertising terms that is used in two senses: It means the total appearance of the advertisement—its overall design and the composition of its elements; it also means the physical rendering of the design of the advertisement—a blueprint for production purposes. You will hear some say: "Here's the layout," handing another person a typed or keyboarded copy and a drawing. Right now, we are talking about the layout as the overall design of the advertisement. The Georgia Gambling Helpline (see Exhibit 17.4) seeks to grab attention with bold colors and illustrations. The images and the copy must function as one. How did the creative team decide to present the "idea" in this manner?

LAYOUT PERSON AS EDITOR

Although the person who creates the visual idea may be the same person who does the layout, the two functions are different. The visualizer translates an idea into visual form; a layout person uses that illustration and all the other elements to make an orderly, attractive arrangement.

Before putting pencil to paper, however, the layout person—usually an art director—and the writer review all of the elements. The first task is to decide what is most important. Is it the headline? The picture? The copy? How important is the

layout
A working drawing (may be computer developed) showing how an advertisement will look. A printer's layout is a set of instructions accompanying a piece of copy showing how it is to be set up. There are also rough layouts, finished layouts, and mechanical layouts, representing various degrees of finish. The term *layout* is used also for the total design of an advertisement.

EXHIBIT 17.4

The images, headline, and logo must work as one to be effective.

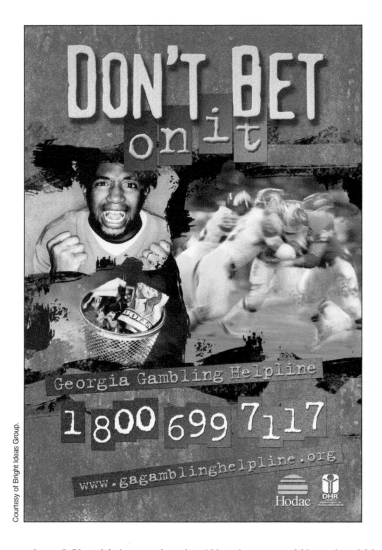

Courtesy of Bright Ideas Group.

package? Should the product itself be shown, and if so, should it be shown in some special environment or in use? Is this advertisement to tell a fast story with a picture and headline, or is it a long-copy advertisement in which illustration is only an incidental feature? The importance of the element determines its size and placement within the advertisement.

THE NEED TO ATTRACT ATTENTION

Disruption. Attracting attention. Getting noticed. High visibility. No matter how you say it, this is the primary creative objective of an advertisement. Today's advertising has to work very hard to get noticed. You cannot rely on strategy alone—the positioning, the product appeals, the demographic and psychographic data that tell you what wavelength the consumer is on—to sell the consumer. Obvious as it sounds, you cannot sell people until you attract their attention. Put another way, people are not going to read the advertisement if they do not see it. Remember, your advertisement is competing with all the advertising clutter and editorial matter in a publication. Unfortunately, most advertisements in most publications are invisible.

All the creative elements—the visual, the headline, the copy—must be strongly executed if the advertisement is to succeed. John Hegarty says, "You're using words and pictures. What you don't want to do is make the pictures do what the words are doing, and the words do what the picture is doing. So you've got to decide which is leading, which is taking you forward, and if it's the picture then you almost certainly will want a

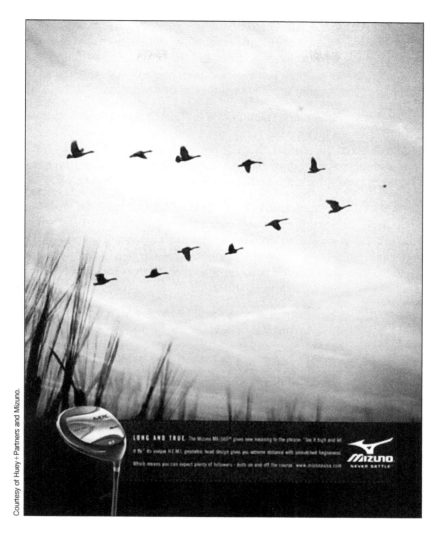

Courtesy of Huey+Partners and Mizuno.

EXHIBIT 17.5

This advertisement depends on the power of the headline twist.

very simple headline. Or it's the other way around—a simple picture and an intriguing headline. So there is a kind of juxtaposition."[9] If the idea is being carried by the headline, it will have a twist, a turn, maybe shock—or some sort of disruption. Huey+Partners (see Exhibit 17.5) uses a humorous and targeted headline to draw attention to a mundane product. The visual will play a straight role. And vice versa if the message is being carried by the picture. Research cannot tell us which creative techniques will work best because creative is not that scientific. Research generally tells us what has been successful, but there are no yardsticks to measure breakthrough advertising ideas. The basic guidelines for writing and designing advertisements are helpful, but there are not really any rules. How do you get an advertisement to stand out? The illustration is usually the key. Either an advertisement grabs people or it does not, and most often it is the illustration that gets them. Of course, many illustrations cannot tell the story alone—they require a headline to complete the communication.

There are three basic means of attracting attention:

1. Using the visual alone

2. Using the headline alone

3. Using a combination of the visual and headline

Do not assume that because we listed the visual first that the art director is more important than the copywriter. Remember, they are a team working together on both visual and language ideas.

BASIC DESIGN PRINCIPLES

5 Identify the principles of design.

There are some general principles that guide design. Some art directors may use different terminology from that used here, but the basic assumptions are the same.

The following design principles, properly employed, will attract the reader and enhance the chances that the message is read or noted.

UNITY   All creative advertising has a unified design. The layout must be conceived in its entirety, with all its parts (copy, art, head, logo, and so forth) related to one another to give one overall, unified effect. If the advertisement does not have unity, it falls apart and becomes visual confusion. Perhaps unity is the most important design principle, but all the principles are necessary for an effective advertisement.

HARMONY   Closely related to unity is the idea that all elements of the layout must be compatible. The art director achieves harmony by choosing elements that go together. This process is similar to dressing in the morning. Some items of clothing go together better than others—for example, stripes, plaids, or paisleys with solid colors. The layout needs harmonious elements to be effective; there should not be too many different typefaces or sizes, illustrations, and so on.

SEQUENCE   The advertisement should be arranged in an orderly manner so it can be read from left to right and top to bottom. The sequence of elements can help direct the eye in a structural or gaze motion. Place the elements so that the eye starts where you want it to start and travels a desired path throughout the advertisement; Z and S arrangements are common.

EMPHASIS   Emphasis involves accenting or focusing on an element (or group of elements) to make it stand out. Decide whether you want to stress the illustration, the headline, the logo, or the copy. If you give all of these elements equal emphasis, your advertisement will end up with no emphasis at all.

CONTRAST   You need some differences in sizes, shapes, and tones to add sparkle so the advertisement will not be visually dull. Altering type to bold or italic or using extended typefaces brings attention to a word or phrase and creates contrast between type elements. Contrast makes the layout more interesting.

BALANCE   By balance, we mean controlling the size, tone, weight, and position of the elements in the advertisement. Balanced elements look secure and natural to the eye. You test for balance by examining the relationship between the right and left halves of the advertisement. There are basically two forms of balance: formal and informal.

FORMAL BALANCE   The poster in Exhibit 17.6 has elements of equal weight, size, and shape on the left and right sides of an imaginary vertical line drawn down the center of the advertisement. Such symmetrical advertisements give an impression of stability and conservatism. Keep in mind that not all formal layouts will have exactly equal weight. For instance, our poster's illustration figures aren't exactly the same size, or in other cases, a logo may be at the lower right corner and not have an equal element on the opposite side, but in general, if all other elements are symmetrical, we would consider it a formal layout.

INFORMAL BALANCE   The optical center of a page, measured from top to bottom, is five-eighths of the way up the page; thus, it differs from the mathematical center. (To test this, take a blank piece of paper, close your eyes, then open them, and quickly place a dot at what you think is the center of the page. The chances are that it will be above the mathematical center.) Imagine that a seesaw is balanced on the optical center. We know that a lighter weight on the seesaw can easily balance a heavier one by being farther away from the fulcrum. (The "weight" of an element in an advertisement may be gauged by its size, its degree of blackness, its color, or its shape.) In informal balance,

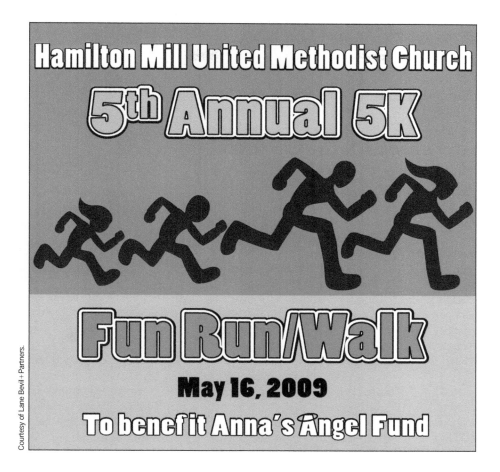

Courtesy of Lane Bevil+Partners.

EXHIBIT 17.6

Formal Balance

If we draw a line down the center, you have basically equal weight on both sides.

objects are placed seemingly at random on the page but in such relation to one another that the page as a whole seems in balance. This type of layout arrangement requires more thought than simple symmetric formal balance, and the effects can be imaginative and distinctive, as illustrated by Exhibit 17.7.

OTHER COMPOSING ELEMENTS

COLOR   One of the most versatile elements of an advertisement is color. It can attract attention and help create a mood. It can aid in selling. Many marketers recognize the incredible power of color and the enormous value of selling the right color at the right time. The Color Marketing Group cites numerous research studies demonstrating the power of color:[10]

- Color increases brand recognition by up to 80 percent.
- Color improves readership as much as 40 percent.
- Color accelerates learning from 55 to 78 percent.
- Color increases comprehension by 73 percent.
- Color ads are read up to 42 percent more than similar ads in black and white.

Psychology of Color   Your personal and cultural associations affect your experience of color. We see colors as warm or cool mainly because of long-held (and often universal) associations. Yellow, orange, and red are associated with the heat of sun and fire; blue, green, and violet with the coolness of leaves, the sea, and the sky. Warm colors seem closer to the viewer than cool colors, but vivid, cool colors can overwhelm light, subtle, warm colors. Using warm colors for foreground and cool colors for background enhances the perception of depth.

KLEPPNER VIEWPOINT 17.2

Jeanne Spencer Partner, Idea Engineering, Inc.,
Santa Barbara, California

GOOD DESIGN = BETTER COMMUNICATION

Jeanne Spencer

How do you evaluate a creative portfolio when selecting an agency or design team? How do you evaluate the work that is developed for you? And why does it matter? Research has shown evidence that the benefits of graphic design include both long- and short-term effects on consumers' psychological influences and buying trends. Effective graphic design aids in memory retention, particularly in the case of qualitative attributes. Good design creates a visual identity that aids in rapid recognition. Structured effectively, graphic design helps to organize information for easy interpretation and understanding of the message. How well your message performs is ultimately decided by the marketplace. However, there are some basic questions you can keep in mind to most effectively evaluate creative work, whatever the medium.

1. **Is It Engaging?** In the context that it will be seen, will it catch your audience's attention and persuade them to pause and learn more? If it's a trade show booth, will it stand out in the convention center? If it's a magazine ad, will someone stop and read it?

   Usually, the most successful creative work is engaging because it connects with your audience's emotions in some way.

   Does what initially attracts attention relate to its overall purpose and message? An ad with a shocking photograph causes us to pause and engages our emotion, but if the message of the ad is that this is the healthiest breakfast cereal available, the disconnect will make us feel unnecessarily manipulated. Similarly, music or a popup ad on a web site can attract attention, but they can also annoy.

   Overall, the creative work needs to be appropriate to its context, while distinct from what surrounds it and relevant to the message. A compelling message and idea are most important. Design choices that help create a distinction include color, scale, and the selection and treatment of images.

2. **Is It Legible?** If your audience can't read it, they're not going to get your message. At first glance, if a headline is in a display font that takes too long to decipher, the reader won't bother. If your audience is seniors, is the type large enough for them to comfortably read it? There are governmental guidelines for designing everything from web sites to signage for visually impaired audiences. But in general, legibility tends to be affected by things like type that is not distinct enough from a background color or image, or that is too small or too crowded. Similarly, images can be evaluated in terms of legibility. Does the diagram clearly communicate its information? Is this photo cropped or colorized in a way that is engaging or simply confusing?

   When reviewing a logo design, consider if it will be legible when reproduced in a small size or a single color.

3. **Does It Have the Appropriate Hierarchy of Information?** When you look at a brochure or ad, is your eye attracted to the most important thing first? Then the next most important? Then the next? This is at the heart of good graphic design—being able to arrange the elements of communication (words, images, choice of materials) to appropriately tell a story. The story starts at the beginning (the image or headline that first catches your eye) then may immediately go to the end (the call to action) or there may be 30 pages that build and support the story in between. But the story is always best told when it follows a planned sequence, and creating a sequence is not possible if everything has the same level of importance. Not every

bit of information on a page can be the biggest, brightest, and most eye-catching. Not if you want your audience to focus on a specific message.

4. **Is It Consistent with Your Brand Identity? If Not, Why Not?** We've been assuming that before you started developing ads or brochures that your basics are in place, including your brand's personality and positioning vis-à-vis your competition. We've also assumed that the visual side of your brand identity is clear: the logo, colors, fonts, and image treatment that are consistently used to create brand recognition. So when you look at a new creative piece in development, besides making sure that it's on target in carrying the personality and core messages of your brand, also look at the visual consistency.

If it's part of a series, inconsistency can be confusing. If it's reaching out to a new audience, stretching the brand's visual identity could be appropriate. If a new product line is being launched, a variation on the main brand will probably be helpful, both internally and for your audience in differentiating from the other product lines.

Consistency is not a holy grail, but brand identities are frequently diffused over time by too many variations. This limits the impact that consistent usage can give, as well as the increase in legibility that comes from familiarity with consistent usage.

5. **Can Any of These Areas Be Improved?** Can the ad be more engaging? More legible? Have better hierarchy? Can it be more consistent with the brand? You don't need to tell your creative team how to accomplish these things, but these are useful ways of describing areas that may need improvement.

A FEW DON'TS

Some things that can seem like good ideas simply don't maximize your results in creative development.

Don't limit design options before discussing them with your creative team: Take advantage of the team's experience and familiarity with creative options. If you know that you want to reach a specific audience and have determined that direct mail is the best method, design considerations can help determine things such as (1) Size: Should an ad be bigger or unusually shaped for more distinctiveness? At what points does size affect production or mailing costs? (2) Should a creative piece be a self-mailer? Or what options for packaging would help it stand out more? (3) What unusual paper or printing process might enhance the impact of the creative piece? (4) Will your audience dislike seeing wasted paper and respond more favorably to a postcard with a link to a web site for more information?

Don't crowd in too much information: If you've heard the term "white space," it's not referring to the value of the color white but to the principle that having some clear space on a page can both help visually balance it and help draw your eye to what is most important. It can be tempting because of limited budgets or a desire to communicate as much as possible to keep adding more to an ad, but after a while, adding more starts to reduce the impact of what is there. It's back to legibility and hierarchy and being engaging.

Don't prioritize your personal preferences . . . unless you are the target audience: Otherwise, the fact that you don't like yellow simply doesn't matter. What does matter is if yellow helps your material be more eye-catching in it's context.

Don't have too many people making final creative decisions: Feedback is great. You don't want to miss something obvious because the schedule was too tight to get key people to review information or buy in to a concept. But the more people involved in creative evaluation, the more likely it is that someone will be involved who doesn't fully understand the marketing goals or how to evaluate creative work. Then things get modified based on personal preference.

Identify whoever is ultimately responsible for decision-making. That person needs to be involved and reviewing at all key points in the process. Keep the group small.

Great creative work depends on great ideas that tell a message in compelling and engaging ways. Beyond that, the talent, technical skills, and experience that graphic designers bring to the process does make a big difference in how that idea takes form. Knowing how to evaluate creative work—and not limit it—can help you find the best team to work with and help you get the most successful results.

Our shared goal is communication, and great design helps you communicate better.

Courtesy of Idea Engineering, Inc.

EXHIBIT 17.7

Informal Balance

This trade publication ad is not symmetrical.

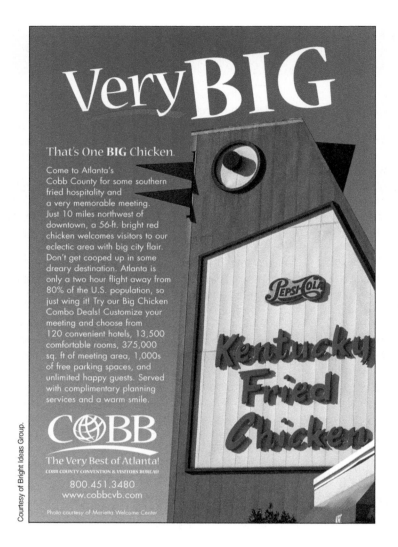

Although red, yellow, and orange, in general, are considered high-arousal colors, and blue, green, and most violets are low-arousal hues, the brilliance, darkness, and lightness of a color can alter the psychological message. Whereas a light blue-green appears to be tranquil, wet, and cool, a brilliant turquoise, often associated with a lush tropical ocean setting, will be more exciting to the eye. The psychological association of a color is often more meaningful than the visual experience.[11]

Depending on the product and the advertising appeal, color can be used for a number of reasons:

▨ It is an attention-getting device. With few exceptions, people notice a color advertisement more readily than one in black and white. Roper Starch research studies indicated color newspaper advertisements were read 61 percent more often than black-and-white advertisements.

▨ Some products can be presented realistically only in color. Household furnishings, food, many clothing and fashion accessories, and cosmetics would lose most of their appeal if advertised in black and white. Studies are done to find the best consumer colors and to spot color trends. For instance, the Pantone Color Institute asked consumers to select their current and future color preferences in specific product categories. In addition, a questionnaire collected data on demographics and placed the respondents into five lifestyle categories: prudent, impulsive, pessimistic, traditional, and confident.

■ Color can highlight specific elements within an advertisement but should be carefully built into the advertisement. Occasionally, an advertiser will use spot color for a product in an otherwise black-and-white advertisement. Any color needs to be an integral part of the advertisement and not an afterthought. We discuss the technique of color production in Chapter 18.

Color can be extremely important in everything from advertising layouts, products, and packaging to the psychological messages consumers perceive. Starch Advertisement Readership Service also has consistently found that bold colors and contrast increase an advertisement's pulling power.

■ In creating for the web, designers must deal with a smaller color palette than that available in print. Advertisers are using bright colors to grab attention on the screen that they would never use in print. This use is making brighter hues more acceptable in our daily lives.

Predicting Popular Colors The Pantone Color Institute conducts color research on color psychology, preferences, and professional color applications. Another organization that predicts colors is the Color Association of America, which forecasts color trends for products and fashion. Another group, the Color Marketing Group (CMG), is a not-for-profit association of some 1,500 designers that forecasts trends 1 to 3 years in advance for all industries, manufactured products, and services. The Color Association of the United States forecasts are released 20 months in advance. Obviously, these predictions have an impact on advertisers. Usually color trends are evolutionary, but that has changed somewhat since 9/11. "In this current retail climate, unique and magical design becomes that much more essential. Designers need to find innovative ways to excite their clients and ignite their passions," said Laurie Pressman, vice president at Pantone.[12]

Most brands are so connected to one or two colors that the brand is evoked just by looking at two swatches side by side. Purple and orange? FedEx, of course. What about Home Depot? What delivery company used "brown" as identification? You get the idea. Would you brand a financial company with a pink and purple color scheme? These colors certainly have their place in communications but a pink/purple color scheme probably would not create an image of a solid, savvy investment company. Each ad's color scheme is important (see Exhibit 17.8).

Color Globalization and Regionalization With the global aspects of today's business and design environment, color is crossing borders and boundaries. Still, strong regional and cultural preferences remain. For example, the bright and sunny colors of tropical areas such as Costa Rica appear out of place and out of context when applied to a setting like New York City; and in Seattle, where the weather is primarily gray all winter, people choose bright colors such as yellow. Many of the same factors affecting the concerns and moods of Americans appear on a global basis, which is unusual.

WHITE SPACE Some layout people and designers become so preoccupied with the illustration that they forget that white space, or blank space, is a very significant design tool. The basic rule for using white space is to keep it to the outside of the advertisement. Too much white space in the middle of an advertisement can destroy unity by pushing the eye in several directions and confusing the reader.

PREPARING THE LAYOUT

The layout is the orderly arrangement of all the copy elements in a print advertisement. It is basically a blueprint that the production people will follow to complete the finished advertisement. An advertisement may go through different levels of roughness as it is developed. These different types of layouts represent different stages of conventional (not electronic) development of the advertisement.

EXHIBIT 17.8

In some instances, art directors believe that color aids in the feel and look of the message. In this case, Bright Ideas Group decided that bright colors would help attract attention to the message.

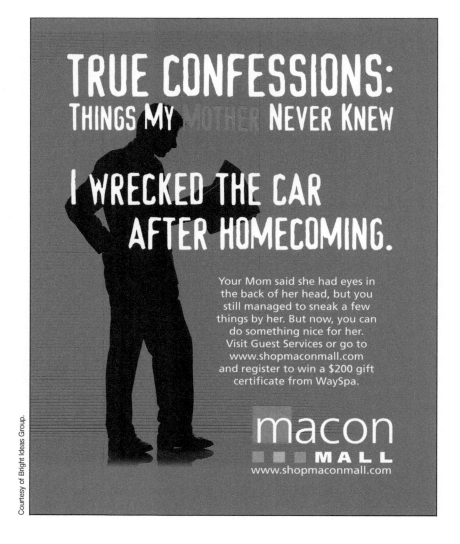

comprehensive
A layout accurate in size, color, scheme, and other necessary details to show how a final advertisement will look; for presentation only, never for reproduction.

- *Thumbnail sketches.* Thumbnail sketches are miniature drawings (actually using markers or pencils) used to try out different arrangements of the layout elements. The best of these will be selected for the next step.

- *Rough layouts.* Rough layouts are usually computer roughs that are equivalent to the actual size of the advertisement. All elements are presented to simulate the way the advertisement is to look (sometimes the copy is fake at this point; see Exhibit 17.9). The best of these will be chosen for the next step.

- *The* **comprehensive** *layout (often simply called the* comp *or the* mechanical*).* All the type set and placed exactly as it is to appear in the printed advertisement comprises the comprehensive layout. Illustrations (or photographs) are drawn and scanned into position. Computer comps look very much like finished advertisements and are used for client approval.

Once the basic advertisement for a campaign has been approved, layouts for subsequent advertisements usually consist of only a comprehensive layout.

COMPUTER DESIGN

Generally, most agency layouts are created in-house by their digital artists. However, there are independent graphic houses or freelance artists who may have a particular expertise in developing designs or illustrations or a particular computer expertise. In some cases, these freelancers simply work as the marketer's design department, or on the project for the agency.

Courtesy of Huey+Partners.

PROUD HOME *of* BROADCASTING'S MOST PRESTIGIOUS PRIZE.

POEMATDIT SCIRE ET NUNQUE VELIM. chartis pretium quotus arroget inter et
dies paternus. Scriptor abhinc annos centum qui decidit, inter perfectos
veteresque referri debet an inter vilis atque novos? Excludat iurgia finis.

Grady College
The University of Georgia

EXHIBIT 17.9

Computer Rough

All of the ad's elements are exactly in place in the layout; however, the included copy is fake at this point.

You know all about being able to do layouts and design on computers. However, let's be sure we're on the same page of information. We define *computer graphics* as the ability to draw or display visual information on a video terminal. Raster scan graphics are the most common computer display. Each spot on the screen, called a **pixel**, represents a location in the computer's memory. The number of individual pixels determines the resolution of the image—this is the difference between poor-quality, computer-set type or visuals and good, reproduction-quality images. The more pixels, the higher the resolution and the more refined the image appears. The resolution of a screen controls its clarity and sharpness. This is probably more than you wanted to know.

In the past, the creation and production processes have been separate. However, with the simplicity of today's computer software, it is possible for one person to do both layout and production, although software expertise may continue to keep these functions specialized. Mastery of layout demands a keen knowledge of art, type, and design as well as photography, computers, and electronic imaging.

pixel
The smallest element of a computer image that can be separately addressed. It is an individual picture element.

TYPE MANAGEMENT

Type may be one of your most valuable assets, and yet it is tricky to manage. You need to understand how your particular computer stores fonts beyond its basic operating system.

Open Type is a font format (you'll learn more about type in the next chapter) jointly developed by Adobe and Microsoft. This font format is superior to *Type 1* and

KLEPPNER VIEWPOINT 17.3

Sheri Bevil Senior Partner, Sheri Bevil Design
and Lane Bevil+Partners

VISUAL DISRUPTION CAN AID IN ATTRACTING READERS

There are those who say the advertising strategy of "disruption" is dead because of new media—and the fact that consumers are in control. But that isn't quite the story of the word. Let's give a simplistic definition of "disruption" as being something that is not supposed to be there. There is disruption when a TV spot shows up in the middle of your favorite program. I'm not talking about media disruption; I'm talking creative disruption.

In new media and old media we must attract attention. They may involve telling a "relevant" story about the product or service or solving a problem of some sort. Disruption simply may be placing an elephant in a cornfield. We are not accustomed to seeing an elephant in a cornfield. It is "disruption" of what is usual or expected. In this case, it is

"visual disruption." No matter what the message is, we often need a treatment that attracts attention. Not a gimmick, but something that relates in some way.

Visually, we may be thinking about something simple like the Chick-fil-A cows on top a billboard (or doing something unusual in a TV commercial—cows standing on top of a car). We usually don't see cows in this manner. Cows are supposed to be in fields. The creators of the Chick-fil-A cows ads, The Richard Group, found that their cow idea was fresh, was adaptive to all media, and would attract attention. They didn't have the money to spend on marketing like a McDonald's. They had to be smarter to be competitive. They were.

To stand out, consider disrupting the way people see things or think by giving them a new approach. Something that is

Sheri Bevil

different from the norm in how messages are presented. Maybe, push consumers' comfort zone buttons. The concept of "ad disruption" can be positive and can be applied to many ad platforms—new and old. So the next time you're looking to connect, stand out, find your elephant in a cornfield.

Courtesy of Sheri Bevil.

TrueType formats because it gives designers more typographic control. It has a greatly expanded character set, which can include thousands; Type 1 and TrueType are limited to 256. A single-font Open Type font provides for many nonstandard characters: true-drawn small caps, extended ligatures sets, swash and alternative characters, dingbats, and symbols, as well as extensive foreign language support in a single font.[13]

Complicating the management of type fonts is the fact that they come in a number of formats that have evolved over the years.

PostScript Type 1. PostScript Type 1 is an earlier bitmap font file that handled on-screen displays; a corresponding PostScript file took care of reproduction. Today's font-management utilities track the pairs when you activate them.

TrueType. Apple developed a system to incorporate the two aspects of PostScript into one file: TrueType. There are actually two TrueType formats, Mac and Windows, but Mac OS X supports both. Windows TrueType font names end in ttf or ttc.

OpenType. The OpenType font also stores all information in one file. It includes either PostScript or TrueType information running on either Mac or Windows and supporting advanced attributes including advanced character sets.

Dfont. Apple introduced the Mac-only Dfont format in the Mac OS X operating system, which is essentially TrueType that plays well with its internal UNIX subsystem.

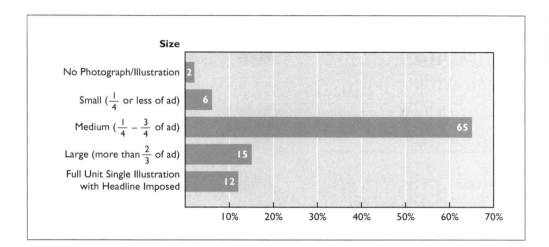

EXHIBIT 17.10

Percentage of Top-Scoring Ads

THE VISUAL

Research indicates that 98 percent of the top-scoring advertisements contain a photograph or illustration, proving that human beings are highly visual creatures, according to Cahners Advertising Performance Studies.[14] In most print advertisements, the photograph or illustration takes between 25 and 67 percent of the layout space (see Exhibit 17.10).

6 Discuss types of visuals.

ART DIRECTING AND PHOTOGRAPHY

Art directing and photography are twin disciplines—each, in theory, raises the other up a notch. Having a great photo in the wrong layout makes for bad advertising. Betsy Zimmerman, art director at Goodby, Silverstein & Partners, says, "The layout's gotta come first. It might look great as a photo, but once you put it in its environment, it is totally different." Jeff Weiss, a noted creative director, says every advertisement contains two things: what you want to say and how you want to say it. What art directing can do is deliver things emotionally, not intellectually. Great art direction takes the selling idea and furthers it without you even knowing it.

Photography can be very expensive. A photo for use in an advertisement may cost between $700 and $10,000, depending on the photographer's reputation and the advertiser's willingness to pay. It costs money to go on location to take photos (see Exhibit 17.11).

EXHIBIT 17.11

Shooting photographs on location can be expensive.

Courtesy of Lane Bevil+Partners.

EXHIBIT 17.12

The shooting of some products requires specialty photographers and sometimes food-preparation people. Here there were two separate photo shots.

Courtesy of Lane Bevil + Partners.

THE ARTIST'S MEDIUM

The tool or material used to render an illustration is called the artist's medium, the term *medium* being used in a different sense than it is in the phrase *advertising medium* (for example, television or magazines). The most popular artist's medium in advertising is photography. Britain's award-winning art director Neil Godfrey says, "I like to use something people can believe in. I rarely use illustration. Nine-tenths of the time, it just doesn't have the impact of photography." Tom Lichtenheld adds, "Even though people are savvy to retouching, they still believe that photographs don't lie." But sometimes there is the cost factor. "Photography, to be any good these days, costs the earth," says writer Malcolm Pryce, "but you can get brilliant illustration comparatively cheaply."[15] A simple product shot can take many hours to shoot the needed images. The banner ad in Exhibit 17.12 has two photos of food, which is always difficult to shoot. Other popular tools are pen and ink, pencil, and crayon (and computer effects). Perhaps a photograph will be used as the main illustration for a print advertisement, but pen and ink will be used for the smaller, secondary illustration. The choice of the artist's medium depends on the effect desired and the medium in which it will be used. If it is a print ad or collateral material, paper and the printing process have to be factored into the equation. Also, you can't take for granted that you can afford the illustrator or that he or she will be available for the project. Exhibit 17.13 shows specialized art that requires a special illustration expertise.

TRADE PRACTICE IN BUYING COMMERCIAL ART

Creating an advertisement usually requires two types of artistic talent: the imaginative person, who thinks up the visual idea with a copywriter or alone and makes the master layout, and an artist, who does the finished art of the illustrations. Large agencies have staff art directors and layout people to visualize and create original layouts, as well as studios and artists to handle routine work.

There are a host of freelance artists and photographers who specialize in certain fields or techniques. There are two important points to observe when buying artwork, especially photographs. First, you must have written permission or a legal release (see Exhibit 17.14) from anyone whose picture you will use, whether you took the picture or got it from an online service. Second, you should arrange all terms in advance. A photographer may take a number of pictures, from which you select one. What will be the price if you wish to use more than one shot? What will be the price if you use the picture in publications, on the web, as a mobile ad, and so forth?

Freelance artists' and photographers' charges vary greatly, depending on their reputation, the nature of the work, in what medium the work is being used, and whether

Courtesy of Chick-fil-A.

EXHIBIT 17.13

This art requires an illustrator who specializes in a specific style.

the advertisement is to run locally, regionally, or nationally. An art illustration may cost $200 if by an unknown artist and up to about $5,000 if by an established artist. A photography session may cost $200 a day for an unknown photographer to about $2,500 for an established photographer. People charge what they think the art or photography is

---

SLRS Advertising MODEL/PERFORMANCE RELEASE

For value received and without further consideration, I HEREBY CONSENT that all pictures/photographs taken of me and/or recording made of my voice or musical or video performances, may be used for advertising purposes, by SLRS Advertising, Inc., and by advertisers SLRS Advertising, Inc., may authorize or represent, in any manner. I understand that illustrations/performances may be edited, changed or reproduced in any manner without my approval. I agree that all reproductions there of and plates, films, and tapes shall remain the property of SLRS Advertising, Inc., or of advertisers represented by SLRS Advertising, Inc.

WITNESS_____   SIGNED_____

                                 SOC. SEC. NO._____

IF SUBJECT IS A MINOR UNDER LAWS OF STATE OF PERFORMANCE

GUARDIAN_____

WITNESS_____   DATE_____

SLRS COMMUNICATIONS, INC./P.O. BOX 5488/ATHENS, GA 30604-5488/(706) 549-2665

EXHIBIT 17.14

Typical Model Release

EXHIBIT 17.15

The selection of models was important because this ad is aimed at a Hispanic audience.

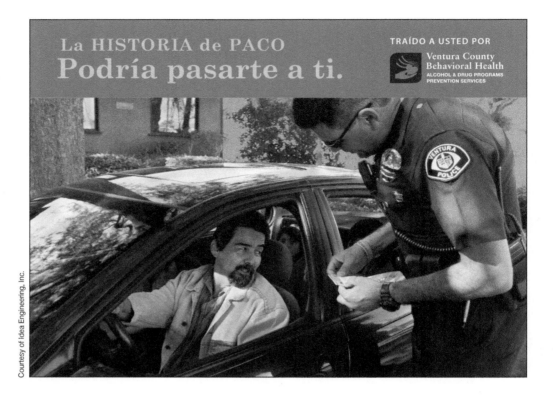

Courtesy of Idea Engineering, Inc.

worth or what the client can or is willing to pay. As a result, the better the reputation of the artist or photographer, the more expensive the final product will likely be. A Ventura County Behavioral Health Hispanic ad required finding subjects including kids in the backseat of a car that fit the concept (see Exhibit 17.15). (In the case of a child's picture, you must obtain a release from the parent or guardian.)

OTHER SOURCES OF ART AND PHOTOGRAPHY

Clients will not always be able to afford the money or time for original advertising art or photography. The basic sources of ready-made images include computer art and stock photos.

ROYALTY-FREE STOCK ILLUSTRATIONS   Royalty-free and stock illustrations (mostly photographs and some art illustrations) are available from a multitude of services. All you have to do is download them to your computer. Almost any kind of image is available, for example, families, men, women, children, business scenes, locations (e.g., farm, beach), and special events. The disadvantage to using these illustrations is that you have to match your idea to available images, and many of the illustrations are rather average. The advantages are the very reasonable costs, extensive choice of images, and no royalty payments. Some art services offer a monthly computer disc (or online service) with a wide variety of images; others offer specialized volumes—restaurant art, supermarket art, or medical art, for example. Once you purchase the service, the art is yours to use as you see fit.

STOCK PHOTOS   As with royalty-free images, there are hundreds of stock-photo libraries available to art directors and advertisers at a cost per photograph. Each library maintains thousands of photographs classified according to the subject categories. A photographer submits photos to the stock company, which are published on the stock company's web site. Clients then browse through the stock company's offerings to research its files for a suitable photo. The art director or advertiser then leases, or contracts, for use of the selected photo to feature in an advertisement. The fee is based on the intended use of the photo.

More than 80 percent of graphic design professionals use stock imagery. There are some fundamental reasons for their popularity:

- *Time pressure.* Meeting tight deadlines and fast turnarounds are possible.
- *Budget restraints.* Stock is less expensive than assignment photography, offering clients cost savings.
- *Quality, choice, variety.* Stock collections have grown in quality, sophistication, and quantity.
- *Ease of accessibility:* There are lots of resources, royalty-free options, digital delivery, and e-commerce sites for easy access.

MOVING TO DIGITAL HAS BEEN HARD FOR MANY COMPANIES

The transition has been more difficult than expected for many advertisers and their agencies. Peter Cowie, managing partner of search consultancy OysterCatchers, observes:[16]

- Digital marketing means different things to different people—web, mobile, gaming, blogs, etc. Clients are learning fast and faster than many agencies.
- Most clients are deeply insecure about all things "digital" and find it hard to know how much digital stuff costs or if they are getting the best value (since it is complex and standards few).
- Traditional agencies still see digital as a new marketing channel; they start with the creative and work backwards [and] integration is hard.
- Digital marketing comprises so many new disciplines and specialties that are like a foreign language to both clients and their agencies—SEO (search engine optimization), SEM (search engine marketing), GUI (graphical user interface), IA (interconnection agreement), experiential design, social networking, mobile, gaming, analytics, etc.

As it has grown, digital has gotten more complex quickly, with new technologies, specialties, and capabilities constantly entering the scene. This is further exacerbated by the rapid change and introduction of new products. Most people haven't had time to become experts at most, if any, of the new disciplines.

COPY AND DESIGN

We talked about expansive information (and copy) in communication in the previous chapter, pointing to the fact that a 30-second spot or a full-page ad may inspire awareness of your product or service, but basically is reductive as the copy because its space or time limitations require you to reduce information. The consumer then goes online to find more information. Advertisers must ensure that key detailed information can be found on their sites—or the consumer user will go elsewhere to find the desired information. There are no space or time constraints in digital. But consumers must be able to easily navigate through your information.

In designing and producing digital material, there is a complex number of software, platforms, and programs to master. The requirements may change from one Internet network or platform to another increasing production costs. It isn't like creating a 30-second TV spot to be used on several television networks. Until standardization (particularly in web video), production can be a challenge.

HEX COLOR CODES   Even the color system is based on a numerical system referred to as the 216 six-digit hexadecimal color codes; they define what are considered safe, nondithering colors for HTML. Hex code uses base-16 math to write a shorthand version of the binary code that is used to represent each of the different colors in the red-green-blue color set. Yes, it is more complex.

KLEPPNER VIEWPOINT 17.4

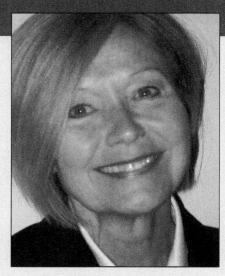

Dr. Parker Middleton Assistant to the Dean
for Advancement, Grady College, University of Georgia

COLLEGES CAN REBRAND TOO

Founded in 1915 and ranked among the oldest and most respected programs for research, teaching, and service for the disciplines of media, the University of Georgia's Henry W. Grady College of Journalism and Mass Communication tapped the creative leadership of advertising alumni to energize its creative and marketing approach for alumni and donor communication and to catalyze internal and external branding efforts. Our alumni are leaders in their fields and want to see their alma mater as a leader in thoughtful, resonant, and forward-looking university branding.

To inaugurate a visual communications and messaging face-lift, Grady turned to advertising alumnus Ron Huey and Huey+Partners to develop a brand anchor for its centennial campaign, first in the form of a logo to contemporize Grady's 100-year history. The centennial campaign logo and other materials were produced as a pro bono gift by Huey+Partners as part of a "By Grady, for Grady" campaign.

The George Foster Peabody Awards, one of the most revered awards in electronic media, was first presented by Grady in 1941. The Peabody Awards is one of the brands in the college's portfolio and the most significant external program of the University of Georgia. To call attention to the Grady-Peabody connection and to leverage its power with alumni and national and international media elite, Grady asked Huey+Partners to develop a campaign to identify the college as home to the Peabodys.

Huey+Partners created a series of ad concepts to accomplish this as the college prepared to launch the Centennial Campaign for Grady and to plan for the seventieth anniversary of the Peabodys in 2011. A first ad, "Applause," appeared in print and online editions of *Broadcasting and Cable Magazine* and in the program of the Annual Peabody Awards banquet at the Waldorf-Astoria in New York City.

Parker Middleton

Other concepts in the Peabody series will work in multiplatform formats for local, national, and other audiences, highlighting the story of the Peabodys' founding at Grady. The Peabodys recognize "excellence on its own terms," observes Peabody director Dr. Horace Newcomb, "and our own messaging about Peabody seeks to honor that." In extensions of the centennial campaign and in efforts to brand Grady as the Peabodys' home, the college will continue to tap the creative power of its alumni.

Courtesy of Dr. Parker Middleton.

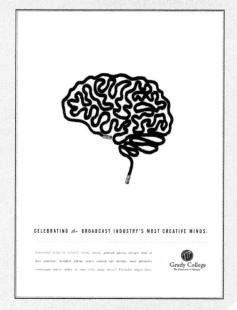

MICROSITE COSTS The cost of building microsites can be staggering. In early 2009, Coca-Cola rolled out the third version of the Happiness Factory, a Flash site with five interactive games that follow the story line of users going to work in a factory that produces happiness. Such a campaign demands high production values and a million-dollar cost. For some agencies, advising a client to skip a $200,000 microsite in favor of a free Facebook page or social network built on Ning for $25 per month might be the right move.

COMPLETE STRATEGY INTEGRATION

When discussing digital ads, designs, and strategy, we have to understand that each communication is designed according to the strength of the medium, each is different, and each has different requirements. They may involve many different kinds of communication tools. Agency Ignitehealth does advertising, web design, interactive animation, e-mail marketing, patient relationship marketing, product collateral, and outdoor advertising for their client Gilead Sciences, a biopharmaceutical company. All of these things have to be integrated into the strategy.

SUMMARY

We have now made the transition from thinking of ideas to making advertisements. We have started with the primary consumer benefit, the most important thing we can say about the product.

In advertising, the total concept is a fresh way of looking at something. A concept is an idea. A big idea is one that expresses the message clearly and combines words and visuals. Another way of looking at it is that a basic idea is an abstract answer to a perceived desire or need. The left brain hemisphere provides reasoning, controls verbal skills and processes information. It thinks in language. It works linearly and methodically. The right hemisphere of the brain provides intuition, processes information in parallel, controls the creative process, thinks in mental images, thinks nonverbally, responds to color, and is artistic. It "sees" the big picture. Usually, a left-brain person and a right-brain person work together to develop concepts.

The creative team, consisting of an art director and a copywriter, next develops the best approach to presenting the executional idea—a rendering in words, symbols, sounds, colors, shapes, and so forth of an abstract answer to a perceived desire or need. Then comes layout preparation (usually done by an art director), in which the various elements of the advertisement are composed into a unified whole. Creating an advertisement that will attract attention is one of the art director's primary concerns. When arranging the elements of an advertisement, the layout artist has to consider the principles of design: unity, harmony, sequence, emphasis, contrast, and balance.

Advertisements usually begin as thumbnail sketches. Subsequent steps include the rough layout, the finished layout, and the comps.

In most cases, art and photography are original executions of the art director's ideas, illustrated or shot according to his or her specifications by freelance artists or photographers. When time or money is short, computer-art services or stock photography may be used.

REVIEW

1. What is the big idea?
2. What is the executional idea?
3. What do art directors and copywriters do?
4. What are the basic means of attracting attention?
5. What is a comp?
6. What are stock photos?

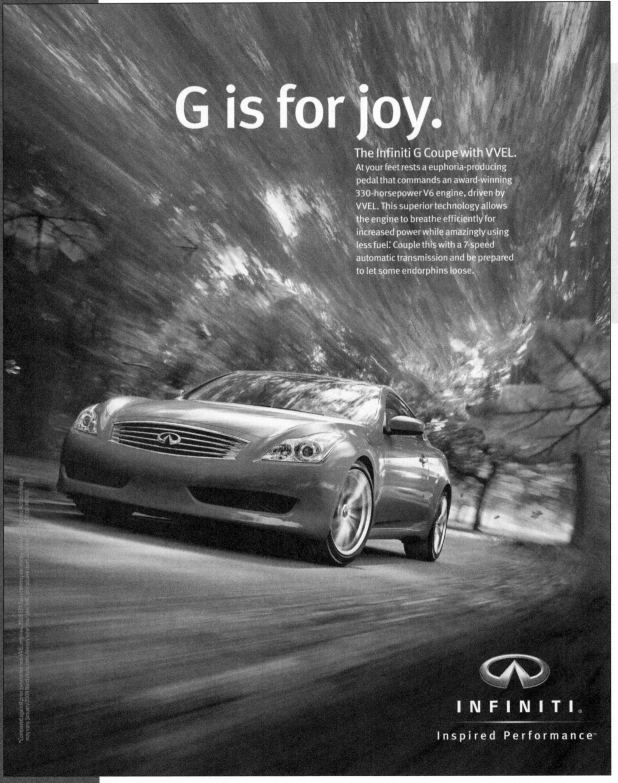

G is for joy.

The Infiniti G Coupe with VVEL.
At your feet rests a euphoria-producing
pedal that commands an award-winning
330-horsepower V6 engine, driven by
VVEL. This superior technology allows
the engine to breathe efficiently for
increased power while amazingly using
less fuel. Couple this with a 7-speed
automatic transmission and be prepared
to let some endorphins loose.

INFINITI.
Inspired Performance

Print Production

A CTUAL PRINTING on presses hasn't changed in decades. The preparation of materials to be printed has become almost all digital. Advertising managers need to understand the new and the old to be effective in their jobs. ▶

CHAPTER LEARNING OBJECTIVES

1 Explain the nature of production departments.

2 Discuss digital and traditional production processes.

3 Discuss the selection of printing processes.

4 Identify mechanicals and artwork.

5 Explain proofing techniques.

It is now time for the print production people to take the ideas and create a finished advertisement for publication. They need the information to get the ad to the publication and/or printer. Because the production process can be complicated and involves quality, time, and cost factors, it is helpful if all advertising and marketing people have some working knowledge of the basics of the production processes. What do we need to send an ad to the publication so it can print the piece? What are the preparation steps and printing procedures for a brochure or insert? How long will this take?

This conversion process, going from the original layout to the finished piece, is the responsibility of the advertiser or agency and is called *print production*. Production requirements differ from advertisement to advertisement. The staff may be producing magazine or newspaper advertisements; collateral brochures; or direct-response, outdoor, or transit advertisements (see Exhibit 18.1). They need a working knowledge of all these production processes, as well as publication mechanical specifications. The planning process may involve a great deal of money and people. Before we get into the organization, let us look at some important issues.

Keep in mind that in most cases digital is only part of the process. Digital presses have limitations for large runs (printing millions of pieces). Most printers have millions of dollars in presses that work fine and will only change when there is a clear quality and economic advantage. Some digital copiers are capable of handling some marketer's small printing jobs. Its paper size is small compared to regular offset presses that take paper sizes three and four times larger than most copiers. You're not going to print your 12-page promotion piece or 700,000 advertising inserts on an office copier. But we talk later in this chapter about the basic printing processes.

Production Data

Production people need to be well versed in the technical aspects of art and type processes, printing methods, and duplicate plates, which we discuss later in the chapter.

1 Explain the nature of production departments.

Courtesy of Bright Ideas.

EXHIBIT 18.1

Ad production people must understand how to get from the computer to the finished piece.

Let's look first at sources of information for print media. As you would expect, most publications have a production or advertising specification link on their web site. Some have pdf downloads for display, classified, and special sections, which include all production specifications.

The SRDS production source—SRDS Print Media Production Data—provides complete data on all critical advertising production specifications for most business and consumer magazines and newspapers. Production, traffic, and graphic design personnel use this resource to confirm essential production information, so they can control production deadlines and budgets. Of course, each publication determines its own advertising due dates and mechanical specifications based on printing requirements. Exhibit 18.2 shows some of the digital advertising specifications for a typical publication and how specific they can be. Knowing these specifications is all-important because they involve cost. The production people may be sending a $50,000 ad or printing a $100,000 run. They better know what they are doing.

Production Planning and Scheduling

To ensure that the creative and production work moves along with the necessary precision, a time schedule is planned at the outset. The closing date is the date or time when all material must arrive at the publication. Once this is known, the advertiser works backward along the calendar to determine when work must begin to meet the date.

Now that we better understand the production environment, let us take a look at the key considerations in a number of production steps.

DIGITAL STUDIOS

Prior to computer-generated layouts for advertisements or promotional printed materials, most art directors only had to design, create accurate mechanicals, and specify color breaks or other information on paper tissues. The production managers were responsible for the remaining production steps and procedures. Today, many art directors and/or digital artists working on their computers perform many production steps.

Some agencies call their computer area an image studio or digital imaging studio, where art directors work on computers to develop the visuals and layout. Some digital production departments are separated into "print" and "interactive"; interactive includes mobile, web, and gaming. In some agencies (especially in small- or medium-size shops), the agency art directors take on part of the production role. They design, typeset, do layouts, create tints, scan, separate colors, produce final pdfs, and, in some cases, transmit the job directly to the press or service bureau. Some production jobs might require the services of outside vendors or service providers. Many agencies rely on outside services for image setting, high-resolution scanning, and proofing. Then there are electronic prepress shops that offer image-setting verification for computer-generated files, which may be required by some publications. If asked to do so, they will use their expertise in taking care of color trapping and other operations necessary to prepare the files for film output. Suppliers can be found for almost every stage of the prepress operation.

Digital Print Production

Despite creating advertisements on a computer, much of the production still involves converting the advertisement from the computer screen to film for the publication or printer according to specifications. To some extent, the advertising person controls only a portion of the advertisement's production efforts. If you have a print advertisement going into a publication, the publication provides its own specification standards as to how advertisements are to be produced and presented (as seen in Exhibit 18.2). The digitally created advertisement on your computer may still have to be converted to a piece of film so that printing plates can be made. Traditional production requires converting all of the advertising elements to film and then to plates for printing. Total digital production involves converting the computer images directly to plates, bypassing the film stage. You have to understand the requirements.

The creation of an advertisement by an agency is probably totally digital. A printer's or publication's prepress operation is a digital process. Once the press has a plate made from either traditional or digital technology, the printing process is generally traditional but it is changing. However, the actual printing changes are moving at a much slower pace than the prepress changes that we've seen over the past decade. Sounds confusing, but we'll outline the process a little later.

2 Discuss digital and traditional production processes.

TECHNICAL CONSIDERATIONS

Problems with digital advertising are often attributed to technology issues, and there can be many of these. Not only must the printer be computer proficient but also the computer artist must be knowledgeable in preparing files so they can output properly. The computer artist must have font and photo files in the proper resolution.

COMPATIBILITY   Even today, file compatibility can also be an issue. The files should be saved in a version common to all parties involved in the process. Today's computer artists, writers, prepress service providers, and publishers work in a variety of computer environments that can lead to file compatibility problems. Often, agencies will send a

DIGITAL DATA REQUIRED FOR AD. Advertising is only accepted in PDF/X1a format. No application files will be accepted.

PRINTING PROCESS: Web Offset

AD SIZES	TRIM	BLEED	LIVE AREA
Page	8-3/8" x 10-1/2"	8-5/8" x 10- 3/4"	7-1/2" x 10"
Spread	16-3/4" x 10-1/2"	17" x 10-3/4"	16" x 10" 1/2
Horizontal spread	16-3/4" x 5-1/4"	17" x 5-1/2"	16" x 4-7/8"
2/3 vertical	5-3/8" x 10-1/2"	5-5/8" x 10-3/4"	4-5/8" x 10
1/2 horizontal	8-3/8" x 5-1/4"	8-5/8" x 5-1/2"	7-1/2" x 4-7/8"
1/2 vertical	4-1/4" x 10-1/2"	4-1/2" x 10-3/4"	3-5/8" x 10"
1/3 vertical	2-7/8" x 10-1/2"	3-1/8" x 10-3/4"	2-1/4" x 10"
1/3 square	4-5/8" x 4-7/8"	n/a	4-5/8" x 4-7/8"

Digital Specifications

Document Construction:
- Build pages to trim size and extend the bleeds 1⁄8" beyond the document page. Supply spread ads as single page files with 1⁄4" gutter safety.
- All high resolution images, artwork and fonts must be included when the PostScript file is written.
- Use only type 1 fonts. Use stylized fonts only. DO NOT apply style attributes to fonts.
- All color must be CMYK unless the color will be printed as a spot color.
- Total area density should not exceed the SWOP standard of 300%.
- Do not nest EPS files within other EPS files.
- All elements must be placed at 100% size. No rotation or cropping of placed images. This must be done in the original application. i.e., Illustrator, Photoshop, etc., prior to placing.
- Place 6mm 5%, 25%, 50%, 75%, 100% C, M, Y, K patch strip on left side of document page.
- Registration offset must be set to 30 pts. Bleed set to .125".
- All required image trapping must be included in the file.

File Formats: (We do not accept any application files.) PDF/X1a (not a standard PDF file) File:
- Careful attention must be paid to the proper creation of PDF/X1a files to ensure that they reproduce correctly. A comprehensive overview may be found online.
- PDF/X1a files must be supplied as composite pages, one ad per file. Files must contain all high resolution images as CMYK or grayscale and have all fonts embedded.

Media Labeling Requirements:
Publication name, issue and date; agency name and phone number; contact person and phone number; advertiser; vendor name; file name/number; print window of the directories on disk.

Electronic Transfer: FTP.
Note: Digital file supplied without corresponding SWOP color proof will forfeit guarantee of color reproduction.

Proofs
Supply digital proofs calibrated to SWOP specifications that represent the digital file at 100% (Kodak Approval is preferred).

All off-press proofs must include a SWOP approved color bar and manufacture ID to be acceptable SWOP proofs. For a list of certified SWOP proofing systems, visit **www.swop.org/certification.html**. Proofs made using digital proofing systems should use a digital control bar having similar content to the hard-dot film control bar. This color control bar should have the following characteristics: Screened areas with rulings of 133 lines per inch with tint values of 25%, 50% and 75% of each of the primary colors in physical proximity to a solid patch. Two-color overprints of the same 25%, 50%, 75% and solids are also recommended. Additional areas such as 1%, 2%, 3%, 5% and 95%, 97%, 98%, 99% may be useful, especially for digital output. A gray balance bar must be included on the proof, designed to match the neutral appearance and weight of black tints of three different values, under standard viewing conditions.

The three-color gray balance portion of the color bar should have the following values:

Black	Cyan	Magenta	Yellow
75%	75%	63%	63%
50%	50%	40%	40%
25%	25%	16%	16%

This color bar could take the form of a manufacturer's color control guide, a GCA/GATF Proof Comparator, or a GATF/SWOP Proofing Bar or their digital equivalents. An exposure control element may also be included where appropriate.

A Digital Proofing Control Bar, provided by the manufacturer, obtained from SWOP, Inc. or created in-house, must be included on all proofs, in order for them to be considered acceptable SWOP proofs. This bar should contain all the elements as described above. Gray balance should appear neutral and similar to that of a SWOP press proof and the substrate should appear similar in hue and brightness to Textweb Proofing Paper. Digital color bars should meet all requirements for color bars contained herein.

SWOP has made color bars meeting the above requirements available as a free download in two different formats. **www.swop.org/downloads.html.** Label color proofs to indicate manufacture ID. If a SWOP certified proof is not supplied, one will be pulled from supplied file for press purposes at our printing facility. Failure to provide this type of proof will result in an $85 production charge applied to advertiser's invoice. Advertiser must provide a ruled proof for position.

4-Color Plate Change: $2,500 (net charge). Matched color and fifth color: $3,500 (net charge).

EXHIBIT 18.2

2010 Mechanical Digital Requirements

test file to determine whether their electronic files can be read correctly. This may avoid unnecessary lost time, frustration, and film costs. Some of the issues are as follows: On which types of digital files should the print workflow be based? Who should be responsible for creating these final exchange formats—the agency, a prepress vendor or service bureau, or the printer? And what tools and best practices should be put in place to ensure file integrity and a job's success? Software developers have created many of the sophisticated tools needed to verify digital file integrity regardless of the format.

INDUSTRY STANDARDS   There are several printing industry organizations that work together to improve quality and technology, for example, SWOP (Specifications Web Offset Publications) and GRACoL (General Requirements for Applications in Commercial Offset Lithography). They set guidelines for production. They promote better communication between print buyers (advertisers and agencies) and print suppliers to improve processes to maintain printing as a competitive force in the communications marketplace. Most publications follow their guidelines.

These organizations have developed production file format standards for the industry. Many believe that the real issues aren't technological but rather financial. The investment can be huge. Printers continue to accept, and even request, everything from native application files to nonstandard Adobe pdf files. It is the production director's job to understand what form or format(s) must be submitted.

PREFLIGHTING   The term *preflight* has been adopted by the graphic arts community to generically refer to file verification at any stage in the print or multimedia workflow. The term was borrowed from the checklist procedures airplane pilots use before taking off. In print production, it is used to make sure digital files will image correctly. But in today's digital workflow, it's common knowledge that the process of controlling digital content file quality occurs at various stages in the production chain. Some production people split the definition of file verification. They define preflighting as the process that happens at the creative stage during document creation in a native application file. This process thoroughly analyzes a design or electronic mechanical for output readiness, regardless of the intended output device. It is a way to discover incomplete or missing digital files or fonts.

POSTFLIGHTING   The term *postflighting* is defined as the verification that takes place at the prepress phase, when the final file format is created and used to drive digital contract proofing, platesetting, or digital printing. So just because you produce an advertisement or collateral material using accepted software, the process of verification of those images is still complex.

On any given job, agency production managers have to check who is responsible for preflighting—the prepress service provider/printer or the agency.

COLOR CALIBRATION   Color calibration is another issue of concern to everyone in the process. All monitors, proofing devices, and printers must be calibrated so that images and hard copy look the same no matter where the files are viewed. Otherwise, a client may output a digital proof on the other side of the country that doesn't match what the prepress or printer is producing.

BIDDING   When the advertiser or agency is producing collateral material, it must find a printer that can efficiently produce the job at a reasonable price. There are online services, such as printbid.com, that assist in getting the best cost. It should be remembered that not every printer can efficiently produce every job—or at the same quality. It becomes the production manager's job to ensure that the "right" printer is chosen. Usually, the advertiser or agency requests three bids from comparable printers.

Prepress Process

What has to be done to the layout design before it can be printed involves the preparation for the act of printing. Then come executions and production. Here we outline the major steps for the traditional and digital methods:

Traditional:	Advertisement concept: copy, layout, and approvals
	Typesetting
	Electronic color separations
	Layout
	Film preparation
	Platemaking
	Printing
Digital:	Advertisement concept: copy, layout, and approvals
	Scanning
	Layout
	Proofing
	Preflight
	Proofing
	Film preparation (if not computer to plate [CTP])
	Platemaking
	Printing

Print Production

The agency's print production group performs the transformation process from the original creative concept to the client's printed communication. This may include magazines, newspapers, outdoor and transit, point of purchase, collateral brochures, and direct response. You probably never thought about it, but most inside and outside restaurant menu boards have to be printed (see Exhibit 18.3). Production personnel must have a working knowledge of all these production processes, as well as publication mechanical specifications, budgetary considerations, and quality requirements. Last but not least, the group must understand the time span available for the execution. All of these factors may be interrelated in a complicated manner.

Print production people are not merely technical people who are knowledgeable. They are also graphic arts consultants, production planners, and production liaison people. They function both internally, with the creative, traffic, media, and account management areas, and externally, with graphic arts vendors and the print media.

The size of a print production group is related to the billing size of the agency. A very small agency may employ a single print production expert. In a very large agency, the print production staff, headed by a print production manager, may consist of a considerable number of people with very specialized expertise. The print operations area includes the following:

- Illustration buyers are versed in various forms of photographic and illustrative techniques. They know the available talent and make all contracts with photographers, illustrators, digital artists, and others in coordination with art directors (see Exhibit 18.4).

- Print producers coordinate all print production activities with the traffic, account management, and creative groups.

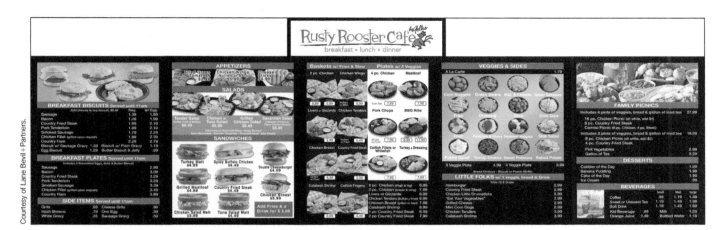

Courtesy of Lane Bevil+Partners.

EXHIBIT 18.3

Most inside and outside restaurant menu boards have to be printed.

Printing buyers specialize in the production planning and buying of outdoor and transit advertising and newspaper and magazine inserts, as well as collateral printed material from brochures to elaborately die-cut direct-mail pieces. A printing buyer's knowledge includes properties of paper and ink as well as the capabilities of printing, binding, and finishing equipment.

In addition to those functions already mentioned, a large production department may include job cost estimators. Generally, clients require an agency to submit a production budget for work to be done. As a rule, a total yearly campaign production budget is estimated to give the client an understanding of approximately how much advertisements and/or collateral will cost to produce. Clients must sign off on each project's production cost in advance of the work being prepared. It is important for the production department to supply accurate production cost estimates.

The production department works closely with the traffic department, which sets and monitors schedules of the operation from creative through final production.

COMPUTER TO PLATE

As the printing industry moves from film to CTP, the production specifications are changing. There has been a growing use of computer-to-plate printing, which eliminates the film traditionally required to make plates for the press. Now it is typical for the agency to give high-resolution pdf files to the printer. This may mean jpegs can be used. But remember that the advertiser or agency doesn't control the specifications for publication. If it is an advertisement for a magazine, the magazine controls how the

EXHIBIT 18.4

Robert Willett is a PhotoShop specialist who sometimes incorporates photos, type, and design elements into special graphics. Here are three complex treatments.

Courtesy of Robert Willett Design.

KLEPPNER VIEWPOINT 18.1

Sheri Bevil

Sheri Bevil Senior Partner, Sheri Bevil Design and Lane Bevil+Partners

"HUGE IMAGES AND FILE-TRANSFER SERVICES"

Most agencies send ads, artwork, layouts, and other electronic image files to printers, media, and clients almost daily. Many medium-to-large-size agencies have their own file transfer protocol (ftp) sites that enable clients (and the agency) to exchange large secure files between them.

If you try to send someone a large design or photo and don't have an ftp site, your file simply may be too large and not suitable for most e-mail systems. There are a number of file-transfer services where you can upload your files. The service then e-mails a link to the recipient, who simply clicks the link to download the file. Some printers and service bureaus have their own upload systems, which makes it easy to send large files. Then, all an advertiser, agency, or designer has to do is upload the files into their system according to the directions. Some services have an iPhone app to keep track of the project and to know whether clients have received the files.

Here are some suggestions for handling large files:

- To eliminate font issues, always "select all" to grab all the type in Illustrator and "create outlines." All your fonts become "art" and the receiver of the file (whether for print production or viewing) will see what you created with the same fonts (*without* your having to send the fonts with the file).
- When sending files to printers for print production via e-mail or the Internet (ftp sites), it's best to "stuff" or "zip" your files to protect them before their trip through cyberspace. There are several great software programs for this. Always check with the receiver of the files to make sure that they can "unstuff" or "unzip" the files once they have received them.
- There are several free or minimal-fee services to use for uploading files that are too big to e-mail (for example: www.yousendit.com and www.mailbigfile.com). Depending on the service, you can upload files as large as 2 gigabits (GB). These services are very easy to use. Simply type in the e-mail address of the recipient; there will be a place to click and

"browse" the files on your computer. Locate the appropriate file and click. Now, it's in the drop down window as the file to send. Then, click "send file." The time it takes to upload depends on the size of the file. You will have to wait for the "your file has been sent successfully" message. Then, the service e-mails the recipient to let them know that there is a file ready for them to download. The recipient simply clicks on the link to go to that file and then downloads the file to their computer. Most services leave this file available for downloading for 7 to 14 days.

Courtesy of Sheri Bevil.

publication will be printed—digital or traditional or a mix. However, digital design is controlled by the agency. If the agency is producing collateral material (brochures, inserts, etc.), the agency controls more of the process. The agency selects the printers and can use those that match its production preferences.

Producing plates directly from computer files rather than film has advantages. Better registration and a crisper dot pattern result in a sharper image on press. The digital workflow reduces both design and printing schedules.

Another advantage of computer-to-plate technology is the proofing and approval process. In traditional printing, if a problem was detected on the job, it could take as long as 16 hours to make corrections, shoot and strip new film, remake plates, and restart the presses. Digital technology allows a printer to pull the plate, correct the digital files, prepare a new plate, and mount the plate in approximately 30 minutes. Now let's look at the printing options.

Selecting the Printing Process

In most cases, the printing process used depends on the medium in which the advertisement is running, not on the advertiser or the agency. However, in some areas, such as sales promotion, advertising inserts, direct mail, and point of sale, the advertiser must make the final decision regarding print production. To deal effectively with printers, the advertiser must have some knowledge of the basic production techniques and which one is the most appropriate for the job at hand.

3 **Discuss the selection of printing processes.**

If the printing process is not predetermined, the first step in production is to decide which process is most suitable. There are three major printing processes:

- Letterpress printing (from a raised surface)
- Offset lithography (from a flat surface)
- Rotogravure (from an etched surface)

Each of these printing processes has certain advantages and disadvantages, and one process may be more efficient than another for a particular job. Once the printing process has been established, the production process has been dictated, for all production work depends on the type of printing used.

As we have indicated, the prepress operation is in transition from traditional to digital operations. Once the advertisement, collateral advertising, or promotion has been created and converted to a printing plate, the printing process is very similar to that which it has been for many decades. The presses are more efficient now than ever before, but the printing concept is not new.

LETTERPRESS PRINTING

Generally, letterpress printing isn't used any more to print publications; however, advertisers have many uses for this printing process, and you should know the basics. In its simplest form, think of the concept of **letterpress** as follows: If you have ever used a rubber ink stamp (with name, address, etc.), you've applied the principle of letterpress printing. You press the rubber stamp against an ink pad. Then, as you press the stamp against paper, the ink is transferred from the stamp to the paper, and the message is reproduced.

In letterpress printing, the area to be printed is raised and inked. The inked plate is pressed against the paper, and the result is a printed impression (see Exhibit 18.5).

Your artwork, photographs, type, and so forth must be converted to a photoengraving (a process of making the plate a raised surface) before printing can occur. The agency must supply the photoengraving or duplicates of such plates to the letterpress printer. In general, this process doesn't reproduce photos as well as offset or gravure. Each of the printing processes has advantages and disadvantages that the advertising

letterpress
Printing from a relief, or raised, surface. The raised surface is inked and comes in direct contact with the paper, like a rubber stamp.

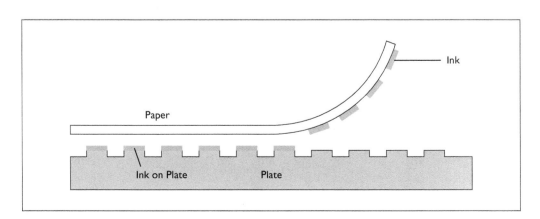

EXHIBIT 18.5

Letterpress Printing

The letterpress printing process involves a plate with a raised surface.

person needs to learn over time. There are several types of letterpress presses. The "job press" plate can print many forms, but it can also die cut (cut shapes in paper), emboss (raise images on paper), perforate, and score (which creases so thicker paper can be folded).

OFFSET LITHOGRAPHY

offset lithography
Lithography is a printing process by which an image was originally formed on special stone by a greasy material; the design was then transferred to the printing paper. Today, the more frequently used process is offset lithography, in which a thin and flexible metal sheet replaces the stone. In this process, the design is "offset" from the metal sheet to a rubber blanket, which then transfers the image to the printing paper.

In its basic description, **offset lithography** is a photochemical process based on the principle that grease and water will not mix. In theory, offset can print anything that can be photographed. In reality, although there are some things that will not print very well by offset, it is the preferred process for most jobs, accounting for 80 to 90 percent of all printing jobs.

Offset lithography is a planographic (flat-surface) process using a thin, flat aluminum plate that is wrapped around a cylinder on a rotary press. The plate is coated with a continuous flow of liquid solution from dampening rollers that repel ink. The inked plate comes in contact with a rubber blanket on another cylinder. The inked impression goes from the plate to the rubber blanket. The inked blanket then transfers or offsets the inked image to the paper, which is on a delivery cylinder. The plate does not come in direct contact with the paper (see Exhibit 18.6).

Because offset is a photographic process, it is very efficient and is the most popular printing process in the United States. It is used to reproduce books (including this text), catalogs, periodicals, direct-mail pieces, outdoor and transit posters, point-of-purchase displays, and most newspapers.

Advertisers or their agencies must supply the artwork and electronic mechanicals or films from which offset plates can be made.

ROTOGRAVURE

rotogravure
The method of printing in which the impression is produced by chemically etched cylinders and run on a rotary press; useful in long runs of pictorial effects.

The image in **rotogravure** printing is etched below the surface of the copper printing plate—the direct opposite from letterpress printing—creating tiny inkwells (tiny depressed printing areas made by means of a screen). The gravure plate is inked on the press and wiped so that only the tiny inkwells contain ink. The plate is then pressed against the paper, causing suction that pulls the ink out of the wells and onto the paper (see Exhibit 18.7).

Gravure is used to print all or parts of many publications, including national and local Sunday newspaper supplements; mail-order catalogs; packaging; newspaper inserts; and large-run magazines, for example, *National Geographic*. The gravure plate is capable of printing millions of copies very efficiently; however, it is not economical for short-run printing. Rotogravure becomes competitive with offset when printing exceeds 100,000 copies. When printing exceeds a million copies, gravure tends to be more efficient than offset. Rotogravure prints excellent color quality on relatively inexpensive

EXHIBIT 18.6

Offset printing press system, showing the image coming off the plate, onto the rubber blanket, and offsetting to paper.

EXHIBIT 18.7
Rotogravure

In the rotogravure process, inkwells fill with ink.

paper, but the preparatory costs are comparatively high, and it is expensive to make major corrections on press.

SHEET-FED VERSUS WEB-FED PRESSES

Letterpress, offset, and gravure printing processes can all use sheet-fed or web-fed presses:

- Sheet-fed presses feed sheets of paper through the press one at a time. The conventional sheet-fed press prints about 6,000 to 7,000 "sheets" per hour.

- Web-fed presses feed paper from a continuous roll, and the printing is rapid—about 1,500 sheets per minute. Most major promotional printing firms use web-fed presses.

SCREEN PRINTING

Another printing process, **screen printing**, which is based on a different principle than letterpress, offset, and rotogravure, is especially good for short runs. This simple process uses a stencil. The stencil of a design (art, type, photograph) can be manually or photographically produced and then placed over a textile (usually silk) or metallic mesh screen (it actually looks like a window screen). Ink or paint is spread over the stencil and, by means of a squeegee, is pushed through the stencil and screen onto the paper (or other surface), as illustrated in Exhibit 18.8.

Screen printing is economical, especially for work in broad, flat colors, as in car cards, posters, and point-of-purchase displays. It can be done on almost any surface: wallpaper, bricks, bottles, T-shirts, and so on. Basically, screen printing is a slow, short-run process (from one copy to 100 or 1,000 or so copies), although sophisticated presses can print about 6,000 impressions per hour and in some cases accommodate billboard-size applications. This expanding printing process is becoming more useful to advertisers.

screen printing
A simple printing process that uses a stencil. It is economical but limited in reproduction quality.

EXHIBIT 18.8
Screen Printing

Courtesy of LKM-Loeffler Ketchum Mountjoy.

EXHIBIT 18.9

This Outward Bound ad uses type not only to communicate but also to interact with the visual.

Understanding Typography

Type has always been an important part of advertisement design. It creates moods, enhances or retards readability, and gives your communication an image. Type is powerful. It is one of the most important design tools. Type creates communication that is friendly and inviting. It keenly focuses attention. It organizes the complex and creates a mood.

It is now more important than ever before for advertising people to understand how to use type because so much of it is being created in-house on the agency or client computer. Before the computer explosion, art directors used specialists—typesetters or typographers—for type. Most agree that few art directors or designers have as good an understanding as they should about type. Getting type up on the screen does not mean that it is typeset effectively. We talk about this again after we learn some of the fundamentals.

typography
The art of using type effectively.

The art of using type effectively is called **typography**. It entails a number of issues: choosing the typeface and size of type; deciding on the amount of space between letters, words, and lines; determining hyphenation use; and preparing type specifications for all the advertisement copy. Charlotte award–winning agency LKM uses type to enhance the visual message with a dramatic photo of a hand and words at the end of each finger (see Exhibit 18.9).

Type and Reading

The objective of text typography is to provide quick and easy communication. Display headlines are supposed to attract the reader's attention and encourage reading of the body copy. Using uppercase typography does not generally accomplish these objectives. Notice the difference in the typefaces in Exhibit 18.10. Which of these would not be good for body copy in a magazine?

More than 95 percent of text is set in lowercase letters. Research has shown that readers are more comfortable reading lowercase letters than all caps. Studies have also proved

Adobe Garamond Pro Bold

Baskerville Semibold

Bradley Hand

Cooper Black

Impact

Jazz LET

Skia

Comic Sans

EXHIBIT 18.10

Examples of different typefaces, each suggesting a different mood or feeling. These examples are all the same size text.

that the varying heights of lowercase letters forming words create an outline shape that is stored in the reader's mind, which aids in recalling the words when they are seen. Words comprised of lowercase characters can be read faster than words set in all caps.

The ideal reading process occurs when the eye is able to scan across a line of copy, grasp groups of three or four words at a time, and then jump to another set of words, then another. The separate stops, or fixational pauses, take about one-quarter of a second each. Words in lowercase letters allow this process to take place. However, words set in all caps force the reader to read individual letters and mentally combine the letters into words, and the words into phrases and sentences. The result is a 10 to 25 percent slowdown in reading speed and comprehension.

There are times when all-cap headlines or subheadlines are, graphically, the right thing to use. Design may take precedence over the "rules of communication," or you may not be able to convince a client or art director that lowercase is a better idea. In these instances, words and lines should be held to a minimum. More than four or five words on a line and more than a couple of lines of all caps become difficult to read.[1]

Typefaces

The typeface selected for a particular advertisement is very important. Exhibit 18.11 illustrates the major classifications of type: text, old Roman, modern Roman, square serif, sans serif, and decorative.

Type Fonts and Families

A type font is all the lowercase and capital characters, numbers, and punctuation marks in one size and face (see Exhibit 18.12). A font may be roman or italic. Roman (with a lowercase *r*) type refers to the upright letterform, as distinguished from the italic form, which is oblique. Roman (capital *R*) denotes a group of serif typeface styles.

Type family is the name given to two or more series of types that are variants of one design (see Exhibit 18.13). Each one, however, retains the essential characteristics of the basic letterform. The series may include italic, thin, light, semibold, bold, medium,

Text   𝕺𝖑𝖉 𝕰𝖓𝖌𝖑𝖎𝖘𝖍
Old Roman   Garamond
Modern Roman   Century
Square Serif   **Lubalin**
Sans Serif   **Avant Garde**
Decorative   Ransom

Optima
abcdefghijklmnopqrstuvwxyz
ABCDEFGHIJKLMNOPQRSTUVWXYZ
1234567890$(&?!%',;)*

**Optima ExtraBlack
abcdefghijklmnopqrstuvwxyz
ABCDEFGHIJKLMNOPQRSTUVWX
YZ1234567890$(&?!%',;)***

condensed, extended, outline, and so forth. Some type families have only a few of these options, whereas others offer a number of styles. The family of type may provide a harmonious variety of typefaces for use within an advertisement.

MEASUREMENT OF TYPE

Typographers have unique units of measurement. It is essential to learn the fundamental units of measure if you are going to interact with production people. The *point* and the *pica* are two units of measure used in print production in all English-speaking countries. Let us take a closer look at these two units of measure.

point (pt)
The unit of measurement of type, about 1/72 inch in depth. Type is specified by its point size, as 8 pt., 12 pt., 24 pt., 48 pt, and so on. The unit for measuring thickness of paper, 0.001 inch.

POINT A **point (pt)** is used to measure the size of type (heights of letters). There are 72 points to an inch. It is useful to know that 36-point type is about one-half inch high and 18-point type is about one-quarter inch high. Exhibit 18.14 illustrates the major terms used in discussing type height. Type can be set from about 6 points to 120 points. Body copy is generally in the range of 6 to 14 points; most publications use type of 9, 10, or 11 points. Type sizes 14 points or larger are referred to as display or headline type. However, these ranges are simply labels—in many newspaper advertisements, the body copy is

Helvetica Thin
Helvetica Light
Helvetica Light Italic
Helvetica
Helvetica Italic
Helvetica Italic Outline
Helvetica Regular Condensed
Helvetica Regular Extended
Helvetica Medium
Helvetica Medium Italic
Helvetica Medium Outline
Helvetica Bold
Helvetica Bold Compact Italic
Helvetica Bold Outline
Helvetica Bold Condensed
Helvetica Bold Condensed Outline
Helvetica Bold Extended
Helvetica Extrabold Condensed
Helvetica Extrabold Condensed Outline
Helvetica Extrabold Ext.
Helvetica Compressed
Helvetica Extra Compressed
Helvetica Ultra Compressed

EXHIBIT 18.13

A family of type retains its basic letterform and style characteristics through all its variations. Some type families consist of only roman, italic, and bold versions. Others, such as the popular Helvetica family, have many variations and different stroke thicknesses.

18 points or so, and there have been advertisements in which the headline was in the body-copy size range. Exhibit 18.15 provides a visual perspective on basic type sizes.

Points also are used to measure the height of space between lines, rules, and borders, as well as the height of the type.

PICA A **pica** is a linear unit of measure. A pica equals 12 points of space, and there are 6 picas to an inch. Picas are used to indicate width or depth and length of line.

AGATE LINE Most newspapers (and some small magazines) sell advertising space in column inches or by the *agate line*, a measure of the depth of space. There are 14 agate lines to a column inch, regardless of the width of the column. Newspaper space is referred to by depth (agate lines) and width (number of columns); for "100 × 2," read "one hundred lines deep by two columns wide."

pica
The unit for measuring width in printing. There are 6 picas to an inch. A page of type 24 picas wide is 4 inches wide.

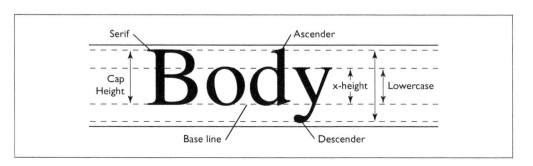

EXHIBIT 18.14

Major Terms for Type Height

EXHIBIT 18.15

**A Visual Perspective
of Type Sizes**

8 point Gill Sans Advertising Production
10 point Gill Sans Advertising Production
12 point Gill Sans Advertising Production
14 point Gill Sans Advertising Production
18 point Gill Sans Advertising Production
36 point Gill Sans Adv
48 point Gill Sans

LINE SPACING   Also called *leading*, line spacing is the vertical space between lines of type and is measured in points from baseline to baseline of type. Lines are said to be set solid when no additional line spacing has been added. Space is added to make type more readable. The rule of thumb is that the extra space should be no more than 20 percent of the type size. Thus, if you are using 10-point type, the maximum extra space between the lines is 2 points, for 12-point leading.

Type specifications are usually determined by art directors, print production personnel, or specialized type directors. The following may be involved in the final decision:

- Type set in lowercase letters is read 13.4 percent faster than type set in all caps.

- Reverse copy—white or light type on a dark background—is read more slowly than black on white. As a result, you should be extra careful in choosing type size and a readable typeface when a reverse is desired. Exhibit 18.16 shows a reverse copy treatment.

Typesetting

Earlier in this chapter, we said that almost all typesetting is performed on a desktop computer. The typographer of the future is an art director or designer—maybe even a copywriter—for whom type is more a means than an end.

GUIDES FOR USING TYPE

- Use only original type. Don't assume the prepress service bureau or printer has the exact same font.

- Remember that as a buyer of a type package you only license the usage rights. You have to acquire a multilicense if the font is to be used on more than one computer.

- Computer artists need to keep a running list of both screen fonts and printer fonts (screen fonts are used by the computer for display on the screen; printer fonts are downloaded to the printer for output).

- Talk to your prepress service provider or printer about fonts being used in electronic mechanicals; otherwise, the advertisement or collateral piece may not look as intended.

- Avoid type smaller than 6 points, especially in serif typefaces (letters having "feet," such as Bodoni). The thin parts of small type characters can disappear when output is of high resolution, making text difficult to read.

- When using reverse type, avoid type that is too small (6 points) or delicate. Sans serif and bold typefaces are better choices. Large blocks of reverse type are difficult to read.

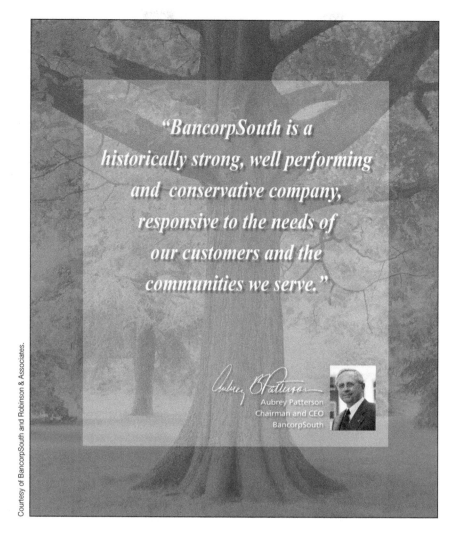

Courtesy of BancorpSouth and Robinson & Associates.

EXHIBIT 18.16

This BancorpSouth advertisement type appears as white ink. It isn't—it is reverse type (white or light type on a dark (green) background).

- When possible, convert type to a graphic (vector objects) in EPS (encapsulated PostScript) files. Common problems for prepress service providers are font substitutions or PostScript errors caused by type in imported EPS graphics.

Electronic Mechanical and Artwork

After the copy has been approved and placed in the advertisement on the desktop system with the rest of the advertisement's material (e.g., illustrations, logos), the advertiser will approve the electronic comp or rough. After approval, the digital file is sent to prepress.

4 **Identify mechanicals and artwork.**

ART FOR PREPRESS SERVICES

Discuss the types of art being used—for example, transparencies (like 35-mm slides or reflective art), line drawings or illustrations, or digital photography—with the prepress service or printer. Agency production people need to ask (or check publication mechanical requirements—see Exhibit 18.17) about what kind of electronic files are preferred. You get the picture—the right files, fonts, and technical requirements are necessary for prepress production to run smoothly. You cannot assume the prepress service, printer, or publication can run your material just because it looks good on your computer. For example, in Exhibit 18.17, a simple printed napkin band has exact specifications.

EXHIBIT 18.17

The mechanical requirements for a printed napkin band.

There are several types of art that production people have to deal with, including line art and halftones in both black and white and color.

LINE ART   Any art, type, or image that is made up of a solid color (and has no tonal value) is called *line art*. If you set type on your computer, it is line art (if it is in solid form). Artwork drawn in pen and ink is line art because the ink has no tonal value. Generally, such art is drawn larger than needed for the mechanical so as to minimize the art's imperfections when it is reduced and printed.

LINE TINT   You can give line art some variation in shades by breaking up the solid color with screen tints or benday screens. Exhibit 18.18 uses a screen tint to give the illusion of gray and contrast. This may be done on the computer layout, or the platemaker can add the screens during the film-stripping stage just prior to platemaking.

LINE COLOR   Artwork does not need to be in color to produce line plates in two, three, or more flat colors. It can be added or changed on the computer. Remember, each color may require a separate plate. Line color provides a comparatively inexpensive method of printing in color with effective results. For example, Exhibit 18.19 uses a black plate and another for the spot color blue—one plate for each color.

Advertising Production
Advertising Production
Advertising Production

EXHIBIT 18.18

The top words are printed in solid (100 percent) color ink. The second line is screened at 50 percent color ink. The third line is screened at 20 percent color ink. The ink color is the same, but the screen gives it another shade. The background is at 20 percent black. Creating tints, as shown here, can change the look and feel of a shape, word, or color.

A solid color (flat or match color) is printed with the exact color. The color is specified with a Pantone Matching System (PMS) color reference number, and the printer mixes an ink that is literally that color. It is like going into a paint store, choosing a color swatch, and having the clerk mix the paint to match your color. The ink is applied to the paper through printing, and the specified color is obtained.

HALFTONES

If you look at black-and-white photographs, you will recognize that they are different from line art—they have tonal value. Such photos have a range of tonal value between pure blacks and pure whites and are called **continuous-tone** artwork.

continuous tone
An unscreened photographic picture or image, on paper or film, that contains all gradations of tonal values from white to black.

Hydroplex XP150

Defining Water Purification Standards

The **XP150**, definitive by design, is the most cost effective, high quality, laboratory point-of-use purification system you will find. Constructed of polypropylene materials housed in a formed acrylic casing, this unit will produce 150 gallons per day, HPLC grade water. Product water meets Type I Laboratory requirements set by ASTM CAP/NCCLS as well as exceeds USP standards.

The **XP150**'s compact design allows for shelf mount, wall mount or counter-top placement. It comes standard with a three (3) gallon conical polypro storage tank, but can be retrofitted to any larger tank to fit your needs. The system can be upgraded to produce 225 gallons per day, and may be plumbed for dispensing at various locations, depending on proximity. It works as stand-alone or may be fitted for polishing larger central water purification systems.

If your laboratory demands a high quality production of purified water for tissue/cell culture, chromatographic procedures (HPLC), media preparation, DNA, RNase, plating and glassware rinse, then you need the micro-process controlled **XP150**.

Contact us for complete specifications. You will be surprised by the **XP150**'s price, performance and low cost maintenance compared to conventional systems on the market today.

(800) 579-6869

Service Centers:
Atlanta, GA
Tampa, FL
Charlotte, NC

Coming Soon:
Nashville, TN
Mobile, AL

admin@hydroinc.net

www.hydroinc.net

HYDRO INC.
Since 1984

EXHIBIT 18.19

This two-color advertisement uses a black plate and another for the spot color blue—one plate for each color. The lighter blue is a tint or screen of the darker blue.

To reproduce the range of tones in continuous-tone art, the art (photo) must be broken up into dots or lines. The art is then called a halftone. Halftones may be reproduced either with a printer's camera (rarely, these days) or digitally; either way breaks the image into dots. Remember that black ink is black ink and not shades of gray, so the production process must create an optical illusion by converting the tonal areas to different-size halftone dots on the printed paper that the eye perceives as gray. If you look at the printed halftone gray areas with a magnifying glass, you will see little black dots. The more dots per inch, the greater the quality of detail reproduced from the original. The quality of the paper must also increase to accommodate the higher dot levels, which drives up paper costs. Again, you may need to check the printer/publisher's specifications on the number of dots or **resolution** that is required.

Resolution is a factor of width and height. In printing, resolution is described as dots per inch or dpi. You can't add resolution if it isn't there in the beginning. If your source image is 72 dpi, as many web images are, you can change its pixel depth but this won't help its apparent resolution. If it started out at low resolution adding pixels simply adds file size but can't make up for the lack of definition. Digital printing requires images that are 300 dpi. There are many pixel-based art file types. Some examples are as follows:

.tif (tagged image file): A pixel-based format with a preview (tag) embedded. A standard print file format.

.jpeg (joint photographic experts group): A pixel-based format with robust compression options. jpegs are often used for web images but are entirely appropriate for printing if they are high resolution, not compressed too much, and CMYK (four-color).

Photoshop EPS (encapsulated PostScript): Not to be confused with Illustrator EPS, Photoshop EPS is a vector art format. Photoshop EPS is like .tif in that it carries a preview (the encapsulated part) with the file.

.gif (graphics interchange format): Almost always used for web images and rarely appropriate for printing.

.png (portable network graphics): First cousin to the.gif and also used mostly for web graphics.

THE HALFTONE FINISH   If you want to make a halftone of a photograph, the computer artist or the platemaker can treat the background in a number of ways; that treatment is called its *finish.* Several techniques that can be applied to halftones include the following:

- *Square halftone.* The halftone's background has been retained.
- *Silhouette.* The background in the photograph has been removed by the photo platemaker or the computer operator.
- *Surprint.* Surprinting involves a combination plate made by exposing line and halftone negatives in succession on the same plate.
- *Mortise.* With mortise, an area of a halftone is cut out to permit the insertion of type or other matter.

LINE CONVERSION   A line conversion transforms a continuous-tone original into a high-contrast image of only black-and-white tones similar to line art. The conversion transfers the image into a pattern of some kind: mezzotint, wavy line, straight line, or concentric circle. Most design software programs offer a number of line conversion choices at the click of the mouse.

TWO-COLOR HALFTONE PLATE   A two-color reproduction can be made from monochrome artwork in two ways. A screen tint in a second color can be printed over (or under) a black halftone. Or the artwork can be photographed twice, changing the screen angle the second time so that the dots of the second color plate fall between those of the first plate. This is called a *duotone.* It produces contrast in both colors of the one-color original halftone.

FOUR-COLOR PROCESS PRINTING   Another printing system is needed when the job requires the reproduction of color photos. This system is called a **four-color process**. The four colors are cyan (blue), magenta (red), yellow, and black. (*C*, *M*, *Y*, and *K* are the letters used to indicate these colors.) These are the least number of colors that can adequately reproduce the full spectrum of natural colors inherent in photography. The first three—cyan, magenta, and yellow—provide the range of colors; the black provides the definition and contrast in the image.

Full-color or process color requires photographic or electronic scanner separation of the color in the photographs (or other continuous-tone copy) into four negatives, one for each of the process colors. This process of preparing plates of the various colors and black is called *color separation* (see Exhibit 18.20). If you examine any of the color advertisements in this text (or any other publication) with a magnifying glass, you will find the halftone dots in four colors.

DIGITAL SCANNERS   Transforming a photograph into a digital file is done using a *scanner*. There are two basic types: flatbed and drum scanners. You probably have used a flatbed scanner. These require little training and their quality varies. Printers or agencies use professional scanners that are capable of creating high-quality images. In general, a drum scanner, in which the original photo or image wraps around a drum that rotates next to a light source, is capable of producing very high-quality results. The important thing to remember is that photographs (whether color or black and white) must be broken up into a dot pattern to print.

COLOR PROOFING   Achieving color reproduction that satisfies advertising agencies and advertisers is one of the most crucial roles of the magazine production manager. Agencies generally demand to see a proof before the job is printed. In today's electronic

four-color process
The process for reproducing color illustrations by a set of plates, one that prints all the yellows, another the blues, a third the reds, and the fourth the blacks (the sequence may vary). The plates are referred to as process plates.

EXHIBIT 18.20

Four-color process printing involves combining four plates—blue (cyan), red (magenta), yellow, and black—to produce the desired colors and contrasts.

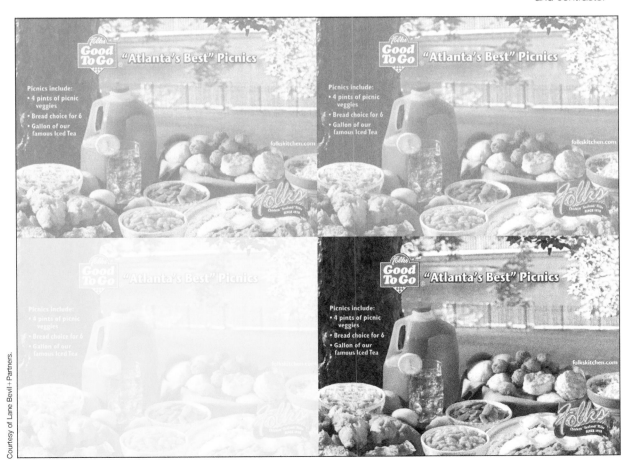

Courtesy of Lane Bevil + Partners.

color production, traditional proofing systems seem to have taken a backseat to digital color proofers, color printers, networked color copiers, and short-run color production devices.

Many proof types are keyed to SWOP/GAA (Gravure Association of America) guidelines, which set standards for inks, density of tones, reverses, and other technical matters.

There are digital hard and soft copy systems that eliminate film to produce continuous-tone proofs. The soft proofing systems allow production and design people to call up a digitized color image and evaluate it before separations are made for an intermediate or position proof. The interactive proofing system gives the agency more flexibility with deadlines and saves time and money for clients.

TYPES OF PROOFS   The choices of types of proof are numerous. Production managers need to decide how accurate a proof is needed or, to put it another way, how much quality they need to pay for. Obviously, they don't want expensive proofs if they are not needed. Here are a number of proof types:

Proof Type	Color Accuracy	Cost
Black-and-white laser	Prints can show color breaks but no color. 300–600 dpi.	Inexpensive
Bluelines	Proofs made by exposing film to light-sensitive paper. They show only a single-color image. Use halftone film.	Inexpensive
Velox	Simple black-and white proofs made from film on photographic paper. Use halftone film.	Moderate
Digital high end	Proofs made from an electronic file. Made by Kodak, 3M, among others. Several processes all meet industry standards. 1800 dpi and higher. Cannot proof actual film.	Moderate
Desktop digital	Usually uses ink jet or thermal wax and gives fairly accurate approximation of color. 300 dpi. Needs color management system to give close approximation of color.	Inexpensive
Laminate/ adhesive	Composite proofs created by exposing the color separations in contact to proofing film and laminating the results. Uses halftone film. Very accurate in color match.	Moderate
Overlay	Made up of layers of acetate attached to a backing substrate. Each overlay film has an image from each separation color. Colors indicate color breaks; not very accurate. Uses halftone film.	Moderate
Press	Proof run on printing press. Uses halftone film. Uses actual printing inks to give most accurate proof.	Expensive

Duplicate Advertisements

Most print advertisements run in more than one publication. Frequently, advertisers have different publications on their schedules, or they need to issue reprints of their advertisements or send material to dealers for cooperative advertising. There are various means of producing duplicate material of magazine or newspaper advertisements. The most common means of sending advertisements to more than one publication is simply sending a digital file to the publication.

Other Production Advances

The changes in technology during the past decade have changed the prepress and printing processes. Future production managers and art directors will continue to have many new options for handling their projects. These new techniques will range from color separation, color management, proofing, and platemaking to printing. The following techniques are of particular interest.

STOCHASTIC SCREENING AND COLOR SEPARATIONS

Computer-to-plate technology has allowed more printers to use a different technique for printing halftones known as frequency modulation (FM) screening, or stochastic printing. Stochastic screening is a process for producing incredible tone and detail that approximates photographic quality. With conventional screens, the dots are spaced equally on a grid (e.g., 110 or 133 lines per inch) and the tonal value is achieved by increasing or decreasing the size of the dots. However, stochastic screening has very tiny dots all of the same size, and their numbers vary according to the tonal value. Used by a quality printer, the image appears to be continuous-tone or of photographic quality and much better than any traditional process. At this time, few companies produce this process. These companies offer an advertiser the ability to produce higher-quality color separations, which in turn allows them to print sharper color advertisements.

HIFI COLOR High-fidelity color is expanding what we know and can do with print reproduction techniques and processes. HiFi color was born out of the limitations of the conventional color printing gamut, which is only a fraction of what the human visual system can see. It is a group of emerging technologies that will expand this printing gamut and extend control by improving and increasing tone, dynamic range, detail, spatial frequency modulation, and other appearance factors of print and other visual media.

HiFi color comprises the technologies of stochastic, or frequency modulation screening; four-plus color process and waterless printing methods; specialty papers, films, coatings, and laminates; and proofing systems, color management systems, software, and hardware.

COLOR MANAGEMENT SYSTEMS (CMS) The ideal—and we have not yet gotten to this point in technology—is seeing an image on a screen and getting an exact printed image, or, as it is touted, what you see is what you get. This is very important in terms of quality control and design. As images go through the production process, the information is transformed in different ways—for example, as photographic data in the original; as pixels of red, green, and blue on the computer screen; or as dots of cyan, magenta, yellow, and black on paper. Software color management systems can bring more consistency to this process, but designers need to know what they can and cannot control. It can be complex even with a color management system.

WATERLESS PRINTING The waterless offset printing technique is popular with environmentalists because it uses less water. Most offset presses use a dampening system of water to cover the plate. Offset is based on the fact that water and grease (ink) don't mix. In waterless printing, a silicone-coated plate is used that rejects ink in the nonimage areas. The result is spectacular detail, high-line screens, richer densities, and consistent quality throughout the press run: in short, great quality. Critics say the plates are far too sensitive, scratch easily, and are temperature sensitive."[2] Offset dominates printing today.

DIGITAL PRINTING Again, we're not talking about your desktop printer. We're talking about printing presses that commercial printers use to print folders, letterheads, and other materials. Generally, digital presses are for short runs. Indigo Press, the first digital printing system, was created in the Netherlands in 1993. Presently, the resolutions and finish of the Indigo Press's digitally printed materials rival offset. It requires a minimum of preflight production tweaking. However, the page size is relatively small to be competitive. The Indigo company merged into Hewlett-Packard. In direct-digital printing workstations send files to the press. Film is not used, and in some cases neither are plates. Today, there are several digital printing systems. Basically, information is transferred

SIMPLE SOLUTIONS

Agency Neathawk Dubuque & Packett (ND&P) had an unusual client come to them seeking help. The Richmond Catholic Diocese needed a program to attract people to the priesthood. After accepting the challenge, the agency came up with some ideas:

Stereotypical challenge—priests don't understand life's complications since they aren't married and aren't out in the real world . . . are out of date . . . how skilled at counseling, then?

Need to show priests aren't "out of touch"—priest with a blog, cell phone, social settings, younger . . .

Creative thoughts: So they are teachers and healers. And counselors. Something visual can be done about the many hats of a priest . . .

You see a man from the back, or just front chest . . . show them changing from construction worker, to

doctor, to teacher, to counselor, to superhero with cape . . . then back up/show neck is collar of a priest . . . because being a priest is about being all these things . . . do something with this on the web site? Transition images?

The solution: Focus on the symbol of the collar.

Two roughs illustrate how the agency's thinking developed early in the process.

A simple solution: a poster and the web site. However, the production of the printed poster was complex. The agency not only had to produce a poster, but also a poster where people could pull off a collar, representing the priesthood. Remember in Chapter 16, we talked about the reduction of ideas and copy.

The web site focused on answering all the anticipated questions for those seeking information. In Chapter 16, we talked about "Expansive" copy. The Richmond Catholic Diocese web site anticipated most every question providing answers.

onto electrophotographic cylinders, instead of plates, and these cylinders use toner to print process color instead of printing ink. There are also other presses that digitize pages onto special plates and are used for short printing runs. It is predicted that digital printing will eventually revolutionize the printing press. Change is in the air.

The computer and digitization are spawning most of the advances in printing and production technology. The day is not far off when the printing and production industry will have a completely filmless, digital process.

The student of advertising production will have to learn these advances in the field, many of which will be both revolutionary and evolutionary, complicating the decision as to which system to use.

SUMMARY

All advertising people need to understand the basics of production. The production terms, concepts, and processes are not easy to learn but are essential to know because they affect budgets, time, and efficiency issues.

Publishers set mechanical requirements for their publications. Advertising production people need to be familiar with sources of information pertaining to print production requirements.

Today, most advertisements are created on the computer (digital). The comps presented to clients appear to be computer finished. The process from the computer screen to a finished advertisement in a publication may be completed digitally or may use a mix of traditional processes. The future will involve more computer-to-plate digital production.

There are three basic kinds of printing processes: letterpress (printing from a raised surface), offset lithography (printing from a flat surface), and gravure (printing from a depressed surface). In addition, silk screen or screen printing offers advertisers additional production applications. The form of printing may affect the type of material sent to the publication to reproduce the advertisement.

Advertisers may use new prepress digital technology or traditional means to prepare advertisements for production. The publication tells the advertiser what type of material is required or accepted. Each method of prepress

has advantages and disadvantages, depending on the degree of quality desired. Typography concerns the style (or face) of type and the way the copy is set. Typefaces come in styles called families. The size is specified in points (72 points per inch). The width of typeset lines is measured in picas (6 picas to an inch). The depth of newspaper space is measured in lines. The space between the lines of type is called leading or line spacing.

The graphics and production processes can be complex because what you see isn't always what really is. Continuous-tone art (a photograph) must be converted into halftone dots (by scanning or using traditional printer's darkroom procedure) so that the tonal values of the original can be reproduced. Line art has no tonal value; it is drawn in black ink on white paper using lines and solid black areas.

Production technology is constantly changing to produce printed materials faster, less expensively, and more efficiently. Achieving color reproduction that satisfies advertising agencies and advertisers is one of the most crucial roles of the magazine production manager. There are a multitude of proofs from which the production manager can choose, as dictated by the need to match colors exactly and the expense involved. "How much quality do we need?" is an often-asked question in terms of which proof to use. Color management systems help advertisers get what you see.

REVIEW

1. Differentiate among the three basic printing processes.
2. What is a digital file?
3. What is continuous-tone copy?
4. What is line art?
5. What are color separations?
6. What colors are used in four-color printing?
7. When is a laminate/adhesive proof used?

CHAPTER 19

Courtesy of Homer LLC.

Video and the Commercial

Video has a lot of connotations today: webisodes, video banners, short or long form, commercials. Here we'll take a look at the development and production of video and television commercials. ▶

CHAPTER LEARNING OBJECTIVES

1. Explain the online environment.
2. Define online ad language.
3. Discuss digital creating and the video/commercial.
4. Discuss producing the video/commercial.

In Chapter 16, we talked about creative thinking and writing. Much of the same thinking applies to all forms of video. Take storytelling or the big idea; blend sight, sound, motion, and technology; and add the ability to impact emotions, build in entertainment, and engage, and you have a very powerful advertising tool. Much of the discussion of television applies to most video production. The length and platform may vary, but the rest is similar to making movies or television spots. Television still reaches multitudes of potential consumers with great impact. There is no doubt video is a powerful means of communication. Just think of all the millions of YouTube brand views. To be specific, people view more than 14 billion videos a month and they have transformed the very nature of web content.

Online Video Environment

In online video advertising, we know what is missing for big-time marketers—standardized video commercial formats and better metrics, perhaps more like those in traditional television commercials. In 2001, major publishers used a similar model for in-page rich media. But publishers such as Yahoo! realized this model didn't allow the ability to drive advertising scale and revenue, and partnered with leading rich-media providers to set standards that led to the growth of in-page rich media. Once standards were in place, revenue and market share for rich media boomed.

Today, web publishers have different sizes, specs, and formats for video, requiring advertisers to create specific ad units for each publisher (in other words, an advertiser may need to reshoot or edit an ad or video many times at great production costs to use a single idea on multiple web networks or platforms); this was not a scalable solution; it was similar to conditions for rich media years ago. However, changing the in-stream video space is more complicated now than in-page rich media was in 2000 because it's more dynamic. For example, there are different video sizes, sequencing issues, proprietary players, and so on.

1. Explain the online environment.

Most online companies agree that standardization is possible. The Interactive Advertising Bureau (IAB) has taken the first steps to standardization by releasing its voluntary Digital Video Ad Serving Template (VAST) and Video Player-Ad Interface Definitions (VPAID) guidelines. These voluntary guidelines provide a framework for advertising inventory and web page design. The goal is to reduce and simplify the amount of work for agencies that may be faced with having to create several assets of a similar size for different publishers, for example, 300×95, 300×100, 300×105 pixels.[1] The IAB ad unit guidelines are for marketers, agencies, and media companies to use in the creating, planning, buying, and selling of interactive marketing and advertising.

Perhaps one of the biggest benefits of the guidelines to publishers is that standardization helps sell video content. If every publisher is selling the same product units, it makes selling as well as buying much easier. Michael Griffin, executive vice president at Eye Wonder, puts it this way, "To put it in context, think of it this way: what if the 30-second TV spot had never been invented? What if advertisers had to build different spots for each station?"[2] That is the situation many advertisers face today using online video.

In video ads, it has been determined that length matters far less than the quality and information provided. Regardless of whether you use an in-banner video ad, a video-enabled profile, or a landing page, research has routinely shown average view rates of 50 to 70 percent of the video, no matter whether it is 30 seconds or 3 minutes long. Doesn't this offer opportunity for great creativity?

INTERACTIVE CAMPAIGNS

In considering the consumer experience, the highly targeted nature of online video means that you can deliver more tailored messaging than on television and engage the consumer in deeper brand conversations. What really sets online video apart from traditional media channels is true interaction. To harness this interactivity to optimum effect, creative execution is key and it is more important than ever that creative and media agencies work together from the early planning stages. The following questions need to be answered:[3]

- *On what journey are you taking the consumer?* What messages do you want to deliver? What do you want the end result to be? What experience do you want the consumer to have?

- *What do you want the consumer to do once they have interacted?* Do you want them to read more in-depth information? View different images of a product? Call you?

- *How do you encourage the user to interact?* Will you offer an incentive? Offer enticing copy?

The Online Language

2 Define online ad language.

There is a new language involving advertising units and technology creative people need to understand. It isn't really all new, but online language is different from everyday language and involves more technical knowledge. If you want an ad that is part text and part video, you have to have some idea of how they work together. It isn't too different a concept from that of your personal web site. You either used one of the standard software formats or templates, or you used a more complex option. The technology continues to give creative people more options, if they understand. Here are a few standard terms for the moment.

- *Banner.* A banner is a long, horizontal, online ad usually found running across the top of a page in a fixed placement.

- *In-banner video ads.* In-banner video ads leverage the banner space to deliver a video experience as opposed to another static or rich media format. The format

Courtesy of Trone.

relies on the existence of a display ad on the page for its delivery (see Exhibit 19.1 for an animated banner).

- *In-page video ads.* Title page video ads are delivered most often as stand-alone ads that do not generally have other streaming content associated with them. The in-page video ad unit allows advertisers to leverage video's sight, sound, and motion on a scale only available through in-page advertising. It is ideal for longer-form advertising, such as branded entertainment, with the ability to reach audiences with an in-stream experience on sites that lack video content.

- *In-stream video ads.* In-stream video ads are played before, during, or after the streaming video content that the consumer has requested. In-stream ads can be played inside short- or long-form video and rely on video content for their delivery.

- *In-text video ads.* In-text video ads are delivered from highlighted words and phrases within the text of web content. The ads are user activated and delivered only when a user chooses to move his or her mouse over a relevant word or phrase.

- *In-banner and in-page expanding video banners.* In-banner and in-page expanding video banners combine the power of video with the scale and targeting of display advertising. Expanding video banners allow advertisers to easily leverage existing video assets and combine them with the creative flexibility of rich media.

- *Overlays.* Overlays are clickable rich media units that display in the bottom third of the video window; they provide advertisers with the opportunity to deliver a brand message during playback without interrupting the user's video experience. Banners increase brand exposure and engagement opportunities.

- *Preroll.* Preroll simply involves taking your television spot and extending usage rights (royalties) to include use on the web, giving you an instant online platform. It becomes an online commercial and could include 15 or 30 online spots. Because there are standard units as with television, there is a lot of discussion both for and against them.

And here are a few related terms:

- *Long-form video.* Long-form video clips are more than 5 minutes in length. When people refer to long-form video, they usually are referring to full-length content, such as TV programs or films.

▨   *Rich media.* Rich media is the collective term given to online advertising formats that use advanced technology to harness broadband to build brands. It uses interactive and audiovisual elements to give rich content and a richer experience for the user when interacting with the ad.

▨   *Short-form video.* Short-form video clips are less than 5 minutes in length. They are usually between 30 seconds and 3 minutes in length. Short-form video makes up the bulk of video content on the Internet today.

Digital Production

Digital production can mean a couple of different things: (1) production of content (videos, photography, animation) that goes into the web and (2) production of code. It involves building the actual web sites (see Exhibit 19.2), including banners, flash pieces, and so on.

In production there are always two issues: cost and quality. When we look at interactive production, there are two extremes at play. Christine Beardsell, creative director at Digitas/Third Act, makes the following observations: "At one extreme you have interactive productions that require the same high-end special effects and quality that television requires. There still is a huge misconception that because the production is going to be on the web, it is going to be cheaper. In fact, the cost will most likely increase because, in addition, you now need to make that content interactive. On the other extreme, you have concepts that require a streamlined, cost-effective method of production. The new term **preditor** (a producer, shooter, editor in one) describes this new emerging group of filmmakers."[4]

preditor
A producer, shooter, and editor in one; it is a term that describes a new emerging group of filmmakers.

Some agencies do all or part of the production in-house. However, most agencies outsource their code and frequently outsource digital concept and design. The main agency generally comes up with a big idea that is expressed across all media, but they'll farm out web ideas to firms such as the Barbarian Group.

PROGRAMMERS AND VISUAL DEVELOPERS

Agencies such as Brunner Digital have programmers and visual developers on staff; therefore, they write most of the code in-house. Other agencies send the ideas to development houses to write the codes. Ernie Mosteller, vice president and creative director says, "As a creative, I find it refreshing, because it means I can think up dang near anything, and I'm pretty sure it's possible in-house. Not everybody has that luxury."[5]

PRODUCTION MANAGER

All of digital production—content and code—is coordinated, policed, scheduled, and managed by a production manager. Large agencies may have several production managers in charge of different accounts.

As for production of content, typically a broadcast producer proficient in any format is in charge and frequently outsources this work. Exhibit 19.3 presents an online storyboard showing the progression of the ad.

BUDGETS

Many production people feel television budgets should cease to exist and should be replaced by "video budgets" that sponsor video content, regardless of the delivery platform. Viewers have become media-agnostic. They are not thinking about watching online or television at any given moment; they're simply watching. However, web networks (or platforms) vary, as we've said. By not having a standard unit or units across web networks, an advertiser has to reshoot or edit an ad or video many times at great production costs to participate on multiple web networks. That said, there has been a movement by the IAB to have some ad formats and sizes standardized by some agencies and web publishers to make it easier on and less costly for marketers.

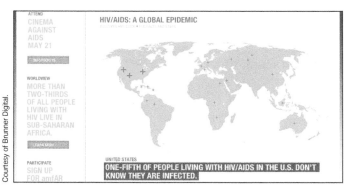

Courtesy of Brunner Digital.

EXHIBIT 19.2

Building major web sites requires planning and knowledge of technology: (a) Consol Energy and (b) AMAR-aids research site.

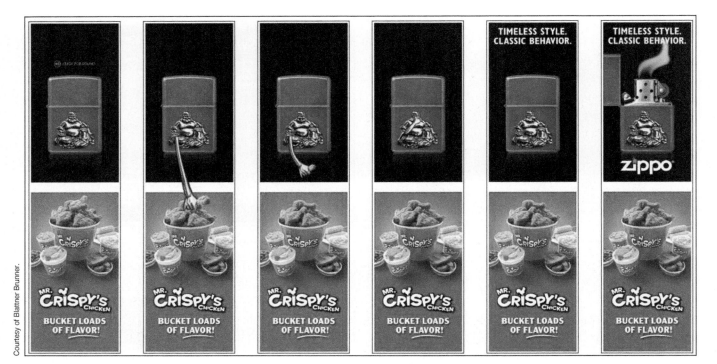

Courtesy of Blattner Brunner.

EXHIBIT 19.3

Zippo Online Storyboard

The Power of the Television Idea

Television is standardized. Television still has power and impact. Some of the characteristics of good television advertising include cutting through clutter and appealing to consumers with humor, intelligence, charm, and emotion. Good ads are like good people. They're smart, funny, and engaging. You tend to remember them long after they're gone. You shouldn't even think about getting into consumers' wallets unless you first get into their lives. If you knew how to do that, you wouldn't have to read the rest of this chapter. However, many people who are supposed to know this don't practice it.

Media-buying agency Starcom Media Services says television advertising drives advertising awareness among viewers. Apparently, the main problem with a television spot is that often nonrelevant ads are shown. So the discussion is not about interruption but rather about relevance of the commercial content.[6]

Here is a convincing example of television's marketing and communication power. Whereas most top-tier banks sell products, BB&T bank preempts respect for the individual in its advertising. Consumer brand-switching intentions increased 300 percent after exposure to BB&T advertising. In one commercial, a lady says, "I'm a great grandmother. Seventy-one and counting. I've danced to the swing. I've danced to the tango. I've seen money wasted. Thrown away. I've seen it used ... to accomplish things ... I never dreamed possible. I will teach my great grandchildren ... to know the difference." The last frame says, "BB&T. You can tell we want your business." That's the way it is supposed to be. Let's look at copy development.

Copy Development and Production Timetable

The creative process is difficult to predict. It isn't always easy to develop new breakthrough copy within the planned timetable or guess the client's reaction to the copy. The agency may love it; the client may hate it. It may take time to develop the right ideas. However, it is important to develop a reasonable timetable for copy development and production. A typical copy development timetable sequence might include the following (of course this can be applied to any video):

- Copy exploratory
- Present ideas to client
- Revisions to client for approval to produce
- Circulate copy for clearance (legal, R&D, management)
- On-air clearance when required
- Prebid meeting (specifications/sets)
- Bid review/award job
- Preproduction meeting
- Shoot
- Postproduction
- Rough cut to client for approval
- Revisions
- Final to client
- Ship date

The advertising agency and the client share responsibility for such a timetable. How long does it take for a 1- to 5-day shoot with 2 to 10 actors to clear this process? Anywhere from 11 to 43 days. This range illustrates the complexity of the process. It isn't easy to generalize.

Creating the Video/Commercial

Many creative people believe it is easier to create a good video or commercial than it is to create a good print ad. After all, the creative person has motion to command more attention, sound, professional actors, producers, directors, and editors. They should be able to communicate with all that support if there is a grain of an idea.

3 Discuss digital creating and the video/commercial.

We'll focus on discussing the television commercial because it is more structured than other video formats. And it has standardized units of time: 15, 30, and 60 seconds. But much of the discussion will apply to online video creation as well. The video commercial has two basic segments: the video (the sight or visual part) and the audio (spoken words, music, or other sounds). The creation process begins with the video because any video is generally better at showing than telling; however, the impact of the words and sounds must be considered. Can you visualize this spot with actors John Hodgman and Justin Long, created by TBWA/Media Arts Lab:

(single and part of series)

Mac: Hello. I'm a Mac.

PC: And I'm a PC.

Mac: Yeah, so what is this PC?

PC: What's that? Oh, this. Yeah well, some people have been having "issues" with Vista, downgrading to XP, some are even switching to Mac, so, yes this will turn the tide however.

(PC presses his button. The words GIVE UP light up)

PC: Oh! That's really unfortunate.

(PC presses his button. The words GIVE UP ON VISTA light up. PC presses his button again and again. GIVE UP and ON VISTA blink on and off. Mac responds with each click)

Mac: No, no, no, no, no. . .

TITLE: (Apple logo) Mac.

Oh, you thought that was a television commercial. Well, no, that was an online video ad. You see, often they come from the same techniques.

KLEPPNER VIEWPOINT 19.1

Ernie Mosteller Vice President, Creative Director/
Emerging Media Brunner

ARE YOU KEEPING UP?

Ernie Mosteller

It's the fall of 2009 as I'm writing this piece about creativity, technology, communications, and advertising. The reason I note the rough date is to be able to offer a frame of reference for future readers. Not because I'm suffering from an overinflated ego. I don't think my words here will live on for generations. In fact, quite the contrary. Because this piece was written for a book (the physically printed and bound kind), I know that whatever I write about creativity, technology, communications, and advertising will be outdated before it even comes off the press.

I'm going to talk about what was. Not in a "Walking to school uphill in the snow" kind of way. But in a "History repeats itself" kind of way. What was, in order to explain what might be. The world of communications changes exceedingly fast and will continue to accelerate its rate of change, matching that of the technology driving it. We are in a revolution—and like all great shifts in the course of history, we can draw some parallels to, and learn from, previous events. If we're smart, we'll do just that.

As revolutions go (scientific, industrial, information, etc.), we are, relatively speaking, in the infancy of the digital revolution. But even at this early stage, the impact has been great. Mass communications techniques have already evolved to resemble something more akin to the interpersonal communications we learned not only in class but also by simply participating in society. As digital delivery systems continue to narrow the audience, the more personal our messaging and tactics will need to become. And, like I said, we're just at the beginning.

Advertising has never been an exercise in permanence. If you're a great artist, you might paint a chapel ceiling that could last a thousand years or more. If you're a great art director, the spot you just launched has to be renewed after 13 weeks. And now, even that is a somewhat outdated and lengthy measure of time. For 50 years or so, the basic vehicles of advertising didn't change. Then the web came along. Since then, the way people communicate, and the way we advertise to them, have done nothing but change.

When television first became ubiquitous, its content was built on lessons producers had learned from other media. News from a single announcer was adapted from radio, and vaudeville acts from the stage became the TV variety show. But as television—both from a production standpoint and from a viewer's perspective—grew in sophistication, so did the content. It took about a decade for programming to evolve into something that was truly of the medium. With the web, that transition has happened much faster. And it continues to evolve at a startlingly rapid pace.

Social media's impact on the way brands interact with customers and

VISUAL TECHNIQUES

There are a number of visual tools for the creative team to use in constructing a video.

TESTIMONIALS   Testimonials can be delivered by known or unknown individuals. Viewers are fascinated with celebrities. Some celebrities (for example, Cindy Crawford) have had staying power for years and years in their ability to grab a viewer's attention. Before his personal problems, Tiger Woods was a successful pitchman. Previously, he pitched for American Express, Accenture, EA Sports, Nike, Rolex, Tag Heuer, Buick, and Titleist. About 20 percent of all TV commercials feature a celebrity. Of course, the superfamous may require long-term deals in the tens of millions of dollars.

There is always a risk with some celebrities of getting into trouble or publicly saying the wrong thing or supporting the wrong cause, but it is worth it because of all the attention they get and the impact they have, according to Total Research Corp.[7] It costs prospects is only beginning to be felt, as I write this. It has already impacted the way brands present themselves on the web. Brand presence on the web has begun to move from a television-derived, entertainment-led structure designed to capture and keep users to one that is more fluid, transparent, conversational, and personal. The web, already the most personalized experience of any media, is becoming more so.

People use the web to connect with other people. And other people is whom they trust for information on just about everything—including, and especially, the things they buy. In the middle of the twentieth century, Bill Bernbach said, "Word of mouth is the best medium of all." If Bill could see the way the average student communicates today, he'd be overwhelmed by the possibilities. As the web becomes more social, brands will realize that what they're dealing with is, essentially, a great big word of mouth machine, connected to an instant-gratification button. Participating effectively within that machine presents a challenge to the next crop of communicators, and to the schools educating them.

There was a time when students went to college not to learn a body of facts, but in fact, to learn how to learn. A classical education in the form of a broad liberal arts degree was once the symbol of a refined and knowledgeable member of society. But somewhere along the way, a degree from a university became a certificate of specialized training in current tactics for any given field. Which is great, if the tactics don't change.

But in communications today, the changes are so many and so rapid that there's no way any established curriculum could ever keep up. Truth is, the participants in the industry can barely keep up.

When I was in college, I learned how to use a lucy to hand-trace headline type. I also learned to make proofreader's marks on copy that came out of a typewriter. Clearly, there is no need for those particular tactical skills—at all—anymore. It took a few years after graduation for those needs to go away. But in today's environment of rapid change, similarly tactical skills, especially in the digital space, meet the same end in much shorter amounts of time. Who needs to know how to build a site in frames? Has anyone reading this even seen a site done in frames? Understanding the tools is important, but the tools change.

There is, however, a constant. Communicating effectively, regardless of the medium, requires a basic understanding of human interaction. How do people communicate with each other? What emotional triggers motivate them? How do they react individually, and as collections of individuals, to different types of messages? Answer these questions and you have the basis for an effective message. It won't matter which tool you use to deliver it.

Students of advertising would be well served to once again focus on learning how to learn. If you want to survive in an environment of rapid tactical change, you, too, must be prepared to change—your tactics, your knowledge base, and your skills—on a regular basis. If I went back to school today to augment my knowledge of advertising, I'd study psychology and sociology. They speak to the essence of human interaction, which is the only constant and is only going to increase in importance as communications become less "mass" and more personal. To keep up with tactics, I send myself to school every day—by constantly seeking out new developments in the digital space. Because there's no catching up; there's only keeping up. Learn to learn. Learn to keep up.

Courtesy of Ernie Mosteller.

an advertiser about $20,000 to research a celebrity to get diagnostic information of not only the personality but also whether the personality fits its product or service. For credibility, Slim-Fast has used satisfied customers showing how much weight they have lost.

SERIALS   Serials are commercials created in a series in which each commercial continues the previous story. The technique was made popular more than a decade ago by the Taster's Choice couple. Beer companies have also tried the serial approach, as have Ragu spaghetti sauce, and Energizer batteries.

OLDIES FOOTAGE   Classic television and film sequences are easily manipulated to create ads that target media-savvy viewers. Audiences have seen John Wayne selling Coors beer, Ed Sullivan introducing the Mercedes M-class sport-utility vehicle, Fred Astaire sweeping with a Dirt Devil, and Lucy Ricardo and Fred Mertz pushing tickets for the California lottery.[8]

SPOKESPERSON   Often this technique features a "presenter" who stands in front of the camera and delivers the copy directly to the viewer. The spokesperson may display and perhaps demonstrate the product. The product should be the hero. The spokesperson should be someone who is likable and believable but not so powerful as to overwhelm the product. In some cases, this is presented with humor.

DEMONSTRATION   The demonstration technique is considered old television. However, creative thinking can make this a modern technique. Product demonstrations have long been a mainstay of advertising because they show what the product can do. When making a demonstration commercial, use close shots so the viewer can see clearly what is happening. Try to make it unexpected, if possible. You may choose a subjective camera view (which shows a procedure as if the viewer were actually doing whatever the product does), using the camera as the viewer's eyes. Make the demonstration relevant and as involving as possible. Do not try to fool the viewer for two important reasons: (1) Your message must be believable, and (2) legally, the demonstration must correspond to actual usage—most agencies make participants in the commercial production sign affidavits signifying that the events took place as they appeared on the TV screen.

CLOSE-UPS   Video is basically a medium of close-ups. The largest screen is too small for extraneous details in the scenes of the video. A fast-food chain may use close-ups to show hamburgers cooking or the appetizing finished product ready to be consumed. With this technique, the audio is generally delivered offscreen (the voiceover costs less than a presentation by someone onscreen).

STORY LINE   The story-line technique is similar to making a miniature movie (with a definite beginning, middle, and end in 30 seconds) except that the narration is done offscreen. In a Mayfield ice cream ad (see Exhibit 19.4), a dad and daughter are walking through the freezer aisle in the supermarket. They notice the Mayfield ice cream freezer floating in the air, tethered only by its electric cord. Amazed, they look through the glass to see that all the Mayfield ice cream cartons are floating to the top of the freezer. As the dad cautiously opens the door to select a flavor, the cartons begin to escape, rising up toward the ceiling. The voiceover says: "Looks like the cream really does come to the top. And you can't get creamier ice cream than Mayfield."

COMPARISONS   Their soft drink has sodium. Our brand is sodium free. Their beer is loaded with carbs. Our beer has next to none. Our sandwich has more meat and less calories. Comparing one product with another can answer questions for the viewer. Usually, the comparison is against the leader in the product category. You could do a user lifestyle comparison between your brand and a competitive brand. In direct product comparisons, you must be prepared to prove in court that your product is significantly superior, as stated, and you must be credible in the way you make your claim, or the commercial may induce sympathy for the competitor.

STILL PHOTOGRAPHS AND ARTWORK   By using still photographs and/or artwork, including cartoon drawings and lettering, you can structure a well-paced commercial. The required material may already exist, to be supplied at a modest cost, or it can be photographed or drawn specifically for your use. Skillful use of the video camera can give static visual material a surprising amount of movement. Zoom lenses provide an inward or outward motion, and panning the camera across the photographs or artwork can give the commercial motion (*panning* means changing the viewpoint of the camera without moving the dolly it stands on).

SLICE-OF-LIFE   Slice-of-life is a dramatic technique in which actors tell a story in an attempt to involve people with the brand. It is a short miniplay in which the brand is the hero. Most slice-of-life commercials open with a problem, and the brand becomes the solution.

"FREEZER"
:30 TV Spot

Story Summary:
As a dad and his daughter walk through the freezer aisle in the grocery store, they notice the Mayfield ice cream freezer floating in mid air, tethered only by the case's electric plug. Amazed, they look through the glass to see that all of the Mayfield cartons are floating to the top of the freezer. As dad cautiously opens the door to select a flavor, the cartons begin to "escape," rising up toward the ceiling.

GIRL: Hey dad. What kind of ice cream is that?

DAD: Oh, that's... Wow!

GIRL: Can we get some?

DAD: You bet.

GIRL: Cool!

SCOTTIE V/O: Looks like the cream really does rise to the top.

Scottie Mayfield

And you can't get creamier ice cream than Mayfield.

Like new Mayfield Cookies & Cream.

It's just not ice cream.

ICE CREAM**IER**

It's ice creamier.

GIRL: What flavor do you want?
DAD: All of 'em!

Courtesy of Mayfield and The Johnson Group.

EXHIBIT 19.4

"Freezer" Spot

This Mayfield ice cream commercial uses a story inside of a supermarket to make a point about its creamier ice cream.

The viewer must see the problem as real, and the reward must fit the problem. Because problem solving is a useful format in almost any commercial, slice-of-life is widely used. Brands selling largely emotional benefits (jeans, soft drinks, beer, greeting cards, athletic gear) have employed the format in great numbers.

CUSTOMER INTERVIEW Most people who appear in television commercials are professional actors, but customer interviews involve nonprofessionals. An interviewer or offscreen voice may ask a housewife, who is usually identified by name, to compare the advertised kitchen cleanser with her own brand by removing two identical spots in her sink. She finds that the advertised product does a better job.

VIGNETTES AND SITUATIONS   Advertisers of soft drinks, beer, candy, and other widely consumed products find techniques involving vignettes and situations useful in creating excitement and motivation. The video usually consists of a series of fast-paced scenes showing people enjoying the product as they enjoy life. The audio over these scenes is often a jingle or song with lyrics based on the situation we see and the satisfaction the product offers. In many cases, it is the music that holds it all together. It can be used effectively to update a brand or sell a lifestyle. It is a challenge to link with the brand and can be costly to produce because you have to shoot 15 or so vignettes (and think about webisodes).

HUMOR   Humor has long been a popular technique with both copywriters and consumers because it makes the commercial more interesting. The dangers are that the humorous aspects of the commercial will get in the way of the sell and that the viewer will remember the humor rather than the product or the benefit. The challenge is to make the humorous copy relevant to the product or benefit.

animation
Making inanimate objects appear alive and moving by setting them before an animation camera and filming one frame at a time.

ANIMATION   Historically, the most common form of **animation** was the cartoon. Today, computer graphics can be extremely realistic and have changed the nature of animation. The cost of animation depends on its style: With limited movement, few characters, and few or no backgrounds, the price can be low.

STOP MOTION   When a package or other object is photographed in a series of different positions, movement can be simulated as the single frames are projected in sequence. Stop motion is similar to artwork photographed in animation. With it, the package can "walk," "dance," and move as if it had come to life.

ROTOSCOPE   In the rotoscope technique, animated and live-action sequences are produced separately and then optically combined. A live boy may be eating breakfast food while a cartoon animal trademark character jumps up and down on his shoulder and speaks to him.

PROBLEM/SOLUTION   The problem/solution technique has been around since the beginning of television. The purpose of many products is to solve the prime prospect's problem— a headache, poor communication, or plaque. You get the idea. The product is selling the solution. Problem/solution is similar to slice-of-life but lacks the depth of story line or plot development. Be sure to let the visuals tell the story. Solve the problem with visuals.

MOOD IMAGERY   The mood imagery technique is expensive and difficult. It often combines several techniques. The main objective is to set a certain mood and image for the product you are trying to sell. Strong imagery can sell ideas (see Exhibit 19.5). Zippo creates mood, mystery, and surprise as a figure moves up metal stairs to music and SFX and then a flash from a Zippo and the torch of the Statue of Liberty lights. The copy reads, "ZIPPO. Use it to start something."

SPLIT AND BOOKEND SPOTS   A variation on the serial commercial is the split spot: Two related (usually 15-second) spots run with a completely unrelated spot between them. The theory behind split and bookend commercials is that breaking out of the expected format will get your product remembered.

INFOMERCIALS   The infomercial is a commercial that looks like a program. These commercials sell everything from woks to make-a-million-in-real-estate programs, and they usually run for 30 minutes. The National Infomercial Marketing Association recommends that every infomercial begin and end with a "paid advertisement" announcement

Courtesy of Zippo and Blattner Brunner.

EXHIBIT 19.5

Zippo

Some ideas naturally lend themselves to mood imagery. Zippo uses a little suspense with sound effects and stark lighting to add mystery.

so that consumers understand what they are watching. The obvious advantage is that the advertiser has an entire program about its product.

COMBINATION   Most commercials combine techniques. A speaker may begin and conclude the message, but there will be close-ups in between. Every commercial should contain at least one or two close-ups to show the package and logo. Humor is adaptable to most techniques. Animation and live action make an effective mixture in many commercials, and side-by-side comparisons may be combined with almost any other technique.

VISUAL VICISSITUDES   Visual vicissitudes are commercials that weave together a string of apparently nonstory-driven scenes, full of talking heads, lush landscapes, or crisp graphic shots. Music and sound can help to serve as a pacing guide.

BUG   Place a "bug" in the lower right-hand corner of the commercial. That's the thing the networks often use that let's you know what network you're watching. And always end your commercial with your brand name prominently on the screen.[9]

VIDEO INFLUENCE

Many visual techniques used in commercials have evolved from the music video industry. These include hyperkinetic imagery, visual speed, and sophistication; ironic, wise-guy attitudes; unexpected humor; quick, suggestive cuts rather than slow segues; narrative implications rather than whole stories; attitudes, not explanations; tightly cropped, partial images instead of whole ones; a mixture of live action, newsreel footage, animation, typography, film speeds, and film quality; and unexpected soundtrack/audio relationships to video.

WHICH TECHNIQUE?

There have been a number of studies over the years to help creatives make up their minds as to what type of commercials to run. However, none provide all the answers. Research found that people who liked a commercial were twice as likely to be persuaded by it compared to people who felt neutral toward the advertising. Perhaps the single most striking finding was the fact that commercial liking went far beyond mere entertainment. People like commercials they believe are relevant and worth remembering. Original or novel approaches alone seem to have little to do with how well a commercial is liked. Like was found to be a function of the product category. A lively, energetic execution also contributed to liking but was less important than relevance. In

KLEPPNER VIEWPOINT 19.2

Gary C. Sain President and CEO, Orlando/Orange County Convention and Visitors Bureau, Inc.

"ORLANDO MAKES ME SMILE"

As the president and CEO of the Orlando/Orange County Convention and Visitors Bureau (Orlando CVB), I often get asked about what role my organization plays in driving leisure and business travel to Orlando. A simple question with a complex answer. I believe there is a general misconception regarding what CVBs do, as well as the services they provide to the destination (and for that matter, to visitors).

Today's CVB is based on a different model from its predecessors of 20 or 30 years ago, when most folks thought of us as an extension of the local chamber of commerce. We now tend to see ourselves as destination marketing associations. In Orlando, this means we strive to brand and market the destination to global travel audiences. Sounds like a mouthful, but it all comes down to increasing visitation while providing in-bound travelers with relevant information about Orlando.

So what does this equate to in real-world terms? Our internal staff and related external agencies reach worldwide audiences with integrated marketing programs and publicity efforts. For leisure domestic travelers, this could result in consumer advertising like our

recent "Orlando Makes Me Smile" campaign. To increase domestic business travel, we developed the "Where Creative Minds Meet" campaign, which targets meeting planners with the message that attendees are more imaginative and creative in Orlando. We market to international consumer audiences, with advertising and promotional programs in Canada, the United Kingdom, Germany, and Latin America, among many other countries.

But that's only the beginning. We work aggressively with the travel trade to provide the industry with information about the latest and greatest leisure options in the destination. The more they know about Orlando, the more valuable they are to their customers. We engage journalists across the globe to help us tell our story to leisure and business travel audiences. Providing current and potential visitors with vacation planning information via VisitOrlando.com is another one of our goals—we pride ourselves on being the destination experts. And we're also a trade association with nearly 1,400 members that represent every facet of travel to the destination.

A tangible example of what we do every day is our previously mentioned "Orlando Makes Me Smile" effort. Launched early in 2009, the consumer advertising campaign was designed to reap the benefits of our "Where Relationships Thrive" brand positioning. Simply, travelers from around the world take an Orlando vacation for essentially the same universal reasons—to bond with and enjoy their

loved ones. Whether it's domestic visitors from Atlanta or international travelers from Brazil, these guests all share the common desire to relax and reconnect with family and friends. In other words, it's all about relationships.

One of the unique challenges of the Smile campaign was to remain connected with the target—families with children—while increasing reach to pre- and postfamilies, such as couples without kids or empty-nesters. The latter groups aren't always associated with travel to Orlando, but the campaign provided an opportunity to showcase the destination and expand awareness to these potential visitors.

So far I have enjoyed a 25-year career in the travel and tourism industry, focusing on sales, marketing, and branding efforts. I previously worked for a well-known and respected advertising agency that specializes in international tourism marketing. I also spent time serving as a marketing executive for several global hotel brands and a cruise line. My passion for the hospitality industry continues to expand each day. Today, I am fortunate to take advantage of my diverse tourism background and apply it to marketing the world's greatest travel destination—Orlando.

Courtesy of Gary C. Sain

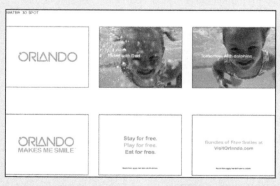

Courtesy of Gary C. Sain, President and CEO, Orlando/Orange County Convention and Visitors Bureau, Inc.

Gary C. Sain

other research findings, Video Storyboard tests reinforce the fact that consumers like commercials with celebrities. Consumer preference for this type of commercial continues to rise. Such commercials are more persuasive than slice-of-life vignettes or product demonstrations; celebrities are bested only by humor and kids as executional elements that characterize persuasive commercials.

Ideas generate production techniques and sometimes thinking of the technique choices generates "ideas." The technology allows you to create almost anything you can visualize. These are your communication tools.

PLANNING THE VIDEO OR COMMERCIAL

Let's review some of the basic principles of writing a video or commercial script. In planning the video, there are many considerations: cost, medium (videotape or film), casting of talent, use of music, special techniques, time, location, and the big idea and its relationship to the advertising and marketing objectives and to the entire campaign.

- You are dealing with sight, sound, and motion. Each of these elements has its own requirements and uses. There should be a relationship among them so that the viewer perceives the desired message. Make certain that when you are demonstrating a sales feature, the audio is talking about that same feature.

- Your audio should be relevant to your video, but there is no need to describe what is obvious in the picture. When possible, you should see that the words interpret the picture and advance the thought.

- Any video generally is more effective at showing than telling; therefore, more than half of the success burden rests on the ability of the video to communicate.

- The number of scenes should be planned carefully. You do not want too many scenes (unless you are simply trying to give an overall impression) because this tends to confuse the viewer. Yet you do not want scenes to become static (unless planned so for a reason). Remember, always know your target, younger audiences digest more scenes quickly than older audiences. Study commercials and time the scene changes to determine what you personally find effective. If you do this, you will discover the importance of pacing the message—if a scene is too long, you will find yourself impatiently waiting for the next one.

- It is important to conceive the video as a flowing progression so that the viewer will be able to follow it easily. You do not have time for a three-act play whose unrelated acts can be tied together at the end. A viewer who cannot follow your thought may well tune you out. The proper use of opticals or transitions can add motion and smoothness to scene transitions.

- Any video is basically a medium of close-ups. The largest screen is too small for extraneous detail in scenes. Long shots can be effective in establishing a setting but not for showing product features.

- The action of the video takes more time than a straight announcer's reading of copy. A good rule is to purposely time the commercial a second or two short. Generally, the action will eat up this time, so do not simply read your script. Act it out.

- You will want to consider the use of *supers* (words on the screen) of the basic theme so that the viewer can see, as well as hear, the important sales feature. Many times, the last scene will feature product identification and the theme line.

- If possible, show the brand name. If it is prominent, give a shot of the package; otherwise, flash its logo. It is vital to establish brand identification.

- Generally, try to communicate one basic idea; avoid running in fringe benefits. Be certain that your words as well as your pictures emphasize your promise. State it, support it, and, if possible, demonstrate it. Repeat your basic promise near the end of a commercial; that is the story you want viewers to carry away with them.

■ Read the audio aloud to catch tongue twisters.

■ As in most other advertising writing, the sentences should usually be short and their structure uncomplicated. Use everyday words. It is not necessary to have something said every second. The copy should round out the thought conveyed by the picture.

■ In writing your video description, describe the scene and action as completely as possible: "Open on husband and wife in living room" is not enough. Indicate where each is placed, whether they are standing or sitting, and generally how the room is furnished.

WRITING THE SCRIPT

Writing a video or TV commercial is very different from writing print advertising. On TV you must be brief. The 30-second commercial has only 28 seconds of audio. In 28 seconds, you must solve your prime prospect's problems by demonstrating your product's superiority. Think of words and pictures simultaneously. You usually divide your script paper into two columns. On the left, you describe the video action, and on the right you write the audio portion, including sound effects and music. Corresponding video and audio elements go right next to each other, panel by panel (see Exhibit 19.6). Longer forms of online videos allow you more time to develop your story.

Write copy in a friendly, conversational style. If you use an off-camera announcer, make certain that his or her dialog is keyed to the scenes in your video portion. Although it is not always possible, matching the audio with the video makes a commercial cohesive and more effective. The audio—words, sound effects, or music—in a script is as important as the video portion. They must work together to bring the viewer the message. You need strong copy and sound and strong visuals. All are vital for an effective commercial.

Some agencies add visuals to their scripts. They use specially designed sheets of paper, usually 8 inches by 11 inches, with boxes down the center for rough sketches of the video portion (see Exhibit 19.7) called photoscripts. For presentations, most agencies use full-size television storyboards.

EXHIBIT 19.6

An Example of a Script Format

VIDEO	AUDIO
	MUSIC: IN AND UNDER (George Winston quiet jazz)
1. MS:BEACHSCENE 3 PEOPLE IN CHAIRS SITTING OUTSIDE OF BEACH HOUSE. BEACH BLANKET IN SAND.	ANNCR: Pawleys is a great
2. CU: CHILD DIGGING IN SAND WITH OCEAN BACKGROUND.	family resort.
3. MS: PEOPLE WALKING ON ALMOST EMPTY BEACH. A FEW HOUSES ARE IN THE BACKGROUND.	It is nature at its best. . .
4. LS: LADY ALONE WALKING INLET WITH DISTANT HOUSE OR TWO.	a beautiful . . . pristine beach
5. WIDE SHOT OF EMPTY BEACH, FEW HOUSES.	Don't come, we're having fun.
6. END FRAME.	
	Pawleys is OUR beach.

EXHIBIT 19.7

**A Television Script
with Storyboard**

TV SCRIPT: Pawleys "Leave Us Alone"

VIDEO		AUDIO
1. MS: BEACH SCENE PEOPLE IN CHAIRS OUTSIDE OF HOUSE		MUSIC: IN AND UNDER (George Winston quiet jazz) ANNCR:Pawleys is a great
2. CU: CHILD DIGGING IN SAND WITH OCEAN BACKGROUND		family resort.
3. MS: PEOPLE WALK-ING ON ALMOST EMPTY BEACH		It is nature at its best....
4. LS: LADY ALONE WALKING INLET		a beautiful pristine...beach
5. WIDE SHOT OF EMPTY BEACH, FEW HOUSES		Don't come, we're having fun.
6. END FRAME	Pawleys *Don't Disturb Us!*	Pawleys is OUR beach.

DEVELOPING THE STORYBOARD

Once the creative art and copy team has developed a script, the next step is to create a **storyboard**, which consists of a series of sketches showing key scenes developed in the script. It is a helpful tool for discussing the concept with other agency or client person-nel, who may not know the background or who may not be able to visualize a script eas-ily. Without a storyboard, each individual may interpret the script's visuals differently.

STORYBOARD VERSUS FINISHED LOOK   It is extremely difficult, if not impossible, to vi-sualize the look of a finished commercial from the storyboard. Most clients are very lit-eral minded and don't visualize storyboards very well. Storyboards should stimulate the imagination of someone's vision prior to shooting. The quality of the storyboards varies from virtual stick figures in limbo to full-color drawings or photos. Keep in mind, using this limited medium, it is a difficult task to show all the details that are necessary to under-stand for production purposes. And for longer form online videos, it becomes even harder.

Storyboards consist of two frames for each scene. The top frame represents the screen (visual). The bottom frame carries a description of the video (as per script) and

storyboard
Series of drawings used to present a proposed commercial. Consists of illustrations of key action (video), accompanied by the audio part. Used for getting advertiser approval and as a production guide.

the audio for that sequence (some storyboards carry only the audio portion). The number of sets of frames varies from commercial to commercial and is not necessarily dictated by the length of the commercial. There may be 4 to 12 or more sets of frames, depending on the nature of the commercial and the demands of the client for detail.

The storyboard is a practical step between the raw script and actual production. It gives the agency, client, and production house personnel a common visual starting point for their discussion. On client approval, the storyboard goes into production.

Assessing the storyboard requires answering a number of questions: Is there a campaign idea? Is it on strategy? Is the campaign idea meaningful? Credible? Provocative? Does the execution showcase the campaign idea? Is the benefit visualized? Does it tell a picture story? Is it clear, credible, and compelling? Does the board represent a single ad or a campaign? Are the ideas communicated clearly in visual-audio elements? Does it sell versus tell?

Exhibit 19.8 is an example of a photoboard. The photoboard is similar to the storyboard but shows the actual frames (photos) that were shot. It is frequently used by

EXHIBIT 19.8

A Television Photoboard

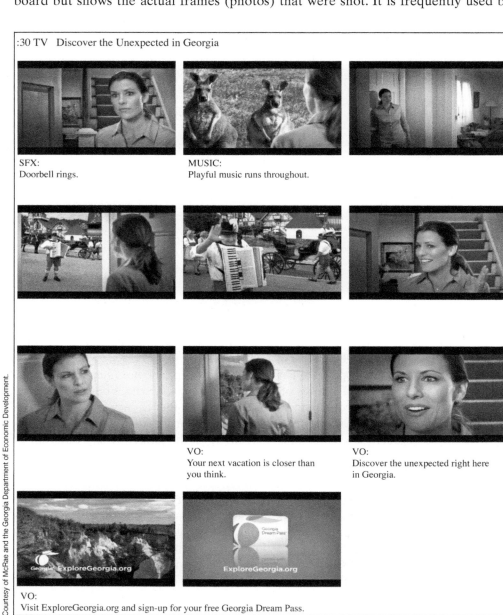

:30 TV   Discover the Unexpected in Georgia

SFX:
Doorbell rings.

MUSIC:
Playful music runs throughout.

VO:
Your next vacation is closer than you think.

VO:
Discover the unexpected right here in Georgia.

VO:
Visit ExploreGeorgia.org and sign-up for your free Georgia Dream Pass.

Courtesy of McRae and the Georgia Department of Economic Development.

companies as a sales tool to show merchants and dealers exactly what kind of advertising support they will be given.

OTHER ELEMENTS OF THE COMMERCIAL

OPTICALS Most commercials contain more than a single scene. Optical devices or effects between scenes are necessary to provide smooth visual continuity from scene to scene. They are inserted during the final editing stage. The actual **opticals** may be one of the director's functions. However, these are used to aid in the transition of getting from one scene to the next scene or establishing a visual. Sometimes which technique is used depends on the importance of a particular scene or the detail that needs to be seen. Exhibit 19.9 illustrates some basic optical decisions. Among the most common are the following:

- *Cut.* One scene simply cuts into the next. It is the fastest scene change because it indicates no time lapse whatsoever. A cut is used to indicate simultaneous action, to speed up action, and for variety. It keeps one scene from appearing on the screen too long.

- *Dissolve.* Dissolve is an overlapping effect in which one scene fades out while the following scene simultaneously fades in. Dissolves are slower than cuts. There are

opticals
Visual effects that are put on a TV film in a laboratory, in contrast to those that are included as part of the original photography.

EXHIBIT 19.9

Examples of Camera Directions

ECU - An Extreme Close Up shows, for example, person's lips, nose, eyes.

CU - The Close Up is a tight shot, but showing face on entire package for emphasis.

MCU - The Medium Close Up cuts to person about chest, usually showing some background.

MS - The Medium Shot shows the person from the waist up. Commonly used shot. Shows much more detail of setting or background than MCU.

LS - The Long Shot shows the scene from a distance. Used to establish location.

fast dissolves and slow dissolves. Dissolves are used to indicate a short lapse of time in a given scene or to move from one scene to another where the action is either simultaneous with the action in the first scene or occurring very soon after the preceding action.

- *Fade-in.* The fade-in is an effect in which the scene actually "fades" into vision from total black (black screen).

- *Fade-out.* The fade-out is the opposite of the fade-in. The scene "fades" into total black. If days, months, or years elapse between one sequence of action and the next, indicate "fade out . . . fade in."

- *Matte.* Matte is when part of one scene is placed over another so that the same narrator, for example, is shown in front of different backgrounds.

- *Super.* The superimposition of one scene or object over another. The title or product can be "supered" over the scene.

- *Wipe.* The new scene "wipes" off the previous scene from top or bottom or side to side with a geometric pattern (see Exhibit 19.10). A wipe is faster than a dissolve but not as fast as a cut. A wipe does not usually connote lapse of time, as a dissolve or fade-out does. There are several types of wipes: flip (the entire scene turns over like the front and back of a postcard), horizontal (left to right or right to left), vertical (top to bottom or bottom to top), diagonal, closing door (in from both sides), bombshell (a burst into the next scene), iris (a circle that grows bigger is an iris out), fan (fans out from center screen), circular (sweeps around the screen—also called clock wipe). Wipes are most effective when a rapid succession of short or quick scenes is desired or to separate impressionistic shots when these are grouped together to produce a montage effect.

- *Zoom.* A zoom is a smooth, sometimes rapid move from a long shot to a close-up or from a close-up to a long shot.

SOUND TRACK   The audio portion of the commercial may be recorded either during the film or videotape shooting or at an earlier or later time in a recording studio. When the sound track is recorded during the shooting, the actual voices of the people

EXHIBIT 19.10

Example of a Wipe

speaking on camera are used in the commercial. If the sound track is recorded in advance, the film or videotape scenes can be shot to fit the copy points as they occur, or if music is part of the track, visual action can be matched to a specific beat. If shooting and editing take place before the sound track is recorded, the track can be tailored to synchronize with the various scenes.

MUSIC Not all commercials need music. But think about it early in the process. Music has the ability to communicate feelings and moods in a unique way. As a result, the use of music can make or break a television commercial. In some commercials, it is every bit as important as the copy or visuals. It is often used as background to the announcer's copy or as a song or jingle that is integral to the ad. Here are some ways you can put music to work:[10]

- *Backgrounds.* In many commercials, background music is used primarily to contribute to the mood. Appropriate music can establish the setting; then it can fade and become soft in the background.

- *Transitions.* Music can be an effective transition device to carry viewers from one setting to another. For example, the music may start out being sedate as the scene is peaceful. As it switches to the product being used, the music changes to rock and the tempo builds, marking the transition from place to place.

- *Movement.* Sound effects (SFX), natural sounds, and music can contribute to movement. Music that moves up the scale, or down, supports something or someone moving up or down.

- *Accents.* Music can punctuate points or actions. The "beat" of the music and visuals can match to hold viewers' attention and drive the commercial. Musical sounds—as little as a single note—can attract attention.

NEW OR OLD MUSIC As mentioned earlier, some advertisers pay big money to professional musicians to develop a special tune or lyrics for a commercial or campaign. The previous wisdom was that original tunes could be cheaper. The cost of an original track ranges from $10,000 to $50,000 not factoring in residuals to singers and musicians. Licensing a hit song from an established act can range from $250,000 to more than $1 million. The superexpensive buys are what people talk about: deals that range from $10 million to $15 million with a superstar. However, there are countless smaller acts available for much less. "You have to have guts to buy songs no one has ever heard before," says Eric Hirschberg at Deutsch.[11]

Music can set the mood for a commercial. General Mills introduced Berry Burst Cheerios with the 1970 pop tune by the Partridge Family, "I Think I Love You." The song set the mood for the humorous television commercials. So we aren't always thinking current music. Licensed music gains instant access to the listener's subconscious.

Whether you're using country, rock, or Latin, the tone of the music can help transfer drama, love, happiness, or other feelings to the viewer. It is a tool to cue the viewer's feelings. Original music can be written and scored for the commercial, or licensing of old or popular songs can be obtained, which can be very expensive. The least expensive music is stock music sold by stock music companies. It is cheap because it is not exclusive.

Producing the Television Commercial

The job of converting the approved storyboard is done by broadcast production. There are three distinct stages to this process:

4 Discuss producing the video/commercial.

1. Preproduction includes casting; wardrobing; designing sets or building props; finding a location or studio; and meeting with agency, client, and production house personnel.

2. Shooting encompasses the work of filming or videotaping (although some digital cameras bypass tape) all scenes in the commercial. Several takes are made of each scene.

3. Postproduction, also known as editing, completion, or finishing, includes selecting scenes from among those shots, arranging them in the proper order, inserting transitional effects, adding titles, combining sound with picture, and delivering the finished commercial. Exhibit 19.11 shows a photoboard with the finished commercial.

In charge of production is the producer, who combines the talents of coordinator, diplomat, watchdog, and businessperson. Some producers are on the staffs of large agencies or advertisers. Many work on a freelance basis. The work of a producer is so all-embracing that the best way to describe it is to live through the entire production process. Let us do that first and pick up the details of the producer's job in the section headed "Role of the Producer."

Let us begin with the problems of shooting the spot, for which a producer appoints a director.

EXHIBIT 19.11

Finished Commercial Photoboard

:30 TV

VO:
Your new house.   It's more than a home.   It's a gathering place.

A sanctuary.   A family bond.   A source of pride.

Your new house is more than a home.   Become part of the Bowen family   Visit Bowen Dream Event.com
It's a Bowen Family Home.   of homeowners.   or call 1-877-MY BOWEN.

Courtesy of McRae and Bowen Homes.

THE DIRECTOR'S FUNCTION

As the key person in the shooting, the director takes part in casting and directing the talent, directs the cameraperson in composing each picture, assumes responsibility for the setting, and puts the whole show together. A director of a regional commercial will earn about $7,500 per day, and a national commercial will double that pay; however, better-known directors may demand $35,000 per spot. The average is $23,000. The Source Maythenyi, an advertising and production database service, estimates there are 4,000 specialized commercial directors and that doesn't include a growing number of feature film directors.[12]

THE BIDDING PROCESS

There is only one way to provide specifications for a commercial shoot when you are seeking bids from production companies, and that is in writing. There is an industry-accepted form for bids. The agency and client provide information for this form. The purpose is to ensure that all production companies are provided with identical job specifications for estimating production costs. It ensures that all bids are based on the same information.

THE PREPRODUCTION PROCESS

A preproduction meeting must be held prior to every production. The agency producer is expected to chair this meeting. The following agency, client, and production company personnel usually attend:

Agency: producer, creative team, account supervisor

Client: brand manager or advertising manager

Production company: director, producer, others as needed

The following points should be covered at every preproduction meeting: direction, casting, locations and/or sets, wardrobe and props, product, special requirements, final script, legal claims/contingencies, and timetable update.

In addition to covering the points just listed, the creative team and the director will likely present shooting boards and the production thinking behind the commercial. The shooting boards should be used for the following purposes:

- To determine camera angles
- To determine best product angles
- To project camera and cast movement and help determine talent status (extra versus principal)
- To determine number of scenes to shoot
- To determine timing of each scene

Role of the Producer

AGENCY PRODUCER

The producer's role begins before the approval of the storyboard. Conferring with the copywriter and/or art director, the producer becomes thoroughly familiar with every frame of the storyboard.

1. The producer prepares the "specs," or specifications—the physical production requirements of the commercial—to provide the production studios with the precise information they require to compute realistic bids. Many advertisers request a further breakdown of the cost of items such as preproduction, shooting, crew, labor,

PRODUCTION SCHEDULE

A typical complex production schedule for a finished computer commercial can cost more than $1.5 million and take 6 months to complete.

Production Schedule

Bidding Studio	Stage or Location Shoot without Special Effects	Special Effects Shoot
Includes: • Screening directors' reels • Sending job specification • Bids (AICP form) returned • Bid comparison by agency • Estimating supplemental costs (music, travel, etc.)	2–3 weeks	3–6 weeks

Preproduction	Stage or Location Shoot without Special Effects	Special Effects Shoot
Includes: • Casting • Location search • Set design • Wardrobe fittings	2–3 weeks	3–6 weeks

Production Schedule

Shoot	Stage or Location Shoot without Special Effects	Special Effects Shoot
Roll camera	1–7 days	1–7 days

Postproduction	Stage or Location Shoot without Special Effects	Special Effects Shoot
Includes: • Edit film • Film color correction • Post–special effects • Casting voiceover talent • Recording voiceover talent • Demo music • Music recording • Final audio mix and masters	2–3 weeks	4–10 weeks

studio, location travel and expenses, equipment, film, props and wardrobe, payroll taxes, studio makeup, direction, insurance, and editing.

2. The producer contacts the studios that have been invited to submit bids based on their specialties, experience, and reputation; meets with them either separately or in one common "bid session"; and explains the storyboard and the specs in detail.

3. The production house estimates expenses after studying specs, the production timetable, and the storyboard. The bids are submitted.

4. The producer arranges for equipment. The studio may own cameras and lights, but more often it rents all equipment for a job. The crew is also freelance, hired by the day. The studio's primary job is to shoot the commercial. For videotape, a few studios own their own cameras and production units; others rent these facilities.

5. Working through a talent agency, the producer arranges, or has the production company arrange, auditions. Final decisions are made on choices of performers.

6. At the preproduction meeting, the producer, creative associates, account executive, and client, together with studio representatives and the director, lay out final plans for production.

7. During the shooting, the producer usually represents both the agency and the client with the director. On the set or location, creative and client people channel comments and suggestions through the producer to avoid confusion.

8. It is the producer's responsibility to arrange for the recording session. Either before or after shooting and editing, he or she arranges for the soundtrack, which may

call for an announcer, actors, singers, and musicians. If music is to be recorded, the producer will have had preliminary meetings with the music contractor.

9. The producer participates in the editing along with the creative team. Editing begins after viewing the dailies and selecting the best takes.

10. The producer arranges screenings for agency associates and clients to view and approve the commercials at various editing stages and after completion of the answer print.

11. Finally, the producer handles the billings and approves studio and other invoices for shooting, editing, and payment to talent.

THE "OUTSIDE" PRODUCER

An **outside producer** is the person representing a production company whose entire business is filmmaking. The agency producer hires him or her to create the commercial.

outside producer
The production company person who is hired by the agency to create the commercial according to agency specifications.

SHOOTING

Most productions consist of the following steps:

1. *Prelight.* This is simply the day (or days) used to set the lighting for specific scenes. To do this exclusively on shoot days would tie up the entire crew.

2. *Shooting.* This phase of the production process is the filming (or taping) of the approved scenes for the commercial. These scenes are then "screened" the next day (dailies) to ensure that the scene was captured as planned.

3. *Wrap.* This signals the completion of production. It is at this stage that most of the crew is released.

4. *Editing.* Editing takes place after the completion of the shoot. Scenes are screened and selected for use in the commercial. The scenes are then merged with a sound track, titles, and opticals, composing a completed or finished commercial.

The role of the client and account service at the shoot is one of advisor. It is really the creative's day, and it is their responsibility to deliver the spot. The producer is generally the liaison between the agency and the director. This chain of command is simple and direct and eliminates confusion on the set, which is an absolute necessity when shooting.

POSTPRODUCTION PROCESS

Postproduction begins after a production company exposes the film in the camera at the shoot. The film that comes out of the camera must be developed and then printed onto a new strip of positive film called the *dailies*. The editor then screens these dailies and selects the good takes from the day's shooting.

The editor edits the scenes and takes selected frames from each scene together to create a *rough cut*, which is a rough rendition of the finished commercial. The agency and client then approve the cut, the editor takes the original film that was shot and developed and pulls the takes from that film that match the selected workprint takes.

Today, virtually all final edits, effects, and opticals are done on videotape using computers. The original camera film takes (35 mm motion-picture film) are transferred electronically to 1-inch videotape. During this transfer of film to videotape, the color is corrected.

The editor then takes this material into a video edit, in which each take is run on videotape. The entire commercial is laid down from the color-corrected videotape master (called the *unedited tape master*). Titles and other special effects are added during this final unedited-tape-to-edited-tape session. Just think of the steps involved in Exhibit 19.12. If you examine this simple script, you see that there is camera movement, a spokesperson shot, a zoom, and a close-up of pouring milk. The sound (which the editor and agency had worked on along with the picture) is then electronically relayed onto the video-edited master, and the spot is finished. Sound complicated? It is.

EXHIBIT 19.12

This simple video required decisions about what angles, zooms, and what part of each shot to use and what kind of transition.

"RECIPE"
:30 TV Spot

Story Summary:
In the process of baking a cake, a woman tastes a bit of Mayfield milk that had spilled on her hand. Surprised by how good the milk tastes, she wants more. Looking around to make sure no one is watching, she picks up the measuring cup and then chugs the delicious Mayfield milk.

SCOTTIE V/O: One taste of Mayfield milk, and it hits you...

...all milks aren't the same.

Only Mayfield has the great taste...

...milk lovers can't resist.

Taste it and you'll see.

There's milk...then there's Mayfield.

Courtesy of The Johnson Group.

Postdirectors are independent contractors in the production mix. They are in the business of cutting film and creatively supervising videotape transfers from film; supervising video edits and special effects; recording narration, sound, music, and sound effects; mixing these sounds together; relaying them onto the picture; and delivering a finished product to the agency.

COMPUTER POSTPRODUCTION TECHNOLOGY

Advances in hardware and software continue to change the creation and production of television commercials and videos. Names such as Silicon Graphics, Avid, Inferno,

Flame, and Quantel's Henry and Harry have been mainstays for a number of years. Terms such as *3-D animation*, *compositing*, *morphing*, *2-D animation*, *nonlinear editing*, *live-action compositing*, and *real time* are common among the professionals who generate visual images and special effects. The systems used for many special effects are still expensive. With any computer, many of the same video effects can be created at a lower cost but usually at a slower speed. Each computer hardware and software system has a plus and a minus.

It is safe to say that today's **computer-generated imagery (CGI)** offers creative minds great new opportunities in production and postproduction. This technology allows creative people to squash, squeeze, stretch, and morph objects in less time than ever before. Computers are turning live action into cartoon action. At production facilities, creative talents can use digital-graphics/animation-compositing systems to top four or five layers of live action with five or six layers of graphics, all simultaneously, allowing the finished visual composite to be seen as it develops.

CGI WIZARDRY Remember the Budweiser Clydesdale who held the pigskin for the point-after attempt in the *Super Bowl*? Or the Aflac duck? These are largely computer-generated (CG) or a mix of special techniques. Animators and software engineers have the ability to make photorealistic animals or monsters, for example. They look real only now they can do things no animal (or monster, for that matter) could be trained to do.

The combination of elements from two or more photographic sources often produces a striking effect. With the advent of computers, the process of combining different layers became much easier, but at the same time it is more complex because the variety of combinations is now seemingly limitless. You may have heard of some of the following electronic production tools and techniques:

- *Compositing.* In the digital realm, *compositing* is the umbrella term for many processes required to technically accomplish image combination in the computer.

- *Matte.* Essentially a silhouette in black and white, matte is the necessary signal for the computer to cut out the part of the image intended to be visible. It can also exist in many other physical forms, such as a painting on glass or a masked-off camera composition.

- *Keying.* Keying is electronically composing one picture over another. The two types of keying are luminance and chroma-keying. This term came from the word *keyhole* and is interpreted by the computer as a signal enabling a hole to be cut in a clip layer.

- *Chroma-keying.* This is another matte derivation method in which the computer sources a specific color (usually green, blue, or red) to create a key signal. This is a way of performing automatic matte extraction, using the colored background. In a weather program that has a map and the weatherperson in front of the map, the map is an electronic image chroma-keyed off of a green screen. The weatherperson can't actually see the map without looking at a monitor. All that is actually behind them is a color screen. The computer interprets it as a hole and replaces the hole with the layer behind it, in this case a map.

- *Keyer.* A keyer is simply an electronic composer.

- *Morphing.* **Morphing** is an industry term for metamorphosing, which means transforming from one object to another. For example, in a Schick shaving spot, a man's head turns into a three-dimensional cube, and for Exxon, a car turns into a tiger. This CG technique allows its operator to move between the real world and the CG by electronically layering visual transitions between live actions.

- *Harry.* The Quantel Henry/Harry online system is an editing device with an optical device tied to it. It allows computer composites to mix with live video. Ninety percent of Harry work can now be created on a Mac.

computer-generated imagery (CGI)
Technology allowing computer operators to create multitudes of electronic effects for TV—to squash, stretch, or squeeze objects—much more quickly than earlier tools could. It can add layers of visuals simultaneously.

morphing
An electronic technique that allows you to transform one object into another object.

■   *Flame.* Flame is an optical device with an editing device tied to it. It functions as a high-capacity, random-access, multilayer compositing system, with video editing, effects, and digital-audio capacity. So you can see that you have to have the right technology for the right job. And, yes, it can be confusing to the nonproduction person in the advertising industry. A Visa "superheroes" spot featured a damsel-in-distress scenario. Thor wields his lightning-charged hammer through the sky. The Flame artist had to create the sky and Thor so it looked like it was going to rain, not storm.

Controlling the Cost of Commercial Production

The cost of producing a TV commercial is of deep concern to both the agency and the advertiser. The chief reason that money is wasted in commercial production is inadequate preplanning. In production, the two major cost items are labor and equipment. Labor—the production crew, director, and performers—is hired by the day, and equipment is rented by the day. If a particular demonstration was improperly rehearsed, if a particular prop was not delivered, or if the location site was not scouted ahead of time, the shooting planned for one day may be forced into expensive overtime or into a second day. These costly mistakes can be avoided by careful planning.

SMALL-BUDGET SPOTS

Bart Cleveland, a well-respected creative director and partner of McKee Wallwork Cleveland in Albuquerque, talks about creating quality commercials on a shoestring budget. Many clients' budgets don't live up to the size of national players. Here are a few of his thoughts.

> Great ideas don't have to cost a lot if you know what ideas cost to produce. Teach your creative people what production costs. If they understand the basic costs of production, they know their scope of possibilities within a budget. They won't waste time on ideas with large casts or incredible special effects. I've learned the hard way that an idea beyond its budget is a bad idea. It's just a brilliant thought lost to bad production quality. Few clients know how good quality happens but they can recognize the difference between good and bad. They will think their agency doesn't know what it's doing when they get bad quality and they will be right."[13]

COST RELATIONSHIP

Several areas that can have a dramatic impact on television production costs are the following:

■   *Location or studio.* Is the commercial planned for studio or location? Location shoots, outside geographic zones, mean travel time and overnight accommodations for the crew, adding a minimum average cost of $7,500 per away day.

■   *Talent.* The number of principals on the storyboard is important and can be expensive. The more people on camera in your commercials, the higher the talent residual bill. The rates for talent are based on the Screen Actors Guild (SAG) union contract. For national commercials, you can roughly estimate your talent cost per on-camera principal as .0015 percent of your media budget for the spot, that is, $15,000 per person per $10 million in exposure. If 20 on-camera people are involved in your spot, expect a $300,000 bill. That chunk of your budget may exceed the entire net cost of production. So it is important to discuss how many on-camera principals are planned for the spot and how many are absolutely necessary.

■   *Residuals.* Another major expense is the residual, or reuse fee, paid to performers—announcers, narrators, actors, and singers—in addition to their initial session fees.

Under union rules, performers are paid every time the commercial is aired on the networks, the amount of the fee depending on their scale and the number of cities involved. If a commercial is aired with great frequency, residuals may actually be more than the production of the commercial itself. This problem is less severe for the local advertiser because local rates are cheaper than national rates. The moral is this: Cast only the number of performers necessary to the commercial and not one performer more.

- *Special effects.* If the board indicated the use of special effects or animation ask how the special effect will be achieved. It is not unusual for complicated CG effects to cost $6,000 to $12,000 per second and more! To prevent surprises, ask questions. What may appear to be a simple execution on the surface may contain extremely expensive elements. Neither the agency nor the client should be satisfied until everyone understands the project. Anything short of this can result in surprise creative expenditures.

- *Estimate costs.* Given the potential complexity of shooting commercials because of a wide range of factors (location, special rigs, special effects, talent, set construction), it is not uncommon to believe a relatively "simple" looking spot presented in storyboard form will be "relatively" inexpensive. This is simply not the case. It is not uncommon for clients to spend 10 percent of their planned media budget in production. As this percentage escalates, the production decision becomes more difficult, particularly in today's economic climate.

- *Editorial fee cost.* There is a creative labor fee for the editor's service. This charge is for the editor's and assistant editor's time. Depending on the editor and the difficulty of the edit, a creative fee can range from $400 to $500 (to supervise sound only, for example, on a single-scene commercial) to more than $10,000 to cut a multi-image, complex spot with special effects manipulations and music.

- *Special effects and titling.* The cost of special effects and titling can range from $100 to make a title art card and include it in the edit session to $10,000 to $30,000 for heavy design, frame-by-frame, picture manipulations.

- *Recording and mixing.* The cost of recording and mixing a voiceover, music, and sound effects together can range from $450 to $4,000 or more.

If you total all these possibilities, from the combined lowest to the combined highest, the cost can be $2,136 to $67,100 to edit a 30-second commercial!

UNIONS AND COST

In March 2009, the SAG and the American Federation of Television and Radio Artists (AFTRA) agreed on 3-year deals that cover performers working in commercials made for and reused on television, radio, the Internet, and new media. Also included in the new deals is an approved pilot study to test the GRP model of restructuring compensation to actors—in effect, paying actors based on how their commercials perform, which is similar to TV marketers' deals with TV networks under its commercial rating, C3 metric. The deal with the ANA and the AAAA went into effect retroactively to April 1, 2009, and will remain in force until March 31, 2012.[14]

We mention this because the agreement affects production, residual payments, and total costs. It is also very complex and complicated. For example, the main session rate for on-camera principals is $592.20, the rate for on-camera groups of three to five is $433.55, and the rate for off-camera groups is $251.15. Here is a snapshot of some of the areas covered, with rates and specifics:[15]

Program Class A Second Use for on-camera principals is $135.80, on-camera groups (three to five) is $125.85. The Third Use for on-camera principals is $107.75.

Program Class B/with New York market is $3,417.10 for on-camera principal, $1,039.30 for the three to five on-camera groups. However, without New York, on-camera

SHOPPING :30 SPOT

ORLANDO

ORLANDO
MAKES ME SMILE

Stay for free.
Play for free.
Eat for free.

Restrictions apply. See Web site for details.

Bundles of Free Smiles at
VisitOrlando.com

Restrictions apply. See Web site for details.

Courtesy of Orlando/Orange Visitors and Convention Bureau and PUSH.

EXHIBIT 19.13

This ad is selling Orlando shopping as part of the city's charm. The title slides also are important.

principals are paid $2,948.30. If it is a Spanish-language program, the on-camera principal rate is $2,138.60. The contract covers Stunt Adjustments, Ad LIB, and Hazard payments. It also states rates for casting and auditions, principals, general extras, hand models, body makeup/oil, costume fitting, interviews, location meal allowances, mileage allowances, meal period violations, and travel time to and from the location. There are also mileage fees based on the vehicle: auto, trailer, motorcycle. It also includes skates, skateboard, bicycle, or moped. It specifies wet, snow, smoke, or dust work as extra compensation. And the advertiser also has to pay additional money toward health and retirement contributions.

As you can see, the union negotiated just about everything. Exhibit 19.13 shows a mother and daughter shopping. So it is easy to calculate using the preceding figures how much this ad will cost for talent. Is it a location shoot? More money. Because almost all the professional talent in this country are members of one of the appropriate unions, an advertiser or agency must abide by these contracts or be blacklisted from all the available talent.

AFTRA represents actors, other professional performers, and broadcasters in television, radio, sound recordings, nonbroadcast/industrial programming, and new technologies, such as interactive programming and CD-ROMs.

A few other union advertisers are involved in one fashion or the other in the United States and Canada:

ACTRA—Alliance of Canadian Television and Radio Artists. ACTRA is a national organization of Canadian performers working in film, television, video, and all other recorded media.

AFM—American Federation of Musicians. AFM is the largest union in the world representing the professional interests of musicians.

ADVANTAGE POINT 19.2

HOW TO KILL YOUR BRAND

INTRO

Put Me Out of My Misery!

Creating, building, extending and managing brands—these are miserable and expensive undertakings. Can one kill a brand and be done with all this? We were surprised to find that there was no useful compilation of murderous branding activities that can be implemented with confidence and ease. So we set upon creating our own handy guide. We believe that brands—unlike Jason of movie fame—can be put to rest once and for all, never to return again.

How, you ask? Turns out that it's quite simple. You can effectively kill your brand by doing any one of the following:

- Not remembering what you said.
- Doing nothing.
- Being just like everyone else.
- And more.

It's true. And anyone can do this. Read on.

— Guy Gabriele, Chief Creative Officer, Idea Engineering

TECHNIQUE #1

Break Your Promise

Remember the trust covenant you established when you launched the brand? The promise of reliability, superior service, corporate responsibility or whatever it was that created the initial bond—well, just forget about all that. Assume that the pesky promise you made way back when has been forgotten. A couple doses of this and you'll be finished.

TECHNIQUE #2

Put On Blinders

Ignore globalization, all new media initiatives, competitors' innovations, and tsunami-like trends. The time and effort it would take to stay on top of these is daunting. Being in denial is a very effective strategy for life in general, so why not use it in business? By doing nothing you gain plausible deniability in that "the competition did me in." Nice!

TECHNIQUE #3

Outsource Everything

If you can get it done cheaper, then why the hell not? How hard is it to answer a few stupid questions, make a billing adjustment or handle a warranty claim? Abdicating responsibility for the brand experience to someone else, when done properly, should lead to a quick and relatively painless demise.

TECHNIQUE #4

Lie!

"If you tell a lie big enough and keep repeating it, people will eventually come to believe it." We couldn't have said it any better. Over-promising is a creative variant on this technique. You might fool them once, try it twice and it's sure to be fatal.

TECHNIQUE #5

Be a Copycat

Your competition has already spent a fortune on R&D, innovation and market research. Why reinvent the wheel? Take their lead and replicate. As the saying goes—"The mediocre are always at their best." The sound of customer indifference will be thunderous, but you won't have to endure it for long.

TECHNIQUE #6

Be Myopic

Manage your company and your brand for the short term only. Keep your eye on that next quarterly report. If the brand comes down with a serious illness in the process, well, at least your job is secure for now. Granted, death will come more slowly with this technique. But take comfort in the knowledge that the end will indeed come.

TECHNIQUE #7

Cheat On Your Spouse

A bit more complex, but if you can find ways to betray your distribution channel, employees, manufacturing or sales partners, you can incite them to attack your brand with deadly force. This takes it out of your hands, and is a bit Kevorkian-esque, but, hey, sometimes you need a little help from your friends.

TECHNIQUE #8

Keep Rebranding

Because variety is the spice of life. Change packaging, graphics, logos, product claims—almost everything—fool the customer. Lead them to believe there's something new here for them. *Caution*: Don't actually make relevant product improvements concurrently, as this may result in a revitalized brand with a longer life.

TECHNIQUE #9

Make Sure That Your Customer Feels Stupid

Shouldn't be hard, right? Actually, this takes some effort. Turns out they aren't all that dumb after all. But, you can do it! Make the packaging very unfriendly and cumbersome. Keep your assembly instructions obtuse. Use billing methods that defy logic. And, this is important, be condescending at all times. They'll leave you for dead. Mission accomplished.

TECHNIQUE #10

Death by MBA

Legend has it that these executives can be the stealthiest, and deadliest brand assassins.

DGA—Director's Guild of America.   DGA represents members in theatrical, industrial, educational, and documentary films, as well as live television, filmed and taped radio, videos, and commercials.

There is a host of other nonunion organizations that may be involved in creating and producing commercials.

ASCAP—American Society of Composers, Authors and Publishers.   ASCAP allows creators and publishers to receive payment for the use of their musical property and provides users of that music with easy and inexpensive legal access to the world's largest and most varied catalog of copyrighted music.

BMI.   BMI is the source for the song titles, writers, and publishers of the world's most popular music—the BMI repertoire—in a searchable database of millions of items, updated weekly, together with the web's most complete fund of information for and about songwriting and music licensing.

TELEVISION PRODUCTION COST AVERAGES

According to the annual 4As Television Production Cost Survey, the average per spot cost of the 1,266 databases of commercials was $318,000. Half of the shoots or more have additional footage shot for web versions, viral spots, or other forms of content. In general, overall costs are pretty much holding steady.

In 2007, advertisers urged everyone from agencies and production companies to find ways of cutting production cost. Commercial production total shooting days in Los Angeles generally range from about 5,650 to a little more than 6,500 per year. The Entertainment Industry Development Corporation (EIDC) tracks this shooting day information. The average cost to edit and finish an original is about $40,000.

SUMMARY

Today, web publishers have different sizes, specs, and formats for video, requiring advertisers to create specific ad units for each publisher (in other words, an advertiser may need to reshoot or edit an ad or video many times at great production costs to use a single idea on multiple web networks or platforms).

Television/video remains the most powerful advertising medium because of its ability to blend sight, sound, and motion to create emotional reactions. In TV, time to communicate is very short—usually 15 seconds to 30 seconds—and creates a challenge for communicating the product story or position. Online video techniques like "Webisodes" have no limitations in terms of time. Digital videos are not standardized and offer the advertiser longer stories and creative opportunities.

There are numerous creative techniques available to the creative team: testimonials, serials, demonstrations, slice-of-life, interviews, humor, animation, infomercials, and so forth. Research can aid the creative decision process in terms of which technique is appropriate for the strategy.

Storyboards are usually created to help communicate the idea to the advertiser and the production company. It is important that everyone clearly visualizes the same commercial before time and money are invested in the idea.

Developing commercials requires some understanding of production terminology such as wipes, dissolves, and close-ups that help communicate the nature of a particular visual or transition from one scene to the next. Writing and visualizing the commercial in simple and easy-to-understand terms are essential to success—it is, after all, a visual medium. Because bad production can destroy a good idea, producing the finished commercial is just as important as conceiving the big idea.

Producing the commercial involves three distinct stages: preproduction, shooting, and postproduction. CGI allows creative people to do almost anything they can imagine—but the cost may be high.

REVIEW

1. What is an in-page video ad?
2. Discuss preroll.
3. What does a "preditor" do?
4. What is the purpose of a storyboard?
5. Who attends the preproduction meeting?

CHAPTER 20

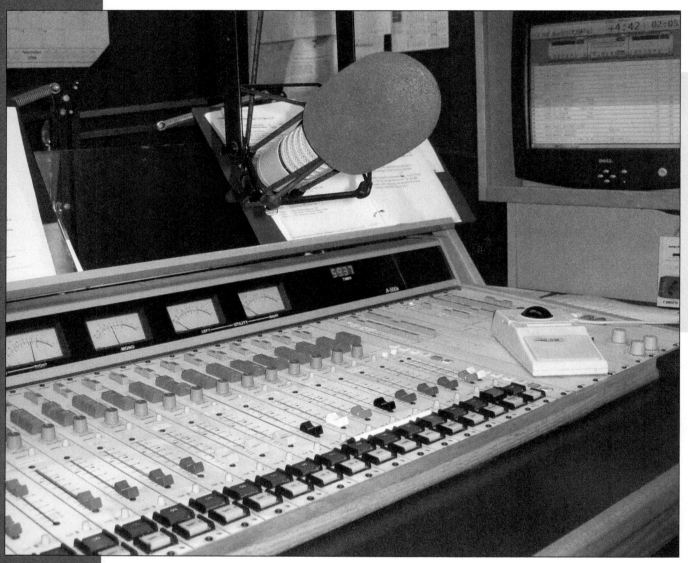

Courtesy of Steven H. Lang.

The Radio Commercial

RADIO HAS BEEN impacted by all the new media changes including the likes of online radio and Sirius. In print and television, visuals are an integral part of communication. Radio is a different medium, one for the ears alone. ▶

CHAPTER LEARNING OBJECTIVES

1. Discuss the nature of the medium.
2. Explain how to create from a strategy.
3. Discuss structuring the commercial.
4. Discuss writing the commercial.
5. Discuss musical commercials.
6. Explain the process of producing radio commercials.
7. Explain unions and talent.

"Radio needs to get better before radio ads can get better," said Bill Wright, creative director at Crispin Porter+Bogusky. "When I read a magazine, all the ads don't annoy me. When I watch TV, all the ads don't annoy me. Even when you do a good radio spot, it's still the best-looking house in a bad neighborhood." This speaks generally to agency attitude toward radio by big agencies. The thought is agency creative people would rather work on interactive or television ads than on radio ads. Despite this attitude, the number of radio listeners is increasing. Streaming radio online and satellite availability are increasing the audience. So radio is changing.

Logic tells you radio advertising should be easy to create. All you have to do is talk to someone about the product. Right? Well, maybe. Great radio advertising is actually very difficult. You need to awaken images in the listener's mind using sound, music, and voices. Some do this simply by talking to the listener.

The Nature of the Medium

Despite being lost in the shuffle of new media, radio still has the power to achieve sales results and market impressions at significant cost savings. Radio gives you the time to tell a story. In print and television advertising, visual images can be powerful in attracting attention and they can be full of emotion. Radio is different. There is no visual image or color to attract people to the message. Yet, sound messages can be powerful. Some would argue that radio is the most visual medium, if you do your job right.

"In radio there's no place to hide anything. No place for mistakes, poor judgment, or weakness. Everything is right there in front of you for 30 or 60 seconds. Everything must be good for the spot to be good. The concept, copy, casting, acting, production—everything. One of them goes wrong, sorry, but it's tune-out time,"[1] says copywriter Tom Monahan. Let us take a closer look at the nature of the medium.

1. Discuss the nature of the medium.

theater of the mind
In radio, a writer paints pictures in the mind of the listener through the use of sound.

Longtime radio advertising expert, Phil Cuttino, often refers to "watching radio—the most misunderstood medium." Before the beginning of widespread viewing of television in the mid-1950s, families used to "watch" the radio. We have all heard excerpts from radio's **theater of the mind**—*Superman, The Lone Ranger, Bulldog Drummon, Inner Sanctum*, and Orson Welles's fabulous spoof, *War of the Worlds*. People watched the radio because the mental imagery that came with every episode was breathtaking or scary or beautiful or just plain funny. However, television's combination of audio and visuals was very compelling and certainly effective as a storyteller and a theater. Television also was, and is, a dynamic advertising medium. Unfortunately, radio was subordinated to the position of music, talk, and other audio-oriented programming. Will its nature change?

Picture a few lines of the commercial below:

MAN: I get up. I take a bath. I get dressed. I eat breakfast.

(Pause)

MAN: I get up. I take a bath. I get dressed,

(Pause)

MAN: I get up.

WOMAN: I give him breakfast.

MAN: I get up.

WOMAN: I get him up. I give him a bath. I get him dressed. I give him breakfast.

ANNCR: Your life changes quickly. Muscular Dystrophy Association.

LOWER PRIORITY AMONG CREATIVES

Despite being attacked as dead, the 30-second television spot remains key in developing impact in many ad campaigns. The short video on the web may be gaining favor, but the fastest way for a creative team to get noticed is probably to create a highly noticed television spot. In major publications, there are commentaries on television commercials, as well as objective and subjective ratings. Television is the closest way that ad people come to "show biz." Another contributing factor to radio's lowly position in the creative pecking order is the fact that most creative teams consist of art directors, designers, and copywriters. Because radio has no material visuals, the visual arts people are out of business when it comes to radio. This tends to lead the creative team to print, television, or interactive media.

Over time, a new type of radio commercial has emerged, which Cuttino calls "print radio." When radio is needed, some copywriters, who are experienced in print advertising but know little about radio, tend to fall back on a familiar copy format. As a result, we hear "print radio." There is a headline, a subhead, body copy, a logo, and a slogan—an audio newspaper ad.

To understand the importance of radio, you need to understand the cynical nature of the American consumer.

No one believes anyone anymore. American consumers are searching for an excuse to disbelieve what you are saying. All they need is a cue that you are trying to sell them something and they will blank you out mentally. They may not change the dial, but this is a case of "the lights are on, but nobody's home." Before you can tell consumers your story, you must disarm them, entertain them, amuse them, and get them on your side.

Radio, like magazines, is a very personal medium. Almost everyone has a favorite radio station. Many consumers listen to Net radio online where some stations use broadband and streaming video content. Consumers get to know the radio personalities; they attend events sponsored by their radio station. It is this kind of listener allegiance, this nonhostile environment, that makes it easy for marketers to approach the listenership. Remember, consumers are not waiting to hear your commercial. They are listening to the radio for entertainment, so entertain them and then sell them. Entertainment is your admission ticket to their consciousness.

The future is uncertain for traditional radio. The Internet has challenged traditional radio in the home and office, but radio has maintained its dominance in the car. Digital satellite radio brings more challenges to local radio and advertisers.[2] Radio is predicted to make a giant leap forward through integration and packaging with digital outdoor, POP, and phone Apps. Here's how it works—you get in the car and hear an ad for a retailer (just like today) but the close says, "go to your live special deal phone App for a special good for the next two hours."

The AP literally drives you to the participating retailer with directions. Digital outdoor does the same thing. When you get in the store the digital POP is there to greet you. Your coupon is scanned off your phone. Radio becomes a backbone for all digital out of home sales. And yes, the measurement to direct sales will greatly improve.

A Google news release on its blog said in 2009 it exited selling radio and was getting out of the radio business. It also said it would explore online streaming audio. This is another example of changes in the media and advertising business and its impact on radio.[3]

Flexibility, Marketability, and Promotionability

Radio offers more than other advertising media. It has the flexibility, the marketability, the promotionability, and the price to fit advertisers' needs to reach their targets—if they choose the right stations and use the right message.

- You have 60 seconds all to yourself. Print ads have to fight for attention with other ads on the page. Television has to contend with channel surfers because viewers have favorite television programs, whereas radio listeners have favorite radio stations. In the time span of a 60-second radio commercial, no other advertising can interfere with your message. The main equalizer in radio is the ability of a locally produced radio spot to be on a level playing field with any national spot. The power of a radio commercial is the idea, the imagery. Unlike television, national-quality production can be easily created for a reasonable cost. Your advertiser can be as big as any other marketer for 60 seconds.

- Radio has the most captive audience of any media. The advent of mass transit has not changed the fact that, in most cities, to get from point A to point B, you still have to get in your car and drive. The heaviest radio listenership occurs during the morning and afternoon drive times. During those times, listeners cannot go to the kitchen for a beer, answer the door, or pick up a magazine. They are trapped in their cars, listening to the traffic report, the news, and your radio commercial.

- Listeners and advertisers have many programming formats to choose from: country, adult contemporary, news/talk/sports/business, oldies, top 40, religion, classic rock, urban rhythm and blues, easy listening, alternative rock, variety, ethnic, classical, gospel, jazz, new age, and preteen. This makes radio a highly selective medium for the advertiser. Reflecting the ethnic multinational nature of our society, there also are foreign-language stations in many markets available to advertisers.

KLEPPNER VIEWPOINT 20.1

Steven H. Lang   Creative Director, Cox Radio/Athens

STAND OUT FROM THE CLUTTER

Steven H. Lang

What makes a good radio commercial? It produces the desired results for the client. That is the only true measure of success. Not awards or compliments. Just results. Anything else is a failure. So how do you create a successful radio commercial? You observe the following methods as a template and build the rest of the ad around them.

Listening to people talk only about themselves can be extremely tedious. You try to get away as quickly as possible, don't you? So why do most radio commercials center on the client rather than on the listener? Radio can be such an engaging medium, yet most clients want to turn it into a brag fest. "We have the biggest this!!! We have the most that!!! We're number one in blah blah!!!" Yawn. Click. So what should you do? Change your focus.

Instead of making the client the subject of the ad, make the listener, or how the listener can benefit, the subject of the commercial. People, by nature, are self-interested. So by speaking about subjects of interest and importance to them, they'll naturally pay more attention. Talking to someone is always better than trying to talk at everyone. This doesn't mean simply using the word *you* all the

time but also fashioning a commercial the listener can identify with by showing both a problem and a solution. However, in our overcommunicated world, simply getting the listener's attention and holding it can be an arduous task. So take them to the theater.

A runaway asteroid in deep space. High noon on the streets of the Old West. A street corner during rush hour. With a few sound effects and a couple minutes in a studio, you can create any environment of sounds from the past, present, or future. Then you sit back and wait for your listeners' imagination to fill in the pictures. By using theater of the mind to involve the listeners in your commercial, they are more apt to follow your message and relate to your product or offer. Video and computer animation can also create these types of environments, but you lose the process of engaging the imagination, and it is much more expensive and time consuming. However, it takes more than only theater of the mind to get your message across. You must also be sure that they'll hear it again and again and again.

Repetition plays a huge part in the success of a radio commercial. Even a poorly written ad can increase effectiveness to some degree by increasing

repetition. Why? "Because sound is intrusive," says Roy H. Williams, a sales and marketing consultant. He notes, "While driving, how many times have you turned down the radio while trying to find a street or turn? How many songs do you know by heart, though you've never set out to learn them?" The intrusive nature of radio, combined with repetition, makes an extremely effective method of getting your message across.

With proper subject focus, theater of the mind, and sufficient repetition, you can stand out from the clutter with radio commercials that get results. As radio programming and sales legend Dan O'Day noted, radio is mass salesmanship.

Courtesy of Steven H. Lang, Creative Director, Cox Radio/Athens.

Creating the Commercial

2 **Explain how to create from a strategy.**

Despite requiring a style, radio commercials are developed through a thought process similar to that used in other media. As with any advertising, you have to understand your target. As Tom Little, award-winning creative director, once said, "People don't buy products. They buy solutions to problems." Last year people bought about 350,000 quarter-inch drill bits in the United States. People didn't want quarter-inch drill bits. They wanted quarter-inch holes.

The radio creative writer has to refer back to the brief for objectives and strategy and to describe the target in both demographic and psychographic terms before beginning the creative process. The writer needs to be sure the message will be believed—that it says the right things to the right people—and needs to ask if the copy strengthens the brand position, the place the advertiser wants to occupy in the consumer's mind. Is it credible? Does the writer have all the copy points that research indicates is needed? Is it human? Is it believable communication? Do people really talk like that? Or is it simply copy lingo? These are some of the things the radio copywriter must think about when sitting down to the blank page or computer screen.

The writer for radio has the opportunity to develop an entire commercial alone (although in some agencies a creative team may work on a project). That means writing the script, picking the talent, and producing the commercial. In radio, the copywriter enjoys the freedom to create scenes in the theater of the listener's imagination by painting pictures in sound—a car starting or stopping, a phone ringing, water running, ice cubes falling into a glass, crowds roaring, a camera clicking. Remember, sound alone has an extraordinary ability to enter people's minds.

Amy Lokken, copywriter for McRae advertising agency, has only 15 seconds to make a point for the Georgia Department of Transportation's 511 program:

15 Radio, Georgia 511, "Thanksgiving"
MUSIC: 1950s instructional movie music underneath
DRAMATIC ANNCR: An important Thanksgiving safety tip. Do *not* drive while in a turkey-induced coma. *Do* drive after alertly calling Georgia 511. 511 is fast, free, real-time traffic information. 511—We'll get you there.

THREE ELEMENTS OF CREATIVE

Let us look at the three elements the copywriter uses to create mental pictures, memorability, and emotion: words, sound, and music and jingles.

WORDS Words are the basic building blocks of effective radio commercials. They are used to describe the product, grab attention, create interest, build desire, and evoke a response from the listener.

Sometimes both the words and the voice are equally important. David Fowler, a creative director from the Richards Group Advertising agency, was driving in Dallas listening to the public radio station when he heard a homey voiced monologue emerge from his radio. It was Tom Bodett. The Richards Group asked him if he'd be willing to use his voice talents as a deadpan radio bullfrog to market a national chain of economy motels. He agreed. Nobody talks one-to-one better than Tom Bodett in commercial after commercial. Bodett's voice has been the voice of Motel 6 for years and years. Ad-libbing the tag line, "We'll Leave the Light on for You," in the very first commercial session gained success for the chain and for Bodett. And the tag has remained the same. He was a regular commentator on National Public Radio's popular news program in the 1980s, *All Things Considered*.[4] You can still find him on the Motel 6 web site and all of his work appears on Bodett's own personal site as well. And the tag remains the same. The campaign is one of the longest-running advertising campaigns, and it continues to win awards for its creativity and effectiveness in the lodging industry. One of his commercials, "Business Talk," makes fun of today's business language and speaks to the business traveler:

> Hi. I'm Tom Bodett for Motel 6, with a word for business travelers. Seems business has its own language these days. Full of buzzwords, like buzzwords. Or Net Net.

The commercial goes on to name a multitude of business speak sayings: *outsource your accommodation needs, deliverables, matrix* of *actionable* items, *cost-effective*, and so on.

> You'll get clean, comfortable rooms at the lowest price, Net Net, of any national chain. . . .

Then he puts an unusual twist on the traditional Motel 6 ending, "*We'll leave the light on for you*": "I'm Tom Bodett for Motel 6. We'll maintain the lighting device in its current state of illumination."

As with the success of Motel 6, the warmth of the human voice may be all that is needed to communicate your message.

Then there was another classic master of words. Stan Freberg—comic, adman, great radio creator—was one of the pioneers of creative radio who created spots for the Radio Advertising Bureau: ". . . okay people, now when I give you the cue, I want the 700-foot mountain of whipped cream to roll into Lake Michigan, which has been drained and filled with hot chocolate. Then the Royal Canadian Air Force will fly overhead towing a 10-ton maraschino cherry." We'll leave the rest to your imagination, or you can hear the rest at http://radiohof.org/comedy/stanfreberg.html.

SOUND   Used properly, sound can unlock the listener's imagination and create feelings. Any sound effect used should be necessary and recognizable; you should never have to explain it for the audience.

The sound has to convey a special message or purpose; it has to attract attention and complement the words. Sound can underscore a point; create feelings of suspense, excitement, or anger; and invoke almost any mood you desire.

There are three basic sources of sound effects: manual, recorded, and electronic. Manual effects are those that are produced live, either with live subjects or with studio props; opening doors, footsteps, and blowing horns are examples. Recorded effects are available from records, tapes, or professional sound libraries. They offer the copywriter almost every conceivable sound—dogs barking, cats meowing, leaves blowing, thunder crashing, cars racing. Electronic effects are sounds that are produced electronically on special studio equipment. Any sound created by using a device that generates an electrical impulse or other electronic sound is an electronic effect.

MUSIC AND JINGLES   It is thought that General Mills used the first jingle in 1926, for the failing Wheaties brand.

> Have you tried Wheaties?
> They're whole wheat with all of the bran.
> Won't you try Wheaties?/For wheat is the best food of man.
> They're crispy and crunchy
> The whole year through
> The kiddies never tire of them
> And neither will you.
> So just try Wheaties,
> The best breakfast food in the land.

Music has proven very powerful in catching the listener's attention and evoking feelings. Thus, music has been called the "universal language." Different kinds of music appeal to different emotions: A minor key is sadder than a major key; an increased tempo creates a sense of anticipation. We'll talk more about music a little later.

Commercials are often set to music especially composed for them or adapted from a familiar song. A few bars of distinctive music played often enough may serve to identify the product instantly. Such a musical logotype usually lasts from 4 to 10 seconds. **Jingles** have been a popular means of making a slogan memorable—think of the music for Coca-Cola, Pepsi, Chevrolet, and McDonald's over the years—but are not as popular at this moment.

Can you sing the Oscar Myer lyrics? "Oh, I wish I had. . . ." You're not alone. When Bob Garfield, the editor-at-large for *Advertising Age*, talks about old advertising jingles, it's not long before he breaks into song. "Oh, I wish I were an Oscar Mayer wiener." "I remember that stupid jingle," he says. "But I don't remember what I had for breakfast, where my car keys are and what my kids' names are." That's the power of the jingle.

jingle
A commercial or part of a commercial set to music, usually carrying the slogan or theme line of a campaign. May make a brand name and slogan more easily remembered.

The popular rock tunes in commercials are making superstar bands richer and creating fame for unknowns. Advertisers have been chasing edgier music to attract the young. As a result jingles are on the wane. Licensing of music rights is now the name of the game. As with most pop culture items, some believe that jingles could return to popularity. Why? Well, for one thing, no one can deny their power.[5]

Plop plop, fizz fizz—oh, what a relief it is!

Folks's Southern Cooking Cous Cous jingle version says:

> Now hold the capers and the sun dried tomatoes
> Hold the Cous Cous and those tarragon potatoes
> When I'm in the mood for some comfort food
> Nobody knows me like my Folks.

Madison Avenue is turning to music stars to pen original ditties for commercials. When Ford executives looked to launch its "Bold Moves," including licensing an old hit for a recent campaign, they explored many musical options, listening to demo tapes of unreleased songs. Ford selected an unreleased song, "Go," co-written by the first *American Idol* winner, Kelly Clarkson, because it fit the mood and tempo the automaker wanted. To date, Clarkson's fans could only download it legally from a Ford-sponsored web site, addictedtokelly.com.

COLLABORATIVE MUSIC ALLIANCES

Advertisers are using current music of all types to try to reach the 18-to-25 market because people this age make brand choices that can influence their buying decisions for life. This group doesn't want in-your-face sales pitches, industry observers said; it wants fresh music.

Ad agency Leo Burnett invited country music star Jo Dee Messina to its offices as part of its "Artist in Residence" program, in the hopes of using her songs in ads. The program was started recently, and it welcomed artists from the entire music spectrum. Gone are the days when signing over song rights to marketers was looked down on by artists and fans alike. "Advertising is the new radio," says Rob Swartyz, executive creative director at TBWA\ Chiat\ Day, in a sentiment echoed around the ad music industry. This new collaborative environment means that the music industry may no longer charge astronomical fees (which ranged from $10,000 into the millions for a popular song), especially if the marketer is willing to work with the artist in many venues, including concert promotion.[6] Simply licensing a top hit probably starts at about $250,000 and can reach into the millions.

CREATE FROM STRATEGY

The Charleston Metro Chamber of Commerce used a strategic creative idea in print, television, and radio. It was the meeting "name tag." The message (reasons to join) was written on the tag along with the name. But the radio copy included the same message.

> Judith. I joined the chamber for lots of reasons. But the one that really attracted me was their Center for Business Research. It provides me with info that I could never afford to track down on my own. Like current economic trends. Economic forecasts. It let me know what's happening and what's about to happen. That helps me make good decisions. Like a magic eight ball that really works.
> Charleston Metro Chamber of Commerce.

It is a simple integrated idea with big results.

Recently, the Slinky coil toy brought the Slinky jingle heard on television since 1963 to radio. The new campaign introduced a different version of the jingle. It begins in the traditional, singsong manner, but then it shifts into a faster rocklike rendition. The lyrics remain basically the same, only shifted around a bit. In an attempt to integrate the brand, the Slinky web site (poof-slinky.com) had downloadable wallpapers and information on the jingle, as well as its advertising and history. Despite limited media exposure, there was an attempt to integrate the brand. The newer version of the Slinky jingle maintains the core feeling of the original. Mom will recognize it from the past, but it is a little more modern so today's kids can better relate to the radio commercial.[7] Here is the new version of the 30-second radio lyrics:

> What walks downstairs
> Alone or in pairs
> And makes the happiest sound?
> Everyone knows it's Slinky
> It's Slinky, it's Slinky
> For fun, it's a wonderful toy
> It's Slinky, it's Slinky
> It's fun for a girl and a boy
> A spring, a spring, a marvelous thing
> It makes a "slinkity" sound
> Everyone knows it's Slinky

Developing the Radio Script

3 **Discuss structuring the commercial.**

You will find some differences in the formats used in the script examples in this chapter. This is because most agencies have their own format sheets for copywriters. Formats also vary according to how the script will be used: If you are going to be in the studio with the producers and talents, you can verbally explain how the script is to be read or answer any questions that come up. If, however, you are going to mail the script to DJs to be read live, you need to be certain that anyone reading it will understand exactly what you want. The guidelines shown in Exhibit 20.1 illustrate explicit script directions.

EXHIBIT 20.1

Example of Radio Form Directions

Length: 60	
Job No. 3364	
LEFT SECTION OF PAGE IS FOR INFORMATION RELATING TO VOICES, ANNOUNCER, MUSIC, SOUND, USUALLY IN CAPS.	The right section of the script consists of copy and directions. It should be typed double-spaced. Pause is indicated by dots (...) or double dash (— —). <u>Underline</u> or use CAPS for emphasis.
MUSIC:	Music is usually indicated by all caps. WILLIAM TELL OVERTURE ESTABLISH AND FADE UNDER. In some cases, music is underlined. Directions may be indicated by parentheses ( ).
VOICE #1:	(LAUGHING LOUDLY) Excuse me sir...
OLD MAN:	Yes... (RAISING VOICE) What do you want?
SFX:	SUPERMARKET NOISES, CRASHING NOISES AS SHOPPING CARTS CRASH. Sound effects indicated by SFX: (:08) BUZZER
SINGERS:	He's bright-eyed and bushy-tailed...
ANNCR:	This indicates announcer talking.
VO:	Voice Over

RADIO, THEATER OF THE MIND

One of the biggest mistakes you can make in creating radio is the failure to recognize the fact that everyone has mental images of sounds that they hear. When no material images exist, sound creates an image in the mind's eye. It is the duty of the radio writer/producer to take control of the listener's imagery and guide it to a positive reaction that seeds the memory with the targeted message and leads to the proper response. For instance, a writer creates a commercial featuring a car dealer who is screaming about a sale, assuming that the tactic will get the listener's attention and will eventually lead the consumer to the dealership because of the "incredible savings." Unfortunately, the mind's eye of the listener doesn't see a sleek new car or the money saved; the listener sees a middle-aged man in a garish plaid suit yelling. In communications, it is important to be concerned about how people feel about your advertisement.

The late creative director Tom Little used to brag about radio's ability to paint pictures in the mind, "I had to spend $40,000 to build an airline set for our television ads, but I could build that same set in the minds of radio listeners for almost nothing."

THE ELEMENTS OF A GOOD RADIO COMMERCIAL

- *Be single-minded, focused.* Don't ask the consumer to take in too much information at one time. Prioritize your copy points. Think of your commercial as a model of our solar system. The major copy point is the sun and all the other copy points are planets of varying degrees of importance, but they all revolve around and support the central idea (see Exhibit 20.2).

- *Research your product or service.* Many clients keep tabs on their competition, but they rarely relate their features and benefits to factual data. Meaningful statistics can give substantial support to your message.

- *Relate to the consumer.* When you tell consumers your story, always relate the brand to their wants and needs. Do not assume they will come to the right conclusion. Exhibit 20.3 attempts to give recyclers a sense that they are helping the environment.

- *Generate extension.* You can multiply the effect of your commercial many times over by achieving extension—consumers picking up phrases from the spot and using them. A clever phrase or execution can have consumers asking other people if they have heard the spot, people requesting the spot to be played on the radio, and even DJs mentioning the spot.

- *Produce an immediate physical, emotional, or mental response.* Laughter, a tug on the heartstrings, or mental exercises of a consumer during a radio spot help seed the memory and aid in message retention.

- *Use plain, conversational English.* Be a clear communicator. Don't force your characters to make unnatural statements. This is not the boardroom—no "execubabble," just clear, plain, simple English. The mild humor and normal dialog in this Ford dealer commercial make the speakers seem like ordinary guys (see Exhibit 20.4).

:15 Radio, Georgia 511, "Football" Amy Lokken	
MUSIC:	Inspirational game-day music underneath
DRAMATIC ANNCR:	Is your nickname "Super Fan"? Are you a tailgating legend? You need Georgia 511. Score fast, free, real-time traffic information on your phone. And get to every game on time. Call 511—We'll get you there.

EXHIBIT 20.2

Georgia 511

This commercial is simply focused on telling people what number to call for traffic information.

EXHIBIT 20.3

ACCR Recycling

This spot promotes a sense of satisfaction that you helped the environment.

Steve Lang

ACCR Recycling
Anncr OK: It's hot! It's intense! It's environmentally friendly! It's Recyclers Gone Wild!
1: Show us your cans!!!
(SFX: cans being poured out) (SFX: whistle)
2: And look at those jugs!
(SFX: plastic jug bouncing)
1: That's a lot of recycling there!
Anncr: Recyclers Gone Wild!
1: Now this one is stacked.
(SFX: dropping newspapers sound)
2: All those newspapers...impressive!
Anncr: Act now; you'll also receive a deep sense of satisfaction that you've helped the environment! Recyclers Gone Wild—so much fun you'll want to do it yourself!
Anncr 2: This message brought to you by the Athens Clark County Recycling Division—show us your cans!

Courtesy of Steven Lang of COX Radio/Athens.

Please review the above script with care and consideration. It is much easier to make changes and corrections before it is produced. Any changes after it has been produced may cause delays in the start of your commercial. Thank you.

EXHIBIT 20.4

Akins Ford Holiday Commercial

The dialog sounds human.

Akins Ford   Steven Lang

Brad: Imagine if Santa left you a shiny new truck this year; what a truly wonderful holiday it would be. Hi. This is Brad Akins.
Peyton: But how would Santa get it down the chimney?
Brad: Santa usually just leaves new trucks in the driveway.
Peyton: Do the elves wrap them?
Brad: Well Peyton, sometimes they put a bow on them, and right now Akins has just announced employee-pricing-plus rebates on the Motortrend truck of the year: the all new two thousand nine Ford F one-fifty.
Peyton: Why couldn't Santa just drive them instead? He could load the back up with the presents and the reindeer could ride upfront with him!
Brad: Umm our trucks are big but not big enough for eight reindeer. So if your wish list includes a new truck, come see us at Akins or visit us at Akins online dot-com.
Peyton: My wish list includes a new pony. Do you have ponies?
Brad: We have Mustangs.
Peyton: But no ponies? Then what do you have?
Brad: I have a very special wish that everyone will have a safe and blessed holidays and that all their wishes will come true; even if they don't wish for trucks.
Peyton: Or ponies?
Brad: Even if. So from all of us at Akins Ford in Winder and Athens. Merry Christmas!

Courtesy of Steven Lang of COX Radio/Athens.

Writing the Commercial

4 Discuss writing the commercial.

Some agencies have a special creative director in charge of radio advertising. For years, the feeling was that agencies assigned junior talent to write radio commercials. It is now hoped that having a specific person in charge of radio will generate enthusiasm for doing great radio. Some agencies have special units that focus only on radio, for example, Hill Holiday Radio, which is a division of Hill Holiday Advertising.

There are radio boutiques that have been used for many years by clients and agencies to help create and produce radio commercials. Some of the most popular boutiques include World Wide Wadio, Radioland, Right Brain Visions, and Funny Farm Radio Hollywood. Funny Farm Radio says, "We encode your existing audio/video, or create and produce with you, create a custom branded MiniRemote to your specs, and stream it on your website or send it to your (clients') customers in emails. And make you look good to gadzillions."

The radio commercial, like the TV commercial, has as its basic ingredient the promise of a significant and distinctive benefit or position. Once the promise has been determined, you are ready to use the arsenal of words and sounds to communicate your product. Ways to vitalize the copy include the following:

- *Simplicity.* The key to producing a good radio commercial is to build around one central idea. Avoid confusing the listener with too many copy points. Use known words, short phrases, and simple sentence structure. Keep in mind that the copy needs to be conversational. Write for the ear, not the eye. Get in the habit of reading your copy out loud.

- *Clarity.* Keep the train of thought on one straight track. Avoid side issues. Delete unnecessary words. (Test: Would the commercial be hurt if the words were deleted? If not, take them out.) Write from draft to draft until your script becomes unmistakably clear and concise. At the end of the commercial, your audience should understand exactly what you have tried to say. Despite having several facts in your commercial, make sure you have the big idea.

- *Coherence.* Be certain that your message flows in logical sequence from the first word to the last; use smooth transitional words and phrases for easy listening.

- *Rapport.* Remember, as far as your listeners are concerned, you are speaking only to them. Try to use a warm, personal tone, as if you were talking to one or two people. Make frequent use of the word *you.* Address the listeners in terms they would use themselves.

- *Pleasantness.* It is not necessary to entertain simply for the sake of entertaining, but there is no point in being dull or obnoxious. Strike a happy medium; talk as one friend to another about the product or service.

- *Believability.* Every product has its good points. Tell the truth about it. Avoid overstatements and obvious exaggerations; they are quickly spotted and defeat the whole purpose of the commercial. Be straightforward; you want to convey the impression of being a trusted friend.

- *Interest.* Nothing makes listeners indifferent faster than a boring commercial. Products and services are not fascinating in themselves; the way you present them makes them interesting. Try to give your customer some useful information as a reward for listening.

- *Distinctiveness.* Sound different from other commercials and set your product apart. Use every possible technique—a fresh approach, a musical phrase, a particular voice quality or sound effect—to give your commercial a distinct character.

SOME TECHNIQUES

Basically a medium of words, radio—more than any other medium—relies heavily on the art of writing strong copy. However, just as print ads and TV commercials include pictures and graphics to add impact to the copy, radio creates mental pictures with other techniques. Radio copywriters can choose among many proven techniques to give more meaning to the copy, to help gain the attention of the busy target audience, and to hold that attention for the duration of the commercial. Some of these techniques parallel those used in television.

- *Humor.* Humor is an excellent technique for service and retail businesses. Consumers never relate an ad to the advertising agency that produced it; they only relate the spot to the advertiser. Therefore, humor can portray a company as friendly, likable, and easy going when negotiating a sale.

Many award-winning radio spots use humor. Tom Little said humorous spots often won awards because they stood out from the hundreds that he had to listen to. If that's true, then the same probably works for consumers. Humor may be part of any writing technique we have discussed. Humor is often appropriate for low-priced packaged products, products people buy for fun, products whose primary appeal is taste, or products or services in need of change-of-pace advertising because of strong competition. Be very careful about making fun of the product or the user or treating too lightly a situation that is not normally funny.

- *Emotion.* Using emotion is an effective method when the topic itself is emotional. Ads for family, health care, donations, mental care, security, and similar products and services use emotion to stimulate the targeted response.

- *Music and sound effects.* Music creates the mood, and sound effects create the imagery in the consumer's mind. Jingles can be very memorable and effective when they relate directly to the product or service.

- *White space. White space* is a term used in print advertising. However, white space in radio can be extremely compelling. A 60-second spot may start with music or sound effects with no copy for 45 seconds, bringing consumers' curiosity into play and leaving them wide open to accept a provocative message.

- *Dialog.* Dialog is a great technique to use in many situations. It doesn't confront the consumer; it allows the listener to eavesdrop on the conversation. Dialog is also very successful when the advertiser has a product that appeals to men and women. Dialog between a man and a woman allows the commercial to play to both targets. Exhibit 20.5 illustrates using multiple voices and an announcer.

EXHIBIT 20.5

Athens Area Men's Baseball League Draft Day Commercial

This ad uses multiple voices and an announcer to promote its message.

Courtesy of Steven Lang of COX Radio/Athens.

A.A. Baseball League   Steve Lang

(SFX: bar/restaurant sounds)
1: Jimmy. It's good to find you here.
2: Uh,…hi guys. W w what's up.
3: Word on the street is that you've gone soft.
2: Ummm.
1: Cause you know, we thought you were one of guys.
3: A real man's man. Please say you didn't go soft on us.
(SFX: music)
Anncr: Guys, don't go soft. Play hardball! Draft day for the Athens Area Men's Baseball League is March 7th, and you can register now at A A M B L dot-com. Play America's past time the way it was meant to be played—nine innings, wooden bats and hard-pitched hard balls! Register now at A A M B L dot-com. It's a 15- to 17-game season with all games played locally. Choose from 18-plus or 28-plus leagues. If you believe in monster home runs, diving catches and head-first slides, this is where you belong—Athens Area Men's Baseball League. To be included on the March 7th draft day sign up now at A A M B L dot-com.

(SFX: bar/restaurant sounds)
2: Me…go soft…? Why would you think that?
1: Jimmy, is that a pink umbrella in your drink?
2: Gulp.
3: You have gone soft. (SFX: knuckles cracking) How very disappointing.

Courtesy of Steven Lang of COX Radio/Athens.

Blount Heating and Cooling   Steve Lang

Do you own a home or business in North Georgia with central heat and air? If so, Blount Heating and Cooling asks for your attention. Because up to $3,000 in rebates and tax credits are now available on new high-efficiency heating and cooling systems from Blount. Three thousand dollars—that's up to 40 percent off cost! And then you'll save up to 50 percent each month on your heating and cooling bills! If you need, or believe you'll soon need, a new heating and air system, please seriously consider this offer. For more details you can call Blount Heating and Cooling at 706–548–5555. With up to $3,000 in rebates and tax credits, *and* savings of up to 50 percent each month, this system will quickly pay for itself, and then start putting money back into your pocket. Service trucks are ready to begin your installation immediately. So call Blount Heating and Cooling at 706–548–5555 and begin to enjoy these savings immediately.

EXHIBIT 20.6

Blount Heating and Cooling Commercial

Straight facts from an announcer are used to sell the message from this company.

- *Sex.* It can sell very well.

- *Straight announcer.* Sometimes the simplest approach works best. In this commonly used and most direct of all techniques, an announcer or personality delivers the entire script. Success depends both on the copy and on the warmth and believability of the person performing the commercial. Tom Bodett for Motel 6 is all these things and one of the reasons the commercials are still so popular. This approach also works particularly well when a positive image has previously been established and a specific event is being promoted, such as a sale. Exhibit 20.6 is an ad selling a heating and air conditioning company with straight facts from the announcer.

- *Combination.* Radio techniques may be mixed in countless ways, combining music, sound effects, an announcer, and a person. You might notice that the advertisement uses the name of the product five times in interesting ways to gain brand recognition. To select the right technique for a particular assignment, follow the guidelines discussed in Chapter 19 for selecting television techniques.

Timing of Commercials

Time is the major constraint in producing a radio commercial. Most radio stations accept these maximum word lengths for live commercial scripts:

- 10 seconds, 25 words
- 20 seconds, 45 words

In prerecorded commercials, you may use as many words as you can fit within the time limit. However, if you use more than 125 words for a 60-second commercial, the commercial will have to be read so rapidly that it may sound unnatural or even be unintelligible. Remember, too, if you insert sound effects, that will probably cut down on the number of words you can use. If you have footsteps running for 5 seconds, you are going to have to cut 10 to 12 words. You need to time the musical introductions and endings or sound effects because each affects the number of words allowable. It is not unusual to go into the recording studio with a script that is a couple of seconds short because the extra time allows the talents to sound more natural. Actors need some breathing room to sound sincere.

Musical Commercials

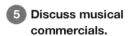**5** **Discuss musical commercials.**

Music can be a powerful tool for getting your product remembered. As musical writer Steve Karman has said, "People don't hum the announcer."[8]

In writing musical commercials, you have to start with an earthquake, then build to something really big. In other words, there is no room for subtlety. The thought process and strategy are different from those in regular songwriting. There are three main elements to writing commercial music:

1. *Intro:* The beginning of the song. The tempo and lyrics may be established here.
2. *Verse:* The middle of the song. This is where the message is developed. There may be several verses.
3. *Theme or chorus:* May be the conclusion of the song.

Often you begin with the chorus to establish your theme, or you may repeat the theme throughout. The theme is what listeners remember. Some musical forms, such as blues, can be thought of as both verse and chorus. A theme may serve as a musical logotype for a product, lasting about 4 seconds to 10 seconds.

Sheri Bevil of Lane Bevil+Partners says, "Folks restaurants hired Jack Turner to do an original score and lyrics for a number of jingles. Usually the radio opens with one of the jingles. Then the promotional message goes over the bed of music (usually an announcer). Then it ends with another jingle. The jingle takes up 28 to 30 seconds leaving another 30 seconds for the specific message." In some cases, Bevil says, "The spot would also end with a 5- to 10-second tag."

> Southern Boy Version: Folks Southern Kitchen
> I've been a southern boy all my life
> Got a Southern drawl and a Southern wife
> When I'm in the mood for some comfort food
> Nobody knows me like my Folks.

Many commercials are composed especially for the advertiser or product. Others are simply adapted from a familiar song. A melody is in the public domain, available for use by anyone without cost, after its copyright has expired. Many old favorites and classics are in the public domain and have been used as advertising themes. But that is one of their detriments: Many others may have used them.

Popular tunes that are still protected by copyright are available only by (often costly) agreement with the copyright owner. An advertiser can also commission a composer to create an original tune, which becomes the advertiser's property and gives the product its own musical personality.

Do you have the talent to write a jingle? Does the typical copywriter have the ability to do so? In general, the job of writing such copy is left to the music experts.

AUDIO TECHNOLOGY

As you use your iPhone or iPod, you are aware of the radical change in the way music and sound are recorded and downloaded. A little more than a decade ago, the world of high-fidelity multitrack recording (and sync-to-picture for television) belonged solely to record companies, postproduction houses, and commercial ventures.

In the early 1990s, software was created for the Macintosh that allowed true four-track recording and simultaneous musical instrument digital interface (MIDI) file play-back. The simple interface was based on the integrated portable studio metaphor and did not require sophisticated knowledge of the software. Today, any computer can use software that creates an entire band and editing studio.

It is easy to record your basic ideas digitally from the very beginning, and add and edit digital audio tracks to your composition. You can then use the software to transfer the master digitally to a digital audiotape (DAT) or compact disk (CD). Today, every step in the multitrack production of digital audio is in the hands of the individual. For example, here are some of the technology options offered by Sound of Music:[9]

> Sound of Music studio houses two rooms. Our "A" studio is centered around a Sony 3036 analogue console from the late 80's. We utilize outboard pre-amps by Neve, API, Fairchild, and Amek; Dynamic effects and processing from Empirical Labs, Alan Smart, DBX, Eventide, Neve, Universal Audio, RADAR II 24-track hard disk recording system, Pro-Tools LE 7.4 via a Digi 002. Mix Ampex ATR 102 / 24bit Masterlink Our "B" studio is used primarily for overdubs, assembly and editing. It features the AMEK Angela console; with RADAR II Hard disk recording system and Pro-tool LE 7.4 via Digi 002.

Methods of Delivery

There are three ways a radio commercial can be delivered: live, by a station announcer, and as a prerecorded announcement.

⑥ Explain the process of producing radio commercials.

THE LIVE COMMERCIAL

A live commercial is delivered in person by the studio announcer, disc jockey, newscaster, or other station personality, or perhaps by a sports reporter from another location. Although generally read from a script prepared by the advertiser, the commercial is sometimes revised to complement the announcer's style. If time allows, the revised script should be approved in advance by the advertiser. Ad-libbing (extemporizing) from a fact sheet should be discouraged because the announcer may inadvertently omit key selling phrases or, in the case of regulated products such as drugs, fail to include certain mandatory phrases.

Some commercials are delivered partly live and partly prerecorded. The prerecorded jingle, for example, can be played over and over with live-announcer copy added. Sometimes the live part (the dealer "tie-up") is left open for the tie-in ad of the local distributor.

One advantage of the live commercial is that the announcer may have a popular following, and listeners tend to accept advice from someone they like. For example, *The Steve and Vikki Morning Show* is the top-rated morning show in Atlanta. Vikki does endorsement commercials for Intimacy. "I'm Vikki Locke. Like most women I spent years wearing the wrong bra size until one day a friend told me about Intimacy. . . ." Steve McCoy talks about how his family breathes better because he installed a Pureatech air treatment system for his home. They both have a big following and bring credibility to their spots. Generally, the other big advantage is cost: Station announcers usually do your commercials free of extra talent costs, although some announcers may demand higher rates.

WORD OF MOUTH: LIVE RADIO ENDORSEMENTS   A new approach of audio product placement is alive and well in radio, and it gets high marks for effectiveness: live radio endorsements. The thought is that polished or scripted commercials don't penetrate the consumer's psyche but that seemingly spur-of-the moment endorsements by personalities will. Let's look at an example of this word-of-mouth type of radio ad:

> DJs Steve and Vikki gab on-air about a comedian. Out of the blue, Steve says, "Maybe you can suggest she could use a Swiffer WetJet at home." Vickie responds

by telling the audience how she sponged up spilled soy sauce last night. "With the Swiffer WetJet," she sings songs, "it was so easy and fast to clean." For 2½ minutes, which included an amusing debate on how long dropped food can linger on the floor before it becomes inedible, they name the product a combined eight times. The WetJet paid the station for a 60-second commercial and compensated the disc jockeys. But they got 90 seconds of freebies.

The media ad placement company Varson Group specializes in word-of-mouth endorsements. The DJs are provided with talking points (copy guide) and with facts and tidbits about the product. Three on-air mentions by name per segment are encouraged. Exaggeration—this shampoo has changed my life—is not as effective with other kinds of product placement, and this technique is not without criticism. However, Vikki Locke says she declines numerous endorsement offers, and her rule of thumb is "If I don't use it, or don't like it, I don't do it." Steve McCoy agrees and adds, "The beauty of live endorsements is that at times they fit right into the show."[10]

STATION ANNOUNCER

For a campaign dealing with a retail offer that will change frequently, advertisers often use a station announcer reading copy written by the agency. This is recorded at the station at no charge to the client—sometimes even with the client's musical theme in the background. This type of delivery allows for frequent changes in copy at no cost.

THE PRERECORDED COMMERCIAL

Advertisers undertaking a regional or national campaign will not know local announcers' capabilities. In any case, it would be impractical to write a separate script to fit each one's particular style. Commercials for these campaigns, therefore, usually are prerecorded. Not only does this assure advertisers that the commercial will be identical each time it is aired but it also allows them to take advantage of techniques that would be impractical in a live commercial. (Actually, in many instances, "live" commercials are recorded by the station so that they can run even when the announcer is not on duty.)

TALENT AND UNIONS

7 Explain unions and talent.

As with television, AFTRA contracts mandate the use of and payment to performers in radio commercials. Talent is paid a session fee when the commercial is recorded. Other requirements for payment based on usage include spot, network, dealer, demo, copy testing, and foreign use. Performer fees are another cost the advertiser must consider.

The complexity of the union contract can be seen in the following table or in its entirety at AFTRA.org. For example, minimum session fees are as follows:

Actor, announcer, sole, duo	$235.40
Group singer/speaker	173.40
Then there are the use fees:	13 weeks
Network program commercial	$1,029.30
Regional network program	770.75
Outside New York, Chicago, or Los Angeles	235.40
New York alone	350.40
Chicago or Los Angeles alone	319.60
Any two of the above	429.80
Demo/copy test	162.20
Additional hour	40.55

Producing the Radio Commercial

Although there are certain broad similarities, producing radio commercials is far simpler and less costly than producing TV commercials. First, the agency or advertiser appoints a radio producer, who converts the script into a recording ready to go on the air. After preparing the cost estimate and getting budget approval, the producer selects a recording studio and a casting director, if necessary. If music is called for, the producer calls a music "house" that usually composes, arranges, and takes all steps necessary to get the finished music. If the music is not a big-budget item, the producer may call for "stock" music (prerecorded and used on a rental basis).

After the cast has been selected, it rehearses in a recording studio, which can be leased by the hour. However, because most commercials are made in short "takes" that are later joined in editing, a formal rehearsal is usually unnecessary. When the producer believes the cast is ready, the commercial is acted out and recorded on tape. Music and sound are taped separately and then mixed with the vocal tape by the sound-recording studio. By double- and triple-tracking music and singers' voices, modern recording equipment can build small sounds into big ones. However, union rules require that musicians and singers be paid extra fees when their music is mechanically added to their original recording. After the last mix, the master tape of the commercial is prepared. When final approval has been obtained, duplicates are made for release to the list of stations.

Steven Lang uses VoiceUnders.com, which is an online audio resource, to get voices from coast to coast and even across the "pond," from the United Kingdom. He sends them a script and they send him an MP3 in return. If necessary, they talk and redo. It is pretty simple.

THINGS TO REMEMBER DURING PRODUCTION

Often the account executive or client will be at the recording session; however, Phil Cuttino has a bias against having either of them at a recording session. He believes their presence creates too many problems, which can inhibit great production. These problems include the talent and engineer tightening up, and everyone being more concerned about time than producing an effective spot. Cuttino suggests that you use a phone patch from the studio to play the spot for the account executive first. Then, with his or her blessing, call the client for the final approval. The engineer and talent should remain in the studio until the final approval is received. Following are some other production thoughts:

- *Call ahead.* Have the studio pull the music and sound effects selections.
- *Studio.* Find a studio that has several talented engineers who will quickly learn your style. Make sure the studio has a good SFX and music library and the latest technology.
- *Brainpower.* During production, use everyone's brain to make the spot better. Ask for input from your engineer and voice talent. Remember, they probably have been involved in more spots in a week than you have in months.
- *Take your time.* Don't push the talent or engineer. Lead them to what you want.
- *Keep up with the technology.* New technology will always broaden your creative envelope.
- *Casting.* Acting professionals usually have the best and most believable voices because they are visualizing the scene. This is particularly true with dialog or group scenes. Go to plays often to find new talent. Do not look at the people who are auditioning for a part in the spot. They will try to sell you with facial expressions, body language, and hand motions—all worthless on radio. At first, allow the talent to give you their own interpretation of the scene. You may be inspired by their rendition.

STEPS IN RADIO PRODUCTION

We may summarize the steps in producing a commercial as follows:

1. An agency or advertiser appoints a producer.

2. The producer prepares cost estimates.

3. The producer selects a recording studio.

4. With the aid of the casting director, if one is needed, the producer casts the commercial.

5. If music is to be included, the producer selects a musical director and chooses the music or selects stock music.

6. If necessary, a rehearsal is held.

7. The studio tapes music and sound separately.

8. The studio mixes music and sound with voices.

9. The producer sees that the master is prepared for distribution on appropriate medium and sent to stations.

You are on the air!

SUMMARY

Radio can be visual, despite its lack of visuals. It paints a picture in the listener's imagination and truly becomes a theater of the mind. Words, sound effects, and music are the tools of the radio copywriter. The biggest limitation is that the radio copywriter is always working against the clock.

It is the duty of the radio writer and producer to take control of the listener's imagination and guide it to a positive reaction that seeds the listener's memory with the targeted message, leading to the anticipated response. The power of a radio commercial is in the idea imagery.

When developing a commercial, it is important to keep it simple and to concentrate on one main idea. Repetition of the main selling ideas is considered necessary, but the main thing is to get the listeners to remember the brand and message. Some of the writing techniques and formats include straight announcer, slice-of-life, jingle-announcer, customer interview, and humor.

As with television, all performers appearing in national commercials are subject to union compensation agreements.

REVIEW

1. Why is radio called the theater of the mind?
2. Briefly summarize the elements of good radio commercials.
3. What is white space in radio?
4. Name four radio station programming formats.
5. What are the three main elements to writing commercial music?
6. What are the steps in radio production?

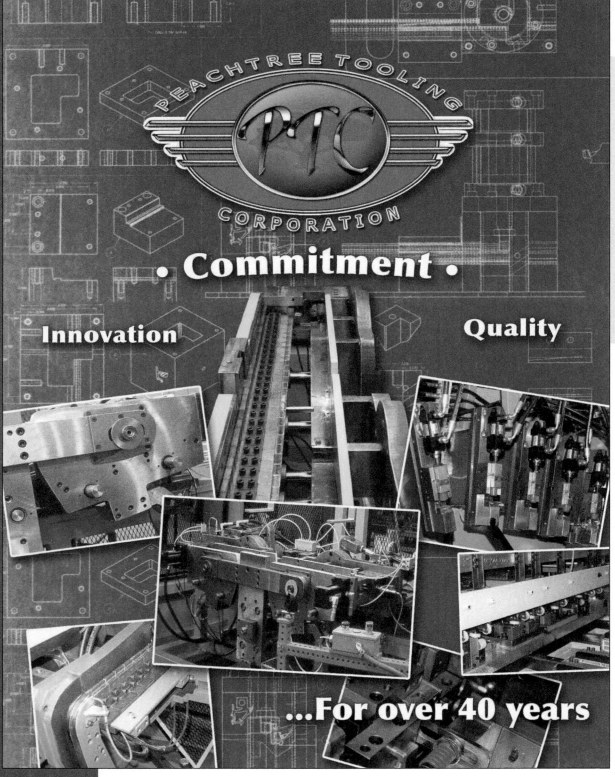

PEACHTREE TOOLING CORPORATION

PTC

• Commitment •

Innovation

Quality

...For over 40 years

Trademarks and Packaging

B RAND NAMES and naming are not to be taken lightly. Product names and trademarks are very important to brand equity, brand identity, and the marketing process. In today's market, advertising and packaging must support each other. ▶

CHAPTER LEARNING OBJECTIVES

1 **Explain what a trademark is.**

2 **Discuss protecting the trademark.**

3 **Discuss forms of trademarks.**

4 **Explain general trademark rules.**

5 **Explain the process for developing memorable names.**

6 **Discuss packaging and marketing.**

7 **Discuss packaging and research.**

Today, naming presents a formidable challenge because legally available names that are clear, distinct, and memorable are in short supply. The brand name is one of the most important assets of a company, and the trademark is the brand's asset. A name communicates the essence of a company, product, or service, forming the foundation of any brand. Peachtree Tooling engineers machines. Many of their clients are automobile companies. Peachtree makes the machines that make the parts. So their logo reflects the brand. Names and trademarks create images and associations in consumers' minds. There are millions of registered trademarks in the United States alone. If you attempt to come up with a corporate or product name, you may decide there are no appropriate new names left to claim. The wrong choice may lead to charges of trademark infringement if you pick a name owned by someone else. Once you have the right name, you must protect it.

Protecting the Name Investment

Consider the financial investment in a name. In only 6 years, Cingular became the largest wireless company with revenues of some $4 billion and hundreds of millions invested to make the name known. In 2007, AT&T merged with Cingular and changed the Cingular brand into the AT&T brand. AT&T had an "old" image but was known internationally; Cingular had a "hip" image but wasn't known globally. The marketing community argued about which was the better name going forward. What appears to be a simple decision is really complex.

Let's look at it in the longer term. Consider the trademark of Coca-Cola, a brand invented in 1886. Think of the corporate and financial loss if Coca-Cola lost the exclusive right to its trademark. It is not impossible for companies to lose that right. This is why they go to great lengths to protect their trademarks. Many companies have with a special legal staff that monitors all uses of the brand(s) to protect their investment. Coke has brand cop lawyers who monitor what's going on in cyberspace. They surf the web, tracking repeat offenders, and writing cease-and-desist letters centered on Coke brand abuses, online and offline. The nature of infractions is studied to determine the need for legal action by the corporate legal department. They ask interlopers to stop using the Coke brand or trademark. Among the most common types of online brand abuses are the following:[1]

- Unauthorized use of logos and images
- Use of a company's name on a competitor's site
- Unauthorized framing, in which a web site appears within another site
- Domain abuse and parody sites
- Unauthorized use of a company's name or product in metatags
- Diverting users away from a web site by hiding key words in background text

All companies face the same threat to their brand and trademark, which we discuss later in this chapter.

From Corporate Identity to Brand Identity

The first book dedicated to trademarks was published in 1924. A trademark established the character of a company and influenced the appearance of a product. Gordon Lippincott, founder of Lippincott & Margulies (now called Lippincott Mercer), coined the term *corporate identity* in 1943 to encompass all the ways a company identifies itself, from a new corporate name and logo to the color of its buildings. Today, the corporate mark is still the cornerstone of an identity program, but it involves much more. Partially because of technology and expanding avenues of communication, corporate identity has become an all-encompassing discipline that embodies the corporate personality, history, reputation, and vision. The best corporate programs closely associate the logo with what a company stands for. The Rusty Rooster Café logo reflects their brand identity and brand image (see Exhibit 21.1).

Today, a brand name not only has to be memorable, distinctive, easy to pronounce, and durable but it also has to work globally. That takes more than a large vocabulary and a thesaurus. There are actually naming specialists who make a science of knowing the origin and esoteric meaning of words. In some cases, they also study the emotional reaction to certain sounds. They study naming trends and clichés, spelling and pronunciation ambiguities, and know expedient ways to conduct legal searches and acquire trademark protection. If it is to be a global name, they look at potential foreign language problems. Graphic experts may participate in the naming process because the graphic expression of the name often determines its success or failure in the marketplace. Although the ultimate reason for settling on a certain name may be purely subjective, it is usually tested to see the reactions of the target or users.

BRAND IDENTITY

Most people associate Volvo with safety, even though nothing in the logo or name (which means "rolling") directly conveys that attribute. A few years ago, research indicated that consumers thought Volvo cars were too boxy and staid. As a result, Volvo began to migrate its branded image by making sleeker cars and adding attributes such as high performance to safety. But the logo hasn't changed. Although a logo can connect a company to its attributes and positioning in the marketplace, it can't do the job alone.

EXHIBIT 21.1

The Rusty Rooster Café logo reflects their brand identity and brand image.

A brand identity system can. The visual identity is the better known part of the brand identity system. It uses the elements of the corporate identity system but is wider and deeper. The building blocks of the system include a company's name, trademarks, tagline, and logo. It also focuses on the elements that come together in almost any communication: imagery, typography, design, color, and consistent message. It may include a system that maps different communication vehicles (e.g., brochure, web site, direct mail, and CD-ROM) to audience content and production values. Education and training may play a part in the system.[2] Without a consistent and cohesive approach to brand identity, a company's communications may not generate the desired results.

There are also digital issues. Lippincott Mercer, a brand-consultant company that currently helps manage identity (including Advanta, Kraft, Nissan, Bayer, Samsung, McDonald's, Borders, Walgreens, Medco, Olive Garden, Coca-Cola, Deloitte Consulting, and Ameriprise Financial), believes that globalization and consolidation will continue as major business trends for many years to come. As a result, advanced communications and information technologies, such as the Internet and company intranets, will provide firms with bold new avenues for delineating and projecting their corporate and brand identities.[3]

A Little History of Trademarks

LANHAM ACT

There were few trademarks used on general merchandise prior to the Civil War. In 1870, the rapid growth in trade identity gave rise to the first federal trademark law. Lacking sufficient legislative safeguards, concerned manufacturers met in 1878 and founded the United States Trademark Association. Its name was changed to the International Trademark Association (INTA) in 1993. This organization promoted the enactment of the Trade-Mark Act of 1881 and its revisions in 1905 and 1920. In 1946, Congress passed the Lanham Act. It defined a trademark and expanded the concept of infringement, permitted the registration of service marks, provided incontestability status for marks in continuous use for 5 years, and provided that federal registration of a trademark would constitute "constructive notice of the registrant's claim of ownership thereof."

In 1996, President Clinton signed the Federal Trademark Dilution Act passed by Congress. It provided owners of famous trademarks with a federal cause of action against those who reduced the distinctiveness of such marks by the use of the same or similar trademarks on similar or dissimilar products or services. Unlike trademark infringement, a dilution action does not require proof or likelihood of consumer confusion. An amendment was added later that year in the form of the Anticounterfeiting Consumer Protection Act of 1996.[4]

PATENT AND TRADEMARK OFFICE AND TECHNOLOGY

In 2000, the agency once known as the Patent and Trademark Office was renamed the United States Patent and Trademark Office (USPTO). The USPTO reviews all trademark applications for federal registration and determines whether an applicant meets the requirements for federal registration. Owning a federal trademark registration on the Principal Register provides several advantages:

- Constructive notice to the public of the registrant's claim of ownership of the mark
- A legal presumption of the registrant's ownership of the mark and the registrant's exclusive right to use the mark nationwide on or in connection with the goods and services listed in the registration
- The ability to bring an action concerning the mark in federal court
- The use of U.S. registration as a basis to obtain registration in foreign countries
- The ability to file the U.S. registration with the U.S. Customs Service to prevent importation of infringing foreign goods

What Is a Trademark?

1 Explain what a trademark is.

trademark
Any device or word that identifies the origin of a product, telling who made it or who sold it. Not to be confused with a trade name.

logotype, or logo
A trademark or trade name embodied in the form of a distinctive lettering or design. Famous example: Coca-Cola.

We have said that brands are among the most valuable assets a marketer has. When a product is manufactured and a brand is created, it must be distinctive from the competition. There are several types of company and product identifications. The **trademark**, also called a brand name, is the name people use to speak of a product. Very often a trademark will include some pictorial or design element. If it does, the combination is called a **logotype** (or simply a **logo**). Exhibit 21.2 shows three distinctive logos.

Trademarks are proper terms that identify the products and services of a business and distinguish them from the products and services of others. Specifically, a trademark is a word, a design, or a combination of the two used by a company to identify its brand and to distinguish it from others, and it may be registered and protected by law. Trademark formats can include letters, numbers, slogans, geometric shapes, pictures, labels, color combinations, product and container shapes, vehicles, clothing, and even sound.

Trademarks can also be termed *service marks* when they are used to identify a service. In general, a trademark for goods appears on the product or its packaging, and a service mark is used in advertising to identify services.

The logo design is an extremely important element in the successful marketing of a product. It is difficult to sell a product until a reasonable level of name recognition is achieved among consumers. The creation of a logo is so important that a number of firms have been established whose primary function is the design of logos, packages, and corporate identity. Most designers attempt to forge a compatible relationship among the package design, logo, and advertising for the product. A strong logo on the package and in product advertising creates an environment of recognition. The process of developing logos is an extensive one involving many ideas and options that are carefully considered. Baker Environmental Nursery involved dozens and dozens of possibilities (see Exhibit 21.3).

Logo designs come in several basic forms including abstract symbols (the apple used by Apple Computer) or logotypes, a stylized rendition of a company's name. You can also use a combination of both. Promoting an abstract symbol can prove very costly and isn't recommended for a small budget. Such logos are also harder to remember. Logotypes or word marks are generally easier to recall. If you use an abstract symbol, it should be used in connection with the business name. Some advertising agencies design logos for clients themselves. Some of the mega-agencies may have sister companies that specialize in this area of brand development and identity. In many cases, the corporation takes responsibility for the process.

DESIGN: AN EXPENSIVE PROCESS

In 2008, Pepsi took 5 months to redesign its logo. The new logo shows a white band in the middle of the Pepsi circle that loosely forms a series of smiles: A smile characterizes

EXHIBIT 21.2

(A) Pax Mondial logo,
(B) Keyworth Bank, and
(C) Max20 ad agency.

EXHIBIT 21.3

The evolution of a logo involves many designs and tweaks.

brand Pepsi, whereas a grin is used for Diet Pepsi and a laugh is used for Pepsi Max. The new logo is Pepsi's eleventh in its 110-year history. Five logos have been introduced in the past 21 years, with the last update in 2002.[5] Experts estimate the cost for a top firm to work 5 months developing a logo to be more than a million dollars. But that's only the beginning. The real cost is in removing the old logo everywhere it appears and putting new material up. For Coke or Pepsi, when you add up all the trucks, vending machines, stadium signage, POP materials, and more around the world, it could easily run several hundred million dollars.[6]

Normally, professional design firms will charge anywhere from $4,000 to $15,000 for a logo alone. However, as with Pepsi, the cost may be many times these figures. Research and development of corporate identity programs may routinely cost as much as $150,000. Keep in mind that there are thousands of independent designers available who charge from $20 to $150 per hour, depending on their experience. As a rule of thumb, a good logo should last at least 10 years. If you look at the amortization of that cost over a 10-year period, it doesn't seem so bad.

Of course, some companies simply get lucky. In 1971, a graphic design student at Portland State University designed the Nike swoosh. Phil Knight, co-founder and chair of Nike asked her to do some work for what was then Blue Ribbon Sports, Inc. Needing to choose a logo in order to meet looming production deadlines, Knight settled on the swoosh, after rejecting various other designs. At the time, he stated of the logo, "I don't love it, but it will grow on me." For her services, she billed the company $35. I suspect he's grown to like it.

Every successful organization tries to develop an intriguing logotype. The Sustainable Cities Institute logo (see Exhibit 21.4) was a challenge for Idea Engineering. This logo had to brand the institute and its sponsor, the Home Depot Foundation. Its goals are different from a product or corporation. Any logo must be applicable to all communication formats—letterheads, envelopes, brochures, web sites, newsletters, and so on. It must work in all integrated marketing formats.

Trademarks should not be confused with trade names, which are corporate or business names. General Motors, for example, is the trade name of a company making automobiles whose trademark (not trade name) is Chevrolet. The terms *trademark* and *trade name* are often confused. **Trade names** are proper nouns. Trade names can be used in the possessive form and do not require a generic form. Many companies, however, use their trade names as trademarks. For example, Reebok International Ltd. is the corporate name, and Reebok may be used as a trade name, as "Reebok's newest line of athletic shoes is for children." Reebok also is used as a trademark: "Are you wearing Reebok athletic shoes or another brand?"

trade name
A name that applies to a business as a whole, not to an individual product.

EXHIBIT 21.4

This logo has to work in all communication formats. It is complex because it has to serve the dual purpose of branding the organization and helping consumers to recognize the sponsor.

Courtesy of Idea Engineering, Santa Barbara.

SUSTAINABLE CITIES INSTITUTE

Built by The Home Depot Foundation

If you're confused, think of yourself as a new product. Your surname is your trade name (e.g., Lane, Smith, Bevil). Your gender is the product classification (Female Lane, Female Smith, or Female Bevil). Your given name then is the brand (Lois Lane, Judy Smith, Sheri Bevil) because it distinguishes you from other family members (like Sarah Bevil).

Some personal names (as with product names) may sound the same but may have different spellings—Sherry, Sherri, or Sheri, or even Cheri (or how about Kwik-Draw, Quick-Draw). Or they may simply be very familiar names—Jennifer, Jane, Jessica, Sarah, Hanna, Emily (or Jeff, Steven, Robert, Tom, Wade, Greg)—or clearly distinctive, like Ruhanna (or unusual like Hudson or McCall). Yet, distinctive names may appear difficult to read or pronounce. Companies and products have similar problems. They want names that easily can become familiar to consumers yet be easy to read, easy to pronounce, and easy to remember.

GENERAL ELECTRIC'S NAMING PROCESS

General Electric (GE) has a simple procedure for developing trademarks for its brands. GE's branding strategy has a number of steps:[7]

1. *Pick a name.* General Electric, for example.
2. *Create a memorable trademark.* The GE monogram is recognized the world over.
3. *Make a promise.* For 60 years, GE promised better living through electricity, which became better living through technology, for the past 30 years.
4. *Effectively communicate the promise.* GE has always had highly imaginative and memorable work produced by its agencies.
5. *Be consistent.* Even as GE grows and modifies its business, it carefully manages the use of its identity worldwide.
6. *Don't get bored.* GE kept the same strategic promise for 30 years before recently changing it to "Imagination at Work."

If you follow this basic strategy, your brand should thrive.

CRITERIA FOR TRADEMARKS

For a firm to qualify for an exclusive trademark, several requirements must be met. If these criteria are not satisfied, the trademark is not legally protected and will be lost to the firm.

The use of a design in an ad does not make it a trademark, nor does having it on a flag over the factory. The trademark must be used in connection with an actual product. It must be applied to the product itself or be on a label or container of that product. If that is not feasible, it must be affixed to the container or dispenser of the product, as on a gas pump at a service station.

The trademark must not be confusingly similar to trademarks on comparable goods. It must not be likely to cause buyers to be confused, mistaken, or deceived as to whose product they are purchasing. The trademark must be dissimilar in appearance, sound, and significance from others for similar goods. In disputes, it is up to a court to decide these issues. The products involved do not need to be identical. For example, Air-O was held in conflict with Arrow shirts. The marks will be held in conflict if the products are sold through the same trade channels or if the public might assume that a product made by a second company is a new product line of the first company.

Trademarks must not be deceptive—that is, they must not indicate a quality the product does not possess. For instance, the word *lemon* was barred from soap that contained no lemon, as was the word *nylon* from sleeping bags that contained no nylon.

Trademarks must not be merely descriptive. For example, when people ask for fresh bread, we cannot trademark our bread Fresh. When people ask for fresh bread, they are describing the kind of bread they want, not specifying the bread made by a particular baker. To prevent such misleading usage, the law does not protect trademarks that are merely descriptive and, thus, applicable to many other products.

TRADEMARK PROTECTION

2 **Discuss protecting the trademark.**

Because a trademark is so valuable, companies go to great lengths to protect their brand names. In recent years, there have been a number of court cases involving allegations that one company has infringed on the trademark of another.

In deciding whether trademark infringement has taken place, several factors are considered by the courts:

1. Distinctiveness of the complainant's mark
2. Similarity of the marks
3. Proximity of the parties' products
4. Likelihood of the complainant's bridging the gap between noncompeting products
5. Similarity of the parties' trade channels and advertising methods
6. Quality of the alleged infringer's products
7. Sophistication of the particular customers

Beware if your trademark is based on a common word. It will be considered legally weak and difficult to protect. Monitor the use of your trademark vigorously, and don't let any competitor use your mark even briefly. If you want to start a trademark infringement suit, don't do it unless you have detailed records and can document lost profits accurately.

TRADEMARK LOSS

In short, if you don't use a trademark properly, you can lose the rights to it. What would happen to Coca-Cola if the courts ruled you or anyone could call a soft drink Coke? You could then make your brew in your bathtub and sell it. Some companies have seen the untimely demise of a trademark. That's right—untimely demise. Many familiar words today were once valid trademarks:

aspirin	cornflakes
yo-yo	nylon
escalator	thermos
lanolin	raisin bran
cellophane	linoleum

To protect a trademark, advertisers must use it with a generic classification so the trademark does not become the name of the product. Advertising writer, Stuart Elliott was asked in his online newsletter, "Why does MasterCard tell you to use your 'MasterCard card?'" The answer, of course, is this becomes a trademark issue. McDonald's sells Big Macs, not "Big Mac burgers." Jon Schwartz, a spokesman for MasterCard International explains, essentially, many times it's because we're driving consumers to use their physical payment card, so we must distinguish between our brand and the MasterCard-branded credit or debit cards that consumers use to make purchases. MasterCard is a trademark name, which should be followed by a generic noun. That is because using a trademark as a noun could weaken its uniqueness, as the trademark lawyers for brands such as Band-Aid, Kleenex, and Xerox could attest.[8]

Originally, Thermos was the trademark owned by the Aladdin Company, which introduced vacuum bottles. In time, people began asking, "What brand of thermos bottle do you carry?" The word *thermos* had come to represent all vacuum bottles, not only those made by Aladdin. The courts held that *Thermos* had become a descriptive word that any manufacturer of vacuum bottles could use because *thermos* (with a lowercase *t*) was no longer the exclusive trademark of the originator. This could be very scary to any brand.

NAME CHANGE RISKS

When America Online announced that it was officially changing its name to AOL, the news caused barely a ripple. The pioneering Internet company unofficially had been known as AOL for years. Most cyberspace brands have yet to generate the kind of emotional bond that many consumers feel for bricks-and-mortar establishments, such as Marshall Field's whose monikers were switched to Macy's with grumblings from consumers. Federated Department Stores Inc. decided to rechristen a number of other regional department store brands with the Macy's brand. The move helps Federated expand Macy's into a national brand and, in the process, helps reduce national advertising costs. When a change sparks vehement objections from longtime customers, it serves as a reminder to marketers that when you rename a company, you might be toying with customer loyalty. But the name changes didn't stop there. Federated then changed its name to Macy's Corporation.

Most companies that serve the business community can adopt a new name with minimal fanfare because, unlike consumer companies, they rarely encounter customers who feel personally betrayed by the brand change. It also is easier for business-to-business firms to communicate the name change to their customers because their target markets tend to be smaller than those of a consumer company. About 90 percent of the name changers nationwide are in the business-to-business arena. For example, Binney & Smith changed their name to help people recognize them, to Crayola (you know Crayola Crayons). Ruth's Chris Steakhouse changed the corporate name to Ruth's. Matsushita Electric Industrial changed their name to Panasonic Corporation because people know the Panasonic name. Technology companies generally lead the pack partly because they are in a young industry with enterprises that sometimes change their focus to keep pace with new technologies. "There is a certain amount of equity that comes with a brand name or company name. In most cases you don't want to risk losing customers who have come to know and trust that name," said Teena Massingill, manager of corporate public affairs for Safeway Stores based in Pleasanton, California.[9]

SELECTING BRAND NAMES

Think about all the possible associations of Mountain Dew. On the one hand, there's the serene, relaxing scenario of a quiet mountain trail or lake. But that wasn't what the folks at Mountain Dew wanted for the brand. They wanted to associate the brand with aggressive, incredibly cool, extreme-sports type activity. The brand is for people who push themselves and consider the outdoors an adventure waiting to happen. The product, as both words and as a brand, has been defined as anything but a serene experience. They managed the brand name. Another challenge in naming is that no word or name exists without both positive and negative connotations. However, a brand can redefine a word. A brand name will be accepted in its ultimate context, if you control the context.[10] A strong brand name will aid branding objectives by helping create and support the brand image. There are several considerations in the brand name selection.[11]

- The name should differentiate the product from the competition. In some product categories, there is a limit to how different brand images can be. In fragrances there has traditionally been one basic image—romance. There is great similarity among some brand names, for example, Caleche, Cacharel, and Chantilly. Consider more distinctive names such as Obsession, Red, Passion, Romance, Eternity, Fracas, and Tiffany. In either direction, creation and support of the brand image—abstract promise rather than actual benefit—are the dominant factors in name selection.

- The name should describe the product, if possible. Brand names such as Post-it, Pudding Pops, Eraser Mate, and Ceco Building Systems (see Exhibit 21.5) are very descriptive. They communicate to consumers exactly what to expect.

- The product should be compatible with the brand name. In other words, do not name a sleeping tablet "Awake."

EXHIBIT 21.5

The name communicates what business the company is in.

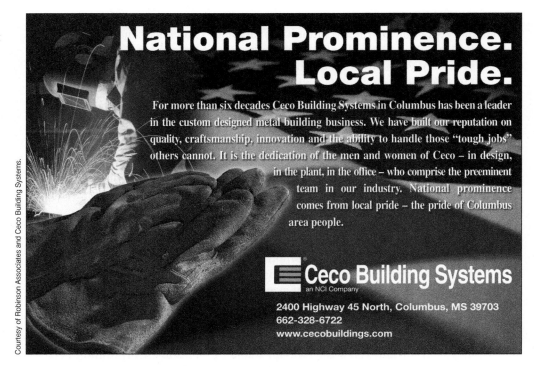

- The name should be memorable and easy to pronounce. One-word, one-syllable brand names are often considered ideal—Fab, Tide, Dash, Bold, Surf, Coke, and Tab. Even though short names may be more memorable, they may be limiting in identifying the type of product or its use.

Al and Laura Ries, brand consultants, recommend the following considerations in naming a brand:[12]

- The name should be short, for instance, Jell-O, Nilla, TheraFlu. Shortness is an attribute that is even more important for an Internet brand.

- The name should be simple. Simple is not the same as short. A simple word uses only a few letters of the alphabet and arranges them in combinations that repeat themselves. Many viral-related names are not simple, but many are distinctive: Flickr, Frappr. ThermaCare is simple and descriptive. Schwab is a short name but not simple because it uses six letters of the alphabet. Coca-Cola is both a short and simple name. Autobytel.com suffers from being too complicated.

- No name is totally unique unless you create it from scratch, such as Acura, Lexus, or Kodak. Remember, a common or generic name is not unique.

- The name should be alliterative. If you want people to remember something, rhyme it for them. Alliteration is another way to improve your brand's memorability: Bed Bath & Beyond, Blockbuster, Volvo, and Weight Watchers.

- The name should be speakable. Try Abercrombie & Fitch and Concierge.com.

FORMS OF TRADEMARKS

3 Discuss forms of trademarks.

Branding experts agree that although still very relevant, the overall value of a company's name has diminished. Convergence, globalization, and the interactive site influx have caused a shift in the branding strategy. The vast majority of the words in the *Oxford English Dictionary* have been registered and trademarked. A recent Interbrand corporate study revealed that 80 percent of naming projects lasted 3 months or less. According to projected naming trends, 19 percent of those surveyed thought "coined" or fabricated names will remain popular because there are not many good dictionary names left; 9 percent of respondents saw a trend toward adopting names that had been part of company heritage (e.g., a founder's name); and 57 percent saw a trend toward more "real" names—either a single or a compound word (e.g., Apple, JetBlue, Black-Berry, Tide).[13] The following are examples of traditional trademark forms.

DICTIONARY WORDS   Many trademarks consist of familiar dictionary words used in an arbitrary, innovative, or fanciful manner. Many common words have already been used, causing advertisers to seek other methods to name a product: Apple computers, Verbatim data disks, Deer Park spring water, Nature Made vitamins, Ivory soap, Dial soap, Equal sweetener, Whopper burgers, Glad plastic bags, Coach leather, Target, Folks restaurant (see Exhibit 21.6), and Pert shampoo. This type of trademark must be used in a merely descriptive sense to describe the nature, use, or virtue of the product: Consider the word *natural* and think of related names such as Natural Blend, Natural Brand, Natural Impressions, Natural Light, Natural Man, Natural Silk, Natural Smoothe, Natural Stretch, Natural Suede, Natural Sun, Natural Touch, Natural Woman, and Natural Wonder; or the prefix *opti* as used in Opti Fonts, Opti Free, Opti-Fry, Opti-Grip, Opti Heat, Opti Pure, Opti-Ray, Opti-Tears, and Opti Twist. A few years ago, OrangeGlo International created a new kind of cleaner using an oxygen booster to remove stains and odors and get laundry whiter. It was called OxiClean. In the beginning it was sold primarily on television directly to consumers, then in specialty stores like Bed Bath & Beyond, and later on grocery shelves. As it began moving more into the mainstream and taking away from established products, competitive products were introduced with their versions of "oxi" or "oxy" products.

Courtesy of Lane Bevil+Partners.

EXHIBIT 21.6

Folks Logo

A name you can find in the dictionary.

EXHIBIT 21.7

Chick-fil-A Logo

Courtesy of Chick-fil-A.

The possible advantage of using dictionary words is that consumers will easily recognize them. The task is to get people to associate the word(s) with the product. Just think what the following real product names using dictionary words are about: Healthy Choice, Oracle, Skin Bracer, Budget Rent-A-Car, Wonder Bra, Computer Associates, Big Mac, Action Plus, Hotmail, and AquaFresh.

At times, a name can be somewhat limiting. For instance, when Burger King moved into a breakfast menu, its name was a limitation because people do not think of burgers as breakfast food.

COINED WORDS   When we run out of dictionary options, we sometimes make up words, such as Google, Avaya, FedEx, Advil, Infiniti, Primerica, Kleenex, Xerox, NYNEX, UNUM, Norelco, Exxon, Delco, Keds, Kodak, Mazola, Häagen-Dazs, Chick-fil-A (see Exhibit 21.7), and Tab. **Coined words** are made up of a new combination of consonants and vowels. The advantage of a coined word is that it is new, and it can be made phonetically pleasing, pronounceable, and short. Coined words have a good chance of being legally protectable. The challenge is to create a trademark that is distinctive. Ocean Spray took the ingredients of cranberries and apples and created the name Cranapple, which is distinctive, descriptive, and relatively easy to pronounce. There is, however, a Cranberry Apple herbal tea. Is this confusing? Probably not.

The simpler coined words are one syllable. It is common to coin trademark words that have a vowel next to a hard consonant or a vowel between two hard consonants, such as Keds. This structure can be expanded—Kodak, Crisco, or Tab.

PERSONAL NAMES   Another traditional form of trademark is the personal name. These may be the names of real people, such as Calvin Klein, Liz Claiborne, Anne Klein, Estée Lauder, Tommy Hilfiger, Perry Ellis, Pierre Cardin, Alexander Julian, Ralph Lauren, L.L.Bean, Jenny Craig, Forbes, and Sara Lee; fictional characters, such as Betty Crocker; historical persons, such as Lincoln cars; or mythological characters, such as Ajax cleanser. A surname alone is not valuable as a new trademark; others of that name may use it. Names such as Ford automobiles, Lipton teas, Heinz foods, and Campbell's soups have been in use for so long, however, that they have acquired what the law calls a "secondary" meaning—that is, through usage, the public recognizes them as representing the product of one company only. However, a new trademark has no such secondary meaning.

There are a lot of names that use Mrs.—Mrs. Fields, Mrs. Winner's, Mrs. Richardson's, Mrs. Allison's, Mrs. Smith's, Mrs. Dash, Mrs. Baird's, Mrs. Butterworth's, Mrs. Lane's, and Mrs. Paul's.

Foreign names have been successfully used to endow a product with an exotic quality. Because the market is now global, these are becoming more common. The argument

coined word
An original and arbitrary combination of syllables forming a word. Extensively used for trademarks, such as PoFolks, Mazola, Gro-Pup, Zerone. (Opposite of a dictionary word.)

against creating foreign names may be the problem of pronunciation or remembering. However, foreign names are part of the global landscape: Toyota, Feni, Gianfranco Ferre, Corneliani, Lubiam, Bertolucci, Giorgia Brutini, Shiseido, Gucci, Volkswagen, Fila, Ferrari, and L'Aimant.

GEOGRAPHICAL NAMES   A geographical name is really a place name: Nashua blankets, Utica sheets, Pittsburgh paints, and Newport cigarettes. These names are old trademarks and have acquired secondary meaning. Often the word *brand* is offered after the geographical name. The law does not look with favor on giving one person or company the exclusive right to use a geographical name in connection with a new product, excluding others making similar goods in that area. However, if the name was chosen because of a fanciful connotation of a geographical setting rather than to suggest that the product was made there, it may be eligible for protection, as with Bali bras and Klondike ice cream bars.

Geographical names can be combined with dictionary words to create trademark names such as Atlanta Bread and Carolina Treat barbecue sauce. The options are many: Georgia Coffee, Texas Instruments, Texas Trails, New York Woman, Florida Queen, Newport Harbor, and Georgia-Pacific, Think of the number of businesses in your community using the city, county, or state name or a geographical region: mountains, coastal, piedmont, tidewater, lake, and so on—Piedmont Hospital, Mountain Man Museum, and Great South Catering.

INITIALS AND NUMBERS   Many fortunes and years have been spent in establishing trademarks such as IBM, IKEA furniture, RCA, GE, AC spark plugs, A&W root beer, J&B whiskey, A.1. steak sauce, and V8 vegetable juice. Hence, these are familiar. In general, however, initials and numbers are the most difficult form of trademark to remember and the easiest to confuse and imitate. How many of these sound familiar: STP, DKNY, S.O.S., AMF, SK, M.O.M.S., S.A.V.E., A.S.A., A&P, 6–12, or 666? There are also combinations of initials and numbers: WD-40 lubricant; numbers and words: 9-Lives cat food, 4 in 1, Formula 44, Formula 409, Formula 28, Formula 36, 4 Most; or dictionary words and initials: LA Gear. In 1949, Mr. Kihachiro Onitsuka began his athletic footwear company (Onitsuka Co., Ltd.) by manufacturing basketball shoes out of his living room in Kobe, Japan. He chose the name ASICS for his company in 1977, based on a famous Latin phrase *Anima Sana in Corpore Sano*, which when translated expresses the ancient ideal of "A Sound Mind in a Sound Body." Taking the acronym of this phrase, ASICS was founded on the belief that the best way to create a healthy and happy lifestyle is to promote total health and fitness.

PICTORIAL   Many advertisers use some artistic device, such as a distinctive lettering style or a design, insignia, or picture. The combination, as mentioned before, is called a logotype or logo. As you can see, names can be categorized into a number of different types and functions.

COLORS   Color is always a factor in ads, trademarks, and packaging. Lippincott, branding and naming experts, indicate blue is a color liked by both men and women, appears on many national flags, and has long associations with trust and stability. In determining a corporate color, blue is often the one color on which all can agree.[14]

THE SUCCESSFUL TRADEMARK

Whatever the form of a specific trademark, it will be successful only if it is distinctive and complements the manufacturer's product and image. As we mentioned earlier in this chapter, the trademark cannot be considered an isolated creative unit. In most cases, it must be adaptable to a package and certainly to other branding communications. It must also be adaptable to many different advertising campaigns, often over a period of many years. The longer a trademark is associated with a brand, the more people recognize it and the greater its value. People are familiar with the Home Depot

EXHIBIT 21.8

Home Depot Foundation Logo

Courtesy of Idea Engineering Inc. and Home Depot Foundation.

trademark, but how many are familiar with the Home Depot Foundation, which is a distinctive extension of the corporate brand (see Exhibit 21.8).

GLOBAL TRADEMARKS

4 **Explain general trademark rules.**

The federal registration of trademarks with the USPTO is not valid outside the United States. However, if you are a qualified owner of a trademark application pending before the USPTO or of a registration issued by the USPTO, you may seek registration in any of the countries that have joined the Madrid Protocol by filing a single application, called an "international application," with the International Bureau of the World Property Intellectual Organization, through the USPTO. Also, certain countries recognize a U.S. registration as the basis for filing an application to register a mark in those countries under international treaties.

GENERAL TRADEMARK RULES

Putting a lock on the ownership of a trademark requires taking the following steps:

1. Always be sure the trademark word is capitalized or set off in distinctive type: KLEENEX, *Kleenex*, **Kleenex**.

2. Always follow the trademark with the generic name of the product, or by using the word *brand* after the mark: Glad disposable trash bags, Kleenex tissues, Apple computers, Tabasco brand pepper sauce.

3. Do not speak of the trademark word in the plural; do not say "three Kleenexes" but rather, "three Kleenex tissues."

4. Do not use the trademark name in a possessive form, unless the trademark itself is possessive, such as Levi's jeans (do not say "Kleenex's new features" but rather "the new features of Kleenex tissues"), or as a verb (do not say "Kleenex your eyeglasses" but rather "wipe your eyeglasses with Kleenex tissues").

It is the advertising person's responsibility to carry out these legal strictures in the ads, although most large advertisers will have each ad checked for legal requirements including trademark protection. Exhibit 21.9 illustrates how a company uses an internal structure to protect their marks.

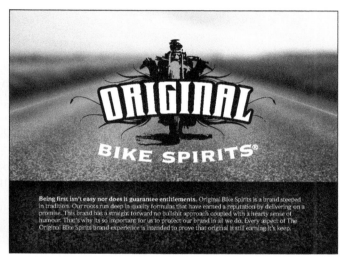

Courtesy of the Arras Group.

Companies should control how the trademark is used in writing ads and so forth. Many companies provide departments and units with written guidelines instructing the use of trademarks. For example, Original Bike Spirits brand guide says,

> **Being first isn't easy nor does it guarantee entitlements.** Original Bike Spirits is a brand steeped in tradition. Our roots run deep in quality formulas that have earned a reputation by delivering on a promise. This brand has a straight forward no bullshit approach coupled with a hearty sense of humour. That's why it's so important for us to protect our brand in all we do. Every aspect of the Original Bike Spirits brand experience is intended to prove that original is still earning its keep.

Kodak has a lengthy document outlining proper use of its trademarks, along with examples of incorrect use. This document includes trademark printing instructions for black-and-white and color use. Blockbuster Corporation warns its employees, "Always use the exact registration or trademark form." You should never change the word or design; never change the upper and lowercase letters; never change the colors; never change the plural or singular form; never add the word *the* to the word or design; never add a design to the word or vice versa; and never make the mark a possessive noun.

EXHIBIT 21.9

Original Bike Spirits has a branding use guide.

DuPont promotes the correct use of its Teflon trademark (see Exhibit 21.10). "Protecting the Teflon trademark is critical to the successful management of a very valuable asset. Improper use of the trademark, or allowing others to use it improperly, lowers its value and can ultimately turn a respected trademark into a common generic term."

EXHIBIT 21.10

Guidelines on the use of the Teflon trademark.

Rule 1: Show Registration.

Show registration status, by using the symbol "®" each and every time the trademark appears.

If there is no ® on a keyboard, as in some electronic mail systems, use parenthesis "R" parenthesis: (R). For countries where the registration symbol is not recognized, use an asterisk (*).

Acceptable	Unacceptable
Teflon® resin	No designation of registration status
Teflon(R) resin	
*Teflon** resin	Teflon resin

IMPORTANT: Regardless of whether "®", (R), or (*) is used, a footnote must be used at least once in each document. Examples of acceptable footnotes:

**Teflon* is a registered trademark of DuPont.

Teflon® is a registered trademark of DuPont for its fluoropolymer resins.

Rule 2: Be Distinctive.

Make the trademark distinctive from the surrounding text each and every time.

Acceptable	Unacceptable
Initial Cap: *Teflon*® resin	Any instance where the trademark is not distinguished from surrounding text, such as: "gaskets with teflon"
All Caps: TEFLON® resin	
Bold: **Teflon®** resin	
Italics: *Teflon*® resin	
Color: Teflon® resin	

Rule 3: Use Correct Generics.

Use the correct generic (common name) for the trademark at least once per package. Generic is the term for the class of goods for which the mark is registered.

Acceptable	Unacceptable
Teflon® resins	*Teflon*® president, *Teflon*® gasket, *Teflon*® cookware, *Teflon*® business
Other acceptable generics: films, fibers, finishes, fabric protector, fluoropolymer, fluoroadditive, micropowder, coating solutions, PTFE, PFA, FEP, ETFE	

NOTE: Although not generics, it is acceptable to refer to the *Teflon*® trademark and the *Teflon*® brand.

Rule 3: Use Correct Generics.

The trademark is the trademark. Don't embellish upon it!

Acceptable	Unacceptable
Wear resistance of *Teflon*®	**Possessives:** *Teflon*®'s wear resistance
Coatings of *Teflon*®	**Hyphens:** *Teflon*®-coated
Fabrics using *Teflon*® wear longer	**Line Breaks** Fabrics using *Teflon*® wear longer
Coat pans with *Teflon*®	**Verbs:** Teflon® your pans
Teflon®	**Coined Words:** *Teflon*® ized

Courtesy of DuPont.

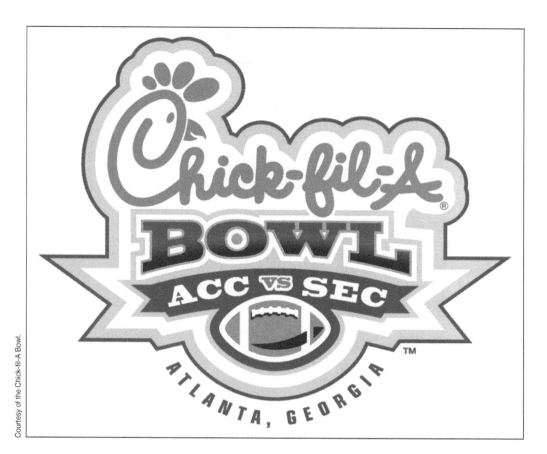

Courtesy of the Chick-fil-A Bowl.

EXHIBIT 21.11

The Chick-fil-A Bowl Game logo uses the "TM" symbol.

REGISTRATION NOTICE

Legal departments at some companies go to great lengths to protect their valuable trademarks. Some common ways of indicating trademark registration follow:

- The "®" symbol after the trademark as a superscript. Example: Mrs. Winner's®

- A footnote referenced by an asterisk in the text.
  Example: McDonald's*
  *A registered trademark of McDonald's Corporation.
  or
  *Reg. U.S. Pat. Tm. Off.
  or
  Registered in the U.S. Patent and Trademark Office.

- A notation of the registration in the text or as a footnote on the same page.

- If a trademark is repeated frequently in an ad, some firms require the registration notice only on the first use.

Most companies require notice of unregistered but claimed words and/or symbols as their trademark by using the "TM" symbol. The football sporting event named "Chick-fil-A Bowl" uses the "TM" symbol (see Exhibit 21.11).

House Marks

As mentioned earlier in this chapter, trademarks are used to identify specific products. However, many companies sell a number of products under several different trademarks. These companies often identify themselves with a **house mark** to denote the firm that produces these products. Kraft is a house mark, and its brand Miracle Whip is a trademark.

house mark
A primary mark of a business concern, usually used with the trademark of its products. General Mills is a house mark; Betty Crocker is a trademark; DuPont is a house mark; Teflon II is a trademark.

Service Marks and Certification Marks

A company that renders services, such as an insurance company, an airline, or even a weight-loss center, can protect its identification mark by registering it in Washington, DC, as a **service mark**. It is also possible to register certification marks, whereby a firm certifies that a user of its identifying device is doing so properly. Teflon is a material sold by DuPont to kitchenware makers for use in lining their pots and pans. Teflon is DuPont's registered trademark for its nonstick finish; Teflon II is DuPont's certification mark for cookware coated with Teflon that meets DuPont's standards. Advertisers of such products may use that mark. The Woolmark symbol (see Exhibit 21.12) is a registered trademark owned by The Woolmark Company. The Woolmark Company controls the use of its trademark by licensing manufacturers who are able to meet the strict performance criteria of the Woolmark program. The Woolmark is a symbol of quality, which denotes that the products concerned meet the specifications laid down by The Woolmark Company and will give the consumer satisfaction for the life of the product, given average wear and usage conditions.

EXHIBIT 21.12
Certification Mark

Company and Product Names

CORPORATE NAME CHANGES

Over the years, thousands of companies have undergone corporate name and identity changes. Corporations can spend millions of dollars to complete the process. Costs include hiring consultants; advertising; and changing logos and designs on such items as stationery, uniforms, trucks, and planes.

In 2001, Accenture spent $175 million to introduce its new name. It was formerly known as Anderson Consulting, a global management and technology consulting company. It hired Landor, a brand identity company owned by Young & Rubicam, to develop a name. They sifted through 5,500 potential options. The original list was pared

NAMING A CHICKEN SANDWICH

Atlanta-based Chick-fil-A® was founded by entrepreneur and restaurateur S. Truett Cathy. His chain has some 1,300 restaurants in 37 states and Washington, DC, generating annual sales of more than $2 billion. Naming a chicken sandwich seems easy but not so if you invented it. However, the development of the brand name—Chick-fil-A—is a prime example of how much thought and care Chick-fil-A founder Cathy put into developing the brand even before the first restaurant opened in 1967.

Having introduced the concept of the chicken sandwich to the restaurant industry, Cathy didn't have much of a point of reference for naming his new product. Originally wanting to trademark the sandwich itself, Cathy initially chose the name "Chicken Steak Sandwich," then "Chicken Steak Burger." Cathy was informed by a patent attorney that he would need to take a "dictionary word" and misspell it, "turn it upside down," to make it unique enough to be registered for a trademark.

Undaunted, Cathy began brainstorming. For him, the chicken fillet was representative of the best part of the chicken and the part he used in his chicken sandwich. Playing with that concept, Truett eventually settled on "Chick-fil-A." Even the capital "A" at the end of the word had significance for Cathy; to him, it represented top quality, sanitary conditions, and excellent service.

ADVANTAGE POINT 21.1

down to 550, then to 50, and then to 10 names. The name didn't actually originate with the brand identity company. An employee from Oslo, Norway, combined *accent* and *future*. It also contains a "greater than" sign (>) hanging over the *t* like an accent mark, but the consonant isn't pronounced differently.[15]

Miles Laboratories ran an ad stating, "After all these years, we think it's time you call us by our first name: Bayer. Today Miles becomes Bayer." The copy started: "You know us as Miles, one of America's largest companies. But in nearly 150 countries, our name is Bayer. Bayer is one of the biggest health care, chemical and imaging technology companies in the world. . . . You already know Bayer for aspirin."

THE PROCESS FOR DEVELOPING MEMORABLE NAMES

There probably isn't a single procedure everyone accepts for selecting names. Ruffell Meyer of Landor Associates says, "The misconception is that you have a couple of people sitting around over a pizza lunch. The first step is to meet with senior management to talk about the direction of the company, its values and image. Does it want to be known for speedy service? Later employees and customers may be included in the discussion."[16]

5 Explain the process for developing memorable names.

Once the information is gathered, the brand identity staff begins the name-generation and image-making processes. The tools are likely to include software packages that can morph word combinations. Landor has a database with more than 50,000 names. A typical list of possibilities can exceed a thousand names. Cingular, the result of the merger of SBC Communications and BellSouth Mobility (now part of AT&T), was created from a list of 6,000 names.

A basic legal search should be made of each name to see if someone else owns the rights to it. Before investing too much time and energy in developing a total identity program around a name, find out if someone else owns it. Naming consultants can refer you to patent attorneys who can conduct a preliminary screening of names registered in the United States. The cost is usually less than $100 per name. A more comprehensive U.S. trademark search typically costs more than $1,000 per name, so you may want to narrow your choice down to a couple of finalists before proceeding to that level.

Private trademark search firms will conduct searches for a fee. The USPTO cannot aid in the selection of a search firm. Search firms are often listed in the Yellow Pages section of telephone directories under the heading "Trademark Search Services" or "Patent and Trademark Search Services." This process reduces the possibilities by about 80 percent. You again analyze the remaining names against the objective and reduce them to a list of about a dozen or so. At this point, you would probably perform a linguistic analysis to determine what happens when the name is translated into foreign languages. Then you might test the names on consumers. You get the idea. Correctly done, the result is a memorable name that is adaptable to a number of advertising formats. Now let us look at the specific steps. First, pull together the basic information:

- *Describe what you are naming.* In your description, include key features and characteristics, competitive advantages, and anything else that differentiates your company, product, or service from the rest of the field.

- *Summarize what you want your name to do.* Should it suggest an important product characteristic (e.g., Blokrot for treated lumber) or convey a particular image (e.g., Pandora's Secrets for an expensive perfume)? Write down the characteristics and images you want your name to convey.

- *Describe whom you are targeting with the name.* Identify your targets and their demographic and lifestyle characteristics. Would they react more positively to a traditional, conservative name or to a liberal, flashy one? List the name qualities you think would appeal to them (name length, sound, and image).

- *List names that you like and dislike.* Try to come up with a few dozen current names in both categories (include your competitors' names). Note words and roots that might work for your new name and jot them down.

■ *Build a list of new name ideas.* Start with the list of names that you like and add to it by pulling ideas from a good thesaurus (e.g., *The Synonym Finder* by Jerome Rodale), a book of names (e.g., *The Trademark Register of the United States*), relevant trade journals, a book of root words (e.g., *Dictionary of English Word Roots* by Robert Smith), or other sources.

■ *Combine name parts and words.* Take words, syllables, and existing name parts and recombine them to form new names.

■ *Pick your favorites.* Select several names that meet all your criteria (just in case your top choice is unavailable or tests poorly).

Next, verify the name's availability and test your favorites:

■ *Conduct a trademark search.* As mentioned previously, before investing too much time and energy in developing a total identity program around a name, find out if anyone else owns it.

■ *Test your name before using it.* Regardless of how fond you are of the new name, others may have different opinions. Solicit reactions to your name from prospective customers, stockholders, and industry experts.

NAME OWNERSHIP   Conducting a trademark search wasn't enough to prevent problems for Cola-Cola's juice drink. They ran into a controversy with Fruitopia's name. Students at Miami University in Ohio came up with a total marketing plan, which included a product name, for a sparkling water and juice drink in development for the Minute Maid brand at Coca-Cola Foods Canada. When they presented it to Coca-Cola, Coca-Cola thought the name Fruitopia was very "iffy." The product rolled out in the United States in 1994 with the Fruitopia name; although there was no question about the legal rights of ownership—Coca-Cola had paid the university a fee for all the students' work—there was a question as to who developed the name. Coca-Cola said that a marketing group, working independently with its advertising agency, came up with the name. This is a reason most companies don't take unsolicited proposals for new products, ads, or product names. If Coca-Cola had not paid for the rights to the students' work, there could have been a legal battle for the name Fruitopia.

NAME ASSISTANCE   The naming of products may be developed by the advertiser or the advertising agency, working independently or together. There are companies and consultants that specialize in helping companies and agencies develop memorable names. Namestormers uses software to help develop product and company names, for example, CarMax (used-car dealer network), Pyramis (medical systems), AutoSource (auto parts network), Spider's Silk (lingerie), CareStream (health care company), and Wavemaker (notebook computer). Goldman & Young uses linguistic architecture to define image strategy and positioning, then creates names, for example, Polaroid Captiva, Nissan Pathfinder, Audi Avant, Clairol Whipsical, Honda Fourtrax ATV, Pep Boys PartsUSA, Pizza Hut QuickStix, Bristol-Myers Squibb Excedrin Migraine, Pfizer Zoloft, and GMC Yukon. Namelab, another company that develops names, used constructional linguistics to create the names Acura, Compaq, Geo, Lumina, and Zapmail. Then there are the large global brand identity companies that also develop names (Landor Associates, Interbrand, Lippincott Mercer, Identica, FutureBrand, etc.). Keep in mind that anyone in the process can create a name.

Packaging

Fully leveraging the power of company brands is contingent on the establishment of meaningful dialog with the customer. Solidifying customer relationships takes time and true marketing strategy. Clear, concise brand communications are an important part of

Courtesy of Arras Group.

EXHIBIT 21.13

Each product's label needs to be true to the brand.

this strategy and should be carefully designed into every product and every product's packaging.

Packaging presents an integral part of every company's brand communications to the customer. Since virtually every product and service in the marketplace is packaged, it is absolutely crucial that companies "get it right." Nothing communicates the brand and its values like packaging. At a time when products enjoy widespread distribution in multiple channels, packaging goes a long way to selling the product.[17]

Product packaging is the most important point-of-purchase merchandising tool. The average package on the supermarket shelf has only about one-seventeenth of a second to attract our attention. After that, the design, color, words, and . . . oh yes . . . the product itself have to interest us enough to put it in our cart and take it home. With the thousands of food products on the shelves, products need to get noticed; otherwise, they become just another fallen casualty in the fickle supermarket arena. The design of Original Bike Spirits individual products requires product labels that are true to the brand (see Exhibit 21.13).

How many times have you bought or almost bought a product simply because you liked the packaging? Some people will only buy milk in the clear plastic jugs instead of the opaque paper containers, even though the paper reduces the damage of nutrients from light. Packaging doesn't only focus on functional aspects such as versatility and food safety anymore. A great deal of the emphasis is directed purely to aesthetics. Revamping new products can be risky. If a product looks too different from before, companies may alienate loyal customers. For example, when Nestlé decided to change the packaging of KitKat candy from foil wrap to plastic, emotionally attached consumers protested the change, even though the new package would keep the product fresh three times longer.

THE PRODUCT PACKAGE

The product package is much more than a container. The package must be designed to take several factors into account. First, it must protect the package contents (see Exhibit 21.14); every other consideration is secondary to the function of the package as a utilitarian container. Second, the package must meet reasonable cost standards. Because the product package is a major expense for most firms, steps must be taken to hold down costs as much as possible.

Once these two requirements of package protection and cost are satisfied, we move to the marketing issues involved in packaging. These include adopting a package that is conducive to getting shelf space at the retail level. A unique package with

EXHIBIT 21.14

The TV commercial touts the milk jug's value of protecting flavor and vitamins.

strange dimensions, protruding extensions, or nonflat surfaces is going to be rejected by many retailers. A package must be easy to handle, store, and stack. It should not take up more shelf room than any other product in that section, as a pyramid-shaped bottle might. Odd shapes are suspect: Will they break easily? Tall packages are suspect: Will they keep falling over? The package should be soil resistant. Does it have ample and convenient space for marking? The product should come in the full range of sizes and packaging common to the field.

For products bought on inspection, such as men's shirts, the package needs transparent facing. The package can make the difference in whether a store stocks the item.

Small items are expected to be mounted on cards under plastic domes, called blister cards, to provide ease of handling and to prevent pilferage. Often these cards are mounted on a large board that can be hung on a wall, making profitable use of that space. Remember, the buyer working for the store judges how a product display will help the store, not the manufacturer.

Once we have considered the requirements of the retail trade, we can turn our attention to designing a container that is both practical and eye-catching. The package is, after all, the last chance to sell to the consumer and the most practical form of point-of-purchase advertising. Therefore, it should be designed to achieve maximum impact on the store shelf. Striving for distinctiveness is particularly critical in retail establishments, such as grocery stores, where the consumer is choosing from hundreds of competing brands.

CHANGING PACKAGE DESIGN AND MARKETING STRATEGIES

Design firms redesign packages to suit changing market strategies for existing consumer products and develop new packaging concepts for product introductions. In 1998, the Swiffer revolution began. Swiffer conveys speed and ease of cleaning, which translates into the same meaning around the globe. Today, there are numerous Swiffer products: Swiffer Wet, WetJet, Max, and Dusters. Procter & Gamble took great care in designing the packaging. The packaging had to attract attention and hold the different

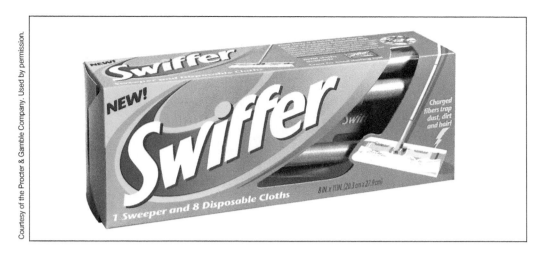

Courtesy of the Procter & Gamble Company. Used by permission.

EXHIBIT 21.15

Packaging for products must stand out on the store shelf to be effective.

content items (see Exhibit 21.15). Several trends in package design can be cited. One is the increasing tendency to use packaging to shore up store brands. Another is the use of sophisticated design approaches or unique packaging to establish the high quality of upscale, private-label brands. There has also been a shift from packaging that suits the convenience of the manufacturer to packaging that is "consumer friendly" in terms of opening, using, and reclosing. In short, package design is responding to a more sophisticated, discerning consumer.

PepsiCo Inc.'s Tropicana Products juice division dropped a new carton design only 6 weeks after rolling out the new package to great fanfare because customers complained that they couldn't differentiate between the company's pulp-free, traditional, and other types of juice. Consumers said that Tropicana's new packaging looked like a generic brand and deemphasized the type of juice inside. The company promised to return the old package design within a month. "We heard our consumers and we listened," Tropicana spokesperson Jamie Stein said.[18] Tropicana listened to their customers' dialogue.

PACKAGING AND MARKETING

At one time, the role of product packages was generally confined to protecting the product. Only the package label was linked with promotional activities. The Uneeda Biscuit package introduced in 1899 is generally considered to be the first that was used for promotion. However, few companies followed Uneeda's lead.

During the Depression of the 1930s, the role of packaging as a promotional tool changed dramatically. Most companies had limited advertising funds during this period so they resorted to using the package as an in-store means of promotion. So successful were their efforts that the role of packaging in the marketing mix became routinely accepted by manufacturers. Faced with a nagging decline in North American sales, Atlanta-based Coke and its bottlers are turning to packaging as a key way to set their products apart and try to generate fresh appeal. Packaging is viewed as a marketing tool. Hendrik Steckhan, head of carbonated soft-drink brands for Coca-Cola North America, admitted the shape of a 2-liter bottle is a problem. Coca-Cola should not be in the same 2-liter bottle as every other brand, he said. They tested and added the 2-liter contour bottle. Consumers will see more sizes and bundles of Coke products at supermarkets and convenience stores over time. The iconic contour shape also will become even more prominent. Here are some of the other planned packaging changes Coca-Cola is using to reach consumers:[19]

The 2-liter contour bottle uses the iconic contour shape. It is being rolled out nationally over several years.

The 50-ounce twin-packs are about 1.5 liters each. They can be shared by friends and families.

6 Discuss packaging and marketing.

ADVANTAGE POINT 21.2

ORIGINAL BIKE SPIRITS

Amrep, a large chemical company asked Costa Mesa–based The Arras Group to come up with a name, look, and marketing campaign for a line of motorcycle care products. The following is a brief outline of the Arras Group's plan.

Courtesy of The Arras Group.

KEY FACTS

- Amrep is introducing a new brand/short line of motorcycle care products.
- Honda is introducing their own full line of chemicals, including Spray Polish and Cleaner. However, they do not have the original chemical formula. We need to quickly assess the quality of the products they are introducing.
- We are expecting to have a 20 percent price advantage over the Honda product.
- We must build the Amrep business within and outside of the Honda dealer network.

TARGET AUDIENCE

We must understand and communicate how we uniquely satisfy the needs and wants of the target audience and then reach them with the right message, in the right way, at the right time and place to move them to the desired action (product purchase).

Dealers	Distributors
Principals	Tucker Rocky
Parts managers	Parts Unlimited
Consumers	Other distributors

OBJECTIVES

- To increase visibility and awareness of Original Bike Spirits (OBS) with key media and opinion leaders in the motorcycle industry
- To transfer the "Honda equity" to the OBS brand to drive business and increase sales
- To broaden OBS appeal to support non-Honda dealers and distribution

STRATEGIES

- Provide Amrep sales personnel and distributor sales personnel with compelling selling tools and training to support a fast launch and a sustained selling effort
- Promote aggressive, ongoing public relations outreach to key media and opinion leaders in the motorcycle industry
- Launch an exciting and effective advertising campaign targeting trade influences and consumers
- Use the power of merchandising to reach and move consumers at the point-of-sale
- Use key trade and consumer shows and events to allow consumer to experience OBS
- Help people to experience OBS products in action
- Reach grassroots enthusiasts

TACTICS

Following is the outline of our recommendations for the use of marketing communications tactics for maximum impact:

- Sales support
- Public relations
- Advertising
- Direct marketing

The 16-ounce bottle, at 99 cents, serves as an entry point when the 20-ounce bottle may be too big and pricey.

The 8.5-ounce aluminum bottle is offered in restaurants, clubs, and upscale hotels.

The package design for most products is developed in much the same way as an advertising campaign. Although each package is developed, designed, and promoted in a unique fashion, there are some common approaches to the successful use of packaging as a marketing tool.

■ Merchandising
- Sales Support
- Product information sheets (4)
  Use existing photography
  4C, 2-sided 8½ × 11
- Samples
  Product event sampling sizes
- Price sheet (1) for all 4 products
- Order form
- Scratch 'n sniff (concept for promotional activities)
- Trade show booth
- Public relations
  To increase visibility and awareness of OBS to key media and opinion leaders in the motorcycle industry, the public relations plan is an integral part of the strategy:
  To retain Honda dealers/customers and attract new dealers/customers, as well as convey the message that OBS is the same tried-and-true product that was previously packaged for Honda
  We are confident that Arras can effectively gain media exposure and valuable impressions in the industry about OBS

1. Public Relations Elements
   PRESS KIT
   - Background folder
   Press releases
   - Development, distribution, media contact
   FEATURE STORY
   - Development, pitching, facilitation
2. Show Participation
   INDY POWERSPORTS EXPO
   - The Indy Powersports Expo is the biggest trade event in the motorcycling industry. It is imperative that Amrep make a splash at this event with Original Bike Spirits. We can effectively reach industry opinion leaders, distributors, and dealers here.
   INTERNATIONAL MOTORCYCLE SHOWS
   - Show booth
   - Sampling/demo program
   - Show-and-shine sponsorship

- Event program ad (scratch 'n sniff?)
- Giveaways (helmet stickers, T-shirts, etc.)

3. Grassroots Program
   In keeping with the motorcycling culture, OBS needs to be where the bikers are. There are several great rallies across the country that make it possible to each consumers in large numbers. The rallies range from full-dress (think Honda Gold Wing), to cruiser, sport bike, and customized beauties, so they cover the range of OBS target demographics. Some of these events attract more than 50,000 motorcyclists. Motorcyclists are passionate and love to take care of their motorcycles. With several key components, OBS can form a lasting impression on our most important consumer . . . the motorcyclist.
   POSSIBLE EVENTS
   - Sturgis Motorcycle Rally—650,000
   - Daytona Bike Week—550,000
   - Laconia Motorcycle Week—400,000
   - Myrtle Beach Bike Week—300,000
   ELEMENTS
   - OBS advocates
   - Show-and-shine sponsorship
   - Sampling/demo
   - Event program ad
   - Advertising
     - TRADE ADVERTISING
       Ad size: full page, 4C; 6x buy
       Recommended publications:
       Motorcycle Product News
       Dealer News
       Power Sport Business
     - CONSUMER ADVERTISING
       Ad size: 1/3 page vertical, 4C; 6x buy
       Consumer media plan will focus on key national publications in several segments:
       - *On-Road*
       - *Rider*
       - *On/Off-Road*
       - *American Motorcyclist*
       - *Cycle News*
       - *Cycle World*
       - *Motorcyclist*
       - *American Iron*

1. *The type of product and function of the package.* Is the product extremely fragile? Do consumers use the product directly from the package? Are there special storage or shipping problems associated with the product?

2. *The type of marketing channels to be used for the product.* If the product is sold in a variety of outlets, will this require some special packaging considerations? Will the package be displayed in some special way at the retail level? Are there special point-of-purchase opportunities for the product?

3. *The prime prospects for the product.* Are adults, children, upper-income families, or young singles most likely to buy the product? What package style would be most appealing to the target market?

4. *Promotion and advertising for the product and its package.* Will the package be used to complement other promotional efforts? Are on-pack coupons or premiums being considered? Can standard package-design ideas be adapted to any special promotional efforts being considered?

5. *The relationship to other packages in a product line.* Will the product be sold in different sizes? Is the product part of a product line that is promoted together? Does the product line use the same brand name and packaging style?

6. *The typical consumer use of the product.* Will the package be stored for long periods in the home? Does the product require refrigeration or freezing? Are only portions of the product from the package used?

The answers to these and other questions can be obtained only through careful research. The package designer must strive for a balance between creativity and function.

PACKAGING AND COLOR

Advertisers are very much aware that colors work on people's subconscious mind and that each color produces a psychological reaction. Reactions to color can be pleasant or unpleasant. Color can inform consumers about the type of product inside the package and influence their perceptions of quality, value, and purity. Thus, color in packaging is an important tool in marketing communications. The Johnson Group designed a series of product packaging for a new Breakfast in a Bag (see Exhibit 21.16).

What kind of consumer perceptions would you encounter if you brewed the same coffee in a blue coffeepot, a yellow pot, a brown pot, and a red pot? Would the perceptions of the coffee be the same? Probably not. Studies indicate that coffee from the blue pot would be perceived as having a mild aroma, coffee from the yellow pot would be thought of as a weaker blend, the brown pot's coffee would be judged too strong, and the red pot's coffee would be perceived as rich and full-bodied.

Kodak is yellow. Fuji is green. United Parcel Service is brown. Home Depot is orange. Color has strong influence and should be considered carefully. Color is one of the main tools that package designers use to influence buying decisions. Consumer reactions to colors are emotional rather than intellectual. Because about 80 percent of

EXHIBIT 21.16

The line of Breakfast in a Bag products uses color to help distinguish one product from another.

Courtesy of The Johnson Group.

consumer choices are made in stores and 60 percent of those are impulse purchases, marketers must consider that package colors can play a major role in the success or failure of a product.

On your next shopping trip, see if you react the way most shoppers do to packages that use these colors:

- Red packaging (or a brand name that is bold and large) makes our hearts beat faster and increases our adrenalin flow. The color communicates power and vitality and stimulates a desire to conquer. Red also conveys a sense of structure, sensibility, practicality, and dependability. By retaining the red roof as an identifying symbol, Landor, branding consultants, helped reinforce the perception of Pizza Hut as a destination. To further differentiate the brand, a freehand typography was used along with an entire palette of icons that symbolized the freshness of its ingredients and ultimately provided Pizza Hut with the brand relevance it desired. It followed through on all the boxes and promotional material.

- Yellow is the most visible of all colors (which is why it is used on road signs) and makes packages look larger. Kodak is yellow. Yellow is also used to convey a cut-rate price image and, if not used properly, can detract from the perceived quality of the product.

- Blue implies cleanliness and purity and induces thoughts of sky and water. Often it conveys feelings of serenity, prestige, confidence, knowledge, and credibility. Think of how Tiffany's blue box has been burned into the consumer's mind.

- White makes us feel fresh and light and is often used on low-fat and diet foods. It is associated with dairy products (milk) and, hence, implies the ultimate in freshness and purity. In Germany, white suggests premium quality, but in England, white suggests budget quality.

- Black is always elegant and sophisticated, and manufacturers use this color to imply a sense of class and quality for their products.

PACKAGE RESEARCH

Extensive research should be done before packaging is developed to uncover the brand's chief assets. Although some assets are overt, others might be dormant, or remain uncovered. Consumer-based research into the brand experiences that impact perception and decision making should then be assessed. The ensuing package design solution can then honestly and directly communicate brand values and, hopefully, create an emotional connection with the consumer.

7 Discuss packaging and research.

Effective packaging is a vital part of marketing a product today. The only absolute in testing a package design is to sell it in a test-market setting. There are several aspects of assessing a package design, including recognition, imagery, structure, and behavior.

- *Recognition.* A package must attract attention to itself so that the consumer can easily identify it in the retail environment. The recognition properties of a package can be measured. Research can determine how long it takes a consumer to recognize the package and what elements are most memorable.

- *Imagery.* Although the package must be easily recognized, it also must project a brand image compatible with the corporate brand-imagery objectives. A package can reinforce advertising or it can negate it.

- *Structure.* The objective is to determine any structural problems consumers pinpoint that may inhibit repeat purchases. Is the package easy to open? Is it easy to close? Is it easy to handle? Is it easy to use?

- *Behavior.* Studying behavior can be the most expensive means of researching packages. Often this approach presents simulated shelf settings to groups of people and monitors whether they pick up or purchase a product.

PACKAGE DIFFERENTIATION

Twelve suburban women sit around a focus group table, psyching themselves up to talk about cat food for 2 hours. Through the course of the evening, only two things really perk them up: the chance to describe their cats and a vacuum-packed foil bag of cat food.

Even before they have examined the nuggets of cat food, most have said they would buy it, intrigued by its high-tech, bricklike bag, which they have come to expect to see in the coffee aisle, certainly, but never spotted before among the cans, boxes, and bags of pet food.

It is a point increasingly driven home to marketers of food, health and beauty product lines, and over-the-counter drugs: The package is the brand.

Marketers are paying more attention to package design because products are so much more at parity these days. When differentiation through taste, color, and other product elements has reached parity, packaging makes a critical difference.[20] A case in point is Pepsi-Cola's changing can designs to attract attention. In 2007, Pepsi decided to take a risk with its Pepsi can design. For 109 years, it fiercely guarded the packaging of Pepsi, but then it decided to create new can designs every 3 to 4 weeks. The new graphics are part of a broader new thematic campaign for Pepsi-Cola that emphasizes the brand's "fun, optimistic, and youthful spirit." Experts say they may risk confusing or alienating consumers who rely on visual cues to find the brand.[21]

BRAND IDENTITY

Brand identity involves a specific combination of visual and verbal elements that helps achieve the following attributes of a successful brand: create recognition; provide differentiation; shape the brand's imagery; link all brand communications to the brand; and—very important—be the proprietary, legal property of the company that owns the brand.

There are surprisingly few components that make up a brand identity. These include name logos, which are the designed versions of a name; symbols; other graphic devices; color; package configuration and permanent support messages—slogans and jingles. Brand identity companies work with an agency, a corporation, or both in developing packaging and may be involved with the total design concept of a corporation or a brand. For example, when you think of McDonald's Corporation—the hamburger people—what comes to mind? Golden arches? Employee uniforms? Cup designs? Paper or box designs? Logo? Paper bags? Premiums? Letterheads? Publications? There are many elements that help identify McDonald's, and every element has its name or logo for starters. The corporate design people help the marketer and sometimes the agency develop strong corporate visual communications.

PACKAGE DESIGN

A product's package is more than a necessary production expense. Therefore, much care needs to be given to the role of packaging in integrated marketing, relationship marketing with its emphasis on quality, and interactive media. In its promotional function, the package does everything a medium should. At the point of purchase, it alone informs, attracts, and reminds the consumer. At the point of use, it reinforces the purchase decision. Quality and value are viewed as relatively new marketing concepts, yet some 18 years ago the Design and Market Research Laboratory showed that quality perception was one of the key criteria for packaging assessment. But quality and value have always been part of the marketing and packaging equation.

Because packaging is such an important weapon in the marketing arsenal, it should be approached as other marketing elements with marketing research, specifically user research with target consumers. Blattner Digital client Zippo has many quality products. The product design is very much part of the package, but it also must be suitable for the web. Exhibit 21.17 shows the animation of an online storyboard.

Courtesy of Brunner Digital and Zippo.

EXHIBIT 21.17

The product design has to be considered in online treatment, if people need to recognize the brand.

Frank Tobolski, president of JTF Marketing/Studios, says research techniques measure the communication strengths and weaknesses of package graphics. They answer such questions as the following: Do the graphics communicate well? Do the graphics reinforce and enhance the image positioning? Do the products and package sell? He reports on a case in which a toy company developed new packaging for a line of products. Perceptual and imagery evaluation in diagnostic laboratory tests was performed, indicating some problems and potential negative sales effects. To obtain behavioral sales data, test quantities of packages were produced for a balanced store test. For 6 weeks during the Christmas season, 18 stores stocked the new test design, and 18 stocked the existing control design. Toy specialty, discount, department store, and mass merchandiser stores were used for the matched store pairings. The bottom line after 6 weeks found the existing control packages sold 63 percent more units than the test packages. Even after adjusting the test stores, the new designs sold 35 percent less.[22] Testing diverted a major loss in sales. Imagine the loss if there had been a full new-package rollout.

Today's packaged-goods marketing managers constantly face the critical task of justifying expenditures in terms of the potential ROI. Although most can instantly give you current sales figures, few know the yield on their latest shelf media or, specifically, packaging design.

Why? There is growing evidence that packaging design has a much stronger impact on sales than is realized.

As any brand manager will tell you, packaging represents a substantial portion of brand equity. When the word *Coke* is uttered, it is more than likely that an image of the trademarked, hourglass-shaped bottle comes to mind.

A Package Value survey suggests that marketers should benchmark new packaging proposals against their own brand equity. The study interviewed a total of 251 men and women, all primary grocery shoppers. Those polled were shown a card with a brand name printed on it and asked to rate the brand on a scale of 1 (agree strongly) to 5 (disagree strongly). Using "top box" methodology, only respondents who said they "agreed strongly" with all statements were included in the final results.

The subjects were then shown photos of actual packaging. The difference between the scores recorded when people were supplied with a brand name and when they were influenced by actual packaging is what makes the study intriguing. For example, when asked to rate the quality of Procter & Gamble's Tide, both the brand name and the packaging got scores of 61.[23]

FUTURE PREDICTIONS   Although predictions are just that, one can usually make an intelligent and reasoned guess about the future by relying largely on the past and current trends that are evolving. With that caveat, Landor's brand identity expert, Allen Adamson, predicts five directions that may influence the future of branding.[24]

1. Consumer perception of a product's performance controls its success. Because a brand represents a promise, one must ensure that the promise is fulfilled at each and every point of contact.

2. Customers interact with brands everywhere. Three-hundred-sixty-degree branding is here to stay. Purchase decisions are not made only at the point of sale so it is critical that you be in your customer's face with a consistent and coordinated expression of identity as often as is feasible.

3. Brands can stretch too far and the result can be jarring: erosion of brand equity. Most brands can probably be stretched into a plethora of categories. But often, brands become stronger when their scope is narrowed.

4. All marketing tactics should be undertaken within the context of a brand being a long-term asset. Partnering with competitors of nontraditional companies or products may enhance the brand's value, but choosing the wrong partner can cause substantial damage. Like people, brands are judged by the company they keep.[25]

5. The brand is the soul of the organization, and understanding its core values becomes the responsibility of everyone within the organization. Every point of contact (not only advertising and promotion) must be on-brand, and every individual within the organization should be charged with the responsibility of knowing exactly what that means.

Once a trend has been assimilated into the culture, it is no longer a trend.

Brands are long-term assets. As such, they need to be managed that way. Considering the future, looking at trends that are currently evolving can help better position brands over the long term. Creating value in tomorrow's brands requires a look at what is changing today.

Change is often subtle. It is rarely an all-of-a-sudden epiphany. Brand stewards must respond as they see trends evolving; they must be cognizant of changes in consumer thinking and observant to even slight changes in consumer behavior because even small changes, over time, can accumulate to become major trends. The challenge is in identifying the change as it is happening and adjusting your branding in concert with that change.

SUMMARY

Packaging is a very important part of the brand equity equation. It has been labeled as the only true method of international branding.

A product's trademark is like a person's name. It gives a product an identity and allows customers to be sure they are getting the same quality each time they purchase it. In addition, the trademark makes advertising and promotion activities possible. For established products, the trademark is one of the company's most valuable assets. It would be very difficult to estimate the value of trademarks such as Coca-Cola, Pepsi-Cola, IBM, and Mercedes. That is why companies take such pains to protect their trademarks.

The trademark can take the form of a word, a design, or a combination of both. Their formats can include letters, numbers, slogans, geometric shapes, color combinations, and so forth. When a trademark is a picture or other design, it is called a logotype. The same principle of trademark protection applies to logos as it does to brand names. Successful trademarks may take many forms; however, they should be easy to pronounce, have something in common with the product, and lend themselves to a variety of advertising and design formats.

The package design is developed in much the same way as an advertising campaign. At the point of purchase, it alone informs, attracts, and reminds the consumer. At the point of use, it reinforces the purchase decision. Packaging is an important marketing tool and should be researched with target groups. Brand identity continues to be an important issue.

REVIEW

1. What is a trademark?
2. What is a service mark?
3. How can you lose a trademark?
4. What are the steps to putting a lock on the ownership of a trademark?
5. Name several marketing issues involved in packaging.

CHAPTER 22

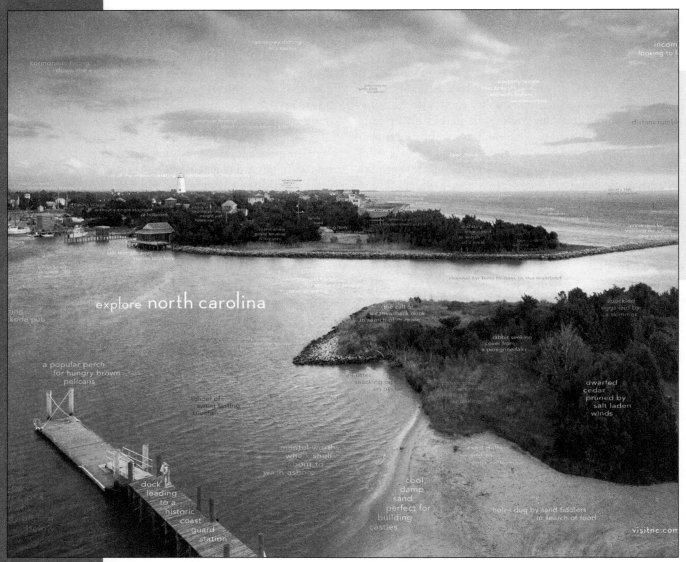

Courtesy of LKM-Loeffler Ketchum Mountjoy.

The Complete Campaign

TODAY'S ADVERTISERS usually create campaigns that fit into their integrated marketing communication program. They don't create only an ad by itself. ▶

CHAPTER LEARNING OBJECTIVES

1. **Define situation analysis.**
2. **Explain creative objectives and strategy.**
3. **Discuss media objectives and strategy.**
4. **Discuss sales promotion plans.**
5. **Explain research posttests.**

Advertising (a broad definition) may not be the first marketing tool used in an integrated marketing campaign for any brand. In Chapter 3, we focused on the premise that a brand is a living entity that is created through communication. It carries a history, which represents its accumulated capital, but it must continue to build new communication by asserting its presence, its sovereignty, and its territory. In doing so it must maintain a consistent identity. The four components (see Exhibit 22.1 as a refresher) are synthesized into an action plan for developing all communications for a brand (integrated marketing), including advertising, promotion, public relations, direct marketing, Internet, mobile, package design, buzz, and so on. There are a lot of options. Most advertisers and agencies view their marketing communications as "media neutral," meaning there won't be a bias toward using advertising or any other specific discipline as the main communication tool in order to receive a maximum return on investment. In some situations, traditional advertising may not be needed in the plan, or, at least it is not what drives the plan. Advertisers' main concern is reaching every consumer's "touch point."

Building a Campaign

In this chapter, we discuss how to specifically build advertising campaigns—*campaign* being defined by *Webster's* as a "series of planned actions."

You've learned about the important components of the advertising process—development of strategy, media, research, print ads, and broadcast—all of which are extremely important. We don't generally think in terms of individual ads because most brand advertising depends on a series of ads run over a period of time—in other words, the campaign.

A Campaign Versus ADs

Marketers should understand brands are rarely built overnight. Success may be measured in years or decades. Coca-Cola wasn't built in a year. BMW has been the ultimate driving machine for more than 30 years. We can't get there with a single ad. Maybe we

EXHIBIT 22.1

A planning process for building a strong brand equity in marketing communications plans.

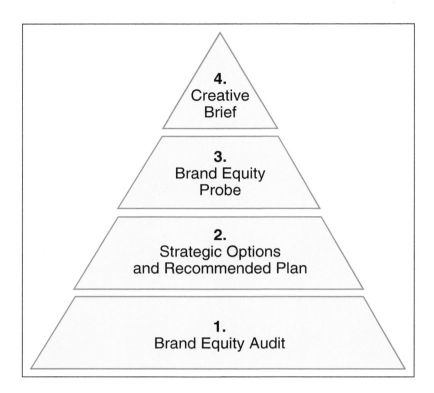

can get there with a strong campaign. More likely we depend on all the integrated communications from the company or brand to dovetail all other messages or impressions about the brand.

There is no magic time frame for a campaign. Yet, as a general rule, campaigns are designed to run over a longer period of time than an individual ad, although there are exceptions. The average length of a regional or national campaign is about 17 months, although it is not uncommon for a campaign to last 3 or 4 years, and a few campaigns have lasted much longer. Certainly, with new interactive capabilities to deliver messages (and efficient measurement), there may be many subcampaigns that may run shorter periods and be directed at "niches" or "mass niches." Remember, the new pioneering stage from Chapter 3.

In 1929, DuPont started using the campaign theme "Better Things for Better Living Through Chemistry." Fifty-five years later it was changed—"Through Chemistry" was dropped. That is building a lot of brand equity. Basically, the messages remained true to its original campaign premise. However, some campaigns need to change. Ford Truck Division dropped their "Ford Country" campaign after only 1 year and returned to its reliable "Built Ford Tough." The automaker's truck division decided that "Built Ford Tough" carried a punch similar to Chevy's "Like a Rock," and "Ford Country" hadn't been able to deliver. The point is that advertisers must understand their product and consumers in a changing marketplace. There is no reason to change an advertising campaign for the sake of change. Many marketing experts believe many advertisers give up on many campaigns too quickly.

Changing Campaigns Risk

There is never a guarantee that the next campaign will be as strong, let alone stronger, than the original. And some companies grope for a better campaign over and over again with little success. For example, in the mid-1970s, Burger King had perhaps its most famous campaign, "Have It Your Way," but decided it was time to change. So it followed with 16 or more different campaigns, looking for success, from "Aren't You Hungry for Burger King Now?" to "We Do It Like You Do It When We Do It at Burger King" to "Get Your Burger's Worth." In 2004, Burger King looked to the marketing— built around a revival of the chain's venerable "Have It Your Way" slogan—and a menu of new products for a much-needed turnaround. Russ Klein, Burger King CMO, says Burger King is no longer flipping marketing strategies as often as burgers— having had new marketing executives and campaigns almost annually for the past 8 years. He says, "This team is absolutely committed to the 'Have it Your Way' brand position and campaign."[1]

Ken Roman, former CEO of Ogilvy & Mather Worldwide, suggests that even the most successful campaigns need refreshing over time. People change, products change, markets change. There are times when campaigns simply wear out because market or competitive changes require a new message.[2]

Pepsi-Cola has been known for advertising to the "Pepsi Generation," but in the process different ad campaigns have been used to generate interest and success. Some are significantly different from previous ones, whereas others are simply tweaks in message or strategy:

Pepsi Generation Advertising Themes

1979 Catch the Pepsi Spirit

1982 Pepsi's Got Your Taste for Life

1984 Pepsi. The Choice of a New Generation

1989 A Generation Ahead

1995 Nothing Else Is Pepsi

1997 GeneratioNext

1999 The Joy of Cola

2000 The Joy of Pepsi

2003 Pepsi. It's the Cola

2007 It's the Cola.

2009 Refresh Everything.com (not officially changed from It's the Cola)

Remember in the advertising spiral in Chapter 3 we said that sometimes companies will try to expand targets with different kinds of promotional efforts. Snickers moved their campaign strategy from "hunger" to "satisfaction" because it is broader. The "Most Satisfying" campaign included television, viral, and outdoor. The television ad featured a troubadour who sang a Snickers ballad in a deadpan manner with an acoustic guitar. He was featured in the viral effort. The web was used as a conduit for devotees to create their own messages and write songs.[3]

Adding online advertising to a television campaign boosts brand awareness, but the inclusion does little to impact sales, according to a study by Dynamic Logic. Although broadcast ads upped the linking of a brand to a message or value proposition by nearly 13 points, the web added 7 points. Television spots increased the ability to influence purchase decisions by nearly 6 points, whereas the web only contributed a mere 0.4 point incremental boost. The web was stronger at raising awareness and association than influencing purchase decisions.[4]

Campaign Diversity

How would you as an advertiser handle diversity issues in a campaign? Separate campaigns for African Americans? Hispanics? Asians? What about for global products? This could become an issue.

In Chapter 4, we discussed targeting to different groups of people. In the 1980s and 1990s, advertisers began to be very conscious of using multiracial faces in their ads, if not targeting exclusively to a specific group—Asian, African American, Hispanic, and so on. Benetton, a global clothing chain, ads had a groundbreaking campaign in the 1980s highlighting models of many races, each one very distinct. Today, there are more than 7 million Americans who identify themselves as members of more than one race—the look of America has changed. Recently, the *New York Times* reported that among art directors and casting agents, there is a growing sense that the demand is weakening for traditional blond-haired, blue-eyed models. Many campaigns have purposely highlighted models with racially indeterminate features. The *New York Times* calls this "Generation E.A.: Ethnically Ambiguous." Any campaign needs to bring together all the advertising elements we have discussed into a unified whole. This calls for an advertising plan. As we have emphasized, good advertising starts with a clear understanding of both short- and long-term marketing goals. These goals are often expressed as sales or share-of-market objectives to be accomplished for a given budget and over a specific time period.

With our marketing goals in mind, we begin to build the advertising plan with a situation analysis.

Situation Analysis

1 Define situation analysis.

To plan and create future advertising, we need to establish a current benchmark or starting point—this is the role of the situation analysis. It has two time orientations: the past and the present. In other words, it asks two basic questions: Where are we today, and how did we get here? The rest of the advertising plan asks the third basic question: Where are we going in the future?

The situation analysis is the first step in developing a campaign. Exhibit 22.2 reminds us of the planning process discussed earlier in Chapter 3. There are strategic steps that must be taken in the planning process. Campaigns are planned; they don't simply happen.

THE PRODUCT

Successful advertising and marketing begin with a good product or service. At this point, we need to analyze our product's strengths and weaknesses objectively. Most product failures stem from an overly optimistic appraisal of a product. Among the questions usually asked are the following:

1. What are the unique consumer benefits the product will deliver?
2. What is the value of the product relative to the proposed price?
3. Are adequate distribution channels available?
4. Can quality control be maintained?

EXHIBIT 22.2

The Planning Cycle

EXHIBIT 22.3

These ads have a similar, but different, look and are obviously part of the same campaign.

BancorpSouth ads provide a sense that they all come from the same company. Each ad is different, but each looks like it is part of the same campaign. Take a look at the two ads in Exhibit 22.3.

PRIME-PROSPECT IDENTIFICATION

The next step is to identify our prime prospects and determine if there are enough of them to market the product profitably. As discussed in Chapter 4, there are a number of ways to identify the primary consumers of our product.

Who buys our product and what are their significant demographic and psychographic characteristics? Can we get a mental picture of the average consumer? Who are the heavy users of the product—the prime prospects? Remember the 80/20 rule; do we need to find those market segments that consume a disproportionate share of our product and determine what distinguishes them from the general population? Finally, we need to examine the prime-prospects' problem. What are their needs and wants in the product or product type?

COMPETITIVE ATMOSPHERE AND MARKETING CLIMATE

We carefully review every aspect of the competition, including direct and indirect competitors. Which specific brand and products compete with our brand, and in what product categories or subcategories do they belong? Is Mountain Dew's competition 7-Up or Sprite, Sun Drop or Crush, or does it extend to colas, iced teas, and milk? If so, to what extent in each case?

During the recession in 2009, Subway, which is the nation's largest restaurant chain, had tremendous growth with a promotion of $5 sandwiches. Because of its success, they made the promotion permanent for a handful of sandwiches. Their pitch to consumers was, "Five, five, five-dollar foot-long." They offered 12-inch sandwiches made right in front of you, just the way you like them, with any kind of bread, and as many toppings as you want. The promotion became the campaign. The success of this strategy became the yardstick for "specials" and sent McDonald's, Arby's, Quiznos, and others into the value mode. McDonald's billboards in some markets featured a Big Mac, fries, and a drink pointing to a full meal at $5.[5] Years ago, Taco Bell started the "Value Menu" in fast food.

Creative Objectives and Strategy

At this point, we begin to select those advertising themes and selling appeals that are most likely to move our prime prospects to action. As discussed in Chapter 16, advertising motivates people by appealing to their problems, desires, and goals—it is not creative if it does not sell. Once we establish the overall objectives of the copy, we are ready to implement the copy strategy by outlining how this creative plan will contribute to accomplishing our predetermined marketing goals:

1. Determine the specific claim that will be used in advertising copy. If there is more than one, the claims should be listed in order of priority.
2. Consider various advertising executions.
3. In the final stage of the creative process, develop the advertising copy and production.

CREATIVE CRITERIA FOR CAMPAIGNS

Most advertising experts agree on the need for similarity between one advertisement and another in developing successful advertising campaigns. Another term, *continuity*, is used to describe the relationship of one ad to another ad throughout a campaign. This similarity or continuity may be visual, verbal, aural, or attitudinal.[6]

VISUAL SIMILARITY   All print ads in a campaign should use the same typeface or virtually the same layout format so that consumers will learn to recognize the advertiser simply by glancing at the ads. This may entail making illustrations about the same size in ad after ad and/or the headline about the same length in each ad. A number of ads in campaigns have appeared throughout this book (e.g., Zippo, Chick-fil-A, Georgia tourism, Folks, Macon Symphony, Rusty Rooster Café, etc.). Each illustration in the Georgia tourism campaign (see Exhibit 22.4) ads is visually treated in the same manner, and there is a similar feel with the photographs, which occupy a similar location in each ad. The same with the "Macon. Discover it" campaign. For a different kind of client and reader, ads may use similar styles, but there is still definite continuity (see Exhibit 22.5). We have the same visual feel from ad to ad. We stress visual continuity—not sameness. These

EXHIBIT 22.4

An effective campaign presents the picture perfect idea and colors and great continuity from ad to ad.

Discover a flourishing panda population
8,600 miles from China.

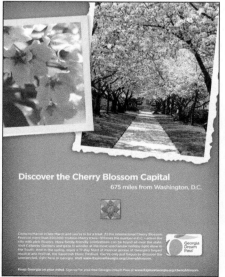

Discover the Cherry Blossom Capital
675 miles from Washington, D.C.

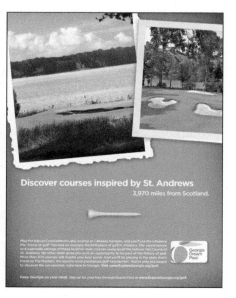

Discover courses inspired by St. Andrews
3,970 miles from Scotland.

Megan Jean Sovern Copywriter,
Goodby, Silverstein & Partners, San Francisco

CAN ART EXIST IN ADVERTISING?

Megan Jean Sovern

Only If You Sneak It in While No One's Looking

My sophomore year in college I did what no parent wants their child to do. I became a poetry major. My mother disowned me, my father turned to the bottle, and then I made a compromise. I declared advertising as my second major and convinced myself I could be a poet in copywriter clothing. And now as a copywriter at Goodby, Silverstein & Partners, I'm still hoping no one finds me out. I keep my poetry books hidden between advertising annuals in my office. And I only wear my beret and drink lattes in the safety of my own home. Is it hard living a double life? Sometimes. But I'm not alone. There are other writers, painters, musicians, and filmmakers doing the same thing. Here's how we (and maybe one day, you) can bring art into advertising.

1. **Know when the time is right OR ELSE.** Not every assignment is an opportunity to "change the world." For example if you try to introduce poetry into a web banner for a financial institution, the conversation will go something like this. Poetry will say, "Hello, I'm poetry and I want to make you beautiful." And the web banner will say, "Shut the hell up. Just tell me if we have free checking." You will be humiliated. And your creative director will tell you not to come out of your office until you've thought about what you've done. But if you're given the chance to create a new campaign for a candy company founded on puns and smart characters with smart dialog, then by all means get on with your bad artistic self.
2. **Know your audience and hug them 'til it hurts.** Men looking for a beer that's great tasting and less filling are not receptive to poetry. Well,

maybe some are, but they're very secretive about it. But don't let that discourage you. Audiences far and wide are looking to connect with something. And they least expect it to be an ad.

Nike brought aspiring athletes a hero by sculpting Michael Jordan into a modern-day David. His voice stands as strong as his figure and people chant his name not only in worship but also in hopes that one day a crowd will chant their own. And they aren't the only ones. Housewives needing appreciation, environmentalists searching for progress, college students looking to lead the culture of cool all need voices and we represent them.

Yes, we sell stuff, but we also have a social responsibility. You're given 30 seconds and an 8½ × 11 sheet of paper, to make an impact, not only on sales numbers but also on your audience. Will they remember your work? Will they feverishly tear out your ad and tape it to a wall? Will they love your work so much they want to become involved in the brand? I hope so because when this happens art has collided with advertising and there's no turning back.

3. **To make artful ads, you must fill the well with art, not ads.** Ad people make the fatal mistake of looking at ads to find inspiration. DO NOT DO THIS. Ad annuals are great for seeing what else is out there. And they make incredible bookends. But they don't hold the answers you're looking for when beginning an assignment. If anything, they will simply piss you off. If you need help getting started, go to the movies. Pay attention to where people laugh, gasp, or

cry. Also mind the parts where they get up and go to the bathroom. Read a book, magazine, or bathroom stall. A professor told me once to read the *New York Times* every Sunday and I try. And if I don't, I leave it on my coffee table so I look incredibly smart when guests are over. You should do the same.

If you're an artist, look to other artists to elevate your thinking. I read more than I write and I'm a stronger writer for it. By studying how other writers use their voices, I've learned how to raise my own.

You're carving out a style, a niche, a something no one else can replace or copy. You're weaving your art into your career and people will want to marry you because you're smart and original and rich. Trust me.

And, well, I guess if I have any other advice, it's to not get too caught up in this great big ad world. Art isn't created under the pressure of deadlines and creative directors. It surfaces when you least expect it. So don't stare at a screen for hours on end. Start with a canvas, a blank page, a note, or a scene. Then open your secret drawer, get out that beret, and create something that will scare your parents. Because it's really about freaking out your parents. Ultimately it always is.

Courtesy Megan Jean Sovern.

I discovered rock 'n' roll.

Leah Yetter, a local photographer, found a whole lot of soul at the Georgia Music Hall of Fame. Just point, click and smile as you explore local interests and make new connections at www.discovermacon.org. The resourceful new website is your expert interactive guide to Macon's community services, organizations and events.

What have you discovered lately? Send us your personal photos, videos and stories about Macon. For inspiration and ideas, find more than you were searching for at www.discovermacon.org.

Macon
Discover it.   www.discovermacon.org

I found my balance.

Ballet teacher Pammie Jimmar keeps kids on their toes in the Bibb County after-school program. You can explore local interests and make new connections at www.discovermacon.org. The resourceful new website is your expert interactive guide to Macon's community services, organizations and events.

What have you discovered lately? Send us your personal photos, videos and stories about Macon. For inspiration and ideas, find more than you were searching for at www.discovermacon.org.

Macon
Discover it.   www.discovermacon.org

I found a sweet spot.

Young executive Jamie Weatherford continues his family's legacy at Crown Candy. You can explore local interests and make new connections at www.discovermacon.org. The resourceful new website is your expert interactive guide to Macon's community services, organizations and events.

What have you discovered lately? Send us your personal photos, videos and stories about Macon. For inspiration and ideas, find more than you were searching for at www.discovermacon.org.

Macon
Discover it.   www.discovermacon.org

(a–c)Courtesy of Bright Ideas; (d–e). Courtesy Adler Chomsky & Warshavsky (Grey Israel) and Delonghi

EXHIBIT 22.5

These ads have a lot of continuity.

examples pertain to print, but the look could easily be carried over to television or direct marketing (see Exhibit 22.6). Strong continuity from medium to medium can strengthen the communication. This also applies to all the elements of integrated communications (promotions, the web, etc.).

Another device is for all ads in a campaign to use the same spokesperson or continuing character in ad after ad. Still another way to achieve visual continuity is to use the same demonstration in ad after ad from one medium to the other. UPS has used the same brown as a way to keep a little continuity.

VERBAL SIMILARITY   It is not unusual for a campaign to use certain words or phrases in each ad to sum up the product's benefits. It is more than a catchy phrase. The proper objective is a set of words that illuminates the advertising and encapsulates the promise that can be associated with one brand only. UPS not only uses the "brown" trucks and uniforms since 1920 but also everyone knows "What brown can do for you." Chevy trucks used "Like a Rock," for more than a dozen years.

Here are a few campaign phrases that have worked:

Mmm mm good.

CAMPBELL'S

The ultimate driving machine.

BMW

EXHIBIT 22.6

There is continuity from one interactive animation to another.

We'll leave a light on for you.

MOTEL 6

Good to the last drop.

MAXWELL HOUSE

Imagination at work.

GE

Pepsi used the words "You're in the Pepsi Generation" to help position it among a younger audience and make Coca-Cola appear to be an old-fashioned brand. But it didn't limit all the upbeat, self-assuring benefits of membership of being part of the Pepsi Generation to people between 13 and 24 years of age; it opened it up to everybody— everybody wanted to be in the Pepsi Generation. It wasn't a point of time in years; it was a point of view. No matter what your age, you could be part of the Pepsi Generation. Today they don't use the same words, but the feeling they are trying to achieve is very similar. In the mid-1970s, Federal Express started their package delivery business. Their tagline (and brand promise) expressed exactly why they were in business, "When it absolutely, positively has to be there overnight.[7]" Great words and great strategy make great campaigns. Here are a few other words and classic campaign strategies:

> **Aren't you glad you use Dial? Don't you wish everybody did?**
> **You're in good hands with Allstate.**
> **American Express. Don't leave home without it.**
> **Have it your way at Burger King.**
> **Is it true blondes have more fun? Be a Lady Clairol blonde and see!**
> **You deserve a break today, at McDonald's.**
> **Nike. Just do it.**

Repeating the benefits, theme, and key copy points in ad after ad bestows continuity across all media and helps to build brand personality.

EXHIBIT 22.7

Each of these ads is introducing a new restaurant and each says so. They also use a lot of continuity so readers can begin recognizing their ads.

We have shown a number of the Rusty Rooster ads earlier in this text to give you a real taste of its campaign. These ads introduce a new restaurant and say so. Ads also use visual, verbal, and attitudinal similarity (see Exhibit 22.7).

Campaigns need to be flexible so they can carry from ad to ad. Baby Gap used a verbal concept that could be endless. Here are a few examples:

Baby Gap is gift.

Baby Gap is newborn. A, B, C

Baby Gap is spring.

AURAL SIMILARITY   You can create aural continuity in broadcast, if you desire. You may use the same music or jingle in commercial after commercial. Using the same announcer's voice in each ad also helps build continuity—a classic is "This is Tom Bodett for Motel 6." The same sound effect can make a campaign very distinctive. Avon used the sound of a doorbell for many years in its "Avon Calling" advertising. Maxwell House used the perking sound for its Master Blend commercials, giving an audible campaign signal. Mazda simply used Zoom Zoom!

ATTITUDINAL SIMILARITY Some campaigns have no theme line that continues from ad to ad. What they do have is an attitude that continues from ad to ad. Each ad expresses a consistent attitude toward the product and the people using it. The commercial's attitude is an expression of brand personality. The "Pepsi Generation" campaign was more than words. It communicated an attitude to younger consumers and older consumers. We cannot leave out the Nike shoe campaign that said, "Just Do It"—or its swoosh campaign.

Everyone agrees that Nike is one of the strongest brand names in the world and not only because it sells great products. Its presence and identity are so strong that many people want to connect with the brand. It signifies status, glamour, competitive edge, and the myriad intricacies of cool. It is this description that is communicated in every message, no matter to whom it is directed. Nike's secret of success resides along a delicate and emotionally charged progression that connects the company, the consumers, and the abiding fantasies that are tethered to sports.[8] In true integrated marketing fashion, its personality is communicated to all—from employees, to stockholders, to consumers. It is conveyed through its corporate culture, as well as through its advertising.

Defining an attitude doesn't have to exclude visual or verbal continuity. The Georgia Film, Music & Digital Entertainment Office today has visual continuity (see Exhibit 22.8) for ads aimed at a niche market.

Media Objectives

Although we have chosen to discuss creative strategy before media objectives, both functions are considered simultaneously in an advertising campaign. Creative planning

EXHIBIT 22.8

These ads were aimed at the film, music, and entertainment industries.

3 **Discuss media objectives and strategy.**

and media planning has the same foundations—marketing strategy and prospect identification—and they cannot be isolated from each other. Media attempts to be "media neutral." The media plan involves three primary areas: strategy, tactics, and scheduling.

MEDIA STRATEGY

At the initial stages of media planning, the general approach and role of media in the finished campaign are determined:

1. *Prospect identification.* The prime prospect is of major importance in both the media and the creative strategy. However, the media planner has the additional burden of identifying prospects. The media strategy must match prospects for a product with users of specific media—both traditional and alternative. This requires that prospects be identified in terms that are compatible with traditional media audience breakdowns.

2. *Timing.* All media, with the possible exception of direct mail, operate on their own schedule, not that of advertisers. The media planner must consider many aspects of timing, including media closing dates, production time required for ads and commercials, campaign length, and the number of exposures desired during the product-purchase cycle.

3. *Creative considerations.* The media and creative teams must accommodate each other. The creative team must know where the ads or messages will go. Media has to be creative in finding a way to reach and engage consumers.

MEDIA TACTICS

At this point, the media planner decides on media vehicles and the advertising weight each is to receive. The question of reach versus frequency may be addressed and appropriate budget allocations made. And media needs to be creative in their efforts. Remember the wedding crashers that dropped cards in the gift boxes? Healthtex supported Kohls with the ads shown in Exhibit 22.9.

MEDIA SCHEDULING

Finally, an actual media schedule and justification are developed, as described in the example in Chapter 7.

THE PROMOTION PLAN

4 Discuss sales promotion plans.

As with any integrated communications planning, the promotion plan for consumers is discussed very early, and its relationship to the advertising plan (and other communications activities) is determined. Promotion activities may involve dealer displays, in-store promotions, premiums, cooperative advertising, and coupon offers.

EXHIBIT 22.9

These ads are mobile.

Courtesy of Trone.

Once a theme for communications has been established, creative work is begun on the promotion material, which is presented along with the consumer advertising material for final approval. Naturally, advertising and promotion materials reinforce each other. Once the promotion material is approved, the production is carefully planned so that all the promotion material will be ready before the consumer advertising breaks.

Other Integrated Elements

Recently Mountain Dew slashed its media budget significantly. It increased its investment in branding subcultures such as action sports (the Dew Tour), *indie* music, and video games. The main focus for Mountain Dew was finding ways to bring the brand to life that go beyond the classic notion of reach and relevance, that is, 30-second spots.[9]

Don't forget the importance of every aspect of your IMC functioning as one voice. You need to maintain focus on the brand or positioning throughout the marketing mix. Toyota introduced its Yaris to 18 to 34 year olds through a lot of platforms hoping 30 percent of the buyers would be younger than 30. To reach the younger audience, the marketer had to make sure the Yaris was everywhere these consumers spent time. Instead of portraying who would be driving it, the communications always featured the car front and center. The media plan was basically a screen-based plan. They launched it over mobile phone service, with 26 episodes of *Prison Break* available to Sprint customers; each 2-minute "mobisode" was preceded by a 10-second ad. Later ads appeared on the web with a contest of consumer-generated commercials, a profile on MySpace.com, a custom community on Facebook.com, video games, and integration of the product into FOX's comedy show *MadTV* through a series of sketches. The target does consume mass media; they just don't consume it in a broad-scale sense.[10] This was a creative media plan involving a series of integrated messages.

So the range of IMC is endless and should be seamless. With packaging, remember Tiffany's blue box—a symbol of luxury. And brand characters may become brand icons and be a part of the program: Ronald McDonald, Wendy, the Exxon Tiger, Jack of Jack-in-the-Box, the Pillsbury Doughboy, and AFLAC's duck. Don't forget endorsers or spokespersons. Every piece of marketing communication can be integrated, including every piece of your web effort.

Getting the Campaign Approved

We now have a complete campaign: the ads, the media schedule, sales promotion material, and costs for everything spelled out, ready for management's final approval. For that approval, it is wise to present a statement of the company's marketing goals. The objectives may be to launch a new product, to increase sales by x percent, to raise the firm's share of the market by z percent, or to promote a specific service of a firm. Next, the philosophy and strategy of the advertising are described, together with the reasons for believing that the proposed plan will help attain those objectives. Not until then are the ads or the commercials presented, along with the media proposal and the plans for coordinating the entire effort with that of the sales department.

What are the reasons for each recommendation in the program? On what basis were these dollar figures calculated? On what research were any decisions based? What were the results of preliminary tests, if any? What is the competition doing? What alternatives were considered? What is the total cost? Finally, how may the entire program contribute to the company's return on its investment? Those people who control the corporate purse strings like to have definite answers to such questions before they approve a total advertising program.

Research—Posttests

5 **Explain research posttests.**

The final part of the campaign entails testing its success. Posttesting falls into two related stages. In the first, the expected results are defined in specific and measurable terms. What do we expect the advertising campaign to accomplish? Typical goals of a campaign are to increase brand awareness by 10 percent or improve advertising recall by 25 percent.

In the second stage, the actual research is conducted to see if these goals were met. In the case of some interactive ads we have almost instant metrics. Regardless of what research technique is used (e.g., test markets, consumer panels, etc.), the problem is separating the results of the advertising campaign from consumer behavior that would have occurred in any case. That is, if we find that 20 percent of the population recognizes our brand at the end of a campaign, the question arises as to what the recognition level would have been if no advertising took place. To answer this question, a research design is often used as a pretest. The pretest is intended not only to provide a benchmark for the campaign but also to determine reasonable goals for future advertising.

CAMPAIGN PORTFOLIO

CENTURY FURNITURE   Furniture ads can only show several pieces of furniture in an ad. How many furniture ads have you seen without furniture peering at you? Not many, I bet. This campaign throws out a lot of "endless possibilities" and "unlimited attention." Driving readers to CenturyFurniture.com. Exhibit 22.10 shows two of the campaign ads.

EXHIBIT 22.10

The dramatic photos and verbal treatment helps communicate verbal benefits.

APPALACHIAN STOVE COMPANY   The Appalachian Stove Company campaign is highly visual, but its humorous copy is large enough to attract readership and lead the eye to the product (see Exhibit 22.11).

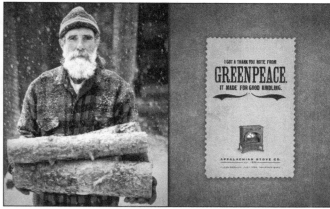

EXHIBIT 22.11

Each of these clever large illustrations and heads attract attention to the stove.

Courtesy of Blattner Brunner.

SUMMARY

The steps in preparing a national campaign for a consumer product are the following:

1 Situation analysis
  a. Product analysis
  b. Prime-prospect identification
  c. Prime-prospects' problem analysis
  d. Competitive atmosphere and market climate

2 Creative objectives and strategy
  a. Determination of specific copy claims
  b. Consideration of various advertising executions
  c. Creation of ads and commercials (and other integrated communications)

3 Media objectives
  a. Media strategy—includes prospect identification, timing, and creative considerations
  b. Media tactics
  c. Media scheduling

4 Promotion plan (and/or other integrated programs)

5 Campaign approval

6 Research posttests

In general, advertising campaigns need to have similarity from ad to ad. It may be visual, verbal, aural, or attitudinal. Campaigns should be designed to last and not be changed simply because you are bored with them.

REVIEW

1. What is the basic purpose of an ad campaign?
2. What is ad continuity?
3. What is involved in the situation analysis?

4. What are some of the means of guaranteeing continuity in a campaign?

Orlando/Orange County Convention and Visitor's Bureau, Inc.: They Use the Symbol in Their Promotions and Logo, "Orlando Makes Me Smile"

BACKGROUND

The home of Walt Disney World Resort; Universal Orlando Resort; SeaWorld Orlando; and world-class golf courses, shopping, and resorts, Orlando is one of the top travel destinations in the world and is famed for its many attractions and sunny Florida weather. Tourism is Orlando's leading industry, with approximately 50 million visitors annually and an economic impact of $29.6 billion.

In 1984, the Orlando/Orange County Convention and Visitors Bureau, Inc. (Orlando CVB) was formed as a private, not-for-profit corporation dedicated to promoting the area as one of the world's premier leisure, convention, and business destinations.

Since its inception, the Orlando CVB has seen Orlando grow and thrive from a one-time city of orange groves with a bright future to a renowned vacation kingdom for adults and families and one of the largest convention locations in the country. As a result of the continuous efforts of the Orlando CVB, Orlando continues to top the charts for travelers worldwide.

OBJECTIVE

Research commissioned by the Orlando CVB in 2008 revealed the need to create an overall positioning strategy for Orlando that focused on the personal connections created and the emotions travelers experienced when visiting the destination.

The Orlando CVB partnered with Push, an advertising, branding, and interactive agency based in Orlando, to create an advertising strategy and creative execution to support the new relationship-centric brand positioning termed "Where Relationships Thrive."

By focusing on the different kinds of relationships between travelers, the Orlando CVB hoped to encourage perceptions of and an increase awareness of Orlando as more than simply a family destination. The plan was to expand its reach to include pre- and postfamilies (such as couples and empty-nesters) in the leisure segment, as well as business travelers, thus showcasing an experience that could be enjoyed by everyone.

According to research conducted by Meredith Corporation Travel Marketing Group, 70 percent of women are key decision makers in travel plans, and four out of five women say a vacation where they travel at least 50 miles from home is a "must have." Based on these facts, women were a main target for the Orlando CVB. Specifically, the campaign's target consumer audience consisted of women, aged 25 to 54, living east of the Mississippi, with a household income of more than $75,000.

BRAND STRATEGY

Push, tasked with developing strategy and creative for the Orlando CVB, turned to the most indicative symbol of the joy one experiences from a thriving relationship—a smile.

The resulting campaign, "Orlando Makes Me Smile," was created to serve as more than simply a tagline; it was to be a timeless statement for Orlando. The personalization of the statement with the word choice of "me" rather than "you" allowed for a greater first-person connection with consumers.

When it came down to developing the campaign into creative executions, Push found inspiration from a surprising source: Mark Twain.

The infamous American author once said, "Wrinkles should merely indicate where smiles have been." Push's chief creative officer, Chris Robb, saw an instant connection for Orlando's new campaign and realized a direction for the creative through a literal interpretation of Twain's famous words.

As a campaign about relationships, "Orlando Makes Me Smile" features images of individuals on their own or with others, each one with a smile on his or her face. Their smiles, and the wrinkles or dimples resulting from them, tell stories of wonderful experiences in Orlando. Each joyful expression is connected to a specific statement about why that person is so happy.

For example, one of the initial print advertisements featuring a young girl lists a number of popular theme park attractions to explain one side of her smile, and on the other side, just one note of great importance . . . a spa day with her mom. Such

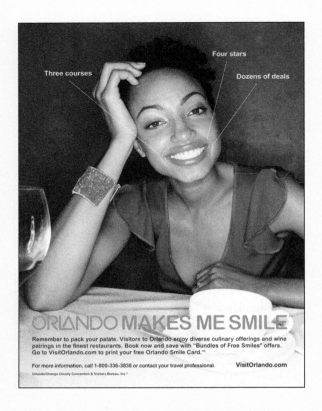

Three courses

Four stars

Dozens of deals

ORLANDO MAKES ME SMILE

Remember to pack your palate. Visitors to Orlando enjoy diverse culinary offerings and wine pairings in the finest restaurants. Book now and save with "Bundles of Free Smiles" offers. Go to VisitOrlando.com to print your free Orlando Smile Card.™

For more information, call 1-800-336-3836 or contact your travel professional.   VisitOrlando.com

Orlando/Orange County Convention & Visitors Bureau, Inc.®

emotional connections are key to the campaign, which is targeted toward women who, as major household decision makers, are the ultimate travel planners.

IMPLEMENTATION

"Orlando Makes Me Smile" officially rolled out on one of the most joyous nights of the year, New Year's Eve 2008, when the campaign was featured for thousands to see on a giant jumbotron screen at Boston's famous "First Night" celebratory event. Concurrently, it went on display in New York's Times Square on a digital outdoor board.

At the start of 2009, a fully integrated plan launched, comprised of co-op magazine, co-op TV, print and interactive online display advertisements, promotions, online marketing, branding of the Orlando CVB web site, publicity initiatives, and cooperative partnerships.

To reach the target audience of women, "Orlando Makes Me Smile" ads ran in popular magazines for the demographic such as *Better Homes and Gardens*, *Ladies Home Journal*, and *Budget Travel*.

Understanding how the U.S. economy affects travel decisions, the Orlando CVB took advantage of the many values the destination has to offer and worked with Push to create a "Bundles of Free Smiles" promotion connected to the campaign. By simply downloading an Orlando Smile Card from the campaign's consumer online splash page, visitors were treated to numerous destination-wide offers, from free hotel night stays to kids eat free programs, free special events, and more. The dedicated "Orlando Makes Me Smile" splash page, which is a microsite on VisitOrlando.com, also featured special campaign-related content to assist visitors in planning an affordable vacation, including information on free and inexpensive activities, a searchable database of affordable places to stay, and an events calendar that highlighted events throughout Central Florida.

RESULTS

Although still a relatively new campaign at the time this case study was composed, significant results have been seen in a short period of time. Not only awareness of, but also interest in, Orlando as a destination has grown—all in only a 4-month period.

The Orlando CVB's web site, which features "Orlando Makes Me Smile" branding, surpassed its unique visitors goal by more than 16 percent. When evaluating its unique visitors month over month, comparing the same time period in 2009 versus that before the campaign in 2008, the increase of unique visitors was more than 27 percent.

Tens of thousands of Orlando Smile Cards have been downloaded, and even more web site–related offers have been printed.

More than 150 of Orlando CVB member companies and organizations participated in the program through related advertising and promotions. As a direct result of their participation, these members received nearly 50,000 more click-throughs from the "Orlando Makes Me Smile" splash page.

With the successful domestic launch of "Orlando Makes Me Smile," the Orlando CVB decided to take the campaign beyond borders throughout the rest of 2009 to reach potential visitors from Brazil, the UK, Ireland, and Canada.

Courtesy of PUSH and the Orlando/Orange County Convention & Visitors Bureau, Inc.

Smokey Bones Bar & Fire Grill

BACKGROUND

Smokey Bones Bar & Fire Grill first opened its doors as Smokey Bones BBQ & Grill in 2000. Darden Restaurants, which owns and operates large brands such as Olive Garden and Red Lobster, launched Smokey Bones with the goal of creating a national barbeque chain.

After 8 years of building and expanding Smokey Bones, Darden Restaurants sold the brand to Sun Capital Partners, a private-equity firm with a restaurant portfolio including Boston Market and Sweet Tomatoes. At the time, Smokey Bones was seeing declining traffic and sales, and Sun Capital Partners wanted to breathe new life into the brand.

INSIGHT AND CHALLENGE

Following the sale from Darden Restaurants to Sun Capital Partners, Smokey Bones searched for an agency to help increase its sales. It hired Orlando-based advertising, branding, and interactive agency, Push, as its agency of record.

Through experiential research, it was determined that Smokey Bones's log cabin theme did not resonate with many guests, nor did it connect well with the barbeque focus. It also was not reflected cohesively across the brand through marketing or advertising initiatives.

Seeing a need for Smokey Bones to change its positioning, Push recommended that the restaurant first work on building a strong brand to increase longevity and growth and then focus on sales as a long-term goal.

Target Audience

Smokey Bones's traditional audience consisted of families or an older demographic that enjoyed barbeque food and discount dining in general. Unfortunately, because of its heavy nature, most diners do not consume barbeque food on a regular basis.

To ensure that Smokey Bones was reaching an audience it could grow with, Push looked to consumers who were motivated by the social aspects of dining, rather than the food itself, and, therefore, were prone to dine out more often.

Consumers with this frame of mind were deemed "social starters" and designated as the ideal target group for Smokey Bones because of their expendable income and propensity to dine out. As per the term (social starters), these individuals are focused on having social lives, meeting people, and appreciating places that cater to the different needs for being social . . . be it a night out or a casual drink.

SOLUTIONS

To remove the heavy barbeque focus from Smokey Bones and cater to social starters by repositioning the brand as an exciting experience with a bar focus, Smokey Bones BBQ & Grill was re-branded as Smokey Bones Bar & Fire Grill.

The following objectives were put in place to kick-start the new brand:

- Open up the bar through design changes and focus on the bar in marketing and advertising materials in order to encourage and increase alcohol sales.

- Use social media tools and recreate the Smokey Bones web site to drive social starters to the site, with the goal of increasing traffic by 20 percent.
- Build Smokey Bones's consumer database and encourage consumer loyalty by increasing membership to the Bones Club (a free-to-join incentives club).

Open Up the Bar

Smokey Bones began rolling out rebranded restaurants, featuring a new atmosphere and a bar focus. A new logo, menu, and signage, among other collateral, were created to showcase this new personality across the board. In addition, Push created a brand training video to educate staff about the brand transition.

Smokey Bones also began sponsoring and partnering with local sports teams and clubs, offering group drink specials on game days.

Social Media and the Web

Since the rebranding of individual Smokey Bones locations was occurring in stages, it was integral that the new brand be implemented through the medium that is most important to social starters. Rather than concentrate on traditional advertising, Smokey Bones aimed to reach its social starter audience through social media. A new web site (SmokeyBones.com) was developed and launched in early 2009. The site was unique in that it localized each visitor's experience, so regardless of whether a local Smokey Bones had been rebranded, it still reached potential guests with the brand's distinct energy. A total of 68 subsites were created, one for each Smokey Bones restaurant in the country. By entering their ZIP codes, visitors were instantly linked to the site for their closest Smokey Bones location.

This localized experience was overseen by a teammate at each Smokey Bones who was designated as "web host" or "web hostess." The web hosts were put in place to infuse their own personality in the brand and control content for local store pages on the main restaurant site, as well as on their own individual Smokey Bones–branded Facebook and MySpace pages (a first for any national restaurant brand).

Bones Club

The Bones Club needed to reach social starters for inclusion in its e-mail and mobile database. Push created a restaurant-use-only iPhone application for the exclusive use of web hosts. The hosts could use the iPhone application to sign up guests for the Bones Club, edit member information, and easily upload images taken with the iPhone to their local Smokey Bones web site.

RESULTS

Smokey Bones Bar & Fire Grill is an all-new Smokey Bones.

The new Smokey Bones experience was created by changing any and all consumer touch points within the brand into something interactive, exciting, and personal. As a result of the new collateral and image projection through social media, this change was evident even in locations that were yet to be fully rebranded. In addition, social starters began hearing the message.

Here are some initial achievements for Smokey Bones at the time of composition of this case study:

- Alcohol sales exceeded Smokey Bones's first quarter 2009 expectations.
- Saint Patrick's Day 2009 was marked by the highest alcohol sales in the brand's 10-year history.
- Traffic increased to SmokeyBones.com by 50 percent, which surpassed the original goal of a 20 percent increase.
- Consumers picked SmokeyBones.com as their favorite restaurant web site, awarding Smokey Bones the esteemed 2009 Webby People's Voice Award.
- Smokey Bones's social networking efforts resulted in a network of thousands of MySpace and Facebook friends across all Smokey Bones locations.
- The Bones Club membership went up by more than 30 percent in only 2½ months.

Thanks to a strong, cohesive brand and a set strategy in place, Smokey Bones is experiencing excellent results and continues to see its social starter audience grow.

Courtesy of Push and Smokey Bones Bar & Fire Grill.

Western Hemisphere Travel Initiative

U.S. Customs and Border Protection (CBP) and the Department of Homeland Security partnered with Elevation, a Washington, DC–based advertising firm, to launch a massive public outreach campaign in late 2008. The campaign was the result of CBP implementing a 9/11 Commission recommendation to create a faster and more reliable way to identify and process the more than 790,000 people crossing the border through U.S. points of entry (land and seaports) each day. The new program, dubbed the Western Hemisphere Travel Initiative, or WHTI for short (pronounced "witty"), created new travel document requirements for Americans and Canadians entering the United States by land or sea from Canada, Mexico, Bermuda, or the Caribbean. The campaign's goal was to educate the traveling public about the new requirements and which compliant documents they would need before the program went into effect in June 2009. The campaign was rolled out in three phases:

1. **"Improving to Keep You Moving"** The "Improving to Keep You Moving" introductory campaign delivered local messages in border-crossing markets about upcoming construction to outfit crossing stations with new technology during the summer of 2008. The purpose was to acknowledge that there would be travel delays associated with the construction but to remind travelers that it would all be worth it to have more efficient and more secure border-crossing stations.

2. **"Let's Get You Home—Phase 1"** Phase 1 of "Let's Get You Home" was a broad, multifaceted national and international campaign that began in the fall of 2008 and sought to introduce the WHTI program to travelers and direct them to a central web site where they could learn which document was right for them and how to apply for it. The campaign used beautiful imagery of travelers in various environments and had a very warm, inviting, and patriotic tone. The goal was to be disarming and not authoritative and to celebrate traveling. By applying for a WHTI travel card, not only were the travelers helping streamline the process for themselves but they were also performing a duty to their country to help further secure our borders.

2. **"Let's Get You Home—Phase 2, A Call to Action"** Using national TV coupled with spot market TV, radio, newspaper, magazine, online, and public relations in border states, the second phase of the "Let's Get You Home" campaign began in spring 2009 and delivered a direct call to action, reminding travelers that it was time to apply in order to meet the June 2009 deadline.

Phase 3 used humor to discern between the "haves," those with compliant WHTI documents, and the "have-nots," those without the documents. The spots showcased the high-tech cards by having cards attached to compliant travelers with their live-action faces seen through the photo window in the cards. The tone of the campaign was often described as very "un-government like." CBP and Homeland Security chose to lead travelers by the hand rather than dragging them in to become compliant.

CAMPAIGN COMPONENTS

Following are some of the campaign components of the WHTI program.

- TV spots ran on NBC and the Travel Channel and were produced with the ability to substitute state-specific enhanced drivers licenses (EDLs) for microtargeted flights.
- Radio in spot market, border-crossing states began to run.
- Print ads ran in *Time*, *Newsweek*, *Travel & Leisure*, *Condé Nast Traveler*, *Budget Travel*, newspapers, and so on.
- Outdoor billboards were placed along the borders.

- Online advertising was placed on travel sites such as Travelocity and Orbitz, including the following:
  - Banners
  - Rich-media banners with geotargeting to pinpoint where the user was logging-in from.
  - Flash video banners where the person inside a travel card would climb out.
- The web site www.GetYouHome.gov was launched.
- The WHTI widget for XP, Vista, and Mac computers was offered.
- Radio public service announcements could be heard in Canada and the United States, including the following:
  - Voice-overs by Shirley Myers and Glenn Frey
- Posters appeared in and on the following:
  - Ports of entry
  - Departments of Motor Vehicles
  - Amtrak stations
  - City buses
- Spanish-language TV (including Telemundo and Univision), radio, microsites, billboards, and tearsheets began running ads.
- The Canada campaign "Know Your Border" included ads on French-language TV, public service announcements, on microsites, and on tearsheets.

RESULTS

Initial indications suggest that the campaign has had great success. There was a strong correlation between ads (flights, insertions, online ads, and outdoor) and the number of web visits to the specially created web site www.GetYouHome.gov. According to Quantcast, web visits went from an insignificant amount in December 2008 to nearly 160,000 monthly visits in April 2009.

Local markets targeted to reach frequent travelers in border markets include the following:

- Northern border
  - Seattle
  - Detroit
  - Buffalo
  - Burlington
  - Bangor
- Southern border
  - San Diego
  - Yuma
  - Tucson
- El Paso
- San Antonio
- Laredo
- Brownsville

Courtesy of Elevations, Ltd., Washington, DC, Credits:, President, CEO: Jim Learned, Account Service: Pablo Izquierdo, Gregg Rappaport, and Tiffany Goodyear, Project Management: Jim Learned, Creative Director: Matt Herath, Creative Director/Copywriter Hispanic: Rodolfo Hernandez, Creative Director Canada: Terry O'Riley, Art Directors: Alex Dobert and Mike Martin, Copywriters: Matt Herath and Mike Martin, Interactive Designer: Alex Dobert, Interactive Flash Design: Toolbox #9, Atlanta, Georgia, TV Director: Sam Crawford, ZOO Pictures Los Angeles, California, TV Producer: Darrin Ball, TV Editor: Jeff Jay, Jam Edit, Atlanta, Georgia, Sound Engineering: Mixology Lab, New York City, Compositing: Pirate Sound, Toronto, Canada, Web Video Production: Magick Lantern, Atlanta, Georgia.

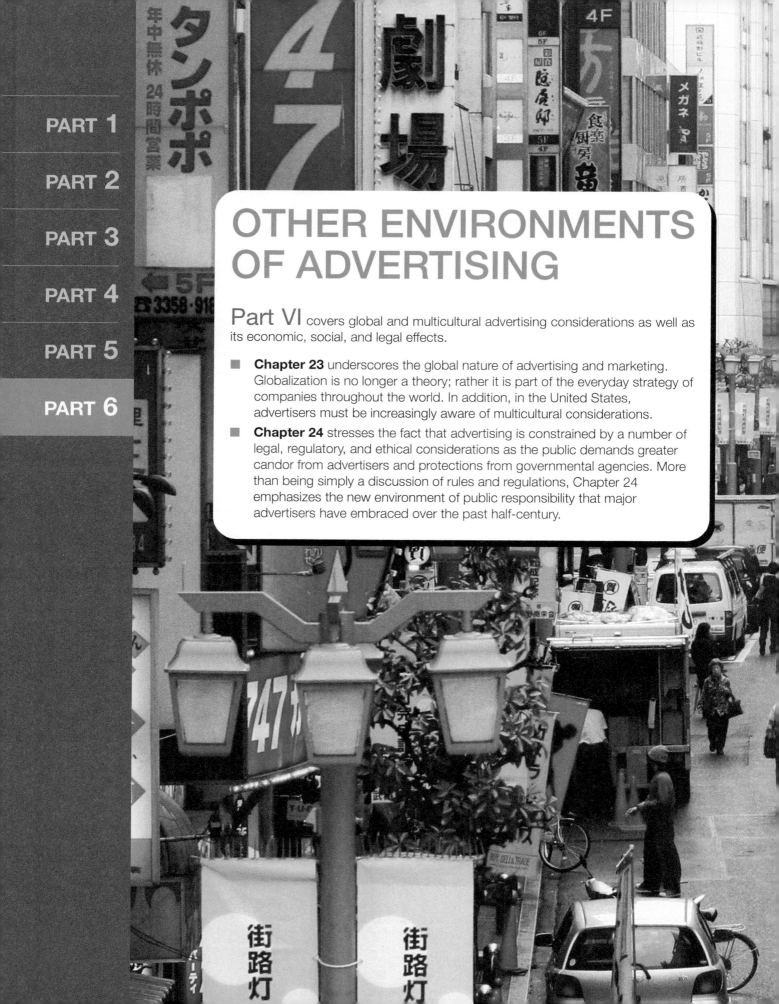

OTHER ENVIRONMENTS OF ADVERTISING

Part VI covers global and multicultural advertising considerations as well as its economic, social, and legal effects.

- **Chapter 23** underscores the global nature of advertising and marketing. Globalization is no longer a theory; rather it is part of the everyday strategy of companies throughout the world. In addition, in the United States, advertisers must be increasingly aware of multicultural considerations.

- **Chapter 24** stresses the fact that advertising is constrained by a number of legal, regulatory, and ethical considerations as the public demands greater candor from advertisers and protections from governmental agencies. More than being simply a discussion of rules and regulations, Chapter 24 emphasizes the new environment of public responsibility that major advertisers have embraced over the past half-century.

עם קטשופ היינץ
האוכל שלך יקבל טעם
שילדים אוהבים

אין ארוחה בלי קטשופ היינץ

Courtesy of Heinz and Adler Chomsky & Warshavsky (Grey Israel).

International Advertising

> " **G**LOCAL" describes how advertisers consider language and culture when tailoring global campaigns to populations around the world—or even, in some respects, within the United States. ▶

CHAPTER LEARNING OBJECTIVES

1. List four obstacles facing U.S. marketers seeking global sales.
2. Explain the concept of glocalization.
3. Describe development of the multinational advertising agency.
4. Describe the creative and cultural considerations of international marketing.
5. Identify three diversity trends influencing marketing.
6. Explain how diversity will influence U.S. advertising.

At one time, U.S. firms considered their international marketing operations separately from domestic sales and promotion. However, in an environment with a Nissan automotive plant in Tennessee, Hondas rolling off an Ohio assembly line, and Mercedes and BMW making luxury cars in the Deep South, the global village is in our own backyard. Globalization is much more than simply doing business abroad. Multinational firms operate in an atmosphere of converging cultural, political, communication, and business issues where companies battle head-to-head for local buyers in what is often worldwide competition. For example, in this ad that ran in Israel, Heinz Ketchup is showcasing its kosher label and extolling its great taste: "A taste that kids would love!" In this chapter, we will examine the challenges facing companies like Heinz and others that must increasingly compete for customers on a global scale.

Going Global

The purchase of goods from abroad is so entrenched in the American economy that we often forget that the global market is a phenomenon of relatively recent vintage. For example, the first Toyota automobile, the Toyopet Crown, was not introduced in the United States until 1957. After selling only 288 cars in the first 14 months, Toyota withdrew from the U.S. market in 1961. In 1965, Toyota launched the Corona with a design more suited to American drivers. By 1972, Toyota reached $1 million annual sales and as of 2009 was the world's leading car manufacturer.[1]

The changing complexion of global advertising and marketing is readily apparent from an examination of how American businesses and advertising agencies are now competing with multinational companies from developed countries throughout the world. For example, a recent global survey of teens asked what brands they found most "likeable." The top three brands were Sony (Japan), Nokia (Finland), and Adidas (Germany)—Coca Cola, in eighth place, was the highest-ranked American brand,

EXHIBIT 23.1

Asia represents much future growth for marketers and advertisers.

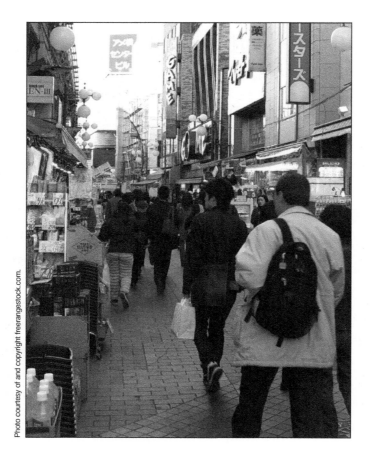

Photo courtesy of and copyright freerangestock.com.

although it rated number one in familiarity.[2] As reflected in the current trade imbalance in the United States, American consumers prefer foreign-made goods in a number of major product categories.

Economies are growing at rates much higher than those found in either North America or Europe providing lucrative areas for expansion. In 1950, New York and London ranked first and second, respectively, among the world's 30 largest cities. In the coming decade, New York will fall to seventh and London will drop off the list altogether. Overall, Asia will be the home of seven of the top ten cities, led by Tokyo with a population of 27 million. Of the top 30 largest cities, only two will be in North America and Europe—New York and Paris.[3] A significant percentage of future growth in marketing and advertising will be more concentrated in the Far East, Middle East, and Latin America as sellers seek new customers for their goods and services (see Exhibit 23.1). This trend has been ongoing for some time as a number of major U.S. companies are spending more than 50 percent of their advertising budgets abroad.

In Chapter 1, we discussed how early advertising in the United States grew as a result of a number of economic, social, and cultural factors. In many respects, today's world marketplace demonstrates many of the same characteristics. Only by understanding these broad issues can we tell the full story of the global economic expansion. It can be argued that the global business revolution of the past decade is fundamentally a communication revolution that, in country after country, has resulted in demands for more open political systems, which inevitably leads to demands for more economic choice. Without an expansion of communication, it is doubtful that the current political and economic environment would exist.

Nowhere is the expansion of global marketing more apparent than in the increase in international advertising spending levels. Rather than the U.S. domination of past years, current spending shows that about half—13 of the top 25 global advertisers—are

EXHIBIT 23.2

Top 25 Global Marketers

Rank		Advertiser	Headquarters	Worldwide Measured Media Spending		
'07	'06			2007	2006	% Change
1	1	Procter & Gamble Co.	Cincinnati	$9,358	$8,419	11.2
2	2	Unilever	London/Rotterdam	5,295	4,535	16.7
3	5	L'Oréal	Clichy, France	3,426	3,060	12.0
4	3	General Motors Corp.	Detroit	3,345	3,375	−0.9
5	4	Toyota Motor Corp.	Toyota City, Japan	3,202	3,129	2.3
6	6	Ford Motor Co.	Dearborn, Mich.	2,902	2,778	4.5
7	7	Johnson & Johnson	New Brunswick, N.J.	2,361	2,192	7.7
8	10	Nestlé	Vevey, Switzerland	2,181	2,046	6.6
9	12	Coca-Cola Co.	Atlanta	2,177	1,909	14.0
10	11	Honda Motor Co.	Tokyo	2,047	1,957	4.6
11	9	Time Warner	New York	2,022	2,048	−1.3
12	21	Reckitt Benckiser	Slough, Berkshire, U.K.	1,983	1,487	33.4
13	8	Sony Corp.	Tokyo	1,886	2,080	−9.3
14	16	Kraft Foods	Northfield, Ill.	1,853	1,682	10.2
15	14	Nissan Motor Co.	Tokyo	1,826	1,770	3.2
16	13	GlaxoSmithKline	Brentford, Middlesex, U.K.	1,802	1,821	−1.0
17	17	McDonald's Corp.	Oak Brook, Ill.	1,740	1,609	8.2
18	18	Volkswagen	Wolfsburg, Germany	1,729	1,585	9.1
19	20	Mars Inc.	McLean, Va.	1,708	1,561	9.4
20	15	Walt Disney Co.	Burbank, Calif.	1,677	1,709	−1.9
21	19	PepsiCo	Purchase, N.Y.	1,553	1,583	−1.9
22	22	Chrysler	Auburn Hills, Mich.	1,319	1,373	−3.9
23	28	Danone Group	Paris	1,306	1,088	20.0
24	26	PSA Peugeot Citroen	Paris	1,292	1,132	14.2
25	23	General Electric Co.	Fairfield, Conn.	1,277	1,318	−3.1

Source: Reprinted with permission from the December 10, 2008 issue of *Advertising Age.* Copyright, Crain Communications Inc. 2008.

headquartered in the United States (see Exhibit 23.2). The expansion of international marketing and advertising is occurring during a period of significant change in global relationships. These alliances cover a continuum from broadly based country and continental connections to aspirations of individual consumers for a better standard of living. Global marketers are faced with the dilemma of dealing with wide-ranging differences among global consumers and at the same time finding some commonality among diverse markets on which to base brand messages. For example, marketers find that although urban Chinese teenagers are a huge potential market, they are conflicted about many of the changes in that country. "This generation has more choices than at any other time in China's history, but they're not entirely comfortable with these choices. They want to express themselves, but only in a safe, socially acceptable context."[4]

As we will discuss throughout this chapter, American companies face another set of obstacles in competing for global sales. Among the major challenges is overcoming significant anti-American opinions abroad. The roots of these attitudes are varied, but many are related to the marketing of American products. For example:

① List four obstacles facing U.S. marketers seeking global sales.

- *Exploitation.* The sense that American companies take more than they give.
- *Corrupting influence.* The view that American brands enhance thinking and behavior that clash with local customs and debase cultural or religious norms.
- *Gross insensitivity and arrogance.* In many cultures there is a perception that Americans believe everyone wants to be like them.
- *Hyper-consumerism.* As we will see in this chapter, a continuing challenge for multinational marketers and their agencies is to find those shared feelings and attitudes that are consistent from country to country to give their brand messages continuity. At the same time, it is imperative that these companies be sensitive to the distinct differences and pride that consumers feel toward their national and cultural heritages.

The Multinational Corporation

An expected consequence of the global economy is the creation of the multinational corporation. Operating in hundreds of countries and selling billions of dollars worth of goods and services, these giant enterprises rival many small countries in terms of economic output. They occupy a place beyond that of a simple seller of merchandise. The CEOs of these firms function as quasi-political and cultural leaders with a scope of influence unknown in earlier times. However, regardless of their influence, the basic motivation of these multinationals is the same as that of the corner pizza shop—to make a profit and expand their customer base.

The fundamental economic model remains the same regardless of the company's size. As companies reach a saturation point within existing markets, they seek new buyers to continue to increase both sales and profitability. It so happens that as the United States and other prosperous countries reached a level of market satiation, the technological means of instant communication and rapid transportation made global trade possible. At the end of World War II, American businesses were at the vanguard of the rebuilding process, first in Western Europe and later in Asia. During these early years of global expansion, multinational marketing was largely confined to U.S. companies, with few competitors headquartered outside the United States. However, since the 1970s, U.S. business has had to share the world market with a number of companies headquartered abroad. In many product categories, such as textiles and electronics, there is virtually no U.S. manufacturing remaining. In other industries, such as automobiles, the U.S. market share has shrunk by more than half in the past 2 decades. Likewise, advertising, long considered a U.S. invention, is truly a global enterprise with many of the icons of U.S. advertising, such as J. Walter Thompson, now controlled by foreign holding companies.

In an ironic twist, the emerging foreign markets that at one time were viewed only as a means of new sales and profits for U.S. and European companies have increasingly become sources of intense competition. Much to the dismay of some major companies, some of this competition comes in the form of products almost identical to those of the originating company. For example, the Chinese Shuanghuan Laibao SRV is virtually the same as the Honda CR-V and, at a 2005 car show, Chinese automaker Red Flag showed a concept car that looked much like the Rolls-Royce Phantom—for half the price. "While Western car makers may be horrified by China's blatant commandeering of their ideas, they are also understandably wary of making enemies in the world's fastest growing car market. Every major car company is desperate to get a slice of the Chinese sales boom. To do this the Chinese government usually requires them to form an alliance with a Chinese company and, although the communist regime may be embracing capitalism, all large investments have to be cleared by the authorities."[5]

Another significant feature of global marketing and advertising is the paradox of a greater ability to communicate across international borders accompanied by growing nationalism and suspicion of outside influences in many countries. Clearly, communication technology, open-trade movements, and improved transportation are making international marketing and advertising more efficient. However, a growing sense of nationalism and increasing protectionism are impeding foreign expansion into many markets. Perhaps people are reacting to a communication revolution that threatens to merge and blur the differences in cultures. Consider that nationalist sentiment in Venezuela, for instance, now requires that all television and radio commercials be produced within that country.[6] This means that a broadcast ad produced in another country must be reshot with Venezuelan production crews. Whatever the reason, a growing sense of isolationism is a factor that international marketers must weigh with great care.

GLOCALIZATION

In some cases, isolationism can be resolved in part by greater sensitivity to other cultures, a willingness to learn local customs, and an openness to new ideas. In an attempt to deal with local culture and at the same time enjoy the advantages and efficiencies of global marketing, many companies have adopted the concept of **glocalization**. The term was popularized by British sociologist Roland Robertson in the 1990s and seeks to combine the twin aims of globalization and localization. The terms usually denote one or both of the following:

glocalization
A hybrid term meaning to adapt global marketing efforts (products and advertising messages) to local markets and cultures.

1. The creation or distribution of products or services intended for a global or trans-regional market but customized to suit local laws or customs.

2. Using electronic communication technologies, such as the Internet, to provide local messages on a global or transregional basis.[7]

2 **Explain the concept of glocalization.**

Glocalization seeks to emphasize the belief that international sales of a product are more likely to succeed when companies adapt the product and/or promotion specifically to a particular locale. For example, Nokia launched the first "kosher phone" when advertising to Orthodox Jews in Israel (see Exhibit 23.3). The increasing presence of McDonald's restaurants throughout the world also demonstrates globalization; at the same time, the menu adaptations and even the architecture of the restaurants themselves on a market-by-market basis show attempts to appeal to local cultures, an example of

EXHIBIT 23.3

Nokia introduced a "kosher phone" when advertising to certain segments of Israelis.

Courtesy of Nokia and Adler Chomsky & Warshavsky (Grey Israel).

glocalization. For promotions in France, McDonald's substituted "Asterix the Gaul" for its familiar Ronald McDonald mascot.[8] The process of glocalization is more a concept than a concrete strategy. However, it reminds us that localized market strategies are both good business and good corporate citizenship.

A greater sense of local country traditions may be more important than business expertise, and even the most astute marketers sometimes misunderstand local customs. For example, Wal-Mart has found that its formula of one-stop discount selling, which is so successful in the United States, does not always translate abroad. In 2006, Wal-Mart withdrew from both Germany and South Korea. The reasons for these withdrawals were numerous, but the core reason was Wal-Mart's failure to adapt to local culture. For example, German customers were uncomfortable with checkout clerks smiling at them—a practice insisted on by Wal-Mart. In addition, German shoppers are more likely to go to a number of stores looking for the best quality and price on individual items rather than making a majority of their purchases at a single store. Korean customers view service as more important than low price, and stores resemble small department stores rather than warehouses are preferred in that country.[9]

In the global arena, it is important to view differences in lifestyle and traditions, as well as consumer behavior, objectively rather than making judgments about customs or cultures in other parts of the world. Despite setbacks, the global economy will continue to grow, fueled by the emergence of middle-class societies in an increasing number of countries. In addition, communication technology is permitting advertisers to reach prospective buyers never before available to them. A growing global demand and a rising standard of living will combine to make advertising even more prevalent throughout the world.

CHINA BECOMES A LEADING GLOBAL MARKET

For many years China has been better known for its exports than its imports, with "Made in China" a seemingly ubiquitous product label. Today, China is recognized for its potential as a growth market. One reason is its size. With more than 1.4 billion people—more than 20 percent of the world's population—China represents a marketer's dream (see Exhibit 23.4). Another reason is the capacity of its growing middle class to buy goods. By 2013, retail sales in China are expected to top $3.2 trillion; a figure that is

EXHIBIT 23.4

China's masses represent a tremendous market for today's brands.

Comstock/Jupiter Images.

astounding when one considers that retail sales in 2007 were $1.2 trillion.[10] As of January 2009, China surpassed the United States to become the largest automotive market. Currently, China represents the leading market for beer and cigarettes, as well as boasting the largest Internet and mobile phone population.[11]

Marketers, however, have been warned to approach this market with caution. Aside from the aforementioned rise in nationalism, China is a very diverse and heterogeneous market. For example, advertising within China has been compared to global marketing because of its more than 22 provinces, 5 time zones, and almost 300 cities with populations greater than 1 million. *Advertising Age* recently published a White Paper, "The Top 10 Things Marketers Need to Know to Succeed in the World's Fastest Growing Market," to help marketers navigate the pitfalls in China and avoid cultural myths. It is clear that as more companies around the world seek growth opportunities, entry into the Chinese domestic market will become an attractive option that will be worth the risk.

The Internet and International Communication

Although a number of factors have fueled international marketing, a necessary element in the expansion of global business activity has been the growth of communication technology, particularly in developing regions. "People in the Third World aspire to First World living standards. They develop that aspiration through watching television, seeing advertisements for First World consumer products sold in their counties, and observing First World visitors to their countries. Even in the most remote villages and refugee camps today, people know about the outside world."[12] Beginning in the 1960s, both print and broadcast media expanded in overseas markets. Sometimes these media were locally produced and, in other cases, U.S. publishers of news magazines such as *Time* and *Newsweek* and of business journals such as the *Wall Street Journal* offered international editions. However, these media were available only in economically developed countries and, even then, only where a free press was established. It wasn't until the introduction of satellite communication that the potential for truly global communication became a reality.

In 1962, NASA engineers transmitted a fuzzy picture over the Telstar satellite to a receiving station in England. Barely 15 years later, in 1976, Home Box Office (HBO) initiated satellite delivery of television programming, which was soon followed by Ted Turner's TBS Superstation, opening the potential for commercial satellite television on a regular basis. Today, viewers throughout the world are able to receive signals via direct broadcast satellite or satellite ground stations owned by a number of cable operators. Since 1975, India has experimented with satellite communication to reach rural areas, and China also has embarked on an ambitious program of reaching rural communities.

The introduction of satellite television brought the possibility of reaching the majority of the world's population with information, entertainment, and advertising. It permitted businesses to expand into a number of countries much faster and efficiently than could have been dreamed of 20 years earlier. However, as impressive as the promise of satellite is, it pales in comparison to the distribution and usage of Internet technology.

WORLDWIDE INTERNET ADOPTION

No communication technology has ever grown at the rate of the Internet. The latest figures indicate that Internet usage has reached 1.6 billion people and will soon pass the 2 billion mark. The penetration of Internet communication is growing in every sector of the globe, with only Africa lagging average usage rates. The potential for future growth is clearly outside the United States and Europe. On the one hand, as is evident in Exhibit 23.5, China represents more than 18 percent of the world's Internet users but only has 22.4 percent penetration among its population. On the other hand, the potential for growth in the United States is slowing because 75 percent of its population already has access to the Internet.

EXHIBIT 23.5

Top 10 Countries with the Most Internet Users

Rank	Country	2008 Population (million)	Internet Penetration	Percent of World Users	2000–2008 Growth
1	China	1,330	22.4%	18.7%	1,244%
2	United States	304	74.7%	14.2%	138%
3	Japan	127	73.8%	5.9%	100%
4	India	1,148	7.1%	5.1%	1,520%
5	Brazil	196	34.4%	4.2%	1,250%
6	Germany	82	67.0%	3.5%	130%
7	United Kingdom	61	71.8%	2.7%	184%
8	France	62	65.7%	2.6%	381%
9	Russia	141	27.0%	2.4%	1,126%
10	South Korea	48	76.1%	2.3%	93%

Source: Adapted from www.InternetWorldStats.com.

The Internet offers marketers immediate access to customers in areas of the world where traditional communication would have been totally impractical. "The interactive and dynamic nature of the Web makes it a powerful tool for marketing. . . . The wonderful thing about Web marketing is that it is right for all types of products and provides a level of interaction with customers that is on a par with personal sales visits."[13]

Today, the technological problems of global communications have been largely overcome. However, the challenge facing both Internet and satellite communication is using the technology in a diverse world community: ". . .despite all the apparent benefits of global Internet marketing, marketers cannot take other countries and their populations for granted. The European countries are a good example. Europeans live on a single continent, have open borders, trade freely, and are moving to a unified economy. Yet each country retains its distinct personality and its own language. And, in the case of marketing, individuals in each country will likely react differently to promotions."[14]

As we will discuss later in this chapter, the key to successful global marketing is finding those common appeals that will work on a universal basis (e.g., a mother's concern for her child's well-being). At the same time, marketers must understand the inherent differences in how these broad appeals may have to be adapted to various markets.

INTERNATIONAL LEGAL ISSUES

In addition to basic differences in consumer language and cultures, multinational marketers also face the problem of country-by-country variances in matters such as privacy and legal and regulatory standards. In South Korea, advertisers can be fined more than $800,000 for failing to identify their messages as promotions and allowing recipients to opt out of future communications. Malaysia has no specific laws regulating e-mail promotions, Germany demands that such promotions be clearly identified as such, and in Spain promotional e-mails are strictly forbidden unless prior consent is obtained from recipients—and even then they must be identified as "publicity." Online marketers must be aware that regulations differ widely by country. Internet promotions sent to an international audience should, at a minimum, include the following elements:

1. Provide opportunities to opt in or opt out of future communications.
2. Give honest and credible information.
3. Prohibit the use of randomly generated addresses.
4. Set standards to prevent relaying e-mail from computers with authorization.[15]

The advantage of communication without borders can be a major problem when offers or advertising themes that are illegal in some countries are widely disseminated. Often, advertisers will carry a statement on their web sites indicating that promotions are specific to a particular country or that offers that are not permitted in particular countries should be considered void. In themselves, these steps may not eliminate the problem, but, at a minimum, they may show good faith on the part of the company and at least reduce any potential legal or regulatory problems. Although the Internet and satellite transmission can provide businesses with instantaneous worldwide communication, there are numerous problems yet to be solved.

The Development of Global Marketing and Advertising

As discussed earlier, during the years shortly after World War II, international business meant American products, marketing, and advertising carried abroad. American companies exported a variety of goods as most of the world began the difficult recovery from the war. Today, America no longer dominates global commerce, and advertising and marketing are truly worldwide. As multinational companies compete on an international stage, we see the effects through the development of universal brands and even a similarity of products and advertising among people in diverse cultures and societies. Many American consumers, like their foreign counterparts, do not know or care whether a brand is made by an overseas company. When American consumers drink a cup of Lipton tea, wash with Dove soap, or make a sandwich with Hellman's mayonnaise, few give a thought to them being products made by a Dutch company, Unilever. Luckily for the American economy, overseas customers of Procter & Gamble's Tide, Pampers, and Charmin feel the same way about these brands.

At one time, whether to enter the international market was a major strategic decision for many American businesses. Today, becoming a player on the international scene is a given for most companies, and the only decision is how best to compete in the global arena. Not only is the success of American businesses more dependent on exporting products abroad but also even American companies that sell only domestically are finding major competition from imported goods in virtually every product category. Firms contemplating entering foreign markets face a number of decisions concerning both the advisability of such a move and the strategy and tactics involved in its execution:

1. Is the company organized from a marketing, production, and financial perspective to successfully compete in international markets?

2. What specific markets offer the greatest chance for success, the lowest risk, and the highest profit potential?

3. How can the firm best enter the global market? Companies use one of three basic means of market entry:

   a. Export goods to independent wholesalers and retailers in host countries. This strategy involves the least risk and, depending on local country contacts, may be the quickest means of gaining entry. However, it usually offers the lowest profit potential and often relinquishes control over marketing strategy, including pricing, promotion, and consumer research. Normally, it is a strategy used by smaller companies with limited product lines or investment.

   b. Begin joint venturing with established local businesses. This approach offers more control over marketing strategy and offers insights into best businesses practices from in-country partners. In a number of countries, joint venturing is the only legal means of establishing a major product presence because some nations will not allow majority ownership of businesses by foreigners.

   c. Establish totally owned enterprises. Some companies establish totally owned subsidiaries in overseas markets, including manufacturing plants, distribution systems, and control over promotion and advertising. This approach has the advantage of being able to fully manage the marketing and production process, but it is the slowest and most expensive means of establishing a presence. Often companies will undertake direct investment only after demonstrating a successful track record in the market. For example, Toyota, Honda, and Nissan imported cars to the United States for many years before building American automotive plants.

4. What is the most efficient marketing program and organization? Can a global theme be imported to local consumers or should localized messages and marketing techniques be used? Should local advertising and promotion agencies be used or should a company develop a coordinated advertising plan across international boundaries?

It is difficult to develop rigid guidelines for global commerce because each company faces unique issues and deals with them in a variety of ways. Traditionally, a major failing of American companies going abroad, especially those with little multinational experience, has been treating a foreign market as if consumers were homogeneous in terms of demography and product preference. Companies accept without question that domestic American markets demonstrate wide variance among different market segments and geographic areas. Yet, they sometimes don't translate this concept to foreign markets. To a degree, this mind-set is based on a lack of research, but more often it shows an appalling ignorance of local cultures and traditions.

Global Marketing and Advertising

global marketing
Term that denotes the use of advertising and marketing strategies on an international basis.

The term **global marketing** was popularized in a classic article by Harvard professor Theodore Levitt entitled "The Globalization of Markets." At the heart of the concept is the assumption that consumer needs are basically alike all over the world and consumers will respond to similar appeals regardless of cultural differences (see Exhibit 23.6). Among other things, Levitt argued that advances in communication technology and marketing efficiencies were making it possible to achieve unprecedented economies of scale by developing and marketing global brands. A fairer reading of Levitt would suggest that he advocated a global approach when it was appropriate, and he encouraged companies to look for such opportunities whenever possible.

Global marketing is a balancing act between keeping costs low through advertising efficiency and communicating effectively with local buyers. In an ideal situation, companies would be able to adopt a single advertising and marketing strategy throughout the world. Product development, advertising themes and media, distribution channels,

EXHIBIT 23.6

The sophistication of markets varies by region and locale.

and target marketing would be identical from one country to another. Such an approach would save large multinational marketers millions of dollars in creative production costs alone. In 2009, Coca-Cola executives sought to do just that during the global introduction of its "Open Happiness" campaign. The company sought to reduce redundancy by creating a "commercial clearinghouse" so that managers facing similar localization obstacles could use the same or similar work instead of creating it from scratch.[16]

Italians drink more bottled water than people in any other country in the world—almost three times as much as Americans. However, most Italians think it is bad manners to eat or drink anywhere but at the table. It is even illegal to sell food or drink at places such as newsstands. Nestlé is attempting to change ingrained habits about out-of-home food consumption, but it is facing major challenges. When asked about the idea of eating on the go, one Italian lawyer said, "It gives me goose bumps to even think about it."[17] During the Muslim holy month of Ramadan, the faithful fast during the day and spend time feasting with family starting at sundown. During the iftar, or evening breaking of the fast, television viewing is a central part of the celebration and ratings remain high well into the night. Many Middle Eastern marketers spend more than half their annual advertising budget during Ramadan, and in Egypt 30-second spots sell for as much as $7,000, double their normal rate.[18]

These and many other examples from around the world point out the difficulty of adopting a true global marketing plan. However, there are times when circumstances dictate a global marketing strategy. For example, in 2006, World Cup soccer matches were broadcast to 189 countries—a rare opportunity for multinational firms to reach a global audience with highly rated programming. Companies such as Anheuser-Busch and MasterCard International adopted television advertising that emphasized brand identification and simple messages that cut across cultural divides. For example, MasterCard's commercials had cheering fans from 30 different countries and a tagline "Football fever. Priceless"—as the account executive explained, its universal appeal worked in any language.[19] Wal-Mart, in an attempt to appeal to Hispanic customers in the United States and expand its sales overseas, developed a number of World Cup–related marketing strategies selling a number of country-specific goods related to the competition.[20] World Cup marketing is an example of using a central theme but adapting it to the interests of customers in diverse markets.

The problems encountered by regional free trade agreements are prime examples of the difficulties inherent in global marketing. The most publicized effort is the **European Union (EU)**, which promised to create a pan-European market that would rival the United States in terms of consumer expenditures and total value of goods. Despite a number of significant steps including introducing the euro in 1998 as a common currency, full implementation of the EU has not been easy. Countries that have been political and economic rivals for centuries are being asked to set aside their differences and make significant compromises for the common good. The EU experienced a setback on May 29, 2005, when almost 55 percent of French voters rejected the EU's proposed constitution and 3 days later the Dutch followed suit in a nonbinding referendum with 62 percent voting no. Similar problems have emerged in trade agreements around the globe. In the United States, the Central America Free Trade Agreement (CAFTA) and the **North American Free Trade Agreement (NAFTA)**, which seek to open borders between the United States and various regions of North and South America, are being condemned in some quarters as antienvironmental and exploitative of workers and small farmers. Likewise, attempts at free trade agreements in the Far East have run afoul of lingering suspicions among long-time political rivals. Whether trying to implement a large-scale program such as free trade or simply introducing a new product abroad, growing nationalistic agendas in many countries make it more imperative than ever to fully understand the global customer.

In developing a successful multinational marketing organization a number of areas must be addressed.

European Union (EU)
The developing economic integration of Europe. Potentially a single market of some 500 million consumers in 2010.

North American Free Trade Agreement (NAFTA)
A treaty designed to eliminate trade barriers among the United States, Mexico, and Canada.

MANAGEMENT

Regardless of a firm's specific marketing strategy, it is invariably coordinated by top management. However, management coordination does not preclude significant latitude for decision making at lower levels. It is unrealistic to think a multinational company, such as Nestlé, can fully manage as many as 7,000 worldwide and local brands, including such disparate products as Polo clothing and Carnation milk, from its Vevey, Switzerland, headquarters. However, Nestlé can create and maintain very sophisticated control centers to market its products according to consistent standards for product quality, advertising and promotion, and distribution. A commonly used management approach by multinational companies involves consolidating strategic management decisions at corporate headquarters and giving local managers flexibility to develop specific tactics within these general principles.

One of the major management challenges for multinational corporations involves developing a strategic plan for branding and advertising themes that can be easily adapted globally. One approach to this problem involves looking at major brands as an umbrella under which a number of related products can be marketed rather than treating each brand as a unique product. For example, Procter & Gamble is beginning to turn its Pampers diaper brand into a baby health care line; SK-II, a dominant Procter & Gamble brand of skin care products in Asia, is being introduced in the United States as a holistic skin care line to be used for virtually any skin problem faced by women; and the company is testing Mr. Clean AutoDry and Mr. Clean Magic Eraser, extending the brand to additional consumer markets.[21] Savvy marketers such as Procter & Gamble know that they must offer products that meet unique needs in different cultures.

However, global brand building allows advertising and promotion to support a number of product adaptations under a central brand and, in many cases, use a focused theme. In 2009, Visa launched its new globally themed campaign, "More People Go With Visa." According to Antonio Lucio, Visa's chief marketing officer, the wording for the campaign could be customized by region or country but the campaign's meaning had to stay the same. "We call it 'golocal' . . . [F]rom the get-go this was a campaign that was supposed to provide freedom with a framework—a very tight framework."[22]

Ironically, marketing concentration, which once featured a consolidation of advertising agencies to service global accounts, is being decentralized among a number of firms. At one time, the trend was for even the largest companies to have no more than four agencies, and this is still the case in many instances. However, other multinational marketers have moved to engaging more local agencies to take advantage of local nuances that cannot be effectively addressed by global agencies operating at some distance from local markets. The execution of international marketing and advertising is divided into two camps. On the one hand, agencies are willing to tolerate the added expense and management headaches to deal with a number of local agencies. On the other hand, efficiencies of centralized control employing a few agencies are worth the potential loss of a local character in advertising. Few companies totally employ either strategy; rather they develop a management style with aspects of both approaches.

ADVERTISING EXECUTION

Regardless of the organizational configuration, a company's international advertising and marketing strategy must adapt in some way to almost every country it enters. However, there are some fundamental decision points that are common to many of these activities. The three problem areas most frequently encountered by multinational firms are as follows:

1. *Language differences.* Language differences present the most obvious starting point for developing global advertising, and it also is the one with some major pitfalls. There are a number of legendary instances when advertising translations

resulted in embarrassment for a brand. Today, major international advertisers use translation firms that go beyond simply word substitution and use experienced in-country language experts who look for language nuances—a process called *language localization* rather than simply translation.

2. *Media research and usage.* In many countries, media research is nonexistent or based on unreliable data. In addition, media usage in many parts of the world is much different from that in the United States. For example, cinema advertising is extremely popular in parts of Europe, and India's newspaper readership is much higher than that in the United States. Likewise, daily television household viewership averages approximately 8 hours in Japan and only 3 hours in Great Britain.

3. *Cultural considerations.* Perhaps the most difficult area of international advertising is dealing with the many cultural components firms attempt to communicate to potential buyers. Advertising needs to demonstrate how products and services solve problems and provide consumer benefits in a context that is comfortable and understandable to consumers in each country. It is gaining an understanding of these cultural elements that often require multinational companies to engage in joint venturing or, at the very least, making use of local employees in each host country.

Technology and more efficient transportation are becoming more readily available to make the *idea* of international advertising and global marketing a reality. However, it is rarely possible to accommodate all the cultural and national differences in any single marketing strategy. Global marketing is such an appealing concept from a cost and efficiency standpoint that companies are tempted to adopt it even with its obvious pitfalls. It can be argued that the misapplication of global marketing places the well-being of the firm ahead of the consumer. Exhibit 23.7 demonstrates the continuum of a one-strategy, one-execution global marketing approach versus a consumer-oriented marketing concept with a different-strategy, different-execution approach in each country.

As shown in Exhibit 23.8, global marketing is rarely an either/or decision. Rather it is a continuum involving a number of steps requiring decisions about both products and marketing strategy that must complement each other. Consider the following situations for example:

1. *Export both the product and the advertising to other countries.* Exporting both the product and the advertising to other countries is the strictest interpretation of global marketing. In this situation, the product (including name and logo) and marketing strategy would be identical in every country. Starbucks is an example of a company that comes close to this model. With more than 11,000 stores in 43 countries, it has kept the basic "coffee house" image that worked so well in the United States. However, only a few companies are as fortunate as Starbucks to have a product that lends itself to this approach. Nevertheless, the advantages in efficiency and cost savings for such a strategy are so obvious that some form of global marketing is the goal that most firms seek and rarely find.

CONTINUUM OF MARKETING/ADVERTISING STRATEGY

Company Oriented   Consumer Oriented

Global
Marketing   Marketing
                                                          Concept

One strategy   Different strategy
One execution   Different execution

EXHIBIT 23.7

Multinational firms usually develop marketing plans that represent a compromise between the needs of consumers and the firm.

EXHIBIT 23.8

These Russian-language ads appeared in Israeli media. The headline reads "More Nokia in your life." Despite language differences, Nokia encourages users to think of its mobile devices as more than simply a phone.

2. *Adapt a product and marketing plan exclusively for the international market or large geographical areas.* It is common for companies to develop specific products, brands, and advertising strategies for regions of the world such as Europe or Asia. This approach is closely related to global marketing, but it recognizes that even broadly marketed products need some localization.

3. *Export the product, but change the name.* Unilever markets its premium-quality detergent under a number of brand names including Wisk in the United States, Skip in parts of Europe, and Omo in its other global markets. While devising a global campaign for the product, the company and its agency, Lowe & Partners, kept the established brand identities but developed a consistent campaign for them using the theme "Dirt is good." Advertising executions emphasized that part of being a child is getting dirty and that rather than having parents worry about it, they should use Unilever detergents to solve the problem. The commercials showed the fun that children have getting dirty and played up the fact that "Kids think differently about getting their clothes dirty" and invited parents to do the same.[23]

4. *Keep the brand name and advertising strategy, but adapt the product country by country.* Australia's Jacob's Creek Wines sells Semillon Chardonnay in Belgium, but it is not available in Brazil. Likewise, Merlot is sold in Canada but not in either Belgium or Brazil. However, the company uses the same brand and packaging globally, changing only the flavor of its wines on a country-by-country basis.

5. *Keep the brand name and product, but adapt the advertising to each country.* Keeping the brand name and product, but adapting the advertising to each country is one of the more common strategies used by multinational firms. Although it is expensive to adopt this plan, it is much less costly than changing the basic product, packaging, and brand name for each country. This approach also allows a company

to emphasize differences in usage and positioning. Global mobile marketer Nokia adapts its advertising to many markets. The ads in Exhibit 23.8 ran in Israel but were specifically crafted to appeal to Russian-speaking Jewish immigrants.

6. *Adapt both the product and the advertising to each country.* Adapting both the product and the advertising to each country is the most expensive plan, but one that fulfills consumer demand for localization of promotions and products. Few companies can afford to fully adopt this approach, and few products would demand such an extreme approach.

There are numerous variations on each of these designs. The important point is that no idea will work for every brand or product category in every country. Even themes that would seem to be universal, demonstrate wide variations of adoption and acceptability from one country to another.

SENSITIVITY

One of the positive aspects of multinational business is that it is bringing people to a greater awareness and understanding of diverse cultures. However, consumer behavior and the aspirations this behavior demonstrates involve fundamental core values of a culture. In recent years, multinational businesses have had to deal with numerous complaints about their operations in developing countries. Even the corporations acknowledge that there is a fine line between opening new markets for their products and exploitation. The problem is not a new one. In 1621, the charter of the Dutch West India Company outlined its responsibility thusly, ". . . for the preservation of the places, keeping good order, police and justice." Few companies are burdened with that level of accountability. However, a primary consideration of globalization and effective management is the development of a sensitivity to the host countries in which they operate. A strict adherence to centralized management makes it difficult for decision makers to effectively manage diverse markets with the same foresight as local executives who share a common culture and perspective with their customers. In recent years, there has been a heightened sensitivity to the responsibilities of companies conducting business as guests in host countries.

Many of the problems in international marketing and business relationships stem from the lack of understanding of how consumers in significantly different cultures view communication and other activities. It is mandatory that messages be reviewed not only for accuracy but also, and equally important, for cultural appropriateness. For example, a major international company wanted to recognize and honor the 24 countries participating in a recent World Cup soccer event. The company distributed promotional displays with flags of each nation. One of the flags was that of Saudi Arabia, which contains a passage about Allah. The display insulted a number of Islamic followers because they feared that the display would eventually be placed in the trash, thus, insulting their religion. Commenting on the flap, one executive commented, "In today's competitive business environment, your company cannot afford to operate with a domestic approach in a global economy. The ability to communicate across cultural borders is a necessity for anyone reaching out to markets made up of different ethnicities."[24]

Marketing sensitivity embraces a range of considerations, and more companies are demonstrating that they understand that there is an important balance to be reached between maximizing sales and profits and being a responsible marketer. Clearly, the notion of global marketing has ethical and philosophical elements that cannot be ignored.

The Multinational Advertising Agency

3 **Describe development of the multinational advertising agency.**

As American business moved into the global marketplace after World War II, their agencies soon followed. In these early years, the basic organization and practice for global agencies was similar to the model developed over the last 100 years in this country. That is, they tended to be full-service agencies executing all aspects of advertising on a country-by-country basis as needed by their clients. The contemporary international agency is much different from those in the pioneering years of the 1940s and 1950s when McCann Erickson and J. Walter Thompson led American agencies into the worldwide arena. They usually started foreign branches on a country-by-country basis with local branch agencies typically responsible for the advertising of a few large U.S. clients in a limited number of countries.

This approach to international advertising was extremely expensive and did not guarantee that the foreign branches would adequately service and coordinate the international marketing needs of their clients. During the 1970s, most U.S. agencies moved from full ownership of foreign offices to some form of joint venture or minority ownership of existing foreign agencies. This plan overcame the long start-up time involved in beginning a new agency and provided advertising plans that reflected local business practices and culture. Joint ventures also recognized the growing expertise of local advertising talent and the fact that around the world many overseas agencies were providing client services on a par with major American agencies. However, until the 1990s, agencies were still responsible for the advertising of their clients, and business was conducted internationally similar to that for domestic clients.

In the past 20 years, there have been a number of significant changes in international advertising on the agency side. Perhaps the most noteworthy is the growing trend for clients to bring much of the marketing communication function in-house. This functional change is apparent in the job titles of personnel in many corporations. Now, the international marketing plans are conducted by executives with such titles as *global brand manager* or *global marketing officer*. In many cases, the agency-client relationship has changed from one of long-term partner to specialist for specific creative or media-buying functions. "The separation of planning from creative and the development of in-house strategic capabilities by clients—who, thanks to database technologies, now know far more about their customers' actual behaviors than any outside partner can tell them—gives marketers the freedom to shop around for creative services."[25] The most significant result of this change is that multinational companies are now calling on small agencies for creative work. In the past, these small agencies would have been out of the mix because they are not staffed to handle full-service accounts.

Another trend is for agencies to eschew large global networks of 100 offices or more, and move toward a smaller number of offices—or micronetworks—strategically located to serve client opportunities. For example, Arnold, with three U.S. offices and a London office, is looking to open up to four offices to match its domestic clients' growth into foreign markets. Prague may be selected because Jack Daniels, the spirits marketer, is a client and experiencing better-than-average sales in that region. Similarly, Crispin Porter+Bogusky is seeking to open a small number of offices in overseas cities so the agency can respond to client needs from any time zone: ". . . our thinking has been we're going to need three, possibly four factories, max, to have a CPB open and available wherever a client might be," said Alex Bogusky.[26]

Let's examine some of the major areas of global advertising from the agency-client perspective.

GROWTH OF MAJOR ADVERTISING CENTERS OUTSIDE THE UNITED STATES

Advertising revenues in the United States account for approximately 40 percent of the world's total. However, much of this advertising is placed by foreign-owned agencies. American dominance of advertising was changed forever on June 26, 1987, when Martin Sorrell bought J. Walter Thompson and placed it under his London-based WPP group. During the next 20 years, he would acquire other American advertising icons such as Ogilvy & Mather, Young & Rubicam, and Grey Global Group.[27] Other long-time U.S. agencies, such as Leo Burnett, also have been bought by overseas holding companies. In

Rank		Agency Company	Headquarters	Worldwide Revenue		
'08	'07			2008	2007	% Change
1	2	WPP	London	$13,598	$12,383	9.8
2	1	Omnicom Group	New York	13,360	12,694	5.2
3	3	Interpublic Group of Cos.	New York	6,963	6,554	6.2
4	4	Publicis Groupe	Paris	6,900	6,393	7.9
5	5	Dentsu	Tokyo	3,296	2,932	12.4
6	6	Aegis Group	London	2,490	2,215	12.4
7	7	Havas	Suresnes, France	2,307	2,094	10.2
8	8	Hakuhodo DY Holdings	Tokyo	1,560	1,392	12.1
9	9	MDC Partners	Toronto/New York	585	534	9.5
10	11	Asatsu-DK	Tokyo	503	454	10.8
11	10	Alliance Data Systems (Epsilon)	Dallas	491	469	4.8
12	12	Media Consulta	Berlin	427	415	3.1
13	13	Microsoft Corp. (Razorfish)	Redmond, Wash.	409	368	11.1
14	15	Photon Group	Sydney	383	314	21.9
15	14	Carlson Marketing	Minneapolis	367	349	5.1
16	16	Chell Worldwide	Seoul	340	300	13.4
17	17	IBM-Corp. (IBM Interactive)	Armonk, N.Y.	313	278	12.6
18	19	Sapient Corp. (Sapient Interactive)	Cambridge, Mass.	306	241	27.0
19	26	InVentiv Health (InVentiv Communications)	Westerville, Ohio	280	204	37.1
20	22	Grupo ABC (ABC Group)	Sao Paulo	280	228	22.6
21	20	STW Group	St. Leonards, Australia	256	235	9.0
22	25	LBI International	Stockholm	241	211	14.2
23	23	Clemenger Group	Melbourne	239	220	8.5
24	24	Cossette Communication Group	Quebec City	238	218	9.6
25	18	George P. Johnson Co.	Auburn Hills, Mich.	238	256	−7.0

EXHIBIT 23.9

World's Top 25 Marketing Agency Companies

Ranked by worldwide revenue, 2008.

Source: Reprinted with permission from the April 27, 2009, issue of *Advertising Age.* Copyright, Crain Communications Inc. 2009.

addition to these acquisitions, the changing landscape of global advertising can be seen in the list of the largest worldwide marketing organizations (see Exhibit 23.9). Only two of the top 10 businesses are headquartered in the United States.

Among these huge enterprises, worldwide revenues often comprise less than half of company totals. More significant is the fact that among the top 10 firms revenue growth is almost always greater outside the United States. As we discussed earlier, the primary motivation for marketers to go abroad is the potential for higher revenues and profits. Likewise, advertising agencies and marketing firms are finding that emerging markets in a number of regions offer more growth potential than the more mature U.S. and Western European economies. It is difficult to predict precise trends among multinational markets. However, it is a certainty that developing regions of the world will continue to offer significant growth potential during the next 2 decades and beyond.

EFFECTS OF INTEGRATED MARKETING COMMUNICATION ON WORLDWIDE AGENCIES

As you will recall, in Chapter 2 we introduced the notion of *integrated marketing communication*. We noted that marketers are much more interested in reaching consumers by the most effective venue rather than pigeonholing their marketing communication into artificial categories of advertising, promotion, and so on. This approach is even more apparent in global marketing where the preferred means of commercial messages covers a wide range of avenues, including out-of-home, product placement, cell phones,

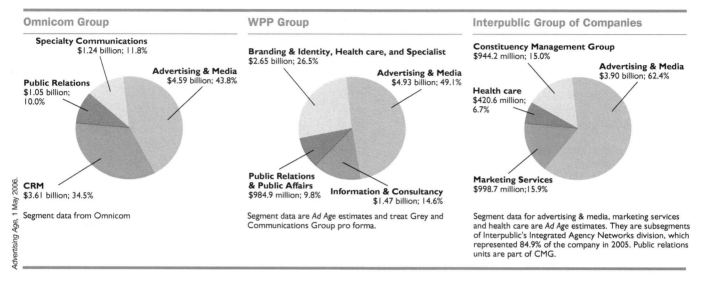

Advertising Age, 1 May 2006.

EXHIBIT 23.10

Worldwide Revenue by Discipline

and other new technologies as well as traditional advertising media. To serve their clients, advertising agencies have had to remake themselves into marketing communication organizations to serve the diverse needs of multinational clients.

The major advertising holding companies passed a watershed in 2001 when the so-called "big three" (Interpublic Group of Companies, Omnicom Group, and WPP Group) derived less than half their gross income from advertising services. The remaining income came from public relations, sales promotion, specialty shops, and research services. Exhibit 23.10 shows the diverse sources of income derived by three of the largest holding companies. Similar results can be seen across a variety of marketing firms. For example, in the future many of these companies will derive significant income from developing Internet and other specialized communication campaigns using video games and other interactive media.

Although the past 20 years has largely been a period of growth and diversification by international agencies, a countertrend toward decentralization has been evident in more recent years. A number of major multinational marketers have opted for using a number of smaller agencies rather than one or two megashops for their global brands. This approach is most evident on the creative side. As companies have brought overall advertising strategy in-house and selected independent media-buying organizations to handle global media placement, they have hired a number of agencies to gain creative alternatives for their global brands.

Rather than creative ideas being dictated from a single global agency, clients are looking for ideas from a number of shops. In some cases, small agencies are developing themes for a particular country, but in a number of instances, these smaller agencies have created advertising executions that have been adopted on a global basis. Motorola, Sony, and Disney all took the decentralized route despite once embracing the single lead-agency concept. These clients appear to prefer choice and a bit of interagency competition to the relative ease of one-stop shopping.[28] The downside of using a multiagency approach is the problem of keeping the brand image and positioning consistent and there are potential difficulties with management control of diverse voices. From a practical standpoint, the major advertising holding companies, after building huge global organizations, find that they may be competing with regional competitors that they never considered rivals before.

RESEARCH AND THE MULTINATIONAL CONSUMER

Nowhere is the changing relationship between international agencies and clients more apparent than in market research. Marketers have long known that understanding the global consumers of a brand presents unique challenges. Multinational research, especially studies attempting to discern common purchase behavior involving a number of countries, deals with issues that domestic marketing research rarely faces. Because of the unique problems involved, during the past decade more multinational marketers are taking primary responsibility for consumer research. Research for multinational brands is one of the primary areas in which centralization works far better than the locally oriented approach found in many creative or media executions and offers efficiencies in both cost and reliability.

Without centralized planning, research will not be comparable from country to country, making global strategy decisions all but impossible. As global marketing becomes more complex, there will be increasing reliance on research data gathered by clients and given to agencies on a project-by-project basis.

Coca-Cola is a multinational company that recently established an internal account planning and research group. The intent of the office is to facilitate global consumer insights by centralizing the planning and research function. This level of centralization will allow Coca-Cola to have a better understanding of how consumers in different countries relate to its various brands and the communication that will resonate within numerous countries. This organization will allow the company to understand "... consumer behavior and consumer insights through data not available to agencies. . . . Marketing is much more the domain of clients and communications is much more the domain of agencies. . . . We [Coke] are looking to have fewer ideas work across the geography."[29] As a major multinational agency CEO commented, "I see more and more businesses asking for a global view of their customers' assets. When you are dealing with Ford Motor Company and IBM Corporation, you cannot have a country or region doing data on their side the way they want . . . [it requires] one person sitting on top of it aligning all the processes and tools."[30]

Although the reliability of global research data has improved immensely in recent years, it is the interpretation of the research that creates the major problems for international marketers. Even developing a logo that is both understood and effective across a number of countries can present major obstacles. The heart of the research process involves finding a means to effectively translate key advertising and marketing information into global advertising executions. Although traditional language translation is important, translation must also include an understanding of the subtle nuances of culture and traditions within a country.

In this sense, **marketing translation** refers to the execution of the basic marketing plan to a number of countries. This translation involves not only language and numerous shades of meaning but also accounting for differences in media usage and availability, legal restrictions on various types of promotion, and basic advertising practices. It is the unusual advertising plan that can be introduced worldwide without numerous adaptations.

A vital element in the translation process is the brand audit. Brand audits are designed to gain consumer perspectives about a specific brand. The brand audit attempts to define what a brand means to consumers worldwide and then develop market strategies that will enhance the brand's future sales potential. Often a brand audit demonstrates that the general perceptions that a company has of its brands don't match those of its customers in specific countries. For example, Tide detergent found that "whiteness" was a common consumer touch point in choosing a cleaning product. Using the whiteness as a product benefit, Procter & Gamble used this across a number of cultures and advertising translations. Similarly, Procter & Gamble created a multinational campaign for Head & Shoulders around the theme of a dandruff treatment that is kind to your hair (see Exhibit 23.11).

Regardless of the function—creative, media, or research—agencies face two major problems in meeting the demands of clients:

1. First, they must accommodate the organizational structure of their clients. An agency with several multinational accounts often finds that the specific needs for

marketing translation
The process of adapting a general marketing plan to multinational environments.

EXHIBIT 23.11

Procter & Gamble has developed global themes for a number of its core brands.

(a) and (e) courtesy of Geller Nessis Leo Burnett Israel and Procter & Gamble; (b), (c), and (d) courtesy of Trio Advertising; (f) courtesy of Bauman Ber Rivnei Saatchi-Saatchi Israel.

account management differs from one client to another. In effect, some agencies find that they need different management organizations for each client.

2. The second major problem faced by multinational agencies is how to manage centrally and communicate locally. The adage "think globally, act locally" is a dilemma for every agency. Agencies must translate broad client marketing strategies to the level of the individual customer in each country they serve.

The Multinational Advertising Plan

As we have seen, international advertising involves much more than simply transporting advertising abroad. It requires a broad range of experience and an ability to deal with subtle nuances. In many cases, advertising decision making in an international environment must be executed with more instinct and less reliable research than in U.S. marketing. Despite these differences, the basic function of advertising remains the same regardless of the arena. All advertising begins with sound planning and an adherence to basic marketing strategy. Although consumer preferences may be more difficult to determine in overseas marketing, differentiated brand benefits still must constitute the central theme of most advertising messages. And like their domestic counterparts, all forms of marketing communication should be coordinated and integrated rather than presented as a series of unrelated advertising and sales promotion messages.

Although advertising basics may be consistent, international advertisers deal with special problems in execution and practices from country to country. The multinational marketer will find that the use and receptivity of advertising as well as its objectives and basic goals demonstrate extraordinary diversity. As firms introduce products on a worldwide basis, problems develop ranging from something as familiar as product category competition to the much more difficult problem of convincing buyers to change established habits or overcoming previously held cultural prohibitions concerning the use of a product.

Regardless of the objective of a particular international campaign, advertisers must deal with a host of situations unique to each country. In this section, we will discuss two areas of primary concern to international agencies and their clients: (1) creative and cultural considerations and (2) media planning and buying procedures, including legal restrictions and regulations.

CREATIVE AND CULTURAL CONSIDERATIONS

International advertising messages involve much more than simply selling products. Although sales and profits remain the primary objective of any promotional message, the creative function for multinational advertisers has changed dramatically in recent years. Multinational marketers are increasingly realizing that there are social, cultural, and, in some cases, political components to their advertising. The proliferation of foreign-based products, especially in developing countries, has led to charges of exploitation and insensitivity to local cultures by international companies. It is no longer sufficient for advertisers to simply introduce new products and depend on latent demand for sales and profits. There is a growing sense of worldwide nationalism where advertising must communicate interesting messages in a vernacular acceptable to local consumers. Advertising is at the forefront of presenting communication that can either dissuade or heighten these concerns among local buyers.

Advertising inadvertently functions on a number of social and cultural levels in addition to selling products and services.

> Advertising exerts a formative influence whose character is both persuasive and pervasive.... Even where adapted to local scenarios and role models, those shown often come from sectors of society, such as the upwardly mobile urban middle class, which embrace or are receptive to Western values and mores.... At

4 Describe the creative and cultural considerations of international marketing.

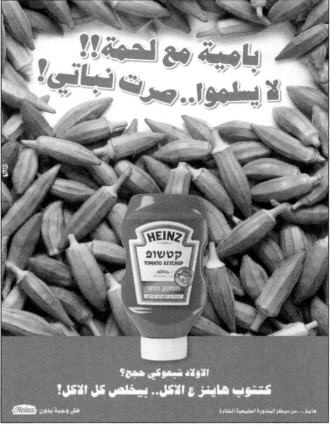

EXHIBIT 23.12

Heinz addresses Arab-speaking parents with creative ads that recognize traditional meals.

the same time, international advertising also acts as an integrating force across national boundaries. It disseminates messages using universal symbols and slogans, and establishes a common mode of communication among target audiences in different parts of the world. . . . Consequently, international advertising can be viewed as a force integrating societies and establishing common bonds, universal symbols, and models of communication among peoples in different parts of the globe.[31]

The failure of advertising to account for local culture can lead to serious problems that may linger for years in the attitudes of local consumers toward a brand. A major problem in exporting U.S. advertising is that Americans, as consumers, tend to be accepting of satire, humor, metaphors, and figures of speech that are viewed with disfavor in other parts of the world. For example, a Nike commercial broadcast in China depicted NBA star LeBron James defeating a cartoon kung fu and a pair of dragons. A number of viewers complained that the commercial showed the Chinese to be weak and incapable of defending themselves. The government's State Administration for Radio, Film and Television banned the ad saying, "all advertisements must uphold national dignity and interest, and respect the motherland's culture."[32] Earlier, Toyota ran afoul of the same authority by placing print advertisements in Chinese publications that showed stone lions, traditional symbols of Chinese power, bowing to a Toyota Land Cruiser Prado.

It is impossible to curtail all cultural missteps in international advertising. However, multinational advertisers today are much more aware of the potential pitfalls than they were in earlier years and are taking steps to prevent them. Many agencies are hiring specialists, such as cultural anthropologists, and making greater use of

EXHIBIT 23.13

Heinz addresses Israeli parents with the kosher seal and points out how much children love ketchup.

in-country research and consultants to more fully understand the consumption habits of buyers. Successful creative executions begin with an in-depth awareness of a country's culture, customs, and buying habits. Sometimes this analysis is as simple as being aware of local holidays, how they are celebrated, and if commercial tie-ins are appropriate.

Consider, for example, how Heinz chose to tailor its message to two different groups in the same area. Insights revealed that among Arab speakers ketchup had high use with "nontraditional" food such as hot dogs and French fries. The campaign in Exhibit 23.12 plays on children's love for ketchup and the excuses they use for not eating traditional foods such as majadara (beans), mnazalah (eggplant stew), and okra with meat. Ads targeted to Israelis featured the kosher seal and kids' love of ketchup (see Exhibit 23.13). From consideration of local diet to worldwide holidays, such as Rosh Hashanah, to country-specific celebrations, such as German Unity Day, advertisers need to know what the local customs are surrounding these events and whether their commercialization is appropriate.

As we have seen, advertising creativity is no longer an American monopoly. Both agencies and clients are open to ideas from around the world. Whereas at one time creative strategy was normally generated in the United States and adapted abroad, we are routinely seeing ideas and advertising executions originating in a foreign market and adopted for global use. The advertising sophistication of overseas markets is increasingly recognized and the idea of U.S.–dictated advertising programs is being quickly replaced by a partnership that acknowledges both the talent level of overseas advertisers and the contribution they can make to a greater understanding of international communication. We are seeing a maturation process that has evolved during the past 30 years in which multinational companies have moved through three basic phases:

1. *Moving into foreign markets.* The first phase involved the decision by companies to move into international markets. Although many large companies had a limited international presence prior to World War II, in the second half of the twentieth century companies began to routinely market their products on a worldwide basis.

2. *Local emphasis in marketing strategy.* Beginning in the 1980s, companies developed more pragmatic, locally oriented marketing and advertising plans. Companies realized that a one-plan-fits-all strategy would not work and began to view markets on a more individualized basis. Unfortunately, these efforts at localization were often based on little solid information and were too often more stereotypical than factual.

3. *Research-supported localization and segmentation.* Currently, we are seeing in many markets the implementation of consumer-based marketing guided by many of the same conceptual foundations found in the United States and other developed advertising economies. Although it may be many years before the majority of countries reach the level of research complexity and consumer understanding enjoyed in the United States, the very fact that marketers sense the need to respect the needs and aspirations of these consumers is a major step in the right direction.

MEDIA PLANNING: A GLOBAL PERSPECTIVE

Historically, the media function has suffered from three primary problems in international advertising:

1. *Media availability and/or usage levels.* Even with the introduction of satellite television, higher worldwide household set penetration, and the distribution of a number of television networks on a global basis, media planning is still a complex problem for multinational companies. However, services such as CNN International, Disney Channels operating in more than 60 countries, and ESPN operating a number of international outlets have made uniform communication much easier for global marketers. However, some countries, notably China, which has tremendously high levels of household television penetration, do not allow foreign programming. The state-controlled CCTV network does allow advertising from overseas companies and receives about 90 percent of its total revenue from advertising, much of it coming from global companies such as Procter & Gamble.[33]

   Media availability may vary for other reasons. For example, Givi Topschishvili, a native of Georgia, of the former Soviet Union, and Russian business consultant, advises media planners to prepare for the unexpected when advertising in Russia: "When putting together a media plan, it would help to account for the risk of the unexpected shutdown of certain media."[34] Aside from the obvious problems, a shutdown can lead to monetary losses and disruption of media goals.

   International services such as these can be combined with local and regional stations and networks to offer advertisers a choice of general channels for global brands and more specialized coverage for brands unique to a single country or region. In addition, the introduction of global television opportunities allows similar brand-building strategies as those used in campaigns originating in more developed countries. Although satellite television adds an important option for media planners, numerous print vehicles, particularly news and business journals such as *Time* and the *Wall Street Journal,* have well-established international editions to reach targeted, upscale consumers.

   The growing availability of international vehicles should not ignore the fact that media usage varies greatly on a country-by-country basis. For example, cinema advertising, regarded as a very minor medium in America, is a primary vehicle in Asia and parts of Europe. Out-of-home and radio advertising also are extremely important in many countries.

2. *Legal prohibitions.* In every country that allows advertising, there is some form of regulation. The degree and type of regulation is usually a function of two issues:

   a. The length of time that advertising has existed and the degree of sophistication that it has attained.

   b. The degree of freedom that business and the press enjoy. The extent of advertising control is directly correlated with a country's level of press freedom. For example, the recent Venezuelan government restrictions on press freedom have affected advertising as well. According to one agency executive in the country, the "gag law castrated the boldness of local advertising.... It is one of the main motives behind the low creative level we are [experiencing]."[35]

Despite differences in advertising regulation and control, there is a good deal of consistency among developed countries in terms of the prevalent types of advertising restraints. In most major advertising markets, advertising is controlled through a combination of self-regulation and legislation. This process is similar to that found in the United States with the FTC and a number of trade and business organizations such as the Council of Better Business Bureaus. For example, in Great Britain the primary self-regulatory entity is the Advertising Standards Authority, which receives complaints about misleading advertising and recommends various voluntary remedies to advertisers. A similar organization, the European Advertising Standards Alliance (EASA), coordinates the efforts of 28 self-regulatory bodies across the continent (see Exhibit 23.14). Underscoring the importance of self-regulation on a worldwide basis, the International Chamber of Commerce announced a revision of its basic code, which was first drafted in 1937. The 2006 version, which is used as the basis of self-regulation in many countries, seeks to define marketing and advertising taking into account new technology and the means of communication.[36]

In addition to formal legal restrictions and broad self-regulatory agencies, there are a number of industry-specific self-regulatory bodies throughout the world similar to those found in the United States. For example, the Union of European Beverage Associations announced a wide-ranging program to limit vending machine sales of soft drinks in primary schools, and a number of other marketing

EXHIBIT 23.14

Self-regulation across Europe is increasingly consistent (Matera, Sicily).

groups adopted similar steps in the face of criticism of targeting children younger than age 12 for the sale of high sugar drinks. In addition, a consortium of food marketers committed to a program to promote "... health, diet, and physical activity."[37] One result of global marketing is that the legal and self-regulatory system founded in the United States has spread to a number of countries as consumers become more sophisticated and empowered to monitor the effects of advertising.

Many of international advertising's limitations are similar to those in the United States. For example, alcohol and tobacco products as well as other categories of products may be limited or excluded from all or certain media. In addition, international media planning must be closely coordinated with creative executions because there are a number of restrictions concerning the type of messages that can be used in various media from country to country. Although space does not allow us to discuss the many advertising restrictions that are imposed by various countries, we can highlight some of the more general restrictions common to advertising regulators throughout the world.

■ *Comparative advertising.* In the United States, advertisers name competitors in their advertising. However, the practice of comparison advertising is strictly regulated or banned outright in numerous other countries where it is considered a form of unfair competition. The prevalence of prohibitions concerning comparative advertising makes it an ill-advised technique in most international advertising campaigns.

■ *Advertising to children.* Again, the United States is among the most permissive countries in the world in terms of children's advertising. Many countries ban any advertising to children and exclude all advertising in children's programming. In other cases, the hours permitted for advertising to children are very limited. The prohibitions against advertising to children cover a wide range of issues. Sweden and Norway ban all television advertising aimed at children. In Holland no celebrity endorsers can be used in broadcast commercials directed at children, and Spain outlaws the use of fictional characters in television food advertising. Outside the United States, a single campaign directed to children using U.S. standards would be very difficult to execute.[38]

■ *Internet advertising.* As more businesses turn to the Internet as a means of product information, promotion, and customer research, it becomes difficult to stay within the rules of international commerce. Because the Internet does not allow a marketer to limit geographic coverage, many advertisers include a statement that all product claims meet U.S. (or whatever countries the promotion is intended for) legal and regulatory standards and are intended for persons residing in those countries. This does not provide a foolproof solution for future liability, but it does provide companies with a defense if challenges are made in foreign jurisdictions. At this point, legal scholars are debating the degree of accountability incurred by Internet marketing. "When a marketer places advertising ... on a server in Chicago, Boston, or New York that advertising ... offer may be accessed throughout the world. From a legal perspective, the question is whether countries other than the United States can exert jurisdiction over advertising ... material that is deemed unlawful by that foreign country."[39]

■ *Standards of truth.* In the United States and much of Western Europe, humor, exaggeration, and hyperbole are accepted formats for advertising. The majority of consumers and regulators alike take the view that creativity can sometimes stray from literal product facts to gain an audience's interest. However, multinational advertisers should err on the side of being extremely conservative in making product claims. Claims touting amazing, stupendous, or marvelous product benefits may be accepted as tolerable puffery in the United States, but they can end up costing a company dearly abroad.

3. *The lack of reliable audience research.* Like all advertising executives, media planners must take a multinational perspective as clients and media move across borders to add market share and audiences. During the past 2 decades, the international media-buying function has changed dramatically. Searching for cost efficiencies and recognizing the unique problems of international media buying, multinational clients have demanded special expertise from their agencies. In this environment, the demands for cross-cultural media research have become crucial.

Outside of a few major advertising markets, media research has traditionally been either nonexistent or the data were notoriously unreliable. Even basic information such as paid circulation for print media is often unavailable or, if numbers exist, they are unaudited. For example, an executive for a major agency doing business in China, commenting on media circulation figures, said, "There is gross exaggeration to a point that would be criminal in any other country."[40] In addition to fundamental media research, media planners also often lack basic information about target audiences including data about their purchase and media usage habits.

Although a lack of audience and market data is a continuing concern to multinational marketers, the problems associated with media planning have improved dramatically in the past decade (see Exhibit 23.15). For example, in recent years availability of television ratings have expanded to countries throughout the world including Kenya, Uganda, Kuwait, Thailand, and even Iran. Although global media planning still presents major challenges, two factors have dramatically improved the ability of advertisers to reach target prospects:

1. *The rapid expansion of efficient global communication.* Cable and satellite television channels, combined with global distribution of movies and the adoption of the Internet and mobile phones, have created practical opportunities for millions of worldwide exposures.

2. *The expansion of global retailers.* As we discussed earlier in the case of Wal-Mart, customers do not always embrace a standard pattern of merchandising and shopping experiences. However, in the long term, global buyers are likely to become more accustomed to similar goods and merchandise with both media and creative strategy becoming more standardized as a result.

Courtesy of Nokia and Adler Chomsky & Warshavsky (Grey Israel).

EXHIBIT 23.15

Expansion of mobile phone use across the globe is enhancing verification of media exposure.

In addition to specific executions of media objectives, media planners must also deal with the special problems of developing and executing a strategic plan on an international basis. Media buying is so complex for large multinational advertisers that the media function is increasingly concentrated in huge multinational media planning companies or brokers that buy for a number of agencies. These media specialists, such as London-based Zenith Optimedia Group, can afford to hire highly trained personnel, conduct multinational audience research, and establish databases that would be beyond the financial reach of most individual advertising agencies. Planners within these organizations also can gain significant media discounts by buying for groups of clients instead of on the basis of single companies or brands.

Advertising and Ethnic Diversity in the United States

As we have discussed, global marketing has become a central strategy for many U.S. companies. However, American firms do not have to go abroad to deal with the challenges of multicultural marketing. Recent data from the U.S. Census Bureau indicates that more than 19 percent of residents prefer a language other than English at home. This trend is more pronounced in the following states: California (42 percent), New Mexico (36 percent), Texas (33 percent), New York (28 percent), and Arizona (27 percent).[41] Although we tend to emphasize the marketing practices of a relatively few global companies, in the United States even the smallest retailers are facing challenges in reaching out to a diverse population and, to a degree, dealing with many of the marketing and promotion problems of companies operating on a worldwide stage. The three major ethnic minorities in the United States are Hispanics, Asian Americans, and African Americans with Native Americans comprising slightly less than 1 percent of the population.

5 **Identify three diversity trends influencing marketing.**

In the past decade, and looking forward over the next 25 years or more, the complexities of ethnic marketing will grow as well as the opportunities offered to those companies that successfully connect with these growing populations. However, the task of marketing to a diverse population is made difficult by three trends:

1. *Majority-minority transition.* The marketplace is changing more quickly than many companies can adapt. Non-Hispanic whites account for less than half the population in Texas, California, New Mexico, and Hawaii. Nine other states, including major regions such as New York and Florida, will soon follow.

2. *Race is more difficult to determine.* In the 2000 Census, almost 7 million respondents listed more than one racial background. This figure included 4 percent of all children. Traditional designations of ethnicity will be significantly less relevant in the future.

3. *Citizens of the world.* Through the Internet and other technology, immigrants more easily stay connected to family and homeland and, consequently, assimilation and acculturation can be a longer process.[42]

As described in Chapter 4, at both the national and local levels, marketers cannot ignore the growing importance of a diverse population. For example, the Hispanic and African American share of the total U.S. population is about 16 percent and 13 percent, respectively. The Hispanic population passed the African American segment in 2003, and it will continue to outpace the population growth of all other ethnic groups in coming decades. Five percent of the U.S. population is Asian American, a group that increased by 30 percent during the 1990s. It is estimated that by 2050 slightly more than 50 percent of the U.S. population will be comprised of these groups with Hispanics making up as much as one-third of the total.

EXHIBIT 23.16

Reaching out to new markets both at home and abroad.

Traditionally, the U.S. ethnic population has been concentrated in a few regions and urban centers of the United States. For example, eight counties in Texas have Hispanic populations of at least 90 percent, whereas 51 percent of Asian Americans live in only three states (California, New York, and Hawaii). Major American companies are aggressively courting Hispanic buyers both in the United States and abroad (see Exhibit 23.16). However, during the past decade, significant growth in the ethnic population has taken place in a number of different places. For example, the three fastest-growing states in terms of Hispanic populations are North Carolina, Georgia, and Arkansas, with some counties in those states demonstrating increases of 500 percent or more from the 1990 to 2000 Census. As shown in Exhibit 23.17, the ethnic population is skewed toward younger age groups accentuating the rapid future increase in the Hispanic population. The rise in multicultural consumers combined with their significant increase in buying power is perhaps the major development in marketing in recent years.

MULTICULTURAL MARKET POWER

Marketers in a number of product categories are taking note of the growing importance of multiethnic consumers. Not only is the multicultural market expanding faster than the general population, but its buying power is also increasing at a greater rate. In a special report, the *Wall Street Journal* explored the challenges and opportunities of diversity. As the report pointed out, "If companies are going to sell products and services globally, they will need a rich mix of employees with varied perspectives and experiences. They will need top executives who understand different countries and cultures."[43] The report went on to explore how Harley-Davidson during the past decade successfully expanded its customer base from almost exclusively white males to include women and people of color. In order to market to these groups, the company increased its vice presidents and managers from 5 percent a decade ago to 25 percent today and its senior managers from 15 percent to 25 percent during the same period. As the company stated, it needs management and marketing teams that reflect the customer base it wants to attract.

6 **Explain how diversity will influence U.S. advertising.**

EXHIBIT 23.17

LifeCycles: The American Consumer

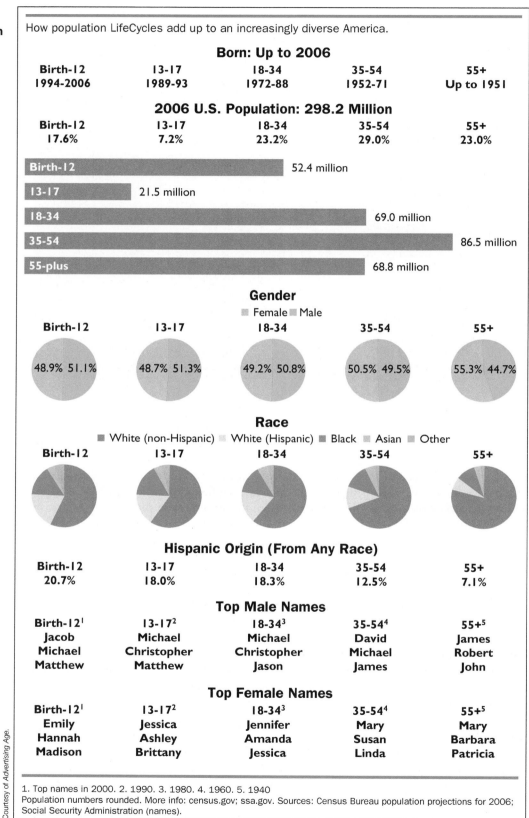

How population LifeCycles add up to an increasingly diverse America.

Born: Up to 2006

Birth-12	13-17	18-34	35-54	55+
1994-2006	1989-93	1972-88	1952-71	Up to 1951

2006 U.S. Population: 298.2 Million

Birth-12	13-17	18-34	35-54	55+
17.6%	7.2%	23.2%	29.0%	23.0%

Birth-12   52.4 million
13-17   21.5 million
18-34   69.0 million
35-54   86.5 million
55-plus   68.8 million

Gender
Female Male

Birth-12	13-17	18-34	35-54	55+
48.9% 51.1%	48.7% 51.3%	49.2% 50.8%	50.5% 49.5%	55.3% 44.7%

Race
White (non-Hispanic) White (Hispanic) Black Asian Other

Birth-12	13-17	18-34	35-54	55+

Hispanic Origin (From Any Race)

Birth-12	13-17	18-34	35-54	55+
20.7%	18.0%	18.3%	12.5%	7.1%

Top Male Names

Birth-12[1]	13-17[2]	18-34[3]	35-54[4]	55+[5]
Jacob	Michael	Michael	David	James
Michael	Christopher	Christopher	Michael	Robert
Matthew	Matthew	Jason	James	John

Top Female Names

Birth-12[1]	13-17[2]	18-34[3]	35-54[4]	55+[5]
Emily	Jessica	Jennifer	Mary	Mary
Hannah	Ashley	Amanda	Susan	Barbara
Madison	Brittany	Jessica	Linda	Patricia

1. Top names in 2000. 2. 1990. 3. 1980. 4. 1960. 5. 1940
Population numbers rounded. More info: census.gov; ssa.gov. Sources: Census Bureau population projections for 2006; Social Security Administration (names).

Companies are coming to realize that it is not enough to simply identify ethnic market segments. Advertisers know that they have to develop both products and messages that realistically meet the special needs of these consumers and are presented in a communication environment that speaks to them in a credible manner. Companies also realize that the market is so large and growing at such a rapid pace that it has to be a major part of virtually any company's future plans. The Hispanic market alone was projected to grow by as much as one-third by 2010 according to the U.S. Census Office. For a number of years, progressive companies such as Bank of America and Burger King have provided an array of services to their Latino customers, such as Spanish-language voice mail, Spanish-fluent employees, and bilingual menus. Today, most major companies are becoming more proactive in their advertising and marketing plans to ethnic customers. For example, a survey by the ANA found that slightly more than half of responding firms had created separate units to handle multicultural marketing with almost one-third of these having autonomous budget responsibility. As the author of the report concluded, "Having a stand-alone department with profit-and-loss objectives was a key factor to organizations really driving their multicultural success."[44]

Companies generally give greater attention to the Hispanic market than either the African American or Asian American market for two reasons. First, the rate of assimilation and acculturation is much higher among Asian Americans and African Americans than among Hispanics. Although there are pockets of large Asian American populations, their relatively low percentage of the general population has forced them to assimilate into U.S. society more rapidly than Hispanics. Statistics such as completion of high school and college, income, and English fluency indicate that Asian Americans are in many ways part of the cultural mainstream. Even though they demonstrate unique product preferences, the overall market size of the Asian American population means that much less market support will be directed toward them. Likewise, the African American population data shows that in many respects they are remarkably similar to the general population. A number of studies have shown that when income is held constant, buying behavior among African Americans and Caucasians is very similar. Notwithstanding these similarities, research reveals that all ethnic minorities tend to respond favorably to companies and brands that direct marketing and advertising messages to their individual needs and preferences.

A second reason for the greater marketing efforts expended in reaching Hispanics is language differences. Whereas virtually every other minority market adopts English very quickly (certainly within one generation), Spanish remains a preference among many Hispanics even when they become fluent in English. One only has to note the number of in-store signs, advertisements, and Spanish-language broadcast and print media to appreciate the slow adoption of English as the preferred language for a sizable proportion of this population. The combination of slower rates of assimilation, higher levels of brand preferences for products with Hispanic themes, and a continually growing market are contributing to companies paying greater attention to this ethnic population. Exhibit 23.18 shows that the major marketers to the Hispanic market are, for the most part, the same as to buyers in general—another indication that this segment is very much on the radar of primary advertisers.

DIVERSITY AND U.S. ADVERTISING

How advertisers deal with U.S. diversity is a matter of both sensitivity and profitability. At one time advertisers thought that a certain percentage of their advertising placed in foreign-language or ethnic-oriented media would provide sufficient accommodation to this market. However, language or media is no longer the defining force in ethnic marketing. Today, it is more important to deal with the texture of cultural differences—differences that cut across age, geography, and language. According to the Pew Hispanic Center, 72 percent of first-generation Hispanic immigrants are Spanish-language dominant, 47 percent of the second generation are bilingual, and 78 percent of third-generation Hispanics are English

EXHIBIT 23.18

Top 25 Advertisers in Hispanic Media

Rank	Marketer	2008 Ad Spending	% Change
1	Procter & Gamble Co.	$183,720	15.4
2	Lexicon Marketing Corp. (Inglés sin Barreras)	138,588	−36.5
3	AT&T	109,411	−8.0
4	Verizon Communications	101,995	27.8
5	McDonald's Corp.	94,300	4.7
6	Johnson & Johnson	93,930	21.3
7	General Motors Co.	92,978	−6.7
8	Broadcasting Media Partners (Univision)	90,869	−18.8
9	Toyota Motor Corp.	88,851	8.3
10	DirecTV Group	78,342	NA
11	State Farm Mutual Auto. Ins. Co.	75,313	NA
12	Walmart Stores	66,878	12.7
13	Sears Holdings Corp.	61,352	−23.4
14	Walt Disney Co.	59,769	−10.1
15	Sprint Nextel Corp.	59,612	12.1
16	SABMiller	58,172	−9.9
17	Deutsche Telekom	52,584	5.1
18	TVAtlas.com	52,268	−5.1
19	America Directo	52,168	−0.6
20	Nissan Motor Co.	52,149	−13.8
21	Target Corp.	49,711	47.2
22	Children International	48,648	NA
23	Ford Motor Co.	47,040	−32.9
24	J.C. Penney Co.	46,528	12.1
25	Allstate Corp.	46,221	−1.6

Dollars in thousands. Media from TNS Media Intelligence and represent the sum of broadcast TV and cable networks, Spanish-language magazines (including four PIB-monitored Spanish-language magazines), Spanish-language newspapers and Spanish-language spot TV and Spanish-language websites. Percent change is computed from 2007 data.

Source: Reprinted with permission from the 2009 Hispanic Fact Pack issue of *Advertising Age.* Copyright, Crain Communications Inc. 2009.

dominant.[45] However, as companies are quickly finding out, language does not define how a person regards his or her cultural roots. Even Hispanics who are English dominant or who speak no Spanish are as likely to have strong values in the Hispanic community as those who speak Spanish.

The emergence of a value-driven, as contrasted to a language-driven, marketing strategy is a primary change in the strategy and execution of ethnic marketing. The debate has shifted from language as a barometer of assimilation to one of self-concept among ethnic populations. As one marketing executive indicated, "The reality that Hispanics have not assimilated and will not assimilate like previous immigrant groups gives rise to a new marketing imperative. Simple translations are no longer acceptable to this increasingly savvy consumer group. Nor is featuring Hispanic faces in general-market advertising effective on its own. Marketing to U.S. Hispanics requires greater consumer insight and cultural and linguistic skills than ever before."[46]

Marketers are facing an interesting dilemma in attempting to reach the U.S. ethnic market. On the one hand, firms know that they have to acknowledge the growing diversity of their buyers to profitably market their products. On the other hand, there is a growing acceptance of diverse cultures among all segments of the population—especially teens—that suggests the future will be one of constant borrowing from a number of cultural identities (see Exhibit 23.19). According to Stephen Palacios, *intraculturalism,* that is, the tendency for American youth to adopt traditions and attitudes of cultures other than its own, is becoming the norm. Another marketing executive points out, ". . . the days of marketing according to vertical lines of ethnicity are fading" and they are being replaced by an appeal to aspirations and lifestyle that can cut across numerous cultural characteristics.[47]

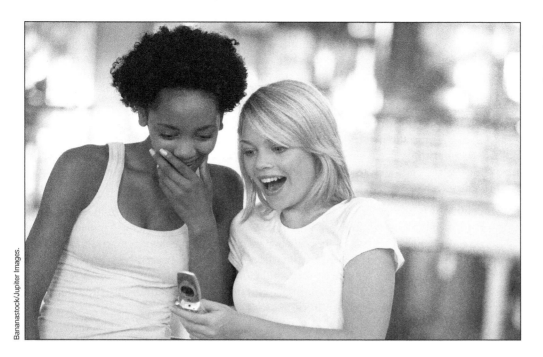

EXHIBIT 23.19

Cultural differences are more blurred for teens and young adults than they are for older citizens.

Each of the major ethnic groups presents special problems and opportunities for marketing and advertising. As we will discuss later in this chapter, there are many sub-cultures within each group. For example, an Asian American of Japanese heritage may have very different product preferences than a person with a Korean or Vietnamese heritage. In the following section, we discuss some of the primary elements in market-ing to various groups.

MEDIA   To a degree, the growth of the ethnic market as well as the degree of its assim-ilation can be gauged by the growth of the ethnic press. The number of foreign-language and ethnic-oriented media outlets demonstrates both the size of these populations and also their potential for marketers. Because of the relatively low-cost entry into the market, ethnic newspapers are the largest medium in terms of number of vehicles (although they are far surpassed by the audiences of ethnic-oriented televi-sion). Exhibit 23.20 offers an overview of the Hispanic media, by far the largest cate-gory of ethnic presses. Every Hispanic medium is growing at a rate far greater than mainstream journalism. In many cases, major publishers and networks have taken full or partial ownership of media within these groups to ensure a means of reaching this lucrative advertising market. The print sector provides a huge range of circulation,

Rank	Medium	U.S. Advertising Spending in Hispanic Media			
		2008	2007	% Change	2006
1	Network/national TV	$1,807.3	$1,789.4	1.00%	$1,733.9
2	Local TV	707.4	707.0	0.05	690.1
3	National radio	221.8	221.3	0.20	214.3
4	Local radio	529.2	524.1	0.98	511.7
5	National newspapers (excl. classified)	124.0	123.8	0.19	120.7
6	Local newspapers (excl. classified)	186.2	185.7	0.25	182.0
7	Internet	225.5	179.9	25.40	132.0
8	Magazines	115.4	110.6	4.34	100.2
9	Out-of-home	86.9	86.2	0.79	83.9
	Total	4,003.7	3,927.9	1.93	3,768.7

EXHIBIT 23.20

Steady Growth on the Horizon

Source: Reprinted with permission from the 2009 Hispanic Fact Pack issue of Advertising Age. Copyright, Crain Communications Inc. 2009.

editorial quality, and advertising sophistication. Ethnic newspapers provide niches for reaching every imaginable target segment.

One can find newspapers aimed at Russian, Chinese, Korean, Filipino, Armenian, and African American readers, to name only a few. They include publications that are issued on a sporadic basis with circulations of a few hundred to major dailies with more than 100,000 readers. Most of the ethnic-targeted publications have demonstrated significant circulation and advertising increases during the past decade. The one exception is the African American press. With few exceptions, newspapers directed to the African American community have shown severe drops in circulation compared to their peak during the 1940s. The decline of the African American press can be attributed to two primary causes:

1. The civil rights movement of the 1960s and 1970s pushed mainstream media, led by local newspapers, to begin more balanced coverage of the African American community. As major newspapers began to gain African American readers, circulation and advertising revenue shifted from the African American press to traditional publications. For example, the century-old *Chicago Defender*, one of the historic luminaries of the African American press, currently has a circulation of 15,000 compared to its peak of 250,000 in the 1960s.[48]

2. Another factor in the decline of the African American press is the fact that it was much easier for major newspapers to assimilate African American readers compared to other ethnic populations. There is no language barrier in reaching the African American community so advertisers don't have to make decisions concerning English versus indigenous languages. Although there are differences of media and product preferences among African Americans, just as among the white majority, they represent a much more homogeneous market than either Asian American or Hispanic American consumers.

In the past, small, independent publishers owned most ethnic newspapers. However, major newspaper chains are aggressively marketing ethnic publications especially to the Hispanic market. Led by *El Nuevo Herald* in Miami, *La Opinion* in Los Angeles, and *Hoy* in both New York and Chicago, these newspapers provide both readers and advertisers with information about news and products directed to the Hispanic market (see Exhibit 23.21). Hispanic-oriented magazines also have been extremely popular with this market. With a fashion, glamour, and celebrity emphasis, the major publications in this segment have been extremely profitable in recent years. With regard to Internet advertising (see Exhibit 23.22), it remains interesting to see that most advertisers on Hispanic web sites are similar to those on mainstream web sites, again demonstrating the importance of this market to general advertisers.

Although print media have had success in reaching the ethnic market, it is television that has attracted the majority of ethnic advertising dollars in the past decade. Reaching the ethnic market is not a new strategy. For almost 3 decades, syndicated television shows such as *Soul Train* have targeted African American audiences. Until the 1990s, ethnic programming was largely confined to syndicated shows and a few locally produced programs in major markets. However, cable brought opportunities to reach segmented audiences that had never been possible through broadcast television. Just as cable made it possible for history buffs, golfers, and chefs to have channels directed to their interests, likewise, it made narrowly focused ethnic programming practical. The introduction of channels such as Black Entertainment Network (BET) furnished entertainment and information to the African American audience not provided by mainstream networks.

The same model is now working for the Hispanic market. The Latino television market is dominated by Univision and Telemundo, a division of NBC Universal. Rather than being niche players among larger television rivals, they have become dominant

Rank	Newspaper	Gross 2008 Ad Revenue	% Change
1	*El Nuevo Herald* (Miami)	$72,776	−19.5
2	*La Opinion* (Los Angeles)	35,193	−23.2
3	*El Diario La Prensa* (New York)	25,732	0.1
4	*El Diario* (Juarez, Mexico)	25,308	−24.9
5	*Hoy* (Chicago)	21,709	8.1
6	*El Norte* (El Paso, Texas/Juarez, Mexico)	12,100	12.5
7	*La Raza* (Chicago)	10,234	−12.1
8	*Hoy* (Los Angeles)	10,150	−21.4
9	*Washington Hispanic*	8,910	−14.3
10	*El Sentinel* (Miami-Fort Lauderdale)	8,189	33.2
11	*La Voz de Phoenix*	8,038	27.4
12	*Al Dia* (Dallas)	6,800	5.8
13	*Hoy* (New York)	6,460	−39.2
14	*Diario Las Americas* (Miami)	6,047	1.3
15	*La Voz de Houston*	4,194	9.6
16	*Prensa Hispana* (Phoenix)	3,792	−2.1
17	*Vida en El Valle* (Fresno, Calif.)	3,568	−5.7
18	*Al Dia* (Philadelphia)	3,534	10.0
19	*TV y Mas* (Phoenix)	3,512	−48.5
20	*Mundo L.A.* (Los Angeles)	3,031	NA
21	*El Latino* (San Diego)	2,799	−11.2
22	*Lawndale News* (Chicago)	2,713	−29.8
23	*El Especial* (New York)	2,522	−11.1
24	*Excelsior* (Orange County, Calif.)	2,185	−3.2
25	*El Mensajero* (San Francisco)	2,153	−10.5

EXHIBIT 23.21

Top 25 Hispanic Newspapers

Dollars are in thousands. Measured newspaper ad spending from TNS Media Intelligence. Figures exclude classified advertising, select local retail categories, internet advertising and circulation revenue. Not all advertising editions are monitored. Percent change is computed from figures.

Source: Reprinted with permission from the 2009 Hispanic Fact Pack issue of *Advertising Age.* Copyright, Crain Communications Inc. 2009.

competitors for younger viewers regardless of language and have won the ratings battle on some occasions. This popularity has not been lost on mainstream broadcasters who have taken a number of steps to compete for the Hispanic audience. For example, ABC decided in 2005 to make its entire primetime lineup bilingual. At considerable expense, the network now subtitles all its shows and dubs four of its highest profile programs including *Desperate Housewives* and *Lost.*[49]

The growth and influence of Hispanic television also is apparent in program development at the major networks. Shows such as *George Lopez* obviously have great appeal to Hispanic audiences, but networks are also going a step further to design shows

Rank	Marketer	2008 Ad Spending	% Change
1	Broadcasting Media Partners (Univision)	$9,463	−55.3
2	Sprint Nextel Corp.	2,613	−43.6
3	CareerBuilder	2,308	6.4
4	IAC/InterActiveCorp	2,280	−10.1
5	Experian Group	2,152	NA
6	Verizon Communications	1,931	−34.9
7	Grupo Televisa	1,801	NA
8	Los Angeles Auto Show	1,769	−59.1
9	Hispanic Credit Solutions	1,367	−3.3
10	L'Oréal	1,297	60.3

EXHIBIT 23.22

Top 10 Advertisers on Hispanic Web Sites

Dollars are in thousands. Measured web ad spending from TNS Media Intelligence. TNS monitors 44 Hispanic sites. Excludes paid search and broadband video. Percent change is computed from 2007 data.

Source: Reprinted with permission from the 2009 Hispanic Fact Pack issue of *Advertising Age.* Copyright, Crain Communications Inc. 2009.

modeled after popular Spanish-language soap operas. Typically, these soaps, unlike the American format that may run for decades, are short form stories or "telenovelas" that run for 13 weeks and wrap up to a conclusion. In developing these shows, the networks hope to attract young female viewers of all backgrounds. However, they also acknowledge that it is a way to connect with the growing Hispanic viewership and to compete with Spanish-language broadcasters.[50]

Language continues to be a major obstacle in reaching the multinational audience. Despite the success of Spanish-language media, we are seeing more English-language programming and advertising directed to the bilingual or English-dominant market. For example, there are two English-language cable outlets for the Hispanic market, SiTV and Mun2. SiTV was launched in 2004 with an all-English format. The objective of SiTV is to reach young Latinos who primarily speak English and secondarily to create crossover appeal to African Americans, Asian Americans, and others who are fans of Latino pop culture but do not speak Spanish.[51] Mun2 (pronounced *mundos* or "two worlds") is a sister outlet to NBC's Telemundo aimed at the Latino youth market with a predominance of English-language programming.

The Asian American market is even more difficult to come to grips with because of the diversity of languages within a relatively small market. Presently, there are two Asian-language networks, ImaginAsian TV and AZN Television. Both are available in limited markets, but the high levels of income and education of the Asian American market make them popular with advertisers attempting to reach this market. A popular strategy for most advertisers is to place advertising in mainstream media but on programs that have high levels of ethnic viewers, listeners, or readers. For example, *Monday Night Football* has high viewership among African Americans and young Hispanic men, whereas shows such as *Desperate Housewives* and *Lost* have a huge following among Hispanic women. Regardless of the advertising plan of a particular advertiser, it is clear that the ethnic market is a fundamental part of the marketing strategy for virtually every major company.

THE MESSAGE   It is important to emphasize that whether advertisers are using English-language or foreign-language media, marketers must be sensitive to the messages and cultural connotations they communicate. Sometimes these problems are as basic as adapting well-known slogans to diverse markets. For example, Taco Bell's tagline, "Think Outside the Bun," designed to lure consumers away from traditional fast-food chains translated "man does not live by bread alone."[52] It is obvious that advertisers are trying a number of approaches to address the problems inherent in reaching these audiences, and they are demonstrating a level of sensitivity that, unfortunately, was missing in earlier years.

As we have seen, advertisers are now able to communicate with ethnic buyers through a number of media outlets. However, reaching the U.S. ethnic markets presents challenges similar to the ones multinational advertisers have found overseas. Advertisers must develop messages that are both sensitive to specific ethnic cultures and, at the same time, provide effective sales messages. Attempts by mainstream advertisers to develop campaigns to reach these markets have resulted in a huge growth in advertising agencies concentrated in ethnic marketing. Exhibit 23.23 lists the largest U.S.–based multicultural advertising agencies by specialty. Dallas-based Dieste brought in more than $44 million in revenue and was recently named top multicultural agency by *Advertising Age* for its work helping clients such as Nissan, Nationwide, Hershey, and Pepsi reach Hispanic customers.

Major advertisers such as Target, Sears, and JCPenney are producing Spanish-language advertising circulars, in-store signage, and some, such as Wal-Mart, even offer Spanish-language magazines distributed free in stores with high levels of Hispanic patronage. Wal-Mart also is using its highly sophisticated inventory tracking system to coordinate merchandising and advertising between its stores in Mexico and those in the United States. For example, Wal-Mart saw the success that its Mexican stores achieved by devoting significant space to baby and children's clothing and stocking a large selection of items with cartoon characters. Based on Mexican sales, the company tweaked its

EXHIBIT 23.23

The Largest Multicultural Agencies

Rank		Agency	Headquarters	U.S. Revenue	
'08	'07			2008	% Change
Hispanic-American					
1	1	Dieste [Omnicom]	Dallas	$44,900	11.1
2	2	Vidal Partnership	New York	35,000	12.9
3	3	Bravo Group [WPP (Y&R)]	Miami	31,500	5.0
4	7	GlobalHue	Southfield, Mich.	28,178	37.2
5	4	Lopez Negrete Communications	Houston	24,150	1.6
6	8	Zubi Advertising Services	Coral Gables, Fla.	21,500	9.7
7	5	Bromley Communications (Publicis)	San Antonio	21,100	−6.6
8	6	Conill [Publicis (Saatchi)]	Miami	19,900	−3.9
9	9	LatinWorks [Omnicom]	Austin, Texas	17,440	1.5
10	12	Alma DDB [Omnicom (DDB)]	Coral Gables, Fla.	14,800	13.0
African-American					
1	4	GlobalHue	Southfield, Mich.	$25,900	31.6
2	1	UniWorld Group [WPP]	New York	25,668	−4.0
3	2	Carol H. Williams Advertising	Oakland, Calif.	23,900	−5.9
4	3	Burrell Communications Group [Publicis]	Chicago	22,000	−4.3
5	5	Sanders/Wingo	El Paso, Texas	14,350	21.5
6	8	Fuse	St. Louis	9,351	14.5
7	9	Images USA	Atlanta	9,253	47.9
8	7	Footsteps [Omnicom]	New York	7,000	−14.6
9	6	Matlock Advertising & Public Relations	Atlanta	5,107	−38.3
10	11	Moroch Partners	Dallas	5,000	6.4
Asian-American					
1	1	Kang & Lee Advertising [WPP (Y&R)]	New York	$15,500	3.3
2	3	Admerasia	New York	10,250	−2.4
3	2	InterTrend Communications	Long Beach, Calif.	10,245	−15.5
4	4	IW Group [Interpublic]	West Hollywood, Calif.	9,085	−10.8
5	7	AdAsia Communications	New York	7,059	22.3
6	5	Time Advertising	Millbrae, Calif.	5,800	−18.3
7	6	PanCom International	Los Angeles	5,103	−13.5
8	9	Global Advertising Strategies	New York	5,000	11.1
9	8	ES Advertising	Los Angeles	4,486	−5.0
10	17	Aaaza	Los Angeles	3,000	71.4

Source: Reprinted with permission from the 2009 Hispanic Fact Pack issue of *Advertising Age.* Copyright, Crain Communications Inc. 2009.

inventory in U.S. stores catering to a Hispanic population. These and other efforts are paying off as a recent survey showed that 36 percent of Hispanic shoppers rated Wal-Mart as their favorite store with no other retailer named by more than 4 percent.[53]

Despite the many positive strides taken by firms during the past 20 years, problems still plague outreach efforts to the ethnic market. As one Hispanic marketing executive said, "Advertisers and their marketing departments are looking at the Hispanic community as a group when in fact there are many factors that make up this 'Group' and they must take into account the diversity which includes the country of origin, whether they are the first or second generation here in the U.S., and their general location . . . a second generation Latino living in Texas would react differently to an ad that is geared toward a second generation Latino living in New York or a second generation Latino living in Miami, Florida."[54] For example, General Motors ran a Saturn commercial in Miami showing a woman in a Mexican dress in front of the Alamo. Unfortunately for GM, the overwhelming majority of the Miami Hispanic community is Cuban American, and the commercial had little or no relevance to them.[55]

While major marketers continue to reach ethnic markets in niche media with messages directed at specific target segments, they also are aware of the growing acculturation of ethnic products, entertainment, and messages into mainstream American

culture and media. Major network portrayals of the ethnic population still lag behind
reality, but, nevertheless, we are seeing entertainment and advertising themes that highlight ethnic subjects (see Exhibit 23.24). In 2005, for the fiftieth anniversary of Crest
toothpaste, Procter & Gamble decided to bring back the "Crest Kid" campaign. It was
last used in 1960 and featured children shouting "Look Mom—no cavities." In the new
version, the advertising featured Cuban-born Enya Martinez who was chosen from
3,000 candidates for her white smile.

During the past several years, a number of major marketers have changed their
product images to reflect a changing population. "In 1989, Aunt Jemima, the matriarch
of the pancake-and-syrup products from PepsiCo's Quaker Oats, had her headband removed, got a new hairstyle and was outfitted with a lace collar and pearl earrings. With
heightened recognition of the buying power of Latinos, African-Americans and other
demographic groups, many advertisers want to make sure their brand accoutrements—
slogans, logos, and spokespersons—match the tenor of the day."[56] The trend toward
both ethnic specific marketing and cultural assimilation into mainstream advertising
will continue as these markets continue to grow in both population and purchasing
power.

Marketers are often creative in conveying cultural diversity to their promotional
mix. For example, brands as diverse as McDonald's, Chrysler, and Jose Cuervo tequila
have initiated promotions celebrating Cinco de Mayo, a minor Mexican holiday com-
memorating a Mexican militia victory over the French army in 1862. "Savvy marketers
with an eye for the burgeoning Hispanic market—and, even more, the cross-ethnicity
appeal of Hispanic culture—have caught on. Homemade Mexican food, mariachis and
sombreros have in the past five years given way to McDonald's-sponsored street festivals, giant Jose Cuervo margaritas and a 900-pound piñata in the shape of a Chrysler
car."[57] More than any particular promotion, events such as Cinco de Mayo underscore
the fact that assimilation is not a one-way street. Just as immigrants to the United States
adopt many U.S. products and customs, American consumers embrace everything from
salsa to Chinese food, and these products become part of the total fabric of the "melt-
ing pot." This assimilation can be traced in the prediction that close to half of third-
generation Latinos marry non-Latinos, which may have major implications for future
marketing strategy.

THE PRODUCT For many years, virtually all multicultural marketing programs consisted of the development of products and brands specifically for various segments of the ethnic market. However, as this population has grown, we are seeing a significant number of brands being introduced from abroad—either by American-based multinational corporations or foreign-based companies exporting popular brands to the U.S. expatriate market. Alen, a major Mexican manufacturer of household cleaning products, exports a number of its brands to the United States. The company believes that there is a ready-made U.S. market of Mexican immigrants who are already familiar with the brand. Likewise, companies such as PepsiCo and Colgate-Palmolive, with strong Mexican subsidiaries, have imported some of their products to the United States. For example, PepsiCo has introduced chili-flavored lollipops with a mango-gum center, and Colgate-Palmolive has imported two of its most popular brands—Suavitel, a fabric softener and Fabuloso, a liquid cleaner. These companies have a dual strategy of primarily appealing to the Hispanic market and at the same time building future sales through crossover purchases by the general population.

Although these brands have the advantage of having been "test marketed" in other countries, there are still challenges to successful importation. Perhaps the biggest hurdle is realizing that even though the brands are the same, the consumers are not. These differences must be reflected in advertising and promotion. As one Hispanic advertising executive commented, importing advertising along with a product is a perfect way to throw away money. "We [immigrants] live a different reality. We're in a foreign land, don't have family around and everything is in a different language. The people get acculturated and have different tastes. Someone may be watching a telenovela but be completely American."[58] Regardless of how a product comes to the U.S. market, the landscape shows numerous examples of how companies are adapting their product offerings to the ethnic markets (see Exhibit 23.25).

Success in the ethnic market is based on relevant communication, delivered through credible media, and backed with products that meet the needs of specific market segments. In other words, profits in the ethnic marketplace are generated according to the same formula found in any other sector. Success is also based on planning using insightful research. In the next section, we discuss how marketers are trying to put the research part of the multicultural puzzle together.

RESEARCH For many years, marketers either ignored the ethnic market or based decisions on invalid research or stereotypes. The lack of reliable research was based on a number of factors including the following:

- Often researchers had little or no experience in ethnic marketing.
- Respondents sometimes were uncooperative with researchers because of language barriers and a lack of full explanations of the research's aims.

Courtesy of the Charleston Metro Chamber of Commerce.

EXHIBIT 23.25

"Muchas Conexiones," welcomes the Charleston Metro Chamber of Commerce.

- Ethnically oriented syndicated research studies were unavailable.
- The weighting of research samples often did not fully consider the ethnic population, especially in some major markets.

Regardless of the reasons, the result was a scarcity of information concerning the multicultural market. Today, that situation is changing, driven primarily by the growth in sales and profitability and the significant investments that are being made in marketing efforts to tap this segment. Research dollars, as is the case with any business expenditure, are driven by the potential return on investment. In the case of advertising research, dollars invested in research are directly correlated with the increasing expenditures in advertising dollars allotted to ethnic audiences. When advertising budgets were relatively small, companies were willing to make advertising decisions more on intuition than hard data. However, firms spending millions of dollars to reach the multicultural market can't risk flawed decision making concerning their advertising investments. The combination of overall population increases and higher levels of buying power continues to make the ethnic market one that is hard to ignore.

Improved research in the ethnic markets also has resulted in a more realistic view of the significant differences exhibited within these groups, and it has helped avoid potentially disastrous stereotyping that often creates ill-will among the very markets a firm is trying to cultivate. Like any market research, the primary objective should be to better serve the needs of a target segment by providing products and advertising messages that most appropriately address their needs. In a major study of Hispanic consumers, *People en Espanol* found significant differences between Hispanic buyers and the general population.[59] Some of these findings include the following:

1. Hispanics are much more likely to go shopping; 56 percent agree with the statement "I love to shop," compared with 39 percent of the general population.

2. Hispanics are much more influenced by advertising than the general population. They are likely to purchase products because of brand image or a perception that a brand is new and trendy (see Exhibit 23.26).

3. They are more likely to pay with cash, with only 15 percent using credit cards compared to 40 percent of the general market.

4. Hispanics are almost 40 percent more likely to download music than the general population. However, overall Internet use is lower (11 percent) among the Spanish-dominant population.

5. Perhaps most significant was the finding that there is a retro acculturation taking place. Even English-dominant Hispanics are returning to their Latin roots in terms of language and media preference.

The latter finding has major implications for the way a company markets to Hispanics. In terms of products, media, and language, there needs to be a significant sensitivity to the way in which this market is approached. From the research, it is clear that the Hispanic population takes increasing pride in their heritage—regardless of their language preference, a fact that needs to be closely watched as advertising executions are developed.

One of the best indicators of the importance of ethnic research is the money invested by both advertisers and media. Nielsen Media Research provides national television ratings through its National Hispanic People Meter sample, and the company

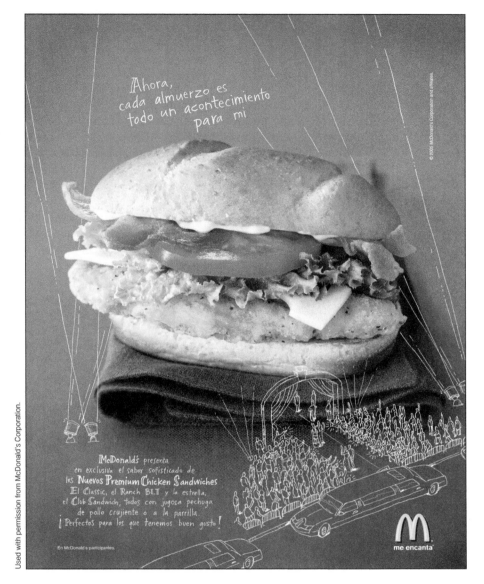

EXHIBIT 23.26

This McDonald's chicken sandwich looks good in any language.

also measures local Hispanic television audiences in 19 of the largest Hispanic markets. Likewise, the Arbitron Hispanic Market Service provides radio ratings for 24 of the largest Hispanic markets. Similar services are available from both rating services for African American broadcast audiences. On the print side, most of the major ethnic print publications are audited by one of the several services that provide guaranteed circulation figures. Multicultural research is underscoring the fact that multicultural consumers have traditional purchasing habits and customs that must be reflected in advertising and promotion. However, research shows that when a brand gains acceptance in the minority community, there is a significant level of brand and company loyalty that makes the effort extremely profitable.

SUMMARY

It is clear that both at home and abroad global and multinational advertising has moved from special niches to an integral part of the promotion plans of the majority of companies. In the United States, even the smallest retailer engages in some form of international marketing—either in the goods it sells or those it buys. As more countries improve both their economic situations and their openness to trade with other nations, we will see even more business conducted on an international basis.

Although multinational marketing has many unique features, the contribution to profitability is the primary objective of all promotional endeavors. The driving force behind multinational marketing is the search for new markets by the countries from the mature economies of the United States, Japan, and Europe to the emerging industrial powers of China and India. In many respects, the search for overseas markets has been the motivation for foreign trade since the days of the early Dutch, English, and Spanish traders in the fifteenth and sixteenth centuries—and, for that matter, the Phoenicians of prehistoric times.

Many of the recent innovations in international advertising have been driven by the introduction of new forms of communication technology. In the 1970s, major U.S. publications began worldwide distribution of foreign-language editions. Print was followed by satellite transmissions of television signals and, more recently, the emergence of the Internet and mobile devices. Each has contributed to a faster pace of advertising and marketing on a worldwide basis.

The potential rewards of marketing in emerging countries can be substantially greater than the same effort invested in domestic marketing. However, multinational companies have learned that overseas marketing and advertising are very different from traditional American advertising. Although the basic functions may be the same, the complexities of dealing in a global economy include testing the planning, research, and the managerial abilities of both companies and their advertising agencies.

One thing is certain: Advertising will play a major role as companies move into more overseas markets. The most successful brands usually will be those that establish the first beachhead in emerging markets by taking pioneering risks. The common criteria for U.S. advertising—CPMs, cost-per-point, audited circulation and verified ratings, and even short-term ROI—are often not applicable in many foreign markets. Instead, experience, judgment, and calculated risk taking must be used to deal with the intricacies of international marketing.

Moreover, even those U.S. businesses that do not participate in multinational advertising will be faced with the challenges of ethnic diversity in the United State. The growth in size and buying power of the African American, Hispanic, and Asian American markets will increasingly require the creative use of media, promotion, and sales messages to reach this eclectic marketplace. Not only business expertise but also sensitivity to the culture, language, and values of other people will be required in this new environment. However, for those willing to devote the time to learn how to operate in this diverse market, the rewards will be great. Clearly, multicultural advertising will continue to undergo a period of dramatic change throughout this decade.

REVIEW

1. What are some of the advantages and disadvantages of the Internet in international marketing?
2. How do legal restrictions affect the execution of multinational marketing?
3. Discuss the marketing concept in terms of global marketing.
4. What are some of the potential advantages and disadvantages of free trade agreements?
5. Discuss the importance of cultural considerations in executing international advertising.
6. Discuss some of the primary means U.S. firms use to enter foreign markets.
7. Discuss the role of product development in meeting the demands of both international marketing and the U.S. ethnic population.
8. What effect has cultural assimilation had on American marketing?
9. Discuss advertising research as a tool for overcoming ethnic stereotyping.

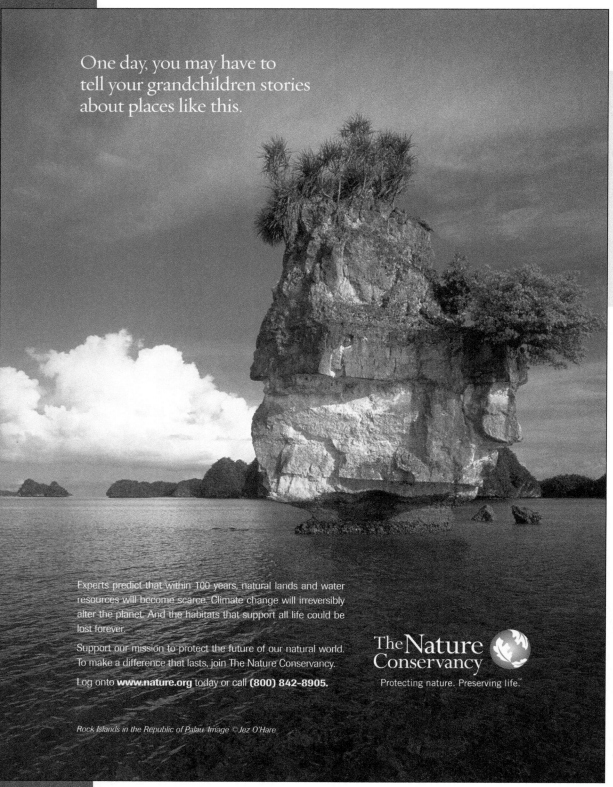

One day, you may have to tell your grandchildren stories about places like this.

Experts predict that within 100 years, natural lands and water resources will become scarce. Climate change will irreversibly alter the planet. And the habitats that support all life could be lost forever.

Support our mission to protect the future of our natural world. To make a difference that lasts, join The Nature Conservancy.

Log onto **www.nature.org** today or call **(800) 842-8905.**

The **Nature** Conservancy

Protecting nature. Preserving life.

Rock Islands in the Republic of Palau. Image © Jez O'Hare

Economic, Social, and Legal Effects of Advertising

A DVERTISING DOESN'T operate in isolation. Marketers, policy makers and advocacy groups work to maintain fair and transparent environments for facilitating exchanges. ▶

CHAPTER LEARNING OBJECTIVES

1. List three eras of advertising criticism.

2. Identify economic arguments for and against advertising.

3. Explain the difference between inadvertent and intentional social roles of advertising.

4. Identify social criticisms of advertising.

5. Explain the difference between issue-advocacy and cause-related advertising.

6. Describe the FTC's role in advertising regulation.

7. Discuss the components of the *Central Hudson Four-Part Test*.

8. List three negative consequences of comparison advertising.

9. Discuss the primary roles of the NARC, NARB, and the CARU in supporting advertising regulation.

Because advertising is such a public element of business, it often comes under greater scrutiny than other elements of the marketing mix. From governmental regulators and the courts to irate consumers writing letters to complain about a television commercial, companies know that the messages they communicate can have significant consequences—both positive and negative. Because it is so pervasive, advertising has a special responsibility to adhere to high ethical and honest business standards as it serves to create economic expansion. Advertising can also advocate social causes, to sway public opinion concerning controversial issues, or underscore a firm's corporate citizenship such as this ad for The Nature Conservancy. This chapter examines the diverse methods that advertisers use as both economic and social communication tools and the constraints under which advertisers work.

Advertising Criticism: A Historical Perspective

Criticism of advertising is not a new phenomenon, but the public's perception of advertising and its expectations have changed markedly during the past 150 years. Before discussing some contemporary areas of advertising evaluation, let's begin by tracing the history of advertising criticism:

1. *The Era of Exaggerated Claims, 1865–1900.* During the era of exaggerated claims (1865–1900), most people accepted advertising as "buyer beware" communication

1 List three eras of advertising criticism.

EXHIBIT 24.1

Magnetic machines and patent medicine were once sold as panaceas for health concerns.

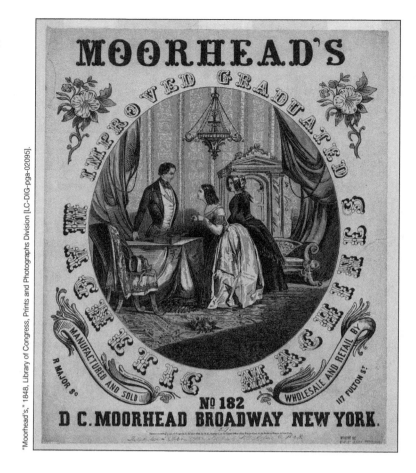

"Moorhead's," 1848, Library of Congress, Prints and Photographs Division [LC-DIG-pga-02095].

in which virtually any claim for a product was allowed. Some advertising claims during this period, especially for patent medicine (see Exhibit 24.1), were so outlandish that one wonders how anyone could have possibly believed them.

2. *The Era of Public Awareness, 1900–1965.* It was during the period from 1900 to 1965 that both the public and governmental regulators began to reject the notion of a laissez-faire, unregulated economic system. By the turn of the twentieth century, legislation such as the Pure Food and Drug Act of 1906 demonstrated Congress's recognition that the public was demanding protection from monopolies as well as of the prevailing untruthful portrayal of products and services. Many responsible advertisers feared for the very existence of the industry as deceptive advertisements became more prevalent during the closing years of the nineteenth century. It was during this period that both enlightened media executives and advertisers realized that there were real opportunities to provide consumers with helpful information that would enhance both their public image and profitability.

3. *The Era of Social Responsibility, 1965–present.* During the past 45 years, advertisers have come to realize that truth alone is not sufficient to meet the demands of ethical advertising. Companies acknowledge that they must meet a higher standard of social responsibility than simply providing literally truthful advertising. Critics of advertising and, for that matter, advertisers deal with a delicate philosophical balancing act. Without totally rejecting the classical economic concept of the rational buyer, both critics and enlightened marketers agree that some level of consumer protection is needed. The concept of consumer protection spawned the consumer movement of the 1960s, oversight of environmental safety, and a heightened awareness of various claims featured in modern advertising.

THE ROLE OF CORPORATE RESPONSIBILITY

During much of the past century there has been a move toward corporations taking more responsibility for noneconomic endeavors supporting humanitarian causes, for being environmentally responsive, and for supporting numerous social issues. In the opinion of some economists, the notion of the corporation as a social organization runs counter to its primary goal as a profit-making institution. They would argue that, rather than being indifferent to an improved society, diverting resources from business to society in the long run harms both.

More than 200 years ago in his classic book *The Wealth of Nations,* Adam Smith popularized the notion that individuals should pursue a selfish course and, in return, society as a whole would be the better for it. The book explored the intellectual framework that explained the benefit of a free market. Smith is most often recognized by the expression "the invisible hand," a term that he coined to demonstrate how self-interest guides the most efficient use of resources in a nation's economy, with public welfare coming as a by-product. To underscore his laissez-faire convictions, Smith argued that state and personal efforts to promote social good are ineffectual compared to unbridled market forces.[1] Smith explained his philosophy, "Every individual is continually exerting himself to find out the most advantageous employment for whatever capital he can command. It is his own advantage, indeed, and not that of the society, which he has in view. But the study of his own advantage naturally, or rather necessarily, leads him to prefer that employment which is most advantageous to the society."[2]

In today's global business environment, the ideas of Adam Smith are not as easily adaptable to a complex business climate. There is no easy answer to the question of the proper role of companies as members of society. One critic of corporate responsibility wrote, "The 20th century proved [Adam Smith to be correct]: Profit seeking corporations, constrained and buttressed by moderate governmental regulation and spending, did far more to increase the welfare of the world than a proliferation of 'socially responsible' governments. And the 21st century is proving it yet again: China's embrace of Adam Smith has yielded the greatest alleviation of poverty in history."[3]

Ilyse Hogue of the Rainforest Action Network expressed a contrary view, "Increasingly, citizens and progressive businesses are recognizing the false divide that the modern-day economic system is struggling to overcome. Should we have to choose between higher quarterly returns or assuring the health of our children's future? More people are saying no. There has to be a way to do both."[4] Clearly, there are no definite answers to the many questions raised by the sometimes-conflicting social responsibilities that the public places on businesses. Likewise, advertising, as the communicator of corporate philosophy, often finds itself the focal point of much of this debate.

Advertising as an Economic and Social Institution

Despite the ongoing debate about the proper social role of business, the majority of both consumers and marketers agree that the social and economic components of advertising are not mutually exclusive. Marketing executives are part of society and benefit from environmental awareness, better education, and other societal issues that are brought to the public's attention through advertising. A number of studies indicate that buyers support those companies and brands that have gained a reputation for being good citizens and actively promote their good works. By the same token, to the extent that advertising contributes to a stronger economy, advertisers and the public gain a higher standard of living.

THE ECONOMIC ROLE OF ADVERTISING

There is little debate that the primary role of advertising is communication. However, there is a major dispute as to whether this information is helpful to consumers. On the one hand, advertising advocates view advertising as providing necessary information to allow consumers to make informed decisions about new products and to choose the best brands to solve a problem (see Exhibit 24.2). On the other hand, the contrary view by those critical of advertising is that it provides consumers with little useful information and that advertisers are much more interested in persuading prospects to buy products they don't need at inflated prices than in offering useful information. The "persuasion versus information" debate is one that will never be resolved because it is a function of two forces: (1) the biases of the proadvertising and antiadvertising camps and (2) the fact that advertising does function in both roles.

We would be extremely naive to think that advertising (or any marketing sales tool) is not trying to influence our behavior. Firms are in business to sell goods and services and to present their products in the most favorable light possible. As long as the message is truthful and accurate, advertising is serving a function that both buyer and seller understand. By the same token, we would expect that the best persuasion is based on solid information about the benefits offered by a particular brand. Another aspect of the information-persuasion debate focuses on the brevity of advertising. That is, a slogan, billboard, or headline—no matter how creatively written—imparts little or no information. Advertisers would argue that their messages need to be considered over the long term, not on an ad-by-ad basis. Brands such as Coca-Cola, Tide, Sony, and Toyota have established such a high degree of familiarity with consumers that much of their advertising is devoted to maintaining top-of-mind awareness as contrasted to selling in a traditional sense.

Some economists expand the criticism of advertising as persuasion to one of "advertising as a detriment to market entry." That is, advertising, by providing little information, works to the detriment of new products entering the market. They see the role of advertising as being one of encouraging brand switching among established products rather than allowing consumers to make informed decisions about new products coming into the marketplace. Within these extreme positions are many specific pros and

EXHIBIT 24.2

Advertising allows consumers to make more informed choices.

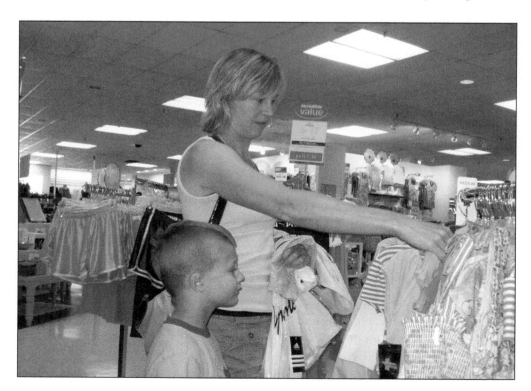

cons about the economic value of advertising. Let's review some of the major arguments for and against the economic role of advertising.

ECONOMIC ARGUMENTS IN FAVOR OF ADVERTISING

1. Advertising provides consumers with information to make informed decisions about new products, availability of products, price, and product benefits. "Brands and advertising are things people can see, touch, and feel, and they know if a company's ads and brands are reliable and can be counted on as is often said, the fastest way to kill a bad product is to advertise it—because consumers will try it and find out firsthand how bad it really is."[5]

2. Advertising supports largely unrestricted media that disseminate news and entertainment. In addition to the social benefits of an independent press, advertising provides employment for the thousands of editorial, production, and administrative workers in these media.

3. By promoting product differentiation, advertising encourages continuing product improvements and the introduction of new and innovative goods and services (see Exhibit 24.3). Competing brands are forced to enhance the benefits of their products to maintain market share.

4. Mass advertising permits companies to achieve economies of scale in production that more than offset the per unit cost of advertising and, combined with competition among opposing brands, results in lower prices.

5. Advertising contributes to increases in the overall economy by increasing generic as well as brand consumption. For example, faced with a steady decline in consumption of cold cereals, a consortium of the big four cereal makers (i.e., Kellogg's, General Mills, Post, and Quaker Foods) devised "The better breakfast" generic campaign to promote the nutrition and convenience of cereals.[6]

2 Identify economic arguments for and against advertising.

ECONOMIC ARGUMENTS AGAINST ADVERTISING

1. The intent of advertising is to persuade, not to inform. Critics dismiss the notion that advertising distributes information on which consumers can base informed decisions. They contend that advertising communicates extravagant product claims and, at best, is guilty of sins of omissions by providing only positive information about a brand.

2. On a macroeconomic basis, advertising spending is largely wasted because it primarily causes consumers to switch from one brand to another without any net economic gain to society.

3. Many economists challenge the notion that advertising lowers the price of products and services. To the contrary, they charge that one of the primary goals of advertising is to insulate a brand from price competition by emphasizing emotional appeals so that price comparisons become less important in purchase decisions.

4. The high rate of advertising expenditures in many product categories makes it difficult, if not impossible, for new products to enter the market. For example, in product categories such as cigarettes, beer, and laundry products in which two or three firms dominate each category, product introductions by other companies are extremely rare.

What conclusions can we draw after reviewing the pros and cons of these arguments concerning the economic role of advertising? The fact is that there is evidence to support each of these claims and counterclaims for advertising. One can find cases in which advertising *was* the catalyst for the introduction of a new and profitable brand or product category. However, there are numerous examples of product categories in which the objective of advertising is to maintain market share and encourage consumers to substitute one brand for another.

EXHIBIT 24.3

Advertising creates competition and enhances product innovation.

Courtesy of Blattner Brunner, Pittsburgh, Atlanta, Washington.

Even in product categories that seem to demonstrate evidence for one side or the other, there is often a middle ground. For instance, there is no question that market share in a number of food and household product segments is dominated by a handful of companies. However, although a few national firms hold dominant market share among these national brands, the emergence of store brands in outlets such as Wal-Mart and Kroger offer consumers many low-price options in products as varied as disposable diapers, batteries, garbage bags, and soft drinks.

It is difficult to deal in generalities when evaluating the economic value of advertising. Advertising's contribution to product sales depends on a host of circumstances unique to each product. The utility of advertising in a market for a relatively new product category, such as satellite radio, is much different from that for beer or cigarettes, which are characterized by flat sales and brand switching. However, if sophisticated, multinational companies are spending billions of dollars on advertising, it is obvious that advertising must be contributing to their profitability.

The Social Role of Advertising

While it is generally agreed that advertising bonds with consumers on both an economic and cultural basis, in recent years it is the effect of advertising on society that has drawn the most attention and controversy to the industry. Perhaps the fundamental question raised in the social context of advertising criticism is whether advertising shapes and defines culture or simply mirrors an evolving society. As we will see, the answer is some of both. Certainly the study and criticism of advertising as a social force has been an ongoing topic of discussion for more than 50 years. A half century ago, David Potter contrasted the economic and cultural roles of advertising:

> The most important effects of this powerful institution are not upon the economics of our distribution system; they are upon the values of our society. If the economic effect is to make the purchaser like what he buys, the social effect is, in a parallel but broader sense, to make the individual like what he gets—to enforce already existing attitudes, to diminish the range and variety of choices, and in terms of abundance, to exalt the materialistic virtues of consumption.[7]

During the past 2 decades, many researchers have significantly changed their approach to the study of culture and advertising. At one time, there was a clear dichotomy between the two major types of cultural effects of advertising on the audience:

1. *Advertising's inadvertent social role.* Those advertising scholars interested in inadvertent social effects often studied advertising from the viewpoint that the ubiquitous, redundant messages presented by advertising through the mass media created various changes in the way the audience responded to their environment. This perspective assumed that advertising conveys largely unintended messages that, nevertheless, impart information about society in general or some segment of the public. By the sheer weight of exposure, advertising sets a social agenda of what is expected, what is fashionable, and what is tasteful for a significant number of people. These influences are particularly true for the young, the undereducated, and the impressionable. More often than not researchers in the so-called "critical-cultural" mode regard these consequences of advertising on society as decidedly negative.

2. *Advertising's overt social role.* A second, less studied area of advertising's social and cultural role deals with advertising as an agent of social change. That is, those campaigns whose primary objective is the promoting of a social agenda. Every day we encounter advertising messages promoting safe driving, adult literacy, environmental causes, and a host of other forms of social activism (see Exhibit 24.4). Given the efficiencies of advertising in selling products, it is not surprising that more special interest groups have recognized the value and effectiveness of advertising.

In the past decade, we have seen a movement to a different view of advertising and cultural effects. A new school of researchers is studying the trend toward advertising adopting techniques that, at one time, were inadvertent effects as an integral part of their advertising strategy. In this view, advertising's cultural dimension is not separated from its economic dimension. In this point of view, consumption cannot be understood outside the societal and group implications in which it is undertaken. Furthermore, advertisers simultaneously incorporate cultural icons in their advertising and, at the same time, use advertising to create new ones. ". . . culture is the accumulation of shared meanings, rituals, norms, and traditions among the members of an organization or society. Consumption choices simply cannot be understood without considering the cultural context in which they are made: culture is the lens through which people view products."[8]

③ Explain the difference between inadvertent and intentional social roles of advertising.

EXHIBIT 24.4

These ads encourage teens to pursue long-term goals and graduate from high school.

This school of research assumes that advertising is no longer promoting products, but, rather, brands are positioned as another part of a person's cultural experience. Products are now bought less for function than as a statement about how people see themselves. In this approach, brands still function as a form of differentiation, but they are used more as audience segmentation strategies than to highlight product distinctions. In this perspective, companies are "... no longer simply branding their own products, but branding the outside culture as well—by sponsoring cultural events, they [can] go out into the world and claim bits of it as brand-name outposts."[9]

Sophisticated research techniques increasingly allow marketers to understand why consumers purchase particular brands by moving beyond the functional benefits of a product and concentrating more on the symbolic meaning that brands convey to particular buyers or market segments. By doing so, advertisers can create both products and, some would argue, images that closely match the worldview of potential buyers. "Good advertisers know how to analyze which properties of a specific product or service will resonate best with consumers. To do this, advertisers must develop a deep understanding of the meanings that are resident in each consumer's culturally constituted world."[10]

Advertising is quickly moving to a point where so-called secondary or inadvertent effects of advertising are becoming part of the primary theme of many advertisers. As products become homogenized, sellers look to advertising and brand image as the principal difference among competing products. As we discussed earlier, differentiation is not found in the product itself but in the mind of the consumer. More importantly, once a brand achieves a dominant position based on image and cultural associations, it is much more difficult for competitors to match than real product differences.

Although the debate continues about the role of advertising and culture, there is no question that advertisers know that effective advertising must mirror social and cultural values by channeling the predispositions of consumers into purchases of particular brands. Advertisers realize that people react in positive or negative ways to the total environment in which a product is presented—including media, message, and presentation—and advertisers must be sensitive to both the intended and inadvertent cues they impart in their marketing.

SOME SOCIAL CRITICISMS OF ADVERTISING

Since the late 1880s, advertising has been the focus of numerous examples of criticism from a host of sources. In recent years, social criticism of advertising has taken precedent over its economic effects. The range of criticism involves advertising strategies, advertising's execution, the targeted audience, and even those groups making use of it. Everyone and everything in advertising's social realm are fair game. Some representative examples of social criticisms of advertising include the following:

4 Identify social criticisms of advertising.

- *Privacy concerns.* In recent years, consumers have become increasingly concerned about privacy issues. This heightened awareness is in large part the result of the development of sophisticated communication technology. The intrusion of spam, other types of unsolicited e-mail, and tracking devices such as radio frequency identification (RFID) tags and cookies have made consumers aware of the numerous techniques used by marketers and others to follow their behavior. The Do Not Call Registry legislation to limit telemarketing is the clearest evidence that both the public and legislative bodies are taking public fears about privacy and intrusiveness issues seriously. In a letter to the FTC, the American Advertising Federation (AAF) affirmed its support of privacy legislation. "The goal of this principle is that personal information should not be used in a way that goes beyond an individual's understanding and consent. If the manner of use of the information is not foreseen, then the consumer has not provided implicit consent."[11]

- *Product placement.* Product placement is not a new technique. Gordon's Gin is said to have had Katharine Hepburn toss its product overboard in *The African Queen.* The technique gained popularity with the sales success of Reese's Pieces after being seen in *ET.*[12] However, as the public has become more resistant to traditional media advertising, advertisers are using various placement techniques as part of their core marketing strategy rather than as a minor component of a marketing plan. Reality shows such as *The Apprentice* build their scripts around featured products. Although many audience members don't seem to be concerned about these activities, critics question the ethics involved. "Product placements are inherently deceptive, because many people do not realize that they are, in fact, advertisements. We're [Commercial Alert] running a campaign to require disclosure of product placement in all media, including TV, movies, videos, video games, books and 'adversongs.'"[13]

- *Advertising's role in obesity.* A number of lawsuits have been filed against fast-food chains charging that their promotions of high-calorie, fatty menu items have led to various health problems. The suits are particularly critical of the chains' longtime emphasis on promotions to children.

SPECIFIC AREAS OF SOCIAL CRITICISM OF ADVERTISING

Space doesn't allow us to fully deal with the uses and criticism of social aspects of advertising. However, companies are being held accountable for both the products and services they provide and the advertising and promotion that support them. Although there are unique features to each of the social criticisms we have analyzed, they tend to focus on four areas:

1. *Advertising content.* By far the most criticized area of advertising is the content of specific advertisements and commercials. Critics point to a spectrum of alleged abuses including the use of sexual themes, exaggerated product claims, debasement of language, the creation of stereotypes, and manipulating children with unrealistic promises. In 1957, Vance Packard's *The Hidden Persuaders* set forth the idea that advertisers were secretly manipulating consumers through "subliminal perception." Using motivational research techniques, Packard alleged that advertising used hidden messages or flashed icons in television shows and movies that operated below the level of conscious perception but, nevertheless, changed the audience's purchase behavior. Although most psychologists agree that Packard greatly overstated the use and value of motivational research, the book did put even greater public scrutiny on advertising. For example, even though there was no evidence that the media were involved in the practice, the major networks issued statements that they would not allow the practice.[14]

   The majority of these objections are directed at alleged exaggerated claims in advertising. Many critics charge that advertising is more likely to provide misinformation, negative content, and in some cases, outright falsehoods than useful consumer information. As we discuss later in this chapter, there are few business enterprises that undergo more governmental and regulatory scrutiny in advertising. But apart from these formal constraints, advertisers know that it is counterproductive to mislead consumers. Although false or misleading advertising may influence a consumer to make an initial purchase, it is rare that an unsatisfied consumer will return.

   One of the long-standing areas of advertising criticism is the portrayal of various segments of society. Many observers claim that advertising deals in objectionable stereotypes in its treatment of the elderly, women, and minorities. In recent years, even advertising's harshest critics agree that most mainstream marketers have made noteworthy strides in portraying these groups in a more realistic and favorable light. However, there are those who see that the advertising has significant room for improvement. "Three decades after the women's movement offered women greater equality and expanded roles, a small chorus of media critics laments what it sees as a one-dimensional portrayal of women by Madison Avenue, characterized by nudity, extreme thinness, sensuality, even bondage. With their dual emphasis on physical perfection and sexuality, such ads, these critics say, can create body dissatisfaction, fuel addictions, and subtly legitimize violence and bondage."[15]

   Ironically, one of the audience segments that seems to have lost ground in the struggle for advertising realism is men. In recent years, a number of voices have been raised about the representation of the "bumbling male" in numerous advertisements and commercials. For example, the theme of many ads is that the simplest household chore, particularly those involving child care, are beyond the capacity of any male. In one commercial, the mother must take care of the family's children (with the appropriate brand of decongestant) after her dim-witted husband allowed them to play in the snow wearing only T-shirts. In other cases, men are portrayed as so hormonally challenged that the very sight of an attractive woman sends them into a state of involuntary lust and ineptitude. Recently, J. Walter Thompson, one of the world's largest agencies addressed the problem: "Men have faded into a collective boob-dom, a sort of *Jackass* meets *The Man Show* meets *The Simpsons*. As result, the way we approach the men's market is ripe for reinvention."[16] The man in this Appalachian Stove ad in Exhibit 24.5 definitely eschews the "bumbling male" stereotype.

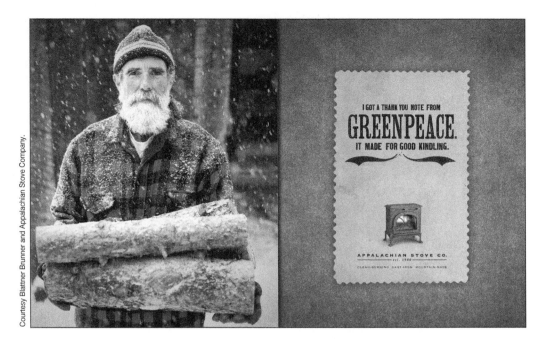

Courtesy Blattner Brunner and Appalachian Stove Company.

EXHIBIT 24.5

Despite criticism, most ads portray healthy images of people, even if the ads occasionally poke fun at environmental organizations.

Beyond simple fairness in the treatment of various segments of the population, there is a growing awareness that advertising should present a more realistic image of reality. For example, recently, advertisers as diverse as Nike and Dove soap have launched campaigns that have moved away from the traditional view of women as wafer-thin models in size one dresses. Critics have long attacked advertising and the media in general for presenting unattainable images of women that contribute to low self-esteem and even eating disorders. Many observers give credit to Dove's "Campaign for Real Beauty" effort, which featured women in all shapes and sizes. As the publisher of *Glamour* magazine commented, "There's a definite trend going on in society and the marketplace of self-acceptance and being comfortable in your own skin."[17] Although, as critics are quick to point out, there is much yet to do in fairly and accurately depicting society, there is growing evidence that the industry is aware of the problem, and it is moving to correct many of the ills of the past.

Despite the real and widespread concerns about stereotyping various segments of the population, most of the complaints about advertising concern executions in specific advertisements and commercials. In recent years, numerous advertising messages have come under attack for their insensitivity to some group or another. For example, in a commercial for Nissan Titan trucks, the theme from the film *The Bridge on the River Kwai*—a film that depicted a ruthless Japanese World War II prison camp—was used. Many viewers thought that using the theme for a Japanese company was insensitive, and the company quickly changed the music.

It is clear that advertisers must be extremely careful how they promote their products. In an environment of greater consumer understanding and awareness of advertising, marketers must be extremely sensitive to a range of subjects that might have potential for upsetting a portion of the audience. The use of inappropriate humor, messages in poor taste (particularly sexual themes), violent content, and stereotyping should be carefully considered in creating advertising messages. At a time when advertisers are acutely aware of these issues, it is paradoxical that the fragmentation of the media and the numerous options for reaching an audience have made content that would be ill-advised in general circulation media acceptable in some narrowly focused venues, such as the Internet.

EXHIBIT 24.6

This ad attempts to counter gambling addiction and promotion.

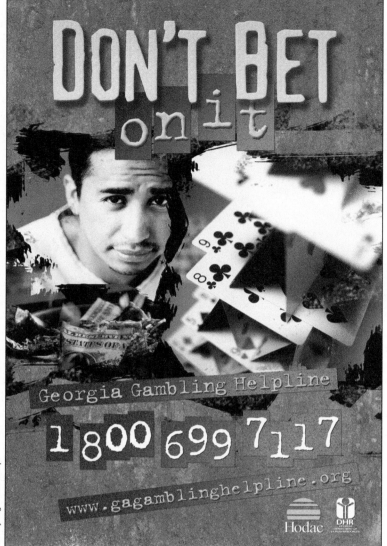

Courtesy Bright Ideas Group.

2. *Advertising of certain product categories.* As we discussed previously, the most frequent criticism of advertising concerns the themes and appeals used in specific advertisements and commercials. However, there are a few product categories that some critics think should not be advertised regardless of how well the ads and commercials are executed (see Exhibit 24.6). In general, the trend is toward a more liberal stance by both advertisers and media in terms of acceptability of advertising. Now that tobacco advertising is virtually nonexistent in mainstream media, some of the remaining products and product categories that garner the most controversy are as follows:

■ *Distilled spirits (as contrasted to beer and wine).* One of the long-standing, self-imposed taboos of advertising was that hard liquor would not be promoted on broadcast media. Until the mid-1990s, liquor advertising was largely confined to magazine ads and outdoor ads. However, the industry was finally able to gain access to cable television and, in a few instances, radio and local television. In 2004, NASCAR agreed for the first time to allow car sponsorship by liquor companies. Because the cars will be featured on television broadcasts of races, many see this as a backdoor method of gaining entry to general television advertising. Nevertheless, there is danger attendant to the NASCAR relationship.

"While spirits marketers see opportunity, there's risk as well. Seeing a whiskey-themed car zipping around the track at 180 mph could raise objections. Also, NASCAR attracts thousands of viewers too young to drink."[18] In the case of tobacco, alcohol, and, more recently, food products with high fat and sugar content, the debate is not so much concerned with advertising executions as it is with the appropriateness of the products themselves. For example, one study indicated that 74 percent of respondents thought that television liquor advertising would encourage teenagers to drink liquor.[19] If an individual or group sees a product category as detrimental to consumers, the evaluation of the advertising for a particular brand is moot.

- *Condoms.* For the past 2 decades, health professionals have advocated widespread promotion of condoms in the battle against sexually transmitted diseases. However, even in light of the AIDS epidemic, most television outlets prohibit the advertising of condoms, a position that many in the public health community think is indefensible. The major networks have been fearful of criticism from conservative media watchdogs and various religious groups. During the 1990s, condom advertising was accepted for some late-night television spots. However, in 2005, led by NBC, advertising for Trojan condoms was accepted for primetime, but the commercials were required to emphasize the health benefits of the product.

- *Advertising to children.* A special category of advertising criticism involves promotional messages to children. There are a number of products such as soft drinks, fast foods, and cereals that are deemed acceptable for general advertising but not in programs directed toward children. Because the audiences of virtually every program have a significant group of youngsters watching, it is very difficult for even the most conscientious advertiser to avoid reaching a sizeable number of children. However, the growing commercial outreach in venues produced solely for a children's market, including online games and videos as well as traditional television shows, is a source of vehement debate among many opponents of children's marketing.

3. *Excessive advertising.* Most of the criticism in this category is directed toward television because print ads are easily ignored by simply turning the page. Approximately 25 percent of television network time is devoted to commercials with higher percentages on local stations and during late-night and daytime periods. Both direct mail and telemarketing have for some time fought critics who wish to impose legal restrictions on them. More recently, Internet spam has come under legislative scrutiny and may soon join telemarketing as an "invitation only" medium. In addition to the nuisance of unwanted and intrusive advertising, new technology, accompanied by sophisticated databases, has increased consumer concerns over privacy issues.

   In addition to the public policy concerns of excessive advertising, there are many within the advertising industry who see it as having the potential to dilute their ROI. Communication research confirms that the number of messages and the order of messages (i.e., first, middle, last) in a commercial block will affect the recall and impact of advertising. In response to advertisers' criticism of excessive clutter, Clear Channel, the country's largest station owner, announced that it was cutting the amount of commercial time on its stations. Early results showed an increase in time spent listening—it remains to be seen if the experiment will be financially viable in the long term.[20] Regardless, it does demonstrate that excessive advertising is a concern of both the audience and the advertising industry.

4. *Advertising's unwanted influences on society.* The harshest critics of advertising are those who think the very existence of persuasive advertising content is contrary to the best interest of consumers. Criticism in this category covers a litany of alleged

abuses. Among the major theses of this school of thought are that advertising *makes* people buy things they don't want or need, lowers morals, and generally exploits the most susceptible segments of society. However, most research shows that mass communication, especially overtly persuasive communication such as advertising, has a very difficult time making even small changes in behavioral intentions or attitudes. The idea that consumers will take some action solely because of advertising is contrary to virtually every theory of communication.

Advertising and Social Causes— the Advertising Council

The most organized effort of social advocacy is the Advertising Council, which has for many years marshaled the advertising industry to support a number of causes. From its World War II beginnings as the War Advertising Council, the Advertising Council recently celebrated its sixtieth anniversary. During those 6 decades, the council has sponsored some of the most well-known public service campaigns and undertaken a number of projects—addressing issues such as racial tolerance, equal rights, job and fair housing opportunities, health awareness, and education (see Exhibit 24.7).

The Ad Council continues to be a major means of disseminating social messages because evidence shows that its efforts work to improve society in a number of significant ways. The council's success stories include the following:

EXHIBIT 24.7

A wide array of organizations use the services of the Advertising Council.

- Applications for Big Brothers and Big Sisters mentors soared from 90,000 a year to 620,000 in 9 months, a sevenfold increase in the number of inquiries to Big Brothers and Big Sisters agencies.

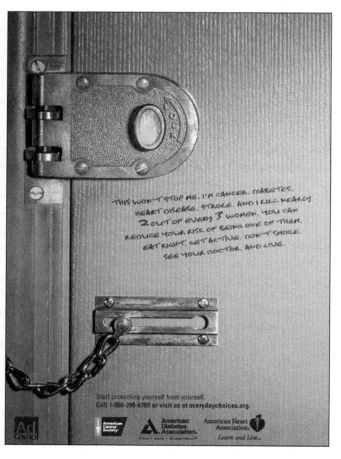

- Ready.gov received more than 18 million unique visitors within the first 10 months of the launch of the Department of Homeland Security's preparedness campaign.

- Safety belt usage is up from 14 percent to 79 percent since the Safety Belt campaign launched in 1985—saving an estimated 85,000 lives and $3.2 billion in costs to society.

- Since 1972, The United Negro College Fund campaign has helped the organization raise more than $2.2 billion to graduate 350,000 minority students from college with the help of the "A Mind Is a Terrible Thing to Waste" slogan.

- Some 6,000 children were paired with a mentor in only the first 18 months of the Ad Council's mentoring campaign.

- Destruction of our forests by wildfires has been reduced from 22 million acres to less than 8.4 million acres per year, since the Forest Fire Prevention campaign began.

- The amount of total waste recycled increased 24.4 percent from 1995 to 2000, and 385.4 percent from the 1980s after the launch of the Environmental Defense campaign.[21]

The council depends on volunteers from across the advertising spectrum. Major agencies produce most of the advertising on a pro bono basis, and the media donate time and space to carry these advertisements and commercials. It is difficult to estimate the equivalent of paid advertising that the council has enjoyed since its founding, but it would certainly be in the billions of dollars.

At one time, the council was the unchallenged organization for idea or public service advertising. However, based largely on its record of success, a number of other organizations have begun to use advertising as a primary tool to deliver social messages. For the past 30 years, a number of organizations including the National Organization for Women (NOW), Mothers Against Drunk Drivers (MADD), and Planned Parenthood have all mounted campaigns that have competed with the Advertising Council for creative services and donated time and space. These private organizations have been joined by a number of companies placing paid advertising promoting some cause related to product marketing. We discuss these marketing promotions in a following section, but they offer another type of alternative to Ad Council public service announcements.

A second challenge for the council involves finding the type of galvanizing topics that were so prevalent in its early years. When the War Advertising Council was conceived, the war effort offered a number of campaigns that the public embraced without question. No one had to convince the public that it was a good idea to conserve tin and fat or to not discuss information about ship movements or factory output. Even after the war, campaigns directed at preventing forest fires and protecting the environment were overwhelmingly accepted by the majority of the public. Unlike the wartime efforts of the War Advertising Council and the early campaigns of the Ad Council, more recent campaigns dealing with the environment, capitalism, the role of the family, the fight against AIDS, and even the proper approach to the "war on terrorism" and support for our troops are topics that engender significant controversy.

Even seemingly inoffensive campaigns such as a recent one to educate parents about the V-chip capability to block unwanted television programming has provoked complaints from child advocates as not going far enough and civil libertarians as a first step toward media censorship. However, despite these problems, the Advertising Council continues to select, define, and address some of the nation's most pressing problems. Council programs will result in the donation of more than $1.5 billion in time and space this year. In many respects, the council created a new role for advertising in the promotion of ideas and opinions. Although some people have reservations about the role of advertising in promoting social institutions and issues, proponents argue that there is no more effective or inexpensive means of getting their messages to the public.

ISSUE-ADVOCACY ADVERTISING

5 Explain the difference between issue-advocacy and cause-related advertising.

Advertising also is used to influence public opinion and legislation regarding a range of political issues from health care reform to energy and trade policy. This form of advertising gained prominence in 1994 when health insurers ran commercials—featuring the likeable characters Harry and Louise—contributing to the defeat of Clinton's health care initiative. In 2009, issue-advocacy advertising is expected to surpass $1 billion as lobbying groups promote issues, attempt to frame them, and engage citizens and policy makers.[22]

Unlike most brand advertising, the tone of many of these ads is negative as groups seek to derail proposed legislation or emphasize shortcomings in an opponent's plan. Recent issues generating advertising both in Washington, DC, and in nationally aired commercials include a Supreme Court nomination as well as health care, environmental, trade, and energy policy. Organizations such as the American Petroleum Institute, Conservation International, and MoveOn.org, among others, can invest millions in a campaign that includes commercials, public relations, and media buying to influence the debate.

ADVERTISING AND CAUSE-RELATED MARKETING

In 1983, American Express sponsored a campaign promising to make a donation to the renovation of the Statue of Liberty each time someone used his or her American Express credit card. This initiative is generally considered to be the introduction of *cause-related marketing*. The days of companies supporting a number of charities with a check and a photo opportunity are nearly over. Today, large corporations are engaging in *strategic philanthropy* in which they market their good deeds in the same way they market their products. As one advertising executive said, "... corporate-social-responsibility initiatives . . . serve as forms of advertising and brand building . . . customers get impressions about products from hundreds of sources, but when they believe a company is a good citizen, they feel more positive about a brand."[23]

Cause-related marketing expenditures have grown from $100 million in 1990 to almost $1.6 billion in 2009. With more than 8 percent annual growth, more major companies are seeing the benefits of engaging in socially related campaigns (see Exhibit 24.8). Companies also are using strategic planning in their philanthropy. "Corporations are focusing their efforts. Instead of volunteering across the spectrum, they're targeting their efforts toward causes that make sense for the vision of the company and the needs of their employees. Companies are looking for high-impact projects where they can really make a difference."[24]

Most research in cause-related marketing indicates that consumers rarely make purchase decisions solely because a company is supporting some favored cause. However, studies do show that such support can be a deciding factor in making choices among similar brands. That is, it becomes another source of product differentiation. For example, a recent Edelman study of 6,000 consumers worldwide revealed that 75 percent say they like to buy brands that donate to good causes. These results are pronounced for products that are of similar quality and price, and continue to hold during an economic downturn.[25]

Companies engaging in cause-related marketing strategically plan these campaigns around several concepts:

UPS focuses its philanthropy on literacy, hunger, and employee volunteerism. In 2005, 43,000 UPS workers engaged in more than 460,000 hours of volunteer projects. The company emphasizes grassroots endeavors to show that it is part of the local community.

McDonald's long association with children makes the support of Ronald McDonald Houses for the families of ill children an excellent fit.

The Home Depot underscores its home-building products with volunteer efforts and financial support for play spaces, affordable housing, and disaster relief.

Avon, like many cause-related efforts, has linked its brand with core concerns of its primary target market through its efforts in the fight against breast cancer.

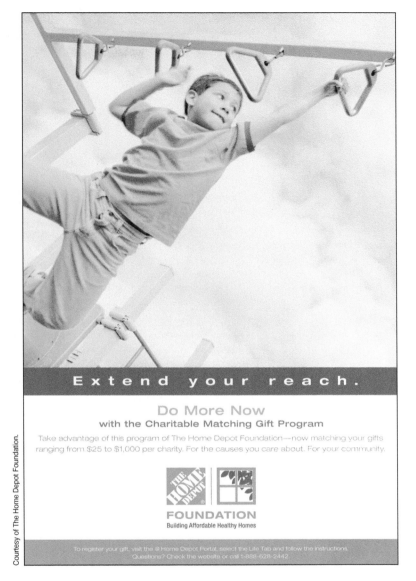

EXHIBIT 24.8

The Home Depot Foundation is one of many corporate-supported nonprofit organizations.

In the past, some companies have refrained from cause-related marketing efforts because they feared that consumers would view their efforts as exploitative. However, a number of research studies indicate that consumers welcome the opportunity to be part of a worthy cause with their purchases, and they reward companies for their efforts. Exhibit 24.9 shows causes that matter most to global consumers. Successful companies are those that are able to creatively support these causes while supporting sales.

Cause marketing generally falls into one of the following tactical categories:[26]

1. *Transactional programs* are programs in which a company contributes to a cause based on consumer purchase of a brand. Mars M&Ms gave 50 cents to the Special Olympics for every specially marked wrapper mailed to the company.

2. *Message promotions* link a brand with information about some cause such as preventing skin cancer. Crest toothpaste supports dental hygiene programs through the Boys and Girls Clubs of America with its "Healthy Smiles 2010" campaign.

3. *Licensing programs* permit companies to use charities' logos in their advertising. For example, ConAgra Foods and America's Second Harvest partnered to focus on the "Feeding Children Better" campaign in many of the companies' promotions.

KLEPPNER VIEWPOINT 24.1

Kelly Caffarelli Executive Director
of The Home Depot Foundation

USING PHILANTHROPY TO ACHIEVE SOCIAL AND CORPORATE GOALS

Kelly Carrafelli

"Doing well by doing good" is a frequently used phrase to explain why businesses give back to their communities. Companies talk about being good corporate citizens and being the neighbors of choice. One can question, though, whether philanthropy is the business of business, as Nobel Prize winner Milton Friedman did in his influential article "The Social Responsibility of Business Is to Increase Its Profits."[1] I think that philanthropy conducted in a strategic way, aligned with the strengths and reputation of a company while engaging a variety of stakeholders, offers a multitude of benefits to corporations.

To be effective in the first instance, the area in which a philanthropic organization focuses must be aligned with the relevant business. Societal efforts must fit with strengths of the for-profit endeavor in order to achieve credibility. To dispute opinions such as Friedman's, the program focus should also directly benefit the corporation. For example, it is easily understandable that the Home Depot Foundation focuses its work on building affordable housing. It makes sense that a company whose business is home improvement should work to help those of modest means achieve the dream of homeownership. The efforts in the community provide an opportunity for the company to put its talents to work for the public good. Moreover, more homeowners mean more customers and higher revenues.

Equally important for the philanthropic efforts is to be focused. Making grants in a scattershot way or merely in response to requests is an ineffective method of impacting a community positively. Moreover, it makes it very difficult for an organization to articulate how it has given back to a community and to create awareness of its philanthropic achievements. In order to be focused, the organization must (a) clearly define a specific unmet need, (b) envision a means of addressing the need, (c) identify the necessary resources and put them to work effectively, and (d) establish the desired outcomes.[2] Only by working through these criteria can an organization say with any confidence that their social investments are actually having an impact. The fact that the issues typically being addressed often require a long-term view makes articulating tangible steps and goals all the more important.

Although it makes sense for the Home Depot Foundation to work in housing, to be focused it needs to narrow its work to create homes that are not only affordable but also "green." The unmet need is available housing units that are affordable for low- to middle-income households to purchase and live in, a well-documented societal need. A means of addressing that need was to increase the production of homes that are moderately priced, are energy and resource efficient, reduce material waste, use durable materials, and provide good indoor air quality. The resources available are funding, volunteer time, training, and technical assistance for those building homes. By partnering with successful nonprofit organizations, the foundation is able to leverage its resources and ensure that the work is completed effectively. The desired outcome is a sufficient number of housing units that are affordable not only to purchase but also to live in and that offer a healthy and sustainable environment for the residents.

The ultimate issue is, of course, the bottom line. Strategic philanthropic investments that create bonds with important stakeholders—shareholders, suppliers, customers, employees, and community leaders—can create financial opportunity, as well as reputational benefits, for a company. More and more, investors are using a social and environmental filter to select mutual funds. For example, in 2005, more than $179 billion in assets were held by such funds.[3] As markets become more global, and therefore more competitive, and the need to attract, motivate, and retain talented employees increases, corporate reputation becomes all the more important. Studies demonstrate that both customers and employees say that they would "recommend" a company for its products and services, or as a place to work, because of good corporate citizenship.[4]

[1]Milton Friedman, "The social responsibility of business is to increase its profits," *New York Times Magazine*, 13 September 1970.

[2]Richard Mittenthal, "Effective philanthropy: The importance of focus," *Briefing,* The Conservation Company, 2002, 2.

[3]Joshua Humphreys, Research Director, "2005 Report on Socially Responsible Investing Trends in the United States," *Social Investment Forum,* 24 January 2006, iv.

[4]Golin Harris Study, "Doing Well by Doing Good."

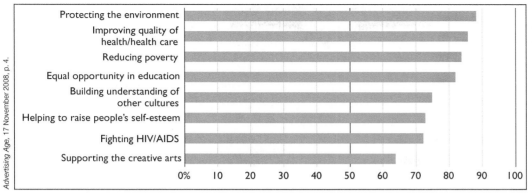

Advertising Age, 17 November 2008, p. 4.

EXHIBIT 24.9

Causes That Matter Most to Global Consumers

Regardless of how cause-related marketing is executed, the public should view it as a more legitimate means of helping accomplish some social need than simply as an extension of a firm's marketing program. "When it comes to cause marketing, businesses walk a fine line between doing the right thing for the right reasons and doing the expected thing to create the right appearance. Marketers that don't get the difference risk breeding cynicism, but many that build social responsibility into their corporate DNA are reaping multilayered benefits."[27]

ADVERTISING INFLUENCE ON EDITORIAL DECISIONS

There are a number of options available to provide financial support for a media system—the government and political parties, church-affiliated organizations, other special interest groups such as labor unions, full payment by the audience, and advertising. Historically, each of these options has been used to support a press system. In the United States, a combination of advertising and subscription charges has been deemed the best approach. The theory behind the adoption of advertising as a primary source of media funding is that, by having economic support spread out over numerous advertisers, it assures that no one entity can exercise undue influence over editorial content.

It would be naive to think that this wall between advertising and editorial has never been breached but, nevertheless, that was the guiding principle. During the modern period of advertising, the first major change in the concept came in the early days of radio, and later in television, when sponsors produced and owned the shows carried by networks and local stations. Most of the audience considered this an acceptable arrangement because the shows were entertainment rather than news and information. However, by the 1970s, it had become prohibitively expensive for single advertisers to bear the total cost of producing a show. This marked the end of "fully sponsored" shows. Programs such as *The Firestone Hour, The United States Steel Hour,* and *The Kraft Music Hall* were replaced by network-controlled programs in which advertisers participated by buying individual spots, but, in theory at least, they had no control over program decisions. The move from single sponsorship to participating commercial buys also was motivated by quiz show scandals during the 1950s in which contestants had been given answers ahead of time. Congress and the public demanded that the networks take more control of content.

Today, we are seeing a limited return to advertiser-controlled programming. Recently, for example, with the CNBC series *dLife,* targeted to diabetes sufferers, an independent producer bought a half-hour slot and then resold time in the form of program participation, segment sponsorship, and onscreen logos. The show was promoted as a combination of medical information, entertainment, and education.[28] Some observers think that such long-form, targeted programming, with its educational component, may replace traditional advertising spots promoting direct-to-consumer drugs, which have come under heavy criticism.

A number of research studies indicate that a large majority of the public believes that advertisers are influencing editorial content. The American Society of Newspaper Editors (ASNE) and the Radio-Television News Directors Association (RTNDA) recently surveyed thousands of citizens and journalists. What they found was disturbing:

- 79 percent of the American public believe that "it's pretty easy for special interest groups to manipulate the press," according to ASNE (55 percent of newspaper journalists agree).

- 84 percent of Americans say, "news reporting on local TV is improperly influenced by advertisers often (51 percent) or sometimes (33 percent)," according to the RTNDA (43 percent of TV news directors agree).[29]

As many observers point out, when the media lose credibility with their audience, it harms both themselves and the advertisers that use them. Unfortunately, there are a number of examples of gray areas between editorial and advertising content. Let's look at some of the ways in which relationships between advertisers and the media are changing:

1. *Withholding advertising as an attempt to control editorial decisions.* One of the most common attempts to control editorial independence is the threat by an advertiser to withhold advertising dollars unless a medium makes editorial decisions favorable to a particular company. In some cases, an advertiser may want favorable coverage of a firm, and in other instances a company demands a medium kill a story critical of a company. In either case, such a demand can involve major ethical as well as financial decisions on the part of the media. In an unusual and highly publicized 2005 case, General Motors pulled all its advertising from the *Los Angeles Times* over what the company characterized as "factual errors and misrepresentations in the editorial coverage" of the company. The company later relented and began placing advertising with the publication. This type of public hostility between a medium and a major advertiser is rare. However, in recent years some companies have asked for prior notification of news stories that concern companies with advertising scheduled in the publication or program. Both BP (formerly British Petroleum) and Morgan Stanley demanded that media notify the companies if negative editorial coverage was planned so that advertising could be withdrawn. As one former editor pointed out, the plan "...raises ethical issues. It can have a chilling effect on editors' judgment and their willingness to do certain stories if they know ... that ads might be pulled."[30] That is often the intention of the advertisers asking for such concessions.

2. *Advertiser-financed productions.* Withholding advertising is an example of an adversarial relationship between the media and advertisers—a situation that is to no one's benefit. In recent years, a number of advertisers have worked with local and network television outlets to jointly produce programming. One of the formal examples of such advertiser involvement is the Family Friendly Forum, a consortium of major advertisers, which underwrites the development of family-oriented network television shows. According to the mission statement of the Forum, it seeks "... to support and promote the development of 'family friendly' television across all programming genres between the hours of 8 and 10 p.m., when adults and children are most likely to watch television together." The Family Friendly Programming Forum has begun a number of different initiatives to carry out this mission:
   - Script Development Fund to help fund family-friendly scripts
   - Scholarship Program for students who work on family-friendly projects
   - Annual Symposium to engage and educate the networks, writers, producers, and press
   - Annual Family Television Awards, which recognize outstanding family television[31]

Although few people question the motives of these companies to bring family entertainment to television, many critics see any involvement between advertising and programming as cause for concern.

The one area of television that has been considered off-limits to product placement has traditionally been news programming. However, in recent years the barriers that shielded news programming from placement deals are falling in the face of competitive pressure for traditional advertising dollars. "Product placement, media and branded entertainment agencies say they are increasingly being pitched opportunities from local stations to integrate their clients' products into news programming in exchange for media buys or integration fees."[32] Although stations are required to disclose the fact that segments are paid for by advertisers, critics worry that busy viewers don't really pay attention to such disclaimers and regard the programs as news and information rather than promotions.

In a similar situation, the *Today* show on NBC was criticized for not revealing that some of the product experts appearing on the show were being paid by the companies whose brands they recommended. In one of the strongest statements about the trend toward nondisclosure of promotional information within a news format, *Advertising Age* editorialized, "It's despicable for journalists to take money to hawk products on TV news and talk shows. Journalists who do so should be fired. And TV stations and networks must disclose to viewers if the TV outlet, staffers, or on-air guests have been paid to make product endorsements."[33]

Some media watchdogs and media trade associations are sufficiently worried about the problem of editorial dilution that they have issued guidelines to stem the expansion of this type of programming and advertising integration in the editorial process. A typical example of these guidelines was developed by the Poynter Institute:

News operations should use press releases and video news releases very selectively and only when journalistically justified. Journalists should clearly inform viewers/ listeners when corporations, public relations agencies, news release services, advertisers or others who are not journalists provide any material you [a medium] are using in a news story. Viewers and listeners should know when a politician, political party, movie studio, theme park or other group or individual pays for satellite, fiber connection or studio time that the journalist uses for presenting a story.[34]

The FCC also has joined the chorus advocating full disclosure. In April 2005, the FCC insisted that broadcasters offer disclaimers when broadcasting so-called video news releases (VNRs). Although the directive was directed specifically at VNRs, there is no question that the spirit of the edict would require disclosure of any third-party, commercial participation in a news show.

3. *Product placement.* In the past decade, the most prevalent type of editorial-promotion alliance was product placement. At one time, product placement was confined to the inclusion of a particular product in a television show or movie. Usually, the placements were no more intrusive than the occasional Coke machine in the background of a scene. However, with the growing antipathy toward advertising by viewers and the glut of commercials vying for prospects, product placement techniques have become more prominent and the relationship to programming more formal. For example, the soap opera *All My Children* worked Enchantment Perfume into a hospital scene on the show, and *General Hospital*'s Jack and Phyllis discussed how GM's OnStar service could get help during a snowstorm.

In the past, product placements were largely confined to movies and television shows. However, in the past few years, there have been a growing number of instances of print media providing promotional opportunities within editorial content. Sometimes the association is overt—the *New York Times* announced plans to superimpose "branded watermarks" over certain editorial content such as stock listings. In other cases, publishers and editors have worked with advertisers to have their products given some exposure such as using a certain brand of appliance in a kitchen scene or a specific make of car in the background of a fashion shot. In rare cases, magazines have provided story lines and product recommendations in exchange for participation fees or advertising. Many publications are feeling pressure from advertisers who are offered numerous opportunities for such placements in television and want the same consideration from major magazines.

The movement to product placement is not confined to traditional media. The popularity of video games has provided a ready-made market for the placement of numerous products, especially those directed toward a young, male audience. Like their television counterparts, video game makers are increasingly weaving product placements into story lines. Marketers such as Jeep, Puma, and Motorola are only a few of the major advertisers using video game placements (see Exhibit 24.10). The growth of video game placements has been phenomenal, rising from $34 million in 2004 to an estimated $562 million by 2009.[35] The latest category of video game advertising is the "advergames" where a video game is created solely to promote a product. These are often offered online in connection with a promotional offer through a fast-food outlet or some children- or teen-oriented product.

We will no doubt see more examples of product placement in the future. With the introduction of digital technology, producers are able to place products in programs at any time. They can change brands for regional buyers, and they can add a product to a program long after the original production of that show. For example, reruns of *Andy Griffith* might someday show the Taylor family sitting down to a meal with a box of Kellogg's Corn Flakes or a bottle of Heinz 57 Sauce on the table.

4. *The advertorial.* For many years, business firms and other organizations have used advertising to express their views about some issue or public policy concern,

EXHIBIT 24.10

Advertising messages and product placement are increasingly featured in video games.

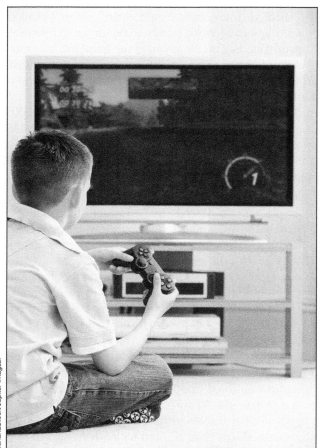

BananaStock/Jupiter Images.

negotiations with labor unions, even potential legal problems faced by a company. These paid advertising messages promoting an opinion rather than a product are known as **advertorials**, that is, a combination of an advertisement and an editorial viewpoint. The expressions, when clearly identified as advertising, are an entirely acceptable means of expressing an opinion and gaining public support.

advertorial
The use of advertising to promote an idea rather than a product or service.

However, since the early 1980s, the use of the advertorial has changed dramatically and its critics would say for the worse. Today, many advertorials are designed to look very much like editorial matter or television programming. Sometimes the advertorials extend the length of several pages and are liberally sprinkled with advertisements giving the section the look of the general publication. Advertising copywriters or public relations specialists produce advertorial sections rather than the editorial staff. The "editorial" matter is an extension of the advertising message, and it is dictated by a sponsor.

The relationship between advertisers and the media they support is often an uneasy truce. Critics point out that with 50 percent to 75 percent of the print media's revenues and virtually 100 percent of broadcast support coming from advertisers, it is unreasonable to expect that at least some publishers and station owners will not be influenced by those who pay the bills. The editorial and programming side wants total control over content with the ability to explore controversial and unpopular topics. Advertisers view the media as a means of reaching their target markets and, not unexpectedly, they often shy away from association with content they think will cause negative connections to their brands.

Advertising's Legal and Regulatory Environment

Successful advertisers know that they depend on consumer trust for their long-term success. To a significant degree, honest and truthful advertising is part of building this consumer trust. Despite philosophical disagreements that we discussed earlier in this chapter, most advertisers are well aware of the ethical dimensions of their messages and strive to act in a principled manner. However, for the past 50 years, a number of governmental, industry, and consumer advocacy groups have monitored and regulated advertising. Today, advertising operates in an environment of regulation and public scrutiny unprecedented in earlier times. For example, Wal-Mart was sued in 2008 by the family of a deceased temporary worker who unfortunately was suffocated by a mad rush of Black Friday shoppers. The family claimed that Wal-Mart's ads were designed to "attract a large crowd and create an environment of frenzy and mayhem."[36]

Whether in the public sector or in the courtroom, studies indicate that the majority of citizens agree that government has a legitimate role in ensuring accurate product information because trustworthy advertising is an important ingredient in a free market economy. When untrue or misleading advertising is disseminated, the implied relationship between the consumer and the advertiser is violated, creating *market failure*.

Today, not only the public but also the advertising industry itself agrees that those companies that use illegal or unethical advertising tactics should be dealt with severely. Not only is deceptive advertising wrong but it also creates a lack of trust in all advertising, making it more difficult for honest businesses to effectively promote their products and services (see Exhibit 24.11). There are three basic constraints on advertising:

1. Laws and regulations of legally constituted bodies such as Congress and the FCC
2. Control by the media through advertising acceptability guidelines
3. Self-regulation by advertisers and agencies using various trade practice recommendations and codes of conduct

EXHIBIT 24.11

Regulation fosters a marketing environment that protects advertisers such as Century Furniture from unscrupulous furniture marketers.

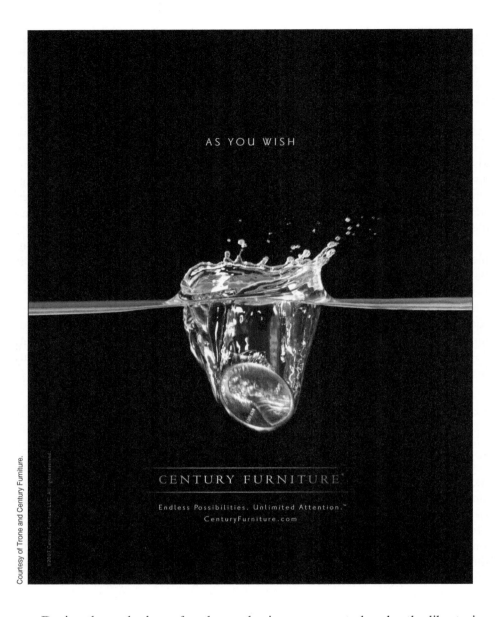

AS YOU WISH

CENTURY FURNITURE

Endless Possibilities. Unlimited Attention.™
CenturyFurniture.com

caveat emptor
Latin for "Let the buyer beware"; represents the notion that there should be no government interference in the marketplace.

During the early days of exchange, businesses operated under the libertarian notion of **caveat emptor**, "let the buyer beware." This concept was based on the classical economic concept of a free marketplace of ideas and assumed perfect knowledge on the part of the participants in that marketplace. That is, buyers and sellers were presumed to have equal information, and it was assumed that both groups, being rational, would make correct economic choices without government interference.

During the past century, the complexities of the marketplace have led to the rejection of many of the principles of caveat emptor. Rather, both businesses and the public realize that buyers have far less information than sellers, and they must be protected by legal guarantees of the authenticity of advertising claims. To shield the public from false and misleading advertising, numerous laws have been passed. Chief among these is the Federal Trade Commission Act, which we discuss first.

The Federal Trade Commission

As we briefly discussed in Chapter 1, the Federal Trade Act was passed in 1914 in reaction to public and congressional concerns over large firms driving out small competitors in a number of industries. Oil, railroads, steel, shipping, and several other core businesses were increasingly dominated by one or two companies. These huge corporations often introduced business practices that today would be considered restraint of trade but were often legal at the time.

The Federal Trade Commission Act declared that "unfair methods of competition are hereby declared unlawful." In its early years, Congress regarded unfair methods of competition as those involving business-to-business transactions, and it did not give the FTC jurisdiction over consumer advertising and other consumer-related activities. The primary mission of the FTC during this period was to protect local retailers from unfair pricing practices by large national chains.

It was not until 1922, in *FTC v. Winsted Hosiery Company,* that the Supreme Court held that false advertising was an unfair trade practice. Then, in 1938, passage of the **Wheeler-Lea Amendments** broadened this mandate to include the principle that the FTC could protect consumers as well as businesses from deceptive advertising. Today, the FTC has sweeping power over advertising for virtually all products sold or advertised in interstate commerce.

Wheeler-Lea Amendments
Broadened the scope of the FTC to include consumer advertising.

THE ROLE OF THE FTC IN REGULATING DECEPTIVE ADVERTISING

Among the several objectives of the FTC is to create a free marketplace based on dissemination of complete, truthful, and nondeceptive advertising (see Exhibit 24.12). In addition to advertising concerns, the FTC also investigates various sales practices and illegal pricing activities. One of the primary concerns of the FTC is to ensure that consumers are protected from deceptive advertising. At the heart of FTC enforcement is the notion that advertisers must be able to **substantiate** their claims. Failure to provide substantiation is the key finding when advertising claims are judged to be deceptive. According to the FTC, the commission uses a three-part test to determine if an advertisement is deceptive or untruthful:

6 **Describe the FTC's role in advertising regulation.**

substantiate
The key to FTC enforcement is that advertisers must be able to prove the claims made in their advertising.

1. *There must be a representation, omission, or practice that is likely to mislead the consumer.* A statement does not have to be untrue to be deceptive. Sometimes advertisers will make a claim that is literally true, but the total impression of the ad is misleading.

2. *The act or practice must be considered from the perspective of a consumer who is acting reasonably.* In other words, the advertiser is not responsible for every possible interpretation, no matter how unreasonable, that might be made by a consumer.

3. *The representation, omission, or practice must be material.* In other words, the claim, even if it is not true, must be judged to have had some influence over a

Courtesy of Homer TLC Inc.

EXHIBIT 24.12

Truthful advertising from the Home Depot fosters trust among consumers.

consumer's decision. For example, the courts have ruled that using plastic ice cubes in a soft drink commercial is not deceptive because no claims are being made about the ice cubes.

In most cases, when the FTC challenges an advertising claim, the company being investigated either provides substantiation or agrees to discontinue the advertising claim in question. For example, the FTC accused the maker of Wonder Bread of unsubstantiated claims that the bread not only built healthy bones but also helped children's memories because it contains extra calcium. The FTC challenged the claims, saying that they had no scientific support. The company, without admitting wrongdoing, agreed to stop the advertising.[37]

METHODS OF FTC ENFORCEMENT

The FTC has a number of means of addressing deceptive advertising. Unless there is evidence of fraud, the first step is for the FTC to work with advertisers to validate a claim or to have advertisers end deceptive practices. In the majority of cases, an advertiser and the FTC will reach a compromise concerning the advertising claims under review, and the investigation will end. However, if an advertiser refuses to discontinue its alleged deceptive practices, there is further recourse for both parties. The following steps outline a typical model for FTC intervention in alleged deception:

1. *There is a claim of deceptive practices to the FTC.* The complaint can come from the general public, special interest groups, competitors (by far the major source of complaints), or the FTC staff.

2. *The FTC begins its investigation with a request for substantiation from the advertiser.* At this point, many advertisers, rather than providing substantiation, voluntarily agree to delete the challenged claim from future advertising. However, if substantiation is provided and the advertising continues, the FTC moves to the next step of evaluating the claims.

3. *If the FTC finds the practice to be unsubstantiated and, therefore, deceptive, a complaint is issued.* At this point, the advertiser is asked to sign a **consent decree** in which the firm agrees to end the deceptive practice or advertising. Most complaints are settled in this manner. An advertiser that continues the practice after signing a consent decree is liable for a fine of $10,000 per day.

4. *If an advertiser refuses to sign a consent decree, the FTC issues a* **cease-and-desist order**. Before such an order can become final, a hearing is held before an administrative law judge. The judge can dismiss the case and negate the cease-and-desist order. If it is upheld, the company may appeal the decision to the full commission.

5. *Even if an advertiser agrees to abide by a cease-and-desist order, the FTC may find that simply stopping a particular practice does not repair past damage to consumers.* To counteract the residual effects of deceptive advertising, the FTC may require a firm to run **corrective advertisements** that are designed to "dissipate the effects of that deception." Orders for corrective advertising are not limited to the FTC. In August 2006, U.S. Judge Gladys Kessler directed the four largest tobacco companies to air spots, run newspapers ads, and produce packaging and in-store signage to counter earlier tobacco advertising that hid the dangers of smoking.[38]

6. *If a company cannot reach agreement with the FTC, its next recourse is the federal courts*—first, to the Federal Court of Appeals and, finally, to the Supreme Court.

It is extremely rare that a case goes beyond the cease-and-desist stage. Companies know that they will incur significant legal costs even if they eventually prevail in the courts. More importantly, most companies don't want the continuing unfavorable publicity that invariably results from extensive disputes with the FTC. Because brand

---

consent decree
Issued by the FTC. An advertiser signs the decree, stops the practice under investigation, but admits no guilt.

cease-and-desist orders
If an advertiser refuses to sign a consent decree, the FTC may issue a cease-and-desist order that can carry a $10,000-per-day fine.

corrective advertising
To counteract the past residual effect of previous deceptive advertising, the FTC may require the advertiser to devote future space and time to disclosure of previous deception. Began around the late 1960s.

equity and brand reputation are so important to most firms, the threat of public embarrassment is a primary concern when an advertisement or sale is challenged.

FTC RULES AND GUIDELINES

The FTC's major responsibility is to protect consumers from deceptive advertising, promotions, and sales techniques. As part of this mission, the FTC engages in a broad program of education for both businesses and consumers to inform them of their rights and, in the case of businesses, to offer advice concerning specific implementation of the FTC's regulations and other legislation that might affect them. Basically, the FTC is responsible for enforcement and education in three areas:

1. *Federal laws passed by Congress.* Dating to the late 1800s, Congress has passed a number of laws concerning fair trade, business practices, and consumer protection. As these laws are enacted, some agency must be given primary responsibility for enforcement. Increasingly, this task has fallen to the FTC. For example, the FTC has established a major program to administer the Fair Debt Collection Practices Act, which provides a number of rights to the public when dealing with debt collectors. These include issues such as the times when calls are permitted (8 A.M. to 9 P.M.), under what circumstances a person can be contacted at work, and so on.

2. *Formal FTC industry rules.* The areas of FTC enforcement are extremely broad. However, no agency can provide complete oversight over all the consumer advertising and trade practices in the marketplace. Consequently, the FTC tends to concentrate its efforts on those areas that affect the most consumers and have demonstrated the highest percentage of buyer complaints. Part of this effort is to issue rules that offer guidance to both consumers and businesses within certain high-profile industries. Some examples of areas where these rules have been issued include:

   - *The Telemarketing Sales Rule.* The FTC is responsible for both the National Do Not Call Registry and the Telemarketing and Consumer Fraud and Abuse Prevention Act. Among the several provisions of the act, callers are required to provide caller identification information, there is demand disclosure of certain information about callers and their companies, and it prohibits unauthorized billing. Modeled after several state laws, the registry went into effect in October 2003 and provided for fines of up to $11,000 per unauthorized call. Telemarketers who run afoul of the FTC can find that it can be a very expensive misstep. For example, in 2005, DirecTV was fined $5.3 million by the FTC for making thousands of calls to households that had been placed on the Do Not Call Registry.[39]

   - *The Used Car Rule.* Over the years, used car sales has been one area that has generated numerous complaints from consumers. According to the FTC, the Used Car Rule is intended to prevent oral misrepresentations and unfair omissions of material facts by used car dealers concerning warranty coverage.

   - *The Contact Lens Rule.* The rules issued by the FTC cover many industries that we would not necessarily think would require this degree of special attention. However, the primary criterion for issuing a rule is the number of complaints from the public and the seriousness with which the FTC regards the problem in terms of consumer safeguards. In the case of the Contact Lens Rule, one of the major problems addressed was patients not being able to get copies of their prescriptions. Among other provisions of the rule, the FTC made the right to obtain such a prescription mandatory.

The commission is constantly monitoring consumer complaints and takes a proactive stance in communicating its expectations and interpretations to the business community and the public. Although there is certainly a punitive dimension to the rules, one of the goals of the FTC is to offer assistance and advice concerning FTC regulations and enforcement criteria before advertisers inadvertently violate FTC rules.

The FTC rules normally apply to a single industry, but the FTC also continually reviews general advertising and marketing practices. For example, the agency recently beefed up rules regarding viral marketing, social media, and blogs. Anyone paid by marketers to spread information by word-of-mouth or other viral elements will "be held liable for any false statements they make about a product they're promoting, along with the product's marketer."[40] As in the case of industry-specific rules, the FTC considers those practices that are most likely to create confusion among consumers as well as those that are clearly deceptive. These general regulations are normally referred to as guidelines as contrasted to the more formal, industry-centric rules. Among the most common areas of FTC inquiry for which guidelines have been issued are the following.[41]

ENVIRONMENTAL CLAIMS   In recent years, a number of companies have made claims about the environmental benefits of their products. The FTC requires that environmentally related claims be qualified and, when such claims are made, the specific nature of the benefits be made clear. For example, a trash bag may be labeled "recyclable." However, because trash bags are not separated from other trash, it is unlikely that the recyclable bag is of any environmental benefit.

THE TERM *FREE* **IN ADVERTISING**   The use of offers such as "buy one, get one free" or "two for one sale" has become so prevalent and abuses so widespread that the FTC issued a four-page guide for nondeceptive usage of the term *free*. The guide emphasizes that when the word *free* is used, a consumer has the right to believe that the merchant will not recoup any cost associated with the purchase of another item. A "two for one" deal requires that the first item is sold at regular price or the lowest price offered within the past 30 days. The commission also requires that any disclosure about the offer price must be made in a conspicuous manner in close conjunction with the offer. In other words, a fine print footnote in an advertisement is not acceptable disclosure.[42]

MADE IN THE U.S.A.   FTC guidelines require that a product has to be "all or virtually all made in the United States" for it to be advertised or labeled as "Made in the U.S.A." This rule excludes products where contents or parts are imported and the product is simply assembled in the United States from carrying the "Made in the U.S.A." designation.

ADVERTISING AS A CONTRACT   One of the many gray areas of advertising is the degree to which an advertisement constitutes a binding, contractual agreement with consumers. For the most part, the courts and the FTC have ruled that it is unreasonable to expect an advertisement or commercial to contain all the details expected in a formal contract. The commission assumes that contractual details will be part of the final sales negotiation, whereas advertising is normally the first step in the transaction. To this end, the courts have been lenient on pricing errors in ads where no deception is intended. For example, a newspaper misprint offering a car for $2,000 would not place the dealer under a legal mandate to sell cars for that price. The courts have held that no reasonable buyer would expect that a sale would be made under those conditions.

However, under certain circumstances advertisements have been regarded as constituting binding offers. For example, when there is a specific commitment, no error in the ad, and the defendant has some control over potential liability, a court may find an obligation to provide a product or service at an advertised price. For example, retailers have been found liable for advertising claims when they offer a product at a certain price but have no intention of selling the product for that price. Instead, sellers attempt to move potential buyers into a more expensive alternative. These so-called "bait-and-switch" tactics have been consistently held to be deceptive, and heavy fines and other penalties have been levied against businesses found guilty of using such tactics. In general, advertisers would be well advised to treat specific advertising claims as if they had the force of a contract.

FACT VERSUS PUFFERY   "Puffery consists of exaggerated opinions, usually at the highest degree of exaggeration, which means superlatives, such as 'the best' or 'superior.' You puff your product. . . . It can be the best tasting, best looking, best lasting . . . or just plain the best."[43] The use and boundaries of puffery are extremely controversial (see Exhibit 24.13). Some critics categorize any statement that is not literally true as deceptive. However, the legal definition of **puffery** is that it is "an exaggeration or overstatement expressed in broad, vague, and commendatory language, and is *distinguishable* from misdescriptions or false representations of specific characteristics of a product and, as such, is not actionable." Advertisers must be wary of pushing the boundaries of puffery. For example, it is easy to cross the line between humor or hyperbole and misleading claims.

puffery
Advertiser's opinion of a product that is considered a legitimate expression of biased opinion.

TESTIMONIALS   A long-held concept in both communication theory and advertising research is that people like to identify with role models and celebrities. This belief is at the heart of testimonial advertising, which seeks to enhance a brand's reputation by having a sports star, entertainment personality, or acknowledged expert endorse a brand. At one time testimonial advertising, especially celebrity endorsements, were viewed very liberally by regulators. However, in recent years, the FTC has taken a much more literal approach to the role of product endorsements. Specifically the FTC has ruled that

■ Endorsements must always reflect the honest opinions, findings, beliefs, or experience of the endorser.

■ In particular, when the advertisement represents that the endorser uses the endorsed product, then the endorser must have been a bona fide user of it at the time the endorsement was given.[44]

The FTC and the courts have held that endorsers who willfully engage in deception can be held liable along with the advertiser for damages. This ruling gives many would-be endorsers pause before they jump into a commercial. Moreover, proposed guidelines in 2009 require celebrities to disclose financial relationships in blogs and talk shows if

Courtesy of The Johnson Group.

EXHIBIT 24.13

Objective facts such as the one in this ad are encouraged in good advertising.

they mention such brands.[45] In recent years, a number of celebrities have introduced their own lines of cosmetics, fragrances, and clothing in concert with major manufacturers. Besides the obvious marketing advantages of name recognition and celebrity appeal of the brands, it removes any potential problems involved with third-party endorsements of the products.

WARRANTIES AND GUARANTEES   The FTC demands that warranty information be available before purchase for consumer products that cost more than $15. The concern with warranties is so great that, even though it is an area of interest across product categories and industries, the FTC has seen fit to issue a rule for the "Pre-Sale Availability of Written Warranty Terms." The guideline also demands that advertising phrases such as "satisfaction guaranteed" or "money-back guarantee" be supported by written terms of these assurances.

THE ROBINSON-PATMAN ACT AND COOPERATIVE ADVERTISING

Robinson-Patman Act
A federal law, enforced by the FTC. Requires a manufacturer to give proportionate discounts and advertising allowances to all competing dealers in a market. Purpose: To protect smaller merchants from unfair competition of larger buyers.

The FTC, through its antitrust division, has responsibility for enforcing another law affecting marketing and advertising, the **Robinson-Patman Act**. The Robinson-Patman Act is part of a three-law "package" that evolved over a period of almost 50 years. These laws and their purposes are as follows:

1. *1890 Federal Sherman Antitrust Act.* The Sherman Antitrust Act was designed to prevent alliances of firms conceived to restrict competition.

2. *1914 Clayton Antitrust Act.* The Clayton Antitrust Act amended the Sherman Act. It eliminated preferential price treatment when manufacturers sold merchandise to retailers.

3. *1936 Robinson-Patman Act.* In turn, the Robinson-Patman Act amended the Clayton Act. It prevents manufacturers from providing a "promotional allowance" to one retailer or wholesaler unless it is also offered to competitors on a proportionally equal basis. Prior to Robinson-Patman, some manufacturers were using a loophole in the Clayton Act to give money back to their bigger customers in the form of promotional allowances. For example, large retailers might be given co-op advertising allowances that were unavailable to small retailers that, in effect, lowered the price of the goods sold by the large retailers to favored customers. Thus, the promotional allowance was a device for under-the-table rebates.

The regulation of co-op allowances has evolved as the media environment has become more complex and the relationships between retailers and manufacturers have changed. At the time Robinson-Patman was passed, the vast majority of retail advertising dollars were placed in newspapers. Today, with a growing number of local advertising options, the FTC requires that retailers must be able to choose from various media and promotional alternatives. For example, a manufacturer may not limit co-op dollars to television, knowing that many retailers in smaller markets might not have practical access to television advertising. Such an offer is known as an *improperly structured program.*

slotting fees
Payments to retailers by manufacturers to gain shelf space.

The evolving relationship between retailers and manufacturers is another aspect of Robinson-Patman that has changed since the act was passed. As in the case of the FTC itself, the primary intent of the act was to protect retailers from manufacturers. Today, many regulators are concerned with the leverage that is wielded by huge retail chains against these same manufacturers. For example, most large retailers charge **slotting fees**, which are payments to retailers by manufacturers to gain shelf space. Retailers argue that prime shelf space is their "product" and stores should receive payments to make this space available.

The FTC has a continuing review of the role of slotting fees because it fears that they have the potential to prevent marketplace entry of new brands or prevent small retailers from gaining access to established brands because of disproportionately high slotting fees. Again, slotting fees, as in the case of other promotional payments, are only illegal if they are administered with the intent to limit competition.

The Federal Food, Drug, and Cosmetic Act

Because of a public outcry over shocking disclosures of unsanitary conditions in meat packing plants and the use of dangerous additives in food as well as continuing scandals concerning patent medicines, the original Food and Drugs Act was passed by Congress on June 30, 1906, and signed by President Theodore Roosevelt. It prohibits interstate commerce in misbranded and adulterated foods, drinks, and drugs. In 1938, Congress passed the Federal Food, Drug, and Cosmetic Act, which established the Food and Drug Administration (FDA). It superseded the original legislation and gave the FDA responsibility for

- Extending control to cosmetics and therapeutic devices.
- Requiring new drugs to be shown safe before marketing—starting a new system of drug regulation.
- Eliminating the Sherley Amendment requirement to prove intent to defraud in drug misbranding cases.
- Providing that safe tolerances be set for unavoidable poisonous substances.
- Authorizing standards of identity, quality, and fill-of-container for foods.
- Authorizing factory inspections.
- Adding the remedy of court injunctions to the previous penalties of seizures and prosecutions.

One of the most active and controversial areas of FDA regulation is consumer prescription drug advertising. Until 1997, pharmaceutical companies could advertise prescription drugs only to doctors. Then, consumer advertising was permitted. By 1999, drug companies were spending more than $1 billion on direct-to-consumer (DTC) prescription drug advertising. By 2005, that figure had grown to $5 billion and many consumer advocates as well as doctors feared that many of the claims did not meet FDA guidelines for such advertising (see Exhibit 24.14). The FDA has begun an aggressive campaign of enforcing promotional regulations, often sending formal letters of warning to drug companies.

In a rare move, the FDA forced Bayer's Yaz brand of birth control to run 6 months of corrective advertising. The agency ruled that Yaz ads were deceptive and made false

Brand X Pictures/Jupiter Images.

EXHIBIT 24.14

Pharmaceutical marketers invest more than $5 billion a year on prescription drug advertising.

claims regarding the brand's effect on acne and premenstrual syndrome.[46] Yaz was required to run $20 million of advertising to correct possible misperceptions—one-third of the previous year's ad budget—and for 6 years must get preapproval for all advertising.

Some drug companies have sharply reduced their advertising budgets and criticized the FDA for overzealous enforcement of a program that it initiated. A spokesperson for the FDA defended its position, "This [the current enforcement campaign] is not a crackdown, it is an enforcement. We're continuing our close monitoring . . . we're prepared to take whatever action necessary to stop misleading promotion."[47]

The jurisdiction of the FDA to control and regulate labeling was enhanced when Congress passed the Nutritional Labeling and Education Act of 1990. Beginning on January 1, 2006, the agency was given greater enforcement authority over labeling, and labeling information was enhanced to include data about trans fat, allergen groups, and whole grain ingredients. Consumer protection groups applauded the new enforcement activity as a step toward more fully informing consumers about food ingredients. With its new authority, the FDA may become much more aggressive in the enforcement of regulations dealing with health claims on labels and packaging, sometimes borrowing strategies from the FTC.

A recent FDA letter to General Mills concerning its Cheerios cereal brand caught the attention of food marketers and the advertising community. Because Cheerios product labeling touted cholesterol-reducing benefits—reducing levels 4 to 6 percent over 6 weeks—the FDA said the cereal is being promoted for health conditions similar to that of a drug.[48] If it continued to use the cholesterol message, the cereal would be subject to much more stringent testing and possible clinical trials.

THE UNITED STATES POSTAL SERVICE

Benjamin Franklin created the forerunner of the United States Postal Service (USPS) in 1772. At the end of the Civil War there was a major outbreak of mail swindles, and in 1872 Congress passed the Mail Fraud Statute, the nation's oldest federal consumer protection statute. Mail fraud is any scheme in which the USPS is used to obtain money by offering a deceptive product, service, or investment opportunity. To obtain a conviction, postal inspectors must prove (1) the offer was intentionally misrepresented and (2) the U.S. mail was used to carry out the fraud. Postal inspectors investigate a number of criminal activities. In particular, the inspectors protect postal customers from mail advertising and promotion schemes involving the elderly and other susceptible groups.

For a number of years, the USPS has been empowered to obtain a mail stop order against a company sending false advertising. However, until recently there was no penalty attached to the stop order. In 1999, the Deceptive Mail Prevention and Enforcement Act (DMPEA) gave the USPS significantly more power to deal with mail fraud. The primary change brought about by DMPEA is that the USPS can impose civil penalties of up to $1 million for the first offense depending on the volume of mail involved.[49]

Advertising and the First Amendment

The wording of the First Amendment makes no distinction between advertising or commercial speech and other forms of expression. However, until the 1970s the courts consistently ruled that advertising had virtually none of the rights guaranteed to other types of speech. The open "marketplace of ideas" was never considered a privilege of advertising, and it was held to a much stricter standard than other forms of expression (see Exhibit 24.15).

In addition to a variety of limitations, advertisers have been frustrated by what they regarded as changing and often contradictory decisions by the Court concerning commercial speech. Although advertising continues to function under regulations that would be unacceptable if applied to other speech, the trend of the past 60 years has been

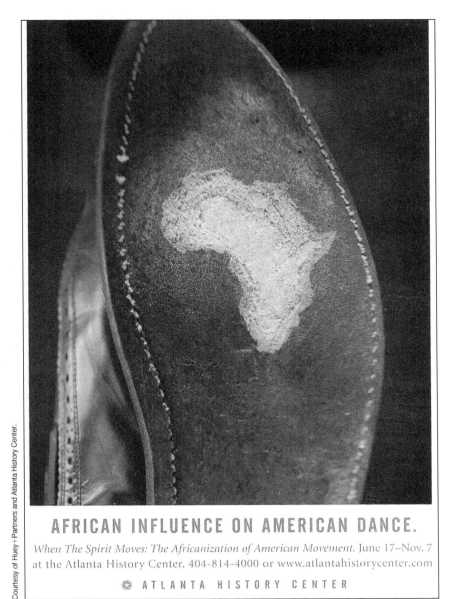

Courtesy of Huey+Partners and Atlanta History Center.

AFRICAN INFLUENCE ON AMERICAN DANCE.

When The Spirit Moves: The Africanization of American Movement. June 17–Nov. 7 at the Atlanta History Center. 404-814-4000 or www.atlantahistorycenter.com

⊛ ATLANTA HISTORY CENTER

EXHIBIT 24.15

The marketplace of ideas allows many organizations to communicate information about their products and services.

toward giving commercial speech greater constitutional protections. Nevertheless, despite a more open environment for commercial messages, judicial opinions supporting commercial speech still deny full First Amendment protection to advertising. In order to understand the legal protections afforded commercial speech, let's outline the major court opinions involving advertising.[50]

1942   The Supreme Court ruled that advertising was not entitled to First Amendment protection. The Court ruled that there were *no* restraints on government's right to prohibit commercial speech.

1964   The Court decided that advertising that expressed an opinion on a *public issue* was protected by the First Amendment but only because it did not contain commercial speech.

1975   The Court gave advertising its first constitutional protection when it overturned a Virginia law making it a criminal offense to advertise out-of-state abortion clinics in Virginia newspapers. However, the ruling left open the question of protection for purely commercial speech that did not deal with opinions or controversial public issues.

1976   In what many advertisers regard as the major breakthrough for commercially protected speech, the Court held in the case of *Virginia State Board of Pharmacy v. Virginia Citizens Consumer Council* that the state of Virginia could not prohibit the advertising of prescription drug prices. It said, in effect, that society benefits from a free flow of commercial information just as it benefits from a free exchange of political ideas.

1979   Advertisers' optimism that they had finally achieved full constitutional protection was short-lived. In the case of *Friedman v. Rogers* the Court upheld the right of the state of Texas to prevent an optometrist from using an "assumed name, corporate name, trade name or any other than the name under which he is licensed to practice optometry in Texas." In its decision, the Court said that First Amendment protection for commercial speech is not absolute and that regulation of commercial speech can be allowed even when the restrictions would be unconstitutional "in the realm of noncommercial expression."

1980   Prior to this year, the Court seemingly ruled on each case involving commercial speech on a purely ad hoc basis. Even as cases were settled, advertisers were left with little if any guidance or precedents. However, in 1980 the Court articulated a set of guidelines concerning the constitutional protection that would be afforded commercial speech. These guidelines were set forth in the case of *Central Hudson Gas & Electric v. Public Service Commission of New York*.

> **7** Discuss the components of the *Central Hudson Four-Part Test.*

This case concerned a prohibition by the New York Public Service Commission against utility advertising. The state's rationale was that the ban was compatible with public concerns over energy conservation. In overturning the prohibition, the Court established a four-part test to determine when commercial speech is constitutionally protected and when regulation is permissible. These guidelines known as the *Central Hudson Four-Part Test* are as follows:

1. *Is the commercial expression eligible for First Amendment protection?* That is, is it neither deceptive nor promoting an illegal activity? No constitutional protection can be provided for commercial speech that fails this test.

2. *Is the government interest asserted in regulating the expression substantial?* This test requires that the stated reason for regulating the advertisement must be of primary interest to the state rather than of a trivial, arbitrary, or capricious nature.

3. *If the first two tests are met, the Court then considers if the regulation of advertising imposed advances the cause of the governmental interest asserted.* That is, if we assume that an activity is of legitimate government concern, will the prohibition of commercial speech further the government's goals?

4. *If the first three tests are met, the Court must finally decide if the regulation is more extensive than necessary to serve the government's interest.* That is, is there a less severe restriction that could accomplish the same goals?

In the *Central Hudson* case, the Court ruled that although the case met the first three guidelines, a total prohibition of utility advertising was more extensive than necessary. Thus, it failed the fourth part of the test and was ruled unconstitutional. The *Central Hudson* guidelines remain the foundation on which most commercial speech cases are considered (see Exhibit 24.16).

1986   Most advertisers thought that *Central Hudson* had provided significant protection in limiting the right of states to ban legitimate advertising. However, in the case of *Posadas de Puerto Rico Associates v. Tourism Company of Puerto Rico,* the Court seemed once again to strengthen the ability of states to regulate advertising. This case involved a Puerto Rican law banning advertising of gambling casinos to residents of Puerto Rico even though casino gambling is legal there and the casinos were permitted to advertise outside of Puerto Rico. In a five to four decision, the Court ruled that the ban met all four standards of the *Central Hudson Four-Part Test.*

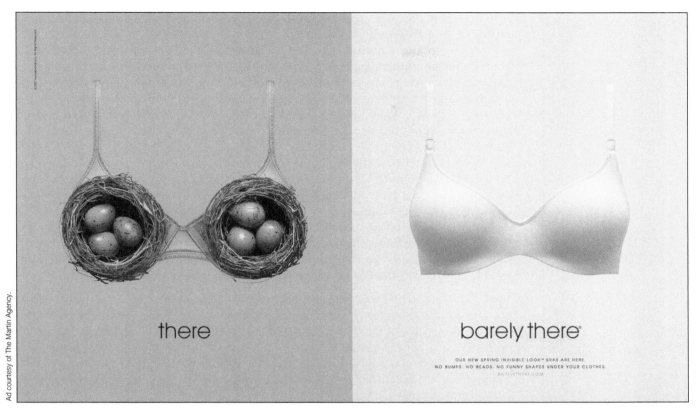

EXHIBIT 24.16

Barely There uses a visual metaphor to emphasize a product attribute.

1988   Many legal scholars believe 1988 marked a significant change in the Court's attitude toward advertising and, just as importantly, a change in its interpretation of *Central Hudson. Board of Trustees of the State University of New York v. Fox* dealt with a college regulation that restricted "private commercial enterprises" on campus. Students challenged the regulation, arguing that at events such as "Tupperware parties" noncommercial subjects were discussed. Because the regulation had the effect of prohibiting both noncommercial and commercial speech, it was too broad and, therefore, did not meet the fourth part of the *Central Hudson* test.

Unfortunately for advocates of commercial speech, the Court upheld the college's regulation. The Court ruled that regulations must be "narrowly tailored," but not necessarily the "least restrictive" option available. Critics of the decision point out that the term *narrowly tailored* is vague and may risk weakening the protections of *Central Hudson.*

1993   In *City of Cincinnati v. Discovery Network,* the Court seemed to offer a clear victory for proponents of First Amendment protection of commercial speech. In a six to three decision, the Court held that the Cincinnati City Council violated the First Amendment by banning newsracks for free promotional publications but allowing them for traditional newspapers. The Court ruled that because the ban was based solely on the content of the publications in the racks, it did not meet the "narrowly tailored" test. The case was widely seen as a victory for commercial speech.

1996   Legal scholars predict that two cases heard in 1996 may provide a significant step in affording more complete constitutional protection to commercial speech. In *44 Liquormart, Inc. v. Rhode Island,* the Court ruled that a Rhode Island ban on price advertising for alcoholic beverages was unconstitutional. The Court referred to the *Central Hudson* case and ruled that the Rhode Island law failed to prove that the ban on price promotions advanced the state's interest in promoting temperance (that is, it failed the third test of *Central Hudson*). Furthermore, the legislation was more extensive than necessary to accomplish the goals of the state (here, it failed the fourth test of *Central Hudson*).

Writing for the majority of the Court, Justice John Paul Stevens said, "Bans that target truthful, nonmisleading commercial messages rarely protect consumers from such harms. Instead, such bans often serve only to obscure an 'underlying governmental policy' that could be implemented without regulating speech."[51] Commenting for the advertising industry, Wally Snyder, president of the AAF, noted, "The Supreme Court ruling represented the strongest opinion to date protecting truthful advertising from government censorship."[52]

In a subsequent case that year, the Court underscored the *Rhode Island* decision by returning to the Fourth Circuit U.S. Court of Appeals case involving a Baltimore ban on alcohol billboard advertising. In *Anheuser-Busch, Inc. v. Schmoke,* the beer maker challenged the city ordinance on constitutional grounds of the denial of the First Amendment right to free speech. However, demonstrating the unpredictability of cases dealing with advertising, the appeals court upheld its original verdict, ruling that because alcoholic beverage companies had other avenues for their advertising, the ban was not as broad as the Rhode Island law and, therefore, was constitutional.

1999   The Greater New Orleans Broadcasters Association sought to overturn a ban on broadcast advertising for gambling enterprises that dated to the Communications Act of 1934. Advocates of the ban argued that the government had a legitimate interest in protecting compulsive gamblers from the temptation that casino gambling fostered. In upholding the ban, the Fifth Circuit Court of Appeals commented that the restriction was appropriate because of the "powerful sensory appeal of gambling conveyed by television and radio."[53]

In June 1999, when the case reached the Supreme Court, the lower court decisions were overturned using the earlier *Central Hudson* guidelines. According to *Central Hudson,* any government restrictions on truthful commercial speech had to be shown to advance some government interest and be no more extensive than necessary. The Court ruled that the casino advertising ban did not sufficiently advance the government's stated interest to protect compulsive gamblers and did not do so in the least intrusive way.[54]

Some advertisers were encouraged that the *New Orleans Broadcasters* case might mean greater First Amendment protection for advertising, perhaps even lifting the prohibition against broadcast tobacco advertising. However, the Court was careful to write its decision narrowly. It "focused on the irrationality of making distinctions among advertisers, while at the same time suggesting that a more uniform and coherent policy of advertising restrictions might well have been upheld. . . . [It] left the door open for the Court to uphold, in future cases, restrictions on the advertising of other lawful products."[55]

ADVERTISING AND THE FIRST AMENDMENT IN THE TWENTY-FIRST CENTURY   During the early years of this century, there were a number of cases dealing with advertising and commercial speech. None appear to have the importance of previous decisions, such as *Central Hudson*, and they appear to continue the trend of unpredictability of decisions dealing with commercial speech. The primary decisions include the following:

1. *Lorillard Tobacco Co. v. Reilly.* In 2000, the attorney general of Massachusetts issued a number of restrictions on tobacco advertising in the state—including banning all outdoor advertising within 1,000 feet of elementary or secondary schools and playgrounds and placed limitations on advertising in retail stores. Several tobacco companies appealed the regulations on the basis that they violated their rights to free speech. The limitations were upheld at the appellate level, but in 2001 the Supreme Court overturned the state regulations on the basis that they "violated tobacco companies' right to free speech."

2. *FDA's role in tobacco marketing.* The Supreme Court ruled in 2002 that the FDA's authority over the marketing communication of drugs and related products must

meet certain First Amendment guidelines. Specifically, the Court ruled that the FDA did not have the authority to impose rules on tobacco marketers that would have prevented the use of certain types of imagery and colors in advertising and point-of-purchase material. The decision was applauded by the advertising industry as a strong statement that regulatory requirement must consider First Amendment implications. However, at this writing, a democratic Congress has granted greater authority to the FDA regarding tobacco control.

3. *Kasky v. Nike.* In the case of *Kasky v. Nike*, the California Supreme Court and the Supreme Court of the United States seemed to send mixed signals for First Amendment protection of commercial speech. For a number of years, detractors charged Nike with tolerating poor working conditions in its overseas plants. In an effort to rebut its critics, Nike sent the news media information offering its side of the debate. Marc Kasky brought suit alleging that the comments were commercial speech and, therefore, did not have full First Amendment protection afforded political discourse and could be challenged on a similar basis to advertising product claims. In 2002, the California Court agreed, ruling four to three that the comments by Nike constituted advertising and, therefore, the company was ordered to establish the truthfulness of its claims under the state unfair practices act. In June 2003, the Supreme Court returned the case to the California Court without comment. In September 2003, Nike and Kasky reached an out-of-court settlement, thereby leaving the legal position of corporate speech and related advertising in limbo.

4. *Kellogg's and the Center for Science in the Public Interest (CSPI).* Potential litigation with a far-reaching impact on the First Amendment rights of advertisers is represented by the threat made by the Center for Science in the Public Interest (CSPI) and other consumer advocates to file a $2 billion lawsuit against Kellogg's for marketing what they regard as unhealthy food to children. A number of marketing and advertising groups sharply criticized the action, many on First Amendment grounds. A 4As spokesperson was quoted as saying, "This action is breathtaking in its willful disregard for the First Amendment protections guaranteed to us all." Meanwhile, a representative of the ANA said the suit was "an extraordinarily radical misconstruction of the First Amendment."[56]

Because of the unique nature of communication, it may be that the Supreme Court will never be able to issue a totally definitive decision that will cover every instance of commercial speech. Instead, most of the decisions considered by the courts involve narrowly defined issues that often pertain to messages dealing with a single industry or product category. These decisions underscore the fact that each case has distinctive elements that don't necessarily provide precedents in other circumstances. Still, there is little question that the Supreme Court will continue to demand that the government meets a high standard of public interest before agreeing to any prohibition of commercial speech.

TARGETING INTERNET SOLICITATION

Taking note of the growing use of the Internet for commercial purposes, Congress passed the Controlling the Assault of Non-Solicited Pornography and Marketing (CAN-SPAM) Act of 2003, which established requirements for those who send commercial e-mail, spells out penalties for spammers and companies whose products are advertised in spam if they violate the law, and gives consumers the right to ask e-mailers to stop spamming them (see Exhibit 24.17).

The law, which became effective January 1, 2004, covers e-mail whose primary purpose is advertising or promoting a commercial product or service, including content on a web site. A "transactional or relationship message"—e-mail that facilitates an agreed-on transaction or updates a customer in an existing business relationship—may not contain false or misleading routing information but otherwise is exempt from most provisions of the CAN-SPAM Act.

EXHIBIT 24.17

CAN-SPAM provides some protection from spam and in appropriate message content.

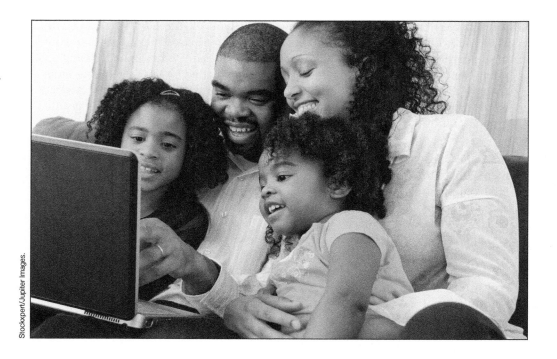

Stockxpert/Jupiter Images.

The FTC enforces the CAN-SPAM Act. CAN-SPAM also gives the Department of Justice (DOJ) the authority to enforce its criminal sanctions. Other federal and state agencies can enforce the law against organizations under their jurisdiction, and companies that provide Internet access may sue violators, as well. Among the major provisions of the act are the following:

- *False or misleading header information is banned.* Your e-mail's "From," "To," and routing information—including the originating domain name and e-mail address—must be accurate and identify the person who initiated the e-mail.

- *Deceptive subject lines are prohibited.* The subject line cannot mislead the recipient about the contents or subject matter of the message.

- *The e-mail must give recipients an opt-out method.* You must provide a return e-mail address or another Internet-based response mechanism that allows a recipient to ask you not to send future e-mail messages to that e-mail address, and you must honor the requests.

- *Commercial e-mail must be identified as an advertisement and include the sender's valid physical postal address.* Your message must contain clear and conspicuous notice that the message is an advertisement or solicitation and that the recipient can opt out of receiving more commercial e-mail from you. It also must include your valid physical postal address.[57]

The regulations concerning spam underscore a central theme of all First Amendment and commercial speech limitations. That is, under no circumstances will the courts offer any level of protection to speech that is untrue or misleading. The advertising industry expects no such exceptions, but it does assume that in the future truthful advertising will be given full protection of the law.

CORPORATE SPEECH AND ADVERTISING

In recent years, we have seen a tremendous growth in corporate advertising espousing some idea or corporate philosophy as contrasted to selling a product or service. Like all other forms of commercial speech, corporate advertising falls into a gray area. Similar to its decisions regarding commercial speech, the Supreme Court has ruled that corporate advertising is protected under certain circumstances. In *First National Bank of*

Boston v. Bellotti, the Court overturned a state law that prohibited national banks from using corporate funds to advocate voting against a state constitutional amendment that would allow the legislature to impose a graduated income tax.

Over the years the Court has delineated several legal principles concerning corporate speech:

1. Spending money to speak does not, in itself, result in the loss of First Amendment rights.

2. Speaking on commercial subjects does not entail loss of First Amendment rights.

3. Speaking for economic interests does not entail loss of First Amendment rights.[58]

We should note that the Court is saying that a commercial aspect to speech does not *necessarily* remove that speech from the rights granted by the First Amendment. However, the converse of this view does not automatically grant these rights to either advertising or corporate speech.

ADVERTISING AND THE RIGHT OF PUBLICITY

A private individual is protected by the right of privacy from having his or her likeness used in an advertisement without permission. Laws vary from state to state, but every state has some legislation that addresses the right of privacy of an individual. In many jurisdictions, the use of a name or picture of a person without prior consent is a misdemeanor. However, civil liability, potentially involving significant monetary judgments, is a much greater concern to advertisers.

Generally, the courts have ruled that public figures, including celebrities, have far less protection than the general public in terms of their right of privacy. However, in recent years the courts have made it clear that this distinction of public versus private persons is related to news, not advertising or other commercial use. Legal precedent makes it clear that public figures are protected from commercial use of their name or likeness by a doctrine of the right of *publicity* (as contrasted with a right of *privacy*).

In the past, most issues of privacy dealt only with living personalities. However, in recent years some states, notably California, have addressed the issue of deceased celebrities. John Wayne, Humphrey Bogart, and other stars from the past have been used in a number of commercials with the permission of their estates. Because state laws vary widely, advertisers should be extremely prudent in using a personality's name or likeness. The normal course of action is that an advertiser or agency will never use a model, personality, or likeness without legal permission. For example, the courts have ruled against a number of advertisers that used impersonators in commercials without permission.

Advertising of Professional Services

One of the most controversial areas of commercial speech involves advertising by professionals, especially attorneys and health care providers. Until the mid-1970s, virtually all forms of professional advertising were banned, often by trade associations such as state medical groups or bar associations. Critics of restrictions on professional advertising claim that one of the overriding concerns of trade associations supporting these bans was to limit competition for established professionals and, in fact, that that constituted restraint of trade (see Exhibit 24.18).

Supporting this claim, research indicates that among doctors those most likely to use advertising are physicians who have been in practice the least amount of time, those who have smaller practices, and females.[59] In part because of concerns that the bans constituted barriers to market entry, absolute prohibition of attorney (and by extension most other professions) advertising was lifted in 1977 in the case of *Bates v. State Bar of Arizona.* The Supreme Court ruled that state laws forbidding advertising by attorneys

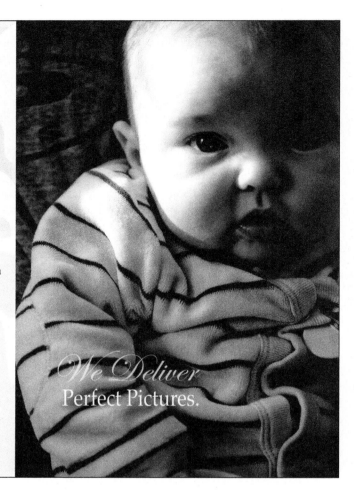

were unconstitutional on First Amendment grounds. The fourth test of the *Central Hudson* case, not an issue in 1977, seems to reinforce the *Bates* decision. That is, most legal scholars think that the total prohibition of a class of advertising will generally not meet the fourth test because any such total ban will be considered broader than necessary. Professional associations still have the right to enforce some regulations over issues such as accuracy and presentation, but they cannot prohibit their members from advertising.

In 1988, the Supreme Court extended the right of attorneys to advertise professional services. A Kentucky lawyer, Richard Shapero, was cited for violating a Kentucky law prohibiting targeted mail solicitations to people who were facing foreclosure. The Court ruled that although personal contact by an attorney could be prohibited, a letter posed no threat of pressure to consumers who are under threat of legal action. The *Shapero* case had the immediate effect of lifting the ban on targeted letters in the 25 states that had previously prohibited them.

In 1993, the Court made an interesting distinction among various types of professional solicitations. The Florida board of accountancy banned personal solicitations for clients, either in person or by telephone. In *Edenfield v. Fane*, the Court overturned the ban and, in doing so, made a clear distinction between lawyers and accountants. The Court held that, unlike lawyers, certified public accountants (CPAs) are not trained in the art of persuasion, they are dealing with clients who probably have had a previous professional relationship with an accountant, and the client of a CPA is probably not under the stress that a lawyer's potential client might be. The Court found that it was

Courtesy of Idea Engineering.

EXHIBIT 24.19

Would this ad be considered an example of professional services advertising?

unlikely that the potential clients of a CPA would be subject to "uninformed acquiescence," which might be the case with a lawyer's client (see Exhibit 24.19).

A 1995 case demonstrated that the courts consider a number of circumstances in ruling on professional solicitations and they are not prepared to issue blanket denials of most state regulations. The Court upheld a Florida Bar Association rule prohibiting lawyers from sending direct mail to accident victims. The Court took the position that an accident victim is in a more vulnerable state of mind than a person facing foreclosure—the circumstance of those solicited by Shapero. Again, referring to the *Central Hudson* guideline, "The state had a substantial interest in protecting the integrity of its legal system."[60]

State and Local Laws Relating to Advertising

Disputes between major corporations and federal agencies such as the FTC garner most of the headlines in the area of advertising regulation. However, most companies are small firms dealing in a local or regional market and, because of limited resources, fly below the radar of federal regulatory bodies. Most federal control of advertising and marketing practices is specifically directed toward intrastate regulation.

During the early 1900s, major advertisers realized that something had to be done to thwart the charlatans and frauds that were preying on an unsuspecting public and causing widespread mistrust of all advertising. However, most of their efforts were directed at the national level with local advertising abuses largely ignored. *Printers' Ink,* a leading trade magazine of the time, proposed state and local advertising regulations to address the growing problem of false advertising. Basically, it sought to regulate "untrue, deceptive, or misleading advertising." However, it has only been in the past decade that enforcement at the local level has become a major force in advertising regulation. Primary local advertising regulation has been undertaken by the National Association of Attorneys General (NAAG), which has become very aggressive in addressing a number of national trade issues, including advertising, as they impact local consumers.

For example, most people probably believe that multibillion-dollar sanctions against major tobacco companies were the result of actions by the federal government. In reality, the 1998 Master Settlement Agreement (MSA) was crafted by a consortium of 46 states and 5 territories. The MSA, much of which addressed the manner in which tobacco could be advertised and promoted, was the most high-profile case brought by members of the NAAG. However, it is only one of a number of suits involving national companies that have been brought by state attorneys general. For example, attorneys general have negotiated a $100 million agreement with a major brokerage house concerning actions by some of its brokers, investigated pharmaceutical industry pricing tactics, and brought suit against major telecommunication companies and health insurance firms.

Today, the NAAG continues to undertake a number of initiatives on a state level as well as frequently having members testify before Congress to offer suggestions for new legislation or to support pending national laws. Among the topics under consideration by the NAAG that have implications for advertising and marketing are the following:

1. Internet and telecom privacy issues
2. Moving company practices
3. Predatory lending concerns
4. Automotive and tire safety
5. Telemarketing fraud

In 2005, Blockbuster settled claims initiated through the NAAG for $630,000. State attorney generals alleged that Blockbuster's "No late fees" campaign did not fully communicate with consumers concerning potential penalties for late or nonreturn of rentals. As part of the settlement with 47 states and the District of Columbia, Blockbuster agreed to reimburse consumers who were charged fees if they did not understand company policies.[61]

On the face of it, no one would question that companies and advertisers should be held accountable for their actions regardless of whether the oversight is conducted by local, state, or national authorities. However, many advertisers have raised questions about the extent that states will be allowed to go beyond or contradict national legislation. Formerly, it appeared the lines between state and federal enforcement were relatively clear. However, in the past decade there has been an obvious shift toward more state control, which creates potential problems for national advertising if it has to meet an array of local standards. However, the NAAG argues that by the cooperative efforts of the various state attorneys general, it is moving to provide standardized regulation across a number of concerns at the state level, but it still leaves potential problems of uneven enforcement from state to state.

Comparison Advertising

One of the most controversial areas of advertising is the comparison of one brand with one or more of its competitors. J. Sterling Getchell is generally credited with the first major use of comparison advertising when the Getchell Agency introduced the Chrysler car in the 1930s by inviting customers to "Try all three."

Comparison advertising began to be widely used after the FTC pushed for more comparative advertising in 1972. The commission urged ABC and CBS to allow commercials that named competitors. Until then, only NBC had permitted such messages, whereas ABC and CBS would allow only "Brand X" comparisons in which competitors were implied but not directly named. The FTC continues to foster comparative advertising, even going so far as to warn trade associations against industry codes that prohibit such comparisons.

Despite the continuing use of the technique, many marketers are concerned that comparison advertising has a number of pitfalls for those using it. The three primary problems often cited in comparison advertising are as follows:

8 **List three negative consequences of comparison advertising.**

- Comparative advertising runs the risk of inadvertently promoting competitive brands and/or appearing to offer credibility to them by including their names. Logic tells us that only those brands that offer genuine competition will be named in a comparison campaign.

- Some comparison advertising techniques may appear unfair to consumers and damage not only the reputation of the brand using it but also advertising in general.

- Firms often fear that comparative advertising claims will precipitate lawsuits by companies that think their brands have been unfairly disparaged. The majority of complaints and lawsuits are brought by competitors who think that a company's comparative claims are deceptive or untrue. When comparison advertising is used, it increases the chances of such objections.

The financial and public relations fallout from such litigation can be extremely serious. For example, as a result of a lawsuit brought by H&R Block in federal court, Intuit, maker of tax-preparation software, TurboTax, agreed to change statements in its advertising. The advertisements claimed "more returns were prepared with TurboTax last year than at all the H&R Block stores combined." A U.S. District Court upheld H&R Block's complaint, and, while Intuit disputed the findings, it agreed to delete the claims.[62]

Comparison advertising also can invite counterattacks from competitive brands. Recently, Campbell's Soup and Progresso waged a "soup war" over taste preference and the healthiness of their respective ingredients. Campbell's fired the first shot with full-page ads comparing ingredients between its Select Harvest line and Progresso's Italian-Style Wedding soup. Progresso responded with ads saying it was removing MSG from its soups but pointed out that 95 Campbell's soups contain the ingredient. Despite observers' claims that the hard-hitting ads would turn off soup consumers, sales of both brands increased.[63] As we noted earlier in this chapter, product substantiation is important in any advertising, but particularly in comparison advertising where, in effect, advertisers must substantiate both the qualities of their brand as well as those of any other brands to which they are making comparisons.

The Advertising Clearance Process

Although advertisers operate in an environment of extensive regulation at both the state and federal level, some of the most effective advertising evaluations are conducted by the industry itself. The vast majority of advertisers not only want to produce truthful advertising but they also are interested in making sure that their peers do likewise. Advertising self-regulation is both philosophical and pragmatic. On the one hand, when consumers are misled by dishonest advertising, all advertisers pay a price in a loss of trust. On the other hand, and just as importantly, if consumers believe deceptive claims for a brand, they can hurt sales and profits of competitors. Advertisers, advertising agencies, and the media that carry their advertising all play a part in the process of ensuring that advertising serves the public interest.

advertising clearance process
The internal process of clearing ads for publication and broadcast, conducted primarily by ad agencies and clients.

The media are a major element in the **advertising clearance process** because they represent an independent reviewer of advertising messages. There are numerous examples of general media prohibitions of specific product categories such as NC-17 movie advertisements, alcohol, and certain types of sexually oriented product categories. In other cases, individual advertisements are refused because they appear to be fraudulent or they may demean a competitor. It is important to remember that in general the media review process is voluntary, and it is up to each medium to set its own standards—the scope and diligence exercised by the various media vary a great deal.

Advertising trade associations, individual media, and media groups often establish their own codes of ethics. Some newspapers and magazines, in varying degree, investigate the reliability of advertisers before accepting their copy. Some publishers have strict rules about acceptable advertising executions to prevent the publication of false or exaggerated claims and to preserve the aesthetic tone of their publications. Most publications clearly label advertisements that might be confused with editorial content.

Radio and television stations generally try to investigate a company and its product before broadcasting advertising messages that might be misleading or controversial. For example, the networks and the National Association of Broadcasters (NAB) have established codes regulating the advertising of medical products and contests, premiums, and other offers. All the networks maintain so-called acceptance departments, which screen both commercial and noncommercial scripts, either rejecting or challenging for substantiation any questionable material.

The American Advertising Federation, an organization of leading national advertisers, has long campaigned for "truth in advertising." Other organizations that promote ethical standards are the 4As and the ANA. The Institute of Outdoor Advertising encourages its members to improve the design of their advertising posters and signs and, more importantly, to make sure they do not erect advertising billboards in locations where they will mar the landscape or otherwise offend the public.[64]

Sometimes it is difficult to predict when a commercial will be turned down. In one case, a network reportedly rejected a commercial because models were not wearing wedding rings even though it was obvious from the context of the commercial that they were living together. In another case, CBS and NBC stopped running commercials for Miller Brewing that they thought unduly disparaged Anheuser-Busch Budweiser and Bud Light brands.[65] The major television networks are particularly vigilant concerning commercials directed to children. For example, toys are one of the most scrutinized advertising categories. The networks take pains to ensure that young children can tell the difference between commercials and programming by limiting advertising time (limiting commercials) during preschool blocks to the beginning and end of programs rather than showing ads in the middle of a program. Basic guidelines for toy commercials include the following:

- Toys must be presented literally and realistically.
- Animation is limited to about 10 seconds a spot.
- Copy must clearly disclose if parts are sold separately and if batteries are not included.[66]

Although many media do a good job of ad screening, the proliferation of media outlets and the resulting competitive pressure for advertising dollars have led to a lowering of review standards on the part of some media. The importance of the media screening process was emphasized in 1998 when the FTC issued a *Guide for the Media,* which stressed the importance of the media in stopping dishonest advertising. In the prologue to the guidelines, the FTC wrote, "Government agencies and self-regulatory groups can step in once the law has been violated, but only the media can stop false ads before they are disseminated."[67]

Lax enforcement of media guidelines or ignoring obviously deceptive and misleading advertising can have significant implications for the media. Media should carefully review advertising they accept as a matter of public trust, but careless acceptance of advertising also can carry legal liability for a medium. If a statement in an advertisement or commercial is false or defamatory, the media can be sued along with the advertiser. This notion was underscored in 2002 when then-FTC chair Timothy Muris introduced the idea that those media that ran clearly misleading advertising were leaving themselves open to legal action. In response, a number of media trade organizations complained that the threatened action was unconstitutional under free speech protections. However, Muris responded that "there is no constitutional right to run false advertising."[68]

CURBING QUESTIONABLE ADVERTISING

A primary emphasis of the FTC has been those media carrying fraudulent diet and weight loss ads. The "get tough" approach to media indifference obviously worked. In a survey conducted by the FTC, the commission found that so-called "red flag" weight loss ads (those with obviously false claims) dropped from 50 percent of total ads in January 2005 to 15 percent in May of that year. Commenting on the results of the survey, FTC chair Deborah Majoras said, "... our overweight population is a societal problem that requires personal responsibility, governmental responsibility, and corporate responsibility."[69]

In 2005, the government demonstrated how serious it is about regulating false advertising when the DOJ launched the latest salvo in its ongoing effort to eliminate online gambling activity in the United States by announcing a $7.2 million settlement with *The Sporting News* in connection with that company's acceptance of advertisements for offshore gambling sites on its web site, in its publications, and on its radio stations. The DOJ has long taken the position that offshore gambling sites are illegal in the United States and, further, that entities that aid and abet the offshore sites in targeting U.S. consumers—including media outlets that accept ads for such sites—are equally liable for the gambling law violations. *The Sporting News* settlement is the latest development in this investigation. *The Sporting News*, while not admitting any liability or violation of law, agreed to pay $7.2 million—a $4.2 million fine and $3 million in corrective advertising in the form of public service ads designed to discourage online gambling activity. The settlement amount reflected the profits that *The Sporting News* reportedly received from spring 2000 through the end of 2003 from the acceptance of Internet gambling ads.[70]

Despite threats of formal legal action, from a practical standpoint, unless a medium knowingly accepts deceptive or libelous advertising, its chances of liability are not great. However, a more practical concern for the media is the loss of goodwill with their audiences if a deceptive ad is cleared for publication or broadcast. No responsible agency or medium would argue that deceptive advertising should be created or run.

Self-Regulation by Industry-Wide Groups

Self-regulation by the advertising industry is not new, but it has become much more evident and effective in the past 25 years. Today, there are a number of initiatives to ensure that advertising is truthful. Some of these efforts are undertaken by groups within specific industries, and others are intended to review more general advertising. Industry self-regulation serves two important purposes beyond ensuring more informative and truthful advertising.

▪ It seeks to overcome the relatively poor public perception of advertising by showing that there is a concerted attempt within the industry to foster responsible advertising.

KLEPPNER VIEWPOINT 24.2

Dr. Peter Cressy President/CEO
of the Distilled Spirits Council

CORPORATE SOCIAL RESPONSIBILITY IN ADVERTISING: A ROAD WELL PAVED BY THE DISTILLED SPIRITS INDUSTRY

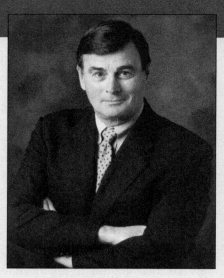

Dr. Peter Cressy

I n an era of corporate mistrust and a growing emphasis on social responsibility, the Distilled Spirits Council (DISCUS) has carved a path to good corporate citizenship through its *Code of Responsible Practices for Beverage Alcohol Advertising and Marketing*. Advertising for many products has come under increased scrutiny by public officials, regulators, and third-party advocacy groups. The distilled spirits industry, however, has been at the forefront of forging good advertising practices and has been repeatedly cited as a model for effective self-regulation of advertising.

For more than 70 years, distilled spirits companies have abided by the DISCUS *Code*, a voluntary set of guidelines issued by the spirits industry trade association for the responsible content and placement of spirits advertising and marketing. These *Code* guidelines have been revised throughout the decades as social mores, the marketplace, and technology have changed.

Throughout its history, the core principle of the *Code* has been and remains to market beverage alcohol products to adults in a responsible and appropriate manner. As an industry, distillers are committed to adhering to a tough advertising and marketing code and holding ourselves to a standard higher than mandated by any law or regulation. Self-regulation is flexible, responsive, and particularly suitable in light of the First Amendment issues that otherwise would be raised by government regulation of advertising.

Unique among other industries, the spirits industry *Code* historically has provided for a Code Review Board, composed of senior member company representatives, which is charged with reviewing complaints about advertising and marketing materials. After receiving a complaint, the board determines whether the advertisement is consistent or inconsistent with the provisions of the *Code*. The board relays its decision to the advertiser and, if a provision of the *Code* has been violated, urges that the advertisement be revised or withdrawn. For DISCUS member company advertisements, the time between receipt of a complaint and Code Review Board action often is a matter of days. There has been 100 percent compliance by DISCUS members with board decisions and a high level of compliance by non-DISCUS members.

■ Strong self-regulation may ward off even stricter government control. For example, two of the most aggressive industry self-regulation initiatives have involved the pharmacy and beverage industries—both under scrutiny by both regulators and consumer protection groups.

The Pharmaceutical Research and Manufacturers of America (PhRMA) instigated a far-reaching code of conduct to address concerns about direct-to-consumer advertising. The code called for prior review by the FDA of all advertising, a discussion of both the risks and benefits of a drug, and clearly identified health conditions for which a drug is intended. Some observers saw the code as a negotiating tool as the FDA begins discussions of drug advertising regulations. "The long-awaited code of conduct issued . . . by a pharmaceutical industry looking to head off government-imposed regulation of direct-to-consumer drug advertising is seen by many as wishy-washy by design, and a mere starting point to bargain for bigger chips."[71] Regardless of whether this cynical view of the industry's motives is correct, it does point out the benefit of implementing such industry codes at a time when it is not in a crisis mode.

For decades the distilled spirits industry has effectively addressed complaints about spirits advertising, but until recently the decisions of the Code Review Board were not made public. As a consequence, the rigor of the board's review process and company adherence to the board's decisions were not widely recognized. To make the industry's review process more transparent and understandable to the public, in 2005, DISCUS began publishing semiannual public reports detailing complaints against specific spirits advertisements, decisions of the Code Review Board, and the responsive actions taken by each advertiser. By providing a public report about complaint decisions, the operation of the distillers' advertising code significantly differs from other industry codes. To the best of our knowledge, DISCUS is the first trade group representing American businesses to issue a public report regarding the proceedings of how an industry regulates itself according to its own internal code. This new transparency provision allows the public at large to better evaluate and appreciate the DISCUS *Code* review process, which the FTC—the lead federal agency with advertising oversight— has repeatedly pointed to as a model of self-regulation and a step above and beyond what others are doing.

Incorporating transparency into the DISCUS *Code* review process has had an immediate and positive impact. Our members continue to achieve full compliance, and we are experiencing a quicker response time and an increased compliance rate among nonmembers. We believe the *Semi-Annual Report* is an important element of our longstanding corporate responsibility efforts, and the distillers' transparent reporting system also has been recognized as a model for other industries by regulators and industry critics and now is receiving acclaim by the business community.

In June 2006, the *Semi-Annual Report* was the recipient of the best "Business Ethics Communications" award by the PR News Corporate Social Responsibility (CSR) Awards. The CSR Awards honor corporations and their partners that have implemented and executed highly successful CSR campaigns in the past 12 months. PR News calls the CSR Awards "the gold standard in corporate citizenship and communications worldwide." DISCUS also was named a finalist in the American Business Awards[SM] "Best Corporate Social Responsibility Program" category for our public reporting system.

Publishers and other media executives also have responded to the distillers' tough voluntary advertising standards. Under a new provision added to the distillers' *Code* in 2003, beverage alcohol advertising and marketing should be placed only in a medium where at least 70 percent of the audience is reasonably expected to be 21 years of age or older. Several trend-setting magazines have established subscription-only editions in response to the distillers' move to a 70 percent adult demographic, which ensure that spirits companies can reasonably expect to meet this standard.

We believe that these efforts have implications beyond the beverage alcohol industry. The distillers' advertising *Code*, with its transparent complaint review process, is a dynamic example of how an industry can effectively regulate itself, promote corporate social responsibility, and raise public confidence.

Dr. Peter Cressy is president/CEO of the Distilled Spirits Council. He is the former chancellor of the University of Massachusetts, Dartmouth, and former president of the Massachusetts Maritime Academy. He is a retired Navy Rear Admiral.

Similarly, beverage companies are facing numerous regulations calling for restrictions or bans on the sale of soft drinks in schools. In addition, there have been calls for government-mandated health warnings on soft drink labels. In the face of this criticism, the American Beverage Association and high-profile members such as Coca-Cola and PepsiCo enacted a voluntary policy to head off stricter legislation. The association spent millions of dollars promoting the voluntary guidelines, which limited the sale of carbonated soft drinks, especially in elementary and middle schools.[72]

Recently, online advertisers announced their own self-policing guidelines in the face of concerns about consumer privacy and behavioral tracking. The guidelines were co-developed by the 4As, the ANA, the Council of Better Business Bureaus, and the DMA. Efforts are designed to both enhance transparency and educate citizens about online behavioral advertising.

We should not suggest that codes of advertising are only enacted by industries in peril. Most major trade associations have guidelines about the marketing and advertising of their products. The advertising industry itself has a long history of promoting truthful advertising (see Exhibit 24.20). In fact, former FTC chair Bob Pitofsky

EXHIBIT 24.20

Advertising agencies take their responsibility for truthful advertising seriously.

Creative Code of the American Association of Advertising Agencies

ADOPTED APRIL 26, 1962

The members of the American Association of Advertising Agencies recognize:

1. That advertising bears a dual responsibility in the American economic system and way of life.

To the public it is a primary way of knowing about the goods and services that are the products of American free enterprise—goods and services that can be freely chosen to suit the desires and needs of the individual. The public is entitled to expect that advertising will be reliable in content and honest in presentation.

To the advertiser it is a primary way of persuading people to buy his goods or services, within the framework of a highly competitive economic system. He is entitled to regard advertising as a dynamic means of building his business and his profits.

2. That advertising enjoys a particularly intimate relationship to the American family.

It enters the home as an integral part of television and radio programs, to speak to the individual and often to the entire family. It shares the pages of favorite newspapers and magazines. It presents itself to travelers and to readers of the daily mails. In all these forms, it bears a special responsibility to respect the tastes and self-interest of the public.

3. That advertising is directed to sizable groups or to the public at large, which is made up of many interests and many tastes.

As is the case with all public enterprises, ranging from sports to education and even to religion, it is almost impossible to speak without finding someone in disagreement. Nonetheless, advertising people recognize their obligation to operate within the traditional American limitations: to serve the interests of the majority and to respect the rights of the minority.

Therefore we, the members of the American Association of Advertising Agencies, in addition to supporting and obeying the laws and legal regulations pertaining to advertising, undertake to extend and broaden the application of high ethical standards. Specifically, we will not knowingly produce advertising that contains:

> **a.** False or misleading statements or exaggerations, visual or verbal.
> **b.** Testimonials that do not reflect the real choice of a competent witness.
> **c.** Price claims that are misleading.
> **d.** Comparisons that unfairly disparage a competitive product or service.
> **e.** Claims insufficiently supported, or which distort the true meaning or practicable application of statements made by professional or scientific authority.
> **f.** Statements, suggestions, or pictures offensive to public decency.

We recognize that there are areas subject to honestly different interpretations and judgment. Taste is subjective and may even vary from time to time as well as from individual to individual. Frequency of seeing or hearing advertising messages will necessarily vary greatly from person to person.

However, we agree not to recommend to an advertiser and to discourage the use of advertising that is in poor or questionable taste or is deliberately irritating through content, presentation, or excessive repetition.

Clear and willful violations of this Code shall be referred to the Board of Directors of the American Association of Advertising Agencies for appropriate action, including possible annulment of membership as provided in Article IV, Section 5, of the Constitution and By-Laws.

Conscientious adherence to the letter and the spirit of this Code will strengthen advertising and the free enterprise system of which it is a part.

remarked, "Today advertising has the best self-regulatory system of any industry in the country."[73] Its efforts offer the public, competitors, and other interested parties a voluntary forum for negotiation without resorting to a formal legal or regulatory body for the adjudication of disagreements. One of the ways in which the business promotes better advertising is through various guidelines and codes of practice promoted by advertising agency groups and media associations as well as trade and professional associations. One of the leading advertising groups promoting truthful and ethical advertising is the AAF. A primary aim of the AAF is to foster truthful and fair advertising through local advertising clubs.

Despite the best efforts of federal regulatory agencies, the media, and individual advertisers, the opinion persists among a large group of consumers that advertising is either basically deceptive or does not provide sufficient information. Given the investment that companies are making in advertising, this perception is a major problem and one that all honest businesses need to address on a united front. As we will see in the next section, the advertising industry is making substantial investments in moving against deceptive advertising.

BETTER BUSINESS BUREAUS

One of the best-known, aggressive, and successful organizations in the fight for honest and truthful advertising is the national network of Better Business Bureaus (BBBs) coordinated by the Council of Better Business Bureaus, Inc. (CBBB). The forerunners of the modern BBBs date to 1905, when various local advertising clubs formed a national association that today is known as the National Advertising Federation. In 1911, this association launched a campaign for truth in advertising coordinated by local vigilance committees. In 1916, these local committees adopted the name Better Business Bureaus, and they became autonomous in 1926. Today, there are approximately 128 local bureaus in the United States and Canada.

In many respects, the work of the CBBB mirrors that of the FTC—without the attending force of law. Some of the key areas of concern for the CBBB and its affiliates are as follows: Internet shopping, warranties and guarantees, comparative price claims, testimonials, and credit fraud. The efforts of the organization are primarily educational with its two-volume *Do's and Don'ts in Advertising* providing the foundation for its efforts. The volumes offer advertisers advice covering most of the basic questions encountered by companies. The "Basic Principles" offers the following overview of the BBBs' philosophy of self-regulation:

- Primary responsibility for truthful and nondeceptive advertising rests with the advertiser. Advertisers should be prepared to substantiate any claims or offers made before publication or broadcast and, on request, present such substantiation promptly to the advertising medium or the Better Business Bureau.

- Advertisements that are untrue, misleading, deceptive, fraudulent, falsely disparaging of competitors, or insincere offers to sell shall not be used.

- An advertisement as a whole may be misleading although every sentence separately considered is literally true. Misrepresentation may result not only from direct statements but also by omitting or obscuring a material fact.[74]

Although the BBBs have no legal authority, they are a major influence on truth and accuracy in advertising. The BBBs are able to exert both the force of public opinion and peer pressure to set up voluntary efforts to address examples of potentially misleading or deceptive advertising.

The NARC Self-Regulation Program

The National Advertising Review Council (NARC) was founded in 1971 in response to the many different consumer movements pushing for more stringent government regulation of advertising and concerns among major advertisers that advertising honesty was not being given enough attention within the industry. The major advertising organizations—the AAF, the 4As, and the ANA—approached the CBBB and together formed the NARC. NARC's primary purpose was to "develop a structure which would effectively apply the persuasive capacities of peers to seek the voluntary elimination of national advertising which professionals would consider deceptive." Its objective was to sustain high standards of truth and accuracy in national advertising through voluntary self-regulation. At the outset, consumers and consumer advocates submitted a number of complaints concerning deceptive advertising. However, in a short time, advertisers became the major watchdogs, lodging the majority of complaints against their competitors—a situation that continues today. "The NARC works because it is tough enough to satisfy consumer advocates, business-minded enough to respect advertising's role in the marketing process and effective enough to keep the Federal Trade Commission off the industry's back."[75]

NARC established a number of units that are administered by the CBBB (see Exhibit 24.21). The primary investigative unit is the **National Advertising Division (NAD)** of the CBBB. The NAD is staffed by full-time lawyers who respond to complaints from competitors and consumers and to referrals from local BBBs. They also monitor national advertising. The unit handled more than 179 cases in 2008. Of those cases, 84 were challenges submitted by advertisers questioning competitors' claims, up 58 percent from the previous year. The National Advertising Review Board (NARB) provides an advertiser with a jury of peers if it chooses to appeal a NAD decision. In

9 **Discuss the primary roles of the NARC, NARB, and the CARU in supporting advertising regulation.**

National Advertising Division (NAD)
The primary investigative unit of the NARC self-regulation program.

EXHIBIT 24.21

The NARC review process is established to ensure fairness and provide an objective examination of advertising.

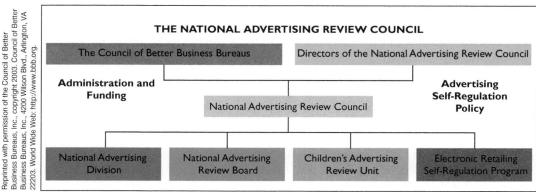

1974, the Children's Advertising Review Unit (CARU) was established to review the special advertising concerns of advertising directed to children. We discuss the CARU in detail later in this section. The Electronic Retailing Self-Regulation Program was developed in 2004 to examine advertising claims in direct-response advertising, including infomercials.

These units "review only national advertisements—those ads disseminated on a nationwide or broadly regional basis. . . . Product performance claims, superiority claims against competitive products and all kinds of scientific and technical claims in national advertising are the types of cases accepted by the NAD. NAD is *not* the appropriate forum to address concerns about the 'good taste' of ads, moral questions about products that are offered for sale or political or issue advertising."[76]

After a complaint is received, the NAD determines the issues, collects and evaluates data, and makes an initial decision as to whether the claims are substantiated. If the NAD finds that substantiation is satisfactory, it announces that fact. If the NAD finds that the substantiation is not adequate, it will recommend that the advertiser modify or discontinue the offending claims. If an advertiser declines to participate in the self-regulatory process, or declines to comply with the terms of an NAD decision, the advertising claims at issue may be referred to the appropriate federal agency for further review. If the advertiser does not agree with an NAD decision, it may appeal to the NARB. NAD decisions are released to the press and also are published in its monthly publication *NAD/CARU Case Reports.*

The NARB is composed of 70 members—40 representing advertisers, 20 representing advertising agencies, and 10 from the public sector. Five members, in the same proportion, are assigned to hear an appeal. If the panel determines the NAD's decision is justified but the advertiser still refuses to correct the deceptive element, the NARB may refer the advertising to the appropriate government agency. Underscoring the competitive nature of advertising claims, competitor challenges are by far the largest source of NAD cases. According to the NAD, there are six primary areas that provide most of the challenges brought to the organization:

1. Product testing
2. Consumer perception studies
3. Taste/sensory claims
4. Pricing
5. Testimonial/anecdotal evidences
6. Demonstrations

In a number of cases, complaints involve comparative advertising. For example, a challenge is often made when product testing or product demonstrations involve other brands' alleged deficiencies. In terms of complaints, the largest product category is health and health aids, followed by food and beverage. It is no coincidence that these are two of the most competitive product categories.

In our examination of the NAD/NARB process, we should understand that it cannot

- Order an advertiser to stop an ad
- Impose a fine
- Bar anyone from advertising
- Boycott an advertiser or a product

What it can do is bring to bear the judgment of an advertiser's peers that a company has produced advertising that is not truthful and is harmful to the industry, to the public, and to the offender. This opinion has great moral weight. It is reinforced by the knowledge that, if the results of an appeal to the NARB are not accepted, the whole matter will be referred to the appropriate government agency and at the same time will be released to the public. This step, unique in business self-regulation machinery, avoids any problem of violating antitrust laws, presents the entire matter to public view, and still leaves the advertiser subject to an FTC ruling on the advertising.

THE CHILDREN'S ADVERTISING REVIEW UNIT OF THE COUNCIL OF BETTER BUSINESS BUREAUS

Both consumer groups and advertisers have long recognized that children's advertising is fundamentally different from commercial messages directed to adults. Because of the special circumstances involved with advertising to children, the NARC, in cooperation with the advertising community, founded the **Children's Advertising Review Unit (CARU)** in 1974. The CARU's work primarily deals with the following areas:

- Product presentations and claims
- Sales pressure
- Disclosures and disclaimers
- Comparative claims
- Endorsements and promotions by program or editorial characters
- Premiums, promotions, and sweepstakes
- Safety
- Interactive electronic media

Children's Advertising Review Unit (CARU) The CARU functions much as the NAD to review complaints about advertising to children.

In general, the CARU's mission is similar to that of the NAD except it considers the special circumstances of the younger audience reached by children-oriented advertising. During the past few years, two of the major areas of concern to children's advocates have been food advertising and the growing use of the Internet as a sales tool to reach children. Effective in April 2000, the Children's Online Privacy Protection Act (COPPA) sought to protect the privacy of children younger than age 13 by requiring parental consent for the collection or use of any personal information by marketers. Among the several provisions of the act, it requires that advertisers include a privacy policy, parental notification of information collected concerning their children, and a requirement that information collected be confidential and secure. The FTC has the primary oversight for COPPA. CARU regularly reviews web sites to assure that the sites comply both with CARU's guidelines and with COPPA. From 2008 through the first half of 2009, CARU issued more than 50 decisions related to web site privacy.

OBESITY CONCERNS   A second major area of concern, food advertising and its alleged contribution to childhood obesity, demonstrates many similarities with the battle over tobacco advertising in the 1990s. The importance of the topic can be seen in the 2005 issuance by NARC of a 92-page white paper entitled "Guidance for Food Advertising Self-regulation." The food industry is coming under blistering attacks by

Congress, consumer advocates, medical and scientific groups, and lawyers threatening legal action akin to that faced by tobacco companies in the past. It was in this environment that CARU announced in 2006 a review of its guidelines, led by Joan Z. (Jodie) Bernstein, a public member of the CBBB board of directors and former director of the Bureau of Consumer Protection at the FTC. At the close of that review process, CARU revised its Guidelines in several significant ways. Further, the CBBB established a Children's Food and Beverage Advertising Initiative to encourage advertisers to promote healthy products and lifestyle choices.

Two of the most vocal detractors of food marketing were Senator Tom Harkin of Iowa and the Institute of Medicine (IOM), an associated organization of the National Academy of Science. Senator Harkin had been specifically critical of the CARU for not having done enough to put teeth in the self-regulatory process. However, the guidelines review and the resulting creation of the Children's Food and Beverage Advertising Initiative won Harkin's praise. In July 2007, Harkin commented, "Recently, many food and beverage companies have stepped up to the challenge and committed to advertising healthier food choices. Just last week, 11 major food and beverage companies pledged to focus their advertising to children under age 12 on more nutritious foods. The companies also agreed to restrict advertising using licensed characters to products that meet nutritional standards."[77]

THE CHILDREN'S FOOD AND BEVERAGE ADVERTISING INITIATIVE

The Children's Food and Beverage Advertising Initiative (CFBAI) was launched by the CBBB in November 2006 to provide transparent and accountable self-regulatory guidelines for companies that advertise foods and beverages to children. The initiative's goal is to ensure that food and beverage advertising messages directed to children younger than age 12 encourage healthy dietary choices and lifestyles. Currently, 15 major food and beverage marketers participate in the initiative, including Burger King, McDonald's, Coca-Cola, and Kraft Foods. It is estimated these companies accounted for more than two-thirds of children's food and beverage advertising expenditures in 2004.[78]

Under the initiative's terms, participating companies promise to devote at least 50 percent of their advertising messages directed to children to promote healthy dietary choices, as well as messages that encourage good nutrition or healthy lifestyles (see Exhibit 24.22). Criteria for determining "better-for-you" products is consistent with established standards, such as USDA Dietary Guidelines, MyPyramid, and FDA standards for health claims. Participating companies also have agreed to the following:[79]

- To reduce the use of third-party licensed characters in advertising primarily directed to children younger than age 12 that does not meet the initiative's product or messaging criteria

- Not to pay for or actively seek food and beverage product placement in editorial or entertainment content that is primarily directed to children younger than age 12

- To change interactive games that are primarily directed to children younger than age 12 that include the company's food or beverage brands to incorporate better-for-you foods or healthy lifestyle messages in the games

In addition, participating companies also agreed not to advertise food or beverage products in elementary schools. CFBAI and CARU work in concert to foster trust in the marketplace by promoting balance in food and beverage marketing and truthful, responsible advertising to children.

As the controversy surrounding food advertising demonstrates, questions concerning children's advertising have few easy answers. To the critics who think that no advertising should be directed to children, even the strictest advertising guidelines are unsatisfactory. However, given the economic support of the media through advertising,

EXHIBIT 24.22

This ad encourages teens to get summer jobs and become active.

it is unlikely that any such ban will ever be invoked. It is imperative that all parties involved (media, advertisers, parents, special interest groups, and government) work to ensure that children's advertising is appropriate to the audience for which it is intended. With public opinion running against them, advertisers must be extremely cautious about the content of all advertising messages directed to children.

SUMMARY

In this chapter, we have discussed the many restraints on the practice of advertising. These include legal, ethical, social, and economic considerations. It is obvious that legal and regulatory bodies are devoting increasing resources to review dishonest and misleading advertising.

However, it is important to remember that the ethical and honest practice of advertising is rarely the result of threats of legislation or punishment. Rather, advertisers, their agencies, and the mainstream media know that attention to the ethical and social problems of content, presentation, and the acceptability of a host of product categories, claims, and advertising practices is good business as well as responsible corporate citizenship. Although legal restraints on advertising are an important part of the advertising environment, it is unusual for major advertisers to develop advertising strategy solely because of governmental regulations.

As we discussed in the beginning of this chapter, advertisers are adopting a much more sensitive perception of their audiences and customers than their counterparts of 25 years ago. The diversity of the marketplace, growing fragmentation of the media, and concerns with public policy issues such as the demand for consumer privacy are topics rarely considered by advertisers only a few years ago. Those advertisers who fail to take account of the current sensitivity of consumers toward social issues run the risk of inadvertently initiating major public relations problems for themselves.

We cannot be certain what the future of advertising holds in terms of social and cultural issues, but we do know that it will be a time of change and adaptation. The public interest will be an increasingly important part of the modern advertiser's agenda—much more important than formal legal restrictions. It is a given that the public will not tolerate untruthful, misleading, and deceptive advertising. But more than simply being truthful, contemporary advertising must incorporate the idea of social responsibility as routinely as it depends on a well thought out marketing plan. As part of this social responsibility, advertising will be used more extensively as a tool for change in society. Rather than simply being confined to selling products and services, advertising will play a large role in presenting ideas and opinions concerning a host of social issues.

Among major advertisers, there is no disagreement that advertising should be fair and truthful and follow both the letter and the spirit of the law. Advertisers are among the most aggressive groups in weeding out the charlatans who make it difficult for all advertisers by eroding public confidence. For the foreseeable future, it is clear that advertisers will have to contend with numerous, sometimes conflicting, and constantly changing advertising regulations.

REVIEW

1. Compare and contrast the social and economic issues involved in the practice of advertising.
2. Discuss two arguments for and against advertising.
3. Discuss the difference between inadvertent and intended social roles of advertising.
4. What is the role of the Advertising Council in encouraging social advertising?
5. Why is substantiation considered the foundation of FTC enforcement?
6. What is the importance of cease-and-desist orders in FTC enforcement?
7. Briefly discuss the *Central Hudson Four-Part Test*.
8. What role does advertising puffery play in enforcing advertising regulations?
9. What is the down side of comparison advertising?
10. Discuss the role of the media clearance process and advertising self-regulation.
11. Describe advertising's overall self-regulation structure at the national level.

Glossary

A

account planner   An outgrowth of the British agency structure in which a planner initiates and reviews research and participates in the creative process. In some agencies, the planner is considered a spokesperson for the consumer.

advertising clearance process   The internal process of clearing ads for publication and broadcast, conducted primarily by ad agencies and clients.

Advertising Council   A nonprofit network of agencies, media, and advertisers dedicated to promoting social programs through advertising.

advertising goals   The communication objectives designed to accomplish certain tasks within the total marketing program.

advertising   Advertising consists of paid notices from identified sponsors normally offered through communication media.

advertorial   The use of advertising to promote an idea rather than a product or service.

American Association of Advertising Agencies (AAAA, 4As)   The national organization of advertising agencies.

amplitude modulation (AM)   Method of transmitting electromagnetic signals by varying the amplitude (size) of the electromagnetic wave, in contrast to varying its frequency. Quality is not as good as frequency modulation but can be heard farther, especially at night.

animation   Making inanimate objects appear alive and moving by setting them before an animation camera and filming one frame at a time.

appeal   The motive to which an advertisement is directed; it is designed to steer a person toward a goal the advertiser has set.

Arbitron Inc.   Syndicated radio ratings company.

audience fragmentation   The segmenting of mass-media audiences into smaller groups because of diversity of media outlets.

audience fragmentation   The segmenting of mass-media audiences into smaller groups because of diversity of media outlets.

Audit Bureau of Circulations (ABC)   The organization sponsored by publishers, agencies, and advertisers for securing accurate circulation statements.

Average Quarter-Hour (AQH)   Manner in which radio ratings are presented. Estimates (AQHE) include average number of people listening (AQHP), rating (AQHR), and share (AQHS) of audience. The Metro Survey Area (MSA) population can be used to determine share.

B

barter syndication   Station obtains a program at no charge. The program has presold national commercials, and time is available for local station spots.

barter   Acquisition of broadcast time by an advertiser or an agency in exchange for operating capital or merchandise. No cash is involved.

behavioral research   Market research that attempts to determine the underlying nature of purchase behavior.

bleed   Printed matter that runs over the edges of an outdoor board or of a page, leaving no margin.

brand   A name, term, sign, design, or a unifying combination of them intended to identify and distinguish the product or service from competing products or services.

brand equity   The value of how such people as consumers, distributors, and salespeople think and feel about a brand relative to its competition over a period of time.

brand extension   These are new product introductions under an existing brand to take advantage of existing brand equity.

brand loyalty   A consumer's preference for and commitment to a specific brand.

brand name   The written or spoken part of a trademark, in contrast to the pictorial mark; a trademark word.

business-to-business advertisers   Advertisers that promote goods through trade and industrial journals that are used in the manufacturing, distributing, or marketing of goods to the public.

C

cable television   Television signals that are carried to households by cable. Programs originate with cable operators through high antennas, satellite disks, or operator-initiated programming.

category manager   A relatively new corporate position, the category manager is responsible for all aspects of the brands in a specific product category for a company, including research, manufacturing, sales, and advertising. Each product's advertising manager reports to the category manager. Example: Procter & Gamble's Tide and Cheer detergent advertising managers report to a single category manager.

caveat emptor   Latin for "Let the buyer beware"; represents the notion that there should be no government interference in the marketplace.

cease-and-desist orders   If an advertiser refuses to sign a consent decree, the FTC may issue a cease-and-desist order that can carry a $10,000-per-day fine.

centralized exchange   A system of trade and marketing through specialized intermediaries rather than the direct exchange of goods between buyers and producers.

Children's Advertising Review Unit (CARU)   The CARU functions much as the NAD to review complaints about advertising to children.

classified advertising   Found in columns so labeled, published in sections of a newspaper or magazine that are set aside for certain classes of goods or services—for example, help wanted positions.

clearance   The percentage of network affiliates that carry a particular network program.

closing date   The date by which all advertising material must be submitted to a publication.

clutter   A proliferation of commercials in a particular medium. This reduces the impact of any single message.

coined word   An original and arbitrary combination of syllables forming a word. Extensively used for trademarks, such as PoFolks, Mazola, Gro-Pup, Zerone. (Opposite of a dictionary word.)

comparative advertising Directly contrasts an advertiser's product with other named or identified products.

compensation The payment of clearance fees by a television network to local stations carrying its shows.

competitive stage The advertising stage a product reaches when its general usefulness is recognized but its superiority over similar brands has to be established in order to gain preference. See pioneering stage, retentive stage.

comprehensive A layout accurate in size, color, scheme, and other necessary details to show how a final advertisement will look; for presentation only, never for reproduction.

computer-generated imagery (CGI) Technology allowing computer operators to create multitudes of electronic effects for TV—to squash, stretch, or squeeze objects—much more quickly than earlier tools could. It can add layers of visuals simultaneously.

concept testing The target audience evaluation of (alternative) creative strategey. Testing attempts to separate good and bad ideas and provide insight into factors motivating acceptance or rejection.

conjoint analysis A research technique designed to determine what consumers perceive as a product's most important benefits.

consent decree Issued by the FTC. An advertiser signs the decree, stops the practice under investigation, but admits no guilt.

consumer advertising Advertising directed to people who will use the product themselves, in contrast to trade advertising, industrial advertising, or professional advertising.

contest A promotion in which consumers compete for prizes and the winners are selected strictly on the basis of skill.

continuous tone An unscreened photographic picture or image, on paper or film, that contains all gradations of tonal values from white to black.

controlled circulation Publications sent without cost to people responsible for making buying decisions. To get on such lists, people must state their positions in companies; to stay on them, they must request it annually. Also known as qualified-circulation publications.

convergence The blending of various facets of marketing functions and communication technology to create more efficient and expanded synergies.

cooperative (co-op) advertising Joint promotion of a national advertiser (manufacturer) and a local retail outlet on behalf of the manufacturer's product on sale in the retail store.

copy approach The method of opening the text of an advertisement. The chief forms are the factual approach, the imaginative approach, and the emotional approach.

copy testing Measuring the effectiveness of advertisements.

corrective advertising To counteract the past residual effect of previous deceptive advertising, the FTC may require the advertiser to devote future space and time to disclosure of previous deception. Began around the late 1960s.

cost per rating point (CPP) The cost per rating point is used to estimate the cost of television advertising on several shows.

cost per thousand (CPM) A method of comparing the cost for media of different circulations. Also, weighted or demographic cost per thousand calculates the CPM using only that portion of a medium's audience falling into a prime-prospect category.

Council of Better Business Bureaus National organization that coordinates a number of local and national initiatives to protect consumers.

coupon Most popular type of sales-promotion technique.

cross-media buy Several media or vehicles that are packaged to be sold to advertisers to gain a synergistic communication effect and efficiencies in purchasing time or space.

customer relationship marketing (CRM) A management concept that organizes a business according to the needs of the consumer.

D

direct premium A sales incentive given to customers at the time of purchase.

direct-response advertising Any form of advertising done in direct marketing. Uses all types of media: direct mail, television, magazines, newspapers, radio. Term replaces mail-order advertising. See direct marketing.

display Newspaper ads other than those text-only ads in the classified columns. Display ads are generally larger and can include color, photos, or artwork to attract reader attention to the product.

distribution channel The various intermediaries, such as retailers, that control the flow of goods from manufacturers to consumers.

dot-coms A generic designation that refers to companies engaged in some type of online commerce.

E

eight-sheet poster Outdoor poster used in urban areas, about one-fourth the size of the standard 30-sheet poster. Also called *junior poster*.

electroencephalography The recording of the brain's electrical activity via electrodes placed on the scalp.

end-product advertising Building consumer demand by promoting ingredients in a product, for example, Teflon and NutraSweet.

engagement The delivery of attentive consumers from a media vehicle to the advertising.

European Union (EU) The developing economic integration of Europe. Potentially a single market of some 500 million consumers in 2010.

exclusionary zones (outdoor) Industry code of conduct that prohibits advertising within 500 feet of churches, schools, or hospitals of any products that cannot be used legally by children.

executional idea A rendering in words, symbols, shapes, forms, or any combination thereof of an abstract answer to a perceived desire or need.

experiential sampling A company's use of specialty vehicles to engage consumers and give them samples to enhance the contact experience.

F

family life cycle Concept that demonstrates changing purchasing behavior as a person or a family matures.

fast-close advertising Some magazines offer short-notice advertising deadlines, sometimes at a premium cost.

Federal Communications Commission (FCC) The federal authority empowered to license radio and television stations and to assign wavelengths to stations "in the public interest."

Federal Trade Commission (FTC) The agency of the federal government empowered to prevent unfair competition and to prevent fraudulent, misleading, or deceptive advertising in interstate commerce.

flat rate A uniform charge for space in a medium, without regard to the amount of space used or the frequency of insertion. When flat rates do not prevail, time discounts or quantity discounts are offered.

flighting Flight is the length of time a broadcaster's campaign runs. Can be days, weeks, or months—but does not refer to a year. A flighting schedule alternates periods of activity with periods of inactivity.

focus group A qualitative research interviewing method using in-depth interviews with a group rather than with an individual.

four-color process The process for reproducing color illustrations by a set of plates, one that prints all the yellows, another the blues, a third the reds, and the fourth the blacks (the sequence may vary). The plates are referred to as process plates.

free-standing inserts (FSIs) Preprinted inserts distributed to newspaper publishers, where they are inserted and delivered with the newspaper.

frequency In media exposure, the number of times an individual or household is exposed to an advertising vehicle for a specific brand within a given period of time.

frequency modulation (FM) A radio transmission wave that transmits by the variation in the frequency of its wave rather than by its size (as in amplitude modulation [AM]). An FM wave is 20 times the width of an AM wave, which is the source of its fine tone. To transmit such a wave, it has to be placed high on the electromagnetic spectrum, far from AM waves with their interference and static, hence its outstanding tone.

fulfillment firm Company that handles the couponing process, including receiving, verification, and payment. It also handles contest and sweepstakes responses.

full-service agency An agency that handles planning, creation, production, and placement of advertising for advertising clients. It may also handle sales promotion and other related services as needed by the client.

G

global marketing Term that denotes the use of advertising and marketing strategies on an international basis.

glocalization A hybrid term meaning to adapt global marketing efforts (products and advertising messages) to local markets and cultures.

gross rating points (GRPs) Each rating point represents 1 percent of the universe being measured for the market. In television, it is 1 percent of the households having television sets in that area.

H

HD radio Offers terrestrial radio stations the ability to deliver additional programming on the same amount of bandwidth with higher-quality sound. It requires a special receiver.

Highway Beautification Act of 1965 Federal law that controls outdoor signs in noncommercial, nonindustrial areas.

hoarding First printed outdoor signs—the forerunner of modern outdoor advertising.

horizontal publication Business publications for people engaged in a single job function regardless of the industry, for example, *Purchasing Magazine*.

house mark A primary mark of a business concern, usually used with the trademark of its products. General Mills is a house mark; Betty Crocker is a trademark; DuPont is a house mark; Teflon II is a trademark.

I

idea advertising Advertising used to promote an idea or cause rather than to sell a product or service.

illuminated posters Seventy to eighty percent of all outdoor posters are illuminated for 24-hour exposure.

in-house agency An arrangement whereby the advertiser handles the total agency function by buying individually, on a fee basis, the needed services (for example, creative, media services, and placement) under the direction of an assigned advertising director.

incentives Sales promotion directed at wholesalers, retailers, or a company's sales force.

industrial advertising Advertising addressed to manufacturers who buy machinery, equipment, raw materials, and the components needed to produce the goods they sell.

infomercial Long-form television advertising that promotes products within the context of a program-length commercial.

institutional advertising Advertising done by an organization speaking of its work views, and problems as a whole, to gain public goodwill and support rather than to sell a specific product. Sometimes called public relations advertising.

integrated marketing communication (IMC) The joint planning, execution, and coordination of all areas of marketing communication.

interactive era Communication will increasingly be controlled by consumers who will determine when and where they can be reached with promotional messages.

interconnects A joint buying opportunity between two or more cable systems in the same market.

J

jingle A commercial or part of a commercial set to music, usually carrying the slogan or theme line of a campaign. May make a brand name and slogan more easily remembered.

L

layout A working drawing (may be computer developed) showing how an advertisement will look. A printer's layout is a set of instructions accompanying a piece of copy showing how it is to be set up. There are also rough layouts, finished layouts, and mechanical layouts, representing various degrees of finish. The term *layout* is used also for the total design of an advertisement.

letterpress Printing from a relief, or raised, surface. The raised surface is inked and comes in direct contact with the paper, like a rubber stamp.

lettershop A firm that not only addresses the mailing envelope but also is mechanically equipped to insert material, seal and stamp envelopes, and deliver them to the post office according to mailing requirements.

lifestyle segmentation Identifying consumers by combining several demographics and lifestyles.

list broker In direct-mail advertising, an agent who rents the prospect lists of one advertiser to another advertiser. The broker receives a commission from the seller for this service.

list manager Promotes client's lists to potential renters and buyers.

logotype, or logo A trademark or trade name embodied in the form of a distinctive lettering or design. Famous example: Coca-Cola.

M

magazine networks Groups of magazines that can be purchased together using one insertion order and paying a single invoice.

make-goods When a medium falls short of some audience guarantee, advertisers are provided concessions in the form of make-goods. Most commonly used in television and magazines.

market A group of people who can be identified by some common characteristic, interest, or problem; use a certain product to advantage; afford to buy it; and be reached through some medium.

market profile A demographic and psychographic description of the people or the households of a product's market. It may also include economic and retailing information about a territory.

market segmentation The division of an entire market of consumers into groups whose similarity makes them a market for products serving their special needs.

marketing communication The communication components of marketing, including public relations, advertising, personal selling, and sales promotion.

marketing concept A management orientation that views the needs of consumers as primary to the success of a firm.

marketing goals The overall objectives that a company wishes to accomplish through its marketing program.

marketing mix Combination of marketing functions, including advertising, used to sell a product.

marketing translation The process of adapting a general marketing plan to multinational environments.

mass communication era The period from the 1700s to the early decades of the twentieth century, in which advertisers were able to reach large segments of the population through the mass media.

mass production A manufacturing technique using specialization and interchangeable parts to achieve production efficiencies.

media buyers Those who execute and monitor the media schedule developed by media planners.

media plan The complete analysis and execution of the media component of a campaign.

media schedule The detailed plan or calendar showing when advertisements and commercials will be distributed and in what media vehicles they will appear.

media/communication planner Person responsible for the overall strategy of the media plan.

merge/purge A system used to eliminate duplication by direct-response advertisers who use different mailing lists for the same mailing. Mailing lists are sent to a central merge/purge office that electronically picks out duplicate names. Saves mailing costs, especially important to firms that send out a million pieces in one mailing. Also avoids damage to the goodwill of the public.

morphing An electronic technique that allows you to transform one object into another object.

N

national advertising Advertising by a marketer of a trademarked product or service sold through different outlets, in contrast to local advertising.

National Advertising Division (NAD) The primary investigative unit of the NARC self-regulation program.

networks Interconnecting stations for the simultaneous transmission of television or radio broadcasts.

Newspaper Association of America (NAA) The marketing and trade organization for the newspaper industry.

niche marketing A combination of product and target market strategy. It is a flanking strategy that focuses on niches or comparatively narrow windows of opportunity within a broad product market or industry. Its guiding principle is to pit your strength against their weakness.

nonwired networks Groups of radio and television stations whose advertising is sold simultaneously by station representatives.

North American Free Trade Agreement (NAFTA) A treaty designed to eliminate trade barriers among the United States, Mexico, and Canada.

O

off-network syndication Syndicated programs that have previously been aired by a major network.

offset lithography Lithography is a printing process by which an image was originally formed on special stone by a greasy material; the design was then transferred to the printing paper. Today, the more frequently used process is offset lithography, in which a thin and flexible metal sheet replaces the stone. In this process, the design is "offset" from the metal sheet to a rubber blanket, which then transfers the image to the printing paper.

open rate In print, the highest advertising rate at which all discounts are placed.

opt-in A form of permission marketing in which online customers are sent messages only after they have established a relationship with a company. Only consumers who have granted permission are contacted.

opt-outs Procedures that recipients use to notify advertisers that they no longer wish to receive advertising messages. A term usually associated with online promotions.

opticals Visual effects that are put on a TV film in a laboratory, in contrast to those that are included as part of the original photography.

Outdoor Advertising Association of America (OAAA) Primary trade and lobbying organization for the outdoor industry.

outside producer The production company person who is hired by the agency to create the commercial according to agency specifications.

P

partial runs When magazines offer less than their entire circulation to advertisers. Partial runs include demographic, geographic, and split-run editions.

penny press Forerunner of the mass newspaper in the United States; first appeared in the 1830s.

per inquiry (PI) Advertising time or space for which medium is paid on a per-response-received basis.

permission marketing Asking consumers for permission or to "opt in" before sending them advertising and other forms of marketing communication.

People meter Device that measures television set usage by individuals rather than by households.

pica The unit for measuring width in printing. There are 6 picas to an inch. A page of type 24 picas wide is 4 inches wide.

pioneering stage The advertising stage of a product in which the need for such a product is not recognized and must be established or in which the need has been established but the success of a commodity in filling that need has to be established. See competitive stage, retentive stage.

pixel The smallest element of a computer image that can be separately addressed. It is an individual picture element.

plant In outdoor advertising, the local company that arranges to lease, erect, and maintain the outdoor sign and to sell the advertising space on it.

point (pt) The unit of measurement of type, about 1/72 inch in depth. Type is specified by its point size, as 8 pt., 12 pt., 24 pt., 48 pt., and so on. The unit for measuring thickness of paper, 0.001 inch.

point-of-purchase Displays prepared by the manufacturer for use where the product is sold.

positioning Segmenting a market by creating a product to meet the needs of a select group or by using a distinctive advertising appeal to meet the needs of a specialized group, without making changes in the physical product.

Potential Rating Index by ZIP Market (PRIZM) A method of audience segmentation developed by Claritas Inc.

preditor A producer, shooter, and editor in one; it is a term that describes a new emerging group of filmmakers.

premarketing era The period from prehistoric times to the eighteenth century. During this time, buyers and sellers communicated in very primitive ways.

premium An item other than the product itself given to purchasers of a product as an inducement to buy. Can be free with a purchase (for example, on the package, in the package, or the container itself) or available with proof of purchase and a payment (self-liquidating premium).

***Printers' Ink* Model Statute (1911)** The act directed at fraudulent advertising, prepared and sponsored by *Printers' Ink*, which was the pioneer advertising magazine.

product advertising manager In package goods, the person responsible for the profitability of a product (brand) or product line, including advertising decisions. Also called a brand manager.

product differentiation Unique product attributes that set off one brand from another.

product life cycle The process of a brand moving from introduction to maturity and, eventually, to either adaptation or demise.

product-user segmentation Identifying consumers by the amount of product usage.

professional advertising Advertising directed at those in professions such as medicine, law, or architecture who are in a position to recommend the use of a particular product or service to their clients.

psychographics A description of a market based on factors such as attitudes, opinions, interests, perceptions, personalities, and lifestyles of consumers comprising that market.

public relations Communication with various internal and external publics to create an image for a product or corporation.

puffery Advertiser's opinion of a product that is considered a legitimate expression of biased opinion.

Pure Food and Drug Act Passed in 1906 by legislation, it was one of the earliest attempts by the federal government to protect consumers.

Q

qualitative research This involves finding out what people say they think or feel. It is usually exploratory or diagnostic in nature.

R

Radio Advertising Bureau (RAB) Association to promote the use of radio as an advertising medium.

Radio's All-Dimension Audience Research (RADAR) Service of Statistical Research, Inc., that is the primary source of network radio ratings.

rate base The circulation level on which advertising rates are based.

rating point The percentage of television households in a market a television station reaches with a program. The percentage varies with the time of day. A station may have a 10 rating between 6:00 and 6:30 P.M. and a 20 rating between 9:00 and 9:30 P.M.

rebate The amount owed to an advertiser by a medium when the advertiser qualifies for a higher space discount.

representative (rep) An individual or organization representing a medium selling time or space outside the city of origin.

research era In recent years, advertisers increasingly have been able to identify narrowly defined audience segments through sophisticated research methods.

response lists Lists of prospects who have previously responded to direct-mail offers.

retail advertising Advertising by a merchant who sells directly to the consumer.

retentive stage The third advertising stage of a product, reached when its general usefulness is widely known, its individual qualities are thoroughly appreciated, and it is satisfied to retain its patronage merely on the strength of its past reputation. See pioneering stage, competitive stage.

return-on-investment (ROI) One measure of the efficiency of a company is the rate of return (profits) achieved by a certain level of investment on various business functions including advertising.

ride-alongs Direct mail pieces that are sent with other mailings, such as bills.

Robinson-Patman Act A federal law, enforced by the FTC. Requires a manufacturer to give proportionate discounts and advertising allowances to all competing dealers in a market. Purpose: To protect smaller merchants from unfair competition of larger buyers.

rotary bulletin (outdoor) Movable painted bulletins that are moved from one fixed location to another in the market at regular intervals. The locations are viewed and approved in advance by the advertiser.

rotogravure The method of printing in which the impression is produced by chemically etched cylinders and run on a rotary press; useful in long runs of pictorial effects.

S

sales promotion (1) Sales activities that supplement both personal selling and marketing, coordinate the two, and help to make them effective. For example, displays are sales promotions. (2) More loosely, the combination of personal selling, advertising, and all supplementary selling activities.

same-day coupons Coupons designed to be used almost instantly, or same day.

sampling The method of introducing and promoting merchandise by distributing a miniature or full-size trial package of the product free or at a reduced price.

satellite radio Available by subscription and contains few, if any, commercials. It requires a special receiver but offers near-CD-quality sound.

scatter plan The use of announcements, over a variety of network programs and stations, to reach as many people as possible in a market.

screen printing A simple printing process that uses a stencil. It is economical but limited in reproduction quality.

selective binding Binding together different material directed to various reader segments in a single issue of a magazine.

self-liquidating premium A premium offered to consumers for a fee that covers its cost plus handling.

service advertising Advertising that promotes a service rather than a product.

service mark A word or name used in the sale of services to identify the services of a firm and distinguish them from those of others, for example, Hertz Drive Yourself Service, Weight Watchers Diet Course. Comparable to trademarks for products.

share of audience The percentage of households using television tuned to a particular program.

short rate The balance advertisers have to pay if they estimated that they would run more advertisements in a year than they did and entered a contract to pay at a favorable rate. The short rate is figured at the end of the year or sooner if advertisers fall behind schedule. It is calculated at a higher rate for the fewer insertions.

Simmons Market Research Bureau (SMRB) and Mediamark Research, Inc. (MRI) Two competing firms that provide audience data for several media. Best known for magazine research.

siquis Handwritten posters in sixteenth- and seventeenth-century England—forerunners of modern advertising.

situation analysis The part of the advertising plan that answers the questions: Where are we today and how did we get here? It deals with the past and present.

slotting fees Payments to retailers by manufacturers to gain shelf space.

social storytelling Storytelling is a powerful way of social bonding. Social storytelling is open-ended. You try to tell a story in a way that leaves room for the consumers to fill in the blanks, to add their own tendrils to the main storyline.

spam Online advertising messages that are usually unsolicited by the recipient.

specialty advertising A gift given to a consumer that encourages a purchase.

spot radio Buying radio time on local stations on a market-by-market basis by national advertisers.

spot television Purchasing of time from a local station, in contrast to purchasing from a network.

Standard Advertising Unit (SAU) Allows national advertisers to purchase newspaper advertising in standard units from one paper to another.

Standard Rate and Data Service (SRDS) *SRDS* publishes a number of directories giving media and production information.

storyboard Series of drawings used to present a proposed commercial. Consists of illustrations of key action (video), accompanied by the audio part. Used for getting advertiser approval and as a production guide.

stripping Scheduling a syndicated program on a 5-day-per-week basis.

substantiate The key to FTC enforcement is that advertisers must be able to prove the claims made in their advertising.

sweepstakes A promotion in which prizewinners are determined on the basis of chance alone. Not legal if purchaser must risk money to enter.

sweeps weeks During these periods, ratings are taken for all television markets.

T

target audience That group that composes the present and potential prospects for a product or service.

target marketing Identifying and communicating with groups of prime prospects.

theater of the mind In radio, a writer paints pictures in the mind of the listener through the use of sound.

time-shift viewing Recording programs on a VCR for viewing at a later time.

total market coverage (TMC) Newspapers augment their circulation with direct mail or shoppers to deliver to all households in the market.

total survey area The maximum coverage of a radio or television station's signal.

trade advertising Advertising directed to the wholesale or retail merchants or sales agencies through whom the product is sold.

trade name A name that applies to a business as a whole, not to an individual product.

trade paper A business publication directed to those who buy products for resale (wholesalers, jobbers, retailers).

trademark Any device or word that identifies the origin of a product, telling who made it or who sold it. Not to be confused with a trade name.

Traffic Audit Bureau for Media Measurement (TAB) An organization designed to investigate how many people pass and may see a given outdoor sign, to establish a method of evaluating traffic measuring a market.

traffic-building premium A sales incentive to encourage customers to come into a store where a sale can be concluded.

TVQ A service of Marketing Evaluations that measures the popularity (opinion of audience rather than size of audience) of shows and personalities.

typography The art of using type effectively.

U

up-front buying The purchase of network television time by national advertisers during the first offering by networks. The most expensive network advertising.

V

value gap The perceived difference between the price of a product and the value ascribed to it by consumers.

value-added opportunities Extra things a medium will do for or provide to an advertiser that adds value to the purchase of time or space in the medium.

Values and Lifestyle System (VALS) Developed by SRI International to cluster consumers according to several variables in order to predict consumer behavior.

vendor program Special form of co-op advertising in which a retailer designs the program and approaches advertisers for support.

vertical publication Business publications dealing with the problems of a specific industry, for example, *Chain Store Age*, *National Petroleum News*, and *Textile World*.

W

War Advertising Council Founded in 1942 to promote World War II mobilization, it later evolved into the Advertising Council.

Wheeler-Lea Amendments Broadened the scope of the FTC to include consumer advertising.

Y

yield management A product pricing strategy to control supply and demand.

Z

zoning Newspaper practice of offering advertisers partial coverage of a market, often accomplished with weekly inserts distributed to certain sections of that market.

Endnotes

CHAPTER 1

1. J. Robert Moskin, *The Case for Advertising* (New York: American Association of Advertising Agencies, 1973), 7.
2. Roland Marchand, *Advertising the American Dream* (Berkeley: University of California Press, 1985), 76.
3. Paul Verna, "A spotlight on UGC participants," *eMarketer,* www.emarkter.com, 19 February 2009.
4. Randall Rothenberg, "The advertising century," *Advertising Age: Special Issue,* 1999, 12.
5. George Burton Hotchkiss, *An Outline of Advertising* (New York: Macmillan, 1957), 10.
6. James Playsted Wood, *Magazines in the United States* (New York: The Ronald Press, 1949), 99.
7. "The Industrial Revolution," www.4.ncsu.edu, 23 August 2005.
8. John McDonough, "From a birth in lower Manhattan to an unmatched global reach," *Advertising Age,* 18 March 2002, C8.
9. Frank Deford, *The Old Ball Game* (New York: Atlantic Monthly Press, 2005), 91, 95.
10. Cynthia Crossen, "Fraudulent claims led U.S. to take on drug makers in 1900s," *Wall Street Journal,* 6 October 2005, B1.
11. James Harvey Young, "The story of the laws behind the labels," www.cfsan.fda.gov, 3–4.
12. From the Federal Trade Commission Mission Statement.
13. Ralph M. Hower, *The History of an Advertising Agency* (Cambridge, MA: Harvard University Press, 1949), 180.
14. Edward Robinson, "Businessman of the century," *Fortune,* 6 September 1999, 227.
15. "Radio captivates a nation," *Advertising Age,* 28 March 2005, 34.
16. Louis Vloedbeld, "The rise of the Bakelite and Catalin radio in the U.S. during the 1930s," www.2.let.uu.nl, 5 January 2006.
17. Lydia Boyd, "Brief history of the radio industry," John W. Hartman Center, Duke University, www.scriptorium.lib.duke.edu/radio, 2.
18. "Brief history of World War Two advertising campaigns: Conservation," John W. Hartman Center for Sales, Advertising and Marketing History, Duke University Library, http://scriptorium.l.b.duke.edu/adaccess/.
19. John McDonough, "Ad Council at 60—Facing a crossroads," *Advertising Age,* 29 April 2002, C–4.
20. Herbert Zeltner, "Proliferation, localization, specialization mark media trends in past 50 years," *Advertising Age,* 30 April 1980, 148.
21. "TV turns on America," *Advertising Age,* 28 March 2005, 44.
22. This section is adapted from Cait Murphy, "Introduction: Wal-Mart rules," *Fortune,* 15 April 2002, www.fortune.com.
23. Alice Z. Cuneo, "Marketers get serious about the 'third screen'," *Advertising Age,* 11 July 2005, 6.
24. "2000s Madison & Vine and ROI," *Advertising Age,* http://adage.com/article?article_id=102708, 28 March 2005.
25. "TV costs and CPM trends," Television Bureau of Advertising Research Central, www.tvb.org/rcentral/adrevenuetrack/media/media.asp?c=1b, 23 March 2009.
26. Bob Garfield, "The chaos scenario," *Advertising Age,* 4 April 2005, 1.

CHAPTER 2

1. Brian Steinberg and Suzanne Vranica, "The ad world's message for 2005: Stealth," *Wall Street Journal,* 30 December 2004, B1.
2. Brian Steinberg, "TV on-demand may make ads more targeted," *Wall Street Journal,* 9 November 2005, B1.
3. Noreen O'Leary, "They want the world, and they want it now," *Adweek.com,* 20 December 2005.
4. Kevin Maney, "A very different future is calling—on billions of cell phones," *USA Today,* 27 July 2005, 3B.
5. Adapted from David W. Schropher, *What Every Account Executive Should Know about a Marketing Plan* (New York: American Association of Advertising Agencies, 1990).
6. Rance Crain, "Emirates' lead agency: A network of partners," *Advertising Age,* 3 April 2006, 14.
7. Jack Neff, "Reckitt Benckiser Ratchets up spending, posts 8% jump in organic sales growth," *Advertising Age,* 11 May 2009, 14.
8. Mathew Creamer, "Engaged: Ad groups take on ROI," *Advertising Age,* 25 July 2005, 4.
9. A term coined in the early 1930s by Professor Neil H. Borden of the Harvard Business School to include in the marketing process such factors as distribution, advertising, personal selling, and pricing.
10. Rich Thomaselli, "Selling drugs: Glaxo's crafty plan," *Advertising Age,* 20 February 2006, 1.
11. Jonah Bloom, "With PR on the rise, here's a refresher course in the basics," *Advertising Age,* 11 May 2009, 22.
12. Bloom, "Agencies that attempt to reinvent via half measures are set up to fail," *Advertising Age,* 27 February 2006, 32.
13. Scott Davis, "Fixing brand bloat: Put focus on consumer-centric portfolio strategy," *Point,* July 2005, 5.
14. Jim Lentz, "Marketing isn't one-size-fits all," *Advertising Age,* 21 February 2005, 22.
15. Matthew Creamer, "Ogilvy looks to the power of one," *Advertising Age,* 31 October 2005, 8.
16. Rance Crain, "Marketers look at new ideas, and PR becomes the closer," *Advertising Age,* 29 July 2002, 15.
17. "The times of our lives: Temporalities of social institutions," www.trinity.edu, 17 January 2006.
18. James W. Carey, "Advertising: An institutional approach," in C. H. Sandage and Vernon Fryburger, *The Role of Advertising* (Homewood, IL: Richard D. Irwin, 1960), 4.
19. David Futrelle, "Are your kids normal about money?" *Money,* December 2005, 55.
20. Susan Linn, "Marketing blitz out of control," *Atlanta Journal-Constitution,* 28 February 2005, A9.
21. Kenneth E. Clow and Donald Baack, *Integrated Advertising, Promotion, and Marketing Communication* (Upper Saddle River, NJ: Prentice Hall, 2004), 80.
22. Michael R. Solomon, *Consumer Behavior* (Upper Saddle River, NJ: Prentice Hall, 2004), 230.
23. Geoffrey A. Fowler, "Buying spree by China firms is a bet on value of U.S. brands," *Wall Street Journal,* 23 June 2005, B1.
24. Scott Leith, "New sodas flood market," *Atlanta Journal-Constitution,* 6 September 2002, F-1.
25. Viewpoint, "No shame in KFC's real name," *Advertising Age,* 2 May 2005, 26.
26. Harper W. Boyd Jr., Orville C. Walker Jr., John W. Mullins, and Jean-Claude Larreche, *Marketing Management* (New York: McGraw-Hill/Irwin, 2002), 267.
27. Mya Frazier, "Big Lots makes big money as land of marketers' misfit ploys," *Advertising Age,* 30 May 2005, 49.
28. Clayton M. Christensen, Scott Cook, and Taddy Hall, "It's the purpose brand, stupid," *Wall Street Journal,* 29 November 2005, B2.

29. "Listening to customers in the electronic age," *Fortune*, 1 May 2000, 318.

30. Gina Chon, "Mercedes seeks to recapture luxury rankings," *Wall Street Journal*, 30 January 2006, B4.

31. "Question of the day," *Wall Street Journal*, 10 January 2006, D6.

32. David J. Pike, "Product by design," *American Demographics*, February 2001, 38.

33. Jack Neff, "P&G kisses up to the boss: Consumers," *Advertising Age*, 2 May 2005, 18.

34. Ann Zimmerman, "Wal-Mart sets out to prove it's in vogue," *Wall Street Journal*, 25 August 2005, B1.

35. Jeffrey McCracken and Joseph B. White, "Ford will shed 28% of workers in North America," *Wall Street Journal*, 24 January 2006, 1A.

36. Lee Hawkins Jr., "GM plan to take toll on sales volume, personnel," *Wall Street Journal*, 28 March 2006, A3.

37. Sarah Ellison, "Colgate's fight for market share will likely erode profit," *Wall Street Journal*, 13 December 2004, C1.

38. Jack Neff, "Why some marketers turn away customers," *Advertising Age*, 14 February 2005, 1.

39. Beth Snyder Bulik, "Cool hunting goes corporate," *Advertising Age*, 1 August 2005, 3.

40. Aaron O. Patrick, "Making P&G's skin products manly," *Wall Street Journal*," 5 August 2005, B4.

41. Gina Chon, "Fuel economy has returned as a marketing tool," *Wall Street Journal*, 26 September 2005, B4.

42. Stephanie Thompson, "Nestle, Hershey figure sticks will be big sellers," *Advertising Age*, 3 October 2005, 3.

43. Kris Oser, "Expecting? Buy those Huggies now," *Advertising Age*, 16 May 2005, 8.

44. Ernest Sander, "Pizza-delivery teams are training hard for Sunday's game," *Wall Street Journal*, 31 January 2006, 1A.

45. Bernard Ryan Jr., *It Works!* (New York: American Association of Advertising Agencies, 1991), 19.

46. Jean Halliday, "Volvo touts models' safety—and style," *Advertising Age*, 5 September 2005, 8.

47. Alice Z. Cuneo, "RAZR," *Advertising Age*, 7 November 2005, S-6.

48. Jack Neff, "Moving to margins in a new marketing age," *Advertising Age*, 24 July 2006, 1.

49. Joyce M. Rosenberg, "Costs, competition help decide prices," *Atlanta Journal-Constitution*, 22 February 2005, C3.

50. Mya Frazier, "Sales may go out like last year's winter coat," *Advertising Age*, 25 April 2005, 16.

51. James B. Arndorfer and Rich Thomaselli, "United to tap draft for part of $60M direct biz," *Advertising Age*, 9 January 2006, 4.

52. Stephanie Thompson, "In-crowd: Paris Hilton, Lucky the Leprechaun," *Advertising Age*, 20 February 2006, 8.

53. Stephanie Thompson, "Frito-Lay defends its snack turf against all comers, salty or sweet," *Advertising Age*, 16 May 2005, 16.

54. Rebecca Weeks, "Buying consumers search for auto research," www.imediaconnection.com, 26 January 2006.

55. Susan Kuchinskas, "Saw it online, paid for it off," www.ecomerce-guide.com, 21 October 2005.

56. "Women's use of Internet affects purchasing decisions," www.microsoft.com/presspass/pass, 26 January 2006.

57. James B. Arndorfer, "Depending on direct: Discipline grows to $161B," *Advertising Age*, 24 October 2005, 6.

58. Michael R. Solomon, *Consumer Behavior* (Upper Saddle River, NJ: Prentice Hall, 2004), 403.

CHAPTER 3

1. Antonio Marraza, "The very tangible value of the brand," www.landor.com, 2000.

2. David Martin, *Romancing the Brand* (New York: Amacon, 1989), xiv.

3. Allen Adamson, "Marketers, don't make promises you can't keep," Forbes.com, 20 January 2009.

4. Norman Berry, "Revitalizing brands," *Viewpoint*, July–August 1987, 18.

5. Allen P. Adamson, *BrandDigital* (New York: Palgrave Macmillan, 2008), 94.

6. Howard, Merrell & Partners, "Introduction," 2000.

7. Allen P. Adamson, *BrandDigital* (New York: Palgrave Macmillan, 2008), 72–73

8. Interbrand.com.

9. Charlie Wrench, "Brand integration: A tough nut to crack," www.landor.com, May 2003.

10. Allen P. Adamson, *BrandSimple* (New York: Palgrave Macmillan, 2006), 10–12.

11. Alan M. Webber, "What great brands do," *Fast Company*, August–September 1997, 96–100.

12. "Retailers cut back on variety, once the spice of marketing," *Wall Street Journal*, 28 June 2009, 1.

13. Robert Berner, "P&G. New and improved," *BusinessWeek*, 7 July 2003, 52–63.

14. Scott Berkun, "The greatest product demo ever and what to learn from it," http://discussionleader.hbsp.com/berkun/2009/01/draft-lessons-from-the-mother.html, 5 January 2009.

15. Laura Petrecca, "PedEgg hatches surprising sales," *USA Today*, 25 August 2008, 7B.

16. Steve Rubel, "Why the print industry should subsidize the Kindle," *Advertising Age*, http://adage.com/article?article_id=135284, 17 March 2009.

17. Steve Smith, "Back to Kindle-garten," *Media Post*, 7 April 2009.

18. Mark McClusky, "The Nike experiment: How the shoe giant unleashed the power of personal metric," *Wired*, 22 June 2009.

19. Bruce Tait, "A brand new idea," *Brand Marketing*, February 2002, 23.

20. Steven Rosenbush, "Verizon's gutsy bet," *BusinessWeek*, 4 August 2003, 53.

21. Bruce Tait, "A brand new idea," *Brand Marketing*, February 2002, 23.

22. "Royal Crown plotting a comeback with new owners' financial support," *Atlanta Journal-Constitution*, 6 March 1994, C8.

23. Stephanie Thompson, "EZ being green: Kids line is latest Heinz innovation," *Advertising Age*, 10 July 2000, 3.

24. Charlotte Moore, "Glowing reports about the health benefits of inexpensive aspirin are still emerging," *Atlanta Journal-Constitution*, 13 May 2003, E1.

CHAPTER 4

1. Rex Briggs and Greg Stuart, *What Sticks* (Chicago: Kaplan, 2006), 218–219.

2. Joe Marconi, "Targets big enough to miss," *American Demographics*, October 1996, 51–52.

3. John McManus, "Street wiser," *American Demographics*, July/August 2003, 32–35.

4. Allison Stein Wellner, "The next 25 years," *American Demographics*, April 2003, 24–31.

5. Christine Bunish, "Multicultural guide," *Advertising Age*, 3 November 2003, M1.

6. William H. Frey, "Revival," *American Demographics*, October 2003, 26–31.

7. Haya El Nasser, "39 million Hispanics largest U.S. minority group," *USA Today*, 19 June 2003, www.usatoday.com/news/nation/census/2003-06-18-Census_x.htm.

8. Marissa Miley, "Don't bypass African-Americans," *Advertising Age*, 2 February 2009, 3, 27.

9. Christine Bunish, "Multicultural guide," *Advertising Age*, 3 November 2003, M1.

10. "Where to find the bright spots in 2009," *Advertising Age*, 12 January 2009, 1, 24–25.

11. Speech by Carl Kravetz, at the Association of National Advertisers Multicultural Marketing Conference, 13 November 2006, at Fairmont Miramar Hotel, Santa Monica, CA.

12. Laurel Wentz, "New data repaints demographic picture of U.S. Hispanics," *Advertising Age*, http://adage.com/article_id=110568, 14 November 2006.

13. Christine Bunish, "Multicultural guide," *Advertising Age*, 3 November 2003, M1.

14. "Disney's Davila: Multicultural 'not a fad,'" *Advertising Age*, 3 November 2003, M3.

15. Marcia Mogelonsky, "America's hottest markets," *American Demographics*, January 1996, 20–27.

16. Michelle Conlin, "The new gender gap," *BusinessWeek*, 26 May 2003, 74–80.

17. Beth Snyder Bulik, "Technology no longer just kid stuff," *Advertising Age*, 2 February 2009, 12.

18. James Morrow, "A place for one," *American Demographics*, November 2003, 24–29.

19. Cheryl Wetzstein, "More homes in U.S. go solo," *Washington Times*, http://washtimes.com/functions/print.php?Story, ID= 20050817-123759-7286r, 17 August 2005.

20. Alison Stein Wellner, "Generational divide," *American Demographics*, October 2000, 52–58.

21. Elwood Carlson, "20th-century U.S. generations," *Population Bulletin*, 64, no. 1, 2009.

22. Natalie Zmuda, "Teens, too, are tightening budgets," *Advertising Age*, 27 April 2009, 6.

23. Edna Gundersen, "Where will teens taste land next?" *USA Today*, 22 September 2000, E1–E2.

24. Sholnn Freeman and Norihiko Shirouzu, "Toyota's gen Y gamble," *Wall Street Journal*, 30 July 2003, B1.

25. Gina Piccalo, "Girls just want to be plugged in—to everything," *Los Angeles Times*, www.latimes.com/business/la-et-polltween11aug11,1,1040639.story?coll=la-headlines-business, 11 August 2006.

26. David F. D'Alessandro, *Brand Warfare* (New York: McGraw-Hill, 2000), 38–39.

27. Philip Kotler, *Marketing Management*, 8th ed. (Upper Saddle River, NJ: Prentice Hall, 1994), 18–21.

28. Frederick E. Webster Jr., "Executing the new marketing concept," *Marketing Management*, 3, no. 1, 9–16.

29. Robert C. Blattberg, Thomas Buesing, and Subrata K. Sen, "Segmentation strategies for new national brands," *Journal of Marketing*, Fall 1980, 60.

30. David J. Lipke, "Head trips," *American Demographics*, October 2000, 38.

31. Rebecca Piirto Heath, "The frontier of psychographics," *American Demographics*, July 1996, 40.

32. Kevin J. Clancy and Robert S. Shulman, *The Marketing Revolution* (New York: Harper Business, 1991), 63.

33. Jack Trout, *Differentiate or Die* (New York: John Wiley & Sons, 2000), 185.

34. Alvin Achenbaum, "Understanding niche marketing," *Adweek*, 1 December 1986, 62.

35. Ira P. Scheiderman, "Niche marketers should follow old rules," *Brand Marketing*, August 2000, 6.

36. Jeff Neff, "Huggies Little Swimmers tests out a new niche," *Advertising Age*, 25 August 1997, 8.

37. Lisa Sanders, "Startup shop Amalgamated targets big-spending bobos," *Advertising Age*, 9 September 2003, 89.

38. Kevin J. Clancy and Robert S. Shulman, *The Marketing Revolution* (New York: Harper Business, 1991), 84–87.

39. Jack Trout and Al Ries, *The Positioning Era* (New York: Ries Cappiello Colwell, 1973), 38–41.

40. David A. Aaker, *Managing Brand Equity* (New York: The Free Press, 1991), 114–115.

41. Philip Kotler, *Kotler on Marketing* (New York: The Free Press, 1999), 57–58.

42. David N. Martin, *Be the Brand* (Richmond: New Marketplace Books, 2000), 88–98.

43. Scott Leith, "For a limited time," *Atlanta Journal-Constitution*, 9 September 2003, C1.

44. "Coffeehouses and donut shops—US—May 2009," Mintel, Market Research Report, May 2009.

45. Jack Neff, "The 80% of sales comes from some 2% of buyers," *Advertising Age*, 8 December 2008, 4.

46. Beth Snyder Bulik, "How personality can predict media use," *Advertising Age*, 4 May 2009, 12.

47. Jeffry Scott, *Atlanta Journal*, July 2, p. 13, 2001.

48. Acxiom, www.acxiom.com/default.aspx?ID=2521& DisplayID=18, 12 November 2006.

CHAPTER 5

1. James Melvin Lee, *History of American Journalism*, rev. ed. (Boston: Houghton Mifflin, 1933), 74.

2. "Crispin, Porter+Bogusky," www.creativereview.co.uk/crblog/, 2009.

3. Ken Roman and Jane Maas, *How to Advertise* (New York: St. Martin's Press, 2003), 216.

4. Ann Cooper, "Bernbach's children come of age," *Adweek*, 25 March 1996, 33–36.

5. Daniel Gross, "The scramble on Mad. Ave.," *Fortune*, 8 August 2005, 63–64.

6. Jeff Weiner, "Anxious ranks," *Agency*, Spring 1994, 42.

7. Jan Larson, "It's a small world, after all," *Marketing Tools*, September 1997, 47–51.

8. Ken Roman and Jane Maas, *How to Advertise* (New York: St. Martin's Press, 2003), 43–44.

9. "How does global marketing benefit consumers?" *Adweek*, 17 November 2003, 96.

10. "Coke seeks ad formula with global appeal," *Atlanta Journal-Constitution*, 18 November 1991, A5.

11. Ashish Banerjee, "Global campaigns don't work; multinationals do," *Advertising Age*, 18 April 1994, 23.

12. Catharine P. Taylor, "Are holding companies obsolete?" *Adweek*, 9 June 2003, 30–31.

13. Jeff Neff, "The newest ad agencies: The major media companies," http://adage.com/agencynews/article?article_id=132190, 3 November 2008.

14. Interview with Kristen Kyle, 5 December 2000.

15. Leon Stafford, "Tourism officials barter to stretch tight advertising budgets," *Atlanta Journal-Constitution*, 15 May 2003, D1.

16. Kal Liebowitz, "Bring barter back: Marketing needs alternative energy," *MediaWorks*, 16 October 2008, p. 13.

17. David Aaker, "The agency as brand architect," *American Advertising*, Spring 1996, 18–21.

18. Jeff Neff, "Coke pushes pay-for-performance model," *Advertising Age*, 27 April 2009, p. 1.

19. Noreen O'Leary, "Agencies in catch-22 over client finances," *Adweek*, 18 May 2009.

20. Terrence Poltrack, "Pay dirt," *Agency*, July/August 1991, 20–25.

21. Stan Beals, "Fresh approaches to agency compensation," *Advertising Age*, 29 August 1994, 20.

CHAPTER 6

1. Ken Bernhardt, "New consumer is a savvy user of new media," *Atlanta Business Chronicle*, 28 July 2006, 3B.

2. Jack Neff, "P&G recategorizes marketing directors," *Advertising Age*, 31 March 2003, 6.

3. Scott Hume, "Integrated marketing: Who's in charge here?" *Advertising Age*, 23 March 1993, 3.

4. William N. Swain, "An exploratory assessment of the IMC Paradigm: Where are we, and where do we go from here?" *Integrated Marketing Communication Research Journal*, 9, Spring 2003, 3–11.

5. Ibid.

6. Interbrand.com, 7 June 2009.

7. Don Schultz, "Managers still face substantial IMC questions," *Marketing News*, 27 September 1993, 10.

8. Ibid.

9. Marian Burk Wood, "Clear IMC goals build strong relationships," *Marketing News*, 23 June 1997, 11.

10. Al Ries, "Why marketing people get it wrong," AdAge.com, 17 March 2003.

11. Leslie H. Moeller, Sharat K. Mathur, and Randall Rothenberg, "The better half: The artful science of ROI marketing," *Strategy+Business*, Spring 2003, 32–45.

12. Rex Briggs and Greg Stuart, *What Sticks* (Chicago: Kaplan, 2006), 213–215.

13. Jack Neff, "Future of Advertising? Print? TV, Online Ads," http://adage.com/article?article_id=136993, 1 June 2009.

14. Steve McKee, "Best foot forward from the start," *BusinessWeek*, 17 April 2006.

15. www.martinowen.tv/whatwedo_brandedcontent.html, July 2, 2009.

16. Louise Story, *New York Times*, www.nytimes.com, 2 November 2006.

17. Christopher Vollmer, John Frelinghuysen, and Randall Rothenberg, "The future of advertising is now," *Strategy+Business*, Summer 2006, 38–51.

18. John Gerzema and Ed Lebar, "The trouble with brands," *Strategy+Business*, Summer 2009, 48–57.

19. Michele Gershberg, "U.S. advertising goes digital to track ads," *USA Today*, www.usatoday.com, 14 February 2005.

20. Joe Mandee, "How far is too far?" *Agency*, May/June 1991, 9.

21. Eleftheria Parpis, "More to come," *Adweek*, 18 September 2000, 28.

22. asoy.com, 6 January 2007.

23. Stuart Elliott, "Advertiser-agency relationships turn a bit brighter," *New York Times*, 6 November 2006, www.nytimes.com, 11 November 2006.

24. Jeff Neff, "Recently named Clorox CEO sets sights on trade marketing," *Advertising Age*, www.adage.com, 31 August 2006.

25. Karen Benezra, "Sea change: Agencies diversify to regain client trust," *Adweek*, 19 April 1999, 42–43.

26. Jennifer Comiteau, "Power play," *Adweek*, 10 June 1996, 33–38.

27. Laura Petrecca, "The year in review: Is it a record pace?" *Advertising Age*, 2 June 1997, 1.

28. Suzanne Vranica, "Marketers shop for fresh creativity," *Wall Street Journal*, 28 July 2003, B3.

29. Russell H. Coilley, *Defining Advertising Goals for Measured Effectiveness* (New York: Association of National Advertisers).

30. Jack Neff, "Half of your advertising isn't wasted—just 37%," *Advertising Age*, 7 August 2006, 1.

31. Tom Patty, "Mastering the new five P's of marketing," TBWA/Chiat/Day web site, 1997.

CHAPTER 7

1. "U.S. ad spending totals by medium," TNS Measured Media Spending, *Advertising Age*, 22 June 2009, 23.

2. Frank Langfitt, "In the Camaro, a glimmer of hope for GM," www.npr.org/templates/story/story.php?storyId=106811668, 21 July 2009.

3. W. Ronald Lane, Karen W. King, and J. Thomas Russell, "An interview with Judy Franks," Viewpoint 7.2, in *Kleppner's Advertising Procedure*, 17th ed. (Upper Saddle River, NJ: Pearson Prentice Hall, 2008), 238.

4. Erwin Ephron, "Preventing dis-engagement," www.ephrononmedia.com, 8 May 2006.

5. Dan Ouellette "Best use of mobile—OMD," *Adweek*, 15 June 2009, 17.

6. Katy Bachman, "Best use of radio—Butler, Shine, Stern & Partners," *Adweek*, 15 June 2009, 14.

7. Erik Sass, "Mag bag: 'Rachael Ray' goes out-of-home," www.mediapost.com/publications/?fa=Articles.san&s=96054&Nid=50073&p=342208, December 2008.

8. Mickey Marks, "Millennial satiation," *Advertising Age,* 14 February 2000, S16.

9. Erwin Ephron, "A new media-mix strategy," *Advertising Age,* 28 February 2000, S10.

10. From www.claritas.com, 15 April 2009.

11. Allen Brivic, *What Every Account Executive Should Know about Media* (New York: American Association of Advertising Agencies, 1989), 14.

1. David Fisher and Marshall Jon Fisher, *Tube: The Invention of Television* (Washington: Counterpoint, 1996), 22.

2. TVB, Nielsen Media Research Custom Survey 2008, www.tvb.org/nav/build_frameset.aspx, 15 June 2009.

3. www.tvb.org/nav/build_frameset.aspx, 7 June 2009.

4. Barry L. Sherman, *The Television Standard* (New York: Gerson Lehrman Group, 1999), 2.

5. TNS Media Intelligence as reported in "U.S. ad spending totals," *Advertising Age*, 22 June 2009, 23.

6. Jane Dalzell, "Who's on first," *Advertising Age, 50 Years of TV Advertising*, Spring 1995, 8.

7. www.tvb.org/rcentral/adrevenuetrack/media/media.asp?c=1b. 30 June 2009.

8. "Marketers claim they can wait until networks drop their upfront prices," http://adage.com/mediaworks/article?article_id=137872, 13 July 2009.

9. Brian Steinberg and Suzanne Vranica, "Madison Avenue sifts through 'clutter,'" *Wall Street Journal Online*, www.wsj.com/article/SB116778101889165317, 7 January 2007.

10. Scott Woolley, "Zap," *Forbes,* 29 September 2003, 77.

11. www.tvb.org/nav/build_frameset.aspx, 30 June 2009.

12. Brian Steinberg and Suzanne Vranica, "Madison Avenue sifts through 'clutter,'" *Wall Street Journal Online*, www.wsj.com/article/SB116778101889165317, 7 January 2007.

13. "Prime-time TV commercial prices plummet, CBS faces biggest drop," www.mediapost.com/publications/?fa=Articles.showArticle&art_aid=99628, 3 February 2009.

14. "What a spot costs," *Advertising Age*, 29 December 2008, 43.

15. The term *scatter plan* has two definitions. The first refers to buying a group of spots across a number of programs. The second refers to those spots that are still available after the up-front buying season is completed.

16. From www.fcc.gov/ownership/rules.html, 15 January 2007.

17. TNS Media Intelligence as reported in "U.S. ad spending totals," *Advertising Age*, 22 June 2009, 23.

18. "2009 TV facts," Cable Television Advertising Bureau, http://thecab.tv/main/resources/tvfacts09/cable-penetration.stml, 3 July 2009.

19. "1995 cable TV facts," a publication of the Cable Advertising Bureau, 72.

20. Fern Siegel, "Magazine rack: *Nick Jr. Family Magazine*," MediaPost Publications e-newsletter, magazinerack@mediapost.com, 16 August 2006.

21. "A guide to cable interconnects 2001/2002," *Advertising Age*, 1 October 2001, A3.

22. Ibid.

23. From www.marketingvox.com/archives/2006/05/04/jupiter_dvr_ad_skipping_threatens_8b_in_advertising/, 5 January 2007.

24. "DVR penetration and growth," http://blog.nielsen.com/nielsenwire/wp-content/uploads/2009/04/dvr_tvlandscape_043009.pdf, 30 April 2009.

25. "Timeshifting lifts *House, The Office*," www.marketingcharts.com/television/us-dvr-penetration-172-timeshifing-lifts-house-lost-the-office-306, 7 May 2007.

26. "Commercials you can't zap," www.nytimes.com/2009/06/07/arts/television/07stan.html?_r=1&emc=eta1&pagewanted=all, 8 June 2009.

27. Ibid.

28. Paul J. Gough, "New TV ratings system tracks product placement, sponsorship," *MediaPost's Media Daily News*, www.mediapost.com, 28 October 2003.

29. Information in this section is from Nielsen Media Research.

CHAPTER 9

1. "Nielsen begins ratings; 'Lux,' 'Lone Ranger' lead," *Advertising Age,* 19 April 1999, 89.

2. http://tvlistings.zap2it.com/ratings/season.html, 16 June 16, 2009.

3. "Arbitron-persons using radio," http://wargod.arbitron.com/scripts/ndb/ndbradio2.asp, 10 June 10, 2009.

4. "Nielsen: Radio still tops with teens," www.mediapost.com/publications/?fa=Articles.showArticle&art_aid=108870, 30 June 2009.

5. "How can I stand out from the competition?" www.rab.com, 24 May 2000.

6. "Radio facts and figures," www.newgeneration.com/radio_resources/info.html, 30 June 2009.

7. "More than 235 million listen to the radio each week reports Arbitron," http://arbitron.mediaroom.com/index.php?s=43&item=599, 12 June 2009.

8. "Radio facts and figures," www.newgeneration.com/radio_resources/info.html, 30 June 2009.

9. "Nielsen: Radio still tops with teens," www.mediapost.com/publications/?fa=Articles.showArticle&art_aid=108870, 30 June 2009.

10. "Radio facts and figures," www.newgeneration.com/radio_resources/info.html, 30 June 2009.

11. TNS Media Intelligence as reported in "U.S. ad spending totals," *Advertising Age*, 22 June 2009, 23.

12. Ibid.

13. www.arbitron.com/downloads/bluebook_sp09.pdf, 22 June 2009.

14. www.mediapost.com/publications/?fa=Article&art_aid=107282, 7 June 2009.

15. http://arbitron.mediaroom.com/index.php?s=43&item=40, 30 June 2009.

16. Ibid.

17. "National advertisers ranked 1 to 25," *Advertising Age*, 22 June 2009, 12.

18. www.arbitron.com/downloads/hispanicradiotoday08.pdf, 29 June 2009.

19. www.arbitron.com/downloads/Black_Radio_Today_08.pdf, 29 June 2009.

CHAPTER 10

1. "Total paid circulation," *Trends and Numbers* (Newspaper Association of America), www.naa.org/TrendsandNumbers/Total+Paid+Circulation.aspx, 7 June 2009.

2. "2008 daily and Sunday newspaper audience report," *Trends and Numbers* (Newspaper Association of America), www.naa.org/TrendsandNumbers/2008_Audience_Report_Active, 7 June 2009.

3. "Total paid circulation," *Editor and Publisher Yearbook, 2009*, www.naa.org/TrendsandNumbers/Total-Paid-Circulation.aspx, 15 June 2009.

4. "Advertising expenditures," *Business Analysis and Research, NAA*, www.naa.org/TrendsandNumbers/Advertising-Expenditures.aspx, 15 June 2009.

5. "U.S. ad-spending totals by medium" (TNS: Measured Media), *Advertising Age*, 22 June 2009.

6. "Advertising spending, annual classified," *Business Analysis and Research, NAA*, www.naa.org/TrendsandNumbers/Advertising-Expenditures.aspx, 15 June 2009.

7. Adapted from Leo Bogart, "Newspapers," *Media Studies Journal*, Spring/Summer 1999, 68.

8. "Advertising expenditures," *Business Analysis and Research, NAA*, www.naa.org/TrendsandNumbers/Advertising-Expenditures.aspx, 15 June 2009.

9. Ibid.

10. CareerBuilder.com, www.careerbuilder.com, 15 June 2009.

11. "The history of ABC," www.accessabc.com/press/Introduction.htm, 15 June 2009.

12. Christine Silk, "Newspaper websites are not keeping viewers reading, says Nielsen Report," www.editorsblog.org/multimedia/2009/05/newspaper_online_sites_are_yet_to_keep_v.php, 5 May 2009.

13. www.mediakit.parade.com, 28 June 2009.

14. www.business.weekend.com/circulation/, 28 June 2009.

CHAPTER 11

1. Unless otherwise noted, the source of information in this chapter is the Magazine Publishers of America, www.magazine.org.

2. "A magazine for everyone," www.magazine.org/handbook_2009/2010, 8, 13 July 2009.

3. Aimee Deeken, "Service upgrades," *Mediaweek*, 2 December 2002, 45–46.

4. "Magazines: The A-list," *Advertising Age*, 6 October 2008, 1.

5. James Playsted Wood, *Magazines in the United States* (New York: The Ronald Press Company, 1949), 104.

6. Hall's Magazine Reports, www.magazine.org/handbook_2009/2010, 2009, 13, 7 July 2009.

7. PriceWaterhouseCoopers Financial Survey, www.magazine.org/handbook, 20, 7 July 2009.

8. Dylan Stableford & Kristina Joukhadar , "Why Wal-Mart cut 1,000 magazine, titles," www.foliomag.com/2008/why-wal-mart-cut-1-000-magazines, 18 January 2008.

9. McPheters & Co. Audience Lab, 2008, www.magazine.org/handbook, 21, 7 July 2009.

10. Dynamic Logic Ad Reaction 4, 2007, and The Futures Company Yankelovich Monitor/Sequent Partners, 2008, www.magazine.org/handbook, 31, 13 July 2009.

11. "A Profile of the National CRMA Audience," www.citymag.org/, 20 July 2009.

12. Hissan Fattah, "Custom publishing grows up," *American Demographics*, July/August 2002, 26.

13. "About the Good Housekeeping Seal," www.goodhousekeeping.com/product-testing/seal-holders/about-good-housekeeping-seal, 15 July 2009.

14. Ann Marie Kerwin, "Time Inc. buys sampling biz to help bolster 'Parenting,'" *Advertising Age*, 2 November 1998, 6.

15. Kate Fitzgerald, "Food magazines rev up event marketing," 16 December 2002; www.adage.com QuikFIND ID:AAO28P, 29 July 2003.

16. Erik Sass, "Mag bag: Rachel Ray goes out-of-home," www.mediapost.com/publications/?fa=Articles.san&s=96054&Nid=50073&p=342208, December 2008.

17. "Elle Magazine Media Kit," www.hfmus.com/media_kits/fashion_beauty/elle/audience/circulation_1, 15 July 2009.

18. "Research brief: B2B media and trade shows most important to executives," Center for Media Research E-Newsletter (research@mediapost.com), 3 August 2006.

19. "The value and role of corporate advertising for business-to-business marketers," *Cahners Advertising Research Report*, #2000.15.

20. *Cahners Advertising Research Report*, www.cahnerscarr.com, #2000.

21. Marc Spiegler, "Hot media buy: The farm report," *American Demographics*, October 1995, 18.

CHAPTER 12

1. Unless otherwise noted, material for this chapter was provided by the Outdoor Advertising Association of America.

2. "Outdoor facts and figures—Mobility," www.oaaa.org/marketingresources/factsandfigures/mobility.aspx, 6 June 2009.

3. Joesph Carroll, "Workers' average commute round-trip is 46 minutes in a typical day," www.gallup.com/poll/28504/workers-average-commute-roundtrip-minutes-typical-day.aspx, 3 July 2009.

4. Eugene Morris, "O-O-H—Media's plain Jane sister," *Inside Out of Home*, January 2000, 7.

5. Carol Krol, "Life after tobacco," *Advertising Age*, 19 April 1999, 48.

6. "Industry Code," www.oaaa.org/about/industrycode.aspx, 7 July 2009.

7. Erwin Ephron, "About the medium," Outdoor Advertising Association of America, www.oaaa.org, 11 November 2003.

8. "Wall to wall walls," *Inside Out of Home*, April 1999, 1.

9. "Creating award winning outdoor," www.oaaa.org, 7 March 2009.

10. "The new audit," www.tabonline.com/thenewaudit.aspx, 7 July 2009.

11. "What Simmons Measures," www.smrb.com/web/guest/what-experian-simmons-measures, 2 July 2009.

12. www.oaaa.org/outdoor/councils/transit.asp.

13. Hoag Levins, "New York subway sells ads on outside of cars," http://adage.com/video/article?article_id=131461, 3 October 2008.

14. "Transit TV: A really mobile medium," http://publications.mediapost.com/index.cfm?fuseaction=Articles.san&s=39071&Nid=18225&p=342208.

15. "Eller goes whole hog to promote transit shelter O-O-H," *Inside Out of Home*, April 1998, 4.

16. "Teens pay attention to mall advertising," www.mediapost.com/publications/?fa=Articles.showArticle&art_aid=107361, 5 June 2009.

17. Eric Sass, "Screenvision adds 675 screens, NCM reports strong results," www.mediapost.com/publications/?fa=Articles.showArticle&art_aid=101883, 5 March 2009.

18. "Place based advertising," www.arbitron.com/downloads/digital_ooh_webinar_1_09.pdf, 13 January 2009.

19. Katy Bachman, "Walmart to roll out 'smart network,'" www.mediaweek.com/mw/content_display/news/out-there/digital/e3i0532517b5fc5d6afaaab1547bd63fc39, 3 September 2008.

20. "Reaching the unreachable," *Marketing Magazine*, 1 August 2005.

21. Michael Bush, "Wedding crashers: Is that a mortgage company by the gift table?" www.adage.com, 12 June 2009.

22. "Charmin rolls out 20 restrooms in Times Square," *USA Today*, 22 November 2006, 6A; and "P&G brings potty to parties," *Advertising Age*, 17 February 2003.

23. "Garbage trucks: The new hot spot for advertisers," http://adage.com/article?article_id=114665, 31 January 2007.

24. "'Desperate' for suds, duds," http://hollywoodreporter.com/thr/television/brief_display.jsp?vnu_content_id=1001021171, 25 August 2005.

25. Abbey Klaassen, "The hottest out-of-home technologies," http://adage.com/mediaworks/article?article_id-112204, 3 October 2006.

CHAPTER 13

1. "First-time vehicle buyers eschew traditional media," www.business-journal.com/AutoMediaObsolete.asp, 31 January 2006.

2. Robert McKim, "Strengthen affinities with spiral branding," *DMNews*, 19 June 2000, 32.

3. Bill Hopkins and Britton Manasco, "The new technologies of marketing," *DMNews*, 22 May 2000, 51.

4. Steve Diller, "Direct marketing's role in a new society," *DMNews*, 1 May 2000, 22.

5. "Top 20 countries with the highest number of internet users," www.internetworldstats.com/top20.htm, 14 August 2009.

6. Joe Mandese, "Ad execs see TV budgets moving into online video," http://publications.mediapost.com/index.cfm?fuseaction=Articles.san&s=51103&Nid=25091&p=342208, 14 November 2006.

7. "Interactive marketers lean on search," *eMarketer.com*, 21 July 2009.

8. Mark Walsh, "eMarketer: Online ad spending growth to slow," http://publications.mediapost.com, 27 February 2007.

9. Jack Neff, "'Passion for digital' pumps P&G's spending," *Advertising Age*, 8 June 2009, 3, 18.

10. Abbey Klaassen, "Why the click is the wrong metric for online ads," *Advertising Age*, 23 February 2009, 4.

11. Abbey Klaassen, "Online CPM prices take tumble," *Advertising Age*, 26 January 2009, 1, 39.

12. "Email marketing and click-through rates: Part II," *eMarketer*, 27 July 2009.

13. Natalie Zmuda, "How e-mail became a direct-marketing rock star in recession," *Advertising Age*, 11 May 2009, 27.

14. H. Robert Wientzen, "Tackling the spam issue," www.the-dma.org/memberguide/tacklingspam.shml, accessed 6 January 2004.

15. Association of National Advertisers (ANA), www.ana.net, 14 October 2003.

16. Zachary Rodgers, "Financial services customers warmed by e-mail," http://cyberatlas.internet.com, 8 December 2003.

17. Jefferson Graham, "Facebook's a great friend to businesses," *USA Today*, 8 May 2009, 3B.

18. Ibid.

19. Emily Bryson York, "DiGiorno turns to Twitter for flatbread-pizza launch," *Advertising Age*, 8 April 2009, http://adage.com/digital/article?article_id=135876.

20. *Social Marketing Playbook*, Interactive Advertising Bureau, 2009.

21. Michael Learmonth, "Why free-ride YouTube is finally winning ad dollars," *Advertising Age*, 13 April 2009, 1, 21.

22. Mary Madden, "The audience for online video-sharing sites shoots up," Pew Internet & American Life Project, 29 July 2009, www.pewinternet.org/Reports/2009/13—The-Audience-for-Online-VideoSharing-Sites-Shoots-Up.aspx, 15 August 2009.

23. Stuart Elliott, "Online, P&G gets a little crazy," www.nytimes.com/2006/12/14/business/media/14adco.html?_r=1&oref=slogin, 14 December 2006.

24. Nate Elliott, "Online video contests can help marketers listen to and energize their customers," *The Forrester Blog for Interactive Marketing Professionals*, 7 July 2009.

25. Ibid.

26. Emma Hall, "How to get the most out of social networks and not annoy users," *Advertising Age*, 27 April 2009, 30.

27. "Monetizing mobile ads," *eMarketer*, 4 August 2009, www.emarketer.com/articles/print.aspx?1007209, accessed 11 August 2009.

28. Rita Chang, "Mobile effort gets more to say 'I can' purchase a Porsche," *Advertising Age*, 9 February 2009, 18.

29. "Kraft provides recipe for mobile-marketing success," *Advertising Age*, 26 January 2009, 12.

30. David Goetzl, "Nissan backs online series *Star Tomorrow*," http://publications.mediapost.com/index.cfm?fuseaction=Articles.san&s=45549&Nid=21709&p=342208, 14 July 2006.

31. "Interact & integrate," *Advertising Age*, 19 June 2000, S40.

32. Rebecca Flass, "Web supplants TV as teen media hub," www.mediaweek.com, 30 August 2003.

33. Rebecca Gardyn, "Born to be wired," *American Demographics*, April 2003, 14.

34. Flass, "Web supplants TV as teen media hub."

35. "New white paper from online publishers association identifies, examines and characterizes Internet dayparts," www.online-publishers.org, 6 February 2003.

36. *Direct Marketing Course Rationale*, a publication of the Direct Marketing Educational Foundation, 1.

37. Jeff Caplan, "Predictive data: It's the real-time thing," *DMNews*, 24 May 1999, 34.

38. Jack Neff, "Wait, there's more! DRTV is gaining mainstream appeal," *Advertising Age*, 23 March 2009, 17.

39. Denny Hatch, "Making DRTV work for you," *Target Marketing*, September 1999, 76.

40. Jack Neff, "Marketing's new red-hot seller: Humble Snuggle," *Advertising Age*, 26 January 2009, 1, 36.

41. Jack Neff, "Amid cutbacks, ShamWow marches on," *Advertising Age*, 23 March 2009, 1, 14.

42. National Trust for Historic Preservation, www.nationaltrust.org/help/mail_order_home.html, 5 January 2003.

43. "Limited Brands reports January 2009, fourth quarter 2008 and fiscal 2008 sales," prnewswire.com, 5 February 2009.

44. Jack Schmid and Steve Trollinger, "Who's making the Net work?" *Target Marketing*, June 1999, 73.

45. "U.S. ad spending totals by medium," *Advertising Age*, 29 December 2008, 10.

46. Lewis Rashmir, "The first compiler was Charles Groves," *DMNews*, 15 February 1993, 35.

47. "E-mail marketers fail the test," *eMarketer*, www.emarketer.com/articles/print.aspx?1007225, 12 August 2009.

CHAPTER 14

1. David Vacek and Richard Sale, "100 years of promotion," *PROMO*, August 1998, 142.

2. Betsy Spethmann, "Is advertising dead?" *PROMO*, September 1998, 32.

3. Peter Breen, "Seeds of change," *PROMO*, May 2000, A5.

4. Russell Bowman and Paul Theroux, "By the book," *PROMO*, March 2000, 95.

5. From www.partnerslevit.com/ConferenceRoom/Sales_Promotions_and_Sweepstak/sales_promotions_and_sweepstak.html. February, 2006.

6. Andrew Hampp, "Mtn Dew banks on branded entertainment," http://adage.com/Madisonandvine/article?, 4 June 2009.

7. Richard Tedesco, "VROOOM!" Promo magazine online, http://promomagazine.com/eventmarketing/sponsoring_nascar_0301/?imw=Y, 1 March 2008.

8. Amy Corr, "If only finding a man was this easy . . . ," *Media Post*, 10 November 2008.

9. Matthew Futterman, "A safety for Giants as the clock counts down on stadium," *Wall Street Journal Online*, http://online.wsj.com/article/SB124519330320920791.html, 17 June 2009.

10. Stephanie Thompson, "Despite tough third quarter, will still emphasize in-store," AdAge.com, 16 October 2006.

11. Steve McClellan, "Study: Sponsorships yield superior ROI," *Adweek*, 8 January 2007, 7.

12. J. Jeffrey Inman and Russell S. Winer, "Where the rubber meets the road: A model of in-store consumer decision making," Working Paper, Marketing Science Institute, October 1998, 25.

13. "Out of sight, out of mind," *PROMO*, March 1996, 16.

14. Richard Sele, "The display police," *PROMO*, March 1999, 80.

15. Kate Bertrand, "Premiums prime the market," *Advertising Age*, May 1998, S6.

16. "Rewarding the faithful," promomagazine.com, 1 April 2006.

17. Patricia Odell, "Promote fruit parfaits," *PROMO*, 1 January 2009, 2.

18. Andrew Scott, "The new frontier," *PROMO*, 1 April 2005, 23.

19. David Goetzl, "Card me: Anheuser-Busch kicks off Bud.TV post-Super Bowl with age verification system," MediaPost.com, 23 January 2007.

20. Patricia Joyce, "NFL players send voice messages," *PROMO*, http://promomagazine.com/news/nfl_players, 24 January 2007.

21. Andrew Hampp, "Chipotle picks its YouTube winners: Inside view of a consumer-generated campaign," AdAge.com, 14 November 2006.

22. Unless otherwise noted, material in this section was provided by the Promotional Products Association International.

23. Research by Louisiana State University and Glenrich Business Studies reported in www.ppai.org, 2005.

24. Christa Hoyland, "KFC scrambles to recover from Oprah coupon nightmare," www.qsrweb.com/article, 7 May 2009.

25. Natalie Zmuda, "Coke: Buy one rival, get our brand free," Adage.com, 9 March 2009.

26. Amy Johannes, "Playing the game," http://promomagazine/research/industry trends/, 9 April 2007.

27. Brian Quinton, "Kleenex seeks artists to design Hispanic-themed packaging," *PROMO*, http://promomagazine.com/contests/109-kleenex-contest-seeks-artists, 1 January 2009.

28. Ira Teinowitz, "Marketers yield to sweepstakes curbs," *Advertising Age*, 24 May 1999, 61.

29. Yellow Pages I.M.A., www.yellowpagesima.org/advertising/aboutcfm, 30 Ocotber 2003.

30. Paul Nolan and Vincent Alonzo, "Making the mark," *Incentive*, August 1999, 30.

CHAPTER 15

1. Sergio Zyman, *The End of Marketing as We Know It* (New York: HarperCollins, 1999), 62.

2. Jon Steel, *Truth, Lies and Advertising* (New York: John Wiley & Sons, 1998), 36.

3. Ibid., 43.

4. David Goetzl, "O&M turns reality TV into research tool," *Advertising Age*, 10 July 2000, 6.

5. Natalie Perkins, "Zeroing in on consumer values," *Advertising Age*, 22 March 1993, 23.

6. "Schwarzenegger campaign uses data on consumer buying habits to identify supporters," www.iht.com/articles/ap/2006/10/26/america/NA_POL_US_Schwarzenegger.php, 27 October 2006.

7. Kenneth Hein, "Study: Obama a BMW, McCain a Ford," *Brandweek*, 21 October 2008.

8. www.us.nielsen.com/products/cps_spectra_apps_hispaniq.shtml, 29 July 2009.

9. James A. Bayton, "Motivation, cognition, learning—Basic factors in consumer behavior," *Journal of Marketing*, January 1958, 282.

10. Jack Neff, "Mucus to maxi pads: Marketing's dirtiest jobs," *Advertising Age*, 16 February 2009, 9.

11. SRI Consulting Business Intelligence, www.sric-bi.com/VALS, 9 September 2006.

12. "MindBase® Attitudinal Segmentation—Who Will Buy—and Why?" www.yankelovich.com/index.php?option=com_content&task=category&sectionid=21&id=42&Itemid=88. 5 July 2009.

13. Christine Hansen, "Brainscan," *Deliver*—a magazine for marketers, November 2006, 18–23.

14. www.nytimes.com/2008/03/31/business/media/31adcol.html?sq=emsense, 31 March 2008.

15. Christine Hansen, "Brainscan," *Deliver*—a magazine for marketers, November 2006, 18–23.

16. Martin Lindstrom, "Why 'Idol' works for Coke—but not for Ford," *Advertising Age*, November 2008, 19.

17. Mark Walsh, "Nielsen: This is your brain on advertising," www.mediapost.com/publications/?fa=Articles.san&s=93319&Nid=48678&p=342208, 23 October 2008.

18. Christine Hansen, "Brainscan," *Deliver*—a magazine for marketers, November 2006, 18–23.

19. Beth Snyder Bulik, "Technology no longer just kids stuff," *Advertising Age*, 2 February 2009, 12.

20. Ben Kunz, "Advertising Outcasts," *Adweek*, 3 August 2009, 1.

21. PACT—Positioning Advertising Copy Testing, The PACT Agencies Report 1982, 6–25.

22. www.gfkamerica.com/practice_areas/brand_and_comm/starch/adnorms.html.en.html, 5 July 2009.

23. Lisa Sanders and Jack Neff, "Copy tests under fire from new set of critics," *Advertising Age*, 9 June 2003, 6.

24. Ibid.

CHAPTER 16

1. Abby Klaassen, "Apple ads breathe new life into online creative," Adage.com. March 30, 2009. http://adage.com/digitalalist09/article?article_id=135592.

2. Gregory Solman, "These Tags are it," *Adweek*, June 9, 2008 www.adweek.com/aw/content_display/creative/news/e3i1751753614c1db7755935f78a85069c5.

3. "Great advertising—It's simply a must," *Viewpoint*, January 1999, 12–13.

4. Scott Scaggs, "8 examples of creative marketing using new media," www.trone.com/index.php/tag/creative/, 9 July 2009.

5. Kenneth Roman and Jane Maas, *How to Advertise*, 3rd ed. (New York: St. Martin's Press, 2003), 215.

6. Jack Myers, "Can the rules of research change?" http://blogs.mediapost.com/tv_board/?p=8, 5 January 2007.

7. Lisa Sanders, "Ignore the research and trust your gut, Euro's David Jones tells Idea Conference to take back creativity from consumers," adage_daily@adage.com, 8 November 2006.

8. Jim Aitchison, *Cutting Edge Advertising* (Singapore: Prentice-Hall, 1999), 31–35.

9. Stefano Hatfield, "World's hot shop is in Paris, and it's Veruroegen's TBWA," *Advertising Age*, 4 August 2003, 16.

10. Jon Steel, *Truth, Lies, and Advertising* (New York: John Wiley & Sons, 1998), 141.

11. Luke Sullivan, *Hey Whipple, Squeeze This: A Guide to Creating Great Ads* (New York: John Wiley & Sons, 1998), 60–65.

12. John Hegarty, "My apologies for this letter being so long. Had I more time it would have been shorter," *Creativity*, March 1997, 12.

13. Jim Aitchison, *Cutting Edge Advertising* (Singapore: Prentice-Hall, 1999), 31–35.

14. Barry Wacksman, "You've got to tell to sell," *Adweek*, 6 October 2008, 14–15.

15. www.theadclass.com/education/storytelling-this-american-life-ira-glass. "American Storytelling-Ira Glass," September 8, 2009.

16. Tom Ehrenfeld, "Starbucks and the power of story" www.strategy-business.com/press/freearticle/08211.

17. Scott Scaggs, "Advertising shouldn't never not be negative. No?" www.trone.com/index.php/tag/creative/, 15 January 2009.

18. Abby Klaassen, "Apple ads breathe new life into online creative," Adage.com, http://adage.com/digitalalist09/article?article_id=135592, 30 March 2009.

19. Ron Huey, interviews by W. Ronald Lane, September 1994, September 1997, August 2003, October 2006.

20. David Martin, *Romancing the Brand* (New York: Amacom, 1989), 134–36.

21. From an American Association of Advertising Agencies speech, 17 May 1980.

22. Dick Costello, "The big picture," *Adweek*, 29 March 1999, 25.

23. The term *copy* is a carryover from the days in printing when a compositor, given a manuscript to set in type, was told to copy it. Before long, the manuscript itself became known as copy. In the creation of a printed advertisement, copy refers to all the reading matter in the advertisement. However, in the production of print advertising, copy refers to the entire subject being reproduced— words and pictures alike. This is one of those instances in advertising when the same word is used in different senses, a practice that all professions and crafts seem to enjoy because it bewilders the uninitiated.

24. Luis Bassar, "Creative paths to great advertising," *Viewpoint*, September/October 1991, 23–24.

25. Steve Lance and Jeff Woll, *The Little Blue Book of Advertising* (New York: Penguin Group, 2006), 189.

26. Ibid.

27. Dean Rieck, "Build consumer confidence with testimonials," *DMNews*, 8 February 1999, 12.

28. Leslie Picot-Zane, "Is advertising too emotional?" www.centerforemotionalmarketing.com, 9 January 2006.

29. From www.ftc.gov/bcp/policystmt/ad-compare.htm.

30. Stuart Elliott, "Dueling brands pick up where politicians leave off," *New York Times*, 3 November 2008. B-1

31. Michael McCarthy, "Imagination at work for GE," *USA Today*, 5 May 2003, 7B.

32. Gregory Solman, "These tags are it," *Adweek*, www.adweek.com/aw/content_display/creative/news/e3i1751753614c1db7755935f78a85069c5, 9 June 2008.

33. *Starch Tested Copy*, a publication of Roper Starch Worldwide.

34. Carnet Williams, "Advertising," http://digital.venturebeat.com/2009/07/15/five-rules-of-thumb-for-social-media-advertising/, 15 July 2009.

35. Gavin O'Malley, "Digital marketer of the year: Nike," *Advertising Age*, 16 October 2006.

36. Maxine Clark, *The Bear Necessities of Business* (Hoboken, NJ: John Wiley & Sons, 2006), 334–336.

37. Jeremy Mullman, "Southern Comfort pours entire media budget into digital," Adage.com, http://adage.com/article?article_id=138202, 30 July 2009.

CHAPTER 17

1. John Butler, "Want to make art?" *Adweek*, 26 May 2003, 20.

2. Noreen O'Leary, "Does creative count?" *Adweek*, 11 December 2000, 32.

3. George Parker, *MadScam* (New York: Entrepreneur Media, 2007), 98.

4. Ryan Underwood, "Ruling the roost," *Fast Company*, April 2005, 70.

5. Al Ries, "Are you a left brainer or a right brainer?" *Advertising Age*, 3 February 2009. http://adage.com/columns/article?article_id=134291.

6. Kate Macarthur, "FCB's Taco Bell success might give it edge in KFC review," *Advertising Age*, 5 August 2003, 2.

7. Roper Starch Worldwide, Inc., *Starch Tested Copy* 5 (no. 3, 4).

8. Jim Aitchison, *Cutting Edge Advertising* (Singapore: Prentice-Hall, 1999), 112–165.

9. Ibid.

10. colormarketing.org, 2009, October 6, 2009.

11. From www.pantone.com/pages/pantone/Pantone.aspx?pg=19382&ca=29, 4 January 2007.

12. www.dexigner.com/design_news/pantone-2010-multi-discipline-forecast.html, October 8, 2009.

13. Ilene Strizver, "Do you believe in magic?" *HOW*, February 2007, 60–63.

14. *Cahners Advertising Research Report* (CARR) No. 118.5 (Newton, MA: Cahners, n.d.), 4.

15. Jim Aitchison, *Cutting Edge Advertising* (Singapore: Prentice-Hall, 1999), 243–244.

16. Augustine Fou, The ClickZ Network, 23 October 2008.

CHAPTER 18

1. Allan Haley, "Using all capitals is a graphic oxymoron," *U & lc*, Fall 1991, 14–15.

2. William Ryan and Theodore Conover, *Graphic Communications Today*, 4th ed. (Clifton Park, NY: Thomson, 2004), 308–309.

CHAPTER 19

1. IAB Guidelines, 2009. www.iab.net/iab_products_and_industry_services/1421/1443/1452.

2. Michael Griffin, "In-stream standardization: publishers, haven't we been here before," MediaPost's Videoinsider, 8 July 2009.

3. Kristof Harling and Camilla Day, "Online video creativity and execution," www.iabuk.net/en/1/onlinevideomarketingcreativityandexecution.html, January 2009.

4. Teressa Iezzi, "Creatives and producers grapple with a new era of production," *Creativity*, 11 August 2008.

5. Interview with Ernie Mosteller, January 2009.

6. "TV advertising still has a future," The Guradian/Adverblog, August 2, 2005.

7. Cyndee Miller, "Celebrities hot despite scandals," *Marketing News,* 28 March 1994, 1–2.

8. Michael Goldman, "Legato's Laboratory," *Millimeter,* September 2005, 31–36.

9. Steve Lance and Jeff Woll, *The Little Blue Book of Advertising* (New York: Penguin Group, 2006), 166–167.

10. *Music—How to Use It for Commercial Production,* a publication of the Television Bureau of Advertising, New York.

11. Stefano Hatfield, "Music to watch sales by," *Creativity,* July 2003, 34–35.

12. Warren Burger, "Action fever," *Creativity,* June 2000, 47–49.

13. Bart Cleveland, "Producing quality TV spots on a shoestring," http://adage.com/small agency, 27 July 2006.

14. SAG & AFTRA News Release, 1 April 2009.

15. AFTRA, www.aftra.org/member/irates.html, 15 January 2004.

CHAPTER 20

1. Tom Monahan, "Advertising," *Communication Arts*, July 1994, 198.

2. Erik Gruenwedel, "Net radio daze," *Adweek*, 1 May 2000, IQ26–27.

3. "Google exits radio but will explore online streaming audio," http://google-tmads.blogspot.com/2009/02/.

4. www.motel6.com/about/bodett.aspx, 2009.

5. J. Patrick Coolican, "Jingles drop out of favor," The Associated Press, 5 September 2006.

6. Aaron Baar, "Advertising saves the radio star," *Adweek*, 6 November 2006, 12–13.

7. Stuart Elliott, "Bringing back the Slinky," www.newyorktimes.com, 3 May 2005.

8. Bruce Bendinger, *The Copy Workshop Workbook* (Chicago: Bruce Bendinger Creative Communications, Inc., 1988), 214.

9. www.soundofmusic.org/, August 16, 2009.

10. Mike Tierney, "Radio ads that fly under the radar," *Atlanta Journal-Constitution*, 17 July 2005, Q1–4.

CHAPTER 21

1. Beth Snyder Bulik, "The brand police," *Business* 2.0, 28 November 2000, 144–148.

2. Roger Sametz, "Moving from corporate identity to brand identity: A great logo only gets you so far," www.sametz.com, 20 January 2004.

3. www.lippincott.com/services/timeline.shtml, 2009.

4. "The Lanham Act: Alive and well after 50 years," International Trademark Association, www.inta.org/lanham.htm, 20 June 2000.

5. Natalie Zmuda, "What went into the updated Pepsi logo," *Advertising Age*, http://adage.com/article?article_id=132016, 27 October 2008.

6. Rupal Parekh, "Breathtaking is one word for purported Arnell Pepsi doc," *Advertising Age*, http://adage.com/agencynews/ article?article_id=134552, 11 February 2009.

7. Richard A. Costello, "Focus on the brand," *The Advertiser*, Spring 1993, 11–18.

8. Stuart Elliott, "Questions and Answers, "www.nytimes.com/2008/ 12/15/business/media/15adnewsletter2.html?8ad&emc=seiaa3, 15 December 2008.

9. Judy Artunian, "Change of name can come with risk," *Chicago Tribune*, 19 May 2006, B-1.

10. Allen P. Adamson, *BrandSimple* (New York: Palgrave Macmillan, 2006) 160.

11. Daniel L. Doden, "Selecting a brand name that aids marketing objectives," *Advertising Age*, 5 November 1990, 34.

12. Al Ries and Laura Ries, *The Immutable Laws of Internet Branding* (New York: HarperBusiness, 2000), 59–70.

13. Julie Cottineau, *Interbrand Special Report: The 'Name Game,'* 2002, August 30, 2009.

14. "Why do so many corporations choose blue?" www.lippincott. com/services/why_so_blue.shtml, September 2, 2009.

15. Richard Linnett, "Anderson's accenture gets $175 mil ad blitz," *Advertising Age*, 4 December 2000, 20.

16. David Goetzl, "Delta flies toward $1 billion in web sales," *Advertising Age*, 11 September 2000, 54–56.

17. www.brandchannel.com/papers_review.asp?sp_id=1270, 12 January 2007.

18. Patrick Conlon, "Tropicana to abandon much-maligned juice carton," *Wall Street Journal,* 23 February 2009; and http://online.wsj .com/article_email/SB123544345146655887lMyQjAxMDI5MzI1 NDQyNDQzWj.html.

19. Joe Guy Collier, "Coca-Cola hands its fans new bottles to hold onto," *Atlanta Journal-Constitution*, 5 July 2009, B-1.

20. www.edf_org/edf/atissue/vol4–1, 22 January 2004.

21. Betsy McKay, "Pepsi's new marketing dance: Can can," *Wall Street Journal*, 12 January 2007, B3.

22. Frank Tobolski, "Package design requires research," *Marketing News*, 6 June 1994, 4.

23. Terry Lofton, "If your brand's number two, get with the package program," *Brandweek*, 27 June 1994, 26.

24. Allen Adamson, "Future of branding based on current trends," Landor.com, 21 January 2004.

25. Allen Adamson, "Future of branding based on current trends," www.landor.com/index.cfm?fuseaction=cBranding.getArticle& storyid=264, 12 March 2004.

CHAPTER 22

1. Theresa Howard, "Burger King appeals to young workers with 'Your Way' ads," *USA Today*, 18 April 2005, M2.

2. Kenneth Roman and Jane Maas, *How to Advertise* (New York: St. Martin's Press, 2003), 48–49.

3. Andrew McMains, "First Snickers work from TBWA/C/D," *Adweek*, 12 June 2006, 8.

4. Ann M. Mack, "Web ads score on recognition factor," *Adweek*, 19 January 2004, 12.

5. Emily Bryson York, "Subway's $5 foot-long becomes the yardstick for fast-food deals," *Advertising Age*, 8 June 2009, 8.

6. Kenneth Roman and Jane Maas, *The New How to Advertise* (New York: St. Martin's Press, 1992), 71–78.

7. Steve Cone, *Powerlines*, (New York: Bloomberg Press, 2008), 12.

8. Lisa Siracuse, "Looks aren't everything: An examination of brand personality," *Integrated Marketing Communications Research Journal*, Spring 1997, 38–39.

9. Andrew Hampp, "Mountain Dew banks on branded entertainment," *Advertising Age*, http://adage.com/madisonandvine/ article?article_id=137086, 4 June 2009.

10. Marc Graser, "Totota hits touch points as it hawks Yaris to youth," *Advertising Age*, 1 May 2006, 28.

CHAPTER 23

1. "The biggest moments in the last 75 years of advertising history," *Advertising Age*, 28 March 2005, 12.

2. Clayton Collins, "Status of U.S. brands slips globally among teens," *Christian Science Monitor*, as reported in *Advertising Age*, 27 February 2006, 26.

3. "The world's largest cities," *Atlanta Journal-Constitution*, 16 November 2005, D3.

4. Normandy Madden, "Reaching China's youth: A balancing act," *Advertising Age*, 6 June 2005, 14.

5. "Invasion of the Chinese clones," www.driving.timesonline.co.uk, 30 January 2006.

6. Valentina Vescovi and Aiza Rocca, "Advertising faces uncertain future under Chavez's rule," *Advertising Age*, 15 June 2009, 12.

7. "Glocalization," www.en.wikipedia.org, 30 January 2006.

8. "Glocalization," www.searchcio.techtarget.com, 30 January 2006.

9. Mark Landler and Michael Barbaro, "No, not always," *New York Times*, 2 August 2006, C1.

10. Normandy Madden, "China's retail sales will reach $3.2 trillion by 2013," *Advertising Age*, http://adage.com/china/article?article_id=137899, 15 July 2009,

11. Normandy Madden, "Looking to grow in China? Ad Age has 10 surefire tips," *Advertising Age*, 4 May 2009, 3, 27.

12. Jared Diamond, *Collapse* (New York: Penguin Books, 2005), 495.

13. "Background: Global Internet solutions," www.tvpress.com, 31 January 2006.

14. Barry Silverstein, "Going global with Internet marketing," www.clickz.com, 30 January 2006.

15. Elizabeth Lloyd, "Marketing to the global inbox," www.imediaconnection.com, 31 January 2006.

16. Natalie Zmuda, "'Open Happiness' opens regional dialogue," *Advertising Age*, 15 June 2009, 4.

17. Deborah Ball, "Italian challenge, water everywhere, but not on the go," *Wall Street Journal*, 23 May 2005, 1A.

18. Eric Pfanner, "On advertising: Ad agencies see revenue in Ramadan," www.nytimes.com, 3 October 2005.

19. Aaron O. Patrick, "World Cup's advertisers hope one size fits all," *Wall Street Journal*, 28 March 2006, B7.

20. Cecilie Rohweddere, "Wal-Mart's big goal," *Wall Street Journal*, 7 June 2006, B1.

21. John Galvin, "The world on a string," *Point*, February 2005, 13.

22. Beth Snyder Bulik, "Visa introduces global campaign with 'golocal' approach," *Advertising Age*, 15 June 2009, 12.

23. Erin White and Sarah Ellison, "Unilever ads offer a tribute to dirt," *Wall Street Journal*, 2 June 2003, B3.

24. "Marketing and image consulting," www.multilingualplanet.com, 1 February 2006.

25. Scott Donaton, "Partners are for dances. To thrive, big agencies need to provide ideas," *Advertising Age*, 9 May 2005, 34.

26. Rupal Parekh, "Agency ambitions: Get global without being everywhere," *Advertising Age*, 15 June 2009, 1, 28.

27. "WPP buys J. Walter Thompson," *Advertising Age*, 21 March 2005, 12.

28. Andrew McMains, "Debunking the consolidation myth," www.adweek.com, 20 February 2006.

29. Kate Macarthur, "This woman scares big agencies," *Advertising Age*, 25 April 2005, 1.

30. Cara B. Dipasquale, "Making data more relevant at Wunderman, byte by byte," *Advertising Age*, 2 September 2002, 24.

31. Susan P. Douglas and C. Samuel Craig, "International advertising," www.pages.stern.nyu.edu, 2 February 2006.

32. Geoffrey A. Fowler, "China bans Nike's LeBron ad as offensive to nation's dignity," *Wall Street Journal*, 7 December 2004, B4.

33. Normandy Madden, "How China buys and sells TV," *Advertising Age*, 8 May 2006, 26.

34. Givi Topschishvili, "How to make it in risky but rewarding Russian market," *Advertising Age*, 15 June 2009, 14.

35. Valentina Vescovi and Aiza Rocca, "Advertising faces uncertain future under Chavez's rule," *Advertising Age*, 15 June 2009, 12.

36. Ira Teinowitz, "International advertising code revised," *Advertising Age*, 23 January 2006, 3.

37. Laurel Wentz, "Pop stops kids' marketing in Europe," *Advertising Age*, 30 January 2006, 8.

38. Doreen Carvajal, "Processed foods? Read this, France says," *International Herald Tribune*, 2 October 2005, www.iht.com, 3 February 2006.

39. Lewis Rose and John Feldman, *Internet Marketing*, quoted at www.usability.com, 3 February 2006.

40. "Tips for tapping China's explosive growth," *Advertising Age*, 16 January 2006, 10.

41. Bradley Johnson, "Looking to experience a foreign culture? Plan a vacation to California," *Advertising Age*, 21 August 2006, 17.

42. Brad Edmondson, "America, new and improved," *Advertising Age*, 2 January 2006, 31.

43. Carol Hymowitz, "In a global economy, it's no longer about how many employees you have in this group and that group. It's a lot more complicated—and if you do it right, a lot more effective," *Wall Street Journal*, 14 November 2005, R1.

44. Laurel Wentz, "Marketers hone focus on minorities," *Advertising Age*, 1 November 2004, 55.

45. Laurel Wentz, "Multicultural? No, mainstream," *Advertising Age*, 2 May 2005, 3.

46. Alex Lopez Negrete, "Marketers, don't assimilate your Hispanic ads," *Advertising Age*, 31 October 2005, 25.

47. Tiffany Meyers, "Cultural mosaic," *Advertising Age*, 13 March 2006, S-1.

48. Jeremy Mullman, *Advertising Age*, 14 August 2006, 11.

49. Brooks Barnes, "Getting 'Housewives' to speak Spanish can turn desperate," *Wall Street Journal*, 13 December 2005, 1A.

50. Brooks Barnes, "U.S. networks try crafting their own Spanish-style soaps," *Wall Street Journal*, 5 January 2006, A13.

51. About Si TV, www.sitv.com/about-us, accessed October 5, 2009.

52. Kate Macarthur, "Taco Bell tries to solve its Hispanic conundrum," *Advertising Age*, 4 September 2006, 36.

53. Ann Zimmerman, "Wal-Mart's Hispanic outreach," *Wall Street Journal*, 31 May 2005, B9.

54. "New age media concepts and Hispanic advertising," www.namct.com, 9 February 2006.

55. Lee Hawkins, Jr., "Behind GM's slide: Bosses misjudged new urban tastes," *Wall Street Journal*, 8 March 2006, 1A.

56. Brian Steinberg, "P&G brushes up iconic image of 'Crest Kid' in new campaign," *Wall Street Journal*, 29 March 2005, B9.

57. Amy Chozick, "Marketers join Cinco de Mayo party," *Wall Street Journal*, 4 May 2005, B8.

58. Laurel Wentz, "Marketers move popular brands north of border," *Advertising Age*, 16 May 2005, 49.

59. Laurel Wentz, "Survey: Hispanics 'passionate' about shopping," *Advertising Age*, 18 July 2005, 29.

CHAPTER 24

1. www.lucidcafe.com, 14 February 2006.

2. www.blupete.com, 14 February 2006.

3. Alan Murray, "Will 'social responsibility' harm business?" *Wall Street Journal*, 18 May 2005, A2.

4. "Corporate social responsibility: Good citizenship or investor rip-off?" *Wall Street Journal*, 9 January 2006, R6.

5. Rance Crane, "Now here's a radical theory: Ads last bastion of honesty," *Advertising Age*, 1 July 2002, 32.

6. Stephanie Thompson, "Cereal consortium tests TV effort," *Advertising Age*, 15 July 2002, 6.

7. David M. Potter, *People of Plenty: Economic Abundance and the American Character* (Chicago: University of Chicago Press, 1954), 188.

8. Michael R. Solomon, *Consumer Behavior* (Upper Saddle River, NJ: Pearson Prentice Hall, 2004), 562.

9. Naomi Klein, *No Logo* (New York: Picador, 2002), 28.

10. Kim Sheehan, *Controversies in Contemporary Advertising* (Thousand Oaks, CA: 2004), 25.

11. www.ftc.gov/bcp/privacy/wkshp97, 15 February 2006.

12. www.howstuffworks.com, 15 February 2006.

13. www.commercialalert.org, 15 February 2006.

14. "Vance Packard's 'hidden persuaders,'" *Advertising Age*, 7 March 2005, 14.

15. Marilyn Gardner, "Body by Madison Avenue," www.csmonitor.com, 24 November 1999.

16. Rosie Murray, "Adland pulls plug on man's lustful ineptitude," www.telegraph.co.uk, 22 August 2005.

17. Rich Thomaselli, "Beauty's new, er, face," *Advertising Age*, 15 August 2005, 1.

18. James B. Arndorfer, "Raising their spirits," *Advertising Age*, 14 February 2005, S-1.

19. Matthew Grimm, "A spirited debate," *American Demographics*, April 2002, 48.

20. Abbey Klaassen, "Clear Channel loses despite gains," *Advertising Age*, 15 August 2005, 8.

21. "Its all about results," www.adcouncil.org, 16 February 2006.

22. Michael Bush, "Boom in issues advertising could net agencies $1 billion," *Advertising Age*, 1 June 2009, 3, 53.

23. Carol Hymowitz, "Asked to be charitable, more CEOs seek to aid their business as well," *Wall Street Journal*, 22 February 2005, B1.

24. Laura Raines, "Corporate citizens," *Atlanta Journal-Constitution*, 20 August 2006, G1.

25. Michael Bush, "Consumers continue to stand by their causes during downturn," *Advertising Age*, 17 November 2008, 4, 49.

26. "Cause market forum," a supplement to *Advertising Age*, 28 July 2003, 2.

27. James Tenser, "The new Samaritans," *Advertising Age*, 12 June 2006, S-1.

28. Rich Thomaselli, "Steady ratings for 'dLife' get marketers' attention," *Advertising Age*, 16 January 2006, 8.

29. www.gradethenews.org/dreamhost, 17 February 2006.

30. Mathew Creamer, "Ad-pull edicts elicit nary a whimper of protest," *Wall Street Journal*, 30 May 2005, 3.

31. "The family friendly programming forum," www.ana.net, 17 February 2006.

32. Gail Schiller, "Advertisers get piece of local news shows," www.hollywoodreporter.com, 16 March 2006.

33. "News is no place for shady shills," *Advertising Age*, 25 April 2005, 32.

34. Al Tompkins, "Balancing business pressure and journalism values," www.poynter.org, 17 February 2006.

35. "Advertisers rush to insert products into video games," *Atlanta Journal-Constitution*, 22 May 2005, F9.

36. Jack Neff, "Marketing blamed in Walmart death," *Advertising Age*, 8 December 2008, 23.

37. Ira Teinowitz, "FTC whacks professor wonder," www.adage.com, 17 April 2002.

38. Ira Teinowitz, "Tobacco firms must air spots, judge says," www.tvweek.com, 18 August 2006.

39. Christopher Conkey, "DirecTV to pay $5.3 million for calling consumers on the 'Do Not Call' list," *Wall Street Journal*, 14 December 2005, D1.

40. Michael Bush, "Bloggers be warned: FTC may monitor what you say," *Advertising Age*, 13 April 2009, 3, 21.

41. For a more complete listing of FTC Rules and Guidelines refer to www.ftc.gov.

42. Arthur Winston, "How to define the concept 'free' via the FTC," *DMNews*, 24 June 1996, 15.

43. Ivan Preston, *The Tangled Web They Weave* (Madison: University of Wisconsin Press, 1994), 103.

44. "FTC guides concerning use of endorsements and testimonials in advertising," www.ftc.gov, 16 April 2000.

45. "Celebrities in ads: FTC proposes new rules," *Consumer Reports*, September 2009, 9.

46. Rich Thomaselli, "What Bayer campaign means for pharma ads," *Advertising Age*, 16 February 2009, 3, 19.

47. Rich Thomaselli, "FDA scrutiny threatens DTC media bonanza," *Advertising Age*, 25 April 2005, 1.

48. Rich Thomaselli, "Cheerios first in FDA firing line. Who's next?" *Advertising Age*, 18 May 2009, 1, 41.

49. Andrew B. Lustigman, "DMPEA gives USPS sweeping powers," *DMNews*, 6 December 1999, 14.

50. Stephen R. Bergerson, "Supreme Court strikes a blow for commercial speech," *American Advertising*, Summer 1993, 24.

51. "High court's hard line on ad bans," *Advertising Age*, 20 May 1996, 57.

52. "Advertising alcoholic beverages," *Advertising Topics*, a publication of the Council of Better Business Bureaus, May 1996, 2.

53. "High court overturns broadcasting ban on gambling advertising," *Advertising Topics*, 14 July 1999, 1.

54. Richard Carelli, "Supreme Court rejects ban on casino ads," www.nytimes.com, 14 June 1999.

55. Linda Greenhouse, "Justices strike down ban on casino gambling ads," www.nytimes.com, 15 June 1999.

56. Ira Teinowitz, "Ad, food groups indignant," *Advertising Age*, 23 January 2006, 25.

57. www.ftc.gov, 13 February 2006.

58. Candiss Baksa Vibbert, "Freedom of speech and corporations: Supreme Court strategies for the extension of the First Amendment," *Communications*, Vol. 12, 1990, 26.

59. Boris Becker and Dennis O. Kaldenberg, "To advertise or not to advertise? Advertising expenditures by professionals," *Proceedings of the American Academy of Advertising*, 1995, Charles S. Madden, ed.

60. Rosalind C. Truitt, "The cases for commercial speech," *Presstime*, March 1996, 31.

61. "Blockbuster to reimburse consumers for late fees," *Advertising Age*, 4 April 2005, 18.

62. *Wall Street Journal*, January 19, 2006, D4.

63. Emily Bryson York, "The gloves are off: More marketers opt for attack ads," *Advertising Age*, 25 May 2009, 4, 22.

64. www.encarta.msn.com/encyclopedia, 13 February 2006.

65. "NBC, CBS to drop some of Miller's ads," *Atlanta Journal-Constitution*, 18 December 2004, F3.

66. Abbey Klaassen, "Toy industry looks to tots for boost," *Advertising Age*, 28 February 2005, 8.

67. "Screen advertisement: A guide for the media," www.ftc.gov, issued September 1998.

68. John R. Wilke, "FTC asks media to reject false ads," *Wall Street Journal*, 20 November 2002, A3.

69. "FTC cites drop in fraudulent diet ads," *Advertising Age*, 7 February 2005, 16.

70. "*The Sporting News* and DOJ agree to $7.2M settlement regarding acceptance of offshore gambling site ads," www.manatt.com, 10 March 2006.

71. Rich Thomaselli, "Drug industry ad code seen as negotiating play," *Advertising Age*, 8 August 2005, 8.

72. Caroline Wilbert, "Beverage industry ads tout new school policy," *Atlanta Journal-Constitution*, 13 October 2005, F1.

73. Rance Crain, "Self-regulation shouldn't be advertising's best-kept secret," *Advertising Age*, 23 February 2009, 11.

74. "Basic principles of the Better Business Bureau Code of Advertising," www.bbb.org, 19 June 2002.

75. "National Advertising Review Council," *Advertising Age*, 28 March 2005, 12.

76. Statement from the NAD, www.narc.org, 14 February 2006.

77. Harkin statement on Better Business Bureau's Children's Food and Beverage Advertising Initiative, http://harkin.senate.gov/pr/p.cfm?i=301493, 29 July 2008.

78. Children's Food and Beverage Advertising Initiative, www.bbb.org/us/children-food-beverage-advertising-initiative/, 6 October 2009.

79. About the Initiative, www.bbb.org/us/about-children-food-beverage-advertising-initiative/, 6 October 2009.

Index